ST/PSCA/1/Add.25*

Department of Political and Peacebuilding Affairs

Repertoire of the Practice of the Security Council

Supplement 2022

United Nations • New York, 2024

* Reissued for technical reasons on 29 May 2025.

Note

The designations employed and the presentation of the material in this publication do not imply the expression of any opinion whatsoever on the part of the Secretariat of the United Nations concerning the legal status of any country, territory, city or area or of its authorities, or concerning the delimitation of its frontiers or boundaries.

ST/PSCA/1/Add.25

United Nations publication
Sales No. E.24.VII.1
ISBN 9789210031820

Contents

Introduction

The present publication constitutes the twenty-fifth supplement to the *Repertoire of the Practice of the Security Council*, 1946–1951, which was issued in 1954. In 2022, despite the continued impact of the outbreak of the coronavirus disease (COVID-19) pandemic, the Council returned to conducting its meetings in person, although with limited participation of the wider membership. For that reason, in accordance with the understanding reached by the Council members, in early 2022, non-Council members continued to submit written statements in connection with open debates, which were compiled in letters from the President of the Security Council.

The twenty-fifth supplement to the *Repertoire* covers the proceedings of the Security Council from the 8943rd meeting, held on 5 January 2022, to the 9234th meeting, held on 22 December 2022. The original *Repertoire* and previous supplements may be consulted online on the Council website (www.un.org/securitycouncil/content/repertoire/structure).

The *Repertoire* was mandated by the General Assembly in its resolution 686 (VII) of 5 December 1952, entitled "Ways and means for making the evidence of customary international law more readily available". It is a guide to the proceedings of the Council and sets forth in a readily accessible form the practices and procedures to which the Council has had recourse. The *Repertoire* is not intended as a substitute for the records of the Council, which constitute the only comprehensive and authoritative account of its deliberations.

The categories employed to arrange the material are not intended to suggest the existence of procedures or practices that have not been clearly or demonstrably established by the Council itself. The Council is at all times master of its own procedure, within the framework of the Charter of the United Nations, its own provisional rules of procedure and the practice established through, inter alia, notes by the President of the Security Council. For ease of reference, this introduction contains a table indicating the membership of the Council during the period under review.

In recording the Council's practice, the headings under which the practices and procedures of the Council were presented in the original volume issued in 1954 have been largely retained. Where necessary, however, adjustments have been made to better reflect the Council's practice. For example, the studies contained in part I of the present publication are organized in chronological order according to region or thematic issues.

The *Repertoire* covers four primary areas: the application of the provisional rules of procedure, the application of Articles of the Charter, the subsidiary organs of the Council, including peacekeeping operations and special political missions, as well as sanctions committees and the associated panels and groups of experts, and an overview of Council activities for each item of which it is seized. From 1946 to 2007, each Supplement to the *Repertoire*, generally covering a period of two to four years, comprised 12 chapters; from 2008 to 2017, each Supplement covered a period of two years and comprised 10 parts. Since 2018, each Supplement, covering a period of one year, has also comprised ten parts.

From 1946 to 2007, the 12 chapters of each Supplement covered the following topics:

Chapter I	Provisional rules of procedure of the Security Council (Articles 28, 30, 98 of the Charter; rules 1–5, 13–36, 40–67 of the rules of procedure)
Chapter II	Agenda (rules 6–12)
Chapter III	Participation in the proceedings of the Security Council (Articles 31, 32, 35 (1); rules 37–39)
Chapter IV	Voting (Article 27; rule 40)
Chapter V	Subsidiary organs of the Security Council
Chapter VI	Relations with other United Nations organs

Chapter VII	Practice relative to recommendations to the General Assembly regarding membership in the United Nations
Chapter VIII	Consideration of questions under the Council's responsibility for the maintenance of international peace and security (overview by agenda item)
Chapter IX	Decisions taken by the Security Council in the exercise of its other functions and powers
Chapter X	Consideration of the provisions of Chapter VI of the Charter
Chapter XI	Consideration of the provisions of Chapter VII of the Charter
Chapter XII	Consideration of the provisions of other Articles (Articles 1 (2), 2 (4), 2 (5), 2 (6), 2 (7), 24, 25, 52–54, 102, 103)

From 2008 onward, the 10 parts of each Supplement covered the following topics:

Part I	Consideration of questions under the responsibility of the Security Council for the maintenance of international peace and security
Part II	Provisional rules of procedure and related procedural developments
Part III	Purposes and principles of the Charter of the United Nations
Part IV	Relations with other United Nations organs
Part V	Functions and powers of the Security Council (Chapter V of the Charter)
Part VI	Consideration of the provisions of Chapter VI of the Charter
Part VII	Actions with respect to threats to the peace, breaches of the peace, and acts of aggression (Chapter VII of the Charter)
Part VIII	Regional arrangements (Chapter VIII of the Charter)
Part IX	Subsidiary organs of the Security Council: committees, tribunals and other bodies
Part X	Subsidiary organs of the Security Council: peacekeeping operations and special political missions

The *Repertoire* is based on published documents of the Council. Symbols of United Nations documents are composed of letters combined with figures. Council documents are indicated by a symbol that includes the year and a sequential number (e.g. S/2022/32). References to the verbatim records of meetings of the Council are given in the form S/PV.9229, meetings being numbered consecutively, starting with the first meeting in 1946. As in previous recent supplements, reference is made in this Supplement only to the provisional verbatim records of Council meetings, as the practice of publishing the meeting records in the *Official Records* has been discontinued.

The resolutions and other decisions adopted by the Council, including statements and notes by the President and relevant exchanges of letters between the President and the Secretary-General, are published in the yearly volumes of *Resolutions and Decisions of the Security Council*. Resolutions are identified by a number followed by the year of adoption in parentheses, for example, resolution 2671 (2022). Since 1994, references to the statements by the President on behalf of the Council are given in the form S/PRST/2022/6, for example. Prior to that date, presidential statements, like other Security Council documents, were circulated under a symbol in the sequential series (e.g. S/25929).

Readers who wish to consult the full record of a meeting or the text of a Council document referred to in the *Repertoire* may do so on the official web page for United Nations documents (www.un.org/en/documents/). Council documents can be accessed on the website by selecting "Official Document System (ODS)" or one of the direct links to specific categories of documents under the heading "Security Council". The volumes of *Resolutions and Decisions* may be accessed by symbol (S/INF/77 for 2022).

Membership of the Security Council, 2022

Albania

Brazil

China

France

Gabon

Ghana

India

Ireland

Kenya

Mexico

Norway

Russian Federation

United Arab Emirates

United Kingdom of Great Britain and Northern Ireland

United States of America

Part I

Consideration of questions under the responsibility of the Security Council for the maintenance of international peace and security

Contents

Middle East

Thematic issues

Introductory note

Part I of the present Supplement to the *Repertoire of the Practice of the Security Council* provides an overview of the proceedings of the Security Council in connection with the items of which the Council is seized that relate to its responsibility for the maintenance of international peace and security.

In 2022, as restrictions related to the coronavirus disease (COVID-19) pandemic were eased, the Council was able to fully resume all in-person activities, including the holding of meetings in person and the adoption of decisions at the Security Council Chamber. The Council also discontinued the use of videoconferences, the written voting procedure and other aspects of the remote working methods established at the outset of the pandemic in March 2020. These changes are reflected in part I.

Part I provides the immediate political context in which the consideration of the items by the Council evolved in 2022, covering the meetings and documents of the Council. Consequently, part I features all items in connection with which meetings were held. Part I constitutes a framework within which the deliberations of the Council expressly related to the provisions of the Charter of the United Nations and the Council's provisional rules of procedure can be considered. For that reason, cross-references to all other relevant parts are included in the narrative sections of part I to facilitate understanding of the structure and content of the Repertoire.

Part I also contains an examination of the substantive aspects of the Council's practice that are not covered in other parts of the Repertoire. For ease of reference, the items are grouped by region, with an additional category of thematic issues. Within each region, items are listed in the order in which they were first included in the list of matters of which the Council is seized. Individual studies highlight significant developments in the Council's consideration of an item that are considered important for contextualizing the decisions taken by the Council.

Each section is followed by a table comprising all procedural information relating to the item, including meetings listed in chronological order, sub-items, documents referred to and speakers. In addition, to illustrate the mainstreaming of thematic issues, sections concerning the items entitled "Children and armed conflict", "Protection of civilians in armed conflict" and "Women and peace and security" are followed by an additional table setting out the relevant provisions of decisions of the Council.

Africa

1. The situation concerning Western Sahara

During the period under review, the Council held one meeting and adopted one resolution in connection with the situation concerning Western Sahara. In that meeting, the Council adopted resolution 2654 (2022).[1] In addition, Council members held one private (closed) meeting with countries contributing troops and police to the United Nations Mission for the Referendum in Western Sahara (MINURSO) pursuant to resolution 1353 (2001).[2] More information on the meeting, including on participants, speakers and outcomes, is provided in the table below. Council members also held informal consultations of the whole in connection with the item.[3]

On 27 October, having considered the report of the Secretary-General,[4] the Council adopted resolution 2654 (2022), by which it extended the mandate of MINURSO for a period of one year, until 31 October 2023.[5] The resolution was adopted with 13 votes in favour and 2 abstentions.[6] In the resolution, the Council expressed its full support for the Secretary-General and his Personal Envoy for Western Sahara to facilitate the negotiations process in order to achieve a solution to the Western Sahara question, building on the progress and framework of the former Personal Envoy.[7] The Council noted with deep concern the breakdown of the ceasefire and, in that regard, called upon the parties to comply fully with the military agreements reached with MINURSO.[8] The Council also called upon the parties to resume negotiations under the auspices of the Secretary-General without preconditions and in good faith, taking into account the efforts made since 2006 and subsequent developments with a view to achieving a just, lasting and mutually acceptable political solution, which would provide for the self-determination of the people of Western Sahara.[9] The Council also noted with deep concern the continued hardships faced by Sahrawi refugees, their dependency on external humanitarian assistance, and the impact of the COVID-19 pandemic, as well as the insufficient funding for those living in Tindouf refugee camps and the risks associated with the reduction of food assistance.[10]

Following the adoption of the resolution, several Council members took the floor to explain their votes. Among those abstaining, the representative of Kenya expressed regret that resolution 2654 (2022) continued a gradual but noticeable shift away from the mandate of MINURSO, which would not assist the parties in achieving a just, lasting and mutually acceptable political solution, as originally intended.[11] He expressed further regret that the proposals made by Kenya during the negotiations had not been taken on board and expressed his concern that the adopted resolution did not substantively reflect the Council's commitment – as reflected in resolution 2602 (2021) and in previous resolutions – to "provide for the self-determination of the people of Western Sahara in the context of arrangements consistent with the principles and purposes of the Charter of the United Nations, and noting the role and responsibilities of the parties in this respect".[12] He further observed that the African Union, which counted both parties as its members, should not be ignored by any United Nations process, if only based on adherence to Chapter VIII of the Charter of the United Nations. He said that the Personal Envoy should make every effort to cooperate with

[1] For more information on the format of meetings, see part II.

[2] The private meeting was held on 10 October in connection with the item entitled "Meeting of the Security Council with the troop- and police-contributing countries pursuant to resolution 1353 (2001), annex II, sections A and B"; see S/PV.9148. See also A/77/2, part II, chap. 21.

[3] See A/77/2, part II, chap. 3.

[4] S/2022/733. See also the letter dated 17 October from the representative of South Africa to the President of the Security Council (S/2022/797).

[5] Resolution 2654 (2022), para. 1. For more information on the mandate of MINURSO, see part X, sect. I.

[6] See S/PV.9168.

[7] Resolution 2654 (2022), para. 3.

[8] Ibid., thirteenth preambular paragraph and para. 6.

[9] Ibid., para. 4.

[10] Ibid., twenty-second preambular paragraph.

[11] See S/PV.9168.

[12] Resolution 2602 (2021), seventh preambular paragraph. Resolution 2654 (2022) contained the language quoted in its sixth preambular paragraph and in paragraph 4.

the African Union to find ways to bring all parties to a common position protective of peace, security and the holding of the agreed referendum. The representative of the Russian Federation echoed the representative of Kenya, stating that the process of preparing and agreeing on the adopted resolution had not been fully consultative, adding that a number of useful proposals by other Council members had also gone unheeded and that, as a result, the resolution was not balanced.[13] He also indicated that, in the past few years, the resolutions on the renewal of the mandate of MINURSO had included amendments that harmed the unbiased and impartial approach needed to resolve the issue of Western Sahara. He added that resolution 2654 (2022) did not reflect the real situation on the ground and was unlikely to facilitate the efforts of the Secretary-General's Personal Envoy to resume the direct negotiation process between Morocco and the Frente Popular para la Liberación de Saguía el-Hamra y de Río de Oro (Frente POLISARIO) in order to reach a mutually acceptable solution. He questioned the vague language used to define the direct participants in the conflict and the Western Sahara peace process. He also considered the numerous references to the round-table format, which was irrelevant and limited the mediation activities of the Personal Envoy, to be misplaced. He added that the text of the resolution did not reflect the continuing issue of access by United Nations entities to the territory of Western Sahara in order to provide humanitarian assistance to the civilian population there. In concluding, he underscored that his delegation's position with respect to the voting was attributable solely to a disagreement with the wording of the resolution and reflected an assessment of the work of the penholder. He reiterated his country's consistent support for MINURSO and its Head and for the key stabilizing role that it played in creating favourable conditions on the ground for the resumption of dialogue between the parties in order to advance the peace process.

Among the delegations voting in favour, the representative of the United States expressed regret that the Council had not been unanimous in support of renewing the mandate of MINURSO, as unity greatly enhanced United Nations efforts to achieve peace. He called upon all concerned to engage with the Personal Envoy in good faith, adding that a political solution was vital to promoting a peaceful and prosperous future for the people of Western Sahara and the region. He further stated that his delegation continued to view the Moroccan autonomy plan as serious, credible and realistic, and one potential approach to satisfying those aspirations. The representative of China expressed the hope that future Council resolutions on the extension of the mandate of MINURSO could reflect the latest changes in the situation, based on in-depth consultations, so as to arrive at a text that was acceptable to the relevant parties and that consensus could be achieved at an early date on the next steps in the political process of the question of Western Sahara. The representative of Brazil noted that, notwithstanding its many virtues, the text could have greatly benefited from a more balanced approach with regard to some of its innovative propositions, which could have proven useful in bridging some of the gaps seen during the negotiations. The representatives of the United Arab Emirates and Gabon expressed their support for the Moroccan autonomy plan, which presented credible prospects that allowed for a solution in line with the Charter, as a way out of the current impasse and also for a mutually acceptable political solution to be reached.

Meeting: the situation concerning Western Sahara, 2022

Meeting record and date	*Sub-item*	*Other documents*	*Rule 37 invitations*	*Rule 39 and other invitations*	*Speakers*	*Decision and vote (for-against-abstaining)*
S/PV.9168 27 October	Report of the Secretary-General on the situation concerning Western Sahara (S/2022/733)	Draft resolution submitted by United States (S/2022/801)			Seven Council members[a]	Resolution 2654 (2022) 13-0-2[b]

[a] Brazil, China, Gabon, Kenya, Russian Federation, United Arab Emirates and United States.
[b] *For*: Albania, Brazil, China, France, Gabon, Ghana, India, Ireland, Mexico, Norway, United Arab Emirates, United Kingdom, United States; *against*: none; *abstaining*: Kenya, Russian Federation.

[13] See S/PV.9168.

2. The situation in Somalia

In 2022, the Council held 12 meetings and adopted six decisions on the situation in Somalia, four of which were under Chapter VII of the Charter. Six meetings took the form of briefings, while the remaining six were convened to adopt decisions.[14] More information on the meetings, including on participants, speakers and outcomes, is provided in the table below. Council members also held informal consultations of the whole to discuss the situation in Somalia.[15]

During the period under review, the Council endorsed the decision of the Peace and Security Council of the African Union to reconfigure the African Union Mission in Somalia (AMISOM) into the African Union Transition Mission in Somalia (ATMIS),[16] and modified the name of the Committee previously known as the "Committee pursuant to resolution 751 (1992) concerning Somalia" to the "Committee pursuant to resolution 751 (1992) concerning Al-Shabaab".[17] For the first time since their introduction in 2008,[18] the Council did not renew the authorizations set out in resolution 2608 (2021) in connection with the fight against piracy and armed robbery at sea off the coast of Somalia, which had expired in March 2022.[19] More information on these and other developments is provided below.

In addition to its consideration of the reports of the Secretary-General on the situation in Somalia,[20] the Council heard regular briefings by the Special Representative of the Secretary-General for Somalia and Head of the United Nations Assistance Mission in Somalia (UNSOM) and the Special Representative of the Chairperson of the African Union Commission for Somalia and Head of ATMIS, as well as the latter's Deputy.[21] The Chair of the Committee pursuant to resolution 751 (1992) concerning Al-Shabaab also provided briefings to the Council.[22] In addition, the Council heard briefings by the Head of the Delegation of the European Union to the United Nations and the Special Representative of the European Union for the Horn of Africa.

In his briefings in 2022, the Special Representative of the Secretary-General provided updates to the Council concerning the political developments in Somalia, including the conclusion of the electoral process in May 2022, the worsening humanitarian conditions and the volatile security situation with a focus on the threat posed by Al-Shabaab and the reconfiguration of AMISOM into ATMIS.

Regarding the political developments, in February, the Special Representative stated that national elections in Somalia were more than one year behind the constitutionally prescribed schedule.[23] In his briefing in May, the Special Representative welcomed the conclusion of the electoral process in Somalia as a major milestone for the country.[24] On 15 May, Hassan Sheikh Mohamud had been elected President in a joint session of Parliament that had been peaceful, orderly and respectful of the rules of procedure. The Special Representative noted, nevertheless, that, contrary to the provisional Constitution of Somalia, the Somali people had not had the opportunity to vote in a one-person, one-vote election and that women had been elected to just 21 per cent of parliamentary seats. Many irregularities in the selection of Members of Parliament had been noted throughout the process, which had been repeatedly marred by violence. In September, the Special Representative reported that the political climate in Somalia was more conducive to addressing key national priorities following the conclusion of its contentious electoral process.[25] In June, the Parliament had unanimously endorsed the nominee for Prime Minister, Hamza Abdi Barre, and in August, confirmed his Cabinet. The Special Representative noted that only 13 per cent

[14] For more information on the format of meetings, see part II.

[15] See A/77/2, part II, chap. 6.

[16] Resolution 2628 (2022), para. 22. For more information on ATMIS, see part VIII, sect. III.

[17] Resolution 2662 (2022), para. 24. For more information on the Committee, see part IX, sect. I.B.

[18] See resolution 1816 (2008). For more information, see *Repertoire*, *Supplement 2008–2009*, part I.

[19] For more information on the authorizations in connection with the fight against piracy and armed robbery at sea off the coast of Somalia, see part VII of previous supplements covering the period from 2008 to 2021.

[20] S/2022/101, S/2022/392 and S/2022/665.

[21] Prior to the adoption of resolution 2628 (2022) on 31 March, the Special Representative of the Chairperson of the African Union Commission provided a briefing to the Council in his capacity as the Head of AMISOM.

[22] For more information, see part VII, sect. III.A, and part IX, sect. I.B.

[23] See S/PV.8965.

[24] See S/PV.9040.

[25] See S/PV.9125.

of Cabinet members were women and called again upon Somali leaders to take further measures to ensure the meaningful participation of women across institutions of government, as well as the inclusion of youth and historically marginalized groups. The Special Representative commended the President on his efforts to improve relations between the central Government and the federal member states in order to advance national priorities, as well as on his outreach to neighbouring countries.

The humanitarian situation remained extremely dire, with 7.7 million Somalis requiring assistance in 2022.[26] In May, the Special Representative reported that the conditions were worsening following the failure of a fourth consecutive rainy season and noted that the number of people affected by the drought had risen to 6.1 million, with the country facing a heightened risk of localized famine in six communities.[27] Later in the year, he noted that nearly half of the country's estimated population had been impacted by the worst drought in at least four decades, exacerbated by climate factors.[28] The Special Representative underscored that the ongoing humanitarian crisis had especially contributed to the vulnerability of displaced women and children.

According to the Special Representative, the security conditions remained volatile in 2022, with Al-Shabaab continuing to pose a major security threat by exploiting local political and security tensions and extensively using improvised explosive devices,[29] with its attacks focused on Mogadishu, South-West State and Hirshabelle.[30] In that context, the Special Representative commended the Somali security forces and ATMIS, who had safeguarded the electoral process and borne the brunt of Al-Shabaab's attacks.[31] On the reconfiguration of the African Union-led Mission, on 15 February, the Special Representative reported on the progress made with regard to the development of the joint African Union-Federal Government of Somalia concept of operations; the joint African Union-United Nations proposal on a reconfigured Mission; and the United Nations logistical options in support of a reconfigured Mission and the Somali security forces going forward, as requested under resolution 2568 (2021).[32] The Special Representative underscored that progress in the implementation of the Somalia Transition Plan was key for both the reconfiguration of AMISOM and to determine the pace of the transfer of responsibilities from AMISOM to the Somali security forces. In his final briefing of the year, the Special Representative reported that the implementation of the transition tasks mandated by resolution 2628 (2022) was advancing, including the request for the Federal Government of Somalia, the African Union, the European Union and the United Nations to identify relevant, clear and realistic benchmarks for progress.[33]

In their briefings, the Special Representative of the Chairperson of the African Union Commission for Somalia and his Deputy informed the Council about the electoral assistance and the security support that the Mission had provided to the Somali authorities, including through joint operations targeting Al-Shabaab.[34] The Special Representative noted that, following the reconfiguration of AMISOM into ATMIS earlier in the year, force generation and adequate and predictable funding and equipment attuned to force activity and mobility were key to degrading Al-Shabaab and ensuring the success of the transition. It was vital to scale up air strategic support with transport and attack helicopters, as well as adequate offensive weapons in all sectors, for both ATMIS and the Somali security forces.[35] Addressing the Council later in the year, the Deputy Special Representative and Acting Head of ATMIS noted that the upcoming drawdown of 2,000 troops by December 2022 would ultimately depend on the ability of the Federal Government to generate forces to fill the gaps left by the reduction of the ATMIS force.[36] A key requirement in that regard was the availability of sustainable, predictable and adequate levels of funding. Given the reluctance to consider a special United Nations meeting on financing for ATMIS and the Somali security forces, she appealed to the Council and all partners to ensure sustainable, predictable and adequate funding for the Mission for the duration of its mandate.

---

[26] See S/PV.8965.
[27] See S/PV.9040.
[28] See S/PV.9125.
[29] See S/PV.8965.
[30] See S/PV.9040.
[31] See S/PV.9040 and S/PV.9125.
[32] See S/PV.8965.
[33] See S/PV.9125.
[34] See S/PV.8965, S/PV.9040 and S/PV.9125.
[35] See S/PV.9040.
[36] See S/PV.9125.

In connection with the above, in her briefing to the Council in September, the Special Representative of the European Union for the Horn of Africa asserted that Al-Shabaab had grown to become the richest and strongest global franchise of Al-Qaida, threatening peace and security, as well as humanitarian efforts, in Somalia and the Horn of Africa.[37] She recalled that the European Union was committed to supporting ATMIS, but that there was no support for more of the same. She urged the Government to provide clarity on the Somalia Transition Plan and the national security architecture and noted that the only exit strategy for ATMIS was to support the Somali security sector.

Regarding the fight against piracy off the coast of Somalia, in his briefing in February, the Head of the Delegation of the European Union to the United Nations expressed the hope that the Council would be able to agree on a revised resolution that better reflected Somali priorities, while also renewing the legal provisions necessary for the continuation of Operation Atalanta of the European Union Naval Force for at least the remainder of the year.[38] If the authorizations set out in the resolution were not extended beyond 3 March, Operation Atalanta would not have the authorization to fight piracy and to protect the deliveries of the World Food Programme and other vulnerable vessels in the Somali territorial waters. At the same meeting, some Council members[39] expressed support for finding a solution for the renewal of the authorizations set out in the resolution on maritime security off the coast of Somalia. The representative of Somalia, however, reiterated that the Federal Government of Somalia would no longer request any renewal or modification of the authorizations set out in the resolution, since it had successfully achieved its intended objectives after nearly 15 years.[40]

During the period under review, Council members' discussions were centred on political developments, including the conduct of elections, the deteriorating humanitarian conditions, the continued threat posed by Al-Shabaab and the reconfiguration of AMISOM into ATMIS.

On the political developments in 2022, Council members welcomed the conclusion of the electoral process and the election of the President, Hassan Sheikh Mohamud,[41] and took note of the formation of a new government led by the Prime Minister, Hamza Abdi Barre.[42] Concerning the representation of women, while several Council members noted that it fell short of the 30 per cent quota, they congratulated Sadia Yasin Haji Samatar on being the first Somali woman elected Deputy Speaker.[43] Throughout the year, several Council members also called for the meaningful participation of women in political processes, including in decision-making.[44] In that regard, the representatives of India and Brazil took note of the increase in the participation of women following the appointment of the Cabinet, while the representative of Ireland indicated that the number of women appointed to the new Cabinet fell short of the country's own commitments.[45] Council members also discussed the constitutional reform process[46] and national reconciliation efforts being made by the Federal Government and the federal member states of Somalia.[47]

Concerning the humanitarian situation, Council members discussed the deteriorating conditions resulting in acute food insecurity and displacement, exacerbated by an unprecedented drought. In that

[37] Ibid.

[38] See S/PV.8965.

[39] United Kingdom, United States, France and Ireland.

[40] See also the letter dated 26 February from the representative of Somalia to the President of the Security Council (S/2022/162) and the report of the Secretary-General on the situation with respect to piracy and armed robbery at sea off the coast of Somalia, in which he stated that the international naval operations within the territorial sea of Somalia had ceased following the expiration on 3 March of the relevant authorizations set out in resolution 2608 (2021) (S/2022/819).

[41] See S/PV.9040.

[42] See S/PV.9125 (Ireland, India, United Arab Emirates, Albania, Mexico and Brazil).

[43] See S/PV.9040 (United Kingdom, Norway, France, Albania, Ireland, Mexico and United States).

[44] See S/PV.9040 (Albania, Ireland and Mexico); S/PV.9071 (Gabon); and S/PV.9125 (Ireland, Norway and Albania).

[45] See S/PV.9125.

[46] See S/PV.8965 (United Kingdom); S/PV.9040 (United Kingdom, Norway, France, Ireland, Gabon (also on behalf of Ghana and Kenya) and India); and S/PV.9125 (Ghana (also on behalf of Gabon and Kenya), Norway, Albania and United States).

[47] See S/PV.8965 (Norway); S/PV.9040 (United Kingdom, Norway, Ireland, Gabon (also on behalf of Ghana and Kenya) and United States); and S/PV.9125 (United Kingdom, Ghana (also on behalf of Gabon and Kenya), Norway, China, United States and Brazil).

context, several Council members noted the growing need for humanitarian assistance,[48] with some also referring to the impact of climate change as a contributing factor.[49] Later in the year, Council members warned about the risk of famine in Somalia and called for the scaling-up of efforts to avert such a scenario.[50]

On the security front, the discussions in the Council were focused on the persistent threat posed by Al-Shabaab, with members condemning the group's terrorist attacks, which continued in 2022. In connection with the reconfiguration of the African Union-led Mission, Council members paid tribute to the efforts of troop- and police-contributing countries that had served in AMISOM and welcomed the establishment of the successor Mission.[51] Noting that it was rare that the Council got the opportunity to help to shape the transition of a mission, the representative of the United States stated that the mandate of ATMIS provided the opportunity to adapt and reinvigorate the African-led international effort against Al-Shabaab. Several Council members underscored the importance of ensuring sustainable and predictable financing for ATMIS to be effective in fulfilling its mandate.[52] The representative of France expressed the view that no new funding for ATMIS, regardless of the amount, would suffice without Somali efforts to generate armed forces, together with the federal states, or without strong support from ATMIS to help Somali forces and conduct offensive operations with them.[53] The representative of the United Kingdom, noting that her country provided funding to ATMIS, encouraged other Member States to join in that endeavour so that Somali forces could develop the capacity and capabilities they needed to end the threat posed by Al-Shabaab.[54]

In 2022, the decisions of the Council were also focused on the issues outlined above, and specifically on the reconfiguration of AMISOM and the review of the mandate of UNSOM.

Concerning the reconfiguration of AMISOM, on 31 March, acting under Chapter VII of the Charter, the Council unanimously adopted resolution 2628 (2022). By that resolution, the Council endorsed the decision of the Peace and Security Council of the African Union to reconfigure AMISOM into ATMIS and authorized, for an initial period of 12 months, the member States of the African Union to take all necessary measures to carry out its mandate to reduce the threat posed by Al-Shabaab, support the capacity-building of the integrated Somali security and police forces, conduct a phased handover of security responsibilities to Somalia and support peace and reconciliation efforts in support of the development of a stable, federal, sovereign and united Somalia.[55] The Council further decided that the strategic objectives of ATMIS would include conducting jointly planned and targeted operations with Somali security forces to degrade Al-Shabaab and affiliates linked to Islamic State in Iraq and the Levant (ISIL/Da'esh); supporting Somali security forces by, inter alia, jointly holding priority population centres and providing protection for the local communities, United Nations personnel and installations; assisting the Federal Government in the implementation of stabilization efforts for all recovered areas; and supporting the capacity development of the Somali security forces.[56] By the same resolution, the Council maintained the number of authorized uniformed personnel at the same level as for AMISOM, at 19,626, inclusive of a minimum of 1,040 police personnel including five formed police units, until 31 December 2022, and endorsed the decision of the Peace and Security Council of the African Union to draw down 2,000 personnel by that date.[57] The Council also authorized the member States of the African Union,

---

48 See S/PV.8965 (United Kingdom, India, Ghana (also on behalf of Gabon and Kenya), United States, Norway, Ireland, Mexico, United Arab Emirates, China and Albania); S/PV.9040 (France and United Arab Emirates); and S/PV.9125 (India, Ghana (also on behalf of Gabon and Kenya), Albania and France).

49 See S/PV.8965 (United Kingdom, France, Norway, Ireland, Mexico, United Arab Emirates and Albania); S/PV.9040 (Norway, Albania, Ireland, Gabon (also on behalf of Ghana and Kenya) and Mexico); S/PV.9071 (Ghana); and S/PV.9125 (Ireland, Ghana (also on behalf of Gabon and Kenya), United Arab Emirates, Mexico and France).

50 See S/PV.9040 (United Kingdom, Norway, China, Albania, Ireland, Gabon (also on behalf of Ghana and Kenya), Mexico, United Arab Emirates, India and United States); and S/PV.9125 (United Kingdom, Ireland, Norway, United Arab Emirates, Mexico, China, United States and Brazil).

51 See S/PV.9009.

52 See S/PV.9040 (China, Gabon (also on behalf of Ghana and Kenya), Russian Federation and India); and S/PV.9125 (Ghana (also on behalf of Gabon and Kenya) and China).

53 See S/PV.9040.

54 See S/PV.9125.

55 Resolution 2628 (2022), para. 22.

56 Ibid., para. 23.

57 Ibid., para. 26.

between 1 January and 31 March 2023, to deploy up to 17,626 uniformed personnel, inclusive of a minimum of 1,040 police personnel including five formed police units.[58]

On 21 December, acting under Chapter VII, the Council unanimously adopted resolution 2670 (2022), in which it noted the African Union request to extend phase 1 of ATMIS for the drawdown of 2,000 ATMIS personnel until 30 June 2023 and exceptionally extended its authorizations and affirmed that paragraph 27 of resolution 2628 (2022) was annulled.[59]

With regard to UNSOM, on 26 May, the Council unanimously adopted resolution 2632 (2022), by which it extended the mandate of the Mission for a period of five months, until 31 October 2022.[60] In the same resolution, the Council welcomed the conclusion of the electoral process, resulting in the election of the President, Hassan Sheikh Mohamud, allowing for the peaceful transition of power, and underscored that the swift formation of an inclusive federal government, with the full, equal and meaningful participation of women, would help to progress critical national priorities, promote national reconciliation and security, and support transition from international security support.[61] The Council also underscored that the mandate of UNSOM was complementary to the mandates of ATMIS, the United Nations Support Office in Somalia (UNSOS) and the United Nations country team, and the support provided by the African Union and international partners.[62] Furthermore, the Council requested the Secretary-General to undertake a strategic review of UNSOM to include recommendations for clearly defined, measurable and realistic benchmarks to track the timely execution and achievement of its mandate and to report to the Council by 30 September 2022.[63]

On 31 October, the Council adopted resolution 2657 (2022),[64] with one abstention, by which it endorsed the proposed benchmarks and recommendations set out in the strategic review and extended the mandate and tasks of UNSOM, for one additional year, until 31 October 2023.[65] It requested UNSOM to maintain and strengthen its presence across Somalia and to continue to strengthen its cooperation with Somalia and ATMIS.[66] Recognizing the renewed operations against Al-Shabaab, the Council encouraged UNSOM to support Somalia (a) to ensure that plans were in place to protect civilians and communities in areas which were the focus of military operations, prior to, during and after engagements; (b) to accelerate implementation of the national stabilization strategy and state-level stabilization plans; (c) to support Somali civilian leadership, ownership and oversight in the planning and coordination of stabilization efforts; (d) to promote expansion of a governance and service delivery to areas and districts where fragility persisted; and (e) to ensure timely, balanced support to areas newly or recently recovered from Al-Shabaab.[67] In explaining the vote, the representative of the United States stated that his country was encouraged by the fact that resolution 2657 (2022) had incorporated recommendations from the strategic review of UNSOM, including further coordination between ATMIS, UNSOS, the United Nations country team and other multilateral and bilateral partners.[68] The representative of China noted that his country had abstained in the voting as it considered that there was still need for improvement in resolution 2657 (2022) on issues such as the protection of civilians, humanitarian access, climate change and the protection of children, and that the future direction of relevant efforts must be clarified.[69] The representative of the Russian Federation said that her delegation had voted in favour, but that it shared the view of China concerning the imbalanced nature of some of the wording of the resolution, including with respect to humanitarian issues, the protection of children in armed conflict and human rights. She also expressed regret that the resolution did not sufficiently reflect the recommendations of the strategic review of UNSOM and its mandate conducted by the Secretariat's independent team.

---

[58] Ibid., para. 27.
[59] Resolution 2670 (2022), second preambular paragraph and para. 1 (a).
[60] Resolution 2632 (2022), para. 1. For more information on the mandate of UNSOM, see part X, sect. II.
[61] Resolution 2632 (2022), third preambular paragraph.
[62] Ibid., fourth preambular paragraph.
[63] Ibid., para. 3. For more information on the report on the independent strategic review of UNSOM, see S/2022/716.
[64] See S/PV.9177.
[65] Resolution 2657 (2022), paras. 2 and 4.
[66] Ibid., para. 6.
[67] Ibid., para. 7.
[68] See S/PV.9177. See also resolution 2657 (2022), para. 3.
[69] See S/PV.9177.

In 2022, the Council also heard three briefings by the Chair of the Committee established pursuant to resolution 751 (1992) and received updates about the Committee's activities in the reporting period. On 24 February, the Chair reported that Committee members welcomed the continued improvement in the relationship between the Panel of Experts and the Federal Government of Somalia, particularly with regard to cooperation on the implementation of the charcoal ban.[70] On 21 June, the Chair noted, inter alia, that the members of the Committee had expressed the view that the successful conclusion of the presidential elections presented a renewed opportunity to cooperate and collaborate with the Federal Government on moving forward with important issues that fell under the Committee's remit.[71] At the same meeting, the representative of Ghana underscored the need for cooperation and unified action within the Council, which was critical to ensuring strict compliance with all the sanctions measures and sustained pressure on all parties to end and prevent all grave violations against children. The representative of Gabon stated that his country supported, inter alia, the recommendation that encouraged the Federal Government of Somalia and its partners to make various efforts in order to dry up the finances of Al-Shabaab, including through restrictions and assets seizure, targeting in particular the money that Al-Shabaab considered essential for carrying out its operations. In his last briefing of the year, held on 19 October, the Chair informed the Council about the Committee's activities in the reporting period, including about the thematic reports received from the Panel of Experts.[72]

The Council adopted two resolutions concerning the sanctions regime relating to Somalia. On 15 November, the Council adopted resolution 2661 (2022), by which it extended resolution 2607 (2021) for two days, until 17 November 2022.[73] On 17 November, acting under Chapter VII, the Council adopted resolution 2662 (2022), with four abstentions.[74] By that resolution, the Council renewed the mandate of the Panel of Experts until 15 December 2023, and expanded the tasks referred to in paragraph 11 of resolution 2444 (2018) to include those contained in paragraphs 32 and 35 of the resolution.[75] By the resolution, the Council also renewed the maritime interdiction of charcoal, weapons or military equipment and improvised explosive devices components until 15 November 2023,[76] and reaffirmed the ban on components of improvised explosive devices.[77] In addition, the Council reaffirmed the partial arms embargo and the exemptions on deliveries on weapons and military equipment or the provision of technical advice, financial and other assistance, and training related to military activities whose beneficiaries were the Somali security and police institutions or those listed in paragraph 21.[78] It further confirmed its commitment to working with Somalia to ensure that the notification procedures were lifted progressively, in the light of the progress made against the benchmarks set out in the technical assessment (S/2022/698).[79] The Council also recalled previous decisions concerning the asset freeze, travel ban and charcoal ban measures, and renewed the humanitarian exemption to the assets freeze without specifying an expiry date.[80] By the same resolution, the Council decided that the name of the Committee established pursuant to resolution 751 (1992) concerning Somalia was to be known as the "Security Council Committee pursuant to resolution 751 (1992) concerning Al-Shabaab".[81]

In the resolution, the Council emphasized that its objective was to establish a consolidated framework to strengthen state- and peace-building in Somalia, defeat Al-Shabaab and complement the mandates of UNSOM and ATMIS, including in particular through: (a) supporting weapons and ammunition management and security sector reform in Somalia (pillar 1); and (b) degrading the threat posed by Al-Shabaab (pillar 2).[82] By the same resolution, the Council requested the Somali Government

---

[70] See S/PV.8976.
[71] See S/PV.9071.
[72] See S/PV.9157.
[73] Resolution 2661 (2022), para. 1.
[74] See S/PV.9196.
[75] Resolution 2662 (2022), para. 44. For more information on the mandate of the Panel of Experts, see part IX, sect. I.B.
[76] Resolution 2662 (2022), para. 41.
[77] Ibid., para. 37.
[78] Ibid., paras. 10, 11, 14, 15, 18 and 21.
[79] Ibid., para. 13.
[80] Ibid., paras. 26, 28 and 34.
[81] Ibid., para. 24. For more information on the mandate of the Committee, see part IX, sect. I.B.
[82] Resolution 2662 (2022), para. 2.

authorities to consider developing and submitting a proposal for consideration by the Committee, for the one-off, complete disposal of charcoal stockpiles to prevent Al-Shabaab from profiting from the sale.[83]

In explanation of their votes, several Council members presented their views on the sanctions regime relating to Somalia.[84] In addition, the representative of the Russian Federation expressed disagreement with several aspects of resolution 2662 (2022), including references to questions relating to bilateral relations between Djibouti and Eritrea and the approach to Al-Shabaab. She said that her delegation continued to be troubled by the ambivalent approach to Al-Shabaab, which blurred the focus of global counter-terrorism efforts. Despite the dangerous nature of that entity and its affiliation with ISIL/Da'esh and Al-Qaida, she added that it continued to be "kept at a distance from the Committees established pursuant to resolutions 1267 (1999), 1989 (2011) and 2253 (2015), respectively". In that regard, she expressed the view that, with the resolution, another erroneous step had been taken by enshrining on paper the notion that Al-Shabaab would be dealt with by the Committee pursuant to resolution 751 (1992), which was in charge of the Somalia sanctions regime. The representative of Kenya explained that his country had voted in favour to demonstrate its backing for the resolution's tougher measures against the Al-Qaida affiliate in Somalia. He added that Kenya and the other African members of the Council were instrumental in ensuring that resolution 2662 (2022) was framed in a way that clarified that the enemy was a terrorist group, Al-Shabaab. He also stated that they had increased pressure on the group by making it easier for the Federal Government to acquire more lethal weapons. The representative of the United Arab Emirates stressed that a critical aspect, which must be part of any discussion on countering terrorism, was the importance of not linking terrorism to religion and welcomed the inclusion of a paragraph jointly put forward by the United Arab Emirates and the three African members of the Council that condemned terrorist groups' attempts to craft distorted narratives based on the misinterpretation and misrepresentation of religion.

Meetings: the situation in Somalia, 2022

Meeting record and date	*Sub-item*	*Other documents*	*Rule 37 invitations*	*Rule 39 and other invitations*	*Speakers*	*Decision and vote (for-against-abstaining)*
S/PV.8965 15 February	Report of the Secretary-General on the situation in Somalia (S/2022/101)		Somalia	Special Representative of the Secretary-General for Somalia and Head of the United Nations Assistance Mission in Somalia, Special Representative of the Chairperson of the African Union Commission for Somalia and Head of the African Union Mission in Somalia, Head of the Delegation of the European Union to the United Nations	13 Council members,[a] all invitees	
S/PV.8976 24 February					One Council member (Ireland)[b]	

[83] Ibid., para. 36 (b).

[84] See S/PV.9196 (United Kingdom, United States, United Arab Emirates, Gabon, Russian Federation, Kenya, China and Ghana). For more information on discussions relating to Article 41, see part VII, sect. III.

Meeting record and date	*Sub-item*	*Other documents*	*Rule 37 invitations*	*Rule 39 and other invitations*	*Speakers*	*Decision and vote (for-against-abstaining)*
S/PV.9009 31 March		Draft resolution submitted by United Kingdom (S/2022/277)	Somalia		Six Council members,[c] invitee	Resolution 2628 (2022) 15-0-0 (adopted under Chapter VII)
S/PV.9040 23 May	Report of the Secretary-General on the situation in Somalia (S/2022/392)		Somalia	Special Representative of the Secretary-General, Special Representative of the Chairperson of the African Union Commission for Somalia and Head of the African Union Transition Mission for Somalia (ATMIS)	13 Council members,[d] all invitees	
S/PV.9044 26 May	Report of the Secretary-General on the situation in Somalia (S/2022/392)	Draft resolution submitted by United Kingdom (S/2022/412)	Somalia		Invitee	Resolution 2632 (2022) 15-0-0
S/PV.9071 21 June					Three Council members (Gabon, Ghana and Ireland)[e]	
S/PV.9125 7 September	Report of the Secretary-General on the situation in Somalia (S/2022/665)		Somalia	Special Representative of the Secretary-General, Deputy Special Representative of the Chairperson of the African Union Commission for Somalia and Acting Head of ATMIS, Special Representative of the European Union for the Horn of Africa	13 Council members,[a] all invitees	
S/PV.9157 19 October	Letters dated 10 and 15 October 2022 from the Chair of the Security Council Committee				One Council member (Ireland)[f]	

Meeting record and date	*Sub-item*	*Other documents*	*Rule 37 invitations*	*Rule 39 and other invitations*	*Speakers*	*Decision and vote (for-against-abstaining)*
	pursuant to resolution 751 (1992) concerning Somalia addressed to the President of the Security Council (S/2022/754 and S/2022/766)					
S/PV.9177 31 October	Letter dated 26 September 2022 from the Secretary-General addressed to the President of the Security Council (S/2022/716) Letter dated 15 October 2022 from the Chair of the Security Council Committee pursuant to resolution 751 (1992) concerning Somalia addressed to the President of the Security Council (S/2022/766)	Draft resolution submitted by United Kingdom (S/2022/812)	Somalia		Six Council members,[g] invitee	Resolution 2657 (2022) 14-0-1[h]
S/PV.9193 15 November	Letter dated 15 September 2022 from the Secretary-General addressed to the President of the Security Council (S/2022/698)	Draft resolution submitted by United Kingdom (S/2022/855)				Resolution 2661 (2022) 15-0-0 (adopted under Chapter VII)
S/PV.9196 17 November		Draft resolution submitted by United Kingdom (S/2022/865)	Somalia		Eight Council members,[i] invitee	Resolution 2662 (2022) 11-0-4[j] (adopted under Chapter VII)

Meeting record and date	Sub-item	Other documents	Rule 37 invitations	Rule 39 and other invitations	Speakers	Decision and vote (for-against-abstaining)
S/PV.9232 21 December		Draft resolution submitted by United Kingdom (S/2022/983)			Six Council members[k]	Resolution 2670 (2022) 15-0-0 (adopted under Chapter VII)

[a] Albania, Brazil, China, France, Ghana (also on behalf of Gabon and Kenya), India, Ireland, Mexico, Norway, Russian Federation, United Arab Emirates, United Kingdom and United States.
[b] The representative of Ireland spoke on behalf of the Chair of the Committee established pursuant to resolution 751 (1992) concerning Somalia.
[c] Albania, China, India, United Arab Emirates, United Kingdom and United States.
[d] Albania, Brazil, China, France, Gabon (also on behalf of Ghana and Kenya), India, Ireland, Mexico, Norway, Russian Federation, United Arab Emirates, United Kingdom and United States.
[e] The representative of Ireland spoke in her capacity as Chair of the Committee established pursuant to resolution 751 (1992) concerning Somalia.
[f] The representative of Ireland spoke in his capacity as Chair of the Committee established pursuant to resolution 751 (1992) concerning Somalia.
[g] China, Kenya, Russian Federation, United Arab Emirates, United Kingdom and United States.
[h] *For*: Albania, Brazil, France, Gabon, Ghana, India, Ireland, Kenya, Mexico, Norway, Russian Federation, United Arab Emirates, United Kingdom, United States; *against*: none; *abstaining*: China.
[i] China, Gabon, Ghana, Kenya, Russian Federation, United Arab Emirates, United Kingdom and United States.
[j] *For*: Albania, Brazil, France, India, Ireland, Kenya, Mexico, Norway, United Arab Emirates, United Kingdom, United States; *against*: none; *abstaining*: China, Gabon, Ghana, Russian Federation.
[k] China, France, Ireland, Norway, United Kingdom and United States.

3. The situation in the Great Lakes region

During the period under review, the Council held two meetings on the situation in the Great Lakes region, both in the form of briefings.[85] The Council did not adopt any decisions under this item in 2022. More information on the meetings, including on participants and speakers, is provided in the table below. Council members also held informal consultations of the whole in connection with the item.[86]

In 2022, the Council heard briefings by the Special Envoy of the Secretary-General for the Great Lakes Region, the Executive Secretary of the International Conference on the Great Lakes Region and a civil society representative. In addition, the Chair of the Peacebuilding Commission submitted written advice, under rule 39 of the provisional rules of procedure, in connection with the two briefings.[87] Further to the two reports of the Secretary-General,[88] during his briefings to the Council, the Special Envoy for the Great Lakes Region focused on the activities of his Office in supporting the implementation of the Peace, Security and Cooperation Framework for the Democratic Republic of the Congo and the Region and the progress achieved on the political and security fronts, as well as the related challenges.

At the meeting held on 27 April, the Special Envoy noted that, since his previous briefing to the Council, the situation in the Great Lakes region had shown an encouraging trend in terms of dialogue, cooperation and integration and, in general, the continued will to tackle the root causes of the instability.[89] However, that positive trend had been disrupted by the security and humanitarian crisis in the eastern Democratic Republic of the Congo, compounded by the resumption of military activities by the Mouvement du 23 mars in the last quarter of 2021, with attacks on several positions of the Armed Forces of the Democratic Republic of the Congo.[90] The Special Envoy expressed regret that the Allied Democratic Forces and other local armed groups continued to commit atrocities against civilians. Despite that

[85] For more information on the format of meetings, see part II.
[86] See A/77/2, part II, chap. 11. See also S/2022/868.
[87] See S/2022/353 and S/2022/789. For more information on written advice submitted in accordance with rule 39, see part II, sect. VII, and part IX, sect. VII.
[88] S/2022/276 and S/2022/735.
[89] See S/PV.9023.
[90] For more information on the situation concerning the Democratic Republic of the Congo, see sect. 4 below.

fragility, he remained convinced that it was still possible to consolidate the significant gains that had been made in the region and to move progressively towards a lasting peace. To that end, the Special Envoy called for efforts to be made on at least three levels: (a) increased cooperation on security matters; (b) direct, standing dialogue at the highest level between the leaders in the region to ease tensions and strengthen trust; and (c) continued support by the international community for the region.

With respect to security cooperation, the Special Envoy noted, inter alia, the joint operations conducted by the Democratic Republic of the Congo and Uganda, the memorandum of understanding between Burundi and the Democratic Republic of the Congo, the establishment of the Contact and Coordination Group on non-military measures, as well as the efforts on devising a counter-terrorism strategy at the level of the International Conference on the Great Lakes Region. With regard to the dialogue aimed at reducing tensions in the region, the Special Envoy welcomed the progress made in normalizing the relations between Rwanda and Uganda and the relations between Burundi and Rwanda. Concerning the support of the international community, the Special Envoy called upon the Council and the International Contact Group for the Great Lakes Region to support regional dialogue efforts and welcomed the close cooperation between the Office of the Special Envoy and the United Nations Organization Stabilization Mission in the Democratic Republic of the Congo (MONUSCO). The Special Envoy further informed the Council about his priority initiatives, which included continuing good offices and diplomatic efforts aimed at improving relations among the countries of the region; supporting the effective deployment of the operational unit of the Contact and Coordination Group on non-military measures; providing technical and logistical support to the Nairobi peace process; promoting enhanced national and regional ownership of the Regional Initiative against the Illegal Exploitation of Natural Resources; promoting the economic empowerment of women as a peacebuilding strategy; and supporting the efforts to combat impunity and promote human rights.

In his briefing to the Council, the Executive Secretary of the International Conference on the Great Lakes Region noted that the region faced various security challenges, emanating mainly from the activities of negative forces and armed groups operating in parts of the Democratic Republic of the Congo, the Central African Republic and South Sudan. An independent expert on the Great Lakes region, Dinesh Mahtani, provided a briefing in which he focused on the increasingly interconnected dynamics of insecurity in the region with other parts of the continent. He noted that the Governments of the Great Lakes and East Africa regions had agreed to possibly launch joint military operations against armed groups in the Democratic Republic of the Congo but indicated that, in addition to the regional trust deficit, there were serious challenges to the implementation of any such proposed force. While the use of force should eventually constitute an important component in any exercise to neutralize armed groups in the eastern Democratic Republic of the Congo, it was crucial that all interested parties first worked together to help to implement the country's strategy on the demobilization of armed groups and rebuild and consolidate trust among the neighbours of the Democratic Republic of the Congo.

During the discussion, Council members expressed concern about the security situation in parts of the Great Lakes region, particularly in the eastern Democratic Republic of the Congo. They also noted the impact of the illicit exploitation of natural resources on the security and stability in the region. Several Council members raised the issue of a growing terrorist threat in the region and the connections between armed groups and terrorist organizations.[91] A number of Council members also expressed concern about the increase of human rights violations and abuses.[92] Among the positive developments, Council members noted the admission of the Democratic Republic of the Congo to the East African Community. Several Council members also welcomed the establishment of the operational cell of the Contact and Coordination Group on non-military measures,[93] as well as the commitment to dialogue that emanated from the meetings of the Regional Oversight Mechanism of the Peace, Security and Cooperation Framework.[94] In addition to Council members, the representatives of Burundi, the Democratic Republic of the Congo and Rwanda also

---

[91] France, Albania, Kenya (also on behalf of Gabon and Ghana), India and Russian Federation.

[92] Albania, Ireland, United States, Norway and United Kingdom.

[93] Albania, India and United States.

[94] Brazil, China, Ireland, India, Norway, Mexico and Russian Federation.

took part in the discussion and expressed their views on the situation in the Great Lakes region, bilateral relations, regional security and economic cooperation and the challenges that were yet to be overcome.

In his second briefing, on 26 October, the Special Envoy said that the Great Lakes region continued to experience instability due to the militancy of armed groups, whose activities fuelled the rekindling of mistrust and tensions among the countries of the region, in particular between the Democratic Republic of the Congo and Rwanda.[95] The illicit exploitation of and trade in natural resources continued to fuel the vicious cycle of intercommunal clashes, the activities of armed groups and the use of such resources by cross-border criminal networks. The humanitarian situation continued to be of concern, with more than 4.9 million refugees and asylum-seekers having fled owing to the violence and climate-related issues. In response to and despite such challenges, the countries of the region remained engaged through various initiatives, including the East African Community peace process on the situation in the eastern Democratic Republic of the Congo, involving both military and non-military efforts. Regarding the deployment of the East African Community Regional Force, the Special Envoy recalled the vital importance of effective coordination with MONUSCO. On non-military initiatives, the Special Envoy reported, inter alia, that his Office had facilitated the first reconnaissance-and-contact mission of the operational cell of the Contact and Coordination Group to South Kivu Province, the goal of which was to engage with local actors to identify opportunities for contact with armed groups and facilitate their disarmament and voluntary repatriation without political preconditions. He highlighted his joint advocacy mission with the Executive Secretary of the International Conference on the Great Lakes Region to Paris and Brussels to increase support for better natural resource governance and announced plans for future missions to the member States of the Conference, aware that national and regional ownership of the Regional Initiative against the Illegal Exploitation of Natural Resources was a prerequisite for its effectiveness. The Office also continued to support efforts to promote greater participation of women in electoral processes and bodies and to conduct activities aimed at increasing the participation of youth in conflict prevention and peacebuilding. The Special Envoy appealed to all the signatory countries to step up their efforts to fully implement the Peace, Security and Cooperation Framework for the Democratic Republic of the Congo and the Region and other regional agreements, solicited the support of Council members, and further appealed to the entire international community to lend more substantial multifaceted support to the regional initiatives and to the United Nations action plan for the Great Lakes region.

In their discussion, Council members deliberated on the security situation in the region, including the threat posed by the activities of the armed groups in the eastern Democratic Republic of the Congo and the question of illicit trade in natural resources as one of the root causes and contributing factors of conflict in the region. Echoing the Special Envoy, Council members called for the implementation of the Peace, Security and Cooperation Framework for the Democratic Republic of the Congo and the Region, as well as other regional agreements. Council members specifically welcomed the progress on the joint road map for peace in the Central African Republic aimed at normalizing the political relations between the Democratic Republic of the Congo and Rwanda, as well as the increasing coordination with the Nairobi process between the countries of the East African Community. Some Council members[96] also commended the States members of the International Conference on the Great Lakes Region on the adoption of the Kinshasa Declaration on Enhancing Regional Judicial Cooperation in the Great Lakes Region in June 2022. On the deployment of the East African Community Regional Force, several Council members[97] underscored the need for effective coordination of its activities with MONUSCO and the national forces. Among those members, some[98] encouraged the regional force to comply with obligations under international law, including international humanitarian law and international human rights law. Council members[99] also discussed the implementation of non-military measures in the region, notably the Disarmament, Demobilization, Community Recovery and Stabilization Programme, with some[100] citing the operationalization of the Contact and Coordination Group, and some[101] the need to combat hate speech, disinformation and misinformation. Several Council members[102] further called for the inclusion of women

---

[95] See S/PV.9165.
[96] France, India, Albania and Mexico.
[97] France, Russian Federation, United States, Norway, United Kingdom, Mexico and Ireland.
[98] France, United States, United Kingdom and Ireland.
[99] France, India, Kenya (also on behalf of Gabon and Ghana), Norway, Brazil, United Kingdom, China and Mexico.
[100] France, India, Kenya (also on behalf of Gabon and Ghana), China and Albania.
[101] Kenya (also on behalf of Gabon and Ghana), United Arab Emirates, Brazil and Albania.
[102] France, United Arab Emirates, Norway, Brazil, Albania and Ireland.

in political and peace processes and their full, equal and meaningful participation at all levels. In addition to Council members, the representatives of Burundi, the Democratic Republic of the Congo, Rwanda and South Africa made statements and expressed their views on the situation in the Great Lakes region.

Meetings: the situation in the Great Lakes region, 2022

Meeting record and date	*Sub-item*	*Other documents*	*Rule 37 invitations*	*Rule 39 and other invitations*	*Speakers*	*Decision and vote (for-against-abstaining)*
S/PV.9023 27 April	Report of the Secretary-General on the implementation of the Peace, Security and Cooperation Framework for the Democratic Republic of the Congo and the Region (S/2022/276)		Burundi, Democratic Republic of the Congo, Rwanda	Special Envoy of the Secretary-General for the Great Lakes Region, Executive Secretary of the International Conference on the Great Lakes Region, independent expert on the Great Lakes region	13 Council members,[a] all invitees[b]	
S/PV.9165 26 October	Report of the Secretary-General on the implementation of the Peace, Security and Cooperation Framework for the Democratic Republic of the Congo and the Region (S/2022/735)		Burundi, Democratic Republic of the Congo, Rwanda, South Africa	Special Envoy of the Secretary-General	13 Council members,[a] all invitees	

[a] Albania, Brazil, China, France, India, Ireland, Kenya (also on behalf of Gabon and Ghana), Mexico, Norway, Russian Federation, United Arab Emirates, United Kingdom and United States.
[b] The Executive Secretary of the International Conference on the Great Lakes Region and the independent expert on the Great Lakes region participated in the meeting by videoconference.

4. The situation concerning the Democratic Republic of the Congo

During the period under review, the Council held eight meetings and adopted three resolutions under Chapter VII of the Charter and one presidential statement in relation to the situation concerning the Democratic Republic of the Congo. Three meetings were convened to adopt a decision of the Council, and five took the form of briefings.[103] More information on the meetings, including on participants, speakers and outcomes, is provided in the table below. The Council also held one private (closed) meeting with countries contributing troops and police to the United Nations Organization Stabilization Mission in the Democratic Republic of the Congo (MONUSCO), pursuant to resolution 1353 (2001).[104] In

[103] For more information on the format of meetings, see part II.
[104] The private meeting was held on 6 December in connection with the item entitled "Meeting of the Security Council with the troop- and police-contributing countries pursuant to resolution 1353 (2001), annex II, sections A and B"; see S/PV.9209. See also A/77/2, part II, chap. 21.

addition, Council members held informal consultations of the whole to discuss the situation concerning the Democratic Republic of the Congo.[105]

In 2022, further to the quarterly reports of the Secretary-General,[106] the Council heard regular briefings by the Special Representative for the Democratic Republic of the Congo and Head of MONUSCO, as well as briefings by representatives of civil society and subregional organizations.[107] The Council also heard briefings by the Special Envoy of the Secretary-General for the Great Lakes Region and the Assistant Secretary-General for Africa in the Departments of Political and Peacebuilding Affairs and Peace Operations.[108] Consistent with prior practice, the Council also heard briefings by the Chair of the Committee established pursuant to resolution 1533 (2004) concerning the Democratic Republic of the Congo.[109] In addition to the representative of the Democratic Republic of the Congo, in 2022, the representatives of Burundi, Rwanda and Uganda also participated in the meetings held under this item.

In her quarterly briefings to the Council, the Special Representative focused on the deteriorating security situation in the east of the country, following the resurgence of the previously dormant Mouvement du 23 mars (M23) and the continued attacks by other armed groups. She provided updates on the regional initiatives aimed at defusing tensions and reported on the political developments, including the progress made on the preparations for the elections scheduled for December 2023. Lastly, the Special Representative provided further information to the Council about the phased drawdown of MONUSCO.

On the security situation, the Special Representative explained that, in addition to the attacks perpetrated by the Allied Democratic Forces and the Coopérative pour le développement du Congo in North Kivu and Ituri, there had been an alarming increase in the activities by the M23 in North Kivu, as well as violence against civilians in South Kivu carried out by the Mai-Mai groups.[110] In North Kivu, the situation was compounded by the disturbing use of improvised explosive devices by the Allied Democratic Forces. In June, the Special Representative stated that the escalation of the M23 attacks and the resulting regional tensions had undermined the positive momentum between the Democratic Republic of the Congo and Rwanda and reported that the resurgence of that group had had broad repercussions for security, human rights and the humanitarian situation in the eastern part of the country, including the possibility that MONUSCO could find itself dealing with a threat that went beyond its current capacities.[111] In her September briefing, the Special Representative reported that MONUSCO remained fully mobilized to address the persistent insecurity created by the criminal activities of armed groups in the eastern Democratic Republic of the Congo.[112] However, the resurgence of M23 had contributed to disinformation about and stigmatization of MONUSCO, which had led to violent new protests and serious incidents that had claimed the lives of dozens of protesters and four Mission employees. In that context, the Special Representative implored the Congolese authorities and members of civil society to continue to focus on easing the tensions to enable the full and unimpeded resumption of the operations of MONUSCO in the eastern Democratic Republic of the Congo. In her last quarterly briefing, the Special Representative stated that the country continued to show resilience despite the immense challenges, notably with regard to the security situation in the eastern part of the country, which had deteriorated dramatically.[113]

On the regional dimension, the Special Representative underscored that the stability of the Democratic Republic of the Congo was tied to the support of its nine neighbouring countries, welcomed the efforts of the President, Félix-Antoine Tshisekedi Tshilombo, in increasing regional cooperation and welcomed the decision of the East African Community to admit the Democratic Republic of the Congo

[105] See A/77/2, part II, chap. 12.
[106] S/2022/252, S/2022/503, S/2022/709 and S/2022/892.
[107] See S/PV.9007, S/PV.9081, S/PV.9142 and S/PV.9215.
[108] See S/PV.9051.
[109] See S/PV.9142 and S/PV.9215.
[110] See S/PV.9007.
[111] See S/PV.9081.
[112] See S/PV.9142.
[113] See S/PV.9215.

as a full member.[114] Following the signing of a status-of-forces agreement in September between the Government of the Democratic Republic of the Congo and the East African Community secretariat for its Regional Force to be deployed in the eastern part of the country for an initial period of six months, the Special Representative stressed the vital importance of effective coordination with MONUSCO in order to enable the Mission to fully carry out its protection of civilians mandate.[115] She further welcomed the adoption of the joint road map for peace in the Central African Republic (Luanda road map) on 6 July, through the mediation of the President of Angola as the current Chair of the International Conference on the Great Lakes Region, aimed at de-escalating tensions between the Democratic Republic of the Congo and Rwanda. In response to increasing insecurity and tensions, regional initiatives had intensified, culminating in a mini-summit, held on 23 November in Luanda, to agree on measures to address the situation in the eastern Democratic Republic of the Congo, including a timetable for the implementation of priority actions to achieve the cessation of hostilities, the immediate withdrawal of M23 from the occupied areas and the coordination of efforts under the Luanda and Nairobi processes.[116] The Special Representative welcomed the meeting of the Armed Forces of the Democratic Republic of the Congo, the East African Community Regional Force and MONUSCO on 29 and 30 November in Goma and reported that the Government of the Democratic Republic of the Congo had formally requested the active involvement of MONUSCO in the implementation of the Luanda mini-summit communiqué, in which an operational role for MONUSCO was envisioned. The Special Representative reiterated the Mission's readiness to leverage its capabilities in support of the regional peace initiatives under way, in line with its mandate. At the same meeting, the Secretary-General of the East African Community outlined the political and military tracks of the Nairobi process and requested the Council to support the East African Community in securing a permanent solution in the eastern Democratic Republic of the Congo, including through cooperation between MONUSCO, the Nairobi process and the East African Community Regional Force.[117]

With regard to political developments in 2022, the Special Representative reported that, in June, the National Assembly and the Senate had enacted revisions to the electoral law, which were expected to increase the transparency of the electoral process and promote the participation of women as candidates.[118] However, the absence of the opposition from the parliamentary debate on those revisions had demonstrated that additional efforts were needed to create the conditions for an inclusive, transparent and peaceful electoral process. In September, the Special Representative reported on the significant progress that had been made in the preparations for the general elections to be held by December 2023 and welcomed the efforts of the Government, the Parliament and the Independent National Electoral Commission to establish the legal framework and conditions for the proper conduct of the elections, while noting that major challenges remained, notably on reaching a broad consensus on the various aspects of the electoral process.[119] In her last quarterly briefing, welcoming the publication of the electoral calendar, which set the presidential and legislative elections for 20 December 2023, the Special Representative reiterated the readiness of MONUSCO to promote a political environment conducive to a transparent, inclusive and peaceful electoral process.[120]

With regard to the phased drawdown of MONUSCO, the Special Representative reported on the progress in the common efforts of the Mission, the United Nations country team and the Government, and added that the implementation of a progressive, responsible and sustainable transition also had advanced at field level.[121] In September, she expressed the Mission's readiness to work closely with the Government to re-evaluate the transition plan in order to step up the pace of the withdrawal of MONUSCO.[122] Concerning the Mission's withdrawal from the remaining provinces of South Kivu, North Kivu and Ituri, in her last briefing of the year, the Special Representative reiterated the readiness of the

---

[114] See S/PV.9007.
[115] See S/PV.9142.
[116] See S/PV.9215.
[117] See S/PV.9215.
[118] See S/PV.9081.
[119] See S/PV.9142.
[120] See S/PV.9215.
[121] See S/PV.9007.
[122] See S/PV.9142.

United Nations to work on the revision of the joint transition plan in order to define concrete actions for the effective implementation of priority benchmarks related to the creation of minimum security conditions for the responsible and sustainable withdrawal of MONUSCO.[123]

In addition to the briefings by the Special Representative and in the light of the deteriorating situation in the eastern Democratic Republic of the Congo, on 31 May, the Council heard briefings by the Assistant Secretary-General for Africa and the Special Envoy of the Secretary-General for the Great Lakes Region.[124] The Assistant Secretary-General reported that the already dire situation was worsening, owing to the recent resurgence of M23 and its hostile activity in North Kivu against the Congolese armed forces and MONUSCO. The Assistant Secretary-General stressed that it was imperative for the Council to lend its full weight to the ongoing regional efforts to defuse the situation and bring an end to the M23 insurgency. She reiterated the Secretary-General's call to local armed groups in the Democratic Republic of the Congo to participate in the political process without preconditions, and to all foreign armed groups to disarm unconditionally and immediately return to their countries of origin. The Assistant Secretary-General also underscored the importance of involving women, including civil society representatives and those affiliated with armed groups, in the ongoing efforts in the search for inclusive and durable solutions. The Special Envoy for the Great Lakes Region called upon all armed groups to stop the violence, immediately lay down their arms and engage resolutely in the Nairobi political dialogue process facilitated by Kenya.[125] He reiterated the importance of non-military measures and encouraged the leaders of the region to continue their high-level dialogue on how to address the threat posed by the armed groups and prevent tensions from escalating between the Democratic Republic of the Congo and its neighbours.

Representatives of civil society also briefed the Council in 2022 with a focus on the deteriorating security situation and its impact on civilians, in particular women and children. In that regard, at the meeting held in June, the Director of the Fund for Congolese Women and the President of Female Solidarity for Integrated Peace and Development shared her views on the reasons for instability in the Democratic Republic of the Congo and the wider region, and recommended strengthening of actions and consultation mechanisms in order to make the protection of the civilian population more effective, especially in the eastern part of the country, as the elections approached.[126] She called for, inter alia, the establishment of international justice for the Democratic Republic of the Congo, the provision of greater medical and psychological assistance to survivors and continuing efforts to address the global food insecurity caused by the war in Ukraine and its ramifications in Africa, especially its impact on women and children. In her briefing in December, a civil society activist and member of the Lutte pour le changement offered her insights into the security situation, the impact of the conflict in the eastern Democratic Republic of the Congo on women and the crucial importance of the political participation of women, as well as the role of MONUSCO.[127] She urged the Council to ensure that MONUSCO provided full protection to the civilians, especially women and girls; that all parties, including the Congolese armed forces, the East African Community Regional Force and MONUSCO, acted within a framework of strict respect for human rights and international humanitarian law; that women participated fully and equally in the electoral and peace processes; that the withdrawal of MONUSCO was gradual, accountable and conditioned on respect for human rights and the protection of civilians; and further called upon Council members to urge the Congolese authorities to begin reforming the security sector, particularly the army.

In 2022, the deliberations among Council members were focused primarily on the worsening security conditions in the eastern Democratic Republic of the Congo and the resulting violations of human rights, as well as the regional initiatives aimed at defusing tensions between the Democratic Republic of the Congo and its neighbours. Council members also discussed political developments, including the preparations for the 2023 elections, as well as the phased drawdown of MONUSCO as set out in the joint transition plan.

---

[123] See S/PV.9215.
[124] See S/PV.9051.
[125] For more information on the situation in the Great Lakes region, see sect. 3 above.
[126] See S/PV.9081.
[127] See S/PV.9215.

With regard to the security situation, Council members expressed concern over the further deterioration of conditions and growing violence, notably in the light of the resurgence of M23 and the activities of other armed groups in the eastern Democratic Republic of the Congo. In this context, several Council members referred to a press statement issued by the Council on 24 May, condemning the attacks by armed groups in the Democratic Republic of the Congo and urging them to lay down their arms.[128] Council members repeatedly called for the cessation of hostilities,[129] requested that all support for armed groups, including external, be stopped,[130] and demanded that the armed groups, particularly M23, withdraw from any occupied areas.[131] Council members also underscored the importance of non-military measures for the stabilization of the eastern parts of the country and in that respect called for the implementation of the disarmament, demobilization and reintegration programme.[132] Concerning the deployment of the East African Community regional force in the Democratic Republic of the Congo, Council members urged it to coordinate its activities closely with MONUSCO and to ensure full respect of international law and human rights.[133] In addition, several Council members continued raising the issue of the human rights situation, including violations and abuses involving conflict-related sexual violence against women and children.[134]

As regards regional dynamics, Council members expressed support for the efforts of regional and subregional stakeholders aimed at defusing tensions, in particular between the Democratic Republic of the Congo and Rwanda, and jointly tackling challenges in the broader Great Lakes region. In this regard, Council members underscored the importance of the Nairobi and Luanda processes,[135] the continued implementation of the Peace, Security and Cooperation Framework for the Democratic Republic of the Congo, as well as the role played by regional and subregional organizations, including the African Union, the East African Community, the International Conference on the Great Lakes Region and the Southern African Development Community.[136]

On the political front, Council members welcomed the progress made towards the preparation of presidential and parliamentary elections scheduled for December 2023.[137] In that regard, Council members underscored the importance of a free, fair, transparent and peaceful electoral process, with several speakers recalling the need for elections to be inclusive.[138] In addition, the representative of Ireland commended the efforts of MONUSCO and the Special Representative in engaging women and young people in electoral processes[139] and the representative of the United Arab Emirates stressed the importance of cooperation between the Mission and political stakeholders in creating an environment conducive to upcoming elections.[140]

Throughout the year, Council members also discussed the gradual withdrawal of MONUSCO and underlined the importance of a conditions-based, responsible and phased drawdown, guided by the situation on the ground and conducted in line with the joint transition plan.[141] The representative of Kenya, speaking also on behalf of Gabon and Ghana, expressed support for the call to MONUSCO by the Government of the Democratic Republic of the Congo to review the joint transition plan and ensure that the benchmarks encompassed strengthening key defence and security institutions, early warning

---

[128] See S/PV.9051 (United Arab Emirates, Albania and China).

[129] See S/PV.9051 (Russian Federation); S/PV.9081 (Ghana (also on behalf of Gabon and Kenya), India, Ireland and Russian Federation); S/PV.9142 (India, United Arab Emirates and Russian Federation); S/PV.9215 (France, United Kingdom, China and Albania).

[130] See S/PV.9215 (United States, United Kingdom, Albania and India).

[131] See S/PV.9215 (France, United States, United Kingdom, China, Kenya (also on behalf of Gabon and Ghana), Albania and Mexico).

[132] See S/PV.9007, S/PV.9051, S/PV.9081, S/PV.9142 and S/PV.9215.

[133] See S/PV.9081, S/PV.9142 and S/PV.9215.

[134] See S/PV.9007, S/PV.9051, S/PV.9081, S/PV.9142 and S/PV.9215.

[135] See S/PV.9142 and S/PV.9215.

[136] See S/PV.9007, S/PV.9051, S/PV.9081, S/PV.9142 and S/PV.9215.

[137] See S/PV.9007, S/PV.9081, S/PV.9142 and S/PV.9215.

[138] See S/PV.9007, S/PV.9081, S/PV.9142 and S/PV.9215.

[139] See S/PV.9081.

[140] See S/PV.9081 and S/PV.9215.

[141] See S/PV.9007, S/PV.9081, S/PV.9142 and S/PV.9215.

initiatives and preventive interventions that could mitigate any relapses into conflict.[142] Taking note of the request made by the Congolese authorities, the representative of Mexico asked for the review exercise to be carried out with prudence, while the representative of India stated that the shortcomings reflected in the update on transition benchmarks needed to be addressed in coordination with the Democratic Republic of the Congo. Following the renewal of the mandate of MONUSCO, the representative of the United Kingdom expressed the hope that resolution 2666 (2022) provided a solid basis for constructive dialogue between the Government of the Democratic Republic of the Congo and the Mission, including on the review of the joint transition plan.[143]

In its decisions in 2022, the Council took action on the issues outlined above. With regard to the political developments in the Democratic Republic of the Congo and the region, on 3 June, the Council adopted a presidential statement welcoming the commitment by the regional Heads of State to implement a two-track approach aimed at finding lasting peace in the Democratic Republic of the Congo and the support provided by MONUSCO and the Office of the Special Envoy of the Secretary-General for the Great Lakes Region to that process.[144] The Council also expressed concern over the increase of armed group activity in the eastern provinces of the Democratic Republic of the Congo and reiterated its condemnation of all armed groups operating in the country and of the recent attacks on the Armed Forces of the Democratic Republic of the Congo and MONUSCO.[145] The Council also expressed concern at the current humanitarian situation in the eastern Democratic Republic of the Congo and remained deeply concerned by the high levels of violations and abuses of human rights and violations of international humanitarian law in parts of the country.[146] The Council encouraged further efforts to de-escalate tensions, to refrain from incendiary statements and incitement to violence and welcomed the engagement of existing regional mechanisms, including the Expanded Joint Verification Mechanism, in bringing to light alleged unauthorized cross-border military activity.[147]

On 20 December, by resolution 2666 (2022), adopted unanimously under Chapter VII of the Charter, the Council extended the mandate of the Mission and the Force Intervention Brigade for one year, until 20 December 2023.[148] In addition to reiterating the strategic priorities of MONUSCO concerning the protection of civilians and the support to the stabilization and strengthening of State institutions and key governance and security reforms,[149] the Council also tasked MONUSCO with the support for the 2023 electoral process in the three provinces where the Mission was still deployed.[150] The Council also authorized MONUSCO to take all necessary measures to carry out its mandate, in line with the basic principles of peacekeeping.[151]

Regarding the Mission's exit strategy, the Council took note of the call by the Government of the Democratic Republic of the Congo to review the transition plan and encouraged the United Nations and the Government, in liaison with civil society, to identify the concrete and realistic steps to be undertaken, as a matter of priority, to create the minimum security conditions to enable the responsible and sustainable exit of MONUSCO.[152] The Council further requested the Secretary-General to provide options for adapting the configuration of the civilian, police and military components of MONUSCO and for the United Nations future configuration in the Democratic Republic of the Congo, once the joint review of the transition plan for MONUSCO had been concluded and no later than July 2023.[153]

In 2022, Council members also deliberated on the work of the Committee established pursuant to resolution 1533 (2004) and took action on the Democratic Republic of the Congo sanctions regime. On 10 June, the Group of Experts on the Democratic Republic of the Congo submitted its final report

---

[142] See S/PV.9142.
[143] See S/PV.9226. See also resolution 2666 (2022), paras. 38, 39 and 42–44.
[144] S/PRST/2022/4, first paragraph.
[145] Ibid., second paragraph.
[146] Ibid., fifth and sixth paragraphs.
[147] Ibid., seventh paragraph.
[148] Resolution 2666 (2022), para. 19.
[149] Ibid., para. 21.
[150] Ibid., para. 26 (a). For more information on the mandate of MONUSCO, see part X, sect. I. For more information on past mandates of MONUSCO, see previous supplements covering the period 2010 to 2021.
[151] Resolution 2666 (2022), para. 21.
[152] Ibid., para. 38.
[153] Ibid., para. 44.

concluding that the security and humanitarian situation in the provinces of North Kivu and Ituri had deteriorated despite a state of siege that had been in force for 11 months in those provinces and despite military operations by the Armed Forces of the Democratic Republic of the Congo, the Uganda People's Defence Forces and MONUSCO.[154] On 30 June, acting under Chapter VII of the Charter, the Council adopted resolution 2641 (2022), with abstentions by China, Gabon, Ghana, Kenya and the Russian Federation,[155] by which it renewed until 1 July 2023 the sanctions measures as set out in resolution 2293 (2016) and extended until 1 August 2023 the mandate of the Group of Experts on the Democratic Republic of the Congo as set forth in resolution 2360 (2017).[156] By the same resolution, the Council decided that the financial and travel measures should also apply to individuals and entities as designated by the Committee for involvement in the production, manufacture or use in the Democratic Republic of the Congo of improvised explosive devices, or in the commission, planning, ordering, aiding, abetting or otherwise assistance of attacks in the Democratic Republic of the Congo with improvised explosive devices.[157]

In the briefing of 30 September, the Chair of the Committee established pursuant to resolution 1533 (2004) gave an overview of its work over the previous 12 months. He informed the Council about the planned visit of a delegation of Committee members to the Democratic Republic of the Congo, Rwanda and Uganda, whose purpose was to gather first-hand accounts concerning the effective implementation of the sanctions measures imposed by resolution 2360 (2017), as reaffirmed by resolution 2641 (2022).[158] Further to the Chair's briefing, the Director of the Angaza Institute called upon the Council to impose sanctions on Member States whose support for armed groups operating in the Democratic Republic of the Congo had been documented and urged that sanctions be imposed with a view to preventing the sale of wood, protected animals and other natural resources by armed rebel groups and governments. The representative of the United States noted that M23 remained designated under the sanctions regime concerning the Democratic Republic of the Congo and that Member States were required to freeze the assets of that armed group and ensure that no funds or economic resources were made available to it. In addition, the representative of the Democratic Republic of the Congo called upon the Council to strengthen sanctions against the mafia networks inside and outside the country that illegally exploited its natural resources and called upon the Council to fully lift the prior notification requirements concerning the shipments of arms or related materiel for the country's armed forces.

At the meeting held on 9 December, the Council heard another briefing by the Chair of the Committee established pursuant to resolution 1533 (2004), during which he provided an overview of his visit to the Democratic Republic of the Congo, Rwanda and Uganda from 7 to 18 November. In the briefing, the Chair reported that during the discussions in Kinshasa, he mainly emphasized that the arms embargo had applied only to armed groups since 2008 and that the notification requirement was binding only on supplier States.[159] Other topics of discussion during the visit included the security situation in the eastern Democratic Republic of the Congo, the activities of armed groups, the alleged links between the Allied Democratic Forces sanctioned armed group and Da'esh, the illegal exploitation of natural resources and human rights violations, including conflict-related sexual violence.

On 20 December, the Council unanimously adopted resolution 2667 (2022) under Chapter VII of the Charter, by which it lifted the notification requirements for arms embargo set out in paragraph 5 of resolution 1807 (2008) and requested the Government of the Democratic Republic of the Congo to provide a confidential report to the Council no later than 31 May 2023 detailing its efforts to ensure the safe and effective management, storage, marking, monitoring and security of the national stockpiles of weapons and ammunition, as well as the efforts to fight arms trafficking and diversion.[160]

---

[154] See the letter dated 10 June from the Group of Experts to the President of the Security Council (S/2022/479).

[155] See S/PV.9084. For more information on the discussion following the vote, see part VII, sect. III.B, case 6.

[156] Resolution 2641 (2022), paras. 1 and 8.

[157] Ibid., para. 3.

[158] See S/PV.9142.

[159] See S/PV.9215.

[160] Resolution 2667 (2022), paras. 2 and 3.

Meetings: the situation concerning the Democratic Republic of the Congo, 2022

Meeting record and date	*Sub-item*	*Other documents*	*Rule 37 invitations*	*Rule 39 and other invitations*	*Speakers*	*Decision and vote (for-against-abstaining)*
S/PV.9007 29 March	Report of the Secretary-General on the United Nations Organization Stabilization Mission in the Democratic Republic of the Congo (MONUSCO) (S/2022/252)		Democratic Republic of the Congo	Special Representative of the Secretary-General for the Democratic Republic of the Congo and Head of MONUSCO, civil society representative	13 Council members,[a] invitee under rule 37, one other invitee (Special Representative)[b]	
S/PV.9051 31 May			Democratic Republic of the Congo, Rwanda, Uganda	Assistant Secretary-General for Africa, Special Envoy of the Secretary-General for the Great Lakes Region	13 Council members,[c] all invitees[d]	
S/PV.9055 3 June						S/PRST/2022/4
S/PV.9081 29 June	Report of the Secretary-General on MONUSCO (S/2022/503)		Burundi, Democratic Republic of the Congo, Rwanda	Special Representative of the Secretary-General, President of Female Solidarity for Integrated Peace and Development	13 Council members,[e] all invitees[f]	
S/PV.9084 30 June	Letter dated 10 June 2022 from the Group of Experts extended pursuant to Security Council resolution 2582 (2021) addressed to the President of the Security Council (S/2022/479)	Draft resolution submitted by France (S/2022/523)			Eight Council members[g]	Resolution 2641 (2022) 10-0-5[h] (adopted under Chapter VII)

Meeting record and date	*Sub-item*	*Other documents*	*Rule 37 invitations*	*Rule 39 and other invitations*	*Speakers*	*Decision and vote (for-against-abstaining)*
S/PV.9142 30 September	Report of the Secretary-General on MONUSCO (S/2022/709)		Burundi, Democratic Republic of the Congo, Rwanda	Special Representative of the Secretary-General, Director of the Angaza Institute	14 Council members,[i] all invitees[j]	
S/PV.9215 9 December	Report of the Secretary-General on MONUSCO (S/2022/892)		Burundi, Democratic Republic of the Congo, Rwanda	Special Representative of the Secretary-General, Secretary-General of the East African Community, activist and member of Lutte pour le changement	14 Council members,[i] all invitees[k]	
S/PV.9226 20 December	Report of the Secretary-General on MONUSCO (S/2022/892)	Draft resolution submitted by France (S/2022/960)			10 Council members[l]	Resolution 2666 (2022) 15-0-0 (adopted under Chapter VII)
		Draft resolution submitted by France (S/2022/964)				Resolution 2667 (2022) 15-0-0 (adopted under Chapter VII)

[a] Albania, Brazil, China, France, India, Ireland, Gabon (also on behalf of Ghana and Kenya), Mexico, Norway, Russian Federation, United Arab Emirates, United Kingdom and United States.

[b] The Special Representative participated in the meeting by videoconference. The civil society representative was unable to deliver remarks at the meeting owing to technical difficulties.

[c] Albania, Brazil, China, France, India, Ireland, Kenya (also on behalf of Gabon and Ghana), Mexico, Norway, Russian Federation, United Arab Emirates, United Kingdom and United States.

[d] The Democratic Republic of the Congo was represented by its Deputy Prime Minister and Minister for Foreign Affairs. The Special Envoy participated in the meeting by videoconference.

[e] Albania, Brazil, China, France, India, Ireland, Ghana (also on behalf of Gabon and Kenya), Mexico, Norway, Russian Federation, United Arab Emirates, United Kingdom and United States.

[f] The President of Female Solidarity for Integrated Peace and Development participated in the meeting by videoconference.

[g] Brazil, China, France, Gabon, Ghana, Kenya, Russian Federation and United Arab Emirates.

[h] *For*: Albania, Brazil, France, India, Ireland, Mexico, Norway, United Arab Emirates, United Kingdom, United States; *against*: none; *abstaining*: China, Gabon, Ghana, Kenya, Russian Federation.

[i] Albania, Brazil, China, France, India, Ireland, Kenya (also on behalf of Gabon and Ghana), Mexico, Norway, Russian Federation, United Arab Emirates, United Kingdom and United States. In addition, the representative of Gabon spoke in his capacity as Chair of the Committee established pursuant to resolution 1533 (2004).

[j] The Director of the Angaza Institute participated in the meeting by videoconference.

[k] The Democratic Republic of the Congo was represented by its Deputy Prime Minister and Minister for Foreign Affairs, who participated in the meeting by videoconference. The Secretary-General of the East African Community and the member of Lutte pour le changement also participated in the meeting by videoconference.

[l] China, Gabon, Ghana, Ireland, Kenya, Norway, Russian Federation, United Arab Emirates, United Kingdom and United States.

5. The situation in the Central African Republic

During the period under review, the Council held five meetings and adopted two resolutions, all under Chapter VII of the Charter of the United Nations, in connection with the situation in the Central African Republic. Three of the meetings took the form of briefings, and the remaining two were held to adopt a decision of the Council.[161] More information on the meetings, including on participants, speakers and outcomes, is given in the table below. The Council held one private (closed) meeting with countries contributing troops and police to the United Nations Multidimensional Integrated Stabilization Mission in the Central African Republic (MINUSCA).[162] In addition to meetings, Council members held informal consultations of the whole in connection with the situation in the Central African Republic.[163]

During 2022, Council members heard three briefings on the reports of the Secretary-General on the Central African Republic by his Special Representative for the Central African Republic, consistent with the four-month reporting schedule established by the Council in resolution 2387 (2017).[164] Council members also heard briefings by the Special Representative of the Chairperson of the African Union for the Central African Republic and Head of the African Union Office in the Central African Republic, the Executive Secretary of the International Conference on the Great Lakes Region and a civil society representative.

The briefings were focused on the political, security, economic, human rights and humanitarian situation in the country. In that regard, they served to continue to update the Council on efforts aimed at revitalizing the Political Agreement for Peace and Reconciliation in the Central African Republic signed by the authorities and 14 armed groups in Bangui on 6 February 2019 and implementing the joint road map adopted under the auspices of the President of Angola on 16 September 2021 by the International Conference on the Great Lakes Region and the republican dialogue launched in March 2022 by the Government with the political parties and key forces. The briefings also served to apprise the Council of preparations for the local elections, the status of the ceasefire of 15 October 2021, the activities of armed groups, including Coalition des patriotes pour le changement, and their impact on security, elections and the provision of humanitarian assistance, efforts to fight impunity for human rights violations and the role of MINUSCA.

At the meeting held on 22 February,[165] the Special Representative of the Secretary-General, congratulating the new Prime Minister of the Central African Republic, said that the Government would have to overcome the challenges of the implementation of the Political Agreement, the organization of the republican dialogue and the restoration of State authority. He gave a briefing to the Council on two visits by representatives of the International Conference on the Great Lakes Region to the Central African Republic, in January and February, to advance the effective implementation of the road map and enable the establishment and development of the terms of reference of a follow-up working group to monitor the road map. He described the ways in which MINUSCA was contributing to advancing the political process through its good offices, through its support for preparations for the local elections and through the establishment of a climate of trust between the Government and the opposition, leading to the return of the opposition to the organizing committee of the republican dialogue, which had resumed its work. He recalled that the security situation remained concerning and was marked by military offensives and continued reports of human rights violations. He commended the efforts of the Government to make operational the Commission on Truth, Justice, Reparation and Reconciliation and welcomed the first public hearing of the Special Criminal Court as signs of progress in fighting impunity.

The African Union Special Representative, taking note of the political tensions surrounding the preparations for the republican dialogue, outlined some issues that remained to be addressed by its organizing committee, including the choice of topics, the presidium and the list of participants. He welcomed the initiatives and efforts of the International Conference on the Great Lakes Region in the

---

[161] For more information on the format of meetings, see part II.

[162] The private meeting was held on 7 November in connection with the item entitled "Meeting of the Security Council with the troop- and police-contributing countries pursuant to resolution 1353 (2001), annex II, sections A and B"; see S/PV.9185. See also A/77/2, part II, chap. 21.

[163] See A/77/2, part II, chap. 13.

[164] See S/PV.8971, S/PV.9074 and S/PV.9156. See also S/2022/119, S/2022/491 and S/2022/762.

[165] See S/PV.8971.

context of the road map to mobilize the subregion in promoting dialogue in the country, including contacts with the leaders of the Coalition des patriotes pour le changement and the regrouping of its combatants. He stated that an offensive by the Armed Forces of the Central African Republic, supported by bilateral forces, to decrease potential trouble-making by armed groups was under way.

The Executive Secretary of the International Conference on the Great Lakes Region focused on the major political, security and humanitarian developments in the Central African Republic. He commended the Government for establishing the organizing committee of the republican dialogue. He stressed that the implementation of the Political Agreement faced challenges, owing to many interlinked factors, and that the Government's institutional capacity to expeditiously implement the Agreement was hampered by both financial and non-financial challenges. He described the obstacles to the holding of the local elections, including those related to voter registration and education. He expressed concerns regarding the humanitarian and security situation, highlighting continued displacement, poverty and unemployment, as well as abuses against civilians and attacks on defence and security forces.

At the meeting held on 22 June,[166] the Special Representative of the Secretary-General updated the Council on efforts to revitalize the political process and reposition MINUSCA. She provided a briefing on her efforts to remobilize the region since she had taken office, culminating, under the leadership of the Government of the Central African Republic and the auspices of Angola and Rwanda, in a strategic review meeting on the political process in Bangui on 4 June. She reported that the authorities had decided to establish a permanent platform for the strategic review, to be convened on a quarterly basis, and called for the Council's unanimous support in carrying out the plan for its monitoring. She suggested that the political commitments previously undertaken separately under the auspices of the Political Agreement guarantors and within the framework of the road map should be part of a single platform and bring together the representatives of the International Conference on the Great Lakes Region, Angola and Rwanda, the African Union, the Economic Community of Central African States and MINUSCA. She urged the Government to expedite the implementation of the recommendations of the republican dialogue, which was one of the components of the road map. Expressing concern about the persistent violations of the ceasefire by all parties, she stated that MINUSCA had readjusted its concept of operations in order to prioritize a preventive approach centred on the civilian populations.

The President of the Network for Women's Leadership in the Central African Republic expressed major concerns regarding the sociopolitical, security, humanitarian and human rights situation in her country, highlighting, inter alia, the killings targeting the populations of the hinterlands and atrocities committed by the Coalition des patriotes pour le changement as well as members of the national army, its allies and the regime militias. She expressed regret that, despite the participation of civil society in the republican dialogue, the nature of the dialogue was non-inclusive. She urged the Council to consider the Central African Republic as a country in an emergency situation for which emergency measures must be taken.

At the meeting held on 19 October,[167] the Special Representative expressed concern regarding the security situation and highlighted the need to critically assess the progress in the implementation of the MINUSCA mandate in four areas: political and security dynamics, safeguarding the Mission's achievements, decentralization of the political and peace process and the extension of State authority. She welcomed the implementation of the shared timetable of the Political Agreement and the joint road map and highlighted the developments that had already emerged in that regard, such as the opening of the President's dialogue with leaders of 11 armed groups. Concerning human rights violations, she informed the Council about the establishment of a framework for constructive dialogue and accountability with regard to the follow-up of documented violations and the implementation of the recommendations made in the public reports of MINUSCA and the Office of the United Nations High Commissioner for Human Rights.

Throughout 2022, discussions in the Council were focused mainly on the topics outlined above. With regard to the political process, Council members took note of the holding of the Executive Monitoring

[166] S/PV.9074.

[167] See S/PV.9156.

Committee meeting on the Political Agreement on 14 February[168] and the subsequent strategic review meeting held on 4 June by the Government of the Central African Republic, with the participation of regional actors, to monitor the implementation of the road map.[169] Council members stressed the need for the implementation of the road map and highlighted its critical importance in restoring peace and security in the country and returning to the commitments under the Political Agreement.[170] The representative of China expressed the hope that the International Conference on the Great Lakes Region would enhance communication with the Government of the Central African Republic in the implementation of the road map and strive to form synergies based on the reality on the ground and its needs.[171] The representative of the Russian Federation underlined the importance for the authorities to commit to the principle of inclusivity when implementing the road map on actualizing the Political Agreement. Other Council members echoed similar sentiments, urging that the process of implementing the road map include women and other social groups.[172]

Concerning the republican dialogue initiated in March, Council members stressed the need for inclusivity, including ensuring the participation of women in the dialogue.[173] The representative of Mexico welcomed the regional mobilization to facilitate the republican dialogue and revitalize the Political Agreement, in particular through the road map, and expressed belief that the region could play an important role in opening channels of communication with the groups linked to the Coalition des patriotes pour le changement in order to bring them back to the negotiating table.[174] The representative of France noted that some of the country's active forces had not been able to participate, emphasizing that only inclusive consultations and consensus surrounding the rules of the democratic process would enable the country to advance towards peace and reconciliation, while the representatives of Gabon (speaking also on behalf of Ghana and Kenya) and Norway emphasized the need for the implementation of the recommendations resulting from the republican dialogue.[175] Council members also welcomed the establishment of the follow-up committee.[176]

Throughout the year, Council members repeatedly expressed concerns regarding the persistent human rights abuses and violations of international humanitarian law,[177] including those committed by the national security forces and the Wagner Group.[178] The representative of the United States recalled that the national defence forces and Wagner Group contractors, referred to as "other security personnel" in the report of the Secretary-General,[179] had perpetrated over 40 per cent of all violations documented during the reporting period, which was why the United States found it hard to consider lifting the arms embargo.[180] In a similar vein, concerned by the alarming reports regarding the conduct of the Central African forces and the brutal methods applied by the Wagner Group and instilled upon the Central African partners, the representative of France stressed that any changes to the embargo must be considered against that backdrop.[181] Council members condemned the massacres allegedly committed by the Wagner Group against

---

[168] See S/PV.8971.

[169] See S/PV.9074 (China, United Arab Emirates, India and Norway).

[170] See S/PV.8971 (France, United Arab Emirates and Brazil); S/PV.9074 (France, Norway, Ireland and Albania); and S/PV.9156 (France, Albania, China, Mexico, Brazil, United Arab Emirates, India, Russian Federation and Gabon (also on behalf of Ghana and Kenya)).

[171] See S/PV.8971.

[172] See S/PV.9156 (France, Albania, Mexico and United Arab Emirates).

[173] See S/PV.8971 (United Arab Emirates, Gabon (also on behalf of Ghana and Kenya) and Norway); S/PV.9074 (France, Brazil, United Arab Emirates and India); and S/PV.9156 (Brazil, United States, United Arab Emirates, Norway, United Kingdom and Gabon (also on behalf of Ghana and Kenya)).

[174] See S/PV.9074.

[175] Ibid.

[176] See S/PV.9156 (Brazil, India and Gabon (also on behalf of Ghana and Kenya)).

[177] See S/PV.8971 (Albania, Gabon (also on behalf of Ghana and Kenya), United Kingdom and Ireland); S/PV.9074 (Brazil); and S/PV.9156 (France, Albania, Norway, Ireland and United Kingdom).

[178] See S/PV.8971 (Albania, Norway and Ireland); S/PV.9074 (France, Norway, United States, Ireland, United Kingdom and Albania); and S/PV.9156 (France, Albania, Ireland, United States, Norway and United Kingdom).

[179] S/2022/119.

[180] See S/PV.8971.

[181] See S/PV.9074.

civilians in January in Aigbando.[182] The representative of Ireland pointed out that State agents were also responsible for 45 per cent of violations and abuses documented between June and October, which was unacceptable.[183] The representatives of Albania and Norway expressed regret that the unilateral ceasefire had not produced the expected results in terms of ending hostilities, and the representative of the United States called upon the authorities to immediately stand up and enforce a ceasefire monitoring mechanism.[184] Council members urged the authorities of the Central African Republic to investigate the allegations of human rights abuses and violations of international humanitarian law and bring those responsible for those acts to account, including through prosecution.[185] The representative of Gabon stressed the need for the implementation of a national special investigation commission to shed light on serious crimes and violations of human rights and humanitarian law.[186] The representative of the United States noted the initial steps taken by the special commission of inquiry, led by the Minister of Justice of the Central African Republic, and the need to follow through on the investigations. Council members welcomed the start of public hearings of the Special Criminal Court.[187]

During the period under review, the Council adopted two resolutions under this item, one in relation to the mandate of MINUSCA and one concerning the sanctions measures for the Central African Republic. Neither of the resolutions was adopted unanimously. With regard to the sanctions measures, by its resolution 2648 (2022) adopted on 29 July, the Council renewed until 31 July 2023 the arms embargo, asset freeze and travel ban,[188] and expanded the list of exemptions to the arms embargo.[189] The Council also removed the requirement of advance notification to the Committee of the intention to acquire arms and related material exempted from the arms embargo by the resolution.[190] Furthermore, the Council extended the mandate of the Panel of Experts until 31 August 2023, requesting it to provide to the Council a final report no later than 30 May 2023.[191] In the resolution, the Council also welcomed the strategic review meeting held in Bangui on 4 June on the operationalization of the road map adopted by the International Conference on the Great Lakes Region on 16 September 2021 to revitalize the implementation of the Political Agreement.[192]

Resolution 2648 (2022) was adopted with 10 votes in favour and five abstentions.[193] Following the adoption, the Minister for Foreign Affairs, Francophonie and Central Africans Abroad of the Central African Republic expressed satisfaction with the first significant step to be made with regard to the embargo on armed groups, but stressed that it remained to be seen how it could be applied to armed groups. She thanked States that had voiced their support for lifting the embargo completely, China and the Russian Federation for their call to take into account the realities on the ground, as well as the three African members of the Council, and expressed regret that the resolution did not respond to her country's legitimate request for a total lifting of the embargo.

Explaining their delegations' abstentions, the representatives of China, Gabon, Kenya and the Russian Federation recalled the requests by the Central African Republic authorities and regional organizations to lift the embargo, which the resolution failed to do. The representative of China said that the resolution still contained a number of restrictive measures that could pose unnecessary obstacles to the defence capacity-building of the Government and that the embargo measures had become increasingly incompatible with developments in the country. The representative of Kenya, recalling provisions of

---

[182] See S/PV.8971 (France, Albania and United States).

[183] See S/PV.9156.

[184] See S/PV.8971.

[185] Ibid. (Albania, Norway, United States, United Kingdom and Ireland); and S/PV.9074 (Norway, Ireland and United Kingdom).

[186] See S/PV.8971.

[187] Ibid. (France, Mexico and Albania); S/PV.9074 (Brazil, India, United States, Ireland, Mexico and Albania); and S/PV.9156 (France, Ireland, Mexico, Brazil and Gabon (also on behalf of Ghana and Kenya)).

[188] Resolution 2648 (2022), paras. 1, 3 and 4. For more information on the sanctions measures concerning the Central African Republic, see part VII, sect. III.

[189] Resolution 2648 (2022), paras. 1 (g) and (h).

[190] Ibid. paras. 1 (a)–(h).

[191] Ibid. paras. 6 and 7. For information on the Committee established pursuant to resolution 2127 (2013) and the Panel of Experts, see part IX, sect. I.B.

[192] Resolution 2648 (2022), third preambular paragraph.

[193] See S/PV.9105.

Chapter VIII of the Charter, expressed the hope that the Council would listen to the voices of people from the Central African Republic and the relevant regional organizations and take the remaining step of removing the notification requirement as soon as possible. The representative of the Russian Federation said that the resolution did not respond fully to the task of stabilizing the situation in the Central African Republic. Noting that the resolution represented the best possible outcome given the prevailing circumstances, the representative of Ghana expressed gratitude for the efforts of France as penholder in trying to accommodate the input of delegations for a responsible release of the levers on the embargo in a way that did not have an adverse impact on the stability of the Central African Republic and its neighbours.

Among the Council members who voted in favour, the representative of France said that the resolution made it even easier for the armed forces of the Central African Republic to acquire all types of weapons and ammunition, sending a strong message to the authorities, whose greater involvement was key to combating the proliferation of weapons in the country. The representative of Albania underscored that the resolution was the closest to a balanced approach. Recognizing the progress made by the authorities in meeting the benchmarks, he noted that the final formula of the resolution kept the focus on the need to improve the ability of the country to safeguard its internal security and improve its compliance with the benchmarks. The representative of the United Kingdom stated that the embargo remained an important tool for supporting the maintenance of peace and stability in the country. The representative of the United States noted that the region was awash with guns, and that it was time to halt that unfettered flow. With effective implementation, which meant a notification requirement, the arms embargo could help to silence the guns. The representative of Brazil said that the resolution kept in place important mechanisms, such as the system of benchmarks and the work of the Panel of Experts, to help to guide the country towards stabilization and durable peace and addressed, although only partially, the assessments and claims of the authorities and regional organizations.

On 15 November, the Council adopted resolution 2659 (2022), by which it extended the mandate of MINUSCA for a period of one year, until 15 November 2023.[194] The Council reiterated that the Mission's mandate should be implemented on the basis of a prioritization of tasks.[195] In that regard, the Council reiterated, with certain modifications, the four priority tasks for MINUSCA, namely, the protection of civilians; the provision of good offices and support for the peace process, including the implementation the Political Agreement and the ceasefire; facilitation of the creation of a secure environment for the delivery of humanitarian assistance; and the protection of United Nations personnel, installations, equipment and goods.[196] In the resolution, the Council also took note of the republican dialogue held in March, and called for further steps from all actors to implement the recommendations contained therein to resolve any arising issues and conclude the electoral process through the organization of local elections.[197] The Council welcomed the strategic review meeting on 4 June, noting the Government's ongoing efforts and the Prime Minister's leadership to coordinate the implementation of the Political Agreement through the road map.[198]

During the meeting at which the Council adopted resolution 2659 (2022), with three abstentions, several Council members took the floor to explain their votes.[199] Explaining her country's abstention, the representative of Gabon emphasized that the text of the resolution did not meet the aspirations of the Central African Republic. She said that it was deplorable that, during the negotiations, the proposals put forward by the three African members of the Council in support of a strong commitment to restoring State authority, which would undoubtedly help to build peace, had been rejected. She expressed regret for the lack of differentiated treatment of the armed groups and the Central African authorities and for the deletion of the well-defined deadline for the strategic review of MINUSCA. She emphasized that the resolution did not take into account the efforts made by the Central African Republic armed forces in defending and securing their territory in difficult conditions. The representative of China emphasized that peacekeeping operations should define their priorities on the basis of the host country's needs. He expressed regret that

[194] Resolution 2659 (2022), para. 29.

[195] Ibid., para. 33.

[196] Ibid., para. 35 (a)–(d). For more information on the mandate of MINUSCA, see part X, sect. I.

[197] Resolution 2659 (2022), seventeenth preambular paragraph.

[198] Ibid., twelfth preambular paragraph.

[199] See S/PV.9190.

the resolution did not reflect the fact that the Government of the Central African Republic continued to recover lost territory and did not take on board the views of China on the security threat posed by armed groups, as well as the Mission's independent strategic review, which left China no other choice but to abstain in the voting. He expressed the hope that the Mission's assistance in extending State authority would be prioritized. The representative of the Russian Federation underscored that her delegation could not accept a text that equated all parties and armed groups to one another, when it was well documented that the latter were responsible for the majority of the violations. She stressed that many points raised by the Russian Federation had not been included in the text, including the proposed wording on the need to effectively investigate the supply chain used to deliver explosive devices and their components deployed to the country.

Among the Council members who voted in favour of the resolution, some[200] expressed support for the inclusion of new language concerning the Mission's freedom of movement and the authorization of night flights. The representative of France said that the abstentions were deplorable and stressed the need for the Council's unanimous support for MINUSCA. The representative of the United States expressed regret that the issue of the "Kremlin-backed Wagner Group" had been left out of the resolution and emphasized that the forces sent by the Russian Federation to the Central African Republic had consistently obstructed the Mission's ability to fulfil its mandate. The representative of the United Kingdom expressed disappointment over the loss of agreed language on the responsibility to protect, stressing that the Government of the Central African Republic remained primarily responsible for the protection of civilians. The representatives of Kenya and Ghana expressed regret that some of the proposals presented by the three African members of the Council, including promoting the extension of State authority, the deployment of security forces and the preservation of territorial integrity from "other tasks" to "priority tasks", had been left out. The representative of Kenya also expressed the hope for stronger language condemning the activities of armed groups and regretted that manifest geopolitical considerations had dictated the positions of certain delegations during the negotiation process.

Meetings: the situation in the Central African Republic, 2022

Meeting record and date	*Sub-item*	*Other documents*	*Rule 37 invitations*	*Rule 39 and other invitations*	*Speakers*	*Decision and vote (for-against-abstaining)*
S/PV.8971 22 February	Report of the Secretary-General on the Central African Republic (S/2022/119)		Central African Republic	Special Representative of the Secretary-General for the Central African Republic and Head of the United Nations Multidimensional Integrated Stabilization Mission in the Central African Republic, Special Representative of the Chairperson of the African Union for the Central African Republic and Head of the African Union Office in the	13 Council members,[a] all invitees[b]	

[200] France, United States and United Kingdom.

Meeting record and date	Sub-item	Other documents	Rule 37 invitations	Rule 39 and other invitations	Speakers	Decision and vote (for-against-abstaining)
				Central African Republic, Executive Secretary of the International Conference on the Great Lakes Region		
S/PV.9074 22 June	Letter dated 1 June 2022 from the Secretary-General addressed to the President of the Security Council (S/2022/449)		Central African Republic	Special Representative of the Secretary General, President of the Network for Women's Leadership in the Central African Republic	13 Council members,[a] all invitees	
	Report of the Secretary-General on the Central African Republic (S/2022/491)					
S/PV.9105 29 July	Letter dated 14 June 2022 from the Secretary-General addressed to the President of the Security Council (S/2022/489)	Draft resolution submitted by France (S/2022/579)	Central African Republic		13 Council members,[c] invitee[d]	Resolution 2648 (2022) 10-0-5[e] (adopted under Chapter VII)
	Letter dated 29 June 2022 from the Panel of Experts on the Central African Republic extended pursuant to resolution 2588 (2021) addressed to the President of the Security Council (S/2022/527)					

Meeting record and date	*Sub-item*	*Other documents*	*Rule 37 invitations*	*Rule 39 and other invitations*	*Speakers*	*Decision and vote (for-against-abstaining)*
S/PV.9156 19 October	Report of the Secretary-General on the Central African Republic (S/2022/762)		Central African Republic, Rwanda	Special Representative of the Secretary-General	13 Council members,[a] all invitees[d]	
S/PV.9190 14 November		Draft resolution submitted by France (S/2022/845)	Central African Republic		11 Council members,[f] invitee[d]	Resolution 2659 (2022) 12-0-3[g] (adopted under Chapter VII)

[a] Albania, Brazil, China, France, Gabon (also on behalf of Ghana and Kenya), India, Ireland, Mexico, Norway, Russian Federation, United Arab Emirates, United Kingdom and United States.

[b] The Central African Republic was represented by its Minister for Foreign Affairs, Francophonie and Central Africans Abroad. The Special Representative of the Chairperson of the African Union for the Central African Republic and the Executive Secretary of the International Conference on the Great Lakes Region participated in the meeting by videoconference.

[c] Albania, Brazil, China, France, Gabon, Ghana, Ireland, Kenya, Norway, Russian Federation, United Arab Emirates, United Kingdom and United States.

[d] The Central African Republic was represented by its Minister for Foreign Affairs, Francophonie and Central Africans Abroad.

[e] *For*: Albania, Brazil, France, India, Ireland, Mexico, Norway, United Arab Emirates, United Kingdom, United States; *against*: none; *abstaining*: China, Gabon, Ghana, Kenya, Russian Federation.

[f] Albania, China, France, Gabon, Ghana, Ireland, Kenya, Norway, Russian Federation, United Kingdom and United States.

[g] *For*: Albania, Brazil, France, Ghana, India, Ireland, Kenya, Mexico, Norway, United Arab Emirates, United Kingdom, United States; *against*: none; *abstaining*: China, Gabon, Russian Federation.

6. Central African region

In 2022, the Council held two meetings under the item entitled "Central African region". Both meetings took the form of briefings.[201] Under this item, the Council considered developments in Burundi, Cameroon, the Central African Republic, Chad, the Congo, the Democratic Republic of the Congo, Gabon and the Gulf of Guinea. More information on the meetings is given in the table below.[202] In 2022, the Secretary-General appointed a new Special Representative for Central Africa and Head of the United Nations Regional Office for Central Africa (UNOCA).[203]

During the period under review, consistent with the six-month reporting period requested by the Council in its presidential statement of 10 August 2018,[204] the Council heard a briefing by the Assistant Secretary-General for Africa in the Departments of Political and Peacebuilding Affairs and Peace Operations and the Special Representative of the Secretary-General for Central Africa and Head of UNOCA further to the reports of the Secretary-General on the situation in the Central African Region.[205] The Assistant Secretary-General and the Special Representative apprised the Council of the activities of UNOCA, its continued cooperation with the Economic Community of Central African States (ECCAS) and the United Nations Office for West Africa and the Sahel (UNOWAS), and its activities as the secretariat for the United Nations Standing Advisory Committee on Security Questions in Central Africa. They updated the Council on the political, human rights and security situation in the region, including on the preparation and conduct of electoral processes in several Central African countries and the subsequent

[201] For more information on the format of meetings, see part II.

[202] See also A/77/2, part II, chap. 24.

[203] See S/2022/582.

[204] S/PRST/2018/17, twentieth paragraph.

[205] S/2022/436 and S/2022/896.

political processes, the continued threats posed by terrorism and violent extremism, in particular in the Lake Chad basin, maritime insecurity in the Gulf of Guinea and the impact of climate change on the security and prosperity of Central African countries. The Council also heard two briefings by the President of the ECCAS Commission and a briefing by the Vice-President of the Coalition des organisations de la société civile d'Afrique centrale pour la préservation de la paix, la prévention des conflits, la resolution et la transformation des crises.

In her briefing to the Council at the meeting held on 8 June 2022,[206] the Assistant Secretary-General recalled that with several countries in the subregion, such as the Congo, Angola, Sao Tome and Principe, Equatorial Guinea, the Democratic Republic of the Congo and Gabon, preparing for crucial electoral processes, all stakeholders should create conditions conducive to credible, inclusive and peaceful elections and the Governments should widen the democratic space through the participation of women and young people in elections. She reported on the security challenges persisting in Cameroon, the Central African Republic, Chad and the Democratic Republic of the Congo, where attacks were exacerbating political and humanitarian crises. The extremist violence in the Lake Chad basin continued to a be concern and in that connection UNOCA and UNOWAS continued their high-level advocacy with Member States to increase coherence in their responses to violent extremism and provide technical support. On climate security, she emphasized the close partnership between UNOCA and ECCAS in better preventing, mitigating and managing the security risks related to climate change. The Assistant Secretary-General also highlighted the women and peace and security agenda as a priority for the subregion and UNOCA, providing support for capacity-building, consultations and public initiatives by civil society focused on women's participation in mediation, peacebuilding, political dialogue and elections in Angola, Chad, the Congo, Equatorial Guinea, Gabon and Sao Tome and Principe. The President of the ECCAS Commission, underlining the Commission's readiness to cooperate with the Council in the spirit of Chapter VIII of the Charter of the United Nations, reported on the positive developments in the region, including an improved security situation and strengthened confidence-building measures. Nonetheless, with the deteriorating security situation on the border between the Democratic Republic of the Congo and Rwanda and the postponement of the Chadian inclusive national dialogue, the President noted that the current political and security situation in the region continued to affect the collective security for which the Council was responsible. The Vice-President of the Coalition des organisations de la société civile d'Afrique centrale pour la préservation de la paix, la prévention des conflits, la resolution et la transformation des crises briefed the Council about the human rights situation and the implementation of the women and peace and security agenda in Central Africa.

In his briefing to the Council on 8 December 2022,[207] the Special Representative of the Secretary-General for Central Africa and Head of UNOCA reported on the electoral progress in the region, highlighting the increased participation and representation of women in political institutions and processes, in particular in Angola and Sao Tome and Principe, with a greater proportion of women in parliamentary assemblies and in government. He emphasized that the States of Central Africa should further open up political and civic space and strengthen the inclusivity, diversity and credibility of political processes, ensuring the legitimacy of the institutions resulting from the elections. In that connection, he urged State authorities to ensure full respect for fundamental rights and freedoms and to avoid any disproportionate use of force in maintaining public order. On the fight against climate change and its effects in Central Africa, the Special Representative noted the commitment of ECCAS and some of its member States during the twenty-seventh session of the Conference of the Parties to the United Nations Framework Convention on Climate Change, held in Sharm El-Sheikh, Egypt, and highlighted the role and capacity of subregional organizations to promote a common vision on key issues and the importance of regular consultations with United Nations entities for greater efficiency in "delivering as one". He concluded his briefing by noting that the year 2023 would be marked by important political processes in several countries in Central Africa and calling for increased support from the Council at the political level. At the same meeting, the President of the ECCAS Commission reported on the security and political situation in Central Africa, taking note of the elections held in the Congo, Angola, Sao Tome and Principe and Equatorial Guinea. Informing the Council about the recent activities of the Commission,

---

[206] See S/PV.9058.

[207] See S/PV.9213.

he reiterated his full support for the Luanda and Nairobi processes set up by the African Union and the East African Community and noted that ECCAS was exploring ways to support the regional force currently deployed in the eastern part of the Democratic Republic of the Congo and serving as an observer and a focal point for the two processes.

In 2022, the Council's deliberations were focused on major political and security challenges and on human rights, humanitarian and socioeconomic situations affecting the Central African region, including the adverse effects of climate change and food security exacerbated by geopolitical conflicts and the lasting impacts of the COVID-19 pandemic. On the political front, Council members welcomed the electoral processes in several countries in the Central African region, including Angola, the Congo, Sao Tome and Principe and Equatorial Guinea, and stressed the importance of delivering democratic elections and inclusive transitional processes and increasing the political participation and representation of women. Council members deliberated on the role of the United Nations and addressed its cooperation with subregional organizations, encouraging UNOCA and ECCAS to continue to assist State authorities in inclusive political processes, electoral reforms and commitment to addressing climate-related security risks. Council members highlighted the key role played by United Nations entities and subregional organizations in advancing the youth and peace and security agenda and promoting women's political participation in the Central African region. Several Council members took note of the improved maritime security situation in the Gulf of Guinea and the cooperation between UNOCA and UNOWAS in that regard.[208] Council members addressed the situation in specific countries, in particular: (a) the ongoing violence in the Central African Republic, including the human rights abuses compounding the existing humanitarian situation and the operations of the United Nations Multidimensional Integrated Stabilization Mission in the Central African Republic and the attacks against humanitarian and peacekeeping personnel, as well as the progress in the republican dialogue;[209] (b) the persisting political tensions in Cameroon, in particular the north-west and south-west regions, and the human rights violations and abuses against civilians;[210] (c) terrorism and violent extremism in the eastern part of the Democratic Republic of the Congo, as well as the emergence of tensions with Rwanda, reiterating the African Union's call for the resolution of disputes through diplomatic means with the mediation of Angola;[211] and (d) progress in the national dialogue and political transitions in Chad, including the signing of the Doha peace agreement and the appointment of an inclusive Government.[212] Council members deliberated on the cross-border threat posed by terrorism in the Lake Chad basin and expressed support for action by the Multinational Joint Task Force to respond to the threats posed by the activities of terrorist groups such as Da'esh, Boko Haram and the Allied Democratic Forces. They also continued to discuss the impact of the geopolitical conflict and socioeconomic and humanitarian crises on women and promoting the active participation of women in political processes and addressing sexual and gender-related violence. In 2021, by an exchange of letters between the Secretary-General and the President of the Security Council dated 3 and 6 August 2021,[213] the Council extended the mandate of UNOCA for three years, until 31 August 2024. In renewing the UNOCA mandate, the Council reiterated, with certain modifications, that the mandate would focus on four core objectives, namely: (a) monitoring political and security developments in Central Africa and carrying out good offices on behalf of the Secretary-General in order to prevent and resolve conflicts, and sustaining peace and advising the Secretary-General and United Nations entities in the area on sustaining peace issues in Central Africa; (b) enhancing subregional capacities for conflict prevention and mediation in countries of the subregion, with due attention to the principles of the Charter, including human rights and gender dimensions; (c) supporting and enhancing

[208] S/PV.9058 (Gabon (also on behalf of Ghana and Kenya), India, United Arab Emirates, Norway and China); and S/PV.9213 (Russian Federation, Brazil, Norway, Ireland and India).

[209] See S/PV.9058 (United Kingdom, Mexico, United States, India, Ireland, China and Albania); and S/PV.9213 (United Kingdom, Mexico, United States and France). For more information on the Central African Republic, see sect. 5 above.

[210] See S/PV.9058 (United Kingdom, Mexico United States, France, Brazil, Russian Federation, Ireland, Norway and Albania); and S/PV.9213 (Gabon (also on behalf of Ghana and Kenya), United Kingdom, United Arab Emirates, Mexico, Brazil, Albania, Norway, United States, France and India).

[211] See S/PV.9058 (Gabon (also on behalf of Ghana and Kenya), India, Norway and China); and S/PV.9213 (Gabon (also on behalf of Ghana and Kenya), Mexico, China and United States).

[212] See S/PV.9058 (Gabon (also on behalf of Ghana and Kenya), United States, France, Brazil and Albania); and S/PV.9213 (Gabon (also on behalf of Ghana and Kenya), Brazil, France and India).

[213] S/2021/719 and S/2021/720.

United Nations efforts in the subregion, as well as regional and subregional initiatives on peace and security, including from human rights and gender perspectives; and (d) enhancing coherence and coordination in the work of the United Nations in the subregion on peace and security.[214]

Meetings: Central African region, 2022

Meeting record and date	*Sub-item*	*Other documents*	*Rule 37 invitations*	*Rule 39 and other invitations*	*Speakers*	*Decision and vote (for- against-abstaining)*
S/PV.9058 8 June	Report of the Secretary-General on the situation in Central Africa and the activities of the United Nations Regional Office for Central Africa (UNOCA) (S/2022/436)			Assistant Secretary-General for Africa, President of the Commission of the Economic Community of Central African States (ECCAS), Vice-President of the Coalition des organisations de la société civile d'Afrique centrale pour la préservation de la paix, la prévention des conflits, la resolution et la transformation des crises	13 Council members,[a] all invitees	
S/PV.9213 8 December	Report of the Secretary-General on the situation in Central Africa and the activities of UNOCA (S/2022/896)			Special Representative of the Secretary-General for Central Africa and Head of UNOCA, President of ECCAS	13 Council members,[a] all invitees[b]	

[a] Brazil, China, France, Gabon (also on behalf of Ghana and Kenya), India, Ireland, Mexico, Norway, Russian Federation, United Arab Emirates, United Kingdom and United States.

[c] The President of the ECCAS Commission participated in the meeting by videoconference.

7. Reports of the Secretary-General on the Sudan and South Sudan

During the period under review, the Council held 22 meetings and adopted six resolutions under the item entitled "Reports of the Secretary-General on the Sudan and South Sudan". Sixteen of the meetings took the form of briefings, and six were convened for the adoption of a resolution.[215] More information on the meetings, including on participants and outcomes, is provided in the tables below. In addition to the meetings, Council members also held informal consultations of the whole in connection with the item.[216] Furthermore, the Council held two private (closed) meetings with countries contributing

[214] S/2021/719, annex, objectives 1–4. For more information on the mandate of UNOCA, see part X, sect. II.

[215] For more information on the format of meetings, see part II.

[216] See A/77/2, part II, chap. 26.

troops and police to the United Nations Mission in South Sudan (UNMISS) and the United Nations Interim Security Force for Abyei (UNISFA) pursuant to resolution 1353 (2001).[217]

Consistent with prior practice, the Council considered several topics under the item, namely: (a) the situation in the Sudan and the mandate of the United Nations Integrated Transition Assistance Mission in the Sudan (UNITAMS); (b) relations between the Sudan and South Sudan, the situation in the Abyei Area and the mandate of UNISFA; and (c) the situation in South Sudan and the mandate of UNMISS.[218] The Council also discussed the work of the Committees and Panels of Experts concerning the Sudan and South Sudan and the implementation of resolution 1593 (2005), by which the Council referred the situation in Darfur to the Prosecutor of the International Criminal Court.

In relation to the Sudan, the Council heard four briefings by the Special Representative of the Secretary-General for the Sudan and Head of UNITAMS further to the periodic reports of the Secretary-General on the situation in the country and the activities of the Mission.[219] The Council also heard one briefing by a civil society representative.[220] The Special Representative focused his statements on the impact of the military takeover of the Government on 25 October 2021 on the political, economic, humanitarian and security situation in the Sudan. He also updated the Council on the work of the African Union, the Intergovernmental Authority on Development (IGAD) and the United Nations in support of the Sudanese-owned and Sudanese-led political dialogue to restore the political transition.

At the meeting held on 28 March,[221] the Special Representative noted that the Sudan remained without a functioning Government since the coup d'état. Furthermore, protests against the coup d'état and the violent repression of them continued, and the economic, humanitarian and security situations in the country were deteriorating. In terms of economic developments, the Special Representative reported on the 45 per cent fall of the Sudanese pound against the United States dollar, the dramatic price increase for basic goods and services, the absence of foreign investment and the dwindling of exports. He added that the combined effects of the conflict, economic crisis and poor harvests would likely double the number of people facing acute hunger to approximately 18 million by the end of 2022. The Special Representative stated that, in the absence of a political solution to the crisis, the security situation had worsened across the country. In Darfur, crime and lawlessness were on the rise and intercommunal conflict had intensified. He welcomed steps taken by the Government of the Sudan and the signatories to the Juba Agreement for Peace in the Sudan to begin the training for and standing up of the joint security-keeping force. He expressed support for the Government's request for international support to implement disarmament, demobilization and reintegration measures. The Special Representative noted that, meanwhile, frequent protests against military rule continued in Khartoum and elsewhere, with protestors continuing to be killed, injured, arrested and subject to criminal charges. He added that it was of particular concern that women were targeted and subjected to violence and intimidation by members of the security forces, mentioning that, as at 22 March, 16 women had reportedly been raped during protests in Khartoum.

The Special Representative announced that the United Nations, the African Union and IGAD had agreed to join efforts in supporting the Sudan through the next phase of the political process by facilitating an inclusive Sudanese-owned and Sudanese-led political process with the full and meaningful participation of women. According to the Special Representative, in order to have a chance of succeeding, the political talks required favourable conditions that entailed an end to the violence and the establishment of the right to hold peaceful demonstrations, the release of political detainees and a firm commitment to phase out the emergency status in the country.

---

[217] The private meetings were held on 3 March and 7 November in connection with the item entitled "Meeting of the Security Council with the troop- and police-contributing countries pursuant to resolution 1353 (2001), annex II, sections A and B"; for UNMISS, see S/PV.8985, and for UNISFA, see S/PV.9186. See also A/77/2, part II, chap. 21.

[218] For more information on the mandates of UNISFA, UNMISS and UNITAMS, see part X.

[219] See S/PV.9006, S/PV.9041, S/PV.9129 and S/PV.9211.

[220] See S/PV.9129.

[221] See S/PV.9006.

At a meeting held on 13 September,[222] the Special Representative noted the announcement on 4 July by the Chair of the Sovereign Council, Lieutenant General Abdel-Fattah Al-Burhan, of the military's intention to withdraw from politics, which generated momentum among civilian forces, resulting in several major initiatives aimed at reaching a common civilian vision. One such initiative was a draft constitutional framework presented by the Sudanese Bar Association, which gathered a broad spectrum of civilian stakeholders. The Special Representative emphasized that, while important differences about the institutional division of powers, in particular the role of the military, remained, there was nevertheless a wide-ranging consensus on, among other things, the need for a civilian Head of State, an independent Prime Minister and Cabinet composed of experts and technocrats, and that transitional justice should be high on the list of priorities. With regard to the security situation, he noted the particularly worrying surge of violence in Darfur and Blue Nile, with UNITAMS documenting 40 incidents of intercommunal violence resulting in the death of more than 300 civilians from 24 May to 28 August. He urged all communities to refrain from hate speech and the authorities to urgently address protection gaps. As a positive step in the implementation of the Juba Peace Agreement, the Special Representative referred to the graduation of the first batch of 2,000 fighters for the joint security-keeping force in Darfur, while also urging the authorities to begin their deployment. He informed Council members that humanitarian needs were at record levels owing to a combination of ongoing political instability, economic crises, a rise in intercommunal violence, poor harvests and floods. Some 11.7 million people were facing acute hunger and the 2022 Humanitarian Response Plan was only 32 per cent funded.

At the meeting held on 7 December,[223] the Special Representative informed the Council that, on 5 December, the military leadership and a broad range of civilian actors signed a political framework agreement to lay the ground for a final political accord and the formation of a new civilian Government, leading the country towards recovery and democratic elections over a two-year transitional phase. The agreement followed negotiations, facilitated by the trilateral mechanism, based on the draft constitutional document prepared under the auspices of the Sudanese Bar Association. While the signing of the framework agreement was an important breakthrough, critical contentious issues such as security sector reform and the merger of forces, transitional justice, the implementation of the Juba Peace Agreement, the status of the dismantling committee and the situation in the east of the Sudan still needed to be addressed. He underlined the importance of a sufficiently inclusive process in the lead-up to a final political agreement in order to safeguard against the influence of those who did not see their interests advanced by a political settlement. He also cautioned that as the Sudan got closer to reaching a final political agreement, those who did not see their interests advanced by a political settlement could escalate attempts to undermine the process.

Reflecting on the challenges during the 13 months since the coup d'état, the Special Representative recalled that over 900 people had reportedly been killed and many more injured in violent conflict and that the resurgence of large-scale violence demonstrated the increasing fragility at the State level, exacerbated by the continued government vacuum. In that regard, he noted that the situation in Blue Nile remained precarious despite the imposition of a state of emergency, while intercommunal violence in the Lagawa locality, West Kordofan, in mid-October had resulted in the killing of at least 19 and displacement of 65,000 people. Furthermore, there was intense fighting in Central Darfur between the Sudan Liberation Army led by Abdul Wahid Al-Nur and the Rapid Support Forces. Across the Sudan, 260,000 people had been displaced since the beginning of 2022 as a result of the conflict. Humanitarian partners estimated that about 15.8 million people, one third of the population, would need humanitarian assistance in 2023, which was an increase of 1.5 million compared with 2022. He concluded by noting that the framework agreement offered a path for realizing the aspirations of Sudanese young people, women and men and that working together with the United Nations, Council members and the larger international community in support of those efforts could help them to move forward on their chosen path.

In his statement to the Council on 13 September,[224] the President of the Sudan Social Development Organization discussed the efforts of civil society under the Sudanese Bar Association initiative to reach

[222] See S/PV.9129.
[223] See S/PV.9211.
[224] See S/PV.9129.

an agreement on a civilian Government. He underscored that a civilian Government could not be established without a unified army and State authority and that such a Government was necessary to stabilize the economic situation, reform the civil service, begin constitutional reform, resolve the issue of transitional justice and address insecurity in Darfur. He highlighted the lack of progress on ensuring the meaningful representation of women during the transition period and noted that, at the initiative of the Sudanese Bar Association, civilian stakeholders agreed that 50 per cent of the Cabinet and the Sovereign Council and more than 40 per cent of the Transitional Legislative Council must be represented by women.

In their discussions in 2022, most Council members expressed concern and disappointment with the negative impact of the military takeover of 25 October 2021 on the political transition, as well as socioeconomic, humanitarian and security conditions in the Sudan. Council members welcomed and expressed support for the African Union-IGAD-United Nations trilateral mechanism and urged all stakeholders to negotiate in good faith with a view to restoring the political transition. Multiple Council members stressed that the transition process must be inclusive and consider the concerns of all stakeholders, in particular women, youth and other marginalized groups.[225] At a meeting held on 11 December, Council members welcomed the signing of the political framework agreement on 5 December, describing it as a good step towards ending the political crisis in the country, with a number of speakers calling upon the parties to work towards a final agreement and the restoration of a civilian Government.[226] Some speakers[227] called on other political stakeholders that had not done so to sign the framework agreement.

Council members condemned the violence and human rights violations against protesters against the military takeover, including acts of sexual violence, and called on the military authorities to create the conditions necessary for political dialogue by lifting the state of emergency, allowing peaceful protests and freedom of expression and releasing all political detainees.[228] With respect to insecurity and violence in Darfur, Blue Nile and Western Kordofan, some speakers urged the Government to ensure the full implementation of the Juba Peace Agreement and the national plan for the protection of civilians.[229] Several delegations stressed the need for the international community to ensure continued support to the Government to ensure the full implementation of the peace agreement and the national plan.[230]

With respect to the economic and humanitarian situation, several delegations expressed concern with the decision of international financial institutions and donors to suspend aid to the Sudan following the military takeover, noting in particular the impact of such measures on the civilian population, and objected to linking such support to progress in the political process.[231] In that regard, the representative of the Russian Federation noted that the politicization of the provision of economic and financial assistance had already led to divisions in society, as well as a loss of civic trust in the transitional authorities, which in turn had led to general instability and new separatist trends in the country.[232] The representatives of Ghana and Kenya, speaking on behalf of the three African members of the Council, echoed the appeal of the Secretary-General for the creation of exceptional modalities to ensure continued

[225] See S/PV.9006 (India, Ireland, Albania, Norway and Mexico); S/PV.9041 (Kenya (also on behalf of Gabon and Ghana), United Arab Emirates, Albania, Brazil, Russian Federation, Norway, Mexico, Ireland and United States); S/PV.9129 (Ireland, Norway, Brazil, India, Gabon (also on behalf of Ghana and Kenya) and Albania); and S/PV.9211 (United Kingdom, Norway, Ireland, United Arab Emirates, Mexico and France).

[226] See S/PV.9211 (United Kingdom, Norway, United States, Albania, United Arab Emirates, Russian Federation, France and India).

[227] Russian Federation, China and Mexico.

[228] See S/PV.9006 (United Kingdom, France, United States, Ireland, Albania and Mexico); S/PV.9041 (United Kingdom, Kenya (also on behalf of Gabon and Ghana), Albania, Norway, France, Mexico, Ireland and United States); S/PV.9129 (United Kingdom); and S/PV.9211 (United Kingdom, Norway, Ireland, Ghana (speaking also on behalf of Gabon and Kenya), United States and France).

[229] See S/PV.9006 (United States, Ghana (also on behalf of Gabon and Kenya), Ireland, Albania, Norway and Mexico); S/PV.9041 (Kenya (also on behalf of Gabon and Ghana), Norway, France, Mexico and Ireland); S/PV.9129 (Ireland and France); and S/PV.9211 (United Kingdom, Ghana (also on behalf of Gabon and Kenya), United States, Albania, Brazil and Mexico).

[230] See S/PV.9041 (Kenya (also on behalf of Gabon and Ghana)); S/PV.9129 (United Arab Emirates and China); and S/PV.9211 (United Arab Emirates).

[231] See S/PV.9006 (India, China and United Arab Emirates); S/PV.9129 (United Arab Emirates, India and China); and S/PV.9211 (India).

[232] See S/PV.9006.

international assistance for the Sudan and called on the international community to reconsider the temporary suspension of aid.[233] Other Council members opined that an inclusive political settlement and the establishment of a civilian Government was the best way to improve socioeconomic and humanitarian conditions in the country.[234] In his remarks at Council meetings, the representative of the Sudan appealed to the international community for financial support for the implementation of the Juba Peace Agreement, in particular the provisions of security sector reform and disarmament, demobilization and reintegration and the resumption of development assistance to mitigate the impact of necessary economic reforms.[235]

By its resolution 2636 (2022) of 3 June, the Council unanimously extended the existing mandate of UNITAMS as contained in resolution 2579 (2021) for a period of one year, until 3 June 2023.[236] After the adoption, the representative of the United Kingdom stated that, as penholder, his delegation's preference would have been for the Council to adopt a substantive resolution that voiced support for the vital efforts of UNITAMS in facilitating a Sudanese-led process to restore a civilian-led transition towards democracy.[237] He added that a substantive resolution would also have enabled the priorities of the Mission to be updated to reflect the request of the Sudan for additional support on disarmament, demobilization and reintegration, transitional justice and civilian protection. A preference for a substantive resolution reflecting the realities on the ground was also expressed by the representatives of Albania, Ireland, Mexico and Norway. The representative of the Russian Federation urged all external players, including UNITAMS, to play a constructive role and recalled that the Mission was deployed at the invitation of the Government to support national efforts in strengthening peace, fulfilling the terms of the Juba Peace Agreement, dealing with issues relating to internally displaced persons and mobilizing assistance for economic development. The representative of China stated that the international community should maintain the patience necessary to create space for the resolution of differences among parties and avoid choosing sides, aggravating tensions and exerting excessive pressure. He recalled that UNITAMS was a political mission established at the request of the Sudan under Chapter VI of the Charter of the United Nations, that it had to abide by the mandate of the Council and respect the sovereignty of the Sudan, and called upon it to strengthen its mandate on mobilizing international development assistance.

Council members also heard four briefings by the Chair of the Committee established pursuant to resolution 1591 (2005) on the work of the Committee and its Panel of Experts.[238] The Chair informed Council members that the Panel had submitted its final report to the Committee in December 2021, after which the Committee had reiterated some of the Panel's recommendations to the Permanent Representatives of the Sudan, the Central African Republic, Chad, Egypt and Libya on 1 March 2022.[239] By its resolution 2620 (2022) of 15 February, acting under Chapter VII of the Charter, the Council unanimously extended the mandate of the Panel of Experts for a period of 13 months, until 12 March 2023.[240] The Council took note of the report of the Secretary-General of 31 July 2021 (S/2021/696), as requested in resolution 2562 (2021), which provided a review of the situation in Darfur and recommending benchmarks to assess the sanctions measures. The Council also expressed its intention to consider by 31 August 2022 adjusting the measures to respond to the situation in Darfur establishing clear, well-identified and realistic key benchmarks.[241] In Council discussions during the reporting period, several Council members, as well as the representative of the Sudan, consistently stressed that the sanctions measures no longer corresponded to the situation in Darfur and impeded the implementation of Juba Peace Agreement and the Government's ability to maintain security and protect civilians.[242]

---

[233] See S/PV.9006 (Ghana); S/PV.9041 (Kenya); and S/PV.9211 (Ghana).

[234] See S/PV.9041 (Albania, Norway and United States); and S/PV.9129 (United Kingdom).

[235] See S/PV.9006, S/PV.9041, S/PV.9129 and S/PV.9211.

[236] Resolution 2636 (2022), para. 1.

[237] See S/PV.9054.

[238] See S/PV.9005, S/PV.9070, S/PV.9128 and S/PV.9210.

[239] See S/PV.9005. See also S/2022/48.

[240] Resolution 2620 (2022), para. 2.

[241] Resolution 2620 (2022), para. 5. The Council did not establish benchmarks to assess the measures in 2022.

[242] See S/PV.8964 (China and Russian Federation); S/PV.9005 (Sudan); S/PV.9006 (Russian Federation and China); S/PV.9041 (China); S/PV.9070 (Russian Federation, China and Gabon); S/PV.9129 (China and Russian Federation); and S/PV.9211 (Russian Federation, China and Sudan).

The representative of China expressed regret that the Council was not able to define benchmarks by 31 August and noted that such benchmarks had to be clear, well defined and realistic.[243]

In addition to the above, pursuant to resolution 1593 (2005), the Prosecutor of the International Court briefed the Council twice in 2022 in relation to Darfur.[244] At a meeting held on 17 January,[245] he expressed concern with the suspension of investigative activities in the Sudan by his office following the military takeover and stressed the need for safe and secure access to the country and the archives. At a meeting held on 23 August,[246] he gave a briefing to the Council by videoconference from Khartoum and reported on his first visit to Darfur and the interaction with Sudanese authorities and internally displaced persons. In terms of procedural developments, he reported that the case against Abd-Al-Rahman ("Ali Kushayb"), the senior Janjaweed militia leader and sole suspect in the Court's custody in relation to the situation in Darfur, had started in April on 31 counts of war crimes and crimes against humanity. Furthermore, he stated that the Government's cooperation with his office had taken a step backwards in recent months and underlined the need for the issuance of multiple entry visa to help with the establishment of an office in Khartoum, the collection of evidence and the building of relationships with the Sudanese authorities and victims.

With respect to the Abyei Area and the situation between the Sudan and South Sudan, Council members heard two briefings by the Special Envoy of the Secretary-General for the Horn of Africa and one each by the Under-Secretary-General for Peace Operations and the Assistant Secretary-General for Africa in the Departments of Political and Peacebuilding Affairs and Peace Operations.[247] At the meeting held on 21 April,[248] the Under-Secretary-General for Peace Operations stated that, while the overall security situation in Abyei remained calm, the trust deficit between the Misseriya and Ngok Dinka communities was still of great concern. He noted several incidents of intercommunal violence since October 2021 in Noong/Annam, Kolom, Leul/Al Luo and the Amiet common market/Faydelzaraf areas that resulted in the killing of 29 people, including two women, and the injury of 30 persons from both communities. He underlined that it was first and foremost for the Governments of the Sudan and South Sudan to renew their engagement on the final status of Abyei and called upon them to use the next meeting of the Abyei Joint Oversight Committee to move forward on the issue. He mentioned that significant progress was made in the development of the Abyei joint programme, through consultations between a team of representatives from the Department of Peace Operations, the Development Coordination Office and the United Nations country teams in the Sudan and South Sudan with women, youth, elders and other community members. The Under-Secretary-General informed the Council that the humanitarian situation had deteriorated, owing largely to the intercommunal violence between the Twic Dinka and Ngok Dinka communities near Agok in February and March. With respect to the other mandated area of UNISFA, he reported an absence of progress on reoperationalizing Joint Border Verification and Monitoring Mechanism team sites 11 and 12 and the headquarters of Sector 1 in Gok Machar after UNISFA was forced to relocate in 2021. Given the three direct attacks against UNISFA patrols in the past two months, the Under-Secretary-General concluded his remarks by strongly emphasizing the need to ensure the safety and security of UNISFA peacekeepers and called on the relevant authorities to investigate those incidents as a matter of priority.

In her statement at the same meeting, the Special Envoy of the Secretary-General for the Horn of Africa stated that, with the removal of the civilian Government in Khartoum, the momentum towards the resolution of outstanding issues between the Sudan and South Sudan had suddenly stopped. Specifically, the meeting of the Joint Political and Security Mechanism, which had been scheduled to take place in January, had not been held and no action had been taken on the decisions reached at the previous meeting, including the withdrawal of Sudanese and South Sudanese forces from the safe demilitarized border zone and the commitment of South Sudan to mediate between communities in Aweil towards the reactivation of the three locations of the Joint Border Verification and Monitoring Mechanism. The Special Envoy

[243] See S/PV.9129. For further detail on the discussion, see part II, sect. VIII.
[244] See S/PV.8948 and S/PV.9113.
[245] See S/PV.8948.
[246] See S/PV.9113.
[247] See S/PV.9020 and S/PV.9170.
[248] See S/PV.9020.

nevertheless highlighted multiple engagements between the two countries in support of each other's peace processes. For example, in March, Lieutenant General Abdel-Fattah Al-Burhan visited Juba to address tensions between the President of South Sudan, Salva Kiir Mayardit, and the First Vice-President, Riek Machar, over the sharing of senior leadership positions in the future national army. South Sudanese officials, meanwhile, continued to shuttle between Juba and Khartoum to facilitate a solution between the military and civilian components of the transitional Government of the Sudan, as well as to exert efforts to convince Abdul Wahid Al-Nur and his faction of the Sudan Liberation Movement/Army to join the peace process and to secure the resumption of negotiations between the Government and the Al-Hilu faction of the Sudan People's Liberation Movement-North. Lieutenant General Al-Burhan and Mr. Kiir also agreed to focus on cooperation along their common border, starting with the development of unitized oil fields, including in the Abyei Area.

At the meeting held on 27 October,[249] the Assistant Secretary-General for Africa highlighted the renewed engagement of the Sudan and South Sudan to address the final status of Abyei and border issues. She welcomed their agreement to enhance cooperation on issues related to Abyei and its final status, as well as their willingness to resume the meetings of the Abyei Joint Oversight Committee, which had not met since 2017. Regarding the security situation, she noted a shift in the conflict dynamics over previous years, with a decrease in intercommunal violence between the Misseriya and Ngok Dinka communities in 2022. However, since February, a new conflict had emerged between the Ngok Dinka and Twic Dinka communities in southern Abyei with the loss of lives and displacement on both sides. In coordination with UNMISS, UNISFA maintained close contact with the Government of South Sudan to support mediation efforts and, in particular, plans for a government-facilitated peace conference in South Sudan. The Assistant Secretary-General expressed concern that, amid the tensions between the two communities, seven attacks on peacekeepers had been recorded, including on 16 October when local community members threatened UNISFA personnel and demanded the removal of Twic Dinka employees and some international staff members from the Mission's headquarters. Finally, the Assistant Secretary-General reported that the reconfiguration of UNISFA into a multinational peacekeeping force was near completion, with 2,567 military personnel out of the authorized 3,250 personnel in place. She expressed the view that, with the Ngok Dinka-Twic Dinka conflict creating new protection needs in the south, the new force must be better equipped to cover a wider area.

In her remarks, the Special Envoy of the Secretary-General for the Horn of Africa noted that, at the meeting of the Joint Political and Security Mechanism on 24 May, the two countries agreed to re-establish the Abyei Joint Oversight Committee, activate river transport, immediately open border crossings and recommit to withdrawing forces from the safe demilitarized border zone. Since May, working with the Chairperson of the African Union High-Level Implementation Panel, the Special Envoy had held separate consultations with the Ngok Dinka and Misseriya communities to find a way out of the stalemate on the final status of Abyei. She added that, on 24 October, the Sudan and South Sudan agreed to jointly expedite the provision of services to the citizens of Abyei and to activate joint mechanisms to provide humanitarian services. She concluded by stating that, notwithstanding the improved bilateral relations, a renewed commitment regarding the implementation of transitional arrangements, as well as the dispute resolution over the final status of Abyei, could not be set apart from the fragile internal situations in both countries.

In their discussions on Abyei and the border during the reporting period, Council members welcomed the improvement in relations between the Sudan and South Sudan and stressed the importance of using that as an impetus to make progress on the final status of the territory. Council members reiterated their calls for the implementation of the agreement of 20 June 2011, in particular through the establishment of the joint institutions provided thereunder, and the regular holding of meetings of the Abyei Joint Oversight Committee and the Joint Political and Security Mechanism. Most Council members expressed serious concern regarding persistent intercommunal violence in Abyei, including the conflict between the Ngok Dinka and Twic Dinka communities. In that regard, a number of speakers highlighted the importance of the role of UNISFA in supporting intercommunal peace initiatives and dialogue.[250]

---

[249] See S/PV.9170.

[250] See S/PV.9020 (United States, Gabon (also on behalf of Ghana and Kenya), United Arab Emirates, Russian Federation, China, Mexico and Norway); and S/PV.9170 (United States, United Arab Emirates, Russian Federation and Ireland).

Regarding the operations of UNISFA, many delegations called on the Governments of the Sudan and South Sudan to ensure the Mission's freedom of movement, including the ability of the Joint Border Verification and Monitoring Mechanism to fully implement its mandate and return to its sector headquarters in Gok Machar.[251] Lastly, several Council members reiterated their calls on the Government of the Sudan to expedite the issuance of visas for Mission staff, including police personnel.[252]

By resolutions 2630 (2022) of 12 May and 2660 (2022) of 14 November, both adopted unanimously, the Council twice extended the mandate of UNISFA to support the Joint Border Verification and Monitoring Mechanism and, acting under Chapter VII of the Charter, the mission's mandate in the Abyei Area.[253] While resolution 2630 (2022) extended the mandate for six months, until 14 November, resolution 2660 (2022) did so for one year, until 15 November 2023. By virtue of both resolutions, the Council urged the Governments of the Sudan and South Sudan to provide full support for UNISFA in the implementation of its mandate and deployment of its personnel.[254] In resolution 2630 (2022), the Council further reiterated that the Abyei Area should be demilitarized from any forces, as well as armed elements of the local communities, and urged the two Governments and the local communities to take all necessary steps in that regard.[255]

In connection with the situation in South Sudan, the Council heard four briefings by the Special Representative of the Secretary-General for South Sudan and Head of UNMISS further to the periodic reports of the Secretary-General on the situation in the country.[256] The Council also heard briefings by the interim Chairperson of the reconstituted Joint Monitoring and Evaluation Commission,[257] a representative of the Office for the Coordination of Humanitarian Affairs[258] and three civil society representatives.[259] In his briefings to the Council, the Special Representative of the Secretary-General focused on the status of the implementation of the Revitalized Agreement on the Resolution of the Conflict in the Republic in South Sudan as the two-year transitional period drew to a close. He also updated Council members on increasing levels of intercommunal violence and humanitarian needs in the country and the role of UNMISS in the protection of civilians and supporting the implementation of the Revitalized Agreement.

In his first briefing of the year on 7 March,[260] the Special Representative stated that the ceasefire in South Sudan continued to largely hold, with civilian casualties significantly reduced over the previous year. On the progress in the implementation of the Revitalized Agreement, he noted the conclusion of executive appointments at the national and state levels and the reconstitution of the Transitional National Legislative Assembly, the Council of States and state parliaments. He was concerned, however, that as the remaining 12 months of the transitional period commenced, an accumulation of unfulfilled commitments remained, with limited time to address them. Key pending benchmarks related to the necessary conducive political and civic space, as well as technical and logistical prerequisites and an agreed timetable for free and fair elections. He also recalled that the constitution-making bill was still pending and that the graduation of unified forces was yet to commence, with no agreement on the command structure.

The Special Representative stressed that the slow implementation of the Revitalized Agreement came at a cost and that peace dividends for the South Sudanese remained elusive. Nowhere was that more clearly reflected than in the frustration of marginalized youth, many of whom had joined tribal militias

---

[251] See S/PV.9020 (United States, Gabon (also on behalf of Ghana and Kenya), India, United Arab Emirates, France, Ireland, China, Mexico, Albania and United Kingdom); and S/PV.9170 (Ghana (also on behalf of Gabon and Kenya), Albania, France, United Kingdom, Brazil, India, Mexico and Ireland).

[252] See S/PV.9020 (United States, India, Ireland, Albania and Norway); and S/PV.9170 (United States, Ghana (also on behalf of Gabon and Kenya), Albania, Norway, India, Mexico and Ireland).

[253] Resolutions 2630 (2022) and 2660 (2022), paras. 1 and 2.

[254] Resolutions 2630 (2022) and 2660 (2022), para. 4.

[255] Resolution 2630 (2022), para. 6.

[256] See S/PV.8987, S/PV.9067, S/PV.9134 and S/PV.9219. See also S/2022/156, S/2022/468, S/2022/689 and S/2022/918.

[257] See S/PV.8987 and S/PV.9219.

[258] See S/PV.9067.

[259] See S/PV.8987, S/PV.9067 and S/PV.9134.

[260] See S/PV.8987.

or channelled their anger at humanitarians and peacekeepers. He noted that subnational violence, which was fuelled by national and local political competition, continued to spread. The conflicts involved the non-signatory armed groups, clashes between factions of the Sudan People's Liberation Movement-Army in Opposition and community disputes over land and resources, including those induced by climate change. He added that humanitarian needs were projected to continue growing, with the third consecutive year of floods, exacerbated by insecurity and the impact of the COVID-19 pandemic, while the appetite of donors to furnish additional resources was trending in reverse. With regard to the efforts of UNMISS, the Special Representative stated that the Mission had established 125 temporary operating bases to prevent and respond to conflict hotspots and had enhanced its capabilities by moving away from static security tasks and maximizing the mobility of the force, which contributed to a 42 per cent decline in the number of civilian casualties over the previous year. He also stated that UNMISS stood ready to provide technical advice on constitutional and electoral matters that were ultimately sovereign choices for the South Sudanese to make.

In his remarks on 20 June,[261] the Special Representative noted that, after the opposition's withdrawal from the transitional security mechanisms amid a tense security situation at the end of March, the parties reached a breakthrough agreement on 3 April on a single joint command structure for the necessary unified forces. It was now expected, according to the Special Representative, for the parties to agree on a road map, recommitting themselves to the Revitalized Agreement, as jointly called for by the African Union, IGAD, the reconstituted Joint Monitoring and Evaluation Commission and the United Nations. He stated that more than 80 per cent of civilian casualties in 2022 had been attributed to intercommunal violence and community-based militias and noted in particular the spread of conflict in Eastern and Central Equatoria, Unity, Warrap and Jonglei States, as well as in the Abyei Area.

At the meeting held on 16 September,[262] the Special Representative informed Council members that on 4 August the signatory parties had agreed on the road map for the remaining tasks, which included revised benchmarks and timelines providing for an extension of the transitional period for 24 months and the holding of elections in December 2024. He added that, while the road map was a welcome development, the extension of the transitional period had met with mixed reactions by many South Sudanese, who had raised concerns about the inclusivity of the process and had called for greater clarity around the Government's commitment to implement the agreement on time.

On 13 December,[263] the Special Representative stated that notable progress had been made in the previous months in the implementation of the Revitalized Agreement, with the adoption of essential bills by the national legislature, including the constitution-making bill, as well as the ratification of the road map of 4 August. He noted that the graduation of the first phase of the necessary unified forces was largely complete and that the second phase required urgent financial, logistical and political support from the Government. While citing some progress in the preparation of the National Elections Act, he expressed concern that the deadlines relating to the Political Parties Act, the Political Parties Council, the reconstituted National Constitution Review Commission and the establishment of the Constitution Drafting Commission had been missed, causing a "domino effect" on subsequent key benchmarks in the road map. He reiterated the position of UNMISS that the first of the two phases recommended by the 2021 electoral needs assessment mission,[264] namely fulfilling the legal requirements and preparing the grounds and environment for the conduct of elections, had to be completed before material assistance for their actual conduct would be contemplated.

With regard to the security situation, he reported that the year-long fracturing of the Sudan People's Liberation Movement-Army in Opposition and the Kit-Gwang splinter group had taken on an ethnic dimension in the Nile River corridor of Upper Nile State, and condemned the resulting human rights violations and abuses, including conflict-related sexual violence. He stated that UNMISS was coordinating with humanitarian partners to accommodate fleeing civilians and engaging politically at the state and national levels to bring needed attention to the conflict and encourage a resolution. Moreover,

---

[261] See S/PV.9067.
[262] See S/PV.9134.
[263] See S/PV.9219.
[264] See S/2021/661.

as tensions continued to simmer and intensify as the electoral date drew closer, the Special Representative underscored that UNMISS was prioritizing the protection of civilians in all aspects of its mandated tasks. He deemed that those efforts would go a long way to support an expansion of civic and political space and a culture of non-violent debate and dispute resolution. With 9.4 million people projected to need humanitarian and protection assistance in 2023, he urged partners to continue to respond generously to the Humanitarian Response Plan. Finally, the Special Representative concluded his remarks by stating that the new road map was a "second mortgage" on the Revitalized Agreement and that, as moral guarantors and partners of the agreement, the international community had a collective task of ensuring that the parties had the best possible international support to fulfil their commitments to the people of South Sudan.

In his statements to the Council, the interim Chairperson of the reconstituted Joint Monitoring and Evaluation Commission focused on the implementation of the Revitalized Agreement, including the development and progress of the road map of 4 August. On 7 March, he observed that the most critical tasks for the conduct of free, fair and credible elections and the fulfilment of the Revitalized Agreement were the unification of forces and their deployment, the enactment of a permanent constitution, the review of the political parties and electoral-related laws and the constitution of the Political Parties Council and the National Election Commission.[265] Concerning the recurring challenges, he cited the lack of sufficient resources, the insufficient political will and commitment of some actors, trust deficits among the parties and capacity gaps, subnational violence and activities of hold-out groups, military defections from one signatory party to another, seasonal flooding and the COVID-19 pandemic. Given the challenges and the timelines provided under the Revitalized Agreement, he noted that the reconstituted Joint Monitoring and Evaluation Commission had tasked the Government of South Sudan with developing a clear road map and strategy on how to implement the outstanding critical tasks. On 13 December, the interim Chairperson provided an update on the implementation of the road map, in particular with respect to governance, permanent ceasefire and transitional security arrangements, humanitarian assistance and reconstruction, resource, economic and financial management, and the making of the permanent constitution.[266] In that context, he recommended to the Council to increase its engagement with the Government to adhere to the road map timelines and prioritize their implementation through the provision of predictable, timely and adequate funding for all tasks. He also recommended that the Council encourage the Government to ensure that civic and political space were guaranteed and protected and to urgently address the root causes of intercommunal violence and insecurity, in particular in Upper Nile and Jonglei States, and that the Council remain seized of the peace process and consider undertaking regular visits to South Sudan as a show of solidarity.

In her remarks on 20 June,[267] the Acting Director in the Operations and Advocacy Division of Office for the Coordination of Humanitarian Affairs informed Council members that, against a backdrop of profound macroeconomic challenges in South Sudan, the drivers of conflict and climate shocks had resulted in a dire humanitarian situation. She noted that 8.3 million people were likely to experience severe food insecurity during the lean season, of whom 2.9 million would likely face emergency levels of hunger and 87,000 would probably face catastrophic and famine-like levels of food insecurity. South Sudan was facing a fourth year of above-average rainfall, which had disrupted the agricultural season and constrained food production. The Acting Director noted that more than 2 million people remained internally displaced and more than 2.3 million were refugees. While underlining the commitment of humanitarian partners to stay and deliver in South Sudan, she reported that four humanitarian workers had been killed so far in 2022. She concluded her briefing with three messages to the Council. First, she stressed that the international response needed humanitarian, development and peacebuilding efforts working together to address the root causes of the crisis. Second, the Government and all parties to the conflict needed to ensure the safety of aid workers and assets. Lastly, with only 26 per cent of the 2022 Humanitarian Response Plan funded, unearmarked and early funding at scale were urgently required to

[265] See S/PV.8987.
[266] See S/PV.9219.
[267] See S/PV.9067.

address the growing humanitarian needs, including to prevent a dangerous deterioration in the food security situation.

In their briefings on South Sudan, civil society representatives discussed the impact of the delays in the implementation of the Revitalized Agreement, particularly increased levels of intercommunal and local conflicts and sexual and gender-based violence. In her remarks on 7 March, Riya Williams Yuyada, a women's human rights and peace activist working with Crown The Woman, a feminist non-governmental organization in South Sudan, addressed the limited progress made in the implementation of the Revitalized Agreement and the increased violence at the local level driven by the exclusionary nature of political and peace efforts.[268] She noted that the denial of protection and justice to survivors of gender-based violence resulting from near total impunity continued to be raised to her organization. In that regard, she urged the Council to follow up on its previous call on the Government to improve the judicial system and establish the Hybrid Court for South Sudan, as well as to swiftly implement the joint action plan for the armed forces on addressing conflict-related sexual violence. On 20 June, Lorna Merekaje, a South Sudanese human rights defender, civil rights activist and peace advocate, expressed similar views to Ms. Yuyada regarding the implementation of the peace agreement, violence and human rights violations against civilians.[269] She stated that the people of South Sudan wanted to be given an opportunity to choose their leaders and participate in the design of a progressive agenda for the country, but that required strengthening the capacity of the institutions and personnel required to conduct a credible election, creating an environment conducive to the operation of free media and civic engagement without intimidation and reprisals and strengthening the necessary legal framework. Furthermore, in order to enhance the contribution of civil society in South Sudan, she recommended that periodic forums be established in which civil society could engage with UNMISS in order to facilitate better in-country interaction and analysis and that the Council authorize the Mission to facilitate or host periodic engagement with the Government and civil society. In her statement on 16 September, the President of the South Sudan Women's Empowerment Network called on the region and the international community to support a broad-based process to ensure inclusivity in the country's transition to peace, democracy and development, and in that regard expressed support for the initiative of Fordham University to convene an inclusive political dialogue to help the South Sudanese to reach a broad consensus on a road map for a new transitional programme.[270]

During their discussions on South Sudan, Council members expressed concern with the delays in the implementation of the Revitalized Agreement. They called upon the parties to fully implement the road map of 4 August in accordance with the timelines established therein and commended the facilitation efforts of IGAD and the African Union in that context. The representative of the United States expressed disappointment with the decision of the parties to extend the transitional period for another two years, despite failing to fully deliver on commitments made in the Revitalized Agreement in 2018.[271] Many speakers underscored the importance of an inclusive transition process with the engagement of civil society, women, youth, persons with disabilities and other marginalized groups, and called on the Government to address the continued shrinking of the civic space and create the conditions necessary for the holding of future elections. Council members condemned the subnational and intercommunal violence over the past year, including acts of sexual and gender-based violence, many of them recalling the primary responsibility of the Government of South Sudan to protect civilians and undertake intercommunal dialogue and reconciliation.[272] Many speakers also called on the Government to investigate and ensure accountability for such crimes. Council members welcomed the graduation of the necessary unified forces, stressing the importance of their urgent deployment to stabilize the security situation.[273] Multiple

[268] See S/PV.8987.

[269] See S/PV.9067.

[270] See S/PV.9134.

[271] See S/PV.9134 and S/PV.9219.

[272] See S/PV.8987 (United States, Kenya (also on behalf of Gabon and Ghana), Brazil, Albania); S/PV.9067 (United States, Mexico, Russian Federation, Ghana (also on behalf of Gabon and Kenya) and France); S/PV.9134 (Ghana (also on behalf of Gabon and Kenya), Norway, Ireland, Albania, Mexico, United Kingdom); and S/PV.9219 (United States, United Kingdom, Mexico, Albania and Norway).

[273] See S/PV.8987 (United States, Kenya (also on behalf of Gabon and Ghana), Albania, United Kingdom and Norway); S/PV.9067 (United States, Ireland, Norway and France); S/PV.9134 (United States, Ghana (also on behalf of Gabon and Kenya), Norway, Ireland, Albania, Mexico, United Kingdom and France); and S/PV.9219 (Mexico, Albania, Norway and Ireland).

delegations called for the review and lifting of the arms embargo imposed on South Sudan and noted that the embargo was hampering the deployment of the necessary unified forces, disarmament, demobilization and demilitarization and security sector reform efforts.[274]

Council members expressed serious concern with the humanitarian conditions in South Sudan, many of them calling on the Government to ensure access for and the safety and security of humanitarian workers. Several speakers called on the international community to strengthen humanitarian support for South Sudan.[275] Furthermore, some Council members made specific reference to the impact of climate change and floods on the situation in the country and underscored the need to define sustainable and long-term solutions to address the consequences of the phenomenon.[276] In his remarks, the representative of South Sudan noted that the new road map and extension of the transitional period were inevitable given that much remained to be implemented in the Revitalized Agreement, but stressed that it was crucial that the parties were able to agree on the way forward on their own and peacefully.[277] He also touched on the need for continued international financial support and the lifting of the arms embargo for the implementation of the agreement, as well as for the international community to fulfil its humanitarian pledges, noting in particular the severe impact of floods.[278]

By its resolution 2625 (2022) of 15 March, acting under Chapter VII of the Charter, the Council extended the mandate of UNMISS for one year, until 15 March 2023, with some modifications, concerning in particular the Mission's support for constitution-drafting, the electoral process, combating and reporting on sexual and gender-based violence and providing risk assessments on the adverse effects of climate change.[279] With respect to the political process, the Council expressed its deep concern about the delays in implementing the Revitalized Agreement and called upon the Government and all relevant actors to take action to fulfil several priority measures, including providing security to redesignated protection of civilians sites, initiating a permanent constitution-making process, making progress on key milestones in the preparations for free and fair elections and completing the graduation of the necessary unified forces.[280]

Resolution 2625 (2022) was adopted with 13 votes in favour and two abstentions (by China and the Russian Federation).[281] In her statement after the vote, the representative of the Russian Federation asserted that the Council and UNMISS did not have the appropriate resources to fulfil the functions of human rights capacity-building, combating sexual violence, defending the rights of women and fighting corruption, which were internal matters for the country. She added that, while the Mission could, at the request of the host country, provide technical and logistical assistance for the conduct of elections, its core function was to stabilize the security situation and assist the South Sudanese authorities in implementing the Revitalized Agreement. The representative of China expressed an objection to the inclusion of human rights-related text in the draft resolution and the assignment of climate change-related mandates to peacekeeping operations without an in-depth analysis of its impacts and a clear understanding of climate change as a driver of security risks. Furthermore, the representatives of China and Ghana expressed criticism of the use of the term "human rights defenders" in the draft text, which was not agreed language and not clearly defined. Although he had voted in favour of the resolution, the representative of India expressed reservations regarding what he described as attempts to "securitize" climate change and added that the place for such discussions was within the framework of the United Nations Framework Convention on Climate Change. As penholder of the draft resolution, the representative of the United States thanked Council members for their efforts to strengthen the mandate

[274] See S/PV.8987 (Kenya (also on behalf of Gabon and Ghana)); S/PV.9067 (Russian Federation and China); S/PV.9134 (China and Russian Federation); and S/PV.9219 (Russian Federation, Ghana (also on behalf of Gabon and Kenya) and China).

[275] See S/PV.8987 (Kenya (also on behalf of Gabon and Ghana), China, India and United Arab Emirates); S/PV.9067 (India, Ghana (also on behalf of Gabon and Kenya) and China); S/PV.9134 (Ghana (also on behalf of Gabon and Kenya), United Arab Emirates, Brazil); and S/PV.9219 (China and India).

[276] See S/PV.8987 (Ireland, Kenya (also on behalf of Gabon and Ghana), Albania, Norway and United Arab Emirates); S/PV.9067 (Mexico, United Arab Emirates, Ghana (also on behalf of Gabon and Kenya) and Albania); S/PV.9134 (Ghana (also on behalf of Gabon and Kenya), Norway and Ireland); and S/PV.9219 (Mexico, Albania, United Arab Emirates and Ireland).

[277] See S/PV.9134.

[278] Ibid. and S/PV.9219.

[279] Resolution 2625 (2022), paras. 1 and 3. For more information on the mandate of UNMISS, see part X, sect. I.

[280] Resolution 2625 (2022), paras. 6 and 9.

[281] See S/PV.8994.

of UNMISS and noted that the renewed mandate reinforced the Mission's core tasks, strengthened its sexual and gender-based violence prevention activities and authorized it to provide electoral assistance.

In addition to the regular briefings relating to South Sudan and UNMISS, Council members heard a briefing on 13 December by the Chair of the Committee established pursuant to resolution 2206 (2015), providing a summary of the work of the Committee in 2022, including its discussions on the final report of the Panel of Experts and the granting of five exemptions with respect to the arms embargo, travel ban and asset freeze.[282] By its resolution 2633 (2022) of 26 May, acting under Chapter VII of the Charter, the Council extended the arms embargo, travel ban and asset freeze for South Sudan until 31 May 2023, as well as the mandate of the Panel of Experts until 1 July 2023.[283] The Council requested the Secretary-General, in close consultation with UNMISS and the Panel of Experts, to conduct, no later than 15 April 2023, an assessment of progress achieved on the benchmarks established in resolution 2577 (2021).[284]

Resolution 2633 (2022) was adopted with 10 votes in favour and five abstentions.[285] In explaining their decision to abstain in the vote, the representatives of China, Gabon, India, Kenya and the Russian Federation expressed regret that the resolution did not take into account the improved situation in South Sudan and the views of the Government, IGAD and the African Union on the need to lift the arms embargo and targeted sanctions, noting that the measures were not effective in supporting the implementation of the Revitalized Agreement and hindered the strengthening of the armed forces. The representative of Kenya added that the resolution also fell short of the Council's own commitment to progressively lift the measures. The representative of China recalled that his delegation put forward constructive amendments to the draft text, including on exempting training and non-lethal equipment, changing the application of exemption requests to reporting, and adjusting the targeted sanctions that, had they been adopted, would have helped the country to respond positively to the concerns of the African Union, enhance the security capacity of South Sudan and encourage the Government to take more substantive steps towards implementing the benchmarks.

For the purposes of facilitating coverage of this item, information on meetings is set out below in three tables under three headings, namely, Sudan (table 1); Sudan and South Sudan and Abyei (table 2); and South Sudan (table 3).

Table 1
Meetings: reports of the Secretary-General on the Sudan and South Sudan – the Sudan, 2022

Meeting record and date	*Sub-item*	*Other documents*	*Rule 37 invitations*	*Rule 39 and other invitations*	*Speakers*	*Decision and vote (for-against-abstaining)*
S/PV.8948 17 January			Sudan	Prosecutor of the International Criminal Court	All Council members, all invitees	
S/PV.8964 15 February	Letter dated 24 January 2022 from the Panel of Experts on the Sudan established pursuant to resolution 1591 (2005) addressed to the President of the Council (S/2022/48)	Draft resolution submitted by United States (S/2022/111)			Three Council members (China, Russian Federation, United States)	Resolution 2620 (2022) 15-0-0 (adopted under Chapter VII)

[282] See S/PV.9219. For further information on the sanctions measures relating to South Sudan, see part VII, sect. III.
[283] Resolution 2633 (2022), paras. 1, 12 and 18. For further information on the Committee established pursuant to resolution 2206 (2015) and the Panel of Experts, see part IX, sect. I.B.
[284] Resolution 2633 (2022), para. 5.
[285] See S/PV.9045.

Meeting record and date	*Sub-item*	*Other documents*	*Rule 37 invitations*	*Rule 39 and other invitations*	*Speakers*	*Decision and vote (for-against-abstaining)*
S/PV.9005 28 March			Sudan		One Council member (Ghana),[a] invitee	
S/PV.9006 28 March	Report of the Secretary-General on the situation in the Sudan and the activities of the United Nations Integrated Transition Assistance Mission in the Sudan (UNITAMS) (S/2022/172)		Sudan	Special Representative of the Secretary-General for the Sudan and Head of UNITAMS	13 Council members,[b] all invitees	
S/PV.9041 24 May	Report of the Secretary-General on the situation in the Sudan and the activities of UNITAMS (S/2022/400)		Sudan	Special Representative of the Secretary-General	13 Council members,[c] all invitees	
S/PV.9054 3 June		Draft resolution submitted by United Kingdom (S/2022/443)			Nine Council members[d]	Resolution 2636 (2022) 15-0-0
S/PV.9070 21 June			Sudan		Five Council members (China, Gabon, Ghana, Russian Federation, United States),[a] invitee	
S/PV.9113 23 August			Sudan	Prosecutor of the International Criminal Court	All Council members, all invitees[e]	
S/PV.9128 13 September			Sudan		One Council member (Ghana),[a] invitee	

Meeting record and date	*Sub-item*	*Other documents*	*Rule 37 invitations*	*Rule 39 and other invitations*	*Speakers*	*Decision and vote (for-against-abstaining)*
S/PV.9129 13 September	Report of the Secretary-General on the situation in the Sudan and the activities of UNITAMS (S/2022/667)		Sudan	Special Representative of the Secretary-General, President of Sudan Social Development Organization	13 Council members,[f] all invitees[g]	
S/PV.9210 7 December			Sudan		One Council member (Ghana),[a] invitee	
S/PV.9211 7 December	Report of the Secretary-General on the situation in the Sudan and the activities of UNITAMS (S/2022/898)		Sudan	Special Representative of the Secretary-General	13 Council members,[b] all invitees[h]	

[a] The representative of Ghana spoke in his capacity as Chair of the Committee established pursuant to resolution 1591 (2005) concerning the Sudan.
[b] Albania, Brazil, China, Ghana (also on behalf of Gabon and Kenya), France, India, Ireland, Mexico, Norway, Russian Federation, United Arab Emirates, United Kingdom and United States.
[c] Albania, Brazil, China, Kenya (also on behalf of Gabon and Ghana), France, India, Ireland, Mexico, Norway, Russian Federation, United Arab Emirates, United Kingdom and United States.
[d] Albania, China, France, Ireland, Mexico, Norway, Russian Federation, United Kingdom and United States.
[e] The Prosecutor of the International Criminal Court participated in the meeting by videoconference.
[f] Albania, Brazil, China, France, Gabon (also on behalf of Ghana and Kenya), India, Ireland, Mexico, Norway, Russian Federation, United Arab Emirates, United Kingdom and United States.
[g] The President of Sudan Social Development Organization participated in the meeting by videoconference.
[h] The Special Representative participated in the meeting by videoconference.

Table 2
Meetings: reports of the Secretary-General on the Sudan and South Sudan – the Sudan, South Sudan and Abyei, 2022

Meeting record and date	*Sub-item*	*Other documents*	*Rule 37 invitations*	*Rule 39 and other invitations*	*Speakers*	*Decision and vote (for-against-abstaining)*
S/PV.9020 21 April	Report of the Secretary-General on the situation in Abyei (S/2022/316)		Sudan, South Sudan	Under-Secretary-General for Peace Operations, Special Envoy of the Secretary-General for the Horn of Africa	13 Council members,[a] all invitees[b]	
S/PV.9031 12 May		Draft resolution submitted by United States (S/2022/387)			One Council member (Russian Federation)	Resolution 2630 (2022) 15-0-0 (adopted under Chapter VII)

Meeting record and date	*Sub-item*	*Other documents*	*Rule 37 invitations*	*Rule 39 and other invitations*	*Speakers*	*Decision and vote (for-against-abstaining)*
S/PV.9170 27 October	Report of the Secretary-General on the situation in Abyei (S/2022/760)		Sudan, South Sudan	Assistant Secretary-General for Africa, Special Envoy of the Secretary-General	13 Council members,[c] all invitees[d]	
S/PV.9191 14 November		Draft resolution submitted by United States (S/2022/839)				Resolution 2660 (2022) 15-0-0 (adopted under Chapter VII)

[a] Albania, Brazil, China, France, Gabon (also on behalf of Ghana and Kenya), India, Ireland, Mexico, Norway, Russian Federation, United Arab Emirates, United Kingdom and United States.
[b] The Under-Secretary-General and the Special Envoy participated in the meeting by videoconference.
[c] Albania, Brazil, China, France, Ghana (also on behalf of Gabon and Kenya), India, Ireland, Mexico, Norway, Russian Federation, United Arab Emirates, United Kingdom and United States.
[d] The Special Envoy participated in the meeting by videoconference.

Table 3
Meetings: reports of the Secretary-General on the Sudan and South Sudan – South Sudan, 2022

Meeting record and date	*Sub-item*	*Other documents*	*Rule 37 invitations*	*Rule 39 and other invitations*	*Speakers*	*Decision and vote (for-against-abstaining)*
S/PV.8987 7 March	Report of the Secretary-General on the situation in South Sudan (S/2022/156)			Special Representative of the Secretary-General for South Sudan and Head of the United Nations Mission in South Sudan, interim Chairperson of the Reconstituted Joint Monitoring and Evaluation Commission, women's human rights and peace activist	13 Council members,[a] all invitees[b]	
S/PV.8894 15 March	Report of the Secretary-General on the situation in South Sudan (S/2022/156)	Draft resolution submitted by United States (S/2022/219)	South Sudan		Five Council members (China, Ghana, India, Russian Federation, United States), invitee	Resolution 2625 (2022) 13-0-2[c] (adopted under Chapter VII)

Meeting record and date	*Sub-item*	*Other documents*	*Rule 37 invitations*	*Rule 39 and other invitations*	*Speakers*	*Decision and vote for-against-abstaining)*
S/PV.9045 26 May		Draft resolution submitted by United States (S/2022/417)	South Sudan		Six Council members,[d] invitee	Resolution 2633 (2022) 10-0-5[e] (adopted under Chapter VII)
S/PV.9067 20 June	Report of the Secretary-General on the situation in South Sudan (S/2022/468)		South Sudan	Special Representative of the Secretary-General, Acting Director in the Operations and Advocacy Division of the Office for the Coordination of Humanitarian Affairs, South Sudanese human rights defender, civil rights activist and peace advocate	13 Council members,[f] all invitees[g]	
S/PV.9134 16 September	Report of the Secretary-General on the situation in South Sudan (S/2022/689)		South Sudan	Special Representative of the Secretary-General, President of the South Sudan Women's Empowerment Network	13 Council members,[f] all invitees	
S/PV.9219 13 December	Report of the Secretary-General on the situation in South Sudan (S/2022/918)		South Sudan	Special Representative of the Secretary-General, interim Chairperson of the Reconstituted Joint Monitoring and Evaluation Commission	13 Council members,[f,h] all invitees[i]	

[a] Albania, Brazil, China, Kenya (also on behalf of Gabon and Ghana), France, India, Ireland, Mexico, Norway, Russian Federation, United Arab Emirates, United Kingdom and United States.

[b] The interim Chairperson of the Reconstituted Joint Monitoring and Evaluation Commission and the civil society representative participated in the meeting by videoconference.

[c] *For*: Albania, Brazil, France, Gabon, Ghana, India, Ireland, Kenya, Mexico, Norway, United Arab Emirates, United Kingdom, United States; *against*: none; *abstaining*: China, Russian Federation.

[d] China, Gabon, Ghana, India, Kenya and Russian Federation

[e] *For*: Albania, Brazil, France, Ghana, Ireland, Mexico, Norway, United Arab Emirates, United Kingdom, United States; *against*: none; *abstaining*: China, Gabon, India, Kenya, Russian Federation.

[f] Albania, Brazil, China, Ghana (also on behalf of Gabon and Kenya), France, India, Ireland, Mexico, Norway, Russian Federation, United Arab Emirates, United Kingdom and United States.

[g] The South Sudanese human rights defender and activist participated in the meeting by videoconference.

[h] The representative of Gabon spoke in his capacity as Chair of the Committee established pursuant to resolution 2206 (2015) concerning South Sudan.

[i] The interim Chairperson of the Commission participated in the meeting by videoconference.

8. Peace consolidation in West Africa

During the period under review, the Council held two meetings in connection with the item entitled "Peace consolidation in West Africa". The meetings took the form of briefings.[286] More information on the meetings, including invitees, speakers and outcomes, is provided in the table below. In addition to the meetings, Council members also held informal consultations of the whole.[287]

On 10 January, Council members heard briefings by the Executive Director of the United Nations Office on Drugs and Crime (UNODC), a lawyer and public policy analyst with Médecins du Monde, on behalf of the People's Coalition for the Sahel, and the Special Representative of the Secretary-General for West Africa and the Sahel and Head of the United Nations Office for West Africa and the Sahel (UNOWAS).[288] In her remarks, the Executive Director of UNODC noted that the Gulf of Guinea region continued to be a priority concern regarding maritime security as incidents in the region accounted for the majority of the global kidnappings of seafarers for ransom. She noted that it was clear that maritime insecurity, illicit flows and the linkages between transnational organized crime and terrorism all represented major obstacles to achieving peace, security and development in West Africa and the Sahel. She informed the Council that the lack of opportunities and frustration were driving more youth to piracy and crime and leaving them more receptive to radicalization narratives, whereas desperate conditions rendered more people vulnerable to human trafficking and migrant smuggling, and more women and girls were at greater risk of exploitation and sexual violence. She said that alongside efforts to provide humanitarian and emergency assistance and to prevent conflict and promote dialogue, there was the need to encourage political will and increased international support to strengthen comprehensive and cooperative crime responses, which needed to be built on international legal and institutional frameworks, regional partnerships and national capabilities. Furthermore, she highlighted various ways in which UNODC had been supporting the countries of the region to advance such actions.

While noting that the entire security strategy had failed, the lawyer and public policy analyst with Médecins du Monde addressed the security and humanitarian situation in the Sahel region. In that context, she proposed a new approach based on "four citizen pillars". First, she noted that States in the Sahel and the international community needed to put civilians at the heart of their response to the crisis. Second, she expressed the view that the international community needed to ensure the implementation of a truly holistic approach addressing the root causes of the crisis. Third, the humanitarian emergency needed to be addressed. Lastly, she stressed the need to fight impunity, as it fuelled the cycle of violence and encouraged recruitment by armed groups.

Presenting the report of the Secretary-General,[289] the Special Representative of the Secretary-General underscored that while there were reasons to celebrate the political progress among various Sahelian countries, the security environment in the region had become more concerning.[290] He noted that one of the major consequences of those security developments was explained by the fact that the region was experiencing a multifaceted humanitarian crisis, characterized by rising food prices, increased poverty due to the COVID-19 pandemic and crop losses due to drought. He made reference to the resurgence of coups d'état, in particular in West Africa, noting that they were frequently attributable to political practices that were completely out of step with the aspirations of the people. In that context, he commended the Economic Community of West African States (ECOWAS) for its active engagement in the crises in Mali and Guinea and noted the support of UNOWAS towards efforts to enable a return to constitutional order. The Special Representative also noted the need for a long-term approach regarding climate change, as well as greater determination in the implementation of the women and peace and security agenda and the youth and peace and security agenda.

Following the briefings, many Council members expressed concern at the security situation in the region, which was characterized by the recurrence of terrorist attacks, including in Burkina Faso, Mali,

---

[286] For more information on the format of meetings, see part II.

[287] See A/77/2, part II, chap. 31.

[288] See S/PV.8944.

[289] S/2021/1091.

[290] See S/PV.8944.

the Niger and Nigeria. Council members also noted that the attacks were expanding to the coastal countries of the Gulf of Guinea/West Africa. In that context, Council members[291] underlined the need for a holistic approach that addressed the root causes of instability, including relating to governance, development and human rights deficits and the impact of climate on security. Some speakers[292] commended the role of regional security mechanisms such as the Joint Force of the Group of Five for the Sahel and the Multinational Joint Task Force and underlined the need for their further support, especially by ensuring predictable and sustainable funding for the Joint Force. With regard to UNOWAS, Council members highlighted its role in supporting regional initiatives to address the issue of terrorism and maintaining peace. Many Council members welcomed the successful holding of presidential elections in Cabo Verde and the Gambia in October and December 2021, respectively. However, some Council members[293] expressed concern at the challenges faced by the political transitions in Mali and Guinea, and took note of the role played by ECOWAS, including through the application of sanctions measures.[294]

On 7 July, Council members heard briefings by the Special Representative of the Secretary-General, the Chair of the Peacebuilding Commission and the Coordinator of the Association Alliance for Peace and Security.[295] Further to the report of the Secretary-General, the Special Representative highlighted the effects of climate change on existing conflicts, noting that extremist and criminal groups in many parts of the Sahel had exploited such weaknesses exacerbated by often inadequate State structures.[296] He said that the southward spread of extremist violence had grown from isolated incidents to a genuine threat in coastal countries and that the announced withdrawal of Mali from the Group of Five for the Sahel and the military redeployments were jeopardizing security arrangements in the subregion. In addition, he underlined that there was no magic formula for effectively combating insecurity, and underscored that it was democratic and accountable governance, including the establishment of decentralized administrations, that would deliver solutions for the daily lives of the population. He noted that ECOWAS had reached agreements to end the crisis with the transitional regimes in Mali and Burkina Faso and the relaunching of dialogue with the transitional authorities in Guinea. Highlighting the accomplishments of the Cameroon-Nigeria Mixed Commission, the Special Representative noted that the Commission would forever remain a concrete model of effective United Nations support for peaceful conflict resolution and peacebuilding.

In her remarks, the Chair of the Peacebuilding Commission shared the Commission's perspective on the situation in West Africa and the Sahel by drawing on its country-specific and regional engagements. In that regard, she stated that the Commission was concerned about the recent military takeovers in the region and the persistence of violent incidents perpetrated by non-State armed groups and terrorist groups. In that context, she elaborated on the Commission's various recommendations, notably: (a) the importance of investing in efforts to address the root causes that aggravated the conflicts, instability and violence in the region; (b) the need for greater support for the objectives of the priority investment plan of the Group of Five for the Sahel; (c) the need for sustained and coordinated support by the United Nations system for building and sustaining peace, including through the implementation of the United Nations integrated strategy for the Sahel; and (d) the need for timely follow-up to and support for the planned joint strategic assessment on the security and governance situation and response initiatives in the region by the African Union, United Nations, ECOWAS and the Group of Five for the Sahel.

Highlighting the deteriorating situation in the Niger, Burkina Faso and Mali, the Coordinator of the Association Alliance for Peace and Security underlined the importance for the international community to "do things differently", namely by putting the protection of the population at the heart of any response to the security crisis in the Sahel. She urged the Council to convince Sahelian leaders and Governments to better protect their citizens by eradicating the reasons that drove young people to take

---

[291] Ghana (also on behalf of Gabon and Kenya), Ireland, Albania, China, France, United Kingdom, United Arab Emirates and United States.

[292] France, United Arab Emirates, India and Norway.

[293] Ghana (also on behalf of Gabon and Kenya), Albania, China, France, United Kingdom, United States and Russian Federation.

[294] Ghana (also on behalf of Gabon and Kenya), France and United States.

[295] See S/PV.9086. See also S/2022/521.

[296] See S/PV.9086.

up arms. To achieve that, she underlined the need to improve governance and access to basic social services and the need to fight against stigmatization and impunity, in particular that enjoyed by certain members of the defence and security forces, which perpetuated the vicious circle of violence.

During the discussions, Council members continued to express concern at the security situation in the region, which had deteriorated since the meeting in January, reflected by ongoing intercommunal conflicts and increased incidents of terrorist threats and attacks, including their expansion to the coastal countries of the Gulf of Guinea and West Africa. While drawing attention to the challenges in the region, they underlined the importance of regional cooperation, with some Council members[297] calling for adequate funding of regional initiatives. Many Council members[298] expressed concern at the humanitarian situation in the region exacerbated by the COVID-19 pandemic, climate shocks and food insecurity. Council members also expressed concern at the abuses and violations of human rights,[299] underlined the need to ensure accountability[300] and called for improved compliance with international human rights standards.[301] Several Council members[302] welcomed the democratic progress in the region, including following the successful parliamentary and local elections in Senegal and the Gambia. Many speakers also noted the agreement with ECOWAS to implement 12-month and 24-month transition timelines, with Burkina Faso and Mali, respectively. In that regard, Council members welcomed the partial lifting of the sanctions measures on Mali by ECOWAS,[303] and further underlined the need to restore constitutional order by holding timely elections.[304] In addition, several Council members[305] underlined the need for the full, equal and meaningful participation of women in political processes, including elections and transitions and in consideration of leadership and decision-making posts. Furthermore, some Council members[306] welcomed the improvement in regional maritime security since the meeting in January.

Meetings: peace consolidation in West Africa, 2022

Meeting record and date	*Sub-item*	*Other documents*	*Rule 37 invitations*	*Rule 39 and other invitations*	*Speakers*	*Decision and vote (for-against-abstaining)*
S/PV.8944 10 January	Report of the Secretary-General on the activities of the United Nations Office for West Africa and the Sahel (UNOWAS) (S/2021/1091)			Special Representative of the Secretary-General and Head of UNOWAS, Executive Director of the United Nations Office on Drugs and Crime (UNODC), lawyer and public policy analyst with Médecins du Monde on behalf of the People's Coalition for the Sahel	13 Council members,[a] all invitees[b]	

[297] Ghana (also on behalf of Gabon and Kenya), India, Albania and China.

[298] Ireland, Ghana (also on behalf of Gabon and Ireland), United Arab Emirates, Albania, Russian Federation and United Kingdom.

[299] Ireland, United States, Albania and United Kingdom.

[300] Ireland and United Kingdom.

[301] United Kingdom.

[302] Ghana (also on behalf of Gabon and Kenya), India, Albania, United Kingdom, Mexico, France and China.

[303] Ghana (also on behalf of Gabon and Kenya), Norway, Albania, Russian Federation, Mexico, China and Brazil.

[304] Ireland, Ghana (also on behalf of Gabon and Kenya), United States, United Kingdom and France.

[305] Ghana (also on behalf of Gabon and Kenya), United Arab Emirates, Albania, United Kingdom, Mexico and France.

[306] Ghana (also on behalf of Gabon and Kenya), Norway, United Arab Emirates, United Kingdom, China and Brazil.

Meeting record and date	*Sub-item*	*Other documents*	*Rule 37 invitations*	*Rule 39 and other invitations*	*Speakers*	*Decision and vote (for-against-abstaining)*
S/PV.9086 7 July	Report of the Secretary-General on the activities of UNOWAS (S/2022/521)			Special Representative of the Secretary-General, Chair of the Peacebuilding Commission, Coordinator of the Association Alliance for Peace and Security	13 Council members,[a] all invitees	

[a] Albania, Brazil, China, France, Ghana (also on behalf of Gabon and Kenya), India, Ireland, Mexico, Norway, Russian Federation, United Arab Emirates, United Kingdom and United States.
[b] The Special Representative, the Executive Director of UNODC and the lawyer and public policy analyst with Médecins du Monde participated in the meeting by videoconference.

9. Peace and security in Africa

During the period under review, the Council held eight meetings in connection with the item entitled "Peace and security in Africa". Three of the meetings took the form of briefings, two took the form of debates, and two were convened for the adoption of decisions.[307] The Council held one private (closed) meeting to discuss the situation in the north of Ethiopia, in relation to which it issued a communiqué.[308] The Council adopted one resolution and a presidential statement. More information on the meetings, including on participants, speakers and outcomes, is provided in the table below. In addition to the meetings, Council members held informal consultations of the whole in connection with the item.[309]

In 2022, the meetings of the Council under the item were focused on the activities and role of the Group of Five for the Sahel, the situation of piracy and armed robbery at sea in the Gulf of Guinea, capacity-building for sustaining peace in Africa and the fight against the financing of armed groups and terrorists through the illicit trafficking of natural resources.

The Council held two meetings on the operations of the Joint Force of the Group of Five for the Sahel on 18 May[310] and 16 November[311] further to the reports of the Secretary-General on the Joint Force.[312] The Council heard briefings by the Assistant Secretary-General for Africa, the Executive Secretary of the Group of Five for the Sahel and two civil society representatives.[313] The briefings were focused primarily on the political and security situation in the subregion and the role of the Group of Five for the Sahel.

At the meeting on 18 May, the Assistant Secretary-General for Africa and the Executive Secretary of the Group of Five for the Sahel both said that the decision of the Malian authorities to withdraw from the Group of Five for the Sahel and its Joint Force was regrettable.[314] The Assistant Secretary-General noted that the security situation in the region had deteriorated and informed the Council that, in the light of the growing complexity of the crisis facing the Sahel, the African Union Commission and the United Nations Secretariat were conducting a joint strategic assessment with a view to strengthening support for the Group of Five for the Sahel and other security and governance initiatives in the region, and exploring innovative ways to mobilize sustainable resourcing for such initiatives. The Executive Secretary said that the Group of Five for the Sahel would participate in that assessment and expressed the hope that its main

[307] For more information on the format of meetings, see part II.
[308] See S/PV.9160.
[309] See A/77/2, part II, chap. 35.
[310] See S/PV.9035.
[311] See S/PV.9194.
[312] S/2022/382 and S/2022/838.
[313] See S/PV.9035 and S/PV.9194.
[314] See S/PV.9035.

components would enable it to define a better security, governance and cooperation architecture in order to ensure the optimal use of resources. Given the way the Joint Force operated and the new context with the ongoing deterioration in the security situation, a review of the concept of its operations had been considered. On the political level, the unconstitutional changes that had taken place in three of the countries of the Group of Five for the Sahel (Burkina Faso, Chad and Mali), as well as the sanctions imposed on some of them, had not contributed to harmony in the subregion. The Coordinator and President of the Rights and Resources Initiative/Group focused her briefing on the links between climate change and the conflict in the Sahel countries, including the ways in which climate change exacerbated conflict, and the impact of climate change and conflict on women and young people. She made several recommendations, including strengthening cooperation with the Group of Five for the Sahel on climate change.

At the meeting on 16 November,[315] the Assistant Secretary-General for Africa said that it was regrettable that, in addition to its financial difficulties, the Joint Force had been weakened by the withdrawal of Mali and the second coup d'état in Burkina Faso, further undermining regional cohesion. The Executive Secretary of the Group of Five for the Sahel underlined the consequences of the withdrawal of Mali. Reaffirming the firm commitment of the Group to continue its mission and of the Heads of State to continue working together, he said that a number of decisions had been taken on the new format of the Joint Force and a road map had been drawn up. He called for the Council to understand the seriousness of the situation in the region, noting the possibility of an even greater threat to international peace and security without a rapid and urgent response. An independent expert on the Joint Force provided an analysis of the threats facing the region, focusing on the threat of terrorism. He said that the results achieved by the Joint Force seemed to be mixed or inadequate, and outlined its limitations and its political, financial, logistical and institutional weaknesses, including the lack of a robust mandate from the Council under Chapter VII of the Charter of the United Nations.

Following the briefings at both meetings, Council members discussed the political, security, socioeconomic, humanitarian and human rights situation in the Sahel countries. Council members called on members of the Group of Five for the Sahel, namely Burkina Faso, Chad and Mali, to restore constitutional order.

Council members addressed security challenges in the Sahel, including the expansion and spread of terrorism to the coastal region of the Gulf of Guinea.[316] Some members discussed the activities of the Wagner Group as another potential source of insecurity in the region.[317] Council members discussed the impact of the conclusion of Operation Barkhane in November 2022 on the security situation in the region.[318] They deliberated ways to combat insecurity in the Sahel, including by improving governance and addressing socioeconomic challenges such as underdevelopment, poverty, inequality and corruption, as well as climate change.[319]

Council members often addressed the role of regional and subregional organizations, most notably the African Union and the Economic Community of West African States (ECOWAS), in the peace and political processes of the countries of the Sahel.[320] Some took note of or welcomed the joint strategic assessment on security and development in the Sahel.[321] The representatives of Norway and Ghana, speaking also on behalf of Gabon and Kenya, underscored that the Independent High-level Panel on Security and Development in the Sahel should build on existing initiatives, including the efforts of the

[315] See S/PV.9194.

[316] See S/PV.9035 (France, China, India and Russian Federation); S/PV.9194 (France, Ireland, China, Brazil, Albania and India).

[317] See S/PV.9194 (France, United States, Ireland, United Kingdom, Albania and Norway).

[318] See S/PV.9194 (France, Mexico, Brazil and Ghana (also on behalf of Gabon and Kenya)).

[319] See S/PV.9035 (Albania, India, United Kingdom, Ireland, Ghana (also on behalf of Gabon and Kenya), United Arab Emirates and United States); and S/PV.9194 (United States, Ireland, Mexico, China, United Arab Emirates, Norway and Ghana (also on behalf of Gabon and Kenya)).

[320] See S/PV.9035 (Albania, India, Mexico, United Kingdom, Ireland, Norway, Ghana (also on behalf of Gabon and Kenya) and United States); and S/PV.9194 (Ireland, Russian Federation, Mexico, United Kingdom and United Arab Emirates).

[321] See S/PV.9035 (Albania, Brazil, China, Mexico, Ireland, Norway, Ghana (also on behalf of Gabon and Kenya) and United Arab Emirates); and S/PV.9194 (France, United States, Ireland, Mexico, United Kingdom, China, Brazil, Albania and Norway).

Group of Five for the Sahel, the Accra Initiative, the Multinational Joint Task Force and the Nouakchott Process.[322]

The activities of the Joint Force of the Group of Five for the Sahel in the context of the regional security architecture were frequently addressed by all Council members in 2022. Council members discussed the consequences of the decision by Mali to withdraw from the Group of Five for the Sahel and its Joint Force.[323] Some emphasized the need for the United Nations Multidimensional Integrated Stabilization Mission in Mali (MINUSMA) to provide support to the Joint Force,[324] and some suggested that the Force would benefit from predictable support through United Nations assessed contributions.[325]

Concerning the issue of piracy and armed robbery at sea in the Gulf of Guinea, at a meeting held on 31 May,[326] the Council adopted resolution 2634 (2022), in which it stressed the primary responsibility of the States of the Gulf of Guinea to counter piracy and armed robbery at sea in the Gulf of Guinea and address the underlying causes[327] and called upon Member States in the region to criminalize piracy and armed robbery at sea under their domestic laws.[328] The Council also requested the Secretary-General to report, within five months and on an exceptional basis in advance of the 10-year anniversary of the Yaoundé Code of Conduct, on the situation of piracy and armed robbery at sea in the Gulf of Guinea and its underlying causes, including any possible and potential linkages with terrorism in West and Central Africa and the Sahel, on United Nations support and contributions, and on any recommendations for further supporting and enhancing national efforts and regional and international cooperation towards combating piracy and armed robbery at sea in the Gulf of Guinea.[329]

On 22 November, the Council held a meeting[330] at which the Assistant Secretary-General for Africa presented the report of the Secretary-General on the situation of piracy and armed robbery at sea in the Gulf of Guinea and its underlying causes,[331] pursuant to the request contained in resolution 2634 (2022). She reported on the steady decline in instances of piracy and armed robbery at sea.[332] She elaborated on the changing dynamics of piracy in the Gulf of Guinea; the underlying causes of piracy, including youth unemployment and inadequate access to public services; and regional and international initiatives aimed at addressing maritime challenges. She emphasized the need to fully operationalize the maritime security architecture set out in the Yaoundé Code of Conduct. While there was no firm evidence to suggest any potential or possible linkages between terrorists and pirate groups, addressing the underlying social, economic and environmental challenges faced by communities in the region would serve to contain both threats. Following the briefing of the Assistant Secretary-General, the Executive Director of the United Nations Office on Drugs and Crime (UNODC) made several recommendations for improving maritime security in the Gulf of Guinea, including helping Member States in the region to develop their capacities and legal frameworks for combating piracy, responding to shifting trends and emerging threats related to piracy in the region by being agile and adaptable, and addressing the root causes of piracy. The Executive Secretary of the Gulf of Guinea Commission then gave a briefing on the achievements in terms of combating piracy in the region, including in the context of the Yaoundé architecture, as well as in terms of bilateral cooperation. She said that other crimes were ongoing in the region that were affecting the well-being of coastal populations and the economic well-being of Governments, including illegal, unreported and unregulated fishing, oil theft and pollution. Lastly, the Maritime Planning Officer of the

---

[322] See S/PV.9194. For discussions on the role of regional and subregional organizations, including the African Union and ECOWAS, in the pacific settlement of disputes, see part VIII, sect. II.B.

[323] See S/PV.9035 (France, Albania, Brazil, India, Mexico, Russian Federation, Ireland and United States); and S/PV.9194 (France, United States, Mexico, Brazil, Albania, India, Norway and Ghana (also on behalf of Gabon and Kenya)).

[324] See S/PV.9035 (France, Albania, Brazil, China and Ghana (also on behalf of Gabon and Kenya)); and S/PV.9194 (Ireland, United Arab Emirates and Ghana (also on behalf of Gabon and Kenya)).

[325] See S/PV.9035 (France, Ireland, India and Ghana (also on behalf of Gabon and Kenya)); and S/PV.9194 (France, India and Ghana (also on behalf of Gabon and Kenya)). For more information on peacekeeping operations led by regional and subregional organizations, see part VIII, sect. III.

[326] See S/PV.9050.

[327] Resolution 2634 (2022), para. 2.

[328] Ibid., para. 3.

[329] Ibid., para. 16.

[330] See S/PV.9198.

[331] S/2022/818.

[332] See S/PV.9198.

African Union Commission gave a briefing on the nature of maritime crime in the region and regional and international efforts aimed at improving maritime security in the areas of information-sharing, joint training and exercises.

Following the briefings, Council members discussed the different threats to peace and security posed by piracy and other crimes at sea in the Gulf of Guinea. Speakers[333] also addressed the humanitarian, socioeconomic and environmental impacts of those crimes and some[334] highlighted their underlying causes, including poverty, unemployment, corruption, climate change and food insecurity. Participants[335] addressed the role played by regional organizations, including the Economic Community of Central African States, ECOWAS and the Gulf of Guinea Commission, in the resolution and prevention of piracy and other maritime crimes. Some[336] said their delegations had taken note of the recommendations provided by the Peacebuilding Commission. The representative of the Russian Federation called for the establishment of a specialized entity under the auspices of the United Nations responsible for addressing the entire spectrum of issues related to combating maritime crime.

On 8 and 9 August, at the initiative of China, which held the presidency for the month,[337] the Council held an open debate on the issue of capacity-building for sustaining peace in Africa.[338] In his briefing, the Commissioner for Political Affairs, Peace and Security of the African Union elaborated on the security threats facing the region, including violent extremism, terrorism, climate change and the illicit exploitation of natural resources, and solutions for addressing those threats.[339] He emphasized the need for demonstrable joint transformative leadership between the Council and the African Union Peace and Security Council and the need to strengthen democracies. The Special Adviser to the Secretary-General on Africa gave a briefing on the internal and external factors that undermined the capacities of African countries to prevent and address violence. She recommended investing in institutional infrastructure to build the capacities needed to tackle the internal causes of violence and strengthening cooperation between peacekeeping missions and national and local authorities, which could, from the perspective of institution-building and security, create opportunities for increasing the presence of the State and enhancing the delivery of services, thereby preventing gaps that could be leveraged by terrorist groups and non-State actors. The Chair of the Peacebuilding Commission focused his briefing on changing conflict dynamics and elaborated on the capacity-building work of the Peacebuilding Commission in Africa.

In the ensuing discussion, speakers addressed the capacity-building challenges facing Africa and identified ways to improve capacity-building to sustain peace. Speakers discussed the roles of regional and subregional organizations, including the African Union,[340] as well as the United Nations, including the Security Council[341] and the Peacebuilding Commission,[342] in efforts to sustain peace in Africa. Many

---

[333] Norway, Gabon, India, Albania, Brazil, United Arab Emirates and European Union.

[334] Gabon, United Kingdom, United States, Brazil, United Arab Emirates, Ireland, China, Mexico and Ghana.

[335] Norway, Gabon, India, United States, France, Albania, Brazil, China and European Union.

[336] Norway, United Kingdom, Kenya, Mexico, Ghana and Germany.

[337] A concept note was circulated by a letter dated 1 August (S/2022/592).

[338] See S/PV.9106 and S/PV.9106 (Resumption 1). For more information on the discussion, see part VIII, sect. II.

[339] For more information on discussions regarding threats to regional and international peace and security, see part VII, sect. I.B.

[340] See S/PV.9106 (Ireland, India, Mexico, Norway, United States, Russian Federation, Ghana, Albania, Senegal, South Africa and Algeria); and S/PV.9106 (Resumption 1) (Republic of Korea, Germany, European Union (also on behalf of Albania, Bosnia and Herzegovina, Montenegro, North Macedonia, Serbia, the Republic of Moldova and Ukraine), Malta, Portugal, Canada, Denmark, Thailand, Italy, Slovenia, Ethiopia, Australia, Tunisia, Equatorial Guinea, Argentina and Bangladesh).

[341] See S/PV.9106 (Switzerland); and S/PV.9106 (Resumption 1) (Ethiopia).

[342] See S/PV.9106 (Kenya, Ireland, United Kingdom, Brazil, Norway, France, Senegal, Egypt, Japan and Algeria); and S/PV.9106 (Resumption 1) (Republic of Korea, Poland, Portugal, Ecuador, Canada, Denmark, Thailand, Italy, Morocco, Rwanda, Australia, Equatorial Guinea and Bangladesh).

members underlined the need to strengthen cooperation between the African Union and the United Nations, including the Council, in the context of capacity-building.[343]

Participants also discussed the nexus between climate change and security,[344] and between sustainable development and peace and security.[345] Among the proposals put forward to strengthen capacity-building for sustaining peace, speakers made reference to increasing funding for peacebuilding;[346] strengthening institution-building and the rule of law;[347] and involving women, young people and civil society in peacebuilding efforts, including in decision-making, public policy implementation and security sector reform.[348] Some speakers commented on the impact of Council-imposed sanctions in relation to maintaining and sustaining peace in Africa.[349]

On 31 August, the Council adopted a presidential statement in relation to capacity-building for sustaining peace, in which it recognized the need to step up capacity-building support to African countries and emphasized the importance of providing capacity support, at the request of and in close consultation with the country in question, to improve the rule of law, strengthen national institutions, extend legitimate State authority, build governance, promote and protect human rights, and enhance social cohesion and inclusiveness.[350] The Council also highlighted the importance of sharing best practices and providing financial support to promote inclusive and effective disarmament, demobilization and reintegration processes; supporting socioeconomic development for sustaining peace in Africa; and providing capacity support and institutional training to address through a holistic approach the underlying conditions conducive to the spread of terrorism and violent extremism.[351] The Council encouraged continued development and application of mechanisms for peaceful settlement of disputes through regional and subregional arrangements, and welcomed the continuing important efforts and enhanced role of the African Union, subregional organizations and regional mechanisms in peace operations in accordance with Council resolutions.[352]

On 6 October, at the initiative of Gabon, which held the presidency for the month,[353] the Council held a high-level debate on strengthening the fight against the financing of armed groups and terrorists through the illicit trafficking of natural resources.[354] In her briefing, the Executive Director of UNODC highlighted the importance of understanding the links between organized crime and terrorism in Africa through data collection. The illegal exploitation of minerals provided armed groups and terrorists with significant sources of revenue. She described the Office's programmes to prevent and respond to crimes against the environment, illegal mining and trafficking, including its youth-driven peacebuilding projects.

---

343 See S/PV.9106 (Gabon, Brazil, Norway, Ghana, Egypt, South Africa and Algeria); and S/PV.9106 (Resumption 1) (Portugal, Denmark (on behalf of the Nordic countries), Italy, Netherlands, Slovenia and Equatorial Guinea). For more information on discussions regarding the relationship between the United Nations and regional and subregional organizations, see part VIII, sect. II.

344 See S/PV.9106 (Kenya, Ireland, Mexico, Ghana, Albania, France and Switzerland); and S/PV.9106 (Resumption 1) (Poland and Canada).

345 See S/PV.9106 (China, Gabon, Mexico, Brazil, United Arab Emirates and Switzerland); and S/PV.9106 (Resumption 1) (Malta, Thailand, Italy, Morocco, Slovenia, Ethiopia, Tunisia, Equatorial Guinea and Argentina).

346 See S/PV.9106 (Kenya, Switzerland, Egypt and South Africa); and S/PV.9106 (Resumption 1) (Germany, European Union (also on behalf of Albania, Bosnia and Herzegovina, Montenegro, North Macedonia, Serbia, the Republic of Moldova and Ukraine), Portugal, Ecuador, Mozambique, Netherlands, Morocco, Slovenia, Rwanda, Australia and Tunisia).

347 See S/PV.9106.

348 See S/PV.9106 (Ireland, Gabon, Mexico, United Kingdom, Brazil, Ghana, Albania, France, Switzerland, South Africa and Algeria); and S/PV.9106 (Resumption 1) (Republic of Korea, European Union (also on behalf of Albania, Bosnia and Herzegovina, Montenegro, North Macedonia, Serbia, the Republic of Moldova and Ukraine), Malta, Portugal, Canada, Denmark (on behalf of the Nordic Countries), Italy, Belgium, Netherlands, Morocco, Slovenia, Slovakia, Tunisia and Bangladesh).

349 See S/PV.9106 (China, Kenya, United States, Russian Federation and France); and S/PV.9106 (Resumption 1) (Equatorial Guinea). For more information on discussions regarding the role of sanctions and their unintended consequences, see part VII, sect. III and IX, respectively.

350 See S/PRST/2022/6, third and fourth paragraphs.

351 Ibid., sixth, thirteenth and sixteenth paragraphs.

352 Ibid., nineteenth and twentieth paragraphs. For more information, see part VIII, sect. II.

353 A concept note was circulated by a letter dated 30 September (S/2022/728).

354 See S/PV.9147.

The Commissioner for Political Affairs, Peace and Security of the African Union then reported on various African Union initiatives, including the establishment of national counter-terrorism fusion centres and national financial intelligence units and strengthened law enforcement at the national level. He underlined the need for enhanced cooperation in terms of capacity-building and the transfer of knowledge in favour of countries in post-conflict situations, and the need to strengthen sanctions regimes against terrorist individuals, groups and organizations through close collaboration with the Council. The Regional Director for East Africa and representative of the Institute for Security Studies to the African Union elaborated on the complex nature of illicit trafficking by non-State and terrorist armed groups and the tools for combating the problem. To strengthen the fight against the income-generating activities of non-State armed groups, including trafficking in natural resources, he suggested modernizing sanctions regimes, breaking up criminal networks within administrations and armed forces, and improving due diligence processes.

Following the briefings, Council members discussed the nature of the threat posed by illicit trafficking in natural resources to finance terrorist activities. Speakers addressed the linkages between the exploitation of natural resources and conflict[355] and the utilization of natural resources to finance terrorism, including through the acquisition of arms, ammunition and mining concessions.[356] Some participants focused on the threats posed by the activities of specific groups, including Islamic State in Iraq and the Levant (ISIL/Da'esh) and Al-Qaida,[357] Al-Shabaab[358] and the Wagner Group.[359] Regarding how to mitigate the problem, speakers focused on international and regional cooperation and support for African countries and on how the United Nations, including the Council,[360] and regional organizations, such as the African Union[361] and the Central African Economic and Monetary Community,[362] could support the fight against the exploitation of natural resources. The role and effectiveness of Council-imposed sanctions as a means of curbing trafficking in natural resources was also addressed by several speakers.[363] Some speakers[364] suggested that there was a need to address shortcomings in governance, institutional frameworks and the rule of law.

Meetings: peace and security in Africa, 2022

Meeting record and date	*Sub-item*	*Other documents*	*Rule 37 invitations*	*Rule 39 and other invitations*	*Speakers*	*Decision and vote (for-against-abstaining)*
S/PV.9035 18 May	Report of the Secretary-General on the Joint Force of the Group of Five for the Sahel (S/2022/382)			Assistant Secretary-General for Africa, Executive Secretary of the Group of Five for the Sahel, Coordinator and President of the Rights and Resources Initiative/Group	13 Council members,[a] all invitees	

[355] Gabon, United States, India, United Arab Emirates, Russian Federation, United Kingdom, Ireland, Norway, Brazil and Central African Republic.
[356] Gabon, Ghana, Russian Federation, Mexico, Norway, Kenya, Brazil and Central African Republic.
[357] United States, India, Norway and Kenya.
[358] United Arab Emirates, China, Russian Federation, United Kingdom, Mexico, Ireland, Kenya and Brazil.
[359] United States, United Kingdom and France.
[360] Gabon, United Kingdom, Kenya and Brazil.
[361] Gabon, India, United Arab Emirates, China and United Kingdom.
[362] India.
[363] United States, United Arab Emirates, Russian Federation, Ireland, Norway, Brazil and Central African Republic.
[364] India, China, United Kingdom, Mexico, Ireland, France, Norway, Kenya, Brazil and Central African Republic.

Meeting record and date	*Sub-item*	*Other documents*	*Rule 37 invitations*	*Rule 39 and other invitations*	*Speakers*	*Decision and vote (for-against-abstaining)*
S/PV.9050 31 May		Draft resolution submitted by 37 Member States[b] (S/2022/62)	28 Member States[c]		Seven Council members[d]	Resolution 2634 (2022) 15-0-0
S/PV.9106 and S/PV.9106 (Resumption 1) 8 and 9 August	Capacity-building for sustaining peace Letter dated 1 August 2022 from the Permanent Representative of China to the United Nations addressed to the Secretary-General (S/2022/592)		30 Member States[e]	Special Adviser to the Secretary-General on Africa, Chair of the Peacebuilding Commission, Commissioner for Political Affairs, Peace and Security of the African Union, Chargé d'affaires a.i. of the Delegation of the European Union to the United Nations	All Council members, all invitees[f]	
S/PV.9122 31 August					One Council member (China)	S/PRST/2022/6
S/PV.9147 6 October	Strengthening the fight against the financing of armed groups and terrorists through the illicit trafficking of natural resources Letter dated 30 September 2022 from the Permanent Representative of Gabon to the United Nations addressed to the Secretary-General (S/2022/728)		Central African Republic, Egypt, Equatorial Guinea, Morocco, Senegal	Executive Director of the United Nations Office on Drugs and Crime (UNODC), Commissioner for Political Affairs, Peace and Security of the African Union, Head of the Delegation of the European Union, Regional Director for East Africa and representative of the Institute for Security Studies to the African Union	All Council members,[g] four invitees under rule 37 (Central African Republic, Egypt, Equatorial Guinea, Morocco), all other invitees[h]	

Meeting record and date	*Sub-item*	*Other documents*	*Rule 37 invitations*	*Rule 39 and other invitations*	*Speakers*	*Decision and vote (for-against-abstaining)*
S/PV.9160 (closed) 21 October			Ethiopia	Director of the Operations and Advocacy Division of the Office for the Coordination of Humanitarian Affairs, African Union High Representative for the Horn of Africa Region	13 Council members,[i] all invitees	
S/PV.9194 16 November	Report of the Secretary-General on the Joint Force of the Group of Five for the Sahel (S/2022/838)			Assistant Secretary-General for Africa, Executive Secretary of the Group of Five for the Sahel, independent expert on the Joint Force	13 Council members,[a] all invitees	
S/PV.9198 22 November	Report of the Secretary-General on the situation of piracy and armed robbery at sea in the Gulf of Guinea and its underlying causes (S/2022/818)		Germany, Nigeria	Assistant Secretary-General for Africa, Executive Director of UNODC, Chargé d'affaires a.i. of the Delegation of the European Union, Executive Secretary of the Gulf of Guinea Commission, Maritime Planning Officer of the African Union Commission	All Council members, all invitees[j]	

[a] Albania, Brazil, China, France, Ghana (also on behalf of Gabon and Kenya), India, Ireland, Mexico, Norway, Russian Federation, United Arab Emirates, United Kingdom and United States.

[b] Albania, Angola, Benin, Brazil, Chad, Denmark, Djibouti, Egypt, Equatorial Guinea, Finland, France, Gabon, Gambia, Ghana, Guinea, Japan, Kenya, Lebanon, Liechtenstein, Luxembourg, Mauritius, Morocco, Netherlands, Nigeria, Norway, Portugal, Republic of Korea, Senegal, Seychelles, Slovakia, Slovenia, South Africa, Sweden, Switzerland, Togo, Tunisia and United States.

[c] Angola, Benin, Chad, Denmark, Djibouti, Egypt, Equatorial Guinea, Finland, Gambia, Guinea, Japan, Lebanon, Liechtenstein, Luxembourg, Mauritius, Morocco, Netherlands, Nigeria, Portugal, Republic of Korea, Senegal, Seychelles, Slovakia, South Africa, Sweden, Switzerland, Togo and Tunisia.

[d] Brazil, China, Ghana, India, Norway, United Kingdom and United States.

[e] Algeria, Argentina, Australia, Bangladesh, Belgium, Canada, Denmark, Ecuador, Egypt, Equatorial Guinea, Ethiopia, Germany, Italy, Japan, Malta, Morocco, Mozambique, Netherlands, Poland, Portugal, Republic of Korea, Rwanda, Senegal, Slovakia, Slovenia, South Africa, Switzerland, Tunisia, Thailand and Ukraine.

[f] The Commissioner and the Special Adviser participated in the meeting by videoconference. The representative of the European Union spoke also on behalf of Albania, Bosnia and Herzegovina, Montenegro, North Macedonia, the Republic of Moldova, Serbia and Ukraine.

[g] Gabon (President of the Council) was represented by its Minister for Foreign Affairs; Ghana was represented by its Minister of National Security; India was represented by its Minister of State for External Affairs; the United Arab Emirates was represented by its Minister for Foreign Affairs and International Cooperation; and the United States was represented by its Permanent Representative to the United Nations and member of the President's Cabinet.

[h] The Executive Director of UNODC, the Commissioner for Political Affairs, Peace and Security of the African Union and the representative of the Institute for Security Studies to the African Union participated in the meeting by videoconference.

[i] Albania, Brazil, China, France, India, Ireland, Kenya (also on behalf of Gabon and Ghana), Mexico, Norway, Russian Federation, United Arab Emirates, United Kingdom and United States.

[j] The representative of Germany spoke on behalf of the Group of Seven Group of Friends of the Gulf of Guinea.

10. The situation in Libya

During the period under review, the Council held 17 meetings concerning the situation in Libya and adopted six resolutions, including two under Chapter VII of the Charter. All the meetings that were not devoted to the adoption of decisions of the Council took the form of briefings.[365] More information on the meetings, including on participants, speakers and outcomes, is given in the table below. In addition to the meetings, Council members held informal consultations of the whole and one informal interactive dialogue to discuss the item.[366] In 2022, the Secretary-General appointed a new Special Representative of the Secretary-General for Libya and Head of the United Nations Support Mission in Libya (UNSMIL).[367]

In 2022, the Council heard briefings by the Under-Secretary-General for Political and Peacebuilding Affairs, the Assistant Secretary-General for Africa and the Special Representative of the Secretary-General for Libya. The briefings focused on the ongoing political, security, humanitarian and socioeconomic challenges facing Libya, including the constitutional review process in preparation for the postponed presidential and parliamentary elections. The briefings also covered the work of UNSMIL towards the implementation of the Libyan-led ceasefire monitoring mechanism, as well as efforts to support the economic reform process and improve the security and humanitarian situation across the country. Other briefers included the Chair of the Committee established pursuant to resolution 1970 (2011) concerning Libya, who gave a briefing on the activities of and developments relating to the work of the Committee and its Panel of Experts; the Prosecutor of the International Criminal Court, who provided updates on the Court's ongoing investigations regarding the situation in Libya; and three civil society representatives. Invitations under rule 37 of the provisional rules of procedure were limited to Libya.

On 24 January, the Council heard a briefing by the Under-Secretary-General for Political and Peacebuilding Affairs, who reported that growing polarization among political actors in disputes over key aspects of the electoral process had resulted in the postponement of the elections scheduled for 24 December 2021.[368] She noted that, on 5 December 2021, the Secretary-General had appointed a Special Adviser on Libya, who was working closely with UNSMIL and who had undertaken wide-ranging consultations in Tripoli, Benghazi, Misratah and Sirte since her arrival in Libya on 12 December. Concerning the political situation in the country, the Under-Secretary-General underlined that the Special Adviser had reiterated to Libyan interlocutors that the focus of the political process should remain the holding of parliamentary and presidential elections in the shortest possible time frame. On the security track, the Under-Secretary-General reported that there had been meetings among various armed groups. On the economic track, she noted that further steps had been taken towards the reunification of the Central Bank of Libya. The Under-Secretary-General welcomed the renewed efforts to advance national reconciliation based on the principles of transitional justice. While the ceasefire had continued to hold,

[365] For more information on the format of meetings, see part II.

[366] See A/77/2, part II, chap. 37.

[367] See S/2022/669 and S/2022/670.

[368] See S/PV.8952.

political uncertainty in the run-up to the elections had had a negative impact on the security situation. The second group of international monitors from the UNSMIL ceasefire monitoring component had deployed to Tripoli in December 2021. Regarding the human rights situation, the Under-Secretary-General said that UNSMIL had documented incidents of election-related violence, attacks against journalists, activists and individuals expressing political views, and hate speech and violence against women and men working to protect and promote the rights of women. She also noted the continued occurrence of arbitrary detention and the inhumane treatment of migrants and refugees in Libya. Nonetheless, the overall humanitarian situation had improved in 2021.

At the same meeting, the Council heard a briefing by the co-founder and Director of Lawyers for Justice in Libya, who warned that focusing on the dates for the elections, instead of a clear process to facilitate them, risked compromising due process for the sake of perceived political expediency. She reported that the systematic crackdown on civil society by all parties in Libya was particularly targeting women human rights defenders and women exercising their right to participate in political or public life. She called upon the Council and Member States to support an electoral process rooted in a legitimate legislative and constitutional framework; to demand accountability of all parties to the conflict, including third States; to apply sanctions fairly, transparently and consistently; to protect women and civil society; and to adopt and implement the recommendations of the independent strategic review of UNSMIL.

On 31 January, the Council unanimously adopted resolution 2619 (2022), by which it extended the mandate of UNSMIL for three months, until 30 April.[369] By the same resolution, the Council recalled that UNSMIL should be led by a Special Envoy and recognized the responsibility of the Secretary-General to appoint such an envoy, as set out in resolution 2542 (2020).[370] Despite the unanimous adoption, most Council members expressed disappointment at the Council's inability to reach an agreement on a substantive renewal of the mandate of UNSMIL.[371] Two Council members[372] supported the three-month extension to allow the Council to respond to developments in the situation in Libya and to agree on the appointment of a Special Envoy.

In her briefing to Council members on 16 March, the Under-Secretary-General for Political and Peacebuilding Affairs, reporting on the political situation in Libya, noted that the Libyan executive was facing a crisis that could lead to instability and parallel Governments in the country.[373] She reported increasingly threatening rhetoric, growing political tensions and divided loyalties among armed groups in western Libya following the 1 March vote of confidence on the new Government. Although the Secretary-General had expressed concern that the vote had fallen short of standards of transparency and procedure, the new Prime Minister had been sworn in by the House of Representatives on 3 March. The Special Adviser on Libya had continued her consultations with a broad cross-section of Libyan political and security actors and civil society. The United Nations was focusing its efforts on building consensus among Libyan institutions regarding the constitutional basis for holding elections as soon as possible. The Under-Secretary-General urged the members of the Council to call for responsible leadership by the Libyan institutions and to remain united in support of United Nations efforts to assist Libya.

At the same meeting, the Council heard a briefing by a member of civil society who was a legal academic, activist and candidate for the parliamentary elections, who conveyed the concerns of the Libyan people regarding the ongoing impasse in the political process, the absence of a permanent constitution, the lack of executive and legislative legitimacy of the State authorities, and the situation of human rights in the country, in particular the rights of women. She called on the Council to support the Libyan electoral process through the international monitoring of elections and to urge the Libyan leadership to honour the commitments of Libya to respect women and ensure a gender perspective in all policies, legislation and national strategies.

---

[369] Resolution 2619 (2022), para. 1.

[370] Ibid., para. 2.

[371] See S/PV.8961.

[372] Russian Federation and China.

[373] See S/PV.8996.

On 29 April, the Council unanimously adopted resolution 2629 (2022), by which it extended the mandate of UNSMIL for three additional months, until 31 July.[374] By the same resolution, the Council requested the Mission to implement the recommendations of the independent strategic review of UNSMIL and decided that the Mission should be led by a Special Representative of the Secretary-General, in Tripoli, supported by two Deputy Special Representatives, and called upon the Secretary-General to appoint a Special Representative promptly.[375] The Council further requested the Secretary-General to report on the implementation of the resolution every 30 days.[376] Many Council members expressed regret that the Council had not been able to secure consensus on a substantive one-year mandate renewal.[377] At the same time, most expressed the hope that the Council would soon be able to agree on a substantive resolution on UNSMIL and called upon the Secretary-General to appoint a Special Representative without delay. Several Council members[378] welcomed the endorsement by the Council of the recommendations of the strategic review, with some[379] citing in particular the reform of the Mission's leadership structure.

On 26 May, the Council heard a briefing by the Under-Secretary-General for Political and Peacebuilding Affairs, who said that the deadlock on the political, security and economic fronts in Libya had persisted, despite the best efforts of the United Nations to facilitate agreement among Libyan actors.[380] The human rights situation had also deteriorated, and she expressed concern about the negative impact of the protracted political impasse on the security situation. While the 2020 ceasefire continued to hold and the activities of the 5+5 Joint Military Commission had resumed, the situation remained fragile, with clashes among armed groups in Tripoli. On the economic front, the reluctance of the Government of National Unity to pay the Libyan National Army's salaries for the first quarter of 2022 had led elements affiliated with the Army to close several oilfields, cutting the country's daily oil output in half.

On 27 June, the Council heard a briefing by the Under-Secretary-General for Political and Peacebuilding Affairs, who said that during the final round of consultations of the House of Representatives and the High State Council regarding the constitutional basis for elections, broad consensus had been reached on most of the contentious issues.[381] She was encouraged that the leaders of both chambers had accepted the invitation of the Special Adviser to meet in Geneva in June to discuss and reach agreement on measures governing the transitional period leading to elections. Nevertheless, she noted that continued political divisions were contributing to a tense security environment in and around Tripoli. The human rights situation remained alarming, with civic space consistently being eroded, arbitrary restrictions imposed on civil society organizations, human rights activists being targeted, and reports of torture in detention facilities and prisons. On the economic front, the suspension of oil revenue transfers could have a negative impact on the ability of the Government of National Unity to pay salaries and meet other spending needs.

Following the briefing by the Under-Secretary-General, the operations manager of Fezzan Libya Organization, a civil society organization, speaking by videoconference from Sabha, Libya, said that there were significant challenges to the political participation of women, who continued to face systemic violence from the Government. While recent Governments had taken positive steps by appointing more women to higher positions, she underlined that achieving the meaningful participation of women also required adopting pro-women legislation.

On 25 July, the Council heard a briefing by the Assistant Secretary-General for Africa, who said that the overall situation in Libya remained highly volatile and that the constitutional and political stalemate persisted, prolonging the tense security environment, with an increased number of clashes in and around Tripoli.[382] Progress had been made on the constitutional track with the agreement between

---

[374] Resolution 2629 (2022), para. 1.

[375] Ibid., para. 2.

[376] Ibid., para. 6.

[377] See S/PV.9025 (Ireland, Albania, Brazil, Mexico, Norway, Gabon, Ghana, Kenya, France, United States and United Kingdom).

[378] United Arab Emirates, Ireland, Albania, Mexico, Norway, France and United Kingdom.

[379] Ireland, Brazil, Mexico and France.

[380] See S/PV.9047.

[381] See S/PV.9078.

[382] See S/PV.9098.

the Speaker of the House of Representatives and the President of the High State Council on some of the transitional measures that would lead to the holding of national elections and on a road map. She reported on the demonstrations held across Libya on 1 July, during which protestors had expressed their frustration with the continuing political divisions and the deterioration of living conditions. Libyan monitors, together with the international monitors of UNSMIL, had conducted two joint workshops to operationalize the Libyan-led and Libyan-owned ceasefire monitoring mechanism. Regarding the economic situation, she expressed concern about the politicization of the National Oil Corporation, emphasizing that the dire economic situation had had a negative impact on people's fundamental right to basic services and access to food, water, sanitation, health care and education.

On 28 July, the Council adopted resolution 2647 (2022), with three abstentions,[383] by which it extended the mandate of UNSMIL for an additional three months, until 31 October 2022, reiterated that the Mission should be led by a Special Representative of the Secretary-General, in Tripoli, supported by two Deputy Special Representatives, and called upon the Secretary-General to appoint a Special Representative promptly.[384] Expressing regret that a number of the deliverables of the Libyan Political Dialogue Forum road map had yet to be achieved, the Council underlined that the objectives and governing principles set out therein were still relevant to the political process and urged the Libyan political institutions and key stakeholders to agree on a pathway to deliver elections as soon as possible through dialogue, compromise and constructive engagement, in a transparent and inclusive manner.[385] In the preambular paragraphs of the resolution, the Council expressed support for the ongoing facilitation of intra-Libyan consultations to create the conditions and circumstances for elections on a constitutional and legal basis, while also encouraging further international support and regional cooperation between Libya, neighbouring countries and relevant United Nations bodies in support of peacebuilding and sustaining peace in the country and the region.[386] The Council recalled that the oil resources of Libya were for the benefit of all Libyans and needed to remain under the exclusive control of the National Oil Corporation and expressed grave concern about the humanitarian situation in the country.[387]

After the vote, the representative of the United Kingdom, the penholder of the resolution, said that resolution 2647 (2022) contained a number of important messages, including on the political and security processes, the integrity of the National Oil Corporation, and human rights.[388] Of particular importance was the message to the Libyan parties on the need to agree on a pathway to deliver presidential and parliamentary elections as soon as possible. However, she shared the frustration of the three African delegations that had abstained due to the short three-month mandate and said that the approach by the Russian Federation of insisting on three-month rollovers in the absence of a Special Representative was short-sighted and undermined the ability of UNSMIL to support Libyan leaders to achieve the political and security objectives required to bring stability to the country. The representative of the Russian Federation said that the adopted resolution was the only possible compromise for all at the current stage and that the tenure of the Special Adviser without an appropriate security mandate had been unjustifiably prolonged. The Secretary-General should promptly submit a worthy and authoritative candidate for the position of Special Representative for Libya and Head of UNSMIL, who would suit the main Libyan actors and regional stakeholders, for subsequent approval by the members of the Council. The insistence of the Russian Federation on appointing a Special Representative was dictated solely by concern for maintaining the effectiveness of United Nations efforts to promote a settlement in Libya. The representative of Gabon explained that her delegation had abstained in the voting on the renewal of UNSMIL as a call for the interests and concerns of Libyans to be put above all other considerations. The Council remained insensitive, despite the gradual deterioration of the security situation on the ground. Short mandates undermined the credibility of the Council. She reiterated her delegation's support for the appointment of an African to the position of Special Representative. Similarly, the representative of Ghana said that the Council had failed to show commitment to the Libyan people by not extending the mandate of UNSMIL for a one-year period in order to consolidate the gains of the peace efforts and foster serious engagement between the Council and the Libyan people through UNSMIL. The failure of the

[383] See S/PV.9103.

[384] Resolution 2647 (2022), paras. 1 and 2.

[385] Ibid., para. 3.

[386] Ibid., second and third preambular paragraphs.

[387] Ibid., sixth and ninth preambular paragraphs.

[388] See S/PV.9103.

Council to find consensus on the Secretary-General's proposed nominee for the vacant position further complicated the Libyan peace process, with the departure of the Special Adviser on Libya. The representative of Kenya said that the resolution and the three-month mandate extension constituted yet another disappointment for the people of Libya and expressed the belief that it was no longer tenable for UNSMIL to operate with such a brief and uncertain mandate. The representative of China expressed support for the appointment of an African candidate and noted that appointing a Special Representative as soon as possible would help to restore the full performance of UNSMIL, strengthen the United Nations capacity for good offices and help to create conditions for UNSMIL to obtain a longer mandate extension in the future. The representative of the United States welcomed the fact that the resolution provided a more substantive mandate, including language in support of the political process and assurances that the oil revenue of Libya was managed transparently for the benefit of the entire Libyan people. She noted the abstentions of the three African members of the Council in protest at the insistence of the Russian Federation on a three-month mandate and said that she shared their frustration. She further rejected the "specious contention" of the Russian Federation that a three-month mandate would assist the Secretariat in securing the Council's full support for a nominee and said that, on the contrary, a short mandate duration only complicated the Secretariat's efforts to recruit the best candidate for the role and made it much harder for UNSMIL to implement long-term plans and develop sustainable solutions to challenges in Libya. The representative of Brazil expressed the view that a candidate from the African continent would be well-suited to the position. He said that the compromise reached within the Council on the duration of the mandate of UNSMIL offered the Secretary-General and Council members a new opportunity to engage in the appointment of the Mission's leadership, with the expectation that a suitable candidate would be appointed as soon as possible, and expressed the hope that subsequent renewals of the mandate would benefit from more predictable time frames.

On 30 August, the Council heard a briefing by the Under-Secretary-General for Political and Peacebuilding Affairs, who reported that the United Nations had continued to engage with Libyan actors at every level to facilitate a resolution to the political impasse.[389] She noted that the ongoing stalemate and continued delays in implementing the electoral process posed a growing threat to security in and around Tripoli, and potentially to all Libyans. Fighting had broken out in Tripoli and its outskirts on 27 August between armed groups supporting Abdul Hamid Dbeibah and Fathi Bashagha respectively. She expressed concern about the limited political progress made during the reporting period and the lack of progress on forging a consensus on a constitutional framework for the elections.

On 24 October, the Council heard a briefing by the newly appointed Special Representative for Libya and Head of UNSMIL, who reported that prior to his arrival in Libya, he had spoken to a range of representatives of Member States and regional organizations and had stressed the importance of ensuring that the international community would support Libyan efforts in a coordinated manner, rally behind the United Nations and refrain from taking any action that could further deepen divisions.[390] Addressing the political situation in the country, he indicated that the deadlock persisted, further delaying the prospects for the holding of inclusive, free and fair elections. He had decided to prioritize consultations with Libyan institutional, political, security and civil society actors from across the country. While significant differences remained among Libyans on how to resolve the crisis, there was near unanimous condemnation across the spectrum of the presence of mercenaries, foreign fighters and foreign forces in Libya and of the incessant foreign interference in the country's affairs. Although the ceasefire continued to hold, the security track needed to be reinvigorated, as it had been adversely affected by the political impasse. He expressed concern regarding the human rights situation, reporting that violations against migrants and asylum-seekers continued with impunity and that arbitrary detention was a common practice. Recalling that the situation in Libya called for a "consensus State re-legitimation process", he stressed the paramount importance of the conduct of legislative and presidential elections and said that he would intensify consultations in that regard.

On 28 October, the Council unanimously adopted resolution 2656 (2022),[391] by which it extended the mandate of UNSMIL until 31 October 2023 and welcomed the appointment of Abdoulaye Bathily as

---

[389] See S/PV.9120.

[390] See S/PV.9162.

[391] See S/PV.9173.

Special Representative of the Secretary-General for Libya and Head of UNSMIL.[392] By the same resolution, the Council reiterated its request for the Mission to implement the recommendations of the independent strategic review of UNSMIL.[393] Recalling the Libyan Political Dialogue Forum road map, the Council urged the Libyan political institutions and key stakeholders to agree on a road map to deliver elections as soon as possible across the country.[394] The Council welcomed the support provided by the United Nations to the Libyan High National Elections Commission.[395] The Council emphasized that there could be no military solution in Libya and called upon all parties to refrain from violence or other actions that could escalate tensions, exacerbate conflicts and undermine the political process or the 23 October 2020 ceasefire.[396] The Council requested the Secretary-General to report on the implementation of the resolution every 60 days.[397]

After the vote, the representatives of Kenya, Brazil, Ghana and Gabon welcomed the substantive renewal of the mandate of UNSMIL for a 12-month period.[398] The representative of Gabon said that, as an African State and one of the three African members of the Council, his delegation felt a sense of having contributed to an important milestone in the stabilization of a major African State. The representative of Kenya said that the Libyan peace process was complex at the national level and made more so by the involvement of competing external interests, and urged all international support to be channelled through the United Nations-led process.

On 15 November, the Council heard a briefing by the Special Representative for Libya, who reported on the various meetings he had held with Libyan stakeholders and representatives of the international community in an effort to bring the country back to peace and stability through a Libyan-Libyan solution to the crisis.[399] He said that UNSMIL continued to provide technical assistance to the High National Elections Commission to maintain readiness for elections. There appeared to be broad agreement that restoring the legitimacy of Libyan institutions across the board was of paramount importance, as was the need to coordinate bilateral and multilateral diplomatic initiatives and to coalesce behind the efforts of the United Nations. He warned that further postponing the elections would make Libya even more vulnerable to political, economic and security instability and could put the country at risk of partition, and urged the Council to send an unequivocal message to obstructionists that their actions would not remain without consequences. On the security track, he reported some progress, including the holding of a meeting of the 5+5 Joint Military Commission, at which the Commission had agreed to establish a subcommittee for the disarmament, demobilization and reintegration of armed groups. The ceasefire continued to hold, despite ongoing escalatory rhetoric and a build-up of forces on both sides. He expressed alarm about the human rights situation and reported that online violence against women was on the rise. On the economic front, he noted that the lack of accountability, transparency and equity in the allocation of resources remained a key cause of tensions.

On 16 December, the Special Representative for Libya gave a briefing on his engagement with Libyan stakeholders and international partners to advance the political process and revive the electoral track, including his visits to Türkiye,[400] Qatar, the United Arab Emirates, Egypt and Tunisia.[401] He called upon the Council, its members and all those with convening power to support the efforts of UNSMIL to bring Libyan political leaders back to the negotiating table and prevent a further deterioration of the situation. On the security and military track, while the ceasefire had continued to hold, the proliferation of weapons under the control of State and non-State actors and the presence of foreign fighters, foreign forces and mercenaries continued to pose security challenges and undermine efforts to unify the country's security institutions. Furthermore, UNSMIL continued to observe a systematic campaign by Libyan security actors attempting to undermine and silence civil society, humanitarian actors, human rights

---

[392] Resolution 2656 (2022), paras. 1 and 2.

[393] Ibid., para. 3.

[394] Ibid., para. 4.

[395] Ibid., para. 5.

[396] Ibid., para. 7.

[397] Ibid., para. 11.

[398] See S/PV.9173.

[399] See S/PV.9192.

[400] Since 2022, "Türkiye" has replaced "Turkey" as the short name used at the United Nations.

[401] See S/PV.9223.

defenders and political activists, including women and young people. He expressed concern about new bureaucratic obstacles and movement restrictions impeding humanitarian access.

During the period under review, the Council also heard regular briefings by the Chair of the Committee established pursuant to resolution 1970 (2011) concerning Libya.[402] During the briefings, the Chair reported on the implementation and violations of the sanctions regime, including the arms embargo, asset freeze, travel ban and the timebound authorizations and measures aimed at preventing the illicit export of petroleum from Libya.[403] The Chair reported on the implementation of the assets freeze, including discussions regarding the preservation of Libyan frozen assets for the benefit of the Libyan people, exemption requests and notifications with respect to the illicit export of petroleum, the travel ban, the assets freeze and the arms embargo, and the consideration of delisting requests by the Committee.

On 13 July, the Council unanimously adopted resolution 2644 (2022) under Chapter VII of the Charter, by which it extended until 30 October 2023 the authorizations and measures contained in resolutions 2146 (2014), 2441 (2018) and 2509 (2020).[404] The Council also extended the mandate of the Panel of Experts established by resolution 1973 (2011) until 15 November 2023 and requested that the Panel closely follow and report to the Committee any information relating to the illicit export from or illicit import to Libya of petroleum, including crude oil and refined petroleum products.[405] The Council also demanded full compliance by all Member States with the arms embargo and called on all Member States not to intervene in the conflict or take measures that exacerbated the conflict.[406]

In 2022, the Prosecutor of the International Criminal Court continued to provide briefings to the Council. He reported twice on the progress and challenges relating to the Court's ongoing investigations regarding the situation in Libya. On 28 April, he gave a briefing on the twenty-third report of the Prosecutor to the Council, pointing out that it was the first time that the Office of the Prosecutor had indicated benchmarks in terms of timelines for certain action, so that the Office could be held to account.[407] At a meeting held on 9 November,[408] the Prosecutor gave a briefing from Libya for the first time. Describing the work performed by forensic experts in various locations, he underlined the need for the international community and the Court to do more to deliver justice for the people of Libya.

In their deliberations in 2022, Council members focused on the political, security and humanitarian situation in Libya and addressed the economic factors that were further destabilizing the country. Many expressed disappointment and concern regarding the postponement of the presidential and parliamentary elections, as well as the deteriorating situation in the country.[409] Council members expressed support for the Libyan-led and owned political process[410] and called on Libyan stakeholders to commit to holding

---

[402] See S/PV.8952, S/PV.8996, S/PV.9047, S/PV.9120 and S/PV.9223. For more information on the work of the Committee and the Panel of Experts, see part IX, sect. I.B.

[403] For more information on the sanctions measures, see part VII, sect. III.

[404] Resolution 2644 (2022), para. 2.

[405] Ibid., paras. 3 and 12.

[406] Ibid., para. 5.

[407] See S/PV.9024.

[408] See S/PV.9187.

[409] See S/PV.8952 (United Kingdom, Brazil, Albania, India, Mexico and Norway); S/PV.8996 (United Kingdom, Ireland, Russian Federation, Gabon (also on behalf of Ghana and Kenya), Mexico, France, China, Norway and United States); S/PV.9162 (United Kingdom, Norway, Mexico, Albania, France, United States, Brazil, China, India, Ireland and United Arab Emirates); S/PV.9192 (Russian Federation, United Kingdom, Norway, Ireland, United States, Brazil, France, Albania, India, China, Mexico and Ghana (also on behalf of Gabon and Kenya)); and S/PV.9223 (United Kingdom, Ireland, Albania and India).

[410] See S/PV.8952 (United Kingdom, United Arab Emirates, Ireland, Kenya (also on behalf of Gabon and Ghana), India, Russian Federation, China, United States and Norway); S/PV.9047 (Kenya (also on behalf of Gabon and Ghana), India and Norway); S/PV.9078 (Ghana (also on behalf of Gabon and Kenya), India, China and Albania); S/PV.9098 (United Kingdom, India, Kenya (also on behalf of Gabon and Ghana), Ireland, Albania and Brazil); S/PV.9120 (Brazil, Russian Federation, India, Albania and China); S/PV.9192 (United Kingdom, Ireland, Brazil, Albania, India, United Arab Emirates, China and Ghana (also on behalf of Gabon and Kenya)); and S/PV.9223 (United Kingdom, Kenya (also on behalf of Gabon and Ghana), China, Brazil, Ireland, United Arab Emirates and India).

free, fair and inclusive elections as soon as possible.[411] Several Council members expressed support for the efforts of the Special Adviser of the Secretary-General on Libya and then the Special Representative of the Secretary-General for Libya to convene consultations between the House of Representatives and the High State Council to establish a constitutional basis for elections.[412] The representative of Gabon, speaking also on behalf of Ghana and Kenya, recommended that the Secretary-General make use of the vast body of African expertise available in the context of the high-level United Nations leadership to achieve progress in the dialogue between the parties and strengthen coordination with States of the region.[413] Council members called for the full implementation of the ceasefire agreement, including the withdrawal of mercenaries and foreign forces from Libya,[414] compliance with the arms embargo,[415] the unification of institutions in Libya,[416] national reconciliation,[417] full and meaningful political participation of women in

[411] See S/PV.8952 (Ireland, Brazil, India, Mexico, France, United States and Norway); S/PV.8996 (Brazil, Gabon (also on behalf of Ghana and Kenya), Mexico, France, China, India, Norway, United States, Albania and United Arab Emirates); S/PV.9047 (United Kingdom, Kenya (also on behalf of Gabon and Ghana), Ireland, Albania, United Arab Emirates, France, India, Norway and United States); S/PV.9078 (Ghana (also on behalf of Gabon and Kenya), India, Norway, France, Ireland, United Arab Emirates and Albania); S/PV.9098 (United Kingdom, India, Kenya (also on behalf of Gabon and Ghana), Mexico, France, Ireland, Norway, China, United Arab Emirates, Albania and Brazil); S/PV.9120 (Norway, Russian Federation, India, United States, Albania, Kenya (also on behalf of Gabon and Ghana), United Arab Emirates, France, Mexico, Ireland and China); and S/PV.9223 (United Kingdom, China, Mexico, France, Ireland, Russian Federation, Norway, Albania, United Arab Emirates, United States and India).

[412] See S/PV.8996 (United Kingdom, Ireland, Brazil, Mexico, India, Norway, United States and Albania); S/PV.9047 (United Kingdom, Albania, China, United Arab Emirates, France, Norway and United States); S/PV.9078 (United Kingdom, Ghana (also on behalf of Gabon and Kenya), Norway, United States, Brazil, France, Mexico, China, Ireland, United Arab Emirates, Russian Federation and Albania); S/PV.9098 (India, Kenya (also on behalf of Gabon and Ghana), United States, Norway and China); S/PV.9192 (China); and S/PV.9223 (China, Mexico, Brazil, Russian Federation, Norway, United Arab Emirates and United States).

[413] See S/PV.8996. See also S/PV.9223 (Kenya (also on behalf of Gabon and Ghana)).

[414] See S/PV.8952 (United Kingdom, United Arab Emirates, Ireland, Kenya (also on behalf of Gabon and Ghana), Brazil, Albania, India, Mexico, France, United States and Norway); S/PV.8996 (France, China, India, Norway, United States, Albania and United Arab Emirates); S/PV.9047 (United Kingdom, Kenya (also on behalf of Gabon and Ghana), Ireland, Russian Federation, India, Norway and United States); S/PV.9078 (United Kingdom, Ghana (also on behalf of Gabon and Kenya), India, Norway, Brazil, France, Mexico, Ireland, United Arab Emirates, Russian Federation and Albania); S/PV.9098 (India, Mexico, France, China, United Arab Emirates, Russian Federation and Albania); S/PV.9120 (Norway, Russian Federation, India, Albania, Kenya (also on behalf of Gabon and Ghana), United Arab Emirates, France, Mexico, Ireland and China); S/PV.9162 (United Kingdom, Norway, Kenya, Mexico, Albania, France, United States, Brazil, China, India, Ireland and United Arab Emirates); S/PV.9192 (United Kingdom, United States, France, Albania, India, United Arab Emirates, China and Ghana (also on behalf of Gabon and Kenya)); and S/PV.9223 (United Kingdom, Kenya (also on behalf of Gabon and Ghana), China, Brazil, France, Russian Federation, Norway, Albania, United Arab Emirates, United States and India).

[415] See S/PV.8952 (Kenya (also on behalf of Gabon and Ghana), India and Mexico); S/PV.8996 (France and United States); S/PV.9047 (United States); S/PV.9078 (Ghana (also on behalf of Gabon and Kenya) and France); S/PV.9098 (United Kingdom, India, Mexico, France, Ireland, Norway and Albania); S/PV.9120 (Brazil, India, United States, France and Mexico); S/PV.9162 (Mexico, France, Brazil and India); S/PV.9192 (Brazil, France, India and Mexico); S/PV.9192 (Brazil, France, India and Mexico); and S/PV.9223 (Brazil, France and India).

[416] See S/PV.8952 (France, Russian Federation, China and United States); S/PV.8996 (United Kingdom, Russian Federation, United States and United Arab Emirates); S/PV.9047 (United Kingdom, United Arab Emirates and France); S/PV.9078 (France); S/PV.9098 (Kenya (also on behalf of Gabon and Ghana), Mexico, France, Norway, Russian Federation and Albania); S/PV.9120 (Kenya (also on behalf of Gabon and Ghana), United Arab Emirates and Mexico); S/PV.9162 (United Kingdom, Mexico, France, Brazil and United Arab Emirates); S/PV.9192 (Ghana (also on behalf of Gabon and Kenya)); and S/PV.9223 (China, Brazil, France, Ireland, Russian Federation and United Arab Emirates).

[417] See S/PV.8952 (Kenya (also on behalf also of Gabon and Ghana) and China); S/PV.8996 (Gabon (also on behalf of Ghana and Kenya) and United Arab Emirates); S/PV.9047 (Kenya (also on behalf of Gabon and Ghana), United Arab Emirates and India); S/PV.9078 (Ghana (also on behalf of Gabon and Kenya), India, Brazil, China, Ireland, United Arab Emirates and Albania); S/PV.9098 (Mexico, United Arab Emirates and Russian Federation); S/PV.9120 (Russian Federation, United Arab Emirates and China); S/PV.9162 (Russian Federation, Kenya (also on behalf of Gabon and Ghana), Brazil, China and United Arab Emirates); S/PV.9192 (Brazil, United Arab Emirates and Ghana (also on behalf of Gabon and Kenya)); and S/PV.9223 (Kenya (also on behalf of Gabon and Ghana), China, Brazil, Russian Federation and United Arab Emirates).

the political process,[418] and for addressing the concerns of Libya regarding the management of its frozen assets.[419] Some Council members addressed the attempts to disrupt oil production at the National Oil Corporation and said that the Corporation should not be politicized and must be allowed to fulfil its duties without interference.[420] Council members expressed concern about the humanitarian and human rights situation in the country, in particular the condition and arbitrary detention of migrants and refugees[421] and incidents of violence against journalists and civil society activists, including women's groups.[422] Some Council members further underscored the importance of ensuring that efforts undertaken for the withdrawal of mercenaries and foreign forces included disarmament, demobilization and reintegration measures in order to prevent instability in neighbouring countries and the Sahel region.[423] Several Council members expressed support for the action plan of the 5+5 Joint Military Commission for the withdrawal of foreign forces and mercenaries.[424] The appointment of a Special Representative for Libya and Head of UNSMIL was discussed extensively by Council members from January to August, both in regular briefings and in meetings for the adoption of decisions.

During his participation in Council meetings on Libya, the representative of Libya said that holding transparent and fair elections based on consensus laws and on a strong constitutional basis was the only genuine guarantee that could return legitimacy to the people, end the conflict and resolve the

---

[418] See S/PV.8952 (United Kingdom, United Arab Emirates, Ireland, Kenya (also on behalf of Gabon and Ghana), Brazil and Norway); S/PV.8996 (France and United Arab Emirates); S/PV.9047 (Ireland, Albania and United Arab Emirates); S/PV.9078 (Ghana (also on behalf of Gabon and Kenya), Mexico and Ireland); S/PV.9098 (Kenya (also on behalf of Gabon and Ghana)); S/PV.9162 (United Kingdom, Kenya (also on behalf of Gabon and Ghana), Mexico, Albania, Brazil, Ireland and United Arab Emirates); S/PV.9192 (United Kingdom, Ireland, Mexico and Ghana (also on behalf of Gabon and Kenya)); and S/PV.9223 (Kenya (also on behalf of Gabon and Ghana), Ireland and United Arab Emirates).

[419] See S/PV.8952, Kenya (also on behalf of Gabon and Ghana) and China; S/PV.8996 (Brazil, Gabon (also on behalf of Ghana and Kenya) and China); S/PV.9047 (Kenya (also on behalf of Gabon and Ghana)); S/PV.9078 (Ghana (also on behalf of Gabon and Kenya) and China); S/PV.9098 (Kenya (also on behalf of Gabon and Ghana), China and Brazil); S/PV.9120 (Brazil, Kenya (also on behalf of Gabon and Ghana), United Arab Emirates and China); S/PV.9162 (Kenya (also on behalf of Gabon and Ghana) and Brazil); S/PV.9192 (Brazil); and S/PV.9223 (Kenya (also on behalf of Gabon and Ghana), Brazil and Russian Federation).

[420] See S/PV.8996 (United Kingdom, France, China, United States and Albania); S/PV.9047 (United Kingdom, Kenya (also on behalf of Gabon and Ghana), Albania, China, France and Norway); S/PV.9078 (France, Mexico, China and Albania); S/PV.9098 (United Kingdom, United States, China and Albania); S/PV.9162 (Kenya (also on behalf of Gabon and Ghana) and Brazil); S/PV.9192 (Russian Federation and Ghana (also on behalf of Gabon and Kenya)); and S/PV.9223 (United States).

[421] See S/PV.8952 (Ireland, Kenya (also on behalf of Gabon and Ghana), Brazil, Albania, Mexico, France, United States and Norway); S/PV.8996 (Ireland, Brazil, Gabon (also on behalf of Ghana and Kenya), Mexico and Norway); S/PV.9047 (United Kingdom, Kenya (also on behalf of Gabon and Ghana), Ireland, Brazil, France and Norway); S/PV.9078 (Ghana (also on behalf of Gabon and Kenya), Mexico and Albania); S/PV.9098 (Kenya (also on behalf of Gabon and Ghana), Ireland and Albania); S/PV.9120 (Kenya (also on behalf of Gabon and Ghana), France, Mexico and Ireland); S/PV.9162 (Norway, Kenya (also on behalf of Gabon and Ghana), Mexico, Albania, France and Ireland); S/PV.9192 (Norway, Mexico and Ghana (also on behalf of Gabon and Kenya)); and S/PV.9223 (Kenya (also on behalf of Gabon and Ghana), Mexico, France, Ireland and United States).

[422] See S/PV.8952 (Brazil); S/PV.8996 (Ireland, Mexico, Norway, United States and Albania); S/PV.9047 (Brazil, Albania, Norway and United States); S/PV.9078 (Norway and Ireland); S/PV.9098 (United Kingdom, Mexico, Ireland and Brazil); S/PV.9162 (United Kingdom, Norway and Ireland); S/PV.9192 (Ireland, Albania and Ghana (also on behalf of Gabon and Kenya)); and S/PV.9223 (United Kingdom, Mexico, France, Ireland, Norway and Albania).

[423] See S/PV.8952 (Kenya (also on behalf of Gabon and Ghana), India, Mexico, France, China and Norway); S/PV.8996 (Gabon (also on behalf of Ghana and Kenya)); S/PV.9047 (Ireland, France, India and Mexico); S/PV.9078 (Ghana (also on behalf of Gabon and Kenya), India, France and Mexico); S/PV.9098 (Kenya (also on behalf of Gabon and Ghana), United States and France); S/PV.9120 (Norway, Kenya (also on behalf of Gabon and Ghana) and France); S/PV.9162 (Kenya (also on behalf of Gabon and Ghana), France, Brazil and China); S/PV.9192 (Brazil and Ghana (also on behalf of Gabon and Kenya)); and S/PV.9223 (Kenya (also on behalf of Gabon and Ghana), China, Mexico, France and India).

[424] See S/PV.8952 (United Kingdom, United Arab Emirates, Kenya (also on behalf also of Gabon and Ghana), Brazil, Albania, India, France, Russian Federation, China and United States); S/PV.9047 (Kenya (also on behalf of Gabon and Ghana), Ireland, France and Mexico); S/PV.9162 (Norway, Kenya (also on behalf of Gabon and Ghana), France and Brazil); and S/PV.9223 (Brazil, Norway and Albania).

situation in the country.[425] He reiterated his request to the United Nations to support, seriously and more effectively, the electoral process and to send its assessment teams, and emphasized the importance of Libyan ownership and leadership of any political process that would lead the country towards stability and impose the State's authority, while excluding all external dictates and intervention.[426] He recalled the need to support the 5+5 Joint Military Commission to ensure the full implementation of the ceasefire agreement and to put an end to any foreign presence on Libyan territories.[427] He said that the people of Libya had become hostage to the disagreements of Council members and some regional Powers, some of which went as far as to intervene directly in Libyan affairs, and recalled the lack of consensus on the mandate of UNSMIL or the appointment of a new Special Envoy of the Secretary-General.[428] He called upon the Council to play a positive and more effective role in supporting Libyan consensus, working to end all interventions in Libya, correcting past mistakes, and supporting all efforts to launch a national reconciliation and transitional justice project.[429] He also called upon the Council to support the strategic vision for national reconciliation[430] and to take additional constructive steps to support stability in Libya and end international division on the issue.[431]

In addition to the decisions outlined above, on 3 June, the Council adopted resolution 2635 (2022) under Chapter VII of the Charter, with one abstention, by which it extended the authorizations concerning the implementation of the arms embargo on the high seas off the coast of Libya, as set out in resolution 2578 (2021), for a further 12 months.[432] After the vote, the representative of the Russian Federation noted that the special inspection regime designed to implement the arms embargo on the high seas off the coast of Libya had failed to decrease the illicit trade in weapons and bring about a political settlement of the protracted conflict in Libya.[433] He said that the European Union military operation in the Mediterranean (Operation IRINI) had in recent years demonstrated low effectiveness in assisting the implementation of the arms embargo and that the work of the European Union Naval Force lacked transparency. The Russian Federation would continue to closely monitor the work of Operation IRINI to ensure full compliance with the arms embargo and would provide a legal assessment of the actions of the European Union Naval Force.

Developments in Libya were also considered under the item entitled "Maintenance of international peace and security".[434]

Meetings: the situation in Libya, 2022

Meeting record and date	*Sub-item*	*Other documents*	*Rule 37 invitations*	*Rule 39 and other invitations*	*Speakers*	*Decision and vote (for-against-abstaining)*
S/PV.8952 24 January	Letter dated 15 December 2021 from the Chair of the Security Council Committee established pursuant to resolution 1970 (2011) concerning Libya addressed to		Libya	Under-Secretary-General for Political and Peacebuilding Affairs, co-founder and Director of Lawyers for Justice in Libya	13 Council members,[a] all invitees	

[425] See S/PV.8996.
[426] See S/PV.8952.
[427] See S/PV.8996 and S/PV.9192.
[428] See S/PV.9078.
[429] See S/PV.8952, S/PV.9192 and S/PV.9223.
[430] See S/PV.9078 and S/PV.9162.
[431] See S/PV.9162.
[432] Resolution 2635 (2022), para. 1.
[433] See S/PV.9053.
[434] For more details, see sect. 35 below.

Meeting record and date	*Sub-item*	*Other documents*	*Rule 37 invitations*	*Rule 39 and other invitations*	*Speakers*	*Decision and vote (for-against-abstaining)*
	the President of the Security Council (S/2021/1058) Report of the Secretary-General on the United Nations Support Mission in Libya (UNSMIL) (S/2022/31)					
S/PV.8961 31 January	Report of the Secretary-General on UNSMIL (S/2022/31)	Draft resolution submitted by United Kingdom (S/2022/69)			13 Council members[b]	Resolution 2619 (2022) 15-0-0
S/PV.8996 16 March			Libya	Under-Secretary-General for Political and Peacebuilding Affairs, activist and candidate for the parliamentary elections	13 Council members,[c] all invitees	
S/PV.9024 28 April			Libya	Prosecutor of the International Criminal Court	All Council members, all invitees	
S/PV.9025 29 April		Draft resolution submitted by United Kingdom (S/2022/356)			14 Council members[d]	Resolution 2629 (2022) 15-0-0
S/PV.9047 26 May	Report of the Secretary-General on UNSMIL (S/2022/409)		Libya	Under-Secretary-General for Political and Peacebuilding Affairs	13 Council members,[a] all invitees	
S/PV.9053 3 June		Draft resolution submitted by France (S/2022/450)			Russian Federation	Resolution 2635 (2022) 14-0-1[e] (adopted under Chapter VII)

Meeting record and date	*Sub-item*	*Other documents*	*Rule 37 invitations*	*Rule 39 and other invitations*	*Speakers*	*Decision and vote (for-against-abstaining)*
S/PV.9078 27 June			Libya	Under-Secretary-General for Political and Peacebuilding Affairs, operations manager of Fezzan Libya Organization	13 Council members,[f] all invitees[g]	
S/PV.9092 13 July	Letter dated 24 May 2022 from the Panel of Experts on Libya established pursuant to resolution 1973 (2011) addressed to the President of the Security Council (S/2022/427)	Draft resolution submitted by United Kingdom (S/2022/548)				Resolution 2644 (2022) 15-0-0 (adopted under Chapter VII)
S/PV.9098 25 July			Libya	Assistant Secretary-General for Africa	13 Council members,[h] all invitees	
S/PV.9103 28 July		Draft resolution submitted by United Kingdom (S/2022/580)			10 Council members[i]	Resolution 2647 (2022) 12-0-3[j]
S/PV.9120 30 August	Report of the Secretary-General on UNSMIL (S/2022/632)		Libya	Under-Secretary-General for Political and Peacebuilding Affairs	13 Council members,[k] all invitees	
S/PV.9162 24 October			Libya	Special Representative of the Secretary-General for Libya and Head of UNSMIL	13 Council members,[h] all invitees[l]	
S/PV.9173 28 October		Draft resolution submitted by United Kingdom (S/2022/803)			Four Council members (Brazil, Gabon, Ghana, Kenya)	Resolution 2656 (2022) 15-0-0
S/PV.9187 9 November			Libya	Prosecutor of the International Criminal Court	All Council members, all invitees[m]	

Meeting record and date	Sub-item	Other documents	Rule 37 invitations	Rule 39 and other invitations	Speakers	Decision and vote (for-against-abstaining)
S/PV.9192 15 November			Libya	Special Representative of the Secretary-General	13 Council members,[f] all invitees[l]	
S/PV.9223 16 December	Report of the Secretary-General on UNSMIL (S/2022/932)		Libya	Special Representative of the Secretary-General	13 Council members,[k] all invitees[l]	

[a] Albania, Brazil, China, France, India, Ireland, Kenya (also on behalf of Gabon and Ghana), Mexico, Russian Federation, Norway, United Arab Emirates, United Kingdom and United States. The representative of India also gave a briefing in his capacity as Chair of the Committee established pursuant to resolution 1970 (2011) concerning Libya.

[b] Albania, Brazil, China, France, Gabon, Ireland, Kenya, Mexico, Norway, Russian Federation, United Arab Emirates, United Kingdom and United States.

[c] Albania, Brazil, China, France, Gabon (also on behalf of Ghana and Kenya), India, Ireland, Mexico, Russian Federation, Norway, United Arab Emirates, United Kingdom and United States. The representative of India also gave a briefing in his capacity as Chair of the Committee established pursuant to resolution 1970 (2011) concerning Libya.

[d] Albania, Brazil, China, France, Gabon, Ghana, Ireland, Kenya, Mexico, Norway, Russian Federation, United Arab Emirates, United Kingdom and United States.

[e] *For*: Albania, Brazil, China, France, Gabon, Ghana, India, Ireland, Kenya, Mexico, Norway, United Arab Emirates, United Kingdom, United States; *against*: none; *abstaining*: Russian Federation.

[f] Albania, Brazil, China, France, Ghana (also on behalf of Gabon and Kenya), India, Ireland, Mexico, Russian Federation, Norway, United Arab Emirates, United Kingdom and United States.

[g] The operations manager of Fezzan Libya Organization participated in the meeting by videoconference.

[h] Albania, Brazil, China, France, India, Ireland, Kenya (also on behalf of Gabon and Ghana), Mexico, Russian Federation, Norway, United Arab Emirates, United Kingdom and United States.

[i] Brazil, China, Gabon, Ghana, Kenya, Mexico, Russian Federation, United Arab Emirates, United Kingdom and United States.

[j] *For*: Albania, Brazil, China, France, India, Ireland, Mexico, Norway, Russian Federation, United Arab Emirates, United Kingdom, United States; *against*: none; *abstaining*: Gabon, Ghana and Kenya.

[k] Albania, Brazil, China, France, India, Ireland, Kenya (also on behalf of Gabon and Ghana), Mexico, Russian Federation, Norway, United Arab Emirates, United Kingdom and United States. The representative of India also gave a briefing in her capacity as Chair of the Committee established pursuant to resolution 1970 (2011) concerning Libya.

[l] The Special Representative participated in the meeting by videoconference.

[m] The Prosecutor of the International Criminal Court participated in the meeting by videoconference.

11. The situation in Mali

During the period under review, the Council held seven meetings and adopted two resolutions under Chapter VII of the Charter of the United Nations in relation to the situation in Mali. Five of the meetings took the form of briefings, and two meetings were convened for the adoption of a resolution.[435] More information on the meetings, including on participants and outcomes, is provided in the table below. The Council also held one private (closed) meeting with countries contributing troops and police to the United Nations Multidimensional Integrated Stabilization Mission in Mali (MINUSMA) pursuant to resolution 1353 (2001).[436] In addition, Council members held informal consultations of the whole in connection with the item.[437]

In 2022, the Council heard four briefings by the Special Representative of the Secretary-General for Mali and Head of MINUSMA in connection with the periodic reports of the Secretary-General on the

[435] For more information on the format of meetings, see part II.

[436] The private meeting was held on 7 June in connection with the item entitled "Meeting of the Security Council with the troop- and police-contributing countries pursuant to resolution 1353 (2001), annex II, sections A and B"; see S/PV.9057. See also A/77/2, part II, chap. 21.

[437] See A/77/2, part II, chap. 38.

situation in Mali.[438] The Council also heard briefings by three civil society representatives[439] and the Chair of the Committee established pursuant to resolution 2374 (2017) concerning Mali.[440] Mali was represented by its Minister for Foreign Affairs and International Cooperation in two of the meetings held under the item.[441]

In 2022, the Special Representative of the Secretary-General updated Council members on the talks between the transitional Government of Mali and the Economic Community of West African States (ECOWAS) to define a new transition timetable for the holding of elections and a return to civilian government, on progress in the implementation of the Agreement on Peace and Reconciliation in Mali, as well as on the security and humanitarian situation in the country amid an increase in violence perpetrated by extremist groups. In his first briefing of the year on 11 January,[442] the Special Representative noted that, at its Extraordinary Summit of Heads of State and Government held on 9 January, ECOWAS had rejected the new timetable proposed by the transitional Government of Mali to extend the political transition and hold elections by the end of 2025, and urged it to focus on a speedy return to constitutional order. ECOWAS had also decided to uphold the individual sanctions imposed on 12 December 2021 and had added new measures, including the closure of land and air borders between member States and Mali. The Special Representative noted that, against that political backdrop, the international mediation for the implementation of the Peace Agreement, led by Algeria and including MINUSMA and other international stakeholders, had called for the early convening of a high-level decision-making meeting between the signatories to allow for overdue progress to be made, most notably on disarmament, demobilization and reintegration. MINUSMA also continued providing structured support for the Malian authorities on the drafting of a comprehensive and politically led strategy for central Mali, as requested by the Council.

The Special Representative observed that 2021 had seen more extremist attacks than ever and that MINUSMA had suffered the highest number of casualties since 2013, which underlined the dangerous environment in which it was operating. The conflict had had a devastating impact on civilians, the number of displaced persons had increased from 216,000 in 2020 to more than 400,000 in 2021, and more than 1.8 million people were expected to need food assistance in 2022 compared to 1.3 million in 2021. The Special Representative also reported on the work of MINUSMA to physically verify the status of schools, protect civilians and ensure the safety and security of peacekeepers.

At the meeting held on 7 April,[443] the Special Representative noted several deadly attacks perpetrated by Islamic State in the Greater Sahara in the Ménaka region and south of Gao and the deployment by MINUSMA of its mobile task force units in response to the incidents. He observed that the attacks had occurred in the context of the withdrawal of Operation Barkhane and Task Force Takuba from Mali and stressed the importance of maintaining the Mission's capabilities and troops and finding adequate responses to its capability shortfalls. While noting that the Malian Defence and Security Forces had stepped up their counter-terrorism efforts in central Mali, the Special Representative emphasized that such operations must be conducted in ways that minimized civilian harm and upheld human rights and international humanitarian law principles, and must be complemented by practical and sustained steps to address the root causes of conflict and violence, including the finalization and implementation of the Government's politically-led strategy. With respect to the political transition, he noted that, at its Extraordinary Summit on 25 March, ECOWAS had endorsed the proposal of its mediator, the former President of Nigeria, Goodluck Jonathan, to extend the transition period for 12 to 16 months as a basis for negotiations on the gradual lifting of sanctions against Mali.

On 13 June,[444] the Special Representative stated that the prolonged uncertainty surrounding the duration of the political transition had made it more difficult to make progress in other areas, leaving little political space for a sustained commitment to the implementation of the Peace Agreement. MINUSMA and Algeria continued to engage with the Government and other signatory parties,

[438] See S/PV.8945, S/PV.9012, S/PV.9061 and S/PV.9154. See also S/2021/1117, S/2022/278/Rev.1, S/2022/446 and S/2022/731.

[439] See S/PV.8945, S/PV.9012 and S/PV.9061.

[440] See S/PV.9200.

[441] See S/PV.9061 and S/PV.9154.

[442] See S/PV.8945.

[443] See S/PV.9012.

[444] See S/PV.9061.

particularly on the organization of the high-level decision-making meeting with the aim of finalizing the details of the disarmament, demobilization and reintegration process on the basis of the Government's offer to integrate 26,000 combatants into State structures and a common understanding of the broad outlines of the necessary institutional reforms. The Special Representative expressed concern regarding the deteriorating security situation in the tri-border area of Liptako-Gourma due to attacks by Islamic State in the Greater Sahara, with consequent effects on Ménaka and Gao. He noted that MINUSMA was enhancing its presence in Ménaka, prioritizing long-range patrols and establishing temporary operating bases in the Gao and Mopti regions. With regard to the centre of Mali, he informed Council members that the campaign by the Malian Defence and Security Forces had undeniably led to an improvement in the situation in some areas and a weakening of the extremist groups. However, he expressed concern that some of the operations were marred by allegations of human rights violations.

In his statement on 18 October,[445] the Special Representative reported that significant progress had been made in the preparations for elections in Mali, following the agreement reached between Mali and ECOWAS in July on a new transition timetable that extended the transition until the end of March 2024. Specifically with regard to the transition, a draft constitution had been presented to the transitional President of Mali, Colonel Assimi Goïta, on 11 October and was expected to be put to a referendum in March 2023. The draft was based on the recommendations of the national dialogue on the reform process, provided for the establishment of a bicameral parliament and included provisions that would greatly facilitate the implementation of the Peace Agreement. He also noted progress in the establishment of the Independent Authority for Election Management and the operationalization of the mechanism for monitoring the transition timetable, which involved the Malian parties, ECOWAS, the African Union and MINUSMA. Furthermore, in his view, the success of the electoral process depended on the availability of financial and logistical resources, the evolution of the security situation and its overall inclusiveness.

The Special Representative also noted some encouraging developments in the implementation of the Peace Agreement and welcomed the Government's adoption of its comprehensive strategy for the stabilization of central Mali on 24 August, which was based on the following four pillars: security and social cohesion; governance and justice; economic and humanitarian recovery; and communication and cooperation.

Notwithstanding those positive developments, the Special Representative noted a sharp increase in the activities of extremist elements affiliated with Islamic State in the Greater Sahara and with Jama'a Nusrat ul-Islam wa al-Muslimin in the Ménaka and Gao regions since March. Regarding humanitarian developments, he informed Council members that the number of internally displaced persons had risen to over 422,000 in the centre and the north, while over 175,000 people were refugees in neighbouring countries. Furthermore, more than 1.8 million people faced severe food insecurity, 1.2 million children under the age of 5 were affected by malnutrition, and more than 600,000 children were affected by school closures due to insecurity. The Special Representative concluded his remarks by echoing the call of the Secretary-General for the urgent provision of missing capabilities for MINUSMA and stressed that its effectiveness depended on the cooperation of the Malian authorities, including with regard to freedom of movement, in conformity with the status-of-forces agreement.

In their briefings in 2022, the three civil society representatives offered their views on the connection between social inequality and the conflict in Mali, challenges to the participation of women in security sector reform and the impact of the political and security situation on the civilian population. At the meeting held on 11 January,[446] the social activist and Executive Director of the Youth Association for Active Citizenship and Democracy, a Mali-wide organization promoting social justice and democratic values, said that after 10 years of failed stabilization strategies, and with the Sahelian crisis at its worst, it was time for a paradigm change. Social, economic, political and environmental inequalities were dangerously fuelling crises and instability and the military response to the security situation was inadequate for overcoming and containing threats. She called on the Council to put its trust in the Malian people and their civil society in order to improve governance, noting that MINUSMA had an important role to play in that regard. In her statement on 7 April,[447] the President of Women in Law and Development in Africa in Mali, a pan-African network for the promotion and protection of women's rights, expressed

[445] See S/PV.9154.
[446] See S/PV.8945.
[447] See S/PV.9012.

the view that the security context in Mali had compounded inequalities and widened the gap that had to be overcome for women and young people to gain access to resources and governance. In the face of those challenges, civil society was planning to coordinate the efforts made by the Council and the Government and promote a legal framework and resources conducive to building a more inclusive, effective, transparent, sustainable and responsible security sector that would serve the people of Mali. In this regard, she outlined several recommendations on overcoming the barriers to women's participation in the security sector, reforming the sector and strengthening the mandate of MINUSMA. She also called on the Council to add a reference to climate change in the Mission's mandate, as a key element that affected the security of the population, specifically women and children. On 13 June,[448] the Director of Mali Musso and writer discussed the consequences of the political stalemate and deteriorating security situation in Mali, including grave violations and abuses against civilians, conflict-related and gender-based violence, the closure of schools and youth unemployment. She underlined that the Council should ensure that its decisions were leading to action on the ground and reiterated the recommendation to bolster the mandate of MINUSMA under Chapter VII of the Charter so that the Mission could fight terrorism alongside the Malian armed forces.

By resolution 2640 (2022) of 29 June, acting under Chapter VII of the Charter, the Council extended the mandate of MINUSMA for a period of one year, until 30 June 2023.[449] While maintaining the overall strategic priorities of MINUSMA to support the implementation of the Peace Agreement and the political transition, and to facilitate the implementation by Malian actors of a strategy that addressed the root causes and drivers of conflict in central Mali, the Council also introduced some modifications, including for the Mission to ensure that its support for the Malian Defence and Security Forces was provided in compliance with the human rights due diligence policy.[450] The Council expressed its support for the proposal of the Secretary-General to conduct an internal review of MINUSMA and requested that the review be conveyed no later than 13 January 2023.[451] In addition to addressing the mandate of MINUSMA, the Council urged the Malian parties to work towards resuming the meetings of all implementing bodies of the Peace Agreement and called on the Government to make tangible progress to achieve the political transition, the swift return to constitutional order and the handover of power to democratically elected civilian authorities.[452] The Council also urged the Malian authorities to prevent, minimize and address civilian harm that might result from operations undertaken by the Malian Defence and Security Forces and called for a cessation of all restrictions on the Mission's freedom of movement by ground and air, disinformation campaigns and other destabilizing activities and for a constructive dialogue between the Malian authorities and the Mission.[453]

Resolution 2640 (2022) was adopted with 13 votes in favour and 2 abstentions.[454] In their statements after the vote, the representatives of France and the United States expressed regret that the resolution had not received unanimous support. The representatives of the United Kingdom and the United States highlighted the importance of the new provisions relating to the Government's responsibility to ensure the Mission's freedom of movement, to protect civilians and to conduct human rights monitoring, and to ensuring that the support given to the Malian Defence and Security Forces complied with the human rights due diligence policy.

The representatives of China, Gabon, Ghana and the Russian Federation disagreed with the addition of new language on human rights. Specifically, the representative of the Russian Federation described the language as "intrusive" and expressed the view that it would not advance the Malian people's exercise of their sovereign right to protect their citizens and investigate incidents. The representative of China stated that the resolution lent too much prominence to human rights issues and stressed that, in fulfilling its human rights mandate, MINUSMA should communicate and cooperate closely with the Government and listen carefully to its views. The representative of Gabon opined that the resolution focused only on human rights, did not support Mali in restoring peace and stability, violated the country's sovereignty and failed to take into account the efforts made by its security forces to defend

[448] See S/PV.9061.
[449] Resolution 2640 (2022), para. 15. For more information on the mandate of MINUSMA, see part X, sect. I.
[450] Resolution 2640 (2022), paras. 18 and 32.
[451] Ibid., para. 58.
[452] Ibid., paras. 1 and 14.
[453] Ibid., paras. 2 and 6.
[454] See S/PV.9082.

their territory. The representative of India criticized the ambiguous nature of terms such as "robust posture", emphasizing that MINUSMA was not mandated to conduct counter-terrorism operations. Together with the representative of Brazil, the representative of India objected to the added language on climate change and the establishment of a link between climate change and security. In contrast to this view, the representatives of Gabon, Ghana and Kenya expressed regret that the resolution did not contain stronger language regarding the impact of climate change on the situation in Mali, in addition to strengthening the Mission's protection of civilians mandate.

On 23 November, the Council heard a briefing by the Chair of the Committee established pursuant to resolution 2374 (2017) concerning Mali, who reported on the work of the Committee during 2022.[455] In this regard, he highlighted the Committee's engagement with the representatives of Mali and of regional States to discuss the challenges in the implementation of the sanctions measures authorized by the Council, and the Committee's consideration on 28 July of the final report of the Panel of Experts and its recommendations.[456] By resolution 2649 (2022) of 30 August, acting under Chapter VII of the Charter, the Council unanimously renewed the travel ban and asset freeze as set out in resolution 2374 (2017) until 31 August 2023 and extended the mandate of the Panel of Experts until 30 September 2023.[457] The Council also expressed its intention to review the mandate of the Panel and to take appropriate action regarding its further extension no later than 31 August 2023.[458]

In their discussions during the periodic briefings in 2022, Council members expressed concern about the political, security and humanitarian situation in Mali. Regarding the political transition, they called for strengthened engagement between the Government of Mali and ECOWAS, welcomed the agreement on the new transition timetable and called for its full implementation for a swift restoration of constitutional order. Many Council members also expressed concern about the negative impact of the 2020 and 2021 coups d'état on the implementation of the Peace Agreement, but nonetheless welcomed the holding of the high-level decision-making meeting in August and the resumption of meetings of the Agreement Monitoring Committee in October 2022. While noting this progress, a number of speakers[459] stressed the need for an inclusive approach to the transition and the peace process, with the full and equal participation of women.

All Council members raised concerns about the increase in terrorist attacks in Mali in 2022 and the impact on the civilian population. Several delegations noted their support for the strengthened counter-terrorism efforts of the Malian Defence and Security Forces since December 2021.[460] Multiple delegations, however, expressed concern regarding the reports of human rights violations committed during those operations and pointed to the responsibility of the Government to protect civilians and ensure accountability for such acts.[461] Several Council members drew attention to the activities of and human rights abuses by foreign mercenaries such as the Wagner Group, including the attacks against civilians in Moura in March during joint operations with the Malian forces[462]. Given these reports, some speakers called on the Government to allow MINUSMA to fully implement its mandate to investigate and report

[455] See S/PV.9200. For more information on the mandate of the Committee established pursuant to resolution 2374 (2017), see part IX, sect I.B.

[456] S/2022/595.

[457] Resolution 2649 (2022), paras. 1 and 4. For more information on the sanctions measures relating to the situation in Mali, see part VII, sect. III.

[458] Resolution 2649 (2022), para. 4.

[459] See S/PV.8945 (United Kingdom, Mexico, Gabon (also on behalf of Ghana and Kenya), United States, Albania, Brazil, Ireland and United Arab Emirates); S/PV.9012 (India, United Arab Emirates, United States, Albania and United Kingdom); S/PV.9061 (Brazil, United States, United Arab Emirates, Ireland, United Kingdom and Mali); and S/PV.9154 (Norway, Ireland, United States, United Arab Emirates, Ghana (on behalf of Gabon and Kenya) Albania, United Kingdom and Mali).

[460] See S/PV.8945 (Russian Federation and China); S/PV.9012 (Mexico, China and Russian Federation); S/PV.9061 (China, Brazil, Mexico and Russian Federation); and S/PV.9154 (China, Brazil and Russian Federation).

[461] See S/PV.8945 (United Kingdom, United States, Albania and Ireland); S/PV.9012 (France, Mexico, United States), Albania, Ireland and Brazil); S/PV.9061 (Brazil, United States, Mexico, Ireland, Norway and United Kingdom); and S/PV.9154 (France, Norway, Ireland, United States, Brazil, Albania and United Kingdom).

[462] See S/PV.9012 (France, Mexico, United States, Albania, Norway, Ireland, Brazil and United Kingdom); S/PV.9061 (United States, Mexico, Norway, United Kingdom and Albania); and S/PV.9154 (France, Norway, Ireland, United States, Albania and United Kingdom).

on human rights violations and abuses.[463] More generally on the deteriorating regional security situation in the Sahel, Council members expressed disappointment at the decision of Mali in May to withdraw from the Joint Force of the Group of Five for the Sahel and stressed the importance of regional cooperation and coordination to address the terrorist threat.[464] Beyond military operations, speakers recognized the need for a holistic approach that addressed the root causes of the conflict and, in that regard, highlighted the importance of the Government's comprehensive politically-led strategy for the stabilization of the centre of the country.[465] In their statements, the representatives of China and the Russian Federation underscored the sovereign right of Mali to establish its own international security cooperation, with the Russian Federation pointing to a significant security vacuum following the withdrawal of Operation Barkhane and Task Force Takuba.[466]

Council members also exchanged views on the challenges MINUSMA faced in the implementation of its mandate, noting in particular an increase in attacks against the Mission's personnel and the Government's restrictions on air and ground movement, with many of them also calling on the Government to abide by its obligations under the status-of-forces agreement. Many speakers stressed the need for MINUSMA to be adequately resourced and equipped to implement its tasks and to ensure the safety and security of its personnel. Furthermore, looking ahead, several delegations called on the Secretariat to ensure that the internal review of the Mission proposed by the Secretary-General, for which the Council expressed support in paragraph 58 of resolution 2640 (2022), took into account the significant changes in the Mission's operational environment.[467] In their remarks to the Council, the Minister for Foreign Affairs and International Cooperation and the representative of Mali provided an overview of the Government's engagement with ECOWAS on the new timetable for the political transition, progress in the implementation of the Peace Agreement, enhancing the capacity of the security forces and counter-terrorism operations, and the restoration of State authority.[468] The Minister for Foreign Affairs and International Cooperation of Mali stated that MINUSMA needed to refocus its work on the foundation of its presence in Mali, which was to support the restoration of State authority and improve its coordination with the Malian authorities.[469] He also listed the key principles that guided the cooperation of Mali with the Council and other international partners, namely, respect for the sovereignty of Mali; respect for its strategic choices and selection of partners; and the need to take the vital interests of the Malian people into account in all decisions.

Meetings: the situation in Mali, 2022

Meeting record and date	*Sub-item*	*Other documents*	*Rule 37 invitations*	*Rule 39 and other invitations*	*Speakers*	*Decision and vote (for-against-abstaining)*
S/PV.8945 11 January	Report of the Secretary-General on the situation in Mali (S/2021/1117) Letter dated 4 January 2022 from the Secretary-General		Mali	Special Representative of the Secretary-General for Mali and Head of the United Nations Multidimensional Integrated Stabilization Mission in Mali, Executive Director	13 Council members,[a] all invitees[b]	

[463] See S/PV.9012 (France, United States, Albania, Norway, Ireland and United Kingdom); S/PV.9061 (France, United States, Mexico, Ireland, Norway, United Kingdom and Albania); and S/PV.9154 (United States, Ghana (also on behalf of Gabon and Kenya) and United Kingdom).

[464] See S/PV.9061 (Ghana (also on behalf of Gabon and Kenya), Mexico, Ireland and India).

[465] See S/PV.8945 (France, Russian Federation, United States, Albania, Brazil and China); S/PV.9012 (France, United Arab Emirates, Albania, China and Brazil); S/PV.9061 (United Arab Emirates and Norway); S/PV.9154 (China, United States, United Arab Emirates and Ghana (also on behalf of Gabon and Kenya)).

[466] See S/PV.9061 and S/PV.9154.

[467] See S/PV.9154 (Norway, Ireland, United States, Ghana (also on behalf of Gabon and Kenya), Russian Federation, Mexico and Albania).

[468] See S/PV.8945, S/PV.9012, S/PV.9061 and S/PV.9154.

[469] See S/PV.9154.

Meeting record and date	*Sub-item*	*Other documents*	*Rule 37 invitations*	*Rule 39 and other invitations*	*Speakers*	*Decision and vote (for-against-abstaining)*
	addressed to the President of the Security Council (S/2022/8)			of the Youth Association for Active Citizenship and Democracy and social activist		
S/PV.9012 7 April	Report of the Secretary-General on the situation in Mali (S/2022/278/Rev.1)		Mali	Special Representative of the Secretary-General, President of Women in Law and Development in Africa in Mali	13 Council members,[c] all invitees[d]	
S/PV.9061 13 June	Report of the Secretary-General on the situation in Mali (S/2022/446) Letter dated 1 June 2022 from the Secretary-General addressed to the President of the Security Council (S/2022/448)		Mali	Special Representative of the Secretary-General, Director of Mali Musso and writer	13 Council members,[c] all invitees[e]	
S/PV.9082 29 June	Report of the Secretary-General on the situation in Mali (S/2022/446) Letter dated 1 June 2022 from the Secretary-General addressed to the President of the Security Council (S/2022/448)	Draft resolution submitted by France (S/2022/517)	Mali		11 Council members,[f] all invitees	Resolution 2640 (2022) 13-0-2[g] (adopted under Chapter VII)
S/PV.9119 30 August	Letter dated 3 August 2022 from the Panel of Experts on Mali established pursuant to resolution 2374 (2017) addressed to the President of the Security Council (S/2022/595)	Draft resolution submitted by France, Mexico (S/2022/650)				Resolution 2649 (2022) 15-0-0 (adopted under Chapter VII)

Meeting record and date	*Sub-item*	*Other documents*	*Rule 37 invitations*	*Rule 39 and other invitations*	*Speakers*	*Decision and vote (for-against-abstaining)*
S/PV.9154 18 October	Report of the Secretary-General on the situation in Mali (S/2022/731)		Mali	Special Representative of the Secretary-General	13 Council members,[c] all invitees[h]	
S/PV.9200 23 November					One Council member (Mexico)[i]	

[a] Albania, Brazil, China, France, Gabon (also on behalf of Ghana and Kenya), India, Ireland, Mexico, Norway, Russian Federation, United Arab Emirates, United Kingdom and United States.

[b] The Special Representative and the Executive Director of the Youth Association participated in the meeting by videoconference.

[c] Albania, Brazil, China, France, Ghana (also on behalf of Gabon and Kenya), India, Ireland, Mexico, Norway, Russian Federation, United Arab Emirates, United Kingdom and United States.

[d] The Special Representative and the President of Women in Law and Development in Africa in Mali participated in the meeting by videoconference.

[e] Mali was represented by its Minister for Foreign Affairs and International Cooperation. The Director of Mali Musso participated in the meeting by videoconference.

[f] Albania, Brazil, China, France, Gabon, Ghana, India, Kenya, Russian Federation, United Kingdom and United States.

[g] *For*: Albania, Brazil, France, Gabon, Ghana, India, Ireland, Kenya, Mexico, Norway, United Arab Emirates, United Kingdom, United States; *against*: none; *abstaining*: China, Russian Federation.

[h] Mali was represented by its Minister for Foreign Affairs and International Cooperation.

[i] The representative of Mexico spoke in his capacity as Chair of the Committee established pursuant to resolution 2374 (2017) concerning Mali.

Americas

12. The question concerning Haiti

During the period under review, the Council held seven meetings and adopted two resolutions under the item entitled "The question concerning Haiti", including resolution 2653 (2022), acting under Chapter VII of the Charter of the United Nations. Five meetings took the form of briefings, and two were convened for the adoption of a resolution.[470] More information on the meetings, including participants and outcomes, is provided in the table below. In addition, Council members held informal consultations of the whole in connection with the item.[471]

In 2022, the Council heard three briefings by the Special Representative of the Secretary-General for Haiti and Head of the United Nations Integrated Office in Haiti (BINUH) in connection with the periodic reports of the Secretary-General on the activities of the Mission and two briefings in emergency meetings convened further to the deterioration of the security and humanitarian situation in the country from September 2022.[472] The Council also heard briefings by the Deputy Secretary-General, the Deputy Executive Director of the World Food Programme (WFP), the Executive Director of the United Nations Office on Drugs and Crime (UNODC) and two representatives of civil society.[473] The Council also heard a briefing by the representative of Gabon in his capacity as Chair of the Committee established pursuant to resolution 2653 (2022) concerning Haiti, which had imposed targeted sanctions.[474] In addition to statements by Haiti, which was represented by its Minister for Foreign Affairs and Worship on four occasions, the meetings under the item also featured statements by the representative of Belize on behalf

[470] For more information on the format of meetings, see part II.

[471] See A/77/2, part II, chap. 8.

[472] See S/PV.8969, S/PV.9066, S/PV.9136, S/PV.9153 and S/PV.9233. See also S/2022/117, S/2022/481 and S/2022/761.

[473] See S/PV.9066, S/PV.9136 and S/PV.9233.

[474] See S/PV.9233.

of the Caribbean Community (CARICOM), the representative of Canada on behalf of the Ad Hoc Advisory Group on Haiti of the Economic and Social Council, the Minister for Foreign Affairs and representative of the Dominican Republic, and the Permanent Observer for the International Organization of la Francophonie to the United Nations.[475]

In her statements to the Council, the Special Representative of the Secretary-General reported on the three intersecting crises in the country, namely, economic, security and political. She gave a briefing on the developments following the decision of the Government of Haiti to reduce regressive subsidies on fuel, the dire security situation, including alarming levels of gang violence, and the blockade of the nation's main fuel terminal and its impact on the socioeconomic and humanitarian situation, including a new cholera outbreak. She also reported on efforts by the Government and stakeholders in Haiti to address the root causes of the crisis.

At the meeting held on 18 February,[476] the Special Representative stated that the situation in Haiti remained fraught and highly polarized, despite some signs of progress. The unveiling of the new Government of Haiti on 24 November 2021 appeared to have eased tensions somewhat and that momentum seemed to be building around an effort to form an inclusive, credible and effective provisional electoral council. Gang violence continued to plunge major urban centres into lawlessness and grief. Criminal armed groups had a strong hold on the economic and social lives of millions of children, women and men, noting in particular their indiscriminate use of abduction and murder, as well as sexual and gender-based violence. The Special Representative stressed that the Haitian National Police could not, on its own, curtail the alarming rise in gang-related insecurity. She expressed the view that the newfound momentum, epitomized by the imminent creation of a United Nations multi-donor basket fund for security assistance for Haiti, must translate into increased Government funding for the police force, as well as additional international financial and technical support.

Beyond the security situation, the Special Representative highlighted the need for socioeconomic projects and reintegration activities in the neighbourhoods most affected by gang violence, to end impunity and to ensure that reform in the judiciary could be sustained over the long term. The lack of impact and effectiveness of development aid over many years required the formulation of a new approach, one premised on a deeper coordination of international efforts and a real partnership with the Haitian authorities and actors. It was imperative for all Haitian leaders to engage constructively in order to steer the country towards elections and for the international community to engage with them to create the security and political conditions necessary for national elections, as well as to ensure urgent structural reforms to tackle gang violence, address impunity and corruption, strengthen the justice system and transform the economy in a sustainable manner.

In her statement on 16 June,[477] the Special Representative drew the attention of Council members to a rapidly deteriorating security situation in Haiti, with gangs expanding their zones of influence. She noted a rise of 36 per cent rise in kidnappings and 17 per cent in intentional homicides, compared with the last five months of 2021, incidents of sexual violence against women and girls, restrictions on the freedom of movement of people and goods, the displacement of at least 17,000 people, and the absence of basic necessities such as food, water and medicine. With respect to efforts to end the ongoing political and institutional vacuum, the Special Representative noted the formation in late March of a civil society-led tripartite committee to enlarge consensus among various political platforms, including the Government, to forge a common path forward. In parallel, the Prime Minister, Ariel Henry, was holding direct talks with the leadership of the Commission for a Haitian Solution to the Crisis (Montana Group), which had proposed new modalities to relaunch formal negotiations.

In his statement at the same meeting, the Executive Director of Volontariat pour le développement d'Haïti provided an overview of what, based on his experience with civil society on the ground, were the most pressing challenges in Haiti and recommendations for addressing them. He underscored the need to broaden consensus on governance, take urgent transnational action against those involved in the illegal arms trade and financial crimes, and provide international support for the Haitian National Police. Furthermore, he encouraged BINUH to work more closely with young people and civil society and opined

---

[475] See S/PV.9066, S/PV.9136, S/PV.9153 and S/PV.9233.

[476] See S/PV.8969.

[477] See S/PV.9066.

that the Mission would be even more effective if it had adequate resources to strengthen its good offices mission and its work of advising and supporting the Haitian National Police.

On 15 July, by resolution 2645 (2022), the Council unanimously extended the mandate of BINUH as set out in resolution 2476 (2019) for a period of one year, until 15 July 2023.[478] The Council acknowledged the letter dated 29 April from the Secretary-General (S/2022/369), in which he provided recommendations for adjustments to the mandate and resources of BINUH,[479] and, on that basis, made several changes to the mission. Specifically, the Council increased the number of civilian and seconded personnel serving as police and corrections advisers in the police and corrections unit from 30 to 42 and provided that the human rights unit would include dedicated capacity to address sexual and gender-based violence, including the identification of women's protection advisers.[480] In terms of tasks, the Council requested BINUH to work with UNODC and other relevant United Nations agencies to support Haitian authorities in combating illicit financial flows and the trafficking and diversion of arms and related materiel, and in enhancing the management and control of borders and ports.[481] With respect to the situation in Haiti, the Council demanded an immediate cessation of gang violence and criminal activities and expressed its readiness to take appropriate measures, as necessary, against those engaged in or supporting gang violence, criminal activities, or human rights abuses or who otherwise took action that undermined the peace, stability and security of Haiti and the region.[482] Lastly, the Council requested the Secretary-General to develop possible options for enhanced security support for the efforts of the Haitian National Police to combat high levels of gang violence, and to submit a written report by 15 October.[483]

At the meeting held on 26 September,[484] the Special Representative noted that gang, economic and political crises in Haiti had begun to intersect in new and frightening ways. She reported that, following the Government's announcement of its decision to reduce regressive subsidies on fuel, roadblocks had been set up throughout the country, which had generated a countrywide lockdown that lasted for five days. On 18 September, one of the largest alliances of criminal gangs in the capital had blocked the nation's main fuel terminal in Varreux, cutting the capital off from its primary source of fuel, creating shortages across the country and closing down hospitals. The chronic situation at the fuel terminal threatened to highlight the very real limits of the Haitian National Police. National stakeholders had begun to re-engage with a renewed sense of urgency, and government representatives, political groups and civil society organizations had launched new consultations on ways to forge a broader consensus on a path to elections. Insecurity had also severely curtailed humanitarian access and the various crises had converged into a humanitarian catastrophe. She called upon the Council to take urgent action to support Haitians in their efforts to build a better future.

In her statement at the same meeting, the Deputy Executive Director of WFP noted that the humanitarian situation in Haiti had reached new levels of desperation. The Food and Agriculture Organization of the United Nations and WFP expected food security to deteriorate further in 2022 and to surpass the record high of 4.5 million people estimated to face crisis levels of food insecurity or worse. Insecurity made it very difficult and dangerous to implement humanitarian and development programmes. Gangs were blocking access to fuel supplies and key logistics hubs and protesters had ransacked and looted humanitarian warehouses throughout the country. In that regard, she looked forward to increased support from Member States to further facilitate humanitarian access and ensure the protection of humanitarian actors, personnel and assets. The Executive Director of UNODC noted that violence and organized crime, as well as the presence of and clashes between armed groups, were compromising stability, security and the rule of law in Haiti, hampering the efforts to achieve peace and the prospects for lasting development. She underscored the need to prioritize supporting services that aimed to uphold and implement the law and criminal justice so as to assist the population and prevent any regional destabilization. In that regard, the Government of Haiti had directly tasked UNODC with supporting its border-management capacity-building endeavours. Investments and efforts in the security sector should

[478] Resolution 2645 (2022), para. 1.

[479] Ibid., fifth preambular paragraph. For more information on the mandate of BINUH, see part X, sect. II.

[480] Resolution 2645 (2022), para. 2.

[481] Ibid., para. 8.

[482] Ibid., para. 5.

[483] Ibid., para. 10. See also S/2022/747.

[484] See S/PV.9136.

be accompanied by similar efforts throughout the entire criminal justice system. She noted the activities planned by UNODC, with the support of BINUH and other organizations, on border management and tracking illicit financial flows.

In her briefing on 17 October,[485] the Special Representative reported that in addition to the three intersecting crises – economic, security and political – Haiti was facing a humanitarian crisis, as a growing number of cholera cases had been confirmed on the island. Gangs continued to blockade the Varreux terminal and, without the free movement of fuel, Haiti would be unable to get ahead of the crisis. Regarding the political situation, the Special Representative noted that resolution 2645 (2022) had generated a sense of urgency and that civil society representatives were attempting to bring all stakeholders around a common proposal, with the support of the good offices of the United Nations. Against a backdrop of insecurity and a humanitarian crisis, on 7 October, the Council of Ministers had authorized the Prime Minister, Ariel Henry, to request the support of a specialized international armed force to help secure the free movement of water, fuel and medical supplies. The Special Representative reiterated the call of the Secretary-General for Haiti's partners to consider that request as a matter of urgency.

On 21 October, by resolution 2653 (2022), acting under Chapter VII of the Charter, the Council unanimously imposed sanctions measures concerning Haiti for an initial period of one year.[486] The measures consisted of a travel ban, asset freeze and targeted arms embargo against individuals and entities designated as responsible for or complicit in, or having engaged in, directly or indirectly, actions that threatened the peace, security or stability of Haiti. By the resolution, the Council established a Committee mandated to monitor implementation of the sanctions measures and to designate individuals and entities subject to the measures, and to consider requests for exemptions.[487] Furthermore, the Council requested the Secretary-General to create, for an initial period of 13 months, a Panel of Experts to support the work of the Committee.[488] The Council also expressed its intent to consider authorizing the Ombudsperson to receive delisting requests.[489]

Explaining her delegation's vote in favour of the resolution, the representative of the United States, as co-penholder together with Mexico, expressed the view that the sanctions measures imposed by resolution 2653 (2022) accomplished the objectives of specifically targeting bad actors in Haiti and allowing humanitarian aid to reach civilians. She added, however, that the measures were only the first step and noted the request from the Government of Haiti and the recommendation of the Secretary-General for the Council to authorize a non-United Nations international security assistance mission to help improve the security situation and enable the flow of humanitarian aid. According to the representative of Mexico, by imposing the sanctions measures, the Council had sent a clear signal that the violence in Haiti could not remain unpunished. He further stressed the importance of the embargo on the transfer of arms to non-State actors that were destabilizing the country. The representative of China, while noting that his country had always called for caution in the use or threat of use of sanctions in international relations, recalled that his delegation had been the first to propose the imposition of measures against the criminal gangs in Haiti, considering the urgency of the situation. In contrast, the representative of the Russian Federation stated that, despite his delegation's support for the resolution, it was not convinced that international restrictive measures would provide an adequate response to the range of problems plaguing Haiti and that a lasting solution should lie in an inclusive political process, socioeconomic development and the eradication of poverty and inequality. Several Council members[490] stressed the importance of humanitarian exemptions in the new sanctions regime. Speakers[491] also welcomed the inclusion in the resolution of specific benchmarks to review the sanctions. Some Council

---

[485] See S/PV.9153.

[486] Resolution 2653 (2022), paras. 3, 6 and 11.

[487] Ibid., paras. 19 (a) and (c).

[488] Ibid., paras. 4 and 21.

[489] Ibid., nineteenth preambular paragraph. For more information on the sanctions measures concerning Haiti, see part VII, sect. III. For more information on the Committee established pursuant to resolution 2653 (2022), see part IX, sect. I.B.

[490] See S/PV.9159 (Norway, United Arab Emirates, Brazil and Ghana).

[491] Kenya, United Arab Emirates, Brazil and Ghana.

members[492] highlighted the Council's recognition of the need for due process safeguards in the resolution, and welcomed its intention to authorize the Ombudsperson to receive delisting requests under the new sanctions regime.

Opening the meeting held on 21 December,[493] the Deputy Secretary-General stated that, at the end of 2022, Haiti was in a deepening crisis of unprecedented scale and complexity that was cause for serious alarm. She noted that Port-au-Prince and the region beyond were suffering the worst human rights and humanitarian emergency in decades. Specifically, the Deputy Secretary-General informed Council members that 90 per cent of cholera cases in Haiti were in areas already suffering high rates of severe acute malnutrition. She condemned the reports of widespread sexual violence by armed gangs. She called for international support and solidarity with Haiti and urged every country with the capacity to do so to urgently consider the Government's request for an international specialized armed force to help restore security and alleviate the humanitarian crisis, in accordance with the letter dated 8 October from the Secretary-General addressed to the President of the Council.[494]

At the same meeting, the Special Representative of the Secretary-General noted that the siege of the main oil terminal in Haiti had come to an end in early November through a concerted effort by the Haitian National Police. Fuel had begun to flow in a number of neighbourhoods in the Port-au-Prince area, allowing hospitals and businesses to open and creating the semblance of a possible return to normalcy. Hope had quickly been dispelled, however, as a new level of gang activity had immediately been felt across the capital, marked by spikes in kidnappings, killings and rapes. The increase in recorded rapes, according to the Special Representative, reflected a horrendous modus operandi of the gangs, which used sexual violence to intimidate and subjugate whole communities. Further compounding the plight of the millions living amid the violence, she added, was the catastrophic economic situation, with some 20,000 people facing famine-like conditions, large levels of displacement, 34 per cent of schools remaining closed and 15,000 suspected cases of cholera.

The Special Representative noted that the adoption of the sanctions measures by the Council under resolution 2653 (2022) was widely welcomed by Haitians, while subsequent bilateral sanctions appeared to have generated a renewed sense of urgency on ways to restore democratically elected institutions. In October and November, civil society groups had launched a new round of inclusive consultations on a transitional road map with members of the Montana Group, private sector associations, trade unions and religious organizations, which had resulted in the development of a national consensus document. The document outlined steps for moving Haiti to elections within an 18-month time frame, with a transitional council and oversight mechanism. She expressed the view that the sanctions measures imposed by the Council would be most effective as part of a comprehensive approach that included both the ongoing political dialogue and enhanced operational security support for the Haitian National Police, as outlined in the letter of the Secretary-General.

In his first briefing to the Council as Chair of the Committee established pursuant to resolution 2653 (2022) concerning Haiti, the representative of Gabon stated that, in accordance with the resolution, the Committee had imposed measures on individuals and entities it designated as being complicit in or having participated, directly or indirectly, in activities that threatened peace, security or stability in Haiti, including a travel ban, assets freeze and a targeted arms embargo. The Chair informed the Council of his expectation that, once appointed, the Panel of Experts would assume its duties in January 2023 and would provide the Council with its interim report no later than 15 March 2023. He echoed resolution 2653 (2022) in urging all Member States, as well as international, regional and subregional organizations, to ensure cooperation with the Panel of Experts.

The editor of *Haiti Liberté* offered the view that previous military interventions in Haiti by the Council following the coups d'états in 1991 and 2004 had cemented an unjust and illegal status quo and noted that Haitians were patently and almost universally opposed to any more United Nations interventions. He questioned the imposition of targeted sanctions by the Council against Jimmy Cherizier, known as "Barbecue", whom he described as a spokesman for a federation of neighbourhoods dedicated

[492] Norway, Ireland and Brazil.

[493] See S/PV.9233.

[494] S/2022/747.

to keeping kidnapping, extortion, rape and other crimes out of their midst. An error of that magnitude, according to the editor, showed how easily misguided, counterproductive and blunt the Council's power under Chapter VII of the Charter could be, especially when it was receiving inaccurate and skewed information. The editor underlined the belief of *Haiti Liberté* that the situation in the country could not be resolved through foreign intervention, military force or even sanctions and that the only thing the United Nations might do was provide disinterested economic support to rebuild the ravaged economy and political institutions. He called on the Council to respect the principles enshrined under Article 2 (7) of the Charter.

In their statements at the meetings held throughout the year, Council members and other Member States[495] focused on the further deterioration in the security situation in Haiti amid rising levels of gang activity and violence, including killings, kidnappings and sexual and gender-based violence, as well as on the socioeconomic conditions and the political impasse and institutional vacuum in the country. They expressed grave concern regarding its impact of the civilian population, particularly women and children.

At the meeting held in June, in anticipation of the renewal of the mandate of BINUH, Council members and other delegations[496] took note of the assessment conducted by the Secretary-General and highlighted the need to strengthen different aspects of the Mission's work that they viewed as essential to addressing the situation on the ground, including good offices and mediation, capacity-building for the Haitian National Police to address gang violence, support for efforts to curb arms trafficking and illicit financial flows, and human rights protection, monitoring and investigation.

In September and October, following the outbreak of protests over the derogation of fuel price subsidies, including the blocking of the Varreux oil terminal, Council members and other speakers expressed deep concern at the increase in violence and the deterioration in the humanitarian situation, including the renewed outbreak of cholera in Haiti. They stressed the need for urgent action by the Council in support of national efforts to curb gang activity and ensure humanitarian access. As a means of addressing the gang problem, multiple speakers[497] called for preventing the supply of arms and illicit financial flows to non-State actors and noted the Council's readiness to take appropriate sanctions measures against those responsible for the instability in Haiti as expressed in resolution 2645 (2022). Some speakers[498] also stressed that economic and humanitarian conditions and the rule of law could not be restored without first stabilizing the security situation.

At the meeting held in December, further to the adoption of resolution 2653 (2022), several delegations[499] welcomed the reopening of the oil terminal, but expressed regret that gang violence and insecurity remained widespread. Multiple delegations[500] called on the Council to effectively utilize the sanctions regime to take action against those responsible for the violence and instability in the country. In this regard, some Council members[501] called on the Committee established pursuant to resolution 2653 (2022) to promptly begin its work and take action against those responsible for the violence and instability. Generally, however, speakers[502] concurred that sanctions alone were insufficient to address the multifaceted crisis in Haiti and therefore underlined the need for national actors, with the support of the international community, to take the steps necessary to end the political impasse and pave the way for undertaking institutional reforms and improving socioeconomic conditions.

---

[495] See S/PV.8969 (United States, Mexico, Ireland, Norway, France, Albania and United Arab Emirates); S/PV.9066 (Mexico, Gabon (also on behalf of Kenya and Ghana), Brazil, China, Ireland, Russian Federation, Albania and Dominican Republic); S/PV.9136 (China, United States, Mexico, Brazil and Russian Federation); S/PV.9153 (Ireland, Norway, United Arab Emirates and China); and S/PV.9233 (Ireland, United Arab Emirates, Norway, Gabon, France, India, Haiti, Dominican Republic and Canada).

[496] See S/PV.9066 (Mexico, Gabon (also on behalf of Kenya and Ghana), Brazil, China, Ireland, Russian Federation, Albania and Dominican Republic).

[497] See S/PV.9136 (China, Mexico, Brazil and Russian Federation); and S/PV.9153 (United States, Brazil, Kenya (also on behalf of Gabon and Ghana) and China).

[498] See S/PV.9136 (United States, Albania and France).

[499] See S/PV.9233 (United States, Ireland, Brazil, Ghana, United Arab Emirates, France and Haiti).

[500] Mexico, United States, Brazil, Kenya, Ghana, China, United Arab Emirates, United Kingdom, Gabon, France, Haiti, Dominican Republic and Canada.

[501] Mexico, Brazil, China and France.

[502] Mexico, United States, Brazil, Ghana, France and Canada.

In October and December, Council members and other Member States exchanged views on the possible deployment of a multinational security force in support of the Haitian National Police, further to the request made by the Government of Haiti and the recommendations of the Secretary-General. Council members held differing views on the approach and benefits of such a deployment. At the meeting held on 17 October,[503] the representative of the United States announced that her delegation was preparing, together with Mexico, a draft resolution that provided for the authorization of a non-United Nations security force, operating under Chapter VII of the Charter. The force would facilitate international support to the police and coastguard and rely on Member State contributions of personnel, equipment and other resources. Multiple Council members and other Member States expressed support for the deployment of the force, particularly considering the Government's request for assistance in that regard,[504] while a number called for more discussions on how best the Council could support the police.[505] Moreover, multiple speakers cautioned the Council against repeating the mistakes of previous international and United Nations interventions in Haiti, with some of them emphasizing the importance of any measures to that effect having the support of Haitians and regional actors.[506]

In their statements at the meetings held in 2022, the representatives of Haiti, including the Minister for Foreign Affairs and Worship, focused on the efforts of the Government of Haiti to stabilize the security and humanitarian situation and engagement with opposition groups to resolve the impasse and pave the way for future elections. The Minister stated that his country had experienced the limits of the United Nations presence in recent decades, yet following the withdrawal of the international forces, local structures could not achieve the same level of performance without receiving adequate training and means.[507] At the meeting held on 26 September,[508] following the outbreak of violent protests, the Minister stressed that Haiti needed very strong support from the international community to support the Haitian National Police in combating armed gangs and welcomed the decision by some countries to consider imposing sanctions on those who participated in criminal activities and insecurity in Haiti. At the meeting held on 21 December,[509] after the Council's imposition of sanctions, the Minister observed that they had had a clear impact and should help facilitate inter-Haitian dialogue and support for a national compromise that could lead to general elections in 2023. He added, however, that without establishing an adequate security environment, it was deceptive to think that Haiti would emerge from the crisis for the long term and stressed that the vast majority of Haitians were in favour of receiving assistance.

Meetings: the question concerning Haiti, 2022

Meeting record and date	*Sub-item*	*Other documents*	*Rule 37 invitations*	*Rule 39 and other invitations*	*Speakers*	*Decision and vote (for-against-abstaining)*
S/PV.8969 18 February	Report of the Secretary-General on the United Nations Integrated Office in Haiti (BINUH) (S/2022/117)		Haiti	Special Representative of the Secretary-General for Haiti and Head of BINUH	13 Council members,[a] all invitees[b]	
S/PV.9066 16 June	Report of the Secretary-General on BINUH (S/2022/481)		Dominican Republic, Haiti	Special Representative of the Secretary-General, Executive Director of	13 Council members,[c] all invitees[d]	

[503] See S/PV.9153.

[504] See S/PV.9153 (United States, Mexico, Kenya (also on behalf of Gabon and Ghana), Albania and Dominican Republic); and S/PV.9233 (United States, Kenya, United Kingdom, France, Dominican Republic and Canada).

[505] See S/PV.9153 (Ireland, Norway, United Kingdom, United Arab Emirates and China); and S/PV.9233 (Ireland, Kenya, Ghana, China, Norway and France).

[506] See S/PV.9153 (Kenya (also on behalf of Gabon and Ghana)); and S/PV.9233 (Kenya, Ghana and India).

[507] See S/PV.9066.

[508] See S/PV.9136

[509] See S/PV.9233.

Meeting record and date	*Sub-item*	*Other documents*	*Rule 37 invitations*	*Rule 39 and other invitations*	*Speakers*	*Decision and vote (for-against-abstaining)*
				Volontariat pour le développement d'Haïti		
S/PV.9095 15 July		Draft resolution submitted by Mexico, United States (S/2022/560)			Seven Council members[e]	Resolution 2645 (2022) 15-0-0
S/PV.9136 26 September			Canada, Dominican Republic, Haiti	Special Representative of the Secretary-General, Deputy Executive Director of the World Food Programme (WFP), Executive Director of the United Nations Office on Drugs and Crime (UNODC)	13 Council members,[a] all invitees[f]	
S/PV.9153 17 October	Letter dated 8 October 2022 from the Secretary-General addressed to the President of the Security Council (S/2022/747) Report of the Secretary-General on BINUH (S/2022/761)		Belize, Dominican Republic, Haiti	Special Representative of the Secretary-General, Permanent Observer for the International Organization of la Francophonie to the United Nations	13 Council members,[a] all invitees[g]	
S/PV.9159 21 October	Letter dated 8 October 2022 from the Secretary-General addressed to the President of the Security Council (S/2022/747) Report of the Secretary-General on the United Nations Integrated Office in Haiti (S/2022/761)	Draft resolution submitted by Mexico, United States (S/2022/765)	Haiti		12 Council members,[h] invitee	Resolution 2653 (2022) 15-0-0 (adopted under Chapter VII)

Meeting record and date	Sub-item	Other documents	Rule 37 invitations	Rule 39 and other invitations	Speakers	Decision and vote (for-against-abstaining)
S/PV.9233 21 December			Canada, Dominican Republic, Haiti	Special Representative of the Secretary-General, editor of *Haiti Liberté*	Deputy Secretary-General, all Council members,[i] all invitees[j]	

[a] Albania, Brazil, China, France, India, Ireland, Kenya (also on behalf of Gabon and Ghana), Mexico, Norway, Russian Federation, United Arab Emirates, United Kingdom and United States.

[b] The Special Representative participated in the meeting by videoconference.

[c] Albania, Brazil, China, France, Gabon spoke (also on behalf of Ghana and Kenya), India, Ireland, Mexico, Norway, Russian Federation, United Arab Emirates, United Kingdom and United States.

[d] Haiti was represented by its Minister for Foreign Affairs and Worship.

[e] Brazil, China, Ghana, Kenya, Mexico, Russian Federation and United States.

[f] The Dominican Republic was represented by its Minister for Foreign Affairs; and Haiti was represented by its Minister for Foreign Affairs and Worship. The Special Representative, the Deputy Executive Director of WFP and the Executive Director of UNODC participated in the meeting by videoconference.

[g] The Dominican Republic was represented by its Minister for Foreign Affairs; and Haiti was represented by its Minister for Foreign Affairs and Worship. The representative of Belize spoke on behalf of the 14 States members of the Caribbean Community (CARICOM). The Special Representative participated in the meeting by videoconference.

[h] Brazil, China, Gabon, Ghana, France, Ireland, Kenya, Mexico, Norway, Russian Federation, United Arab Emirates and United States.

[i] The representative of Gabon spoke twice, once in his capacity as Chair of the Committee established pursuant to resolution 2653 (2022) and once in his national capacity.

[j] The Dominican Republic was represented by its Minister for Foreign Affairs; and Haiti was represented by its Minister for Foreign Affairs and Worship. The representative of Canada spoke on behalf of the Ad Hoc Advisory Group on Haiti of the Economic and Social Council. The Special Representative participated in the meeting by videoconference.

13. Identical letters dated 19 January 2016 from the Permanent Representative of Colombia to the United Nations addressed to the Secretary-General and the President of the Security Council (S/2016/53)

During the period under review, the Council held five meetings and adopted one resolution under the item entitled "Identical letters dated 19 January 2016 from the Permanent Representative of Colombia to the United Nations addressed to the Secretary-General and the President of the Security Council (S/2016/53)". Four of the meetings took the form of briefings, and one was convened for the adoption of a resolution.[510] More information on the meetings, including participants and outcomes, is provided in the table below. In addition, Council members held informal consultations of the whole in connection with the item.[511]

In 2022, the Council heard four briefings by the Special Representative of the Secretary-General for Colombia and the Head of the United Nations Verification Mission in Colombia in connection with the periodic reports of the Secretary-General on the Verification Mission.[512] In addition, the Council heard briefings by a former combatant of the Fuerzas Armadas Revolucionarias de Colombia-Ejército del Pueblo (FARC-EP), the President of the Truth Commission of Colombia, the Chair of the Peacebuilding Commission and two representatives of civil society.[513] At the meetings, Colombia was represented by its President, its Presidential Adviser for Stabilization and Consolidation, its Vice-President and Minister for Foreign Affairs, and its Minister for Foreign Affairs.

[510] For more information on the format of meetings, see part II.

[511] See A/77/2, part II, chap. 40.

[512] See S/PV.8951, S/PV.9015, S/PV.9094 and S/PV.9151. See also S/2021/1090, S/2022/267, S/2022/513 and S/2022/715.

[513] See S/PV.8951, S/PV.9094 and S/PV.9151.

In his briefings, the Special Representative of the Secretary-General updated Council members on the progress made in the implementation of the Final Agreement for Ending the Conflict and Building a Stable and Lasting Peace and remaining challenges, the conduct of legislative and presidential elections and the priorities of the newly inaugurated Administration led by its President, Gustavo Petro Urrego, in relation to the peace process. In his first briefing of the year on 20 January,[514] the Special Representative stated that the fifth anniversary of the Final Agreement provided an opportunity to celebrate its achievements, acknowledge the persistent challenges and recommit to its comprehensive implementation. The visit of the Secretary-General to Colombia in November 2021 had served to reaffirm the commitment of the United Nations to the success of the peace process, for which the support of the Council had been instrumental. In preparation for the congressional elections in March, the Colombian authorities were taking steps to ensure that the overall conditions for the process were peaceful and that all candidates were secure and protected. An enhanced implementation of the security guarantees provisions of the Final Agreement was critical for the elections, especially in regions prioritized for implementation that continued to be hit by violence. While noting that political reintegration was at the core of the peace process, he called on the Colombian authorities to ensure the political rights and protection of people who had laid down their arms, especially in the light of persistent insecurity and stigmatization.

More generally, on security, the Special Representative acknowledged the reduction in the number of killings of ex-combatants in 2021 but underscored the need to secure conflict-affected areas where illegally armed actors continued to take advantage of the limited presence of the State. Beyond security, the Special Representative stated that 2022 would also be a critical year for the transitional justice system, highlighting the work of the Unit for the Search for Persons Deemed as Missing to find thousands of persons disappeared during the conflict, the Truth Commission's preparation of its final report and the issuance of its first sentences. With the peace agreement setting down ever deeper roots, the period ahead would be crucial for the parties and Colombian society.

A former combatant of FARC-EP shared with Council members some of the views and concerns of the signatories to the Final Agreement and their families regarding the political process in Colombia. Noting the grievances and stigmatization of the families and children of killed former combatants, she stressed the need to ensure that they received differentiated yet equal treatment to ensure access to higher education, effective health-care systems, the job market, the financial system and comprehensive social security systems and rights. The widows and orphaned children of former combatants were a special population who needed a robust plan with a differentiated and gender focus to prevent them from falling into poverty, being objectified or being victims of stereotypes, gender violence or discrimination. The notion of family, which was mentioned 92 times in the Final Agreement, should not remain a dead letter and, together with women, girls, boys and social leaders who were being killed or suffering, it had to be a comprehensive part of the concept of security.

At the meeting held on 12 April,[515] the Special Representative of the Secretary-General reported that the congressional elections held in March had been mostly free of violence. The elections had seen an increase in the number of women elected to Congress and the opportunity to elect, for the first time, representatives of 16 new electoral districts established under the peace agreement in conflict-affected regions. Regarding the social and economic reintegration of former combatants, the vast majority of the more than 13,000 who were accredited remained engaged with the peace process and almost two thirds of former FARC-EP members were taking part in collective and individual income-generating activities. Nevertheless, the sustainability of the peace process remained contingent on halting the violence that continued to jeopardize the plans of former combatants to build a new life. If implemented in a coordinated manner, the security guarantees provisions of the Final Agreement had the potential to boost key areas such as reintegration, political participation and transitional justice. The Special Representative also highlighted the importance of further progress in rural reform and in combating illegal drugs through crop-substitution programmes and the effective use of the institutions devised by the Government and the former FARC-EP. Lastly, he welcomed all the efforts made by the Government, led by its President, Iván Duque Márquez, in the implementation of the Final Agreement and noted that that responsibility would soon pass to a new Administration following the presidential elections to be held in May.

---

[514] See S/PV.8951.

[515] See S/PV.9015.

Speaking after the Special Representative, the President of Colombia stated that the peace process launched in 2016 presented Colombia with both challenges and opportunities. His Government's policy of "Peace with Legality" was comprehensive in nature and aimed at ensuring progress in all areas, while maintaining a critical view in order to improve areas in which improvement was needed. In terms of successes, he cited the processes of reintegration, restitution, reparation and political inclusion in relation to victims, development programmes with a territorial focus and comprehensive rural reform, as well as truth, reconciliation, non-repetition and justice. The President underlined that the position of his Government was to establish institutional stability so that Colombia could ensure the right to peace, a duty that was enshrined in its Constitution.

In his briefing on 14 July,[516] echoing the Secretary-General, the Special Representative welcomed the mostly peaceful presidential elections held in May and June, which had resulted in the election of Gustavo Petro Urrego as President and Francia Márquez Mina as Vice-President. He noted the significant contribution that the Final Agreement had made to widening and deepening Colombian democracy and that the electoral outcomes increasingly reflected the diversity of the country's vibrant society. The Special Representative expressed the hope that the new Congress would make considerable progress in adopting the more than 30 pending peace-related norms, including on key matters such as comprehensive rural reform and guarantees for political participation. Despite the reasons for optimism stemming from the elections, the Verification Mission had recorded the killing of 331 former combatants since the Final Agreement had been signed. He stated that Indigenous and Afro-Colombian communities were among those most seriously affected by the violence and insecurity and expressed disappointment that the implementation of the ethnic provisions of the Final Agreement remained comparatively weak. As a milestone in the implementation of the Agreement, he welcomed the publication of the final report of the Truth Commission on 28 June, which, in addition to shedding light on the causes and effects of the conflict, provided a wealth of recommendations for advancing peacebuilding and reconciliation as a national project. Furthermore, he noted that the Special Jurisdiction for Peace had held its first hearings of truth and acknowledgment of responsibility and was also moving towards the imposition of its first sanctions.

At the same meeting, the President of the Truth Commission reported that, in the four years since its establishment, the Commission had heard more than 30,000 individual and collective testimonies from all sides in a conflict that had affected more than 10 million people in various ways, including 450,000 killed between 1985 and 2018, 80 per cent of whom were unarmed civilians. The Commission had also heard multiple testimonies of the 50,000 kidnapped and of the many thousands of children brought into the war, primarily by the guerrillas. It had also visited the sites of more than 4,000 massacres where entire communities had been destroyed. The work of the Commission included the search for answers as to the reason for the damage done to life, democracy and culture and to understand why the conflict sought to persist. In doing so, the Commission had established that it was necessary to change the security system and called for an end to the war against drug trafficking and armed prohibitionism. At the end of the meeting, the Vice-President and Minister for Foreign Affairs of Colombia provided an overview of the efforts of the outgoing Administration with respect to the peace process. She stressed that the incoming Administration must continue along the same path, strengthening institutions and the economy, providing legal guarantees and effective and efficient policies for all Colombians, supporting victims, continuing with reincorporation and the voluntary substitution of illicit crops, comprehensive rural development, humanitarian demining and the implementation of the cross-cutting perspectives of gender and ethnicity.

At the meeting held on 12 October,[517] the Special Representative of the Secretary-General stated that Colombia was experiencing a moment of renewed expectations as a result of the "total peace" approach advanced by Mr. Petro Urrego, a policy anchored in the comprehensive implementation of the Final Agreement. In addition, he noted that the Government was seeking to deepen peace through the resumption of dialogue with the Ejército de Liberación Nacional (ELN) and rapprochement with other armed actors. The search for "total peace" was also an opportunity to continue building on the foundations of resolution 1325 (2000), while ensuring the broad and effective participation of women. He also noted the concerns of community representatives about the threat posed by illegal armed actors and the frustration at unmet expectations regarding the State's slow delivery of basic services and development opportunities. He therefore expressed confidence that some of the new measures taken by the Government,

[516] See S/PV.9094.

[517] See S/PV.9151.

notably the development of an emergency plan for the protection of social leaders, human rights defenders and ex-combatants, would result in improvements in terms of security and quality of life.

In his remarks, the Chair of the Peacebuilding Commission noted that, at the request of the Government of Colombia, the Commission was mobilizing support for the country's peacebuilding efforts since the ratification of the Final Agreement in 2016. He described Colombia as a successful example of inclusive peacemaking. He commended the President and his Government for their commitment to peace and to the full implementation of the Final Agreement, as well as to reducing inequality, governing with and for women, ensuring zero tolerance for corruption and holding regional dialogues, as critical steps towards building lasting peace. He also commended the President for appointing a gender-equal Cabinet and creating a Ministry of Equality to address issues related to gender, ethnic communities, youth and children, among others. The Chair encouraged the full and effective use of mechanisms that drew on the inputs of civil society actors, victims and former combatants in order to build consensus towards the success of peace efforts. He welcomed the support that the Verification Mission and the United Nations country team provided to peacebuilding in Colombia, as well as the catalytic contribution of the Peacebuilding Fund through the multi-partner trust fund for sustaining peace and reiterated the Commission's commitment, within its mandate, to continue to accompany the country in its peacebuilding efforts.

At the same meeting, the legal representative of the Community General Council of San Juan spoke about what she termed the process of "physical and cultural extinction" of the Black, indigenous and peasant communities throughout the Colombian Pacific as a result of the violation of their economic, social, cultural and environmental rights, and the armed conflict. She stated that those communities nevertheless had hope, particularly with the election of Márquez Mina as Vice-President, who was a Black woman, born poor and a victim of the armed conflict, and expressed trust that the Government would guarantee human dignity and allow ethnic peoples to decide how to live their lives, individually and collectively. She asked the international community to strengthen the direct presence of United Nations agencies and other humanitarian organizations in the territories most affected by war and violence. In addition, she asked for more resources to be allocated to strengthen grass-roots organizations and human right defenders, especially for initiatives that allowed communities to build economic self-sufficiency in balance with the environment and to combat climate change.

On 27 October, the Council unanimously adopted resolution 2655 (2022), by which it extended the mandate of the Verification Mission for a period of one year, until 31 October 2023, without any modification.[518] In the resolution, the Council acknowledged the request from the Minister for Foreign Affairs of Colombia for an extension of the mandate of the Mission and for the Council to consider tasking the Mission to verify the implementation of section 1, on comprehensive rural reform, and section 6.2, on the ethnic chapter, of the Final Agreement.[519] In that regard, the Council requested the Secretary-General to provide detailed recommendations on how those additional tasks would be carried out and to confirm any implications for the configuration of the Mission, and expressed its intent to consider those recommendations swiftly.[520]

In terms of challenges, Council members maintained their serious concern regarding threats, attacks and killings targeting former FARC-EP members and community and social leaders, including women and members of Indigenous and Afro-Colombian communities. They called on the Government to increase security and the presence of the State in conflict-affected areas, to swiftly adopt the public policy on the dismantling of illegal armed groups, to strengthen judicial institutions to ensure accountability for the crimes committed and to implement the action plan of the Comprehensive Programme for Safeguards for Women Leaders and Human Rights Defenders. Moreover, while reiterating the need for further accelerated progress, Council members welcomed the advancements made by the Government in the socioeconomic reintegration of the more than 13,000 demobilized former combatants, including through rural reform, crop replacement and development projects. With regard to inclusivity, multiple speakers highlighted the election of representatives from the 16 special districts and the highest-ever number of

---

518 Resolution 2655 (2022), para. 1. See S/PV.9169.

519 Resolution 2655 (2022), ninth preambular paragraph. See also S/2022/787.

520 Resolution 2655 (2022), para. 2. See also the letter dated 9 December from the Secretary-General addressed to the President of the Council, providing recommendations regarding the additional tasks of the Verification Mission (S/2022/940).

women to Congress.[521] Nevertheless, they also widely expressed concern about the slow implementation of the ethnic and gender provisions of the Final Agreement, which they described as essential for lasting peace.[522]

Meetings: identical letters dated 19 January 2016 from the Permanent Representative of Colombia to the United Nations addressed to the Secretary-General and the President of the Security Council (S/2016/53), 2022

Meeting record and date	*Sub-item*	*Other documents*	*Rule 37 invitations*	*Rule 39 and other invitations*	*Speakers*	*Decision and vote (for-against-abstaining)*
S/PV.8951 20 January	Report of the Secretary-General on the United Nations Verification Mission in Colombia (S/2021/1090)		Colombia	Special Representative of the Secretary-General for Colombia and Head of the United Nations Verification Mission in Colombia, former combatant of the Fuerzas Armadas Revolucionarias de Colombia-Ejército del Pueblo	All Council members, all invitees[a]	
S/PV.9015 12 April	Report of the Secretary-General on the United Nations Verification Mission in Colombia (S/2022/267)		Colombia	Special Representative of the Secretary-General	13 Council members,[b,c] all invitees[d]	
S/PV.9094 14 July	Report of the Secretary-General on the United Nations Verification Mission in Colombia (S/2022/513)		Colombia	Special Representative of the Secretary-General, President of the Truth Commission, Nasa Indigenous community leader and human rights defender	13 Council members,[b] all invitees[e]	
S/PV.9151 12 October	Report of the Secretary-General on the United Nations Verification Mission in Colombia (S/2022/715)		Colombia	Special Representative of the Secretary-General, Chair of the Peacebuilding Commission, legal representative of the Community General Council of San Juan	13 Council members,[f] all invitees[g]	

[521] See S/PV.9015 (Kenya (also on behalf of Gabon and Ghana), Albania, United Arab Emirates, United States, Brazil, Mexico, Ireland, India and Norway).

[522] See S/PV.8951 (Kenya and United States); S/PV.9015 (Albania, United States and Norway); S/PV.9094 (Norway, United States, Albania and Kenya (also on behalf of Gabon and Ghana)); and S/PV.9151 (Gabon (also on behalf of Ghana and Kenya), Norway, United Kingdom, Ireland and Albania).

Meeting record and date	Sub-item	Other documents	Rule 37 invitations	Rule 39 and other invitations	Speakers	Decision and vote (for-against-abstaining)
S/PV.9169 27 October	Report of the Secretary-General on the United Nations Verification Mission in Colombia (S/2022/715)	Draft resolution submitted by Mexico, United Kingdom (S/2022/804)			Five Council members (Brazil, Kenya, Mexico, United Kingdom, United States)	Resolution 2655 (2022) 15-0-0

[a] Colombia was represented by its Presidential Adviser for Stabilization and Consolidation.
[b] Albania, Brazil, China, France, India, Ireland, Kenya (also on behalf of Gabon and Ghana), Mexico, Norway, Russian Federation, United Arab Emirates, United Kingdom and United States.
[c] The United Kingdom (President of the Council) was represented by its Minister of State for South and Central Asia, North Africa, the United Nations and the Commonwealth, and the Prime Minister's Special Representative for Preventing Sexual Violence in Conflict.
[d] Colombia was represented by its President.
[e] Colombia was represented by its Vice-President and Minister for Foreign Affairs. The Nasa Indigenous community leader and human rights defender participated in the meeting by videoconference.
[f] Albania, Brazil, China, France, Gabon (also on behalf of Ghana and Kenya), India, Ireland, Mexico, Norway, Russian Federation, United Arab Emirates, United Kingdom and United States. Gabon (President of the Council) and Norway were represented by their respective Ministers for Foreign Affairs.
[g] Colombia was represented by its Minister for Foreign Affairs. The legal representative of the Community General Council of San Juan participated in the meeting by videoconference.

Asia

14. The situation in Afghanistan

During the period under review, the Council held seven meetings under the item entitled "The situation in Afghanistan". One meeting was convened for the adoption of a decision, and six took the form of briefings.[523] More information on the meetings, including on participants, speakers and outcomes, is provided in the table below. In addition, in 2022, Council members held informal consultations of the whole to discuss this item.[524]

During 2022, the Special Representative of the Secretary-General for Afghanistan and Head of the United Nations Assistance Mission in Afghanistan (UNAMA) and the Deputy Special Representatives provided quarterly briefings in meetings further to the reports of the Secretary-General on the situation in Afghanistan.[525] The Council also heard remarks by the Secretary-General,[526] as well as briefings by the Under-Secretary-General for Humanitarian Affairs and Emergency Relief Coordinator.[527] The Chair of the Committee established pursuant to resolution 1988 (2011) provided briefings twice in 2022.[528] In addition, the Executive Director of the United Nations Office on Drugs and Crime (UNODC) gave a briefing to Council members once in 2022.[529] In 2022, Council members also heard briefings by seven civil society representatives.[530] The representative of Afghanistan delivered statements at six of the seven meetings held.[531]

[523] For more information on the format of meetings, see part II.
[524] See A/77/2, part II, chap. 8.
[525] S/2022/64, S/2022/485, S/2022/692 and S/2022/916.
[526] See S/PV.8954.
[527] See S/PV.9075, S/PV.9118 and S/PV.9227.
[528] See S/PV.8954 and S/PV.9227.
[529] See S/PV.9137.
[530] See S/PV.8954, S/PV.8984, S/PV.9075, S/PV.9118, S/PV.9137 and S/PV.9227.
[531] Ibid.

At the outset of 2022, on 26 January, the Council held a high-level meeting.[532] In addition to the Special Representative, Council members heard remarks by the Secretary-General as well as briefings by the Chair of the Committee established pursuant to resolution 1988 (2011) and by the Afghan women human rights defender and Executive Director of the Afghan Women Skills Development Centre.

During his remarks, the Secretary-General stated that over half of all Afghans were facing extreme levels of hunger, that the country was facing its worst drought in two decades and that the economy was also in dire straits.[533] Human rights were also losing ground, with women and girls being shut out of offices and classrooms, and reports of arbitrary arrests and abductions of women activists. In that context, the Secretary-General urged the Taliban to work closely with the global community and the Council to suppress the global terrorist threat in Afghanistan, to build institutions that promoted security and to recognize and protect the fundamental human rights that every person shared. He reiterated his appeal for an increase in humanitarian operations, the suspension of rules and conditions that constricted not only the economy of Afghanistan but also life-saving operations, and international funding to pay the salaries of public sector workers.

Following the Secretary-General, the Special Representative emphasized that it was past time for the Taliban to initiate a wider dialogue on a process for national reconciliation. While welcoming the recent statements by the de facto authorities' leaders that girls of all ages would be educated nationwide, she added that future incentives from some international donors would likely be determined by whether the de facto authorities delivered on their stated commitments. The United Nations had provided life-saving assistance to almost 18 million people by the end of 2021, but the humanitarian needs continued to be pressing, and more assistance funds were needed for 2022. In that context, the adoption of resolution 2615 (2021), on a humanitarian exemption to the United Nations sanctions regime for Afghanistan, and the issuing of new general licences by the United States in December 2021 had provided some welcome assurances that had facilitated the humanitarian activities of the Mission. In addition, the Special Representative announced the launch of a comprehensive and system-wide strategy called the United Nations Transitional Engagement Framework for Afghanistan, aimed at preventing a further deterioration of the humanitarian situation and generating sufficient economic stability to reverse the increase in poverty. However, donors were reluctant to show more flexibility until they had a better idea of what kind of government the de facto Administration intended to create.

The Chair of the Committee established pursuant to resolution 1988 (2011) provided a briefing during which he reiterated that the main goal of the sanctions regime had been to facilitate conditions that promoted dialogue between the Taliban and the Government of Afghanistan intended to result in a peaceful and stable country. The Committee had once again extended the three-month travel ban exemption, on 22 December 2021, for 14 listed Taliban members so that they could continue to attend talks in the interest of promoting peace and stability in Afghanistan. He urged Member States to respect the annexes to resolutions including resolution 2611 (2021), to consult in confidence with the monitoring team with a view to facilitating the sharing of information and to strengthen implementation of sanctions measures.

In her briefing, the Afghan women human rights defender and Executive Director of the Afghan Women Skills Development Centre stated that the hasty exit of the international community from Afghanistan in August 2021 had undermined the achievements of the people of Afghanistan, especially women and girls, and had dashed their hopes for a democratic nation. While urging the Council, the international community and the United Nations to do everything in their power to provide life-saving assistance in order to avert further suffering, she noted that it was in the collective interest of ordinary Afghans to ensure a robust international presence through UNAMA, monitoring developments in the country and ascertaining whether the Taliban were following through on their commitments, which was especially important at a time when civil society, the media and international non-governmental organizations were unable to do so.

---

[532] See S/PV.8954. For more information on high-level meetings and videoconferences, see part II.

[533] See S/PV.8954.

On 2 March, the Council held a meeting[534] at which it heard briefings by the Special Representative of the Secretary-General and the Executive Director of the Organization for Policy Research and Development Studies. In her briefing, the Special Representative stated that the worst fears of famine and widespread starvation had perhaps been avoided. However, providing short-term relief was not the same as giving hope or preparing a strong foundation for Afghan self-reliance. Explaining that UNAMA could not truly assist the Afghan people without working with the de facto authorities, she also acknowledged that there remained an enduring distrust between the Taliban and much of the international community and that the Taliban complained that the Mission's reports did not reflect the reality as they saw it. In that regard, UNAMA had addressed issues through constructive engagement and cooperation with the de facto authorities, both on humanitarian delivery as well as on some of the sensitive issues.

The Executive Director of the Organization for Policy Research and Development Studies focused on priorities for the new mandate of UNAMA, the humanitarian crisis and the political path forward for Afghanistan. Stressing that the Mission must have the resources and capacity to extend its reach and support local organizations to carry out their human rights work, she urged the Council to ensure that UNAMA prioritized gender equality and the rights of women in terms of both their protection and their participation. The participation of women was essential in delivering humanitarian assistance, and the humanitarian response must be carried out in partnership with Afghan civil society, which was ready to provide support if given the resources. The Taliban wanted an Islamic emirate, a form of Government in which power is consolidated in a leader selected by a council, whereas in the past 20 years, Afghans had experienced life under a democracy, in which citizens choose their leaders through elections. The international community could play an important role in facilitating discussions between Afghans and the Taliban, as well as in monitoring progress towards that goal. To do so effectively, it must unite and set clear benchmarks on fundamental issues such as women's rights, freedom of the press, inclusive governance and the equal representation of men, women, young people, civil society, victims and LGBTQI+ individuals from all ethnic and religious communities, which could then be supported and monitored through UNAMA.

On 17 March, the Council adopted (with one abstention) resolution 2626 (2022), by which it extended the mandate of UNAMA for one year.[535] The Council further decided that UNAMA and the Special Representative of the Secretary-General would continue to carry out their mandate in close consultation with all relevant Afghan political actors and stakeholders, including relevant authorities as needed, in support of the people of Afghanistan in a manner consistent with Afghan sovereignty, leadership and ownership.[536] Following the adoption of the resolution, nine Council members provided explanations of their vote.[537] While welcoming the adoption of the resolution and affirming that it provided a clear and unambiguous foundation upon which UNAMA could engage with all relevant Afghan stakeholders in support of a better future for Afghanistan and its people, the representative of Ireland expressed regret that the Council could not agree to include a reference to climate insecurity. The representative of the Russian Federation stated that his country was compelled to abstain in the voting on the resolution because the reference to the importance of achieving the agreement of the host country on the presence of the United Nations had been met with opposition during the discussions on the draft. He also expressed regret regarding the ignorance of the new realities in the country and the promotion of irrelevant approaches, as well as the omission of more substantive cooperation between the special political mission and the Taliban authorities, which could jeopardize the effectiveness of the Mission in achieving its mandate and, on the whole, undermine international efforts to stabilize the situation.

On 23 June, the Council held a meeting,[538] at which members heard briefings by the Deputy Special Representative of the Secretary-General and Resident Humanitarian Coordinator for Afghanistan, the Under-Secretary-General for Humanitarian Affairs and Emergency Relief Coordinator, an international correspondent and news presenter for BBC News and a consultant for VOICE Amplified. In his briefing,

---

[534] See PV.8984.

[535] Resolution 2626 (2022), para. 4.

[536] Ibid., para. 5. For more information on the mandate of UNAMA, see part X, sect. II.

[537] See S/PV.8997 (Norway, United Kingdom, United States, Ireland, Albania, Brazil, Russian Federation, China and the United Arab Emirates).

[538] See S/PV.9075.

the Deputy Special Representative focused on the recent deadly earthquake in Afghanistan, with search-and-rescue operations ongoing, and on other emergencies that the population in Afghanistan faced. The de facto authorities had increasingly restricted the exercise of basic human rights, including the freedom of peaceful assembly and freedom of expression, limiting the rights and freedoms of Afghan women and girls in particular, most prominently through the ban on secondary schooling for girls and the decision to impose a face covering on women. He also reported on the economic crisis and the ongoing humanitarian emergency and underscored the need for continued engagement with the de facto authorities.

Reporting on his visits to Afghanistan, the Under-Secretary-General for Humanitarian Affairs stated that poverty was the most common reason for which people were leaving their homes in the country and that a lack of money was the main barrier to accessing basic services such as health care and electricity. The humanitarian exception approved by the Council through its adoption of resolution 2615 (2021) had been critical to ensuring that humanitarian partners continued to receive funds and do their work.

In her briefing, the international correspondent and news presenter for BBC News shared observations drawn from her years of reporting on Afghanistan. The Taliban takeover of Afghanistan on 15 August 2021 had had a transformative impact on the position of women and girls in Afghan society. Afghanistan was now the only country in the world where girls were prevented from receiving an education, and millions of Afghan girls across Afghanistan had been forced to contemplate a life without formal education. In that regard, what was happening in Afghanistan was unique. It was the most sudden and significant change in the position of women to take place anywhere in the world in modern history.

The consultant of VOICE Amplified noted that UNAMA had the potential to meaningfully serve the Afghan people going forward. In that context, she called upon UNAMA to prioritize the participation of diverse Afghan women's organizations and politicians in exile, to resume regular public reporting immediately and to ensure that its reports provided accurate and unvarnished information reflecting the realities on the ground. She urged the Council to end all exemptions for the sanctioned Taliban leaders if there was no progress on women's rights in 60 days and to call upon UNAMA to prioritize facilitating an inclusive intra-Afghan dialogue as soon as the new Special Representative of the Secretary-General had been appointed.

On 29 August, the Council held a meeting,[539] at which it heard briefings by the Under-Secretary-General for Humanitarian Affairs and Emergency Relief Coordinator, the Deputy Special Representative of the Secretary-General (Political) for Afghanistan and an independent researcher and author. The Under-Secretary-General reported that close to 19 million people were facing acute levels of food insecurity and that more than half of the population needed humanitarian assistance. The malnutrition crisis had been fuelled by recurrent droughts, and some 25 million people were living in poverty. Large-scale development assistance had been halted for a year. In that context, it was imperative that the international community, as reflected in the Council, stay and deliver for the people of Afghanistan and that the de facto authorities of Afghanistan also do their part. Female humanitarian aid workers – national and international – must be allowed to work unhindered and in safety, and girls must be allowed to continue their education.

In his briefing, the Deputy Special Representative stated that the current regime in Afghanistan had not been recognized by any member of the international community. With regard to the economic situation, there was no question that the sanctions on the Taliban had affected the Afghan economy since the Taliban had taken control. The de facto authorities were faced with a growing number of governance challenges, including the practice of governing by decree and through policy decisions, which had further curtailed fundamental human rights and freedoms. The previous three weeks had seen the highest number of civilian casualties in a one-month period since 15 August 2021, in a series of improvised explosive device attacks in Kabul, most of them claimed by Islamic State in Iraq and the Levant-Khorasan (ISIL-K). It was important for the Taliban to understand that their neighbours, regional partners and the wider Islamic world wanted them to be part of the international community.

The independent researcher and author said that the rapid disintegration of Afghanistan following the departure of the international community in 2021 was no surprise and that, to know why that

[539] See S/PV.9118.

catastrophic failure had occurred, it was necessary to understand what the main characteristics of what she termed the post-2001 Western intervention of Afghanistan had encompassed. In her briefing, she addressed a series of factors that indicated the extreme deception about what had been at the heart of the 20-year Western occupation of Afghanistan and what had prompted the sudden withdrawal.

On 27 September, the Council held a meeting[540] further to the report of the Secretary-General on the situation in Afghanistan and its implications for international peace and security.[541] In addition to the Deputy Special Representative of the Secretary-General (Political) for Afghanistan, the Council heard briefings by the Executive Director of UNODC and the former Deputy Speaker of the Afghan Parliament.[542] The Deputy Special Representative reported that the ongoing ban on secondary education for girls and growing restrictions on women's rights were signals that the Taliban were indifferent to more than 50 per cent of the population and were willing to risk international isolation. The economic situation in Afghanistan remained tenuous, with part of the enduring economic downturn due to liquidity problems related to the isolation of Afghanistan from the international banking system. In that context, humanitarian assistance alone could not replace essential service delivery systems, such as health and water, nor prevent an economic collapse, and there was a continued lack of political inclusiveness and transparency in decision-making. In addition to the significant curtailment of the rights of women and girls, as well as potential violations of international human rights, UNAMA continued to record violations of the amnesty declaration that the Taliban had laudably declared but inconsistently enforced.

The Executive Director of UNODC explained that, with an alarming increase in methamphetamine production, the Taliban de facto authorities had announced a complete ban on the cultivation and production of all narcotics while granting a grace period that had practically exempted the most recent major opium-poppy harvest, which had ended in July 2022. Severe droughts had destroyed food harvests at a time when the Afghan economy was collapsing, and it remained unclear to what extent the ban could or would be enforced by the de facto authorities, considering the economic and political realities in Afghanistan and the presence of at least a dozen armed groups challenging the authorities' rule across 18 provinces. UNODC was conducting its opium cultivation surveys remotely and would publish estimates of how much heroin had been produced from the most recent harvest.

In her briefing, the former Deputy Speaker of the Afghan Parliament noted that Afghanistan had yet again become a safe haven for international military extremist groups in the region. A wave of violence had taken on a new form, including through targeted extrajudicial and mass killings of different segments of the population, amounting to war crimes and crimes against humanity. She emphasized that the only solution to the question of Afghanistan was political dialogue and requested that the Council initiate and facilitate a stronger mechanism and collectively use all leverage over the Taliban towards a meaningful and genuine commitment to dialogue and a peace process.

On 20 December, further to the report of the Secretary-General on the situation in Afghanistan and its implications for international peace and security,[543] the Council held the final meeting of the year in relation to that item.[544] In addition to the new Special Representative, who gave her first briefing since her appointment in September,[545] the Council heard briefings by the Under-Secretary-General for Humanitarian Affairs and Emergency Relief Coordinator, the Chair of the Committee established pursuant to resolution 1988 (2011) and an Afghan women's rights activist. In her briefing, the Special Representative assessed that the Taliban remained essentially in control of the country but unable to satisfactorily address the problem of terrorist groups operating inside Afghanistan. She expressed concern about the recent activity of ISIL-K, as well as the attacks on the embassies of the Russian Federation and Pakistan and a hotel hosting many Chinese nationals resulting in significant civilian casualties. Moreover, the media and civil society, which were already suffering from serious financial constraints, continued to be stifled through intimidation by the de facto security institutions and at times through repressive actions. The social space of women was being restricted as much as their political space, and the banning of secondary education would mean that no girls would be entering university in two years. On the economic front, the Special Representative

---

[540] See S/PV.9137.

[541] S/2022/692.

[542] See S/PV.9137.

[543] S/2022/916.

[544] See S/PV.9227.

[545] See S/2022/671 and S/2022/672.

reported some positive developments, including that corruption had significantly decreased compared to the days of the Republic. Nonetheless, there had been worrying signs of an uptick in the previous six months. UNAMA was undertaking an internal review to assess effectiveness in the implementation of its mandate, which would yield recommendations for its future mandate. Engagement with the de facto authorities must continue in some form.

The Under-Secretary-General for Humanitarian Affairs reported that 97 per cent of Afghans lived in poverty and that two thirds of the population needed humanitarian assistance to survive. The humanitarian community in Afghanistan was fully mobilized to address the most urgent needs. In that regard, he discussed the challenges, including the routine interference and restrictions with the de facto authorities, the continued bank de-risking, the daunting financial challenge to fund humanitarian assistance, and the paucity of progress on restarting urgently needed development initiatives, without which the humanitarian situation was likely to further deteriorate, resulting in more people requiring emergency assistance.

In his briefing, the Chair of the Committee established pursuant to resolution 1988 (2011) reported that the number of United Nations-sanctioned individuals occupying Cabinet and senior positions in the Taliban Administration had risen from 41 to more than 60, conveying concerns that the Taliban had reversed policies and gone back on commitments. ISIL-K remained a primary threat in Afghanistan and the neighbouring countries. He concluded by reiterating the goal of the Committee's sanctions measures to promote a peaceful, stable and prosperous Afghanistan by deterring support to terrorist entities and by supporting peace and stability discussions. In that context, he emphasized the need for Member States to further support and assist the work of the Committee and the monitoring team, as outlined in paragraph 1 of resolution 2255 (2015) and the annex to resolution 2611 (2021).

In her briefing, the Afghan women's rights activist provided reflections in comparison to those in her briefing to the Council in January. The situation had only worsened since then, as Afghanistan was the only country in the world where girls were banned from going to school, and minorities had vanished and been banished from public and social life in Afghanistan. International terrorist groups had also been wreaking havoc with impunity. She requested that the Council continue to provide life-saving aid to the Afghan people, provide support to reinvigorate the economy and make sure to keep the interests of the people of Afghanistan in mind when engaging with the Taliban.

Throughout 2022, many Council members and participants continued to call for formation of inclusive governance and for inclusive dialogue with the full, equal and meaningful participation of women as well as ethnic and religious minorities.[546] Given the lack of progress, several Council members and participants reiterated their call for an inclusive intra-Afghan dialogue and affirmed that a broad-based, inclusive and representative government in Afghanistan was necessary for both domestic and international engagement;[547] in that context, the representative of China stated that constructive engagement must be strengthened to support Afghanistan in realizing autonomous and effective State governance. Participants at Council meetings also argued that continued engagement with the de facto authorities was necessary to advance peace in Afghanistan.[548]

Concerning security in the country, Council members and participants at one meeting called upon the Taliban to put an end to reprisal killings and forced disappearances and to respect freedom of expression, including for members of the media, and freedom of peaceful assembly,[549] while the representative of Kenya urged the Taliban to also engage with other regional countries to address and resolve any tensions and security incidents along border areas with a view to enhancing a collective security approach. In that connection, at another meeting, some speakers highlighted the role of regional countries and Islamic countries including the Organization of Islamic Cooperation, which they believed played a special part in

[546] See S/PV.8954 (Norway, Ireland, Mexico, France, United Kingdom, United Arab Emirates, Albania, Brazil, Afghanistan and Pakistan).

[547] See S/PV.9075 (India, Ghana, Mexico, United Kingdom, Brazil, Albania, Islamic Republic of Iran and Uzbekistan).

[548] See S/PV.9227 (Norway, China, United Arab Emirates, Brazil, Mexico, Russian Federation, Islamic Republic of Iran, Uzbekistan, Kazakhstan and Pakistan).

[549] See S/PV.8984 (United States, Ghana and Afghanistan).

relation to engagement with the Taliban.[550] In Council meetings throughout the period, speakers condemned the terrorist attacks in the country, emphasizing the need to prevent terrorism from taking hold in Afghanistan and prevent attacks from being planned or financed from the country. Specifically, some Council members noted their concerns about the security situation, in particular the intensification of terrorist attacks, including those by ISIL-K.[551] The discussions in the Council were also focused on the need for the Taliban to intensify efforts aimed at combating terrorism and protecting the population, deemed their responsibility, as well as to meet their commitments to ensuring principled, unhindered humanitarian access across the country and upholding basic human rights, most pressingly for women and girls.[552]

The question of the gravity of the deteriorating humanitarian situation in the country was addressed by Council members throughout 2022 with a particular focus on the situation of women and girls. Council members highlighted the expectation for the Taliban to follow through on their promise regarding the rights of women and girls, including to receive an education and access employment.[553] Many Council members also deplored the continued denial of the access of girls to education by the Taliban, as well as the restrictions on women's participation in public life. Some participants condemned the announcement at the end of the year by the Taliban to ban women from public and private universities.[554]

Regarding the mandate of UNAMA, speakers reiterated their support for the efforts and mandate of UNAMA with regard to good offices, human rights monitoring reporting functions, its humanitarian coordination role, child and civilian protection activities and its work to promote the full, equal and meaningful participation of women in all aspects of public life.[555] Highlighting the importance of engagement, the representative of Norway stated that the Special Representative of the Secretary-General and her team needed a strong mandate to promote political dialogue and engage with the Taliban, monitor and report on human rights and facilitate the provision of humanitarian and basic human needs. The representative of India underscored that his country was working constructively with other members of the Council to ensure that UNAMA's new mandate focused on the welfare, well-being and expectations of the Afghan people.

Regarding sanctions, Council members welcomed the unanimous adoption of resolution 2615 (2021) to facilitate conditions for continuing the humanitarian assistance without violating the United Nations sanctions regime.[556] Speakers recalled that Afghan financial institutions must have access to the country's assets which were subject to unilateral sanctions and that the unfreezing of the assets was of importance if Afghanistan was to have a chance at preventing a severe economic downturn and a dreadful rise in poverty and hunger.[557] In addition, a few speakers expressed regret that the Council could not reach a consensus on renewing exceptions to the travel ban for some of the individuals listed by the Committee established pursuant to resolution 1988 (2011);[558] in that context, the representative of the Russian Federation called upon the countries concerned to take a constructive stance by supporting the extension of the existing exemption. A number of participants recalled the issue of the management and distribution of Afghan frozen assets to the benefit of the Afghan people.[559]

Developments in Afghanistan were also considered elsewhere under the item entitled "Threats to international peace and security caused by terrorist acts".[560]

---

550 See S/PV.9118 (Russian Federation, United Arab Emirates and Pakistan).
551 Ibid. (Ghana, Kenya, Gabon, Russian Federation and France).
552 Ibid. (Norway, Gabon, United Kingdom, Albania, France, Kenya and Afghanistan).
553 Ibid. (Norway, Ghana, Ireland, China, United Kingdom, Mexico, Kenya, Gabon, Albania, United Arab Emirates, United States and France).
554 See S/PV.9227 (United States, United Kingdom, Afghanistan, Uzbekistan, Pakistan and United Arab Emirates).
555 See S/PV.8984 (France, United Kingdom, United States, Albania, Ghana, Kenya, Mexico, Gabon and United Arab Emirates).
556 See S/PV.8954 (Norway, United States, Mexico, France, Russian Federation, China, Ghana, United Arab Emirates, Brazil and India).
557 Ibid. (Russian Federation, China, Brazil, Uzbekistan and Pakistan). For further information on the sanctions measures concerning the Taliban, see part VII, sect. III.
558 See S/PV.9118 (Brazil and Pakistan).
559 See S/PV.9227 (Gabon, China, Kenya, Ghana, Russian Federation, Afghanistan, Islamic Republic of Iran and Pakistan).
560 For more information, see sect. 30 below.

Meetings: the situation in Afghanistan, 2022

Meeting record and date	*Sub-item*	*Other documents*	*Rule 37 invitations*	*Rule 39 and other invitations*	*Speakers*	*Decision and vote (for-against-abstaining)*
S/PV.8954 26 January			Afghanistan, Iran (Islamic Republic of), Pakistan, Uzbekistan	Special Representative of the Secretary-General for Afghanistan and Head of the United Nations Assistance Mission in Afghanistan, Afghan women human rights defender and Executive Director of the Afghan Women Skills Development Centre	Secretary-General, all Council members,[a] all invitees[b]	
S/PV.8984 2 March	Report of the Secretary-General on the situation in Afghanistan and its implications for international peace and security (S/2022/64)		Afghanistan, Iran (Islamic Republic of), Pakistan	Special Representative of the Secretary-General, Executive Director of the Organization for Policy Research and Development Studies	All Council members, all invitees	
S/PV.8997 17 March	Report of the Secretary-General on the situation in Afghanistan and its implications for international peace and security (S/2022/64)	Draft resolution submitted by Norway (S/2022/237)			Nine Council members[c]	Resolution 2626 (2022) 14-0-1[d]
S/PV.9075 23 June	Report of the Secretary-General on the situation in Afghanistan and its implications for international peace and security (S/2022/485)		Afghanistan, Iran (Islamic Republic of), Pakistan, Uzbekistan	Deputy Special Representative of the Secretary-General (Political) for Afghanistan, Resident and Humanitarian Coordinator for Afghanistan, Under-Secretary-General for	All Council members, all invitees[e]	

Meeting record and date	*Sub-item*	*Other documents*	*Rule 37 invitations*	*Rule 39 and other invitations*	*Speakers*	*Decision and vote (for-against-abstaining)*
				Humanitarian Affairs and Emergency Relief Coordinator, international correspondent and news presenter for BBC News, consultant for VOICE Amplified		
S/PV.9118 29 August			Afghanistan, Iran (Islamic Republic of), Pakistan	Under-Secretary-General for Humanitarian Affairs, Deputy Special Representative of the Secretary-General, independent researcher and author	All Council members, all invitees[f]	
S/PV.9137 27 September	Report of the Secretary-General on the situation in Afghanistan and its implications for peace and security (S/2022/692)		Afghanistan, Iran (Islamic Republic of), Kyrgyzstan, Pakistan	Deputy Special Representative of the Secretary-General, Executive Director of the United Nations Office on Drugs and Crime (UNODC), former Deputy Speaker of the Afghan Parliament	All Council members, all invitees[g]	
S/PV.9227 20 December	Report of the Secretary-General on the situation in Afghanistan and its implications for peace and security (S/2022/916)		Afghanistan, Iran (Islamic Republic of), Kazakhstan, Pakistan, Uzbekistan	Special Representative of the Secretary-General, Under-Secretary-General for Humanitarian Affairs, Afghan women's rights activist	All Council members,[h] all invitees[i]	

[a] Norway (President of the Council) was represented by its Prime Minister. Gabon was represented by its Minister for Foreign Affairs. The representative of India spoke in his capacity as Chair of the Committee pursuant to resolution 1988 (2011).

[b] The Special Representative participated in the meeting by videoconference.

[c] Norway, United Kingdom, United States, Ireland, Albania, Brazil, Russian Federation, China and United Arab Emirates.

[d] *For*: Albania, Brazil, China, France, Gabon, Ghana, India, Ireland, Kenya, Mexico, Norway, United Arab Emirates, United Kingdom, United States; *against*: none; *abstaining*: Russian Federation.

[e] The Deputy Special Representative and the Under-Secretary-General participated in the meeting by videoconference.

[f] The Under-Secretary-General for Humanitarian Affairs, the Deputy Special Representative and the independent researcher and author participated in the meeting by videoconference.
[g] The Executive Director of UNODC participated in the meeting by videoconference.
[h] The representative of India spoke in his capacity as Chair of the Committee pursuant to resolution 1988 (2011).
[i] The Under-Secretary-General participated in the meeting by videoconference.

15. The situation in Myanmar

During the period under review, the Council held one public meeting and two private (closed) meetings under the item entitled "The situation in Myanmar".[561] At the only public meeting in 2022, the Council also adopted a resolution, which was the first resolution adopted under this item. More information on the meetings. including on participants and speakers, is provided in the table below. In addition, Council members held informal consultations of the whole in connection with this item.[562]

On 28 January and 27 May, the Council held private meetings during which it heard briefings by the Special Envoy of the Secretary-General for Myanmar and the Acting Assistant Secretary-General for Humanitarian Affairs and Deputy Emergency Relief Coordinator. In addition, the Deputy Prime Minister and Minister for Foreign Affairs of Cambodia provided briefings to the Council in his capacity as Special Envoy of the Association of Southeast Asian Nations (ASEAN) Chair on Myanmar.[563]

On 21 December, the Council held a meeting at which it adopted resolution 2669 (2022), with three abstentions.[564] By resolution 2669 (2022), the Council demanded an immediate end to all forms of violence throughout Myanmar and urged restraint and de-escalation of tensions and for all parties to respect human rights, fundamental freedoms and the rule of law, while also urging the Myanmar military to immediately release all arbitrarily detained prisoners, including the President, Win Myint, and State Counsellor, Aung San Suu Kyi.[565] The Council further acknowledged the central role of ASEAN in helping to find a peaceful solution to the crisis in Myanmar in the interests of the people of Myanmar and encouraged the international community to support the ASEAN-led mechanism and process in that regard, including efforts to implement the five-point consensus agreed on 24 April 2021.[566] The Council also called for concrete and immediate actions to effectively and fully implement the consensus. In addition, it requested the Secretary-General, or through his Special Envoy, to report orally to the Council by 15 March 2023 on United Nations support on the implementation of the consensus.[567] The Council further underscored the need to address the root causes of the crisis in Rakhine State and to create conditions necessary for the voluntary, safe, dignified and sustainable return of Rohingya refugees and internally displaced persons.[568]

After the vote, the representative of the United Kingdom, the penholder of the resolution, affirmed that, with the adoption of resolution 2669 (2022), the Council had responded to the calls of ASEAN leaders for United Nations support for their efforts.[569] The briefing of the Secretary-General in March 2023, mandated under the resolution, would be an important opportunity to assess developments on the ground. The representative of France welcomed the adoption of the resolution and underlined that, faced with the continuous deterioration of the situation, it was essential that the Council express its concerns and its demands to the junta, in support of the Burmese people. The representative of Norway, while emphasizing the importance of the adoption of the resolution, expressed regret that it was not possible to agree on a more substantial text that would send an even stronger signal to the actors in Myanmar to abstain from violence and engage constructively towards building a peaceful, reform-oriented and

---

[561] For further information on past proceedings and decisions adopted in connection with this item, see *Repertoire, Supplements 2004–2007* to *2021*.
[562] See A/77/2, part II, chap. 32.
[563] For more information on participation in meetings of the Council, see part II.
[564] See S/PV.9231.
[565] Resolution 2669 (2022), paras. 1, 2 and 4.
[566] Ibid., para. 5.
[567] Ibid., para. 6.
[568] Ibid., para. 10.
[569] See S/PV.9231.

prosperous Myanmar. Norway had advocated stronger language, including on the protection of children and education in armed conflict, combating sexual and gender-based violence and ending impunity, as well as language on preventing the flow of arms and financial assets of the military. Resolution 2669 (2022) should be followed by other, more substantial resolutions, including Chapter VII provisions, should the situation warrant it. The representative of Ireland recalled his country's position that Council action in response to the violence suffered by the Myanmar people since the military coup in 2021 had been inadequate, and he emphasized that the Council could and should have done more. Ireland had voted in favour of the resolution in order to combat the cycle of violence and impunity that the Myanmar military relied upon. The resolution should have gone further by recognizing and condemning the continued sale and transfer of weapons to Myanmar and the widespread sexual and gender-based violence and grave violations against children in Myanmar and by recognizing the importance of accountability mechanisms such as the Independent Investigative Mechanism for Myanmar and directly calling upon the Myanmar military to halt its relentless assault on the people of Myanmar. He reiterated the need for the Council to maintain a dedicated focus on the situation in Myanmar, to do so in open meetings and to keep at the heart of its work the needs and interests of the Myanmar people. The representative of the United Arab Emirates welcomed the adoption of the resolution and noted that the text sent an important message about the need to address the challenges faced by the Rohingya, the crisis in Rakhine State and the dangers that it posed to the situation in the region, at a time when international attention on the Rohingya crisis was waning. She considered, however, that the language contained in the resolution was insufficient and that the text failed to address the scope of the current challenges on the ground. The representative of the United States welcomed the adoption of the resolution but similarly stressed that the resolution did not go far enough and that it had failed to directly address the regime's severe violations of the freedom of religion and belief, to call for the regime to face justice for the crimes that it had reportedly committed, to acknowledge General Assembly resolution 75/287, in support of an arms embargo, and to pursue a mechanism to prevent the flow of financial resources to the regime. The representative of Ghana underscored that, through resolution 2669 (2022), the Council had responded to the call of ASEAN upon the United Nations to support the organization's efforts in the implementation of the five-point consensus. The representative of Brazil expressed appreciation for the positive engagement of all Council members, which had allowed the Council to speak on the situation in Myanmar, and for the involvement of and consultations with ASEAN in the process. She further commended the United Kingdom, as penholder, for the inclusive and transparent manner in which it had conducted the process to arrive at the text that had been adopted. The representative of Albania underscored that the adoption of resolution 2669 (2022) demonstrated the ability of the Council to respond to the growing calls for supporting Myanmar in finding a peaceful solution to the deep crisis in the country, noting that the Council would have the opportunity to remain seized of the developments in Myanmar. The representative of Mexico explained that his country had voted in favour of the resolution because it conveyed an unequivocal message that reaffirmed the need for an immediate cessation of violence, respect for human rights and the need for an inclusive dialogue to resume the process towards democratic transition in the interest of the people of Myanmar. However, Mexico would have preferred that the resolution include references to the importance of preventing the flow of arms. The representative of Gabon indicated that his vote in favour of the resolution reflected a message of solidarity with the people of Myanmar and against violence on the civilian population as well as a call for a resolution of the Rohingya crisis. Gabon would continue to support the quest for a solution based on dialogue while encouraging the prioritization of the regional dynamic and the guiding role of ASEAN.

The representative of China, which had abstained from the vote, expressed continued concerns about the resolution that had just been adopted. In terms of the format, a presidential statement would have been more appropriate under the circumstances. In terms of the content, even after amendments, the tone of the text lacked balance. The Council must always act with caution; blindly using the Council to exert pressure or threaten sanctions would only intensify confrontation and antagonism, complicate the situation and prolong the crisis. The representative of the Russian Federation explained that his country had abstained in the voting as it was the country's principled position that the situation in Myanmar did not pose a threat to international peace and security. The contents of the resolution were focused mostly on human rights aspects, which should be addressed by the Third Committee of the General Assembly rather than the Council. He expressed dissatisfaction with the penholder, stating that the concerns regarding the text that other delegations had raised had been ignored, in particular the proposal to include a point about the counterproductiveness of unilateral restrictive measures that had a negative effect on the socioeconomic situation in the country. He also warned against the Council playing into the hands of those who would benefit from a destabilization of the situation on the ground, undermining the mediation efforts of ASEAN and creating divisions in the Council. The effect of the non-consensual resolution was going to be rather limited, thus the Russian Federation had decided not to veto it, notwithstanding its clearly provocative nature. The situation in Rakhine State was the only aspect of the situation in Myanmar that should be addressed by the Council. The representative of India, which had also abstained from the vote, praised the delegation of the United Kingdom for having negotiated the text of resolution 2669 (2022) in a transparent and consultative manner by taking into account the views of neighbouring countries, and in particular those of ASEAN. However, under the current circumstances, a Council resolution might entrench the parties in their inflexible positions rather than encourage them to pursue an inclusive political dialogue.

Meetings: the situation in Myanmar, 2022

Meeting record and date	*Sub-item*	*Other documents*	*Rule 37 invitations*	*Rule 39 and other invitations*	*Speakers*	*Decision (for-against-abstaining)*
S/PV.8959 (closed) 28 January			Cambodia	Special Envoy of the Secretary-General for Myanmar, Acting Assistant Secretary-General for Humanitarian Affairs and Deputy Emergency Relief Coordinator	All Council members, all invitees[a]	
S/PV.9049 (closed) 27 May			Cambodia	Special Envoy of the Secretary-General	All Council members, all invitees[a]	
S/PV.9231 21 December		Draft resolution submitted by United Kingdom (S/2022/980)			14 Council members[b]	Resolution 2669 (2022) 12-0-3[c]

[a] Cambodia was represented by its Deputy Prime Minister and Minister for Foreign Affairs, who spoke in his capacity as Special Envoy of the Association of Southeast Asian Nations Chair on Myanmar.
[b] Albania, Brazil, China, France, Gabon, Ghana, India, Ireland, Mexico, Norway, Russian Federation, United Arab Emirates, United Kingdom, United States.
[c] *For*: Albania, Brazil, France, Gabon, Ghana, Ireland, Kenya, Mexico, Norway, United Arab Emirates, United Kingdom, United States; *against*: none; *abstaining*: China, India, Russian Federation.

16. Letter dated 13 September 2022 from the Permanent Representative of Armenia to the United Nations addressed to the President of the Security Council (S/2022/688)

During the period under review, the Council held two meetings under the item entitled "Letter dated 13 September 2022 from the Permanent Representative of Armenia to the United Nations addressed to the President of the Security Council (S/2022/688)". Both meetings took the form of briefings.[570]

[570] For more information on the format of meetings, see part II.

More information on the meetings, including on participants and speakers, is provided in the table below. In addition, in 2022, Council members held informal consultations of the whole to discuss this item.[571]

During 2022, the Council heard two briefings from the Assistant Secretary-General for Europe, Central Asia and the Americas in the Departments of Political and Peacebuilding Affairs and Peace Operations. The representatives of Armenia and Azerbaijan also participated in both meetings and delivered statements.

During his briefing, on 15 September, the Assistant Secretary-General referred to the reports of the authorities in Armenia and Azerbaijan about heavy fighting on their international border.[572] According to reports, heavy artillery, drones and large-calibre weapons were used on 13 and 14 September, and a ceasefire starting on 14 September, at 8 p.m. local time, had been agreed. Both countries had written to the Secretary-General and the Council, alleging violations of the ceasefire agreement brokered by the Russian Federation in 2020 and of their territorial integrity.[573] Ongoing mediation efforts in the region, in particular those of the Russian Federation and the European Union, could lay the groundwork for enabling the parties to resume a dialogue aimed at a long-term peace.[574] The escalation underscored the urgent need for the parties to advance the process of delimitation and demarcation within the framework of their mutual recognition of their respective territorial integrity and sovereignty and was a reminder of the potential that the tensions had to destabilize the region. In the immediate term, the parties must abide by their obligations to fully implement the trilateral statement on the ceasefire of 9 November 2020, and the Assistant Secretary-General urged them to return to the negotiating table and take steps towards the signing of a lasting peace treaty. It was important for the Council to send a similar united message in order to enable the parties to focus on a diplomatic solution.

Following the briefing, discussions were focused on the opportunities for negotiation between the parties. Council members welcomed the ceasefire agreement on 14 September and called for a lasting peace settlement between Armenia and Azerbaijan. They expressed concern regarding the clashes at the border and strongly condemned the attacks on civilians and the destruction of critical infrastructure in the region. In addition, they welcomed international efforts in helping to advance negotiations between the two countries. Most Council members called in particular for the preservation of and compliance with the trilateral statements brokered by the Russian Federation in 2020. Some members[575] also expressed support for the mediation efforts of the Organization for Security and Cooperation in Europe, especially the Co-Chairs of the Minsk Group, as well as the mediation efforts of the European Union. Several countries[576] highlighted and supported the progress made during the high-level meetings held on 31 August, in Brussels, mediated by the President of the European Council.

The representative of the Russian Federation described his country's involvement with both parties to reduce tensions and to achieve a sustainable ceasefire and the return of Azerbaijani and Armenian soldiers to their previous positions. The Collective Security Council of the Collective Security Treaty Organization (CSTO) had met on 13 September, resulting in an agreement by the CSTO secretariat and the joint staff to send a mission to Armenia in order to study the situation in various areas on the border between Armenia and Azerbaijan and make appropriate recommendations and proposals to be reviewed by the CSTO Heads of State. While noting the difficult path to reconciliation, the representative said that his country was making every effort to normalize relations between the two countries on the basis of the three trilateral statements of the leaders of the Russian Federation, Azerbaijan and Armenia dated 11 January 2021, 26 November 2021 and 31 October 2022. The first statement had ended the hostilities and defined the parameters for the deployment of a Russian peacekeeping contingent along the Lachin corridor and the line of contact in the Nagorno-Karabakh conflict area, the second had concerned the unblocking of all economic and transportation links in the region, and the third had been focused on establishing mechanisms for border demarcation and delimitation.[577]

---

[571] See A/77/2, part II, chap. 41.
[572] See S/PV.9132.
[573] See S/2020/996 and S/2022/688.
[574] See S/PV.9132.
[575] Ireland, Kenya, Mexico, Ghana, Albania, Norway and France.
[576] Ireland, Albania and United Kingdom.
[577] For more information on the discussion, see part VI, sect. IV.

The representatives of Armenia and Azerbaijan spoke after all Council members had spoken. With regard to the heavy fighting at the international border, the representative of Armenia stated that, on 13 September, Azerbaijan had initiated an attack on the eastern and south-eastern regions of Armenia. He highlighted the destruction of civilian settlements and infrastructure, emphasizing that civilian homes had been affected by the violence, and noted that densely populated towns had come under heavy fire. He called upon the Council to uphold its responsibility in maintaining international peace and security and to condemn the attack against the sovereign territory of Armenia, as well as to demand the withdrawal of the military forces of Azerbaijan. He also urged the Council to demand that Azerbaijan refrain from future acts of aggression, comply with international commitments, engage in peaceful negotiations, including in relation to the Nagorno-Karabakh conflict, and release and repatriate all Armenian prisoners of war.

By contrast, the representative of Azerbaijan said that, on the night of 12 to 13 September, the armed forces of Armenia had committed a large-scale act of military provocation in the direction of the Azerbaijani districts of the State border, resulting in the deaths of servicemen and damage to military infrastructure. Armenia had continued attacks in border areas after the ceasefire agreement had come into effect on the morning of 13 September, and the military escalation had been provoked by Armenia with the goal of destabilizing the normalization process. The countermeasures taken in response to the actions of Armenia had been limited and targeted at legitimate military objects. He called upon the international community to persuade Armenia to reciprocate the offer of Azerbaijan, cease its political and military provocations, abandon its aggressive rhetoric and actions and engage in good faith in direct negotiations to find peaceful diplomatic solutions to all issues pertaining to inter-State relations between Azerbaijan and Armenia.

On 20 December, the Council held a meeting[578] further to the letters received from Armenia and Azerbaijan.[579] At the meeting, the Council heard a briefing by the Assistant Secretary-General for Europe, Central Asia and the Americas, who reported that, regrettably, despite the promising diplomatic engagements over the previous months, the tensions both on the Armenia-Azerbaijan border and around areas under the control of the Russian peacekeeping forces had not abated.[580] In the latest sign of escalating tensions, protests had emerged near a Russian peacekeeping post on the Lachin road, a vital artery for the people living in the area. It had been reported that the protests had been against what was claimed to be the illegal exploitation of mineral resources and its environmental impact on the surrounding area. In the letters submitted by Armenia and Azerbaijan to the Secretary-General and the Council, both sides alleged violations of the trilateral statement of 9 November 2020. The potential human toll of a resumption of the conflict could be considerable, and any renewed conflict would impact not only the people of Armenia and Azerbaijan but also likely those in the wider South Caucasus region and beyond. The parties must abide by their obligation to fully implement the trilateral statement on the ceasefire of 9 November 2020 and the subsequent agreed statements and commitments, as well as to redouble their diplomatic efforts to achieve a negotiated, lasting and peaceful settlement.

Following the briefing, the discussions were focused on the opportunities for mediation as a pacific means of resolving the ongoing conflict. Council members expressed concern regarding the interference with the Lachin corridor and heightened tensions between the neighbouring countries and called for the immediate reopening of the corridor to allow for the natural flow of traffic and the delivery of goods, supplies and services. Most Council members[581] encouraged Armenia and Azerbaijan to resolve all disputes through diplomacy and dialogue and build upon the progress made. Many Council members[582] also encouraged Armenia and Azerbaijan to fully abide by and implement the trilateral statement of 9 November 2020. Some members[583] stressed the importance of adhering to all previously reached agreements, including the trilateral statements, as they laid the groundwork for achieving peace and

[578] See S/PV.9228.

[579] S/2022/979 and S/2022/988.

[580] See S/PV.9228.

[581] France, Albania, China, United States, Russian Federation, United Kingdom, Brazil, Norway, Ghana, Ireland, Gabon and India.

[582] France, United Arab Emirates, Russian Federation, Mexico, Norway, Ghana and Ireland.

[583] Albania, United Arab Emirates, Russian Federation, Kenya and India.

stability in the region. A number of Council members[584] acknowledged and supported ongoing mediation efforts in the region, whether of the Russian Federation, the European Union or other Member States. Many members[585] further encouraged the international community's role in facilitating dialogue and normalizing relations between the two countries. In that regard, several Council members[586] supported the delineation and delimitation of the border between the two countries.[587]

The representatives of Armenia and Azerbaijan spoke after all Council members had spoken. While the representative of Armenia stated that the humanitarian crisis had been created by Azerbaijan as a result of its imposition of an illegal blockade on the population of Nagorno-Karabakh in direct breach of its existing commitments, the representative of Azerbaijan accused Armenia of engaging in illegal military activities, including the planting of mines, in violation of the trilateral statement of 9 November 2020. Notwithstanding their disagreements, Azerbaijan underscored the commitment to achieving regional peace and stability and the establishment of good-neighbourly relations between Armenia and Azerbaijan. The representative of Armenia called for the deployment of a fact-finding mission to Nagorno-Karabakh and the Lachin corridor to assess the humanitarian situation on the ground and ensure humanitarian access for United Nations agencies to Nagorno-Karabakh.

Meetings: letter dated 13 September 2022 from the Permanent Representative of Armenia to the United Nations addressed to the President of the Security Council (S/2022/688), 2022

Meeting record and date	*Sub-item*	*Other documents*	*Rule 37 invitations*	*Rule 39 and other invitations*	*Speakers*	*Decision and vote (for-against-abstaining)*
S/PV.9132 23 September			Armenia, Azerbaijan	Assistant Secretary-General for Europe, Central Asia and the Americas	All Council members, all invitees	
S/PV.9228 20 December			Armenia, Azerbaijan	Assistant Secretary-General for Europe, Central Asia and the Americas	All Council members, all invitees	

Europe

17. The situation in Cyprus

During the period under review, the Council held two meetings, at which it adopted two resolutions concerning the situation in Cyprus.[588] More information on the meetings, including on participants and speakers, is given in the table below. Council members also held two private (closed) meetings with countries contributing troops and police to the United Nations Peacekeeping Force in Cyprus (UNFICYP) pursuant to resolution 1353 (2001).[589] In addition, Council members held informal consultations of the whole to discuss the item.[590]

---

[584] France, United Arab Emirates, United States, Russian Federation, Brazil, Norway, Ghana and India.

[585] United Arab Emirates, China, United States, Ghana, Norway, Ghana and Gabon.

[586] France, Russian Federation, Ghana and Gabon.

[587] For more information on the discussion, see part VI, sect. IV.

[588] For further information on the format of meetings, see part II.

[589] The private meetings were held on 12 January and 13 July in connection with the item entitled "Meeting of the Security Council with the troop- and police-contributing countries pursuant to resolution 1353 (2001), annex II, sections A and B"; see S/PV.8947 and S/PV.9093. See also A/77/2, part II, chap. 21.

[590] See A/77/2, part II, chap. 1.

On 27 January, further to the reports of the Secretary-General on his mission of good offices in Cyprus and on the United Nations operation in Cyprus,[591] the Council unanimously adopted resolution 2618 (2022), by which it extended the mandate of UNFICYP for a period of six months, until 31 July 2022.[592] Concerning the mission's mandate and within its limits and area of operations, the Council requested the Secretary-General to implement a series of activities and existing obligations in the planning and conduct of the mission's operations relating to, among other things, women and peace and security requirements under resolution 1325 (2000) and all resolutions addressing women and peace and security, peacekeeping performance requirements under resolutions 2378 (2017) and 2436 (2018) and youth and peace and security requirements under resolutions 2250 (2015), 2419 (2018) and 2535 (2020).[593]

In the resolution, recalling the status of Varosha as set out in its relevant decisions and expressing deep regret at the unilateral actions contrary to them, the Council called for the immediate reversal of this course of action, reiterated that no actions should be carried out in relation to Varosha that were not in accordance with its resolutions, and stressed the need to avoid any unilateral actions that could raise tensions on the island and undermine the prospects for a peaceful settlement.[594] The Council also expressed concern at the continued tensions in the Eastern Mediterranean and called upon the leaders of the two Cypriot communities and all parties involved to refrain from any actions and rhetoric that could damage the settlement process.[595]

As in previous resolutions,[596] the Council called upon the two leaders to reinvigorate their efforts to provide the necessary support and overall guidance to free the Technical Committees from political obstructions in their work, ensure effective coordination and cooperation on criminal matters, intensify efforts to promote peace education across the island, improve the atmosphere for negotiation to secure a settlement, and increase their support to civil society engagement in peace efforts.[597] The Council urged the sides to engage actively and with an increased sense of urgency with the Secretary-General and his team to that end, including by reaching an agreement regarding the proposal of the Secretary-General to appoint a United Nations envoy.[598] In addition, it requested the Secretary-General to report on his good offices, as well as on the implementation of the resolution by 5 July 2022.[599] In that regard, the Council also requested that the report on his good offices include the contents of the written updates of the leaders of the two communities to the good offices mission. The Council further requested that the report on the implementation of the resolution provide integrated, evidence-based and data-driven analysis, strategic assessments and frank advice to the Council, drawing on data collected and analysed through the Comprehensive Planning and Performance Assessment System, the mission's implementation of the integrated peacekeeping performance and accountability framework and other strategic planning and performance measurement tools to describe the mission's impact and overall performance.

On 28 July, further to the subsequent reports of the Secretary-General on the United Nations operation in Cyprus and on his mission of good offices in Cyprus,[600] the Council unanimously adopted resolution 2646 (2022), by which it again extended the mandate of UNFICYP for a period of six months, until 31 January 2023.[601] As with resolution 2618 (2022), in resolution 2646 (2022), the Council requested the Secretary-General to submit by 3 January 2023 a report on his good offices and on the implementation of the resolution.[602]

---

[591] S/2021/1109 and S/2021/1110.

[592] Resolution 2618 (2022), para. 10.

[593] Ibid., para. 16.

[594] Ibid. para. 3. See also resolutions 550 (1984) and 789 (1992), as well as S/PRST/2021/13. For further information on the mandate of UNFICYP, see part X, sect. I.

[595] Resolution 2618 (2022), para. 4.

[596] See, for example, resolution 2587 (2021), para. 4.

[597] Resolution 2618 (2022), para. 5.

[598] Ibid., para 2.

[599] Ibid., para. 19. For background information on UNFICYP, see previous supplements covering the period 1963 to 2021.

[600] S/2022/533 and S/2022/534.

[601] Resolution 2646 (2022), para. 10.

[602] Ibid., para. 20.

Meetings: the situation in Cyprus, 2022

Meeting record and date	*Sub-item*	*Other documents*	*Rule 37 invitations*	*Rule 39 and other invitations*	*Speakers*	*Decision and vote (for-against-abstaining)*
S/PV.8956 27 January	Report of the Secretary-General on his mission of good offices in Cyprus (S/2021/1109) Report of the Secretary-General on the United Nations operation in Cyprus (S/2021/1110)	Draft resolution submitted by United Kingdom (S/2022/52)				Resolution 2618 (2022) 15-0-0
S/PV.9102 28 July	Report of the Secretary-General on the United Nations operation in Cyprus (S/2022/533) Report of the Secretary-General on his mission of good offices in Cyprus (S/2022/534)	Draft resolution submitted by United Kingdom (S/2022/578)				Resolution 2646 (2022) 15-0-0

18. Items relating to the situation in the former Yugoslavia

A. The situation in Bosnia and Herzegovina

During 2022, the members of the Council held two meetings and adopted one resolution under Chapter VII of the Charter of the United Nations in connection with the situation in Bosnia and Herzegovina. The two meetings took the format of a debate.[603] More information on the meetings, including on participants and speakers, is provided in the table below.[604]

At a meeting held on 11 May 2022,[605] the Council heard a briefing by the High Representative for the Implementation of the Peace Agreement on Bosnia and Herzegovina. At the outset of the meeting, prior to the briefing, the representatives of the Russian Federation and China asked to take the floor. The representative of the Russian Federation said that his delegation did not consider Christian Schmidt to be the legitimate High Representative for Bosnia and Herzegovina, as the Council had not approved his appointment to that position. The argument that his appointment had allegedly taken place in accordance with the decision of the Steering Board of the Peace Implementation Council did not stand up to criticism, and his delegation believed that the post of the High Representative remained vacant. In that connection, the Russian Federation saw no basis for inviting Mr. Schmidt to meetings of the Council as High Representative, and his presence in the Chamber in that capacity undermined the authority of the Council and of the United Nations in general. At the same time, the Council had a practice that allowed individuals to brief the Council in their personal capacity in order to determine whether their further participation was required, and that this was how his delegation viewed the presence of Mr. Schmidt at the meeting. The representative of China stated that, according to the Dayton Peace Agreement, the role of the Council in appointing a High Representative was indispensable and had been established practice. In the light of the fact that the appointment of Mr. Schmidt had not been endorsed by the Council, China believed that

[603] For more information on the format of meetings, see part II.

[604] See also A/77/2, part II, chap. 7.A.

[605] See S/PV.9029.

it was inappropriate for him to brief the Council in the capacity as High Representative for Bosnia and Herzegovina.[606]

In his briefing, the High Representative provided updates on developments in connection with his latest report.[607] At the outset, he noted that, as in the previous period, authorities of the Republika Srpska continued to embrace rhetoric and actions, including the adoption of legislation, that could undermine the constitutional framework of Bosnia and Herzegovina.[608] In that regard, what the Republika Srpska authorities were pursuing through the unilateral withdrawal from agreements on the transfer of competencies to the State would, if followed through, achieve a de facto secession of the entity by opting out of the constitutional framework and assuming the competencies of a State. The entities of Bosnia and Herzegovina existed by virtue of the Constitution and were a constitutional part of the State, but they had no right to secede. Announced moves by the Republika Srpska authorities undermined the sovereignty of Bosnia and Herzegovina, and as a representative of the Steering Board of the Peace Implementation Council, he was committed to preserving the country's sovereignty and territorial integrity. In that regard, with the support of the Steering Board, he had used his executive authority as High Representative to issue decisions as a countermeasure to the illegal and destabilizing actions taken by the Republika Srpska authorities. If constitutional order was to be amended or improved, that must be done by elected representatives working to find a legal solution. While an agreement on electoral reforms had not been reached notwithstanding two years of negotiations, the elections could and would be held on schedule in October, just as general elections had been conducted on schedule in 2018, and the holding of regular, fair and free elections was a requirement under the General Framework Agreement for Peace. In addition, the High Representative reported having met with those responsible for Western Balkans policy in several capitals, especially those of the assembled members of the Steering Board, not only because of the urgency of the current situation but also because of the necessity of re-engaging the capitals in completing the tasks at hand. In that regard, he noted that the Russian Federation, as a member of the Peace Implementation Council, had suspended its participation. The fulfilment of the 5 plus 2 agenda and the European Union recommendations would not only resolve certain grievances but also contribute to lasting peace and stability.

During the discussion that ensued, Council members expressed concern with the continuing political stalemate and instability in Bosnia and Herzegovina. Speakers condemned in particular the deeply divisive ethnic rhetoric from political leaders and the increase in reported inter-ethnic tensions, fuelled by hate speech, genocide denial and glorification of war criminals. In that connection, several Council members[609] noted that the recent initiatives by the Republika Srpska leadership to withdraw from State-level institutions in violation of the national Constitution and the Dayton Agreement were likely to undermine the security and territorial integrity of Bosnia and Herzegovina. In addition, the representative of the United States noted that calls to obstruct elections or create a new territorial organization by Bosnian Croat leaders were also dangerous and could undermine peace and security in the region. In that context, a number of speakers[610] expressed support for the presence of the European Union military operation in Bosnia and Herzegovina (EUFOR-Althea) in maintaining stability in the country. More specifically, the representatives of the United Kingdom and Norway welcomed the increased presence of EUFOR-Althea as a precautionary measure. The representative of the Russian Federation, on the other hand, noted with particular concern the increase of the EUFOR-Althea military contingent, which had been doubled in March. Such behaviour raised serious questions about the added value of the continued presence of EUFOR-Althea, which had gone from being a source of stability to an element of intimidation and political confrontation.

In view of the general elections scheduled for early October 2023, Council members expressed concern about the lack of progress on the electoral and constitutional reforms due to the political divergencies, as well as the fact that no government had been established in the Federation after the 2018 elections. In that context, several members[611] expressed support for the work of the High Representative

---

[606] For more information on the discussion concerning the High Representative for Bosnia and Herzegovina, see part II, sect. VII.

[607] S/2022/374.

[608] See S/PV.9029.

[609] Brazil, United Kingdom, Gabon, Albania, France, Mexico and United States.

[610] United Kingdom, Gabon, France, China, Norway, Mexico and European Union.

[611] United Kingdom, Ireland, Albania, France, Kenya, United Arab Emirates, India, Norway, and United States.

and called upon all the relevant actors to ensure dialogue, cooperation and full respect for national institutions. Some members[612] expressed support for the use of the executive powers attributed to the Office of the High Representative, as decided by the Peace Implementation Council. The representative of the Russian Federation, on the other hand, expressed the view that attempts to invoke the Bonn powers were unlawful and legally null and void, as there was no agreement on their use by the international community and because those emergency tools had been granted personally to the High Representative, whose post remained vacant. In that regard, a frank discussion was needed on practical ways to close the Office of the High Representative as soon as possible, as it had exhausted its positive functions. In that connection, some Council members[613] said that it was important that any disagreement among members of the Steering Board of the Peace Implementation Council be resolved through consensus and constructive engagement, in line with the Peace Agreement. Furthermore, several Council members[614] called upon all Bosnian authorities to fulfil the 5 plus 2 agenda as a prerequisite for the closure of the Office of the High Representative.

On 2 November, the Council held its second semi-annual debate on the situation in Bosnia and Herzegovina.[615] At the outset of the meeting, the Council unanimously adopted resolution 2658 (2022) under Chapter VII of the Charter. By the resolution, the Council renewed the authorization of EUFOR-Althea and the continued presence of the North Atlantic Treaty Organization in the country for a period of 12 months, starting from the date of the adoption of the resolution.[616]

In the ensuing debate, Council members discussed the most recent report of the High Representative.[617] Council members welcomed the unanimous adoption of resolution 2658 (2022) as well as the renewal of the mandate of EUFOR-Althea and stressed the importance of the role of the European Union military operation in maintaining post-conflict stability and security in Bosnia and Herzegovina.[618] In that regard, the representative of the Russian Federation said that, while her delegation was pleased that the document voted upon had been depoliticized and purely technical, it was concerned with the doubling of the size of the EUFOR-Althea contingent, especially as the command of the operation had stated that there were no immediate threats to peace and stability in Bosnia and Herzegovina. On the other hand, the representative of Ghana, stated that a substantive resolution would have better helped advance the peace agenda in Bosnia and Herzegovina, and he called for the Council's future efforts in that direction.

The majority of speakers welcomed the successful holding of general elections on 2 October. At the same time, a number of speakers[619] acknowledged that the country still faced serious challenges, including the continuation of the ethnic-based and divisive rhetoric, and in that context, they called upon all political representatives to ensure the swift formation of a new Government in order to put an end to the political stalemate and paralysis of State institutions. The representative of the United States expressed deep concern about the allegations of fraud in the election, in particular in the Republika Srpska presidential race, and encouraged Bosnian institutions to fully address the shortcomings raised by election observers while urging all stakeholders and citizens to pursue any grievances through established channels. With regard to the outcome of the elections, the representative of the Russian Federation noted that an overwhelming majority of voters had opted for the ethnic-oriented and Dayton-based concept of statehood and its fundamental premise about the central role of the constituent peoples.

A number of speakers[620] expressed support for the mandate of the High Representative in overseeing the implementation of the civilian aspects of the General Framework Agreement for Peace. Some Council members[621] expressed further support for the use of the executive powers of the High Representative, should the situation require it. The representative of the Russian Federation, on the other

---

[612] United Kingdom, Albania and Norway.

[613] Kenya and India.

[614] Brazil, Ireland, Albania, Kenya, India, Ghana, Norway, Mexico and United States.

[615] See S/PV.9179.

[616] Resolution 2658 (2022), paras.1 and 2.

[617] S/2022/806.

[618] See S/PV.9179.

[619] Ireland, Mexico, Norway, France, United States, Albania, Gabon, Brazil, United Kingdom, Ghana and European Union.

[620] Ireland, Norway, France, United States, Albania, United Arab Emirates, United Kingdom, Ghana and European Union.

[621] United States, Albania and United Kingdom.

hand, stated that the increased activity of the Office of the High Representative posed additional threats to the peace and stability in the country, which was in direct contradiction to the tasks originally assigned to it. The representative of China also expressed concern that the use of the Bonn powers had become rather controversial and added that they were a special arrangement out of a specific era. In addition, the representative of India stated that the disagreement over the Office of the High Representative needed to be resolved through constructive engagement, in line with the Agreement for Peace. Finally, the President of the Council expressed regret about the inability of the High Representative to participate in the meeting owing to the lack of consensus on the matter. In that connection, he stated that the collaborative exchanges between the Council and the Office of the High Representative, through the briefings of the High Representative, helped members to better appreciate the complex political situation that pertained to Bosnia and Herzegovina, and he expressed the hope that, in the future, the Council would be able to resume its established format for the meeting. Several speakers[622] encouraged the authorities of Bosnia and Herzegovina to continue progress on the implementation of the 5 plus 2 agenda by which the Office of the High Representative could complete its mission and the international supervision of Bosnia and Herzegovina would be no longer needed.

Meetings: the situation in Bosnia and Herzegovina, 2022

Meeting record and date	*Sub-item*	*Other documents*	*Rule 37 invitations*	*Rule 39 and other invitations*	*Speakers*	*Decision and vote (for-against-abstaining)*
S/PV.9029 11 May	Letter dated 3 May 2022 from the Secretary-General addressed to the President of the Security Council (S/2022/374)		Bosnia and Herzegovina, Croatia, Serbia	High Representative for the Implementation of the Peace Agreement on Bosnia and Herzegovina, Deputy Head of the Delegation of the European Union to the United Nations	All Council members, all invitees[a]	
S/PV.9179 2 November	Letter dated 25 October 2022 from the Secretary-General addressed to the President of the Security Council (S/2022/806)	Draft resolution submitted by Ireland (S/2022/809)	Bosnia and Herzegovina, Croatia, Serbia	Deputy Head of the Delegation of the European Union	All Council members,[b] all invitees	Resolution 2658 (2022) 15-0-0 (adopted under Chapter VII)

[a] Bosnia and Herzegovina was represented by the Chair of its Presidency.
[b] Ireland was represented by its Minister of State for European Affairs.

B. Security Council resolutions 1160 (1998), 1199 (1998), 1203 (1998), 1239 (1999) and 1244 (1999)

In 2022, the Council held two meetings in connection with the item entitled "Security Council resolutions 1160 (1998), 1199 (1998), 1203 (1998), 1239 (1999) and 1244 (1999)". Both meetings took the form of briefings.[623] More information on the meetings, including on participants and speakers, is

[622] Ireland, Mexico, Norway, France, United Kingdom and Kenya.
[623] For more information on the format of meetings, see part II.

given in the table below.[624] No decisions were adopted in connection with this item during the period under review.

Council members heard briefings by the newly appointed Special Representative of the Secretary-General for Kosovo and Head of the United Nations Interim Administration Mission in Kosovo (UNMIK),[625] further to the reports of the Secretary-General pursuant to resolution 1244 (1999).[626] In line with established practice, statements were also delivered by the Minister for Foreign Affairs of Serbia and the Deputy Prime Minister and Minister for Foreign Affairs of Kosovo during the meetings.

At a meeting held on 20 April,[627] the Special Representative gave a briefing to the Council following the elections in Serbia conducted on 3 April, noting that developments in Ukraine had inevitably influenced and would continue to influence all issues of European security. Despite the international community urging the Pristina and Belgrade authorities to agree on modalities to facilitate eligible voters' participation in Kosovo, a solution had not been identified to permit that. The Special Representative expressed regret about the polarizing effects of that decision, since it had divided public opinion sharply along ethnic lines. Nevertheless, the election process had gone smoothly and without incident.

The Special Representative drew attention to the incidents of serious concern in northern Kosovo, with attacks directly targeting Kosovo police patrols, and called upon the leaders of both Pristina and Belgrade to be very judicious in their actions and their rhetoric at the political level and in the public arena, recalling that those leaders bore the main responsibility for reducing tensions. Even on extremely technical subjects, progress remained tentative and slow, and she reemphasized the principle that, however difficult the path towards agreements and solutions, unilateral actions by any side had the potential to damage the real interests of the people of both sides. Dramatic shocks to the economy of Kosovo and to other regional economies had been building up well before the onset of events in Ukraine. In that context, finding practical modes of economic cooperation among Belgrade, Pristina and all the neighbours of the region assumed greater urgency. Any region-wide initiatives that could help towards promoting that objective should be welcomed.

At the outset of her mandate, the Special Representative wished to clarify two important points. First, she indicated that her responsibility was to provide objective information to the Secretary-General and the Council, and in that regard, the contents of the Secretary-General's reports were not the subject of negotiation. Secondly, she referred to inaccurate perceptions regarding the mandate of UNMIK, namely that the Mission, in and of itself, represented either an obstacle or a vehicle for the outcome preferred by one or the other side or that the Mission harboured a particular agenda to forward or favour outside the bounds of its mandate. Neither of those inaccurate perceptions contained any demonstrable truth, yet both had too frequently been allowed to gain currency in local public discourse. Accordingly, the Mission would continue its work in the areas where it was genuinely able to help advance the common objectives held by the authorities, communities and institutions in Kosovo, and the Mission's legacy of institutional support, its trust among communities and political actors and its work with the full spectrum of multilateral and bilateral actors would drive the agenda. The Council's support to the Mission remained essential, as was its attention to the state of relations between Pristina and Belgrade.

Following the briefing by the Special Representative and the statements by the Minister for Foreign Affairs of Serbia and the representative of Kosovo, Council members discussed the latest developments as reported by the Secretary-General. Council members noted the slow progress in a constructive Belgrade-Pristina dialogue and urged all actors to engage fully and constructively. Most representatives expressed support and appreciation for the work of UNMIK and underlined its important role in promoting peace and security, stability and respect for human rights. Some Council members, however, differed in their views on the role of the Mission. The representative of Brazil underlined that substantial autonomy for Kosovo had been generally achieved, but the conditions for a peaceful and normal life for all communities in the region had not yet been accomplished, and the main objective of UNMIK remained unfulfilled. The representative of China said that, given the standstill in bilateral talks and the ongoing tensions on the ground, maintaining the Mission's presence was crucial. The representative

[624] See also A/77/2, chap. 7.B.

[625] See S/2021/963 and S/2021/964.

[626] S/2022/313 and S/2022/739.

[627] See S/PV.9019.

of the United Arab Emirates argued that the support for the important role played by the United Nations in Kosovo should continue, as it undertook many activities and projects that supported Government institutions as well as initiatives aimed at building trust between religious and ethnic communities and providing economic empowerment and support for the search for missing persons. Similar support to UNMIK was expressed by the representatives of Gabon, France and Ghana. Nevertheless, the representative of the United Kingdom stated that conditions on the ground were unrecognizable from 1999, and a review of the Mission's role and responsibilities was needed. The representative of Norway affirmed that, while the Mission pursued important work in various areas, his delegation would support a close look at possible efficiency improvements. Finally, the representatives of Albania and the United States expressed the view that UNMIK had already fulfilled its mandate. The representative of the United States added that it was time to reduce the frequency of briefings to an annual basis.

Following the statements by Council members, the representatives of the Russian Federation and Albania took the floor twice to make further statements. The Minister for Foreign Affairs of Serbia and the Deputy Prime Minister and Minister for Foreign Affairs of the Republic of Kosovo took the floor three times.

At the meeting held on 18 October, the briefing of the Special Representative of the Secretary-General was focused on the report of the Secretary-General on UNMIK and the latest developments on the ground.[628] She reported that there had been several escalations in political rhetoric between Pristina and Belgrade, as well as a few moments of acute tension on the ground. Amid all challenges, there had been positive examples of leadership and cooperation. Her goal was for UNMIK to focus on those areas where the continued presence, in concert with the entire United Nations family – as well as other partners in Kosovo – contributed consistently, with positive effects. That included participating in and promoting effective communication across ethnic and political lines at all levels of society, redoubling the Mission's commitment to supporting trust-building actors from across all parts of Kosovan society and helping to promote broad awareness about the interdependence and shared problems and interests of people across Kosovo and throughout the region.

Following the briefing by the Special Representative and the statements by the Minister for Foreign Affairs of Serbia and the representative of Kosovo, Council members discussed the latest developments as reported by the Secretary-General. In their statements, many Council members focused on the increased tensions in northern Kosovo and reiterated their concern at the slow progress in dialogue between Kosovo and Serbia.

Several delegations[629] welcomed the meetings held between the parties in Brussels in August and the agreement reached on free movement between Kosovo and Serbia. The representative of Ireland added that the agreement was a positive step in the right direction and proof that acceptable, pragmatic solutions were possible when leaders engaged openly and constructively in the Belgrade-Pristina dialogue. The European Union-facilitated dialogue was the channel through which to resolve tensions between Serbia and Kosovo. Similarly, the representative of the United States underlined that the European Union-facilitated dialogue continued to be the principal mechanism for reconciling issues. The representatives of the United Kingdom and Kenya urged both parties to uphold their commitments made in the framework of the dialogue, while the representative of Ghana called upon both sides to recommit to the full implementation of their respective obligations under previous and future agreements to be reached in the context of the European Union-facilitated dialogue.

Concerning the role of UNMIK, Council members expressed overall praise and support for its work on different fronts and specifically on confidence and trust-building efforts,[630] women and peace and security and youth and peace and security agendas,[631] the return of missing persons,[632] strengthening of the rule of law[633] and the promotion of social cooperation and cohesion in Kosovo.[634] As in April, Council members discussed the continuity of the Mission and the continued value of its mandate.

[628] See S/PV.9155. See also S/2022/739.

[629] Ireland, Brazil, Ghana, India, China and France.

[630] Ireland, Kenya, Ghana and Gabon.

[631] Ireland, United Arab Emirates, Kenya, Ghana and Gabon.

[632] Ireland, India and Gabon.

[633] Norway, Kenya, Brazil, France and Gabon.

[634] Ireland, United Arab Emirates and Ghana.

While representatives of Albania, the United Kingdom and the United States advocated a thorough review of UNMIK given the change of circumstances in Kosovo and its institutions, other Council members[635] supported the continuity of the Mission and its mandate. The representative of the United States expressed disappointment that the Council had not moved towards sunsetting UNMIK, including by developing a plan to close the Mission. Briefings were no longer needed on a six-month basis and should be reduced to annual meetings, as the Council had far more pressing priorities to address, and its resources were limited. The representative of Albania also expressed the view that it was time to reduce Council meetings to only one a year in recognition of the progress made and as encouragement for the parties to pursue dialogue with more determination. By contrast, the representative of the Russian Federation expressed full support for UNMIK, as the most important guarantor of security in the province. While understanding the difficult circumstances in which the Mission must operate, his delegation expected UNMIK to make realistic rather than neutral rosy assessments of the situation in the province. The representative of China affirmed that the Special Representative and UNMIK should continue to work actively in accordance with resolution 1244 (1999), effectively carrying out its mandates and playing a constructive role in maintaining regional stability, promoting national reconciliation and facilitating dialogue between the two sides. Following the statements by Council members, the representatives of Serbia and Kosovo took the floor to make further statements.

Meetings: Security Council resolutions 1160 (1998), 1199 (1998), 1203 (1998), 1239 (1999) and 1244 (1999), 2022

Meeting record and date	*Sub-item*	*Other documents*	*Rule 37 invitations*	*Rule 39 and other invitations*	*Speakers*	*Decision and vote (for-against-abstaining)*
S/PV.9019 20 April	Report of the Secretary-General on the United Nations Interim Administration Mission in Kosovo (UNMIK) (S/2022/313)		Serbia	Special Representative of the Secretary-General for Kosovo and Head of UNMIK, Donika Gërvalla-Schwarz	All Council members, all invitees[a]	
S/PV.9155 18 October	Report of the Secretary-General on UNMIK (S/2022/739)		Serbia	Special Representative of the Secretary-General, Donika Gërvalla-Schwarz	All Council members, all invitees[a]	

[a] Serbia was represented by its Minister for Foreign Affairs.

19. Items relating to Ukraine

A. Letter dated 28 February 2014 from the Permanent Representative of Ukraine to the United Nations addressed to the President of the Security Council (S/2014/136)

During the period under review, the Council held eight meetings under the item entitled “Letter dated 28 February 2014 from the Permanent Representative of Ukraine to the United Nations addressed to the President of the Security Council (S/2014/136)” and adopted one resolution.[636] Resolution 2623 (2022) was the first resolution of the Council in 40 years in which the Council decided to call an emergency special session of the General Assembly.[637] In addition, the Council failed to adopt one draft

[635] Mexico, Russian Federation, Ghana and China.

[636] Resolution 2623 (2022).

[637] For more information regarding the relations between the Council and the General Assembly, see part IV, sect. I.C. For more details on the discussion, see part V, sect. I.

resolution owing to the negative vote of a permanent member.[638] All the meetings that were not devoted to the adoption of decisions of the Council took the form of briefings.[639] More information on the meetings, including on participants, speakers and outcomes, is provided in the table below. Council members also held informal consultations of the whole under the item to discuss the situation in Ukraine.[640]

In 2022, the Council heard four briefings by the Under-Secretary-General for Political and Peacebuilding Affairs[641] and two briefings by the Under-Secretary-General for Humanitarian Affairs and Emergency Relief Coordinator.[642] The briefings were focused on the ongoing political and security developments and the humanitarian situation in Ukraine. Briefings were also given by the United Nations High Commissioner for Refugees, who addressed the Council on the challenges faced by the civilian population and humanitarian actors and on the growing number of displaced people and refugees;[643] the Director General of International Atomic Energy Agency (IAEA), who provided updates on the military developments in the vicinity of the Zaporizhzhia nuclear power plant;[644] the Assistant Secretary-General for Humanitarian Affairs and Deputy Emergency Relief Coordinator, who reported on the humanitarian crisis in Ukraine and the global impact of the war;[645] and the Executive Director of the World Food Programme (WFP), who spoke about the decimating consequences of the war in Ukraine and the worsening food crisis around the world.[646] While most invitations under rule 37 of the provisional rules of procedure were limited to Germany and Ukraine, on 25 February, 75 Member States were invited to participate in the meeting of the Council.[647] The Head of the Delegation of the European Union to the United Nations was invited once under rule 39 of the provisional rules of procedure.[648]

On 21 February, the Council convened an emergency meeting[649] during which it heard a briefing by the Under-Secretary-General for Political and Peacebuilding Affairs following the decree of the Russian Federation to recognize certain areas of Donetsk and Luhansk as independent regions. During her briefing, the Under-Secretary-General expressed concern about the possible implications of the latest developments for the existing negotiation frameworks and emphasized the importance of pursuing dialogue. She noted the decision to order a mass evacuation of civilians of Donetsk and Luhansk into the Russian Federation and expressed regret about the deployment of Russian troops into eastern Ukraine, reportedly on a peacekeeping mission. She also expressed concern about the escalating shelling across the contact line and the targeting of critical civilian infrastructure and called for an immediate cessation of hostilities. Underlining that the risk of major conflict was real and needed to be prevented at all costs, the Under-Secretary-General reiterated the full commitment of the United Nations to the sovereignty, independence and territorial integrity of Ukraine.

During the meeting, while only some participants[650] condemned the decision of the Russian Federation to recognize non-government-controlled areas as independent entities, others spoke of the political and security developments as an attack on the sovereignty and territorial integrity of Ukraine[651] and a violation of the principles of the Charter of the United Nations and the Minsk agreements.[652] The representative of the Russian Federation recalled that the Luhansk People's Republic and the Donetsk People's Republic had declared their independence from Ukraine in 2014, and affirmed the high level of support for recognizing that independence, both in the Republics themselves and in Russian society. He also

[638] See S/PV.8980. See also S/2022/155.
[639] For more information on the format of meetings, see part II.
[640] See A/77/2, part II, chap. 39.B.
[641] See S/PV.8970, S/PV.8974, S/PV.8986 and S/PV.9011.
[642] See S/PV.8983 and S/PV.9011.
[643] See S/PV.8983.
[644] See S/PV.8986.
[645] See S/PV.9008.
[646] Ibid.
[647] See S/PV.8979.
[648] See S/PV.9011.
[649] See S/PV.8970.
[650] Albania, France, Kenya, Norway and Germany.
[651] United States, Albania, France, United Kingdom, Mexico, Ireland, Kenya, Ghana, Gabon, Norway and Ukraine.
[652] Albania, France, United Kingdom, Ireland, Ghana, Norway and Ukraine.

reminded Council members that, at the time when the Minsk agreements were signed, the Republics had already declared their independence, and underlined that the Russian decision to recognize them on 21 February in no way changed the make-up of parties to the Minsk agreements, as Russia had not been a party to them. In his statement, the representative of Ukraine emphasized the responsibility of the Council to maintain international peace and security, in accordance with the Article 24 of the Charter,[653] and called on the members to make recommendations or decide what measures should be taken to maintain or restore international peace and security.[654]

On 23 February, the Council held a meeting[655] to hear a briefing from the Under-Secretary-General for Political and Peacebuilding Affairs. At the outset of the meeting, the Secretary-General delivered opening remarks, followed by the briefing by the Under-Secretary-General. In his statement, the Secretary-General called on the President of the Russian Federation to stop his troops from attacking Ukraine. The Under-Secretary-General informed the Council that the Ukrainian authorities had declared a nationwide state of emergency and announced other related defence and security measures, including the mobilization of reservists. She added that the Ukrainian authorities had reported a new large-scale cyberattack targeting several State and financial institutions. In that regard, she encouraged the efforts of the President of Ukraine and the President of the Russian Federation to continue dialogue and diplomacy and gave assurance that United Nations staff remained on the ground to provide humanitarian assistance to the people of Ukraine.

Following the briefing, several participants[656] condemned the decision by the President to send Russian troops into the Donetsk and Luhansk regions and the announcement of a military operation. Some Council members[657] called on the Russian Federation to de-escalate and withdraw its troops from the territory of Ukraine, others[658] urged it to refrain from any action that might further increase tensions on the ground and others[659] emphasized the importance of the peaceful settlement of disputes. Council members[660] were concerned about the high-intensity ceasefire violations and urged all parties to protect civilians and civilian infrastructure and to guarantee unimpeded access for humanitarian assistance, in accordance with their obligations under international law. Some members[661] continued to emphasize the responsibility of the Council to maintain international peace and security. The representative of the Russian Federation announced that, during the course of the meeting, the President of the Russian Federation had made an address announcing his decision to launch a special military operation in Donbas. He noted that the occupation of Ukraine was not part of his country's plans. Rather, the purpose of the special operation was to protect people who had been subjected to abuse and genocide by the Kyiv regime for eight years. He added that the decision had been made in accordance with Article 51 of the Charter,[662] with the approval of the Federation Council of the Russian Federation and pursuant to the Treaty of Friendship and Mutual Assistance signed with the Donetsk People's Republic and the Luhansk People's Republic.[663] In her second statement at the meeting, further to the statement by the representative of the Russian Federation about the launching of the special military operation, the representative of the United States announced that her delegation would be putting a draft resolution on the table the following day. Condemning the start of the military operation, the representatives of the United Kingdom and France both expressed support for the preparation of a Council resolution. The representative of Ukraine called on the representative of the Russian Federation to relinquish his responsibilities as President of the Council. Underscoring the responsibility of the Council, he called on members to convene an emergency meeting to consider all necessary draft decisions and do everything possible to stop the war.

---

[653] For further details on the discussion, see part V, sect. I.B.

[654] See S/PV.8970.

[655] See S/PV.8974.

[656] France, Norway, Germany, Albania and Ireland.

[657] Albania, United Kingdom, France, India, United Arab Emirates, Norway, Gabon and Germany.

[658] Ireland, India, China, Brazil, United Arab Emirates, and Ghana.

[659] India, United Arab Emirates, Norway, China, Brazil, Ghana and Gabon.

[660] United Arab Emirates, Norway, Ghana and Gabon.

[661] Ireland, Brazil, Mexico, Ukraine and United States.

[662] For more information on Article 51, see part VII, sect. X.

[663] See S/PV.8974.

On 25 February, the Council voted on a draft resolution[664] submitted by Albania and the United States and sponsored by a further 80 Member States. Before the vote, the representatives of the United States and Albania explained the text of the draft resolution.[665] In addition, four other Council members made statements before the vote. The draft resolution was not adopted owing to the negative vote of one permanent member, namely, the Russian Federation. According to the draft resolution, the Council would have condemned the declaration by the Russian Federation on 23 February of a "special military operation" in Ukraine and deplored in the strongest terms its aggression against Ukraine in violation of Article 2 (4), of the Charter, as well as the decision of 21 February related to the status of certain areas of the Donetsk and Luhansk regions of Ukraine as a violation of the territorial integrity and sovereignty of Ukraine and inconsistent with the principles of the Charter.[666] In addition, according to the draft resolution, the Council would have decided that the Russian Federation should immediately cease its use of force against Ukraine; refrain from any further unlawful threat or use of force against any Member State; immediately, completely and unconditionally withdraw all of its military forces from the territory of Ukraine within its internationally recognized borders; and immediately and unconditionally reverse the decision related to the status of certain areas of the Donetsk and Luhansk regions of Ukraine.[667]

Following the vote, most Council members who voted in favour expressed regret about the decision of the Russian Federation to veto the draft resolution.[668] The representative of France welcomed the mobilization of all members of the Council who, by voting in favour of the draft resolution, had expressed their commitment to international law and their support for Ukraine. The representative of the United Kingdom stated that a large majority of Council members had voted in favour of the draft resolution aimed at stopping the war, yet it had not been adopted only because of the single veto of the permanent member of the Council who was perpetrating that conflict. The representative of Norway stated that a veto cast by the aggressor undermined the purpose of the Council, adding that it was a violation of the very foundation of the Charter and that in the spirit of the Charter, as a party to a dispute, the Russian Federation should have abstained from voting on the draft resolution.[669] Some members[670] condemned what they termed an aggression by the Russian Federation, while others[671] called on the parties to immediately cease hostilities. The representative of Gabon called on the parties to resume dialogue, while the representative of Ghana called on the Russian Federation to immediately withdraw its forces from Ukraine and to recommit to dialogue and diplomacy.

In explaining his country's abstention, the representative of China noted that, faced with the highly complex and sensitive situation, the Council should make the necessary response, while cautioning that actions should be truly conducive to defusing the crisis rather than adding fuel to the fire. He added that the legitimate security aspirations of the Russian Federation should receive attention and be addressed properly, and Ukraine should become a bridge between the East and the West, not an outpost for confrontation between major powers. While affirming that Member States needed to honour the principles of sovereignty and territorial integrity, the representative of India affirmed, in explaining his vote, that dialogue was the only answer to settling differences and disputes, however daunting it appeared at that moment. The representative of the United Arab Emirates expressed support for the draft resolution's emphasis on the need to adhere to the principles of international law and the Charter, which she said must be the basis for the resumption of dialogue and the pathway forward.

Explaining his country's negative vote, the representative of the Russian Federation stated that the draft resolution was anti-Russian and anti-Ukrainian and ran counter to the fundamental interests of the Ukrainian people. He concluded his statement by emphasizing that the Russian Federation was not waging a war against Ukraine or the Ukrainian people but was carrying out a special operation against nationalists to protect the residents of Donbas and for the purposes of denazification and demilitarization.

---

[664] S/2022/155.
[665] See S/PV.8979.
[666] See S/2022/155, sixth preambular para. and paras. 2 and 5.
[667] Ibid., paras. 3, 4 and 6.
[668] See S/PV.8979 (Albania, Norway and Ireland).
[669] For more information, see part II, sect. VIII.C.
[670] United Kingdom, Mexico, Albania, Norway and Ireland.
[671] Gabon, Mexico, Brazil and United Arab Emirates.

Speaking after Council members, the representative of Ukraine stressed that the Russian Federation had violated the provisional rules of procedure of the Security Council, namely rule 20 in relation to the President of the Security Council, by presiding over the Council during the consideration of a question with which it was directly connected.[672]

On 27 February, the Council held a meeting at which, despite the negative vote of the Russian Federation, it adopted resolution 2623 (2022), calling an emergency special session of the General Assembly, having taken into account that the lack of unanimity of its permanent members at the 8979th meeting had prevented it from exercising its primary responsibility for the maintenance of international peace and security.[673] Following the adoption, the representatives of Albania, Ireland and Mexico explained their votes in favour of convening an emergency special session as a means for the Assembly to condemn the aggression.

The representative of Albania underlined the historic significance of resolution 2623 (2022), which had opened the doors to the General Assembly for the world to speak out and condemn an unprovoked and unjustified pure act of aggression. The representative of the United States noted that the Council had called for an emergency special session of the Assembly for the first time in decades as an extraordinary action. Welcoming the results of the vote on the resolution, the representative of the United Kingdom urged all Member States to use their voice to call for the immediate withdrawal of Russian forces from Ukraine and end the war. Other members[674] elaborated on the use of the veto by the Russian Federation, by which a permanent member prevented the Security Council from fulfilling its primary responsibility for the maintenance of international peace and security. The representative of France asserted that his country would remain poised within the Council to ensure that it assumed its primary responsibility for the maintenance of international peace and security. He added that, together with Mexico, France would submit a draft resolution to guarantee unhindered humanitarian access to meet the urgent needs of the people remaining in Ukraine. The representative of Mexico reiterated that the exercise of the veto by the permanent members of the Security Council should not be a privilege and that, in every situation, it constituted an enormous and highly sensible responsibility. The representative of Ireland underlined that the Council had failed to exercise the responsibility to act in the face of conflict and called on the Assembly to step up where the Council had failed. In contrast, the representative of Brazil asserted that the Council had not yet exhausted its instruments and mechanisms to contribute to a negotiated and diplomatic solution towards peace and that the Council and the Assembly must work together.

Expressing regret about the worsening of the situation in Ukraine, the representatives of India and the United Arab Emirates, whose delegations had abstained together with China, reiterated their call to cease hostilities and return to the path of diplomacy and dialogue. In that regard, they also welcomed the latest announcement by both sides about the commencement of talks on the Ukraine-Belarus border. The representative of China expressed support for discussions on an equal footing between the European Union and the Russian Federation on security issues to establish a balanced, effective and sustainable European security mechanism. He added that the Council should play a constructive role in resolving the Ukraine issue and that the United Nations should help to calm the situation and facilitate diplomatic solutions to avoid an escalation of tensions.

Elaborating on his vote, the permanent representative of the Russian Federation stated that he had voted against resolution 2623 (2022) because it placed on record that the Council was unable to uphold its primary responsibility for maintaining international peace and security. He underlined that the right of veto was granted to the permanent members of the Council as a tool for ensuring the balance of interests that ensured global stability, and any attempt to circumvent or disregard the position of the Russian Federation undermined the bedrock of the Charter.

On 28 February, the Council heard a briefing by the Under-Secretary-General for Humanitarian Affairs, who reported on the latest civilian casualties, damage to critical civilian infrastructure and

[672] For more information on the role of the presidency, see part II, sect. IV.

[673] See S/PV.8980. For more information on the emergency special session and the relations between the Council and the General Assembly, see part IV, sect. I.C. For more information on the discussion, see part II, sect. VIII.C, and part V, sect. I.

[674] France, Ireland, Mexico, Norway and Ghana.

growing humanitarian needs in the hardest hit areas of the conflict in Ukraine.[675] He underscored that the ongoing fighting had constrained the humanitarian movement of the United Nations and the work of humanitarian workers on the ground, stressing the need for the parties to the conflict to provide assurances that humanitarian workers would be protected and that the rapid and unimpeded passage of impartial humanitarian relief would be ensured.

The United Nations High Commissioner for Refugees reported that, in addition to the grave situation inside Ukraine, hundreds of thousands were seeking refuge in the neighbouring countries of Poland, Hungary, the Republic of Moldova, Romania, Slovakia and the Russian Federation. Commending the Governments of the receiving countries, he encouraged them to maintain access for all who were fleeing and underlined that there could be no discrimination against any person or any group. While noting that the challenges to admit, register and ensure the protection of those fleeing so far had been met, he expressed concern about the likelihood of a further escalation in the number of arrivals. In that regard, he spoke of the bilateral support to the receiving countries offered by the European Union and its member states and other Governments. He elaborated on the scaled-up efforts by the Office of the United Nations High Commissioner for Refugees with its United Nations partner agencies and national and international non-government organizations. He explained that the Office was planning for up to 4 million refugees in the following days and weeks and that such a rapid increase would be a huge burden for receiving States and would no doubt stress reception systems and related resources. He added that, like any country hosting refugees around the world, such countries could not be left alone to shoulder that responsibility, and welcomed the support expressed by many European States at the European Union Justice and Home Affairs Council meeting to activate the temporary protection directive for people fleeing Ukraine, which would enable the provision of immediate temporary refuge in the European Union and facilitate the sharing of responsibility among States members of the European Union for people fleeing Ukraine.

During the discussion, in their remarks on the humanitarian situation and the protection of civilians and civilian infrastructure, Council members[676] welcomed the growing humanitarian efforts of the United Nations in Ukraine. Members called on both parties to immediately and unconditionally cease hostilities,[677] respect international humanitarian law at all times,[678] exercise self-restraint,[679] refrain from attacks on civilians and civilian infrastructure[680] and ensure safe and unimpeded access for humanitarian actors and their movements.[681] While the representatives of Ireland and the United Kingdom spoke about the indiscriminate attacks and use of explosives weapons by the Russian Federation in populated areas, the representatives of the United States, Albania and Ukraine stressed the need to document and address all violations of international humanitarian law and human rights law. Against the backdrop of a humanitarian situation that was worsening with each passing hour, the representative of Mexico explained that, together with France, his country would present a draft resolution aimed at achieving a general cessation of hostilities, the protection of civilians and guaranteed access to humanitarian aid. In response, the representative of the Russian Federation underlined that the Russian special operation did not have an impact on civilian infrastructure and that civilians in the areas under the control of the Russian armed forces were not encountering acute humanitarian issues. With regard to the draft resolution, he said that his delegation needed to study the text closely before making any assessments and that, in any case, the Russian military would provide any necessary humanitarian assistance to the people of Ukraine in the territories that had been freed from what he referred to as "the radicals".

In connection with the refugee and displacement crisis, Council members commended the neighbouring countries for receiving refugees[682] and called for borders to be kept open.[683] While some

[675] See S/PV.8983.
[676] Albania, India and China.
[677] France, Ireland, India, Ghana, Gabon and United Arab Emirates.
[678] France, Mexico, United Arab Emirates and Brazil.
[679] United Arab Emirates and China.
[680] Ireland, Ghana, Gabon and United Arab Emirates.
[681] France, Mexico, Norway, Ghana, Gabon and Brazil.
[682] Kenya, United States, Ireland, Norway, Albania and Gabon.
[683] Mexico, Ireland and Norway.

members[684] commented on the reported accounts of discrimination experienced by Africans and people of African descent as they were fleeing the war, several[685] echoed the High Commissioner for Refugees in urging the international community to provide support to all, without discrimination based on race or nationality. Members also expressed differing views on the economic sanctions adopted against the Russian Federation and Belarus. In that connection, the representative of France assured the Council that the sanctions would be implemented with full regard for international humanitarian law and with no impact on the humanitarian response. The representative of Kenya cautioned that sanctions might lead to an escalation of the conflict rather than opening the path to peace. The representative of Brazil also warned that the severe economic sanctions being imposed might have ripple effects on the world's economy.

On 4 March, the Council heard a briefing by the Under-Secretary-General for Political and Peacebuilding Affairs and the Director General of IAEA, who focused on the latest developments in the area of the Zaporizhzhia and Chernobyl nuclear power plants and the deteriorating humanitarian situation in Ukraine.[686] During her briefing, the Under-Secretary-General underscored that attacks on nuclear power facilities were contrary to international humanitarian law. Welcoming the statements and actions of IAEA in connection with the establishment of an appropriate framework that would ensure the safe, secure and reliable operation of Ukrainian nuclear power plants, she emphasized the need for safe and urgent passage for IAEA personnel. She added that the United Nations was significantly increasing its humanitarian assistance in response to the escalating crisis and welcomed the agreements between Ukrainian and Russian negotiators on the establishment of humanitarian corridors to allow safe passage for civilians and the delivery of humanitarian assistance.

The Director General of IAEA reported that the Russian forces had taken charge of the Chernobyl nuclear site. Their advance towards the perimeter of the Zaporizhzhia nuclear power plant, however, had been met by opposition and groups of civilians who had blocked access to the facility. He confirmed that, although a projectile had impacted a building adjacent to the Zaporizhzhia nuclear plant facility, no security or safety systems had been compromised and the operations at both plants had continued normally. On the establishment of a framework to ensure the observance of the basic principles of safety and security, he underlined that the basic elements of the proposal had already been shared with the Ukrainian counterpart and the Russian authorities. He clarified that the mission of IAEA would be restricted and circumscribed to the safety and security of the nuclear installations in Ukraine.

During the discussion, Council members expressed concern about the situation at both the Chernobyl and Zaporizhzhia nuclear sites. Members continued to call on the Russian Federation to abide by its international obligations,[687] to halt the use of force near any power plant[688] and to end violence and withdraw its troops from the territory of Ukraine.[689] The representative of Kenya urged the need to observe international conventions regulating the conduct of armed conflict and called on the leadership of Ukraine and the Russian Federation to reduce the targeting of and threat to critical infrastructure. Referring to Chapter VI of the Charter and to the first resolution adopted by the General Assembly in the context of the eleventh emergency special session,[690] the representative of Brazil urged all members of the Council to engage truly and actively to promote dialogue and rebuild trust.[691] The representatives of India, Ghana, China and the United Arab Emirates welcomed the second round of talks on the establishment of a safe humanitarian corridor.[692] Participants also expressed support for the work of IAEA in Ukraine and called for the urgent and unhindered access of its personnel to monitor the conditions and ensure nuclear safety. The representative of the Russian Federation denounced the statements about Russian troops attacking the Zaporizhzhia nuclear power plant that were part of an unprecedented campaign of lies and disinformation against his country and were untrue. According to the representative,

---

[684] Kenya and Gabon.
[685] Norway, United States, Ghana and Gabon.
[686] See S/PV.8986.
[687] United States, Ireland, Norway and Mexico.
[688] Albania, United States, France, Ireland and Ghana.
[689] United Kingdom, Albania, United States, Ireland and Norway.
[690] Resolution ES-11/1.
[691] For more details on Chapter VI, see part VI.
[692] See S/PV.8986.

an agreement to place the power plant under the protection of the Russian military had been reached with the management of the plant to ensure its security and prevent interruptions in power supply to the population of Ukraine and European consumers. He asserted that the current situation was similar to that in the area of the Chernobyl power plant and that the security of those facilities was being ensured jointly by the Russian armed forces and the Ukrainian operators of the nuclear installations. Stating that Russia had deliberately undertaken an armed attack against a nuclear power site, an action that had violated all international agreements with IAEA, the representative of Ukraine demanded that Russian forces withdraw from the Zaporizhzhia nuclear power plant. He called on the international community to respond adequately to the actions of the Russian Federation by closing the skies over Ukraine, supporting Ukraine in terms of security and humanitarian assistance and expelling Russians from international institutions.

On 29 March, the Council heard a briefing by the Assistant Secretary-General for Humanitarian Affairs and Deputy Emergency Relief Coordinator,[693] who informed the Council about the scaling up of the humanitarian system. Highlighting the risk of human trafficking, as well as sexual violence, exploitation and abuse in Ukraine and the region, in particular for children fleeing the war, she announced the scaling up of protection services at the border and within the country in order to offer information on safe options and routes and access to helplines and safe shelters. In that connection, she reported that humanitarian partners were coordinating to provide swift and specialized services to survivors. She also stressed the need for detailed, realistic agreements on humanitarian ceasefires and pauses to ensure the safe and unhindered passage of aid and indicated that, following the request from the Secretary-General, the Under-Secretary-General for Humanitarian Affairs and Emergency Relief Coordinator had been engaging with both parties on possible arrangements for a humanitarian ceasefire.

The Executive Director of WFP gave a briefing on the impact of the war on global food insecurity. He stressed the need not to neglect other regions such as the Sahel, North Africa, the rest of Africa and the Middle East to prevent massive migration from all sides of Europe. He explained the risk of a pricing problem due to the increase in fuel, food and shipping costs and an availability problem due to the lack of fertilizer-based products from Belarus and the Russian Federation, calling it a crisis on top of a crisis. In closing, he appealed to everyone involved to deconflict, provide the access necessary for the safe delivery of aid and minimize the impact globally and in Ukraine.

Council members discussed the humanitarian impact of the conflict in Ukraine. While some members[694] attributed the responsibility for the humanitarian crisis inside and outside Ukraine to the Russian Federation, others[695] commended the neighbouring countries for receiving refugees. Council members and other participants discussed the massive displacement and refugee crisis created by the conflict, the threats of human trafficking and gender-based violence as well as the challenges faced by civilians and humanitarian organizations. In this regard, most Council members called for safe and unhindered access for humanitarian aid and safe passages for civilians in besieged cities. The representatives of Norway and the United Arab Emirates welcomed the Secretary-General's initiative to request the Under-Secretary-General for Humanitarian Affairs to work directly with the parties on a possible agreement for a humanitarian ceasefire. Council members and other participants discussed the negotiations taking place between the parties in Istanbul, Türkiye, at the time. While the representative of China underlined that the international community should encourage and support continued direct negotiations between the Russian Federation and Ukraine until a positive outcome was achieved and peace was restored, the representative of the United Arab Emirates stressed the important role of women in conflict resolution and peace negotiations, including to ensure their sustainability and durability. Council members also discussed the impact of the economic sanctions adopted in response to the conflict in Ukraine. While some Council members[696] denied an impact of the sanctions on the global food supply chains, others[697] argued that sanctions exacerbated food shortages and price distortions, having a detrimental impact on developing countries.

[693] See S/PV.9008.

[694] United States, United Kingdom and France.

[695] United States, Kenya, Norway and Gabon.

[696] France and United States.

[697] Kenya, Russian Federation, Brazil and China.

On 5 April, the Council held a meeting during which it heard briefings by the Secretary-General, the Under-Secretary-General for Political and Peacebuilding Affairs and the Under-Secretary-General for Humanitarian Affairs and Emergency Relief Coordinator.[698] In his remarks, the Secretary-General said that Ukraine was one of the greatest challenges ever to the international order and the global peace architecture, founded on the Charter, because of its nature, intensity and consequences. He added that the world was dealing with the full-fledged invasion, on several fronts, of one Member State, Ukraine, by another, the Russian Federation – a permanent member of the Security Council – in violation of the Charter and with several aims, including redrawing the internationally recognized borders between the two countries. He also focused on the humanitarian consequences of the conflict, including the massive devastation in urban centres and the destruction of civilian infrastructure, rapes and sexual violence, as well as the displacement of more than 10 million people in just one month. In addition, he spoke about the massive increases in the prices of food, energy and fertilizers, disrupting supply chains and increasing cost of transportation, putting even more pressure on the developing world. Regretting the divisions that had prevented the Council from acting not only on Ukraine, but on other threats to peace and security around the world, he urged the Council to do everything in its power to end the war and mitigate its impact, both on the suffering people of Ukraine and on vulnerable people and developing countries around the world.

In her briefing, the Under-Secretary-General focused on the ongoing military operations, noting that cities continued to be pounded, the number of civilians killed had more than doubled and hundreds of thousands of people remained trapped in encircled cities. She expressed grave concern about the persistent use of explosive weapons with a wide impact in or near populated areas and underlined that such indiscriminate attacks were prohibited under international humanitarian law. She also expressed concern about reports of cases of arbitrary arrests and enforced disappearances, as well as emerging allegations of conflict-related sexual violence. Against that backdrop, she reported that, according to the International Organization for Migration, suspected and verified cases of human trafficking were surfacing in the surrounding countries, and expressed grave concern about the heightened risk for displaced persons and refugees. She reported that, away from the fighting, diplomatic efforts to end the war, including direct talks between Ukrainian and Russian representatives, had continued, and commended, in that regard, the Government of Türkiye. The Under-Secretary-General noted the reported withdrawal of Russian forces from around the Chernobyl nuclear site and reemphasized that all nuclear sites in Ukraine must be fully protected and secured. Noting the reported reduction of Russian troops and attacks around Kyiv and Chernihiv, she reiterated the call by the General Assembly for Russian forces to withdraw entirely from Ukrainian territory and cease all military operations. In closing, the Under-Secretary-General cautioned that the war had damaged the European security architecture, noting that the longer the war continued, the greater the risk that it would further weaken the global institutions and mechanisms dedicated to preserving peace and security.

In his statement, the Under-Secretary-General for Humanitarian Affairs and Emergency Relief Coordinator spoke about the humanitarian needs and what was being done to meet them. He also reported on his actions further to the Secretary-General's instruction to bring both sides together on humanitarian grounds to explore specific and sustained ways to reduce humanitarian suffering, including the pursuit of a humanitarian ceasefire. In this regard, he spoke about his meetings with the Russian authorities and his forthcoming meetings with Ukrainian authorities. While expressing gratitude for the generous contributions from donors, he stressed that funding to support the needs in Ukraine must not be diverted from other crises and called on all Council members and Member States to support all efforts in the pursuit of peace and the alleviation of human suffering.

During the deliberations, Council members exchanged views on the reported violence and attacks against civilian and humanitarian infrastructure. Council members and other participants emphasized the responsibility of the Council to end the war and to maintain international peace and security,[699] urged the parties to the conflict to comply with international humanitarian law[700] and condemned the atrocities and

---

[698] See S/PV.9011.

[699] Ireland, Brazil, Mexico and Norway. For more information on functions and powers of the Council, see part V, sect. I.

[700] Albania, Gabon, Ireland, Brazil, China, France, United Arab Emirates and European Union (also on behalf of Albania, Bosnia and Herzegovina, Georgia, Iceland, Liechtenstein, Monaco, Montenegro, North Macedonia, Republic of Moldova and San Marino).

abuses committed on the territory of Ukraine.[701] Some Council members and participants expressed support for an investigation by the International Criminal Court[702] and by the Independent International Commission of Inquiry on Ukraine established by the Human Rights Council.[703] In this connection, the representative of the United States announced that her country, in coordination with Ukraine and many other Member States, would seek the suspension of the Russian Federation from the Human Rights Council.

In addition to this item, during the period under review, the Council discussed developments in the situation in Ukraine under the following items: "Letter dated 13 April 2014 from the Permanent Representative of the Russian Federation to the United Nations addressed to the President of the Security Council (S/2014/264)",[704] "Maintenance of peace and security of Ukraine"[705] and "Threats to international peace and security".[706]

Meetings: letter dated 28 February 2014 from the Permanent Representative of Ukraine to the United Nations addressed to the President of the Security Council (S/2014/136), 2022

Meeting record and date	*Sub-item*	*Other documents*	*Rule 37 invitations*	*Rule 39 and other invitations*	*Speakers*	*Decision and vote (for-against-abstaining)*
S/PV.8970 21 February			Germany, Ukraine	Under-Secretary-General for Political and Peacebuilding Affairs	All Council members, all invitees	
S/PV.8974 23 February			Germany, Ukraine	Under-Secretary-General for Political and Peacebuilding Affairs	Secretary-General, all Council members, all invitees	
S/PV.8979 25 February		Draft resolution submitted by 82 Member States[a] (S/2022/155)	75 Member States[b]		All Council members, one invitee (Ukraine)	Not adopted 11-1-3[c]
S/PV.8980 27 February		Draft resolution submitted by Albania, United States (S/2022/160)	Ukraine		14 Council members,[d] invitee	Resolution 2623 (2022) 11-1-3[e]
S/PV.8983 28 February			Ukraine	Under-Secretary-General for Humanitarian Affairs and Emergency Relief Coordinator, United Nations High	All Council members, all invitees[f]	

[701] Ireland, Kenya, Mexico, India, France, Ghana and European Union (also on behalf of Albania, Bosnia and Herzegovina, Georgia, Iceland, Liechtenstein, Monaco, Montenegro, North Macedonia, Republic of Moldova and San Marino).

[702] Ireland, Mexico, Norway, United Kingdom and European Union (also on behalf of Albania, Bosnia and Herzegovina, Georgia, Iceland, Liechtenstein, Monaco, Montenegro, North Macedonia, Republic of Moldova and San Marino).

[703] Mexico, France, Norway and European Union (also on behalf of Albania, Bosnia and Herzegovina, Georgia, Iceland, Liechtenstein, Monaco, Montenegro, North Macedonia, Republic of Moldova and San Marino).

[704] For more information, see sect. 19.B below.

[705] For more information, see sect. 19.C below.

[706] For more information, see sect. 34 below.

Meeting record and date	*Sub-item*	*Other documents*	*Rule 37 invitations*	*Rule 39 and other invitations*	*Speakers*	*Decision and vote (for-against-abstaining)*
				Commissioner for Refugees		
S/PV.8986 4 March			Ukraine	Under-Secretary-General for Political and Peacebuilding Affairs, Director General of International Atomic Energy Agency (IAEA)	14 Council members,[g] all invitees[h]	
S/PV.9008 29 March			Ukraine	Assistant Secretary-General for Humanitarian Affairs and Deputy Emergency Relief Coordinator, Executive Director of the United Nations World Food Programme (WFP)	All Council members,[i] all invitees[j]	
S/PV.9011 5 April			Ukraine	Under-Secretary-General for Political and Peacebuilding Affairs, Under-Secretary-General for Humanitarian Affairs, Head of the Delegation of the European Union to the United Nations	Secretary-General, all Council members, all invitees[k]	

[a] Albania, Andorra, Antigua and Barbuda, Australia, Austria, Bahamas, Barbados, Belgium, Belize, Bosnia and Herzegovina, Botswana, Bulgaria, Canada, Chile, Colombia, Costa Rica, Croatia, Cyprus, Czechia, Denmark, Dominican Republic, Ecuador, Estonia, Fiji, Finland, France, Gambia, Georgia, Germany, Greece, Grenada, Guatemala, Haiti, Hungary, Iceland, Ireland, Italy, Jamaica, Japan, Kiribati, Kuwait, Latvia, Lesotho, Liberia, Liechtenstein, Lithuania, Luxembourg, Malta, Marshall Islands, Micronesia (Federated States of), Monaco, Montenegro, Netherlands, New Zealand, Niger, North Macedonia, Norway, Palau, Panama, Papua New Guinea, Paraguay, Peru, Poland, Portugal, Republic of Korea, Republic of Moldova, Romania, Samoa, San Marino, Singapore, Slovakia, Slovenia, Spain, Suriname, Sweden, Switzerland, Timor-Leste, Trinidad and Tobago, Türkiye, Ukraine, United Kingdom and United States.

[b] Andorra, Antigua and Barbuda, Australia, Austria, Bahamas, Barbados, Belgium, Belize, Bosnia and Herzegovina, Botswana, Bulgaria, Canada, Chile, Colombia, Costa Rica, Croatia, Cyprus, Czechia, Denmark, Dominican Republic, Ecuador, Estonia, Fiji, Finland, Gambia, Georgia, Germany, Greece, Grenada, Guatemala, Haiti, Hungary, Iceland, Italy, Jamaica, Japan, Kiribati, Kuwait, Latvia, Lesotho, Liberia, Liechtenstein, Lithuania, Luxembourg, Malta, Marshall Islands, Micronesia (Federated States of), Monaco, Montenegro, Netherlands, New Zealand, Niger, North Macedonia, Palau, Panama, Papua New Guinea, Paraguay, Peru, Poland, Portugal, Republic of Korea, Republic of Moldova, Romania, Samoa, Singapore, Slovakia, Slovenia, Spain, Suriname, Sweden, Switzerland, Timor-Leste, Trinidad and Tobago, Türkiye and Ukraine.

[c] *For*: Albania, Brazil, France, Gabon, Ghana, Ireland, Kenya, Mexico, Norway, United Kingdom, United States; *against*: Russian Federation; *abstaining*: China, India, United Arab Emirates.

[d] Albania, Brazil, China, France, Gabon, Ghana, India, Ireland, Mexico, Norway, Russian Federation, United Arab Emirates, United Kingdom, United States.

[e] *For*: Albania, Brazil, France, Gabon, Ghana, Ireland, Kenya, Mexico, Norway, United Kingdom, United States; *against*: Russian Federation; *abstaining*: China, India, United Arab Emirates.

[f] The Under-Secretary-General for Humanitarian Affairs and the High Commissioner participated in the meeting by videoconference.

[g] Albania, Brazil, China, France, Ghana, India, Ireland, Kenya, Mexico, Norway, Russian Federation, United Arab Emirates, United Kingdom, United States.
[h] The Director General of IAEA participated in the meeting by videoconference.
[i] The United States was represented by its Deputy Secretary of State.
[j] The Executive Director of WFP participated in the meeting by videoconference.
[k] Ukraine was represented by its President, who participated in the meeting by videoconference. The representative of the European Union spoke also on behalf of Albania, Bosnia and Herzegovina, Georgia, Iceland, Liechtenstein, Monaco, Montenegro, North Macedonia, the Republic of Moldova and San Marino.

B. Letter dated 13 April 2014 from the Permanent Representative of the Russian Federation to the United Nations addressed to the President of the Security Council (S/2014/264)

During the period under review, the Security Council held two public meetings in connection with the item entitled “Letter dated 13 April 2014 from the Permanent Representative of the Russian Federation to the United Nations addressed to the President of the Security Council (S/2014/264)”, which took the form of a briefing and adoption, respectively.[707] The Council failed to adopt a draft resolution in connection with this item, having failed to obtain the required number of votes. More information on the meetings, including on participants and speakers is given in the table below.[708]

On 17 February, Council members heard briefings by the Under-Secretary-General for Political and Peacebuilding Affairs, the Special Representative of the Organization for Security and Cooperation in Europe (OSCE) Chairperson-in-Office, the Chief Monitor of the OSCE Special Monitoring Mission and a Ukrainian civil society representative.[709]

Drawing attention to the fragile security situation, the Under-Secretary-General cautioned that tensions in and around Ukraine were running higher than at any point since 2014. She explained that the issues underpinning the crisis were complex and long-standing, tying together the eight-year conflict in eastern Ukraine with larger issues relating to the European security architecture, and she noted with regret that there had been little, if any, meaningful progress in the implementation of the Minsk agreements. She also said that both the talks in the Normandy Four format and the discussions led by the Trilateral Contact Group remained deadlocked. Against that backdrop, she noted with concern the reports of ceasefire violations across the contact line and called on all sides to refrain from any unilateral measures that could go against the letter and spirit of the Minsk agreements or undermine their implementation. She added that it was incumbent on all Member States to fully respect the key principles of the Charter, to settle disputes by peaceful means and to refrain from the threat or use of force against the territorial integrity or political independence of any State. She welcomed the efforts by France and Germany to host the recent Normandy Four discussions to break the current impasse and the recent diplomatic talks, including between Heads of State, and urged more tangible steps on the ground and an end to inflammatory rhetoric in order to defuse tensions. The Under-Secretary-General further reported that, owing to COVID-19-related restrictions, millions of people were unable to travel freely across the contact line and, as a consequence of increased isolation and the abrupt loss of access to basic services and livelihoods, the needs of the already vulnerable population had been exacerbated. She called for safe and unimpeded access for humanitarian actors and early and adequate funding to continue to meet the needs of vulnerable people in both government-controlled and non-government-controlled areas. The Under-Secretary-General pointed out that, despite the persistent tensions, the Office of the United Nations High Commissioner for Human Rights had, the previous year, document the lowest number of civilian casualties since the beginning of the conflict and underlined that the overall adherence to the ceasefire had been an important factor in that trend that had to continue. In concluding, she said that the world was looking to the collective security mechanisms in Europe, as well as to the Council, to help to ease tensions.

The Special Representative of the OSCE Chairperson-in-Office said that it was impossible to address the Donbas issue without paying attention to the bigger context, which was the tense security situation

[707] For more information on the format of meetings, see part II.
[708] See also A/77/2, part II, chap. 39.C.
[709] See S/PV.8968.

around Ukraine and in the region, as well as intensive, high-level diplomacy. He noted that, while the bigger context had a strong interlinkage with the work of the Trilateral Contact Group, the positions of the participants to the discussions were too far from each other, affirming that it was not possible to resolve the conflict related to eastern Ukraine within the Contact Group. He observed that none of the elements of the Minsk agreements had been implemented or, at least, fully implemented, while emphasizing that everyone involved in the discussions of the Contact Group needed to bear responsibility for carrying out what had been agreed. Highlighting that the security situation along the contact line in eastern Ukraine was one of the key focuses of the work of the Contact Group, he stressed that it was important to continue to stay calm along the contact line and avoid provocations. In this regard, the Special Representative informed the Council about recent political, military and humanitarian developments on the ground, emphasizing that all participants needed to remain committed to the goal of restoring Ukrainian sovereignty over the totality of its territory. He added that the unprecedented international focus on Ukraine and the region should be used as an opportunity to unblock the work of the Contact Group, which he noted had been meeting by videoconference for almost two years. He expressed resolve to return to the face-to-face meetings, bringing together Ukraine, the Russian Federation and OSCE, as well as representatives of certain areas of the Donetsk and Luhansk regions.

The Chief Monitor of the OSCE Special Monitoring Mission in Ukraine updated the Council on the impact of the eight-year conflict on the civilian population and the Mission's increasingly challenging operational environment. He reported that the situation remained fraught with tension and expressed deep concern that the Mission had been deprived of its operational freedom and independence. In this context, he explained that the Mission had been vilified in public rhetoric, that its technical monitoring tools had been subjected to intense interference and that it had suffered temporary blockades in the Donetsk and Luhansk regions. He noted that, since the last briefing to the Council, the security situation in eastern Ukraine remained volatile, with an increase in the level of armed conflict and kinetic activity, including destructive weapons, and a high number of ceasefire violations on both sides of the contact line, resulting in civilian casualties and damage to infrastructure. The Chief Monitor emphasized that in such challenging circumstances it was imperative for the sides to strictly adhere to the ceasefire, reduce tensions and allow space for negotiations. Expressing hope that the recent resumption of the Normandy Four consultations and other confidence-building efforts under the auspices of OSCE would provide much-needed political impetus for the conflict-resolution process to move forward, he called for the signatories of the Minsk agreements to adhere to all their commitments and urged the restoration of the Mission's freedom of movement.

The Ukrainian civil society representative affirmed that the authorities in Kyiv had never had the intention of implementing the first package of the Minsk agreement and, to an even lesser degree, the subsequent Minsk package of measures agreement. She added that there was absolutely no explanation for the "Western hysteria" about the Russian Federation being about to invade and stated that "the West" wanted a war with the Russian Federation and that it wanted that war to take place on Ukrainian territory.

Following the briefing, Council members discussed the security situation in and around Ukraine and its connection with the European security architecture. Reaffirming support for the Minsk agreements, Council members expressed concerns at the military build-up by the Russian Federation at the border with Ukraine. Council members[710] also expressed diverging views on the likelihood of a military invasion while affirming their support for the sovereignty and territorial integrity of Ukraine. In this regard, a majority of Council members[711] called on both parties to de-escalate and engage instead in diplomacy and dialogue. Most Council members[712] affirmed that the Minsk agreements remained the framework for achieving a negotiated solution through the Normandy format and the Trilateral Contact Group. The representative of the Russian Federation recalled, however, that the Normandy format, according to annex II to resolution 2202 (2015), was a mechanism to oversee implementation and not a discussion forum on new decisions.

---

[710] United States, United Kingdom, Norway, Ireland, Kenya, Ghana, Albania and France.

[711] United States, United Kingdom, Norway, Ireland, India, United Arab Emirates, Mexico, France and Gabon.

[712] United States, United Kingdom, Norway, Brazil, Ireland, India, Kenya, United Arab Emirates, Ghana, France and Gabon.

Council members[713] also expressed concern at the resolution of the Russian State Duma calling on the President of the Russian Federation to recognize the self-declared Luhansk People's Republic and Donetsk People's Republic as independent States. In response, the representative of the Russian Federation encouraged Council members to concentrate on the implementation of the Minsk agreements instead of speculating about the initiative – an appeal from the members of the State Duma.

Council members also exchanged views about the dire humanitarian situation after eight years of conflict. The representative of Norway stressed that civilians were increasingly losing access to essential life-saving services and humanitarian assistance and that any escalation of the conflict would lead to devastating humanitarian consequences. Some delegations[714] called for the removal of obstacles to the flow of humanitarian aid and freedom of movement of civilians in conflict areas, and some[715] also expressed concern at the obstacles to the freedom of movement of the OSCE Special Monitoring Mission, which impeded the implementation of its mandate.

In addition to Council members, the representatives of Ukraine and Germany participated in the meeting and delivered statements. In his statement, the representative of Ukraine underscored that the recognition by the Russian Federation of the so-called Donetsk People's Republic and Luhansk People's Republic was tantamount to withdrawal from the Minsk agreements. He called on the Russian Federation to take a constructive stance towards achieving progress within the framework of the existing negotiation formats and warned that the Russian Federation would bear full responsibility for undermining the Minsk agreements and the process of peaceful settlement of the armed conflict. With reference to the Charter, the representative of Germany underscored that the Russian State Duma resolution ran counter to the Minsk agreement and constituted a further breach of Ukrainian sovereignty and territorial integrity. She said that the failure of the Russian Federation to provide any satisfactory explanation for the military build-up on the Ukrainian border was deplorable and called on the Russian Federation to immediately withdraw its troops in a substantial and verifiable manner.[716]

On 23 March, the Council voted on a draft resolution[717] submitted by Belarus, the Democratic People's Republic of Korea, the Russian Federation and the Syrian Arab Republic. The draft resolution was not adopted, having failed to obtain the required number of votes.[718] Among other aspects contained in the draft resolution, the Council would have demanded that civilians, including humanitarian personnel and persons in vulnerable situations, including women and children, were fully protected and that provisions of international humanitarian law in connection with objects indispensable to the survival of the civilian population and civilian infrastructure were fully respected by all parties.[719] It would have also called upon Member States to fund the flash appeal launched by the United Nations for the humanitarian response in Ukraine, as well as the regional refugee response plan for Ukraine.[720] In addition, the Council would have called upon all parties concerned to allow safe and unhindered passage to destinations outside of Ukraine, including to foreign nationals without discrimination, and to facilitate safe and unhindered access of humanitarian assistance to those in need in and around Ukraine.[721]

Before the vote, the representative of the Russian Federation took the floor to reject the assertion that the Council could not adopt a resolution on the Ukrainian humanitarian dossier.[722] He affirmed that his delegation was submitting for a vote a draft resolution, based on the French-Mexican draft text, that was not politicized in any way, adding that it was analogous to other humanitarian draft resolutions adopted by the Council. The representative of the United States, also speaking before the vote, said that it was unconscionable that the Russian Federation would have the audacity to put forward a draft resolution asking the international community to solve a humanitarian crisis that it alone had created.

---

[713] Norway, Ireland and France.
[714] Brazil, United Arab Emirates, Ghana and Mexico.
[715] Ireland, Mexico, Ukraine and Germany.
[716] For more information on the discussion, see part III, sect. II.
[717] S/2022/231.
[718] See S/PV.9002.
[719] S/2022/231, paras. 1 and 3.
[720] Ibid., para. 6.
[721] Ibid., para. 4.
[722] See S/PV.9002.

She explained that the United States intended to abstain in the voting on the text because, to state the obvious, the Russian Federation did not care about the deteriorating humanitarian conditions.

After the vote, some delegations[723] explained their abstentions by pointing out the lack of reference to the immediate and unconditional cessation of hostilities in the draft resolution. The representative of France explained that France and Mexico had negotiated, in good faith, a draft resolution in the Council with the objective of obtaining an immediate cessation of hostilities and providing a concrete response to the humanitarian catastrophe unfolding in Ukraine. He added that, given the reality of Russian obstruction, together they had decided to take that initiative to the General Assembly, where a transregional group had developed a draft resolution.[724] In this regard, the representative of the United Kingdom added that the Assembly would soon vote on a draft resolution that made clear that the only way to end the humanitarian crisis was for the Russian Federation to end the war. The representative of Ghana explained the abstention, affirming that his delegation did not believe that the draft resolution reflected the position of the international community on the course of the humanitarian catastrophe or address the requirement for an immediate and unconditional cessation of hostilities. Explaining his delegation's vote, the representative of Mexico clarified that, following the announcement that Mexico and France had made on 14 March that they were going to take the initiative to the Assembly, which had the item under consideration on its agenda pursuant to its resolution 377 (V), the Russian Federation had decided, without prior warning, to submit an alternative draft text to be voted upon the following day. He argued that such conduct stood in contradiction with the willingness to engage in a dialogue with which Mexico and France had led the process from the start.[725] The representative of Ireland explained that his country could not vote in favour of a draft resolution that purported to address the humanitarian situation, but which did not recognize the cause of the humanitarian crisis that was engulfing Ukraine. In this connection, the representative of Norway said that a party to a conflict could not expect to be perceived as neutral. She added that, in the spirit of the Charter, a party to a conflict should not be the author of Council draft resolutions and should not take part in voting on the conflict to which it was a party. The representative of Gabon explained the abstention, indicating that his delegation would abstain every time it believed that humanitarian issues were being instrumentalized for hidden purposes, adding that humanitarian issues should be the permanent consensus of the social compact of humankind. The representative of the United Arab Emirates explained that, while agreement was not possible, the Council could not abrogate its responsibility for maintaining international peace and security. The representative of the United States took the floor again after the vote to underline that it was not necessary to veto the draft resolution; 13 members of the Council had abstained, which was all that was required to defeat the draft resolution.

The representative of China explained that his country's vote in favour was based on its call for the international community to attach high importance to the humanitarian issue in Ukraine and for the parties concerned to strengthen coordination on humanitarian issues so as to effectively protect the safety of civilians. The representative of the Russian Federation said that the vote had exposed all those for whom politicizing the humanitarian file was more important than helping the United Nations to provide humanitarian aid to Ukrainians in need.

[723] France, Ghana, Mexico, Ireland, Brazil and United Arab Emirates.

[724] For more information on the relations between the Council and the General Assembly, see part IV, sect. I.

[725] For more information on the discussion, see part II, sect. VII.

Meetings: letter dated 13 April 2014 from the Permanent Representative of the Russian Federation to the United Nations addressed to the President of the Security Council (S/2014/264), 2022

Meeting record and date	*Sub-item*	*Other documents*	*Rule 37 invitations*	*Rule 39 and other invitations*	*Speakers*	*Decision and vote (for-against-abstaining)*
S/PV.8968 17 February			Germany, Ukraine	Under-Secretary-General for Political and Peacebuilding Affairs, Special Representative of the Organization for Security and Cooperation in Europe (OSCE) Chairperson-in-Office in Ukraine and in the Trilateral Contact Group, Chief Monitor of the OSCE Special Monitoring Mission in Ukraine, Ukrainian civil society representative.	All Council members,[a] all invitees[b]	
S/PV.9002 23 March		Draft resolution submitted by Belarus, Democratic People's Republic of Korea, Syrian Arab Republic (S/2022/231)	Belarus, Democratic People's Republic of Korea, Syrian Arab Republic		13 Council members,[c] all invitees	Not adopted 2-0-13[d]

[a] The Russian Federation (President of the Council) was represented by its Deputy Minister for Foreign Affairs; the United Kingdom was represented by its Minister of State for Europe and North America; and the United States was represented by its Secretary of State.

[b] The Special Representative of the OSCE Chairperson-in-Office in Ukraine and in the Trilateral Contact Group, the Chief Monitor of the OSCE Special Monitoring Mission in Ukraine and the civil society representative participated in the meeting by videoconference.

[c] France, United Kingdom, Albania, Ghana, Mexico, Ireland, Norway, Brazil, China, Gabon, Russian Federation, United Arab Emirates, United States and Mexico.

[d] *For*: China and Russian Federation; *against*: none; *abstaining*: Albania, Brazil, France, Gabon, Ghana, India, Ireland, Kenya, Mexico, Norway, United Arab Emirates, United Kingdom, United States.

C. Maintenance of peace and security of Ukraine

During the period under review, on 11 April, the Council introduced a new item entitled "Maintenance of peace and security of Ukraine".[726] In connection with this item, the Council held 18 public meetings in 2022, most of which took the form of briefings. In addition, the Council issued one presidential statement[727] and failed to adopt a draft resolution,[728] owing to the negative vote of a permanent member. More information on the meetings, including on participants, speakers and outcomes,

[726] For more information, see part II, sect. II.A.

[727] See S/PV.9028 and S/PRST/2022/3.

[728] See S/PV.9143.

is provided in the table below. Council members also held informal consultations of the whole in connection with this item.[729]

At the first meeting under this item, held on 11 April,[730] Council members discussed the scope of the item. The representative of the Russian Federation said that his delegation was not against adding the item to the agenda of the Council's meeting, having concluded that it covered all kinds of aspects of the situation in Ukraine and was, therefore, in essence universal in character. In this regard, he proposed deleting the two other items pertaining to Ukraine from the matters of which the Council is seized, namely the letters from the Russian Federation and Ukraine dating from 2014 (S/2014/264 and S/2014/136, respectively), which reflected common sense, as well as the current situation. Bearing in mind the foregoing, he called on the presidency of the Council to take the procedural steps necessary to formalize adding the new item and deleting the two older ones. By contrast, the representative of the United States clarified that the meeting had been proposed without prejudice to the items in relation to the letters of 2014. She added that, while the scope of the situation in Ukraine had grown far beyond the circumstances in 2014, it was important to recognize its history, and it was possible that Member States would wish to focus on Crimea during future meetings. Against that backdrop, she said that the earlier items must remain in place. In response, she noted that the process for removing items was normally governed by the Council's latest note by the President (S/2017/507) on its working methods and usually took three years. Given the split views heard, she proposed that the issue be discussed separately and that agreement be sought on a way forward in the coming days.[731]

Briefings and deliberations under this item were focused on a broad range of topics, principally the political, security and humanitarian aspects of the conflict in Ukraine, including the political process to end the conflict; the deteriorating humanitarian situation in the country; the reports of attacks on nuclear facilities; and the implementation and extension of the Initiative on the Safe Transportation of Grain and Foodstuffs from Ukrainian Ports and the impact of the war on global food insecurity. Briefings and discussions also covered the mass displacement of population and the refugee crisis, allegations of war crimes, human rights violations and atrocity crimes. In addition to Council members, Ukraine participated in most of the meetings under this item under rule 37 of the provisional rules of procedure. Also invited under rule 37 of the provisional rules of procedure were the following Member States: Belarus, Czechia, Estonia, Germany, Greece, Italy, Latvia, Lithuania, Poland, Republic of Moldova, Romania, Slovakia, Sweden and Türkiye.

In 2022, the Council heard three briefings by the Secretary-General,[732] eight briefings by the Under-Secretary-General for Political and Peacebuilding Affairs[733] and two briefings by the Under-Secretary-General for Humanitarian Affairs and Emergency Relief Coordinator.[734] The Council also heard briefings by the Executive Director of the United Nations Entity for Gender Equality and the Empowerment of Women (UN-Women), the Director of the Office of Emergency Programmes of United Nations Children's Fund (UNICEF), the United Nations Deputy High Commissioner for Refugees, the Director General of the International Organization for Migration (IOM), the United Nations High Commissioner for Human Rights, the Assistant Secretary-General for Humanitarian Affairs and Deputy Emergency Relief Coordinator, the Deputy Executive Director for Programmes at UNICEF, the Special Representative of the Secretary-General on Sexual Violence in Conflict, the Special Adviser on the Prevention of Genocide, the Assistant Secretary-General for Human Rights, the Prosecutor of the International Criminal Court and the United Nations Resident and Humanitarian Coordinator in Ukraine. During the period under review, the Council also heard briefings from six civil society representatives during five of its meetings.[735]

[729] See A/77/2, part II, chap. 39.A.

[730] See S/PV.9013.

[731] In 2022, all three items remained on the list of matters of which the Council was seized. For more information, see part II, sect. II.

[732] See S/PV.9027, S/PV.9115 and S/PV.9135.

[733] See S/PV.9080, S/PV.9104, S/PV.9115, S/PV.9126, S/PV.9138, S/PV.9161, S/PV.9195 and S/PV.9202.

[734] See S/PV.9027 and S/PV.9208.

[735] See S/PV.9013, S/PV.9027, S/PV.9056, S/PV.9069 and S/PV.9126.

At the meeting held on 11 April,[736] the Executive Director of UN-Women reported on her recent visit to the Republic of Moldova and on the impact of the war on civilians, women and children specifically. She also described the efforts of neighbouring countries and civil society partners in receiving Ukrainian refugees to ensure that basic needs were met and services provided. The Executive Director highlighted that women continued to serve and lead their communities and support internally displaced persons and stressed that it was vital that they be consulted and engaged in all decisions related to the crisis and to peace. At the same meeting, the Director of the Office of Emergency Programmes of UNICEF said with reference to his recent mission to Ukraine that he had rarely seen so much damage caused in so little time, adding that the attack on Kramatorsk train station had been particularly horrifying. The station had been a critical route for thousands of families fleeing Donetsk oblast, an area that had seen some of the worst violence and destruction of the war. When the station was attacked, it was filled with families desperate to escape, which he denounced as a blatant disregard for civilian lives and international humanitarian law. He said that children, families and communities were under attack, adding that of the 3.2 million children estimated to have remained in their homes nearly half could be at risk of not having enough food. Attacks on the water system infrastructure and power outages had left an estimated 1.4 million people without access to water in Ukraine, and another 4.6 million people had only limited access. He reported that hundreds of schools and educational facilities had been attacked or used for military purposes and expressed concern about the widespread presence of explosive remnants of war, which exposed children to the risk of death and horrendous injury.

In her briefing at the meeting held on 19 April,[737] the United Nations Deputy High Commissioner for Refugees provided an update on the situation of Ukrainian refugees in receiving countries and displaced persons within Ukraine. The Deputy High Commissioner reported that in Ukraine the vast majority of people on the move were women and children and the risk of gender-based violence, trafficking and sexual exploitation and abuse was high. At the same meeting, the Director General of IOM expressed concern about the continued deterioration of the humanitarian situation in Ukraine and appealed to the parties to the conflict to honour all their obligations under international humanitarian law to protect civilians and their homes and civilian infrastructure. He highlighted specific risks for internally displaced persons, refugees and third-country nationals, including a negative psychological impact and mental health problems, and the concerning situation of women and children vulnerable to trafficking, violence, including sexual violence, exploitation and abuse.

At the meeting held on 5 May,[738] the Secretary-General addressed the Council on his recent visit to the Russian Federation and Ukraine, during which he met with the President of the Russian Federation on 26 April and the President of Ukraine on 28 April. He explained that, as part of his visit, he had also held discussions with the President of Türkiye in Ankara and the President of Poland in Rzeszów, stating that he had said the same thing in Moskow, Kyiv and New York, namely that the Russian invasion of Ukraine was a violation of its territorial integrity and of the Charter. He emphasized the importance of humanitarian access and evacuations and the establishment of safe corridors and discussed the global impact of the war on energy markets and financial systems, leading to the establishment of the Global Crisis Response Group on Food, Energy and Finance to address those challenges. Following the Secretary-General, the Under-Secretary-General for Humanitarian Affairs and Emergency Relief Coordinator focused on the increased threat of gender-based violence and allegations of sexual violence. He also highlighted the efforts of the United Nations and its partners in responding to humanitarian needs, including assisting displaced persons, restoring basic services and negotiating aid delivery and safe evacuations for civilians in active conflict areas. At the same meeting, the United Nations High Commissioner for Human Rights gave a briefing to the Council on the allegations of violations of international human rights law and international humanitarian law in the context of the Russian armed attack on Ukraine. She also reported to the Council on the arbitrary detention and possible forced disappearances of civilians and the ill-treatment and summary execution of prisoners of war committed

[736] See S/PV.9013.

[737] See S/PV.9018.

[738] See S/PV.9027.

by both parties, and urged the parties to the conflict to investigate all violations of international human rights law and international humanitarian law allegedly committed by their armed forces.

At the meeting held on 12 May,[739] the Assistant Secretary-General for Humanitarian Affairs and Deputy Emergency Relief Coordinator provided an update on joint efforts by the United Nations to negotiate humanitarian pauses to allow safe passage for civilians trapped in the fighting. She stressed that, under international humanitarian law, the parties must respect all civilians and essential infrastructure, and she urged them to remove any barriers to the movement of humanitarian staff to ensure the continued delivery of life-saving assistance across Ukraine. At the same meeting, the Deputy Executive Director for Programmes at UNICEF said that, like all wars, the war in Ukraine was a child protection and child rights crisis. In that regard, he informed the Council about the verified cases of child death, injuries, displacement and grave child rights violations and attacks on schools and critical infrastructure, including hospitals and water and sanitation systems.

In her briefing at the meeting held on 6 June,[740] the Special Representative of the Secretary-General on Sexual Violence in Conflict described the mounting allegations of conflict-related sexual violence, occurring against women, girls, men and boys. In that regard, she acknowledged and commended the leadership of the Ukrainian authorities in their agreement on a framework of cooperation with the United Nations on the prevention and response to conflict-related sexual violence. The framework would serve as the basis for a comprehensive and multifaceted preventive and service response and more effective coordination of all stakeholders, including the United Nations agencies in Ukraine and neighbouring countries. It was aimed at strengthening the rule of law, accountability and the capacity of the security and defence sector to prevent sexual violence. It was also focused on ensuring that survivors of sexual violence and their children had access to comprehensive services, that sexual violence was addressed in the framework of a ceasefire agreement and that such crimes were ultimately reflected in the specific provisions of any peace agreement. She also stressed the equal and meaningful participation of women in all political processes, including negotiations for peace. In connection with other aspects of the framework, she emphasized the action required to address conflict-related trafficking in persons for the purposes of sexual exploitation and prostitution. She drew attention to the human trafficking dimensions of women and children fleeing the conflict, who were targeted for trafficking and exploitation, and protection challenges to address the pace and volume of displacement. Underlining that the framework of cooperation made women and girls in conflict settings an explicit priority, she called for the solidarity of the Council and the international donor community to support the Ukrainian authorities and relevant United Nations entities to implement the framework.

At the meeting held on 21 June,[741] the Special Adviser on the Prevention of Genocide provided a briefing on the topic of incitement to violence, leading to atrocity crimes. In that regard, she informed Council members about serious allegations, including indications of the possible commission of genocide and war crimes, in Ukraine. She reminded the Council that the prevention of genocide, crimes against humanity and war crimes was a legal obligation for States under international law.

The Under-Secretary-General for Political and Peacebuilding Affairs did not address the Council until June. During her eight briefings, she focused on the ongoing political, security and humanitarian challenges facing Ukraine and the multidimensional threats beyond its borders. She also provided updates in connection with the attacks on civilians and critical civilian infrastructure and the mass displacement of the population.

During her briefing at the meeting held on 28 June,[742] the Under-Secretary-General emphasized that the work of the Independent International Commission of Inquiry on Ukraine established by the Human Rights Council, the Prosecutor of the International Criminal Court and other fact-finding efforts were essential to establishing accountability for the crimes and atrocities committed during the war and to prevent such violations in the future. On 29 July, the Under-Secretary-General focused on, among other topics, developments relating to the Black Sea Initiative, noting that it was a sign of possible

---

[739] See S/PV.9032.

[740] See S/PV.9056.

[741] See S/PV.9069.

[742] See S/PV.9080.

dialogue between the parties.[743] She also underlined that despite the encouraging developments on grain and fertilizer, the lack of prospects for a shift towards a meaningful resumption of diplomatic efforts to end the war remained concerning and the escalatory rhetoric from any side was not consistent with the constructive spirit demonstrated at the signing of the agreement in Istanbul.

At the meeting held on 24 August,[744] the Secretary-General provided an update on the progress of the Black Sea Initiative, commending Ukraine, the Russian Federation and Türkiye for their constructive approach and efforts and calling for a significant increase in support for developing countries to capitalize on the opportunities of the Initiative. He expressed concern about the ongoing fighting in Ukraine and the situation surrounding the Zaporizhzhia nuclear power plant and highlighted allegations of violations of international humanitarian law and violations of abuses of human rights related to armed conflict. Following the Secretary-General, the Under-Secretary-General for Political and Peacebuilding Affairs said that the war was weakening the foundations of the international system and voiced concern at the reports of human rights violations and the arbitrary detention and forced disappearances of civilians, including local authorities, journalists and civil society activists.

At the meeting held on 7 September,[745] the Under-Secretary-General for Political and Peacebuilding Affairs focused during her briefing on the large-scale displacement of the population, highlighting that Ukrainian women, who constituted half the refugees, continued to face significantly increased security risks, including sexual and gender-based violence, trafficking, exploitation and abuse. At the same meeting, she expressed concern at the reports of attacks in the vicinity of the Zaporizhzhia nuclear power plant and urged all concerned to provide maximum cooperation with IAEA. Following the Under-Secretary-General, the Assistant Secretary-General for Human Rights reported that armed attacks by the Russian Federation in Ukraine, along with human rights violations in territories occupied by Russian or controlled by affiliated armed forces groups, had led to people fleeing to various regions, including territories under Russian control and to the Russian Federation itself. Her briefing highlighted credible allegations of forced transfers of unaccompanied children to Russian occupied areas and concerns about granting Russian citizenship to such children without parental consent, in violation of the Geneva Convention relative to the Protection of Civilian Persons in Time of War. Civilians were subjected to so-called filtration, a system of security checks and personal data collection, resulting in numerous human rights violations, including arbitrary detention, torture, ill-treatment and enforced disappearance. She urged the Russian Federation to provide unimpeded access to international monitors for all places of detention under their control and to allow representatives of human rights and humanitarian organizations to safely access conflict-affected individuals in the Russian Federation and occupied areas in Ukraine.

At a meeting held on 22 September,[746] the Secretary-General expressed concern at the reports of plans to organize so-called referendums in areas of Ukraine that were not under government control at that time. He underlined that any annexation of a State's territory by another State resulting from the threat or use of force was a violation of the Charter and international law. Following the Secretary-General, the Prosecutor of the International Criminal Court briefed the Council on the ongoing investigations in Ukraine. He underlined the fact that 43 States parties to the Rome Statute, one third of the Assembly of States Parties, referred the matter to the Court signifying not only the nature of the crisis and the concern expressed but also an understanding that the law had an important role to play.

During her briefing at the meeting held on 27 September,[747] the Under-Secretary-General reported on the so-called referendums conducted by de facto authorities in the Donetsk, Luhansk, Kherson and Zaporizhzhia regions, underlining that given that those exercises had been held during active armed conflict they could not be called a genuine expression of the popular will and could not be regarded as legal under international law. She noted the alarming rhetoric regarding the use of nuclear weapons, which she deemed inconsistent with the joint statement of the leaders of the five nuclear weapon States on preventing nuclear war and avoiding an arms race.

[743] See S/PV.9104.
[744] See S/PV.9115.
[745] See S/PV.9126.
[746] See S/PV.9135.
[747] See S/PV.9138.

At the meeting held on 21 October,[748] the Under-Secretary-General for Political and Peacebuilding Affairs informed the Council that the Russian Federation had launched a series of attacks on cities and towns across the country and expressed grave concern about the destruction of critical energy infrastructure. She reported that, based on the report to the General Assembly submitted by the Independent International Commission of Inquiry on Ukraine, there were grounds to conclude that war crimes and violations of human rights and international humanitarian law had been committed in Ukraine since 24 February. She also expressed concern about the announcements of the Russian Federation to introduce martial law in the regions of Ukraine under its temporary military control and about the evacuation in Kherson amid intensified fighting on the ground. On the Black Sea Initiative, she noted that the agreement had helped to lower and stabilize global food prices and to move grain from one of the world's breadbaskets to those in need and emphasized the critical nature of its extension for the maintenance of food security worldwide. Following the Under-Secretary-General, the United Nations Resident and Humanitarian Coordinator in Ukraine provided a briefing about the human toll of the war, the new dimensions of the humanitarian crisis and the challenge of access to non-government-controlled areas. With particular emphasis on the urgent need for humanitarian assistance and greater access to deliver aid, she underlined that, despite the challenges, humanitarian efforts had been made to provide assistance, but more support was needed to alleviate the suffering of the affected population.

At the meeting held on 16 November,[749] the Under-Secretary-General for Political and Peacebuilding Affairs said that Ukrainians had suffered some of the most intense bombardments of the war, noting that Russian missiles and drones had rained down on Kyiv, Mykolayiv, Chernihiv, Cherkasy, Zhytomyr, Sumy, Kharkiv, Lviv, Poltava and elsewhere, destroying or damaging homes and severely disrupting critical services. She added that the military dynamics on the ground continued to evolve, with no end to the war in sight. She also said that allegations of atrocities and human rights violations in Ukraine during the war were extensive and highlighted grave concerns about the rights, safety and security of the youngest Ukrainians, including reports of forced transfers of children, including of some under institutionalized care, to Russian-occupied territory or to the Russian Federation. She also expressed concern at the conditions of prisoners of war and affirmed that the extension of the Black Sea Initiative remained critical in order to avoid a food crisis for millions of people. She added that the risk of a nuclear incident in the context of the open hostilities in Ukraine remained an unacceptable danger, and echoed the serious concerns expressed by numerous Member States in that regard.

During her briefing at the meeting held on 23 November,[750] the Under-Secretary-General reported on a new wave of missile and drone strikes in Ukraine. She said that attacks targeting civilians and civilian infrastructure were prohibited under international humanitarian law, as well as attacks on military objectives that might be expected to cause harm to civilians that would be excessive in relation to the concrete and direct military advantage anticipated. In that regard, she said that the United Nations strongly condemned the attacks and demanded that the Russian Federation immediately ceased such actions. She also expressed the deep remaining concern about the situation at the Zaporizhzhia nuclear power plant and said that the reported shelling at the plant the previous weekend had been reckless and deplorable. Amid the dark news, she mentioned a positive development, namely that the parties had reported yet another prisoner exchange. At the last meeting under this item in 2022, held on 6 December,[751] the Under-Secretary-General for Humanitarian Affairs and Emergency Relief Coordinator focused on the widespread death, destruction, displacement and suffering caused by the war, the ongoing humanitarian operations and the challenges that the humanitarian community continued to face amid winter temperatures. Gender-based violence targeting women and girls continued to be pervasive and underreported. While there had been an improvement in humanitarian access in eastern and southern oblasts, the biggest challenge remained the impediments to reaching areas in Donetsk, Luhansk, Kherson and Zaporizhzhia.

In 2022, the deliberations in the Council under this item were focused principally on the political, security and humanitarian developments in the context of the armed conflict in Ukraine as well as on the

[748] See S/PV.9161.

[749] See S/PV.9195.

[750] See S/PV.9202.

[751] See S/PV.9208.

possible accountability concerning the alleged war crimes and violations and abuses of human rights and violations of international humanitarian law committed in Ukraine.

Insofar as it concerns the political situation, Council members called for de-escalation and peaceful resolution of the conflict by returning to diplomacy and political dialogue. On 6 May, the Council held a meeting to issue a presidential statement,[752] in which it expressed deep concern regarding the maintenance of peace and security of Ukraine, recalled that all Member States had undertaken, under the Charter, the obligation to settle their international disputes by peaceful means and expressed strong support for the efforts of the Secretary-General in the search for a peaceful solution. In addition, Council members addressed the so-called referendums conducted by the Russian Federation in eastern and southern Ukraine. In this connection, on 30 September, the Council voted on a draft resolution[753] submitted by Albania and the United States. In the text of the draft resolution, the Council would have condemned the illegal referendums, called upon all States not to recognize any alteration of the status of the Ukrainian regions of Luhansk, Donetsk, Kherson or Zaporizhzhia and decided that the Russian Federation should immediately withdraw its troops from Ukraine. The draft resolution was not adopted owing to the negative vote of a permanent member of the Council.[754] Speaking prior to the vote as co-penholder of the draft resolution, together with Albania, the representative of the United States underlined that that was exactly what the Council was made to do – defend sovereignty, protect territorial integrity and promote peace and security – and urged all members to vote in favour.[755] The representative of the United Kingdom also spoke before the vote, urging condemnation of Russian actions and a vote in favour of the draft resolution as members of the Council with the responsibility of maintaining international peace and security. In reference to the draft resolution, the representative of the Russian Federation argued instead that such openly hostile actions on the part of the West were a refusal to engage and cooperate within the Council. He noted that the Council had had the opportunity to adopt a truly balanced and useful document. He also stated that the authors of the draft resolution were prepared to devalue the efforts of the Council as the principal organ for the maintenance of peace and security and brazenly used the forum as a dress rehearsal before their main performance in the General Assembly. After the vote, some members[756] criticized the use of the veto by the Russian Federation, while most also expressed support for and commitment to the sovereignty and territorial integrity of Ukraine. In explaining their abstentions, the representatives of India, China, Brazil and Gabon expressed support for a diplomatic and negotiated solution to the conflict. The representative of China also recalled his country's position on the conflict, including that the legitimate security concerns of all parties should be taken seriously. He added that any action taken by the Council should be truly conducive to easing the situation and resolving the crisis, rather than intensifying conflict and exacerbating confrontation. He also expressed the view that facts had shown that political isolation, sanctions and pressure, stoking tensions and bloc confrontation would not bring about peace. The representative of Brazil explained that the scope and language of the draft resolution did not favour an environment conducive to a solution to the conflict in Ukraine. Having voted in favour, the representative of Kenya acknowledged that the draft resolution, whether in the Council or the Assembly, would not solve the crisis, adding that his country's affirmative vote was based on his country's principled defence of the Charter and, in particular, its protection of the principle of the sovereignty and territorial integrity of all Member States. Council members also deliberated on the implications of the war vis-à-vis the Charter during other meetings. Some delegations underlined that the situation in Ukraine was a violation of Article 2 of the Charter[757] and stressed the role of the Council in

[752] See S/PRST/2022/3. For more information concerning the decisions of the Council relating to Chapter VI of the Charter in 2022, see part VI, sect. IV.

[753] S/2022/720.

[754] Pursuant to General Assembly resolution 76/262 of 26 April 2022, the Council submitted a special report to the Assembly on the use of the veto at the meeting (A/77/551). For more information, see part IV, sect. I.F.

[755] See S/PV.9143.

[756] Norway, United Kingdom, Ireland, Ghana and France.

[757] See S/PV.9104 (Albania, United States, Norway, Mexico and Latvia); S/PV.9115 (Mexico); S/PV.9135 (Mexico and Ireland); and S/PV.9138 (Mexico and Norway). For more information on the discussions concerning Article 2 (4) of the Charter, see part III, sect. II.

conflict resolution[758] and its responsibility to maintain international peace and security.[759] Several delegations also drew attention to the situation in Ukraine as a threat to international peace and security[760] and to the right of Ukraine to self-defence, under Article 51 of the Charter.[761] Several Council members also recognized the negotiation efforts of the United Nations and its partners with the parties to the conflict, in particular the Secretary-General's visits to Moscow and Kyiv, to create conditions for a solution to the ongoing security and humanitarian situation.[762]

Regarding the security and humanitarian situation, Council members discussed during the year the protection of civilians and critical infrastructure and human rights in the context of the war in Ukraine. Members underlined that attacks against civilians and critical infrastructure were in violation of international law,[763] and those responsible for the committed war atrocities must be held accountable.[764] On 16 November, after the latest launch of air and missile bombardments against critical civilian infrastructure in Ukrainian cities, some delegations emphasized the responsibility of the Russian Federation in creating the current humanitarian and displacement crisis and called on the country to cease hostilities.[765] Focusing attention on the deepening humanitarian catastrophe in Ukraine, speakers urged the parties to guarantee access to humanitarian aid for people in need and to essential services, which had been disrupted by the conflict.[766] Council members also focused on addressing and preventing national, racial or religious hatred as potential triggers for the commission of atrocity crimes in a debate on disinformation campaigns, propaganda and hate speech online and in the mainstream media.[767]

In their discussions concerning the alleged war crimes and violations and abuses of human rights and violations of international humanitarian law committed in Ukraine, in 2022, Council members stressed the importance of establishing facts and ensuring accountability. They expressed support for the investigation launched by national authorities and the International Criminal Court,[768] for the establishment by the Human Rights Council of the Independent International Commission of Inquiry and for the establishment by the Secretary-General of the fact-finding mission to Olenivka.[769] On 12 May, Council members pointed out severe conflict-related effects on education and expressed concern about the risks of human trafficking, sexual exploitation and abuse faced by unaccompanied children seeking refuge.[770] Many speakers condemned attacks against schools[771] and called on the Secretary-General and his Special Representative for Children in Armed Conflict to record the situation in Ukraine in the forthcoming report on children and armed conflict, listing those responsible for violations against children.[772] On 6 June, during

---

[758] See S/PV.9018 (Ukraine); S/PV.9135 (Ghana); S/PV.9138 (United Arab Emirates); and S/PV.9143 (China).

[759] See S/PV.9018 (Kenya and Ukraine); S/PV.9032 (Kenya); S/PV.9080 (Ukraine and Poland); S/PV.9104 (United Arab Emirates and Ghana); S/PV.9115 (United Kingdom and United Arab Emirates); S/PV.9135 (Norway, Mexico, United States, Ireland, Brazil, Czechia and Poland); S/PV.9143 (United States, United Kingdom and Ukraine); and S/PV.9161 (Ireland). For more information on the functions and powers of the Council, see part V.

[760] See S/PV.9056 (Ukraine); S/PV.9104 (Kenya); S/PV.9115 (Russian Federation); S/PV.9126 (Kenya); S/PV.9135 (Ukraine); and S/PV.9143 (Norway). For information on threats to international peace and security considered by the Council in 2022, see part VII, sect. I.

[761] See S/PV.9135 (Norway, United States, Ghana and Ukraine); S/PV.9138 (France); S/PV.9161 (France); S/PV.9080 (United Kingdom); and S/PV.9195 (United States, France, United Kingdom and Estonia). For more details on Article 51 of the Charter, see part VII, sect. X.A.

[762] See S/PV.9027 (Albania, Mexico, Ghana, China, Kenya, Brazil, Ireland, United Arab Emirates, Gabon, Norway and India); S/PV.9115 (Albania, Norway, United Kingdom, Brazil, Kenya, United Arab Emirates, Ghana, Mexico and China); and S/PV.9135 (Norway, Mexico, United States, China, Ireland).

[763] See S/PV.9161 (Mexico, France, Kenya, United States, Ireland, Ghana and Norway); and S/PV.9208 (France, Brazil, Norway, Ghana and Albania).

[764] See S/PV.9161 (France, Ireland, Ghana and Norway); S/PV.9069 (United States, United Kingdom, Norway, Kenya, Ireland, Mexico, United Arab Emirates, Gabon and Ghana); and S/PV.9208 (Mexico, Norway, Ireland and Albania).

[765] See S/PV.9195 (Albania, United Kingdom, Ireland, Ghana, Ukraine and European Union).

[766] Ibid. (Mexico, Ireland, Ghana, Norway, Gabon, Ukraine, Estonia and European Union).

[767] See S/PV.9069 (United Kingdom, Norway, France, Kenya, Ireland, Mexico and Ghana).

[768] See S/PV.9027 (Mexico, France, Ireland, Norway and United States).

[769] See S/PV.9069 (United States, Mexico and United Arab Emirates). For more details on the discussion, see part VI, sect. II.

[770] See S/PV.9032 (Mexico, Norway, Brazil and China).

[771] Ibid. (France, Ghana, Kenya, Russian Federation, Poland and Slovakia).

[772] Ibid. (Mexico, France, Albania, Ireland, United States and Ukraine).

a discussion focused on conflict-related sexual violence and human trafficking, most Council members expressed support for the new framework of cooperation on preventing and responding to conflict-related sexual violence, signed by the United Nations and the Government of Ukraine.[773] In their remarks on forced displacement and deportations of Ukrainian civilians and "filtration" operations by the Russian and Russian-affiliated forces on 7 September, most members called for access for United Nations agencies to the so-called filtration centres and to places of forced deportation and relocation for an investigation to ensure accountability and to provide humanitarian assistance.[774]

In addition to the deliberations in the Council on the political, security and humanitarian situation in Ukraine, in 2022, Council members also focused on the effect of the conflict beyond the borders of Ukraine in the light of the mass displacement of the population and the impact on the global food supply. Against the backdrop of mass displacement in Ukraine, the influx of refugees in neighbouring countries and Ukrainians returning home, most delegations commended the neighbouring countries and welcomed the efforts of the United Nations and its partners in assisting the affected people,[775] and expressed support for the Secretary-General's call for an urgent humanitarian pause to enable humanitarian corridors.[776] At the same meeting, some Council members[777] stressed the need for the host countries to ensure protection for third-country nationals and avoid discrimination based on race and ethnicity. Concerning the global food insecurity resulting from the conflict, most Council members highlighted the signing of the Black Sea Initiative, encouraging the parties in support of its renewal and implementation and expressing hope for continuing dialogue and negotiations.[778] At a meeting on 19 April, members also exchanged views about the implications of unilateral sanctions imposed on the Russian Federation on food insecurity and on the energy crisis worldwide, bringing attention to the negative impact on countries in the developing world.[779] Referring to the findings of the Global Crisis Response Group on Food, Energy and Finance established by the Secretary-General to mobilize United Nations agencies, multilateral development banks and other international institutions to help countries faced with such challenges, the representative of India welcomed the recommendations of the Group on exempting purchases of food for humanitarian assistance by WFP from export restrictions,[780] while the representative Kenya stated that States should resist export restrictions and make reserves available to countries with serious food insecurity.[781] On 29 July, the representative of Kenya underlined that the recommendations and solutions of the Group should receive sufficient financial and operational support and be a bridge to longer-term ambitious reforms and initiatives.[782]

In 2022, Council members also deliberated on the military and security situation in and around Ukrainian nuclear sites, in particular the Zaporizhzhia and Chernobyl nuclear power plants, and the work of IAEA in preventing the risks of nuclear accidents.[783] On 24 August, the representatives of France and Ireland called on the Russian Federation to withdraw its forces from the Zaporizhzhia power plant and the representative of Gabon called on the parties to comply with nuclear security rules and cooperate with IAEA.[784] On 23 November, several members expressed support for the establishment of a security zone

[773] See S/PV.9056 (Mexico, United States, China, Norway, Gabon, Kenya, United Arab Emirates and Ireland).

[774] See S/PV.9126 (Albania, United States, United Kingdom, Ghana, Kenya, Mexico, Ireland, Gabon and France).

[775] See S/PV.9018 (Mexico, Gabon, Norway, Ghana, Albania, Kenya, United Arab Emirates, Ukraine and Estonia).

[776] Ibid. (Mexico, France, Norway, China, United States, Albania, Ghana, United Arab Emirates, United Kingdom, Ukraine, Sweden, Estonia and Slovakia).

[777] Ibid. (Ireland, Mexico, France, Gabon, Norway, United States, Brazil and Ghana).

[778] See S/PV.9104 (Ireland and Gabon); S/PV.9115 (Norway, Brazil, Gabon, Kenya, Ghana, Mexico and China); S/PV.9135 (Norway, Mexico and Ghana); S/PV.9138 (China and Kenya); S/PV.9161 (Mexico, France, China, United States, United Kingdom and Norway); S/PV.9195 (United States, Albania, France, United Kingdom, United Arab Emirates, Mexico, Kenya, India, Ireland, Brazil, China, Norway and Ghana); S/PV.9202 (Norway, United Arab Emirates, Mexico, Kenya, China and Ghana); and S/PV.9208 (Mexico, Gabon, China, Norway and United Arab Emirates).

[779] See S/PV.9018 (Russian Federation, China, Brazil and Kenya).

[780] See S/PV.9018, S/PV.9027 and S/PV.9080.

[781] See S/PV.9032.

[782] See S/PV.9104.

[783] See S/PV.9115 (France, Ireland, Brazil and Gabon); S/PV.9126 (China); S/PV.9135 (Russian Federation); S/PV.9195 (France and Mexico); and S/PV.9102 (China, Russian Federation and Ghana).

[784] See S/PV.9115 (France, Ireland and Gabon).

in and around the Zaporizhzhia power plant as recommended by IAEA,[785] while the representative of the United States underlined that Russian attacks on infrastructure supporting the safety of the Ukrainian nuclear power plants cast doubts on the seriousness with which it was engaging on the prospects of a protection zone around the Zaporizhzhia nuclear power plant.

Developments in Ukraine were also considered under the items "Letter dated 28 February 2014 from the Permanent Representative of Ukraine to the United Nations addressed to the President of the Security Council (S/2014/136)", "Letter dated 13 April 2014 from the Permanent Representative of the Russian Federation to the United Nations addressed to the President of the Security Council (S/2014/264)" and "Threats to international peace and security".[786]

Meetings: maintenance of peace and security of Ukraine, 2022

Meeting record and date	*Sub-item*	*Other documents*	*Rule 37 invitations*	*Rule 39 and other invitations*	*Speakers*	*Decision and vote (for-against-abstaining)*
S/PV.9013 11 April			Germany, Poland, Romania, Ukraine	Executive Director of the United Nations Entity for Gender Equality and the Empowerment of Women (UN-Women), Director of the Office of Emergency Programmes of the United Nations Children's Fund (UNICEF), President of La Strada-Ukraine	All Council members,[a] all invitees[b]	
S/PV.9018 19 April			Six Member States[c]	United Nations Deputy High Commissioner for Refugees, Director General of the International Organization for Migration (IOM)	All Council members,[d] all invitees[e]	
S/PV.9027 5 May			Seven Member States[f]	Under-Secretary-General for Humanitarian Affairs and Emergency Relief Coordinator, United Nations High Commissioner for Human Rights, Advocacy Coordinator at Right to Protection	Secretary-General, all Council members, all invitees[g]	
S/PV.9028 6 May						S/PRST/2022/3

[785] See S/PV.9202 (Albania, Norway, Mexico and Ghana).

[786] See sects. 19.A and 19.B. above and sect. 34 below.

Meeting record and date	*Sub-item*	*Other documents*	*Rule 37 invitations*	*Rule 39 and other invitations*	*Speakers*	*Decision and vote (for-against-abstaining)*
S/PV.9032 12 May			Estonia, Poland, Slovakia, Ukraine	Assistant Secretary-General for Humanitarian Affairs and Deputy Emergency Relief Coordinator, Deputy Executive Director for Programmes at UNICEF	All Council members, all invitees[h]	
S/PV.9056 6 June			Six Member States[i]	Special Representative of the Secretary-General on Sexual Violence in Conflict, President of the European Council, co-founder and Director on Strategic Development of the Ukrainian Women's Fund, President of Sesame Workshop	All Council members, all invitees[j]	
S/PV.9069 21 June			Lithuania, Slovakia, Ukraine	Special Adviser on the Prevention of Genocide, Head of the Centre for Strategic Communication and Information Security, Chief Executive Officer of Jigsaw and Adjunct Senior Fellow at the Council on Foreign Relations	All Council members, all invitees[k]	
S/PV.9080 28 June			Estonia, Poland, Ukraine	Under-Secretary-General for Political and Peacebuilding Affairs	All Council members, all invitees[h,l]	
S/PV.9104 29 July			Seven Member States[m]	Under-Secretary-General for Political and Peacebuilding Affairs, Chargé d'affaires a.i. of the Delegation of the European Union to the United Nations	All Council members, all invitees[n]	
S/PV.9115 24 August			Ukraine	Under-Secretary-General for Political and Peacebuilding Affairs, Chargé d'affaires a.i. of the Delegation of the European Union	Secretary-General, all Council members, all invitees[l]	Procedural vote (rule 37) 13-1-1[o]

Meeting record and date	*Sub-item*	*Other documents*	*Rule 37 invitations*	*Rule 39 and other invitations*	*Speakers*	*Decision and vote (for-against-abstaining)*
S/PV.9126 7 September			Italy, Latvia, Poland, Slovakia, Ukraine	Under-Secretary-General for Political and Peacebuilding Affairs, Assistant Secretary-General for Human Rights, Coordinator for International Cooperation at the Center for Civil Liberties	All Council members, all invitees[n,p]	
S/PV.9135 22 September			Seven Member States[q]	Prosecutor of the International Criminal Court, High Representative of the European Union for Foreign Affairs and Security Policy	Secretary-General, all Council members,[r] six invitees under rule 37,[s] all other invitees	
S/PV.9138 27 September			Ukraine	Under-Secretary-General for Political and Peacebuilding Affairs	All Council members, all invitees[l]	
S/PV.9143 30 September		Draft resolution submitted by Albania, United States (S/2022/720)	Ukraine		All Council members, invitee	Not adopted 10-1-4[t]
S/PV.9161 21 October			Germany, Greece, Poland, Slovakia, Ukraine	Under-Secretary-General for Political and Peacebuilding Affairs, United Nations Resident and Humanitarian Coordinator in Ukraine, Head of the Delegation of the European Union	All Council members, all invitees[u]	
S/PV.9195 16 November			Estonia, Poland, Slovakia, Ukraine	Under-Secretary-General for Political and Peacebuilding Affairs, Head of the Delegation of the European Union	All Council members, all invitees[h]	
S/PV.9202 23 November			Republic of Moldova, Romania, Ukraine	Under-Secretary-General for Political and Peacebuilding Affairs	All Council members, all invitees[l]	

Meeting record and date	*Sub-item*	*Other documents*	*Rule 37 invitations*	*Rule 39 and other invitations*	*Speakers*	*Decision and vote (for-against-abstaining)*
S/PV.9208 6 December			Germany, Latvia, Poland, Ukraine	Under-Secretary-General for Humanitarian Affairs, Head of the Delegation of the European Union	All Council members, all invitees[n]	

[a] The United Kingdom (President of the Council) was represented by its Minister of State for South and Central Asia, North Africa, United Nations and the Commonwealth, and the Prime Minister's Special Representative on Preventing Sexual Violence in Conflict.

[b] The President of La Strada-Ukraine participated in the meeting by videoconference.

[c] Estonia, Italy, Poland, Slovakia, Sweden and Ukraine.

[d] Ireland was represented by its Minister for Foreign Affairs and Defence.

[e] The representative of Estonia spoke on behalf of the three Baltic states; and the representative of Sweden spoke on behalf of the Nordic countries. The Deputy High Commissioner and the Director General of IOM participated in the meeting by videoconference.

[f] Germany, Greece, Italy, Latvia, Poland, Slovakia and Ukraine.

[g] Poland was represented by its Deputy Prime Minister and Minister of Culture and National Heritage. The representative of Latvia spoke on behalf of the three Baltic states. The Under-Secretary-General, the High Commissioner and the Advocacy Coordinator at Right to Protection participated in the meeting by videoconference.

[h] The representative of Estonia spoke on behalf of the three Baltic states.

[i] Germany, Italy, Latvia, Poland, Slovakia and Ukraine.

[j] The representative of Latvia spoke on behalf of the three Baltic states. The Special Representative and the co-founder and Director on Strategic Development of the Ukrainian Women's Fund participated in the meeting by videoconference.

[k] The representative of Lithuania spoke on behalf of the three Baltic states. The Head of the Centre for Strategic Communication and Information Security participated in the meeting by videoconference.

[l] Ukraine was represented by its President, who participated in the meeting by videoconference.

[m] Germany, Italy, Latvia, Poland, Romania, Slovakia and Ukraine.

[n] The representative of Latvia spoke on behalf of the three Baltic states.

[o] *For*: Albania, Brazil, France, Gabon, Ghana, India, Ireland, Kenya, Mexico, Norway, United Arab Emirates, United Kingdom, United States; *against*: Russian Federation; *abstaining*: China.

[p] The Assistant Secretary-General for Human Rights and the Coordinator for International Cooperation at the Center for Civil Liberties participated in the meeting by videoconference.

[q] Belarus, Czechia, Germany, Lithuania, Poland, Türkiye and Ukraine.

[r] Norway was represented by its Prime Minister. Albania and France (President of the Council) were represented by their respective Ministers for Europe and Foreign Affairs; Brazil, Gabon, Kenya, Mexico and the Russian Federation were represented by their respective Ministers for Foreign Affairs; China was represented by its State Councillor and Minister for Foreign Affairs; Ghana was represented by its Minister for Foreign Affairs and Regional Integrations; Ireland was represented by its Minister for Foreign Affairs and Defence; India was represented by its Minister for External Affairs; Kenya was represented by its Director General, Bilateral and Political Affairs; the United Arab Emirates was represented by its Minister of State for International Cooperation in the Ministry of Foreign Affairs and International Cooperation; the United Kingdom was represented by its Secretary of State for Foreign, Commonwealth and Development Affairs; and the United States was represented by its Secretary of State.

[s] Belarus, Czechia, Germany, Lithuania, Poland and Ukraine were represented by their respective Ministers for Foreign Affairs. The representative of Lithuania spoke on behalf of the three Baltic states. The delegation of Türkiye did not make a statement.

[t] *For*: Albania, France, Ghana, Ireland, Kenya, Mexico, Norway, United Arab Emirates, United Kingdom, United States; *against*: Russian Federation; *abstaining*: Brazil, China, Gabon, India.

[u] The Under-Secretary-General for Political and Peacebuilding Affairs participated in the meeting by videoconference.

Middle East

20. The situation in the Middle East

During the period under review, the Council held 39 meetings in relation to the item entitled "The situation in the Middle East". Consistent with prior practice, most meetings held under the item took the form of briefings.[787] More information on the meetings, including on participants, speakers and outcomes, is given in the tables below. Under the item, Council members considered a variety of topics, principally, the conflict in the Syrian Arab Republic, the conflict in Yemen, the mandate of the United Nations Disengagement Observer Force (UNDOF) and the mandate of the United Nations Interim Force in Lebanon (UNIFIL). In 2022, the Council also held three private (closed) meetings with countries contributing troops and police to UNDOF and UNIFIL.[788] In addition to the meetings, Council members held informal consultations of the whole to discuss the item.[789]

In 2022, the Council adopted a total of six resolutions in connection with the item. On 13 July, the Council extended the mandate of the United Nations Mission to Support the Hudaydah Agreement (UNMHA) for one year, until 14 July 2023.[790] On 28 February, the Council renewed the sanctions measures in relation to the situation in Yemen until 28 February 2023 and extended the mandate of the Panel of Experts on Yemen for 13 months, until 28 March 2023.[791] The Council also renewed twice the mandate of UNDOF for periods of six months each,[792] and extended the mandate of UNIFIL for a period of 12 months, until 31 August 2023.[793]

During the period under review, the meetings in relation to the conflict in the Syrian Arab Republic continued to be focused on three main aspects: the implementation of the Syrian-led and Syrian-owned political process to end the conflict; the humanitarian situation in the country, including issues related to the protection of civilians, the worsening economic crisis and humanitarian access; and the proliferation and use of chemical weapons. Briefings concerning the political process and the humanitarian situation in the Syrian Arab Republic were often given during the same meeting, whereas those on the proliferation and use of chemical weapons were given separately, in dedicated meetings.[794]

Regarding the political process, Council members heard regular monthly briefings by the Special Envoy and the Deputy Special Envoy of the Secretary-General for Syria on the efforts to reach a political solution to the conflict.[795] In that connection, in 2022, the briefings and discussions continued to be focused on the progress of the Constitutional Committee in drafting a constitutional text and on the elements necessary for the implementation of resolution 2254 (2015), such as a lasting nationwide ceasefire, the issue of detainees, abductees and missing persons, engagement with civil society representatives and women's groups, especially the Syrian Women's Advisory Board, to ensure their meaningful participation in the political process, and step-by-step confidence-building. In March, the Special Envoy, giving a briefing to the Council on the fourth day of the seventh session of the small body of the Syrian Constitutional Committee, noted that there were significant differences between the parties.[796] Furthermore, the Special Envoy continued to call for a nationwide ceasefire and a focus on

---

[787] For more information on the format of meetings, see part II.

[788] The private meetings were held on 9 June, 16 August and 7 December in connection with the item entitled "Meeting of the Security Council with the troop- and police-contributing countries pursuant to resolution 1353 (2001), annex II, sections A and B". For UNDOF, see S/PV.9060 and S/PV.9212; and for UNIFIL, see S/PV.9111. See also A/77/2, part II, chap. 21.

[789] See A/77/2, part II, chap. 2.B.

[790] Resolution 2643 (2022), para. 1.

[791] Resolution 2624 (2022), paras. 4 and 15.

[792] Resolutions 2639 (2022) and 2671 (2022), para. 15.

[793] Resolution 2650 (2022), para. 1.

[794] For more information on the format of meetings in relation to the item, see *Repertoire, Supplements 2018 to 2021*, part II.

[795] See S/PV.8955, S/PV.8978, S/PV.9003, S/PV.9022, S/PV.9083, S/PV.9117, S/PV.9130, S/PV.9163, S/PV.9204 and S/PV.9230.

[796] See S/PV.9003.

supporting the political process.[797] In August, he expressed concerns about troubling signs of a military escalation and mounting challenges in implementing resolution 2254 (2015).[798] He also reported on developments in and the status of the issue of detainees, abductees and missing persons.[799] In that regard, on 25 October, the Special Envoy stated that his team had continued to receive reports of arbitrary arrests throughout the country and that there had been nothing new to report six months after the presidential amnesty decree, despite the continued engagement of his team.[800] He urged all stakeholders to engage in step-by-step confidence-building measures to help to advance the implementation of resolution 2254 (2015), and reported that he was seeking to work with the parties and the Co-Chairs of the Constitutional Committee to unblock obstacles to reconvening the Committee and to ensure that there would be the political will to engage in a spirit of compromise and at a faster pace, with better working methods and more substance. At the end of 2022, the Special Envoy cautioned against an increase in mutual strikes and violence across northern Syrian Arab Republic and reiterated the call by the Secretary-General for all parties to exercise maximum restraint and avoid escalation. He called for all actors to engage in serious efforts to move towards a nationwide ceasefire and expressed concern regarding the fact that the Constitutional Committee had not met for six months, underlining the need for all parties to resume and make more substantive the meetings of the Committee in Geneva.[801] Noting that 2022 had seen no tangible progress in the political process, the Special Envoy appealed to all members to get behind the agenda, as the Syrian Arab Republic needed sustained international attention, starting with unity in the Council.[802]

In relation to the humanitarian situation in the Syrian Arab Republic, Council members heard briefings by the Under-Secretary-General for Humanitarian Affairs and Emergency Relief Coordinator, the Assistant Secretary-General for Humanitarian Affairs and Emergency Relief Coordinator, and the Director of the Operations and Advocacy Division of the Office for the Coordination of Humanitarian Affairs.[803] The briefings were focused on the findings of the reports of the Secretary-General on the implementation of relevant resolutions, including resolutions 2585 (2021) and 2642 (2022), by which the Council extended the authorization for cross-border humanitarian operations.[804] The briefers provided regular updates on the humanitarian conditions in different parts of the country, in particular Idlib in north-western Syrian Arab Republic and the Rukban and Hawl refugee camps. During the year, the briefers also reported on the effects of the continued economic crisis on access to basic services such as water, sanitation, health and education, and highlighted the need for funding for early recovery and resilience programmes. In addition, they reported to the Council on the status of the cross-border and cross-line humanitarian deliveries in northwestern Syrian Arab Republic and highlighted that cross-border assistance remained the central part of the humanitarian response.

Ahead of the expiration of the humanitarian aid delivery mechanism on 10 July,[805] at a meeting held on 20 June,[806] the Secretary-General noted that the United Nations cross-border operation in Syria was one of the most heavily scrutinized and monitored aid operations in the world, and emphasized the importance of maintaining and expanding access to aid, including through cross-line and cross-border operations, in order to save lives.

With respect to the use of chemical weapons in the Syrian Arab Republic, Council members heard regular briefings by the High Representative for Disarmament Affairs on progress in the implementation of resolution 2118 (2013) on the elimination of the Syrian chemical weapons programme. Except during

[797] See S/PV.9083, S/PV.9117 and S/PV.9130.
[798] See S/PV.9117.
[799] See S/PV.9130.
[800] See S/PV.9163.
[801] See S/PV.9204 and S/PV.9230.
[802] See S/PV.9230.
[803] See S/PV.8957, S/PV.8978, S/PV.9003, S/PV.9022, S/PV.9038, S/PV.9068, S/PV.9117, S/PV.9130, S/PV.9163, S/PV.9204 and S/PV.9230.
[804] Resolutions 2585 (2021) and 2642 (2022), para. 2.
[805] See resolution 2585 (2021), para. 2.
[806] See S/PV.9068.

the months of May, June and August, the Council heard monthly briefings by the High Representative.[807] In her briefings, the High Representative reported on the activities of the Organisation for the Prohibition of Chemical Weapons (OPCW) and informed the Council about the work carried out by the Declaration Assessment Team, the fact-finding mission and the Investigation and Identification Team. The OPCW Technical Secretariat had been unable to conduct a planned deployment of the Declaration Assessment Team to the Syrian Arab Republic and maintained its assessment that the declaration submitted by the Syrian Arab Republic could not be considered accurate or complete.[808] In that regard, the High Representative reiterated the importance of resolving the remaining outstanding issues regarding the initial declaration of the Syrian Arab Republic. On 29 April, the High Representative noted that, while significant progress towards the elimination of chemical weapons had been achieved through the implementation of the Convention on the Prohibition of the Development, Production, Stockpiling and Use of Chemical Weapons and on Their Destruction over the past 25 years, those accomplishments had been challenged by the use of chemical weapons in the Syrian Arab Republic, despite that country's accession to the Convention.[809] In that context, the High Representative noted that efforts to clarify the outstanding issues regarding the initial and subsequent declarations by the Syrian Arab Republic had not progressed, and that the Syrian Arab Republic continued to place conditions on the work of OPCW, violating its obligations under the Convention.[810] In the light of the continued gaps and inconsistencies and the failure of the Syrian Arab Republic to provide sufficient technical information, the High Representative called upon the Syrian Arab Republic to respond with urgency to the Technical Secretariat's requests.[811]

In 2022, in addition to the briefings by the Special Envoy of the Secretary-General for Syria and the Under-Secretary-General for Humanitarian Affairs and Emergency Relief Coordinator, the Council heard briefings by the Under-Secretary-General of the Office of Counter-Terrorism, the Assistant Secretary-General of the League of Arab States and seven civil society representatives concerning the political and humanitarian situation in the country, specifically on the topics of detainees, abductees and missing persons, the participation of women in the political process, the growing humanitarian needs in the country, the voices of the Syrian people, including women, and the restoration of sovereignty in the Syrian Arab Republic.[812] On 27 January, the Under-Secretary-General of the Office of Counter-Terrorism reported on the attack by Da'esh on Sina'ah prison in Hasakah city in north-eastern Syrian Arab Republic and the ongoing fighting, which had affected the civilian population.[813] On 24 March, the Assistant Secretary-General of the League of Arab States, giving a briefing to the Council against the backdrop of the eleventh anniversary of the Syrian crisis, elaborated on the decision adopted by the Council of the League of Arab States on 9 March, which formed the basis for the Arab position on the humanitarian crisis in the country.[814] He highlighted the League's genuine concern about the consequences of the war in Ukraine on the Syrian crisis, and expressed the hope that the humanitarian aid mechanism would continue to function across borders to the Syrian Arab Republic and would be renewed in July, free from any politicization of the issue.

In connection with the conflict in Yemen, the Council continued to focus on three distinct areas, namely, the implementation of the nationwide truce and the need for a political process to find a solution to the conflict; the humanitarian situation in the country; and the sanctions measures in place against individuals and entities designated as engaging in or providing support for acts that threatened peace, security and stability in Yemen.

---

[807] See S/PV.8943, S/PV.8982, S/PV.8990, S/PV.9026, S/PV.9097, S/PV.9141, S/PV.9164, S/PV.9184 and S/PV.9207.

[808] See S/PV.8943, S/PV.8982, S/PV.8990, S/PV.9026, S/PV.9097, S/PV.9141, S/PV.9164, S/PV.9184 and S/PV.9207.

[809] See S/PV.9026.

[810] See S/PV.9097 and S/PV.9141.

[811] See S/PV.9164, S/PV.9184 and S/PV.9207.

[812] See S/PV.8955, S/PV.8957, S/PV.8958, S/PV.9003, S/PV.9022, S/PV.9038, S/PV.9068, S/PV.9083 and S/PV.9130.

[813] See S/PV.8958.

[814] See S/PV.9003.

Regarding the political process, the Council heard regular briefings by the Special Envoy of the Secretary-General for Yemen.[815] The briefings were focused on updating the Council on the truce and its extensions, the status of the Agreement on the City of Hudaydah and the Ports of Hudaydah, Salif, and Ra's Isa towards an inclusive political settlement and the implementation of the Riyadh Agreement, including the outcomes of consultations between the parties. In January, the Special Envoy emphasized that the military escalation had accelerated as the parties had doubled down on military options.[816] He added that, seven years down the road of war, the prevailing belief of all warring sides seemed to be that inflicting sufficient harm on the other would force them into submission. He stressed that there was no sustainable long-term solution to be found on the battlefield and that the warring parties should talk, even if they were not ready to put down their arms. During the subsequent briefing, in February, the Special Envoy noted that the attacks on the United Arab Emirates and Saudi Arabia indicated how the conflict in Yemen risked spiralling out of control unless serious efforts were urgently made by the Yemeni parties, the region and the international community to end the conflict.[817] He also reported on his continuous engagement with the parties on possible mutually agreeable compromises and said that he would continue working towards the establishment of a multitrack process that could produce durable solutions to the conflict, while seeking opportunities for de-escalation. In April, the Special Envoy announced that the parties had agreed to a United Nations initiative for a two-month nationwide, renewable truce, which was the first nationwide truce in six years.[818] He discussed obstacles faced in the implementation of the truce and outlined a way forward, including extending, consolidating and expanding the truce to reach a political settlement.[819] He reported a significant decline in civilian casualties, with the first week of August seeing the lowest civilian casualty count since the beginning of the war.[820] The Special Envoy welcomed the parties' restraint following the expiration of the truce on 2 October, noting that only sporadic exchanges of artillery and small arms fire had been witnessed in front-line areas in Ta'izz, Ma'rib, Hudaydah and Dali'.[821] He also emphasized the need for the parties to demonstrate the leadership, compromise and flexibility required to urgently reach an agreement on the renewal and expansion of the truce. In November, he noted that, despite incidents of concern and the expiration of the truce, there had not been a return to full-fledged war.[822] Nonetheless, attacks on civilian infrastructure continued, raising the risk of military and economic escalation and undermining current mediation efforts.

Regarding the humanitarian situation in Yemen, the Council heard briefings by the Under-Secretary-General for Humanitarian Affairs and Emergency Relief Coordinator, by the Assistant Secretary-General for Humanitarian Affairs and Deputy Emergency Relief Coordinator, and by the Director or Acting Director of the Operations and Advocacy Division of the Office for the Coordination of Humanitarian Affairs, often in conjunction with the Special Envoy.[823] The briefers focused on the devastating consequences of the conflict for civilians and civilian infrastructure, food insecurity and the declining economy, all of which had deepened the humanitarian crisis in the country. They also focused on the impact of the conflict in Ukraine given that one third of the wheat consumed in Yemen originated in the Russian Federation and Ukraine. The briefers emphasized the need to ensure safe and unimpeded humanitarian access and the safety and security of humanitarian workers, and for efforts to find a just, lasting end to the conflict. The representatives of the Office for the Coordination of Humanitarian Affairs reported on the work of the United Nations to find a pragmatic and workable solution to the grave danger posed by the *FSO Safer* tanker.[824]

The Council also heard briefings by two civil society representatives, who spoke about various aspects of the peace talks and the humanitarian situation in the country and made specific proposals to the Council aimed at ensuring the participation of women, young people and civil society and ameliorating the humanitarian crisis.[825]

---

[815] See S/PV.8946, S/PV.8966, S/PV.8995, S/PV.9017, S/PV.9063, S/PV.9110, S/PV.9152 and S/PV.9199.
[816] See S/PV.8946.
[817] See S/PV.8966.
[818] See S/PV.9017.
[819] See S/PV.9063.
[820] See S/PV.9110.
[821] See S/PV.9152.
[822] See S/PV.9199.
[823] See S/PV.8946, S/PV.8966, S/PV.8995, S/PV.9017, S/PV.9063, S/PV.9088, S/PV.9110, S/PV.9152 and S/PV.9199.
[824] See S/PV.8946 and S/PV.9063.
[825] Ibid.

Council members also heard a briefing by the Chair of the Committee established pursuant to resolution 2140 (2014) in connection with the activities of the Committee and the Panel of Experts.[826]

In its decisions in 2022, the Council also addressed the issues outlined above concerning the conflicts in the Syrian Arab Republic and Yemen and the mandates of UNDOF and UNIFIL.

In connection with the Syrian Arab Republic and against the backdrop of the expiration of the authorization for the cross-border operations mechanism, which had been last renewed on 9 July 2021 by resolution 2585 (2021), the Council held a meeting to consider two competing draft resolutions,[827] one submitted by Ireland and Norway and one submitted by the Russian Federation. At the meeting, held on 8 July, the Council failed to adopt either draft resolution.[828] The draft resolution submitted by Ireland and Norway, which was voted on first was not adopted due to the negative vote of a permanent member, the Russian Federation, while the draft resolution submitted by the Russian Federation was not adopted owing to the failure to obtain the required number of votes.[829] Four days later, on 12 July, a new draft resolution submitted by Ireland and Norway was adopted as resolution 2642 (2022), with France, the United Kingdom and the United States abstaining from the voting.[830] By that resolution, the Council extended the authorizations of paragraphs 2 and 3 of Council resolution 2165 (2014) for a period of six months, until 10 January 2023, but only for the border crossing at Bab al-Hawa.[831] The Council also provided for an additional extension of six months, until 10 July 2023, subject to a separate resolution confirming the extension, and requested the Secretary-General to provide a special report on humanitarian needs in the Syrian Arab Republic no later than 10 December 2022.[832] By the same resolution, the Council encouraged the convening of an informal interactive dialogue every two months, with the participation of donors, interested regional parties and representatives of the international humanitarian agencies operating in th e Syrian Arab Republic, in order to regularly review and follow up on the implementation of the resolution, including progress in early recovery projects.[833]

Prior to the adoption of resolution 2642 (2022), the representative of Ireland, speaking also on behalf Norway, its co-penholder, noted that the draft resolution represented a delicate balance between the different positions of the members of the Council and that the primary focus of the Council was to keep the cross-border mechanism open and operating.[834] Speaking on behalf of the 10 elected members of the Council, the representative of Kenya stated that, while those members supported a 12-month renewal, as that would give humanitarian organizations more certainty in their operations, their fundamental interest was for the Council to meet the grave needs of the Syrian people, and they therefore supported the draft resolution. After the adoption of the resolution, most of the Council members took the floor. Having abstained from the voting, the representatives of France, the United Kingdom and the United States said that the resolution fell short of providing the operational certainty for the provision of humanitarian aid, in particular during the winter, and did not heed the call by the Secretary-General and the humanitarian community to renew the mechanism for 12 months. Nonetheless, they reiterated their commitment to working with partners to ensure that the Council met the needs of the people at the time of the renewal. Having voted in favour of the resolution, the representative of the Russian Federation explained that the informal interactive dialogues offered opportunities to monitor progress in implementing the resolution so as to decide on the ultimate fate of the cross-border mechanism. The representative of India reiterated his country's call for enhanced and effective humanitarian assistance without discrimination, politicization or preconditions and noted that cross-border operations could not exist in perpetuity.

---

[826] See S/PV.8966. For more information on the Committee and the Panel of Experts, see part IX, sect. I.B, and for more information on the sanctions in Yemen, see part VII, sect. III.

[827] S/2022/538 and S/2022/541.

[828] See S/PV.9087.

[829] Pursuant to General Assembly resolution 76/262 of 26 April 2022, the Council submitted a special report to the Assembly on the use of the veto at the meeting (see A/76/905). For more information, see part IV, sect. I.F.

[830] See S/PV.9089.

[831] Resolution 2642 (2022), para. 2.

[832] Ibid.

[833] Ibid., para. 6. In 2022, informal interactive dialogues were held pursuant to the resolution on 26 September, 21 November and 16 December (see A/77/2).

[834] See S/PV.9089.

With regard to the conflict in Yemen, on 13 July, the Council unanimously adopted resolution 2643 (2022) concerning UNMHA. The Council extended the mandate of the Mission for a period of 12 months, until 14 July 2023.[835] The representative of Ireland stated that, despite having voted in favour of the resolution, his country wished to put on record its view that Council resolutions should remain grounded in evidence-based reporting that was available to all Council members.[836] He said that the language in the resolution "expresses concern at accounts of the military use" of the ports of Hudaydah, Salif and Ra's Isa was based on assessments to which not all Council members had access and therefore strayed from the usual precedent and practice at the Council. His country would have preferred for the text to remain fully aligned with that of the original Hudaydah Agreement, on which the Mission's capacity was based and its focus remained.

Regarding the sanctions measures imposed in connection with the conflict in Yemen, on 28 February, the Council adopted resolution 2624 (2022) under Chapter VII of the Charter of the United Nations, with Brazil, Ireland, Mexico and Norway abstaining from the voting. By that resolution, the Council renewed the sanctions measures in place until 28 February 2023 and extended the mandate of the Panel of Experts on Yemen, for 13 months, until 28 March 2023.[837] In explanation of their votes, the representatives of Albania, China, India and the United Arab Emirates welcomed the renewal of the sanctions and condemned Ansar Allah for its attacks on the United Arab Emirates and Saudi Arabia.[838] Having abstained from the voting, the representatives of Brazil, Ireland, Mexico and Norway stressed that, while they condemned the actions of the Ansar Allah leadership and welcomed the implementation of the arms embargo, impediments to humanitarian aid reaching people in need must be avoided, and expressed the concern that designation might result in unintended negative humanitarian and political consequences. Noting that there were no internationally agreed definitions of the terms "terrorism" and "terrorist group", they expressed concern about the fact that the use of those terms in a Council resolution concerning sanctions on Yemen might have unintended negative consequences for the Yemeni people living under Ansar Allah control. The representative of Kenya stated that sanctions would be necessary to impede the capacity of Ansar Allah to carry out indiscriminate attacks and to signal that no political legitimacy could be achieved while carrying out such acts. The representative of Mexico expressed concern about the implications of the designation for the United Nations-facilitated political process and for the efforts to resolve the critical situation regarding the *FSO Safer* tanker and noted that Mexico did not consider it appropriate that the mechanism for the designation of terrorist groups should pass through resolutions relating to sanctions regimes. The representatives of Ghana and the Russian Federation stated that the sanctions regime should not have the effect of exacerbating the critical humanitarian situation.

In 2022, the mandate of UNDOF was renewed by resolution 2639 (2022) and resolution 2671 (2022) for periods of six months each, until 31 December 2022 and 30 June 2023, respectively.[839] Both resolutions were adopted unanimously.

In connection with Lebanon, the Council unanimously adopted resolution 2650 (2022), by which it extended the mandate of UNIFIL for one year, until 31 August 2023.[840]

For the purposes of facilitating the coverage of this item, information on the meetings is set out in the tables below, under four headings, namely: (a) Syrian Arab Republic; (b) Yemen; (c) United Nations Disengagement Observer Force; and (d) United Nations Interim Force in Lebanon.

[835] Resolution 2643 (2022), para. 1. For more information on the mandate of UNMHA, see part X, sect. II.

[836] See S/PV.9091.

[837] Resolution 2624 (2022), paras. 4 and 15. For more information on the sanctions measures, see part VII, sect. III, and for more information on the Committee established pursuant to resolution 2140 (2014) and the Panel of Experts, see part IX, sect. I.B.

[838] See S/PV.8981.

[839] Resolutions 2639 (2022) and 2671 (2022), para. 15. For more information on the mandate of UNDOF, see part X, sect. I.

[840] Resolution 2650 (2022), para. 1. For more information on the mandate of UNIFIL, see part X, sect. I.

Table 1
Meetings: the situation in the Middle East – Syrian Arab Republic, 2022

Meeting record and date	*Sub-item*	*Other documents*	*Rule 37 invitations*	*Rule 39 and other invitations*	*Speakers*	*Decision and vote (for-against-abstaining)*
S/PV.8943 5 January	Letter dated 28 December 2021 from the Secretary-General addressed to the President of the Security Council (S/2021/1103)		Iran (Islamic Republic of), Syrian Arab Republic, Türkiye	High Representative for Disarmament Affairs	All Council members, all invitees	
S/PV.8955 26 January			Iran (Islamic Republic of), Syrian Arab Republic, Türkiye	Special Envoy of the Secretary-General for Syria, Director of the Release Me project in northern Syrian Arab Republic	All Council members, all invitees	
S/PV.8957 27 January			Iran (Islamic Republic of), Syrian Arab Republic, Türkiye	Under-Secretary-General for Humanitarian Affairs and Emergency Relief Coordinator, Secretary-General of the Norwegian Refugee Council	14 Council members,[a] all invitees	
S/PV.8958 27 January			Iran (Islamic Republic of), Iraq, Syrian Arab Republic, Türkiye	Under-Secretary-General of the Office of Counter-Terrorism	All Council members, all invitees	
S/PV.8978 25 February	Report of the Secretary-General on the implementation of Security Council resolutions 2139 (2014), 2165 (2014), 2191 (2014), 2258 (2015), 2332 (2016), 2393 (2017), 2401 (2018), 2449 (2018),		Iran (Islamic Republic of), Syrian Arab Republic, Türkiye	Special Envoy of the Secretary-General, Assistant Secretary-General for Humanitarian Affairs and Deputy Emergency Relief Coordinator	13 Council members,[b] all invitees	

Meeting record and date	Sub-item	Other documents	Rule 37 invitations	Rule 39 and other invitations	Speakers	Decision and vote (for-against-abstaining)
	2504 (2020), 2533 (2020) and 2585 (2021) (S/2022/135)					
S/PV.8982 28 February	Letter dated 31 January 2022 from the Secretary-General addressed to the President of the Security Council (S/2022/76)		Iran (Islamic Republic of), Syrian Arab Republic, Türkiye	High Representative for Disarmament Affairs	13 Council members,[c] all invitees	
S/PV.8990 10 March	Letter dated 4 March 2022 from the Secretary-General addressed to the President of the Security Council (S/2022/181)		Iran (Islamic Republic of), Syrian Arab Republic, Türkiye	High Representative for Disarmament Affairs	13 Council members,[c] all invitees	
S/PV.9003 24 March			Iran (Islamic Republic of), Syrian Arab Republic, Türkiye	Special Envoy of the Secretary-General, Under-Secretary-General for Humanitarian Affairs, Assistant Secretary-General of the League of Arab States	13 Council members,[b] all invitees	
S/PV.9022 26 April	Report of the Secretary-General on the implementation of Security Council resolutions 2139 (2014), 2165 (2014), 2191 (2014), 2258 (2015), 2332 (2016), 2393 (2017), 2401 (2018), 2449 (2018), 2504 (2020), 2533 (2020) and 2585 (2021) (S/2022/330)		Iran (Islamic Republic of), Syrian Arab Republic, Türkiye	Special Envoy of the Secretary-General, Assistant Secretary-General for Humanitarian Affairs, Regional Director for the Middle East and North Africa of CARE International	12 Council members,[d] all invitees	

Meeting record and date	*Sub-item*	*Other documents*	*Rule 37 invitations*	*Rule 39 and other invitations*	*Speakers*	*Decision and vote (for-against-abstaining)*
S/PV.9026 29 April	Letter dated 30 March 2022 from the Secretary-General addressed to the President of the Security Council (S/2022/281)		Iran (Islamic Republic of), Syrian Arab Republic, Türkiye	High Representative for Disarmament Affairs	12 Council members,[e] all invitees	
S/PV.9038 20 May			Iran (Islamic Republic of), Syrian Arab Republic, Türkiye	Under-Secretary-General for Humanitarian Affairs, obstetrician gynaecologist from the Syrian American Medical Society	12 Council members,[f] all invitees	
S/PV.9068 20 June	Report of the Secretary-General on the implementation of Security Council resolutions 2139 (2014), 2165 (2014), 2191 (2014), 2258 (2015), 2332 (2016), 2393 (2017), 2401 (2018), 2449 (2018), 2504 (2020), 2533 (2020) and 2585 (2021) (S/2022/492)		Iran (Islamic Republic of), Syrian Arab Republic, Türkiye	Under-Secretary-General for Humanitarian Affairs, Coordinator of North west Syria NGO Forum (Gaziantep, Türkiye)	Secretary-General, 12 Council members,[g] all invitees[h]	
S/PV.9083 29 June			Iran (Islamic Republic of), Syrian Arab Republic, Türkiye	Special Envoy of the Secretary-General, representative of the Syrian Emergency Task Force	13 Council members,[c] all invitees	
S/PV.9087 8 July		Draft resolution submitted by Ireland, Norway (S/2022/538)	Syrian Arab Republic		13 Council members,[i] invitee	S/2022/538 not adopted 13-1-1[j]

Meeting record and date	*Sub-item*	*Other documents*	*Rule 37 invitations*	*Rule 39 and other invitations*	*Speakers*	*Decision and vote (for-against-abstaining)*
		Draft resolution submitted by Russian Federation (S/2022/541)				S/2022/541 not adopted 2-3-10[k]
S/PV.9089 12 July		Draft resolution submitted by Ireland, Norway (S/2022/546)	Syrian Arab Republic		11 Council members,[l] invitee	Resolution 2642 (2022) 12-0-3[m]
S/PV.9097 20 July	Letter dated 30 June 2022 from the Secretary-General addressed to the President of the Security Council (S/2022/530)		Iran (Islamic Republic of), Syrian Arab Republic, Türkiye	High Representative for Disarmament Affairs	13 Council members,[c] all invitees	
S/PV.9117 29 August	Report of the Secretary-General on the implementation of Security Council resolutions 2139 (2014), 2165 (2014), 2191 (2014), 2258 (2015), 2332 (2016), 2393 (2017), 2401 (2018), 2449 (2018), 2504 (2020), 2533 (2020), 2585 (2021) and 2642 (2022) (S/2022/635)		Iran (Islamic Republic of), Syrian Arab Republic, Türkiye	Special Envoy of the Secretary-General, Assistant Secretary-General for Humanitarian Affairs	13 Council members,[n] all invitees	
S/PV.9130 14 September			Iran (Islamic Republic of), Syrian Arab Republic, Türkiye	Deputy Special Envoy of the Secretary-General for Syria, Under-Secretary-General for Humanitarian Affairs, Director of the Syrian Center for Media and Freedom of Expression	13 Council members,[c] all invitees[o]	

Meeting record and date	*Sub-item*	*Other documents*	*Rule 37 invitations*	*Rule 39 and other invitations*	*Speakers*	*Decision and vote (for-against-abstaining)*
S/PV.9141 29 September	Letter dated 30 August 2022 from the Secretary-General addressed to the President of the Security Council (S/2022/658)		Iran (Islamic Republic of), Syrian Arab Republic, Türkiye	High Representative for Disarmament Affairs	13 Council members,[c] all invitees	
S/PV.9163 25 October	Report of the Secretary-General on the implementation of Security Council resolutions 2139 (2014), 2165 (2014), 2191 (2014), 2258 (2015), 2332 (2016), 2393 (2017), 2401 (2018), 2449 (2018), 2504 (2020), 2533 (2020), 2585 (2021) and 2642 (2022) (S/2022/775)		Iran (Islamic Republic of), Syrian Arab Republic, Türkiye	Special Envoy of the Secretary-General, Director for Operations and Advocacy of the United Nations Office for the Coordination of Humanitarian Affairs	13 Council members,[n] all invitees	
S/PV.9164 25 October	Letter dated 30 September 2022 from the Secretary-General addressed to the President of the Security Council (S/2022/727)		Iran (Islamic Republic of), Syrian Arab Republic, Türkiye	High Representative for Disarmament Affairs	13 Council members,[n] all invitees	
S/PV.9184 7 November	Letter dated 2 November 2022 from the Secretary-General addressed to the President of the Security Council (S/2022/828)		Iran (Islamic Republic of), Syrian Arab Republic, Türkiye	High Representative for Disarmament Affairs	13 Council members,[c] all invitees	

Meeting record and date	*Sub-item*	*Other documents*	*Rule 37 invitations*	*Rule 39 and other invitations*	*Speakers*	*Decision and vote (for-against-abstaining)*
S/PV.9204 29 November			Iran (Islamic Republic of), Syrian Arab Republic, Türkiye	Special Envoy of the Secretary-General, Under-Secretary-General for Humanitarian Affairs	13 Council members,[b] all invitees	
S/PV.9207 5 December	Letter dated 30 November 2022 from the Secretary-General addressed to the President of the Security Council (S/2022/897)		Iran (Islamic Republic of), Syrian Arab Republic, Türkiye	High Representative for Disarmament Affairs	13 Council members,[c] all invitees	
S/PV.9230 21 December	Report of the Secretary-General on humanitarian needs in the Syrian Arab Republic (S/2022/933) Report of the Secretary-General on the implementation of Security Council resolutions 2139 (2014), 2165 (2014), 2191 (2014), 2258 (2015), 2332 (2016), 2393 (2017), 2401 (2018), 2449 (2018), 2504 (2020), 2533 (2020), 2585 (2021) and 2642 (2022) (S/2022/956)		Iran (Islamic Republic of), Syrian Arab Republic, Türkiye	Special Envoy of the Secretary-General, Under-Secretary-General for Humanitarian Affairs	13 Council members,[n] all invitees	

[a] Albania, Brazil, China, France, Gabon, Ghana, India, Kenya, Mexico, Norway (also on behalf of Ireland, its co-penholder on the humanitarian situation in the Syrian Arab Republic), Russian Federation, United Arab Emirates, United Kingdom and United States.

[b] Albania, Brazil, China, France, India, Ireland, Kenya (also on behalf of Gabon and Ghana), Mexico, Norway, Russian Federation, United Arab Emirates, United Kingdom and United States.

[c] Albania, Brazil, China, France, Ghana (also on behalf of Gabon and Kenya), India, Ireland, Mexico, Norway, Russian Federation, United Arab Emirates, United Kingdom and United States.

[d] Albania, Brazil, China, France, Gabon (also on behalf of Ghana and Kenya), India, Ireland (also on behalf of its co-penholder, Norway), Mexico, Russian Federation, United Arab Emirates, United Kingdom and United States.

[e] Albania, China, France, Ghana (also on behalf of Gabon and Kenya), India, Ireland, Mexico, Norway, Russian Federation, United Arab Emirates, United Kingdom and United States.
[f] Albania, Brazil, China, France, Ghana (also on behalf of Gabon and Kenya), India, Mexico, Norway (also on behalf of its co-penholder, Ireland), Russian Federation, United Arab Emirates, United Kingdom and United States.
[g] Albania, Brazil, China, France, Ghana (also on behalf of Gabon and Kenya), India, Ireland (also on behalf of its co-penholder, Norway), Mexico, Russian Federation, United Arab Emirates, United Kingdom and United States.
[h] The Coordinator of the Northwest Syria NGO Forum participated in the meeting by videoconference.
[i] Albania, Brazil, China, France, Ghana, Ireland, Kenya (on behalf of the 10 elected members of the Council), Mexico, Norway, Russian Federation, United Arab Emirates, United Kingdom and United States.
[j] *For*: Albania, Brazil, France, Gabon, Ghana, India, Ireland, Kenya, Mexico, Norway, United Arab Emirates, United Kingdom, United States; *against*: Russian Federation; *abstaining*: China.
[k] *For*: China, Russian Federation; *against*: France, United Kingdom, United States; *abstaining*: Albania, Brazil, Gabon, Ghana, India, Ireland, Kenya, Mexico, Norway, United Arab Emirates.
[l] Albania, China, France, India, Ireland, Kenya (on behalf of the 10 elected members of the Council), Norway, Russian Federation, United Arab Emirates, United Kingdom and United States.
[m] *For*: Albania, Brazil, China, Gabon, Ghana, India, Ireland, Kenya, Mexico, Norway, Russian Federation, United Arab Emirates; *against*: none; *abstaining*: France, United Kingdom, United States.
[n] Albania, Brazil, China, France, Gabon (also on behalf of Ghana and Kenya), India, Ireland, Mexico, Norway, Russian Federation, United Arab Emirates, United Kingdom and United States.
[o] The Director of the Syrian Center for Media and Freedom of Expression participated in the meeting by videoconference.

Table 2
Meetings: the situation in the Middle East – Yemen, 2022

Meeting record and date	*Sub-item*	*Other documents*	*Rule 37 invitations*	*Rule 39 and other invitations*	*Speakers*	*Decision and vote (for-against-abstaining)*
S/PV.8946 12 January			Yemen	Special Envoy of the Secretary-General for Yemen, Acting Assistant Secretary-General for Humanitarian Affairs and Deputy Emergency Relief Coordinator, co-founder and Chief Executive Officer of the Sheba Youth Foundation for Development	All Council members, all invitees	
S/PV.8966 15 February	Letter dated 25 January 2022 from the Panel of Experts on Yemen addressed to the President of the Security Council (S/2022/50)		Yemen	Special Envoy of the Secretary-General, Under-Secretary-General for Humanitarian Affairs and Emergency Relief Coordinator	All Council members, all invitees	

Meeting record and date	*Sub-item*	*Other documents*	*Rule 37 invitations*	*Rule 39 and other invitations*	*Speakers*	*Decision and vote (for-against-abstaining)*
S/PV.8981 28 February	Letter dated 25 January 2022 from the Panel of Experts on Yemen addressed to the President of the Security Council (S/2022/50)	Draft resolution submitted by United Kingdom (S/2022/158)			11 Council members[a]	Resolution 2624 (2022) 11-0-4[b] (adopted under Chapter VII)
S/PV.8995 15 March			Yemen	Special Envoy of the Secretary-General, Under-Secretary-General for Humanitarian Affairs	All Council members, all invitees	
S/PV.9017 14 April			Yemen	Special Envoy of the Secretary-General, Under-Secretary-General for Humanitarian Affairs	All Council members, all invitees	
S/PV.9063 14 June			Yemen	Special Envoy of the Secretary-General, Acting Director of the Operations and Advocacy Division of the Office for the Coordination of Humanitarian Affairs, Protection and Advocacy Officer from Peace Track Initiative	All Council members, all invitees	
S/PV.9088 11 July			Yemen	Special Envoy of the Secretary-General, Assistant Secretary-General for Humanitarian Affairs	All Council members, all invitees[c]	

Meeting record and date	*Sub-item*	*Other documents*	*Rule 37 invitations*	*Rule 39 and other invitations*	*Speakers*	*Decision and vote (for-against-abstaining)*
S/PV.9091 13 July	Letter dated 13 June 2022 from the Secretary-General addressed to the President of the Security Council (S/2022/484)	Draft resolution submitted by United Kingdom (S/2022/549)				Resolution 2643 (2022) 15-0-0
S/PV.9110 15 August			Yemen	Special Envoy of the Secretary-General, Acting Director of the Operations and Advocacy Division	All Council members, all invitees[c]	
S/PV.9152 13 October			Saudi Arabia, Yemen	Special Envoy of the Secretary-General, Assistant Secretary-General for Humanitarian Affairs	All Council members, all invitees[d]	
S/PV.9199 22 November			Saudi Arabia, Yemen	Special Envoy of the Secretary-General, Director of the Operations and Advocacy Division	All Council members, all invitees	

[a] Albania, Brazil, China, Ghana, India, Ireland, Kenya, Mexico, Norway, Russian Federation and United Arab Emirates.
[b] *For*: Albania, China, France, Gabon, Ghana, India, Kenya, Russian Federation, United Arab Emirates, United Kingdom, United States; *against*: none; *abstaining*: Brazil, Ireland, Mexico, Norway.
[c] The Special Envoy participated in the meeting by videoconference.
[d] The Special Envoy and the Assistant Secretary-General for Humanitarian Affairs participated in the meeting by videoconference.

Table 3
Meetings: the situation in the Middle East – United Nations Disengagement Observer Force, 2022

Meeting record and date	*Sub-item*	*Other documents*	*Rule 37 invitations*	*Rule 39 and other invitations*	*Speakers*	*Decision and vote (for-against-abstaining)*
S/PV.9076 27 June	Report of the Secretary-General on the United Nations Disengagement Observer Force (UNDOF) (S/2022/447)	Draft resolution submitted by Russian Federation, United States (S/2022/512)				Resolution 2639 (2022) 15-0-0
S/PV.9234 22 December	Report of the Secretary-General on UNDOF (S/2022/887)	Draft resolution submitted by Russian Federation, United States (S/2022/986)				Resolution 2671 (2022) 15-0-0

Table 4
Meeting: the situation in the Middle East – United Nations Interim Force in Lebanon, 2022

Meeting record and date	*Sub-item*	*Other documents*	*Rule 37 invitations*	*Rule 39 and other invitations*	*Speakers*	*Decision and vote (for-against-abstaining)*
S/PV.9121 31 August	Letter dated 9 August 2022 from the Secretary-General addressed to the President of the Security Council (S/2022/607)	Draft resolution submitted by France (S/2022/654)			Four Council members (Brazil, India, United Arab Emirates, United States)	Resolution 2650 (2022) 15-0-0

21. The situation in the Middle East, including the Palestinian question

During the period under review, the Council held 13 meetings in connection with the item entitled "The situation in the Middle East, including the Palestinian question". No decisions were adopted by the Council during the period under review. In 2022, during the meetings held under the item, the Council continued its practice of holding monthly briefings and quarterly open debates.[841] In addition to the regular meetings under the item, the Council held a previously unscheduled meeting on 8 August following the ceasefire agreed between Israel and Palestinian Islamic Jihad on 7 August.[842] More information on the meetings, including on participants and speakers, is given in the table below. In addition to the meetings, Council members held informal consultations of the whole.[843] Under the item, the Council also considered developments in Lebanon, the Syrian Arab Republic and Yemen and the overall situation in the Middle East region.[844]

[841] For more information on the format of meetings, see part II.
[842] See S/PV.9107.
[843] See A/77/2, part II, chap. 2.A.
[844] See also sect. 20 above.

During the period under review, Council members heard regular briefings by the Special Coordinator for the Middle East Peace Process and Personal Representative of the Secretary-General to the Palestine Liberation Organization and the Palestinian Authority. The Council also heard one briefing by the Deputy Special Coordinator for the Middle East Peace Process, United Nations Resident Coordinator and Humanitarian Coordinator for the Occupied Palestinian Territory.[845] In addition, the Commissioner-General of the United Nations Relief and Works Agency for Palestine Refugees in the Near East (UNRWA) delivered one briefing.[846] Council members also heard briefings by five civil society representatives.[847]

In his monthly briefings, in February, May, August and November, the Special Coordinator focused on developments in the occupied Palestinian territory, including the situation in Gaza, the situation in the West Bank, specifically the violence by the Israeli security forces, the attacks by Israeli settlers and other civilians against Palestinians and by Palestinians against Israeli civilians, the settlement expansion and the demolition, seizure or forced eviction of Palestinian-owned structures. The Special Coordinator also provided updates to Council members on the engagement between Israeli and Palestinian officials and on the fiscal and financial situation of the Palestinian Authority.[848] In addition, he raised concerns over the funding for UNRWA, reiterating the Secretary-General's call to provide UNRWA with predictable, sustainable and sufficient funding to provide essential assistance to Palestinian refugees in the region.[849] Beyond the Israeli-Palestinian conflict, the Special Coordinator addressed other topics in the region, including developments in the occupied Golan and Lebanon.[850]

At the meeting in May,[851] the Special Coordinator focused on the killing of the Palestinian-American journalist Shireen Abu Akleh. He reiterated the Secretary-General's condemnation of all attacks on journalists and his call on the relevant authorities to carry out an independent and transparent investigation. In August, in addition to the regular meeting on 25 August, the Council held an emergency, previously unscheduled, meeting on 8 August,[852] during which it heard a briefing by the Special Coordinator on the escalation of violence in the Gaza Strip between 5 and 7 August. At that meeting, the Special Coordinator reported on the hundreds of air strikes carried out by the Israeli Defense Forces against targets in Gaza, including against a senior commander of Palestinian Islamic Jihad, who was killed in the attack. He also reported on the launching by Palestinian Islamic Jihad and other militant factions of thousands of rockets and mortars into Israel. He informed the Council that, as a result of the escalation of violence, 46 Palestinians had been killed and 360 injured, hundreds of residential housing units in the Gaza Strip had been damaged or destroyed, together with other civilian infrastructure, and 70 Israelis had been injured, with damage to residential and other civilian structures in Israel. The Special Coordinator welcomed the ceasefire but cautioned that it was fragile and that any resumption of hostilities would have devastating consequences for both sides. At the regular monthly meeting less than three weeks later, on 25 August,[853] the Special Coordinator noted that the dire humanitarian situation in Gaza had been partly mitigated by the ceasefire, together with the economic relief delivered to the people of Gaza, reinstating a "fragile calm" in the region. He reminded Council members that the humanitarian response across the occupied Palestinian territory continued to face chronic funding gaps and that maintenance of the status quo through short-term fixes was not a viable substitute for real political progress. Following the Special Coordinator, the Commissioner-General of UNRWA reported that more than 80 per cent of Palestine refugees in Lebanon, the Syrian Arab Republic and Gaza lived below the poverty line and alerted the Council to the decrease in funding allocated to UNRWA. He maintained that adequate funding was crucial for the Agency to provide much-needed relief to Palestinian refugees and to protect their right to a dignified life. The President of the US/Middle East Project subsequently addressed the Council and proposed rethinking and reappraising some of the assumptions and beliefs that

[845] See S/PV.9099.
[846] See S/PV.9116.
[847] See S/PV.8950, S/PV.8973, S/PV.9046 and S/PV.9116.
[848] See S/PV.8973 and S/PV.9046.
[849] See S/PV.8973.
[850] See S/PV.8973, S/PV.9046 and S/PV.9116.
[851] See S/PV.9046.
[852] See S/PV.9107.
[853] See S/PV.9116.

might inadvertently contribute to the intractability of the conflict. He cautioned that, in the absence of unprecedentedly far-reaching action to implement the partition plan established 75 years previously, Council members would be debating the challenge of achieving equality under a reality of non-partition. At the meeting on 28 November,[854] the Special Coordinator stated that freezing the conflict or managing it permanently were not viable options. He cautioned that, as the violence mounted, settlement expansion and restrictions continued to squeeze the economic and physical space for developing a viable Palestinian State. He said that political leadership was required to reset a trajectory towards a two-State solution, which still garnered support among Israelis and Palestinians.

During the monthly meetings held in February, May, August and November, Council members, while reiterating the calls for dialogue and their support for a two-State solution, expressed concern at the disproportionate use of force against civilians by the Israeli authorities.[855] Some Council members requested investigations into those incidents.[856] At the meeting in May,[857] a number of Council members[858] condemned the killing of the Palestinian-American journalist Shireen Abu Akleh, and several members[859] expressed concern at the excessive and disproportionate use of force at her funeral by the Israeli police. Some Council members[860] made reference to the press statement issued by the Council on 13 May, in which the Council condemned the killing of the journalist. In addition, most Council members[861] called for an immediate, thorough, transparent and impartial investigation into the killing and for full accountability for those found responsible. Some Council members[862] also made reference to resolutions 2222 (2015) and 1738 (2006) relating to the protection of journalists, media professionals and associated personnel. At the emergency meeting in August,[863] most Council members welcomed the ceasefire reached between the parties, calling on them to fully respect the agreement and to exercise restraint, and emphasized the need for efforts to prevent further escalation.

On a quarterly basis, in March, June, September and December, the monthly briefings were used to report on the implementation of resolution 2334 (2016). Consistent with prior practice, in 2022, two reports of the Secretary-General on the implementation of resolution 2334 (2016) were submitted in writing: the twenty-second report in June and the twenty-fourth report in December.[864] During the briefings, the Special Coordinator continued to report on the limited progress in the implementation of the main provisions of the resolution, namely, those relating to: the settlement activities of Israel; violence against civilians, including acts of terror, incitement, provocation and inflammatory rhetoric; steps and efforts to advance the peace process; and actions by all States to distinguish in their relevant dealings between the territory of the State of Israel and the territories occupied since 1967. The Special Coordinator also continued to express his concern about the deterioration of the security situation in the occupied Palestinian territory, the continued loss of life and injuries, settler-related violence and the continued settlement advancement by Israel in the West Bank, including in and around East Jerusalem.[865] He reaffirmed that settlement expansion continued to fuel violence in the occupied Palestinian territory, further entrenching the occupation and undermining the right of the Palestinian people to self-determination and independent statehood, and eroding the possibility of establishing a continuous and viable Palestinian State.[866]

---

[854] See S/PV.9203.

[855] See S/PV.8973 (France, Ireland, Gabon and Russian Federation); S/PV.9046 (Russian Federation, Ireland, United Kingdom and Brazil); S/PV.9116 (Mexico, Ireland and China); and S/PV.9203 (China, Russian Federation and Ireland).

[856] See S/PV.8973 (France, Ireland and United Kingdom); S/PV.9046 (United Kingdom, Ireland and China); and S/PV.9203 (United Kingdom, China and Albania).

[857] See S/PV.9046.

[858] United States, Ireland, Norway and Mexico.

[859] Ireland, United Kingdom, France, Gabon, Mexico, Ghana and Brazil.

[860] China, Kenya and United Arab Emirates.

[861] United States, China, Russian Federation, Ireland, Norway, Kenya, United Kingdom, Albania, France, United Arab Emirates, Gabon, Mexico and Brazil.

[862] Ireland, Mexico and Brazil.

[863] See S/PV.9107.

[864] S/2022/504 and S/2022/945.

[865] See S/PV.9000, S/PV.9077, S/PV.9139 and S/PV.9224.

[866] See S/PV.9000, S/PV.9139 and S/PV.9224.

At the meeting held in March,[867] the Special Coordinator asserted that the possible excessive use of force by Israeli security forces, in particular the use of live ammunition, continued to raise serious concerns and to result in the injuring and killing of children. He urged the Israeli authorities to conduct effective and transparent investigations into those killings and injuries. In his conclusion, he noted that the absence of a meaningful peace process to end the Israeli occupation was fuelling a dangerous deterioration that was destabilizing the situation across the occupied Palestinian territory. At the same meeting, most Council members urged Israel to uphold its responsibilities in accordance with international law and the relevant United Nations resolutions. In their remarks, the majority of Council members[868] underlined the importance of implementing resolution 2334 (2016) and expressed their support for the two-State solution, with the State of Palestine living side by side with Israel, in peace and security, on the basis of the 1967 borders and with Jerusalem as the capital of both States.

During the meeting held in June,[869] the Special Coordinator maintained that the Israeli settlement expansion in the occupied West Bank, including East Jerusalem, remained deeply troubling, as settlements constituted a flagrant violation of United Nations resolutions and international law. Noting that he was appalled by the killing of journalist Shireen Abu Akleh and disturbed by the behaviour of some members of the Israeli security services in the context of her funeral, the Special Coordinator reiterated the Secretary-General's call for an independent and transparent investigation into her killing and the need to ensure that those responsible were held accountable. During the discussion that ensued, several Council members[870] called for an effective investigation into the killing. Most Council members criticized the continued violations and limited progress in the implementation of resolution 2334 (2016), while urging increased compliance. In that connection, some members[871] recalled that the Council must do more to address the issue and had an obligation to ensure the implementation of the resolution. At the same meeting, some members[872] urged the full lifting of the blockade of Gaza, in accordance with resolution 1860 (2009), so that humanitarian aid could be distributed.

During the meeting held in September,[873] the Special Coordinator noted that settlement expansion in the occupied Palestinian territory, as well as violence against civilians, had escalated, effectively constituting a violation of paragraph 2 of resolution 2334 (2016), in which the Council called for the immediate cessation of all Israeli settlement activity. He expressed concern at the advancement of construction plans for housing units in East Jerusalem and the emergence of new illegal outposts across the West Bank, as well as at the high rate of demolitions, evictions and seizures of Palestinian-owned structures. He also expressed concern at the deaths and injuries of civilians, including children, caused by the most recent escalation in Gaza, the deteriorating security situation in the occupied West Bank and the high levels of settler-related violence against Palestinians in the occupied West Bank. Nevertheless, the Special Coordinator commended the statements made by the Prime Minister of Israel, Yair Lapid, and the President of the State of Palestine, Mahmoud Abbas, during the high-level week of the seventy-seventh session of the General Assembly, in which they reaffirmed their commitment to a peaceful resolution. Regarding the lack of progress towards the implementation of resolution 2334 (2016), the Special Coordinator maintained that negotiations could no longer be put off indefinitely and that meaningful initiatives were needed to turn the trajectory around, with the collective objective of ending the occupation and realizing the two-State solution. Following the statement by the Special Coordinator, speakers reiterated their support for a two-State solution, encouraging the two parties to engage in meaningful peace negotiations and urging the Council to fulfil its responsibility by ensuring compliance with resolution 2334 (2016). Some Council members[874] underscored the importance of mitigating the impact of the conflict not only on civilian lives, but also on the economy.

[867] See S/PV.9000.

[868] Ireland, France, India, Mexico, Kenya, Ghana, Albania, China and United Arab Emirates.

[869] See S/PV.9077.

[870] France, China, Ireland, Mexico and Albania.

[871] Ireland and Kenya.

[872] Gabon, Ireland and Kenya.

[873] See S/PV.9139.

[874] Ireland, Russian Federation, Kenya, Brazil and United Kingdom.

During the period under review, the Council fully resumed its practice of holding quarterly open debates in the Security Council Chamber.[875] All open debates held in 2022 involved the participation of large numbers of Member States, effectively restoring the practice existing prior to the COVID-19 outbreak. In his briefings during the quarterly open debates, in January, April, July and October, the Special Coordinator updated the Council on the most recent developments in the situation in the occupied Palestinian territory, including the fiscal situation of the Palestinian Authority, the settlement expansion by Israeli security forces, demolitions and seizures of Palestinian-owned structures and the overall situation in Gaza. He also addressed developments in the region, including in Lebanon and the Syrian Arab Republic. At the open debate in January, the Special Coordinator cautioned that, without a realistic prospect of an end to the occupation and the realization of a two-State solution based on United Nations resolutions, international law and previous agreements, it was only a matter of time before there would be an irreversible, dangerous collapse and widespread instability.[876] In April, the Special Coordinator informed the Council that, following the outbreak of the conflict in Ukraine, rising prices and market disruptions threatened the food security levels of vulnerable families in the occupied Palestinian territory.[877] In July, the Deputy Special Coordinator for the Middle East Peace Process delivered the briefing on behalf of the Special Coordinator.[878] She noted that, while the specific developments of the conflict fluctuated, the structural reality had not changed and that her office continued to witness concerning levels of violence against civilians, which exacerbated mistrust and undermined a peaceful resolution of the conflict. She added that, despite the worrisome backdrop, the visit by the President of the United States, Joseph Biden, to the region had signalled renewed consensus for a two-State solution based on the 1967 lines. She informed the Council that, on 30 June, the Israeli Knesset had voted to dissolve itself and had called for new parliamentary elections to be held on 1 November. In October, the Special Coordinator informed the Council that 2022 was on course to be the deadliest year for Palestinians in the West Bank since 2005.[879] He encouraged action from both parties towards a peaceful resolution with the support of the international community and stressed the importance of empowering the Palestinian Authority to build towards a return to a political process. He also reported on the signing on 13 October of the Algiers Declaration by 14 Palestinian factions, including Fatah and Hamas. In the Declaration, the factions agreed to recognize the Palestinian Liberation Organization as the sole legitimate representative of the Palestinian people and to hold elections for the presidency of the Palestinian Authority, the Palestinian Legislative Council and the Palestinian National Council. Finally, in December, the Special Coordinator expressed deep concern over the high levels of violence and the Israeli settlement expansion in the occupied West Bank.[880] He noted that, although there had been no advancements of housing units in the occupied West Bank, including East Jerusalem, from 21 September to 7 December, the total number of settlement housing units advanced in 2022 remained high. Expressing concern about the fragility of the political and security dynamics, he noted that the increase in violence and the absence of a political horizon had empowered extremists. Concerning Gaza, he emphasized the need for political solutions, calling for a return of the legitimate Palestinian Government to the Strip, a full lifting of Israeli closures in line with resolution 1860 (2009) and an end to the militant build-up.

In addition to the briefings by the Special Coordinator, in January, the Palestine Director and the Israel Director of EcoPeace Middle East reported on their proposed "Green Blue Deal" for the Middle East, calling on the Council to consider it as a practical and attainable path towards achieving climate security and water diplomacy, which needed to be an integral part of the Middle East peace process in order to advance the two-State solution within the 1967 borders.[881] The Israel Director called upon the Council to recognize globally that climate change was a threat to peace within the meaning of Article 39 of the Charter of the United Nations.[882]

---

[875] In accordance with the understanding reached among Council members in the light of the extraordinary circumstances caused by the COVID-19 pandemic, the official record of the January open debate (S/PV.8950 and S/PV.8950 (Resumption 1)) was supplemented by a compilation of statements submitted by eight non-members of the Council (see S/2022/39). For more information on the procedures and working methods developed during the pandemic, see part II.

[876] See S/PV.8950.

[877] See S/PV.9021. For more information on items relating to Ukraine, see sect. 19 above.

[878] See S/PV.9099.

[879] See S/PV.9174.

[880] See S/PV.9224.

[881] See S/PV.8950.

[882] For more information on the practice of the Council in relation to Article 39 of the Charter, see part VII, sect. I.

At the quarterly open debates, held in January, April, July, and October, Council members and invitees under rule 37 of the provisional rules of procedure expressed concern at the deteriorating humanitarian crisis in Gaza, the advancement of the settlement activities in the West Bank and the security situation in Israel and the occupied Palestinian territory. Council members expressed concern about the continued tensions and violence between the two sides and called upon both parties to protect civilians, including children. Several members of the Council emphasized the need for an end to the settlement expansion, urging Israel to stop building new settlements and demolishing Palestinian-owned structures.[883]

Most Council members expressed support for the peace process, including through the Middle East Quartet. In that regard, the mediation efforts of Egypt, Jordan and Qatar to de-escalate the situation in the region were recognized by a number of Council members during the open debates.[884] In April, the representative of the United Arab Emirates urged for more decisions to be taken to create a stable and sustainable situation that would allow Palestinians and Israelis to sit together at the negotiating table and revive the Middle East peace process.[885] At the same meeting, the representative of China called upon the international community to make greater efforts in accordance with relevant United Nations resolutions and international consensus, including the principle of land for peace, to advance the Middle East peace process. In October, the mediation efforts of Algeria were acknowledged, and most Council members welcomed the internal reconciliation agreement reached by the Palestinian political factions in Algiers, pointing to intra-Palestinian reconciliation as essential to finding a durable solution to the conflict.[886] During the open debates, Council members reiterated the calls made during the monthly meetings for the international community to provide more assistance to Palestine, in particular through financial contributions to UNRWA. Regarding the tensions between the two sides during the holy month of Ramadan in April, most Council members raised concerns over the violent acts in and around holy sites, notably the Aqsa and Al-Ibrahimi mosques and the Holy Esplanade, and called upon both parties to protect the historical and legal status quo.[887] Those concerns were reiterated in October by some Council members.[888]

Meetings: the situation in the Middle East, including the Palestinian question, 2022

Meeting record and date	*Sub-item*	*Other documents*	*Rule 37 invitations*	*Rule 39 and other invitations*	*Speakers*	*Decision and vote (for-against-abstaining)*
S/PV.8950, S/PV.8950 (Resumption 1) and S/2022/39 19 January			18 Member States[a]	Seven invitees[b]	All Council members,[c] all invitees[d]	
S/PV.8973 23 February			Israel	Special Coordinator for the Middle East Peace Process and Personal Representative of the Secretary-General to the Palestine Liberation Organization and the Palestinian	All Council members, all invitees	

[883] See S/PV.8950 (Norway, China and France); and S/PV.9021 (Russian Federation, Ireland, France, Mexico and China).

[884] See S/PV.8950 (United Arab Emirates and China); S/PV.9021 (Mexico, Gabon and Albania); S/PV.9099 (Russian Federation); and S/PV.9174 (Ireland, United Arab Emirates and Kenya).

[885] See S/PV.9021.

[886] See S/PV.9174 (Ireland, Russian Federation, Albania, China, Norway, Kenya, Mexico, Brazil and Gabon).

[887] See S/PV.9021.

[888] See S/PV.9174 (Ireland, Albania, United Arab Emirates, Brazil and Gabon).

Meeting record and date	*Sub-item*	*Other documents*	*Rule 37 invitations*	*Rule 39 and other invitations*	*Speakers*	*Decision and vote (for-against-abstaining)*
				Authority, Permanent Observer of the State of Palestine to the United Nations		
S/PV.9000 22 March				Special Coordinator for the Middle East Peace Process	All Council members, invitee	
S/PV.9021 and S/PV.9021 (Resumption 1) 25 April			26 Member States[e]	Special Coordinator for the Middle East Peace Process, Vice-Chair of the Committee on the Exercise of the Inalienable Rights of the Palestinian People, Permanent Observer of the State of Palestine, Deputy Head of the Delegation of the European Union to the United Nations, Permanent Observer of the League of Arab States to the United Nations	All Council members, all invitees[f]	
S/PV.9046 26 May			Israel	Special Coordinator for the Middle East Peace Process, Permanent Observer of the State of Palestine, Executive Director of Musalaha, spokesperson of Parents Circle	All Council members, all invitees	

Meeting record and date	*Sub-item*	*Other documents*	*Rule 37 invitations*	*Rule 39 and other invitations*	*Speakers*	*Decision and vote (for-against-abstaining)*
S/PV.9077 27 June				Special Coordinator for the Middle East Peace Process	All Council members, invitee	
S/PV.9099 and S/PV.9099 (Resumption 1) 26 July			24 Member States[g]	Seven invitees[h]	All Council members, all invitees[i]	
S/PV.9107 8 August			Egypt, Israel, Jordan	Special Coordinator for the Middle East Peace Process, Permanent Observer of the State of Palestine	All Council members, all invitees	
S/PV.9116 25 August				Special Coordinator for the Middle East Peace Process, Commissioner-General of the United Nations Relief and Works Agency for Palestine Refugees in the Near East, President of the US/Middle East Project	All Council members, all invitees	
S/PV.9139 28 September				Special Coordinator for the Middle East Peace Process	All Council members, invitee	
S/PV.9174 and S/PV.9174 (Resumption 1) 28 October			28 Member States[j]	Special Coordinator for the Middle East Peace Process, Vice-Chair of the Committee on the Exercise of the Inalienable Rights of the Palestinian People, Permanent Observer of the State of Palestine, Head of the	All Council members, all invitees[k]	

Meeting record and date	*Sub-item*	*Other documents*	*Rule 37 invitations*	*Rule 39 and other invitations*	*Speakers*	*Decision and vote (for-against-abstaining)*
				Delegation of the European Union, Permanent Observer of the League of Arab States		
S/PV.9203 28 November				Special Coordinator for the Middle East Peace Process	All Council members, invitee	
S/PV.9224 19 December				Special Coordinator for the Middle East Peace Process	All Council members, invitee	

[a] Argentina, Bahrain, Chile, Cuba, Egypt, Hungary, Indonesia, Iran (Islamic Republic of), Israel, Japan, Jordan, Kuwait, Malaysia, Morocco, Saudi Arabia, South Africa, Syrian Arab Republic and Türkiye.
[b] The Special Coordinator for the Middle East Peace Process; the Vice-Chair of the Committee on the Exercise of the Inalienable Rights of the Palestinian People; the Minister for Foreign Affairs and Expatriates of the State of Palestine; the Head of the Delegation of the European Union; the Permanent Observer of the League of Arab States; the Palestine Director of EcoPeace Middle East; and the co-founder and Israel Director of EcoPeace Middle East.
[c] Ghana was represented by its Minister for Foreign Affairs and Regional Integration; Norway (President of the Council) was represented by its Minister for Foreign Affairs; the United Arab Emirates was represented by its Permanent Representative to the United Nations and Assistant Minister for Foreign Affairs and International Cooperation; and the United States was represented by its Permanent Representative to the United Nations and member of the President's Cabinet.
[d] The representative of Egypt spoke on behalf of the Group of Arab States.
[e] Algeria, Bahrain, Bangladesh, Cuba, Egypt, Indonesia, Iran (Islamic Republic of), Israel, Japan, Jordan, Kuwait, Lebanon, Malaysia, Maldives, Morocco, Oman, Pakistan, Peru, Qatar, Republic of Korea, Saudi Arabia, South Africa, Syrian Arab Republic, Tunisia, Türkiye and Venezuela (Bolivarian Republic of).
[f] The Special Coordinator participated in the meeting by videoconference.
[g] Algeria, Argentina, Azerbaijan, Bahrain, Bangladesh, Cuba, Egypt, Indonesia, Iran (Islamic Republic of), Israel, Japan, Jordan, Kuwait, Lebanon, Malaysia, Morocco, Pakistan, Qatar, Republic of Korea, Saudi Arabia, South Africa, Syrian Arab Republic, Türkiye and Venezuela (Bolivarian Republic of).
[h] The Deputy Special Coordinator for the Middle East Peace Process, United Nations Resident Coordinator and Humanitarian Coordinator for the Occupied Palestinian Territory; the Vice-Chair of the Committee on the Exercise of the Inalienable Rights of the Palestinian People; the Permanent Observer of the State of Palestine; the Chargé d'affaires a.i. of the Delegation of the European Union to the United Nations; the Permanent Observer of the League of Arab States; the Chargé d'affaires a.i. of the Permanent Observer Mission of the Organization of Islamic Cooperation to the United Nations; and the Permanent Observer of the Holy See to the United Nations.
[i] The representative of Azerbaijan spoke on behalf of the Movement of Non-Aligned Countries.
[j] Algeria, Azerbaijan, Bahrain, Brunei Darussalam, Cuba, Ecuador, Egypt, Hungary, Indonesia, Iran (Islamic Republic of), Iraq, Israel, Japan, Jordan, Kuwait, Lebanon, Malaysia, Morocco, Pakistan, Qatar, Republic of Korea, Saudi Arabia, South Africa, Syrian Arab Republic, Tunisia, Türkiye, Venezuela (Bolivarian Republic of) and Viet Nam.
[k] The representative of Pakistan spoke on behalf of the Organization of Islamic Cooperation.

22. The situation concerning Iraq

During the period under review, the Council held five meetings in relation to the item entitled "The situation concerning Iraq". On 26 May, through the unanimous adoption of resolution 2631 (2022), the Council extended the mandate of the United Nations Assistance Mission for Iraq (UNAMI) until 31 May 2023.[889] All other meetings under the item during the period under review took the form of briefings.[890]

[889] For more information on the mandate of UNAMI, see part X, sect. II.
[890] For more information on the format of meetings, see part II.

More information on the meetings, including on participants, speakers and outcomes, is given in the table below. In addition to the meetings, Council members held informal consultations of the whole to discuss the item.[891]

In 2022, the Council heard regular briefings by the Special Representative of the Secretary-General for Iraq and Head of UNAMI on the situation concerning Iraq. In addition, on 26 July, at the request of the representative of Iraq,[892] the Council held an emergency meeting to discuss the attack of 20 July on a tourist resort in Dahuk Governorate in the Kurdistan Region of Iraq. The Council heard one briefing by a civil society representative, human rights defender and civil society activist, the co-founder and Chair of the Iraqi Al-Amal Association.[893] In addition, the representative of Iraq participated in four meetings and the representative of Türkiye participated in one meeting, under rule 37 of the rules of procedure.

In connection with the reports of the Secretary-General,[894] the Special Representative provided, in February, May and October, briefings focused on the political developments in the country, including the parliamentary elections held in October 2021 and their aftermath, and the participation of women in the political process. She also reported on the relations between Baghdad and Erbil and within the Kurdistan Region, and on the status of the implementation of economic reforms by the federal Government, the adoption of a federal budget and efforts to combat corruption. She informed the Council about the security situation in Iraq, including the attacks committed by Da'esh and the Iranian and Turkish shelling in the north. In addition, the Special Representative described the environmental challenges facing Iraq, including water scarcity and desertification. She also reported throughout the period on the camps and prisons along the border of north-eastern Syrian Arab Republic, warning that children were at risk of exploitation and forced recruitment by terrorist groups. Lastly, she discussed progress on the repatriation and return of missing Kuwaiti and third-country nationals and their remains and of Kuwaiti property.

At the emergency meeting held on 26 July,[895] the Special Representative provided an update on the shelling that had taken place in the Zakhu district of Dahuk Governorate on 20 July, as a result of which 9 civilians had lost their lives and 33 had been injured. She informed the Council that, following the attack, the Prime Minister of Iraq, Mustafa Al-Kadhimi, had established a committee, which had visited the site of the attack, collected evidence and engaged with witnesses and local authorities. On the basis of the committee's assessment of the evidence collected, the Government of Iraq had attributed the tragic events to the Turkish Armed Forces. In the meantime, the Ministry of Foreign Affairs of Türkiye had issued a press statement in which it condemned the attack and denied involvement. The following day, the Turkish Embassy in Baghdad had stated on social media that the Kurdistan Workers' Party (PKK) had been responsible for the attack. On 20 July, PKK had issued a statement in which it denied being present in the area and blamed Türkiye for the attack. The National Security Council of Iraq had held an emergency session the same day, during which it had strongly condemned the attack and rejected the use of Iraqi territory as a base to attack neighbouring countries and settle accounts. On 23 July, during a meeting of the Council of Representatives that had been convened to discuss the incident, the Parliamentary Security and Defence Committee had recommended the expulsion of PKK elements from Iraq, the withdrawal of all Turkish forces, the redeployment of federal forces along the border with Türkiye, the abolition of any security agreements with Türkiye and a review of the defence budget to enhance the military capabilities of Iraq. The Special Representative clarified that Iraq was demanding that Türkiye withdraw its military forces from all Iraqi lands and calling for an investigation. She emphasized that it was of the greatest importance that all attacks on Iraqi territory ceased, as such aggression not only recklessly heightened national and regional tensions but also caused grave human tragedies.

Following the briefing, the representative of Iraq welcomed the press statement issued by the Council on 25 July, in which the Council had condemned the attack. He stated that, on 20 July, the Turkish army had committed an act of aggression against the territory and sovereignty of Iraq and the lives of its

[891] See A/77/2, part II, chap. 28.
[892] See S/2022/574.
[893] See S/PV.9034.
[894] S/2022/100, S/2022/366 and S/2022/696. See also S/2022/103, S/2022/368 and S/2022/714.
[895] See S/PV.9100.

citizens in Dahuk Governorate. He condemned in the strongest terms that aggression against innocent civilians, underscoring that the attack constituted a threat to regional and international peace and security. He demanded that Türkiye withdraw its military forces from Iraqi territories and recalled that the matter was a recurring issue that had been documented in numerous letters from the representative of Iraq to the Secretary-General and the President of the Council over the years. He condemned the illegal presence of Turkish military forces on Iraqi territories and, in accordance with Article 35 of the Charter of the United Nations, called upon the Council to adopt a resolution to compel Türkiye to withdraw, under the Council's supervision, its occupying military forces from Iraqi territory.[896] The representative of Iraq also called upon the Council to introduce an item entitled "The situation concerning Iraq and Türkiye" to the list of matters of which it was seized.[897] He accused Türkiye of failing to uphold Article 51 of the Charter and reaffirmed that there was no security agreement between Iraq and Türkiye that allowed for an incursion into Iraq by Turkish forces to chase PKK. He called upon the Council to establish an international independent panel of inquiry to investigate the attack on Dahuk Governorate and asserted that the people of Iraq hoped that the Council would play a decisive and effective role in finding solutions to prevent any future repercussions of the crisis.

The representative of Türkiye expressed his condolences to the people and Government of Iraq and informed the Council that, immediately after the attack, Türkiye had been in touch with the Government of Iraq and the Kurdistan Regional Government to make it clear that Türkiye was ready to take all steps to unveil the truth. He added that the sovereignty and territorial integrity of Iraq had been breached by terrorist organizations, not by Türkiye. He stated that the Government of Iraq could not exercise effective sovereignty over certain parts of its territory in the north, including in Sinjar, where, he claimed, the presence of PKK was still tolerated. He emphasized that it was the obligation of the Iraqi authorities to stop PKK from using the territory of Iraq and underscored that a State could not castigate its neighbour for using its right to self-defence. He noted that, in the absence of the ability and willingness of Iraq to deal with the presence of terrorist organizations in its country, Türkiye was obliged to take appropriate measures and would continue to exercise its inherent right to self-defence in accordance with Article 51 of the Charter.[898]

During the period under review, the Council focused on the evolving political situation in Iraq, the security situation in the country and on its borders, and the remaining questions relating to the invasion of Kuwait in 1990, namely, compensation for the invasion and the issues of missing Kuwaiti and third-country nationals and missing Kuwaiti property.

During their deliberations, Council members expressed concern about the post-electoral political impasse,[899] and called upon Iraqi leaders to form an inclusive Government that reflected the will and met the needs and aspirations of the Iraqi people.[900] Several Council members welcomed the national dialogue facilitated by the Prime Minister of Iraq to overcome the deadlock.[901] Some Council members endorsed the implementation of the Agreement for Restoring Stability and Normalizing Conditions in the Sinjar District by the Government of Iraq and the Kurdistan Regional Government.[902] Some Council members emphasized the importance of the full and meaningful participation and representation of women in the process of

[896] For more information on the referral of disputes and situations pursuant to Article 35 of the Charter, see part VI, sect. I.

[897] For more information on the introduction of new items to the list of matters of which the Council is seized, see part II, sect. II.

[898] For more information on the discussion, see part VII, sect. X.

[899] See S/PV.8975 (Albania, Gabon (also on behalf of Ghana and Kenya), France and India); S/PV.9034 (United Arab Emirates, United Kingdom, Mexico, Russian Federation, France, Gabon (also on behalf of Ghana and Kenya), Norway and Brazil); and S/PV.9145 (India, United Kingdom, Ireland, Albania, Brazil, Mexico, Norway and France).

[900] See S/PV.8975 (United States, Albania, Gabon (also on behalf of Ghana and Kenya), Brazil, Norway, Ireland, France, United Kingdom, India, Mexico, United Arab Emirates and Russian Federation); S/PV.9034 (United Arab Emirates, China, United Kingdom, Mexico, Russian Federation, Ireland, India, France, Gabon (also on behalf of Ghana and Kenya), Norway, Brazil, Albania and United States); and S/PV.9145 (United States, Ireland, Albania, Mexico, United Arab Emirates, Norway, France and Gabon (also on behalf of Ghana and Kenya)).

[901] See S/PV.9145 (India, Ireland, Brazil, Mexico, Russian Federation and France).

[902] See S/PV.8975 (Mexico); S/PV.9034 (France); and S/PV.9145 (United States and Mexico).

government formation.[903] Several Council members expressed concern about the incidence of political violence in the country,[904] in particular the escalation of tensions and clashes in Sinjar.[905] Regarding the security situation in Iraq and the region, Council members expressed concern regarding the threat of terrorist groups and the continued attacks perpetrated by Da'esh in Iraqi territory.[906] Several Council members condemned the ballistic missile attacks of the Islamic Republic of Iran on Erbil on 13 March[907] and the Islamic Revolutionary Guard Corps air strikes in the Kurdistan Region on 28 September.[908] At the emergency meeting on 26 July,[909] Council members condemned the attack of 20 July in Dahuk Governorate and expressed support for the investigation to ensure accountability. Several Council members[910] expressed the concern that the attack could exacerbate the political and security crisis in the country, and many members[911] called for respect for the sovereignty and territorial integrity of Iraq.

Several Council members commended Iraq for fulfilling its obligations regarding compensation for the unlawful invasion of Kuwait in 1990 through the United Nations Compensation Commission.[912] When addressing the issue of civilians stranded in detention facilities, some Council members emphasized the importance of treating children primarily as victims.[913] On the issue of missing Kuwaiti and third-country nationals and missing Kuwaiti property, many Council members welcomed the progress and the cooperation between the two countries.[914] Most Council members discussed the impact of climate change on Iraq,[915] and some of them expressed their support for the work of the United Nations in assisting Iraq to address that impact.[916] The representative of Brazil asked what specific conceptual and scientific evidence there was to link sandstorms with climate change, as opposed to sandstorms being merely localized climatological events.[917]

During his interventions in Council meetings in 2022, among other matters, the representative of Iraq reiterated his call for the territories of Iraq not to be used as an arena for settling scores or for advancing political interests under the pretext of combating terrorism and called upon the Council to give serious consideration to the issue of respect for the principles of the Charter, in particular the sovereignty of Member States, good-neighbourly relations and the promotion of cooperation.[918]

---

[903] See S/PV.8975 (Albania, Gabon (also on behalf of Ghana and Kenya), Norway, Ireland, France, United Kingdom, Mexico and United Arab Emirates); S/PV.9034 (Mexico, Ireland, India, France, Gabon (also on behalf of Ghana and Kenya), Norway and Albania); and S/PV.9145 (Ireland, Albania, Mexico, Norway, France and Gabon (also on behalf of Ghana and Kenya)).

[904] See S/PV.8975 (Albania and United Kingdom).

[905] See S/PV.9034 (Mexico, Ireland, France and Norway).

[906] See S/PV.8975 (United States, Gabon (also on behalf of Ghana and Kenya), Norway, Ireland, France, United Kingdom, China, India, Mexico, United Arab Emirates and Russian Federation); S/PV.9034 (United Arab Emirates, China, Mexico, Russian Federation, Ireland, India, France, Gabon (also on behalf of Ghana and Kenya) and Albania); and S/PV.9145 (India, Mexico, United Arab Emirates, Russian Federation, China, France and Gabon (also on behalf of Ghana and Kenya)).

[907] See S/PV.9034 (United Arab Emirates, United Kingdom, Mexico, Ireland and France).

[908] See S/PV.9145 (United States, United Kingdom, Ireland, Albania, Brazil, Mexico, France, Gabon (also on behalf of Ghana and Kenya)).

[909] See S/PV.9100.

[910] United Arab Emirates, Kenya, Russian Federation and United Kingdom.

[911] United States, United Arab Emirates, Ireland, India, Norway, Ghana, France, Kenya, Russian Federation, United Kingdom, China, Albania and Brazil.

[912] See S/PV.8975 (Gabon (also on behalf of Ghana and Kenya), Brazil, Ireland, France, United Arab Emirates and Russian Federation). For more information on the United Nations Compensation Commission, see sect. 23 below.

[913] See S/PV.8975 (Norway and Ireland); and S/PV.9145 (Norway).

[914] See S/PV.8975 (Gabon (also on behalf of Ghana and Kenya), Ireland, France, United Kingdom, China, India and United Arab Emirates); S/PV.9034 (United Arab Emirates, United Kingdom, Mexico, India, France and Gabon (also on behalf of Ghana and Kenya)); and S/PV.9145 (India, United Kingdom, Ireland, Albania, Mexico, United Arab Emirates, China, France and Gabon (also on behalf of Ghana and Kenya)).

[915] See S/PV.9034 (China, United Kingdom, Ireland, France, Gabon (also on behalf of Ghana and Kenya), Norway, Brazil, Albania and United States); and S/PV.9145 (United States, United Kingdom, Albania, Norway, Gabon (also on behalf of Ghana and Kenya)).

[916] See S/PV.9034 (China, United Kingdom, Ireland, Norway, Albania and United States).

[917] See S/PV.9034.

[918] See S/PV.8975, S/PV.9034 and S/PV.9145.

In 2022, the Council unanimously adopted resolution 2631 (2022), by which it extended the mandate of UNAMI until 31 May 2023.[919] In the resolution, the Council commended the Government of Iraq and the Independent High Electoral Commission for executing a technically well-managed and generally peaceful election on 10 October 2021 and called for the swift and peaceful formation of a new Government to deliver on national priorities for the Iraqi people, including through economic reform, regional cooperation, stabilization, development and the promotion and protection of human rights.[920] In the resolution, the Council also recognized the threat of explosive ordinance and its impact on civilians, including children,[921] and condemned in the strongest terms the assassination attempt of 7 November 2021 against the Prime Minister of Iraq.[922] In the resolution, the Council noted the importance of the Government of Iraq urgently delivering meaningful reform, recognized the Government's efforts to that effect and called for State institutions to redouble efforts to pursue accountability for those responsible for crimes involving the killing, serious injury, abduction or disappearance of demonstrators and journalists, and to safeguard and respect the right to freedom of expression.[923] The Council recognized that the adverse effects of climate change, ecological changes and natural disasters, among other factors, could contribute to desertification and drought, have an adverse impact on the humanitarian situation and aggravate any existing instability, and acknowledged the United Nations Framework Convention on Climate Change and the Paris Agreement.[924] The Council reiterated and made several additions to the tasks of UNAMI and modified the requirement for the Secretary-General to report to the Council on the progress made towards the fulfilment of all the responsibilities of UNAMI from every three months to every four months.[925] Following the vote on the resolution, the representative of India expressed appreciation for the work of UNAMI and its close cooperation with the Government of Iraq.[926] He emphasized, however, the need to ensure that UNAMI not be distracted by additional responsibilities that either duplicated or could otherwise be efficiently executed by the competent agencies in Iraq. He reiterated that climate change issues should be addressed holistically through the United Nations Framework Convention on Climate Change and the Paris Agreement, and that no artificial link should be drawn between climate change and security-related issues without any firm scientific basis.

In addition, developments in 2022 relating to the United Nations Investigative Team to Promote Accountability for Crimes Committed by Da'esh/Islamic State in Iraq and the Levant, established pursuant to resolution 2379 (2017), were dealt with under the item entitled "Threats to international peace and security"[927] and those relating to the United Nations Compensation Commission were dealt with under the item entitled "The situation between Iraq and Kuwait".[928]

Meetings: the situation concerning Iraq, 2022

Meeting record and date	*Sub-item*	*Other documents*	*Rule 37 invitations*	*Rule 39 and other invitations*	*Speakers*	*Decision and vote (for-against-abstaining)*
S/PV.8975 24 February	Thirty-third report of the Secretary-General on the implementation of paragraph 4 of Security Council resolution 2107 (2013) (S/2022/100)		Iraq	Special Representative of the Secretary-General for Iraq and Head of the United Nations Assistance Mission for Iraq (UNAMI)	13 Council members,[a] all invitees	

[919] Resolution 2631 (2022), para. 1.
[920] Ibid., sixth and seventh preambular paragraphs.
[921] Ibid., third preambular paragraph.
[922] Ibid., fourth preambular paragraph.
[923] Ibid., eighth preambular paragraph.
[924] Ibid., eleventh preambular paragraph.
[925] Ibid., para. 5. For more information on the mandate of UNAMI, see part X, sect. II.
[926] See S/PV.9043.
[927] For more information, see sect. 34 below and part IX, sect. III.
[928] For more information, see sect. 23 below.

Meeting record and date	*Sub-item*	*Other documents*	*Rule 37 invitations*	*Rule 39 and other invitations*	*Speakers*	*Decision and vote (for-against-abstaining)*
	Report of the Secretary-General on the implementation of resolution 2576 (2021) (S/2022/103)					
S/PV.9034 17 May	Thirty-fourth report of the Secretary-General on the implementation of paragraph 4 of Security Council resolution 2107 (2013) (S/2022/366)		Iraq	Special Representative of the Secretary-General, co-founder and Chair of the Iraqi Al-Amal Association	13 Council members,[a] all invitees	
	Report of the Secretary-General on the implementation of resolution 2576 (2021) (S/2022/368)					
S/PV.9043 26 May	Thirty-fourth report of the Secretary-General on the implementation of paragraph 4 of Security Council resolution 2107 (2013) (S/2022/366)	Draft resolution submitted by United States (S/2022/426)			One Council member (India)	Resolution 2631 (2022) 15-0-0
	Report of the Secretary-General on the implementation of resolution 2576 (2021) (S/2022/368)					
S/PV.9100 26 July			Iraq, Türkiye	Special Representative of the Secretary-General	All Council members, all invitees[b]	
S/PV.9145 4 October	Thirty-fifth report of the Secretary-General on the implementation of paragraph 4 of Security Council resolution 2107 (2013) (S/2022/696)		Iraq	Special Representative of the Secretary-General	13 Council members,[a] all invitees[c]	

Meeting record and date	Sub-item	Other documents	Rule 37 invitations	Rule 39 and other invitations	Speakers	Decision and vote (for-against-abstaining)
	Report of the Secretary-General on the implementation of resolution 2631 (2022) (S/2022/714)					

[a] Albania, Brazil, China, France, Gabon (also on behalf of Ghana and Kenya), India, Ireland, Mexico, Norway, Russian Federation, United Arab Emirates, United Kingdom and United States.
[b] Iraq was represented by its Minister for Foreign Affairs.
[c] The Special Representative participated in the meeting by videoconference.

23. The situation between Iraq and Kuwait

During the period under review, the Security Council held one meeting in relation to the item entitled "The situation between Iraq and Kuwait", at which it adopted one resolution.[929] It was the first meeting held by the Council in relation to the item since February 2019.[930] More information on the meeting, including on participants, speakers and outcomes, is given in the table below.[931]

On 22 February, acting under Chapter VII of the Charter of the United Nations, the Council adopted resolution 2621 (2022), in which it decided that the United Nations Compensation Commission had fulfilled its mandate under resolutions 687 (1991) and 692 (1991), and reaffirmed that Iraq had fulfilled its international obligations to compensate all claimants awarded compensation by the Commission for direct loss, damage, including environmental damage and the depletion of natural resources, or injury to foreign Governments, nationals and corporations as a result of its unlawful invasion and occupation of Kuwait, as set out in resolutions 687 (1991), paragraphs 16 and 18, and 692 (1991).[932] By the same resolution, the Council decided to terminate the mandate of the Commission and to conclude its consideration of compensation by the Commission for liability as set out in resolutions 687 (1991), paragraphs 16 and 18, and 692 (1991).[933]

At the meeting,[934] following the vote on the resolution, the President of the Governing Council of the United Nations Compensation Commission noted that the Commission was the first successful example of a system giving individuals recourse to seek compensation from an aggressor State and recalled that, on 9 February, the Governing Council had adopted decision 277, its final decision, in which the Governing Council had marked the fulfilment of the mandate of the Commission and had declared that the Government of Iraq had fulfilled its international obligations to compensate for losses and damages suffered as a direct result of its unlawful invasion of Kuwait. He stated that the Commission had completed its work and would be winding down all activities in 2022. He added that a final administrative Governing Council session would be held following the closure of the accounts for the return of any remaining funds in the United Nations Compensation Fund to Iraq and the issuance of all audit reports. Following the final session, the Commission would be dissolved, and a report would be sent to the Council.[935] He underscored that the Commission demonstrated what multiple States with different interests could achieve through positive cooperation at the United Nations, and that post-war reconstruction and reconciliation by Member States acting through the United Nations were possible.

[929] For more information on the format of meetings, see part II.
[930] For more information on prior meetings on the item, see *Repertoire, Supplement 2019*, part I, sect. 23.
[931] See also A/77/2, part II, sect. 5.
[932] Resolution 2621 (2022), paras. 1–2.
[933] Ibid., paras. 7 and 8.
[934] See S/PV.8972.
[935] See S/2022/104.

At the same meeting,[936] the representative of the United Kingdom, the penholder of the resolution, said that the Commission represented an important success for the international rules-based order and that its work was a historic achievement for multilateralism in terms of post-conflict reconciliation and solutions to large-scale and complex problems related to conflict. She added that the successful completion of the mandate of the Commission served as not only a reminder of the consequences of breaching international law but also an example of what could be achieved through positive cooperation at the United Nations. The representative of the United States noted that the Commission had been a successful mechanism for post-conflict management, made possible by the Council's collective commitment to multilateralism and the maintenance of international peace and security. He underlined that, while the completion of the work of the Commission was a success, it was also a reminder that the impact of war extended for decades. He stressed that the Council, consistent with its role under the Charter, must continue to take actions to prevent the outbreak of armed conflict and advance international peace and security. The representative of France noted that the closure of the Commission was a major achievement in post-conflict reconstruction and reconciliation and marked the beginning of a new chapter in relations between Iraq and Kuwait. The representative of the United Arab Emirates stated that the conclusion of the work of the Commission represented a historic moment for the item entitled "The situation between Iraq and Kuwait". The representative of India said that the episode served as a good model of how Member States could come together to achieve post-conflict reconciliation through positive cooperation. The representative of Ireland emphasized that the fulfilment of the mandate of the Commission marked an unprecedented achievement in the history of international claims resolution and the first case of individuals having recourse to seek compensation from an aggressor State. She added that the joint efforts, commitment and perseverance of the Governments of Iraq and Kuwait, acting through the United Nations, were a reminder of the enduring value of dialogue and multilateralism. The representative of Norway referred to the conclusion of the mandate of the Commission as a historic and significant achievement. Similarly, the representative of China said that the completion of the work of the Commission was very significant and expressed the hope that Iraq and Kuwait would deepen cooperation and jointly promote regional stability, peace and prosperity. The representative of Albania noted that the Commission remained a model for post-conflict reconstruction and reconciliation, demonstrating the value and importance of international law and respect for Member States. He added that the occasion should serve as a reminder of the catastrophic costs of war and a lesson on the importance of showing resolve in efforts to prevent conflicts, discourage illegal acts of aggression and end wars. The representative of Ghana was pleased to note that the Commission had lived up to and successfully completed its mandate, thus reinforcing her country's conviction that meaningful post-conflict reconstruction and reconciliation could be achieved by Member States through constructive cooperation in a multilateral setting. The representative of Kenya indicated that the day marked a momentous occasion for the United Nations and for multilateralism. The representative of the Russian Federation noted that the dissolution of the Commission was a historic event and expressed his belief that the resources that would be available to Iraq would make a tangible contribution to improving the socioeconomic situation of Iraqi society, which had endured the humanitarian consequences of sanctions pressure since the outbreak of the crisis in the Persian Gulf in 1990.

Many Council members[937] asserted that Iraq had fulfilled its obligations in relation to the measures under Chapter VII of the Charter concerning its unlawful invasion and occupation of Kuwait in 1990, and most Council members[938] commended Iraq for its commitment to make its payments, often in challenging circumstances. Some Council members[939] expressed their appreciation to the Government of Kuwait for its commitment to the Commission. Several Council members[940] called for further progress on the issues of missing Kuwaiti and third-country nationals and missing Kuwaiti property, including items from the national archives.

---

[936] See S/PV.8972.

[937] United Kingdom, United States, France, Mexico, India, Gabon, Norway, China, Albania and Kenya.

[938] United Kingdom, United States, France, United Arab Emirates, Mexico, India, Ireland, Norway, China, Ghana, Brazil, Kenya and Russian Federation.

[939] United States, France, United Arab Emirates, Mexico, Ireland, Norway, China, Albania, Ghana, Brazil and Kenya.

[940] United Arab Emirates, India, Gabon and Ireland.

The Minister for Foreign Affairs of Iraq stressed that the cooperation of his Government with the Commission and the Council was a successful model of multilateral action that reinforced confidence in international mechanisms and measures to resolve crises confronting the world. He added that the fulfilment by Iraq of its obligations to the international community and to Kuwait was a major development that would strengthen its relations with the region and the world, as well as its historical ties with Kuwait. He clarified that, following the fulfilment by Iraq of its obligations, the international community and the United Nations now had a legal and moral obligation towards Iraq that included ending the application of measures under Chapter VII of the Charter against Iraq; preserving the rights, assets and international legal privileges of Iraq; and shielding Iraq from any future claims, in line with United Nations-led international efforts and in accordance with the Charter and the norms of international law ensuring justice and fairness. The representative of Kuwait welcomed the unanimous adoption of resolution 2621 (2022) and underscored that the fulfilment by mechanisms and subsidiary organs established by the Council of their tasks and responsibilities and the readiness to follow up on their implementation to achieve the desired outcomes of the relevant resolutions enhanced the credibility and effectiveness of the Council. He praised the Council on the historic achievement in its work on the issue of compensation and congratulated Iraq on fully meeting its obligations related to the issue of compensation and on ceasing to be subject to its most important obligations under Chapter VII. The representative of Kuwait reiterated his country's commitment to working and cooperating with the Government of Iraq to finalize the outstanding issues and obligations relating to missing Kuwaitis and third-country nationals and the return of property, including the national archives, as stipulated in resolution 2107 (2013).

Meeting: the situation between Iraq and Kuwait, 2022

Meeting record and date	*Sub-item*	*Other documents*	*Rule 37 invitations*	*Rule 39 and other invitations*	*Speakers*	*Decision and vote (for-against-abstaining)*
S/PV.8972 22 February	Letter dated 10 February 2022 from the President of the Governing Council of the United Nations Compensation Commission addressed to the President of the Security Council (S/2022/104)	Draft resolution submitted by United Kingdom (S/2022/136)	Iraq, Kuwait	President of the Governing Council of the United Nations Compensation Commission	All Council members, all invitees[a]	Resolution 2621 (2022) 15-0-0 (adopted under Chapter VII)

[a] Iraq was represented by its Minister for Foreign Affairs.

Thematic issues

24. United Nations peacekeeping operations

During the period under review, the Council held four meetings and adopted one resolution and one presidential statement under the item entitled "United Nations peacekeeping operations". Two of the meetings took the form of briefings, one took the form of an open debate, and one was convened for the adoption of a decision.[941] More information on the meetings, including on participants, speakers and outcomes, is provided in the table below.[942]

[941] For more information on the format of meetings, see part II.

[942] See also A/77/2, part II, chap. 4.

In 2022, the Council continued to hold the annual briefings on the Action for Peacekeeping initiative and its implementation strategy, Action for Peacekeeping Plus, pursuant to resolution 2378 (2017) and on the work of United Nations police components. The Council also held a high-level open debate on the importance of strategic communications for efficient peacekeeping, during which it adopted a presidential statement and resolution 2668 (2022) concerning mental health and psychosocial support for United Nations peace operations personnel. During those meetings, the Council heard two briefings by the Under-Secretary-General for Peace Operations and one briefing each by the Secretary-General, the Force Commander of the United Nations Organization Stabilization Mission in the Democratic Republic of the Congo (MONUSCO), the police commissioners of MONUSCO and the United Nations Mission in South Sudan (UNMISS), the Director of Research at the International Peace Institute and a representative of the Kofi Annan International Peacekeeping Training Centre.[943]

On 12 July, at the initiative of Brazil, which held the presidency of the Council for the month,[944] the Council held a high-level open debate on the role of strategic communications in efficient peacekeeping.[945] Opening the meeting, the Secretary-General stated that strategic communications were critical across the mandates of peacekeeping operations, including the mandates to protect civilians and prevent violence, to secure ceasefires and safeguard political settlements, to investigate and report on human rights abuses and violations, to advance the women and peace and security agenda and promote the role of women as peacekeepers, peacemakers and peace leaders, and to ensure the safety and security of personnel and the communities they served.[946] The Secretary-General noted that disinformation was not just misleading but also dangerous and potentially deadly, fuelling open violence against United Nations personnel and their partners. The best and most cost-effective instruments for countering that threat, according to the Secretary-General, were credible, accurate and human-centred strategic communications, which not only defused harmful lies but also enabled tailored two-way communication that built trust and political and public support. Such communication could strengthen understanding among local populations of United Nations missions and mandates and in return strengthen the understanding of peacekeepers of the concerns, grievances, expectations and hopes of those populations.

The Secretary-General observed that, to be effective, strategic communications must be grounded in evidence, based on verified data, open to dialogue, rooted in storytelling and delivered by credible messengers. He noted that, as a means of improving strategic communications in peacekeeping, the United Nations was adopting a whole-of-mission communications approach, holding mission leaders accountable to own and lead those efforts, providing guidance and training to missions, working with technology and media companies and Member States, monitoring and evaluating the efficacy of information campaigns, and deploying communications to strengthen accountability and to end misconduct by personnel and partners, including sexual exploitation and abuse. The Secretary-General concluded by emphasizing that the United Nations must take a deliberate stand as a trusted information actor in conflict environments by providing engaging and factual content, facilitating inclusive dialogue, demanding the removal of harmful speech, holding leaders to account and promoting peace and unity.

Following the Secretary-General, the Force Commander of MONUSCO shared his perspective on the utility of strategic communications in countering the overall poor perception among the population in the Democratic Republic of the Congo of the relevance of the Mission in improving the security situation. The Force Commander noted that one part of the Mission's strategy was to communicate in person with stakeholders, from the village chief to the media and up to the national and regional armed forces leadership, all of whom played a critical role in countering the criticism of the Mission, explaining the aim and the limits of the mandate and acknowledging the validity of the human rights due diligence policy on United Nations support to non-United Nations security forces. In terms of challenges, he highlighted the need for more female translators, better predeployment training for units, qualified public information and information operation staff officers and a specialized military psychological operational unit. Furthermore, he stressed the need for synergy between the military campaign plan and the strategic communications plan, noting that strategic communication was a command duty and a mission leadership endeavour.

---

[943] See S/PV.9090, S/PV.9090 (Resumption 1), S/PV.9123 and S/PV.9189.

[944] A concept note was circulated by a letter dated 5 July (S/2022/539).

[945] See S/PV.9090 and S/PV.9090 (Resumption 1). For more information on high-level meetings, see part II.

[946] See S/PV.9090.

In her remarks, the Director of Research of the International Peace Institute discussed the role of strategic communications in enhancing the protection of civilians, how to ensure that communication was not only gender sensitive but also gender transformative, and the importance of active listening in order to place the experiences of communities in peacekeeping at the forefront. With respect to the protection of civilians, she stated that strategic communications were not limited to managing expectations by communicating the limitations of a mission's protection work but also included messaging on how to improve the access of populations to the protection interventions that were available. Strategic communications could also be used to counter hate speech and misinformation or disinformation that was used to incite violence, inflame identity-based divisions or mobilize individuals to join armed groups. The Director of Research explained that gender-transformative communications used narratives and storytelling to promote gender equality and combat harmful stereotypes and behaviours by, for example, highlighting stories and images that expanded traditional understandings of gender roles, addressing harmful gender practices and using information to increase women's access to power and resources. Finally, she emphasized that strategic communications should move beyond a unidirectional flow of relaying information to a dynamic dialogue between missions and communities. In that regard, she suggested using, in addition to data and analytics, storytelling as a means of persuading people and inspiring them to act for the sake of peace.

In their discussion, members and participating non-members of the Council highlighted the importance of strategic communications for the effectiveness of peacekeeping operations in the face of increasingly complex and hostile operating environments and a significant increase in the dissemination of misinformation, disinformation and hate speech through digital technologies. They pointed out the role of effective strategic communications in implementing protection of civilians mandates and ensuring the safety and security of peacekeeping personnel. In terms of practical steps, speakers recommended implementing communications strategies across all missions and all their respective components, ensuring the ownership of such strategies by mission leadership, improving communication capabilities through the deployment of specialized personnel, training and the use of technology, and ensuring two-way communication between peacekeepers, communities, host Governments and other stakeholders on the ground. Many speakers also emphasized the utility of strategic communications in advancing the women and peace and security agenda.

In the presidential statement adopted during the meeting, the Council underscored the importance of strategic communications to the implementation of the mandates of United Nations peacekeeping operations and to the safety and security of peacekeepers.[947] The Council recognized that strategic communications and the provision of accurate content helped to strengthen the understanding of peacekeeping mandates, managed the expectations of and garnered trust and support among relevant stakeholders, notably host Governments and local communities, and contributed to countering disinformation and misinformation.[948] Moreover, the Council stressed the need to improve the culture of strategic communications across all mission components and called upon peacekeeping operations, in the implementation of protection of civilians mandates, to enhance community engagement and awareness about the protection needs and capacities of local communities.[949] Finally, the Council requested the Secretary-General to provide, no later than 15 April 2023, a strategic review of strategic communications across all peacekeeping operations and to ensure that his regular reports on individual peacekeeping operations included, as applicable, information on the actions and impact of strategic communications for mandated activities.[950]

On 6 September, the Under-Secretary-General for Peace Operations gave a briefing to the Council on the implementation of resolution 2378 (2017) and the progress and challenges in the implementation of the Action for Peacekeeping initiative and the Action for Peacekeeping Plus strategy.[951] Noting the increasingly complex geopolitical environment, the Under-Secretary-General stressed the need to do everything possible to preserve space for United Nations peacekeeping operations, which continued to

[947] S/PRST/2022/5, fifth paragraph.
[948] Ibid.
[949] Ibid., sixth and seventh paragraphs.
[950] Ibid., sixteenth and seventeenth paragraphs.
[951] See S/PV.9123.

visibly manifest a multilateral system in action on the ground. He provided an overview of the implementation of some of the priorities of Action for Peacekeeping Plus. With regard to the second priority, on strategic and operational integration, the Under-Secretary-General reported that 11 out of 12 missions had developed either integrated mission plans or results frameworks for the Comprehensive Planning and Performance Assessment System, most of which took into account gender considerations and the women and peace and security agenda. Noting that missions could fulfil their mandates only if they had the appropriate capacities at the right time, he called for the support of Council members to fill the critical capacity gaps, especially in utility and armed helicopters. With regard to the fourth priority, on safety and security, the Under-Secretary-General expressed his regret over the doubling of peacekeeper deaths in 2021 compared with 2020 and noted that the trend had continued in 2022, in particular with attacks using explosive ordnance and improvised explosive devices.

On the sixth priority, the Under-Secretary-General stated that missions were working to fully integrate strategic communications into planning and decision-making and were proactively communicating on the tangible impact of peacekeeping in a compelling, human-centred way through social media and United Nations-operated radio networks. Regarding the participation of women in peacekeeping, he noted that, except in relation to military contingents, most of the targets set in the uniformed gender parity strategy 2018–2028 had been met and surpassed. The Under-Secretary-General stated that efforts to create more gender-responsive working and living environments continued and that gender analysis was being used to inform decision-making. Nevertheless, he highlighted constraints related to inadequate resources and personnel, including a shortage of gender advisers. While acknowledging that notable progress had been made in addressing the priorities outlined in Action for Peacekeeping Plus, the Under-Secretary-General called for stronger and more united support from the Council for advancing the political efforts of peacekeeping operations, and for ongoing support from the Council for missions that were facing undue restrictions and obstacles from the parties to the conflict, including violations of status-of-forces agreements.

In their exchanges following the briefing, Council members widely recognized the improvements made in the performance of peacekeeping operations since the launch of the Action for Peacekeeping initiative, but also outlined a number of challenges. Most Council members stressed that effective mandate implementation required tailored, realistic and properly resourced mandates that formed part of an overall strategy to achieve a political solution to the conflict. Several Council members[952] expressed concern over the increasingly broad nature of mandates and stressed that focus should remain on supporting political processes. Several speakers[953] raised the need to engage and improve relations with host Governments. Some Council members[954] urged host Governments to avoid imposing restrictions on missions and to abide by their obligations under status-of-forces agreements. A number of Council members[955] pointed to the increasing tensions between some missions and local communities and called for greater use of strategic communications to rebuild and maintain trust. In terms of other priorities for improving peacekeeping performance, speakers highlighted the importance of partnerships with regional organizations and regional missions on the ground, additional resources and capacities to ensure the safety and security of peacekeeping personnel, the use of data and technology, the implementation of the women and peace and security agenda, and the creation of conditions conducive to the participation of women in missions.

On 14 November, the Council held its annual briefing with selected police commissioners of United Nations peacekeeping operations.[956] In his introductory remarks, the Under-Secretary-General for Peace Operations provided an overview and examples of the work of the Secretariat and United Nations police personnel in support of political transitions, including work to increase the links between long-term strategic planning and operational decision-making, align predeployment training with in-mission training, conduct performance assessments, develop police-related impact indicators within the Comprehensive Planning and Performance Assessment System, employ strategic communications and improve cooperation with host

[952] Ghana, China and Russian Federation.

[953] China, Gabon, Russian Federation, Kenya, India and France.

[954] Ghana, United Kingdom, United States and France.

[955] Norway, United Arab Emirates, Kenya, Albania and Brazil.

[956] See S/PV.9189.

countries during transitions. The Under-Secretary-General stated that gender-responsive policing efforts ensured that the different security needs of women, men, girls and boys were considered, including through a robust network of gender advisers and police gender focal points. He added that the gender parity targets for United Nations police for 2025 had already been achieved, with women comprising almost one in five police officers and heading five out of nine police components.

In their remarks, the police commissioners of UNMISS and MONUSCO described the work of their police components to protect civilians and improve performance. The Police Commissioner of UNMISS noted that, as part of its mandate, the police component participated in whole-of-mission efforts to foster protection through dialogue and engagement, participated in integrated civilian-military-police patrols and deployments to temporary operating bases near conflict hotspots, and contributed to the creation of a protective environment through its support to rule of law institutions. As a means of improving performance, she highlighted the need for a more enabling environment for the participation of women, additional capacity for joint and integrated planning, proactive and resourceful police officers with a good education and predeployment training, and additional formed police units. The Police Commissioner of MONUSCO noted that efforts had been made to improve the performance of the Mission's police component, in particular through communication with police-contributing countries on the quality of formed police units and specialized teams, training, the use of monitoring and measurement systems, such as the Comprehensive Planning and Performance Assessment System, and the implementation of an annual workplan as a monitoring and assessment mechanism. He also referred to the deployment of police teams to measure and help to improve the performance of the Congolese National Police in combating urban and organized crime.

Following the Police Commissioners, a representative of the Kofi Annan International Peacekeeping Training Centre spoke about the influence of decisions, norms, ideas and policies implemented at the multilateral level of United Nations peacekeeping on the decision-making of peacekeeping stakeholders at the national level. Specifically, she expressed the view that peacekeeping had a democratizing effect on the security sector in host communities and troop-contributing countries and strengthened the legitimacy and effectiveness of domestic security relations. She noted that police in peacekeeping brought mutually reinforcing benefits to the women and peace and security agenda in peacekeeping theatres and at the domestic level. While noting the critical contribution of police components to the Action for Peacekeeping priorities, she highlighted the need for improvements in innovation, adaptability, operational readiness, strategic and operational integration and accountability for peacekeepers in missions of which fragile States were often the beneficiaries. She added that police-contributing countries had maximized their participation in peacekeeping beyond fragile host countries in order to benefit their own societies and strengthen the legitimacy and effectiveness of domestic security relations.

In their statements following the briefings, Council members recognized the important work of police components, in particular in conflict prevention and early warning, the protection of civilians, peacekeeping transitions, capacity-building, the implementation of the women and peace and security agenda and strategic communications. Council members[957] underscored that ensuring effective and accountable police components was a key requirement under the Action for Peacekeeping Plus strategy. While noting some improvements, Council members stressed the need to ensure that police officers were provided with specialized and tailored training relevant to their operational environment and had the right mindset and necessary equipment, including technology, to successfully perform their duties. Council members acknowledged the important role of women police officers, in particular in community engagement, and called for additional progress in increasing their participation in police components and improving their working conditions. As a key element of increasing the effectiveness of police, speakers called for stronger partnerships between police components and stakeholders such as local communities, host countries, United Nations country teams, civil society and regional organizations. Furthermore, some members[958] underscored the need for greater coordination among the Council, the Secretariat, police-contributing countries and host States, in particular with respect to planning, mandate design and exit strategies.

[957] Kenya, Ireland, United States, Mexico, United Kingdom and Ghana.

[958] China, India and Russian Federation.

On 21 December, the Council unanimously adopted resolution 2668 (2022), in which it recognized the need to raise awareness of the importance of mental health and psychosocial support to United Nations peace operations personnel.[959] The Council encouraged troop- and police-contributing countries, including Member States and the Secretariat, to provide mental health services to support personnel during predeployment training, to continue to foster a culture of well-being and care during deployment, and to continue to provide peace operations personnel at the post-deployment stage with adequate mental health and psychosocial support services.[960] Furthermore, the Council requested the Secretary-General to include information on the implementation of aspects of the 2018 United Nations System Mental Health and Well-being Strategy, as appropriate, in his comprehensive reports to the Council under resolution 2378 (2017).[961]

Following the vote on the resolution, the representatives of India and the Russian Federation, while expressing their support for the resolution, questioned whether the Council was the appropriate forum to address the issue of mental health and psychosocial support for peacekeeping personnel.[962] Specifically, the representative of the Russian Federation stated that the Special Committee on Peacekeeping Operations of the General Assembly was the specialized platform bringing together all interested parties, including troop contributors and Secretariat experts, for a comprehensive review of all aspects of peacekeeping operations and added that the Council lacked the necessary competence, data and analysis to consider the mental health issues of peacekeeping personnel.[963] The representative of the Russian Federation expressed the view that personnel selection and performance issues in special political missions fell under the responsibility of the Secretariat and that mixing the notions of "peacekeeping operations" and "special political missions" under the single term "peace operations" introduced uncertainty regarding the responsibility for the appropriate selection of personnel, their mental health support, funding and the overall scope of the efforts needed. Similarly, the representative of India stressed that any serious deliberations on the issue should be premised on data and studies conducted in consultation with troop- and police-contributing countries and noted that the Special Committee was giving due consideration to the mental health of peacekeeping personnel, as a result of which there had been consistent improvement in recent years in the operating environment, living conditions, casualty evacuation and medical facilities, among other areas. As the penholder of the resolution, the representative of Mexico expressed the view that the Council should give due importance not only to the physical well-being of uniformed and civilian personnel, but also to their mental health before, during and after their deployment.

Meetings: United Nations peacekeeping operations, 2022

Meeting record and date	*Sub-item*	*Other documents*	*Rule 37 invitations*	*Rule 39 and other invitations*	*Speakers*	*Decision and vote (for-against-abstaining)*
S/PV.9090 and S/PV.9090 (Resumption 1) 12 July	The key role of strategic communications for efficient peacekeeping Letter dated 5 July 2022 from the Permanent Representative of Brazil to the United Nations addressed to the Security Council (S/2022/539)		23 Member States[a]	Force Commander of the United Nations Organization Stabilization Mission in the Democratic Republic of the Congo (MONUSCO), Head of the Delegation of the European Union to the	Secretary-General, all Council members,[b] all invitees[c]	S/PRST/2022/5

[959] Resolution 2668 (2022), para. 1.

[960] Ibid., paras. 2–4.

[961] Ibid., para. 5.

[962] See S/PV.9229.

[963] For more information on the relations between the Council and the General Assembly, including its subsidiary organs, see part IV.

Meeting record and date	*Sub-item*	*Other documents*	*Rule 37 invitations*	*Rule 39 and other invitations*	*Speakers*	*Decision and vote (for-against-abstaining)*
				United Nations, Director of Research at the International Peace Institute		
S/PV.9123 6 September				Under-Secretary-General for Peace Operations	All Council members, invitee	
S/PV.9189 14 November	Police Commissioners			Under-Secretary-General for Peace Operations, Police Commissioner of the United Nations Mission in South Sudan (UNMISS), Police Commissioner of MONUSCO, representative of the Kofi Annan International Peacekeeping Training Centre	All Council members, all invitees[d]	
S/PV.9229 21 December		Draft resolution submitted by 52 Member States[e] (S/2022/977)	45 Member States[f]		Three Council members (India, Mexico, Russian Federation)	Resolution 2668 (2022) 15-0-0

[a] Algeria, Australia, Bangladesh, Belgium, Denmark, Ecuador, Egypt, Germany, Guatemala, Indonesia, Israel, Japan, Lithuania, Malta, Morocco, Philippines, Portugal, Republic of Korea, Slovakia, South Africa, Switzerland, Thailand and Uruguay.

[b] Brazil (President of the Council) was represented by its Minister for Foreign Affairs; Ghana was represented by its Minister for Foreign Affairs and Regional Integration; India was represented by its Secretary (East) in the Ministry of External Affairs; and the United Arab Emirates was represented by its Permanent Representative to the United Nations and Assistant Minister for Foreign Affairs and International Cooperation for Political Affairs.

[c] The representative of Denmark spoke on behalf of the Nordic countries; and the representative of Indonesia spoke on behalf of the Group of Friends on the Safety and Security of United Nations Peacekeepers.

[d] The Police Commissioners of UNMISS and MONUSCO participated in the meeting by videoconference.

[e] Albania, Algeria, Australia, Belgium, Botswana, Bulgaria, Canada, Colombia, Costa Rica, Croatia, Cyprus, Czechia, Denmark, Djibouti, Dominican Republic, Ecuador, Estonia, Finland, Gabon, Georgia, Germany, Greece, Guatemala, Hungary, Ireland, Israel, Italy, Japan, Kazakhstan, Kenya, Latvia, Lithuania, Luxembourg, Malta, Mexico, Netherlands, New Zealand, Norway, Portugal, Republic of Korea, Republic of Moldova, Serbia, Sierra Leone, Slovakia, Slovenia, Suriname, Sweden, Switzerland, Thailand, Türkiye and United Arab Emirates.

[f] Algeria, Australia, Austria, Belgium, Botswana, Bulgaria, Canada, Colombia, Costa Rica, Croatia, Cyprus, Czechia, Denmark, Djibouti, Dominican Republic, Ecuador, Estonia, Finland, Georgia, Germany, Greece, Guatemala, Hungary, Israel, Italy, Japan, Kazakhstan, Latvia, Lithuania, Luxembourg, Malta, Netherlands, New Zealand, Portugal, Republic of Korea, Republic of Moldova, Serbia, Sierra Leone, Slovakia, Slovenia, Suriname, Sweden, Switzerland, Thailand and Türkiye.

25. International Residual Mechanism for Criminal Tribunals

In 2022, the Council held four meetings related to the work of the International Residual Mechanism for Criminal Tribunals.[964] Of the four meetings, two took the form of debates, and two were convened for the adoption of a decision.[965] The Council adopted one resolution under Chapter VII of the Charter of the United Nations in connection with the item. More information on the meetings, including on participants, speakers and outcomes, is given in the table below.[966]

On 31 March, the Council adopted a presidential statement in which it requested the Mechanism to submit, by 14 April, a report on the progress of its work since June 2020, including detailed schedules for the ongoing proceedings and factors related to projected completion dates for the remaining cases.[967] In the presidential statement, the Council also requested the Informal Working Group on International Tribunals to carry out a thorough examination of the Mechanism's report and of the report on the evaluation of the methods and work of the Mechanism by the Office of Internal Oversight Services (OIOS), which was due by 31 March.[968] The Council asked the Informal Working Group to present in its review its views and any findings or recommendations for the Council's consideration by 13 May.[969] Furthermore, the Council noted with concern that, despite reaching an earlier agreement, the Mechanism continued to face problems in the relocation of acquitted persons and convicted persons who had completed their sentences. The Council emphasized the importance of the successful relocation of such persons and stressed its ongoing determination to combat impunity for those responsible for serious violations of international humanitarian law and the necessity for all persons indicted by the International Tribunal for the Former Yugoslavia and the International Criminal Tribunal for Rwanda, including the remaining fugitives, to be brought to justice.[970]

On 14 June, the Council held a meeting in which it heard the first semi-annual briefings by the President of the Mechanism and by its Prosecutor.[971] At the meeting, the President and the Prosecutor presented their latest reports on the work of the Mechanism, submitted pursuant to paragraph 16 of resolution 1966 (2010). Addressing the Council for the last time before stepping down as President of the Mechanism, Judge Carmel Agius expressed his satisfaction with the significant progress accomplished during the reporting period, noting that there were only three main cases left, which represented a markedly reduced judicial workload compared with early 2019, and that appeal case proceedings were on track for completion within the projected time frames. In addition, the President highlighted the advances in the tracking of fugitives of the International Criminal Tribunal for Rwanda and their decisive impact on the Mechanism's operations and outlook. He said that, as a result of the efforts of the Prosecutor, only four fugitives were left, all of whom were expected to be tried in Rwanda. The President also highlighted progress in the enforcement of sentences and in the monitoring of cases referred to national jurisdictions, the number of which had been reduced from seven to two. The President noted that, parallel to the results, some setbacks had been experienced during the reporting period. In that connection, he reported that the binding agreement signed between the United Nations and the Niger to

[964] For more information on the International Residual Mechanism for Criminal Tribunals, see previous supplements covering the period 2018 to 2021; for further information on issues considered under the item, see also previous supplements covering the period 1996 to 2007.

[965] For more information on the format of meetings, see part II.

[966] See also A/77/2, part II, chap. 10.

[967] S/PRST/2022/2, fifth paragraph.

[968] Ibid., sixth paragraph.

[969] Ibid.

[970] Ibid., ninth and tenth paragraphs.

[971] See S/PV.9062.

relocate the acquitted and released persons to the territory of the Niger had not been honoured. He also mentioned the failure of Serbia to fulfil the international obligations under resolution 1966 (2010), as illustrated by the contempt case against Petar Jojić and Vjerica Radeta. In closing, the President stated that, like its predecessor tribunals, the Mechanism was part of a broader system that reflected a shared vision of justice and a determination that the crucial work of those tribunals would be seen through to the very end. He added that, after almost a decade of operations, the Mechanism was far closer to realizing the Council's vision of a small and temporary institution. He emphasized, nonetheless, that many of the Mechanism's activities, including a number of judicial functions, would extend into the foreseeable future and for long after the main cases had concluded, unless the Council decided otherwise. In that connection, it would be for the Council to determine the scope of the Mechanism's mandate and to decide if and when certain duties should more appropriately be discharged by others.

In his statement, the Prosecutor informed the Council that, in the previous two years, his Office had accounted for half of the fugitives who had remained at large following the closure of the International Criminal Tribunal for Rwanda, with only four fugitives remaining. He reported that, after several challenging years, progress was being made with South Africa and that an operational task team had recently been established to assist his Office in bringing the flight from justice of Fulgence Kayishema to an end. He added that his Office's goal was to account for all four outstanding fugitives by the time the Council next reviewed the work of the Mechanism. In addition, the Prosecutor provided updates on his Office's continuing efforts to complete the *Kabuga*, the *Fatuma et al.* and the *Stanišić and Simatović* cases. With regard to the mandate given by the Council to his Office to respond to requests for assistance from domestic investigators and prosecutors around the world, the Prosecutor affirmed that assisting national jurisdictions prosecuting international crimes committed in the former Yugoslavia and Rwanda continued to be a priority. He added that, as his Office moved closer to completing the last cases and accounting for the final fugitives, it was important to remember that thousands of cases still needed to be completed in national courts and that his Office's assistance was essential to completing that work. Furthermore, national prosecutors still faced other critical challenges, with regional judicial cooperation remaining the most significant issue in the former Yugoslavia. In that connection, the Prosecutor urged the countries concerned to significantly increase their cooperation in the search for missing persons, which was a humanitarian imperative. With respect to Rwanda, the Prosecutor said that the challenge was about, fundamentally, priorities and resources and, sometimes, a lack of political will. More broadly, in relation to both Rwanda and the countries of the former Yugoslavia, he said that genocide denial and the glorification of war criminals persisted and that there could be no tolerance for such behaviour, which insulted the victims and sowed the seeds for future conflict. In closing, the Prosecutor outlined the main findings of the ongoing review process and of the OIOS report and reported on the steps that had been taken to deliver on the mandate of his Office during the review period, including securing convictions in the trials in the *Stanišić and Simatović* and the *Nzabonimpa et al.* cases and in the *Mladić* appeal.

Following the briefings, the Council discussed the progress achieved by the Mechanism during the reporting period. At the outset, the representative of Gabon stated that, as requested in the statement by the President of the Council adopted on 31 March,[972] the President and the Prosecutor had in their status update attempted to show that the Council had been right to trust and invest in the Mechanism to bring justice to victims of international crimes in Rwanda and the former Yugoslavia.[973] He added that the Mechanism had made considerable progress during the biennium despite the many challenges it had faced from the health crisis caused by the COVID-19 pandemic, a statement that was echoed by several Council members.[974] By contrast, the representative of the Russian Federation expressed the view that the Mechanism had not made any progress in the planned completion of its activities and that there had been no real downsizing over the previous five years. He said that the results of the biennial review that was under way would determine the parameters of the further functioning of the Mechanism and that that process would help the leadership of the Mechanism to undertake the efforts necessary to draw down its work as soon as possible. Other Council members[975] acknowledged the progress achieved by the Mechanism in judicial matters and its working methods during the reporting period, while encouraging the Mechanism to take the measures necessary to follow the projected timelines and to implement the remaining

[972] S/PRST/2022/2, fifth paragraph.
[973] See S/PV.9062.
[974] India, France, Ghana, United Kingdom, United States, Mexico, Kenya and Ireland.
[975] India, France, United Kingdom, Mexico, United Arab Emirates, China and Albania.

recommendations in line with its mandate. In that regard, several members[976] acknowledged the progress in the *Kabuga* case and said that they were looking forward to the completion of the trial. Some members[977] were also looking forward to the judgments in the *Stanišić and Simatović* and the *Fatuma et al.* cases. Most Council members underscored the importance of judicial cooperation among national jurisdictions and between the States concerned, and of full cooperation with the Mechanism to enable it to complete its mandate. In that connection, several members[978] expressed concern about the non-compliance by Serbia with the Mechanism's arrest warrant for the *Jojić and Radeta* case, and others[979] urged States to help in the arrest and surrender of the four remaining fugitives indicted by the International Criminal Tribunal for Rwanda. Furthermore, many Council members[980] expressed concern about the issue of the relocation of the acquitted or released persons and called upon the States concerned and the Mechanism to urgently find an appropriate solution. Members and non-members of the Council[981] condemned the denial of atrocity crimes committed in the former Yugoslavia and Rwanda and the glorification of their perpetrators.

At the meeting on 22 June,[982] the Council adopted, with one abstention, resolution 2637 (2022) under Chapter VII of the Charter, by which it appointed the Prosecutor of the Mechanism with effect from 1 July 2022 until 30 June 2024.[983] In the resolution, the Council continued to urge all States to intensify their cooperation with and render all necessary assistance to the Mechanism, in particular to achieve the arrest and surrender of all remaining fugitives indicted by the International Criminal Tribunal for Rwanda as soon as possible.[984] The Council noted with concern that, despite having reached an earlier agreement, the Mechanism continued to face problems in the relocation of acquitted persons and convicted persons who had completed their sentence, and emphasized the importance of finding expeditious and durable solutions to those problems, including as part of a reconciliation process.[985] In that regard, the Council noted that decisions on the relocation of persons who had been acquitted or had completed their sentences should take into account, inter alia, the readiness of the State of origin to accept its nationals, the consent or any objections raised by the individuals to be relocated and the availability of other relocation States.[986] The Council welcomed the report submitted by the Mechanism to the Council and the OIOS report on the evaluation of the methods and work of the Mechanism.[987] In that regard, the Council requested the Mechanism to implement the recommendations made by the Informal Working Group on International Tribunals and to continue to take steps to further enhance its efficiency and effective and transparent management, including the production of clear and focused projections of completion timelines at the earliest stage possible and disciplined adherence thereto.[988] The Council reiterated its request to the Mechanism to include in its six-monthly reports to the Council information on progress achieved in implementing the resolution.[989] With a view to strengthening independent oversight of the Mechanism, the Council recalled that, as set out in its presidential statement of 31 March 2022, future reviews carried out pursuant to paragraph 17 of resolution 1966 (2010) should include evaluation reports sought from OIOS with respect to the methods and work of the Mechanism.[990]

On 12 December, Council members heard the second semi-annual briefings by the President of the Mechanism and by its Prosecutor, in which they presented the latest progress report on the work of the

---

[976] Gabon, France, United Kingdom, United States, Mexico, United Arab Emirates, China, Kenya, Norway, Ireland and Albania.
[977] United Kingdom, United States, Mexico, Norway and Albania.
[978] United Kingdom, United States, Norway, Ireland and Albania.
[979] France, Ghana, United States, Mexico, Kenya, Norway and Ireland.
[980] India, Ghana, United Kingdom, United States, Mexico, United Arab Emirates, Norway and Ireland.
[981] Gabon, Russian Federation, United Kingdom, United States, Ireland, Albania and Bosnia and Herzegovina.
[982] See S/PV.9072.
[983] Resolution 2637 (2022), para. 1.
[984] Ibid., para. 3.
[985] Ibid., para. 4.
[986] Ibid., para. 5.
[987] Ibid., para. 8. See also S/2022/148 and S/2022/319.
[988] Resolution 2637 (2022), para. 10.
[989] Ibid., para. 12.
[990] Ibid., para. 16.

Mechanism.[991] During the meeting,[992] the President of the Mechanism reported that, after disposing of the *Fatuma et al.* contempt case on 29 June, in line with the original projection, the Mechanism had been left with only two main cases in its pending judicial caseload. In that regard, she reported that the trial against Félicien Kabuga had commenced at The Hague on 29 September and was proceeding apace, and that the projection for the completion of its trial phase remained by September 2024. She also reported that the appeals procedure in the *Stanišić and Simatović* case continued to be on track and said that she was confident that the appeal judgment would be delivered by June 2023. In addition, she reported that the Mechanism had made important strides in its other continuous judicial activities, such as the protection of victims and witnesses, assistance to national jurisdictions and the monitoring of cases referred to national courts, and the enforcement of sentences. She added that those matters regularly called for decisions by Mechanism judges or the President and required sustained effort and resources to see the full cycle of justice through to the end. Regarding the eight relocated persons who had been acquitted or had completed their sentences, the President affirmed that the best way to resolve the situation would be for the existing agreement between the United Nations and the Niger to be observed and that the collective inability to find a durable solution reflected negatively not only on the Organization but also on the credibility of international justice as a whole. She stated that State assistance in identifying and implementing an acceptable solution to that crisis would help the Mechanism to move ahead with its transition plans. In connection with the request by the Council for the Mechanism to provide options regarding the transfer of its remaining activities in due course, the President stated that developing a strategy for the future had become one of the priorities of her presidency and that she had presented the Informal Working Group with a road map for developing a Mechanism-wide scenario-based workforce plan. With the road map as a first point of reference, the Mechanism would provide updates on the development of a comprehensive strategy to guide its continued transition to a truly residual court. The President underscored that any delay in addressing current challenges such as the enforcement of sentences would have an impact on the transition plans. In that connection, she urgently appealed to States to share the burden of enforcing the sentences of people convicted by the International Tribunal for the Former Yugoslavia, the International Criminal Tribunal for Rwanda or the Mechanism and added that, unless additional States came forward, the Mechanism would struggle to continue to fulfil its duties in that important area. Finally, the President stated that, despite the Council's continued emphasis on ensuring that the Mechanism remained guided by the premise of operating as a small, temporary and efficient structure, the scope of its responsibilities and the volume of its activities extended far beyond what had been envisaged when the ad hoc tribunals had been established. In that sense, its mandated residual functions, including judicial functions, remained essential. Even after the completion of its pending caseload, the Mechanism would be left with a number of long-term responsibilities, including the enforcement of sentences, the protection of witnesses and assistance to national jurisdictions. In closing, the President underscored the need to redouble efforts to counter genocide denial, revisionism and the glorification of war criminals.

Following the President of the Mechanism, the Prosecutor reported on the progress of the two remaining core crime cases: the *Kabuga* trial and the *Stanišić and Simatović* appeal. He also highlighted his Office's work under its mandate to investigate and prosecute contempt-of-court crimes. With regard to the search for the remaining fugitives, he reported that only four remained at large. In that connection, he thanked the President of South Africa for establishing a dedicated national investigative team to work directly with the Prosecutor's tracking team in the search for Fulgence Kayishema. He added that important results had been achieved and that the investigation in South Africa was progressing quickly. The Prosecutor highlighted the fact that over a thousand fugitives were still wanted by Rwandan prosecutors for crimes committed during the genocide and said that, while tracking the fugitives, his Office had discovered some fugitives who were enjoying impunity in third countries. In that context, he stated that his Office would work with the national authorities of the countries that were responsible for extraditing or prosecuting those individuals and that Rwanda would continue to need assistance from the international community to account for the many other fugitives suspected of genocide. Recalling that the Council had mandated his Office to respond to requests for assistance from domestic investigators

[991] S/2022/583.

[992] See S/PV.9217.

and prosecutors around the world, the Prosecutor affirmed that meeting that mandate continued to be his priority. He reminded the Council that, while his Office moved closer to completing the last cases and accounting for the final fugitives, thousands of cases had yet to be completed in national courts and that his Office's assistance remained essential for investigating and prosecuting the thousands of perpetrators of war crimes, crimes against humanity and genocide who had yet to be investigated and prosecuted in the former Yugoslavia. In that regard, he anticipated that requests for assistance would increase in number as well as in complexity and significance. Concerning regional cooperation in the Balkans, the Prosecutor stated that, despite important signs of positive progress, local prosecutors reported that they did not receive the cooperation they needed from Croatia in cases involving Croatian suspects. In that context, his Office would continue to engage with Croatian authorities to find mutually acceptable solutions. The Prosecutor also referred to issues related to the continued denial of war crimes and glorification of convicted war criminals in the countries of the former Yugoslavia.

Council members acknowledged the progress achieved by the Mechanism towards the completion of its work during the reporting period and welcomed the initiative of the President to devise a drawdown strategy for the Mechanism. The representative of the Russian Federation thanked the President of the Mechanism for her intention to transform the Mechanism from a judicial body into a genuine residual structure. In that context, he said that the Russian Federation had taken note of the plans to close the pretrial detention facility in Arusha and the Sarajevo office as from 1 April 2023 and considered that decision to be a step in the right direction. He added that, given the residual nature of the Mechanism, its leadership should regularly review its functions, departments and offices for redundancies and diminishing relevance, and that the relevant practical recommendations of OIOS were much needed. The Russian representative expressed the view that the Mechanism should follow the best practices of other similar structures, in particular the Special Tribunal for Lebanon.

Council members continued to call upon all States to cooperate fully with the Mechanism in tracking all the remaining fugitives to enable the completion of the judicial process. The representative of Gabon stated that the credibility and effectiveness of the Mechanism would continue to depend largely on the assistance provided by States, especially their support to the Prosecutor to facilitate the arrest of the fugitives at large, and that the purpose and effectiveness of the Mechanism would be called into question if the fugitives were not arrested and then tried according to the required legal procedures. With regard to cooperation, several Council members[993] expressed their regret that the situation of the eight acquitted or released individuals remained unresolved. In that context, some members[994] called on the Niger and the States concerned to abide by the terms of the relocation agreement. The representative of Ghana recalled resolution 2529 (2020), in which the Council emphasized the importance of expeditiously and durably relocating those persons. He stressed that the international justice community had to pay attention to and resolve that situation, and called upon the Council to critically discuss the matter with an outcome that would assist the Mechanism in line with paragraph 5 of resolution 2637 (2022). Emphasizing the importance of cooperation between the Mechanism and the Member States concerned, a number of Council members[995] urged Serbia to promptly execute the outstanding arrest warrants of Petar Jojić and Vjerica Radeta, while others[996] expressed their regret about the continued need to confront the denial of crimes and the glorification of war criminals.

During the period under review, the Council took note of the intention of the Secretary-General to appoint a new President of the Mechanism and to reappoint the 25 judges and the Prosecutor of the Mechanism, all with effect from 1 July 2022 to 30 June 2024.[997]

[993] United Arab Emirates, Ireland, Norway and India.
[994] Ireland, Norway and India.
[995] United States, Ireland, Norway, Albania and United Kingdom.
[996] United States, Ireland, Albania, France, Mexico and United Kingdom.
[997] See S/2022/486 and S/2022/487. See also S/2022/511. For more information on actions of the Council concerning the judges of the Mechanism, see part IV, sect. I.D, and part IX, sect. IV.

Meetings: International Residual Mechanism for Criminal Tribunals, 2022

Meeting record and date	*Sub-item*	*Other documents*	*Rule 37 invitations*	*Rule 39 and other invitations*	*Speakers*	*Decision and vote (for-against-abstaining)*
S/PV.9010 31 March						S/PRST/2022/2
S/PV.9062 14 June			Bosnia and Herzegovina, Croatia, Rwanda, Serbia	President of the International Residual Mechanism for Criminal Tribunals, Prosecutor of the Mechanism	All Council members, all invitees[a]	
S/PV.9072 22 June		Draft resolution submitted by Gabon (S/2022/501)				Resolution 2637 (2022) (adopted under Chapter VII) 14-0-1[b]
S/PV.9217 12 December	Note by the Secretary-General on the International Residual Mechanism for Criminal Tribunals (S/2022/583)		Bosnia and Herzegovina, Croatia, Rwanda, Serbia	President of the Mechanism, Prosecutor of the Mechanism	All Council members, all invitees	

[a] Serbia was represented by its Minister of Justice.
[b] *For*: Albania, Brazil, China, France, Gabon, Ghana, India, Ireland, Kenya, Mexico, Norway, United Arab Emirates, United Kingdom, United States; *against*: none; *abstaining*: Russian Federation.

26. Children and armed conflict

During the period under review, the Council held one open debate in connection with the item entitled "Children and armed conflict".[998] More information on the meeting, including on participants and speakers, is provided in table 1 below.[999]

The open debate, held on 19 July, was convened at the initiative of Brazil, which held the presidency for the month,[1000] in connection with the annual report of the Secretary-General on children and armed conflict.[1001] The open debate was chaired by the Vice-Minister for Foreign Affairs of Brazil and featured briefings by the Special Representative of the Secretary-General for Children and Armed Conflict, the Executive Director of the United Nations Children's Fund (UNICEF) and the founder and Executive Director of the non-governmental organization Similar Ground.[1002]

In her remarks, the Special Representative of the Secretary-General for Children and Armed Conflict noted that the abuses that children had been subjected to the previous year had been as grievous as they had been many. She reported that, in 2021, a total of 23,982 grave violations against over 19,165 children had been verified in the 21 country situations and one regional monitoring arrangement covered by her mandate. She added that, in 2021, 8,000 children had been either killed or maimed, making killing

[998] For more information on the format of meetings, see part II.
[999] See also A/77/2, part II, chap. 14.
[1000] A concept note was circulated by a letter dated 5 July (S/2022/540).
[1001] S/2022/493.
[1002] See S/PV.9096 and S/PV.9096 (Resumption 1).

and maiming the most prevalent of all grave violations. With more than 6,300 verified cases, the recruitment and use of children for, in and by parties to armed conflict had been the second most prevalent violation, followed by the denial of humanitarian access to children, with more than 3,900 incidents. The Special Representative expressed concern over the increase in cases of abduction, rape and other forms of sexual violence and the steady increase in violations against girls, especially killing and maiming, sexual violence and abduction. She also noted a general rise in attacks on schools and hospitals and a verified increase in the military use of schools. She added that the Secretary-General had included the situations of Ethiopia, Mozambique and Ukraine in the children and armed conflict agenda due to the severity of the armed violence, conflict and war in those places and would begin monitoring to report on those situations by 2023. With regard to positive developments, she highlighted the implementation of 17 joint action plans with parties to conflict, the adoption of 40 new commitments and agreed measures, and the release of over 12,200 children from armed groups and forces in 2021, following advocacy by the United Nations. In addition, progress had been made in analysis, policy development and partnerships and in prevention mechanisms in line with resolution 2427 (2018), including the launch of a guidance note on the violation of abduction, the publishing of studies on the impact of the COVID-19 pandemic on grave violations against children in armed conflict and the issuance of a report consolidating the results of the four regional consultations conducted to identify challenges and collect lessons learned to strengthen the monitoring and reporting mechanism on children and armed conflict. In conclusion, the Special Representative highlighted three of the recommendations outlined in the report of the Secretary-General: first, ensuring that United Nations operations on the ground were adequately mandated, staffed and funded to continue to carry out their mandate in relation to the protection of children; second, safeguarding humanitarian spaces and ensuring safe, timely and unimpeded humanitarian access to all children; and third, ensuring sustainable financial support and technical assistance for timely, gender-, age- and disability-sensitive, survivor-centred and inclusive reintegration programmes for children, which were critical for breaking cycles of violence and allowing child survivors a second chance at a constructive life. In concluding, she stressed that the best way to protect children and prevent violations against them in situations of armed conflict was to promote and champion peace.

While lamenting the continued proliferation of conflicts and grave violations against children, and the addition of three new situations to the report of the Secretary-General, the Executive Director of UNICEF underscored the progress made, in particular the removal of eight situations from the report and the release of over 10,000 children from armed forces and groups, bringing the total number of children documented to have been released since 2000 to more than 186,000. She emphasized the continued commitment of the United Nations to protecting children in accordance with humanitarian principles, while underlining that Member States had enormous power to drive progress to protect children. She called upon Member States not only to insist on compliance with international humanitarian law but also to use their power to issue military orders with zero-tolerance policies on grave violations against children, to endorse and implement the Safe Schools Declaration, to use their influence to urge States and non-State armed groups to prevent and end grave violations against children, to protect children who had survived grave violations from stigma and revictimization, and to support United Nations efforts through the allocation of resources and a commitment to supporting the agenda.

In his briefing, the founder and Executive Director of the non-governmental organization Similar Ground shared with the Council his personal experience, first being forced to become a child soldier when he was growing up, then escaping to Uganda to become a refugee, eventually joining the War Child programme known as VoiceMore, a youth-led advocacy programme, and running a project for orphans and separated children, and finally setting set up, together with friends, a community-based organization, Similar Ground, to help hundreds of children to recover from stress and trauma. On the basis of his experience, he proposed four recommendations to the Council, relating to the reintegration of children, longer-term funding for projects and local organizations and community groups, greater participation in decision-making for children and young people, and greater accountability for violations of humanitarian law, including the Convention on the Rights of the Child, the Geneva Conventions and relevant Council resolutions concerning the protection of children.

In their statements, Council members and other delegations expressed concern at the growing number of children subjected to all six grave violations against children in armed conflict, as defined in the relevant Council resolutions. Speakers also stressed that children associated with armed or terrorist groups should be treated not as criminals but rather as victims.[1003] The representative of Kenya expressed his belief that human rights-sensitive and effective counter-terrorism was a key tool in the protection of children and called for a more robust and consistent counter-terrorism regime to protect children.[1004] Many speakers welcomed the inclusion of Ukraine, Mozambique and Ethiopia as situations of concern in the annual report of the Secretary-General on children and armed conflict, given the severity of the armed violence in the countries.[1005]

On the way forward, many speakers underscored that impunity for grave violations against children was unacceptable and called for full accountability through national and international justice mechanisms.[1006] Some speakers underlined that all parties to armed conflict must comply with international humanitarian law, international human rights law and international refugee law and act to prevent and end grave violations against children.[1007] In that connection, speakers encouraged all Member States to commit to the Safe Schools Declaration, the Paris Principles and the Vancouver Principles on Peacekeeping and the Prevention of the Recruitment and Use of Child Soldiers and to ratify the Optional Protocol to the Convention on the Rights of the Child on the involvement of children in armed conflict.[1008]

Speakers said that the children and armed conflict agenda should be mainstreamed into all efforts and discussions concerning conflict, including conflict prevention, mediation, peacebuilding and post-conflict reconstruction, and that child protection provisions and capacities should be incorporated adequately into all relevant mandates of United Nations peacekeeping operations and political missions.[1009] To facilitate responses to threats against children, speakers urged full support for the allocation of targeted and rapid resources to provide safe accommodation and enhanced protection for displaced refugees and stateless children victims of the six grave violations against children in conflict, and to enable the safe and meaningful participation of victims and survivors in legal proceedings to end impunity.[1010] The majority of speakers noted that the fight against grave violations should not end with the release of children but should also include their reintegration into society.

Affirming the important role of the listing mechanism of the annual report of the Secretary-General in child protection, speakers maintained that clear, objective, impartial, transparent and measurable listing criteria were critical.[1011] Noting with concern that the report of the Secretary-General included situations that were not situations of armed conflict or threats to the maintenance of international peace

---

1003 See S/PV.9096 (Brazil, Norway, Ghana, China, Canada (on behalf of the Group of Friends of Children and Armed Conflict) and Switzerland); and S/PV.9096 (Resumption 1) (Slovenia, Italy, Andorra and Chile).

1004 See S/PV.9096

1005 See S/PV.9096 (United States, United Kingdom, Ireland, Albania, Canada and Ukraine); and S/PV.9096 (Resumption 1) (Italy, Germany, European Union (also on behalf of Albania, Andorra, Bosnia and Herzegovina, Georgia, Monaco, Montenegro, North Macedonia, Republic of Moldova, San Marino and Ukraine), Belgium, Poland, Slovakia, Australia and Bulgaria).

1006 See S/PV.9096 (Brazil, Norway, France, India, Gabon, Mexico, United Kingdom, Albania, United States, Canada, Malta, Liechtenstein and Uruguay); and S/PV.9096 (Resumption 1) (Slovenia, Estonia, Denmark, Italy, European Union (also on behalf of Albania, Andorra, Bosnia and Herzegovina, Georgia, Monaco, Montenegro, North Macedonia, Republic of Moldova, San Marino and Ukraine), Slovakia, Republic of Korea, Lebanon, State of Palestine and Morocco).

1007 See S/PV.9096 (Canada (on behalf of the Group of Friends of Children and Armed Conflict) and Malta); and S/PV.9096 (Resumption 1) (Denmark (on behalf of the Nordic countries), Czechia, Poland, Slovakia, Republic of Korea and Georgia).

1008 See S/PV.9096 (France, India, United Arab Emirates, Kenya, Gabon, Mexico, Ireland, China, Canada (on behalf of the Group of Friends of Children and Armed Conflict), Malta, Liechtenstein, Switzerland, Uruguay and Ecuador); and S/PV.9096 (Resumption 1) (Slovenia, Denmark (on behalf of the Nordic countries), Italy, Germany, Botswana (on behalf of the Group of Friends of Children and Armed Conflict), Slovakia, New Zealand, Spain, Andorra, Malaysia, Georgia, Portugal, Chile and Bulgaria).

1009 See S/PV.9096 (Brazil, Ghana, United States, India, Kenya, Ireland, Albania and Switzerland); and S/PV.9096 (Resumption 1) (Poland, Thailand, Malaysia, Bulgaria and Türkiye).

1010 See S/PV.9096 (Ghana, Canada (on behalf of the Group of Friends of Children and Armed Conflict), Liechtenstein and Switzerland; and S/PV.9096 (Resumption 1) (Thailand, Türkiye, South Africa and Bangladesh).

1011 See S/PV.9096 (Ireland, China, Canada (also on behalf of the Group of Friends of Children and Armed Conflict), Malta, Liechtenstein and Switzerland); and S/PV.9096 (Resumption 1) (Slovenia and Belgium).

and security, the representative of India cautioned that attempts to selectively expand the mandate would only politicize it.[1012] The representative of Canada expressed concern about the decision to list the Government of the Syrian Arab Republic in annex I.B to the report of the Secretary-General and said that such a decision had set a troubling precedent and should have been taken only on the basis of a significant decrease in serious violations and respect for specific time-bound commitments.

In 2022, the Council addressed the children and armed conflict agenda in several of its country- and region-specific decisions and in decisions relating to thematic items. Selected provisions of decisions in which the Council explicitly referenced actions or measures concerning that agenda in 2022 are listed in table 2. In 2022, the Council, inter alia: (a) condemned and demanded the cessation of violations and abuses against children, including attacks on schools and the deprivation of access to education, and called for accountability and compliance with international instruments; (b) called for the implementation of action plans and programmes on children and armed conflict, with new emphasis on preventing and responding to sexual violence against children; (c) underscored the importance of taking into account child protection concerns in the demobilization, disarmament and reintegration processes and security sector reform; (d) requested monitoring, analysis and reporting on violations and abuses against children; (e) mandated United Nations peacekeeping operations and special political missions with child protection tasks; (f) imposed or called for the imposition of measures against perpetrators of violations against children; and (g) building on resolution 2601 (2021),[1013] called for the protection, respect and promotion of the right to education in armed conflict.

Table 1
Meetings: children and armed conflict, 2022

Meeting record and date	*Sub-item*	*Other documents*	*Rule 37 invitations*	*Rule 39 and other invitations*	*Speakers*	*Decision and vote (for-against-abstaining)*
S/PV.9096 and S/PV.9096 (Resumption 1) 19 July	Report of the Secretary-General on children and armed conflict (S/2022/493) Letter dated 5 July 2022 from the Permanent Representative of Brazil to the United Nations addressed to the Secretary-General (S/2022/540)		56 Member States[a]	Special Representative of the Secretary-General for Children and Armed Conflict, Executive Director of the United Nations Children's Fund, Chargé d'affaires a.i. of the Delegation of the European Union to the United Nations, Permanent Observer of the State of Palestine to the United Nations; founder and Executive Director of Similar Ground	All Council members,[b] all invitees[c]	

[a] Algeria, Andorra, Argentina, Armenia, Australia, Azerbaijan, Bangladesh, Belgium, Botswana, Bulgaria, Canada, Chile, Czechia, Denmark, Ecuador, Egypt, Estonia, Ethiopia, Georgia, Germany, Greece, Guatemala, Hungary, Iran (Islamic Republic of), Iraq, Israel, Italy, Japan, Lebanon, Liechtenstein, Lithuania, Luxembourg, Malaysia, Malta, Morocco, Myanmar, New Zealand, Pakistan, Philippines, Poland, Portugal, Republic of Korea, Romania, Saudi Arabia, Slovakia, Slovenia, South Africa, Spain, Sudan, Switzerland, Syrian Arab Republic, Thailand, Türkiye, Ukraine, Uruguay and Yemen.
[b] Brazil (President of the Council) was represented by its Vice-Minister for Foreign Affairs.

[1012] See S/PV.9096.
[1013] For more information, see *Repertoire*, *Supplement 2021*, part I, sect. 24.

[c] Hungary was represented by its Minister for Foreign Affairs and Trade. The representative of Botswana spoke on behalf of the Group of Friends of the Responsibility to Protect; the representative of Canada spoke also on behalf of the Group of Friends of Children and Armed Conflict; the representative of Denmark spoke on behalf of the Nordic countries; and the representative of the European Union spoke also on behalf of Albania, Andorra, Bosnia and Herzegovina, Georgia, Monaco, Montenegro, North Macedonia, the Republic of Moldova, San Marino and Ukraine.

Table 2
Selection of provisions relevant to children and armed conflict, by theme and item

	Item	*Decision*	*Paragraph*
Condemnation and demands for the cessation of violations and abuses against children and calls for accountability and compliance with international instruments			
Country- and region-specific	The situation in the Central African Republic	Resolution 2659 (2022)	26, 27, 56
	The situation concerning the Democratic Republic of the Congo	Resolution 2666 (2022)	9, 10
	The question concerning Haiti	Resolution 2653 (2022)	1
	The situation in Mali	Resolution 2640 (2022)	5, 12, 47
	The situation in Somalia	Resolution 2628 (2022)	14, 14 (a), (b) and (d)
		Resolution 2657 (2022)	10, 10 (a) (i) and (iv)
	Reports of the Secretary-General on the Sudan and South Sudan	Resolution 2625 (2022)	17
Thematic	Threats to international peace and security caused by terrorist acts	S/PRST/2022/7	fifth
Action plans and programmes on children and armed conflict			
Country- and region-specific	Peace and security in Africa	S/PRST/2022/6	nineteenth
	The situation in the Central African Republic	Resolution 2659 (2022)	26, 27
	The situation concerning the Democratic Republic of the Congo	Resolution 2666 (2022)	8, 10, 24 (i) (e)
	The situation in Mali	Resolution 2640 (2022)	48, 49
	The situation in Somalia	Resolution 2628 (2022)	14 (e)
		Resolution 2657 (2022)	10 (b), 13 (b)
	Reports of the Secretary-General on the Sudan and South Sudan	Resolution 2625 (2022)	16, 20 (m)
Child protection in disarmament, demobilization and reintegration processes and security sector reform			
Country- and region-specific	Peace and security in Africa	S/PRST/2022/6	sixth
	The situation in the Central African Republic	Resolution 2659 (2022)	11, 36 (e) (i)
	The situation concerning the Democratic Republic of the Congo	S/PRST/2022/4 Resolution 2666 (2022)	fourth 11, 24 (ii) (g), (h) and (k)
Thematic	Threats to international peace and security caused by terrorist acts	S/PRST/2022/7	thirteenth

	Item	*Decision*	*Paragraph*
Monitoring, analysis and reporting on violations and abuses against children			
Country- and region-specific	The situation in Afghanistan	Resolution 2626 (2022)	5 (g)
	The situation in the Central African Republic	Resolution 2659 (2022)	36 (b) (ii)
	The situation in Mali	Resolution 2640 (2022)	26 (d) (ii)
	The situation in Somalia	Resolution 2662 (2022)	48
	Reports of the Secretary-General on the Sudan and South Sudan	Resolution 2625 (2022)	3 (d) (ii)
		Resolution 2633 (2022)	21
Child protection mandates in United Nations peacekeeping operations and special political missions[a]			
Country- and region-specific	The situation in Afghanistan	Resolution 2626 (2022)	5 (a), (f) and (j)
	The situation in the Central African Republic	Resolution 2659 (2022)	35 (a) (iv), 36 (b) (ii) and (e) (i), 43, 48
	The situation concerning the Democratic Republic of the Congo	Resolution 2666 (2022)	24 (i) (e) and (ii) (g), (h) and (k), 28
	The situation concerning Iraq	Resolution 2631 (2022)	2 (c) (ii) and (f)
	The situation in Mali	Resolution 2640 (2022)	26 (c) (iii) and (d) (ii), 41
	Reports of the Secretary-General on the Sudan and South Sudan	Resolution 2625 (2022)	3 (a) (i) and (v)
Measures against the perpetrators of violations and abuses against children			
Country- and region-specific	The question concerning Haiti	Resolution 2653 (2022)	16 (a) and (e)
	The situation in the Middle East	Resolution 2624 (2022)	12
Calls for the protection, respect and promotion of the right to education in armed conflict			
Country- and region-specific	The situation in Afghanistan	Resolution 2626 (2022)	5 (f)
	The situation in the Central African Republic	Resolution 2659 (2022)	56

[a] For additional information on mandates and decisions relevant to peacekeeping and political missions, see part X.

27. Protection of civilians in armed conflict

In 2022, the Council held three meetings in connection with the protection of civilians in armed conflict. Two of the meetings took the form of open debates, and one took the form of a briefing.[1014] No decisions were adopted under the item during the period under review. More information on the meetings, including on participants and speakers, is given in table 1 below.[1015]

On 25 January, at the initiative of Norway, which held the presidency of the Council for the month,[1016] the Council held a high-level open debate under the sub-item entitled "War in cities: protection of

[1014] For more information on the format of meetings, see part II.

[1015] See also A/77/2, part II, chap. 15.

[1016] A concept note was circulated by a letter dated 10 January (S/2022/23).

civilians in urban settings".[1017] At the meeting, the Council heard briefings by the Secretary-General, the President of the International Committee of the Red Cross (ICRC) and the Chair and co-founder of the Mwatana Organization for Human Rights in Yemen.[1018] In his briefing, the Secretary-General remarked on the devastating harm suffered by civilians and civilian infrastructure when hostilities took place in urban settings, especially when explosive weapons were used in populated areas. In that regard, he mentioned some examples of conflict zones in which the urban civilian population had been heavily impacted, including in Afghanistan, Iraq, Libya, the Syrian Arab Republic, Yemen and the State of Palestine. The Secretary-General then outlined some prevention and mitigation measures against the impact of urban war and urged States to follow good practices to reduce the humanitarian impact of the use of explosive weapons in populated areas. Furthermore, he welcomed efforts towards a political declaration to address the harm arising from the use of those weapons and urged all Member States to commit themselves to avoiding the use of wide-area explosive weapons in populated areas. Finally, the Secretary-General urged all Member States to use their influence over their partners and allies to ensure respect for international humanitarian law and the adoption of good practices and underlined the Council's vital role in that regard.

The President of ICRC pointed to the negative impacts of the urbanization of conflict and attacks on interconnected infrastructure on populations in urban areas, with no major improvements despite repeated calls for action. He voiced the Committee's concerns about the extensive use of heavy explosive weapons in urban and other populated areas, which was a particular cause of civilian harm in current armed conflicts. In that regard, he announced the issuance of a new ICRC report on heavy explosive weapons in populated areas with over a decade of analysis. According to the President, the report, in which ICRC outlined practices and recommendations for political authorities and armed forces on a range of mitigating measures, could serve as a tool to inform ongoing negotiations on a political declaration on explosive weapons in populated areas. ICRC continued to urge Member States to act more decisively to improve their own action and leverage their special relationship with allies and partners to enhance respect for international humanitarian law, and highlighted the urgent need to adopt and implement measures to protect essential services as the world confronted the double vulnerability of conflict and the COVID-19 pandemic. In that regard, the President urged States to fully and swiftly implement resolution 2573 (2021) and stressed the need for Council members to ensure that sanctions did not hinder the work of humanitarian actors to prevent the implosion of basic social service systems.

The Chair of the Mwatana Organization for Human Rights, speaking from Sana'a, reported that civilians continued to suffer in the conflict in Yemen and that all warring parties had committed violations of international humanitarian law and international human rights law. In that regard, she provided a summary of figures documented by her organization, including the number of air and ground attacks, mine explosions and civilians killed or wounded since the outbreak of the conflict in 2014. She noted that, in a large number of those attacks, either no military target had been identified or the documented civilian harm was beyond any apparent military benefit, concluding that those attacks had happened because the parties to the conflict had confidently relied on impunity. She also noted that it was not sufficient to name and shame the warring parties and their behaviour, and that the Council should refer the situation in Yemen to the International Criminal Court.

During the debate that ensued, Member States shared their perspectives on the impact of armed conflict in urban areas. Participants reflected on the major complexities of the prevailing wars at the time, including the embedding of non-State actors and armed groups in the infrastructure of urban areas in contravention of international humanitarian law. The Prime Minister of Norway stated that warfare in urban areas, in particular in protracted conflicts, caused civilian deaths and human suffering beyond what was acceptable and stressed that civilians must be protected whether or not an individual military attack was considered legal. He added that it was not just a question of complying with international humanitarian law and made a number of proposals for actions that should be taken for the effective

[1017] See S/PV.8953 and S/PV.8953 (Resumption 1). In accordance with the understanding reached among Council members in the light of the extraordinary circumstances caused by the COVID-19 pandemic, five non-Council members also participated by submitting written statements (see S/2022/54). For more information on the procedures and working methods developed during the pandemic, see part II.

[1018] See S/PV.8953.

protection of civilians and civilian objects in urban settings. The Minister for Foreign Affairs of Gabon stated that recent partial data revealed that an average of eight times more civilians were killed in urban warfare than in conflicts in rural areas. He added that the complexity of urban theatres was a major challenge for military and humanitarian operations owing to the density of the population and the overlap of civilians and combatants. Member States stressed the need for parties to conflict to avoid the use of explosive weapons with wide-area impacts in densely populated areas and to strengthen compliance with international humanitarian law and all relevant instruments. A number of delegations highlighted concerns about the devastating impact of armed conflicts on civilian populations that had been reflected in the latest report of the Secretary-General on the protection of civilians in armed conflict.[1019] In that regard, several delegations recalled the unanimous adoption of, or urged compliance with, resolution 2573 (2021) concerning the protection of civilians and essential civilian infrastructure.[1020] In addition, several Member States proposed concrete actions, including the use of sanctions to coerce or deter perpetrators;[1021] strengthening the participation and leadership of women in humanitarian and reconstruction processes and initiatives;[1022] and documenting civilian harm as a means to assess whether the predicted casualties of military operations corresponded to the damage actually caused to civilians.[1023] Some Member States underscored the need for United Nations peacekeeping operations to better integrate the protection of civilians into mission planning and for their mandates to better reflect the realities on the ground.[1024] The representative of Canada pointed out that action to condemn a State or an armed group that flouted the law was taken less frequently due to the Council often being obstructed by the veto.[1025] He noted that, since 2011, the Council had been blocked 16 times from taking urgently needed action on the Syrian Arab Republic, including to address some of the most pressing humanitarian aspects of the civil war. Moreover, he stated that it was incumbent upon all Member States to challenge the Council when its will was blocked by the veto and to pressure it to achieve its mandate or find alternative avenues of collective address under the Charter.

On 25 May, the Council held its annual open debate on the protection of civilians in armed conflict to discuss the latest report of the Secretary-General.[1026] At the meeting, the Council heard briefings by the Director of Coordination in the Office for the Coordination of Humanitarian Affairs, the Director General of ICRC, the President and Chief Executive Officer of the International Rescue Committee and the Country Director of Women for Women International in the Democratic Republic of the Congo.[1027]

The Director of Coordination in the Office for the Coordination of Humanitarian Affairs highlighted some of the key concerns set out by the Secretary-General in his annual report, including the fact that when explosive weapons had been used in populated areas, such as in Afghanistan, the Syrian Arab Republic, Yemen and Gaza, about 90 per cent of the casualties had been civilians, compared with 10 per cent in other areas. Other concerns that he voiced included attacks against schools and health-care facilities and damage to the natural environment and essential infrastructure. He noted that conflict-driven hunger had worsened, leading to acute food insecurity among millions of people in 24 States, including Ethiopia, Nigeria, South Sudan and Yemen. Moreover, humanitarian operations had continued to face complex access challenges that had deprived people of the assistance that they needed to survive in Somalia, the Central African Republic and Myanmar. In that connection, he stated that sanctions and broadly conceived counter-terrorism measures had impeded principled humanitarian activities and that

[1019] See S/PV.8953 (Ireland, Mexico, Albania, India, Liechtenstein, Switzerland (on behalf of the Group of Friends on the Protection of Civilians in Armed Conflict), Austria, Egypt, Islamic Republic of Iran and Poland); S/PV.8953 (Resumption 1) (Ecuador, Slovakia, Luxembourg, Holy See and Georgia); and S/2022/54 (Azerbaijan, Republic of Korea, Rwanda and San Marino). See also S/2021/423.

[1020] See S/PV.8953 (United States, Mexico, Liechtenstein, Switzerland, Austria, Malta, Italy, Germany and Poland); S/PV.8953 (Resumption 1) (Japan, Ecuador, Sweden, Holy See and Belgium); and S/2022/54 (Republic of Korea and San Marino).

[1021] See S/PV.8953 (United Arab Emirates and France); and S/2022/54 (Myanmar).

[1022] See S/PV.8953 (Norway, United Arab Emirates, Switzerland (on behalf of the Group of Friends on the Protection of Civilians in Armed Conflict) and Germany); and S/PV.8953 (Resumption 1) (Indonesia).

[1023] See S/PV.8953 (Brazil).

[1024] See S/PV.8953 (Ireland, France and Slovenia); and S/PV.8953 (Resumption 1) (Guatemala and Philippines).

[1025] See S/PV.8953 (Resumption 1).

[1026] See S/PV.9042 and S/PV.9042 (Resumption 1). See also S/2022/381.

[1027] See S/PV.9042.

misinformation and disinformation had eroded trust, putting humanitarians at risk of harm and ultimately jeopardizing humanitarian operations. Turning to the conflict in Ukraine, he said that the war had effectively ended Ukrainian food exports and that the humanitarian impacts were being felt far beyond Ukraine, with price increases for staple foods threatening people in countries across Africa and the Middle East, exacerbating suffering in other conflict situations and planting the seeds for further political instability and unrest worldwide. The Director of Coordination concluded by mentioning a few practical steps that States and non-State armed groups should take to fully comply with international humanitarian law, as repeatedly stated by the Secretary-General. Such steps included tracking reports of civilian harm to gauge the impact of military operations and shift course, if necessary; increasing understanding of the effects of conflict on the natural environment and integrating legal protection for the environment into military training, doctrine and policy and legal frameworks; engaging in political dialogue, training and joint operational planning with security allies, including non-State armed groups, and withholding arms transfers where there was a clear risk that the arms would be used to commit serious violations of international humanitarian law; ensuring that humanitarian operations were shielded from the political dynamics of conflict and supporting humanitarian engagement with all parties to conflict; facilitating humanitarian activities and excluding them from the scope of counter-terrorism and sanctions measures; investigating alleged war crimes, prosecuting perpetrators, ensuring reparations for victims and strengthening other States' capacity to investigate and prosecute; and developing policy frameworks and building upon good policies and practices.

The Director General of ICRC stated that, while certain progress had been made on the normative and policy fronts on the issue of the protection of civilians, the reality on the ground continued to tell a very different story, with deliberate attacks on civilians and civilian objects, frequent indiscriminate and disproportionate attacks, and the politicization of humanitarian action while political solutions to end conflict remained elusive. He added that States were falling short of their primary responsibility to respect and ensure respect for international humanitarian law. To that end, he urged States to take decisive action in three areas, namely, making the protection of civilians a strategic priority in the planning and conduct of all military and security operations in populated areas; working to avoid and prevent the spread of misinformation and disinformation in armed conflicts and to mitigate their impact on affected people; and refraining from making operational humanitarian organizations such as ICRC responsible for sharing data from international humanitarian law monitoring. In that regard, the Director General stated that there was a need to bridge the wide gap between the ever-growing protection and assistance needs of conflict-affected people and the ability of humanitarian organizations to deliver an adequate response. That meant removing obstacles such as restrictive measures that criminalized aid, denied access, politicized funding or imposed requirements compromising humanitarian principles. He concluded by stating that the responsibility for removing those obstacles and for ensuring protection lay first and foremost with States, including the members of the Council.

The President of the International Rescue Committee said that the system for protecting civilians was not succeeding and that no failure was greater than the denial of access for innocent civilians to the legal right to receive life-saving aid. In that context, he stated that every year the delivery of aid became harder in conflict zones, not because the natural geography was more difficult but because the human-made obstacles were more significant. He said that, while the Council was not responsible for the tactics of those laying siege to communities or targeting civilians or aid workers, it was responsible for the failure to hold those actors to account and to curb their illegal excesses, and that was what needed to change. He added that the denial of humanitarian access should be a permanent item at the Council and that the Council should set a standard for defending United Nations officials who called out violations of international law, noting that those officials should be backed by independent assessments of access violations that left no room for political pressure. He stressed the importance of early warning mechanisms and suggested that resolution 2417 (2018) on conflict-induced hunger could be an effective indicator of food insecurity and famine and a tool to fight it if it were not undermined by weak and inconsistent implementation, data and reporting. Lastly, he said that, where the Council had direct power over access to aid, such as in the upcoming vote on renewing cross-border access to the Syrian Arab Republic, such votes should be based on facts and law alone to ensure that humanitarian aid reached those in need by the most direct and effective routes. When the Council was divided, the General Assembly could continue to play a critical role in establishing independent mechanisms to gather evidence on international humanitarian law violations.

The Country Director of Women for Women International in the Democratic Republic of the Congo focused her briefing on the challenges faced by the women and other marginalized populations affected by conflict in the eastern part of the Democratic Republic of the Congo and on how gender-transformative approaches and local women's organizations like hers must be part of the strategy from the start to ensure better humanitarian access and the protection of all civilians. In that regard, she said that there must be closer coordination among humanitarian country teams, government authorities, peacekeeping missions and civil society across the planning and implementation phases of humanitarian responses.

Following the briefings, delegations discussed the deterioration of the humanitarian situation in various conflict zones around the world and the unprecedented challenges to global efforts for the protection of civilians. In that connection, a number of delegations underscored the need for the full and effective implementation of relevant Council resolutions concerning the protection of civilians.[1028] The representative of Brazil expressed the view that it was clear that the problem was not the absence of norms but rather the lack of their implementation and of respect for them.[1029]

In terms of the most pressing protection challenges, speakers pointed to the use of heavy explosives in densely populated areas and the widespread availability of weapons; conflict-related sexual violence and the increased vulnerabilities faced by women, children, refugees, internally displaced persons and persons with disabilities; the shrinking of the humanitarian space due to deliberate attacks on humanitarian and medical personnel, schools and medical facilities; and the rapid spread of misinformation and disinformation. Several delegations also raised concerns about the unintended consequences of sanctions and counter-terrorism measures on humanitarian assistance.[1030] In that regard, some delegations underscored the need to consider safeguards or humanitarian carveouts, such as the one established by resolution 2615 (2021) concerning Afghanistan, in order to exclude the application of sanctions to humanitarian activities. The representative of France stressed the need to sanction violations of international humanitarian law with regard to the protection of civilians by making better use of the tool of sanctions against those responsible for those violations.[1031] A number of speakers also touched upon the fact that the world faced unprecedented levels of food insecurity due to the widespread and protracted armed conflicts. In that regard, several delegations expressed the view that the adverse effects of the conflict in Ukraine on food and energy prices had exacerbated an already critical humanitarian situation in conflict zones.[1032]

Member States drew attention to the instrumental role played by peacekeepers in the protection of civilians and to the increasing challenges faced by United Nations missions around the world in executing their protection mandates. In that connection, many delegations advocated more adequate training and resources to enable peacekeepers to effectively implement their protection mandates.[1033] In addition, a number of speakers stressed the importance of preventing the outbreak of armed conflicts as the most effective way to protect civilians.[1034] While most delegations called for compliance with international

---

[1028] See S/PV.9042 (Gabon, United Kingdom, Ireland, Norway, Albania, China, Mexico and Switzerland (on behalf of the Group of Friends on the Protection of Civilians in Armed Conflict)); and S/PV.9042 (Resumption 1) (Luxembourg, Malta, Portugal, New Zealand, Austria, Yemen, South Africa, Japan, Morocco, Poland, Italy, Nepal, Bangladesh, Maldives, Argentina, Republic of Korea and Belgium). For more information on the discussion concerning the obligation of Member States to accept and carry out the decisions of the Council in the context of the protection of civilians in armed conflict, see part V, sect. II.

[1029] See S/PV.9042.

[1030] See S/PV.9042 (Brazil, Ireland, France, Norway, United Arab Emirates, Mexico and Switzerland (on behalf of the Group of Friends on the Protection of Civilians in Armed Conflict)); and S/PV.9042 (Resumption 1) (European Union (also on behalf of Albania, Bosnia and Herzegovina, Georgia, Monaco, Montenegro, North Macedonia, Republic of Moldova, San Marino and Ukraine) and Islamic Republic of Iran).

[1031] See S/PV.9042.

[1032] See S/PV.9042 (United States, Albania, Mexico and Türkiye); and S/PV.9042 (Resumption 1) (Ecuador, European Union (also on behalf of Albania, Bosnia and Herzegovina, Georgia, Monaco, Montenegro, North Macedonia, Republic of Moldova, San Marino and Ukraine), Portugal, Liechtenstein, Slovakia, Greece and Denmark (on behalf of the Nordic countries)).

[1033] See S/PV.9042 (India, Norway, China, United Arab Emirates and Egypt); and S/PV.9042 (Resumption 1) (New Zealand, Estonia, Australia, Nepal, Bangladesh, Costa Rica, Argentina, Indonesia, Guatemala, Malaysia and Chile).

[1034] See S/PV.9042 (United Kingdom, Brazil, Albania, United Arab Emirates and Egypt); and S/PV.9042 (Resumption 1) (Slovenia, Viet Nam, Qatar, Maldives, Uruguay, Croatia (on behalf of the Group of Friends of the Responsibility to Protect) and Chile).

humanitarian law and accountability, some participants also underscored the necessity of embedding civilian protections into national laws.[1035] The representative of New Zealand said that improved integration with the United Nations peacebuilding architecture would better protect civilians at all stages of conflict.[1036]

On 15 September, at the request of Brazil and Ireland, as co-focal points on food security and armed conflict, the Council held a meeting further to a white note sent to the Council by the Office for the Coordination of Humanitarian Affairs on 24 August in accordance with resolution 2417 (2018).[1037] In that resolution, the Council requested the Secretary-General to report swiftly to the Council when the risk of conflict-induced famine and widespread food insecurity in armed conflict contexts occurred. Accordingly, the situations in the following four regions were detailed in the white note: northern Ethiopia, north-east Nigeria, South Sudan and Yemen. At the meeting, the Council heard briefings by the Under-Secretary-General for Humanitarian Affairs and Emergency Relief Coordinator, the Chief Economist of the Food and Agriculture Organization of the United Nations (FAO) and the Executive Director of the World Food Programme (WFP).

Recalling the request of the Council in resolution 2417 (2018), the Under-Secretary-General for Humanitarian Affairs reported on the recent assessments in the four regions in which such a risk was clear.[1038] In that regard, the Under-Secretary-General reported that, according to the Integrated Food Security Phase Classification system for monitoring food security worldwide, hundreds of thousands of people in those regions were facing catastrophic levels of hunger – the equivalent of phase 5 of the system, which was the ultimate, most devastating phase. Elaborating on the main drivers of hunger due to the direct and indirect impact of conflict and violence, he noted that, in each context, a similar pattern recurred, characterized by forced displacement, the disruption of access to markets, agricultural production and income generation by explosive remnants of war, the destruction of essential civilian infrastructure and equipment, the deliberate suspension of access to commercial supplies and essential services, and the eventual use of hunger as a tactic of war. Humanitarian organizations faced impediments and attacks that prevented them from reaching people in need and made their suffering worse. After providing a snapshot of the situation in each of the regions in crisis, the Under-Secretary-General recommended four specific steps to be taken by Member States with regard to each area, namely, to pursue peaceful and negotiated resolutions to conflicts and other situations of violence; to remind and encourage States and armed groups to abide by their obligations under international humanitarian law and international human rights law; to support an integrated response to address the underlying drivers of acute food insecurity; and to sustain humanitarian financing for those crises. Before concluding, the Under-Secretary-General pointed to the impact of climate change and how it was felt variously by those who did little to create it. Drawing attention to the risk of famine in Somalia specifically, he called upon the climate community and Member States to ensure that money pledged for climate financing reached its destination.

In his briefing, the Chief Economist of FAO underscored that conflict had immediate and lasting effects on every dimension of agrifood systems and severely hampered humanitarian access to civilians. Before describing the situations in the four contexts addressed in the white note, he said that, although not included in detail in the white note, it was important to describe the dire situation in Somalia and to draw the Council's attention to Afghanistan, where the humanitarian situation remained highly fragile. In closing, he said that preventing conflict was the most effective means of preventing famine and that immediate action was essential to minimize potential calamities.

In his briefing, the Executive Director of WFP stated that the world was facing a global emergency of unprecedented magnitude, with the threat of mass starvation and famine growing constantly. He echoed the assessments of the situations in Ethiopia, north-east Nigeria, South Sudan and Yemen by previous briefers and urged the Council to show the leadership the world needed to facilitate political solutions to end those wars.

[1035] See S/PV.9042 (United Kingdom, France and Mexico); and S/PV.9042 (Resumption 1) (Canada, South Africa, Italy and Croatia (on behalf of the Group of Friends of the Responsibility to Protect)).

[1036] See S/PV.9042 (Resumption 1).

[1037] See S/PV.9133. See also resolution 2417 (2018), paras. 1 and 12.

[1038] See S/PV.9133.

In the ensuing debate, Council members emphasized that armed conflict and violence remained primary drivers of the risk of conflict-induced famine and widespread food insecurity in parts of South Sudan, Yemen, north-east Nigeria and northern Ethiopia, as highlighted in the white note, as well as in Somalia and Afghanistan. A number of participants[1039] highlighted the Council's preventive role in averting conflict, as envisaged in resolution 2417 (2018), and called for the full implementation of that resolution. In that connection, the representatives of Mexico and the United States underscored the importance of the white note as a useful early warning tool. Many delegations[1040] expressed the view that the conflict in Ukraine had exacerbated the already precarious situation in those regions. In contrast, the representative of the Russian Federation stated that the causes of food crises in any country needed specific analysis without hasty generalizations. He added that the Secretary-General had recently warned of the risk of mass famine in five countries, four of which had been the subject of items of the Council for years. In that context, the Russian representative said that it was regrettable that the subject of food security was being manipulated for geopolitical ends and that "Western countries continue[d] to blame Russia for every problem", including the food crisis, even as they acknowledged that it had preceded the special military operation in Ukraine.

Throughout 2022, the Council continued the practice of hearing briefings by the Office for the Coordination of Humanitarian Affairs concerning the protection of civilians in armed conflict under country- and region-specific items.[1041] The Council also included protection-related provisions in most of its decisions in relation to both country- and region-specific items and thematic ones during the year. The Council focused on multiple aspects of the protection of civilians agenda and used a variety of language formulas to address the protection of civilians in its decisions. Selected provisions of those decisions are listed in table 2 below. In particular, the Council: (a) strongly condemned all forms of violence and abuses committed against civilians, in particular against women and children, and demanded the cessation of attacks against humanitarian and medical personnel and civilian infrastructure, including attacks against schools, hospitals and humanitarian facilities;[1042] (b) demanded that all parties to armed conflict ensure rapid, safe and unhindered access for the delivery of humanitarian assistance to populations in need and ensure the safety of humanitarian and medical personnel; (c) called upon all relevant parties to comply with their obligations under international humanitarian law, human rights law and refugee law and called for accountability measures against perpetrators of such crimes; (d) emphasized the primary responsibility of States to comply with their relevant obligations and called for their action to protect civilians; (e) requested additional monitoring and response mechanisms to threats and attacks against civilians and reporting arrangements in order to improve the protection of civilians in armed conflict; and (f) adopted or expressed its intention to adopt targeted measures, including sanctions, against individuals or entities who violated international humanitarian and human rights law. In that regard, the Council also decided on humanitarian exemptions and urged Member States to minimize and mitigate the unintended adverse humanitarian consequences of targeted measures, as decided later in the year by resolution 2664 (2022).[1043] In addition, the Council's practice of strengthening the mandates of United Nations peace operations with a view to protecting civilians continued to evolve. During the reporting period, the Council continued to request several missions to make the protection of civilians under threat of physical violence a specific priority and benchmark of their mandates, with particular attention on, but not limited to, women, children, refugees and internally displaced persons, including by creating a secure environment for the safe delivery of humanitarian assistance, strengthening local community engagement and empowerment and early warning mechanisms, and using strategic communications to counter disinformation and misinformation.[1044]

[1039] Brazil, Ireland, United Arab Emirates, Norway, Albania, United States and France.

[1040] Brazil, Ireland, United Arab Emirates, Mexico, Norway, India, Albania, United States, France and Italy.

[1041] In 2022, the Council heard briefings by the Office for the Coordination of Humanitarian Affairs 35 times at public meetings and 20 times at either private meetings or informal consultations, for a total of 55 briefings. For more information on briefings on those items prior to 2022, see *Repertoire, Supplement 2021*, part I, sect. 25.

[1042] For more information on the decisions of the Council concerning children and armed conflict, and specifically the protection of schools and education facilities, see sect. 26 above. For more information on the decisions of the Council concerning conflict-related sexual violence and gender-based violence, see sect. 29 below.

[1043] Resolution 2664 (2022), para. 7. For more information on the discussion related to preventing humanitarian consequences of sanctions, see sect. 28 below. For more information on the economic problems arising from the implementation of sanctions by the Council, see part VII, sect. IX.

[1044] For more information on the mandates of peacekeeping and special political missions, see part X.

Table 1
Meetings: protection of civilians in armed conflict, 2022

Meeting record and date	*Sub-item*	*Other documents*	*Rule 37 invitations*	*Rule 39 and other invitations*	*Speakers*	*Decision and vote (for-against-abstaining)*
S/PV.8953, S/PV.8953 (Resumption 1) and S/2022/54 25 January	War in cities: protection of civilians in urban settings Letter dated 10 January 2022 from the Permanent Representative of Norway to the United Nations addressed to the Secretary-General (S/2022/23)		33 Member States[a]	President of the International Committee of the Red Cross (ICRC), Head of the Delegation of the European Union to the United Nations, Permanent Observer of the Holy See to the United Nations, Chair and co-founder of the Mwatana Organization for Human Rights	Secretary-General, all Council members,[b] all invitees[c]	
S/PV.9042, S/PV.9042 (Resumption 1) 25 May	Report of the Secretary-General on the protection of civilians in armed conflict (S/2022/381)		50 Member States[d]	Seven invitees[e]	All Council members, all invitees[f]	
S/PV.9133 15 September			Italy	Under-Secretary-General for Humanitarian Affairs and Emergency Relief Coordinator, Chief Economist of the Food and Agriculture Organization of the United Nations, Executive Director of the World Food Programme	All Council members, all invitees	

[a] Argentina, Armenia, Austria, Belgium, Canada, Chile, Ecuador, Egypt, Georgia, Germany, Guatemala, Indonesia, Iran (Islamic Republic of), Italy, Japan, Jordan, Liechtenstein, Lithuania, Luxembourg, Malta, Morocco, Pakistan, Philippines, Poland, Portugal, Slovakia, Slovenia, South Africa, Sweden, Switzerland, Türkiye, Ukraine and Yemen.

[b] Ghana was represented by its Vice-President and Minister for Foreign Affairs; and Norway (President of the Council) was represented by its Prime Minister. Gabon was represented by its Minister for Foreign Affairs; the United Arab Emirates was represented by its Permanent Representative to the United Nations and Assistant Minister for Foreign Affairs and International Cooperation for Political Affairs; and the United States was represented by its Permanent Representative to the United Nations and member of the President's Cabinet.

[c] The Chair and co-founder of the Mwatana Organization for Human Rights participated in the meeting with audio only. The representative of Sweden spoke on behalf of the Nordic countries; the representative of Switzerland spoke on behalf of the Group of Friends on the Protection of Civilians in Armed Conflict; and the representative of the European Union spoke also on behalf of Albania, Bosnia and Herzegovina, Georgia, Montenegro, North Macedonia, Serbia, Türkiye and Ukraine.

[d] Algeria, Argentina, Armenia, Australia, Austria, Azerbaijan, Bangladesh, Belgium, Canada, Chile, Costa Rica, Croatia, Cyprus, Denmark, Ecuador, Egypt, Estonia, Georgia, Germany, Greece, Guatemala, Indonesia, Iran (Islamic Republic of), Israel, Italy, Japan, Liechtenstein, Luxembourg, Malaysia, Maldives, Malta, Morocco, Nepal, New Zealand, Nigeria, Pakistan, Poland, Portugal, Qatar, Republic of Korea, Slovakia, Slovenia, South Africa, Spain, Switzerland, Türkiye, Ukraine, Uruguay, Viet Nam and Yemen.

[e] The Director of Coordination in the Office for the Coordination of Humanitarian Affairs; the Director General of ICRC; the Head of the Delegation of the European Union to the United Nations; the Permanent Observer of the State of Palestine to the United Nations; the Permanent Observer of the Holy See; the President and Chief Executive Officer of the International Rescue Committee; and the Country Director of Women for Women International in the Democratic Republic of the Congo.

[f] Germany was represented by its State Secretary at the Federal Foreign Office. The representative of Croatia spoke on behalf of the Group of Friends of the Responsibility to Protect; the representative of Denmark spoke on behalf of the Nordic countries; the representative of Switzerland spoke on behalf of the Group of Friends of the Protection of Civilians in Armed Conflict; and the representative of the European Union spoke also on behalf of Albania, Bosnia and Herzegovina, Georgia, Montenegro, Monaco, North Macedonia, the Republic of Moldova, San Marino and Ukraine.

Table 2
Selection of provisions relevant to the protection of civilians in armed conflict, by theme and item, 2022

	Item	*Decision*	*Paragraph*
Condemnation and demands for the cessation of attacks and acts of violence against civilians and civilian infrastructure and humanitarian and medical personnel			
Country- and region-specific	The situation in the Central African Republic	Resolution 2659 (2022)	3, 25, 56
	The situation concerning the Democratic Republic of the Congo	Resolution 2666 (2022)	7, 9, 10
	The question concerning Haiti	Resolution 2653 (2022)	1
	The situation in Somalia	Resolution 2628 (2022)	16–18
	Reports of the Secretary-General on the Sudan and South Sudan	Resolution 2625 (2022)	11
Thematic	Threats to international peace and security caused by terrorist acts	S/PRST/2022/7	fifth, sixth
Demands on parties to allow immediate humanitarian access and ensure the safety of humanitarian and medical personnel and facilities			
Country- and region-specific	The situation in the Central African Republic	Resolution 2659 (2022)	54, 55
	The situation concerning the Democratic Republic of the Congo	Resolution 2666 (2022)	31
	The situation in Myanmar	Resolution 2669 (2022)	9
	The situation in Somalia	Resolution 2657 (2022)	11, 11 (a) and (a) (iii)
	Reports of the Secretary-General on the Sudan and South Sudan	Resolution 2625 (2022)	10, 12

	Item	Decision	Paragraph
Calls for compliance with and accountability under applicable international humanitarian law, human rights law and refugee law and relevant Council resolutions by all parties			
Country- and region-specific	The situation in the Central African Republic	Resolution 2659 (2022)	14, 22
	The situation concerning the Democratic Republic of the Congo	Resolution 2666 (2022)	5
	The situation in Mali	Resolution 2640 (2022)	31, 46, 47
	The situation in Myanmar	Resolution 2669 (2022)	4, 10
	The situation in Somalia	Resolution 2657 (2022)	9
	Reports of the Secretary-General on the Sudan and South Sudan	Resolution 2625 (2022)	9
Thematic	Threats to international peace and security caused by terrorist acts	S/PRST/2022/7	thirteenth
Affirmation of the primary responsibility of States and parties to conflict to protect civilians and calls for action to protect civilians			
Country- and region-specific	The situation in the Central African Republic	Resolution 2659 (2022)	10, 24
	The situation concerning the Democratic Republic of the Congo	S/PRST/2022/4	fifth, sixth
		Resolution 2666 (2022)	5, 6
	The situation in Mali	Resolution 2640 (2022)	2, 12, 25, 45
	The situation in Somalia	Resolution 2628 (2022)	6, 9, 14 (c), 19
		Resolution 2657 (2022)	13 (a) and (b)
	Reports of the Secretary-General on the Sudan and South Sudan	Resolution 2625 (2022)	5, 13, 17, 20 (g)
		Resolution 2630 (2022)	4
Requests for specific monitoring and analysis of and reporting on protection of civilians			
Country- and region-specific	The situation in the Central African Republic	Resolution 2659 (2022)	36 (b) (i), 43
	The situation concerning the Democratic Republic of the Congo	Resolution 2666 (2022)	30, 43
	The situation in Mali	Resolution 2640 (2022)	57 (i) and (iv)
	The situation in the Middle East	Resolution 2642 (2022)	2, 5
	The situation in Somalia	Resolution 2628 (2022)	11, 53 (f)
	Reports of the Secretary-General on the Sudan and South Sudan	Resolution 2625 (2022)	20 (a)
		Resolution 2633 (2022)	23

	Item	*Decision*	*Paragraph*
Imposition of targeted measures against perpetrators of violations against civilians in armed conflict			
Country- and region-specific	The situation in the Central African Republic	Resolution 2648 (2022)	5
		Resolution 2659 (2022)	4
	The question concerning Haiti	Resolution 2645 (2022)	5
		Resolution 2653 (2022)	13, 16 (e) and (g)
	The situation in Mali	Resolution 2649 (2022)	2
	The situation in Somalia	Resolution 2657 (2022)	11 (d)
	Reports of the Secretary-General on the Sudan and South Sudan	Resolution 2625 (2022)	18
		Resolution 2633 (2022)	13
Stressing of the need to minimize adverse humanitarian consequences of sanctions measures and humanitarian exemptions			
Country- and region-specific	Peace and security in Africa	S/PRST/2022/6	eighth
	The question concerning Haiti	Resolution 2653 (2022)	10, 17
	The situation in the Middle East	Resolution 2624 (2022)	6, 16
	The situation in Somalia	Resolution 2662 (2022)	28
Thematic	General issues relating to sanctions	Resolution 2664 (2022)	1, 7
	Threats to international peace and security caused by terrorist acts	S/PRST/2022/7	seventh, seventeenth
Inclusion of mission-specific protection mandates and benchmarks[a]			
Country- and region-specific	The situation in the Central African Republic	Resolution 2659 (2022)	35 (a) (i)–(iv) and (c), 36 (b) (i) and (iii) and (f) (i), (iv) and (vii), 41
	The situation concerning the Democratic Republic of the Congo	Resolution 2666 (2022)	21, 24, 24 (i), 24 (i) (a), (e) and (f), 25, 26 (b) and (c)
	The situation concerning Iraq	Resolution 2631 (2022)	2 (c) (i) and (ii)
	The situation in Mali	Resolution 2640 (2022)	26 (b) (i) and (iii), (c) (i) and (ii), (d) (i) and (ii) and (e)
	The situation in Somalia	Resolution 2657 (2022)	7 (a)
	Reports of the Secretary-General on the Sudan and South Sudan	Resolution 2625 (2022)	3 (a) (i)–(iii), (v), (vii), (viii) and (x), (b), (c) (v) and (d) (i) and (iv), 20 (j), 25
Thematic	United Nations peacekeeping operations	S/PRST/2022/5	seventh, fifteenth

[a] For additional information on mandates and decisions relevant to peacekeeping and political missions, see part X

28. General issues relating to sanctions

During the period under review, the Council held two meetings in connection with the item entitled "General issues relating to sanctions". The Council had last held a meeting under this item in 2017.[1045] One of the meetings took the form of a debate, while the other was convened to adopt a resolution. More information on the meeting, including on participants, speakers and outcomes, is provided in the table below.[1046]

On 7 February, at the initiative of the Russian Federation, which held the presidency of the Council for the month,[1047] the Council held a debate focused on preventing the humanitarian and unintended consequences of sanctions.[1048] The Council was given briefings by the Under-Secretary-General for Political and Peacebuilding Affairs and the Under-Secretary-General for Humanitarian Affairs and Emergency Relief Coordinator. The Under-Secretary-General for Political and Peacebuilding Affairs pointed out that sanctions remained a vital tool for the Council to ensure the maintenance of international peace and security. To be effective, sanctions should be part of a comprehensive political strategy. They were no longer the blunt instrument that they once had been, and they had undergone considerable changes since the 1990s to minimize their possible adverse consequences on civilian populations and third States. Notwithstanding those changes, some concerns remained about unintended consequences and adverse effects of Council sanctions. De-risking policies and overcompliance were probably two of the most important problems facing humanitarian actors. In that regard, more could be done to reduce the possible adverse consequences of sanctions. She welcomed the adoption of resolution 2615 (2021), which carved out a humanitarian exemption to the sanctions regime on Afghanistan, adding that similar standing exemptions in other sanctions regimes could go a long way to responding to the critical needs of civilian populations and that Member States could further minimize the burden on humanitarian actors by keeping their domestic legislation as close as possible to Council language. The continued monitoring by sanctions committees of the possible humanitarian impact of sanctions was vital, and it was essential to increase cooperation with humanitarian actors and the private sector. She highlighted the role of the Office of the Ombudsperson for individuals and entities seeking to be removed from the Islamic State in Iraq and the Levant (ISIL/Da'esh) and Al-Qaida sanctions list, adding that providing fair and clear procedures to all other designated entities and individuals would render the sanctions tool even more effective.

Noting the evolution of sanctions and the progress in the design of sanctions to limit unintended consequences, the Under-Secretary-General for Humanitarian Affairs and Emergency Relief Coordinator summarized some concerns over the use of sanctions in countries already affected by humanitarian crises. Humanitarian access and principles could be put under pressure by the demands of sanctions, making it harder for humanitarian agencies to engage and transact with listed individuals or entities that held significant control over the lives of entire populations. In addition, banks and other commercial operators, aiming to avoid any risk of penalty or prosecution, could effectively deny services to humanitarian customers, sever commercial relationships or make routine transactions excessively slow and bureaucratic, even when they were well within the permitted rules. Furthermore, commercial operators that traded food, fuel and other necessities could also decide to err on the side of caution or to overcomply, which could lead to shortages and price rises. When ministries and departments were run by listed individuals, sanctions aimed at political movements and figures could limit the provision of social services and economic stability. In that regard, mitigating the humanitarian impact of sanctions required continuing to review the way in which sanctions were designed, how they were implemented and how they had an impact. In that connection, he suggested some priorities. He urged the Council and Member

[1045] The previous meeting on the item was held on 3 August 2017 (see S/PV.8018). For more information, see *Repertoire*, *Supplement 2016-2017*, part I, sect. 32. As no meetings on the item were held in the three years following, and in accordance with the procedure set out in document S/2017/507, the item was deleted from the list of agenda items of which the Council was seized (see S/2021/10 and S/2021/10/Add.10). For more information on the format of meetings, see part II.

[1046] See also A/77/2, part II, chap. 16.

[1047] A concept note was circulated by a letter dated 2 February (S/2022/86).

[1048] See S/PV.8962.

States to ensure that sanctions applicable in armed conflict did not impede the assistance and protection activities of impartial humanitarian organizations for persons who were not fighting, irrespective of their allegiance or designation. The Council and other jurisdictions should build comprehensive humanitarian carveouts into the original legislation rather than through case-by-case authorization procedures, which could be cumbersome and inefficient. In closing, he said that it was a collective responsibility to ensure that sanctions were used to improve compliance with international humanitarian law and international human rights law and, equally, to ensure that they would not have unintended consequences for civilians already caught up in humanitarian crises.

Following the briefings, Council members discussed the role of sanctions imposed by the Council in the maintenance of international peace and security.[1049] Council members also focused on the humanitarian impact of sanctions and specifically on their unintended consequences, including overcompliance.[1050] In that regard, Council members made observations and proposals with a view to mitigating the detrimental impact of sanctions. In addition to Council members, the representatives of Iraq, Mali, the Sudan, South Sudan and Venezuela (Bolivarian Republic of) participated in the meeting and expressed concern at the impact of sanctions in their respective countries and regions. The representative of Iraq said that sanctions should be targeted, smart and able to achieve their goals without exposing an entire society to shortages and need because that could lead to violent extremism, the militarization of society or an increase in organized crime.

On 9 December, the Council held a meeting[1051] at which it adopted resolution 2664 (2022) under Chapter VII of the Charter of the United Nations.[1052] Through the resolution, which was adopted with 14 votes in favour and one abstention, the Council created a humanitarian carveout for all asset freeze measures imposed by the Council or any of its sanctions committees.[1053] By the resolution, the Council requested the Emergency Relief Coordinator to provide or arrange a briefing for each relevant Committee 11 months from the date of adoption of the resolution and every 12 months thereafter on the delivery of humanitarian assistance and other activities supporting basic human needs.[1054] Also by the resolution, the Council requested the Secretary-General to issue a written report on unintended adverse humanitarian consequences of Council sanctions measures within nine months of the adoption of the resolution and that the report include recommendations on ways to minimize and mitigate such unintended adverse consequences.[1055]

Speaking before the adoption, as one of the penholders of the draft resolution, the representative of the United States explained that the humanitarian community had asked for a clear, standard carveout of humanitarian assistance and activities to meet basic human needs for all United Nations sanctions regimes and that that was exactly what Council members were voting on that day.[1056] Following the adoption of resolution 2664 (2022), Council members welcomed the adoption of the resolution, underscoring its role in providing clarity for humanitarian actors and diminishing the unintended adverse consequences of sanctions. The representative of Ireland, as co-penholder of the resolution with the United States, underscored that the resolution, while significant, was not a panacea and that it might take some time for its effects to be implemented by States and executed by all relevant stakeholders. Explaining her country's abstention during the vote, the representative of India said that her delegation's concerns emanated from proven instances of terrorist groups taking full advantage of such humanitarian carveouts and making a mockery of sanctions regimes. She mentioned several cases of terrorist groups reincarnating themselves as humanitarian organizations and civil society groups precisely to evade such sanctions. Humanitarian exemptions must not facilitate the mainstreaming of terror entities in the political space, and due diligence and extreme caution in the implementation of resolution 2664 (2022)

[1049] For more information on the discussion, see part VII, sect. III.

[1050] See S/PV.8962.

[1051] See S/PV.9214.

[1052] The draft resolution (S/2022/925) was submitted by Ireland and the United States and sponsored by a further 51 Member States.

[1053] Resolution 2664 (2022), para. 1.

[1054] Ibid., para. 5.

[1055] Ibid., para. 7. For more information on sanctions regimes, see part VII, sect. III.

[1056] See S/PV.9214.

were an absolute must. She expressed regret that her delegation's proposal for a proactive role for the Coordinator, Analytical Support and Sanctions Monitoring Team coupled with robust reporting standards and mechanisms had not been fully addressed in the final text and expressed the hope that the shortcoming would be corrected in the future when the implementation of the resolution was reviewed. The representative of the United Arab Emirates noted that, although most aid providers were covered by the resolution, some genuine humanitarian organizations might be left out. While the resolution constituted a milestone in the Council's support for people in need of humanitarian assistance, his delegation saw some potential for overcompliance and believed that it was important to regularly review how the resolution was being implemented on the ground and adjust it as needed. The representative of the Russian Federation said that her delegation was pleased that its many calls had finally been heeded by those who, for years and under various pretexts, had kept postponing the resolution of that issue. The resolution did not resolve many of the issues that existed when it came to Council sanctions, but if it could help humanitarians in certain countries to be more effective in providing assistance to the most vulnerable people, that already in itself was a worthwhile result. Similarly, the representative of China expressed appreciation that the co-penholders had responded to the appeals and demands of all parties and had introduced the resolution on humanitarian exemptions. He also expressed the hope that States Members of the United Nations and international humanitarian agencies would actively implement the humanitarian exemptions provided for in the resolution and prevent an expanded interpretation or excessive implementation of sanctions.

Meetings: general issues relating to sanctions, 2022

Meeting record and date	*Sub-item*	*Other documents*	*Rule 37 invitations*	*Rule 39 and other invitations*	*Speakers*	*Decision and vote (for-against-abstaining)*
S/PV.8962 7 February	Preventing their humanitarian and unintended consequences Letter dated 2 February 2022 from the Permanent Representative of the Russian Federation to the United Nations addressed to the Secretary-General (S/2022/86)		Iraq, Mali, South Sudan, Sudan, Venezuela (Bolivarian Republic of)	Under-Secretary-General for Political and Peacebuilding Affairs, Under-Secretary-General for Humanitarian Affairs and Emergency Relief Coordinator	All Council members, all invitees[a]	
S/PV.9214 9 December		Draft resolution submitted by 53 Member States[b] (S/2022/925)	33 Member States[c]		10 Council members[d]	Resolution 2664 (2022) 14-0-1[e] (adopted under Chapter VII)

[a] The representative of the Bolivarian Republic of Venezuela spoke on behalf of the Group of Friends in Defence of the Charter of the United Nations.

[b] Albania, Andorra, Australia, Austria, Bahamas, Belgium, Brazil, Bulgaria, Canada, Chile, Croatia, Cyprus, Czechia, Denmark, Dominican Republic, Ecuador, Estonia, Fiji, Finland, France, Georgia, Germany, Greece, Guinea, Guyana, Hungary, Iceland, Ireland, Italy, Latvia, Lesotho, Liechtenstein, Luxembourg, Malta, Marshall Islands, Montenegro, Netherlands, New Zealand, Norway, Poland, Portugal, Republic of Moldova, Romania, Samoa, San Marino, Slovakia, Slovenia, Spain, Sweden, Switzerland, Ukraine, United Kingdom and United States.

[c] Australia, Austria, Bahamas, Belgium, Bulgaria, Canada, Croatia, Cyprus, Czechia, Denmark, Dominican Republic, Estonia, Fiji, Finland, Germany, Greece, Iceland, Italy, Latvia, Lesotho, Liechtenstein, Luxembourg, Malta, Marshall Islands, New Zealand, Portugal, Romania, Samoa, San Marino, Slovenia, Spain, Switzerland and Ukraine.

[d] Albania, Brazil, China, India, Ireland, Norway, Russian Federation, United Arab Emirates, United Kingdom and United States.

[e] *For*: Albania, Brazil, China, France, Gabon, Ghana, Ireland, Kenya, Mexico, Norway, Russian Federation, United Arab Emirates, United Kingdom, United States; *against*; none; *abstaining*: India.

29. Women and peace and security

In 2022, the Council held five high-level meetings under the item entitled "Women and peace and security", all of which took the form of open debates.[1057] More information on the meeting, including on participants and speakers, is given in table 1 below.[1058] The Council did not adopt any decisions in relation to this item during the year.

In 2022, Council members heard briefings by the Executive Director of the United Nations Entity for Gender Equality and the Empowerment of Women (UN-Women) three times.[1059] The Council also heard briefings by the United Nations High Commissioner for Human Rights,[1060] the Managing Director of the International Monetary Fund[1061] and the Special Representative of the Secretary-General on Sexual Violence in Conflict.[1062] In addition, Council members heard briefings by representatives of regional and subregional organizations, namely, the Special Envoy on Women, Peace and Security of the Chairperson of the African Union Commission,[1063] the Secretary-General of the Organization for Security and Cooperation in Europe, the European Union Ambassador for Gender and Diversity and the Assistant Secretary-General and Head of Social Affairs Sector at the League of Arab States.[1064] Council members also heard briefings by civil society representatives in four of the five meetings held under this item.

On 18 January, at the initiative of Norway, which held the presidency for the month,[1065] the Council held a high-level open debate under this item, on the sub-item entitled "Protecting participation: addressing violence targeting women in peace and security processes".[1066] The Minister for Foreign Affairs of Norway presided over the meeting, during which the Council heard briefings by the United Nations High Commissioner for Human Rights, the Executive Director of the Women and Children Legal Research Foundation and the Executive Director of the non-governmental organization Working Group on Women, Peace and Security. The Council also invited 34 Member States to deliver statements in accordance with rule 37 of the provisional rules of procedure.

In her briefing to the Council, the United Nations High Commissioner for Human Rights noted that women's safe and meaningful participation was necessary to address not only the root causes of conflict but also its full impact, including gender-based violence and the use of sexual violence as a weapon of war.[1067] The Office of the High Commissioner had documented patterns of attacks against women working on gender equality, sexual and reproductive health and rights, corruption, labour rights and environmental and land issues, and reprisals by State and non-State actors against people who cooperated with the United Nations remained high, including in countries associated with matters addressed by the Council, significantly undermining global efforts to prevent conflict and sustain peace

[1057] For more information on the format of meetings, see part II.

[1058] See A/77/2, part II, chap. 17.

[1059] See S/PV.8989, S/PV.9064 and S/PV.9158.

[1060] See S/PV.8949.

[1061] See S/PV.8989.

[1062] See S/PV.9016.

[1063] See S/PV.9064 and S/PV.9158.

[1064] See S/PV.9064.

[1065] A concept note was circulated by a letter dated 10 January (S/2022/22).

[1066] See S/PV.8949 and S/PV.8949 (Resumption 1). In accordance with the understanding reached among Council members in the light of the extraordinary circumstances caused by the COVID-19 pandemic, 10 delegations also participated by submitting written statements (see S/2022/38). For more information on the procedures and working methods developed during the pandemic, see part II.

[1067] See S/PV.8949.

because they deterred women from participation and leadership. Calling for more action to provide safe spaces for women human rights defenders to interact with the Council and its subsidiary bodies without fear of retribution, the High Commissioner requested the Council to consider harmonizing approaches to ensure the safe involvement of women in peace processes, as well as their participation in the Council's work. She suggested that peace operation mandates could explicitly include provisions for the protection of all civil society actors and United Nations interlocutors from threats and reprisals, in particular women peacebuilders. The Executive Director of the Women and Children Legal Research Foundation focused on the situation in Afghanistan, highlighting the important role of the United Nations Assistance Mission in Afghanistan (UNAMA). She urged Council members, as they considered renewing its mandate, to ensure that UNAMA continued to monitor the human rights situation and to protect and promote human rights as well as ensuring that education was supported as part of the humanitarian efforts and that it also fell under the new UNAMA mandate. The Council must call for an inclusive, negotiated peace process that enjoyed the full, equal and meaningful participation of diverse women from across the country at all stages of planning, negotiation and implementation. The Executive Director of Working Group on Women, Peace and Security underlined the pattern of reprisals and intimidation against female civil society representatives who had briefed the Council, which had increased exponentially in recent years. She called upon all Members States, the leadership of the United Nations and the Council members to stop such attacks, end impunity and ensure that all perpetrators were held accountable and urged the Council to call upon the Secretary-General to ensure that the leadership of the United Nations publicly champion the role of women human rights defenders. Further to the briefings, participants in the open debate expressed concerns about intimidation, violence and reprisals against women civil society representatives and women human rights defenders and highlighted the importance of making tangible progress in the participation of women in peace processes, including in negotiations and peacekeeping.[1068] Calling for more effective protection mechanisms, several delegates also requested the allocation of rapid funding resources and policies to respond to threats against women peacebuilders. The Minister for Europe and Foreign Affairs of Albania and the representative of the United Arab Emirates underscored their shared commitments on women and peace and security to make the issue a top priority during their respective Council presidencies.[1069]

On 8 March, at the initiative of the United Arab Emirates, which held the presidency for the month,[1070] the Council held a high-level open debate under this item, on the sub-item entitled "Women's economic inclusion and participation as a key to building peace".[1071] The Minister for Climate Change and Environment of the United Arab Emirates presided over the meeting, during which the Council heard briefings by the Executive Director of UN-Women, the Managing Director of the International Monetary Fund and a civil society representative representing the Network of Women Economic Agents in the Ségou region of Mali. The Council invited 43 Member States to deliver statements in person in accordance with rule 37 of the provisional rules of procedure.

Welcoming the focus placed in the open debate on the role of the private sector and private-public partnerships as an underexplored area for innovation, the Executive Director of UN-Women called upon the Council to say much more about women's economic inclusion and pointed out that some resolutions covering women and peace and security contained paragraphs that tended to be gender-blind on economic security, development issues and the illegal exploitation of resources.[1072] In that connection, she called upon the Council to use such resolutions to prioritize women-led businesses and support for the care economy in all reconstruction and recovery initiatives. The Managing Director of the International Monetary Fund commended the Council's decision to focus on the role of women in peace and security on International Women's Day, noted the impact of gender equality in significantly increasing economic growth, enhancing financial stability and reducing income inequality and highlighted the importance of

[1068] See S/PV.8949 (Ghana, Albania, United Arab Emirates, United Kingdom, Gabon, Norway, Canada and European Union); and S/PV.8949 (Resumption 1) (Portugal, Australia, Jordan and Egypt).

[1069] See S/PV.8949.

[1070] A concept note was circulated by a letter dated 1 March (S/2022/175).

[1071] See S/PV.8989 and S/PV.8989 (Resumption 1). In accordance with the understanding reached among Council members in the light of the extraordinary circumstances caused by the COVID-19 pandemic, five delegations participated by submitting written statements (see S/2022/207).

[1072] See S/PV.8989.

a country-tailored approach in empowering women and girls as powerful agents of change that helped society to transition from fragility to stability. Other briefers highlighted the importance of economic development and inclusion, with an explicit focus on the role of gender equality, as a precondition for lasting peace and societal transition for a better future for all. Following the briefings, participants in the open debate addressed the disproportionate impact of the COVID-19 pandemic on the social and economic participation of women and noted that providing access to entrepreneurship, finance and job opportunities to women not only created a societal wealth but also generated long-term sustainable peace. Some Council members and Member States highlighted the important role played by public-private partnership in advancing skills development and business environment, thereby strengthening women's full, equal and meaningful participation in conflict prevention, peacebuilding and post-conflict reconstruction.[1073]

On 13 April, at the initiative of the United Kingdom, which held the presidency for the month,[1074] the Council held a high-level open debate under this item, on sub-items entitled "Accountability as prevention" and "Ending cycles of sexual violence in conflict".[1075] The Prime Minister's Special Representative on Preventing Sexual Violence of the United Kingdom presided over the meeting, during which the Council heard briefings by the Special Representative of the Secretary-General on Sexual Violence in Conflict, a Nobel Peace Prize laureate and United Nations Office on Drugs and Crime (UNODC) Goodwill Ambassador, a co-founder of Huquqyat and an Ethiopian female civil society representative. The Council also invited 54 Member States to deliver statements in accordance with rule 37 of the provisional rules of procedure.

Presenting the annual report of the Secretary-General on conflict-related sexual violence,[1076] the Special Representative emphasized the importance of accountability, including prosecution as a form of prevention that could help to convert the culture of impunity for such crimes.[1077] All Council members could lead the way in reflecting that prohibition of sexual violence in their military manuals, international humanitarian law dissemination and training, codes of conduct and military disciplinary measures at all levels of the chain of command. The Nobel Peace Prize laureate and UNODC Goodwill Ambassador noted that accountability could be a crucial component of prevention only by including meaningful justice and the services and support needed by survivors, calling upon everyone in the Chamber to make it a reality by choosing to act. Other briefers spoke about the situation of sexual violence and entrenched discrimination against women and girls in Ethiopia and the Syrian Arab Republic. They urged the Council and Member States to refer the situation in the Syrian Arab Republic to the International Criminal Court and to champion the work of the recently established International Commission of Human Rights Experts on Ethiopia and demanded that all parties ensure full and safe humanitarian access to Tigray. Following the briefings, most participants in the open debate noted the deeply traumatizing nature of conflict-related sexual violence and underscored that justice and accountability should be at the core of the international response and that survivors should be kept at the centre of its approach.[1078] They called upon the international community to fight impunity for sexual violence against women.

On 15 June, at the initiative of Albania, which held the presidency for the month,[1079] the Council held a high-level open debate under this item, on the sub-item entitled "Keeping the promises: the role of regional organizations in implementing the women and peace and security agenda in the face of

[1073] See S/PV.8989 (United Arab Emirates, Ireland, Mexico and Brazil); and S/PV.8989 (Resumption 1) (Ecuador, Liechtenstein, Peru, South Africa, Costa Rica, Lebanon and Bangladesh).

[1074] A concept note was circulated by a letter dated 5 April (S/2022/293).

[1075] See S/PV.9016 and S/PV.9016 (Resumption 1).

[1076] S/2022/272.

[1077] See S/PV.9016.

[1078] See S/PV.9016 (United Kingdom, India, Brazil, Albania, Ireland, France, Mexico, Ghana, Gabon, Colombia, Jordan, Malta and Canada (also on behalf of 64 States members of the Group of Friends of Women, Peace and Security); and S/PV.9016 (Resumption 1) (Australia, Netherlands, Slovenia, Lithuania, New Zealand, Argentina, South Africa, Luxembourg, Estonia, Morocco, Switzerland, European Union (also on behalf of Albania, Andorra, Bosnia and Herzegovina, Georgia, Montenegro, North Macedonia, the Republic of Moldova, San Marino and Ukraine), Türkiye, Croatia, Poland, Islamic Republic of Iran, Belgium, Italy, Liechtenstein, Germany, Denmark (also on behalf of Finland, Iceland, Norway and Sweden), Czechia, Malaysia, Spain, Slovakia, Georgia, Holy See, Costa Rica, Cyprus, Sierra Leone, Indonesia, Sri Lanka, Austria, Nepal, Chile, Sweden, Republic of Korea and Algeria).

[1079] A concept note was circulated by a letter dated 4 June (S/2022/457).

political turmoil and seizures of power by force".[1080] The Minister for Europe and Foreign Affairs of Albania presided over the meeting, during which the Council heard briefings by the Secretary-General, the Executive Director of UN-Women, the Secretary-General of the Organization for Security and Cooperation in Europe, the Special Envoy of the Chairperson of the African Union Commission on Women, Peace and Security, the European Union Ambassador for Gender and Diversity and the Assistant Secretary-General and Head of Social Affairs Sector at the League of Arab States. The Council also invited 36 Member States to deliver statements in accordance with rule 37 of the provisional rules of procedure.

In his statement, the Secretary-General pointed out that, while the Council met several times a year on the issue, with consensus among Member States on the importance of the women and peace and security agenda, the situation on the ground was regressing because of the political deadlocks and entrenched conflicts based on enduring power imbalances and patriarchy.[1081] He emphasized the role of neighbouring countries and regional organizations, including the European Union, the African Union, the League of Arab States and the Organization for Security and Cooperation in Europe, in implementing the commitments of the women and peace and security agenda, noting the centrality of women and girls in security policies in his proposed New Agenda for Peace, included in the report entitled "Our Common Agenda".[1082] The Executive Director of UN-Women, applauding the efforts of 12 regional organizations that had adopted action plans on women and peace and security, observed that, when regional organizations made such commitments, national actions often followed.[1083] She underscored the key role of regional organizations in the development of networks of women mediators, such as the registry of women experts in peace and mediation of the Association of Southeast Asian Nations, the African Women Leaders Network, the Network of African Women in Conflict Prevention and Mediation and the Arab Women Mediators Network. She called upon the regional organizations to ensure the presence of women when convening negotiations and encourage legislative and administrative reforms among their member States. The representatives of the Organization for Security and Cooperation in Europe, the African Union, the European Union and the League of Arab State focused on their respective commitments and contributions to advancing the women and peace and security agenda and expanding their cooperation with the Council. Following the briefings, Council members and other Member States stressed the critical role of regional partners in supporting safe and enabling environments for women peacebuilders, civil society activists and human rights defenders and emphasized that gender perspectives should be mainstreamed into regional peacebuilding efforts by promoting the inclusion of women in key political processes and decision-making and in governance.[1084]

On 20 October, at the initiative of Gabon, which held the presidency for the month,[1085] the Council held a high-level open debate under this item, on the sub-item entitled "Strengthening women's resilience and leadership as a pathway to peace in regions plagued by armed groups".[1086] The Council heard briefings by the Deputy Secretary-General, the Executive Director of UN-Women, the Special Envoy on Women, Peace and Security of the Chairperson of the African Union Commission and the Editor-in-Chief of *Zan Times*.[1087] The Head of the Delegation of the European Union to the United Nations, the Special Representative of the Secretary-General of the North Atlantic Treaty Organization for Women, Peace and Security and the Head of the Policy and Humanitarian Diplomacy Division of the International Committee of the Red Cross participated in the meeting in accordance with rule 39 of the Council's provisional rules of procedure. The Council also invited 56 Member States to deliver statements in accordance with rule 37 of the provisional rules of procedure.

[1080] See S/PV.9064 and S/PV.9064 (Resumption 1).
[1081] See S/PV.9064.
[1082] A/75/982.
[1083] See S/PV.9064.
[1084] See S/PV.9064 (Albania, Ghana, Gabon, Kenya, Mexico, Finland and Canada (also on behalf of the Group of Friends of Women, Peace and Security)); and S/PV.9064 (Resumption 1) (Türkiye, Malta, Bulgaria, South Africa, Germany, Namibia, Austria, Ecuador, Poland, Guatemala and Bolivarian Republic of Venezuela.
[1085] A concept note was circulated by a letter dated 4 October (S/2022/743).
[1086] See S/PV.9158 and S/PV.9158 (Resumption 1).
[1087] See S/PV.9158.

The Deputy Secretary-General, emphasizing the slow progress of women's participation in peace processes and the consistent underfunding for women peacebuilders, reaffirmed five transformative actions identified by the Secretary-General for the decade ahead on women's rights. She urged everyone to implement them without delay and to pay special attention to protecting women human rights defenders. Noting that the women and peace and security agenda was not just an answer to historic wrongs and marginalization but an opportunity to do things differently, she highlighted the need for full gender parity, including through special quotas to accelerate the inclusion of women across election monitoring, security sector reform, disarmament, demobilization and justice systems. The Executive Director of UN-Women, presenting the annual report of the Secretary-General on women and peace and security,[1088] focused her briefing on women human rights defenders and the need to strengthen reporting and coordination within the United Nations, build partnerships with Member States, regional organizations and civil society and provide material and political support.[1089] She called upon the Member States to demand that women be properly represented in peace processes and urged everyone to make the smart decision on funding and prioritize resources. The Special Envoy of the Chairperson of the African Union Commission on Women, Peace and Security called upon the Council to strengthen its collaboration with the African Union Peace and Security Council to align priorities and actions on the ground in support of women's full participation in peace processes. She emphasized the importance of access to predictable and flexible funding for women's organizations and the need for taking deliberate measures to increase women's participation in peace processes and for combining peacebuilding efforts with women's economic survival as mutually reinforcing strategies owing to the impact of climate change, the coronavirus pandemic and conflicts. In her briefing, the Editor-in-Chief of *Zan Times*, a woman-led newsroom covering human rights violations in Afghanistan, warned Council members of the disturbing reports of war crimes that continued to emerge in Afghanistan and said that the Council had overwhelming evidence that the Taliban were terrorizing women, girls and marginalized groups. She urged the Council to call upon the Taliban to respect the human rights of all Afghans, including women, girls, lesbian, gay, bisexual and transgender people and all ethnic and religious groups, and to stop the targeting and abuse of protesters, human rights defenders, journalists and their families. The Council should ensure the full, equal and meaningful participation of Afghan women civil society in any decision-making regarding the future of Afghanistan, including its own decisions. Following the briefings, participants in the open debate deliberated on women's leadership in achieving progress in peace and security by strengthening the global response to conflict-related sexual violence and making meaningful progress in women's participation in peace processes. Several Council members and Member States urged the Secretary-General and the Council to take concrete actions to fight in solidarity against destabilization, terrorism and armed groups and the protection of women and girls from attacks on their right to education.[1090]

During the period under review, the Informal Expert Group on Women and Peace and Security continued to be convened in accordance with paragraph 5 (a) of resolution 2242 (2015), including to address country- and region-specific situations in Afghanistan; the Central African Republic; Iraq; Lebanon; the Middle East; the Middle East, including the Palestinian question; and Myanmar.[1091]

In 2022, Council members submitted communications to the President of the Council in connection with the women and peace and security agenda. By a letter dated 3 February,[1092] the representatives of Ireland, Kenya and Mexico transmitted a handover and summary report on a Council Presidency Trio for Women, Peace and Security. By a letter dated 12 October,[1093] the representative of Norway transmitted, ahead of the open debate held on 20 October, a summary report entitled "Protecting women human rights defenders in conflict" resulting from the civil society consultations on the issue of reprisals against women human rights defenders in conflict-affected countries, including as a result of cooperation with

[1088] S/2022/740.

[1089] See S/PV.9158.

[1090] See S/PV.9158 (Gabon, Albania, United Arab Emirates, United Kingdom, Ireland, China, Mexico, France, Norway and Finland); and S/PV.9158 (Resumption 1) (South Africa, Greece, Slovakia, Dominican Republic, Indonesia, Mali, Morocco, Kuwait and International Committee of the Red Cross).

[1091] See S/2022/171, S/2022/258, S/2022/557, S/2022/593, S/2022/815, S/2022/816 and S/2022/1005.

[1092] S/2022/91.

[1093] S/2022/756.

the United Nations. In addition, by a letter dated 27 December,[1094] the representative of Norway transmitted, on behalf of the 15 signatories (former, then current and incoming Council members, namely, Albania, Brazil, Ecuador, France, Gabon, Ireland, Japan, Kenya, Malta, Mexico, the Niger, Norway, Switzerland, United Arab Emirates and United Kingdom), the statement of shared commitments on women and peace and security, which had been launched in December 2021, building on the trio initiative of September 2021 by Ireland, Kenya and Mexico.

The Council referred to issues related to women and peace and security under multiple items in 2022. As summarized in table 2 below, the Council addressed in its decisions various measures concerning the specific implementation of the women and peace and security agenda and, in particular, in relation to the following categories: (a) the representation and participation of women in public affairs and decision-making, as well as in peacebuilding, conflict prevention and resolution; (b) the participation of women in peacekeeping operations, including through the appointment of women's protection and gender advisers; (c) the development and inclusion of gender mainstreaming, gender expertise and gender-sensitive responses by Member States and United Nations entities, including socioeconomic empowerment, the participation of women in security sector reforms and counter-terrorism efforts; and (d) combating sexual violence through measures such as monitoring, analysing and reporting on conflict-related sexual violence and gender-based violence as well as its accountability mechanisms, including prosecutions of the perpetrators of sexual violence and the use of targeted sanctions.

Table 1
Meetings: women and peace and security, 2022

Meeting record and date	*Sub-item*	*Other documents*	*Rule 37 invitations*	*Rule 39 and other invitations*	*Speakers*	*Decision and vote (for-against-abstaining)*
S/PV.8949, S/PV.8949 (Resumption 1) and S/2022/38 18 January	Protecting participation: addressing violence targeting women in peace and security processes Letter dated 10 January 2022 from the Permanent Representative of Norway to the United Nations addressed to the Secretary General (S/2022/22)		34 Member States[a]	United Nations High Commissioner for Human Rights, Head of the Delegation of the European Union to the United Nations, Executive Director of the Women and Children Legal Research Foundation, Executive Director of Working Group on Women, Peace and Security	All Council members,[b] all invitees[c]	
S/PV.8989, S/PV.8989 (Resumption 1) and S/2022/207 8 March	Women's economic inclusion and participation as a key to building peace Letter dated 1 March 2022 from the Permanent Representative of the United Arab Emirates to the United Nations addressed to the		43 Member States[d]	Executive Director of the United Nations Entity for Gender Equality and the Empowerment of Women (UN-Women), Managing Director of the International Monetary Fund, Deputy Head of the Delegation of the European Union,	All Council members,[e] all invitees[f]	

[1094] S/2022/1009.

Meeting record and date	*Sub-item*	*Other documents*	*Rule 37 invitations*	*Rule 39 and other invitations*	*Speakers*	*Decision and vote (for-against-abstaining)*
	Secretary-General (S/2022/175)			representative of the Network of Women Economic Agents in the Ségou region of Mali		
S/PV.9016 and S/PV.9016 (Resumption 1) 13 April	Accountability as prevention Ending cycles of sexual violence in conflict Letter dated 5 April 2022 from the Permanent Representative of the United Kingdom of Great Britain and Northern Ireland to the United Nations addressed to the Secretary-General (S/2022/293)		54 Member States[g]	Seven invitees[h]	All Council members,[i] all invitees[j]	
S/PV.9064 and S/PV.9064 (Resumption 1) 15 June	Keeping the promises: the role of regional organizations in implementing the women and peace and security agenda in the face of political turmoil and seizures of power by force Letter dated 4 June 2022 from the Permanent Representative of Albania to the United Nations addressed to the Secretary-General (S/2022/457)		36 Member States[k]	Executive Director of UN-Women, Secretary-General of the Organization for Security and Cooperation in Europe, Special Envoy of the Chairperson of the African Union Commission on Women, Peace and Security, European Union Ambassador for Gender and Diversity, Assistant Secretary-General and Head of Social Affairs Sector at the League of Arab States	Secretary-General, all Council members,[l] all invitees[m]	
S/PV.9158 and S/PV.9158 (Resumption 1) 20 October	Strengthening women's resilience and leadership as a pathway to peace in regions plagued by armed groups		56 Member States[n]	Seven invitees[o]	Deputy Secretary-General, all Council members,[p] all invitees[q]	

Meeting record and date	Sub-item	Other documents	Rule 37 invitations	Rule 39 and other invitations	Speakers	Decision and vote (for-against-abstaining)
	Report of the Secretary-General on women and peace and security (S/2022/740) Letter dated 4 October 2022 from the Permanent Representative of Gabon to the United Nations addressed to the Secretary-General (S/2022/743)					

[a] Argentina, Australia, Austria, Belgium, Bulgaria, Canada, Chile, Denmark, Ecuador, Egypt, Estonia, Fiji, Georgia, Germany, Greece, Indonesia, Iran (Islamic Republic of), Italy, Japan, Jordan, Latvia, Liechtenstein, Lithuania, Malaysia, Malta, Morocco, New Zealand, Poland, Portugal, Rwanda, Slovakia, Slovenia, Switzerland and Türkiye.

[b] Albania was represented by its Minister for Europe and Foreign Affairs; Ghana was represented by its Minister for Foreign Affairs and Regional Integration; Norway (President of the Council) was represented by its Minister for Foreign Affairs; the United Arab Emirates was represented by its Permanent Representative to the United Nations and Assistant Minister for Foreign Affairs and International Cooperation for Political Affairs; and the United States was represented by its Under Secretary of State for Civilian Security, Democracy and Human Rights.

[c] The representative of Belgium spoke also on behalf of Luxembourg and the Netherlands; the representative of Canada spoke on behalf of the Group of Friends of Women, Peace and Security; and the representative of Denmark spoke on behalf of the Nordic countries.

[d] Argentina, Bahrain, Bangladesh, Barbados, Canada, Chile, Costa Rica, Czechia, Dominican Republic, Ecuador, Egypt, Georgia, Germany, Greece, Guatemala, Indonesia, Iraq, Iran (Islamic Republic of), Israel, Italy, Japan, Jordan, Lebanon, Liechtenstein, Malaysia, Maldives, Malta, Morocco, Nepal, Pakistan, Peru, Poland, Portugal, Qatar, South Africa, Sri Lanka, Switzerland, Sweden, Thailand, Türkiye, Ukraine, Uruguay and Viet Nam.

[e] India was represented by its Secretary (West) in the Ministry of External Affairs; Ireland was represented by its Minister for Foreign Affairs and Minister for Defence; Mexico was represented by its Vice-Minister for Multilateral Affairs and Human Rights; the United Arab Emirates (President of the Council) was represented by its Minister for Climate Change and Environment; and the United States was represented by its Permanent Representative to the United Nations and member of the President's Cabinet.

[f] Maldives was represented by its Minister of State for Foreign Affairs. The representative of Barbados spoke on behalf of the Caribbean Community; the representative of Canada spoke on behalf of the Group of Friends of Women, Peace and Security. The representative of Sweden spoke on behalf of the Nordic and Baltic countries (Denmark, Estonia, Finland, Iceland, Latvia, Lithuania, Norway and Sweden).

[g] Algeria, Argentina, Australia, Austria, Bangladesh, Belgium, Bulgaria, Canada, Chile, Colombia, Costa Rica, Croatia, Cyprus, Czechia, Denmark, Ecuador, Estonia, Ethiopia, Georgia, Germany, Greece, Indonesia, Iraq, Iran (Islamic Republic of), Italy, Japan, Jordan, Latvia, Lebanon, Liechtenstein, Lithuania, Luxembourg, Malaysia, Maldives, Malta, Morocco, Nepal, Netherlands, New Zealand, Poland, Portugal, Republic of Korea, Sierra Leone, Saudi Arabia, Slovakia, Slovenia, South Africa, Spain, Sri Lanka, Sweden, Switzerland, Türkiye, Ukraine and Yemen.

[h] The Special Representative of the Secretary-General on Sexual Violence in Conflict; the Head of the Delegation of the European Union; the Head of the North Atlantic Treaty Organization (NATO) Liaison Office to the United Nations; the Permanent Observer of the Holy See to the United Nations; a Nobel Peace Prize laureate and United Nations Office on Drugs and Crime Goodwill Ambassador; the co-founder of Huquqyat; and an Ethiopian civil society representative.

[i] The United Kingdom (President of the Council) was represented by its Minister of State for South and Central Asia, North Africa, the United Nations and the Commonwealth, and the Prime Minister's Special Representative for Preventing Sexual Violence in Conflict; and the United States was represented by its Permanent Representative and member of the President's Cabinet.

[j] Colombia was represented by its Vice-President and Minister for Foreign Affairs. The representative of Canada spoke on behalf of the Group of Friends of Women, Peace and Security; the representative of Denmark spoke on behalf of the Nordic countries; the representative of Sweden spoke on behalf of the LGBTI Core Group; and the representative of the European Union spoke also on behalf of Albania, Andorra, Bosnia and Herzegovina, Georgia, Montenegro, North Macedonia, the Republic of Moldova, San Marino and Ukraine. The civil society representative participated in the meeting by videoconference.

[k] Algeria, Argentina, Austria, Bulgaria, Canada, Chile, Croatia, Czechia, Ecuador, Egypt, Finland, Georgia, Germany, Greece, Guatemala, Italy, Indonesia, Jordan, Liechtenstein, Luxembourg, Malta, Morocco, Namibia, Poland, Republic of Korea, Portugal, Slovakia, Slovenia, Spain, South Africa, Switzerland, Thailand, Türkiye, Ukraine, Uruguay and Venezuela (Bolivarian Republic of).

[l] Albania (President of the Council) was represented by its Minister for Europe and Foreign Affairs; Ghana was represented by its Deputy Minister of Finance; Norway was represented by its State Secretary; the United Arab Emirates was represented by its Permanent Representative and Assistant Minister for Foreign Affairs and International Cooperation for Political Affairs; and the United States was represented by its Permanent Representative and member of the President's Cabinet.

[m] Finland was represented by its Minister for Development Cooperation and Foreign Trade and spoke on behalf of the Nordic countries. The representative of Canada spoke on behalf of the Group of Friends of Women, Peace and Security; the representative of Luxembourg spoke on behalf of the Benelux countries; and the representative of Germany spoke on behalf of the Group of Friends of the African Women Leaders Network.

[n] Australia, Austria, Bangladesh, Belgium, Bulgaria, Canada, Central African Republic, Chile, Colombia, Costa Rica, Croatia, Democratic Republic of the Congo, Dominican Republic, Ecuador, Egypt, Estonia, Finland, Georgia, Germany, Greece, Guatemala, Guyana, Indonesia, Iran (Islamic Republic of), Israel, Italy, Japan, Jordan, Kuwait, Latvia, Lebanon, Liechtenstein, Lithuania, Luxembourg, Malaysia, Mali, Malta, Morocco, Namibia, Netherlands, New Zealand, Niger, Philippines, Poland, Portugal, Republic of Korea, Romania, Slovakia, Slovenia, South Africa, Spain, Switzerland, Thailand, Türkiye, Ukraine, Viet Nam and Yemen.

[o] The Executive Director of UN-Women; the Special Envoy on Women, Peace and Security of the Chairperson of the African Union Commission; the Head of the Delegation of the European Union; the NATO Secretary-General's Special Representative for Women, Peace and Security; the Head of Policy and Humanitarian Diplomacy Division of the International Committee of the Red Cross; the Permanent Observer of the State of Palestine to the United Nations; and the Editor-in-Chief of *Zan Times*.

[p] Albania was represented by its Deputy Minister for Europe and Foreign Affairs; the United Arab Emirates was represented by its Permanent Representative and Assistant Minister for Foreign Affairs and International Cooperation for Political Affairs; and the United States was represented by its Permanent Representative and member of the President's Cabinet.

[q] The Central African Republic was represented by its Minister for Foreign Affairs, Francophonie and Central Africans Abroad; the Democratic Republic of the Congo was represented by its Minister of Gender, Family and Infants; and Finland was represented by its State Secretary to the Minister for Foreign Affairs, who spoke on behalf of the Nordic countries. The representative of Canada spoke on behalf of the Group of Friends of Women, Peace and Security; the representative of Türkiye spoke also on behalf of Australia, Indonesia, Mexico and the Republic of Korea; the representative of Germany spoke on behalf of the Group of Friends of the African Women Leaders Network; and the representative of Croatia spoke on behalf of the Group of Friends of the Responsibility to Protect.

Table 2
Selection of provisions relevant to women and peace and security, by theme and item

	Item	*Decision*	*Paragraph*
Representation and participation of women in political processes at all levels, including decision-making			
Country- and region-specific	The situation in Afghanistan	Resolution 2626 (2022)	5 (c), 5 (f)
	Peace and security in Africa	S/PRST/2022/6	Fifth
	The situation in the Central African Republic	Resolution 2659 (2022)	9, 49
	The situation concerning the Democratic Republic of the Congo	Resolution 2666 (2022)	2, 29
	The question concerning Haiti	Resolution 2645 (2022)	3
	The situation concerning Iraq	Resolution 2631 (2022)	2 (e)
	The situation in Libya	Resolution 2647 (2022)	4
		Resolution 2656 (2022)	6
	The situation in Mali	Resolution 2640 (2022)	3, 14, 26 (a) (vi), 48
	The situation in the Middle East	Resolution 2650 (2022)	27
	The situation in Somalia	Resolution 2628 (2022)	3
		Resolution 2657 (2022)	8 (c)

	Item	*Decision*	*Paragraph*
	Reports of the Secretary-General on the Sudan and South Sudan	Resolution 2625 (2022)	3 (c) (v), 7–8, 24
Thematic	United Nations peacekeeping operations	S/PRST/2022/5	Eighth
Participation of women in peacebuilding and in conflict prevention and resolution			
Country- and region-specific	The situation in Afghanistan	Resolution 2626 (2022)	5 (f)
	Peace and security in Africa	S/PRST/2022/6	Fifth
	The situation in the Central African Republic	Resolution 2648 (2022)	4
		Resolution 2659 (2022)	2, 7, 11, 35 (b) (iii)–(vi), 49
	The situation in Cyprus	Resolution 2618 (2022)	5 (e), 6
		Resolution 2646 (2022)	5 (e), 6
	The situation concerning the Democratic Republic of the Congo	Resolution 2666 (2022)	16
	The question concerning Haiti	Resolution 2645 (2022)	3
	The situation concerning Iraq	Resolution 2631 (2022)	2 (a)
	The situation in Libya	Resolution 2647 (2022)	4
		Resolution 2650 (2022)	27
	The situation in Mali	Resolution 2640 (2022)	9, 26 (a) (v), 48
	The situation in Somalia	Resolution 2628 (2022)	3
		Resolution 2657 (2022)	8 (c)
	Reports of the Secretary-General on the Sudan and South Sudan	Resolution 2625 (2022)	3 (c) (ii), 6, 14, 24
	The situation concerning Western Sahara	Resolution 2654 (2022)	14
Thematic	Cooperation between the United Nations and regional and subregional organizations in maintaining international peace and security	S/PRST/2022/1	Fifteenth
	United Nations peacekeeping operations	S/PRST/2022/5	Seventh
Socioeconomic environment for the meaningful participation and empowerment of women and funding of national programmes			
Country- and region-specific	Peace and security in Africa	S/PRST/2022/6	Ninth, fourteenth
	The situation in Cyprus	Resolution 2618 (2022)	5 (e)
		Resolution 2646 (2022)	5 (e)
	The situation concerning Iraq	Resolution 2631 (2022)	2 (e)
	The situation concerning the Democratic Republic of the Congo	Resolution 2666 (2022)	7, 29

	Item	Decision	Paragraph
Conflict-related sexual violence and gender-based violence			
Country- and region-specific	The situation in Afghanistan	Resolution 2626 (2022)	5 (e)
	The situation in the Central African Republic	Resolution 2659 (2022)	26–27, 35 (a) (iv), 35 (a) (vi), 35 (b) (iv)–(vi), 36 (b) (ii), 36 (f) (vii), 44, 49
	The situation in Cyprus	Resolution 2618 (2022)	16 (e), 17
		Resolution 2646 (2022)	17 (c), 18
	The situation concerning the Democratic Republic of the Congo	S/PRST/2022/4	Sixth
		Resolution 2666 (2022)	7, 9, 24 (i) (e), 29–30, 37
	The question concerning Haiti	Resolution 2645 (2022)	2
		Resolution 2653 (2022)	1, 16 (a), 16 (f), 25 (b)
	The situation concerning Iraq	Resolution 2631 (2022)	2 (e)
	The situation in Mali	Resolution 2640 (2022)	7, 26 (c) (iii), 26 (d) (ii), 41, 45, 49–51
	The situation in the Middle East	Resolution 2624 (2022)	12
		Resolution 2639 (2022)	14
		Resolution 2650 (2022)	26
		Resolution 2671 (2022)	14
	The situation in Somalia	Resolution 2628 (2022)	14, 15, 15 (a)–(e), 34
		Resolution 2657 (2022)	8 (f), 9, 13 (a)–(c)
		Resolution 2662 (2022)	48
	Reports of the Secretary-General on the Sudan and South Sudan	Resolution 2625 (2022)	3 (a) (iv), 3 (a) (vii)–(viii), 3 (d) (ii), 11, 15, 17, 20 (h), 20 (o), 26
		Resolution 2633 (2022)	13, 21
	The situation concerning Western Sahara	Resolution 2654 (2022)	16
Thematic	Cooperation between the United Nations and regional and subregional organizations in maintaining international peace and security	S/PRST/2022/1	Fifteenth
	Threats to international peace and security caused by terrorist acts	S/PRST/2022/7	Fifth
	United Nations peacekeeping operations	S/PRST/2022/5	Seventh, ninth
Role of women in countering terrorism and violent extremism			
Thematic	Threats to international peace and security caused by terrorist acts	S/PRST/2022/7	Eighth

	Item	*Decision*	*Paragraph*
Gender mainstreaming, gender expertise and gender-sensitive responses			
Country- and region-specific	The situation in Afghanistan	Resolution 2626 (2022)	5 (f)
	The situation in the Central African Republic	Resolution 2659 (2022)	11, 35 (a) (iv), 36 (e) (i)–(ii), 43, 49
	The situation in Cyprus	Resolution 2618 (2022)	5 (e), 6, 16 (a), 18
		Resolution 2646 (2022)	5 (e), 6, 17 (a), 19
	The situation concerning the Democratic Republic of the Congo	Resolution 2666 (2022)	24 (ii) (g)–(h), 29, 43
		S/PRST/2022/4	Fourth
	The situation concerning Haiti	Resolution 2653 (2022)	24
	The situation concerning Iraq	Resolution 2631 (2022)	2 (e)
	The situation in Mali	Resolution 2640 (2022)	26 (c) (iii), 47
	The situation the Middle East	Resolution 2639 (2022)	13
		Resolution 2650 (2022)	27
	The situation in Somalia	Resolution 2662 (2022)	23, 44
	Reports of the Secretary-General on the Sudan and South Sudan	Resolution 2625 (2022)	3 (a) (v)–(vi), 3 (b) (i), 20 (a), 20 (k), 24–25
		Resolution 2633 (2022)	19
Thematic	International Residual Mechanism for Criminal Tribunals	Resolution 2637 (2022)	10
	Threats to international peace and security caused by terrorist acts	S/PRST/2022/7	Thirteenth
	United Nations peacekeeping operations	Resolution 2668 (2022)	4
Protection of women and women's protection advisers			
Country- and region-specific	Peace and Security in Africa	S/PRST/2022/6	Nineteenth
	The situation in the Central African Republic	Resolution 2659 (2022)	11, 35 (a) (iv), 49
	The situation concerning the Democratic Republic of the Congo	Resolution 2666 (2022)	29
	The situation in Haiti	Resolution 2645 (2022)	2
	The situation in Mali	Resolution 2640 (2022)	12, 26 (c) (iii), 48
	The situation in Somalia	Resolution 2628 (2022)	15 (a)
	Reports of the Secretary-General on the Sudan and South Sudan	Resolution 2625 (2022)	3 (a) (i), 3 (a) (v)
Participation of women in peacekeeping operations			
	Peace and security in Africa	S/PRST/2022/6	Nineteenth

	Item	*Decision*	*Paragraph*
Country- and region-specific	The situation in the Central African Republic	Resolution 2659 (2022)	35 (a) (iv), 35 (b) (iii), 43, 49
	The situation in Cyprus	Resolution 2618 (2022)	16 (a), 18
		Resolution 2646 (2022)	17 (a), 19
	The situation concerning the Democratic Republic of the Congo	Resolution 2666 (2022)	29
	The situation in Mali	Resolution 2640 (2022)	44
		Resolution 2659 (2022)	2
	The situation in the Middle East	Resolution 2639 (2022)	13, 21
		Resolution 2650 (2022)	28
		Resolution 2671 (2022)	13
	The situation in Somalia	Resolution 2628 (2022)	35
	Reports of the Secretary General on the Sudan and South Sudan	Resolution 2625 (2022)	20 (k), 25
	The situation concerning Western Sahara	Resolution 2654 (2022)	12
Thematic	United Nations peacekeeping operations	S/PRST/2022/5	Eighth
Participation of women in the security sector and in security sector reform			
Country- and region-specific	The situation in the Central African Republic	Resolution 2659 (2022)	12, 36 (d) (iv)
	The situation concerning the Democratic Republic of the Congo	Resolution 2659 (2022)	12, 35 (b) (iii), 36 (d) (iv), 36 (e) (i)
		Resolution 2666 (2022)	13, 24 (iii) (l), 29
	The situation in Mali	Resolution 2640 (2022)	48
	The situation in the Middle East	Resolution 2650 (2022)	27
	The situation in Somalia	Resolution 2628 (2022)	24 (i), 35
		Resolution 2657 (2022)	8 (c)

30. Threats to international peace and security caused by terrorist acts

During the period under review, the Council held four meetings under the item entitled “Threats to international peace and security caused by terrorist acts”. Three of the meetings held in 2022 took the form of briefings, and the remaining meeting was convened for the adoption of a decision.[1095] Indeed, the Council adopted one resolution, under Chapter VII of the Charter, and one presidential statement.[1096] More information on the meetings, including on participants, speakers and outcomes, is provided in the table below.[1097]

[1095] For more information on the format of meetings, see part II.

[1096] Resolution 2665 (2022) and S/PRST/2022/7.

[1097] See also A/77/2, part II, chap. 22.

In 2022, Council members heard briefings by the Under-Secretary-General of the Office of Counter-Terrorism and the Acting Executive Director of the Counter-Terrorism Committee Executive Directorate. In addition, Council members heard briefings by two civil society representatives; a senior researcher at the Institute for Security Studies and a survivor of the Mumbai terror attacks of 26 November 2008. Briefings during the reporting period were focused on the expansion of affiliates of Da'esh and Al-Qaida throughout the African continent, the increase in terrorist attacks based on xenophobia, racism and intolerance, the humanitarian and security situation of thousands of individuals suspected of having links with Da'esh held in detention facilities, and the activities of the Counter-Terrorism Committee Executive Directorate in support of the counter-terrorism efforts of Member States. Briefers and Council members also discussed the manner in which developments in Afghanistan continued to affect counter-terrorism efforts in the region,[1098] and the importance of countering the use of new and emerging technologies for terrorist purposes.

On 9 February, Council members heard a briefing by the Under-Secretary-General of the Office of Counter-Terrorism on the fourteenth report of the Secretary-General on the threat posed by Da'esh to international peace and security.[1099] The Under-Secretary-General reported that Al-Qaida, Da'esh and their various affiliates remained serious threats and that terrorist attacks based on xenophobia, racism and intolerance were increasing.[1100] He urged the Council and all Member States to use every available tool at their disposal to sustain important gains against the threat posed by Da'esh in order to prevent its regional expansion and curtail its capabilities to launch attacks and recruit new members. He emphasized the need to focus on restoring human dignity, trust and social cohesion, starting by addressing the desperate situation in displacement camps and detention facilities across the Syrian Arab Republic and Iraq, where tens of thousands of people, including children, remained stranded at growing risk of further radicalization and recruitment. It was essential to ensure humanitarian access to those locations to alleviate suffering and reduce security concerns. In Iraq and the Syrian Arab Republic, Da'esh continued to operate as an entrenched rural insurgency, while its regional affiliates beyond those two countries continued to expand at an unsettling scale and pace, in particular in Central, East and West Africa. In connection with the security landscape in Afghanistan following the Taliban takeover, the Under-Secretary-General reiterated the repeated calls by the Secretary-General for collective work to prevent Afghanistan from once again becoming a safe haven for terrorist activity. In Europe, online terrorist radicalization and recruitment remained a foremost concern during the reporting period. He urged the Council to sustain its consensus in counter-terrorism cooperation.

At the same meeting, the Acting Executive Director of the Counter-Terrorism Committee Executive Directorate stated that the global terrorist landscape continued to present a range of complex challenges for Member States. The threat of Da'esh persisted, with a resurgence of violence in Iraq and the Syrian Arab Republic, and supporters notably emerging and expanding their operations in the battlefields of West, East, Southern and Central Africa while also seeking to exploit recent developments in Afghanistan. Da'esh and other terrorist groups had sought to exploit fault lines arising from social restrictions, political tensions and economic downturns exacerbated by the pandemic. Against that backdrop, the Directorate continued to coordinate closely with the Office of Counter-Terrorism and other key partners to ensure that the recommendations of the Counter-Terrorism Committee served as the basis for relevant capacity-building activities. The Directorate had recently issued its updated global survey of the implementation by Member States of resolution 1373 (2001) and other resolutions, as well as its updated global survey of the implementation of resolution 1624 (2005) and a number of other reports and studies on the challenges faced by Member States. The Directorate had continued to work closely with the Office on a series of activities aimed at enhancing the capacities of Member States on, inter alia, countering terrorist travel; the creation of fusion cells; countering the trafficking of small arms and light weapons; the protection of vulnerable targets; countering the financing of terrorism; and prosecution, rehabilitation and reintegration.

On 19 August, Council members heard a briefing by the Under-Secretary-General of the Office of Counter-Terrorism on the fifteenth report of the Secretary-General on the threat posed by Da'esh to

[1098] For more information on the situation in Afghanistan, see sect. 14 above.

[1099] See S/PV.8963. See also S/2022/63.

[1100] See S/PV.8963.

international peace and security.[1101] The Under-Secretary General reported that Da'esh had continued to pose a threat to international peace and security that had been rising since the onset of the COVID-19 pandemic, with Da'esh and its affiliates continuing to exploit pandemic-related restrictions and misuse digital spaces to intensify their efforts to recruit sympathizers and attract resources.[1102] Da'esh had significantly increased the use of unmanned aerial systems and had managed to do so in part by resorting to a largely decentralized internal structure centred around a so-called general directorate of provinces and associated offices. The offices operated not only in Iraq and the Syrian Arab Republic but also outside the core conflict zone, with those most active being reported in Afghanistan, Somalia and the Lake Chad basin, and he underscored the importance of understanding better and continuously monitoring that structure in order to counter and prevent the threat posed by Da'esh and its affiliates. That threat remained higher in societies affected by conflict, such as the border between Iraq and the Syrian Arab Republic and Afghanistan, and Da'esh had expanded in Central, South and West Africa. He expressed concern about the potential impact of climate-related challenges and global food insecurity in West Africa and the Sahel. With regard to Europe, Da'esh had called upon sympathizers to carry out attacks by exploiting the easing of pandemic-related restrictions and the conflict in Ukraine. Despite the persistent threat, joint efforts by Member States had continued to yield positive results, and the diversity of resources used by Da'esh to finance terrorist activities and exert control over affiliated groups and fighters underlined the importance of sustained efforts to counter the financing of terrorism. He expressed deep concern about the limited progress achieved in repatriating foreign terrorist fighters and their family members from camps in the north-east of the Syrian Arab Republic. The persistent threat posed by Da'esh, as well as the magnitude of the challenges that it presented, underlined the importance of non-military measures to counter terrorism and address its consequences. He emphasized the importance of addressing the vulnerabilities, societal grievances and inequality that were exploited by the group. In that regard, he also emphasized the importance of promoting and protecting human rights and the rule of law.

During his briefing, the Acting Executive Director of the Counter-Terrorism Committee Executive Directorate asserted that the threat posed by Da'esh and its affiliates remained both global and evolving. Despite its recent leadership losses, Da'esh continued to take advantage of conditions conducive to the spread of terrorism to recruit as well as to organize and execute complex attacks. The situation in Africa, in particular in West and Central Africa and in Mozambique, had become more concerning. During 2022, the Directorate had been able to resume its on-site assessment visits on behalf of the Counter-Terrorism Committee. The Directorate had issued several analytical and research products, such as a report on key trends and developments in relation to Da'esh in Africa, a study on the interrelationship between counter-terrorism frameworks and international humanitarian law, and a joint report with the International Peace Institute on the relationship between masculinities and violent extremism conducive to terrorism. He informed the Council about the forthcoming special meeting of the Committee on the use of emerging technologies for counter-terrorism purposes, to be held from 28 to 30 October in New Delhi and Mumbai, India.

At the same meeting, a senior researcher at the Institute for Security Studies, a think tank on human security in Africa, provided his reflection on and analysis of why the threat posed by Da'esh to Africa was growing day by day and why the continent could be the future of the caliphate. He noted with concern that at least 20 countries in Africa had directly experienced Da'esh activity, with more than 20 others being used for logistics and to mobilize funds and other resources. There were regional hubs that had become corridors for instability in Africa. The Lake Chad basin continued to serve as the group's biggest area of operations, the Sahel had become ungovernable, and Somalia remained the hotspot for the Horn of Africa. Factors that had made Da'esh successful in Africa included the presence of natural resources in connection with the battle over the continent's resources, the lingering grievances about global injustices and the lack of political will to deal with the Palestinian problem as a main source of the radicalization of young people in Africa, the ability of Da'esh to work with other terror and criminal groups on the continent, the inconsistency in State responses to terrorism, the ailing war on terrorism in Africa, and the divorce between the fight against transnational organized crime and counter-terrorism in Africa. The Council could mobilize support for counter-terrorism in Africa, be closer and more involved and find a way to ensure that the resolutions that it adopted were communicated to those concerned on

[1101] See S/PV.9108. See also S/2022/576.

[1102] See S/PV.9108.

the ground, in particular at the community level. He called upon the Council to work closely with the African Union and regional economic communities in the fight against terrorism in Africa.

On 15 December, at the initiative of India, which held the presidency for the month,[1103] the Council held a high-level meeting[1104] under the sub-item entitled "Global counter-terrorism approach – principles and the way forward". At the meeting, the Council heard briefings by the Under-Secretary-General of the Office of Counter-Terrorism, the Acting Executive Director of the Counter-Terrorism Committee Executive Directorate and a civil society representative.

The Under-Secretary-General asserted that, despite continuing leadership losses by Al-Qaida and Da'esh, terrorism in general had become more prevalent and more geographically widespread. He emphasized the urgency of the situation in West Africa and the Sahel, where terrorist groups strove to expand their areas of operation, and added that the activities of such groups had also contributed to the deteriorating security situation in Central and Southern Africa. Regarding the situation in Afghanistan, the sustained presence of terrorist groups in the country continued to pose serious threats to the region and beyond, as some groups had ambitions to conduct external operations. The de facto authorities had failed to sever long-standing ties with terrorist groups sheltering in the country, despite the Council's demands to do so. He expressed concern about the manner in which terrorist groups misused and abused developments in technological innovation, including online video games, to advance their agendas. In that regard, he welcomed the adoption of the Delhi declaration on countering the use of new and emerging technologies for terrorist purposes at the special meeting of the Counter-Terrorism Committee held in India in October 2022. He also expressed concerned about the increase in terrorist attacks based on xenophobia, racism and other forms of intolerance, or in the name of religion or belief. He enumerated four principles for guiding collective action in countering terrorism going forward, namely, ensuring prevention; applying community-based and conflict- and gender-sensitive whole-of-society approaches; keeping human rights at the centre of effective counter-terrorism responses; and leveraging regional arrangements.

During his briefing to the Council at the same meeting, the Acting Executive Director of the Counter-Terrorism Committee Executive Directorate stated that the threat of terrorism had become diffuse and diverse in nature, with battlefields emerging in the Sahel, in West, East, Southern and Central Africa and in parts of Asia. Da'esh was also persisting in regrouping in its traditional geographical centre, and threats from terrorism based on xenophobia, racism and other forms of intolerance had been increasing. Terrorists continued to exploit online platforms to recruit and radicalize, raise funds, plan and coordinate operations and disseminate propaganda. In that connection, the Counter-Terrorism Committee had held a special meeting in India on 28 and 29 October, with the support of the Directorate, on the topic of countering the use of new and emerging technologies for terrorist purposes. At that meeting, the Committee had adopted the Delhi declaration to reaffirm its commitment to working with Member States in achieving the full implementation of all relevant Council resolutions to address the threats posed by terrorism. The Directorate would support the Committee in developing a set of non-binding guiding principles consistent with international human rights law and humanitarian law, with a view to assisting Member States in countering the threat posed by the use of new and emerging technologies for terrorist purposes. At the present meeting, the Council also heard a briefing by a civil society representative, a staff nurse at the Cama and Albless Hospital in Mumbai who had survived the terrorist attack on the hospital on 26 November 2008. She gave a briefing to the Council on her experience of terrorism, asserting that the victims and survivors of such attacks lived the rest of their lives in trauma and urging the international community, through the Council, to bring to justice the sponsors of the Mumbai attacks and give closure to the families of the victims.

At the end of the meeting, the Council adopted a presidential statement by which it reaffirmed that terrorism in all forms and manifestations constituted one of the most serious threats to international peace and security and condemned in the strongest terms terrorism and all terrorist acts, including those on the basis of xenophobia, racism and other forms of intolerance, or in the name of religion or belief, further

---

[1103] A concept note was circulated by a letter dated 5 December (S/2022/906).

[1104] See S/PV.9221.

reaffirming that terrorism should not be associated with any religion, nationality, civilization or group.[1105] The Council also stressed the need to promote and protect rights of victims of terrorism, including women and children, and reaffirmed that Member States must ensure that any measures taken to counter terrorism complied with all their obligations under international law, emphasizing that effective counter-terrorism measures and respect for human rights, fundamental freedoms and the rule of law were complementary and mutually reinforcing and an essential part of a successful counter-terrorism effort.[1106] The Council further underscored the importance of whole-of-government and whole-of-society approaches in increasing awareness about the threats of terrorism and violent extremism conducive to terrorism and effectively tackling them and urged Member States to continue efforts to ensure the full, equal and meaningful participation and leadership of women and the inclusion of youth in approaches and strategies to counter terrorism and violent extremism conducive to terrorism.[1107] The Council reiterated its call upon Member States to, inter alia, take actions to address the threat posed by foreign terrorist fighters and prevent and suppress the financing of terrorist acts and the movement of terrorists or terrorist groups through effective border controls and other measures.[1108] The Council also urged Member States, when designating and applying measures to counter the financing of terrorism, to take into account the potential effect of those measures on exclusively humanitarian activities, including medical activities carried out by impartial humanitarian actors in a manner consistent with international humanitarian law.[1109] The Council expressed deep concern that the threat of terrorism in all its forms and manifestations had increased and become more diffuse in various regions of the world, aided by the use of new and emerging technologies for terrorist purposes, while recognizing that innovations in technology could also offer significant opportunities for countering terrorism and, in that regard, welcomed the adoption of the Delhi Declaration on countering the use of new and emerging technologies for terrorist purposes.[1110]

On 16 December, the Council unanimously adopted resolution 2665 (2022), under Chapter VII, by which it decided that all States should continue to take the measures required under paragraph 1 of resolution 2255 (2015) with respect to individuals and entities designated prior to the date of adoption of resolution 1988 (2011) as the Taliban, as well as other individuals, groups, undertakings and entities associated with the Taliban in constituting a threat to the peace, stability and security of Afghanistan as designated by the Committee established pursuant to resolution 1988 (2011) in the sanctions list established pursuant to resolution 1988 (2011).[1111] The Council also decided to extend for a period of 12 months, until December 2023, the mandate of the Analytical Support and Sanctions Monitoring Team in support of the Committee established pursuant to resolution 1988 (2011).[1112]

In 2022, the discussions at the Council were focused on many of the topics covered by the briefers and the decisions adopted during the meetings featured above. Council members expressed concern about the continued activity of Da'esh and its expansion in other regions, in particular throughout Africa.[1113] Several Council members also expressed concern regarding the situation of foreign nationals, including many women and children, stranded in displaced persons camps and detention facilities[1114] and emphasized the importance of the repatriation, rehabilitation and reintegration of women and children[1115] and the

[1105] See S/PRST/2022/7, first and second paragraphs.
[1106] Ibid., fifth and seventh paragraphs.
[1107] Ibid., eighth paragraph.
[1108] Ibid., thirteenth, fourteenth, fifteenth and sixteenth paragraphs.
[1109] Ibid., seventeenth paragraph.
[1110] Ibid., twenty-third paragraph.
[1111] Resolution 2665 (2022), para. 1.
[1112] Ibid., para. 2. For more information on the Analytical Support and Sanctions Monitoring Team and the Committee established pursuant to resolution 1988 (2011), see part IX, sect. I.B.
[1113] See S/PV.8963 (United States, United Kingdom, United Arab Emirates, Albania, China, Norway, France, Gabon, Ireland, Ghana, India, Brazil, Kenya and Russian Federation); S/PV.9108 (United States, Norway, France, Ghana, Gabon, Brazil, United Arab Emirates, United Kingdom, Kenya, Russian Federation, Ireland, Albania, India, Mexico and China); and S/PV.9221 (Ireland, United Arab Emirates, Kenya, Norway, France, China and Gabon).
[1114] See S/PV.8963 (United States and Albania); S/PV.9108 (United States, Brazil, United Arab Emirates, Albania and China); and S/PV.9221 (United States).
[1115] See S/PV.8963 (United States, Albania, United Arab Emirates, Mexico, Ireland and Brazil); S/PV.9108 (United States, Brazil, United Arab Emirates and China); and S/PV.9221 (United States).

prosecution of foreign terrorist fighters.[1116] Furthermore, Council members discussed the importance of tackling terrorism financing,[1117] and the misuse of new technologies by terrorists.[1118] Some Council members continued to emphasize the need for the international community to prevent Afghanistan from becoming a safe haven for terrorism.[1119] Council members also discussed the importance of holistic approaches to countering terrorism, including addressing its root causes,[1120] and the need for the full, equal and meaningful participation of women in counter-terrorism efforts.[1121]

Developments concerning threats to international peace and security caused by terrorist acts were also considered under the item entitled "Briefings by Chairs of subsidiary bodies of the Security Council".[1122]

Meetings: threats to international peace and security caused by terrorist acts, 2022

Meeting record and date	*Sub-item*	*Other documents*	*Rule 37 invitations*	*Rule 39 and other invitations*	*Speakers*	*Decision and vote (for-against-abstaining)*
S/PV.8963 9 February	Fourteenth report of the Secretary-General on the threat posed by ISIL (Da'esh) to international peace and security and the range of United Nations efforts in support of Member States in countering the threat (S/2022/63)			Under-Secretary-General of the Office of Counter-Terrorism, Acting Executive Director of the Counter-Terrorism Committee Executive Directorate	All Council members, all invitees	
S/PV.9108 9 August	Fifteenth report of the Secretary-General on the threat posed by ISIL (Da'esh) to international peace and security and the range of United Nations efforts in support of Member States in countering the			Under-Secretary-General of the Office of Counter-Terrorism, Acting Executive Director of the Counter-Terrorism Committee Executive	All Council members, all invitees[a]	

[1116] See S/PV.8963 (United States, Norway and Ireland); S/PV.9108 (United States); and S/PV.9221 (United States).

[1117] See S/PV.8963 (United States, France, Gabon, Ireland, Ghana, India and Kenya); S/PV.9108 (France, Ghana, Gabon, Kenya, Albania, India and China); and S/PV.9221 (India, United Arab Emirates, United States, United Kingdom, Ghana and France).

[1118] See S/PV.8963 (United Kingdom, United Arab Emirates, France and India); S/PV.9108 (Ghana, United Arab Emirates, Albania, India and China); and S/PV.9221 (India, Ireland, United Arab Emirates, United States, United Kingdom, Kenya, Norway, France, Albania, China and Brazil).

[1119] See S/PV.8963 (United States, United Kingdom, United Arab Emirates, China, France, India and Russian Federation); S/PV.9108 (United States, Norway, France, United Kingdom, Ireland, Albania, India, Mexico and China); and S/PV.9221 (Ireland, United Kingdom and France).

[1120] See S/PV.8963 (Albania, Norway, Mexico, Ireland, Ghana and Brazil); S/PV.9108 (Norway, France, Ghana, Gabon, Brazil, Ireland, Albania, China and Mexico); and S/PV.9221 (Ireland, United Arab Emirates, United States, United Kingdom, Kenya, Norway, France, Albania, China, Mexico, Brazil and Gabon).

[1121] See S/PV.8963 (United States, United Arab Emirates, Norway and Ireland); S/PV.9108 (Ireland); and S/PV.9221 (Ireland, United Arab Emirates, United States, United Kingdom, Norway and Brazil).

[1122] See sect. 31 below.

Meeting record and date	*Sub-item*	*Other documents*	*Rule 37 invitations*	*Rule 39 and other invitations*	*Speakers*	*Decision and vote (for-against-abstaining)*
	threat (S/2022/576)			Directorate, senior researcher at the Institute for Security Studies		
S/PV.9221 15 December	Global counter-terrorism approach – principles and the way forward Letter dated 5 December 2022 from the Permanent Representative of India to the United Nations addressed to the Secretary-General (S/2022/906)			Under-Secretary-General of the Office of Counter-Terrorism, Acting Executive Director of the Counter-Terrorism Committee Executive Directorate, Nursing Officer at the Cama and Albless Hospital in Mumbai	All Council members,[b] all invitees	S/PRST/2022/7
S/PV.9222 16 December		Draft resolution submitted by United States (S/2022/955)				Resolution 2665 (2022) 15-0-0 (adopted under Chapter VII)

[a] The senior researcher at the Institute for Security Studies participated in the meeting by videoconference.
[b] Ghana was represented by its Permanent Secretary of the Ministry of Foreign Affairs and Regional Integration; India (President of the Council) was represented by its Minister for External Affairs; Ireland was represented by its Minister for Foreign Affairs and Defence; Kenya was represented by its Principal Secretary for Foreign Affairs; the United Arab Emirates was represented by its Minister of Culture and Youth and member of Cabinet; the United Kingdom was represented by its Minister of State for the Middle East, North Africa, South Asia, the United Nations and the Commonwealth, and the Prime Minister's Special Representative for Preventing Sexual Violence in Conflict; and the United States was represented by its Under Secretary for Political Affairs.

31. Briefings

As with previous supplements, briefings by different speakers not explicitly connected to a specific item before the Council are featured in this section. In 2022, the Council held five such meetings, four of which were public.[1123] More information on the meetings, including on participants and speakers, is provided in the tables below.[1124]

In 2022, the Council held one meeting under the item "Briefing by the Chairperson-in-Office of the Organization for Security and Cooperation in Europe".[1125] On 14 March, the Minister for Foreign Affairs of Poland, in his capacity as Chairperson-in-Office of the Organization for Security and Cooperation in Europe (OSCE), provided a briefing to the Council focused on the developments in Ukraine.[1126] In that regard, he addressed the Council with a sense of urgency and moral imperative to

[1123] For more information on the format of meetings, see part II.
[1124] See also A/77/2, part II, chaps. 18-20 and 23.
[1125] See S/PV.8992.
[1126] For more information on discussions relating to Ukraine, see also part I, sects. 19.A-C and 36.

make every possible effort to stop the military aggression of the Russian Federation against Ukraine, noting that close cooperation between OSCE and the United Nations was even more needed when the basic principles of the Charter and international law were being flagrantly violated in the very heart of Europe. The international community had rightly condemned the invasion by the Russian Federation and called upon Moscow to withdraw its forces from Ukraine, and it was hard to ignore 141 countries assembled in the General Assembly asking the President of the Russian Federation to stop the war. Any sustainable, political solution must fully respect the sovereignty, territorial integrity and independence of Ukraine within its internationally recognized borders. With regard to the broader implications of the developments in Ukraine, the aggression by the Russian Federation threatened the very existence of OSCE, and its non-compliance with OSCE principles and commitments was forcing OSCE to put on hold or delay some of the issues that were important for its daily operation. Furthermore, the changing situation on the ground would probably determine the scope and character of the future engagement of the OSCE Special Monitoring Mission to Ukraine. OSCE would continue to call upon all sides to military conflicts to abide by humanitarian law and refrain from activities directed against the civilian population and civilian infrastructure. In concluding, he asserted that it was true that OSCE might evolve as a result of the current experience and that the celebrations of the fiftieth anniversary of the Helsinki Final Act could turn out to be dedicated to finding a solution to the deep crisis of multilateralism.

At the same meeting, the Council heard a briefing by the Under-Secretary-General for Political and Peacebuilding Affairs, in which she reflected on the complementarity and cooperation between the United Nations and OSCE in line with Chapter VIII of the Charter, citing the examples of joint work in Central Asia, the Western Balkans, the Caucasus, Nagorno-Karabakh and Moldova. The war in Ukraine was the most severe test that OSCE and related regional frameworks had faced since their creation, and the Russian invasion had shaken the foundations of the European security architecture. Any questioning of the sovereignty and territorial integrity of Ukraine within its internationally recognized borders would be inconsistent with the Charter of the United Nations and the relevant Council and General Assembly resolutions.

During the discussion, Council members took note of the commitment of the Polish chairship of OSCE to finding peaceful solutions to protracted conflicts in the OSCE area and recalled the importance of the principles of the prohibition of the use or threat of the use of force,[1127] the peaceful settlement of disputes[1128] and respect for sovereignty and territorial integrity. In response to some of the comments expressed by Council members, the OSCE Chairperson-in-Office took the floor for a second time.[1129]

In accordance with previously established practice, the Council heard one briefing by the President of the International Court of Justice at a private (closed) meeting held on 26 October.[1130]

In addition, on 2 November, the Council heard the yearly briefing by the United Nations High Commissioner for Refugees.[1131] At the meeting, the High Commissioner reflected on the impact of growing conflicts, the climate emergency, pandemics, and energy and food crises on more than 103 million refugees and displaced people.[1132] With regard to Ukraine, the Russian invasion had driven the fastest and largest displacement witnessed in decades, with some 14 million people forced from their homes since 24 February. In addition to Ukraine, the Office of the United Nations High Commissioner for Refugees had responded to 37 emergencies around the world in the previous 12 months, including in Ethiopia, Myanmar, the Democratic Republic of the Congo, Afghanistan and the Syrian Arab Republic. In addition, the High Commissioner highlighted the intersection between climate change and displacement, which in many situations included a clear connection with conflict. In that regard, he cited the examples of Somalia and the Sahel. He concluded by drawing the attention of the Council to four areas: (a) the need for more resources for humanitarian aid; (b) the need to strengthen peacebuilding by reinforcing the capacity of the police, the judiciary, local government and overall rule of law in fragile

[1127] For more information on the prohibition of the threat or the use of force, see part III.
[1128] For more information on the peaceful settlement of disputes, see part VI.
[1129] For more information on invitees under rule 39 and their interventions, see part II.
[1130] See S/PV.9166. For more information on relations with the Court, see part IV.
[1131] See S/PV.9178. The previous briefing by the United Nations High Commissioner for Refugees to the Council was held on 7 December 2021 (see S/PV.8919). See also *Repertoire*, *Supplement 2021*, part I, sect. 29.
[1132] See S/PV.9178.

countries; (c) the need to safeguard humanitarian action, including by ensuring that international humanitarian law was upheld and by contributing to preserving the civilian character of refugee settings; and (d) the need for the international community, starting with Council members, to overcome its divisions and disagreements, at least on humanitarian issues.

Following the briefing, Council members underscored the importance of addressing the root causes of forced displacement, in particular armed conflicts, with many speakers[1133] raising the issue of climate change as a contributing factor in that regard. In response to some of the questions raised by Council members, the High Commissioner took the floor for a second time.

In 2022, the Council held two meetings under the item entitled "Briefings by Chairs of subsidiary bodies of the Security Council". On 23 November, the Council heard a joint briefing[1134] by the Chairs of the three committees related to counter-terrorism and non-proliferation, namely, the Committee pursuant to resolutions 1267 (1999), 1989 (2011) and 2253 (2015) concerning Islamic State in Iraq and the Levant (Da'esh), Al-Qaida and associated individuals, groups, undertakings and entities, the Committee established pursuant to resolution 1373 (2001) concerning counter-terrorism and the Committee established pursuant to resolution 1540 (2004). At the meeting, the Chairs provided an overview of the work of the three committees, noting that the three subsidiary bodies had continued to cooperate and coordinate their work to ensure an effective and efficient approach to counter-terrorism and to prevent the proliferation of weapons of mass destruction and their means of delivery by non-State actors. The representative of Norway, speaking on behalf of the three committees, and the representative of India, in her capacity as Chair of the Counter-Terrorism Committee, further reported that the Counter-Terrorism Committee had convened a special meeting on 28 and 29 October in Mumbai and New Delhi, India, on countering the use of new and emerging technologies for terrorist purposes, at which it had adopted the Delhi declaration on that matter. In addition, Council members[1135] underscored the value of field visits, including joint visits, with some[1136] citing in particular the sharing of information among the committees. Council members[1137] also raised the issue of the evolving nature of the threat of terrorism in several parts of Africa, Asia and the Middle East, and others[1138] discussed the conclusion of the comprehensive review of the status of the implementation of resolution 1540 (2004).[1139]

In line with established practice, on 12 December, the Council heard the end-of-year briefing by the outgoing Chairs of the various subsidiary bodies who were concluding their terms at the end of 2022.[1140] In their briefings, the Chairs presented the key activities undertaken during their tenure and offered their recommendations for the incoming elected members of the Council. Several Chairs[1141] reflected on the need for effective implementation of sanctions regimes and underscored the importance of the humanitarian carveout to minimize the unintended consequences of sanctions measures. The Chair of the Committee pursuant to resolution 2713 (2023) concerning Al-Shabaab outlined the innovative elements that Ireland had introduced, including broadening the scope of Committee discussions by inviting new briefers and holding joint meetings with other sanctions committees. The Chair of the Working Group on Children and Armed Conflict stated, inter alia, that it had been important to her as Chair to consistently strive for conclusions that were fit for purpose, practical, and instruments for real action. The Working Group had received and reviewed regular global horizontal notes to stay alert of recent developments, and she urged the Council to continue to mainstream child protection throughout its work. The representative of India, speaking in her capacity as Chair of several committees, noted that

---

[1133] Kenya, France, Brazil, Ireland, Gabon, Albania, United Arab Emirates, Mexico, Norway, United Kingdom and Ghana.

[1134] See S/PV.9201.

[1135] Norway, India, Mexico, United States, China, Russian Federation, Brazil and Ireland.

[1136] Mexico, United States, China, Gabon and Ireland.

[1137] Norway, India, Russian Federation, France, Ireland and Ghana.

[1138] Mexico, China, United Arab Emirates, Norway, Brazil, United Kingdom and Ireland.

[1139] For more information on the committees, see part IX, sect. I.B. For more information on the comprehensive review of the status of the implementation of resolution 1540 (2004), see sect. 34.A below.

[1140] See S/PV.9218. For more information on the subsidiary organs, see part IX.

[1141] Ireland (as Chair of the Committee pursuant to resolution 2713 (2023) concerning Al-Shabaab), Norway (as Chair of the Working Group on Children and Armed Conflict) and Mexico (as Chair of the Committees established pursuant to resolution 1540 (2004) and resolution 2374 (2017) concerning Mali).

it was important for the five permanent members of the Council to respect the consensus of the 10 elected members and to take their preferences for chairing a particular subsidiary body seriously. Furthermore, the function or dysfunction of a subsidiary body depended on the cooperation of its members, there was a need to bring predictability to the scheduling of committee meetings and to enhance the transparency of their functioning, and the credibility of a committee also depended on how objective and fair its decisions were perceived to be.[1142] The representative of Kenya, speaking on behalf of the Chair of the Ad Hoc Working Group on Conflict Prevention and Resolution in Africa, noted that the Working Group was a good platform that could be utilized for horizon-scanning briefings on emerging global issues that impinged on peace and security in Africa. The Working Group should consider utilizing field visits, including with other committees, to enrich its deliberations. The Chair of the Committee established pursuant to resolution 1540 (2004) stated that the Committee had undertaken a review of the lessons learned over the past five years and had formulated proposals for its future mandate. The same representative, speaking in his capacity as Chair of the Committee established pursuant to resolution 2374 (2017) concerning Mali, noted that greater support was needed from the Committee and the Secretariat in order to ensure that the countries of the region had the technical tools to fully implement sanctions. He reported better coordination of activities with government authorities, including through the provision of access to the final reports of the group of experts prior to their publication.

Table 1

Meeting: briefing by the Chairperson-in-Office of the Organization for Security and Cooperation in Europe, 2022

Meeting record and date	*Sub-item*	*Other documents*	*Rule 37 invitations*	*Rule 39 and other invitations*	*Speakers*	*Decision and vote (for-against-abstaining)*
S/PV.8992 14 March			Ukraine	Chairperson-in-Office of the Organization for Security and Cooperation in Europe and Minister for Foreign Affairs of Poland, Under-Secretary-General for Political and Peacebuilding Affairs	All Council members, all invitees	

Table 2

Meeting: briefing by the President of the International Court of Justice, 2022

Meeting record and date	*Sub-item*	*Other documents*	*Rule 37 invitations*	*Rule 39 and other invitations*	*Speakers*	*Decision and vote (for-against-abstaining)*
S/PV.9166 26 October (closed)			President of the International Court of Justice	Council members, invitee		

Table 3

Meeting: briefing by the United Nations High Commissioner for Refugees, 2022

Meeting record and date	*Sub-item*	*Other documents*	*Rule 37 invitations*	*Rule 39 and other invitations*	*Speakers*	*Decision and vote (for-against-abstaining)*
S/PV.9178 2 November			United Nations High Commissioner for Refugees	All Council members, invitee		

Table 4

[1142] For more information on Council committees, see part IX, sect. I.B.

Meetings: briefings by Chairs of subsidiary bodies of the Council, 2022

Meeting record and date	*Sub-item*	*Other documents*	*Rule 37 invitations*	*Rule 39 and other invitations*	*Speakers*	*Decision and vote (for-against-abstaining)*
S/PV.9201 23 November					All Council members, Chair of the Committee pursuant to resolutions 1267 (1999), 1989 (2011) and 2253 (2015) concerning Islamic State in Iraq and the Levant (Da'esh), Al-Qaida and associated individuals, groups, undertakings and entities, Chair of the Committee established pursuant to resolution 1373 (2001) concerning counter-terrorism, Chair of the Committee established pursuant to resolution 1540 (2004)[a]	
S/PV.9218 12 December					Chairs of eight committees and two working groups[b]	

[a] Before her briefing as Chair of the Committee pursuant to resolutions 1267 (1999), 1989 (2011) and 2253 (2015) concerning Islamic State in Iraq and the Levant (Da'esh), Al-Qaida and associated individuals, groups, undertakings and entities, the representative of Norway delivered a joint statement on behalf of that Committee, the Committee established pursuant to resolution 1540 (2004) and the Committee established pursuant to resolution 1373 (2001) concerning counter-terrorism. All three Chairs spoke twice, once in their capacity as Chair and once in their national capacity.

[b] Chair of the Committee established pursuant to resolution 751 (1992) concerning Al-Shabaab; Chair of the Committee established pursuant to resolution 1718 (2006) concerning the Democratic People's Republic of Korea and the Working Group on Children and Armed Conflict; Chair of the Committee established pursuant to resolution 1373 (2001) concerning counter-terrorism, the Committee established pursuant to resolution 1988 (2011) and the Committee established pursuant to resolution 1970 (2011) concerning Libya; Chair of the Ad Hoc Working Group on Conflict Prevention and Resolution in Africa; Chair of the Committee established pursuant to resolution 1540 (2004) and the Committee established pursuant to resolution 2374 (2017) concerning Mali; and Chair of the Committee pursuant to resolutions 1267 (1999), 1989 (2011) and 2253 (2015) concerning Islamic State in Iraq and the Levant (Da'esh), Al-Qaida and associated individuals, groups, undertakings and entities.

32. Items relating to non-proliferation

A. Non-proliferation of weapons of mass destruction

During the period under review, the Council held three meetings in connection with the item entitled "Non-proliferation of weapons of mass destruction". One meeting took the form of a briefing, and two meetings were convened for the adoption of resolutions.[1143] In 2022, the Council unanimously adopted two resolutions under Chapter VII of the Charter.[1144] More information on the meetings, including on participants, speakers and outcomes, is provided in the table below.[1145]

On 14 March, the Council held a meeting under the item, focused on the implementation of resolution 1540 (2004).[1146] At the meeting, Council members heard a briefing by the Chair of the

[1143] For more information on format of meetings, see part II.

[1144] Resolutions 2622 (2022) and 2663 (2022).

[1145] See also A/77/2, part II, chap. 25.

[1146] See S/PV.8993.

Committee established pursuant to resolution 1540 (2004), on its activities in 2021. In his briefing, the Chair underscored that the resolution remained a vital component of the global non-proliferation architecture aimed at preventing non-State actors, including terrorists, from gaining access to weapons of mass destruction. States had made significant progress in the full implementation of the resolution, despite the gaps remaining for its full and effective implementation. He stated that 185 Member States had already submitted their first reports containing information on measures taken to comply with their obligations under the resolution, and 136 Member States had informed the Committee of their national points of contact for its implementation. Noting that 35 Member States had submitted voluntary national implementation action plans to the Committee since 2007, he said that, during the reporting period, the Committee had supported Botswana and Mongolia in the process of developing their own plans. The Committee would continue to support States that wished to conduct peer reviews, through which Member States could identify effective national practices and share them with the Committee and other partners. Emphasizing the important role of the Committee in facilitating assistance to Member States, the Chair noted that the Committee had received four new requests for assistance in 2021 and assured the Council that the Committee would include new programmes and updated information regarding available assistance on its website. As one of its main priorities, the Committee continued to conduct the comprehensive review of resolution 1540 (2004) as provided for in resolution 1977 (2011), pursuant to the extension of its mandate under resolution 2622 (2022). The review of the status of the implementation of resolution 1540 (2004) by Member States was a central theme of the comprehensive review.

After the briefing, Council members reaffirmed that resolution 1540 (2004) remained an essential component of the international disarmament and non-proliferation architecture in preventing non-State actors from gaining access to weapons of mass destruction and recalled the central role played by the Committee and its group of experts in that regard. Noting the importance of approving the Committee's mandate, the representative of the Russian Federation stated that the mandate should be based on the unifying principles of resolution 1540 (2004) and be aimed at maintaining the fundamental principles of the Committee's work, without endowing it with intrusive or attributive powers. Some Council members expressed concern over the evolving risks of proliferation posed by non-State actors, with the representative of the United Kingdom citing the risks posed by their attempted use of crude toxin weapons such as ricin and the representatives of China and the United Arab Emirates their exploitation of modern and new technologies, such as unmanned aerial vehicles, synthetic biology and artificial intelligence. Several Council members[1147] expressed support for enhanced cooperation and coordination of the Committee with international organizations and other United Nations committees, such as those dealing with terrorism in delivering its mandate. Regarding the ongoing comprehensive review of resolution 1540 (2004), Council members[1148] underlined the importance of inclusiveness of the process and encouraged broad consultations with, inter alia, Member States, international, regional and subregional organizations, civil society and the private sector.

On 25 February and 30 November, the Council convened meetings at which it adopted resolutions 2622 (2022) and 2663 (2022), respectively. Both resolutions were adopted unanimously, and both were adopted under Chapter VII of the Charter.

By its resolution 2622 (2022), the Council decided to extend the mandate of the Committee established pursuant to resolution 1540 (2004) until 30 November 2022, with the continued assistance of its group of experts, as specified in paragraph 5 of resolution 1977 (2011).[1149] It also decided that the Committee, while continuing its work pursuant to its mandate, would continue to conduct and complete the comprehensive review on the status of implementation of resolution 1540 (2004) and submit to the Council a report on the conclusion of the review.[1150] Explaining his delegation's vote after the adoption of resolution 2622 (2022), the representative of the Russian Federation expressed concern that the Council had once again limited itself to a strictly technical rollover of the Committee's mandate, in the interests of ensuring that the comprehensive review of the resolution's implementation could be concluded swiftly.[1151] He underlined the importance of undertaking the review appropriately and allowing

[1147] France, India and Gabon.

[1148] France, Ghana, Ireland, Norway, Brazil, United Kingdom, Russian Federation, United States and United Arab Emirates.

[1149] Resolution 2622 (2022), para. 1.

[1150] Ibid., para. 2. For more information on the mandate of the Committee, see part IX, sect. I.B.

[1151] See S/PV.8977.

substantive contributions to be made by key participants. He also underscored that failing to do so would lead to the added value of the review process being largely wasted. The representative of China expressed the hope that the Committee would elaborate plans to advance its work in an orderly manner, including with regard to the comprehensive review of the status of the implementation of resolution 1540 (2004), adding that the legitimate concerns of all parties should be accorded equal attention and be properly addressed in that process. Noting the comments made with respect to the process of a technical renewal of the mandate, the representative of Mexico, recalling his position as Chair of the Committee, clarified that consultations had been conducted in good faith, transparently and in response to all concerns expressed. He added that the great majority of members had expressed their preference for a technical renewal as the most viable way of undertaking the broad review mandated in resolution 1977 (2011). The representative of the United States stated that the technical extension would allow the Committee and its group of experts to continue their important work. During the upcoming comprehensive review and mandate renewal, his delegation would prioritize the full implementation of States' obligations under resolution 1540 (2004) by striving to improve the functionality and credibility of the Committee, empowering its group of experts and enhancing support for assistance- and outreach-related activities. Expressing strong support for the adoption of resolution 2622 (2022), the representative of the United Kingdom applauded the efforts of the Chair to secure an extension of the mandate.

In its resolution 2663 (2022), the Council endorsed the 2022 comprehensive review of the status of the implementation of resolution 1540 (2004) and took note of its results as contained in its final report (S/2022/899). By the same resolution, the Council extended the mandate of the Committee for a period of 10 years, until 30 November 2032,[1152] and reiterated the mandate of the Committee in promoting the implementation of resolution 1540 (2004), emphasizing in particular those aspects relating to outreach and technical assistance to Member States. After the adoption, 11 Council members delivered statements.[1153] Some Council members emphasized the importance of the full, equal and meaningful participation of women in global disarmament and non-proliferation efforts and welcomed its inclusion in the resolution, encouraging the Committee to give due consideration to the matter in all its activities.[1154] Council members also welcomed the strengthening of the Committee's cooperation with international, regional and subregional organizations and other committees.[1155] Some Council members underlined the central role of the group of experts in monitoring and supporting the work of the Committee,[1156] with the representatives of Norway and the United States highlighting the call for the Committee to review its internal guidelines on matters regarding its group of experts.[1157] The representatives of the United Kingdom and the United States expressed disappointment that the new mandate did not go further in strengthening the Committee's support to Member States in implementing the resolution, with the former citing the issue of proliferation financing and the latter expressing regret that the Committee and its group of experts had not been given the tools they would need to work efficiently and effectively. The representative of China opined that the unfair and unreasonable aspects of the international non-proliferation regime remained striking, while the right of the majority of developing countries to the peaceful use of science and technology continued to be subject to many restrictions.

In 2022, the Council also heard an additional briefing by the Chair of the Committee established pursuant to resolution 1540 (2004) under the item entitled "Briefings by Chairs of subsidiary bodies of the Security Council".[1158]

1152 Resolution 2663 (2022), para. 2.

1153 See S/PV.9205.

1154 Ibid. (Ireland, Albania, United Arab Emirates, Norway, Mexico and Ghana). See also resolution 2663 (2022), nineteenth preambular paragraph.

1155 See S/PV.9205 (Ireland, Albania, India and Ghana). See also resolution 2663 (2022), eleventh, fifteenth to seventeenth and twenty-first preambular paragraphs and paras. 21–23, 25 and 26.

1156 See S/PV.9205 (Ireland, United Kingdom, United Arab Emirates, Norway and United States).

1157 Resolution 2663 (2022), para. 5.

1158 See S/PV.9201. For more information, see sect. 31 above.

Meetings: non-proliferation of weapons of mass destruction, 2022

Meeting record and date	*Sub-item*	*Other documents*	*Rule 37 invitations*	*Rule 39 and other invitations*	*Speakers*	*Decision and vote (for-against-abstaining)*
S/PV.8977 25 February		Draft resolution submitted by Mexico (S/2022/147)			Five Council members (China, Mexico, Russian Federation, United Kingdom, United States)	Resolution 2622 (2022) 15-0-0 (adopted under Chapter VII)
S/PV.8993 14 March					All Council members[a]	
S/PV.9205 30 November		Draft resolution submitted by Mexico (S/2022/881)			11 Council members[b]	Resolution 2663 (2022) 15-0-0 (adopted under Chapter VII)

[a] The representative of Mexico spoke in his capacity as Chair of the Committee established pursuant to resolution 1540 (2004).
[b] Albania, China, Ghana, India, Ireland, Mexico, Norway, Russian Federation, United Arab Emirates, United Kingdom and United States.

B. Non-proliferation

During the period under review, the Council held two meetings under the item entitled "Non-proliferation". Both meetings took the form of briefings.[1159] More information on the meetings, including on participants and speakers, is provided in the table below.[1160]

Under the item, the Council heard briefings by the Under-Secretary-General for Political and Peacebuilding Affairs, by representatives of the Delegation of the European Union to the United Nations, speaking on behalf of the High Representative of the Union for Foreign Affairs and Security Policy, in his capacity as Coordinator of the Joint Commission of the Joint Comprehensive Plan of Action, and by representatives of Ireland, speaking as Security Council Facilitator for the implementation of resolution 2231 (2015). Representatives of Germany and Iran (Islamic Republic of) participated in both meetings under rule 37 of the provisional rules of procedure and delivered statements.

On 30 June, the Council heard a briefing by the Under-Secretary-General for Political and Peacebuilding Affairs on the thirteenth report of the Secretary-General on the implementation of Security Council resolution 2231 (2015).[1161] During the briefing, the Under-Secretary-General noted that diplomatic engagements in and around the Joint Commission with a view to restoring the Joint Comprehensive Plan of Action resumed in November 2021.[1162] Nevertheless, despite their determination to resolve political and technical differences, the participants and the United States had yet to return to the full and effective implementation of the Plan and resolution 2231 (2015). She reiterated her appeal to the United States to lift or waive its sanctions, as outlined in the Plan, and to extend the waivers regarding the trade in oil with the Islamic Republic of Iran, while also calling upon the latter to reverse the steps it had taken that were not consistent with its nuclear-related commitments under the Plan. She added that the bilateral and regional initiatives to improve relationships with the Islamic Republic of Iran remained key and should be encouraged and built upon. In addition to the issues with regard to the implementation of the commitments under the Plan, it was also important for the Islamic Republic of Iran to address the concerns raised by participants in the Plan and by other Member States in relation to annex B to resolution 2231 (2015). Emphasizing that the Plan was at a critical juncture, she expressed the hope that the Islamic

[1159] For more information on the format of meetings, see part II.
[1160] See also A/77/2, part II, chap. 30.
[1161] See S/PV.9085. See also S/2022/490.
[1162] See S/PV.9085.

Republic of Iran and the United States would continue to build on the momentum of the previous few days of talks, facilitated by the European Union, to resolve the remaining issues. Speaking on behalf of the High Representative, in his capacity as Coordinator of the Joint Commission, the Head of the Delegation of the European Union reported that, after more than one year of intense multilateral negotiations, very tough political choices had had to be made by all participants in the Plan and the United States to reach the delicate balance in the text. With the deal almost finalized and the space for further significant changes exhausted, it was therefore important to show the necessary political will and pragmatism to restore the Plan on the basis of the text on the table. While acknowledging the strong sense of urgency, he emphasized the importance of avoiding escalatory steps and preserving sufficient space for diplomatic efforts to succeed. He urged all Member States to refrain from actions and statements that would increase regional and international tensions and thereby escalate a military build-up in the region and beyond. The Security Council Facilitator thanked all Council members for their constructive engagement and flexibility in approving the thirteenth six-month report of the Facilitator on the implementation of the Security Council resolution 2231 (2015).[1163] Elaborating on some aspects of that report, she mentioned that the Council had held one meeting in the "2231 format", on 23 June 2022.[1164] She also highlighted the importance of the role of the International Atomic Energy Agency (IAEA) in conducting verification and monitoring activities in the Islamic Republic of Iran, as requested under resolution 2231 (2015), as well as for providing confidence for the international community that the country's nuclear programme was for exclusively peaceful purposes. She added that the reports of the Director General of IAEA had played a key role in that regard.

After the briefings, representatives discussed the findings and recommendations set out in the thirteenth report of the Secretary-General, prior to its public release. They also discussed the ongoing diplomatic efforts to restore the Plan, the ballistic missile and space vehicle launches by the Islamic Republic of Iran, and issues related to implementation of resolution 2231 (2015). Many Council members[1165] reiterated their ambition and call for a mutual return to the full implementation of the Plan and resolution 2231 (2015). In that context, several speakers[1166] expressed concerns about the impediments to the verification and monitoring activities by IAEA in the Islamic Republic of Iran, including the removal of surveillance cameras and monitoring equipment. Some Council members[1167] called for the reconsideration of unilateral coercive measures imposed on the Islamic Republic of Iran, and for the United States to lift all relevant unilateral sanctions on the country so that it could fully benefit from the economic dividends of the Plan.

On 19 December, the Council held its second briefing for the year pursuant to the relevant report of the Secretary-General.[1168] In her statement, the Under-Secretary-General reported on the status of the negotiations, noting that the space for diplomacy appeared to be shrinking rapidly since her prior briefing.[1169] She encouraged all parties and the United States to resume their efforts to resolve the outstanding issues, to prevent the gains achieved by the Plan after years of painstaking efforts from being completely lost. The Under-Secretary-General expressed regret about the reporting by IAEA on the intention of the Islamic Republic of Iran to install new centrifuges at the Natanz fuel enrichment plant and to produce more uranium enriched up to 60 per cent at the Fordow fuel enrichment plant, which would bring the country's estimated stockpile to more than 18 times the allowable amount under the Plan. Speaking on behalf of the High Representative, in his capacity as Coordinator of the Joint Commission, the Chargé d'affaires a.i. of the Delegation of the European Union stressed that the restoration of the Plan remained the only way for the Islamic Republic of Iran to reap the full benefits of the Plan and reach its full economic potential, as it would result in a comprehensive lifting of sanctions that would encourage greater cooperation by the entire international community with the Islamic Republic of Iran. Noting that the process to conclude a deal and bring the Plan back on track had been seriously challenged by various developments over the previous months, he reiterated that diplomacy and restoring the full

[1163] S/2022/510, annex.

[1164] See S/PV.9085.

[1165] United States, Mexico, France, Norway, Ghana, Kenya, United Arab Emirates and Ireland.

[1166] United States, United Kingdom, Norway, Ghana, United Arab Emirates, Ireland, Albania and Germany.

[1167] Mexico, Gabon, China, Ghana, Ireland and Russian Federation.

[1168] See S/PV.9225. See also S/2022/912. For the reports of the Joint Commission and the Facilitator, see S/2022/919, annex, and S/2022/937, annex, respectively.

[1169] See S/PV.9225.

implementation of the Plan was still the best option for preventing the country from developing a nuclear weapon, which was also instrumental to the security of the whole region. The Facilitator emphasized the importance of the full restoration of the Plan as soon as possible and the need for all parties to the agreement to uphold it in both letter and spirit, avoid actions that undermined the implementation of commitments and ensure its full and effective operation.

During the deliberations, some Council members[1170] reiterated the need to resume negotiations with all parties, with a view to returning to the full implementation of the resolution. Other Council members[1171] expressed their continued concern about the nuclear enrichment by the Islamic Republic of Iran. Several Council members[1172] called for further progress in the dialogue between the Islamic Republic of Iran and IAEA, to enable the Agency to provide assurances of the exclusively peaceful nature of the country's nuclear programme.

Concerning the implementation of paragraphs 3 and 4 of annex B to resolution 2231 (2015), several speakers[1173] raised concerns about the findings in the report of the Secretary-General concerning the transfer and use of unmanned aerial vehicles from the Islamic Republic of Iran to the Russian Federation and encouraged an inspection of those vehicles recovered in Ukraine. In that regard, the representative of Brazil stated that he would await an independent assessment of such allegations. The representative of the Russian Federation reiterated its assertion that any results of a "pseudo-investigation" were null and void from a legal standpoint, and that references to any alleged practice in the conduct of inspections were irrelevant. The representative of China expressed the hope that the parties concerned, including the Secretariat, would accurately interpret Council resolutions and documents, prudently handle issues such as the space launch by the Islamic Republic of Iran and the so-called transfer of unmanned aerial vehicles systems, and avoid influencing negotiations on resuming compliance.

Developments relating to the implementation of resolution 2231 (2015) were also considered by the Council under the item entitled "Maintenance of international peace and security".[1174]

Meetings: non-proliferation, 2022

Meeting record and date	*Sub-item*	*Other documents*	*Rule 37 invitations*	*Rule 39 and other invitations*	*Speakers*	*Decision and vote (for-against-abstaining)*
S/PV.9085 30 June	Letter dated 10 June 2022 from the Security Council Facilitator for the implementation of resolution 2231 (2015) addressed to the President of the Security Council (S/2022/482) Thirteenth report of the Secretary-General on the implementation of Security Council resolution 2231 (2015) (S/2022/490)		Germany, Iran (Islamic Republic of)	Under-Secretary-General for Political and Peacebuilding Affairs, Head of the Delegation of the European Union to the United Nations	All Council members,[a] all invitees[b]	

[1170] Gabon, Ghana, China and Kenya.

[1171] Ireland, Mexico, France, Albania, Norway and United Kingdom.

[1172] Gabon, United Arab Emirates and India.

[1173] Ireland, France, Norway, United Kingdom and Germany.

[1174] See S/PV.9167. For more information, see sect. 35 below.

Meeting record and date	*Sub-item*	*Other documents*	*Rule 37 invitations*	*Rule 39 and other invitations*	*Speakers*	*Decision and vote (for-against-abstaining)*
	Letter dated 23 June 2022 from the Security Council Facilitator for the implementation of resolution 2231 (2015) addressed to the President of the Security Council (S/2022/510)					
S/PV.9225 19 December	Fourteenth report of the Secretary-General on the implementation of Security Council resolution 2231 (2015) (S/2022/912) Letter dated 6 December 2022 from the Security Council Facilitator for the implementation of resolution 2231 (2015) addressed to the President of the Security Council (S/2022/919) Letter dated 12 December 2022 from the Security Council Facilitator for the implementation of resolution 2231 (2015) addressed to the President of the Security Council (S/2022/937)		Germany, Iran (Islamic Republic of)	Under-Secretary-General for Political and Peacebuilding Affairs, Chargé d'affaires a.i. of the Delegation of the European Union	All Council members,[c] all invitees[b]	

[a] The representative of Ireland spoke twice, once in her capacity as the Security Council Facilitator for the implementation of resolution 2231 (2015) and once in her national capacity.
[b] The representative of the European Union spoke on behalf of the High Representative of the Union for Foreign Affairs and Security Policy, in his capacity as Coordinator of the Joint Commission of the Joint Comprehensive Plan of Action.
[c] The representative of Ireland spoke twice, once in his capacity as Facilitator and once in his national capacity.

C. Non-proliferation/Democratic People's Republic of Korea

During the period under review, the Security Council held six meetings under this item. Five meetings took the form of briefings and one was convened to adopt a decision.[1175] The Council adopted one resolution, under Chapter VII of the Charter, by which it extended the mandate of the Panel of Experts established pursuant to resolution 1874 (2009) in support of the Committee established pursuant to resolution 1718 (2006).[1176] The Council failed to adopt one draft resolution due to the negative vote of two permanent members. More information on the meetings, including on participants, speakers and outcomes, is provided in the table below. In addition to the meetings, Council members held informal consultations of the whole in connection with the item.[1177]

During the period under review, Council members heard briefings by the Under-Secretary-General for Political and Peacebuilding Affairs and the Assistant Secretary-General for the Middle East, Asia and the Pacific of the Departments of Political and Peacebuilding Affairs and Peace Operations.[1178] Their briefings were focused on the unprecedented number of ballistic missile launches by the Democratic People's Republic of Korea during the year and the risk of a significant escalation of tension in the region and beyond.[1179] Also in their briefings, they reaffirmed the Secretary-General's commitment to working with all the parties for sustainable peace and a complete denuclearization of the Korean peninsula, reiterating that the unity of the Council was essential to ease tensions and overcome the diplomatic impasse.[1180] Noting the negative action-reaction cycle of missile launches and military exercises, the briefers stressed the importance of strengthening communication channels, including inter-Korean and military-to-military ones, in de-escalating tensions and lowering the risk of miscalculation.[1181] On the grave humanitarian situation in the country, the briefers expressed the readiness of the United Nations to assist people in need and reiterated the Secretary-General's call for the unimpeded entry of international staff and humanitarian supplies.[1182] In addition to Council members, Japan and the Republic of Korea participated in all meetings of the Council, under rule 37 of the provisional rules of procedure.

At those meetings, Council members held differing views regarding the approach to the actions of the Democratic People's Republic of Korea. For example, at the meeting held on 21 November,[1183] many Council members[1184] considered that the continued development and testing of nuclear weapons undermined the non-proliferation regime and raised tensions in the region and beyond, posing a threat to international peace and stability. Some speakers[1185] criticized the continued silence of the Council. Considering the absence of consensus on the adoption of a draft resolution on the situation, the representative of the United States expressed his delegation's intention to propose a draft presidential statement to hold the Democratic People's Republic of Korea accountable for its dangerous rhetoric and destabilizing actions. Several Council members[1186] called on all parties to demonstrate restraint and to reaffirm in practice their readiness to renew dialogue. While also expressing concern over the rising tensions and intensifying confrontation on the Korean peninsula, the representatives of China and Russian Federation expressed opposition to any military activity threatening the security of the peninsula. They argued that the draft resolution proposed jointly by China and the Russian Federation would help to ease the humanitarian situation in the Democratic People's Republic of Korea, create an atmosphere for dialogue and promote the realization of a political statement.

[1175] For more information on the format of meetings, see part II.
[1176] For more information on the mandate of the Committee and its Panel of Experts, see part IX, sect. I.B.
[1177] See A/77/2, part II, chap. 33.
[1178] See S/PV.9004, S/PV.9030, S/PV.9146, S/PV.9183 and S/PV.9197.
[1179] See, for example, S/PV.9004, S/PV.9146 and S/PV.9183.
[1180] See S/PV.9004, S/PV.9030 and S/PV.9146.
[1181] See S/PV.9183 and S/PV.9197.
[1182] See S/PV.9004, S/PV.9030, S/PV.9146, S/PV.9183 and S/PV.9197.
[1183] See S/PV.9197.
[1184] United States, Albania, Ireland, Gabon, India, Kenya, Brazil and United Arab Emirates.
[1185] Albania, France, Ireland, Norway, United Kingdom, Mexico and Republic of Korea.
[1186] Albania, France, Ireland, Norway, United Kingdom, Gabon, Mexico, Kenya and United Arab Emirates.

Also at those meetings, Council members discussed the role of sanctions in addressing the peace and security issues on the Korean peninsula. Some Council members affirmed the effectiveness of sanctions in slowing advancements by the Democratic People's Republic of Korea in connection with weapons of mass destruction and ballistic missiles,[1187] and some underlined the importance of sanctions compliance by all Member States and the full implementation of relevant Security Council resolutions.[1188] Some Council members expressed concern regarding the evasion of sanctions by the Democratic People's Republic of Korea allowing continued funding to its illegal weapons of mass destruction programmes, including through cyberactivity,[1189] and some opined that all reasonable measures should be taken to prevent evasion, that the current sanctions regime should be updated to cover the new areas and that stricter sanctions should be imposed.[1190] At the meeting held on 11 May, the representative of China, stressing that sanctions were only a means to an end, stated that sanctions should not be equated with, or used to replace, diplomatic efforts and that furthering sanctions by means of a resolution, as proposed by the United States, was an inappropriate way to address the situation.[1191] At the same meeting, the representative of the Russian Federation asserted that seeking mutually acceptable political and diplomatic solutions was the only way to peacefully resolve the issues concerning the Korean peninsula and expressed regret that the Council had only tightened the sanctions while ignoring positive signals from the Democratic People's Republic of Korea in the past few years. Her delegation believed that the further strengthening of sanctions against the Democratic People's Republic of Korea exceeded the scope of the measures needed to cut off channels for funding nuclear missile programmes and exposed its people to unacceptable socioeconomic and humanitarian turmoil. At the meeting held on 5 October, the representative of Brazil called on the Council to seriously explore alternative avenues to reducing tensions on the peninsula and breaking the deadlock.[1192] He expressed the view that, while multilateral sanctions might be part of a comprehensive response, they alone could not address the peace and security issue of the peninsula.[1193]

In their deliberations, Council members also addressed the grave humanitarian situation in the Democratic People's Republic of Korea. Some Council members expressed the belief that the Democratic People's Republic of Korea itself had worsened the situation of its own people, by diverting resources from humanitarian needs to illegal military and ballistic missile programmes, and called upon the country to prioritize the needs of its people over costly military ventures and to allow the entry of relief organizations and the flow of humanitarian aid into the country.[1194] In response to the concern that sanctions exacerbated the humanitarian situation, the representative of Norway, who chaired the Committee established pursuant to resolution 1718 (2006) in 2022, stated at various meetings that sanctions were not intended to have adverse humanitarian consequences for the civilians and that members of the Council continued to show that they had taken the humanitarian situation in the country seriously, with requests for humanitarian exemptions swiftly processed by the Committee.[1195]

In addition, in 2022, the Council convened two meetings to adopt decisions in connection with the item. On 25 March, under Chapter VII of the Charter, the Council unanimously adopted resolution 2627 (2022), by which it extended the mandate of the Panel of Experts established pursuant to resolution 1874 (2009) for a period of 12 months, until 30 April 2023.[1196] After the adoption of the resolution, several Council members made statements, in which they noted with concern the leaks of the 2021 interim and final reports of the Panel of Experts and the potential damage to the credibility of the work of the Committee and stressed the need for the Panel to improve its working methods.[1197] The representative of Mexico expressed regret that Council members could not reach agreement on explicit instructions to the

[1187] See S/PV.9030 (United States); and S/PV.9183 (Norway and United Arab Emirates).

[1188] See S/PV.9030 (United Arab Emirates and India); and S/PV.9146 (United States, Albania, Ireland, Norway, India and United Arab Emirates).

[1189] See S/PV.9030 (Albania, Ireland, United Kingdom, France and Norway); and S/PV.9183 (France).

[1190] See S/PV.9030 (France and United States); and S/PV.9183 (France and United Arab Emirates).

[1191] See S/PV.9030.

[1192] See S/PV.9146.

[1193] For more information on the imposition of sanctions by the Council, see part VII, sect. III.

[1194] See S/PV.9146 (Albania, France, United Arab Emirates and Republic of Korea); S/PV.9183 (United Kingdom and United Arab Emirates); and S/PV.9197 (Ireland, Kenya and United Arab Emirates).

[1195] See, for example, S/PV.9183 and S/PV.9197.

[1196] Resolution 2627 (2022), para. 1.

[1197] See S/PV.9004 (United States, Norway, China and Russian Federation).

Panel of Experts to investigate and report, in a timely manner, on incidents relating to the launch of ballistic missiles, in addition to its interim and final reports. Despite having voted in favour of the resolution, the representative of China expressed regret and discontent that the concerns of his delegation, which had been supported by a large number of Council members, had not been taken on board by the penholder.

On 26 May, the Council voted on a draft resolution[1198] submitted by the United States. As penholder of the draft resolution, the representative of the United States made a statement before the vote, in which she affirmed that the launch of six intercontinental ballistic missiles since the beginning of 2022, including on 25 May, constituted a threat to the peace and security of the entire international community.[1199] She noted that the Council had not issued a response to any of the six intercontinental ballistic missiles launches, despite the commitment made in resolution 2397 (2017). With regard to the argument by some Council members that a presidential statement was the appropriate response, she recalled that her delegation had proposed press elements and a statement to the press following many of those launches, but had been told that any such statement could lead to escalation or could destabilize the Korean peninsula. She argued that the exact opposite had happened, and that the Democratic People's Republic of Korea had taken the Council's silence as a green light to act with impunity and escalate tensions on the peninsula. With the adoption of the draft resolution, a message could be sent to all proliferators that Council members would not stand for any actions aimed at undermining international peace and security. She added that, if adopted, the resolution would restrict the ability of the Democratic People's Republic of Korea to advance its unlawful weapons of mass destruction and ballistic missile programmes, streamline sanctions implementation and further facilitate the delivery of humanitarian aid. The draft resolution was not adopted due to the negative vote of two permanent members.[1200]

After the vote, 13 Council members made statements.[1201] The representative of China stated that, with regard to the peninsula issue, the Council should play a positive and constructive role, and its actions should help to de-escalate the situation and prevent it from deteriorating and even spiralling out of control. He added that reliance on sanctions would not help to resolve the issue, as they would not only fail to resolve the problem but would lead to further negative consequences and an escalation of the confrontation. His delegation had repeatedly expressed the hope that the United States would consider issuing a presidential statement instead, as the best way to garner consensus among Council members and avoid confrontation. Explaining his country's vote, the representative of the Russian Federation said that the penholder had ignored the frequent clarifications made during the drafting process and that his delegation's appeals for it to be issued as a presidential statement instead had gone unheeded. According to the representative, strengthening the sanctions pressure on Pyongyang was not only futile, but extremely dangerous, considering the humanitarian consequences of such measures. The quest for mutually acceptable political and diplomatic solutions was the only possible way to reach a peaceful solution to the Korean peninsula question and establish robust security mechanisms in North-East Asia. Other speakers[1202] stated that the continued launches by the Democratic People's Republic of Korea of ballistic missiles, including of intercontinental range, had been a clear violation of Security Council resolutions and of the nuclear disarmament and non-proliferation regime and expressed regret that the draft resolution had not been adopted because of the veto by two permanent members. Some speakers[1203] expressed concern that the veto would send a wrong signal of impunity and embolden the authorities of the Democratic People's Republic of Korea. In that connection, several Council members[1204] called for the swift issuance of a special report by the Council to the General Assembly explaining the veto, in accordance with Assembly resolution 76/262 of 26 April 2022.

[1198] See S/2022/431.

[1199] See S/PV.9048.

[1200] Pursuant to General Assembly resolution 76/262, the Council submitted a special report to the Assembly on the use of the veto at the meeting (see A/76/853). For more information on such reports, see part IV, sect. I.F.

[1201] See S/PV.9048.

[1202] Kenya, Mexico, Albania, Ireland, Ghana, Norway, Brazil, United Kingdom, Gabon, France, United States, Japan and Republic of Korea.

[1203] Brazil, United Kingdom, France, United States and Republic of Korea.

[1204] Mexico, Ireland and Norway.

Meetings: non-proliferation/Democratic People's Republic of Korea, 2022

Meeting record and date	*Sub-item*	*Other documents*	*Rule 37 invitations*	*Rule 39 and other invitations*	*Speakers*	*Decision and vote (for-against-abstaining)*
S/PV.9004 25 March		Draft resolution submitted by United States (S/2022/263)	Japan, Republic of Korea	Under-Secretary-General for Political and Peacebuilding Affairs	All Council members, all invitees	Resolution 2627 (2022) 15-0-0 (adopted under Chapter VII)
S/PV.9030 11 May			Japan, Republic of Korea	Assistant Secretary-General for the Middle East, Asia and the Pacific	All Council members, all invitees	
S/PV.9048 26 May		Draft resolution submitted by United States (S/2022/431)	Japan, Republic of Korea		13 Council members,[a] all invitees	Not adopted 13-0-2[b]
S/PV.9146 5 October			Japan, Republic of Korea	Assistant Secretary-General for the Middle East, Asia and the Pacific	All Council members, all invitees	
S/PV.9183 4 November			Japan, Republic of Korea	Assistant Secretary-General for the Middle East, Asia and the Pacific	All Council members, all invitees	
S/PV.9197 21 November			Japan, Republic of Korea	Under-Secretary-General for Political and Peacebuilding Affairs	All Council members, all invitees	

[a] Albania, Brazil, China, France, Gabon, Ghana, Ireland, Kenya, Mexico, Norway, Russian Federation, United Kingdom, United States.

[b] *For*: Albania, Brazil, France, Gabon, Ghana, India, Ireland, Kenya, Mexico, Norway, United Arab Emirates, United Kingdom, United States; *against*: China, Russian Federation; *abstaining*: none.

33. Peacebuilding and sustaining peace

During the period under review, the Council held two meetings under the item entitled "Peacebuilding and sustaining peace" which took the form of a briefing and an open debate.[1205] More information on the meetings, including on participants and speakers, is provided in the table below.[1206] In 2022, no decisions were adopted in connection with this item.

On 27 July, the Council held its annual briefing to discuss the report of the Peacebuilding Commission. At the meeting, the Council heard briefings by the representative of Egypt in his capacity as former Chair of the Commission for 2021 and by the representative of Bangladesh, in his capacity as Chair of the Commission for 2022.[1207]

[1205] For more information on the format of meetings, see part II.

[1206] See also A/77/2, part II, chap. 27.

[1207] See S/PV.9101.

During his briefing, the former Chair of the Peacebuilding Commission focused on the annual report of the Commission on its fifteenth session,[1208] under the chairmanship of Egypt. The former Chair stated that, throughout 2021, the Commission had led efforts towards the operationalization of the review outcome, as contained in the twin resolutions adopted by the Council and the General Assembly in 2020,[1209] including by exploring avenues to strengthen the Commission's advisory, bridging and convening roles, with a focus on enhancing the impact of peacebuilding in the field.[1210] He reported that in 2021, the Commission had engaged in support for 13 country- and region-specific settings, including by holding meetings for the first time on the Gulf of Guinea and on the transition in Chad, and with a total of 23 different countries and regions – the highest number since its inception. In terms of thematic engagements, the Commission had considered new themes, including interlinkages between peacekeeping and peacebuilding, disarmament, demobilization and reintegration and security sector reform. Regarding its advisory and bridging roles, the Commission had further expanded and strengthened its relations with the Security Council, the General Assembly and the Economic and Social Council, through the designation of informal coordinators for the Commission's relations with those organs and better alignment of their programmes of work. The Commission had provided advice nine times to the Security Council in 2021, including, for the first time, on the Great Lakes region. The current Chair gave a briefing on the Commission's programme of work for 2022 and its implementation status for the year. He noted that the Commission planned to engage with at least 12 different countries and five different regions during the year, in addition to its ongoing thematic priorities. He informed the Council that the Chair of the Liberia configuration of the Commission had conducted a field visit to the country, country-specific meetings had been held at the request of Burkina Faso, the Central African Republic, Colombia, Guinea-Bissau and Liberia, and regional meetings had been held on the Lake Chad basin, the Pacific islands and the Sahel. He emphasized that the programme of work for the year prioritized national ownership and inclusivity and a coherent United Nations approach to peacebuilding. He indicated that the Commission had continued its efforts to enhance its advisory and bridging role with the General Assembly, the Security Council and the Economic and Social Council and reported that, for the first time, the Commission had shared its programme of work with the Assembly and the Security Council, through formal communications from the Chair.[1211] He highlighted that the Chair of the Commission and the President of the Security Council had requested that the Secretary-General liaise with the Commission in advance of relevant reporting to the Council and underlined that the Commission had submitted advisories to the Council on such topics as the situations in Burkina Faso, the Central African region and the Great Lakes region, women and peace and security and the impact of the COVID-19 pandemic on peacebuilding and had given a briefing to the Council on the United Nations Office for West Africa and the Sahel.[1212]

Council members welcomed the briefings by the former and current Chairs and discussed the advisory role of the Peacebuilding Commission with regard to the Council and approaches for enhancing the relationship between the two organs.[1213] The representative of Kenya, the delegation of which had served as informal coordinator between the two bodies, emphasized the critical need to ensure that the Commission remained well-positioned to provide timely, relevant and actionable advice to the Council, whether thematic, country-specific or region-specific. Recognizing that the alignment of the programmes of work of the Council and the Commission remained a challenge, the representative also stressed the need for early focus and planning around the already scheduled Council meetings, in particular in regard to peace operation transitions and mandate renewals. He called for the establishment of a follow-up mechanism to ensure that the Council integrated and followed up on the Commission's advice in its work. Similarly, the representative of Mexico suggested that the Commission's recommendations to the Council should reach the latter in time for them to be duly considered. The representative of Brazil called for more meaningful collaboration between the two bodies, including through consultations on issues relating to peacebuilding and sustaining peace ahead of the formation, review, drawdown and transition of peace operations; through the regular submission by the Commission of written advice on issues addressed by

[1208] S/2022/89.

[1209] Council resolution 2558 (2020) and Assembly resolution 75/201.

[1210] See S/PV.9101.

[1211] See S/2022/202 and S/2022/250.

[1212] See S/PV.9101.

[1213] For more on the relationship between the Council and the Peacebuilding Commission, see part IX, sect. VII.

both bodies; through the submission of advice on how peacebuilding planning could concretely address the needs of children affected by conflict; through further alignment of the work programmes of the two bodies and greater interaction between their respective penholders; and by enhancing the Council's working methods regarding interaction with the Commission. The representative of China encouraged the Council to invite the Chair of the Commission to give more frequent briefings, in order to strengthen communication, and the representative of Gabon welcomed the efforts made by the Commission to establish more coordinated action with the Council.

The representative of the United Arab Emirates encouraged Council members to further engage with the Peacebuilding Commission, including by continuing to invite it to give briefings and provide written advisories to the Council on relevant matters. She suggested that Council members could coordinate with the Commission before and during their assumption of the Council presidency. She also called for the Council to draw upon the perspectives and recommendations of the Commission in the design and implementation of mandates for peace operations and their transitional arrangements and proposed that the Commission be included in the initial stages of exit strategies in order to foster peace in local contexts. The representative of Ghana welcomed the Commission's practice of submitting letters or notes of advice ahead of Council meetings, underscoring that, if further established, that practice would undergird relations between the two bodies in a manner that would enable the Commission to contribute to addressing the underlying causes of the conflicts considered by the Council. The representative of Norway noted that the Council should request, deliberate and draw upon the targeted advice of the Commission more often, especially in the formation of mandates, renewals and transitions. The representative of the United Kingdom acknowledged the potential of the Commission and indicated that, by continuing to deepen its follow-up on the countries with which it engaged and by rallying collective responses to peacebuilding challenges, the Commission would continue to grow in value.

The representative of India expressed the view that the advisory role of the Peacebuilding Commission should be exercised judiciously and only when warranted. The representative of the Russian Federation believed that there was room for improvement in the quality of the Commission's recommendations to the Council and emphasized that the value of the Commission was that it could pass the peacebuilding priorities of host countries along to the Council, which could be a useful addition to the reports of the Secretary-General. She added that the value and pertinence of the Commission's recommendations played a fundamental role in it being taken into account in the work of the Council and that, in order to improve the quality of the cooperation between the two organs in some cases, there was no need to wait for a planned Council meeting for the head of a country-specific configuration to issue a formal statement. If the matter was urgent, then a letter could be written to the Council to that effect. Highlighting the advisory role of the Commission, the representative of Ireland called upon the Council to turn that advice into action and to ensure that the Commission and the Member States it represented were empowered to fulfil their important roles.

Emphasizing the importance of the work of the Peacebuilding Commission on thematic and cross-cutting subjects, in particular in promoting the women and peace and security and the youth and peace and security agendas, the representative of France noted that such work needed to be placed in specific geographical contexts. She suggested that the Commission support preparations for the withdrawal of peacekeeping operations and that, before the renewal of peacekeeping operation mandates and in anticipation of dialogue with Council penholders, it should produce complementary, targeted and operational recommendations to the Council, while respecting the mandates of the two bodies.

On 3 November, at the initiative of Ghana, which held the presidency for the month,[1214] the Council convened a high-level open debate under the sub-item entitled, "Integrating effective resilience-building in peace operations for sustainable peace".[1215] Council members heard introductory remarks by the Secretary-General and briefings by the Assistant Secretary-General for Africa of the Departments of Political and Peacebuilding Affairs and Peace Operations, the Commissioner for Political Affairs, Peace and Security of the African Union, the Chair of The Elders and the Executive Director of Security Council Report.[1216]

[1214] A concept note was circulated by letter dated 24 October (S/2022/799).

[1215] See S/PV.9181 and S/PV.9181 (Resumption 1).

[1216] See S/PV.9181.

During his briefing, the Secretary-General indicated that the local and global contexts in which United Nations peace operations were deployed were becoming increasingly challenging. Geopolitical tensions were growing, and insecurity was becoming widespread. Emphasizing that the drivers of conflict were fuelling political tensions, economic despair and social unrest, he warned that the peacebuilding gains on the African continent and elsewhere were being reversed. He stressed the need to ensure a sharper focus on prevention and on building resilience and for peace operations to be empowered and equipped to play a greater role in sustaining peace at all stages of conflict and in all its dimensions. The Secretary-General encouraged engagement with local communities and noted that peace operations could help to promote more responsive and inclusive governments and institutions. He advocated in favour of the participation and leadership of women and young people in conflict prevention and resolution efforts. Regarding resilience-building and sustaining peace, he recommended a holistic and integrated approach involving strengthened partnerships between the United Nations and regional organizations, including the African Union, as well as with international and regional financial institutions. He also suggested better integrating the work of United Nations country teams with the mandates of peace operations, including in transition contexts. Lastly, he noted that funding by the international community must be scaled up in support of the Peacebuilding Fund.

The Assistant Secretary-General for Africa addressed the need to adapt United Nations peace operations to fast-changing conflict dynamics and called for holistic and integrated approaches and for inclusive strategies in which the entire spectrum of peace was considered in order to ensure the success of such operations. She underlined the importance of mobilizing and engaging international, regional and national actors working cooperatively and collaboratively on conflict prevention and resolution. Noting that security-oriented responses alone were insufficient, she emphasized that peace operations needed clear, realistic and topical mandates. She also emphasized the need for inclusive strategies in peacebuilding efforts, including acknowledging the contributions and concerns of women and young people, and encouraged meaningful engagement with communities at the local level. She also stressed the importance of complementarity and collaboration among peace and security efforts, the protection of human rights and development and humanitarian work. In relation to sustaining peace, she emphasized the critical role of the United Nations country teams in supporting countries, especially during United Nations transitions.

In his briefing, the Commissioner of Political Affairs, Peace and Security stressed that the Security Council could ensure that peace operations in Africa facilitated a pathway to addressing the underlying causes of conflict by adopting a whole-of-Organization approach in implementing mandates. He also underscored the need to align programmes for complementing critical political transitions with exit strategies for peace support operations, in order to build relevant institutional and normative capacities towards resilience. He noted that the African Union was working closely with the United Nations Development Programme to support political transitions and requested the Council's support for the African Union-United Nations regional governance facility for managing inclusive transitions in Africa. He called for a common purpose between the African Union and the United Nations in addressing existing and emerging threats to regional and international peace, with increased collaboration and coordination.

In her briefing, the Chair of The Elders emphasized that security, sustainable development and human rights should be the foundation for resilient peace operations. She stated that peace operations should address the root causes of conflict and insecurity, not just the immediate symptoms, and called upon the Council to play a more proactive role and promote a whole-of-United Nations approach in support of just and sustainable peace, while ensuring that peace operations drew on and complemented the work of staff at the country level. She also expressed the support of The Elders for the principle of enabling regional organizations to take a leading role in conflict prevention and resolution and emphasized that the Council should cooperate closely with those organizations and step in when they were unable to take effective action. She also stressed the importance of ensuring the fair and meaningful participation of women and girls in peace processes, including by increasing the representation of women in defence and security structures and in peacebuilding and mediation. She further underlined that the climate crisis was a threat multiplier and driver of conflict and recommended integrating an environmental analysis into the work of the Council and the Peacebuilding Commission.

The Director of Security Council Report noted the Council's acknowledgement of previously unaddressed structural factors of conflict and non-traditional threats, including, for example, in discussions on the effects of gang violence in Haiti, alongside the recent establishment of a sanctions regime. She also recalled the Council's support for transitional justice initiatives in mandating peace operations in the Central African Republic and Colombia. She suggested that the Council could consider additional steps to protect its investments in peace through peace operations by, inter alia, signalling its strong interest in sustaining peace, in tandem with the work of the Peacebuilding Commission, and periodically following up with countries after mission closures, including through visits by the Council. Although no peace operation was expected to address every last issue, the full and intricate context in which those operations intervene should be considered.

After the briefings, some Council members and other participants conveyed their support for the Secretary-General's Action for Peacekeeping initiative and its implementation strategy, Action for Peacekeeping Plus.[1217] Numerous speakers underscored that military interventions by peace operations were insufficient for achieving sustainable peace and emphasized the need for a holistic approach, including non-military measures, to identify and address the root causes and drivers of conflicts. In that regard, some participants asserted that the humanitarian-development-peace nexus needed to be strengthened in order to address the root causes of conflict.[1218] A number of Council members and other participants pointed towards the need to integrate resilience-building into peace operations, especially during transition planning.[1219] Numerous speakers defended initiatives centred on inclusion and the meaningful participation of women and young people. Some Council members and other participants also highlighted the importance of addressing the underlying factors exacerbating the threat of terrorism in conflict situations.[1220] Several Council members and other participants similarly acknowledged the existence of climate-related security risks and emphasized the need to address them.[1221] The representative of the Russian Federation said that political solutions must be based on a common understanding of the causes of conflict, without which it would be impossible to agree on realistic mandates, gain the confidence of host States or ensure regional support. Some Council members stated that the Council should concentrate on the core mandate of peace operations and work more closely with national Governments and authorities in determining strategies and priorities for maintaining peace and creating space for finding solutions to conflicts.[1222]

With regard to strengthening the nexus between peacekeeping and peacebuilding, most speakers expressed support for greater coordination and collaboration between the Council and the Peacebuilding Commission, as well as with other United Nations bodies, regional organizations and country teams in the context of transitions and for informing Council decision-making concerning mandate renewals. In that regard, Council members and participants acknowledged the fundamental role of the Commission as a bridge within and outside the United Nations system, in particular in helping to mobilize attention and commitments to international peacebuilding efforts. In that connection, many speakers emphasized the importance of sustainable and predictable funding for peacebuilding efforts, including through contributions to the Peacebuilding Fund. Some participants also welcomed the emerging practice of the Commission to provide written advice and recommendations to inform Council discussions, including on peace operations and resilience-building.[1223]

[1217] See S/PV.9181 (United States, Kenya, Albania, Italy, Austria and Sweden (on behalf of the Nordic countries)); and S/PV.9181 (Resumption 1) (Netherlands, Rwanda and Portugal).

[1218] See S/PV.9181 (Ghana and Republic of Korea); and S/PV.9181 (Resumption 1) (European Union (also on behalf of Albania, Bosnia and Herzegovina, Georgia, North Macedonia, Montenegro, the Republic of Moldova, Serbia and Ukraine), Poland and Morocco).

[1219] See S/PV.9181 (Ghana, Gabon, Ireland, Mexico, Albania, Brazil, United Arab Emirates and Slovenia); and S/PV.9181 (Resumption 1) (Bangladesh and Lebanon).

[1220] See S/PV.9181 (Ghana, Ireland, India, Kenya, United Arab Emirates, Republic of Korea and Malta); and S/PV.9181 (Resumption 1) (Tunisia, Algeria, Bangladesh, Portugal, Nigeria and Germany).

[1221] See S/PV.9181 (Ghana, Ireland, Mexico, Norway, Albania, France, United Arab Emirates, Slovenia, Austria, Malta and Sweden (on behalf of the Nordic countries)); and S/PV.9181 (Resumption 1) (European Union (also on behalf of Albania, Bosnia and Herzegovina, Georgia, North Macedonia, Montenegro, the Republic of Moldova, Serbia and Ukraine), Chile, Tunisia, Bangladesh, Poland, Lebanon, Portugal, Nigeria and Germany).

[1222] See S/PV.9181 (India, China and Russian Federation).

[1223] See S/PV.9181 (Kenya, Norway and Switzerland); and S/PV.9181 (Resumption 1) (Japan and Germany).

Meetings: peacebuilding and sustaining peace, 2022

Meeting record and date	*Sub-item*	*Other documents*	*Rule 37 invitations*	*Rule 39 and other invitations*	*Speakers*	*Decision and vote (for-against-abstaining)*
S/PV.9101 27 July		Annual report of the Peacebuilding Commission on its fifteenth session (S/2022/89)		Former Chair of the Peacebuilding Commission, Chair of the Peacebuilding Commission	All Council members, all invitees	
S/PV.9181 and S/PV.9181 (Resumption 1) 3 November	Integrating effective resilience-building in peace operations for sustainable peace Letter dated 24 October 2022 from the Permanent Representative of Ghana to the United Nations addressed to the Secretary-General (S/2022/799)		32 Member States[a]	Assistant Secretary-General for Africa, Commissioner for Political Affairs, Peace and Security of the African Union, Chargé d'affaires a.i. of the Delegation of the European Union to the United Nations, Chair of The Elders, Executive Director of Security Council Report	Secretary-General, all Council members,[b] all invitees[c]	

[a] Algeria, Argentina, Austria, Bangladesh, Canada, Chile, Ecuador, Egypt, Germany, Indonesia, Italy, Japan, Lebanon, Malta, Morocco, Netherlands, Nigeria, Peru, Poland, Portugal, Republic of Korea, Rwanda, Sierra Leone, Slovakia, Slovenia, South Africa, Sudan, Sweden, Switzerland, Thailand, Tunisia and Ukraine.

[b] Gabon was represented by its Deputy Minister for Foreign Affairs; Ghana (President of the Council) was represented by its Minister for Foreign Affairs and Regional Integration; India was represented by its Foreign Secretary; Ireland was represented by its Minister of State for European Affairs; and the United States was represented by its Permanent Representative to the United Nations and Member of the President's Cabinet.

[c] The Commissioner for Political Affairs, Peace and Security participated in the meeting by videoconference. The representative of Sweden spoke on behalf of the Nordic countries; and the representative of the European Union spoke also on behalf of Albania, Bosnia and Herzegovina, Georgia, North Macedonia, Montenegro, the Republic of Moldova, Serbia and Ukraine.

34. Threats to international peace and security

In 2022, the Security Council held 22 meetings under the item entitled "Threats to international peace and security", of which 21 were public (open) meetings and 1 was a private (closed) meeting. Among the public meetings, 17 took the form of briefings, 2 were convened to adopt a decision, and the remaining 2 were held in a debate format.[1224] The Council adopted one decision under the item and failed to adopt one draft resolution, owing to the lack of the required number of votes. More information about the meetings, including on participants, speakers and outcomes, is provided in the table below. In addition, Council members held informal consultations of the whole to discuss different topics under the item.[1225]

[1224] For more information on the format of meetings, see part II.

[1225] See A/77/2, part II, chap. 29.

During the period under review, various topics were considered under the item. Most of the meetings held under the item in 2022 were focused on the conflict in Ukraine and its implications on the humanitarian situation in the country as a result of the war, the alleged use and manufacturing of biological weapons in Ukraine (in connection with which a draft resolution was proposed, but the Council failed to adopt it), the safety of nuclear facilities in the context of the armed conflict and the Initiative on the Safe Transportation of Grain and Foodstuffs from Ukrainian Ports (Black Sea Initiative).[1226] In addition, one meeting held under the item was focused on the gas leaks detected in the Nord Stream submarine pipelines in the Baltic Sea, one was focused on the investigation conducted into the forced landing of Ryanair flight FR-4978 by Belarus on 23 May 2021, and two were focused on Africa, one with regard to climate and security and one with regard to counter-terrorism. Lastly, consistent with prior practice, the Council held three meetings and adopted one resolution under the item, in connection with the United Nations Investigative Team to Promote Accountability for Crimes Committed by Da'esh/Islamic State in Iraq and the Levant (UNITAD), established pursuant to resolution 2379 (2017).[1227]

In 2022, a total of 15 meetings convened under the item were devoted to the conflict in Ukraine, including with regard to tensions prior to the outbreak of war. On 31 January, at the request of the United States, the Council held a meeting to discuss the threat to international peace and security posed by the build-up of Russian forces on the border of Ukraine.[1228] Upon request by the Russian Federation, the provisional agenda was put to the vote and adopted, with 10 votes in favour, 2 votes against and 3 abstentions.[1229] During the meeting, the Council heard a briefing by the Under-Secretary-General for Political and Peacebuilding Affairs, who expressed great concern over the tensions that continued to escalate, in a dangerous military build-up in the heart of Europe, citing reports of more than 100,000 troops and heavy weaponry from the Russian Federation positioned along the border with Ukraine, with unspecified numbers also reportedly deployed to Belarus ahead of large-scale joint military exercises in February on the borders with Ukraine, Poland and the Baltic States. She added that members of the North Atlantic Treaty Organization (NATO) were reportedly planning additional deployments in its Eastern European member States and that 8,500 troops were currently on high alert. The Under-Secretary-General conveyed the Secretary-General's strong belief that there should not be any military intervention in that context, that diplomacy should prevail and that any such intervention by one country in another would be against international law and the Charter of the United Nations. She reiterated the full commitment of the United Nations to the sovereignty, political independence, unity and territorial integrity of Ukraine within its internationally recognized borders, in accordance with relevant General Assembly resolutions, and stressed the Secretary-General's appeal to all concerned to take immediate steps to de-escalate tensions and continue on the diplomatic path.

In the discussion, most speakers expressed concern about the situation on the borders of Ukraine and urged respect for the principles set out in the Charter, in particular the principles of sovereignty, independence and territorial integrity and the prohibition on the threat or use of force. Council members called for de-escalation and the peaceful resolution of the situation through preventive diplomacy and political dialogue. The representative of the United States expressed the view that the aggression by the Russian Federation threatened not only Ukraine, but also Europe and the international order that the Council was charged with upholding. If the Russian Federation further invaded Ukraine, the consequences would be horrific and the current dire humanitarian situation in eastern Ukraine would pale in comparison to the impact of the full-scale land invasion that it was currently planning. She expressed the belief that there was a diplomatic path out of the crisis and noted that, if the situation was truly about security concerns, the United States was offering the Russian Federation an opportunity to address those concerns at the negotiating table. The representative of China opposed the holding of the public meeting, noting that it was not conducive to creating a favourable environment for dialogue or defusing tensions. The representative of the Russian Federation rejected the allegations of a planned military invasion of Ukraine and noted that the Russian troops had been deployed within the territory of the Russian Federation. Among his country's security concerns were that Ukraine should not join NATO and that no foreign troops should be deployed on its territory. He said that his delegation agreed with the calls for a

[1226] For more information on the items relating to Ukraine, see sect. 19 above.

[1227] For more information on the establishment of UNITAD, see *Repertoire*, *Supplement 2016–2017*.

[1228] See S/PV.8960.

[1229] For more information about the procedural vote on the provisional agenda, see part II.

settlement of the crisis surrounding Ukraine, but noted that it was an internal matter. The representative of Ukraine stated that the situation at the border of his country, where the Russian Federation continued its military build-up, constituted a grave threat to international peace and security. He reiterated the absence of any aggressive intention from the Government of Ukraine and noted that the Council needed to take into account the information it heard at the meeting to make an informed decision, when appropriate, on acting swiftly and decisively in employing preventive diplomacy under Chapter VI of the Charter.

Following the outbreak of war, in two additional briefings in March,[1230] the Under-Secretary-General for Political and Peacebuilding Affairs reported on the growing number of casualties and the attacks on civilian infrastructure, including through the use of cluster munitions, noting that such acts were prohibited under international law and calling for investigations and accountability. In both briefings, she appealed for a cessation of hostilities to allow for the safe passage of civilians and humanitarian aid and welcomed diplomatic efforts aimed at ending the war. At the second briefing, the Council also heard updates from the Assistant High Commissioner for Operations of the Office of the United Nations High Commissioner for Refugees (UNHCR), who reported that the number of refugees from Ukraine in neighbouring countries had risen to more than 3.1 million, in what had become the fastest-growing refugee crisis in Europe since the Second World War.[1231] More than 90 per cent of the refugees fleeing Ukraine were women and children, and at least 2 million people were believed to have been displaced internally. Despite all its efforts, UNHCR was unable to respond to the sheer scale of the rapidly growing needs of the Ukrainian people and systematically deliver much-needed life-saving assistance. He called for civilians and civilian infrastructure to be protected, for international humanitarian law to be upheld and for safe passage to be enabled for civilians. At the same meeting, the Director General of the World Health Organization urged the Council to work towards an immediate ceasefire and a political solution and for all donors to support the response to humanitarian and health needs in Ukraine and neighbouring countries. Although Ukraine was rightly the focus of the world's attention, the Director General urged Council members not to lose sight of the many other crises in which people were suffering.

In their discussions during both of the aforementioned meetings in March, Council members focused on the humanitarian crisis in Ukraine and the attacks on civilians and civilian infrastructure.[1232] At the meeting on 17 March, members also discussed the order issued the previous day by the International Court of Justice, in which the Court requested, inter alia, the suspension of military operations by the Russian Federation in Ukraine.[1233]

In addition, in 2022, the Council heard six briefings by the High Representative for Disarmament Affairs and her Deputies concerning allegations of a biological weapons programme in Ukraine[1234] and reports of supplies of lethal weapons to Ukraine.[1235] In four of those briefings, the High Representative and her Deputies, as representatives of the Office for Disarmament Affairs, reiterated that the United Nations was not aware of biological weapons programmes in Ukraine.[1236] They recalled on those occasions that the Convention on the Prohibition of the Development, Production and Stockpiling of Bacteriological (Biological) and Toxin Weapons and on Their Destruction of 1972 contained several measures to which concerned States parties could have recourse for addressing situations in which States parties had concerns or suspicions about the activities of their peers, such as the possibility of convening a formal consultative meeting to consider such matters or lodging a complaint with the Council to initiate an investigation. In their briefings, the representatives of the Office continued to note that the Convention needed to be operationalized and institutionalized and to recall that the ninth Review Conference of the States Parties to the Biological Weapons Convention, to be held in November and December 2022, presented an opportunity for States parties to strengthen the Convention. In his briefing in October, the Director and Deputy to the High Representative reported that the Office was aware that the Russian Federation, pursuant its earlier request for the convening of a formal consultative meeting under article V

[1230] See S/PV.8991 and S/PV.8998.
[1231] See S/PV.8998.
[1232] See S/PV.8991 and S/PV.8998.
[1233] See S/PV.8998.
[1234] See S/PV.8991, S/PV.8999, S/PV.9033 and S/PV.9171.
[1235] See S/PV.9127 and S/PV.9216.
[1236] See S/PV.8991, S/PV.8999, S/PV.9033 and S/PV.9171.

of the Convention, had filed an official complaint, in line with the provisions of its article VI, regarding the allegations of biological weapons programmes in Ukraine.[1237] He noted that the provisions of article VI had not been invoked since the entry into force of the Convention, which did not contain any guidance on the type of investigation that the Council might initiate. Were the Council to initiate an investigation, the Office stood ready to support it.

At a meeting held on 2 November, a draft resolution submitted by the Russian Federation was not adopted, owing to the lack of the required number of votes.[1238] Under the draft resolution, the Council would have established a commission consisting of all Council members to investigate the claims against the United States and Ukraine contained in the complaint by the Russian Federation (see S/2022/796) regarding compliance with obligations under the Biological Weapons Convention in the context of the activities of biological laboratories in the territory of Ukraine.[1239] In explaining their votes, Council members exchanged views on the conditions for an investigation by the Council, as laid out in article VI of the Convention.[1240]

In her briefings in September and December, the High Representative focused on the reported supply of lethal weapons to Ukraine and their consequences and noted that, since the invasion of Ukraine by the Russian Federation on 24 February, a number of States had transferred weapons systems and ammunition to Ukraine for its defence forces, which was a matter of public record.[1241] The High Representative noted that any large-scale influx of weapons into any armed conflict situation raised many concerns, including the possible diversion of those weapons and, in that context, referred to the available mechanisms for enhancing transparency of arms transfers and measures to mitigate risks of weapons and ammunition diversion.

During the discussions concerning the allegations of a biological weapons programme, Council members underscored the importance of the Biological Weapons Convention as a key mechanism for dealing with that topic.[1242] The representative of the Russian Federation continued to raise concerns about the possible use of such programmes by Ukraine with the support of the United States, while the representatives of Ukraine and the United States continued to reject those allegations and to deny any involvement in such activities. At a meeting held on 9 December,[1243] on the reported transfer of weapons systems and ammunition to Ukraine, speakers[1244] also addressed other topics, such as arms control and the importance of the Arms Trade Treaty, with some Council members[1245] also raising the issue of weapons from the Islamic Republic of Iran being used by the Russian Federation in contravention of resolution 2231 (2015). In the context of the war in Ukraine, several speakers[1246] also addressed the issue of the right to self-defence as enshrined in Article 51 of the Charter.[1247]

During the year, the Council also heard two briefings by the Under-Secretary-General for Humanitarian Affairs and Emergency Relief Coordinator, once in March, jointly with the Executive Director of the United Nations Children's Fund (UNICEF), and once in October, jointly with the Secretary-General of the United Nations Conference on Trade and Development (UNCTAD).[1248] In his briefing in March, the Emergency Relief Coordinator noted that, as the unthinkable had become the reality, the United Nations and its humanitarian partners had started a scalable and agile, adaptable and resilient humanitarian operation fit for the changing situation.[1249] He outlined the three priorities that he had conveyed to the Ukrainian and Russian authorities, namely, for the parties to take constant care to spare

[1237] See S/PV.9171.
[1238] See S/PV.9180. See also S/2022/821.
[1239] For more information, see part IX, sect. VIII.
[1240] See S/PV.9180. For more information on the discussion and about investigative and fact-finding functions acknowledged by the Council, see part VI, sect. II.
[1241] See S/PV.9127 and S/PV.9216.
[1242] See S/PV.8991, S/PV.8999, S/PV.9033, S/PV.9171 and S/PV.9180.
[1243] See S/PV.9216.
[1244] Russian Federation, China, United Arab Emirates, United States, Mexico, Brazil and Ukraine.
[1245] Norway, United Kingdom, France, Albania, United States and Ireland.
[1246] Norway, United Kingdom, Ghana, Albania, United States, Mexico, Brazil, Ireland and Ukraine.
[1247] For more information about discussions relating to Article 51 of the Charter, see part VII, sect. X.
[1248] See S/PV.8988 and S/PV.9176.
[1249] See S/PV.8988.

civilians and civilian homes and infrastructure in their military operations, including by allowing safe passage for civilians to leave areas of active hostilities on a voluntary basis, in the direction they chose; for them to enable safe passage for humanitarian supplies into areas of active hostilities; and for a system of constant communication with parties to the conflict to be to put in place, with assurances to enable the delivery of humanitarian aid. In her briefing, the Executive Director of UNICEF focused on the impact of the conflict on children and called upon Council members to remind all parties of their legal and moral obligation to protect children and spare them from attack and to refrain from targeting civilian infrastructure. In that regard, she appealed to all parties to avoid the use of explosive weapons in populated areas. She also asked the Council to send a strong message to all parties of their obligation to ensure the safety of humanitarian personnel and equipment and to ensure that sanctions and other restrictive measures did not impede humanitarian action. She added that UNICEF had renewed its call for an immediate suspension of ongoing military actions in Ukraine. After the briefings, Council members discussed the humanitarian impact of the war, the question of ensuring safe humanitarian corridors and the protection of civilians and the need for the cessation of hostilities.

In his briefing in October, in the aftermath of reports of the Sevastopol attacks and damage to Russian military vessels and infrastructure, the Emergency Relief Coordinator focused on the implementation of the Black Sea Initiative in the light of the decision of the Russian Federation to suspend its participation.[1250] On the alleged connection between those attacks and the Initiative, he underscored that military vessels, aircraft and assets belonging to any party were prohibited from approaching closer than 10 nautical miles to the cargo ships and that the corridor provided neither cover for nor protection from offensive or defensive military action. Turning to the alleged misuse of cargo vessels in the Initiative for military purposes, the Emergency Relief Coordinator affirmed that none had been in the corridor on the night of 29 October, when the reported attacks had taken place. Expressing readiness to consider an inquiry into any evidence, he stated that all sides had decided, within the Joint Coordination Centre, that the Initiative would be entirely civilian in nature and that the safety of shipping was protected by the commitments of Ukraine and the Russian Federation not to attack ships and related port facilities.

In her briefing, the Secretary-General of UNCTAD noted that the impact of two initiatives – the Black Sea Initiative and the Memorandum of Understanding between the Russian Federation and the Secretariat of the United Nations on promoting Russian food products and fertilizers to world markets – had been made clear in a short period of time, with massive effects on global welfare. She referred to the chilling effect of sanctions on the private sector and noted that transaction costs on insurance premiums, financial payments, shipping costs and transport costs for Russian food and fertilizer exports were very high, leading to continued high global food and fertilizer prices. Adding that a lot of work remained to be done even with clear exemptions to the sanctions, she urged all parties to make every effort to resume and extend the Black Sea Initiative and implement both agreements to their fullest extent.

During the discussion that followed, the representative of the Russian Federation stated that his country had suspended its participation in the Black Sea Initiative following the air and sea strikes against its fleet and infrastructure. He added that the implementation of the Initiative was not possible and that the decisions made by the Joint Coordination Centre without the participation of the Russian Federation were not binding. In the discussion that ensued, Council members exchanged views on the decision of the Russian Federation to suspend its participation the agreement and urged the continued implementation of the Initiative, noting its importance for global food security.

In connection with the reported attacks on nuclear facilities in Ukraine, the Council heard one briefing by the Under-Secretary-General for Political and Peacebuilding Affairs in August[1251] and three briefings by the Director General of the International Atomic Energy Agency (IAEA), in August, September and October, the last of which was conducted during a private meeting.[1252] In her briefing in August, the Under-Secretary-General stated that, despite numerous calls and appeals, instead of de-escalation, alarming incidents involving the Zaporizhzhia nuclear plant continued to be reported on a near-daily basis.[1253]

[1250] See S/PV.9176.
[1251] See S/PV.9114.
[1252] See S/PV.9109, S/PV.9124 and S/PV.9172.
[1253] See S/PV.9114.

She urged the parties to provide the IAEA mission with immediate, secure and unfettered access to the site and noted that any potential nuclear incident would have catastrophic consequences not only for the immediate vicinity, but for the region and beyond. The Under-Secretary-General further underscored that it was imperative to receive the express commitment of the parties to stop any military activities around the plant to enable its continued safe and secure operations.

In his open briefings in August and September, the Director General of IAEA reported on the situation at the nuclear facilities in Ukraine, focusing on the Zaporizhzhia nuclear power plant and called for any military actions that would jeopardize nuclear safety to be stopped immediately.[1254] Since 24 February, IAEA had activated its Incident and Emergency Centre, had established regular contact with the Ukrainian authorities and had closely monitored both the situation at the facilities and activities involving radioactive sources and nuclear material in Ukraine.[1255] In the wake of the shelling of the Zaporizhzhia nuclear power plant on 5 August, the Director General asked both sides to cooperate with IAEA and allow a mission to the site to proceed as soon as possible, so that the Agency could corroborate facts and develop and provide an independent assessment of the nuclear safety and security risks. In September, the Director General reported on the mission conducted by IAEA to the plant, including on the proposed establishment of a nuclear safety and security protection zone.[1256] He reported that IAEA inspectors had remained at the site, to be able to directly and immediately evaluate the situation on the ground as it developed. At the same meeting, the Secretary-General delivered remarks, in which he welcomed the IAEA mission and requested the Russian and Ukrainian forces to commit not to engage in any military activity towards or from the plant site. He also called for an agreement on a demilitarized perimeter, which would include a commitment by Russian forces to withdraw all military personnel and equipment from that perimeter and a commitment by Ukrainian forces not to move into it. The Secretary-General expressed regret about the failure of the tenth Review Conference of the Parties to the Treaty on the Non-Proliferation of Nuclear Weapons to reach consensus on its outcome document, which had been intended to address the issue of the safety and security of nuclear power plants in armed conflict zones, including in Ukraine.

In their discussions concerning the reported attacks involving the nuclear facilities in Ukraine, Council members expressed concern about the risks of nuclear incidents and called for the demilitarization of the areas around all nuclear sites in Ukraine.[1257] Council members also discussed the need for a cessation of hostilities, the importance of avoiding any actions that could lead to nuclear disasters and of pursuing dialogue to end the conflict. They expressed support for the seven pillars of nuclear safety and security and both support for an IAEA mission to Ukraine and appreciation for its having been conducted in September, as well as for the continued presence of its inspectors on the ground. Several Council members urged the Russian Federation to withdraw its troops from the territory of Ukraine and to return full control of nuclear facilities to the Ukrainian authorities.[1258]

On 30 September, the Council held a meeting under the item focused on the gas leaks detected in the Nord Stream submarine pipelines in the Baltic Sea.[1259] At the meeting, the Council heard briefings by the Assistant Secretary-General for Economic Development in the Department of Economic and Social Affairs, the official spokesperson for Gazprom and the Director of the Centre for Energy and Climate of the French Institute of International Relations.

The Assistant Secretary-General emphasized that the United Nations was not in a position to verify or confirm any of the reported details related to the incident and noted that, while the causes of the incident were being investigated, it was equally urgent to address the consequences of those leaks. The damage to the Nord Stream pipelines raised concerns regarding the uncertainty in the global energy markets, the potential environmental impact and the vulnerability of critical energy infrastructure. He concluded that the

[1254] See S/PV.9109 and S/PV.9124.

[1255] See S/PV.9109.

[1256] See S/PV.9124.

[1257] See S/PV.9109, S/PV.9114 and S/PV.9124.

[1258] See S/PV.9109 (United States, Norway, Albania, France, Ireland and United Kingdom); S/PV.9114 (Norway, United States, Ireland, Ghana, United Kingdom, France and Albania); and S/PV.9124 (United States, United Kingdom, Albania, Ireland, Norway and France).

[1259] See S/PV.9144.

incident must not be allowed to further increase tensions or deepen divisions in an already tense regional context. The other two briefers noted, inter alia, that the ruptures in the Nord Stream pipelines were unprecedented and were affecting energy supplies to Europe.

After the briefings, the representative of the Russian Federation argued that the damage to the Nord Stream pipelines was an act of sabotage that benefited neither European States nor the Russian Federation, noting that, instead, it benefited the United States. He added that his country endorsed a comprehensive investigation to shed light on the true circumstances of the incident, adding that any international investigation could claim to be objective only if the Russian Federation was included in it. The representative of the United States categorically denied any involvement in the incident. Most Council members[1260] also noted that the available information indicated that the damage to the pipelines was the result of an act of sabotage, and several[1261] underscored the importance of an independent and impartial investigation to be conducted about the incident, with some[1262] expressing support for the ongoing investigation led by Denmark, Germany and Sweden. Some Council members[1263] also addressed the broader context of the war in Ukraine, with several among them also calling for an end to the conflict.

On 31 October, the Council held a meeting under the item focused on the findings of an investigation conducted into the forced landing of Ryanair flight FR-4978 by Belarus on 23 May 2021.[1264] At the meeting, the Council heard a briefing by the President of the Council of the International Civil Aviation Organization (ICAO), in which he reported on the findings of an investigation conducted by his organization into the matter of Ryanair flight FR-4978, which had been diverted over Belarus airspace on 23 May 2021 to land in Minsk while travelling from Athens to Vilnius. The investigation had led to the conclusion that senior officials of Belarus had orchestrated the deliberate diversion of the flight under the false pretext of a bomb threat. The ICAO Council had decided that the actions of the Government of Belarus amounted to an infraction of the Convention on International Civil Aviation (Chicago Convention), to be reported to the ICAO Assembly. Having acknowledged that there had been an infraction of the Convention by Belarus, the ICAO Assembly adopted resolution A41-1, in which it condemned the actions of the Government of Belarus in committing an act of unlawful interference that had deliberately endangered the safety and security of Ryanair flight FR-4978 and the lives of those on board.[1265]

After the briefing, Council members and other meeting participants acknowledged having taken note of the report on the ICAO fact-finding mission, with many expressing concern over the implication of the Belarusian authorities in the incident, which they viewed as a violation of the relevant international aviation norms.[1266] In that regard, most speakers[1267] also addressed the detention of a Belarusian journalist, who had been arrested following the forced landing of the Ryanair flight in Minsk. Some speakers[1268] also raised the issue of complicity of Belarus in the war in Ukraine. The representative of the Russian Federation expressed the view that the ICAO report carried little credibility and expressed doubts about the organization's impartiality, because no objective and transparent investigation into the incident involving the Ryanair flight had been conducted. The representative of China recalled his country's objection to the ICAO report and noted that different parties had different views on it and had concerns about the source and authenticity of some key information contained therein. The representative of Belarus stated that his country would never accept the conclusions of the report, which it considered to be based on incomplete information. Some Council members[1269] also questioned whether the Council was the appropriate body to discuss the matter.

[1260] Norway, Mexico, Ireland, United Kingdom, United States, China, United Arab Emirates, Albania and France.

[1261] Mexico, Gabon, China, United Arab Emirates, India and Ghana.

[1262] Norway, Ireland, United Kingdom, United States, Albania and France.

[1263] Mexico, Gabon, United States, United Arab Emirates, Albania, Kenya and India.

[1264] See S/PV.9175.

[1265] For more information on the discussion, see part VI, sect. II. For more information on the incident, see S/2021/608 and S/2022/802.

[1266] See S/PV.9175 (Albania, United Kingdom, United States, France, Ireland, Norway, Brazil, Kenya, Mexico, Ghana, Lithuania, Poland, Latvia (also on behalf of Czechia and Estonia), Greece and Germany).

[1267] Albania, United Kingdom, United States, France, Ireland, Mexico, Lithuania, Poland, Latvia (also on behalf of Czechia and Estonia) and Germany.

[1268] Albania, United Kingdom, France, Ireland, Norway, Poland, Latvia (also on behalf of Czechia and Estonia) and Germany.

[1269] Russian Federation, Brazil, Mexico and China.

In 2022, consistent with prior practice, the Council held two meetings under the item to heard briefings on the work of UNITAD, and a third meeting to adopt a resolution to extend the mandate of the Investigative Team. On 8 June and 5 December, pursuant to the two biannual reports on the activities of the Investigative Team,[1270] the Council heard briefings by the Special Adviser and Head of UNITAD, in which he reported on the progress made in the investigative activities of the Team, including with regard to witness interviews, the digitization of documentary evidence and the drafting of case files.[1271] Investigations had progressed into the provision of financial support to Da'esh by the Bayt al-Mal, the development and use of chemical and biological weapons, the case concerning the Christian community in the Ninawa plains and the cases involving the destruction of cultural heritage sites in Iraq. The Special Adviser also provided updates on cases involving the crimes committed against the Yazidi community and those committed against the personnel of Tikrit Air Academy, as well as the case of the Badush prison. He added that UNITAD had expanded and further operationalized arrangements with the Iraqi judiciary and increased its support to ongoing domestic proceedings in several Member States, in consultation with the Government of Iraq. In that context, in addition to the landmark conviction of a Da'esh member in Frankfurt, Germany, in 2021, for the crime of genocide, the Special Adviser noted that the Team had also supported the Joint Investigation Team, consisting of the national prosecution authorities of Belgium, France and Sweden, in cases involving international crimes connected with Da'esh. In his briefing in December, the Special Adviser noted that the sharing of evidence with the Iraqi judiciary for criminal proceedings could take place only once the respective legal requirements and standards were met in terms of substantive and procedural law.[1272] He emphasized that promoting accountability for international crimes committed by Da'esh in Iraq meant delivering tailored assistance in accordance with the needs of the respective investigative court or judge.

After the briefings, at both meetings, Council members expressed their support for the work of UNITAD and welcomed the cooperation between the Investigative Team and the Iraqi authorities.[1273] Specifically, several Council members noted the importance of a gender-responsive approach to the Team's investigation of Da'esh crimes.[1274] Some Council members reiterated the need to ensure full respect for the sovereignty of Iraq and its jurisdiction over crimes committed in its territory,[1275] with several members also pointing to the importance of handing over the collected evidence to the Iraqi authorities.[1276] In that regard, some Council members underscored the need for progress on developing the relevant domestic legislation to enable the prosecution of those crimes in Iraq, including as regards the aspects related to the capital punishment.[1277]

On 15 September, pursuant to the request of the Government of Iraq (S/2022/687), the Council unanimously adopted resolution 2651 (2022), by which it extended the mandate of the Special Adviser and the Investigative Team for a period of one year, until 17 September 2023.[1278] In the resolution, the Council underscored the importance of sharing evidence collected by the Investigative Team with the relevant Iraqi authorities, in a timely manner, for eventual use in fair and independent criminal proceedings, consistent with applicable international law and the terms of reference of the Investigative Team.[1279] It also requested the Special Adviser to continue to submit and present reports to the Council on the Team's activities every 180 days.[1280]

In 2022, under the item, the Council also held two meetings focused on Africa, one on climate and security and one on counter-terrorism.[1281]

[1270] S/2022/434 and S/2022/836.
[1271] See S/PV.9059 and S/PV.9206.
[1272] See S/PV.9206.
[1273] See S/PV.9059 and S/PV.9206.
[1274] See S/PV.9059 (United Kingdom, United Arab Emirates, Gabon, Kenya, Norway, Ireland and France); and S/PV.9206 (France, Norway, Ireland and Kenya).
[1275] See S/PV.9059 (Gabon, China and Brazil) and S/PV.9206 (Brazil).
[1276] See S/PV.9059 (Russian Federation, Ghana, China, Brazil and India); and S/PV.9206 (United Arab Emirates, China, Ghana, Russian Federation, Brazil, Kenya and India).
[1277] See S/PV.9059 (Mexico, Norway, Ireland and France); and S/PV.9206 (Albania, France, Norway, Mexico, United States and Ireland).
[1278] Resolution 2651 (2022), para. 2.
[1279] Ibid., seventh preambular paragraph.
[1280] Ibid., para. 3. For more information, see part IX, sect. III.
[1281] See S/PV.9150 and S/PV.9188.

On 12 October, at the initiative of Gabon, which held the presidency for the month,[1282] the Council convened a high-level open debate under the sub-item entitled, "Climate and security in Africa".[1283] At the meeting, the Council heard briefings by the Assistant Secretary-General for Africa in the Departments of Political and Peacebuilding Affairs and Peace Operations, the former Chair of the African Group of Negotiators on Climate Change and the Regional Director for Africa at the International Committee of the Red Cross (ICRC).

The Assistant Secretary-General stated that the climate emergency was a danger to peace and added that climate change exacerbated existing risks and created new ones. To support the African continent in addressing the impact of climate change on peace and security, action was needed on multiple fronts. For that reason, she added, multidimensional partnerships connecting the work of the United Nations, regional organizations, Member States, international financial institutions, civil society, the private sector and international and local researchers were vital.

The former Chair of the African Group of Negotiators on Climate Change outlined the links between climate change and peace and security in Africa, examined the resources available to Africa in addressing the threat of climate change to peace and security in Africa and explored ways to maximize the international community's support for Africa in order to minimize the effects of climate change on peace and security.

The Regional Director for Africa at ICRC noted that the convergence of climate risk, environmental degradation and armed conflict threatened people's lives and health and worsened food, economic and water insecurity. He added that climate change multiplied existing vulnerabilities and inequalities in conflict zones and that the impact of such overlap could shape human mobility and access to resources on a regional scale, citing examples of situations – and ICRC responses – in several countries in the Sahel, as well as in Mali, the Niger and Somalia.

After the briefings, Council members and other speakers discussed the impact of climate change on peace and security in Africa and the steps that the Council and the broader international community could take to address that question. Speakers exchanged views on the extent to which climate change was a contributing factor to or threat multiplier in various conflict situations and deliberated on the role of the Council in addressing it.[1284]

On 10 November, at the initiative of Ghana, which held the presidency for the month,[1285] the Council held a high-level debate under the sub-item entitled, "Counter-terrorism in Africa: an imperative for peace, security and development".[1286] During the meeting, the Council heard briefings by the Deputy Secretary-General, the Chairperson of the African Union Commission, the Managing Director for Common Security and Defence Policy and Crisis Response of the European External Action Service and the President and Chief Executive Officer of the International Crisis Group.

In her briefing, the Deputy Secretary-General noted that terrorists and violent extremists had exploited instability and conflict to increase their activities and intensify attacks across Africa, with women and girls bearing the brunt of insecurity and inequality. Countering international terrorism required effective multilateral responses, which needed to address terrorism together with concurrent and converging threats, including the worsening climate emergency, armed conflict, poverty and inequality, lawless cyberspace and uneven recovery from the COVID-19 pandemic.

The Chairperson of the African Union Commission stated that, in Africa, terrorism and the increasingly frequent use of violence as a means of gaining and maintaining power were fragmenting societies and causing dozens of deaths and significant physical and psychological damage. He said that Somalia, Libya, Mali, Burkina Faso, the Lake Chad basin, Mozambique and the eastern Democratic Republic of the Congo were all theatres and preferred areas for the proliferation of deadly terrorist

[1282] A concept note was circulated by a letter dated 3 October (S/2022/737).
[1283] See S/PV.9150.
[1284] For more information on Council members' discussions on whether the issue of climate change was within the purview of the Council's mandate, see part V, sect. I.
[1285] A concept note was circulated by a letter dated 1 November (S/2022/822).
[1286] See S/PV.9188.

activities, adding that the defeat of terrorism in Africa was necessary to cut its chances of metastasizing elsewhere.

The Managing Director for Common Security and Defence Policy and Crisis Response of the European External Action Service highlighted that West Africa required immediate attention to stem the risks of spillover from advancing terrorist actors.

The President and Chief Executive Officer of the International Crisis Group asserted that conflicts involving non-State armed groups would be a source of instability in Africa for some time to come. Robust, African-led missions were well positioned to counter those threats, but required proper and reliable resources, and stabilizations missions alone could not stem the threat of non-State armed groups, which required broader responses, including projects to provide basic services and better governance. Expressing the view that conflicts that destabilized several African regions were not only about counter-terrorism, she stressed that they were often rooted in concrete grievances with State authorities and elites whose level of public legitimacy was dismal and that the use of force should always be part of a wider political strategy.

In their discussion, Council members focused on the role of regional and subregional organizations and initiatives, such as the African Union and the Economic Community of West African States, in countering terrorism in different regions of Africa, including in the Sahel, West Africa and the Horn of Africa. They also discussed the threat posed by various terrorist groups, focusing on Al-Qaida and Da'esh and their local offshoots. Other topics addressed during the discussion included preventive efforts aimed at tackling the underlying causes of terrorism and drivers of instability, the impact of climate change and the extent to which the United Nations peace operations could tackle the challenges of terrorism in Africa.

Meetings: threats to international peace and security, 2022

Meeting record and date	*Sub-item*	*Other documents*	*Rule 37 invitations*	*Rule 39 and other invitations*	*Speakers*	*Decision and vote (for-against-abstaining)*
S/PV.8960 31 January			Belarus, Lithuania, Poland, Ukraine	Under-Secretary-General for Political and Peacebuilding Affairs	All Council members, all invitees[a]	Procedural vote (rule 9) 10-2-3[b]
S/PV.8988 7 March			Ukraine	Under-Secretary-General for Humanitarian Affairs and Emergency Relief Coordinator, Executive Director of the United Nations Children's Fund	All Council members, all invitees	
S/PV.8991 11 March			Ukraine	Under-Secretary-General for Political and Peacebuilding Affairs, High Representative for Disarmament Affairs	14 Council members,[c] all invitees	

Meeting record and date	*Sub-item*	*Other documents*	*Rule 37 invitations*	*Rule 39 and other invitations*	*Speakers*	*Decision and vote (for-against-abstaining)*
S/PV.8998 17 March			Poland, Ukraine	Under-Secretary-General for Political and Peacebuilding Affairs, Assistant High Commissioner for Operations of the Office of the United Nations High Commissioner for Refugees, Director General of the World Health Organization	All Council members, all invitees	
S/PV.8999 18 March				High Representative for Disarmament Affairs	All Council members, invitee	
S/PV.9033 13 May				Director and Deputy to the High Representative for Disarmament Affairs	All Council members, invitee	
S/PV.9059 8 June			Iraq	Special Adviser and Head of the United Nations Investigative Team to Promote Accountability for Crimes Committed by Da'esh/Islamic State in Iraq and the Levant (UNITAD)	All Council members, all invitees	
S/PV.9109 11 August			Ukraine	Director General of the International Atomic Energy Agency (IAEA)	All Council members,[d] all invitees[e]	
S/PV.9114 23 August			Ukraine	Under-Secretary-General for Political and Peacebuilding Affairs	All Council members, all invitees	

Meeting record and date	*Sub-item*	*Other documents*	*Rule 37 invitations*	*Rule 39 and other invitations*	*Speakers*	*Decision and vote (for-against-abstaining)*
S/PV.9124 6 September			Germany, Ukraine	Director General of IAEA	Secretary-General, all Council members, all invitees[e]	
S/PV.9127 8 September			Ukraine	High Representative for Disarmament Affairs, Director of the Center for Geostrategic Studies	All Council members, all invitees	
S/PV.9131 15 September		Draft resolution submitted by United Kingdom (S/2022/693)				Resolution 2651 (2022) 15-0-0
S/PV.9144 30 September				Assistant Secretary-General for Economic Development, spokesperson for Gazprom, Director of the Centre for Energy and Climate of the French Institute of International Relations	All Council members, all invitees[f]	
S/PV.9150 12 October	Climate and security in Africa Letter dated 3 October 2022 from the Permanent Representative of Gabon to the United Nations addressed to the Secretary-General (S/2022/737)		10 Member States[g]	Assistant Secretary-General for Africa, Regional Director for Africa at the International Committee of the Red Cross, former Chair of the African Group of Negotiators on Climate Change	All Council members,[h] all invitees[i]	
S/PV.9171 27 October			Ukraine	Director and Deputy to the High Representative for Disarmament Affairs	All Council members, all invitees	

Meeting record and date	*Sub-item*	*Other documents*	*Rule 37 invitations*	*Rule 39 and other invitations*	*Speakers*	*Decision and vote (for-against-abstaining)*
S/PV.9172 27 October (closed)			Ukraine	Director General of IAEA	Council members, all invitees	
S/PV.9175 31 October			Six Member States[j]	President of the Council of the International Civil Aviation Organization	All Council members, all invitees[k]	
S/PV.9176 31 October			Germany, Romania, Türkiye, Ukraine	Under-Secretary-General for Humanitarian Affairs and Emergency Relief Coordinator, Secretary-General of the United Nations Conference on Trade and Development, Deputy Head of the Delegation of the European Union to the United Nations	All Council members, all invitees	
S/PV.9180 2 November		Draft resolution submitted by Russian Federation (S/2022/821)			14 Council members[l]	Not adopted 2-3-10[m]
S/PV.9188 10 November	Counter-terrorism in Africa: an imperative for peace, security and development Letter dated 1 November 2022 from the Permanent Representative of Ghana to the United Nations addressed to the Secretary-General (S/2022/822)			Chairperson of the African Union Commission, Managing Director for Common Security and Defence Policy and Crisis Response of the European External Action Service, President and Chief Executive Officer of the International Crisis Group	Deputy Secretary-General, all Council members,[n] all invitees[o]	

Meeting record and date	Sub-item	Other documents	Rule 37 invitations	Rule 39 and other invitations	Speakers	Decision and vote (for-against-abstaining)
S/PV.9206 5 December	Letter dated 7 November 2022 from the Special Adviser and Head of UNITAD addressed to the President of the Security Council (S/2022/836)		Iraq	Special Adviser and Head of UNITAD	All Council members, all invitees	
S/PV.9216 9 December			Ukraine	High Representative for Disarmament Affairs, civil society representative	All Council members, all invitees	

[a] The representative of Lithuania spoke also on behalf of Estonia and Latvia.
[b] *For*: Albania, Brazil, France, Ghana, Ireland, Mexico, Norway, United Arab Emirates, United Kingdom, United States; *against*: China, Russian Federation; *abstentions*: Gabon, India, Kenya.
[c] Albania, Brazil, China, France, Ghana, Gabon, India, Ireland, Kenya Mexico, Norway, Russian Federation, United Kingdom, United States.
[d] The United States was represented by its Under Secretary of State for Arms Control and International Security.
[e] The Director General of IAEA participated in the meeting by videoconference.
[f] The spokesperson for Gazprom and the Director of the Centre for Energy and Climate of the French Institute of International Relations participated in the meeting by videoconference.
[g] Colombia, Egypt, Germany, Italy, Morocco, Namibia, Niger, Poland, South Africa and Ukraine.
[h] Gabon (President of the Council) and Norway were represented by their respective Ministers for Foreign Affairs; the United Arab Emirates was represented by its Permanent Representative to the United Nations and Assistant Minister for Foreign Affairs and International Cooperation; and the United States was represented by its Permanent Representative to the United Nations and member of the President's Cabinet.
[i] The representative of Germany spoke on behalf of the Group of Friends on Climate and Security.
[j] Belarus, Germany, Greece, Latvia, Lithuania and Poland.
[k] The representative of Latvia spoke also on behalf of Czechia and Estonia.
[l] Albania, Brazil, China, France, Ghana, India, Ireland, Kenya Mexico, Norway, Russian Federation, United Arab Emirates, United Kingdom, United States.
[m] *For*: China, Russian Federation; *against*: France, United Kingdom, United States; *abstaining*: Albania, Brazil, Gabon, Ghana, India, Ireland, Kenya, Mexico, Norway, United Arab Emirates.
[n] Ghana (President of the Council) was represented by its President. Gabon was represented by its Deputy Minister for Foreign Affairs; the United Arab Emirates was represented by its Minister of State in the Ministry of Foreign Affairs and International Cooperation; and the United States was represented by its Assistant to the President for Homeland Security.
[o] All invitees participated in the meeting by videoconference.

35. Maintenance of international peace and security

During the period under review, the Council held eight meetings in connection with the item entitled "Maintenance of international peace and security". Four of the meetings took the form of briefings, three took the form of open debates, and one was convened to adopt a decision of the Council.[1287] The Council adopted one resolution, under Chapter VII of the Charter of the United Nations. More information on the meetings, including on participants, speakers and outcomes, is provided in the table below. In addition, Council members held informal consultations of the whole to discuss different topics under the item.[1288]

[1287] For more information on the format of meetings, see part II.
[1288] See also A/77/2, part II, chap. 34.

In 2022, as in previous periods, a broad range of new and existing sub-items were discussed in connection with the item.[1289] The thematic sub-items addressed during the period under review were as follows: (a) implementation of resolutions 2532 (2020) and 2565 (2021); (b) conflict and food security; (c) technology and security; (d) strengthening accountability and justice for serious violations of international law; (e) promoting common security through dialogue and cooperation; and (f) a new orientation for reformed multilateralism. The meetings in which the above sub-items were addressed are described below in chronological order. The Council also adopted a resolution in connection with the report of the Secretary-General on the implementation of resolution 2491 (2019) relating to the smuggling of migrants and trafficking in persons in the Mediterranean Sea off the coast of Libya.

On 11 April, the Council held a meeting under the sub-item entitled "Implementation of resolutions 2532 (2020) and 2565 (2021)".[1290] At the meeting, Council members heard briefings by the Global Lead Coordinator for COVID-19 Vaccine Country Readiness and Delivery, the Senior Adviser to the Office of the Director General of the International Committee of the Red Cross (ICRC) and the Health and Nutrition Coordinator at CARE South Sudan.

The Global Lead Coordinator for COVID-19 Vaccine Country Readiness and Delivery asserted that the pandemic was still far from over and highlighted the urgency of raising COVID-19 vaccination rates in countries that did not have that opportunity in 2021. He pointed out that more than 11.1 billion doses of COVID-19 vaccines had been administered globally, but that the vaccination rate in low-income countries was only 11 per cent. Through strong political leadership, country coordination and planning, as well as the implementation of mass vaccination campaigns, countries could quickly pick up their vaccination rates and coverage. To address the significant vaccine equity gap that continued to pose a threat to global health security, he called for continued strong support and actions to implement resolutions 2532 (2020) and 2565 (2021), with a particular focus on ensuring that countries continued to prioritize COVID-19 vaccinations. He expressed appreciation for the $4.8 billion in pledges made at the COVID-19 Vaccine Global Access (COVAX) Advance Market Commitment Summit and stated that commitments must be turned into tangible support for lower income countries with COVID-19 vaccination needs and with a priority on a delivery system. He stressed the need to advocate in favour of, and help to guarantee, full, safe and unhindered access, including through ensuring the safety of health and humanitarian personnel administering vaccines in humanitarian settings. He asked that Member States ensure strong national vaccination planning that addressed the needs of all populations living within the national territory, regardless of nationality or migration or refugee status. Lastly, he emphasized the need to engage in important conversations on the global health emergency architecture and to advocate in favour of strong governance and investment in the basics of primary health care as a key element of future pandemic preparedness.

The Senior Adviser to the Office of the Director General of ICRC stated that successes in the development and production of vaccines meant that many countries were starting to regain a sense of normalcy. However, to end the pandemic, vaccination needed to occur everywhere, and that was not the case in conflict-affected areas. To raise vaccination rates in conflict settings, she requested that the international community first ensure that international humanitarian law was respected, in particular with regard to the protection of hospitals and other medical facilities, as well as medical personnel, from attacks. She also stressed the importance of integrating COVID-19 vaccinations into a broader health strategy and, in tandem, strengthening the health system to address renewed outbreaks of other highly contagious and lethal diseases. She advocated in favour of involving the community in vaccination activities and of adequately resourcing community engagement. She emphasized that equitable access to COVID-19 vaccination was a humanitarian imperative.

The Health and Nutrition Coordinator at CARE South Sudan described the work carried out by his organization in providing humanitarian assistance to various parts of the country in multiple sectors, including health care, nutrition, gender and protection, food security and livelihoods. He urged Council members to call on the United Nations system, the international donor community and host Governments to take a number of actions, namely, to ensure safe and unhindered humanitarian access to all people in

[1289] For more information on new sub-items, see part II, sect. II.A.

[1290] See S/PV.9014.

need; to ensure that COVID-19 vaccine costing models and budgets covered all aspects of delivery and reflected the real-world costs of rolling out vaccines to the last mile; to ensure that non-governmental organizations (NGOs), women-led organizations and front-line health-care workers had meaningful roles in the COVID-19 vaccine roll-out; to invest in community-driven, bottom-up approaches that included the meaningful and consistent participation of local NGOs, community groups and women's groups; and to make concrete investments to ensure an equitable COVID-19 vaccine roll-out that left no one behind.

During the discussion, Council members expressed concern regarding the global vaccine equity gap, while stressing the need for a concerted effort by the international community to work on ensuring equitable access to COVID-19 vaccinations, especially in conflict-affected areas. In that context, they underscored the need to strengthen the capacity of national health systems and safeguard humanitarian access for vaccine distribution and called for continued support and actions to implement resolutions 2532 (2020) and 2565 (2021). Making reference to the COVAX Facility, many Council members underlined the need to strengthen and support the mechanism to ensure equitable access to vaccines. In that connection, some Council members[1291] expressed support for initiatives to waive intellectual property rights for COVID-19 vaccines. Several Council members[1292] also discussed the vital role of the African Union in the distribution of vaccines to vulnerable countries.[1293]

On 19 May, at the initiative of the United States, which held the presidency for the month,[1294] the Council held a high-level open debate under the sub-item entitled "Conflict and food security".[1295] Council members heard opening remarks by the Secretary-General and briefings by the Executive Director of the World Food Programme (WFP), the Director General of the Food and Agriculture Organization of the United Nations (FAO) and the founder and Chief Executive Officer of Gro Intelligence.[1296]

In his opening remarks, the Secretary-General noted that 60 per cent of the world's undernourished people lived in areas affected by conflict. He emphasized that armed conflict created hunger, adding that the impact of conflicts was magnified by the climate crisis and economic insecurity, which had been compounded by the pandemic. Consequently, decades of progress in combating hunger were being undone. He stated that 49 million people in 43 countries were at emergency levels of hunger, known as Integrated Phase Classification 4, which was just one step away from famine, and women and girls were the worst affected. Addressing the situation in Ukraine, he stated that the war was adding a frightening new dimension to that picture of global hunger. He suggested four actions that countries could take to break the deadly dynamic of conflict and hunger. First, they should invest in political solutions to end conflicts, prevent new ones and build sustainable peace. Second, referring to international humanitarian law as reflected in resolution 2417 (2018), he emphasized that the Council had a critical role to play in demanding adherence to international humanitarian law and pursuing accountability when the law was breached. Third, he called for greater coordination and leadership to address the interconnected risks of food insecurity, energy and financing. Fourth, underscoring that feeding the hungry was an investment in global peace and security, he urged donors to fund humanitarian appeals in full and to demonstrate to all other countries in need the same generosity that had been shown to Ukraine.

Citing the crises in Afghanistan, Ethiopia and Ukraine, the Executive Director of WFP underscored that the world was facing an unprecedented perfect storm caused by conflict, climate change and the COVID-19 pandemic. He drew attention to the increasing number of people who were at the verge of starvation, struggling to find food and living from hand to mouth on a daily basis. He identified food prices as the number one problem in 2022, but predicted that, in 2023, it would likely be replaced by issues of food availability. He urged the international community to help to stabilize food markets to prevent a further deterioration of the situation, by, inter alia, opening ports and increasing production around the world.

[1291] China, Mexico, Gabon and India.

[1292] United Kingdom, Ghana, Gabon and Kenya.

[1293] For more information on discussions regarding cooperation with regional and subregional organizations, see part VIII, sect. I.

[1294] A concept note was circulated by a letter dated 12 May (S/2022/391).

[1295] See S/PV.9036 and S/PV.9036 (Resumption 1).

[1296] See S/PV.9036.

The Director General of FAO reported that there had been a spike in the global level of acute hunger in the previous five years. He warned about the risk of famine in Afghanistan, Somalia, South Sudan and Yemen and asserted that conflict remained the single-greatest driver of hunger. He described the steps that FAO had taken to strengthen agrifood systems, save lives and protect the agricultural livelihoods of the world's most vulnerable. He stated that Member States needed to urgently transform their agrifood systems to be more efficient, inclusive, resilient and sustainable. Noting that technology, good policies and management were solutions to alleviate the food crisis, he encouraged Member States to invest more in innovation and new technologies, especially water management, irrigation systems and high-quality agricultural inputs, including fertilizer, and in more transparent market information systems.

The founder and Chief Executive Officer of Gro Intelligence provided insights from data collected by her organization on the state of the global food systems. She noted that the conflict between the Russian Federation and Ukraine had not started the food security crisis, but had simply added fuel to a fire that had long been burning. She listed five major challenges occurring simultaneously that had already started to unravel decades of global economic progress, namely, a lack of fertilizer, climate disruptions, record low inventories of cooking oils, record low inventories of grains and logistical bottlenecks. She underscored the need for substantial, immediate and aggressive coordinated global actions to prevent further human suffering and economic damage.

Following the briefings, speakers discussed the challenges of conflict-driven global food insecurity, including ways to mitigate those impacts on the most vulnerable groups, such as women and children, especially in developing countries.[1297] Recalling Council resolution 2417 (2018), by which it had established the link between armed conflict and violence and conflict-induced food insecurity and the threat of famine, participants urged the Council to ensure its implementation. Many speakers noted the grave consequences of conflict on food security, citing the impact of the war in Ukraine, climate change and the COVID-19 pandemic among other factors contributing to the worsening global food crises. Notably, speakers drew attention to the alarming food security situations in countries in Africa, Asia and the Middle East, highlighting the risk of famine posed by the blockade of Ukrainian ports, which had prevented shipments of grains from leaving Ukraine. Participants also raised concerns about rising food prices and the increasing number of people in need of assistance, in particular in developing countries.

On 23 May, the Council held a meeting under the sub-item entitled "Technology and security".[1298] Council members heard briefings by the Under-Secretary-General for Political and Peacebuilding Affairs, the Director of Advox – the digital rights project of Global Voices and an adjunct professor at the McGill University Centre for International Peace and Security Studies and non-resident Fellow at the International Peace Institute.

The Under-Secretary-General highlighted various benefits of digital technologies for the maintenance of international peace and security. Technological developments had improved the ability to detect crises, to better pre-position humanitarian stocks and to design data-driven peacebuilding programming. She affirmed that the use of digital technologies could improve the safety and security of peacekeeping and civilian staff on the ground and noted that the launch of the Strategy for the Digital Transformation of United Nations Peacekeeping represented an essential step towards that goal, as well as towards more effective mandate implementation, thereby increasing early-warning capacities. Digital tools made it possible to visualize information and convey data-rich analysis to support Council decision-making. The Under-Secretary-General indicated, however, that advances in technology had also created significant new risks that could affect conflict dynamics for the worse and expressed concern about the increasing number of State- and non-State-sponsored incidents of malicious use of digital technologies for political or military ends, in particular through activities targeting essential infrastructure. She added that digital technologies had raised major human rights concerns, from artificial intelligence systems that might be discriminatory to the widespread availability of surveillance technologies that could be deployed to target communities or individuals, as well as concerns regarding the increasing use of Internet shutdowns. She highlighted several actions that had been undertaken to mitigate those risks, driven by

[1297] See S/PV.9036 and S/PV.9036 (Resumption 1).

[1298] See S/PV.9039.

the United Nations Strategy and Plan of Action on Hate Speech, launched by the Secretary-General. She urged Member States to fully embrace the opportunities offered by digital technologies to advance peace and to mitigate the risks that such technologies posed and promote their responsible use by all actors.

The Director of Advox, cautioning listeners against interpreting her remarks on digital technology in relation to peace and security as an invitation for the militarization and securitization of the Internet, urged the Council to instead commit to preserving the Internet as a global public good. Recalling the Council's mandate to preserve peace and security, she urged it to take a multilateral, transnational and generational approach to addressing the challenges of human rights in the digital age. To achieve such an approach, she elaborated on three key principles that, in her view, would create opportunities for action to safeguard peace and security. First, she noted that digital rights were human rights and that any effort to address those challenges must begin with the protection of human beings from the excesses of the power of the State and private corporations. Second, the power of the Internet could and must be harnessed for the greater good as a global public good, without allowing the interests of security or profit to drown out the interests of peace. Lastly, whatever actions the Council chose to take must extend beyond the moment to protect the aspirations of future generations.

The adjunct professor at the McGill University Centre for International Peace and Security Studies shared his perspective on three interlinked topics concerning technology and security. In addressing how digital technologies were reshaping the conflicts on which the Council was engaged, he urged it to demand that social media companies apply their content moderation resources equally across their global reach. He commented on how those technologies and their use by parties to conflict and the United Nations itself had affected the Organization's efforts to prevent and resolve violence. He then elaborated on ways in which the United Nations peace and security toolkit, especially its peace operations, could be adapted to the impacts of digital technologies on conflict, mitigate the negative impacts of those technologies on its own operations and use digital technologies to work more effectively and responsibly in those evolving contexts.

Following the briefings, Council members outlined the benefits of digital technology in conflict management, while raising concerns about the risks posed by technology in exacerbating conflicts. Many Council members underscored the threat posed by digital technology when used for malicious purposes by both State and non-State actors, including through misinformation and the suppression of human rights. In that context, some Council members[1299] expressed concern about the increasing use of Internet shutdowns to prevent freedom of expression and political participation, while noting that such practice was a violation of human rights. Several Council members[1300] also specifically emphasized the need to combat misinformation and disinformation campaigns on social media platforms, including in the context of peace operations and humanitarian activities.

On 2 June, at the initiative of Albania which held the presidency for the month,[1301] the Council held a high-level open debate under the sub-item entitled "Strengthening accountability and justice for serious violations of international law".[1302] Council members heard briefings by the President of the International Court of Justice, the United Nations High Commissioner for Human Rights and a professor of Public International Law at the University of Oxford.[1303]

The President of the International Court of Justice highlighted the special role played by the Court in strengthening the accountability of States in the context of armed conflict and widespread abuses of human rights. She recalled that the Court's judgments and orders on the indication of provisional measures were legally binding on the parties to a case. She explained that, before addressing the merits of any contentious case brought before it, the Court had to satisfy itself that it had the jurisdiction to do so. She reminded Member States that the Court could promote accountability only to the extent that Member States accorded it the jurisdiction to do so. She added that the adoption of a convention on crimes against humanity would be one way to promote accountability for violations of some of the most

[1299] United States, Albania, France and Norway.

[1300] United States, Mexico, United Arab Emirates, Brazil, Norway and United Kingdom.

[1301] A concept note was circulated by a letter dated 24 May (S/2022/418/Rev.1).

[1302] See S/PV.9052 and S/PV.9052 (Resumption 1).

[1303] See S/PV.9052.

fundamental obligations found in international law and that the Court would be ready to decide any disputes over which it would have jurisdiction on the basis of such a convention.

Focusing her briefing on three key initiatives by her Office, the High Commissioner first underlined that the Human Rights Council had stepped up its response to serious human rights violations that might also amount to international crimes, including by creating mechanisms with mandates to establish the facts and circumstances of violations, by collecting, consolidating, preserving and analysing information and evidence, by identifying those responsible and by making recommendations towards establishing future accountability. Second, she stated that her Office was working with the Executive Office of the Secretary-General and the wider United Nations system to enhance the Organization's support for national transitional justice mechanisms, including truth commissions and reparations programmes. Third, she added that her Office had been strengthening its focus on gender sensitivity in all phases of justice and accountability processes. Addressing the issue of accountability, she asserted that the adoption of a convention on the prevention and punishment of crimes against humanity would fill a significant gap and would facilitate international cooperation in that area. She emphasized that Council support for efforts promoting independent and impartial investigations, justice and accountability was essential. Lastly, she underlined that placing victims at the centre of accountability strategies would contribute to the sustainability of accountability and justice efforts.

The professor of Public International Law at the University of Oxford stated that, in order to strengthen accountability and bring about justice for international crimes, progress needed to be made on two levels. He first underlined the importance of developing some of the rules that underpinned the prevention, investigation and punishment of such crimes. Although crimes against humanity were clearly prohibited under customary international law, there was no corresponding treaty that established obligations of prevention and punishment regarding that category of international crime; he urged States to begin negotiations to adopt such a treaty. Second, he emphasized the need to strengthen institutional mechanisms for delivering accountability for international crimes. He suggested that the Council had a special role to play in strengthening accountability, given its primary responsibility for maintaining international peace and security. Beyond issuing referrals to the International Criminal Court, the Council could, inter alia, promote cooperation by States and consider imposing targeted sanctions on individuals wanted by the Court. In the case of situations that had not been referred to the Court, he emphasized the need to ensure that credible investigations of international crimes were conducted in a way that provided future opportunities for prosecution at either the international or the domestic levels, including through the creation of United Nations investigative support mechanisms.

During the discussion, Council members and other participants reaffirmed the need to strengthen and further develop accountability mechanisms for the most serious violations of international law at the national, regional and international levels, including by urging States to take collective measures in the maintenance of international peace and security and by enhancing efforts by the Council to ensure accountability and justice for serious violations of international law in conflict situations under its consideration.[1304] Several speakers welcomed and highlighted the importance of the adoption of General Assembly resolution 76/262 of 26 April 2022, which provided for the convening of the General Assembly following the exercise of the right of veto in the Security Council.[1305] In that context, the representatives of France and Mexico made reference to their joint initiative on the suspension of the veto in situations of mass atrocities.[1306] Some speakers also underlined the important role of the International Court of Justice in issuing advisory opinions on legal questions referred to it by authorized United Nations organs and specialized agencies.[1307]

[1304] See S/PV.9052 and S/PV.9052 (Resumption 1).

[1305] See S/PV.9052 (Ireland, Kenya and Malaysia); and S/PV.9052 (Resumption 1) (Switzerland, Denmark (on behalf of the Nordic countries), Latvia, Bulgaria, European Union (also on behalf of Albania, Andorra, Bosnia and Herzegovina, Georgia, Montenegro, North Macedonia, the Republic of Moldova, San Marino and Ukraine), Estonia and Türkiye).

[1306] See S/PV.9052.

[1307] See S/PV.9052 (India, Mexico and Luxembourg); and S/PV.9052 (Resumption 1) (Philippines). For discussions concerning the relationship between the Council and the International Court of Justice, see part IV, sect. III.

On 22 August, at the initiative of China, which held the presidency for the month,[1308] the Council held a meeting under the sub-item entitled "Promote common security through dialogue and cooperation".[1309] Council members heard briefings by the Secretary-General and by the President of the tenth Review Conference of the Parties to the Treaty on the Non-Proliferation of Nuclear Weapons.

During his briefing, the Secretary-General informed the Council of his trip to Ukraine, Türkiye and the Republic of Moldova, where he had witnessed the Initiative on the Safe Transportation of Grain and Foodstuffs from Ukrainian Ports in action. The Initiative, together with the Memorandum of Understanding between the Russian Federation and the Secretariat of the United Nations on promoting Russian food products and fertilizers to world markets, formed a comprehensive plan that represented a concrete example of how dialogue and cooperation could deliver hope, even in the midst of conflict. He added that the same commitment to dialogue and results must be applied to the critical situation at the Zaporizhzhia nuclear power plant. He stressed the need to reforge a global consensus around the cooperation required to ensure collective security, including the work of the United Nations. He renewed his call upon all States parties to the Treaty on the Non-Proliferation of Nuclear Weapons to demonstrate flexibility and a willingness to compromise across all negotiations during the tenth Review Conference.

The President of the tenth Review Conference stated that, since its entry into force in 1970, the Treaty had proven to be a bulwark of international peace and security and a key facilitator of the benefits of nuclear energy and nuclear applications. Despite the challenges resulting from the geopolitical turmoil that had begun in February 2022, State parties had come together, resolved to strengthen the global regime that spanned the three pillars of the Treaty, namely, nuclear disarmament, non-proliferation and the peaceful uses of nuclear energy. He said that, for the States parties to be able to make progress and strengthen the implementation of all three pillars, they needed to reach agreement on several key areas, namely, action on nuclear disarmament, confidence-building and de-escalation; risk reduction and strengthened security assurances; and strengthening the non-proliferation regime against emerging challenges.

Following the briefings, Council members presented ideas on how the multilateral system should evolve to meet present and future challenges to international peace and security through dialogue and cooperation. In that regard, Council members discussed the tools at the Council's disposal to exercise its mandate. In the context of the final week of the Review Conference, most Council members emphasized the importance of nuclear non-proliferation. Some Council members[1310] also stressed the importance of comprehensive approaches that addressed the root causes of conflict. Collaboration with regional organizations in prevention of conflicts was also highlighted by several Council members.[1311]

On 26 October, the Council held a meeting with the participation of the Under-Secretary-General for Legal Affairs, the United Nations Legal Counsel, pursuant to a request for the Legal Counsel to give a briefing to the Council on Article 100 of the Charter, in connection with the work performed by the Secretary-General and the Secretariat with respect to Council resolution 2231 (2015).[1312] The Legal Counsel explained that the obligations of the Secretary-General and the staff of the Secretariat with regard to the conduct of their work and corresponding obligations on the part of Member States vis-à-vis the Secretariat were set out in Article 100. He added that paragraph 2 of the Article contained two corresponding obligations on the part of Member States, namely, to respect the exclusively international character of the responsibilities of the Secretary-General and the staff and not to seek to influence them in the discharge of their responsibilities. He recalled the note dated 16 January 2016,[1313] in which the President of the Security Council had set forth practical arrangements and procedures for the Council with regard to carrying out tasks relating to the implementation of resolution 2231 (2015) and in which the Secretary-General had been requested to appoint the Security Council Affairs Division of the Department of Political and Peacebuilding Affairs as a point of contact and to support the work of the Council and of its facilitator and, as envisaged in annex B to resolution 2231 (2015), to report to the

---

[1308] A concept note was circulated by a letter dated 12 August (S/2022/617).

[1309] See S/PV.9112.

[1310] Brazil and Ireland.

[1311] United Arab Emirates, Brazil, Gabon, Kenya and Norway. For more information on discussions regarding the pacific settlement of disputes and cooperation with regional and subregional organizations, see part VIII, sect. II.

[1312] See S/PV.9167.

[1313] S/2016/44.

Council every six months on the implementation of the resolution. The Legal Counsel further informed Council members that, since the first report prepared pursuant to the resolution,[1314] in which the Secretariat had reported on the implementation of the restrictive measures in annex B in force during the reporting period concerned, including on information voluntarily brought to its attention by Member States in writing and through meetings at United Nations Headquarters or in capitals, the Secretary-General had not received any request, pursuant to paragraph 6 (g) of the note by the President or otherwise, that supplemented or modified the nature and scope of the work done by the Division in the preparation of the his reports submitted to the Council every six months.[1315] Therefore, absent further guidance by the Council, the Secretary-General would continue to prepare those reports in the same manner in which they had been prepared to date.

Following the briefing, Council members discussed the interpretation and application of Article 100 of the Charter. The discussion was focused specifically on the mandate of the Secretariat and the Secretary-General in relation to the implementation of Council resolution 2231 (2015) concerning the Joint Comprehensive Plan of Action on the Iranian nuclear issue, in the context of the reported transfer from the Islamic Republic of Iran to the Russian Federation of unmanned aerial vehicles being used in the conflict in Ukraine. Representatives of the Islamic Republic of Iran and Ukraine also participated in the meeting and delivered statements.[1316] In the lead-up to the meeting, the representatives of France, Germany, the United Kingdom and the United States, in letters dated 21 October,[1317] had expressed concern with respect to the transfer of unmanned aerial vehicles from the Islamic Republic of Iran to the Russian Federation, in violation of resolution 2231 (2015) and had requested an investigation of the issue by the Secretariat team responsible for monitoring the implementation of the resolution. In response, also in a letter dated 21 October,[1318] the representative of the Russian Federation expressed concerns regarding attempts by certain Member States to give instructions to the Secretariat in violation of Article 100. In his view, the Secretariat had no authority to conduct an "investigation" with regard to claims of an alleged breach of resolution 2231 (2015) and requested the Secretariat to abstain from any engagement in any form in any "investigation" relating to the matter.

On 14 December, at the initiative of India which held the presidency for the month,[1319] the Council held a high-level open debate under the sub-item entitled "New orientation for reformed multilateralism",[1320] at which Council members heard briefings by the Secretary-General and the President of the General Assembly.[1321]

In his briefing, the Secretary-General informed the Council that his report entitled "Our Common Agenda"[1322] had led to the initiation of a process aimed at reinvigorating multilateralism to deal with current interconnected threats.[1323] Notwithstanding the important progress achieved since the inception of the United Nations in maintaining collective security, the international community was still grappling with many of the same challenges, notably, inter-State wars, limits to peacekeeping abilities, terrorism, a divided collective security system and evolving conflicts, fuelled by the negative implications of digital technologies and the climate crisis. The Secretary-General stated that his New Agenda for Peace would serve to address the full range of new and old local, national, regional and international security challenges and would help in examining ways to update existing tools for mediation, peacekeeping, peacebuilding and counter-terrorism. Through the New Agenda for Peace, the United Nations would articulate a vision for its work in peace and security; set out a comprehensive approach to prevention, linking peace, sustainable development, climate action and food security; consider how the United Nations adapted its peace and security instruments to an era of cyberthreats, information warfare and other forms of conflict; and look to Member States for new frameworks to reinforce multilateral solutions and manage intense geopolitical competition. Emphasizing that many Member States were aware that the

---

[1314] See S/2016/589.
[1315] See S/PV.9167.
[1316] For more information on the discussion, see part II, sect. V, and part VI, sect. II.
[1317] S/2022/781 and S/2022/782.
[1318] S/2022/783.
[1319] A concept note was circulated by a letter dated 25 November (S/2022/880).
[1320] See S/PV.9220 and S/PV.9220 (Resumption 1).
[1321] For discussions concerning the relationship between the Council and the General Assembly, see part IV, sect. I.
[1322] A/75/982.
[1323] See S/PV.9220.

Council should be reformed to reflect contemporary geopolitical realities, the Secretary-General expressed the hope that regional groups and Member States would work together to achieve greater consensus on the way forward and on the terms of the reform and noted that the Secretariat was ready to provide the necessary support. He also noted the calls of Member States for the revitalization of the work of the General Assembly and the strengthening of the Economic and Social Council in the framework of a reformed multilateralism. To that end, he stated that the Secretariat was also ready to provide support in connection with any decision by Member States to streamline the practices of the Assembly.

The President of the General Assembly underlined that the international rules, norms, instruments and institutions that had guided inter-State relations for over 75 years were facing deep and existential questions of relevance at a time when the world needed them most. Stating that global challenges such as the COVID-19 pandemic, the climate crisis, protracted debt and food and energy emergencies were far too great for any one nation to handle alone, he expressed the hope that the international community would find a multilateral solution, designed in line with the Charter and international law to address those issues. He added that, just as the actions taken in the United Nations had profound effects across the globe, so did inaction in the Assembly or the Council. He recalled that the 193 States Members of the Assembly had placed their trust in the 15 Council members and emphasized that each Council member was expected to act for the good of all and to uphold the Charter. He maintained that, although Council members had done so on countless occasions, there had also been examples of failed collective action, citing specifically the lack of consensus that had led to Council's inability to adopt any resolutions concerning the war in Ukraine to mitigate the exact type of crisis that the United Nations had been created to prevent. He underlined that the so-called veto initiative had opened an important door for a new form of collaboration and accountability between the two bodies. He added that Member States were participating in 15 negotiating processes on a range of issues, including the ongoing intergovernmental negotiations on Council reform, and noted that, despite having been a mandated duty of the Assembly for many years, the outcome was still less than what had been expected. Lastly, he urged the Council to prioritize dialogue and diplomacy and to trade political differences for genuine political will.

During the discussion, speakers focused on the need to strengthen the multilateral system and on the need for Council reform, in order to effectively address evolving threats to international peace and security.[1324] In that connection, many participants expressed support for Council reform, while highlighting the important role of the intergovernmental negotiations in the General Assembly on such reform. Participants also exchanged views on the Council's primary responsibility for the maintenance of international peace and security and on the impact of the use of the veto on the Council's ability to discharge its functions.[1325] Numerous participants addressed the question of limiting the use of the veto and enhancing accountability and transparency regarding its use.[1326] In that context, some Member States welcomed the adoption of General Assembly resolution 76/262.[1327] While many speakers welcomed the report of the Secretary-General entitled "Our Common Agenda", including his proposal for the New Agenda for Peace, the representatives of Brazil and Kenya expressed the view that the New Agenda for Peace had to include Security Council reform if it were to truly offer a new chapter for multilateralism.[1328] Some Council members also stressed the importance of strengthening partnerships between the Council and regional organizations and of leveraging the key role of regional organizations in preventing conflict and addressing crises.[1329]

In 2022, the Council adopted one resolution in connection with the item. On 29 September, the Council unanimously adopted resolution 2652 (2022), in which it welcomed the report of the Secretary-General (S/2022/655), including his observations on the plight of migrants and refugees in Libya, and

---

[1324] See S/PV.9220 and S/PV.9220 (Resumption 1).

[1325] For more information on this aspect of the discussion, see part V, sect. I.

[1326] For more information on this aspect of the discussion, see part II, sect. VIII.

[1327] See S/PV.9220 (Ireland, Japan and Poland); and S/PV.9220 (Resumption 1) (Switzerland, Singapore, Estonia, Bulgaria, Malta, Liechtenstein, Lebanon and Romania).

[1328] See S/PV.9220.

[1329] See S/PV.9220 (China and Albania); and S/PV.9220 (Resumption 1) (Philippines, Egypt, South Africa, European Union (also on behalf of Albania, Bosnia and Herzegovina, Montenegro and the Republic of Moldova), Indonesia, Spain, Thailand, Chile, Viet Nam (on behalf of the Association of Southeast Asian Nations), Kazakhstan and Portugal). For more information on discussions regarding cooperation with regional and subregional organizations, see part VIII, sect. I.

condemned all acts of migrant smuggling and human trafficking into, through and from Libyan territory and off the coast of Libya.[1330] Acting under Chapter VII of the Charter, the Council renewed the authorizations regarding acts of migrant smuggling and human trafficking in the territorial sea of Libya, as set out in paragraphs 7 to 10 of resolution 2240 (2015), for a further 12-month period. The Council also renewed the reporting requests set out in paragraph 17 of its resolution 2240 (2015) and requested the Secretary-General to report to the Council 11 months after the adoption of resolution 2652 (2022) on its implementation, in particular with regard to the implementation of paragraphs 7 to 10 of its resolution 2240 (2015).[1331]

Meetings: maintenance of international peace and security, 2022

Meeting record and date	*Sub-item*	*Other documents*	*Rule 37 invitations*	*Rule 39 and other invitations*	*Speakers*	*Decision and vote (for-against-abstaining)*
S/PV.9014 11 April	Implementation of resolutions 2532 (2020) and 2565 (2021)			Global Lead Coordinator for COVID-19 Vaccine Country Readiness and Delivery, Senior Adviser to the Office of the Director-General of the International Committee of the Red Cross, Health and Nutrition Coordinator at CARE South Sudan	All Council members,[a] all invitees[b]	
S/PV.9036 and S/PV.9036 (Resumption 1) 19 May	Conflict and food security Letter dated 12 May 2022 from the Permanent Representative of the United States of America to the United Nations addressed to the Secretary-General (S/2022/391)		56 Member States[c]	Director General of the Food and Agriculture Organization of the United Nations, Executive Director of the World Food Programme, Head of the Delegation of the European Union to the United Nations, representative of the Observer Mission of the Holy See to the United Nations, founder and Chief Executive Officer of Gro Intelligence	Secretary-General, all Council members,[d] all invitees[e]	

[1330] Resolution 2652 (2022), third preambular paragraph and para. 1.
[1331] Ibid., paras. 2 and 3.

Meeting record and date	*Sub-item*	*Other documents*	*Rule 37 invitations*	*Rule 39 and other invitations*	*Speakers*	*Decision and vote (for-against-abstaining)*
S/PV.9039 23 May	Technology and security			Under-Secretary-General for Political and Peacebuilding Affairs, Director of Advox – the digital rights project of Global Voices, adjunct professor at the McGill University Centre for International Peace and Security Studies and non-resident Fellow at the International Peace Institute	All Council members, all invitees	
S/PV.9052 and S/PV.9052 (Resumption 1) 2 June	Strengthening accountability and justice for serious violations of international law Letter dated 24 May 2022 from the Permanent Representative of Albania to the United Nations addressed to the Secretary-General (S/2022/418/Rev.1)		48 Member States[f]	President of the International Court of Justice, United Nations High Commissioner for Human Rights, professor of Public International Law at the University of Oxford, Chargé d'affaires a.i. of the Delegation of the European Union, Permanent Observer of the State of Palestine to the United Nations	All Council members,[g] all invitees[h]	
S/PV.9112 22 August	Promote common security through dialogue and cooperation Letter dated 12 August 2022 from the Permanent Representative of China to the United Nations addressed to the Secretary-General (S/2022/617)			President of the tenth Review Conference of the Parties to the Treaty on the Non-Proliferation of Nuclear Weapons	Secretary-General, all Council members, invitee	

Meeting record and date	*Sub-item*	*Other documents*	*Rule 37 invitations*	*Rule 39 and other invitations*	*Speakers*	*Decision and vote (for-against-abstaining)*
S/PV.9140 29 September	Report of the Secretary-General on the implementation of Security Council resolution 2598 (2021) (S/2022/655)	Draft resolution submitted by 29 Member States[i] (S/2022/718)	25 Member States[j]			Resolution 2652 (2022) 15-0-0 (adopted under Chapter VII)
S/PV.9167 26 October			Iran (Islamic Republic of), Ukraine	Under-Secretary-General for Legal Affairs, the United Nations Legal Counsel	All Council members, all invitees	
S/PV.9220 and S/PV.9220 (Resumption 1) 14 December	New orientation for reformed multilateralism Letter dated 25 November 2022 from the Permanent Representative of India to the United Nations addressed to the President of the Security Council (S/2022/880)		48 Member States[k]	President of the General Assembly, Head of the Delegation of the European Union	Secretary-General, all Council members,[l] 47 invitees under rule 37,[m] all other invitees[n]	

[a] The United Arab Emirates was represented by its Minister of State for Advanced Technology; the United Kingdom (President of the Council) was represented by its Minister of State for South and Central Asia, North Africa, the United Nations and the Commonwealth, and the Prime Minister's Special Representative for Preventing Sexual Violence in Conflict; and the United States was represented by its Permanent Representative to the United Nations and member of the President's Cabinet.

[b] All invitees participated in the meeting by videoconference.

[c] Algeria, Australia, Bangladesh, Belarus, Belgium, Bulgaria, Canada, Chile, Croatia, Cyprus, Dominican Republic, Ecuador, Egypt, Ethiopia, Fiji, Germany, Greece, Guatemala, Hungary, Indonesia, Iran (Islamic Republic of), Italy, Japan, Jordan, Liechtenstein, Lithuania, Luxembourg, Malta, Maldives, Mauritius, Morocco, Myanmar, Namibia, Nepal, Netherlands, New Zealand, Niger, Pakistan, Panama, Peru, Poland, Portugal, Qatar, Republic of Korea, Romania, Slovenia, Spain, South Africa, Sweden, Switzerland, Thailand, Türkiye, Ukraine, Uruguay, Venezuela (Bolivarian Republic of) and Viet Nam.

[d] Albania was represented by its Minister for Europe and Foreign Affairs; Gabon was represented by its Minister for Foreign Affairs; Ghana was represented by its Minister for Foreign Affairs and Regional Integration; India was represented by its Minister of State for External Affairs; Ireland was represented by its Minister of State for Overseas Development Aid and Diaspora; Kenya was represented by its Cabinet Secretary for Foreign Affairs; Mexico was represented by its Minister of Agriculture and Rural Development; Norway was represented by its Minister of International Development; the United Arab Emirates was represented by its Permanent Representative to the United Nations and Assistant Minister for Foreign Affairs and International Cooperation for Political Affairs; and the United States (President of the Council) was represented by its Secretary of State.

[e] Bangladesh and Japan were represented by their respective State Ministers for Foreign Affairs; Canada, Guatemala, Pakistan and Romania were represented by their respective Ministers for Foreign Affairs; Croatia was represented by its State Secretary for Political Affairs; Hungary was presented by its Minister for Foreign Affairs and Trade; Lithuania, Panama and Uruguay were represented by their respective Deputy Ministers for Foreign Affairs; Luxembourg was represented by its Minister for Foreign and European Affairs; and Sweden was represented by its State Secretary for International Development Cooperation. The representative of the Dominican Republic spoke also on behalf of the Group of Friends of Action on Conflict and Hunger; the representative of Fiji spoke also on behalf of the members of the Pacific Islands Forum; the representative of Lithuania spoke on behalf of the Baltic countries; and the representative of Sweden spoke on behalf of the Nordic countries.

[f] Argentina, Armenia, Australia, Austria, Azerbaijan, Belgium, Bulgaria, Canada, Chile, Colombia, Croatia, Cyprus, Czechia, Denmark, Ecuador, Estonia, Georgia, Germany, Guatemala, Iran (Islamic Republic of), Italy, Japan, Jordan, Latvia, Liechtenstein, Lithuania, Luxembourg, Malaysia, Malta, Marshall Islands, Morocco, Myanmar, Netherlands, North Macedonia, Pakistan, Philippines, Poland, Republic of Korea, Romania, Sierra Leone, Slovakia, Slovenia, South Africa, Spain, Switzerland, Türkiye, Ukraine and Venezuela (Bolivarian Republic of).

[g] Albania (President of the Council) was represented by its Prime Minister. India was represented by its Minister of State for External Affairs; Ireland was represented by its Attorney-General; the United Arab Emirates was represented by its Permanent Representative and Assistant Minister for Foreign Affairs and International Cooperation for Political Affairs; and the United States was represented by its Under Secretary of State for Civilian Security, Democracy and Human Rights.

[h] The President of the Court and the High Commissioner participated in the meeting by videoconference. The representative of Austria spoke on behalf of Group of Friends of the Rule of Law; the representative of Denmark spoke on behalf of the Nordic countries; the representative of the Marshall Islands spoke on behalf of the Group of Friends of Accountability following the Aggression against Ukraine; and the representative of the European Union spoke also on behalf of Albania, Andorra, Bosnia and Herzegovina, Georgia, Montenegro, North Macedonia, the Republic of Moldova, San Marino and Ukraine.

[i] Albania, Austria, Belgium, Bulgaria, Croatia, Cyprus, Czechia, Denmark, Estonia, Finland, France, Germany, Greece, Hungary, Ireland, Italy, Latvia, Lithuania, Luxembourg, Malta, Netherlands, Norway, Poland, Portugal, Romania, Slovakia, Slovenia, Spain and Sweden.

[j] Austria, Belgium, Bulgaria, Croatia, Cyprus, Czechia, Denmark, Estonia, Finland, Germany, Greece, Hungary, Italy, Latvia, Lithuania, Luxembourg, Malta, Netherlands, Poland, Portugal, Romania, Slovakia, Slovenia, Spain and Sweden.

[k] Algeria, Argentina, Armenia, Australia, Austria, Azerbaijan, Bangladesh, Bulgaria, Chile, Cuba, Ecuador, Egypt, Estonia, Ethiopia, Georgia, Germany, Guatemala, Indonesia, Iran (Islamic Republic of), Italy, Japan, Kazakhstan, Kuwait, Latvia, Lebanon, Liechtenstein, Lithuania, Malta, Morocco, Nepal, Nigeria, Pakistan, Philippines, Poland, Portugal, Qatar, Republic of Korea, Romania, Saint Vincent and the Grenadines, Singapore, Slovenia, South Africa, Spain, Switzerland, Thailand, Türkiye, Ukraine and Viet Nam.

[l] Ghana was represented by its Permanent Secretary of the Ministry of Foreign Affairs and Regional Integration; India (President of the Council) was represented by its Minister for External Affairs; the United Arab Emirates was represented by its Minister of Culture and Youth and member of Cabinet; and the United States was represented by its Permanent Representative and member of the President's Cabinet.

[m] Armenia, Japan and Pakistan were represented by their respective Ministers for Foreign Affairs; Azerbaijan and Poland were represented by their respective Deputy Ministers for Foreign Affairs; and Kuwait was represented by its Assistant Foreign Minister for International Organizations. The representative of Saint Lucia spoke in place of a representative of Saint Vincent and the Grenadines on behalf of a group of like-minded countries; and the representative of Viet Nam spoke on behalf of the Association of Southeast Asian Nations.

[n] The representative of the European Union spoke also on behalf of Albania, Bosnia and Herzegovina, Montenegro and the Republic of Moldova.

36. Cooperation between the United Nations and regional and subregional organizations in maintaining international peace and security

During the period under review, the Security Council held four meetings and adopted one presidential statement under the item entitled "Cooperation between the United Nations and regional and subregional organizations in maintaining international peace and security". Two of the meetings took the form of briefings and two took the form of debates.[1332] More information on the meetings, including on participants, speakers and outcomes, is provided in the table below.[1333]

In 2022, the Council continued to hold its annual meetings on cooperation with the African Union and European Union, while also meeting to discuss relations with the Collective Security Treaty Organization (CSTO) and the League of Arab States. The Council also adopted a presidential statement, in which it addressed its cooperation with the League. The four meetings featured briefings by the Secretary-General of the United Nations, the Secretary-General of CSTO, the Secretary-General of the League of Arab States, the High Representative of the European Union for Foreign Affairs and Security Policy and the Chairperson of the African Union Commission.[1334] At the meeting on cooperation between the United Nations and the League of Arab States, the Council also heard a briefing by a civil society representative on peace and security challenges in the Arab region.[1335]

[1332] For more information on the format of meetings, see part II.

[1333] See also A/77/2, part II, chap. 36.

[1334] See S/PV.8967, S/PV.9001, S/PV.9065 and S/PV.9149.

[1335] See S/PV.9001.

Addressing the Council in the context of a debate held on 16 February on cooperation between the United Nations and CSTO,[1336] the Secretary-General of the United Nations stated that the two organizations were continuously strengthening their ties and deepening their responses to regional challenges in Central Asia since the signing of the Joint Declaration on United Nations-CSTO Secretariat Cooperation in 2010. He reflected on three priorities for strengthening their relations across the peace and security spectrums that had been identified at the tenth anniversary of the Joint Declaration. First, on conflict prevention, counter-terrorism and counter-narcotics, he stated that the good working relations between CSTO and the United Nations Regional Centre for Preventive Diplomacy for Central Asia enabled constructive early warning exchanges and regular contact during security-related events in the region. Second, with regard to peacekeeping, the Secretary-General expressed the view that further cooperation would help to advance the Action for Peacekeeping initiative and its implementation strategy, Action for Peacekeeping Plus, and noted that he looked forward to receiving more pledges from CSTO members to the Peacekeeping Capability Readiness System of the United Nations. Third, the Secretary-General opined that close coordination with CSTO was critical in helping to defuse evolving threats from terrorism and illicit drugs and arms flows stemming from the situation in Afghanistan, preventing spillover, promoting stability and saving lives. Recalling that one of the main goals set out in his report entitled "Our Common Agenda"[1337] was to build, by encouraging partnerships, a more inclusive and effective multilateralism that operated like a network, he stated his intention to continue to hold annual meetings with all leaders of regional organizations.[1338]

The Secretary-General of CSTO observed that, in the year of the thirtieth anniversary of the signing of the Treaty on Collective Security within the framework of the Commonwealth of Independent States and the twentieth anniversary of the establishment of his organization, CSTO had become an effective international body that protected its member States from existing threats on a collective basis. He underlined that the United Nations was the main international partner of CSTO and expressed interest in further developing relations in all areas, on the basis of the Joint Declaration, including counter-terrorism and peacekeeping. The Secretary-General noted that CSTO had developed practices to deprive international terrorist organizations of their "breeding grounds" by cutting off channels of recruitment and financing and combating the spread of terrorist ideology and propaganda. Under the auspices of the United Nations, the organization aimed to develop universal rules, norms and principles for proper conduct in the information sphere. He expressed his organization's readiness to share its experience in conducting rapid response prevention operations to combat international terrorism and extremism and encouraged international and regional organizations and individual States to participate in its activities. He recalled that, in December 2021, the United Nations and CSTO had established a joint working group on peacekeeping and that CSTO had received beneficial assistance in conducting certification procedures for various programmes and methodology for the training of its peacekeepers. CSTO was also reviewing the possibility of having its peacekeepers join United Nations peacekeeping operations. The Secretary-General reaffirmed his organization's commitment to developing friendly and mutually acceptable relations with third countries and international organizations with a view to maintaining peace and stability on the basis of the principles of international law, the rejection of confrontation and an embrace of lasting solutions through political and diplomatic means, in line with the provisions and aims of the Charter of the United Nations.

In the subsequent discussion, Council members and participating Member States exchanged views on the challenges facing the Central Asian region, ways of strengthening cooperation between the United Nations and CSTO and the principles that should underlie such cooperation.[1339] They further reflected on the deployment of the CSTO peacekeeping forces following the civil unrest in Kazakhstan in January 2022 and the security threats emanating from the conflict in Afghanistan. Many speakers opined that the United Nations and CSTO could further develop their joint work on conflict prevention, early warning, peacekeeping, peacebuilding, counter-terrorism and countering the trafficking in persons, arms and

[1336] See S/PV.8967.

[1337] A/75/982.

[1338] See S/PV.8967.

[1339] For more information on the discussion in this meeting on the principles of cooperation between the United Nations and regional and subregional organizations under Chapter VIII of the Charter, see part VIII, sect. I.B.

narcotics. In terms of concrete proposals, several speakers[1340] called for increased engagement, consultation and information-sharing between the two organizations. The representative of Ghana opined that regular consultations could help to bridge conceptual differences in the understanding of the security challenges of the Eurasian region and improve harmonized responses. He added that the wealth of experience of the United Nations in preventive diplomacy should be enhanced in its engagement with CSTO, in particular through the United Nations Regional Centre for Preventive Diplomacy. The representative of Kenya recommended that the two organizations undertake joint horizon-scanning and analysis to inform strategic actions that drew support from Member States in the region. The representative of the Russian Federation expressed the shared desire of CSTO member States to resolve emerging problems through political and diplomatic means under international law.

At the meeting on cooperation between the United Nations and the League of Arab States held on 23 March,[1341] the Secretary-General of the United Nations stated that strengthening cooperation with regional organizations was a sine qua non for strengthening multilateralism globally. He observed that the League was critical across the spectrum of the work of the United Nations and that the two organizations remained united in their pursuit of multilateral answers to the cascading challenges that the Arab world and the world beyond were facing. Those efforts had an added urgency in the face of the profound global ramifications of the war in Ukraine, which were affecting the poorest the hardest and planting the seeds for political instability and unrest across the globe. The Secretary-General highlighted the joint engagement of the United Nations and the League of Arab States to address the situations in Iraq, Lebanon, Libya, the Sudan, the Syrian Arab Republic and Yemen and between Israel and the State of Palestine. He noted that ever-closer cooperation was vital to achieving all the goals relating those situations and that the United Nations looked forward to strengthening those ties, including through its liaison office to the League. He further noted that the two organizations were expanding their cooperation on youth and peace and security, women and peace and security, and disarmament, mediation and peacebuilding.

In his briefing, the Secretary-General of the League of Arab States stated that the international order was perhaps at its most critical juncture since the end of the cold war and that the escalation of conflict between global Powers was bringing several security, political and economic risks. He expressed the hope that that situation would not have a negative impact on the Council's attention to other issues and crises worldwide, in particular in the Arab region. In that regard, he noted that the region continued to suffer from the significant shock of 2011 and that internal conflicts continued in the Syrian Arab Republic, Libya and Yemen. Furthermore, noting that developments in the international arena had led many in the Arab region to consider the suffering of the Palestinian people differently, he reminded the Council that it had endorsed the principle of land for peace and the two-State solution as a basis for resolving that historic conflict. He called on all international powers to shoulder their responsibilities, as set forth in the Charter of the United Nations, to address all issues and crises alike, in full respect for international law and the purposes and principles of the Charter. The Secretary-General also referred to what he described as Iranian intervention in the internal affairs of Arab States, stressing the need for an agreement to establish a zone free from nuclear and other weapons of mass destruction in the Middle East and for good and neighbourly relations with the Islamic Republic of Iran, on the basis of respect for sovereignty and non-interference. Regarding overall cooperation with the United Nations and the Council, the Secretary-General welcomed the convening of the ministerial-level meeting with the Arab Summit Troika on the margins of the high-level segment of the seventy-sixth session of the General Assembly in September 2021, in accordance with the statement by the President adopted by the Council on 29 January 2021.[1342] He also called for the implementation of other provisions of the presidential statement, such as conducting field visits and working to increase the participation of women and young people in international peace and security efforts, and reiterated the League's commitment to its strategic partnership with the Council in order to achieve their common goals.[1343]

The civil society representative, noting that she spoke on behalf of Arab youth, who represented 60 per cent of the population in the Arab region, presented several recommendations to the Council.

[1340] Ghana, Kenya, Mexico and United Arab Emirates.

[1341] See S/PV.9001.

[1342] See S/PRST/2021/2.

[1343] See S/PV.9001.

Specifically, she stressed the need to ensure the participation of young people at all levels of the United Nations, including in all three pillars of the work of the Organization, and in the formulation and implementation of national and regional policies. She noted that youth participation could never be complete without the participation of women in all efforts. She also pointed to the need to address the main Arab challenges that were before the Council so that financial and human resources could be directed towards the development and implementation of the 2030 Agenda for Sustainable Development. In that regard, the roles of the Council and the League of Arab States were pivotal.

Following the briefings, Council members and the representative of Yemen, speaking on behalf of the Group of Arab States, exchanged views on how to strengthen the cooperation between the United Nations and the League of Arab States with a view to addressing the conflicts in the Arab region, as well as cross-cutting issues such as counter-terrorism, climate and security, women and peace and security, youth and peace and security, and children and armed conflict.[1344] Speakers called for institutionalizing the relationship through regular consultations and information exchange. Multiple delegations also underlined the importance of further strengthening the trilateral cooperation between the United Nations, the League and the African Union.

At the conclusion of the meeting, the Council adopted a statement by the President, in which it reiterated its intention to consider further steps to promote closer cooperation and strategic coordination between the United Nations and the League of Arab States in the fields of conflict early warning and prevention, peacekeeping, peacebuilding, sustaining peace, promoting respect for international law and the Charter of the United Nations, addressing root causes of conflicts and enhancing safety and security at sea, preventing and countering terrorism and violent extremism and building resilience to resist incitement.[1345] The Council also recognized the importance of cooperation in sustainable development, comprehensive risk assessments and risk management strategies, including poverty eradication, food security and water management, disaster risk reduction, and desertification and drought management in the Arab region.[1346] The Council reaffirmed the important and positive contribution of youth to the efforts for the maintenance and promotion of peace and security and stressed the importance of creating policies for young people that would positively contribute to peacebuilding efforts in the Arab region.[1347] The Council expressed its intention to consider holding further joint consultative meetings with the Council of the League and requested the Secretary-General of the United Nations to provide a brief report on the implementation of the presidential statement and on further ways of strengthening institutional relations and cooperation between the two organizations.[1348]

At the annual briefing on cooperation with the European Union, held on 16 June,[1349] the High Representative of the Union for Foreign Affairs and Security Policy noted that the multilateral system was under pressure as never before, especially as there was a strong demand for an approach to global problems based on multilateralism, but an insufficient supply, given the scale of cooperation needed to manage the global commons. Stating that the war against Ukraine by the Russian Federation was an attack on the foundations of the United Nations and the Council by one of its permanent members, he urged all Council members to help to end the war, restore the sovereignty of Ukraine and ensure that the global fallout was contained, especially with regard to the increasing food crisis affecting millions of people around the world. The European Union fully supported the efforts of the United Nations in ensuring that Ukraine could resume its deliveries of grain to the world and in dealing with the global consequences of the war.

Beyond the war in Ukraine, the High Representative noted that the United Nations and the European Union worked closely together at the headquarters and field levels in a number of areas, starting with crisis management operations such as the European Union military operation in the Mediterranean in support of the implementation of the Council's arms embargo on Libya; the European Union military operation to contribute to the deterrence, prevention and repression of acts of piracy and armed robbery off the coast of

[1344] For more information on the discussion within the framework of Chapter VIII of the Charter, see part VIII, sect. I.B.

[1345] S/PRST/2022/1, seventh paragraph.

[1346] Ibid., eighth paragraph.

[1347] Ibid., sixth paragraph.

[1348] Ibid., ninth and twenty-first paragraphs.

[1349] See S/PV.9065.

Somalia; and the European Union military operation in Bosnia and Herzegovina. He noted that the European Union made large contributions to the work of the United Nations on mediation, peacebuilding and transitions and underlined the strategic nature of cooperation on peace and security between the European Union and the African Union. Lastly, the High Representative commented on the efforts of the European Union, together with the United Nations, to address the crises in the Syrian Arab Republic, the Sahel and Afghanistan and with respect to the nuclear programme of the Islamic Republic of Iran.

In the subsequent discussion, Council members widely recognized the contribution of the European Union to international peace and security and multilateralism, including in cooperation with the United Nations. In particular, they noted and called for strengthened cooperation in conflict prevention, crisis management and humanitarian assistance, peacekeeping, counter-terrorism, development, human rights and climate and security, as well as in the implementation of the women and peace and security and children and armed conflict agendas. Most Council members expressed grave concern regarding the war in Ukraine and its geopolitical and humanitarian impact in Europe and beyond. Council members [1350] recognized the role of the European Union in efforts to alleviate the consequences of the conflict, in particular with regard to ensuring global food security. The representative of the United States stated that the European Union had clearly demonstrated its support for the values enshrined in the Charter of the United Nations, through its actions to uphold the principles of sovereignty and territorial integrity after the war launched by the Russian Federation on Ukraine. The representative of Norway underlined the need for a strong European Union, working together with the United Nations and the Council, to contribute to advancing the causes of peace and prosperity. The representatives of China and Ghana further encouraged the European Union to play a mediation role to end the conflict.

The representative of the Russian Federation took a different view regarding the role of the European Union in relation to the war in Ukraine, maintaining that the organization was circumventing the Council by imposing illegitimate unilateral sanctions. He added that a collective Western policy on sanctions had helped to provoke the food and energy crisis. The representative of Brazil urged the European Union to consider in advance the possible consequences of unilateral sanctions. In contrast, several Council members[1351] asserted that the sanctions imposed by the European Union did not affect the provision of humanitarian aid or the ability of the Russian Federation to export agricultural products and that the negative impact on global food security was the result of the actions of the Russian Federation. The representative of France stated that the one objective of the sanctions measures was to bring the Russian Federation back into compliance with the Charter.

More generally, the representative of China stated that the European Union should take the lead in upholding the purposes and principles of the Charter of the United Nations, by complying with international law and the universally recognized fundamental norms of international relations, earnestly respecting the sovereignty and political independence of all countries and committing to the principle of non-interference. The European Union was expected to play an active and constructive role in international affairs by rejecting any revival of the idea of confrontation between camps or blocs and by encouraging all countries to strengthen unity and to achieve shared progress under the banner of multilateralism. With respect to peacekeeping, the representative of Brazil stated that European Union missions should always be aligned with the mandates established by the Council and act in accordance with the principles enshrined in the Charter.

At the debate held on 11 October,[1352] the Secretary-General presented his annual report on strengthening the partnership between the United Nations and the African Union, including the work of the United Nations Office to the African Union.[1353] In his briefing, he noted that, in the year of the twentieth anniversary of the creation of the African Union, cooperation between the two organizations had never been stronger, although challenges remained.[1354] Observing that the use of force was too often seen as the only method of resolving disputes, he noted the rise of unconstitutional changes of

[1350] United States, Ghana, Ireland, India, United Arab Emirates and United Kingdom.

[1351] France, Ireland and United Kingdom.

[1352] See S/PV.9149.

[1353] S/2022/643.

[1354] See S/PV.9149.

government, efforts by Da'esh and its Al-Qaida affiliates to extend its reach in the Sahel, protracted conflicts in the Horn of Africa, Ethiopia, the eastern part of the Democratic Republic of the Congo, Mali, the Sudan and Libya, violence against women and the use of misinformation and hate speech as weapons of war. In order to address those challenges, the Secretary-General stressed the need for States to develop the capacity to detect and pre-empt conflicts at the earliest signs and to address the governance deficit, and for the Council to ensure predictable funding for African Union operations that had it authorized. He stated that climate change was a matter of survival for countries in Africa and urged leaders, especially those of the Group of 20 (G20) countries, which were responsible for 80 per cent of greenhouse gas emissions, to finally take the urgent action needed. He recalled his appeal for a Sustainable Development Goals stimulus, led by the G20, to massively boost development assistance, stressing the need for international financial institutions and multilateral banks to remove the barriers that prevented developing countries from accessing the financing they needed, and called for an effective global debt relief mechanism. Lastly, the Secretary-General called upon all leaders – within the Council, on the African continent and beyond – to spare no effort in supporting the African Union in achieving its goals for an integrated, peaceful and prosperous continent.

In his statement, the Chairperson of the African Union Commission indicated that the main issue that the African Union and United Nations faced in their cooperation no longer had to do with normative mechanisms but with the need to consider the profound transformations that had occurred throughout African development and the conservatism that had governed the doctrine in force at the United Nations since the Second World War. Given that Africa was home to 1.4 billion people, that 70 per cent of United Nations peacekeeping missions were in Africa and that African issues were at the forefront of debates conducted at the Organization, the Chairperson questioned why it was the only true continent excluded from the benefits of permanent membership in the Council. He called for a specific time frame to discuss and decide on the role of Africa in that forum for world peace. He emphasized the need to ensure the primacy of establishing and safeguarding peace in the mandates of African missions; to secure funds and financial structures for preventing and combating pandemics; to ensure that investment on climate issues was no longer a small portion of the financing allotted to Africa; and to ensure that the unlimited universe of science and new technologies was generously opened to Africa. According to the Chairperson, if the Council chose that path, it would find the entire continent mobilized around it; if not, its credibility could suffer irreversibly. Commending the achievements in cooperation between the two organizations, he called for deepening partnerships between their specialized agencies and special envoys and, especially, between the Security Council of the United Nations and the Peace and Security Council of the African Union.

In their statements, Security Council members and participating non-members of the Council underscored the importance of cooperation between the United Nations and regional and subregional organizations under Chapter VIII of the Charter of the United Nations and discussed progress made in and challenges to relations between the Organization and the African Union since the signing, in 2017, of the Joint United Nations-African Union Framework for Enhanced Partnership in Peace and Security. In that regard, several speakers[1355] underlined the importance of the principles of subsidiarity, complementarity and the use of comparative advantages in their cooperation. In particular, speakers noted their joint efforts to prevent and address conflict, especially through mediation, in the Central African Republic, Libya, Somalia, the Sudan and the Sahel region, as well as the important role of the African Union in the resolution of the conflict in Ethiopia. Highlighting existing cooperation between the two organizations on conflict prevention, early warning, mediation, disarmament, counter-terrorism, countering maritime piracy and security sector reform, participants called for strengthened joint action on peacebuilding, on addressing the root causes of conflict, on matters relating to climate and security, on countering misinformation and on countering the proliferation of small arms, among other areas.[1356]

[1355] Gabon, India, Egypt and South Africa.

[1356] For more information on the discussion within the framework of Chapter VIII of the Charter, see part VIII, sect. I.B.

Meetings: cooperation between the United Nations and regional and subregional organizations in maintaining international peace and security, 2022

Meeting record and date	*Sub-item*	*Other documents*	*Rule 37 invitations*	*Rule 39 and other invitations*	*Speakers*	*Decision and vote (for-against-abstaining)*
S/PV.8967 16 February	Collective Security Treaty Organization (CSTO)		Armenia, Belarus, Kazakhstan, Kyrgyzstan, Tajikistan	Secretary-General of CSTO	Secretary-General, all Council members,[a] all invitees[b]	
S/PV.9001 23 March	League of Arab States Letter dated 17 March 2022 from the Permanent Representative of the United Arab Emirates to the United Nations addressed to the Secretary-General (S/2022/240)		Yemen	Secretary-General of the League of Arab States, civil society representative	Secretary-General, all Council members,[c] all invitees[d]	S/PRST/2022/1
S/PV.9065 16 June	European Union			High Representative of the European Union for Foreign Affairs and Security Policy	All Council members,[e] invitee[f]	
S/PV.9149 11 October	African Union Report of the Secretary-General on strengthening the partnership between the United Nations and the African Union on issues of peace and security in Africa, including the work of the United Nations Office to the African Union (S/2022/643)		Seven Member States[g]	Chairperson of the African Union Commission	Secretary-General, all Council members,[h] all invitees[i]	

Meeting record and date	*Sub-item*	*Other documents*	*Rule 37 invitations*	*Rule 39 and other invitations*	*Speakers*	*Decision and vote (for-against-abstaining)*
	Letter dated 3 October 2022 from the Permanent Representative of Gabon to the United Nations addressed to the Secretary-General (S/2022/736)					

[a] The Russian Federation (President of the Council) was represented by its Deputy Minister for Foreign Affairs.
[b] The Secretary-General of CSTO participated in the meeting by videoconference.
[c] India was represented by its Foreign Secretary; and the United Arab Emirates (President of the Council) was represented by its Minister of State in the Ministry of Foreign Affairs and International Cooperation.
[d] The representative of Yemen spoke on behalf of the Group of Arab States.
[e] Albania (President of the Council) was represented by its Minister for Europe and Foreign Affairs.
[f] The High Representative of the European Union participated in the meeting by videoconference.
[g] Egypt, Germany, Japan, Morocco, Namibia, Senegal and South Africa.
[h] Gabon (President of the Council) was represented by its Minister for Foreign Affairs; the United Arab Emirates was represented by its Permanent Representative to the United Nations and Assistant Minister for Foreign Affairs and International Cooperation for Political Affairs; and the United States was represented by its Permanent Representative to the United Nations and member of the President's Cabinet.
[i] The Chairperson of the Commission participated in the meeting by videoconference.

Part II
Provisional rules of procedure and related procedural developments

Contents

Introductory note

Part II of the present Supplement covers the practice of the Security Council in relation to its provisional rules of procedure and relevant Articles of the Charter of the United Nations. Since the provisional rules of procedure are routinely applied by the Council at its formal meetings, the focus of part II is on special applications of the rules in the proceedings of the Council, rather than on the standard applications of the rules.

Part II is divided into 10 sections, in the order of the relevant chapters of the provisional rules of procedure, as follows: section I, meetings and records (Article 28 of the Charter and rules 1–5 and 48–57); section II, agenda (rules 6–12); section III, representation and credentials (rules 13–17); section IV, presidency (rules 18–20); section V, Secretariat (rules 21–26); section VI, conduct of business (rules 27, 29, 30 and 33); section VII, participation (Articles 31 and 32 and rules 37 and 39); section VIII, decision-making and voting (Article 27 and rules 31, 32, 34–36, 38 and 40); section IX, languages (rules 41–47); and section X, status of the provisional rules of procedure (Article 30).

The remaining rules are covered in other parts of the present Supplement, as follows: rule 28, concerning subsidiary organs of the Council, in parts IX and X, and concerning Security Council missions, in part VI; and rule 61, concerning relations with other United Nations organs, in part IV.

During the period under review, there were no instances of the application of rules 58 to 60 concerning the admission of new Members, and the present Supplement therefore contains no material relating to those rules.

* * *

During the period under review, the Council held 292 meetings, of which 276 were public (open) and 16 were private (closed). The members of the Council held 127 informal consultations of the whole in 2022. Council members continued to hold informal interactive dialogues and Arria-formula meetings. Council members also continued the practice of holding informal "wrap-up" sessions at the end of the month.

In 2022, the Council was seized of 68 items. The Council added two new items to the list of matters of which it was seized, namely, "Maintenance of peace and security of Ukraine" and "Letter dated 13 September 2022 from the Permanent Representative of Armenia to the United Nations addressed to the President of the Security Council (S/2022/688)". Although it was seized of 68 items, the Council considered only 47, of which 26 concerned country-specific and regional situations and 21 dealt with thematic and other issues.[1]

During the period under review, the Council adopted 54 resolutions and 7 statements by the President. The Council also issued 19 notes by and 27 letters from the President. Three draft resolutions were not adopted owing to the lack of the required nine affirmative votes, and four draft resolutions were not adopted because of the negative vote of one or more permanent members. In 2022, objections to the adoption of the agenda and to the extension of invitations pursuant to rule 37 of the provisional rules of procedure led to procedural votes on two occasions. The Council also adopted resolution 2623 (2022), by which it called for an emergency special session of the General Assembly, and which was adopted despite the negative vote of a permanent member of the Council consistent with General Assembly resolution 377 A (V).

In 2022, with the continued improvement of the situation regarding the coronavirus disease (COVID-19) pandemic in New York City, the Council fully resumed all in-person activities, including the holding of meetings in person and the adoption of decisions at the Security Council Chamber. The Council also discontinued the use of videoconferences, the written voting procedure and all other aspects of the remote working methods established at the outset of the pandemic in March 2020.[2] Consequently,

---

[1] See S/2023/10.

[2] For more information on the working methods developed by Council members in response to the COVID-19 pandemic in 2020 and 2021, see *Repertoire*, *Supplements 2020* and *2021*, part II, sect. I.

Council members did not hold any videoconferences or adopt any decisions using the written voting procedure during the year.

This notwithstanding, in a letter dated 17 January addressed to the Permanent Representatives of the members of the Council,[3] the President of the Council for the month (Norway) noted that it would strive to continue to maintain the regular conduct of business, while indicating that if the situation related to the pandemic deteriorated, the Council could consider reverting to the working methods outlined in the letter dated 7 May 2020 from the President of the Council addressed to the Permanent Representatives of the members of the Council.[4] Similarly, in a letter dated 7 March,[5] the President of the Council for the month (United Arab Emirates) outlined several recommended restrictions and precautions for the conduct of the Council's work given that the pandemic continued to evolve and change around the world, including in New York City. In both letters, the Presidents reiterated that, as in previous cases, the working methods and guidelines outlined therein were a response to the exceptional and unprecedented circumstances and would not set a precedent for the future. The practice of circulating letters outlining the agreed upon interim working methods for the month was subsequently discontinued by presidencies of the Council. In addition to the views expressed at Council meetings, in particular at the annual open debate on the working methods of the Council held on 28 June,[6] in a letter dated 29 December,[7] the five outgoing elected members of the Council transmitted their views on the procedures adopted during the COVID-19 pandemic and recommendations on how to ensure continuity in the work of the Council in future extraordinary circumstances.

Aspects relating to the working methods of the Council continued to be raised and discussed by Council members, in particular at the annual open debate on the working methods of the Council, held under the item entitled "Implementation of the note by the President of the Security Council (S/2017/507)" (see cases 1, 3, 4, 5 and 6).[8] The discussions were focused on how to ensure transparency, efficiency and effectiveness in the work of the Council, particularly as it related to the format of Council meetings, the agenda, the role of the Council presidency, the Secretariat, participation in Council meetings and other activities, inclusivity in the decision-making process, the practice of penholdership and the use of the veto.

In a letter dated 25 January addressed to the President of the Council,[9] the representative of Saint Vincent and the Grenadines, in her capacity as Chair of the Informal Working Group on Documentation and Other Procedural Questions in 2020 and 2021, shared her reflections and recommendations on the work of the Informal Working Group during her tenure. In an annex to the letter, the representative submitted a demonstration of an index that set out the location of key words and phrases contained in the note by the President dated 30 August 2017[10] and the subsequently issued notes by the President on working methods, which was intended to enhance the user-friendliness of those documents. She explained that, by making it easier to manoeuvre within those texts, the index would assist in the preparation of written monthly commitments and contribute to members' acquaintance with the note by the President dated 30 August 2017 and subsequently issued notes and thereby support their implementation.[11]

In a letter dated 30 December addressed to the President of the Council,[12] the Chair of the Informal Working Group on Documentation and Other Procedural Questions transmitted the first annual report of the Informal Working Group since its establishment in 1993, covering the period from 1 January to 31 December 2022. During the period under review, the Informal Working Group held five meetings and

[3] S/2022/32.

[4] S/2020/372.

[5] S/2022/196.

[6] See S/PV.9079 and S/PV.9079 (Resumption 1).

[7] S/2022/1011.

[8] See S/PV.9079 and S/PV.9079 (Resumption 1).

[9] S/2022/88.

[10] S/2017/507.

[11] For subsequently issued notes by the President on the working methods of the Council, see S/2019/990, S/2019/991, S/2019/992, S/2019/993, S/2019/994, S/2019/995, S/2019/996, S/2019/997, S/2021/645, S/2021/646, S/2021/647, S/2021/648 and S/2021/1074.

[12] S/2022/1032.

conducted an informal retreat in Tirana from 5 to 7 October. In 2022, among other issues, the Informal Working Group discussed the status of the implementation of the note by the President dated 30 August 2017 and the 13 subsequently issued notes by the President on working methods, mainstreaming gender in the work of the Council, the division of labour on subsidiary bodies and penholdership, cooperation with other principal organs of the United Nations, access for elected members to confidential documents of the Council predating their membership, and the participation of civil society representatives in Council meetings. As a standing agenda item in its meetings, the Informal Working Group also discussed the extent of their implementation of the note by the President dated 30 August 2017 through regular briefings by Council members on their respective presidencies and on their respective responsibility as penholders.

I. Meetings and records

Note

Section I covers the practice of the Council concerning meetings, publicity and the records of the Council, in relation to Article 28 of the Charter of the United Nations and rules 1 to 5 and 48 to 57 of the provisional rules of procedure of the Council.

Article 28

1. The Security Council shall be so organized as to be able to function continuously. Each member of the Security Council shall for this purpose be represented at all times at the seat of the Organization.

2. The Security Council shall hold periodic meetings at which each of its members may, if it so desires, be represented by a member of the government or by some other specially designated representative.

3. The Security Council may hold meetings at such places other than the seat of the Organization as in its judgment will best facilitate its work.

Rule 1

Meetings of the Security Council shall, with the exception of the periodic meetings referred to in rule 4, be held at the call of the President at any time he deems necessary, but the interval between meetings shall not exceed fourteen days.

Rule 2

The President shall call a meeting of the Security Council at the request of any member of the Security Council.

Rule 3

The President shall call a meeting of the Security Council if a dispute or situation is brought to the attention of the Security Council under Article 35 or under Article 11 (3) of the Charter, or if the General Assembly makes recommendations or refers any question to the Security Council under Article 11 (2), or if the Secretary-General brings to the attention of the Security Council any matter under Article 99.

Rule 4

Periodic meetings of the Security Council called for in Article 28 (2) of the Charter shall be held twice a year, at such times as the Security Council may decide.

Rule 5

Meetings of the Security Council shall normally be held at the seat of the United Nations.

Any member of the Security Council or the Secretary-General may propose that the Security Council should meet at another place. Should the Security Council accept any such proposal, it shall decide upon the place and the period during which the Council shall meet at such place.

Rule 48

Unless it decides otherwise, the Security Council shall meet in public. Any recommendation to the General Assembly regarding the appointment of the Secretary-General shall be discussed and decided at a private meeting.

Rule 49

Subject to the provisions of rule 51, the verbatim record of each meeting of the Security Council shall be made available to the representatives on the Security Council and to the representatives of any other States which have participated in the meeting not later than 10 a.m. of the first working day following the meeting.

Rule 50

The representatives of the States which have participated in the meeting shall, within two working days after the time indicated in rule 49, inform the Secretary-General of any corrections they wish to have made in the verbatim record.

Rule 51

The Security Council may decide that for a private meeting the record shall be made in a single copy alone. This record shall be kept by the Secretary-General. The representatives of the States which have participated in the meeting shall, within a period of ten days, inform the Secretary-General of any corrections they wish to have made in this record.

Rule 52

Corrections that have been requested shall be considered approved unless the President is of the opinion that they are sufficiently important to be submitted to the representatives on the Security Council. In the latter case, the representatives on the Security Council shall submit within two working days any comments they may wish to make. In the absence of objections in this period of time, the record shall be corrected as requested.

Rule 53

The verbatim record referred to in rule 49 or the record referred to in rule 51, in which no corrections have been requested in the period of time required by rules 50 and 51, respectively, or which has been corrected in accordance with the provisions of rule 52, shall be considered as approved. It shall be signed by the President and shall become the official record of the Security Council.

Rule 54

The official record of public meetings of the Security Council, as well as the documents annexed thereto, shall be published in the official languages as soon as possible.

Rule 55

At the close of each private meeting the Security Council shall issue a communiqué through the Secretary-General.

Rule 56

The representatives of the Members of the United Nations which have taken part in a private meeting shall at all times have the right to consult the record of that meeting in the office of the Secretary-General. The Security Council may at any time grant access to this record to authorized representatives of other Members of the United Nations.

Rule 57

The Secretary-General shall, once each year, submit to the Security Council a list of the records and documents which up to that time have been considered confidential. The Security Council shall decide which of these shall be made available to other Members of the United Nations, which shall be made public, and which shall continue to remain confidential.

The present section comprises five subsections: A. Meetings, concerning the convening of meetings pursuant to rules 1 to 5 and rule 48; B. Informal consultations of the whole; C. Other informal meetings of the members of the Security Council; D. Discussions concerning meetings; and E. Records, maintained pursuant to rules 49 to 57.

During the period under review, the Council held 292 meetings, compared with 164 in 2021 and 81 in 2020. Of the 292 meetings, 276 were public and 16 were private. The Council also held a total of 127 informal consultations of the whole (also known as consultations or informal consultations), compared with 67 in 2021 and 46 in 2020. The number of Council meetings and informal consultations combined was the highest since 2018. The significant increase of meetings and informal consultations in 2022 is explained, in part, by the discontinuation of the use of videoconferences, which were not considered meetings of the Council and were introduced in lieu of meetings as part of the working methods developed during the COVID-19 pandemic.

During the period under review, the Council continued the practice of conducting wrap-up sessions at the end of the month, except for the months of February and September, and most of those sessions followed the "Toledo-style" format, whereby, in addition to the President of the Council, members of the Council presented jointly the activity of the Council for the relevant month as a panel and in an interactive manner. Council members also held five informal interactive dialogues and 21 Arria-formula meetings. Figure I shows the total number of meetings and informal consultations held from 2013 to 2022.

Figure I
Number of meetings, consultations and videoconferences, 2013–2022

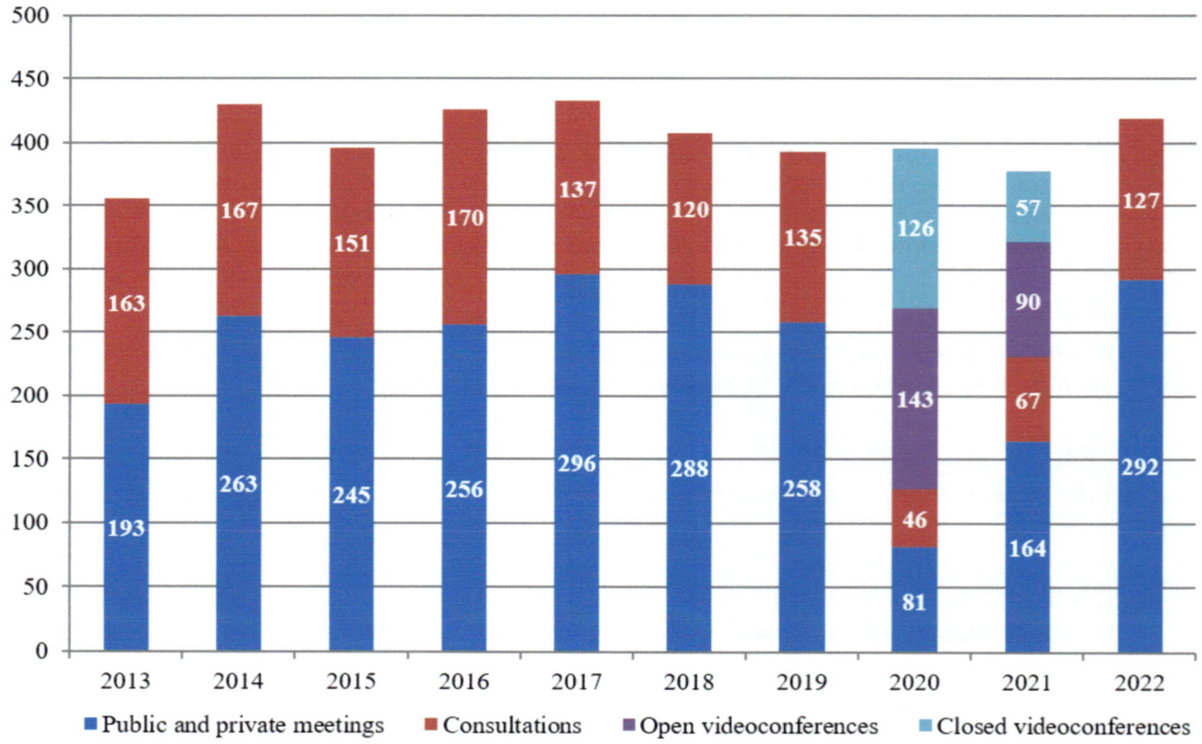

A. Meetings

1. Application of rules relating to meetings

During the period under review, there were no intervals exceeding 14 days between meetings of the Council as established under rule 1 of the provisional rules of procedure. The Council continued to convene more than one meeting a day on occasion.

In 2022, the Council held no periodic meetings pursuant to rule 4 or meetings away from Headquarters in accordance with rule 5.

During the reporting period, no communications were received from Member States requesting the Council to convene a meeting that explicitly cited rule 2 or 3 as the basis of the request. Table 1 below lists eight communications in which an urgent or special meeting was requested by either explicitly or implicitly invoking Article 35 of the Charter, under which Member States or States that are not members of the United Nations may refer disputes to the Council.[13]

Table 1
Letters in which Member States requested an urgent or special meeting, 2022

Letter addressed to the President of the Security Council	*Summary*	*Meeting convened (item and date)*
Letter dated 19 February 2022 from the Permanent Representative of Ukraine to the United Nations addressed to the Secretary-General (S/2022/133)	Requesting to hold an urgent meeting of the Council on the escalation of the conflict on the State border of Ukraine	S/PV.8970 Letter dated 28 February 2014 from the Permanent Representative of Ukraine to the United Nations addressed to the President of the Security Council (S/2014/136) 21 February
Letter dated 24 March 2022 from the Permanent Representative of Japan to the United Nations addressed to the President of the Security Council (S/2022/261)	Requesting the President of the Council to convene an urgent meeting of the Council to consider the ballistic missile launch by the Democratic People's Republic of Korea, under the item entitled "Non-proliferation/Democratic People's Republic of Korea"	S/PV.9004 Non-proliferation/Democratic People's Republic of Korea 25 March
Letter dated 9 May 2022 from the Permanent Representative of Japan to the United Nations addressed to the President of the Security Council (S/2022/379)	Requesting the President of the Council to convene an urgent meeting of the Council to consider the ballistic missile launch by the Democratic People's Republic of Korea, under the item entitled "Non-proliferation/Democratic People's Republic of Korea"	S/PV.9030 Non-proliferation/Democratic People's Republic of Korea 11 May
Letter dated 22 July 2022 from the Permanent Representative of Iraq to the United Nations addressed to the President of the Security Council (S/2022/574)	Submitting an urgent complaint to the Council and calling upon it to fulfil its role under the Charter of the United Nations and hold an emergency meeting to discuss the aggression by Türkiye, and calling upon the Council to form a committee to follow up on the situation between Iraq and Türkiye and to add an item on the repeated Turkish attacks	S/PV.9100 The situation concerning Iraq 26 July
Letter dated 13 September 2022 from the Permanent Representative of Armenia to the United Nations addressed to the President of the Security Council (S/2022/688)	Requesting to convene an emergency meeting of the Council, on the basis of Article 35 (1) of the Charter	S/PV.9132 Letter dated 13 September 2022 from the Permanent Representative of Armenia to the United Nations addressed to the President of the Security Council (S/2022/688) 15 September

[13] For more information on Article 35 of the Charter, see part VI, sect. I.

Letter addressed to the President of the Security Council	*Summary*	*Meeting convened (item and date)*
Letter dated 4 October 2022 from the Chargé d'affaires a.i. of the Permanent Mission of Japan to the United Nations addressed to the President of the Security Council (S/2022/742)	Requesting the President of the Council to convene an urgent meeting of the Council to consider the ballistic missile launch by the Democratic People's Republic of Korea, under the item entitled "Non-proliferation/Democratic People's Republic of Korea"	S/PV.9146 Non-proliferation/Democratic People's Republic of Korea 5 October
Letter dated 3 November 2022 from the Permanent Representative of Japan to the United Nations addressed to the President of the Security Council (S/2022/829)	Requesting the President of the Council to convene an urgent meeting of the Council to consider the ballistic missile launches by the Democratic People's Republic of Korea, under the item entitled "Non-proliferation/Democratic People's Republic of Korea"	S/PV.9183 Non-proliferation/Democratic People's Republic of Korea 4 November
Letter dated 18 November 2022 from the Permanent Representative of Japan to the United Nations addressed to the President of the Security Council (S/2022/870)	Requesting the President of the Council to convene an urgent meeting of the Council to consider the ballistic missile launch by the Democratic People's Republic of Korea, under the item entitled "Non-proliferation/Democratic People's Republic of Korea"	S/PV.9197 Non-proliferation/Democratic People's Republic of Korea 21 November

Complaints raised by Member States concerning the application of rule 2 or 3

During the period under review, Council members exchanged contrasting views regarding the application of rules 2 and 3 of the provisional rules of procedure in the context of two sets of requests for a meeting on the conflict in Ukraine in April and June 2022.

In a letter dated 4 April addressed to the President of the Council,[14] the representative of the Russian Federation expressed his delegation's protest of and disappointment with a "clear abuse" by the United Kingdom of its prerogatives as the President of the Council. In that regard, the representative stated that, on 3 April, following reports of what he termed a "Ukrainian provocation" in Bucha, Ukraine, the Russian Federation had called for a Council meeting to be convened on 4 April under the item entitled "Letter dated 13 April 2014 from the Permanent Representative of the Russian Federation to the United Nations addressed to the President of the Security Council (S/2014/264)" to discuss the issue. He added that, even though the request had been filed under rule 2 of the provisional rules of procedure, which made it necessary for the presidency to take action as requested by a Council member, the presidency had denied the right of a member to call for a meeting and instead had suggested postponing the discussion until the next scheduled meeting on Ukraine, which was to be held on 5 April under a different item. Further noting that a second request for a meeting filed by his delegation on 4 April had also been rejected, the representative of the Russian Federation stated that the presidency should not impose its view regarding the urgency of meetings and block an initiative to hold a Council meeting by a Council member, and that, in so doing, the presidency had "trampled on the Council's rules of procedure".

At the meeting described in the letter, held on 5 April under the item entitled "Letter dated 28 February 2014 from the Permanent Representative of Ukraine to the United Nations addressed to the President of the Security Council (S/2014/136)",[15] before the adoption of the provisional agenda, the representative of the Russian Federation protested the manner in which the United Kingdom, as the President for the month of April, had handled his delegation's two requests to convene an emergency Council meeting in connection with the "Ukrainian provocation" in Bucha. According to the representative, the first request of the Russian Federation, made on 3 April, had been for a Council meeting to be held on Monday, 4 April, at 3 p.m. After that request had been denied, the Russian

[14] S/2022/286.

[15] See S/PV.9011.

Federation had then requested an emergency meeting to be held on 4 April at 12 p.m. The representative of the Russian Federation questioned on what grounds, and without coordinating with anyone else, had the presidency decided that it would be better to discuss the topic at the meeting on 5 April. He further noted that, in cases where the presidency did not agree with the proposal of his delegation, it should convene a meeting and put the issue to a vote. He also demanded a guarantee that, in the future, the presidency would not challenge the right of Council members to request meetings, as enshrined in rule 2 of the provisional rules of procedure. Responding to the Russian Federation, the President of the Council underscored that her delegation had not rejected the requests but had proposed either scheduling the meeting alongside the meeting of 5 April or sequentially, one after the other. She stated that the two proposals, both of which had been rejected by the Russian Federation, had been well within the 48-hour limit that was the convention of the Council and had involved a deferral of less than 24 hours. She added that the presidency shared the view that it was an urgent situation and had done everything in line with the provisional rules of procedure and precedent.

In a letter dated 11 April,[16] further elaborating upon the issue and in response to the letters of the Russian Federation dated 4 and 5 April, the representative of the United Kingdom stated that the presidency of the Council had not blocked the request of the Russian Federation for a meeting nor questioned its urgency. She explained that, while the provisional rules of procedure obligated the presidency to hold a meeting when requested, rule 1 was clear that the presidency retained discretion over timing. She noted that convention suggested that a request for an "urgent meeting" was usually scheduled within 48 hours. According to the representative, upon receipt of the request from the delegation of the Russian Federation, the presidency had proposed for the meeting to be combined with an existing meeting on the same topic already scheduled within a 48-hour window, an approach for which there were multiple precedents and for which a number of Council members had expressed support.

In a letter dated 14 April,[17] the representative of the Russian Federation rejected the description of "convention" in the letter from the United Kingdom and stated that the practice of the Council, at least for the past five years, clearly indicated that an urgent meeting was to be convened in three hours' time. He added that, by claiming that it had the right to schedule the requested meeting at a moment up to 48 hours after the request of the Russian Federation, the presidency had denied the right to request a meeting, in a clear breach of rule 2 of the provisional rules of procedure.

In another instance, in a letter dated 29 June,[18] the representative of the Russian Federation objected to the decision of the presidency of the Council, held by Albania for that month, to convene a meeting of the Council on 28 June pursuant to a request from Ukraine.[19] Noting the protracted discussion among Council members on the application of rule 3 of the provisional rules of procedure, he stated that there were multiple examples of situations in which a request from a Member State for a meeting had not been granted given that no Council member had called for it. The representative added that in such cases, or in a situation in which it was applying rule 1 of the provisional rules of procedure, the presidency should consult the members of the Council.

In a letter dated 18 July,[20] in response to the letter from the Russian Federation, the representative of Albania stated that rule 3 of the provisional rules of procedure mandated the President of the Council to call a meeting if a dispute or a situation was brought to the attention of the Council under Article 35 of the Charter. Noting that the practice of the Council offered multiple examples in that regard, the representative stated that rule 3 did not contain any requirement for consultations upon receiving a request for a meeting, despite the fact that this had occasionally happened, nor did it require the President to wait for a request from a Council member to call the meeting.

Similarly, in a letter dated 19 July,[21] the representative of the United States emphasized that the use of the word "shall" in rule 3 indicated that the President of the Council had no discretion regarding calling a meeting of the Council at the request of a Member State. Furthermore, while noting that there

[16] S/2022/309.
[17] S/2022/320.
[18] S/2022/528.
[19] See S/PV.9080.
[20] S/2022/565.
[21] S/2022/567.

had been a few rare and exceptional instances in which the Council had determined that the best course of action would be to hold closed consultations after receiving a request for a Council meeting from a Member State, the representative stated that there was no requirement for the presidency to wait for a concurring request from a Council member prior to calling the formal meeting. She further expressed the view that the course of action taken by the presidency of Albania had been consistent with the letter and spirit of rule 3.

2. Format

Public meetings

The Council continued to convene meetings in public as provided for in rule 48 of the provisional rules of procedure, mainly for the purposes of: (a) hearing briefings on country-specific or regional situations or thematic issues under its consideration; (b) holding debates on particular items;[22] and (c) adopting decisions.[23] In 2022, the Council held a total of 292 meetings, of which 276, or 94.5 per cent, were public.

During the period under review, Council members held 23 meetings at which two or more Council members were represented at the ministerial or higher levels. A total of 17 of those meetings were held in connection with thematic items and 6 were held in connection with regional and country-specific situations. In addition, the Council held five meetings at which one or more Council members were represented at the level of Head of State or Government.

Table 2 lists all high-level meetings and videoconferences held in 2022 at which two or more Council members were represented at ministerial or higher levels.

Table 2
High-level meetings, 2022

Meeting record and date	*Item*	*Sub-item/topic*	*High-level participation*
S/PV.8949, S/PV.8949 (Resumption 1) and S/2022/38 18 January	Women and peace and security	Protecting participation: addressing violence targeting women in peace and security processes	**Ministerial level (5)** **Albania** (Minister for Europe and Foreign Affairs), **Ghana** (Minister for Foreign Affairs and Regional Integration), **Norway** (Minister for Foreign Affairs), **United Arab Emirates** (Permanent Representative to the United Nations and Assistant Minister for Foreign Affairs and International Cooperation), **United States** (Under Secretary for Civilian Security, Democracy and Human Rights)
S/PV.8950, S/PV.8950 (Resumption 1) and S/2022/39 19 January	The situation in the Middle East, including the Palestinian question		**Ministerial level (4)** **Ghana** (Minister for Foreign Affairs and Regional Integration), **Norway** (Minister for Foreign Affairs), **United Arab Emirates** (Permanent Representative to the United Nations and Assistant Minister for Foreign Affairs and International Cooperation), **United States** (Permanent Representative to the United Nations and member of the President's Cabinet)

[22] In 2022, the Council continued the practice of holding meetings from 10 a.m. to 1 p.m. and from 3 to 6 p.m., with resumptions in the case of several open debates (see, for example, S/PV.8949, S/PV.8949 (Resumption 1), S/PV.9016, S/PV.9016 (Resumption 1), S/PV.9099, S/PV.9099 (Resumption 1), S/PV.9174, S/PV.9174 (Resumption 1), S/PV.9181, S/PV.9181 (Resumption 1), S/PV.9220 and S/PV.9220 (Resumption 1)).

[23] On the formats of public meetings, see also S/2017/507, annex, sect. II.C.1.

Meeting record and date	Item	Sub-item/topic	High-level participation
S/PV.8953, S/PV.8953 (Resumption 1) and S/2022/54 25 January	Protection of civilians in armed conflict	War in cities: protection of civilians in urban settings	**Heads of State or Government (2)** **Ghana** (Vice-President), **Norway** (Prime Minister) **Ministerial level (3)** **Gabon** (Minister for Foreign Affairs), **United Arab Emirates** (Permanent Representative to the United Nations and Assistant Minister for Foreign Affairs and International Cooperation), **United States** (Permanent Representative to the United Nations and member of the President's Cabinet)
S/PV.8954 26 January	The situation in Afghanistan		**Heads of State or Government (1)** **Norway** (Prime Minister) **Ministerial level (1)** **Gabon** (Minister for Foreign Affairs)
S/PV.8968 17 February	Letter dated 13 April 2014 from the Permanent Representative of the Russian Federation to the United Nations addressed to the President of the Security Council (S/2014/264)		**Ministerial level (3)** **Russian Federation** (Deputy Minister for Foreign Affairs), **United Kingdom** (Minister of State for Europe and North America), **United States** (Secretary of State)
S/PV.8989, S/PV.8989 (Resumption 1) and S/2022/207 8 March	Women and peace and security	Women's economic inclusion and participation as a key to building peace	**Ministerial level (5)** **India** (Secretary (West), Ministry of External Affairs), **Ireland** (Minister for Foreign Affairs and Defence), **Mexico** (Vice-Minister for Multilateral Affairs and Human Rights), **United Arab Emirates** (Minister for Climate Change and the Environment), **United States** (Permanent Representative to the United Nations and member of the President's Cabinet)
S/PV.9001 23 March	Cooperation between the United Nations and regional and subregional organizations in maintaining international peace and security	League of Arab States	**Ministerial level (2)** **India** (Foreign Secretary), **United Arab Emirates** (Minister of State, Ministry of Foreign Affairs and International Cooperation)
S/PV.9014 11 April	Maintenance of international peace and security	Implementation of resolutions 2532 (2020) and 2565 (2021)	**Ministerial level (3)** **United Arab Emirates** (Minister of State for Public Education and Advanced Technology), **United Kingdom** (Minister of State for South and Central Asia, North Africa, the United Nations and the Commonwealth, and the Prime Minister's Special Representative for Preventing Sexual Violence in Conflict), **United States** (Permanent Representative to the United Nations and member of the President's Cabinet)

Meeting record and date	*Item*	*Sub-item/topic*	*High-level participation*
S/PV.9016 and S/PV.9016 (Resumption 1) 13 April	Women and peace and security	Accountability as prevention Ending cycles of sexual violence in conflict	**Ministerial level (2)** **United Kingdom** (Minister of State for South and Central Asia, North Africa, the United Nations and the Commonwealth, and the Prime Minister's Special Representative for Preventing Sexual Violence in Conflict), **United States** (Permanent Representative to the United Nations and member of the President's Cabinet)
S/PV.9036 and S/PV.9036 (Resumption 1) 19 May	Maintenance of international peace and security	Conflict and food security	**Ministerial level (10)** **Albania** (Minister for Europe and Foreign Affairs), **Gabon** (Minister for Foreign Affairs), **Ghana** (Minister for Foreign Affairs and Regional Integration), **India** (Minister of State for External Affairs), **Ireland** (Minister of State for Overseas Development Aid and Diaspora), **Kenya** (Cabinet Secretary for Foreign Affairs), **Mexico** (Minister of Agriculture and Rural Development), **Norway** (Minister of International Development), **United Arab Emirates** (Permanent Representative to the United Nations and Assistant Minister for Foreign Affairs and International Cooperation), **United States** (Secretary of State)
S/PV.9052 and S/PV.9052 (Resumption 1) 2 June	Maintenance of international peace and security	Strengthening accountability and justice for serious violations of international law	**Heads of State or Government (1)** **Albania** (Prime Minister) **Ministerial level (4)** **India** (Minister of State for External Affairs), **Ireland** (Attorney General), **United Arab Emirates** (Permanent Representative to the United Nations and Assistant Minister for Foreign Affairs and International Cooperation), **United States** (Under Secretary for Civilian Security, Democracy and Human Rights)
S/PV.9064 and S/PV.9064 (Resumption 1) 15 June	Women and peace and security	Keeping the promises: the role of regional organizations in implementing the women and peace and security agenda in the face of political turmoil and seizures of power by force	**Ministerial level (5)** **Albania** (Minister for Europe and Foreign Affairs), **Ghana** (Deputy Minister of Finance), **Norway** (State Secretary), **United Arab Emirates** (Permanent Representative to the United Nations and Assistant Minister for Foreign Affairs and International Cooperation), **United States** (Permanent Representative to the United Nations and member of the President's Cabinet)
S/PV.9090 and S/PV.9090 (Resumption 1) 12 July	United Nations peacekeeping operations	The key role of strategic communications for efficient peacekeeping	**Ministerial level (3)** **Brazil** (Minister for Foreign Affairs), **Ghana** (Minister for Foreign Affairs and Regional Integration), **India** (Secretary (East), Ministry of External Affairs), **United Arab Emirates** (Permanent Representative to the United Nations and Assistant Minister for Foreign Affairs and International Cooperation)

Meeting record and date	Item	Sub-item/topic	High-level participation
S/PV.9135 22 September	Maintenance of peace and security of Ukraine		**Heads of State or Government (1)** **Norway** (Prime Minister) **Ministerial level (14)** **Albania** (Minister for Europe and Foreign Affairs), **Brazil** (Minister for Foreign Affairs), **China** (State Councillor and Minister for Foreign Affairs), **France** (Minister for Europe and Foreign Affairs), **Gabon** (Minister for Foreign Affairs), **Ghana** (Minister for Foreign Affairs and Regional Integration), **India** (Minister for External Affairs), **Ireland** (Minister for Foreign Affairs and Defence), **Kenya** (Director General, Bilateral and Political Affairs), **Mexico** (Minister for Foreign Affairs), **Russian Federation** (Minister for Foreign Affairs), **United Arab Emirates** (Minister of State for International Cooperation, Ministry of Foreign Affairs and International Cooperation), **United Kingdom** (Secretary of State for Foreign, Commonwealth and Development Affairs), **United States** (Secretary of State)
S/PV.9147 6 October	Peace and security in Africa	Strengthening the fight against the financing of armed groups and terrorists through the illicit trafficking of natural resources	**Ministerial level (5)** **Gabon** (Minister for Foreign Affairs), **Ghana** (Minister of National Security), **India** (Minister of State for External Affairs), **United Arab Emirates** (Minister for Foreign Affairs and International Cooperation), **United States** (Permanent Representative to the United Nations and member of the President's Cabinet)
S/PV.9149 11 October	Cooperation between the United Nations and regional and subregional organizations in maintaining international peace and security	African Union	**Ministerial level (3)** **Gabon** (Minister for Foreign Affairs), **United Arab Emirates** (Permanent Representative to the United Nations and Assistant Minister for Foreign Affairs and International Cooperation), **United States** (Permanent Representative to the United Nations and member of the President's Cabinet)
S/PV.9150 12 October	Threats to international peace and security	Climate and security in Africa	**Ministerial level (4)** **Gabon** (Minister for Foreign Affairs), **Norway** (Minister for Foreign Affairs), **United Arab Emirates** (Permanent Representative to the United Nations and Assistant Minister for Foreign Affairs and International Cooperation), **United States** (Permanent Representative to the United Nations and member of the President's Cabinet)
S/PV.9151 12 October	Identical letters dated 19 January 2016 from the Permanent Representative of Colombia to the United Nations addressed to the		**Ministerial level (2)** **Gabon** (Minister for Foreign Affairs), **Norway** (Minister for Foreign Affairs)

Meeting record and date	*Item*	*Sub-item/topic*	*High-level participation*
	Secretary-General and the President of the Security Council (S/2016/53)		
S/PV.9158 and S/PV.9158 (Resumption 1) 20 October	Women and peace and security	Strengthening women's resilience and leadership as a path to peace in regions plagued by armed groups	**Ministerial level (3)** **Albania** (Deputy Minister for Europe and Foreign Affairs), **United Arab Emirates** (Permanent Representative to the United Nations and Assistant Minister for Foreign Affairs and International Cooperation), **United States** (Permanent Representative to the United Nations and member of the President's Cabinet)
S/PV.9181 and S/PV.9181 (Resumption 1) 3 November	Peacebuilding and sustaining peace	Integrating effective resilience-building in peace operations for sustainable peace	**Ministerial level (5)** **Gabon** (Deputy Minister for Foreign Affairs), **Ghana** (Minister for Foreign Affairs and Regional Integration), **India** (Foreign Secretary), **Ireland** (Minister of State for European Affairs), **United States** (Permanent Representative to the United Nations and member of the President's Cabinet)
S/PV.9188 10 November	Threats to international peace and security	Counter-terrorism in Africa: an imperative for peace, security and development	**Heads of State or Government (1)** **Ghana** (President) **Ministerial level (3)** **Gabon** (Deputy Minister for Foreign Affairs), **United Arab Emirates** (Minister of State, Ministry of Foreign Affairs and International Cooperation), **United States** (Assistant to the President for Homeland Security)
S/PV.9220 and S/PV.9220 (Resumption 1) 14 December	Maintenance of international peace and security	New orientation for reformed multilateralism	**Ministerial level (4)** **Ghana** (Permanent Secretary of the Ministry of Foreign Affairs and Regional Integration), **India** (Minister for External Affairs), **United Arab Emirates** (Cabinet member and Minister of Culture and Youth), **United States** (Permanent Representative to the United Nations and member of the President's Cabinet)
S/PV.9221 15 December	Threats to international peace and security caused by terrorist acts	Global counter-terrorism approach – principles and the way forward	**Ministerial level (7)** **Ghana** (Permanent Secretary of the Ministry of Foreign Affairs and Regional Integration), **India** (Minister for External Affairs), **Ireland** (Minister for Foreign Affairs and Defence), **Kenya** (Principal Secretary for Foreign Affairs), **United Arab Emirates** (Cabinet member and Minister of Culture and Youth), **United Kingdom** (Minister of State for the Middle East, North Africa, South Asia, the United Nations and the Commonwealth, and the Prime Minister's Special Representative for Preventing Sexual Violence in Conflict), **United States** (Under Secretary for Political Affairs)

Private meetings

During the period under review, the Council continued to hold meetings in private, in accordance with rule 48 of the provisional rules of procedure. Private meetings continued to constitute a small percentage of all Council meetings, with 16 private meetings (5.5 per cent) out of a total of 292 meetings held in 2022 (see figure II).[24] As indicated in table 3, 11 of those meetings were held with troop- and police-contributing countries under the item entitled "Meeting of the Security Council with the troop- and police-contributing countries pursuant to resolution 1353 (2001), annex II, sections A and B".

Figure II
Public and private meetings, 2022

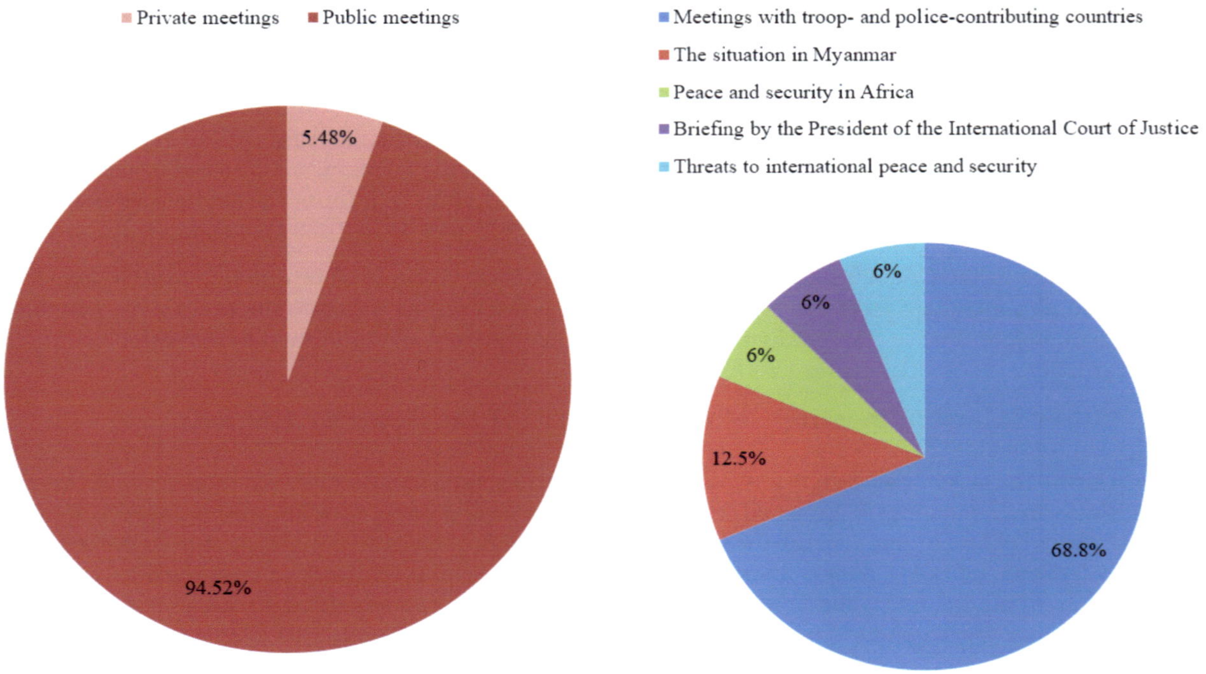

Table 3
Private meetings, 2022

Item	*Meeting record and date*
Meeting of the Security Council with the troop- and police-contributing countries pursuant to resolution 1353 (2001), annex II, sections A and B	S/PV.8947, 12 January S/PV.8985, 3 March S/PV.9057, 7 June S/PV.9060, 9 June S/PV.9093, 13 July S/PV.9111, 16 August S/PV.9148, 10 October S/PV.9185, 7 November S/PV.9186, 7 November S/PV.9209, 6 December S/PV.9212, 7 December
The situation in Myanmar	S/PV.8959, 28 January S/PV.9049, 27 May

[24] On the formats of private meetings, see also S/2017/507, annex, sect. II.C.2.

Item	*Meeting record and date*
Peace and security in Africa	S/PV.9160, 21 October
Briefing by the President of the International Court of Justice	S/PV.9166, 26 October
Threats to international peace and security	S/PV.9172, 27 October

B. Informal consultations of the whole

Informal consultations of the whole are not official meetings of the Council. The members gather in private for the purpose of holding discussions and receiving briefings from the Secretariat and representatives of the Secretary-General. These meetings are normally held in the Consultations Room, adjacent to the Security Council Chamber. During the period under review, with the continued easing of the health and safety restrictions related to the COVID-19 pandemic, Council members gradually resumed the holding of informal consultations in the Consultations Room in April 2022. Most frequently, informal consultations continued to be held immediately after public meetings on the same issue. In 2022, with the return to in-person activities of the Council, the number of informal consultations increased significantly, with 127 held in 2022, compared with 67 in 2021 and 46 in 2020 (see figure I).

Pursuant to the Council's established practice, no official records of informal consultations were issued, and non-members were not invited. Frequently, however, statements to the press were issued or elements to the press were read out by the President of the Council after informal consultations.

C. Other informal meetings of the members of the Security Council

During the period under review, Council members continued to hold informal interactive dialogues and Arria-formula meetings.[25] Informal interactive dialogues and Arria-formula meetings are convened at the initiative of one or more members of the Council. Informal interactive dialogues are convened with the participation of all Council members, while Arria-formula meetings are convened with the participation of all or some Council members. While informal interactive dialogues are presided over by the President of the Council, Arria-formula meetings are not. Frequently, the member or one of the members of the Council convening the Arria-formula meeting also serves as the Chair. Neither of the two types of meetings are considered formal meetings of the Council. They are not announced in the *Journal of the United Nations* or in the Council's programme of work, and no official records are prepared. Invitees to informal interactive dialogues and Arria-formula meetings include Member States, relevant organizations and individuals. In past practice, Arria-formula meetings were closed to the public; more recently, however, they have been open and broadcast. Informal interactive dialogues are not open to the public or broadcast.

Informal interactive dialogues

According to the note by the President dated 30 August 2017, when it deems appropriate, the Council may utilize informal dialogues to seek the views of Member States that are parties to a conflict and/or other interested and affected parties.[26] In addition, on 12 July and in relation to the humanitarian situation in the Syrian Arab Republic, the Council adopted resolution 2642 (2022), in which it encouraged the convening of a Security Council informal interactive dialogue every two months with the participation of donors, interested regional parties and representatives of the international humanitarian agencies operating in the country in order to regularly review and follow up on the implementation of the resolution, including progress in early recovery projects.[27] As shown in table 4, the Council held five

[25] For more information on informal interactive dialogues and Arria-formula meetings, see S/2017/507, annex, paras. 92, 95 and 97–99.

[26] S/2017/507, annex, para. 92.

[27] Resolution 2642 (2022), para. 6. For more information on the situation in the Middle East, see part I, sect. 20.

informal interactive dialogues in 2022, all of which concerned country-specific or regional situations, and three of which related to the humanitarian situation in the Syrian Arab Republic.[28]

Table 4
Informal interactive dialogues, 2022

Date	*Subject*	*Participants (including non-members of the Council)*
24 May	The situation in Libya (European Union military operation in the Mediterranean (Operation IRINI))	All Council members; Director for Integrated Approach for Peace and Security, European Union
26 September	The situation in the Middle East (humanitarian situation in the Syrian Arab Republic)	All Council members; Under-Secretary-General for Humanitarian Affairs and Emergency Relief Coordinator; Resident and Humanitarian Coordinator for the Syrian Arab Republic, United Nations Development Programme; Deputy Regional Humanitarian Coordinator for the Syria Crisis, Office for the Coordination of Humanitarian Affairs; Regional Humanitarian Coordinator for the Syria Crisis, Office for the Coordination of Humanitarian Affairs; Ecuador; Japan; Malta; Mozambique; Switzerland; Canada; Germany; Sweden; European Union; Islamic Republic of Iran; Syrian Arab Republic; Türkiye
28 September	Peace and security in Africa (Ethiopia/Tigray)	All Council members; Special Envoy of the Secretary-General for the Horn of Africa; Permanent Representative of Ethiopia to the United Nations
21 November	The situation in the Middle East (humanitarian situation in the Syrian Arab Republic)	All Council members; Deputy Director for the Middle East and North Africa, Office for the Coordination of Humanitarian Affairs; Regional Humanitarian Coordinator for the Syria Crisis, Office for the Coordination of Humanitarian Affairs; Resident and Humanitarian Coordinator ad interim for the Syrian Arab Republic, United Nations Development Programme; Syrian Arab Republic; Türkiye; Islamic Republic of Iran; Sweden; Germany; Canada; European Union
16 December	The situation in the Middle East (humanitarian situation in the Syrian Arab Republic)	All Council members; Acting Director of Operations and Advocacy, Office for the Coordination of Humanitarian Affairs; Regional Humanitarian Coordinator for the Syria Crisis, Office for the Coordination of Humanitarian Affairs; Resident and Humanitarian Coordinator ad interim for the Syrian Arab Republic, United Nations Development Programme; Syrian Arab Republic; Türkiye; Islamic Republic of Iran; Sweden; Germany; Canada; European Union

Arria-formula meetings

As provided for in the note by the President dated 30 August 2017, Arria-formula meetings are utilized by members of the Council as a flexible and informal forum for enhancing their deliberations and contact with civil society and non-governmental organizations.[29] In accordance with the note, Council members may invite, on an informal basis, any Member State, relevant organization or individual to participate in Arria-formula meetings.

In 2022, Council members held 21 Arria-formula meetings, compared with 32 in 2021 and 22 both in 2020 and in 2019. In terms of publicity, 20 were open and broadcast on United Nations Web TV and 1 was closed. In some instances, members and non-members of the Council transmitted concept notes,

[28] For information on the evolution of informal interactive dialogues, see *Repertoire*, *Supplements 2008–2009* to *2021*.

[29] S/2017/507, annex, para. 98.

summaries and compilations of statements made by participants in Arria-formula meetings, as well as other communications concerning the meetings.[30] Arria-formula meetings held during the period under review are listed in table 5.

Table 5
Arria-formula meetings, 2022

Date	*Subject*	*Organizer(s) and sponsor(s)*	*Concept note*	*Summary or compilation of statements*
9 March	Climate finance for sustaining peace and security	United Arab Emirates	–	–
25 March	Ensuring access to mental health and psychosocial support in conflict, post-conflict and humanitarian settings	Mexico	–	S/2022/456
6 April	Threats to international peace and security emanating from military biological activities in regions across the globe	Russian Federation	–	–
21 April	Conflict and hunger	Ireland	S/2022/338	–
27 April	Ensuring accountability for atrocities committed in Ukraine	Albania, Australia, Austria, Belgium, Bosnia and Herzegovina, Bulgaria, Canada, Colombia, Croatia, Czechia, Denmark, Estonia, Finland, France, Georgia, Germany, Iceland, Ireland, Italy, Japan, Latvia, Liechtenstein, Lithuania, Luxembourg, Marshall Islands, Micronesia (Federated States of), Montenegro, Netherlands, New Zealand, North Macedonia, Norway, Poland, Republic of Korea, Romania, Slovakia, Sweden, Ukraine, United Kingdom, United States, European Union	S/2022/352	S/2022/375
6 May	Systematic and mass grave violations of the international humanitarian law as well as other war crimes committed by the Ukrainian military personnel and militia and discovered in the course of ongoing special military operation of the Russian armed forces	Russian Federation	S/2022/363	S/2022/990
24 May	Protection of journalists	Ireland	S/2022/406	S/2022/564
3 June	Syrian women's voices on detainees and the disappeared in the Syrian Arab Republic	Albania, Belgium, Canada, France, Germany, Netherlands, Qatar, Türkiye, United Kingdom, United States, Syrian Negotiation Commission	–	–

[30] See, for example, a note verbale from the Bolivarian Republic of Venezuela concerning the Arria-formula meeting held on 2 November on the topic of ongoing protests in the Islamic Republic of Iran (S/2022/830).

Date	Subject	Organizer(s) and sponsor(s)	Concept note	Summary or compilation of statements
24 June	Twentieth anniversary of the entry into force of the Rome Statute: reflections on the relationship between the International Criminal Court and the Security Council	Albania, Ecuador, France, Gabon, Ghana, Ireland, Japan, Malta, Mexico, Norway, Switzerland, United Kingdom	S/2022/494	S/2022/705
11 July	Neo-Nazism and radical nationalism: exploring root causes of the crisis in Ukraine	Russian Federation	–	S/2022/626
14 July	A milestone year for a peaceful future: transitional justice in Colombia	Colombia, Ireland, Norway	S/2022/553	–
15 July	Destruction of cultural heritage as a consequence of the Russian aggression against Ukraine	Albania, Poland, Ukraine	S/2022/551	–
27 July	Collective security through equitable burden sharing: strengthening regional arrangements for the maintenance of international peace and security	Ghana	–	S/2022/629
11 August	Implementation of the note by the President of the Security Council dated 30 August 2017 (S/2017/507): penholdership	Russian Federation	–	–
31 August	Threats to international peace and security caused by transnational activities of terrorist groups	Kenya, United Arab Emirates	–	–
24 October	Engaging Afghanistan (closed)	Norway	–	–
2 November	Ongoing protests in the Islamic Republic of Iran	Albania, United States	–	–
17 November	Preventing economic collapse and exploring prospects for recovery and development in Afghanistan	Russian Federation	–	–
29 November	Climate, peace and security: opportunities for the United Nations peace and security architecture	Albania, France, Gabon, Germany, Ghana, Ireland, Japan, Kenya, Malta, Mozambique, Nauru, Norway, Switzerland, United Arab Emirates, United Kingdom, United States	S/2022/999	S/2022/999
12 December	Marking the seventh anniversary of the youth, peace and security agenda	Ecuador, Ghana, Ireland	S/2023/13	S/2023/13
22 December	Transitioning from protracted conflict and fragility into peace through sustainable development	Brazil, China, Ecuador, Ireland, Kenya, Sierra Leone, United Kingdom	S/2022/949	–

Other informal meetings

Following the practice started in 2007, the Security Council and the Peace and Security Council of the African Union held their seventh informal joint seminar and sixteenth annual joint consultative meeting in New York on 14 October.[31]

D. Discussions concerning meetings

During the period under review, questions pertaining to meetings were raised in communications and meetings of the Council. In a letter dated 16 February addressed to the President of the Council,[32] the representative of Finland transmitted the report on the nineteenth annual workshop for newly elected members of the Council, which had been held on 18 and 19 November 2021. It was noted in the report that the workshop participants had reflected upon, among other issues, the balance between transparency, effectiveness and efficiency, and the use of videoconferences and contingency procedures for the Council in future crisis situations such as the COVID-19 pandemic.

Council members and the wider membership also discussed issues pertaining to the format of meetings and other informal gatherings during the annual open debate on the working methods of the Council, held on 28 June under the item entitled "Implementation of the note by the President of the Security Council (S/2017/507)" (case 1). They also discussed issues concerning the frequency of meetings at a meeting held on 29 September under the item entitled "The situation in the Middle East", specifically with regard to the implementation of resolution 2118 (2013) (case 2).

Case 1
Implementation of the note by the President of the Security Council (S/2017/507)

On 28 June, at the initiative of Albania, which held the presidency of the Security Council for the month and whose Permanent Representative chaired the Informal Working Group on Documentation and Other Procedural Questions in 2022,[33] the Council convened an open debate on its working methods under the item entitled "Implementation of the note by the President of the Security Council (S/2017/507)" and the sub-item entitled "Working methods of the Security Council".[34] In their discussions, members and non-members of the Council exchanged views on how different formats of meetings and other Council activities affected the efficiency, effectiveness and transparency of the Council's work. Following the Council's full return to in-person conduct of business in 2022, participants also discussed the lessons learned from the remote working methods developed during the COVID-19 pandemic and how to ensure continuity in its work in future extraordinary circumstances.

In that regard, several delegations underlined that the Council needed to strike a balance between open and closed meetings.[35] The representative of Malta expressed the view that striking the right balance between effectiveness and transparency was not easy and noted that open briefings allowed Council members to make their positions known and gave the opportunity to non-Council members and the public to follow the discussions. On the other hand, the representative noted that closed consultations served an important purpose, in particular when dealing with more sensitive and polarized issues. The representative of Switzerland, speaking on behalf of the Accountability, Coherence and Transparency Group, stated that all available formats should be used by the Council in order to forge consensus.

Some participants called upon the Council to convene more open meetings as a means of ensuring transparency.[36] The representatives of Cuba, Italy and Pakistan expressed the view that closed meetings

[31] See A/77/2. For information on prior practice concerning the informal joint meetings of the Security Council and the Peace and Security Council of the African Union, see *Repertoire*, *Supplements 2008–2009* to *2021*. For more information on cooperation with regional and subregional organizations pursuant to Chapter VIII of the Charter, see part VIII.

[32] S/2022/128.

[33] A concept note was circulated by a letter dated 21 June (S/2022/499).

[34] See S/PV.9079 and S/PV.9079 (Resumption 1). See also S/2022/842.

[35] See S/PV.9079 (Russian Federation, Ireland (on behalf of the elected members of the Council), France and Austria).

[36] See S/PV.9079 (Republic of Korea, Pakistan and Morocco); and S/PV.9079 (Resumption 1) (Italy and Egypt).

should be restricted to a minimum and should be the exception and not the rule.[37] The representative of Egypt stated that all meetings should be public, with the exception of those that addressed issues relating to the national security of States.[38] The representative of Germany welcomed the increase in open and public debates and called upon Council members to stop blocking certain topics from being discussed publicly, as a matter of principle. Conversely, the representative of France stated that some issues had to be preserved for confidential discussions and negotiations, as they allowed Council members to adjust their positions and reach a compromise.[39] Similarly, the representative of the United Kingdom stated that some discussions had to be held in private to ensure that the Council could solve problems through interactive debate, consensus-building, responsible penholdership and decision-making.

The representative of Switzerland underlined the need for open debates to be more effective and inclusive. The representative of Ecuador stated that participants in discussions and meetings should be able to rely on a prior and solid base of information, including real statistics, projections and proposals for solutions, not just the general information provided in concept notes. The representative of Singapore called upon the Council to improve the focus and interactivity of open debates. The representative of the Syrian Arab Republic stated that it was essential to limit the length of statements in open debates involving the participation of many delegations to ensure that all Member States had an equal opportunity to speak.[40] The representative of Kuwait called for allowing Member States to submit written statements in connection with open debates.[41]

Some delegations addressed the issue of transparency and the modalities of informal consultations. The representative of Pakistan noted that much of the Council's real work increasingly took place behind closed doors in informal meetings, which had no records and therefore did not assign responsibility or provide explanations for most of the decisions taken by the Council. The representatives of Cuba and Singapore called upon the Council to issue and circulate records from informal consultations. The representative of China stated that, when giving briefings to the media on the proceedings of closed consultations, some Council members distorted the positions of other members by quoting them out of context. He expressed the view that that undermined the consultations, affected their outcomes and eroded unity among the members. The representative of Malta stated that closed consultations should be frank, interactive and aimed at finding mutually acceptable solutions and should not be just another forum in which Council members delivered written statements and reiterated well-known positions.

Regarding Arria-formula meetings, the representative of Liechtenstein noted that they served to bring to the attention of the Council topics and voices that it had otherwise not heard. He added that, if used as intended, Arria-formula meetings could do a great deal to enhance the Council's inclusivity and relevance and expressed hope that they would be used consistently in accordance with their original intent and purpose. The representative of Malta stated that Arria-formula meetings allowed the Council to consider issues from a specific angle and provided non-Council members the opportunity to participate in discussions. The representative of Peru stated that the Arria-formula meetings needed to provide for some kind of follow-up. The representative of Kuwait suggested that, in order to promote transparency, Arria-formula meetings should be included in the *Journal of the United Nations*. The representative of France, while acknowledging the importance of Arria-formula meetings, pointed out that they were too numerous and sometimes misused. She called upon Council members to find a way to limit their number and ensure that they were genuinely inclusive by providing interpretation in a systematic manner. The representative of China stated that Arria-formula meetings should be better managed in accordance with their original purpose, which was to provide Council members with an opportunity to know more about the issues on its agenda and exchange views in an informal setting. He went on to encourage presidencies of the Council to demonstrate good leadership in steering Arria-formula meetings towards a more rational track.

A number of speakers shared their views regarding the remote working methods developed during the COVID-19 pandemic, including the use of videoconferences. The representative of the United States stated that videoconferences should be considered formal meetings of the Council, under the provisional

[37] See S/PV.9079 (Pakistan and Cuba); and S/PV.9079 (Resumption 1) (Italy).

[38] See S/PV.9079 (Resumption 1).

[39] See S/PV.9079.

[40] See S/PV.9079 (Resumption 1).

[41] See S/PV.9079.

rules of procedure, so that the Council could adopt draft resolutions through a virtual correspondence process. The representative of the Republic of Korea expressed the view that the innovative adaptation of working methods during the pandemic provided a unique opportunity to look critically at how the Council had been conducting its work and to explore how to further improve the transparency, efficiency and effectiveness of its work. More specifically, the representative of Liechtenstein stated that the Council should bear in mind the use of videoconference technology to improve inclusiveness. The representative of Peru stated that the practice of broadcasting Council meetings on the United Nations audiovisual system was a genuine democratic opening. The representative of Cyprus stated that, while technology could add value in cases where briefers could not attend a meeting physically, its use should be measured by its contribution to the core function of the Council.[42]

Several speakers addressed the need for the Council to codify the best practices developed during the COVID-19 pandemic and for contingency planning for future extraordinary circumstances.[43] The representative of Peru stated that the Council must be prepared for new challenges, such as those posed by the pandemic, so that it could continue to discharge its functions and so that dialogue could remain open, inclusive and transparent. The representative of Cyprus stated that the Council must ensure that it could take all necessary action without delay, that it could enforce its decisions, that its work was transparent and accessible to non-members of the Council and that it could effectively interact with those Member States that were directly affected by its work.[44] She also said that a contingency plan did not need to be overly prescriptive but did need to include the ability to physically gather a representative from each Council member for decisions to be made and did need to designate a location beyond the Security Council Chamber for meetings to be held in case Headquarters was affected by a disaster. In contrast, the representative of the Russian Federation stated that there was no need to institutionalize the temporary measures developed during the pandemic and that, in case of future crises, the Council could turn to the procedures enshrined in the letters from the President of the Council that were circulated each month.[45]

Case 2
The situation in the Middle East

At a meeting held on 29 September under the item entitled "The situation in the Middle East",[46] the Security Council heard a monthly briefing by the High Representative for Disarmament Affairs on the implementation of resolution 2118 (2013), regarding the elimination of the chemical weapons programme of the Syrian Arab Republic. In his remarks, the representative of the Russian Federation expressed "bewilderment" at the decision of the presidency of the Council not to grant his delegation's urgent request to convene, that same day, a meeting on the situation regarding the Nord Stream pipeline.[47] Instead, the Council was discussing the report of the Director General of the Organisation for the Prohibition of Chemical Weapons (OPCW) on the implementation of resolution 2118 (2013) – a report that had been issued in August and that, according to the representative, had no urgency. He stated that there was no point in discussing the Syrian chemical weapons issue in the Council every month, as discussions were going around in circles, and that open meetings once every quarter would be sufficient to ensure a transparent discussion of the subject. In a similar vein, the representative of Brazil said that it was incontrovertible that the frequency of the meetings on the issue had to change. He noted that, while regular OPCW reports continued to be a valuable tool for monitoring the file, holding monthly meetings with the Council when the reports pointed to little or no relevant new developments on the ground did not seem efficient in terms of both time and resources. The representative of China, echoing that view, stated that like most members of the Council, his delegation would like to see the Council meet less

[42] See S/PV.9079 (Resumption 1).

[43] See S/PV.9079 (Ireland (on behalf of the elected members of the Council), United States, Switzerland (on behalf of the Accountability, Coherence and Transparency Group), Japan, Austria, Portugal, Indonesia, Bahrain and Slovenia).

[44] See S/PV.9079 (Resumption 1).

[45] See S/PV.9079.

[46] See S/PV.9141.

[47] For more information concerning the Nord Stream pipeline discussed under the item entitled "Threats to international peace and security", see part I, sect. 34.

frequently to consider the Syrian chemical weapons issue. In contrast, the representative of France emphasized that the repetitive nature of meetings should not make the Council members lose sight of what was important and that the perpetrators of the chemical weapons attack on the outskirts of Damascus in August 2013 must be identified and held to account. The representative of Norway expressed concern that the Council must convene amid no progress made on the file for the entirety of 2022, underlining the lack of fulfilment by the Syrian Arab Republic of its obligations in line with the Chemical Weapons Convention and resolution 2118 (2013). The representative of the United States noted that the desire to end the outrageous behaviour of the Al-Assad regime and its "Russian enablers" was what brought the Council to those meetings each month, to speak truth and urge the regime to comply with its international obligations. The representative of Ireland said that until the Council saw real assurance by the Syrian Arab Republic that its chemical weapons programme was verifiably and definitively destroyed, the Council should uphold the international legal norm against chemical weapons by holding the Syrian Arab Republic to its obligations under resolution 2118 (2013) and the Chemical Weapons Convention and by supporting OPCW in its mandated tasks.

At another briefing, held on 7 November under the same item,[48] the representative of the Russian Federation pointed out that there were no other subjects within the Council's mandate-reporting cycle that had been considered with such frequency, underlining that the previous meeting on the implementation of resolution 2118 (2013) had been held less than two weeks prior. He further stated that it was "simply absurd" given that there had been no developments on the situation at all. The representative of China strongly appealed to the Council to reduce the frequency of deliberations on the Syrian issue or consider combining issues related to the Syrian Arab Republic to economize on meeting resources and improve the Council's efficiency. In a similar vein, the representative of the United Arab Emirates pointed out that the Council was meeting only several days after the most recent meeting on the same file without any developments that warranted the holding of the meeting and that the meetings were unfortunately still scheduled every month without regard for their usefulness. In that connection, she stressed the importance of using the time and resources of the Council wisely. While expressing support for the convening of a meeting on the dossier following any relevant developments, the representative underlined the shared responsibility of Council members to reconsider the meetings that the Council held on the issue to ensure the efficiency of the Council. The representative of Brazil said that his delegation did not believe that holding successive Council meetings when there were few or no developments on the ground was efficient in terms of time or resources. He also explained that his delegation's position on readdressing the frequency of meetings on the item was strictly with regard to the efficiency of the Council's work, as recognized by most Council members. The representative of Ghana, speaking also on behalf of Gabon and Kenya, expressed concern over the lack of tangible progress in addressing the issue in accordance with the Chemical Weapons Convention and called into question the propriety of the frequency with which the Council met on the Syrian chemical weapons file. He joined other members of the Council in calling for a review of the status quo to enable the Council to focus its attention and resources on other existing challenges facing the Syrian people. The representative of India also stated that discussions on the Syrian Arab Republic and chemical weapons should reflect progress on the ground, which had remained at a standstill for several months. The representative of the United States said that as long as there remained discrepancies in the chemical weapons statement of the Syrian Arab Republic, the monthly meetings remained necessary and fully appropriate. The representative of the United Kingdom, acknowledging that there was an understandable frustration in the Council about the lack of progress, underlined that the problem was not how many meetings the Council held but the behaviour of the "Syrian regime" in breach of core international norms, including resolutions of the Council. The representative of Albania stated that the cooperation of the Syrian Arab Republic by answering the questions put forward in the report of the Declaration Assessment Team should precede the call for fewer meetings on its chemical weapons programme. The representative of Ireland stated that actions by the Syrian Arab Republic were important to closing the file and that it was only through the country's genuine engagement that OPCW would be able to provide the necessary assurance that the chemical weapons programme was a thing of the past. Until then, she added that the Council could not

[48] See S/PV.9184. For more information on meetings held under the item entitled "The situation in the Middle East" relating to the Syrian Arab Republic, see part I, sect. 20.

"simply shrug its shoulders" and that regular discussions were needed to show that the lack of cooperation by the Syrian Arab Republic would not go unanswered.

E. Records

During the period under review, verbatim records were issued following each public meeting of the Council, in accordance with rule 49 of the provisional rules of procedure, while communiqués were issued following private meetings, in accordance with rule 55. No explicit reference was made at Council meetings to rules 49 to 57 in connection with the preparation, access to and issuance of verbatim records, communiqués or other documents. Nevertheless, the content and preparation of records was raised at the annual open debate on the working methods of the Council held on 28 June under the item entitled "Implementation of the note by the President of the Security Council (S/2017/507)".[49] In his statement at the meeting, the representative of Liechtenstein welcomed the fact that the Council had been able to follow up on the working methods aspects of General Assembly resolution 76/262 of 26 April 2022, which provided for the President of the Assembly to convene a debate within 10 working days of the casting of a veto by one or more permanent members of the Council.[50] He also noted that that it was essential to have records of relevant Council meetings produced as expeditiously as possible in the future in order to ensure maximum flexibility for the scheduling of an Assembly meeting.

Notwithstanding the Council's full return to in-person conduct of business, at the beginning of 2022, the front page of the verbatim records of in-person open debates provided that, in accordance with the procedure set out in the letter dated 7 May 2020 from the President of the Council, which had been agreed in the light of the extraordinary circumstances created by the COVID-19 pandemic, the official record of the Council would be supplemented by a compilation of statements submitted by interested non-Council members who were unable to participate in person.[51] The last open debate to feature a compilation of statements in addition to verbatim records was held on 8 March.[52] The practice was discontinued thereafter.

II. Agenda

Note

Section II deals with the practice of the Council concerning the agenda, in relation to rules 6 to 12 of the provisional rules of procedure.

Rule 6

The Secretary-General shall immediately bring to the attention of all representatives on the Security Council all communications from States, organs of the United Nations, or the Secretary-General concerning any matter for the consideration of the Security Council in accordance with the provisions of the Charter.

Rule 7

The provisional agenda for each meeting of the Security Council shall be drawn up by the Secretary-General and approved by the President of the Security Council.

---

[49] See S/PV.9079 and S/PV.9079 (Resumption 1).

[50] See S/PV.9079. For more information on General Assembly resolution 76/262, see part IV, sect. I.B.

[51] See, for example, S/PV.8949, S/PV.8949 (Resumption 1), S/PV.8950, S/PV.8950 (Resumption 1), S/PV.8953, S/PV.8953 (Resumption 1), S/PV.8989 and S/PV.8989 (Resumption 1) and the corresponding compilations of written statements submitted by Member States, S/2022/38, S/2022/39, S/2022/54 and S/2022/207.

[52] See S/PV.8989, S/PV.8989 (Resumption 1) and S/2022/207.

Only items which have been brought to the attention of the representatives on the Security Council in accordance with rule 6, items covered by rule 10, or matters which the Security Council had previously decided to defer, may be included in the provisional agenda.

Rule 8

The provisional agenda for a meeting shall be communicated by the Secretary-General to the representatives on the Security Council at least three days before the meeting, but in urgent circumstances it may be communicated simultaneously with the notice of the meeting.

Rule 9

The first item of the provisional agenda for each meeting of the Security Council shall be the adoption of the agenda.

Rule 10

Any item on the agenda of a meeting of the Security Council, consideration of which has not been completed at that meeting, shall, unless the Security Council otherwise decides, automatically be included in the agenda of the next meeting.

Rule 11

The Secretary-General shall communicate each week to the representatives on the Security Council a summary statement of matters of which the Security Council is seized and of the stage reached in their consideration.

Rule 12

The provisional agenda for each periodic meeting shall be circulated to the members of the Security Council at least twenty-one days before the opening of the meeting. Any subsequent change in or addition to the provisional agenda shall be brought to the notice of the members at least five days before the meeting. The Security Council may, however, in urgent circumstances, make additions to the Agenda at any time during a periodic meeting.

The provisions of rule 7, paragraph 1, and of rule 9, shall apply also to periodic meetings.

During the period under review, the Secretary-General continued the practice of distributing communications from States, organs of the United Nations or himself concerning any matter for the consideration of the Council, in accordance with the provisions of the Charter of the United Nations and pursuant to rule 6 of the provisional rules of procedure. The Secretary-General also continued to draw up a provisional agenda for each meeting of the Council and to communicate the provisional agenda to the representatives on the Council, in accordance with rules 7 and 8. No periodic meetings were held in 2022, and rule 12 was not applied. The present section is focused on the practice and discussion regarding rules 9 to 11 and is organized under the following three main headings: A. Adoption of the agenda (rule 9); B. Matters of which the Security Council is seized (rules 10 and 11); and C. Discussions concerning the agenda.

A. Adoption of the agenda (rule 9)

In accordance with rule 9 of the provisional rules of procedure, the first item of the agenda for each meeting of the Council is the adoption of the agenda.

Voting on the adoption of the agenda

In 2022, an objection was raised to the adoption of the provisional agenda that led to a procedural vote on one occasion. At a meeting of the Council held on 31 January under the item entitled "Threats to international peace and security", despite the objection raised, the procedural vote resulted in the adoption of the provisional agenda.[53]

Newly introduced items

During the period under review, the Council added two new items to the list of matters of which it was seized. The Council held a total of 18 meetings under the new item entitled "Maintenance of peace and security of Ukraine", the first of which was held on 11 April.[54] The Council also convened two meetings under the new item entitled "Letter dated 13 September 2022 from the Permanent Representative of Armenia to the United Nations addressed to the President of the Security Council (S/2022/688)", the first of which was held on 15 September.[55]

From 2000 to 2007, the Council added between 8 and 23 new items to its agenda every year. Since 2008, however, the number of new items introduced each year has decreased significantly, with no more than three new items introduced in any given year. Figure III provides information on the number of items newly introduced per year since 2000.

Figure III
Number of newly introduced items per year, 2000–2022

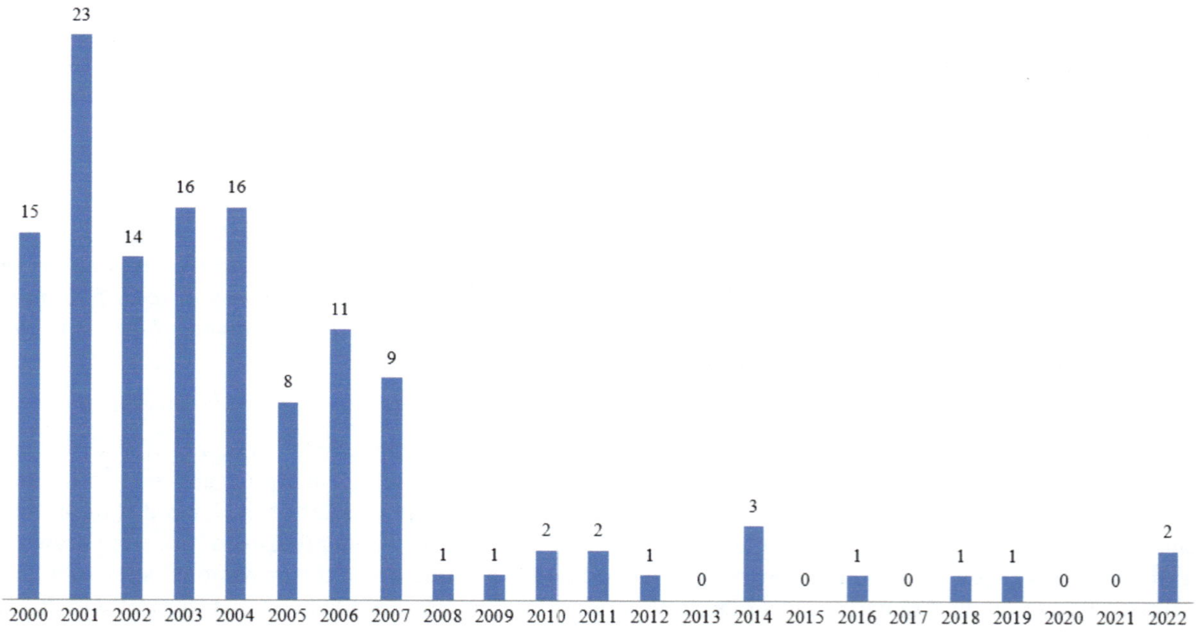

Consideration of country-specific situations under existing items of a regional nature and region-specific situations under existing thematic items

During the period under review, the Council continued the practice of using existing items of a regional nature for the consideration of evolving country-specific situations. For example, Council members continued to consider the situations in Lebanon, the Syrian Arab Republic and Yemen under the items entitled "The situation in the Middle East" and "The situation in the Middle East, including the

[53] See S/PV.8960. For further details on the discussion, see sect. II.C below and part I, sect. 34.

[54] See S/PV.9013. For more information, see part I, sect. 19.C.

[55] See S/PV.9132. For more information, see part I, sect. 16.

Palestinian question".[56] The Council also considered the situation in Ethiopia under the item entitled "Peace and security in Africa".[57]

The Council continued to utilize thematic items to discuss country- and region-specific situations. For example, under the item entitled "Threats to international peace and security", Council members continued to deliberate on the work of the United Nations Investigative Team to Promote Accountability for Crimes Committed by Da'esh/Islamic State in Iraq and the Levant, established pursuant to resolution 2379 (2017).[58] In 2022, the Council also utilized the item to regularly discuss the situation in Ukraine,[59] and also convened meetings under the item to discuss climate and security in Africa[60] and counter-terrorism in Africa.[61] Under the item entitled "Cooperation between the United Nations and regional and subregional organizations in maintaining international peace and security", the Council deliberated on its cooperation with regional organizations, such as the African Union,[62] the Collective Security Treaty Organization,[63] the European Union[64] and the League of Arab States.[65] Furthermore, Council members discussed the implementation of resolution 2231 (2015) and the Joint Comprehensive Plan of Action under the items entitled "Maintenance of international peace and security"[66] and "Non-proliferation".[67]

Inclusion of new sub-items under existing items

During the period under review, the Council continued the practice of adding new sub-items to existing items for the consideration of evolving threats to international peace and security. Table 6 provides a list of new sub-items introduced in 2022 in chronological order of their introduction.[68]

Table 6
New sub-items added to existing items at formal meetings, 2022

Meeting record and date	Item	New sub-item
S/PV.8949 18 January[a]	Women and peace and security	Protecting participation: addressing violence targeting women in peace and security processes
S/PV.8953 25 January[a]	Protection of civilians in armed conflict	War in cities: protection of civilians in urban settings
S/PV.8962 7 February	General issues relating to sanctions	Preventing their humanitarian and unintended consequences
S/PV.8989 8 March[a]	Women and peace and security	Women's economic inclusion and participation as a key to building peace
S/PV.9014 11 April	Maintenance of international peace and security	Implementation of resolutions 2532 (2020) and 2565 (2021)

[56] For more information, see part I, sects. 20 and 21.
[57] For more information, see part I, sect. 9.
[58] See, for example, S/PV.9059 and S/PV.9206.
[59] See, for example, S/PV.8960, S/PV.8988, S/PV.9124 and S/PV.9216.
[60] See S/PV.9150.
[61] See S/PV.9188.
[62] See S/PV.9149.
[63] See S/PV.8967.
[64] See S/PV.9065.
[65] See S/PV.9001.
[66] See S/PV.9167.
[67] See S/PV.9085 and S/PV.9225.
[68] The table excludes cases of routine sub-items relating to briefings on Council missions, briefings by Chairs of subsidiary bodies, letters addressed to the President of the Council, reports of the Secretary-General and meetings of the Council with troop- and police-contributing countries pursuant to resolution 1353 (2001), annex II, sects. A and B.

Meeting record and date	Item	New sub-item
S/PV.9016 13 April[a]	Women and peace and security	Accountability as prevention Ending cycles of sexual violence in conflict
S/PV.9036 19 May[a]	Maintenance of international peace and security	Conflict and food security
S/PV.9039 23 May	Maintenance of international peace and security	Technology and security
S/PV.9052 2 June[a]	Maintenance of international peace and security	Strengthening accountability and justice for serious violations of international law
S/PV.9064 15 June[a]	Women and peace and security	Keeping the promises: the role of regional organizations in implementing the women and peace and security agenda in the face of political turmoil and seizures of power by force
S/PV.9090 12 July[a]	United Nations peacekeeping operations	The key role of strategic communications for efficient peacekeeping
S/PV.9106 8 August[a]	Peace and security in Africa	Capacity-building for sustaining peace
S/PV.9112 22 August	Maintenance of international peace and security	Promote common security through dialogue and cooperation
S/PV.9147 6 October	Peace and security in Africa	Strengthening the fight against the financing of armed groups and terrorists through the illicit trafficking of natural resources
S/PV.9150 12 October	Threats to international peace and security	Climate and security in Africa
S/PV.9158 20 October[a]	Women and peace and security	Strengthening women's resilience and leadership as a path to peace in regions plagued by armed groups
S/PV.9181 3 November[a]	Peacebuilding and sustaining peace	Integrating effective resilience-building in peace operations for sustainable peace
S/PV.9188 10 November	Threats to international peace and security	Counter-terrorism in Africa: an imperative for peace, security and development
S/PV.9220 14 December[a]	Maintenance of international peace and security	New orientation for reformed multilateralism
S/PV.9221 15 December	Threats to international peace and security caused by terrorist acts	Global counter-terrorism approach – principles and the way forward

[a] The 8949th, 8953rd, 8989th, 9016th, 9036th, 9052nd, 9064th, 9090th, 9106th, 9158th, 9181st and 9220th meetings were resumed in the afternoon of the same day or the following day (see S/PV.8949 (Resumption 1), S/PV.8953 (Resumption 1), S/PV.8989 (Resumption 1), S/PV.9016 (Resumption 1), S/PV.9036 (Resumption 1), S/PV.9052 (Resumption 1), S/PV.9064 (Resumption 1), S/PV.9090 (Resumption 1), S/PV.9106 (Resumption 1), S/PV.9158 (Resumption 1), S/PV.9181 (Resumption 1) and S/PV.9220 (Resumption 1)).

B. Matters of which the Security Council is seized (rules 10 and 11)

During the period under review, pursuant to rule 11 of the provisional rules of procedure and the note by the President dated 30 August 2017,[69] the Secretary-General continued to communicate each week to the members of the Council a summary statement of matters of which the Council was seized and of the stage reached in their consideration.[70] The practice of including an agenda item in the summary statement upon its adoption at a formal meeting of the Council remained unchanged.

In 2022, the Council added the items entitled "Maintenance of peace and security of Ukraine" and "Letter dated 13 September 2022 from the Permanent Representative of Armenia to the United Nations addressed to the President of the Security Council (S/2022/688)" to the summary statement, which were considered for the first time at meetings held on 11 April and 15 September, respectively.[71]

In accordance with the note by the President dated 30 August 2017, the preliminary annual summary statement of matters of which the Council is seized, issued in January each year by the Secretary-General, identifies the items that have not been considered by the Council during the preceding three calendar years and that are therefore subject to deletion. An item is deleted unless a Member State notifies the President of the Council, by the end of February, of its request that the item be retained on the list, in which case the item will remain on the list for an additional year. If no Member State requests the item's retention on the list, the first summary statement issued in March of that year reflects its deletion.[72]

During the period under review, in accordance with rule 11 of the provisional rules of procedure and the note by the President dated 30 August 2017, the Council continued the practice of reviewing the summary statement at the beginning of each year in order to determine whether the Council had concluded its consideration of any items.[73] In 2022, of the 16 items identified for deletion in January, the item entitled "The situation in Liberia" was deleted, while the other 15 items were retained for one additional year at the request of Member States, as illustrated in table 7.[74]

Table 7
Items proposed for deletion from the summary statement, 2022

Item	*Date of first and last consideration*	*Status in March 2022*
The India-Pakistan question	6 January 1948; 5 November 1965	Retained
The Hyderabad question	16 September 1948; 24 May 1949	Retained
Letter dated 20 February 1958 from the representative of the Sudan addressed to the Secretary-General	21 February 1958; 21 February 1958	Retained
Letter dated 11 July 1960 from the Minister for Foreign Affairs of Cuba addressed to the President of the Security Council	18 July 1960; 5 January 1961	Retained
Letter dated 31 December 1960 from the Minister for External Affairs of Cuba addressed to the President of the Security Council	4 January 1961; 5 January 1961	Retained
The situation in the India/Pakistan subcontinent	4 December 1971; 27 December 1971	Retained
Letter dated 3 December 1971 from the Permanent Representatives of Algeria, Iraq, the Libyan Arab Republic and the People's Democratic Republic of Yemen to the United Nations addressed to the President of the Security Council	9 December 1971; 9 December 1971	Retained

[69] S/2017/507, annex, paras. 15 and 16.
[70] See, for example, S/2022/10/Add.1 and S/2022/10/Add.2.
[71] See S/2022/10/Add.16 and S/2022/10/Add.38. See also S/PV.9013 and S/PV.9132.
[72] S/2017/507, annex, paras. 15 and 16.
[73] See S/2022/10.
[74] See S/2022/10/Add.10.

Item	*Date of first and last consideration*	*Status in March 2022*
Complaint by Cuba	17 September 1973; 18 September 1973	Retained
The situation between Iran and Iraq	26 September 1980; 31 January 1991	Retained
Letter dated 1 October 1985 from the Permanent Representative of Tunisia to the United Nations addressed to the President of the Security Council	2 October 1985; 4 October 1985	Retained
Letter dated 19 April 1988 from the Permanent Representative of Tunisia to the United Nations addressed to the President of the Security Council	21 April 1988; 25 April 1988	Retained
Letter dated 2 February 1990 from the Permanent Representative of Cuba to the United Nations addressed to the President of the Security Council	9 February 1990; 9 February 1990	Retained
The situation in Liberia	22 January 1991; 19 April 2018	Deleted
The situation in Georgia	8 October 1992; 15 June 2009	Retained
The situation in the Democratic People's Republic of Korea	22 December 2014; 11 December 2017	Retained
Letter dated 13 March 2018 from the Chargé d'affaires a.i. of the Permanent Mission of the United Kingdom of Great Britain and Northern Ireland to the United Nations addressed to the President of the Security Council (S/2018/218)	14 March 2018; 6 September 2018	Retained

Items considered at Security Council meetings

Following the deletion of one item in March 2022, the Council was seized of 68 items during the review period.[75] Of the 68 items, the Council considered 47 items at its formal meetings, of which 26 were country- or region-specific and 21 were thematic. Table 8 provides an overview of the items of which the Council was seized and the items considered at formal meetings of the Council.

Table 8
Items of which the Council is seized and items considered at formal meetings, 2022

Item	*Considered at a formal meeting*
Country-specific and regional situations	
Africa	
Peace and security in Africa	Yes
The situation in Burundi	No
Central African region	Yes
The situation in the Central African Republic	Yes
The situation concerning the Democratic Republic of the Congo	Yes
The situation in the Great Lakes region	Yes
The situation in Guinea-Bissau	No
The situation in Libya	Yes

[75] See S/2022/10, S/2022/10/Add.10 and S/2022/10/Add.49.

Item	Considered at a formal meeting
The situation in Mali	Yes
The situation in Somalia	Yes
Letter dated 20 February 1958 from the representative of the Sudan addressed to the Secretary-General	No
Reports of the Secretary-General on the Sudan and South Sudan	Yes
Letter dated 1 October 1985 from the Permanent Representative of Tunisia to the United Nations addressed to the President of the Security Council	No
Letter dated 19 April 1988 from the Permanent Representative of Tunisia to the United Nations addressed to the President of the Security Council	No
Peace consolidation in West Africa	Yes
The situation concerning Western Sahara	Yes
Americas	
Identical letters dated 19 January 2016 from the Permanent Representative of Colombia to the United Nations addressed to the Secretary-General and the President of the Security Council (S/2016/53)	Yes
Complaint by Cuba	No
Letter dated 11 July 1960 from the Minister for Foreign Affairs of Cuba addressed to the President of the Security Council	No
Letter dated 31 December 1960 from the Minister for External Affairs of Cuba addressed to the President of the Security Council	No
Letter dated 2 February 1990 from the Permanent Representative of Cuba to the United Nations addressed to the President of the Security Council	No
The question concerning Haiti	Yes
The situation in the Bolivarian Republic of Venezuela	No
Asia	
The situation in Afghanistan	Yes
Letter dated 13 September 2022 from the Permanent Representative of Armenia to the United Nations addressed to the President of the Security Council (S/2022/688)	Yes
The situation in the Democratic People's Republic of Korea	No
The Hyderabad question	No
The India-Pakistan question	No
The situation in the India/Pakistan subcontinent	No
The situation in Myanmar	Yes
Europe	
The situation in Bosnia and Herzegovina	Yes
The situation in Cyprus	Yes
The situation in Georgia	No
Maintenance of peace and security of Ukraine	Yes

Item	Considered at a formal meeting
Letter dated 28 February 2014 from the Permanent Representative of Ukraine to the United Nations addressed to the President of the Security Council (S/2014/136)	Yes
Letter dated 13 April 2014 from the Permanent Representative of the Russian Federation to the United Nations addressed to the President of the Security Council (S/2014/264)	Yes
Letter dated 13 March 2018 from the Chargé d'affaires a.i. of the Permanent Mission of the United Kingdom of Great Britain and Northern Ireland to the United Nations addressed to the President of the Security Council (S/2018/218)	No
Security Council resolutions 1160 (1998), 1199 (1998), 1203 (1998), 1239 (1999) and 1244 (1999)	Yes
Middle East	
Letter dated 3 December 1971 from the Permanent Representatives of Algeria, Iraq, the Libyan Arab Republic and the People's Democratic Republic of Yemen to the United Nations addressed to the President of the Security Council (S/10409)	No
The situation between Iran and Iraq	No
The situation concerning Iraq	Yes
The situation between Iraq and Kuwait	Yes
The situation in the Middle East	Yes
The situation in the Middle East, including the Palestinian question	Yes
Total, country-specific and regional situations	**26 items**
Thematic and other issues	
Briefing by the Chairperson-in-Office of the Organization for Security and Cooperation in Europe	Yes
Briefing by the President of the International Court of Justice	Yes
Briefing by the United Nations High Commissioner for Refugees	Yes
Briefings by Chairs of subsidiary bodies of the Security Council	Yes
Children and armed conflict	Yes
Consideration of the draft report of the Security Council to the General Assembly	Yes
Cooperation between the United Nations and regional and subregional organizations in maintaining international peace and security	Yes
General issues relating to sanctions	Yes
Implementation of the note by the President of the Security Council (S/2017/507)	Yes
International Residual Mechanism for Criminal Tribunals	Yes
Maintenance of international peace and security	Yes
Meeting of the Security Council with the troop- and police-contributing countries pursuant to resolution 1353 (2001), annex II, sections A and B	Yes
Non-proliferation	Yes
Non-proliferation/Democratic People's Republic of Korea	Yes
Non-proliferation of weapons of mass destruction	Yes
Peacebuilding and sustaining peace	Yes

Item	Considered at a formal meeting
Protection of civilians in armed conflict	Yes
Security Council mission	No
Small arms	No
The promotion and strengthening of the rule of law in the maintenance of international peace and security	No
Threats to international peace and security	Yes
Threats to international peace and security caused by terrorist acts	Yes
United Nations peacekeeping operations	Yes
Women and peace and security	Yes
Total, thematic and other issues	**21 items**
Total number of items[a]	**68 items**
Total number of items considered	**47 items**

[a] In 2022, the Council also considered the item entitled "Date of election to fill a vacancy in the International Court of Justice" (see S/PV.9073), which was not on the list of items of which it was seized.

C. Discussions concerning the agenda

During the period under review, Council members discussed the agenda and matters of which the Council was seized in several meetings.

At a meeting held on 31 January under the item entitled "Threats to international peace and security",[76] the representative of the Russian Federation requested a procedural vote on the provisional agenda. Explaining his request, the representative expressed his delegation's objection to the view of the United States, which had proposed the holding of the meeting, that the deployment of troops of the Russian Federation on its own territory was a threat to international peace and security. He stated that it was tantamount to unacceptable interference in the domestic affairs of the Russian Federation and an attempt to mislead the international community on the situation. He reminded Council members that the Russian Federation, as the President of the Council for February 2022, planned to hold an annual discussion on the situation in Ukraine, at which the United States delegation could add any information concerning the situation in question. In response, the representative of the United States explained that her delegation's request for the meeting was based on the actions of the Russian Federation on the border with Ukraine and that the meeting was about the protection of the peace and security of a Member State, in accordance with the Charter. She underlined that it was time to hold a public meeting, noting the numerous private meetings that the United States had had with officials of the Russian Federation and in consultation with European and Ukrainian colleagues. The provisional agenda was put to a vote and adopted.[77]

At the first meeting convened under the new item entitled "Maintenance of peace and security of Ukraine", held on 11 April,[78] following the adoption of the provisional agenda, the representative of the Russian Federation, while noting that his delegation was not against adding the new item to the agenda of the Council, suggested deleting the two other existing items pertaining to the situation in Ukraine, entitled "Letter dated 28 February 2014 from the Permanent Representative of Ukraine to the United Nations addressed to the President of the Security Council (S/2014/136)" and "Letter dated 13 April 2014 from the Permanent Representative of the Russian Federation to the United Nations addressed to the

[76] See S/PV.8960.

[77] The provisional agenda received 10 votes in favour (Albania, Brazil, France, Ghana, Ireland, Mexico, Norway, United Arab Emirates, United Kingdom and United States), 2 against (China and Russian Federation) and 3 abstentions (Gabon, India and Kenya).

[78] See S/PV.9013.

President of the Security Council (S/2014/264)". He stated that, since the new item covered all kinds of aspects of the situation in Ukraine, it was universal in character and the deletion of the previous two items would reflect common sense and the current situation. He called upon the presidency of the Council to take the necessary procedural steps to formalize the new item and delete the two previous items at an early date so that future presidencies would not have problems on agreeing on the Council's programme of work. The representative of the United States said that the meeting under the new item was proposed by her delegation without prejudice to the two existing items. She expressed the view that the existing items had to remain in place because, while the scope of the situation in Ukraine had grown far beyond the circumstances in 2014, it was important to recognize its history and it was possible that Member States would wish to focus on Crimea during future meetings. The representative of the United Kingdom, in her capacity as President of the Council, recalled that the process for removing items from the list of items of which the Council was seized was governed by the note by the President dated 30 August 2017[79] and usually took three years. Given the split views among Council members, she proposed discussing the issue separately and seeking to agree on a way forward. In his remarks, the representative of Ukraine underscored that the title of the new item, "Maintenance of peace and security of Ukraine", was exceptional for conflict-specific issues, which mostly referred to "situations in" specific countries or "questions concerning" them. According to the representative, such language was an acknowledgment that the peace and security of Ukraine had been violated from abroad and that the Council would remain seized of the matter until they were restored.

At a meeting held on 26 July under the item entitled "The situation concerning Iraq",[80] the Minister for Foreign Affairs of Iraq called upon the Council to include the item entitled "The situation concerning Iraq and Türkiye" on its agenda, considering the repeated Turkish violations of Iraqi territories and airspace for several years as Türkiye was illegally expanding its military presence.

In 2022, the agenda of the Council was also discussed in more detail during the annual open debate on the working methods of the Council, held on 28 June under the item entitled "Implementation of the note by the President of the Security Council (S/2017/507)" (case 3).

Case 3
Implementation of the note by the President of the Security Council (S/2017/507)

On 28 June, at the initiative of Albania, which held the presidency of the Security Council for the month and whose Permanent Representative chaired the Informal Working Group on Documentation and Other Procedural Questions in 2022,[81] the Council convened an open debate on its working methods under the item entitled "Implementation of the note by the President of the Security Council (S/2017/507)" and the sub-item entitled "Working methods of the Security Council".[82] In their statements, Council members exchanged views on the content and scope of the Council's agenda.

In her remarks, the representative of the Russian Federation cautioned against the practice of individual members using the Council to expand its agenda through domestic, political, human rights, climate or other questions.[83] The representative argued that the practice ignored the fact that the Council, under the Charter of the United Nations, should not be a venue for, and could not help with the resolution of, those problems. The representative of China stated that the Council had seen a steady increase in the number of emerging issues and a continuous proliferation of cross-cutting issues on its agenda, some of which were clearly beyond its core mandate. He said that the Council should focus on the major pressing issues that threatened international peace and security and avoid taking on new topics without due consideration, which did not produce the desired effects and took up too much of its resources. Furthermore, the representative stated that there should be a reasonable division of labour between the Council and other bodies on cross-cutting issues to avoid overlap and redundancy. Citing the Council's discussions on the Syrian Arab Republic as an example, he added that issues on the agenda and arrangements for deliberations should be adjusted as and when the situation on the ground changed.

[79] S/2017/507.
[80] See S/PV.9100.
[81] A concept note was circulated by a letter dated 21 June (S/2022/499).
[82] See S/PV.9079 and S/PV.9079 (Resumption 1). See also S/2022/842.
[83] See S/PV.9079.

The representative of the Islamic Republic of Iran emphasized that the Council should exercise caution when introducing new topics for consideration and avoid duplication of efforts and encroaching on the mandate of the General Assembly. The representative of the Sudan underscored that the reform of the Council's working methods under Article 24 of the Charter required the Council to adhere to its Charter-mandated functions, adding that a quick glance at the agenda of the Council revealed that it was rapidly expanding, necessitating a pause for reflection and meaningful review.[84] In a similar vein, speaking also on behalf of India, the representative of Brazil stated that there were items on the agenda of the Council on which discussion had not been held since the creation of the United Nations and suggested that members begin a discussion on the review of items on the list of matters of which the Council was seized in accordance with the note by the President dated 30 August 2017.[85]

III. Representation and credentials

Note

Section III covers the practice of the Council concerning representation and the credentials of its members, in relation to rules 13 to 17 of the provisional rules of procedure.

Rule 13

Each member of the Security Council shall be represented at the meetings of the Security Council by an accredited representative. The credentials of a representative on the Security Council shall be communicated to the Secretary-General not less than twenty-four hours before he takes his seat on the Security Council. The credentials shall be issued either by the Head of the State or of the Government concerned or by its Minister of Foreign Affairs. The Head of Government or Minister of Foreign Affairs of each member of the Security Council shall be entitled to sit on the Security Council without submitting credentials.

Rule 14

Any Member of the United Nations not a member of the Security Council and any State not a Member of the United Nations, if invited to participate in a meeting or meetings of the Security Council, shall submit credentials for the representative appointed by it for this purpose. The credentials of such a representative shall be communicated to the Secretary-General not less than twenty-four hours before the first meeting which he is invited to attend.

Rule 15

The credentials of representatives on the Security Council and of any representative appointed in accordance with rule 14 shall be examined by the Secretary-General who shall submit a report to the Security Council for approval.

Rule 16

Pending the approval of the credentials of a representative on the Security Council in accordance with rule 15, such representative shall be seated provisionally with the same rights as other representatives.

Rule 17

Any representative on the Security Council, to whose credentials objection has been made within the Security Council, shall continue to sit with the same rights as other representatives until the Security Council has decided the matter.

[84] See S/PV.9079 (Resumption 1).

[85] See S/PV.9079. See also S/2017/507.

During the period under review, in accordance with rule 13 of the provisional rules of procedure, the credentials of the representatives of the members of the Council were communicated to the Secretary-General. The Secretary-General subsequently submitted his report to the Council pursuant to rule 15. Such reports were transmitted to the Council when there were changes in the representation of the members of the Council,[86] as well as when representatives of the newly elected members of the Council were designated prior to the beginning of each term.[87]

No discussions regarding the interpretation and application of rules 13 to 17 arose during the period under review. However, the issue of authorization to represent a Member State was raised on one occasion. At a meeting held on 29 March under the item entitled "Letter dated 28 February 2014 from the Permanent Representative of Ukraine to the United Nations addressed to the President of the Security Council (S/2014/136)",[88] the representative of Ukraine said that, while he recognized the representative of the "aggressor State" in the permanent seat of the Soviet Union, the representative of the Russian Federation was not authorized to speak on behalf of the Ukrainian people.

IV. Presidency

Note

Section IV covers the practice of the Council concerning the monthly rotation of the presidency, the role of the President and the temporary cession of the chair by the President during the consideration of a particular question with which the Member State he or she represents is directly connected, in relation to rules 18 to 20 of the provisional rules of procedure.

Rule 18

The presidency of the Security Council shall be held in turn by the members of the Security Council in the English alphabetical order of their names. Each President shall hold office for one calendar month.

Rule 19

The President shall preside over the meetings of the Security Council and, under the authority of the Security Council, shall represent it in its capacity as an organ of the United Nations.

Rule 20

Whenever the President of the Security Council deems that for the proper fulfilment of the responsibilities of the presidency he should not preside over the Council during the consideration of a particular question with which the member he represents is directly connected, he shall indicate his decision to the Council. The presidential chair shall then devolve, for the purpose of the consideration of that question, on the representative of the member next in English alphabetical order, it being understood that the provisions of this rule shall apply to the representatives on the Security Council called upon successively to preside. This rule shall not affect the representative capacity of the President as stated in rule 19, or his duties under rule 7.

The present section comprises two subsections, namely: A. The role of the President of the Security Council (rules 18 and 19); and B. Discussions concerning the presidency of the Security Council. In 2022, there were no instances of the application of rule 20.

A. Role of the President of the Security Council (rules 18 and 19)

During the period under review, in accordance with rule 18 of the provisional rules of procedure, the presidency of the Council was held in turn for one calendar month by the members of the Council in English

---

[86] See, for example, S/2022/27, S/2022/238, S/2022/262, S/2022/778 and S/2022/784.
[87] See S/2022/1020.
[88] See S/PV.9008.

alphabetical order. In addition to continuing to preside over meetings of the Council, informal consultations of the whole and informal interactive dialogues, the President of the Council continued to perform several other functions under the authority of the Council, including: (a) briefing non-members of the Council and the media on the monthly programme of work at the beginning of the month and holding "wrap-up" sessions with non-Council members and briefings with the media at the end of the presidency; (b) representing the Council and delivering statements on its behalf, including the presentation of the annual report of the Council to the General Assembly;[89] (c) holding monthly meetings with the Secretary-General and the President of the General Assembly; and (d) delivering statements or elements to the press following informal consultations of the whole or whenever Council members reached an agreement on a text.[90]

The presidency of the Council continued the practice of holding wrap-up sessions with the wider membership of the United Nations, except during the months of February and September. The wrap-up sessions were held in accordance with the note by the President dated 27 December 2019,[91] following the "Toledo-style" format, whereby members of the Council presented jointly the activity of the Council for the month as a panel and in an interactive manner.[92] In December, as President of the Council for the month, India held a joint wrap-up session with Ireland, Kenya, Mexico and Norway, the four other outgoing elected members of the Council, to provide a briefing to the wider membership on the Council's activities during the month and reflect on their two-year tenure.[93] Council members also continued to submit, in their national capacities, monthly assessments providing an overview of the work of the Council during their presidencies.[94]

Consistent with the note by the President dated 12 July 2021,[95] in 2022, Council presidencies continued the practice of circulating written monthly commitments providing a list of priorities and measures to enhance the effectiveness, efficiency and transparency of the Council. Monthly commitments were circulated among Council members at the beginning of the month and on an informal basis. In some cases, monthly commitments were submitted jointly by a set of successive or like-minded presidencies. In their monthly commitments, Council members would indicate the priorities of the presidency in terms of working methods, focusing, inter alia, on the following: convening of briefings on the informal programme of work and wrap-up sessions for the wider membership, establishing a good balance between public meetings and informal consultations, requesting speakers to deliver their statements in five minutes or less in public meetings, encouraging interactivity and dialogue in informal consultations and the use of elements to the press, further strengthening the participation of civil society in Council meetings and ensuring zero tolerance for any reprisals against them, regularly seeking the views of affected Member States and regional and subregional organizations on the Council's informal programme of work, and enhancing coordination with the other principal organs of the United Nations and the Peacebuilding Commission.

During their respective presidencies of the Council, in January and March, Norway and the United Arab Emirates developed and launched digital platforms for the Council's monthly programme of work, featuring all formal and informal activities, which were published on the websites of their respective permanent missions. The United Arab Emirates made available the programme of work in a digital form in both English and Arabic.

Council presidencies also continued to implement and further build upon the joint working methods commitments entitled "Security Council Presidency Trio for Women, Peace and Security", originally developed by the delegations of Ireland, Kenya and Mexico in September 2021. In a letter dated 3 February addressed to the President of the Council,[96] the representatives of those three former

[89] At a meeting held on 20 May (see S/PV.9037), the Council issued a note by the President (S/2022/403), in which it indicated that it had adopted its report to the General Assembly covering the period from 1 January to 31 December 2021 (A/76/2). The report was introduced to the Assembly at the 79th plenary meeting of its seventy-sixth session, on 9 June, by the President of the Council for the month of June (Albania). See also part IV, sect. I.F.

[90] Not all statements to the press are issued as a result of informal consultations. Council presidencies referred to the practice of delivering statements and elements to the press in their respective monthly assessments (see, for example, S/2022/924, S/2022/917, S/2022/868, S/2023/40, S/2022/989, S/2023/82 and S/2023/107).

[91] S/2019/994.

[92] See, for example, S/2022/924, S/2022/917, S/2022/1017 and S/2022/989.

[93] See S/2023/107.

[94] As at the time of writing, 8 of the 12 monthly presidencies had submitted monthly assessments for 2022: S/2022/924, S/2022/917, S/2022/868, S/2022/1017, S/2023/40, S/2022/989, S/2023/82 and S/2023/107.

[95] S/2021/647.

[96] S/2022/91.

elected members of the Council submitted a handover and summary report from the so-called "Presidency Trio", in which they also outlined several recommendations for future presidencies. In a letter dated 27 December,[97] the representative of Norway submitted an updated statement of shared commitments on women and peace and security on behalf of the following 15 signatories: Albania, Brazil, Ecuador, France, Gabon, Ireland, Japan, Kenya, Malta, Mexico, Niger, Norway, Switzerland, United Arab Emirates and United Kingdom.[98] Among the priorities outlined in the document, the signatories committed to: (a) the full, equal and meaningful participation of women in meetings of the Council; (b) including gender perspectives in Council meetings and products; and (c) transparency in advancing the women and peace and security agenda in the Council.

In 2022, some Council presidencies continued the convening of "sofa talks" at the level of permanent representatives to the United Nations, a practice initiated in 2019 for Council members to raise issues of concern regarding international peace and security in an informal setting. On 13 January, as the President of the Council for the month, Norway organized a President's retreat, also referred to as the "Mini Oslo Forum", on preventive diplomacy and mediation in Manhasset, New York, which was held in the format of extended "sofa talks" for the 15 Security Council ambassadors.[99]

Following previous practice, and in accordance with the note by the President dated 30 August 2017, the introduction to the annual report of the Council to the General Assembly for 2021 was prepared under the coordination of the President of the Council for the month of July 2021 (France).[100]

In 2022, Council presidencies continued to bring to the attention of the Council emerging and evolving issues related to international peace and security by organizing meetings under thematic items, sometimes adding new sub-items or proposing new topics. In most cases, Council presidencies transmitted concept notes in their national capacities to guide the discussion.[101] In a letter dated 21 June,[102] the representative of Albania transmitted a concept note for the annual open debate on the Council's working methods, which was held on 28 June under the item entitled "Implementation of the note by the President of the Security Council (S/2017/507)".[103] Furthermore, during a meeting held on 22 August under the item entitled "Maintenance of international peace and security" and the sub-item entitled "Promote common security through dialogue and cooperation", the President of the Council took the floor ahead of the briefers invited under rule 39 of the provisional rules of procedure to draw the attention of Council members to the concept note and explain the purpose and objectives of the meeting.[104]

B. Discussions concerning the presidency of the Security Council

In 2022, the role of the presidency was discussed in multiple instances in communications and meetings of the Council.

---

[97] S/2022/1009.

[98] The Niger held the presidency in December 2021; Albania, Brazil, France, Gabon, Norway, the United Arab Emirates and the United Kingdom held the presidency in 2022; and Albania, Brazil, Ecuador, Japan, Malta, Switzerland, the United Arab Emirates and the United Kingdom were to hold the presidency in 2023.

[99] See S/2022/924.

[100] See S/2017/507, annex, para. 127.

[101] See, for example, the concept note on the sub-item entitled "Protecting participation: addressing violence targeting women in peace and security processes" (S/2022/22, annex), circulated by the representative of Norway prior to a high-level meeting of the Council held on 18 January (see S/PV.8949 and S/PV.8949 (Resumption 1)); the concept note on the sub-item entitled "League of Arab States" (S/2022/240, annex), circulated by the representative of the United Arab Emirates prior to a high-level meeting held on 23 March (see S/PV.9001); the concept note on the sub-item entitled "Strengthening women's resilience and leadership as a path to peace in regions plagued by armed groups" (S/2022/743, annex), circulated by the representative of Gabon prior to a high-level meeting held on 20 October (see S/PV.9158 and S/PV.9158 (Resumption 1)); and the concept note on the sub-item entitled "Global counter-terrorism approach – principles and the way forward" (S/2022/906, annex), circulated by the representative of India prior to a high-level meeting held on 15 December (see S/PV.9221).

[102] S/2022/499.

[103] See S/PV.9079 and S/PV.9079 (Resumption 1). An analytical summary of the debate was circulated after the meeting by the representative of Albania (S/2022/842, annex).

[104] See S/PV.9112. See also S/2022/617.

Communications

During the period under review, in seven letters submitted to the President of the Council and the Secretary-General, the representatives of Albania, the Russian Federation and the United States exchanged competing views on the role of the presidency and the alleged misuse of its prerogatives in, among other issues: (a) addressing requests for Council meetings under rules 2 and 3 of the provisional rules of procedure; (b) the participation of a Member State by videoconference under rule 37; and (c) the participation of a civil society representative under rule 39.[105] Furthermore, in a letter dated 12 September addressed to the President of the Council,[106] the representative of Ethiopia expressed deep concern about the decision of the delegation of France, which held the presidency of the Council during the month, to circulate a letter from a non-State actor, a group designated as a terrorist under the laws of Ethiopia. The representative stated that it went against the fundamental tenets of the Charter of the United Nations, which established a State-centred and intergovernmental multilateral system founded on the respect for the sovereignty of Member States. He further stated that the action of the President of the Council was "unprecedented and highly regrettable" and urged France to rectify it.

In a letter dated 16 February,[107] the representative of Finland transmitted the report on the nineteenth annual workshop for the newly elected members, which had been held on 18 and 19 November 2021. In the report, it was noted that participants had discussed the modalities for the preparation of press elements following informal consultations and the role of the President of the Council in delivering them. In that regard, during the discussion, it had been noted that press elements allowed the Council to convey a message of unity and that they did not need to be extensive. Some speakers had expressed the belief that press elements had become more serious than they should be, with members negotiating them as though they were press statements. It had been suggested that the presidency of the Council needed some flexibility in speaking on behalf of the Council; otherwise, they could become so cautious that they might tell the press nothing. Several participants, however, had favoured caution in that regard, noting that the President should not deliver press elements without securing the agreement of the entire membership. One participant had said that presidencies needed to be careful in answering questions on behalf of the Council and that differences among members in consultations on sensitive issues should not be shared with the press. Several speakers had said that they were willing to try the practice whereby the President, after reading the press elements, could leave the stake-out without answering questions. Participants had also reflected on the role of Council presidencies in promoting priorities through joint initiatives such as the working methods commitments. In that regard, several speakers had welcomed the "Security Council Presidency Trio for Women, Peace and Security", with one noting in particular that, given that elected members were limited to two-year terms, promoting joint priorities across presidencies was a good way to address the challenge of sustaining priorities.

Meetings

On 18 January, at a meeting held under the item entitled "Women and peace and security", the representative of the United Arab Emirates said that her delegation, alongside Albania, the Niger and Norway, had committed to remaining vigilant with Council briefers and taking a zero-tolerance approach towards reprisals, as reflected in their shared working methods commitments on women and peace and security.[108] The representative of the European Union, urging the members of the Council to continue to invite more women human rights defenders and civil society leaders to give briefings to the Council, while taking all the necessary precautions to ensure their safety, said that the innovative shared commitments regarding women and peace and security, launched by the "Trio Presidency" of Ireland, Kenya and Mexico in 2021 and continued by Albania, the Niger, Norway and the United Arab Emirates, were positive steps in that regard.

---

[105] For more information on requests for a meeting of the Council and on participation, see sects. I above and VII below, respectively. See also S/2022/286, S/2022/292, S/2022/309, S/2022/320, S/2022/528, S/2022/565 and S/2022/567.

[106] S/2022/686.

[107] S/2022/128.

[108] See S/PV.8949.

At a meeting held on 25 February under the item entitled "Letter dated 28 February 2014 from the Permanent Representative of Ukraine to the United Nations addressed to the President of the Security Council (S/2014/136)", the representative of Ukraine said that the Russian Federation, by occupying the seat of a Council member in 1991, had violated not only the Charter but also rule 20 of the provisional rules of procedure, as it should not have presided over the Council during the consideration of a particular matter with which it was directly connected.[109] At a meeting held on 27 February under the same item, the representative of Ukraine expressed regret that, once again, rule 20 had not been properly applied by the presidency.[110]

At a meeting held on 5 April under the same item, before the adoption of the provisional agenda, the representative of the Russian Federation protested the manner in which the presidency of the Council, held by the United Kingdom, had handled the requests of his delegation to convene a Council meeting in connection with what he termed provocation by Ukrainian radicals in Bucha.[111]

At a meeting held on 29 April under the item entitled "The situation in the Middle East", the representative of the Russian Federation, taking the floor to make a further statement at the end of the meeting and noting that it was the last meeting of the month, expressed his regret that the presidency of the Council had considerably undermined both written and unwritten rules on which the trust and cooperation in the Council was based.[112] The President assured Council members that the United Kingdom would continue to uphold the Charter and the Council's provisional rules of procedure in its future terms as President, just as it had done during the current presidency.

At a meeting held on 27 July under the item entitled "Peacebuilding and sustaining peace", the representative of the United Arab Emirates, encouraging Council members to further engage with the Peacebuilding Commission, including by continuing to invite it to provide briefings and written advice to the Council on relevant matters, suggested that Council members could coordinate with the Commission before and during their assumption of the Council presidency.[113] According to the representative, such coordination would not only allow for the identification of issues pertinent to the Commission but would also allow enough time for it to make the necessary preparations in an effective manner ahead of Council meetings and consultations.

The role of the President of the Council was also discussed in greater detail at the annual open debate on the working methods of the Council, held on 28 June under item entitled "Implementation of the note by the President of the Security Council (S/2017/507)" (case 4).

Case 4
Implementation of the note by the President of the Security Council (S/2017/507)

On 28 June, at the initiative of Albania, which held the presidency of the Security Council for the month and whose Permanent Representative chaired the Informal Working Group on Documentation and Other Procedural Questions in 2022,[114] the Council convened an open debate on its working methods under the item entitled "Implementation of the note by the President of the Security Council (S/2017/507)" and the sub-item entitled "Working methods of the Security Council".[115] In their statements, participants discussed different aspects of the work of the President of the Council, including its engagement with the wider membership and other principal organs of the United Nations, the preparation of monthly assessments and the practice of circulating monthly working methods commitments.

Speaking on behalf of the elected members of the Council, the representative of Ireland stressed the important role of the presidency in the engagement with the other principal organs of the United Nations.[116]

[109] See S/PV.8979.
[110] See S/PV.8980.
[111] See S/PV.9011. For more information on the discussion, see part I, sect. 19.A. For more information about the referral of a dispute or situation to the Council by States, see sect. I.A above.
[112] See S/PV.9026.
[113] See S/PV.9101.
[114] A concept note was circulated by a letter dated 21 June (S/2022/499).
[115] See S/PV.9079 and S/PV.9079 (Resumption 1). For an analytical summary of the discussion, see S/2022/842.
[116] See S/PV.9079.

In that regard, she noted that the organization of briefings on the informal programme of work to Member States, the media and civil society were useful tools and encouraged the holding of interactive monthly wrap-up sessions. The representatives of Austria, Liechtenstein and Slovenia underlined the need for those sessions to be more interactive. Recalling the non-paper presented by the Accountability, Coherence and Transparency Group on the subject in 2021, the representative of Austria expressed hope that Council members would consider those meetings as an opportunity to further shape public opinion at the United Nations in order to render them more substantial. The representative of Peru said that dialogue under the "Toledo format" should continue to be conducted jointly and interactively in wrap-up sessions, with a view to a more analytical exchange to enhance the transparency of and information regarding the Council's work. Beyond wrap-up sessions, the representative of the Syrian Arab Republic singled out the role of the President in communicating with non-Council members that were being discussed as part of the Council's agenda.[117] The representative of Egypt called for more briefings to all Member States in order to hear their views on the programme of work and to keep them informed about Council visits and various activities.

Participants also discussed the monthly assessments of Council presidencies. In her briefing at the beginning of the meeting, the Director of Security Council Procedure and co-author of the fourth edition of *The Procedure of the UN Security Council* recalled that the note by the President dated 12 June 1997,[118] by which monthly assessments were launched, stated that those documents were to be prepared by Council members "under their own responsibility" and should not be considered as representing the views of the Council.[119] Noting the decrease in the number of assessments submitted since 2015 as a result of the view expressed by some Council members that the assessments had to be agreed by consensus, she appealed to all Council members to return to the letter and spirit of the 1997 note by the President, so that publication could return to 100 per cent. The representative of Ireland said that monthly assessments, which were prepared under the authority of each presidency, constituted useful records of the Council's action and inaction. She highlighted the importance of the assessments being timely and frank in their analysis and assessment of the work of the Council, and added that Member States, civil society and academia should be able to consult such documents and find accurate reflections of the realities of the Council, rather than lists of meetings.

Several speakers discussed the importance of the monthly working methods commitments circulated by Council members at the beginning of their presidencies. The representative of Ireland stated that the growing practice was a step towards the implementation of the note by the President dated 30 August 2017[120] and the subsequent 13 notes by the President and towards greater transparency and accountability. Speaking on behalf of the Accountability, Coherence and Transparency Group, the representative of Switzerland stated that the monthly working methods commitments offered a way to promote agility and institutionalize commitments towards greater effectiveness and transparency.[121] The representatives of Luxembourg (speaking also on behalf of Belgium and the Netherlands), Malta and Switzerland specifically welcomed the commitment to the women and peace and security agenda initiated by the presidencies of Ireland, Kenya and Mexico in 2021, joined by a growing number of presidencies, highlighting that they had made tangible contributions to its implementation across the Council's agenda. Similarly, the representative of Slovenia pointed out that the use of shared thematic commitments to the women and peace and security agenda was an important and innovative step towards promoting its implementation. She added that a similar approach could be useful to advance other issues on the Council's agenda.

[117] See S/PV.9079 (Resumption 1).
[118] S/1997/451.
[119] See S/PV.9079.
[120] S/2017/507.
[121] See S/PV.9079.

V. Secretariat

Note

Section V covers the practice of the Council concerning the functions and powers of the Secretary-General in connection with meetings of the Council, in relation to rules 21 to 26 of its provisional rules of procedure.[122]

Rule 21

The Secretary-General shall act in that capacity in all meetings of the Security Council. The Secretary-General may authorize a deputy to act in his place at meetings of the Security Council.

Rule 22

The Secretary-General, or his deputy acting on his behalf, may make either oral or written statements to the Security Council concerning any question under consideration by it.

Rule 23

The Secretary-General may be appointed by the Security Council, in accordance with rule 28, as rapporteur for a specified question.

Rule 24

The Secretary-General shall provide the staff required by the Security Council. This staff shall form a part of the Secretariat.

Rule 25

The Secretary-General shall give to representatives on the Security Council notice of meetings of the Security Council and of its commissions and committees.

Rule 26

The Secretary-General shall be responsible for the preparation of documents required by the Security Council and shall, except in urgent circumstances, distribute them at least forty-eight hours in advance of the meeting at which they are to be considered.

During the period under review and in accordance with previous practice, the Secretary-General and senior officials of the Secretariat continued to attend Council meetings and provide oral briefings and written reports to the Council, as requested. The Council continued to request briefings by senior officials from the Secretariat.

The various functions of the Secretariat were addressed in several communications of the Council, in particular with respect to its role under resolution 2231 (2015), on the nuclear programme of the Islamic Republic of Iran. In a letter dated 21 October addressed to the Secretary-General and the President of the Council,[123] the representatives of France, Germany and the United Kingdom expressed their deep concern at the transfer of unmanned aerial vehicles from the Islamic Republic of Iran to the Russian Federation in violation of resolution 2231 (2015), which were being used by the Russian Federation in its "war of aggression" against Ukraine. The representatives stated that they would welcome an investigation by the Secretariat team responsible for monitoring the implementation of resolution 2231 (2015). Expressing a similar concern, in a letter issued on the same day and addressed to the President of the Council,[124] the representative of the United States requested the Secretariat team responsible for monitoring the implementation of resolution 2231 (2015) to conduct a technical and impartial

[122] For specific instances in which the Secretary-General was requested or authorized by the Council to carry out other functions in accordance with Article 98, see part VI.

[123] S/2022/781.

[124] S/2022/782.

investigation. The representative also urged the Council to meet in its "2231 format" to review the information and determine an appropriate response.

In another letter dated 21 October,[125] the representative of the Russian Federation expressed concerns regarding the attempts of certain Member States to give instructions to the Secretariat in violation of Article 100 of the Charter of the United Nations, as demonstrated in the letter from the representatives of France, Germany and the United Kingdom[126] and the statements of some Secretariat officials about their intention to accept those instructions. He stressed that no mandate had ever been given to the Secretariat by the Council for any investigation in the context of resolution 2231 (2015) and called upon the Council to request the Secretariat to abstain from any engagement in any investigation with regard to claims of alleged violation of the resolution.

The role of the Secretariat with respect to the implementation of resolution 2231 (2015) was further discussed at a meeting held on 26 October under the item entitled "Maintenance of international peace and security".[127]

VI. Conduct of business

Note

Section VI covers the practice of the Council concerning the conduct of business at its meetings, in relation to rules 27, 29, 30 and 33 of its provisional rules of procedure.

Rule 27

The President shall call upon representatives in the order in which they signify their desire to speak.

Rule 29

The President may accord precedence to any rapporteur appointed by the Security Council.

The Chairman of a commission or committee, or the rapporteur appointed by the commission or committee to present its report, may be accorded precedence for the purpose of explaining the report.

Rule 30

If a representative raises a point of order, the President shall immediately state his ruling. If it is challenged, the President shall submit his ruling to the Security Council for immediate decision and it shall stand unless overruled.

Rule 33

The following motions shall have precedence in the order named over all principal motions and draft resolutions relative to the subject before the meeting:

1. *To suspend the meeting;*
2. *To adjourn the meeting;*
3. *To adjourn the meeting to a certain day or hour;*
4. *To refer any matter to a committee, to the Secretary-General or to a rapporteur;*
5. *To postpone discussion of the question to a certain day or indefinitely; or*
6. *To introduce an amendment.*

---

[125] S/2022/783.
[126] S/2022/781.
[127] See S/PV.9167. For a detailed overview of the discussion, see part VI, sect. II.B.

Any motion for the suspension or for the simple adjournment of the meeting shall be decided without debate.

In 2022, no explicit reference was made to rules 27, 29 and 30 in the meetings of the Council. The President of the Council continued to request speakers to limit their statements in Council meetings in accordance with the note by the President dated 30 August 2017 which, as a general rule, encourages all participants, both members and non-members of the Council, in Council meetings to deliver their statements in five minutes or less.[128] For example, at a meeting held on 25 April, before giving the floor to non-Council members, the President reminded all speakers to limit their statements to no more than four minutes and noted that the flashing lights on the collar of the microphone would prompt speakers to bring their remarks to a close.[129] Following previous practice, during the period under review, joint statements were delivered by Council members[130] and non-Council members invited to participate in Council meetings.[131] Moreover, briefers were also encouraged to be succinct and to limit their remarks to 7 to 10 minutes.[132] Similarly, at a meeting held on 28 September, during the remarks of the briefer, the President of the Council requested him to provide the factual segment of his statement in written form and to move on to the substance of the briefing.[133]

According to the note by the President dated 30 August 2017, as a general practice, the speaking order for meetings of the Council is established by a draw. In addition, the President of the Council delivers his or her national statement last of all Council members.[134] However, in certain cases, the speaking order is established by the use of a sign-up sheet, and the President may make his or her national statement before the other members take the floor.[135] Also in certain cases, the President may adjust the list of speakers and inscribe first the delegation or delegations responsible for the drafting process in order to allow them to make an introductory or explanatory presentation.[136] When an unscheduled or emergency meeting is convened, the President may adjust the list of speakers so that the delegation that requested the meeting can

[128] S/2017/507, annex, para. 22.

[129] See S/PV.9021 and S/PV.9021 (Resumption 1). See also S/PV.9016, S/PV.9016 (Resumption 1), S/PV.9042, S/PV.9042 (Resumption 1), S/PV.9052, S/PV.9052 (Resumption 1), S/PV.9079, S/PV.9079 (Resumption 1), S/PV.9096, S/PV.9096 (Resumption 1), S/PV.9106 and S/PV.9106 (Resumption 1).

[130] In a number of instances, the representatives of Gabon, Ghana and Kenya delivered joint statements on behalf of the three African members of the Council (referred to as the "A3") (see, for example, S/PV.9012 and S/PV.9141). In several instances, Council members delivered joint statements as co-penholders on a particular issue (see, for example, S/PV.9038 and S/PV.9068). At a meeting held on 28 June under the item entitled "Implementation of the note by the President of the Security Council (S/2017/507)", the representative of Ireland delivered a statement on behalf of the 10 elected members of the Council, while the representative of Brazil delivered a statement also on behalf of India (see S/PV.9079).

[131] For example, at a meeting held on 19 April under the item entitled "Maintenance of peace and security of Ukraine", the representative of Sweden spoke on behalf of the Nordic countries (see S/PV.9018); at a meeting held on 25 May under the item entitled "Protection of civilians in armed conflict", the representative of Switzerland delivered a joint statement on behalf of the Group of Friends on the Protection of Civilians in Armed Conflict (see S/PV.9042) and the representative of Croatia delivered a joint statement on behalf of the Group of Friends of the Responsibility to Protect (see S/PV.9042 (Resumption 1)); and, at a meeting held on 12 July under the item entitled "United Nations peacekeeping operations", the representative of Indonesia spoke on behalf of the Group of Friends on the Safety and Security of United Nations Peacekeepers (see S/PV.9090).

[132] See, for example, S/PV.8943, S/PV.8952 and S/PV.8955.

[133] See S/PV.9139. At public and private meetings, briefers are encouraged to limit initial remarks to 15 minutes, unless otherwise decided by the Council (S/2017/507, annex, para. 56).

[134] S/2017/507, annex, paras. 24 and 25.

[135] Ibid. For example, at a meeting held on 7 February under the item entitled "General issues relating to sanctions", the representative of the Russian Federation (President of the Council) took the floor and delivered his national statement after the briefers but before the other members of the Council (see S/PV.8962); at a meeting held on 23 May under the item entitled "Maintenance of international peace and security", the representative of the United States (President of the Council) took the floor and delivered her national statement after the briefers but before the other members of the Council (see S/PV.9039).

[136] S/2017/507, annex, para. 26. For example, at a meeting held on 27 October under the item entitled "The situation concerning Western Sahara", the representative of the United States, as penholder of resolution 2654 (2022), which was adopted at the meeting, took the floor first after the vote to provide explanatory remarks (see S/PV.9168).

speak before other Council members in order to present the rationale for convening the meeting.[137] The President may also inscribe first the Chairs of the subsidiary bodies of the Council when they present their work, as was the case on several occasions during the period under review.[138]

According to established practice and the note by the President dated 30 August 2017, the list of speakers was adjusted according to protocol when high-level officials were representing Council members at a meeting.[139] In 2022, consistent with past practice under these items and in accordance with the note by the President dated 30 August 2017, non-members of the Council having a direct interest in the matter under consideration spoke before Council members in meetings held under the items entitled "Security Council resolutions 1160 (1998), 1199 (1998), 1203 (1998), 1239 (1999) and 1244 (1999)" and "The situation in the Middle East, including the Palestinian question".[140]

The Council continued to use videoconferencing technology to facilitate participation at its in-person meetings.[141] In 2022, Council members received briefings from speakers participating by videoconference in 127 out of 292 meetings (43.5 per cent).[142]

At a meeting held on 5 April under the item entitled "Letter dated 28 February 2014 from the Permanent Representative of Ukraine to the United Nations addressed to the President of the Security Council (S/2014/136)", at the request of the President of Ukraine, invited under rule 37 of the provisional rules of procedure, an audiovisual recording showing the situation in Ukraine was played in the Security Council Chamber.[143]

VII. Participation

Note

Section VII covers the practice of the Council concerning the extension of invitations to non-members of the Council to participate in meetings of the Council. Articles 31 and 32 of the Charter of the United Nations and rules 37 and 39 of the provisional rules of procedure describe circumstances

---

[137] S/2017/507, annex, para. 26. For example, at a meeting held on 4 March under the item entitled "Letter dated 28 February 2014 from the Permanent Representative of Ukraine to the United Nations addressed to the President of the Security Council (S/2014/136)", the representative of the United Kingdom, having requested the Council meeting, delivered a statement after the briefers but before the other members of the Council (see S/PV.8986).

[138] S/2017/507, annex, para. 27. For example, at a meeting held on 21 June under the item entitled "The situation in Somalia", the representative of Ireland spoke before the other members of the Council and provided a briefing to the Council in her capacity as Chair of the Committee pursuant to resolution 751 (1992) concerning Somalia (see S/PV.9071). Pursuant to resolution 2662 (2022), in November 2022, the Council modified the name of the Committee to "Security Council Committee pursuant to resolution 751 (1992) concerning Al-Shabaab" (resolution 2662 (2022), para. 24). For more information, see part VII, sect. III.A, and part IX, sect. I.B.1.

[139] S/2017/507, annex, paras. 29 and 30. For example, at a meeting held on 25 January under the item entitled "Protection of civilians in armed conflict", the Prime Minister of Norway (President of the Council) took the floor after the briefers but before the other Council members (see S/PV.8953); at a meeting held on 8 March under the item entitled "Women and peace and security", the Minister for Climate Change and the Environment of the United Arab Emirates (President of the Council) took the floor after the briefers but before the other Council members (see S/PV.8989); and, at a meeting held on 11 October under the item entitled "Cooperation between the United Nations and regional and subregional organizations in maintaining international peace and security", the Minister for Foreign Affairs of Gabon (President of the Council) took the floor after the briefers but before the other Council members (see S/PV.9149). At a meeting held on 29 July under the item entitled "The situation in the Central African Republic", the Minister for Foreign Affairs, Francophonie and Central Africans Abroad of the Central African Republic took the floor first after the adoption of resolution 2648 (2022), before the members of the Council (see S/PV.9105). At a meeting held on 26 July under the item entitled "The situation concerning Iraq", the Minister for Foreign Affairs of Iraq took the floor after the briefer and before the representative of Türkiye and the Council members (see S/PV.9100). For more information on high-level meetings, see sect. I.A above.

[140] S/2017/507, annex, para. 33. See, for example, S/PV.9019, S/PV.9021, S/PV.9099, S/PV.9107 and S/PV.9155.

[141] S/2017/507, annex, para. 60.

[142] For more information on participation by videoconference, see sect. VII below.

[143] See S/PV.9011. For more information about discussions in Council meetings and communications regarding the participation of rule 37 invitees by videoconference, see sect. VII below.

in which invitations can be extended to non-members of the Council to participate, without a vote, when the Council so decides.

Article 31

Any Member of the United Nations which is not a member of the Security Council may participate, without vote, in the discussion of any question brought before the Security Council whenever the latter considers that the interests of that Member are specially affected.

Article 32

Any Member of the United Nations which is not a member of the Security Council or any state which is not a Member of the United Nations, if it is a party to a dispute under consideration by the Security Council, shall be invited to participate, without vote, in the discussion relating to the dispute. The Security Council shall lay down such conditions as it deems just for the participation of a state which is not a Member of the United Nations.

Rule 37

Any Member of the United Nations which is not a member of the Security Council may be invited, as the result of a decision of the Security Council, to participate, without vote, in the discussion of any question brought before the Security Council when the Security Council considers that the interests of that Member are specially affected, or when a Member brings a matter to the attention of the Security Council in accordance with Article 35 (1) of the Charter.

Rule 39

The Security Council may invite members of the Secretariat or other persons, whom it considers competent for the purpose, to supply it with information or to give other assistance in examining matters within its competence.

During the period under review, the Council continued to invite non-members of the Council to participate in its meetings. The invitations were extended by the President of the Council at the beginning of or during Council meetings, either under the "relevant provisions" of the Charter without an explicit reference to a specific Article or rule of the provisional rules of procedure, or under rule 37 or rule 39. Specifically, Member States continued to be invited under rule 37, while representatives of the Secretariat, other United Nations organs, specialized agencies, funds and programmes and regional and other intergovernmental organizations, or other invitees, including representatives of non-governmental organizations and civil society, were invited under rule 39. While Member States requested invitations in letters addressed to the President, in most cases these were not circulated as documents of the Council. In addition, in 2022, the President requested written advice from the Peacebuilding Commission under rule 39 of the provisional rules of procedure in connection with a number of Council meetings.

During the period under review, in accordance with the notes by the President dated 30 August 2017 and 27 December 2019, the Council invited newly elected members to observe all meetings of the Council and informal consultations of the whole, including consultations on Council outcome documents, as from 1 October 2022, for the three months immediately preceding their term of membership.[144]

The present section is divided into four subsections, namely: A. Invitations extended under rule 37; B. Invitations extended under rule 39; C. Invitations not expressly extended under rule 37 or rule 39; and D. Discussions relating to participation.

A. Invitations extended under rule 37

In accordance with the relevant Articles of the Charter and provisional rules of procedure, all States, whether Members of the United Nations or not, can be invited to participate in Council meetings when: (a) the interests of a Member State are "specially affected" (Article 31 of the Charter and rule 37);

[144] S/2017/507, annex, paras. 140 and 141, and S/2019/993.

(b) a Member State or a non-Member State is a party to a dispute under consideration by the Council (Article 32 of the Charter); and (c) a Member State of the United Nations brings a matter to the attention of the Council in accordance with Article 35 (1) of the Charter (rule 37).[145]

In 2022, with the continued improvement of the situation regarding the COVID-19 pandemic in New York City and the full resumption of Council meetings, restrictions on the participation of non-Council members were progressively removed. During the first months of the year, several aspects of the remote working methods developed during the pandemic that related to the participation of non-Council members continued to be implemented. In a letter dated 17 January addressed to the Permanent Representatives of the members of the Council,[146] the President of the Council (Norway) outlined the working methods agreed upon by the members for the month. While noting that the presidency planned to hold Council meetings in person in the Security Council Chamber, the President indicated that non-Council members would continue to be able to participate in open debates through the submission of written statements. In a letter dated 7 March,[147] the President (United Arab Emirates) further indicated that non-Council members could participate in open debates either in person or through the submission of written statements. Accordingly, Council members continued the practice of having the President circulate a compilation of statements submitted by interested non-Council members who were not able to participate in person, until March 2022, when the practice was discontinued. Despite the restrictions described above, there were no changes to the procedure for extending invitations to Member States to participate in the proceedings of the Council.

Consistent with previous practice, Member States invited under rule 37 of the provisional rules of procedure continued to speak on occasion in other capacities. For example, at private meetings held on 28 January and 27 May under the item entitled "The situation in Myanmar", the Deputy Prime Minister and Minister for Foreign Affairs and International Cooperation of Cambodia participated under rule 37 in his capacity as Special Envoy of the Association of Southeast Asian Nations Chair on Myanmar.[148] In addition, there were several instances of representatives of Member States participating under rule 37 who delivered statements on behalf of groups of States.[149] In 2022, there were several instances of representatives of non-Council members invited in accordance with rule 37 who participated in meetings by videoconference.[150]

---

[145] For more details on the referral of a dispute or situation to the Council by States, see sect. I.A above and part VI, sect. I.A.

[146] S/2022/32.

[147] S/2022/196.

[148] See S/PV.8959 and S/PV.9049.

[149] For example, at a meeting held on 18 January under the item entitled "Women and peace and security", the representative of Canada spoke on behalf of the Group of Friends of Women, Peace and Security, the representative of Switzerland spoke on behalf of the Human Rights and Conflict Prevention Caucus, the representative of Belgium spoke also on behalf of Luxembourg and the Netherlands and the representative of Denmark spoke on behalf of the Nordic countries (see S/PV.8949 and S/PV.8949 (Resumption 1)). At a meeting held on 19 July under the item entitled "Children and armed conflict", the representative of Canada spoke on behalf of the Group of Friends of Children and Armed Conflict and the representative of Botswana spoke on behalf of the Group of Friends of the Responsibility to Protect (see S/PV.9096 and S/PV.9096 (Resumption 1)). At a meeting held on 28 October under the item entitled "The situation in the Middle East, including the Palestinian question", the representative of Pakistan spoke on behalf of the Organization of Islamic Cooperation, the representative of Saudi Arabia spoke on behalf of the Gulf Cooperation Council and the representative of Azerbaijan spoke on behalf of the Movement of Non-Aligned Countries (see S/PV.9174 and S/PV.9174 (Resumption 1)).

[150] The Deputy Prime Minister and Minister for Foreign Affairs and International Cooperation of Cambodia at meetings held on 28 January and 27 May under the item entitled "The situation in Myanmar" (see S/PV.8959 and S/PV.9049); the President of Ukraine at a meeting held on 5 April under the item entitled "Letter dated 28 February 2014 from the Permanent Representative of Ukraine to the United Nations addressed to the President of the Security Council (S/2014/136)" (see S/PV.9011); and the President of Ukraine at meetings held on 28 June, 24 August, 27 September and 23 November under the item entitled "Maintenance of peace and security of Ukraine" (see S/PV.9080, S/PV.9115, S/PV.9138 and S/PV.9202).

At two meetings held in 2022, Council members raised issues of concern regarding invitations extended to Member States pursuant to rule 37 of the provisional rules of procedure. First, an objection to the extension of an invitation pursuant to rule 37 led to a procedural vote on one occasion. At a meeting held on 24 August under the item entitled "Maintenance of peace and security of Ukraine",[151] the representative of the Russian Federation expressed his delegation's objection to the participation of the President of Ukraine in the meeting by videoconference. Speaking ahead of the procedural vote, the representative clarified that his delegation was not opposing the participation of the President of Ukraine or his representative, but underlined that such participation must be in person in the Security Council Chamber, in accordance with the rules that governed the work of the Council. While noting that the President of Ukraine had already spoken to the Council twice by videoconference in 2022, instances that had been described as exceptions by certain other Council members, the representative stated that, while a precedent was not set after one or two times, a third time was no longer an exception. He further noted that the meeting had been announced a week in advance and that the President of Ukraine had had the opportunity to travel to New York. In response, the representative of Albania, while agreeing that virtual participation under rule 37 should be an exception in the post-pandemic situation, reiterated that the justification for the exception remained unchanged from the previous times that the Council had agreed that the President of Ukraine could address the Council by videoconference. He added that, when a full military attack on Ukraine was ongoing, the Council could not reasonably demand that the President of Ukraine travel to New York. The proposal to invite the President of Ukraine to participate in the meeting was put to a vote and adopted by majority.[152]

Second, at a meeting held on 31 October under the item entitled "Threats to international peace and security" and in relation to the diversion of Ryanair flight FR-4978 over the airspace of Belarus,[153] the representative of the Russian Federation expressed his delegation's surprise and disappointment at the decision of the President of the Council to allow representatives of several States of the European Union to participate in the meeting, as they had no connection with the item.

In 2022, Member States continued to submit communications in which they raised issues of concern regarding invitations pursuant to rule 37 of the provisional rules of procedure. In a letter dated 5 April addressed to the President of the Council,[154] the representative of the Russian Federation protested the decision of the President of the Council (United Kingdom) to grant under rule 37 the participation by videoconference of the President of Ukraine in a meeting on Ukraine held on the same day under the item entitled "Letter dated 28 February 2014 from the Permanent Representative of Ukraine to the United Nations addressed to the President of the Security Council (S/2014/136)".[155] The representative stated that it ran contrary to established practice and that the President of the Council had ignored the principle that all Member States invited to address the Council should do so in person. In a letter dated 11 April addressed to the Secretary-General,[156] the representative of the United Kingdom recalled that the presidency of the Council had explained in advance the exceptional nature of the approach to allow the President of Ukraine to participate by videoconference, on the basis that he had been unable to travel to New York given the circumstances in Ukraine, which had been in line with precedent and for which there had been broad support in the Council.

In a letter dated 29 June,[157] the representative of the Russian Federation once again objected to the participation of the President of Ukraine by videoconference at a meeting held on 28 June,[158] which he maintained ran counter to established practice. The representative further noted that similar requests for participation by videoconference from other Member States had been declined by previous presidencies

[151] See S/PV.9115.

[152] The proposal received 13 votes in favour (Albania, Brazil, France, Gabon, Ghana, India, Ireland, Kenya, Mexico, Norway, United Arab Emirates, United Kingdom and United States), 1 against (Russian Federation) and 1 abstention (China).

[153] See S/PV.9175.

[154] S/2022/292.

[155] See S/PV.9011.

[156] S/2022/309.

[157] S/2022/528.

[158] See S/PV.9080.

and that the presidency of Albania had denied such participation to at least one other Member State. He added that such an approach by the presidency demonstrated that it had exploited its prerogatives in a biased manner. In a letter dated 18 July,[159] the representative of Albania recalled that the presidency had clearly specified that the participation of the President of Ukraine by videoconference had been an exceptional case that would not constitute a precedent. Moreover, he added that granting the President of Ukraine the possibility to remotely address the Council, when his country remained under invasion, could not, by any reasonable standard, be called biased or selective, considering that the presidency had not received any request from any other country under similar circumstances. The representative further recalled that, before taking such a decision, the presidency had consulted across the Council and had found wide support for the proposal.

In a letter dated 15 August,[160] the representative of Pakistan stated that, in relation to the briefing of the Council held on 9 August under the item entitled "Threats to international peace and security caused by terrorist acts",[161] his delegation, not being a member of the Council, had not had the opportunity to participate and, considering that the item was of vital interest to Pakistan, was submitting its comments for circulation as an annex. In a letter dated 21 October,[162] the representative of Lithuania, transmitting a joint statement by Estonia, Latvia, Lithuania and Czechia in connection with the Council briefing held on the same day under the item entitled "Maintenance of peace and security of Ukraine",[163] expressed the delegation's disappointment with the decision of the President of the Council to reverse its previously communicated decision to allow Lithuania to participate and deliver a statement.

Furthermore, during the period under review, a number of Member States requested the circulation of their own individual or joint statements with other Member States in connection with meetings in which they did not participate. The majority of these meetings were held in the briefing format under items related to Ukraine.[164]

B. Invitations extended under rule 39

In accordance with rule 39 of the provisional rules of procedure, members of the Secretariat or other persons may be invited to supply the Council with information or give other assistance in examining matters within its competence.

---

[159] S/2022/565.

[160] S/2022/620.

[161] See S/PV.9108.

[162] S/2022/790.

[163] See S/PV.9161.

[164] For example, in separate letters dated 7 March addressed to the President of the Council, the representatives of eight Member States submitted their statements in connection with a briefing held on the same day under the item entitled "Threats to international peace and security" concerning the humanitarian situation in Ukraine, in which they did not participate (see S/2022/185, S/2022/187, S/2022/188, S/2022/189, S/2022/190 and S/2022/195). See also S/2022/127, S/2022/138, S/2022/153, S/2022/165, S/2022/166, S/2022/184, S/2022/241, S/2022/242, S/2022/245, S/2022/273, S/2022/289, S/2022/290, S/2022/305, S/2022/306, S/2022/311, S/2022/615, S/2022/640, S/2022/717, S/2022/790 and S/2022/792. In another example, in letters dated 14 March, the representatives of Estonia, Latvia and Lithuania, jointly, as well as Romania and Slovakia, individually, transmitted their statements in relation to the Council's meeting held on the same day under the item entitled "Briefing by the Chairperson-in-Office of the Organization for Security and Cooperation in Europe" (see S/2022/221, S/2022/224 and S/2022/228). In letters dated 19 and 20 May, the representatives of Slovakia and Georgia, respectively, transmitted statements in relation to the open debate of the Council held on 19 May under the item entitled "Maintenance of international peace and security", in which they did not participate (see S/2022/407 and S/2022/408). In a letter dated 28 June, the representative of Saint Vincent and the Grenadines transmitted a statement in relation to the Council's annual open debate on its working methods held on the same day under the item entitled "Implementation of the note by the President of the Security Council (S/2017/507)", in which she did not participate (see S/2022/519).

Following previous practice, an invitation under rule 39 was extended to a representative of a Member State, on an exceptional basis, if his or her participation was in a role other than that of a representative of a State, for example, as Chair of the Peacebuilding Commission.[165]

In 2022, a total of 445 invitations were extended under rule 39, in comparison with 354 in 2021 and 304 in 2020 (see figure IV).

Figure IV
Invitations under rule 39, 2013–2022

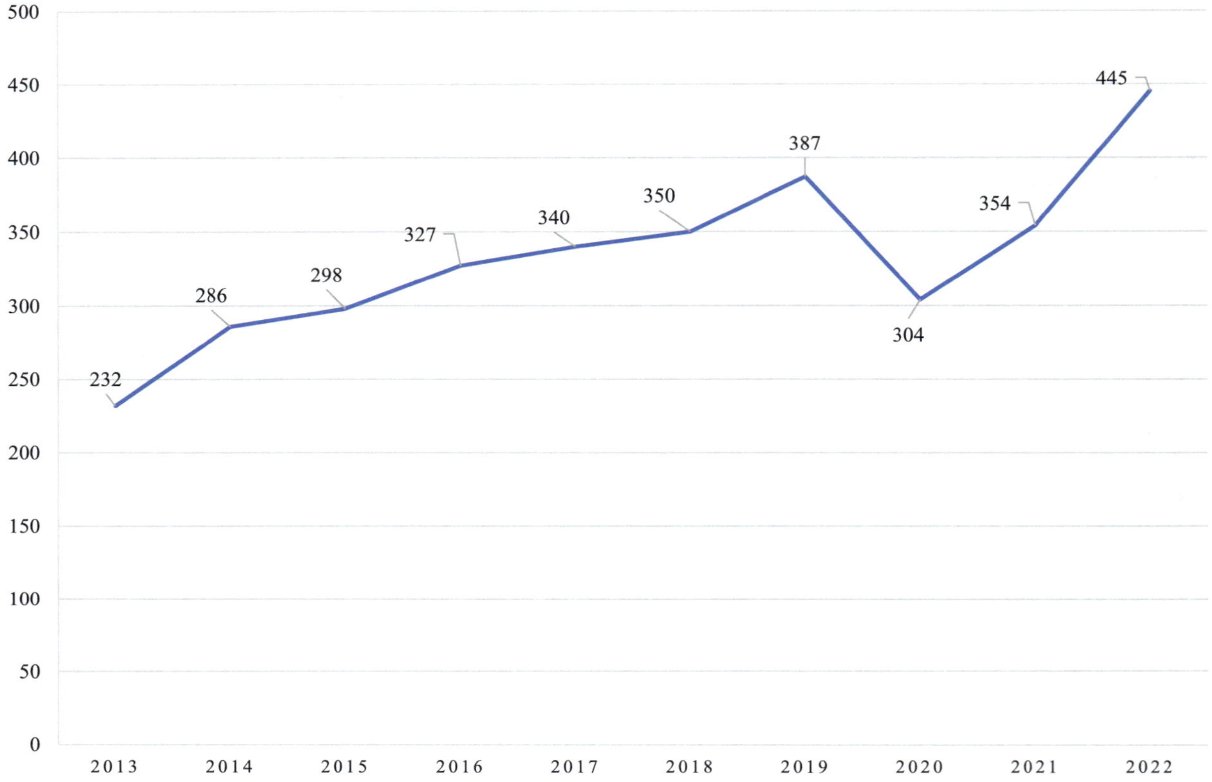

Of the 445 invitees under rule 39, a total of 242 were men and 203 were women. As shown in figure V, in recent years, both the total number and percentage of female speakers invited to Council meetings under rule 39 has increased, with the latter being 45.6 per cent in 2022 compared with 43.8 per cent in 2021. Moreover, in 2022, as part of their monthly working methods commitments, several presidencies of the Council continued to place specific emphasis on ensuring the participation of women briefers in the meetings of the Council.[166]

---

[165] For example, at meetings held on 7 and 27 July, 8 August and 12 October, under the items entitled "Peace consolidation in West Africa" (see S/PV.9086), "Peacebuilding and sustaining peace" (see S/PV.9101), "Peace and security in Africa" (see S/PV.9106) and "Identical letters dated 19 January 2016 from the Permanent Representative of Colombia to the United Nations addressed to the Secretary-General and the President of the Security Council (S/2016/53)" (see S/PV.9151), respectively, representatives of Bangladesh gave briefings to Council members in the capacity as Chair of the Peacebuilding Commission.

[166] For more information on the monthly working methods commitments of Council presidencies, see sect. IV above.

Figure V
Invitees under rule 39, 2013–2022

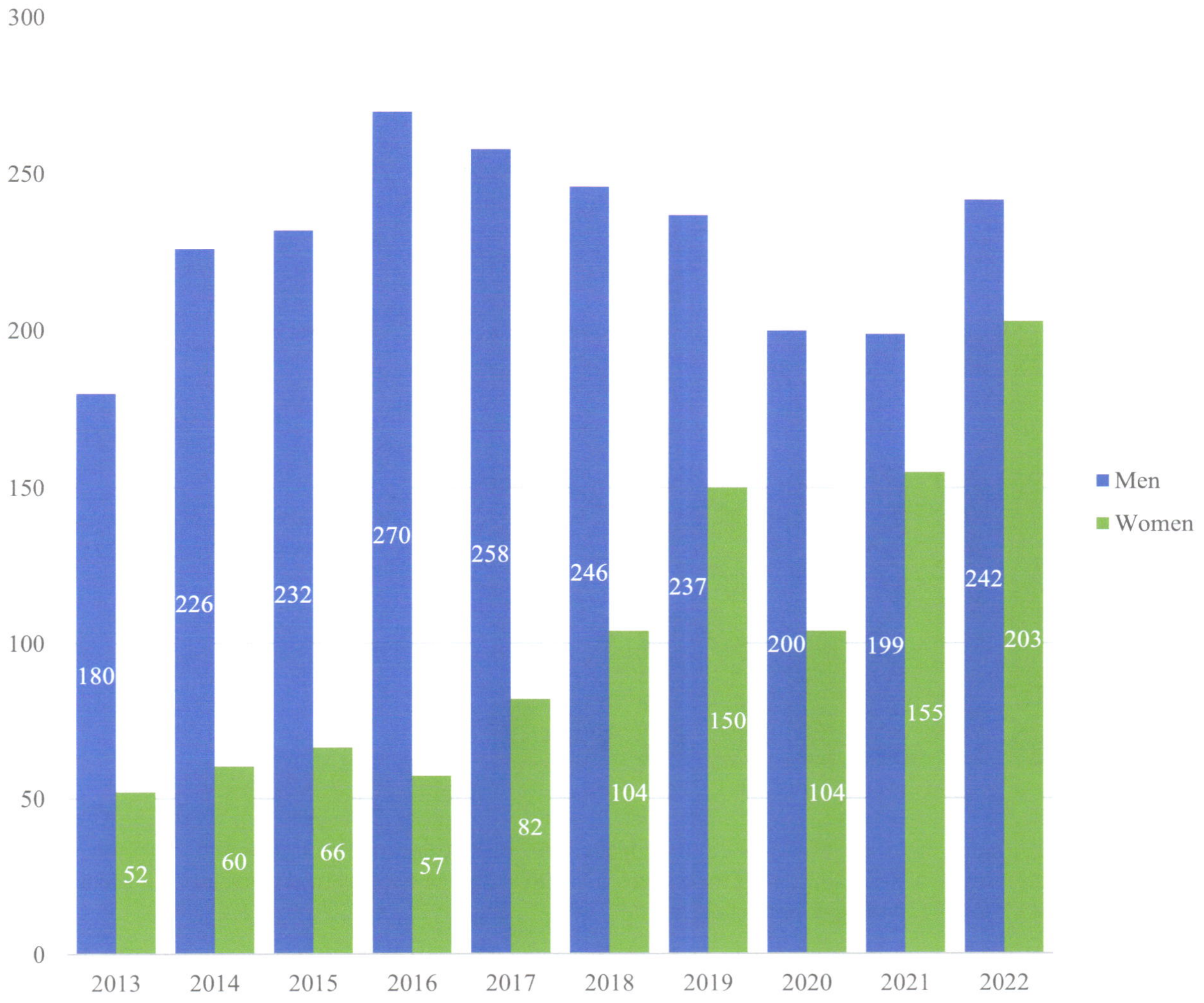

For the purposes of this part of the *Repertoire*, invitations extended under rule 39 are classified according to four main categories, namely:[167] (a) officials of the United Nations system; (b) invitees from international organizations other than the United Nations; (c) officials representing regional intergovernmental organizations; and (d) representatives of other entities such as non-governmental and civil society organizations. As shown in figure VI, invitations under rule 39 were most often extended to officials of the United Nations system and non-governmental and civil society organizations. The number of civil society representatives increased from 86 in 2021 to 89 in 2022, which was the highest number of invitees recorded in this category. In terms of sex-disaggregated data for each category, of the 272 invitations to United Nations officials, 150 (55 per cent) were extended to men and 122 (45 per cent) to women. Of the 70 invitations to officials representing regional intergovernmental organizations, 58 (83 per cent) were extended to men and 12 (17 per cent) to women. Of the 14 invitations to representatives of international organizations other than the United Nations, 10 (71 per cent) were extended to men and 4 (29 per cent) to women. Finally, of the 89 invitations to representatives of other entities such as non-governmental organizations and civil society, 24 (27 per cent) were extended to men and 65 (73 per cent) to women.

[167] In earlier supplements, separate categories were used for invitees of the Secretariat and Council subsidiary bodies and those representing other United Nations organs, subsidiary bodies or agencies. Since the *Repertoire*, *Supplement 2016–2017*, these two categories have been subsumed under the category "United Nations system".

Figure VI
Breakdown of invitations under rule 39, by category, 2013–2022

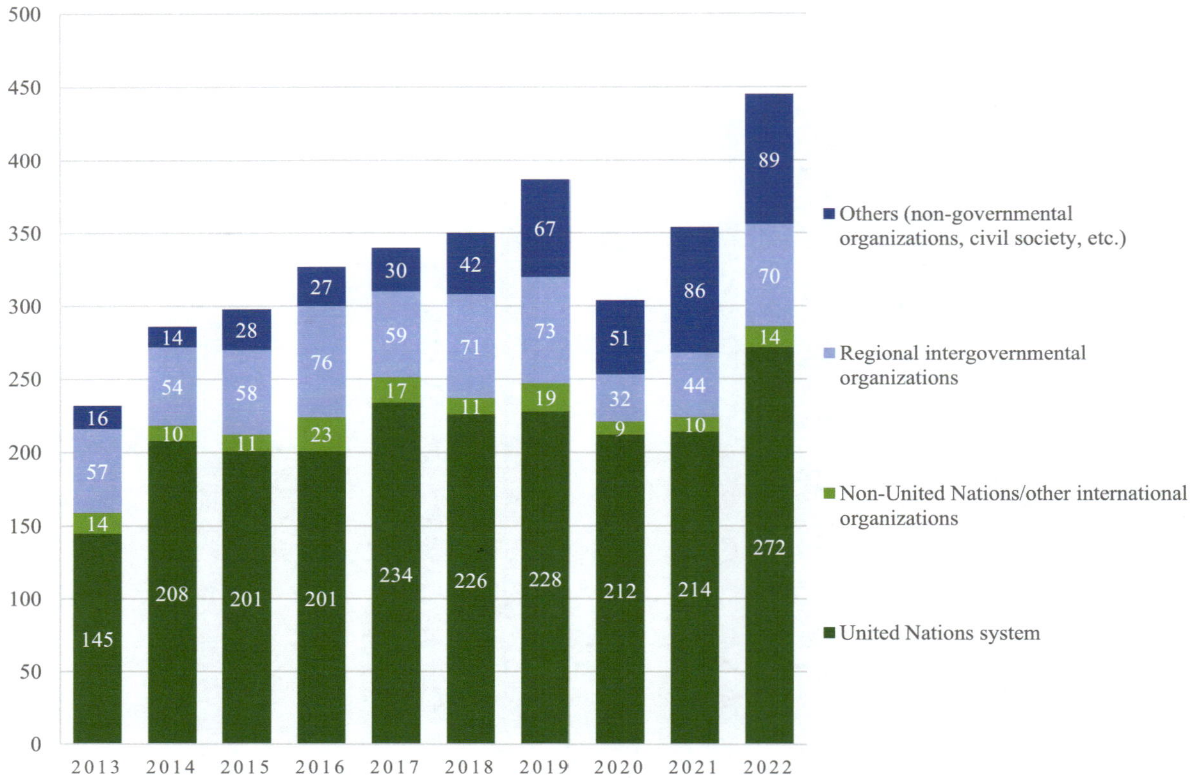

In 2022, there were no changes to the procedure for extending invitations under rule 39 to participate in meetings of the Council. There were also no instances wherein an invitation extended to participate in a Council meeting was put to a vote.

Nevertheless, invitations under rule 39 were discussed in several communications submitted to the Council. In a letter dated 29 June addressed to the President of the Council,[168] the representative of the Russian Federation objected to the choice of a civil society briefer by the Council presidency (Albania) at a meeting held on the Syrian Arab Republic on the same day.[169] The representative stated that it was unacceptable that the briefer had used foul language, insulted Member States and addressed unfounded accusations, adding that that "actor-like" behaviour had not contributed to the discussion. He concluded that this was a clear indication of the need to reconsider the approach to the question of the presence of civil society representatives at Council meetings in order to exclude such incidents. In a letter dated 18 July,[170] the representative of Albania acknowledged the concern of the delegation of the Russian Federation regarding the inappropriate tone and language used by the civil society briefer on 29 June and underlined the need for everyone to respect the decorum of the Council. He added that his delegation strongly supported the free and unimpeded participation of representatives of civil society in the work of the Council, as it enriched its deliberations and common efforts to advance and preserve international peace and security.

During the period under review, the Chair of the Peacebuilding Commission submitted written advice in response to the invitation by the President of the Council to do so under rule 39 of the provisional rules of procedure in connection with a number of meetings held under regional and thematic items.[171]

[168] S/2022/528.
[169] See S/PV.9083.
[170] S/2022/565.
[171] For more information on the Peacebuilding Commission, see part IX, sect. VII.

C. Invitations not expressly extended under rule 37 or rule 39

During the period under review, the Council extended several invitations not expressly under rule 37 or rule 39 (see table 9).

Invitations to representatives of the Holy See and the State of Palestine to participate in meetings of the Council were routinely extended "in accordance with the provisional rules of procedure and the previous practice in this regard", without specification of any rules.

Table 9
Invitations not expressly extended under rule 37 or rule 39, 2022

Invitee	*Meeting record and date*	*Item*
Holy See	S/PV.8953 and S/PV.8953 (Resumption 1), 25 January	Protection of civilians in armed conflict
	S/PV.9042 and S/PV.9042 (Resumption 1), 25 May	
	S/PV.9016 and S/PV.9016 (Resumption 1), 13 April	Women and peace and security
	S/PV.9099, 26 July	The situation in the Middle East, including the Palestinian question
State of Palestine	S/PV.8973, 23 February	The situation in the Middle East, including the Palestinian question
	S/PV.9021, 25 April	
	S/PV.9046, 26 May	
	S/PV.9099, 26 July	
	S/PV.9107, 8 August	
	S/PV.9174, 28 October	
	S/PV.9042 and S/PV.9042 (Resumption 1), 25 May	Protection of civilians in armed conflict
	S/PV.9052 and S/PV.9052 (Resumption 1), 2 June	Maintenance of international peace and security
	S/PV.9096 and S/PV.9096 (Resumption 1), 19 July	Children and armed conflict

D. Discussions relating to participation

During the period under review, when non-members of the Council were invited to participate in a meeting, Council members generally spoke before Member States invited under rule 37 of the provisional rules of procedure and before those not expressly invited under any rule, except on some occasions when parties directly involved in the matter under consideration took the floor before Council members.[172] The practice of the Council with regard to invitees under rule 39 was less consistent, and the order of speakers depended on whether or not they were participating to give a briefing to the Council. In 2022, matters concerning participation in Council meetings were raised in meetings of the Council.

[172] For more information on the order of speaking, see sect. VI above.

For example, at a meeting held on 28 February under the item entitled "The situation in the Middle East", the representative of the Russian Federation expressed disappointment that the Director General of the Organisation for the Prohibition of Chemical Weapons (OPCW) had declined to participate in the meeting, even though the Council had extended an invitation to him, and expressed regret that he had been unable to find time to schedule a briefing to the Council, which was the second time that had happened since May 2021.[173] At a meeting held on 20 July under the same item, the representative of the Russian Federation said that his delegation had expected to see the Director General of OPCW among the briefers and expected the Director General to find an opportunity to address the members of the Council at the next meeting.[174]

At a meeting held on 11 May under the item entitled "The situation in Bosnia and Herzegovina", the representative of the Russian Federation expressed reservations regarding the participation of Christian Schmidt in accordance with rule 39 of the provisional rules of procedure, as his delegation did not consider him to be the legitimate High Representative for the Implementation of the Peace Agreement on Bosnia and Herzegovina.[175] The representative of the Russian Federation asserted that Mr. Schmidt's appointment had not been approved by the Council and highlighted that the situation in Bosnia and Herzegovina was on the Council's agenda under Chapter VII of the Charter. He underscored that Mr. Schmidt did not have the right to speak on behalf of the international community or to submit documents to the Council and that there was no basis for inviting him to meetings of the Council as High Representative, as his presence in the Chamber in that capacity undermined the authority of the Council and of the United Nations in general. The representative of the Russian Federation added, however, that the Council had a practice that allowed individuals to provide a briefing to the Council in their personal capacity to determine whether their further participation was required, which was how the Russian Federation viewed Mr. Schmidt's presence at the meeting in question. Similarly, the representative of China stated that, in the light of the fact that the appointment of Mr. Schmidt had not been endorsed by the Council, his delegation believed that it was inappropriate for him to give a briefing to the Council in the capacity as High Representative.

Participation in Council meetings was also discussed in greater detail during the annual open debate on the working methods of the Council held on 28 June under the item entitled "Implementation of the note by the President of the Security Council (S/2017/507)" (case 5).

Case 5
Implementation of the note by the President of the Security Council (S/2017/507)

At a meeting held on 28 June at the initiative of Albania, which held the presidency of the Security Council for the month and whose Permanent Representative held the Chair of the Informal Working Group on Documentation and Other Procedural Questions in 2022,[176] the Council convened an open debate on its working methods under the item entitled "Implementation of the note by the President of the Security Council (S/2017/507)" and the sub-item entitled "Working methods of the Security Council".[177] In their statements, participants discussed the importance and modalities of participation in Council meetings, with a focus on the wider membership and civil society representatives.

Members and non-members of the Council widely agreed on the need to ensure the participation of the wider United Nations membership in Council meetings. Speaking on behalf of the Accountability, Coherence and Transparency Group, the representative of Switzerland argued that the Council should return to a more inclusive approach on the acceptance of requests for participation under rule 37 of the provisional rules of procedure.[178] The representative of Liechtenstein stated that there should be timely and regular opportunities to address the Council under rule 37. The representative of Germany stated that Council presidencies should, to the greatest extent possible, give affected countries the opportunity to participate in meetings, in accordance with rule 37 and in line with paragraph 74 of the note by the

[173] See S/PV.8982.
[174] See S/PV.9097.
[175] See S/PV.9029.
[176] A concept note was circulated by a letter dated 21 June (S/2022/499).
[177] See S/PV.9079 and S/PV.9079 (Resumption 1).
[178] See S/PV.9079.

President dated 30 August 2017.[179] He added that artificially limiting the number of participants in Council meetings would seriously undermine the Council's inclusivity and legitimacy. The representative of Slovakia echoed that view and called for interaction and dialogue between the Council and other Member States, in particular those directly concerned and affected by a specific situation, stating that such interaction and dialogue needed to be further enhanced and widened through a continued thorough application of rule 37. The representative of Cyprus suggested that establishing an informal channel through the presidency of the Council might help the Council to account for the perspectives of Member States primarily involved in a situation under discussion and that such States could be invited to offer their perspectives in closed consultations, before the Council began its closed deliberations.

Specifically regarding participation in different formats of Council meetings, the representative of the Syrian Arab Republic stated that, even though it was essential to limit the length of statements given during open debates to ensure that all Member States had an equal opportunity to speak, restricting the right of States concerned under an item to express their positions during meetings at which their countries' situations were being discussed thwarted their ability to present their national perspectives and respond to concerns raised. The representative of Guatemala stated that the continuation of the practice of open debates was conducive to the greater participation of non-Council members.[180] The representative of Algeria noted the importance of ensuring that open debates that were held in a virtual format allowed for the broadest possible participation of Member States.[181] The representative of Bahrain said that the regular meetings on the working methods of the Council were of importance to all Member States and made it possible to review the progress and developments made in adapting them to continual changes.[182] The representative of the Russian Federation reiterated her delegation's support for discussing the working methods of the Council in an open format with the participation of all interested Member States, which was an opportunity to increase the Council's coordination with a broad number of them.

Speakers also reflected on the participation of briefers, in particular representatives of civil society, under rule 39 of the provisional rules of procedure. The representative of Ireland, speaking on behalf of the elected members of the Council, stated that Council presidencies should strive for gender balance and diversity when selecting briefers. The representative of France called for more to be done to achieve parity for women and young people at Council meetings. Moreover, participants called for more civil society representatives as briefers in Council meetings,[183] including female briefers and youth representatives.[184] The representative of Malta called upon the Council to ensure that civil society and non-governmental organizations were given adequate space to make their voices heard, as they had a crucial role to play in providing a clear and factual picture of the situation on the ground. The representative of Germany expressed concern over cases in which civil society briefers had faced threats after making statements in the Council.[185] He underlined the importance of civil society briefers being able to speak openly in the Council and of countering all forms of pressure on them. The representative of the Syrian Arab Republic stated that the participation of representatives of civil society and non-governmental organizations should bring added value to the Council's work and that they should benefit the Council with their experience on the subject matter. He added that their participation should in no way constitute an attack on or offend any Member State, promote biased points of view or convey a false or non-objective picture of the situation discussed. In a similar vein, the representative of China encouraged Council presidencies to strengthen the screening process during the selection of civil society briefers to ensure that they were truly well informed on the topics discussed and that their positions were objective and impartial in order to facilitate the Council's discussions and search for solutions.[186] The representative of Indonesia stated that as conflict became more regionalized, the Council needed to ensure the inclusion of regional and subregional organizations in discussions related to their region. He emphasized that regional organizations

[179] See S/PV.9079 (Resumption 1). See also S/2017/507.
[180] See S/PV.9079.
[181] See S/PV.9079 (Resumption 1).
[182] See S/PV.9079.
[183] See S/PV.9079 (China, Luxembourg (also on behalf of Belgium and the Netherlands), Republic of Korea and Liechtenstein); and S/PV.9079 (Resumption 1) (Italy).
[184] See S/PV.9079 (Republic of Korea and Malta).
[185] See S/PV.9079 (Resumption 1).
[186] See S/PV.9079.

could help to mend fractured relationships between United Nations missions and their respective host countries by bridging the two and constructively responding to the situation on the ground.

Several participants emphasized the importance of in-person participation in Council meetings. The representative of Luxembourg, speaking also on behalf of Belgium and the Netherlands, strongly encouraged the Council to ensure that all Member States and all relevant stakeholders were involved, with a particular focus on the participation of civil society representatives in Council meetings, and underlined the importance of in-person participation of Member States and observer States in open meetings of the Council. The representative of Liechtenstein stated that the Council should prioritize in-person access for all States and civil society. The representative of the Russian Federation stated that there was no alternative to in-person discussions and personal interaction among Council Members.

VIII. Decision-making and voting

Note

Section VIII covers the practice of the Council with regard to decision-making, including voting. Article 27 of the Charter of the United Nations and rule 40 of the provisional rules of procedure govern the voting in the Council. They provide that decisions on procedural matters require an affirmative vote of 9 of the 15 Council members, while decisions on substantive matters require an affirmative vote of 9 Council members, including all of the permanent members.

The present section also covers rules 31, 32, 34 to 36 and 38 of the provisional rules of procedure, which govern the conduct of business with regard to voting on draft resolutions, amendments and substantive motions.

Article 27

1. Each member of the Security Council shall have one vote.

2. Decisions of the Security Council on procedural matters shall be made by an affirmative vote of nine members.

3. Decisions of the Security Council on all other matters shall be made by an affirmative vote of nine members including the concurring votes of the permanent members; provided that, in decisions under Chapter VI, and under paragraph 3 of Article 52, a party to a dispute shall abstain from voting.

Rule 31

Proposed resolutions, amendments and substantive motions shall normally be placed before the representatives in writing.

Rule 32

Principal motions and draft resolutions shall have precedence in the order of their submission.

Parts of a motion or of a draft resolution shall be voted on separately at the request of any representative, unless the original mover objects.

Rule 34

It shall not be necessary for any motion or draft resolution proposed by a representative on the Security Council to be seconded before being put to a vote.

Rule 35

A motion or draft resolution can at any time be withdrawn so long as no vote has been taken with respect to it.

If the motion or draft resolution has been seconded, the representative on the Security Council who has seconded it may require that it be put to the vote as his motion or draft resolution with the same right of precedence as if the original mover had not withdrawn it.

Rule 36

If two or more amendments to a motion or draft resolution are proposed, the President shall rule on the order in which they are to be voted upon. Ordinarily, the Security Council shall first vote on the amendment furthest removed in substance from the original proposal and then on the amendment next furthest removed until all amendments have been put to the vote, but when an amendment adds to or deletes from the text of a motion or draft resolution, that amendment shall be voted on first.

Rule 38

Any Member of the United Nations invited in accordance with the preceding rule, or in application of Article 32 of the Charter, to participate in the discussions of the Security Council may submit proposals and draft resolutions. These proposals and draft resolutions may be put to a vote only at the request of a representative on the Security Council.

Rule 40

Voting in the Security Council shall be in accordance with the relevant Articles of the Charter and of the Statute of the International Court of Justice.

The present section comprises five subsections, namely: A. Decisions of the Security Council; B. Penholdership and sponsorship in accordance with rule 38; C. Decision-making by voting; D. Decision-making without a vote; and E. Discussions concerning the decision-making process.

In 2022, rule 31 of the provisional rules of procedure was routinely applied in Council meetings. There were no instances of motions or amendments requiring voting, withdrawal of draft resolutions or requests for separate voting on parts of a draft resolution. Consequently, there were no instances in which rules 32, 34 and 36 were explicitly invoked. Nonetheless, there were instances of competing draft resolutions submitted, which were voted upon in their order of submission pursuant to rule 32, as described in section A below.

A. Decisions of the Security Council

During the period under review, the Council continued to adopt resolutions and statements by the President of the Council at its meetings, in addition to making procedural decisions. Decisions of the Council also took the form of notes by the President and letters from the President, which were not adopted at meetings but were issued as documents of the Council.

In 2022, the Council adopted a total of 54 resolutions and 7 presidential statements. The Council also issued 19 notes by and 27 letters from the President. The number of letters from the President issued in 2022 constituted a significant decrease compared with the 170 and 242 letters issued in 2021 and 2020, respectively. The decrease is largely explained by the progressive return to the working methods existing prior to the COVID-19 pandemic, namely, the return to the practice of adopting resolutions at in-person meetings, thereby ending the use of the written voting procedure, and the return to in-person meetings, thereby reducing the compilations of written statements submitted by interested non-Council members who were unable to participate in person.[187] Figure VII shows the total number of resolutions and presidential statements adopted and notes and letters from the President issued during the past decade (2013–2022).

[187] For more information on the written voting procedure and compilations of written statements, see *Repertoire, Supplements 2020* and *2021*, part II, sect. I. For more information on the compilations of written statements in 2022, see sect. I.E above.

Figure VII
Resolutions and presidential statements adopted and notes by and letters from the President issued, 2013–2022

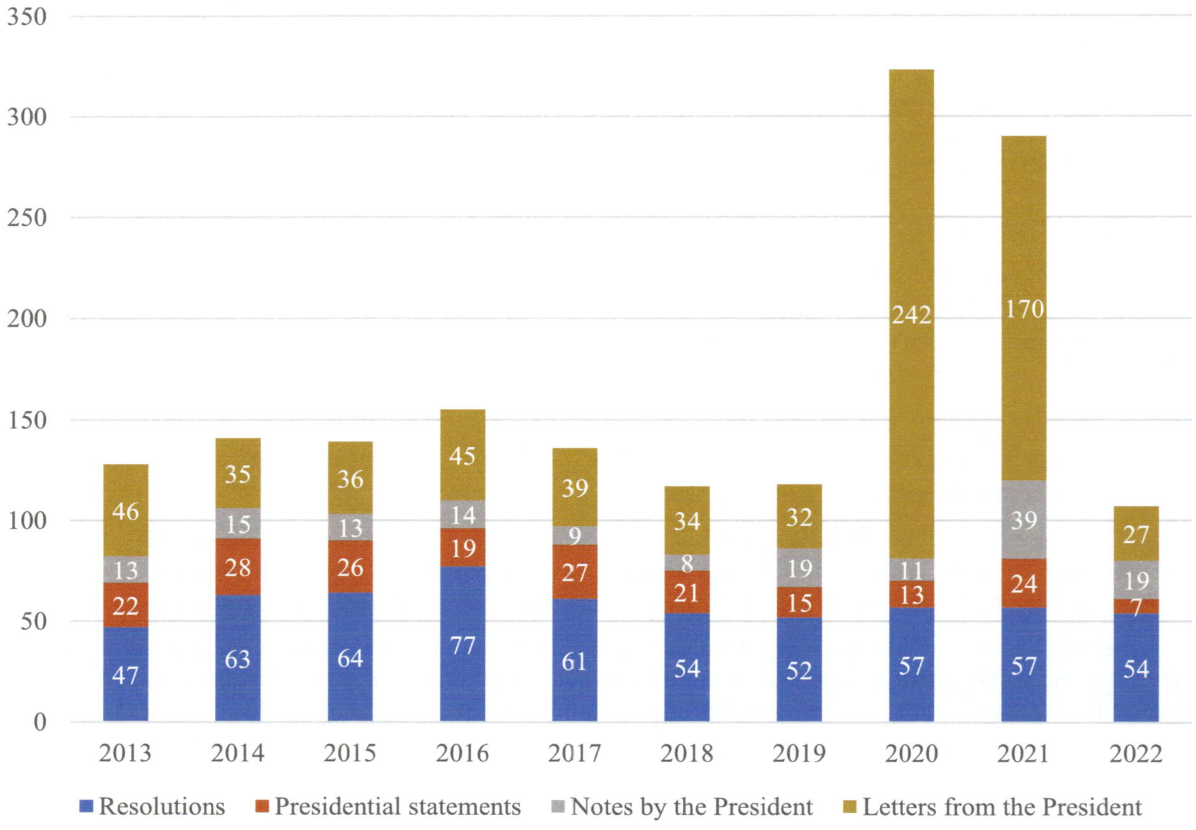

Multiple decisions in one meeting

During 2022, the Council continued the standard practice of adopting a single decision in a meeting, with one exception. At a meeting held on 20 December under the item entitled "The situation concerning the Democratic Republic of the Congo", the Council unanimously adopted resolutions 2666 (2022) and 2667 (2022).[188] There was also one instance in which more than one draft resolution was put to a vote at a single meeting. At a meeting held on 8 July under the item entitled "The situation in the Middle East", the Council failed to adopt a draft resolution submitted by Ireland and Norway owing to the negative vote of a permanent member of the Council.[189] The Council also failed to adopt a second draft resolution, submitted by the Russian Federation, as the draft resolution did not obtain the required number of votes.[190]

B. Penholdership and sponsorship in accordance with rule 38

A draft resolution may be submitted by any member of the Council. The note by the President dated 30 August 2017 provides that the members of the Council support, where appropriate, the informal arrangement whereby one or more Council members, as penholder(s), initiate and chair the informal drafting process. In accordance with the note, any member of the Council may be a penholder, and more than one Council member may act as co-penholders, when it is deemed to add value, taking into account

[188] See S/PV.9226.
[189] See S/PV.9087. See also S/2022/538.
[190] See S/2022/541.

as appropriate the expertise and/or contributions of Council members on the subject. In the note, Council members reaffirmed that all members of the Council should be allowed to participate fully in the preparation of, inter alia, resolutions, presidential statements and press statements of the Council and that the drafting of all documents such as resolutions and presidential statements and press statements should be carried out in an inclusive manner that would allow participation of all members of the Council. The members of the Council also encouraged the penholder or co-penholders, depending on the subject as well as the urgency of the situation on the ground, to provide reasonably sufficient time for consideration by all Council members when draft resolutions, presidential statements and press statements were placed under a silence procedure.[191] In 2022, while the majority of the decisions of the Council continued to be drafted by permanent members, 14 out of 53 resolutions (26.4 per cent) were drafted or co-drafted by one or more elected members.[192]

Pursuant to rule 38 of the provisional rules of procedure, any Member of the United Nations invited in accordance with rule 37 or in application of Article 32 of the Charter to participate in the discussions of the Council may also submit proposals and draft resolutions, but proposals and draft resolutions may be put to a vote only at the request of a Council member. The Member States that submit a draft resolution become sponsors of the draft resolution. A draft resolution is described as a presidential text if all the Council members agree to be co-sponsors. In 2022, no presidential texts were submitted, compared with six in 2021 and one in 2020.[193]

During the period under review, the Council considered a total of 60 draft resolutions, 6 of which were co-sponsored by non-members of the Council, as shown in table 10.

---

[191] S/2017/507, annex, paras. 78–82.

[192] Draft resolution S/2022/147, drafted by Mexico in connection with the item entitled "Non-proliferation of weapons of mass destruction", was adopted as resolution 2622 (2022) on 25 February; draft resolution S/2022/160, co-drafted by Albania and the United States in connection with the item entitled "Letter dated 28 February 2014 from the Permanent Representative of Ukraine to the United Nations addressed to the President of the Security Council (S/2014/136)", was adopted as resolution 2623 (2022) on 27 February; draft resolution S/2022/237, drafted by Norway in connection with the item entitled "The situation in Afghanistan", was adopted as resolution 2626 (2022) on 17 March; draft resolution S/2022/62, co-drafted by Ghana and Norway in connection with the item entitled "Peace and security in Africa", was adopted as resolution 2634 (2022) on 31 May; draft resolution S/2022/501, drafted by Gabon in connection with the item entitled "International Residual Mechanism for Criminal Tribunals", was adopted as resolution 2637 (2022) on 22 June; draft resolution S/2022/546, co-drafted by Ireland and Norway in connection with the item entitled "The situation in the Middle East", was adopted as resolution 2642 (2022) on 12 July; draft resolution S/2022/560, co-drafted by Mexico and the United States in connection with the item entitled "The question concerning Haiti", was adopted as resolution 2645 (2022) on 15 July; draft resolution S/2022/650, co-drafted by France and Mexico in connection with the item entitled "The situation in Mali", was adopted as resolution 2649 (2022) on 30 August; draft resolution S/2022/765, co-drafted by Mexico and the United States in connection with the item entitled "The question concerning Haiti", was adopted as resolution 2653 (2022) on 21 October; draft resolution S/2022/804, co-drafted by Mexico and the United Kingdom in connection with the item entitled "Identical letters dated 19 January 2016 from the Permanent Representative of Colombia to the United Nations addressed to the Secretary-General and the President of the Security Council (S/2016/53)", was adopted as resolution 2655 (2022) on 27 October; draft resolution S/2022/809, drafted by Ireland in connection with the item entitled "The situation in Bosnia and Herzegovina", was adopted as resolution 2658 (2022) on 2 November; draft resolution S/2022/881, drafted by Mexico in connection with the item entitled "Non-proliferation of weapons of mass destruction", was adopted as resolution 2663 (2022) on 30 November; draft resolution S/2022/925, drafted by Ireland and the United States in connection with the item entitled "General issues relating to sanctions", was adopted as resolution 2664 (2022) on 9 December; and draft resolution S/2022/977, drafted by Mexico in connection with the item entitled "United Nations peacekeeping operations", was adopted as resolution 2668 (2022) on 21 December.

[193] For more information on past practice concerning presidential texts, see *Repertoire*, *Supplements 2008–2009* to *2021*, part II.

Table 10
Draft resolutions co-sponsored by non-members of the Council, 2022

Draft resolution	*Item*	*Meeting record and date*	*Resolution*	*Council member sponsors*	*Non-Council member co-sponsors*
S/2022/62	Peace and security in Africa	S/PV.9050 31 May	2634 (2022)	8 Council members (Albania, Brazil, France, Gabon, Ghana, Kenya, Norway, United States)	29 Member States[a]
S/2022/155	Letter dated 28 February 2014 from the Permanent Representative of Ukraine to the United Nations addressed to the President of the Security Council (S/2014/136)	S/PV.8979 25 February	Not adopted owing to the negative vote of a permanent member of the Council	6 Council members (Albania, France, Ireland, Norway, United Kingdom, United States)	76 Member States[b]
S/2022/231	Letter dated 13 April 2014 from the Permanent Representative of the Russian Federation to the United Nations addressed to the President of the Security Council (S/2014/264)	S/PV.9002 23 March	Not adopted owing to an insufficient number of affirmative votes	1 Council member (Russian Federation)	3 Member States (Belarus, Democratic People's Republic of Korea, Syrian Arab Republic)
S/2022/718	Maintenance of international peace and security	S/PV.9140 29 September	2652 (2022)	4 Council members (Albania, France, Ireland, Norway)	25 Member States[c]
S/2022/925	General issues relating to sanctions measures	S/PV.9214 9 December	2664 (2022)	7 Council members (Albania, Brazil, France, Ireland, Norway, United Kingdom, United States)	46 Member States[d]
S/2022/977	United Nations peacekeeping operations	S/PV.9229 21 December	2668 (2022)	7 Council members (Albania, Gabon, Ireland, Kenya, Mexico, Norway, United Arab Emirates)	45 Member States[e]

[a] Angola, Benin, Chad, Denmark, Djibouti, Egypt, Equatorial Guinea, Finland, Gambia, Guinea, Japan, Lebanon, Liechtenstein, Luxembourg, Mauritius, Morocco, Netherlands, Nigeria, Portugal, Republic of Korea, Senegal, Seychelles, Slovakia, Slovenia, South Africa, Sweden, Switzerland, Togo and Tunisia.

[b] Andorra, Antigua and Barbuda, Australia, Austria, Bahamas, Barbados, Belgium, Belize, Bosnia and Herzegovina, Botswana, Bulgaria, Canada, Chile, Colombia, Costa Rica, Croatia, Cyprus, Czechia, Denmark, Dominican Republic, Ecuador, Estonia, Fiji, Finland, Gambia, Georgia, Germany, Greece, Grenada, Guatemala, Haiti, Hungary, Iceland, Italy, Jamaica, Japan, Kiribati, Kuwait, Latvia, Lesotho, Liberia, Liechtenstein, Lithuania, Luxembourg, Malta, Marshall Islands, Micronesia (Federated States of), Monaco, Montenegro, Netherlands, New Zealand, Niger, North Macedonia, Palau, Panama, Papua New Guinea, Paraguay, Peru, Poland, Portugal, Republic of Korea, Republic of Moldova, Romania, Samoa, San Marino, Singapore, Slovakia, Slovenia, Spain, Suriname, Sweden, Switzerland, Timor-Leste, Trinidad and Tobago, Türkiye and Ukraine.

[c] Austria, Belgium, Bulgaria, Croatia, Cyprus, Czechia, Denmark, Estonia, Finland, Germany, Greece, Hungary, Italy, Latvia, Lithuania, Luxembourg, Malta, Netherlands, Poland, Portugal, Romania, Slovakia, Slovenia, Spain and Sweden.

[d] Andorra, Australia, Austria, Bahamas, Belgium, Bulgaria, Canada, Chile, Croatia, Cyprus, Czechia, Denmark, Dominican Republic, Ecuador, Estonia, Fiji, Finland, Georgia, Germany, Greece, Guinea, Guyana, Hungary, Iceland, Italy, Latvia, Lesotho, Liechtenstein, Luxembourg, Malta, Marshall Islands, Montenegro, Netherlands, New Zealand, Poland, Portugal, Republic of Moldova, Romania, Samoa, San Marino, Slovakia, Slovenia, Spain, Sweden, Switzerland and Ukraine.

[e] Algeria, Australia, Austria, Belgium, Botswana, Bulgaria, Canada, Colombia, Costa Rica, Croatia, Cyprus, Czechia, Denmark, Djibouti, Dominican Republic, Ecuador, Estonia, Finland, Georgia, Germany, Greece, Guatemala, Hungary, Israel, Italy, Japan, Kazakhstan, Latvia, Lithuania, Luxembourg, Malta, Netherlands, New Zealand, Portugal, Republic of Korea, Republic of Moldova, Serbia, Sierra Leone, Slovakia, Slovenia, Suriname, Sweden, Switzerland, Thailand and Türkiye.

C. Decision-making by voting

According to Article 27 (2) and (3) of the Charter, decisions of the Council on procedural matters shall be made by an affirmative vote of nine Council members. On all other matters, that is, substantive or non-procedural matters, an affirmative vote of nine Council members is required, including the concurring votes of the permanent members.

The result of a vote in the Council often does not in itself indicate whether the Council considers the matter voted upon to be procedural or substantive. For example, whether a vote is procedural or not cannot be determined when a proposal is: (a) adopted by a unanimous vote; (b) adopted by an affirmative vote of all permanent members; or (c) not adopted as a result of having failed to obtain the nine affirmative votes required. When a proposal is adopted as a result of having obtained nine or more affirmative votes, with one or more permanent members casting a negative vote, that indicates that the vote is considered procedural. Conversely, if the proposal is not adopted, the matter voted upon is considered to be substantive. On certain occasions, in its early years, the Council found it necessary to decide, by vote, the question of whether the matter under consideration was procedural within the meaning of Article 27 (2). This procedure is known as the "preliminary question", after the language used in the San Francisco Statement on Voting Procedure. However, in recent years, including during the period under review, there have been no instances of the Council deciding to examine the preliminary question. Furthermore, procedural motions, such as the adoption of the agenda, the extension of invitations to participate in meetings and the suspension or adjournment of a meeting, have generally been decided upon by the Council without a vote. When such motions were voted upon, the vote was considered procedural.

In 2022, procedural matters were put to a vote on two occasions, compared with none in 2021 and one in 2020. At a meeting held on 31 January under the item entitled "Threats to international peace and security", pursuant to an objection raised, Council members held a procedural vote and adopted the provisional agenda.[194] At a meeting held on 24 August under the item entitled "Maintenance of peace and security of Ukraine", pursuant to an objection raised, Council members voted on whether to extend an invitation under rule 37 of the provisional rules of procedure to the President of Ukraine and adopted the proposal.[195] In addition, at a meeting held on 27 February, the Council adopted resolution 2623 (2022), by which it decided to call an emergency special session of the General Assembly to examine the question concerning "Letter dated 28 February 2014 from the Permanent Representative of Ukraine to the United Nations addressed to the President of the Security Council (S/2014/136)".[196] Pursuant to Assembly resolution 377 A (V), the Council adopted the resolution, with 11 votes in favour and 3 abstentions, despite the negative vote of a permanent member of the Council, taking into account that the lack of unanimity of its permanent members at the meeting held on 25 February had prevented it from exercising its primary responsibility for the maintenance of international peace and security.[197]

---

[194] See S/PV.8960. For further details on the discussion, see sect. II.C above and part I, sect. 34.

[195] See S/PV.9115. For further details on the discussion, see sect. VII.A above.

[196] See S/PV.8980. For more information, see part IV, sect. I.C. The Council had previously adopted a total of seven resolutions in which it had called for an emergency special session of the General Assembly, the last of which was adopted as resolution 500 (1982) on 28 January 1982 (see S/PV.2330). For more information, see *Repertoire*, *Supplement 1981–1984*, chap. VI, part I, sect. B.

[197] At the meeting held on 25 February, owing to the negative vote of a permanent member, the Council failed to adopt a draft resolution by which the Council would have decided that the Russian Federation must immediately, completely and unconditionally withdraw all of its military forces from the territory of Ukraine within its internationally recognized borders (see S/2022/155). The draft resolution received 11 votes in favour (Albania, Brazil, France, Gabon, Ghana, Ireland, Kenya, Mexico, Norway, United Kingdom and United States), 1 against (Russian Federation) and 3 abstentions (China, India and United Arab Emirates) (see S/PV.8979).

Adoption of resolutions

During the period under review, of the 54 resolutions adopted, 36 (66.7 per cent) were adopted unanimously, compared with 48 out of 57 (84.2 per cent) in 2021 and 44 out of 57 (77.2 per cent) in 2020. A total of 18 resolutions were adopted without a unanimous vote (see table 11).

Table 11
Resolutions adopted without a unanimous vote, 2022

Resolution	*Item*	*Meeting record and date*	*Votes in favour*	*Votes against*	*Abstentions*
2623 (2022)	Letter dated 28 February 2014 from the Permanent Representative of Ukraine to the United Nations addressed to the President of the Security Council (S/2014/136)[a]	S/PV.8980 27 February	11 (Albania, Brazil, France, Gabon, Ghana, Ireland, Kenya, Mexico, Norway, United Kingdom, United States)	1 (Russian Federation)[b]	3 (China, India, United Arab Emirates)
2624 (2022)	The situation in the Middle East[c]	S/PV.8981 28 February	11 (Albania, China, France, Gabon, Ghana, India, Kenya, Russian Federation, United Arab Emirates, United Kingdom, United States)	–	4 (Brazil, Ireland, Mexico, Norway)
2625 (2022)	Reports of the Secretary-General on the Sudan and South Sudan[d]	S/PV.8994 15 March	13 (Albania, Brazil, France, Gabon, Ghana, India, Ireland, Kenya, Mexico, Norway, United Arab Emirates, United Kingdom, United States)	–	2 (China, Russian Federation)
2626 (2022)	The situation in Afghanistan[e]	S/PV.8997 17 March	14 (Albania, Brazil, China, France, Gabon, Ghana, India, Ireland, Kenya, Mexico, Norway, United Arab Emirates, United Kingdom, United States)	–	1 (Russian Federation)
2633 (2022)	Reports of the Secretary-General on the Sudan and South Sudan[d]	S/PV.9045 26 May	10 (Albania, Brazil, France, Ghana, Ireland, Mexico, Norway, United Arab Emirates, United Kingdom, United States)	–	5 (China, Gabon, India, Kenya, Russian Federation)
2635 (2022)	The situation in Libya[f]	S/PV.9053 3 June	14 (Albania, Brazil, China, France, Gabon, Ghana, India, Ireland, Kenya, Mexico, Norway, United Arab Emirates, United Kingdom, United States)	–	1 (Russian Federation)
2637 (2022)	International Residual Mechanism for Criminal Tribunals[g]	S/PV.9072 22 June	14 (Albania, Brazil, China, France, Gabon, Ghana, India, Ireland, Kenya, Mexico, Norway, United Arab Emirates, United Kingdom, United States)	–	1 (Russian Federation)

Resolution	*Item*	*Meeting record and date*	*Votes in favour*	*Votes against*	*Abstentions*
2640 (2022)	The situation in Mali[h]	S/PV.9082 29 June	13 (Albania, Brazil, France, Gabon, Ghana, India, Ireland, Kenya, Mexico, Norway, United Arab Emirates, United Kingdom, United States)	–	2 (China, Russian Federation)
2641 (2022)	The situation concerning the Democratic Republic of the Congo[i]	S/PV.9084 30 June	10 (Albania, Brazil, France, India, Ireland, Mexico, Norway, United Arab Emirates, United Kingdom, United States)	–	5 (China, Gabon, Ghana, Kenya, Russian Federation)
2642 (2022)	The situation in the Middle East[c]	S/PV.9089 12 July	12 (Albania, Brazil, China, Gabon, Ghana, India, Ireland, Kenya, Mexico, Norway, Russian Federation, United Arab Emirates)	–	3 (France, United Kingdom, United States)
2647 (2022)	The situation in Libya[f]	S/PV.9103 28 July	12 (Albania, Brazil, China, France, India, Ireland, Mexico, Norway, Russian Federation, United Arab Emirates, United Kingdom, United States)	–	3 (Gabon, Ghana, Kenya)
2648 (2022)	The situation in the Central African Republic[j]	S/PV.9105 29 July	10 (Albania, Brazil, France, India, Ireland, Mexico, Norway, United Arab Emirates, United Kingdom, United States)	–	5 (China, Gabon, Ghana, Kenya, Russian Federation)
2654 (2022)	The situation concerning Western Sahara[k]	S/PV.9168 27 October	13 (Albania, Brazil, China, France, Gabon, Ghana, India, Ireland, Mexico, Norway, United Arab Emirates, United Kingdom, United States)	–	2 (Kenya, Russian Federation)
2657 (2022)	The situation in Somalia[l]	S/PV.9177 31 October	14 (Albania, Brazil, France, Gabon, Ghana, India, Ireland, Kenya, Mexico, Norway, Russian Federation, United Arab Emirates, United Kingdom, United States)	–	1 (China)
2659 (2022)	The situation in the Central African Republic[j]	S/PV.9190 14 November	12 (Albania, Brazil, France, Ghana, India, Ireland, Kenya, Mexico, Norway, United Arab Emirates, United Kingdom, United States)	–	3 (China, Gabon, Russian Federation)
2662 (2022)	The situation in Somalia[l]	S/PV.9196 17 November	11 (Albania, Brazil, France, India, Ireland, Kenya, Mexico, Norway, United Arab Emirates, United Kingdom, United States)	–	4 (China, Gabon, Ghana, Russian Federation)
2664 (2022)	General issues relating to sanctions[m]	S/PV.9214 9 December	14 (Albania, Brazil, China, France, Gabon, Ghana, Ireland, Kenya, Mexico, Norway, Russian Federation, United Arab Emirates, United Kingdom, United States)	–	1 (India)

Resolution	Item	Meeting record and date	Votes in favour	Votes against	Abstentions
2669 (2022)	The situation in Myanmar[n]	S/PV.9231 21 December	12 (Albania, Brazil, France, Gabon, Ghana, Ireland, Kenya, Mexico, Norway, United Arab Emirates, United Kingdom, United States)	–	3 (China, India, Russian Federation)

[a] For more information on the discussion, see part I, sect. 19.A.
[b] At the meeting held on 27 February, the Council adopted resolution 2623 (2022), by which it called for an emergency special session of the General Assembly to examine the question concerning the situation in Ukraine. The resolution was adopted despite the negative vote of a permanent member of the Council.
[c] For more information on the discussion, see part I, sect. 20.
[d] For more information on the discussion, see part I, sect. 7.
[e] For more information on the discussion, see part I, sect. 14.
[f] For more information on the discussion, see part I, sect. 10.
[g] For more information on the discussion, see part I, sect. 25.
[h] For more information on the discussion, see part I, sect. 11.
[i] For more information on the discussion, see part I, sect. 4.
[j] For more information on the discussion, see part I, sect. 5.
[k] For more information on the discussion, see part I, sect. 1.
[l] For more information on the discussion, see part I, sect. 2.
[m] For more information on the discussion, see part I, sect. 28.
[n] For more information on the discussion, see part I, sect. 15.

Draft resolutions not adopted

In accordance with Article 27 (3) of the Charter, a draft resolution on non-procedural matters is not adopted when it fails to obtain the nine affirmative votes required or when a negative vote is cast by a permanent member. During the period under review, there were three instances in which a draft resolution was not adopted because it failed to obtain the nine affirmative votes required, compared with one instance in 2021 and four instances in 2020. Furthermore, there were four instances in which a draft resolution was not adopted owing to a negative vote cast by one or more permanent members, compared with one instance in 2021 and three instances in 2020 (see table 12).

Table 12
Draft resolutions not adopted owing to the negative vote of a permanent member or for lack of the requisite number of votes, 2022

Draft resolution	Item	Meeting record and date	Votes in favour	Votes against	Abstentions
S/2022/155	Letter dated 28 February 2014 from the Permanent Representative of Ukraine to the United Nations addressed to the President of the Security Council (S/2014/136)[a]	S/PV.8979 25 February	11 (Albania, Brazil, France, Gabon, Ghana, Ireland, Kenya, Mexico, Norway, United Kingdom, United States)	1 (Russian Federation)	3 (China, India, United Arab Emirates)

Draft resolution	Item	Meeting record and date	Votes in favour	Votes against	Abstentions
S/2022/231	Letter dated 13 April 2014 from the Permanent Representative of the Russian Federation to the United Nations addressed to the President of the Security Council (S/2014/264)[b]	S/PV.9002 23 March	2 (China, Russian Federation)	–	13 (Albania, Brazil, France, Gabon, Ghana, India, Ireland, Kenya, Mexico, Norway, United Arab Emirates, United Kingdom, United States)
S/2022/431	Non-proliferation/ Democratic People's Republic of Korea[c]	S/PV.9048 26 May	13 (Albania, Brazil, France, Gabon, Ghana, India, Ireland, Kenya, Mexico, Norway, United Arab Emirates, United Kingdom, United States)	2 (China, Russian Federation)	–
S/2022/538	The situation in the Middle East[d]	S/PV.9087 8 July	13 (Albania, Brazil, France, Gabon, Ghana, India, Ireland, Kenya, Mexico, Norway, United Arab Emirates, United Kingdom, United States)	1 (Russian Federation)	1 (China)
S/2022/541	The situation in the Middle East[d]	S/PV.9087 8 July	2 (China, Russian Federation)	3 (France, United Kingdom, United States)	10 (Albania, Brazil, Gabon, Ghana, India, Ireland, Kenya, Mexico, Norway, United Arab Emirates)
S/2022/720	Maintenance of peace and security of Ukraine[e]	S/PV.9143 30 September	10 (Albania, France, Ghana, Ireland, Kenya, Mexico, Norway, United Arab Emirates, United Kingdom, United States)	1 (Russian Federation)	4 (Brazil, China, Gabon, India)
S/2022/821	Threats to international peace and security[f]	S/PV.9180 2 November	2 (China, Russian Federation)	3 (France, United Kingdom, United States)	10 (Albania, Brazil, Gabon, Ghana, India, Ireland, Kenya, Mexico, Norway, United Arab Emirates)

[a] For more information on the discussion, see part I, sect. 19.A.
[b] For more information on the discussion, see part I, sect. 19.B.
[c] For more information on the discussion, see part I, sect. 32.C.
[d] For more information on the discussion, see part I, sect. 20.
[e] For more information on the discussion, see part I, sect. 19.C.
[f] For more information on the discussion, see part I, sect. 34.

D. Decision-making without a vote

A procedural or substantive motion may be adopted in the Council without a vote or by consensus. In 2022, there was one instance of a resolution being adopted without a vote. At a meeting held on 22 June under the item entitled "Date of election to fill a vacancy in the International Court of Justice",[198] the Council adopted resolution 2638 (2022) without a vote and by consensus, by which it decided that the election to fill the vacancy in the Court would take place on 4 November 2022, at a meeting of the Council and at a meeting of the General Assembly at its seventy-seventh session.

Presidential statements continued to be adopted by consensus. A total of seven presidential statements were adopted during the period under review.[199]

Following past practice, during the period under review, notes by and letters from the President were adopted by consensus and issued as documents of the Council. In 2022, the Council issued 19 notes by and 27 letters from the President.[200]

Notes by and letters from the President are rarely adopted during Council meetings. During the period under review, consistent with past practice, one note by the President, concerning the adoption of the draft annual report of the Council to the General Assembly for the period from 1 January to 31 December 2021, was adopted during a meeting of the Council.[201]

E. Discussions concerning the decision-making process

Council members discussed issues pertaining to the decision-making process of the Council at several meetings. For example, at a meeting held on 26 May under the item entitled "Reports of the Secretary-General on the Sudan and South Sudan",[202] the Council adopted resolution 2633 (2022), by which it extended the sanctions measures on South Sudan. The draft resolution, submitted by the United States, received 10 votes in favour (Albania, Brazil, France, Ghana, Ireland, Mexico, Norway, United Arab Emirates, United Kingdom and United States) and 5 abstentions (China, Gabon, India, Kenya and Russian Federation). In explaining the decision of her delegation to abstain in the vote, the representative of the Russian Federation expressed regret that the penholder of the draft resolution had ignored not only the views of South Sudan but also the agreed position of African countries and the views of other Council members, including the Russian Federation. She added that there was an increasing number of questions regarding the working methods of penholders and reminded Council members that the note by the President dated 30 August 2017[203] stipulated that penholders must provide their colleagues with the opportunity to participate fully in the drafting of resolutions and conduct consultations in a spirit of openness and flexibility. In a similar vein, the representative of China, highlighting that the responsibility of the penholder was to help the Council to come up with a text that had the broadest possible consensus, expressed regret that the fairness and inclusiveness that a penholder should demonstrate had been absent.[204]

At a meeting held on the same day under the item entitled "Non-proliferation/ Democratic People's Republic of Korea",[205] the Council voted on a draft resolution submitted by the United States, by which it would have condemned in the strongest terms the intercontinental ballistic missile launch conducted by the Democratic People's Republic of Korea and would have decided to expand the sanctions measures

[198] See S/PV.9073.

[199] For a list of presidential statements adopted during the period under review, see part I, chap. 2, of the report of the Council to the General Assembly at its seventy-seventh session (A/77/2).

[200] For a list of notes by the President of the Council issued in 2022, see part I, chap. 13, of the report of the Council to the General Assembly at its seventy-seventh session (A/77/2). For a list of letters from the President of the Council issued in 2022, see part I, chap. 3, of the same report.

[201] See S/2022/403, adopted at a meeting held on 20 May (see S/PV.9037). For more information on the annual report of the Council to the General Assembly, see part IV, sect. I.F.

[202] See S/PV.9045.

[203] S/2017/507.

[204] See S/PV.9045.

[205] See S/PV.9048.

specified in resolution 1718 (2006).[206] The draft resolution was not adopted owing to the negative votes of two permanent members of the Council.[207] Following the vote, the representative of Ireland, expressing regret about the use of the veto to block Council action, noted that her frustration was shared by the wider United Nations membership, as demonstrated by the consensus adoption of the "veto initiative" by the General Assembly in its resolution 76/262 of 26 April 2022, and looked forward to the swift issuance of a special report on the matter by the Council.[208] The representative of Norway called upon the Secretariat to produce such a report in consultation with the Chair of the Informal Working Group on Documentation and Other Procedural Questions. The representative of France, deeply deploring the result of the voting, said that the use of the veto amounted to protecting the regime of the Democratic People's Republic of Korea and giving it a blank cheque to launch even more weapons. The representative of the United States stated that the text of the draft resolution had been circulated for nine weeks and that, in that time, the countries that had vetoed the draft resolution had refused to engage on it. She further remarked that, before that day, the Council had had a remarkable record of consensus and collective action on the issue by unanimously responding to the provocations of the Democratic People's Republic of Korea with resolutions that imposed sanctions and brought collective condemnation. The representative of Japan, expressing deep regret for the result of the voting, said that despite the continued destabilizing nuclear and missile activities of the Democratic People's Republic of Korea, which gravely threatened the peace and security of the region and beyond, no Council resolutions had been adopted as a result. Nonetheless, he emphasized that the veto did not negate the need for the strict implementation of the Council resolutions that continued to be in effect. The representative of China stated that if the United States had accepted the proposals of China and some other members of the Council, the situation could easily have been averted. He also said that solving the issue of the Korean Peninsula did not hinge on whether or not the Council adopted a new draft resolution. The representative of the United States said that the draft resolution had failed because of the veto of China and the Russian Federation and that, despite some discussion over several days about a proposal for a presidential statement submitted by China, the United States delegation had never seen any draft of that proposal. She further stated that when pressed, China had said that the only acceptable provision was to update the weapons-control list, which the Council already had authorization to do pursuant to previous resolutions.

At a meeting held on 22 June under the item entitled "The situation in the Central African Republic",[209] the representative of the Central African Republic, speaking on behalf of the Minister for Foreign Affairs, Francophonie and Central Africans Abroad of the Central African Republic, raised the question as to whether, in order to better address priorities and situations in Africa, in particular in the Central African Republic and the subregion, it would be advisable for the penholder to be one of the three African members of the Council or the country concerned, in line with paragraphs 78 and 79 of the note by the President dated 30 August 2017.

At a meeting held on 27 June under the item entitled "The situation in Libya",[210] the representative of Libya expressed reservations regarding the procedure for the adoption of draft resolutions and presidential statements. In that regard, he stated that the Council failed to take into account the position of the State concerned because Council members and penholders were not obliged to include the State concerned in their consultations or discussions and that his delegation was only consulted informally.

At a meeting held on 13 September under the item entitled "Reports of the Secretary-General on the Sudan and South Sudan",[211] the representative of China, highlighting the impact of sanctions measures imposed by the Council on the ability of the Government of the Sudan to maintain stability and protect civilians in Darfur, expressed regret that the Council had not been able to set benchmarks to adjust the sanctions before 31 August, as required by the relevant resolutions. He urged the penholder to fulfil

---

[206] See S/2022/431.

[207] The draft resolution received 13 votes in favour (Albania, Brazil, France, Gabon, Ghana, India, Ireland, Kenya, Mexico, Norway, United Arab Emirates, United Kingdom and United States) and 2 against (China and Russian Federation). For more information, see part I, sect. 32.C.

[208] See S/PV.9048.

[209] See S/PV.9074.

[210] See S/PV.9078.

[211] See S/PV.9129.

its responsibilities, resume consultations as soon as possible and spare no effort to achieve consensus. He noted that the Government of the Sudan had stated its position on the benchmarks, which deserved a positive response from the penholder and other Council members. The representative of India emphasized that in its ongoing deliberations on the benchmarks, the Council must consider the complex interplay of local factors without resorting to an overly prescriptive approach and welcomed the decision of the penholder to keep a decision on sanctions benchmarks in abeyance, which kept the Council united on a sensitive issue. The representative of the Russian Federation expressed her delegation's disappointment by the decision of the penholder to end work on the Council document on benchmarks for the lifting of the arms embargo, which her delegation considered to be an irresponsible approach, by which the Council had sabotaged its own decisions on the review of the Sudanese sanctions for the second year in a row.

At a meeting held on 11 October under the item entitled "Cooperation between the United Nations and regional and subregional organizations in maintaining international peace and security", [212] in connection with the cooperation between the United Nations and the African Union, the representative of Kenya stated that more could be done to make the Council inclusive and responsive to Africa through reforms of its working methods, including penholdership, which needed to change in response to African responsibility, knowledge and ownership. He added that it would bring extra life to the Chapter VIII linkage to the African Union. The representative of China, calling for increased cooperation between the United Nations and the African Union in the maintenance of peace and security in Africa, affirmed that the Council should support more African members serving as penholders on African issues.

Council members and the wider membership also discussed issues pertaining to the decision-making of the Council, penholdership and the use of the veto by permanent members at the annual open debate on the working methods of the Council, held on 28 June under the item entitled "Implementation of the note by the President of the Security Council (S/2017/507)" (case 6), and at a meeting held on 14 December under the item entitled "Maintenance of international peace and security" (case 7).

Case 6
Implementation of the note by the President of the Security Council (S/2017/507)

On 28 June, at the initiative of Albania, which held the presidency of the Security Council for the month and whose Permanent Representative held the Chair of the Informal Working Group on Documentation and Other Procedural Questions in 2022,[213] the Council convened an open debate on its working methods under the item entitled "Implementation of the note by the President of the Security Council (S/2017/507)" and the sub-item entitled "Working methods of the Security Council".[214] As part of the discussion, members and non-members of the Council exchanged views on how to increase inclusivity and transparency in the decision-making of the Council, including in the practice of penholdership and through consultations with affected countries, as well as the use of the veto by permanent members.

With regard to inclusivity, multiple delegations called for a more equal division of responsibilities between permanent and elected members of the Council and the need for more elected members to serve as penholders and co-penholders on Council decisions and outcomes.[215] In that regard, the representative of the Russian Federation recalled that, in accordance with the note by the President dated 30 August 2017,[216] any Council member could be a penholder and more than one Council member could act as co-penholder.[217] According to the representative, revisiting the issue of informal penholdership would help to improve the effectiveness of the Council. The representative of China stated that penholdership was an informal arrangement that was supposed to reflect shared responsibility and collective engagement. He advocated a systematic restructuring of the arrangement whereby, as a general principle, there should be two or

[212] See S/PV.9149.

[213] A concept note was circulated by a letter dated 21 June (S/2022/499).

[214] See S/PV.9079 and S/PV.9079 (Resumption 1). See also S/2022/842.

[215] See S/PV.9079 (Ireland (on behalf of the elected members of the Council), China, Republic of Korea, Poland, Liechtenstein, Costa Rica, Thailand, Singapore, Kuwait and Portugal); and S/PV.9079 (Resumption 1) (Italy and Central African Republic).

[216] S/2017/507.

[217] See S/PV.9079.

three co-penholders per topic, to be shared between permanent and elected members. The representative of the Central African Republic maintained that having one or a very limited number of penholder countries resulted in decisions that were imposed unilaterally and served the national agenda of penholders, instead of addressing the reality on the ground and helping to find solutions.[218] Underscoring that it was critical for the Council's tasks and responsibilities to be distributed democratically, the representative of the Sudan expressed the view that the reform of penholdership was but an actualization of the principle of the sovereign equality of Member States. The representative of the United Kingdom stated that penholdership was a flexible practice that supported consistency.[219] Echoing the need for a fair distribution of responsibilities between elected and permanent members of the Council, the representative of Brazil, who spoke also on behalf of India, stated that the process for the distribution of penholdership must be open, transparent, based on exhaustive consultations and informed by a more integrated perspective.

More broadly, speakers also called for greater inclusivity and transparency in the Council's decision-making, both among Council members and vis-à-vis the wider membership. For example, the representative of Poland stated that elected members of the Council could play a key role in the decision-making process, making it more transparent and effective. The representative of the Central African Republic stated that all Council members should have the same opportunities to participate fully and meaningfully in the drafting of Council documents on an equal and equitable footing.[220] He added that, with regard to African affairs, special attention must be paid to the views of the three African members of the Council. The representative of Ireland stated that the Chairs of sanctions committees should be more involved in the initial consultations on sanctions renewals led by the penholders.[221]

Multiple delegations stressed that the views and concerns of countries on the Council's agenda had to be taken into consideration in the preparation of Council decisions.[222] The representative of China stated that penholders should engage closely with the countries concerned, Council members and the competent departments of the Secretariat to maximize consensus and avoid confrontation.[223] The representative of Cuba called for an elimination of exclusive practices to ensure genuine participation in, and the democratization of, the work of the Council, including in decision-making processes. He stated that the Council had to ensure that States directly involved in or particularly affected by an issue under the Council's consideration could participate in discussions and decision-making on matters that affected them, in accordance with Article 31 of the Charter of the United Nations. The representative of Libya called for proper consultation by penholders with the countries concerned and for their views to be reflected in the draft resolutions related to them.[224] The representative of the Central African Republic stated that the lack of consultations with countries on the Council's agenda during the drafting of Council documents by penholders had a negative impact on efforts to resolve crises and implement the mandates of United Nations missions. The representative of Indonesia stated that the process of involving troop- and police-contributing countries should not be a mere formality but an important avenue for the Council to hear their views.[225] He noted that such a process often took place very close to the adoption of a peacekeeping mandate, which hindered the proper consideration of the troop- and police-contributing countries' concerns and inputs in the process of the drafting of the mandate.

Several speakers discussed the use of the veto in the Council's decision-making, with some delegations calling for limitations or restraints in its use,[226] in particular in cases of mass atrocities.[227] In that regard, speakers encouraged all Member States, but particularly permanent Council members, to join

[218] See S/PV.9079 (Resumption 1).
[219] See S/PV.9079.
[220] See S/PV.9079 (Resumption 1).
[221] See S/PV.9079.
[222] See S/PV.9079 (Russian Federation, China and Cuba); and S/PV.9079 (Resumption 1) (Syrian Arab Republic, Egypt, Central African Republic, Libya and Sudan).
[223] See S/PV.9079.
[224] See S/PV.9079 (Resumption 1).
[225] See S/PV.9079.
[226] Ireland (on behalf of the elected members of the Council), Republic of Korea and Cuba.
[227] See S/PV.9079 (Ireland (on behalf of the elected members of the Council), Morocco and Malta); and S/PV.9079 (Resumption 1) (Italy and Germany).

the French and Mexican initiative for the voluntary and collective suspension of the use of the veto in cases of mass atrocities and the code of conduct regarding Council action against genocide, crimes against humanity or war crimes of the Accountability, Coherence and Transparency Group.[228] The representative of France expressed the view that permanent members must use the veto sensibly and that the threat of using the veto at any time as a negotiating tool was unacceptable.[229] While calling upon the members of the Council to fulfil all obligations to enable the Council to discharge its responsibilities, the representative of Switzerland, speaking on behalf of the Accountability, Coherence and Transparency Group, recalled that Article 27 of the Charter limited the participation of Council members that were directly involved in a dispute in decisions relating to the peaceful settlement thereof. Conversely, the representative of the Russian Federation underscored that the issue of the veto did not pertain to working methods of the Council but was rather the linchpin of the entire architecture of the Council and the key to achieving balance in its decisions.

Many delegations welcomed the adoption of General Assembly resolution 76/262 of 26 April 2022, by which the Assembly mandated an Assembly meeting following the casting of a veto by a permanent Council member.[230] Some described the resolution as an important mechanism for ensuring accountability and transparency in the use of the veto.[231] The representative of the United States stated that the Assembly meeting had provided an opportunity for those casting a veto to explain themselves and for Member States to react to its use. The representative of Singapore said that permanent members should explain how their decision to use the veto was consistent with the Charter and international law. The representative of Liechtenstein stressed that the special reports of the Council to the Assembly submitted pursuant to resolution 76/262 should provide a more substantive analysis of the reasons for each veto cast and that the records of relevant Council meetings must be produced as expeditiously as possible to ensure maximum flexibility for the scheduling of the Assembly meeting. The representative of Portugal encouraged the Council to enclose a special report in its next annual report to the Assembly, together with a summary of the debate in the Assembly, in accordance with resolution 76/262. The representative of Guatemala urged the Council and the Secretariat to include in the verbatim records of the meetings the cases in which a veto was cast by a permanent member, in accordance with resolution 76/262.

Case 7
Maintenance of international peace and security

On 14 December, at the initiative of India, which held the presidency of the Security Council for the month,[232] the Council held a high-level open debate under the item entitled "Maintenance of international peace and security" and the sub-item entitled "New orientation for reformed multilateralism".[233] In their statements, members and non-members of the Council discussed the impact of the use of the veto on the ability of the Council to implement its mandate to maintain international peace and security. Speakers also exchanged views on how to improve inclusivity and transparency in the Council's decision-making and the practice of penholdership.

A number of delegations expressed the view that the use of the veto prevented the Council from implementing its mandate and taking action to maintain international peace and security, with several delegations noting that the Council's failure to adopt a decision on the conflict in Ukraine was a clear

[228] See S/PV.9079 (France, Switzerland (on behalf of the Accountability, Coherence and Transparency Group), Luxembourg (also on behalf of Belgium and the Netherlands), Austria, Singapore, Morocco, Kuwait, Portugal, Malta and Slovenia); and S/PV.9079 (Resumption 1) (Italy, Slovakia and Germany).

[229] See S/PV.9079.

[230] See S/PV.9079 (United States, United Kingdom, Switzerland (on behalf of the Accountability, Coherence and Transparency Group), Luxembourg (also on behalf of Belgium and the Netherlands), Republic of Korea, Poland, Japan, Liechtenstein, Austria, Morocco and Kuwait); and S/PV.9079 (Resumption 1) (Italy, Slovakia and Germany). For more information, see part IV, sect. I.B. For more information on the adoption of General Assembly resolution 76/262 and the special reports from the Council to the Assembly submitted pursuant to it, see part IV, sect. I.F.

[231] See S/PV.9079 (United Kingdom, Switzerland (on behalf of the Accountability, Coherence and Transparency Group), Peru and Slovenia).

[232] A concept note was circulated by a letter dated 25 November (S/2022/880).

[233] See S/PV.9220 and S/PV.9220 (Resumption 1).

example in that regard.[234] The representative of Estonia stated that any permanent member that exercised the veto to defend its own acts of aggression against another Member State most seriously undermined the credibility of the Charter of the United Nations, the United Nations and the entire multilateral international rules-based system.[235] The representative of the European Union, also on behalf of Albania, Bosnia and Herzegovina, Montenegro and the Republic of Moldova, stated that Council members must fulfil the highest standards of conduct by upholding international law, including international humanitarian law. He added that, for permanent members of the Council, it meant refraining from using the veto when there was a risk of mass atrocity crimes and not abusing the veto power when they were party to a conflict. The representative of Liechtenstein underscored the need to ensure that the right of the veto was no longer exercised in a way that was at odds with the purposes and principles of the Charter and expressed interest in examining the application of Article 27 (3) of the Charter, whereby parties to a dispute had to abstain from voting. The representative of Ireland expressed the view that the veto was an anachronism that prevented the Council from implementing its mandate and allowed aggressors to evade accountability.[236]

Multiple speakers exchanged views on how to restrict and ensure accountability for the use of the veto. In that regard, delegations expressed support for the French and Mexican initiative for the voluntary suspension of the use of the veto in cases of mass atrocities,[237] as well as for the code of conduct regarding Council action against genocide, crimes against humanity or war crimes of the Accountability, Coherence and Transparency Group.[238] The representative of France explained that, being of a voluntary nature, the French and Mexican initiative did not require a revision of the Charter but only the political commitment of the permanent members of the Council.[239] Having led this initiative at the General Assembly, the representative of Liechtenstein stated that resolution 76/262 of 26 April 2022 was an essential step towards addressing the challenges that the use of the veto posed to the effectiveness of the Council and the public perception of the United Nations as a whole.[240] While agreeing with the general intention behind initiatives such as the French and Mexican initiative, the representative of Brazil stated that the veto was an expression of the great divide that stalled the Council rather than the main reason why the organ had become ineffective.[241] Moreover, he added that a veto was cast only after diplomacy and dialogue had not prospered.

More generally on the reform of the Council, the Minister for Foreign Affairs of Pakistan stated that it would not serve the purposes of the United Nations to add more members to the elitist club and expand the power of the veto, as it would multiply the possibility of paralysis in the Council. Similarly, the representative of Liechtenstein presented the view that adding more members to those who held the veto power was counter-intuitive, given the vast negative impact that the use of the veto already had on the effectiveness of the Council and its decision-making.[242] The representative of Egypt stated that Council reform and the redress of historical injustices imposed on Africa could only be achieved through the "Ezulwini Consensus," which called for, inter alia, abolishing the right of veto or granting it to new permanent members of the Council.

Speakers also highlighted the need to improve the working methods of the Council, in particular with respect to decision-making and the practice of penholdership. The representative of China called for a systematic change to the penholder system.[243] According to the representative, through the creation of co-penholderships, jointly held and regularly rotated among permanent and elected members, the voices of small and medium-sized countries could be enhanced. The representative of Ecuador reaffirmed that

---

[234] See S/PV.9220 (Ireland); and S/PV.9220 (Resumption 1) (Italy, Liechtenstein, Spain, Australia, Lithuania, Georgia and Ukraine).

[235] See S/PV.9220 (Resumption 1).

[236] See S/PV.9220.

[237] See S/PV.9220 (Brazil, France, Albania and Japan); and S/PV.9220 (Resumption 1) (Austria, Ecuador, Malta, European Union (also on behalf of Albania, Bosnia and Herzegovina, Montenegro and the Republic of Moldova), Latvia and Lebanon).

[238] See S/PV.9220 (Albania and Norway); and S/PV.9220 (Resumption 1) (Switzerland, Austria, Estonia, Ecuador, European Union (also on behalf of Albania, Bosnia and Herzegovina, Montenegro and the Republic of Moldova), Liechtenstein, Latvia and Lebanon).

[239] See S/PV.9220.

[240] See S/PV.9220 (Resumption 1).

[241] See S/PV.9220.

[242] See S/PV.9220 (Resumption 1).

[243] See S/PV.9220.

elected members should work to achieve a fair distribution of responsibilities with regard to the subsidiary bodies and penholdership.[244] The representative of Kenya stated that, while existing penholders often did a commendable job, a strong perception that they used the pen to sustain the history of its use to pursue national interests was almost inevitable, even when that was not the case.[245] He stated that the immediate reform needed to address that issue was to ensure that all penholders were sensitive to that reality, and that existing penholders should be subjected to a review by Council members. Moreover, he urged for one of the three African members of the Council, or the collective, to serve as penholders on all new files from Africa, which would enable the drafting of mandates and statements that were more in keeping with the required solutions and that would enjoy greater confidence among African members and their citizens. The representative of Norway expressed support for the request of the African members of the Council to be penholders or co-penholders on African dossiers and encouraged them, as well as all elected members of the Council, to approach relevant permanent members for a more active role on files that concerned them and encouraged the permanent members to welcome that constructively.

IX. Languages

Note

Section IX covers rules 41 to 47 of the provisional rules of procedure of the Council, which relate to the official and working languages of the Council, interpretation and the languages of meeting records and published resolutions and decisions.

Rule 41

Arabic, Chinese, English, French, Russian and Spanish shall be both the official and the working languages of the Security Council.

Rule 42

Speeches made in any of the six languages of the Security Council shall be interpreted into the other five languages.

Rule 43

[Deleted]

Rule 44

Any representative may make a speech in a language other than the languages of the Security Council. In this case, he shall himself provide for interpretation into one of those languages. Interpretation into the other languages of the Security Council by the interpreters of the Secretariat may be based on the interpretation given in the first such language.

Rule 45

Verbatim records of meetings of the Security Council shall be drawn up in the languages of the Council.

Rule 46

All resolutions and other documents shall be published in the languages of the Security Council.

[244] See S/PV.9220 (Resumption 1).

[245] See S/PV.9220.

Rule 47

Documents of the Security Council shall, if the Security Council so decides, be published in any language other than the languages of the Council.

During the period under review, rules 41 to 47 were applied consistently in meetings of the Council. At several meetings, speakers delivered their statements in a language other than the six official languages of the United Nations, as provided in rule 44.[246] The matter of working languages of the Council was addressed in meetings and communication submitted to the Council.

For example, at a meeting held on 20 May under the item entitled "Consideration of the draft report of the Security Council to the General Assembly", the representative of France, as the drafter of the introduction to the annual report on the activities of the Council in 2021, emphasized the importance of multilingualism, which, he noted, had suffered greatly during the COVID-19 pandemic.[247] He added that it was essential to ensure that all the work of the Council, including of its subsidiary bodies and at Arria-formula meetings, benefited from interpretation into the six official languages of the United Nations.

At a meeting held on 28 June under the item entitled "Implementation of the note by the President of the Security Council (S/2017/507)", the representative of France, expressing the view that there were too many Arria-formula meetings and that they were sometimes misused, encouraged the Council to find a way to limit the number of meetings in that format and ensure that they were genuinely inclusive by providing interpretation.[248]

By a letter dated 29 December addressed to the President of the Council,[249] the representatives of India, Ireland, Kenya, Mexico and Norway, as elected members of the Council in 2021 and 2022, transmitted a note on the working methods developed by the Council during the COVID-19 pandemic. In that regard, they expressed the view that upholding multilingualism during that period had been a significant challenge. While noting that a solution had eventually been implemented in August 2020 by using a remote interpretation platform for open videoconferences, the representatives explained that in some instances the platform had experienced technical challenges and it had not been agreed by all Council members for use in closed or informal discussions, which had largely been conducted in English only. As part of their recommendations for future consideration by the Council should physical meetings again become impossible, the representatives stressed the need for solutions to be found to ensure multilingualism in line with the note by the President dated 12 July 2021.[250]

By a letter dated 20 December addressed to the President of the Council,[251] the Chair of the Committee pursuant to resolution 751 (1992) concerning Al-Shabaab transmitted the report on the Committee's activities from 1 January to 31 December 2022, in which he noted that, owing to the lack of interpretation services, the members of the Committee had agreed, on an exceptional basis, to hold a virtual meeting, in the form of a closed videoconference, on 27 May.[252]

---

[246] For example, at a meeting held on 5 April under the item entitled "Letter dated 28 February 2014 from the Permanent Representative of Ukraine to the United Nations addressed to the President of the Security Council (S/2014/136)", the President of Ukraine spoke in Ukrainian and the interpretation was provided by the delegation of Ukraine (see S/PV.9011). At meetings held on 28 June, 24 August, 27 September and 23 November under the item entitled "Maintenance of peace and security of Ukraine", the President of Ukraine spoke in Ukrainian and the interpretation was provided by the delegation of Ukraine (see S/PV.9080, S/PV.9115, S/PV.9138 and S/PV.9202). At a meeting held on 11 May under the item entitled "The situation in Bosnia and Herzegovina", the Chair of the Presidency of Bosnia and Herzegovina spoke in Bosnian and the interpretation was provided by the delegation (see S/PV.9029). At a meeting held on 15 December under the item entitled "Threats to international peace and security caused by terrorist acts", a briefer invited under rule 39 of the provisional rules of procedure spoke in Hindi and the interpretation was provided by the delegation of India, which held the presidency of the Council for the month (see S/PV.9221).

[247] See S/PV.9037.

[248] See S/PV.9079.

[249] S/2022/1011

[250] S/2021/648.

[251] S/2022/995.

[252] For more information on the Committee, see part VII, sect. III.A, and part IX, sect. I.B.1.

X. Status of the provisional rules of procedure

Note

Section X covers the deliberations of the Council concerning its provisional rules of procedure. Article 30 of the Charter of the United Nations provides that the Council shall adopt its own rules of procedure. Since their adoption by the Council at its first meeting, held on 17 January 1946, the provisional rules of procedure have been amended 11 times, with the last amendment being adopted in 1982.[253] On 27 December 2019, the Council issued a note by the President providing that, in line with the efforts of the United Nations and its Member States to promote the advancement of women and greater gender inclusivity and equality in their policies and practices, the members of the Council confirmed that, as a matter of existing practice, any reference to a male person in the Council's provisional rules of procedure was deemed not to be limited to male persons and also constituted a reference to a female person, unless the context clearly indicated otherwise.[254]

Article 30

The Security Council shall adopt its own rules of procedure, including the method of selecting its President.

During the period under review, the question of the status of the provisional rules of procedure, including in connection with Article 30 of the Charter, was raised at the annual open debate on the working methods of the Council, held on 28 June under the item entitled "Implementation of the note by the President of the Security Council (S/2017/507)".[255] In his remarks, the representative of Thailand pointed out that while the Council's provisional rules of procedure allowed the Council flexibility in its work, adopting permanent rules of procedure would bring about greater predictability and transparency.[256] He suggested that, with various amendments and a number of documents supplementing its working methods, the Council could better function with standing rules in place. The representative of Cuba called upon the Council to adopt its rules of procedures to put an end to the provisional status that its rules had had since the establishment of the organ.

By a letter dated 25 January,[257] the representative of Saint Vincent and the Grenadines transmitted her reflections as Chair of the Informal Working Group on Documentation and Other Procedural Questions in 2020 and 2021, in which she stated that the Council should consider the issue of the status of virtual meetings and the application of the provisional rules of procedure therein and further build on the provisions of the note by the President dated 22 December 2021.[258] In a letter dated 29 December addressed to the President of the Council,[259] the representatives of India, Ireland, Kenya, Mexico and Norway, as elected members of the Council in 2021 and 2022, transmitted a note providing their reflections and recommendations on the working methods developed by the Council during the COVID-19 pandemic. They noted that the Council's provisional rules of procedure had not been applied in videoconferences and that, therefore, procedural voting in virtual meetings had not been possible. In that regard, they recommended that the Council should agree on parameters for virtual meetings to be considered as formal meetings of the Council and agree to apply the provisional rules of procedure, even when meeting virtually, to the fullest extent possible, including the possibility of undertaking procedural votes.

---

[253] The provisional rules of procedure of the Council were amended: five times during the Council's first year, at its 31st, 41st, 42nd, 44th and 48th meetings, held on 9 April, 16 and 17 May and 6 and 24 June 1946; twice in its second year, at its 138th and 222nd meetings, held on 4 June and 9 December 1947; and subsequently at its 468th meeting, on 28 February 1950; 1463rd meeting, on 24 January 1969; 1761st meeting, on 17 January 1974; and 2410th meeting, on 21 December 1982. The provisional rules were issued under the symbols S/96 and S/96/Add.1, with subsequent versions being issued as revisions, the latest of which was issued under the symbol S/96/Rev.7.

[254] See S/2019/996.

[255] See S/PV.9079 and S/PV.9079 (Resumption 1).

[256] See S/PV.9079.

[257] S/2022/88.

[258] S/2021/1074.

[259] S/2022/1011.

Part III
Purposes and principles of the Charter of the United Nations

Contents

Introductory note

Part III covers the consideration by the Security Council of Articles contained in Chapter I of the Charter of the United Nations relating to the purposes and principles of the United Nations, namely Articles 1 (2), 2 (4), 2 (5) and 2 (7). Part III consists of four sections. Section I features material relating to the principle of self-determination of peoples under Article 1 (2) of the Charter. Section II covers material relevant to the prohibition of the use of force or the threat of the use of force as enshrined in Article 2 (4). Section III deals with the obligation of States to refrain from assisting a target of the Council's enforcement action as stipulated in Article 2 (5). Section IV highlights the Council's consideration of the principle of non-intervention by the United Nations in the internal affairs of States, as regulated by Article 2 (7).

In 2022, Council members and other participants in Council discussions deliberated on the principle of self-determination in the context of the Palestinian question, the situation concerning Western Sahara and the referendums held in the occupied regions of Ukraine. Council members addressed the application and interpretation of Article 2 (4) of the Charter concerning the prohibition of the use or threat of use of force and non-interference in the internal affairs of other States at meetings held in connection with the escalation of hostilities on the Armenia-Azerbaijan border and the situations in Iraq, the Golan, Libya, the Syrian Arab Republic and Ukraine, as well as in the context of promoting common security through dialogue and cooperation. Council members also discussed the obligation of States to refrain from giving assistance to any State or non-State actor against which the United Nations was taking preventive or enforcement action pursuant to Article 2 (5) in connection with the situations in the Democratic Republic of the Congo, Libya, Ukraine and Yemen. Furthermore, Council members reflected on the principles enshrined in Article 2 (7) during discussions concerning the renewals of the mandate of the United Nations Multidimensional Integrated Stabilization Mission in Mali and of the sanctions regime imposed on the Democratic Republic of the Congo, as well as during a high-level open debate focused on strengthening accountability and justice for serious violations of international law.

During the period under review, the Council did not adopt any decision containing explicit references to Articles 1 (2), 2 (4), 2 (5) or 2 (7) of the Charter. Nonetheless, part III includes Council decisions featuring language relating to the principles enshrined in those Articles. In addition, it includes explicit invocations of Articles 1 (2), 2 (4) and 2 (7) found in the correspondence addressed to the Council during the period under review.

I. Principle of equal rights and self-determination of peoples under Article 1, paragraph 2

Article 1, paragraph 2

[The Purposes of the United Nations are:]

To develop friendly relations among nations based on respect for the principle of equal rights and self-determination of peoples, and to take other appropriate measures to strengthen universal peace.

Note

Section I concerns the practice of the Council regarding the principle of equal rights and self-determination of peoples as enshrined in Article 1 (2) of the Charter of the United Nations. Subsection A features decisions relevant to the principle enshrined in Article 1 (2). Subsection B describes the references made to the principle of self-determination in Council discussions during the reporting period. Subsection C sets out instances in which the principle of self-determination was invoked in communications addressed to the Council.

A. Decisions relating to Article 1 (2)

During the period under review, the Council did not explicitly invoke Article 1 (2) of the Charter in its decisions. However, language found in one Council decision, adopted in connection with the envisaged referendum in Western Sahara, is of relevance to the interpretation and application of Article 1 (2) (see table 1).

Table 1
Decisions containing implicit references to Article 1 (2) of the Charter, 2022

Decision and date	*Provision*
The situation concerning Western Sahara	
Resolution 2654 (2022) 27 October	Reaffirming its commitment to assist the parties to achieve a just, lasting and mutually acceptable political solution, based on compromise, which will provide for the self-determination of the people of Western Sahara in the context of arrangements consistent with the principles and purposes of the Charter of the United Nations, and noting the role and responsibilities of the parties in this respect (sixth preambular paragraph)
	Calls upon the parties to resume negotiations under the auspices of the Secretary-General without preconditions and in good faith, taking into account the efforts made since 2006 and subsequent developments with a view to achieving a just, lasting and mutually acceptable political solution, which will provide for the self-determination of the people of Western Sahara in the context of arrangements consistent with the principles and purposes of the Charter of the United Nations, and noting the role and responsibilities of the parties in this respect (para. 4)

B. Discussions relating to Article 1 (2)

During the period under review, Article 1 (2) of the Charter was not explicitly invoked in deliberations at meetings of the Council. Nevertheless, the principle of self-determination was addressed by Council members in the context of both thematic and country-specific discussions, as elaborated upon below.

In 2022, Council members and other Member States and entities continued to express support for the right of the Palestinian people to self-determination at meetings held under the item entitled "The situation in the Middle East, including the Palestinian question".[1] At one of those meetings, the representative of Kenya stated that the right of self-determination of Palestinians was closely linked to the right to the free exercise of religion.[2] That interlinkage, he added, inevitably had to form part of the underpinnings of lasting peace between Israelis and Palestinians.

In relation to the question concerning Western Sahara, at a meeting held on 27 October,[3] at which the Council adopted resolution 2654 (2022) extending the mandate of the United Nations Mission for the Referendum in Western Sahara (MINURSO), the representative of Kenya, who had abstained from the vote on the resolution, expressed regret that progress in returning MINURSO to its core objective of implementing a referendum for the self-determination of the people of Western Sahara had been limited. He noted that resolution 2654 (2022) continued a gradual but noticeable shift away from that mandate and would not assist the parties in achieving a just, lasting and mutually acceptable political solution. He also explained that, unfortunately, the proposals that had been made by his delegation during the negotiations had not been taken on board, which was why Kenya had abstained in the vote. He expressed concern that the resolution did not substantively reflect the Council's commitment, as had been the case in previous resolutions, to provide for the self-determination of the people of Western Sahara in the context of arrangements consistent with the principles and purposes of the Charter. He also emphasized that, underlying the United Nations recognition of the right to self-determination through a properly implemented referendum was the Charter, which held that all peoples have the unquestionable and inalienable right to self-determination. The representative of the Russian Federation, who had also abstained from voting, stressed that the formula for a final settlement should be based on mutually acceptable outcomes that would contribute to a fair political resolution of the situation in Western Sahara for both Morocco and the Frente Popular para la Liberación de Saguía el-Hamra y de Río de Oro and should provide for the self-determination of the people of Western Sahara in the framework of procedures that were consistent with the purposes and principles of the Charter.

With respect to the situation in Ukraine, on 27 September, at a meeting held under the item entitled "Maintenance of peace and security of Ukraine", Council members deliberated on the right to self-determination in the context of the referendums carried out by authorities of the Russian Federation in the occupied regions of Donetsk, Luhansk, Kherson and Zaporizhzhia (see case 1).

Case 1
Maintenance of peace and security of Ukraine

On 27 September, the Security Council held a meeting under the item entitled "Maintenance of peace and security of Ukraine".[4] Council members heard a briefing by the Under-Secretary-General for Political and Peacebuilding Affairs, who informed the Council that the de facto authorities in the regions of Donetsk, Luhansk, Kherson and Zaporizhzhia had conducted so-called referendums in which Ukrainians had been asked whether they approved their regions joining the Russian Federation. She added that voting had taken place in polling centres while the de facto authorities accompanied by soldiers had also gone door to door with ballot boxes. She emphasized that those exercises, which had been held during active armed conflict

[1] See S/PV.8950 (Mexico and Egypt (on behalf of the Group of Arab States)); S/PV.8950 (Resumption 1) (Committee on the Exercise of the Inalienable Rights of the Palestinian People, Cuba, Indonesia, Malaysia and Argentina); S/2022/39 (Azerbaijan (on behalf of the Movement of Non-Aligned Countries), Organization of Islamic Cooperation and Qatar); S/PV.9021 (Kenya, Ireland, Jordan, Lebanon and Algeria); S/PV.9021 (Resumption 1) (Malaysia, Pakistan, Bolivarian Republic of Venezuela, Committee on the Exercise of the Inalienable Rights of the Palestinian People and Cuba); S/PV.9099 (Algeria and Jordan); S/PV.9099 (Resumption 1) (Pakistan, Bolivarian Republic of Venezuela, Cuba, Malaysia, Committee on the Exercise of the Inalienable Rights of the Palestinian People, Qatar, Indonesia, Azerbaijan (on behalf of the Movement of Non-Aligned Countries), Argentina and Organization of Islamic Cooperation); S/PV.9174 (China, Lebanon, Egypt, Jordan and Algeria); S/PV.9174 (Resumption 1) (Islamic Republic of Iran, Malaysia, Indonesia, Bolivarian Republic of Venezuela, South Africa, Iraq (on behalf of the Group of Arab States), Committee on the Exercise of the Inalienable Rights of the Palestinian People, Cuba and Azerbaijan (on behalf of the Movement of Non-Aligned Countries)).

[2] See S/PV.9021.

[3] See S/PV.9168.

[4] See S/PV.9138.

in areas under the control of the Russian Federation and outside the legal and constitutional framework of Ukraine, could not be called a genuine expression of the popular will.

During the ensuing discussion, several Council members stated that they considered the referendums carried out by the Russian Federation in regions of Ukraine to be a "sham", "illegal" or "illegitimate".[5] A number of Council members emphasized that the referendums had no legal effect or impact on the status of the regions in question and on the sovereignty of Ukraine within its internationally recognized borders,[6] nor did they reflect the will of the Ukrainian people.[7]

Some Council members referred to the right to self-determination in the context of those referendums. In that regard, the representative of Brazil, expressing concern about the holding of the referendums, underscored that the Charter of the United Nations and other international treaties recognized the inalienable right of all peoples to self-determination and to freely decide their political status, and stated that the right to self-determination was a fundamental principle of international law, which was the very basis of the legitimacy of States. He further stated that, while many times in the past, in particular in the context of decolonization, the holding of referendums had been the means chosen for peoples to express their free will and that Council resolutions had established the use of that instrument as a legitimate practice to decide on issues of sovereignty and territorial integrity, its validity depended on certain conditions. On that note, he explained that it was unreasonable to assume that populations in areas of conflict were able to freely express their will, and recalled that international practice recommended that referendums on questions of sovereignty be conducted in a transparent manner, without restrictions on the freedom of expression and with the possibility of monitoring by independent observers, which did not seem to have been the case for the regions of Donetsk, Luhansk, Kherson and Zaporizhzhia in Ukraine. The representative of Mexico expressed support for the right to self-determination of peoples as stated in General Assembly resolution 2625 (XXV), in which the Assembly had also stipulated, in the annex to the resolution, that the enjoyment and exercise of that right was not to be construed "as authorizing or encouraging any action which would dismember or impair, totally or in part, the territorial integrity ... of sovereign and independent States". Given the gravity of the context in which those so-called referendums had taken place, he further reiterated his delegation's call for urgent dialogue between the parties, as well as for the strengthening of diplomatic channels to promote confidence-building measures.

By contrast, the representative of the Russian Federation underscored that the referendums had been held under exceptionally transparent conditions, with all electoral norms being fully observed, and stated that soldiers had been protecting the participants in the referendums from likely provocations on the Ukrainian side. He maintained that self-determination was considered a democratic choice only if the West approved of it, and added that, when denying the people of Donbas and the liberated territories of Ukraine their right to self-determination, Western delegations were demonstrating egregious double standards, given that those criticizing the referendum in the Donbas, Kherson and Zaporizhzhia regions had supported the independence of Kosovo and had argued that the territory of Kosovo had had the right to "remedial secession" from Serbia in the case of a real threat to the rights of Kosovar Albanians. He pointed out that, while the Charter stipulated the principle of respect for territorial integrity, such respect under international law was not unconditional. In that regard, he recalled the interpretation of the principle of territorial integrity provided by the General Assembly in its Declaration on Principles of International Law concerning Friendly Relations and Cooperation among States in accordance with the Charter of the United Nations, according to which all States should respect the sovereignty and territorial integrity of any State whose Government respected the principle of self-determination of peoples and represented all peoples within its territory.

On 30 September, at a meeting held under the same item,[8] following the announcement by the Russian Federation of the results of the referendums in support of the integration of the Donetsk, Luhansk, Kherson and Zaporizhzhia regions into the Russian Federation, Council members voted on a draft resolution submitted by Albania and the United States, in which the Council would have condemned

---

[5] United States, Albania, Ireland, United Kingdom and France.

[6] Ireland, Norway and France.

[7] United States, Albania, Ireland, Ghana and France.

[8] See S/PV.9143.

the "illegal so-called referenda in regions within Ukraine's internationally recognized borders".[9] The Council failed to adopt the draft resolution owing to the negative vote of the Russian Federation.[10] Prior to the vote, the representative of the Russian Federation informed the Council that treaties had been signed on the accession of those regions into the Russian Federation, adding that there would be no turning back, as the draft resolution had tried to impose.[11] He further recalled that the Russian Federation had constructively proposed amendments that many Council members would have supported concerning the fact that it was necessary to respect both the territorial integrity of all Member States and the principle of the self-determination of peoples, in accordance with the Charter. He also indicated that members of the Council had different assessments of the outcome of the referendums, adding that no one could argue with the fact that the free expression of the will of the people was an essential element of a democratic society. After the vote, the representative of the United Arab Emirates, who had voted in favour of the draft resolution, underscored that the referendums held over the past week and the announcement regarding the incorporation of the four regions into the Russian Federation were serious developments in the conflict, which made finding a peaceful resolution more difficult and implicated the territorial integrity, sovereignty and independence of a State Member of the United Nations. While noting that those were core principles of the Charter that were central to peaceful, cooperative and productive relations between States and essential for the security and stability of all, she emphasized that the principle of self-determination was also a fundamental principle enshrined in the Charter, and that any tensions between that principle and the principles of territorial integrity, sovereignty and independence did not need to amount to a zero-sum game.

C. Invocations of the principle enshrined in Article 1 (2) in communications

During the period under review, two explicit references to Article 1 of the Charter were made in letters from the representative of the Russian Federation addressed to the President of the Security Council or circulated as a Council document, referring to the principle of self-determination enshrined in Article 1 (2).

In a letter dated 24 February, the representative of the Russian Federation transmitted an address made by the President of the Russian Federation on 24 February, in which the President emphasized that, while the outcomes of the Second World War were sacred, they did not override the right of nations to self-determination as enshrined in Article 1 of the Charter.[12] He added that neither at the founding of the Soviet Union nor after the Second World War had the people living in any of the territories that made up present-day Ukraine been asked how they themselves wanted to build their lives, and underscored that the policy of the Russian Federation was based on the freedom of choice for all to determine their own future and that of their children.

In a letter dated 3 October, the representative of the Russian Federation transmitted an address made by the President of the Russian Federation on 30 September, on the occasion of the signing of the treaties on the accession of the Donetsk, Luhansk, Kherson and Zaporizhzhia regions into the Russian Federation.[13] In the address, the President reported that referendums had been held, ballots had been counted and the results had been announced, and that the people had made their unequivocal choice. He stated that, following the signing of the treaties, he had no doubt that the Federal Assembly would support the constitutional laws on the accession into the Russian Federation and the establishment of four new regions, as new constituent entities of the Russian Federation, because that was the will of millions of people. According to the President, it was undoubtedly their right, an inherent right sealed in Article 1 of the Charter, which directly stated the principle of equal rights and self-determination of peoples.

During the period under review, the principle of self-determination was invoked in numerous communications addressed to or brought to the attention of the Council, including communications from

[9] S/2022/720, para. 2.
[10] For more information, see part I, sect. 19.
[11] See S/PV.9143.
[12] See S/2022/154, annex.
[13] See S/2022/738, annex.

Member States relating to Cyprus,[14] the India-Pakistan question,[15] the Middle East, including the Palestinian question,[16] Nagorno-Karabakh,[17] Ukraine[18] and Western Sahara.[19] In addition, in communications addressed to the President of the Security Council or brought to the attention of the Council, Member States made reference to referendums that were of relevance to the right of self-determination. For example, such references were found in letters from Georgia, concerning "the so-called referendum on unification with Russia recently announced by the Tskhinvali occupation regime",[20] and Ukraine, concerning the preparations for the holding of "pseudo-referendums by the occupying administrations of the Russian Federation in the temporarily occupied territories of Ukraine".[21]

Moreover, in his reports to the Council regarding the situation in Mali,[22] the State of Palestine,[23] the situation concerning Western Sahara[24] and the situation in the Sudan and the activities of the United Nations Integrated Transition Assistance Mission in the Sudan,[25] the Secretary-General made reference to the principle of self-determination. In addition, references to the right to self-determination were made in a letter from the representatives of China and the Russian Federation, transmitting a joint statement dated 4 February 2022 by the Russian Federation and China on international relations entering a new era and global sustainable development,[26] a letter from the representative of the Russian Federation, transmitting a report of the Republika Srpska on recent political developments in Bosnia and Herzegovina,[27] and a note verbale from the Permanent Mission of the Bolivarian Republic of Venezuela, transmitting a statement of the Group of Friends in Defence of the Charter of the United Nations for the Arria-formula meeting on the theme "Ongoing protests in Iran", held on 2 November.[28]

II. Prohibition of the threat or use of force under Article 2, paragraph 4

Article 2, paragraph 4

All Members shall refrain in their international relations from the threat or use of force against the territorial integrity or political independence of any state, or in any other manner inconsistent with the Purposes of the United Nations.

Note

Section II covers the practice of the Council concerning the principle of the prohibition of the threat or use of force under Article 2 (4) of the Charter of the United Nations. Subsection A includes implicit references to Article 2 (4) in decisions adopted by the Council. Subsection B highlights discussions relating to the threat or use of force. Subsection C features explicit references to Article 2 (4) in communications to the Council.

[14] See S/2022/599.
[15] See S/2022/90, annex; S/2022/295, annexes I and II; S/2022/296, annex; S/2022/600, annex; S/2022/620, annex; S/2022/759, annex; and S/2022/807, annex.
[16] See S/2022/25; S/2022/114; S/2022/236; S/2022/283; S/2022/364, annex; S/2022/372, enclosure; S/2022/377; S/2022/452; S/2022/466; S/2022/589; S/2022/628; S/2022/662; S/2022/719; S/2022/879; S/2022/905; and S/2022/1035.
[17] See S/2022/37; S/2022/168, annex; and S/2022/988, annex.
[18] See S/2022/337, annex.
[19] See S/2022/339, annex; S/2022/414, annex; S/2022/473; S/2022/555; and S/2022/797, annex.
[20] See S/2022/308, annex.
[21] See S/2022/604, annex.
[22] See S/2022/446.
[23] See S/2022/504 and S/2022/945.
[24] See S/2022/733.
[25] See S/2022/898.
[26] See S/2022/212, annex.
[27] See S/2022/823, annex.
[28] See S/2022/830, annex.

A. Decisions relating to Article 2 (4)

During the period under review, the Council did not adopt any decision containing explicit references to Article 2 (4) of the Charter. In a number of its decisions, however, the Council underlined the principles of Article 2 (4) by: (a) reaffirming the prohibition of the threat or use of force in international relations; (b) reiterating the importance of good-neighbourliness and non-interference by States in the internal affairs of others; (c) calling for the cessation of support by States to armed groups engaged in destabilizing national and regional peace and security; and (d) calling upon parties to withdraw all military forces from a disputed area or occupied territories. The four themes are covered below.

In addition, two draft resolutions in relation to the conflict in Ukraine that the Council put to a vote and failed to adopt contained references to Article 2 (4)[29] and Article 2[30] of the Charter.

Affirmation of the prohibition of the threat or use of force in international relations

In 2022, the Council stressed the prohibition of the threat or use of force against other Member States in a few of its decisions, in particular concerning the future status of Abyei and the situation in the Middle East (see table 2).

Table 2
Decisions affirming the prohibition of the threat or use of force in international relations, 2022

Decision and date	*Provision*
The situation in the Middle East	
Resolution 2639 (2022) 27 June	Stressing that both parties must abide by the terms of the disengagement of forces agreement of 31 May 1974 between Israel and the Syrian Arab Republic and scrupulously observe the ceasefire (third preambular paragraph)
	See also resolution 2671 (2022), third preambular paragraph
	Stresses the obligation on both parties to scrupulously and fully respect the terms of the disengagement of forces agreement of 31 May 1974, calls upon the parties to exercise maximum restraint and prevent any breaches of the ceasefire and the area of separation, encourages the parties to take full advantage of the liaison function of the United Nations Disengagement Observer Force (UNDOF) regularly to address issues of mutual concern, as appropriate, and to maintain their liaison with UNDOF to prevent any escalation of the situation across the ceasefire line, as well as to support the enhancement of the UNDOF liaison function, and underscores that there should be no military activity of any kind in the area of separation, including military operations by the Syrian Arab Armed Forces (para. 2)
	See also resolution 2671 (2022), para. 2
Reports of the Secretary-General on the Sudan and South Sudan	
Resolution 2630 (2022) 12 May	Reiterating that the territorial boundaries of States shall not be altered by force, and that any territorial disputes shall be settled exclusively by peaceful means, affirming the priority it attaches to the full and urgent implementation of all outstanding issues from the Comprehensive Peace Agreement, underscoring that the future status of Abyei shall be resolved by negotiations between the parties in a manner consistent with the Agreement and not by the unilateral actions of either party, and recalling prior agreements on the administration and security of the Abyei Area (third preambular paragraph)

[29] See S/2022/155, para. 2.

[30] See S/2022/155, first preambular paragraph; and S/2022/720, first preambular paragraph.

Reiteration of the principles of good-neighbourliness, non-interference and regional cooperation among States

During the period under review, the Council reiterated in several of its decisions the principles enshrined in Article 2 (4) of the Charter of good-neighbourliness, non-interference and regional cooperation with regard to the situations in the Central African Republic, the Democratic Republic of the Congo, Libya, South Sudan and the Sudan, as well as more broadly under the item entitled "Peace and security in Africa" (see table 3). Furthermore, the Council consistently reaffirmed, in many of its decisions concerning country-specific situations, its respect for or commitment to the sovereignty, unity, independence and territorial integrity of States.

Table 3
Decisions affirming the principles of good-neighbourliness, non-interference and regional cooperation among States, 2022

Decision and date	*Provision*
Peace and security in Africa	
S/PRST/2022/6 31 August	The Security Council reaffirms its commitment to the sovereignty, territorial integrity and political independence of all States in accordance with the Charter of the United Nations and the principles of good-neighbourliness, non-interference and regional cooperation (first paragraph)
The situation in the Central African Republic	
Resolution 2659 (2022) 14 November	Reaffirming its strong commitment to the sovereignty, independence, unity and territorial integrity of the Central African Republic, and recalling the importance of the principles of non-interference, good-neighbourliness and regional cooperation (second preambular paragraph)
The situation concerning the Democratic Republic of the Congo	
Resolution 2641 (2022) 30 June	Reaffirming its strong commitment to the sovereignty, independence, unity and territorial integrity of the Democratic Republic of the Congo as well as all States in the region, and emphasizing the need to respect fully the principles of non-interference, good-neighbourliness and regional cooperation (second preambular paragraph)
	See also resolution 2666 (2022), third preambular paragraph
The situation in Libya	
Resolution 2644 (2022) 13 July	Expresses serious concern over continued violations of the arms embargo, demands full compliance by all Member States with the arms embargo, calls upon all Member States not to intervene in the conflict or take measures that exacerbate the conflict, and reiterates that individuals and entities determined by the Committee established pursuant to resolution 1970 (2011) concerning Libya to have violated the provisions of resolution 1970 (2011), including the arms embargo, or assisted others in doing so, are subject to designation (para. 5)
Reports of the Secretary-General on the Sudan and South Sudan	
Resolution 2625 (2022) 15 March	Reaffirming its strong commitment to the sovereignty, independence, territorial integrity and national unity of South Sudan, and recalling the importance of the principles of non-interference, good-neighbourliness and regional cooperation (second preambular paragraph)
Resolution 2630 (2022) 12 May	Reaffirming its strong commitment to the sovereignty, independence, unity and territorial integrity of the Sudan and South Sudan, and to the purposes and the principles of the Charter of the United Nations, and recalling the importance of the principles of good-neighbourliness, non-interference and regional cooperation (second preambular paragraph)

Calls for the cessation of support by States to armed groups engaged in destabilizing national and regional peace and security

During the period under review, the Council adopted decisions in which it called upon States to refrain from or prevent the provision of any form of support or assistance to armed groups, including through the financing of their activities, in relation to the situations in the Democratic Republic of the Congo and Libya (see table 4).

Table 4
Decisions calling for the cessation of support by States to armed groups engaged in destabilizing national and regional peace and security, 2022

Decision and date	*Provision*
The situation concerning the Democratic Republic of the Congo	
Resolution 2666 (2022) 20 December	Recalls that the elimination of the threat posed by armed groups requires an integrated regional approach and strong political engagement by the Government of the Democratic Republic of the Congo, the African Union, the East African Community, the International Conference on the Great Lakes Region and the Southern African Development Community, reaffirms its support to national and regional efforts to promote peace and stability in the Democratic Republic of the Congo and the region, building on the commitments made by the countries of the region under the Peace, Security and Cooperation Framework for the Democratic Republic of the Congo and the Region, which remains an essential mechanism to achieve durable peace and stability, stresses the commitments undertaken by the region under the Framework to neither tolerate nor provide assistance or support of any kind to armed groups, strongly condemns all external support to non-State armed actors, including the Mouvement du 23 mars, and calls for an immediate end to such support (para. 15)
The situation in Libya	
Resolution 2644 (2022) 13 July	Recalling that providing support for armed groups or criminal networks through the illicit exploitation of crude oil or any other natural resources in Libya may constitute acts that threaten the peace, stability and security of Libya (ninth preambular paragraph)
	Further reiterating its concern about activities which could damage the integrity and unity of Libyan State financial institutions and the National Oil Corporation, and stressing the need for the unification of Libya's institutions, and, in this regard, calling upon Member States to cease support to and official contact with parallel institutions outside of the authority of the Government of Libya (tenth preambular paragraph)
	Calls upon all parties to implement the ceasefire agreement of 23 October 2020 (S/2020/1043) in full and urges Member States to respect and support the full implementation of the agreement, including through the withdrawal of all foreign forces and mercenaries from Libya without further delay (para. 6)
Resolution 2647 (2022) 28 July	Calls upon all parties to implement the ceasefire agreement of 23 October 2020 in full, including the action plan agreed by the 5+5 Joint Military Commission in Geneva on 8 October 2021, which is to be implemented in a synchronized, phased, gradual and balanced manner, and urges Member States to respect and support its full implementation, including through the withdrawal of all foreign forces, foreign fighters and mercenaries from Libya without further delay (para. 8)
	See also resolution 2656 (2022), para. 10

Calls upon parties to withdraw all military forces from a disputed area or occupied territories

During the period under review and consistent with past practice, the Council urged the Government of Israel to expedite the withdrawal of its army from northern Ghajar, located on the border between Israel and Lebanon.[31]

[31] Resolution 2650 (2022), para. 20.

B. Discussions relating to Article 2 (4)

During the period under review, Article 2 (4) of the Charter was explicitly invoked 11 times at nine Council meetings. References to this provision were made in connection with country- and region-specific as well as thematic items, as elaborated upon below.

A total of 6 of the 11 explicit references to Article 2 (4) of the Charter were made during meetings held under items concerning Ukraine.[32] Three additional explicit references were also made to Article 2 (4) relating to the conflict in Ukraine in the context of the following thematic items: "Maintenance of international peace and security"[33] and "Threats to international peace and security".[34]

The remaining two explicit references to Article 2 (4) of the Charter were made in connection with the item entitled "Protection of civilians in armed conflict"[35] and the newly introduced item entitled "Letter dated 13 September 2022 from the Permanent Representative of Armenia to the United Nations addressed to the President of the Security Council (S/2022/688)" regarding the escalation of hostilities at the Armenia-Azerbaijan border.[36]

In addition, Article 2 of the Charter was referred to more broadly eight times during seven meetings held by the Council in 2022. Six of the eight references were made at meetings held in connection with items concerning Ukraine.[37] The remaining two references were made in connection with the item entitled "Maintenance of international peace and security".[38]

Furthermore, language that may be considered of relevance to the application and/or interpretation of Article 2 (4) of the Charter was used at various meetings held in connection with Bosnia and Herzegovina, the Golan, Iraq, Libya and the Syrian Arab Republic.[39]

---

[32] See, in connection with the item entitled "Letter dated 28 February 2014 from the Permanent Representative of Ukraine to the United Nations addressed to the President of the Security Council (S/2014/136)", S/PV.8979 (Mexico and Ghana); in connection with the item entitled "Letter dated 13 April 2014 from the Permanent Representative of the Russian Federation to the United Nations addressed to the President of the Security Council (S/2014/264)", S/PV.9002 (Mexico); and in connection with the item entitled "Maintenance of peace and security of Ukraine", S/PV.9104 (Mexico), S/PV.9115 (Mexico) and S/PV.9138 (Mexico).

[33] See S/PV.9220 (Resumption 1) (Austria).

[34] See S/PV.9127 (Ireland and Ukraine).

[35] See S/PV.8953 (Resumption 1) (Canada).

[36] See S/PV.9132 (Armenia).

[37] See, in connection with the item entitled "Letter dated 28 February 2014 from the Permanent Representative of Ukraine to the United Nations addressed to the President of the Security Council (S/2014/136)", S/PV.8970 (Ukraine) and S/PV.8979 (Kenya and Ukraine); and in connection with the item entitled "Maintenance of peace and security of Ukraine", S/PV.9104 (Albania), S/PV.9135 (Mexico) and S/PV.9138 (Norway).

[38] See S/PV.9052 (India); and S/PV.9112 (Albania).

[39] See, for example, in connection with the item entitled "The situation in Bosnia and Herzegovina", S/PV.9029 (United Kingdom, Gabon, Ireland, Albania, China, United Arab Emirates, Russian Federation, Norway, United States, Bosnia and Herzegovina, European Union, Serbia and Croatia); in connection with the item entitled "The situation concerning Iraq", S/PV.9034 (United Arab Emirates, China, Russian Federation, Ireland, India, France, Brazil and Iraq) and S/PV.9100 (Iraq, Türkiye, United States, Ireland, India, Norway, Ghana, Kenya, Russian Federation, United Kingdom, China, Albania and Brazil); in connection with the item entitled "The situation in Libya", S/PV.8952 (United Kingdom, United Arab Emirates, Kenya (also on behalf of Gabon and Ghana), India and Libya) and S/PV.9162 (Norway, Russian Federation, Kenya (also on behalf of Gabon and Ghana), Mexico, France, China and United Arab Emirates); in connection with the item entitled "The situation in the Middle East", S/PV.8978 (United Arab Emirates, Kenya (also on behalf of Gabon and Ghana), China, Russian Federation and Islamic Republic of Iran), S/PV.9003 (Russian Federation, France, China, Kenya, Brazil, United Arab Emirates and Islamic Republic of Iran), S/PV.9083 (Russian Federation, United States, China, Brazil, Mexico, Ghana (also on behalf of Gabon and Kenya), France and India) and S/PV.9117 (United States, Mexico, China and Syrian Arab Republic); and in connection with the item entitled "The situation in the Middle East, including the Palestinian question", S/PV.8950 (Russian Federation, China and Islamic Republic of Iran) and S/PV.8950 (Resumption 1) (Cuba, Syrian Arab Republic and Argentina). For more information on discussions held under the item entitled "The situation in the Middle East" in the context of the right to self-defence under Article 51 of the Charter, see part VII, sect. X.A, case 12.

Concerning thematic items, Council members and other delegations addressed the principles enshrined in Article 2 (4) of the Charter, specifically the need to respect the sovereignty and territorial integrity of States and the prohibition of the threat or use of force, at various meetings held during the reporting period.[40]

Featured below are the most relevant discussions held by the Council in 2022 on the prohibition of the threat or the use of force against the territorial integrity of other States and the inadmissibility of the acquisition of territory by force, whether by means of explicit or implicit references to Article 2 (4) of the Charter. During the period under review, the Council held numerous meetings to address developments in the conflict in Ukraine under the following items: "Threats to international peace and security",[41] "Letter dated 28 February 2014 from the Permanent Representative of Ukraine to the United Nations addressed to the President of the Security Council (S/2014/136)",[42] and "Maintenance of peace and security of Ukraine",[43] featured in cases 2 to 4 below.[44] In addition, case 5 focuses on a discussion concerning the escalation of hostilities at the Armenia-Azerbaijan border held under the item entitled "Letter dated 13 September 2022 from the Permanent Representative of Armenia to the United Nations addressed to the President of the Security Council (S/2022/688)".

Case 2
Threats to international peace and security

On 31 January, at the initiative of the United States, the Security Council held a meeting under the item entitled "Threats to international peace and security" focused on the situation in Ukraine,[45] to address actions of the Russian Federation on the border with Ukraine. At the outset of the meeting, the representative of the Russian Federation requested a procedural vote on the proposal of the United States to hold the meeting. The representative of the Russian Federation recalled that, in explaining its proposal to convene the meeting, the United States had underscored that it considered the deployment of Russian troops on Russian territory to be a threat to international peace and security, which, he said, was not only tantamount to unacceptable interference in the domestic affairs of the Russian Federation but also an attempt to mislead the international community on the actual situation in the region and on the reason for current global tensions. At the request of the Russian Federation, the provisional agenda was put to a vote and adopted with 10 votes in favour (Albania, Brazil, France, Ghana, Ireland, Mexico, Norway, United Arab Emirates, United Kingdom and United States), 2 against (China and Russian Federation) and 3 abstentions (Gabon, India and Kenya).[46]

Following the adoption of the agenda, the Council heard a briefing by the Under-Secretary-General for Political and Peacebuilding Affairs, who expressed great concern over the continuing escalation of tensions and the reports that more than 100,000 troops and heavy weaponry from the Russian Federation were positioned along the border with Ukraine. She conveyed the Secretary-General's strong belief that

---

[40] See, in connection with the item entitled "Briefing by the Chairperson-in-Office of the Organization for Security and Cooperation in Europe", S/PV.8992 (Norway, Ghana, United Kingdom, France, Brazil, United States, China, Ireland and United Arab Emirates); in connection with the item entitled "Cooperation between the United Nations and regional and subregional organizations in maintaining international peace and security", S/PV.9065 (High Representative of the European Union for Foreign Affairs and Security Policy, United States, China, Mexico, India and United Kingdom); and in connection with the item entitled "Maintenance of international peace and security", S/PV.9112 (Brazil, Gabon, France, United States, United Kingdom, Norway, Ghana, Ireland, India, Albania, Mexico and China), S/PV.9220 (Ghana, Albania, Pakistan, Armenia and Poland) and S/PV.9220 (Resumption 1) (Egypt, Estonia, Ethiopia, Ecuador, Malta, Saint Lucia (also on behalf of Bahamas, Barbados, Bhutan, Brazil, Cabo Verde, Gambia, Grenada, Guyana, India, Jamaica, Malawi, Mauritius, Federated States of Micronesia, Mongolia, Nauru, Nigeria, Palau, Papua New Guinea, Rwanda, Saint Kitts and Nevis, Saint Vincent and the Grenadines, Samoa, South Africa, Timor-Leste and Vanuatu), Liechtenstein, Indonesia, Islamic Republic of Iran, Latvia, Viet Nam (on behalf of the Association of Southeast Asian Nations) and Morocco).

[41] For more information on the item, see part I, sect. 34.

[42] For more information on the item, see part I, sect. 19.A.

[43] This item was added in 2022 to the list of matters of which the Council is seized. For more information on the item, see part I, sect. 19.C. For more information on the Council agenda, see part II, sect. II.

[44] In addition to the meetings featured below, developments in connection with Ukraine were also discussed under the item entitled "Letter dated 13 April 2014 from the Permanent Representative of the Russian Federation to the United Nations addressed to the President of the Security Council (S/2014/264)".

[45] See S/PV.8960.

[46] For more information about the procedural vote on the provisional agenda, see part II.

there should not be any military intervention in that context and that diplomacy should prevail, adding that any such intervention by one country in another would be against international law and the Charter of the United Nations. The Under-Secretary-General reiterated the full commitment of the United Nations to the sovereignty, political independence, unity and territorial integrity of Ukraine within its internationally recognized borders.

In the ensuing discussion, Council members and other Member States expressed support for the sovereignty and territorial integrity of Ukraine.[47] Some participants also underlined more broadly the importance of the principles enshrined in the Charter, including the respect for the sovereignty and territorial integrity of States and the prohibition of the use of force.[48]

Without explicit reference to Article 2 (4) of the Charter, many Council members deliberated on the significance of the prohibition of the use or threat of use of force. The representative of the United States underscored that the actions of the Russian Federation were a threat not only to Ukraine but also to Europe and the international order. She emphasized that Ukraine was a sovereign country and a sovereign people, entitled to determine their own future, without the threat of force, which was a right enshrined by the Charter. She added that if the Russian Federation further invaded Ukraine, the consequences would be horrific. She further pointed out that if former empires had licence to start reclaiming territory by force, it would set the world down a dangerous path. The representative of Albania warned that it would be wrong to consider the threat of a military attack by the Russian Federation against Ukraine as another crisis between the Russian Federation and the West, as it was rather a challenge to the European security order and to the whole international security architecture, which was based on the Charter. He further called upon the Russian Federation and the Council to expressly confirm respect for the sovereignty and territorial integrity of Ukraine. The representative of the United Kingdom stressed that any invasion or act of aggression by the Russian Federation against Ukraine would be a gross breach of international law and of the commitments of the Russian Federation under the Charter, and urged the Russian Federation to make clear in the Council that it would abide by its obligations under the Charter, that it had no plans to invade Ukraine, that it would abstain from the threat or use of force against its neighbour, that it would not further undermine the sovereignty or territorial integrity of Ukraine by military or any other means and that it would stand down its troops. The representative of France underscored that the accumulation of significant military capabilities on the border of a neighbouring sovereign State constituted threatening behaviour and that it raised legitimate questions about the intentions of the Russian Federation, especially since that country had already undermined the territorial integrity of Ukraine in the past. He added that dialogue efforts to address the situation must respect the fundamental principles on which European security was based, as set out in the Charter and the founding documents of the Organization for Security and Cooperation in Europe, including the sovereign equality and territorial integrity of States, the inviolability of borders, non-recourse to the threat or use of force and the freedom of States to choose or modify their own security arrangements. The representative of Mexico said that there were basic principles when addressing the issue, in accordance with the Charter, including the prohibition on the threat or use of force in international relations, the principle of non-intervention and the peaceful settlement of disputes. He explained that, with regard to the first principle, the mere escalation of tensions in Eastern Europe was a potential threat to international peace and security, and that it was therefore within the purview of the Council, pursuant to Article 39 of the Charter.[49] For that reason, he stressed the importance of trying to avoid any type of action that could be considered hostile by any of the parties, however slight it might seem. He said, however, that the remarks made by the representative of the Russian Federation had been encouraging, as he had been very clear in reiterating that there was no planned invasion of Ukraine, which was a unilateral statement of non-aggression. The representative of Ukraine stated that his country strongly rejected any attempt to use the threat of force as an instrument of pressure to make Ukraine and its partners accept illegitimate demands and emphasized the country's inherent sovereign right to choose its own security arrangements, which, he added, could not be questioned by the Russian Federation. The representative of Lithuania condemned the continued aggressive actions and threats of the Russian Federation against Ukraine and called upon the Russian Federation to de-escalate the situation and abide by international law, immediately stop fuelling the conflict by providing financial and military support to

---

[47] Albania, United Kingdom, France, Ireland, Kenya, Mexico, Norway and Lithuania (also on behalf of Estonia and Latvia).

[48] Brazil, United Arab Emirates and Poland.

[49] For more information, see part VII, sect. I.

the armed formations that it backed and to withdraw its military troops and materiel from the eastern border of Ukraine and the Crimean peninsula.

By contrast, the representative of the Russian Federation indicated that the deployment of Russian troops within its own territory was being interpreted by the West as a planned military action and even an act of aggression about to be launched without proof to uphold that accusation, and in turn accused the West of whipping up tensions and rhetoric and provoking escalation, as the discussion about the threat of war was provocative in itself.[50]

Case 3
Letter dated 28 February 2014 from the Permanent Representative of Ukraine to the United Nations addressed to the President of the Security Council (S/2014/136)

On 25 February, following the invasion of Ukraine by the Russian Federation, the Security Council met to vote on a draft resolution submitted by 82 Member States.[51] The Council failed to adopt the draft resolution owing to the negative vote of the Russian Federation.[52] Under the draft resolution, the Council would have recalled the obligation of all States under Article 2 of the Charter of the United Nations to refrain in their international relations from the threat or use of force against the territorial integrity or political independence of any State, would have deplored in the strongest terms the aggression of the Russian Federation against Ukraine in violation of Article 2 (4) of the Charter, and would have decided that the Russian Federation was to immediately cease its use of force against Ukraine, refrain from any further unlawful threat or use of force against any Member State and immediately, completely and unconditionally withdraw all of its military forces from the territory of Ukraine within its internationally recognized borders.[53] Furthermore, the Council would have deplored the decision of 21 February 2022 of the Russian Federation related to the status of certain areas of the Donetsk and Luhansk regions of Ukraine as a violation of the territorial integrity and sovereignty of Ukraine and inconsistent with the principles of the Charter and would have decided that the Russian Federation was to immediately and unconditionally reverse that decision.[54]

Against that backdrop, during the meeting, Council members discussed the prohibition of the use of force in relation to the events unfolding in Ukraine.[55] In that regard, two Council members made two explicit references to Article 2 (4) of the Charter during the discussion. Speaking before the vote, the representative of Mexico pointed out that the invasion of one sovereign country by another constituted a flagrant violation of Article 2 (4) of the Charter and also constituted an act of aggression under the terms of General Assembly resolution 3314 (XXIX). He added that since the establishment of the United Nations, his country had defended the prohibition of the threat or use of force in international relations and would continue to do so in the Organization and in all other forums. He further condemned the acts of aggression that the Russian Federation had perpetrated against Ukraine and stated that his country recognized the sovereignty, political independence and territorial integrity of Ukraine. Speaking after the vote, the representative of Ghana said that his country had voted in favour of the draft resolution because the invasion of Ukraine by the Russian Federation breached the obligation of the Russian Federation to respect the provisions of Article 2 (4). He further underscored that, by not refraining from the use of force in its relations with Ukraine, the Russian Federation had chosen to violate without justification the sovereignty, political independence and territorial integrity of Ukraine. He added that the actions of the Russian Federation, which had assailed the purposes and principles of the Charter, had threatened the global order and the balance of peace and security. The representative of Ghana also stated that his delegation had taken note of the letter from the Russian

---

[50] For more information on the discussions held under this item in the context of Article 51 of the Charter, see part VII, sect. X.A. For information on all meetings held under this item concerning the conflict in Ukraine, see part I, sect. 34.

[51] See S/2022/155.

[52] The draft resolution received 11 votes in favour (Albania, Brazil, France, Gabon, Ghana, Ireland, Kenya, Mexico, Norway, United Kingdom and United States), 1 against (Russian Federation) and 3 abstentions (China, India and United Arab Emirates). See S/PV.8979.

[53] S/2022/155, first preambular paragraph and paras. 2–4.

[54] Ibid., paras. 5 and 6.

[55] See S/PV.8979.

Federation submitted to the Council,[56] in which the Russian Federation sought to indicate that its use of force against Ukraine was in self-defence while dismissing its all-out military action against Ukraine. He noted that, in his assessment, Ukraine presented no immediate threat to the Russian Federation.[57] He also stressed that the use of force as a basis for securing international agreement had no place in the modern international order and was unacceptable. He expressed regret that, at a time when the world looked to the Council to send a strong message that threats and use of force against other States were unacceptable, the Council had been unable to do so.

In addition to the above, two broader references to Article 2 of the Charter in relation to the prohibition of the threat or use of force were made during the meeting. Speaking after the vote, the representative of Kenya said that his country had voted in favour of the draft resolution to affirm Article 2, according to which all Members were to refrain in their international relations from the threat or use of force against the territorial integrity or political independence of any State, and to register his country's opposition to the breach by the Russian Federation of the territorial integrity of Ukraine. In summarizing the content of the draft resolution, the representative of Ukraine referred to the obligation of all States under Article 2 to refrain in their international relations from the threat or use of force against the territorial integrity or political independence of any State.

Other speakers discussed the importance of the prohibition of the use of force enshrined in Article 2 (4) of the Charter without explicitly referring to that Article. Speaking before the vote, the representative of the United States, as co-penholder of the draft resolution together with Albania, pointed out that the Russian Federation had chosen to invade its neighbour and to violate the sovereignty of Ukraine, international law and the Charter. She emphasized that Council members should vote in favour of the draft resolution if they believed in upholding the Charter and supported the right of Ukraine or any State to sovereignty and territorial integrity. Conversely, she said that Council members should vote against or abstain in the voting if they did not uphold the Charter and if they aligned themselves with the aggressive and unprovoked actions of the Russian Federation. The representative of Albania, highlighting the unprovoked aggression by the Russian Federation, said that the Russian Federation not only was inflicting untold pain and causing an unprecedented humanitarian situation in Europe, but also had "stained the Charter of the United Nations with innocent blood" and was "burying the Charter under the rubble of destruction" in Kyiv and other cities in Ukraine. He called upon the members of the Council to support the draft resolution in order to say no to aggression, to unprovoked war and to the domination of a country by a more powerful one. Before the vote, expressing grave concern about the military operations of the Russian Federation against targets in sovereign Ukrainian territory, the representative of Brazil expressed the view that a line had been crossed and called upon the Council to react swiftly to the use of force against the territorial integrity of a Member State. He recalled that during the negotiations on the draft resolution, Brazil had attempted to seek balance and to maintain a space for dialogue while still signalling that the use of force against the territorial integrity of a Member State was not acceptable. After the vote, he added that the framing of the use of force against Ukraine as an act of aggression in the draft resolution, a precedent that had seldom been used in the Council, signalled to the world the gravity of the situation but could also downplay other times when force had been used against the territorial integrity of Member States with no equivalent reaction from the Council. No country, he said, elected or non-elected, with or without veto power, should be able to use force against the territorial integrity of another State with no Council reaction. The representative of the United Kingdom dismissed the claims of the Russian Federation that its invasion of Ukraine was in self-defence as absurd and expressed her country's intention to hold the Russian Federation accountable for its aggression. The representative of Norway expressed deep regret about the veto of the draft resolution by the Russian Federation. She stressed that preventing and ending acts of aggression was a direct responsibility of the Council and that a veto cast by the aggressor undermined the purpose of the Council and was a violation of the very foundation of the Charter. She further asserted that, in the spirit of the Charter, as a party to a dispute, the Russian Federation should have abstained from voting on the draft resolution. She said that the aggression of the Russian Federation not only violated the independence, sovereignty and territorial integrity of Ukraine but also constituted a serious breach of international peace and security, and called

[56] S/2022/154.
[57] See S/PV.8979.

upon the Russian Federation to immediately, completely and unconditionally stop all fighting, withdraw all of its forces from the territory of Ukraine and respect the principles and purposes of the Charter. The representative of Ireland said that his country had voted in favour of the draft resolution in response to the flagrant violation by the Russian Federation of the Charter, international law and the sovereignty and territorial integrity of Ukraine. He added that the Russian Federation had launched an unjustified and unprovoked attack on Ukraine and that its use of the veto in blatant defence of its military aggression was reprehensible. The representative of Ukraine said that the Russian Federation could not justify the offensive and emphasized that the Russian Federation should show respect for the core principles enshrined in the Charter, namely, sovereign equality and the prohibition of the use or threat of use of force against the territorial integrity and political independence of States.

Case 4
Maintenance of peace and security of Ukraine

At a high-level meeting held on 22 September under the item entitled "Maintenance of peace and security of Ukraine",[58] the Secretary-General gave a briefing to the Security Council on the most recent developments in relation to the conflict between the Russian Federation and Ukraine. The Secretary-General expressed deep concern about the reports of plans to organize so-called referendums in areas of Ukraine that were not at the time under government control, adding that any annexation of a State's territory by another State resulting from the threat or use of force was a violation of the Charter of the United Nations and international law.

During the discussion that followed, a number of Council members emphasized that the so-called referendums were inconsistent with the principles enshrined in Article 2 (4) of the Charter. The Minister for Europe and Foreign Affairs of France asserted that the aggression that the Russian Federation had decided to launch alone against Ukraine constituted a flagrant violation of the fundamental norms of the Charter, adding that the principles of the non-use of force, the peaceful resolution of disputes and the respect for the sovereignty and territorial integrity of States had each been blatantly violated. The Prime Minister of Norway underlined that the war of aggression of the Russian Federation against Ukraine constituted a gross violation of international law and the Charter. He condemned the planned so-called referendums in the occupied regions of Ukraine and emphasized that they would have no legal standing or legitimacy and further pointed out that the referendums would in no way affect the sovereignty of Ukraine within its internationally recognized borders. The Secretary of State of the United States indicated that the President of the Russian Federation, Vladimir Putin, had chosen not to work towards achieving a diplomatic solution but instead to render such a solution impossible by seeking to annex more Ukrainian territory through sham referendums. He further emphasized that defending the sovereignty and territorial integrity of Ukraine was about much more than standing up for one nation's right to choose its own path; it was also about protecting an international order in which no nation could redraw the borders of another by force. The Minister for Europe and Foreign Affairs of Albania condemned the new path of confrontation taken by the Russian Federation by supporting the organization of illegal referendums in four currently occupied Ukrainian territories and stated that those sham referendums were another blatant violation of the independence, sovereignty and territorial integrity of Ukraine and a serious violation of the Charter. The Minister for Foreign Affairs and Defence of Ireland pointed out that the invasion of Ukraine by the Russian Federation was the antithesis of the principles of the Charter, a grave violation of international law and an attempt to change internationally recognized borders by the use of force.

Other speakers recognized the importance of the principles enshrined in Article 2 (4) of the Charter, including the prohibition of the use of force, more broadly in the context of the invasion of Ukraine by the Russian Federation. In that regard, the Minister for Foreign Affairs of Mexico reiterated his country's position on the conflict, which was based on the constitutional principles of its foreign policy, namely, non-intervention, the peaceful settlement of disputes and a ban on the use or threat of use of force, all of which were in line with the purposes and principles of the Charter. He added that there was no room for ambiguity, that the peaceful coexistence of States depended precisely on respect for all of those principles and that there could be no exceptions. He further noted that, in the preceding few months, Mexico had been clear in reiterating the importance of Article 2 of the Charter, which prohibited the use of force

[58] See S/PV.9135.

against the territorial integrity and political independence of any State, and underlined the importance of the basic guarantee of being able to live without the threat of being invaded by another country. He stressed that any action that violated that principle was illegal and illegitimate. Recalling that the aggression towards Ukraine disregarded the norms of international law and the principles of the Charter, the Minister for Foreign Affairs and Regional Integration of Ghana emphasized that Ghana did not, and would not, recognize any territory that was unilaterally and forcefully acquired or dismembered from a sovereign entity. She reiterated the call upon the Russian Federation to immediately and unconditionally cease its operations, withdraw its troops from the internationally recognized borders of Ukraine and respect its neighbour's sovereignty and political independence. The Secretary of State for Foreign, Commonwealth and Development Affairs of the United Kingdom recalled that the Members of the United Nations had agreed that the solemn principles of the Charter were vital to international peace and security and had undertaken to refrain from the use or threat of use of force against the territorial integrity or political independence of any State, and yet, he added, Mr. Putin had invaded Ukraine illegally and without justification. The Minister for Foreign Affairs of Ukraine underlined the principle that no country was allowed to change internationally recognized borders by force, which, he added, the Russian Federation had badly damaged. The Federal Minister for Foreign Affairs of Germany stressed the need to live up to the spirit of the Charter, which clearly stated that all Members were to refrain from the threat or use of force against the territorial integrity or political independence of any State.

Case 5
Letter dated 13 September 2022 from the Permanent Representative of Armenia to the United Nations addressed to the President of the Security Council (S/2022/688)

In response to the request for an emergency meeting by Armenia,[59] the Security Council held its first meeting under the item entitled "Letter dated 13 September 2022 from the Permanent Representative of Armenia to the United Nations addressed to the President of the Security Council (S/2022/688)", on 15 September.[60]

During the meeting, several Council members and the Member States parties to the conflict addressed the recent escalation between Armenia and Azerbaijan in the context of the principles contained in Article 2 (4) of the Charter of the United Nations. In that regard, the representative of Armenia underlined that acts of criminal aggression had been perpetrated by Azerbaijan against the territorial integrity of Armenia, in flagrant violation of international law and the Charter. He recalled that Armenia had repeatedly brought to the attention of the Council the fact that Azerbaijan had engaged in the illegal practice of acquisition of territories by force. He further noted that the most recent attacks demonstrated that, in the absence of proper accountability measures, policies of aggression were likely to continue and even increase in scope and scale. He added that, emboldened by the results of the use of force in the past, Azerbaijan sought to normalize violence and aggression to capture territories by force, and indicated that over the preceding two days Azerbaijan had intruded on and occupied more than 10 km^2 of the sovereign territory of Armenia. He underscored that the actions of Azerbaijan were in blatant violation of the purposes and principles of the Charter, in particular Article 2 (4), and indicated that the military aggression of Azerbaijan went against the letter and spirit of the trilateral statements of 9 November 2020 and 26 November 2021, on the establishment of a ceasefire and cessation of hostilities and the agreement to take steps to increase the level of stability and security on the Azerbaijani-Armenian border, respectively.[61]

The representative of Azerbaijan recalled that the meeting was taking place in the aftermath of a serious military escalation along the undelimited border between Armenia and Azerbaijan and that it had been recklessly provoked by Armenia with the aim of torpedoing the fragile post-conflict normalization process being pursued with the active engagement of relevant international actors, including the members of the Council.[62] He categorically rejected the allegations made by the representative of Armenia and

---

[59] See the letter dated 13 September from the representative of Armenia (S/2022/688), by which he transmitted a letter from the Minister for Foreign Affairs of Armenia to request that an emergency meeting of the Security Council be convened, on the basis of Article 35 (1) of the Charter of the United Nations, in relation to the large-scale aggression of Azerbaijan against Armenia launched on 13 September. For more information on the practice of the Council under Article 35 of the Charter, see part VI, sect. I.A. For more information on the item, see part I, sect. 16.

[60] See S/PV.9132.

[61] See S/2020/1104, annex; and S/2021/985, annex.

[62] See S/PV.9132.

added that the Armenian armed forces had committed a large-scale act of military provocation in the direction of the Dashkesan, Kelbajar and Lachin Districts along the Azerbaijan-Armenia border, attempting to plant mines on the roads between the military positions of the Azerbaijani army while taking advantage of the night-time and difficult terrain. He added that the positions of the armed forces of Azerbaijan had been subjected to intense fire and that Azerbaijan had taken adequate and proportionate measures to neutralize the threat against its sovereignty and territorial integrity that were limited and targeted at legitimate military objects. He also expressed the view that the lack of adequate attention and targeted measures to implement the demands of the Council had encouraged Armenia to consolidate the results of its unlawful use of force against Azerbaijan and that the consequences of its aggression therefore remained unaddressed and were being further aggravated.

In that context, several Council members condemned or considered unacceptable the use of force to settle international disputes.[63] The representative of Ghana called for the intensification of negotiations on all unresolved issues in order to move the parties closer to a conclusive resolution based on the principles of international law, with due regard to the Charter and its provisions relating to the mutual recognition of territorial integrity, the non-use or threat of use of force in the acquisition of territory and the pacific settlement of disputes. The representative of Ireland stressed that all forces must urgently return to the positions that they had held before the regrettable escalation of hostilities and that no forces should remain on the territory of another sovereign State. Similarly, the representative of the United Kingdom urged an immediate and sustained cessation of all military activity and the withdrawal of armed forces to their original positions before the escalation. The representative of France called upon Azerbaijan to maintain its forces in their original positions, stressing that the delimitation of the border must be decided exclusively through negotiations and that the territorial integrity of Armenia must be respected in the context of the advance of Azerbaijani forces beyond certain segments of the border.

C. Invocations of the principle enshrined in Article 2 (4) in communications

In 2022, six communications from Member States addressed to or brought to the attention of the Council included explicit references to Article 2 (4) of the Charter (see table 5). In addition, communications addressed to the Secretary-General or the President of the Security Council and circulated as documents of the Council made reference to Article 2 in relation to the dispute between Armenia and Azerbaijan,[64] the situation in Cyprus[65] and the conflict in Ukraine.[66]

Table 5
Communications containing explicit references to Article 2 (4) of the Charter, 2022

Symbol	*Title*	*Relevant extract*
S/2022/173	Identical letters dated 2 March 2022 from the Permanent Representative of Georgia to the United Nations addressed to the Secretary-General and the President of the Security Council	The obligation of the occupying power arising from the international law, to ensure the well-being of the population living in the occupied territories is continuously violated by the Russian Federation that has been exercising effective control over Abkhazia and Tskhinvali regions of Georgia. Consequently, these regions suffer from the extreme deterioration of the humanitarian situation and increased human rights violations occurring on daily basis. In full disregard for international law, primarily in violation of article 2 (4) of the United Nations Charter – stating that "all Members shall refrain in their international relations from the threat or use of force against the territorial integrity or political independence of any state, or in any other manner inconsistent with the Purposes of the United Nations" – the Russian Federation is undertaking steps towards the de-facto annexation of Georgia's two regions.

[63] Gabon, Ireland and Russian Federation.

[64] See S/2022/688, annex; S/2022/729; and S/2022/808.

[65] See S/2022/317 and S/2022/944.

[66] See S/2022/966, annex.

Symbol	*Title*	*Relevant extract*
S/2022/225	Letter dated 14 March 2022 from the Permanent Representative of the Islamic Republic of Iran to the United Nations addressed to the Secretary-General and the President of the Security Council	At that meeting, the Israeli regime's representative misused the Security Council forum, deviated from the Council's main agenda item and, in flagrant violation of international law and the Charter of the United Nations, specifically its Article 2 (4), explicitly threatened to use force against Iran and its peaceful nuclear programme.
S/2022/294	Letter dated 6 April 2022 from the Permanent Representative of Pakistan to the United Nations addressed to the President of the Security Council	Reaffirming the need for strict observation by all states of those principles and their international obligations in the conduct of their international relations, including Article 2 (4) of the United Nations Charter. (Resolution No. 60/48-POL, on peace and security in South Asia, of the Council of Foreign Ministers of the Organization of Islamic Cooperation, second preambular paragraph)
S/2022/432	Letter dated 25 May 2022 from the Permanent Representative of Greece to the United Nations addressed to the Secretary-General	In light of the above, Greece solemnly calls upon Turkey to stop questioning Greece's sovereignty over its Aegean islands, in particular through legally baseless and historically false assertions, to abstain from threatening Greece with war in case it extends its territorial waters beyond the present width of 6 nautical miles, in full contravention of Article 2, paragraph 4, of the Charter of the United Nations, and to refrain from illegal activities in violation of Greece's sovereignty and sovereign rights in the Aegean and the Eastern Mediterranean. Such practices by Turkey, in addition to betraying adherence to a revisionist mentality totally disconnected from the basic principles governing relations between States, as reflected in the Charter, pose a serious threat to peace and stability in the broader region.
S/2022/483	Identical letters dated 13 June 2022 from the Permanent Representative of the Syrian Arab Republic to the United Nations addressed to the Secretary-General and the President of the Security Council	I should also like to inform you that the Civil Aviation Authority of the Syrian Arab Republic will be filing a formal complaint with the International Civil Aviation Organization (ICAO) for the necessary measures to be taken in accordance with its regulations and obligations. The request filed by the Syrian Arab Republic with ICAO is based on well-established legal principles and provisions that criminalize the targeting of civilian airports and aviation rights under international instruments, notably the Charter of the United Nations, the Convention on International Civil Aviation (Chicago Convention) and annexes thereto, and international humanitarian law. These include the following: I. Article 2, paragraph 4, of the Charter of the United Nations. That Article states that all Members shall refrain in their international relations from the threat or use of force against the territorial integrity or political independence of any State, or in any other manner inconsistent with the purposes of the United Nations.
S/2022/694	Letter dated 13 September 2022 from the Permanent Representative of Armenia to the United Nations addressed to the Secretary-General	The actions of Azerbaijan are in blatant violation of the purposes and principles of the Charter of the United Nations, in particular Article 2 (4) of the Charter, in violation of the Helsinki Final Act and in violation of international humanitarian law. Moreover, the military aggression of Azerbaijan goes against the letter and spirit of the trilateral statements signed by the leaders of Azerbaijan, Armenia and the Russian Federation on 9 November 2020, 11 January 2021 and 26 November 2021. The statement of 26 November 2021 in particular stipulates that the sides agreed to "take steps to increase the level of stability and security on the Azerbaijani-Armenian border...". It is obvious that Azerbaijan attempts to undermine the agreements reached in the trilateral statements.

III. Obligation under Article 2, paragraph 5, to refrain from assisting the target of enforcement action

Article 2, paragraph 5

All Members shall give the United Nations every assistance in any action it takes in accordance with the present Charter, and shall refrain from giving assistance to any state against which the United Nations is taking preventive or enforcement action.

Note

Section III covers the practice of the Council with regard to the principle enshrined in Article 2 (5) of the Charter of the United Nations, in particular the obligation of Member States to refrain from providing assistance to a State against which the United Nations has taken preventive or enforcement action.[67] Subsection A features implicit references made to Article 2 (5) in the decisions of the Council, and subsection B features discussions held by the Council which may be considered relevant to the interpretation of Article 2 (5). Communications addressed to the Council in 2022 did not contain any references to Article 2 (5).

A. Decisions relating to Article 2 (5)

In 2022, the Council did not explicitly invoke Article 2 (5) of the Charter in its decisions. The Council, however, included language that may be considered of relevance to the interpretation of Article 2 (5) in decisions concerning the situations in the Central African Republic,[68] Libya,[69] Somalia,[70] South Sudan[71] and Yemen.[72]

B. Discussions relating to Article 2 (5)

In 2022, Article 2 (5) of the Charter was not explicitly invoked in any of the Council's meetings. However, implicit references that may be considered of relevance to the interpretation of Article 2 (5) were made at several meetings of the Council during the period under review in connection with the Democratic Republic of the Congo, Libya, Ukraine and Yemen, as elaborated upon below.

At a meeting held on 29 June under the item entitled "The situation concerning the Democratic Republic of the Congo",[73] the representative of Rwanda pointed out that the Armed Forces of the Democratic Republic of the Congo was fighting the Mouvement du 23 mars alongside the Forces démocratiques de libération du Rwanda, an alliance which was sanctioned by the Council pursuant to resolution 2078 (2012). He called upon the Council to condemn the alliance and urged the United Nations Organization Stabilization Mission in the Democratic Republic of the Congo, through its due diligence, to avoid any military cooperation with the Armed Forces of the Democratic Republic of the Congo, as long as the latter was allied with negative forces.

In 2022, at meetings of the Council held under the item entitled "The situation in Libya", Council members continued to express concern about, or stress the need to cease or refrain from, all actions in violation of the arms embargo, including the provision of military support that was inconsistent with the embargo.[74]

---

[67] For the practice of the Council relating to assistance by Member States to United Nations action in accordance with the Charter, see part V, sect. II (Article 25), and part VII, sects. V and VII (Articles 43, 45 and 48).

[68] Resolution 2648 (2022), para. 1.

[69] Resolution 2644 (2022), tenth preambular paragraph and para. 9.

[70] Resolutions 2628 (2022), para. 21, and 2662 (2022), paras. 10 and 37.

[71] Resolutions 2625 (2022), para. 18, and 2633 (2022), para. 8.

[72] Resolution 2624 (2022), para. 21.

[73] See S/PV.9081.

[74] See, for example, S/PV.8952 (Kenya (also on behalf of Gabon and Ghana) and Mexico); and S/PV.9120 (United States and Mexico).

Council members also expressed concern regarding the continued presence of mercenaries in the territory of Libya in contravention of relevant resolutions of the Council.[75] In that regard, at meetings held under the same item,[76] the representative of India, who at the time served as Chair of the Committee established pursuant to resolution 1970 (2011) concerning Libya, expressed serious concern about the repeated violations of the arms embargo and cited the report of the Panel of Experts on Libya, in which the Panel had noted the continuous presence of Turkish-backed Syrian fighters in Government of National Unity-Affiliated Forces military camps in Tripoli and had indicated that some of the training provided by Türkiye to the Government of National Unity-Affiliated Forces was military or naval in nature and thus a violation of paragraph 9 of resolution 1970 (2011).[77]

In connection with the conflict in Ukraine, at meetings held under the item entitled "Threats to international peace and security", Council members expressed concern regarding the use by the Russian Federation of military equipment originating from the Islamic Republic of Iran and the Democratic People's Republic of Korea, in contravention of Council resolutions. In that regard, at a meeting held on 8 September,[78] the representative of the United Kingdom said that, as the Russian Federation was struggling to maintain stocks of equipment, exacerbated by component shortages resulting from the international sanctions aimed at ending the war in Ukraine, it was turning to the Islamic Republic of Iran to supply unmanned aerial vehicles and, in a clear violation of United Nations sanctions, to the Democratic People's Republic of Korea to supply ammunition. In a similar vein, the representative of the United States accused Moscow of purchasing millions of rockets and artillery shells from the Democratic People's Republic of Korea for use on the battlefield in Ukraine, which, he stated, would be a clear and unequivocal violation of Council resolutions. At a meeting held on 9 December,[79] the representative of the United Kingdom again pointed out that the Russian Federation was perpetrating the war in Ukraine with weapons sourced from the Islamic Republic of Iran, in violation of resolution 2231 (2015), and was almost certainly seeking to source weaponry from other United Nations-sanctioned States, such as the Democratic People's Republic of Korea. The representative of France expressed a similar view that the Russian Federation sought to obtain supplies by any means, including in violation of Council resolutions, by using combat drones supplied by the Islamic Republic of Iran as part of its strategy to systematically target the Ukrainian civilian population and its infrastructure. He called upon the Secretariat of the United Nations to investigate those transfers as it was mandated to do, as they constituted a violation of resolution 2231 (2015), and to report back to the Council. During the same meeting, the representatives of Albania, Ireland and the United States also brought to the attention of the Council the issue of the transfer of unmanned aerial vehicles to the Russian Federation by the Islamic Republic of Iran, in violation of the same resolution.

In connection with Yemen, at meetings held under the item entitled "The situation in the Middle East", speakers continued to express concern about or condemn the illicit transfer of weapons of Iranian origin to the Houthis in violation of the arms embargo.[80]

IV. Non-intervention in the internal affairs of States by the United Nations under Article 2, paragraph 7

Article 2, paragraph 7

Nothing contained in the present Charter shall authorize the United Nations to intervene in matters which are essentially within the domestic jurisdiction of any state or shall require the Members to submit such matters to settlement under the present Charter; but this principle shall not prejudice the application of enforcement measures under Chapter VII.

---

[75] See, for example, S/PV.9192 (Norway, United States, France, India, United Arab Emirates, China and Ghana (also on behalf of Gabon and Kenya)).
[76] See S/PV.9098 and S/PV.9120.
[77] S/2022/427, paras. 30 and 77.
[78] See S/PV.9127.
[79] See S/PV.9216.
[80] See, for example, S/PV.8946 (United Arab Emirates, United States, Mexico and Yemen).

Note

Section IV concerns the practice of the Council in relation to the principle of non-intervention by the United Nations in the internal affairs of States enshrined in Article 2 (7) of the Charter of the United Nations. Subsection A features references to that Article in the decisions of the Council. Subsection B covers the deliberations of the Council touching upon the principle enshrined in Article 2 (7). Subsection C features references to Article 2 (7) in communications brought to the attention of the Council.

A. Decisions relating to Article 2 (7)

In 2022, the Council did not explicitly refer to Article 2 (7) of the Charter in its decisions. Nonetheless, language used in some Council decisions under country- and region-specific as well as thematic items may be considered of relevance to the interpretation and application of Article 2 (7) (see tables 6 and 7).

Table 6
Decisions containing implicit references to Article 2 (7) of the Charter, by region and country, 2022

Decision and date	*Provision*
The situation in Afghanistan	
Resolution 2626 (2022) 17 March	Decides further that the United Nations Assistance Mission in Afghanistan and the Special Representative of the Secretary-General for Afghanistan will continue to carry out their mandate in close consultation with all relevant Afghan political actors and stakeholders, including relevant authorities as needed, in support of the people of Afghanistan in a manner consistent with Afghan sovereignty, leadership and ownership, with a particular focus on the priorities laid out below (para. 5)
Peace and security in Africa	
Resolution 2634 (2022) 31 May	Stresses the primary responsibility of the States of the Gulf of Guinea to counter piracy and armed robbery at sea in the Gulf of Guinea and address their underlying causes, in close cooperation with regional and subregional organizations and their international partners (para. 2)
S/PRST/2022/6 31 August	The Security Council reiterates its support for the work of the Peacebuilding Commission, acknowledges the importance of strong coordination, coherence and cooperation with the Peacebuilding Commission and commends the Peacebuilding Commission's continued engagement with the countries and regions in Africa in enhancing capacity in the areas of inclusive peacebuilding, socioeconomic development, disarmament, demobilization and reintegration, security sector reform and institutions of justice and national reconciliation in line with national peacebuilding priorities, emphasizes that such engagement should continue to be guided by the principles of national ownership and meaningful partnerships with subregional and regional organizations, and all effort must be put to ensure that these projects, while complementing Peacebuilding Fund activities, are appropriately financed and judiciously utilized to ensure sustainability and optimal benefit to the local communities (seventh paragraph)
The situation in the Central African Republic	
Resolution 2659 (2022) 14 November	Reaffirming the basic principles of peacekeeping, such as consent of the parties, impartiality and non-use of force except in self-defence and defence of the mandate, recognizing that the mandate of each peacekeeping mission is specific to the need and situation of the country concerned, underlining that the mandates that it authorizes are consistent with the basic principles, reiterating that the Security Council expects full delivery of the mandates it authorizes, and recalling in this regard its resolution 2436 (2018) (third preambular paragraph)
	Recalling that the Central African Republic authorities have the primary responsibility to protect all populations in the Central African Republic, including from international crimes, recognizing the persistent security challenge threatening civilians, also underlining the importance of national efforts to restore State authority in all parts of the country to overcome the threats posed by armed groups (fourth preambular paragraph)

Decision and date	*Provision*
The situation concerning the Democratic Republic of the Congo	
Resolution 2666 (2022) 20 December	Reaffirming the basic principles of peacekeeping, including consent of the parties, impartiality and non-use of force except in self-defence and defence of the mandate (second preambular paragraph)
	Recalling that the Government of the Democratic Republic of the Congo bears the primary responsibility to protect civilians within its territory and subject to its jurisdiction, including from international crimes, recognizing the persistent security challenge threatening civilians, also underlining the importance of national efforts to restore State authority in all parts of the country to overcome the threats posed by armed groups (fourth preambular paragraph)
The question concerning Haiti	
Resolution 2645 (2022) 15 July	Stressing the primary responsibility of the Government of Haiti to address long-standing drivers of instability and inequality, and to engage with other stakeholders, including civil society, youth and the private sector, and the full, equal and meaningful participation of women, to deliver durable solutions to Haiti's immediate and long-term challenges (penultimate preambular paragraph)
Resolution 2653 (2022) 21 October	Stressing the primary responsibility of the Government of Haiti to address long-standing drivers of instability and inequality (fifth preambular paragraph)
The situation concerning Iraq	
Resolution 2631 (2022) 26 May	Requests that the Special Representative of the Secretary-General for Iraq and the United Nations Assistance Mission for Iraq, at the request of the Government of Iraq, shall:
	...
	(d) Promote accountability and the protection of human rights, and judicial and legal reform, with full respect for the sovereignty of Iraq, in order to strengthen the rule of law and improve governance in Iraq, in addition to supporting the work of the United Nations Investigative Team to Promote Accountability for Crimes Committed by Da'esh/Islamic State in Iraq and the Levant established in resolution 2379 (2017) (para. 2 (d))
The situation in Libya	
Resolution 2644 (2022) 13 July	Reaffirming its strong commitment to a Libyan-led and Libyan-owned political process, facilitated by the United Nations, to create a path to hold free, fair and inclusive national presidential and parliamentary elections in Libya as soon as possible, and, in this regard, expressing support for the ongoing facilitation of intra-Libyan consultations to create the conditions and circumstances for elections on a constitutional and legal basis (third preambular paragraph)
The situation in Mali	
Resolution 2640 (2022) 29 June	Reaffirming its strong commitment to the sovereignty, unity and territorial integrity of Mali, emphasizing that the Malian authorities have primary responsibility for the provision of stability, security and protection of civilians throughout the territory of Mali, urging the Malian authorities to uphold their efforts to meet their obligations in that regard, and expressing great concern at the violent and unilateral actions taken by non-State actors hampering the return of State authority and basic social services (second preambular paragraph)
	Reaffirming the basic principles of peacekeeping, including consent of the parties, impartiality and non-use of force except in self-defence and defence of the mandate, recognizing that the mandate of each peacekeeping mission is specific to the need and situation of the country concerned, and recalling its presidential statement of 14 May 2018 (S/PRST/2018/10) (third preambular paragraph)
	Reiterates that the Malian authorities have primary responsibility to protect civilians in Mali, urges these authorities to take expedited action to protect civilians throughout the country and to prevent, minimize and address civilian harm that might result from operations undertaken by the Malian Defence and Security Forces (para. 2)

Decision and date	Provision
Resolution 2649 (2022) 30 August	Reaffirming its strong commitment to the sovereignty, unity and territorial integrity of Mali, emphasizing that the Malian authorities have primary responsibility for the provision of stability and security throughout the territory of Mali, and underscoring the importance of achieving national ownership of peace- and security-related initiatives (second preambular paragraph)

The situation in the Middle East

Decision and date	Provision
Resolution 2650 (2022) 31 August	Further requests the United Nations Interim Force in Lebanon, in line with resolution 1701 (2006) and following the letter of the Government of Lebanon of 15 March 2022 addressed to the President of the Security Council as well as per the recommendations of the Secretary-General (S/2022/556), to exceptionally extend temporary and special measures, that should not be considered as a precedent in the future nor a long-term solution, to support and assist the Lebanese Armed Forces with the provision of relevant additional non-lethal material (fuel, food and medicine) and logistical support for a period of six months and no longer than 28 February 2023, within existing resources and without implications for the increase of the budget level, for the joint activities of the Lebanese Armed Forces and the Force and in compliance with the United Nations human rights due diligence policy, and without prejudice to the mandate and its implementation, the concept of operations and rules of engagement of the Force, while fully respecting Lebanese sovereignty and at the request of the Lebanese authorities, and that such support be subject to appropriate and immediate oversight and scrutiny (para. 11)
	Urges all parties to cooperate fully with the Head of Mission and the Force in the implementation of resolution 1701 (2006), as well as to ensure that the freedom of movement of the Force in all its operations and its access to the Blue Line in all its parts is fully respected and unimpeded, in conformity with its mandate and its rules of engagement, including by avoiding any course of action which endangers United Nations personnel, reaffirms that, pursuant to the status-of-forces agreement between the Government of Lebanon and the United Nations, the Force does not require prior authorization or permission to undertake its mandated tasks and that it is authorized to conduct its operation independently, condemns in the strongest terms all attempts to deny access or restrict the freedom of movement of Force personnel and all attacks on Force personnel and equipment as well as acts of harassment and intimidation of Force personnel and disinformation campaigns against the Force, calls upon the Government of Lebanon to facilitate prompt and full access of the Force to sites requested by the Force for the purpose of swift investigation, including all relevant locations north of the Blue Line related to the discovery of tunnels crossing the Blue Line which the Force reported as a violation of resolution 1701 (2006), in line with resolution 1701 (2006), while respecting Lebanese sovereignty (para. 16)

The situation in Somalia

Decision and date	Provision
Resolution 2628 (2022) 31 March	Recalling that the Federal Government of Somalia has the primary responsibility for ensuring security in Somalia, and recognizing Somalia's request for continued international support to enable it to achieve progressively its aim of a secure, stable, peaceful, united and democratic country (second preambular paragraph)
	Underscores the primary responsibility for protecting civilians of the Somali authorities, and further underscores the importance of protecting civilians in accordance with relevant provisions of international human rights law and international humanitarian law (para. 6)
	Endorses the African Union Peace and Security Council's decision to reconfigure the African Union Mission in Somalia into the African Union Transition Mission in Somalia, and authorizes, for an initial period of 12 months, the States members of the African Union to take all necessary measures, in full compliance with the obligations of participating States under international law, including international humanitarian law and international human rights law, and in full respect for the sovereignty, territorial integrity, political independence and unity of Somalia, to: … (para. 22)

Reports of the Secretary-General on the Sudan and South Sudan

Decision and date	Provision
Resolution 2620 (2022) 15 February	Reaffirming the primary responsibility of the Government of the Sudan to protect civilians across its territory, and acknowledging in this regard the Government of the Sudan's national plan for civilian protection (S/2020/429) and the weapons-collection programme (fifth preambular paragraph)

Decision and date	Provision
Resolution 2625 (2022) 15 March	Strongly condemning all human rights violations and abuses and violations of international humanitarian law by all parties, including armed groups and national security forces, as well as the incitement to commit such abuses and violations, including those in Tambura, Western Equatoria State, further condemning the harassment, targeting and censorship of civil society, humanitarian personnel and journalists, emphasizing that those responsible for violations of international humanitarian law and violations and abuses of human rights must be held accountable, and that South Sudan's Government bears the primary responsibility to protect its populations from genocide, war crimes, ethnic cleansing and crimes against humanity, and expressing concern that despite the signing of the Revitalized Agreement, violations and abuses, including rape and sexual violence, continue to occur, which may amount to international crimes, including war crimes and crimes against humanity (fifteenth preambular paragraph)
	Recalls its resolution 2086 (2013), reaffirms the basic principles of peacekeeping, as set forth in presidential statement S/PRST/2015/22, including consent of the parties, impartiality and non-use of force except in self-defence and defence of the mandate, and recognizes that the mandate of each peacekeeping mission is specific to the need and situation of the country concerned, and that the Security Council expects full delivery of the mandates it authorizes (para. 19)
Resolution 2660 (2022) 14 November	Urges the Governments of the Sudan and South Sudan to provide full support to the United Nations Interim Security Force for Abyei in the implementation of its mandate and the deployment of Force personnel, including to facilitate the smooth functioning of all Force bases and Joint Border Verification and Monitoring Mechanism team sites, in line with their primary responsibility as host States and the status-of-forces agreements, and further reiterates that the Abyei Area shall be demilitarized from any forces, as well as armed elements of the local communities, other than the Force and the Abyei Police Service when it is gradually established, and urges the Governments of the Sudan and South Sudan and the local communities to take all necessary steps in this regard (para. 4)

Table 7
Decisions containing implicit references to Article 2 (7) of the Charter, by thematic issue, 2022

Decision and date	Provision
United Nations peacekeeping operations	
S/PRST/2022/5 12 July	The Security Council underscores the importance of peacekeeping as one of the most effective tools available to the United Nations in the promotion and maintenance of international peace and security, and reaffirms the basic principles of peacekeeping, such as consent of the parties, impartiality and non-use of force except in self-defence and defence of the mandate (second paragraph)

B. Discussions relating to Article 2 (7)

During the period under review, Article 2 (7) of the Charter was explicitly invoked once in the Council's deliberations. At a meeting held on 21 December under the item entitled "The question concerning Haiti",[81] the Editor of *Haiti Liberté* emphasized that the situation in Haiti could not be resolved through foreign intervention, military force or even sanctions, and that the Haitian people, acting with full sovereignty, must be allowed to sort out their own problems. He further called upon the Council to respect the principles enshrined in the Charter, in particular Article 2 (7), which stated that nothing contained in the Charter should authorize the United Nations to intervene in matters which were essentially within the domestic jurisdiction of any State.

[81] See S/PV.9233.

In addition, during several meetings of the Council in 2022, held under both country- and region-specific items, its members and other speakers discussed the principle of non-intervention by the United Nations in the domestic affairs of States enshrined in Article 2 (7) of the Charter without explicitly referring to that Article, as described below.

At a meeting held on 29 June under the item entitled "The situation in Mali",[82] the representative of the Russian Federation, explaining her country's abstention in the voting on resolution 2640 (2022) concerning the renewal of the mandate of the United Nations Multidimensional Integrated Stabilization Mission in Mali (MINUSMA), said that the resolution's intrusive language on the human rights mandate of MINUSMA would not advance the Malian people's exercise of their sovereign right to protect their citizens and investigate incidents. The representative of China, who had also abstained, underscored that Member States bore the primary responsibility for the protection and promotion of human rights, and recalled that the Mission's main task was to assist the Government of Mali in implementing the Agreement on Peace and Reconciliation in Mali and restoring the State's authority in the north. He added that, in fulfilling its human rights mandate, the Mission should communicate and cooperate closely with the Government and listen carefully to its views. Elaborating on the reasons behind his country's abstention, he further indicated that resolution 2640 (2022) excessively emphasized the Mission's human rights-related mandate and did not reflect full respect for the Government's ownership. The representative of Gabon underscored that the resolution violated the sovereignty of Mali, as it did not take into account the efforts made by the Malian defence forces in honour of their sovereign duty to defend their territory, in conditions that were very often challenging. The representative of Mali recalled that his country had always cooperated in good faith with MINUSMA since its establishment in 2013 but stressed that, in line with the principle of respect for the country's sovereignty, as well as for coordination and security reasons, the movements of MINUSMA could take place only with the agreement of the competent Malian authorities. He added that Mali was not in a position to guarantee the freedom of movement of MINUSMA in its investigations without the prior agreement of the Government. In that context, he stressed that Mali did not intend to implement the related provisions of resolution 2640 (2022), as the Government of Mali believed that allegations concerning human rights violations were the primary responsibility of the Malian authorities, adding that the Mission's role was to provide them with the necessary assistance in that regard, rather than replace the Government of Mali.

At a meeting held on 30 June under the item entitled "The situation concerning the Democratic Republic of the Congo",[83] the Council adopted resolution 2641 (2022), by which it renewed the sanctions measures and extended the mandate of the Group of Experts on the Democratic Republic of the Congo.[84] After the vote, the representative of Ghana, who had abstained from voting, underscored that the remaining notification requirement on certain shipments of arms and related materiel for the Democratic Republic of the Congo, as expressed in resolution 2641 (2022), did not respond to the imperatives for peace in the country, nor was it reflective of its sovereignty.[85] The representative of Gabon, who had also abstained from voting, expressed regret about the lack of consensus among Council members, emphasizing that it was essential that the international community recalibrated its priorities in the Democratic Republic of the Congo and focused, above all, on the interests of the people, taking into account the national sovereignty of the country.

Council members and other Member States also stressed the need to respect the sovereignty and national ownership of States in the context of the operations of United Nations peacekeeping and special political missions in Somalia and the Sudan, at meetings held under the items entitled "The situation in Somalia"[86] and "Reports of the Secretary-General on the Sudan and South Sudan",[87] as well as in relation

---

[82] See S/PV.9082.
[83] See S/PV.9084.
[84] Resolution 2641 (2022), paras. 1, 5 and 8.
[85] See S/PV.9084.
[86] See, for example, S/PV.8965 (Ghana (also on behalf of Gabon and Kenya), China and Russian Federation); and S/PV.9177 (Russian Federation and Somalia).
[87] See, for example, S/PV.9006 (China and United Arab Emirates); and S/PV.9041 (United Arab Emirates).

to the cross-border humanitarian mechanism in the Syrian Arab Republic at meetings held under the item entitled "The situation in the Middle East".[88]

In 2022, in connection with thematic items, Council members and other Member States also continued to underline the importance of the principles of sovereignty, territorial integrity, political independence and consent of the host States enshrined in Article 2 (7) of the Charter, without making explicit reference to that Article, as described below.

At a high-level open debate held on 2 June under the item entitled "Maintenance of international peace and security",[89] Council members and other Member States addressed the principles enshrined in Article 2 (7) of the Charter in the context of a discussion on strengthening accountability and justice for serious violations of international law. The Minister of State for External Affairs of India stated that the responsibility to protect could not be invoked to address all violations of human rights and humanitarian law but must rather be confined to four major crimes – genocide, war crimes, ethnic cleansing and crimes against humanity.[90] He recalled that practice had shown that the default response of the international community should not be the use of coercive measures imposed on the basis of Chapter VII of the Charter. He also added that the responsibility to protect should not be seen as a pretext for humanitarian intervention and stressed the need to refrain from imposing universal jurisdiction on acts of atrocities alleged to have been committed on the territory of a sovereign State. In his conclusion, he pointed out that accountability for serious violations of international law was a noble objective that should be pursued with due respect for the sovereign equality of States. Stressing that accountability measures should respect the judicial sovereignty of the States concerned, the representative of China noted that States had the primary responsibility for punishing serious crimes, ending impunity and achieving justice, and that adherence to the principle of State ownership was not only an important manifestation of the principles of sovereign equality and non-interference in internal affairs, but also a crucial assurance for the smooth advancement of accountability and the achievement of the desired results.

In addition, those same principles were discussed at meetings held under the item entitled "Protection of civilians in armed conflict" in relation to the delivery of humanitarian assistance,[91] as well as under the item entitled "Peacebuilding and sustaining peace" in connection with the annual report of the Peacebuilding Commission.[92] Speakers also continued to address the need for the United Nations to uphold the principles of peacekeeping, including the respect for the sovereignty and consent of the host States, at meetings held under the item entitled "United Nations peacekeeping operations".[93]

C. Invocations of the principle enshrined in Article 2 (7) in communications

In 2022, two communications brought to the attention of the Council included explicit references to Article 2 (7) of the Charter (see table 8). It should be noted, however, that Article 2 (7) concerns the practice of the Council in relation to the principle of non-intervention by the United Nations in the internal affairs of States and not the intervention by Member States in the internal affairs of other States.[94]

---

[88] See, for example, S/PV.8957 (China and Syrian Arab Republic).

[89] See S/PV.9052 and S/PV.9052 (Resumption 1).

[90] See S/PV.9052.

[91] See S/PV.8953 (China, India and Egypt); S/2022/54 (Azerbaijan); S/PV.9042 (India, China and Algeria); and S/PV.9042 (Resumption 1), (Viet Nam, Georgia and Azerbaijan).

[92] See S/PV.9101 (China and Russian Federation). For more information on the activities of the Peacebuilding Commission, see part IX, sect. VII.

[93] See, for example, S/PV.9090 (India, Russian Federation, China, Morocco and Guatemala).

[94] For information on the practice of the Council in relation to Article 2 (4) of the Charter, see sect. II above.

Table 8
Communications containing explicit references to Article 2 (7) of the Charter, 2022

Symbol	*Title*	*Relevant extract*
S/2022/372	Identical letters dated 28 April 2022 from the Permanent Representative of Lebanon to the United Nations addressed to the Secretary-General and the President of the Security Council	Request the Group of Arab States in New York to take the necessary action to transmit the present resolution to the relevant United Nations bodies and have it issued as a document of the United Nations, and to request that they include the question on their respective agendas, in accordance with the Charter of the United Nations, Article 2, paragraph 7, which prohibits interference in the internal affairs of States. (Resolution 8749, on Iranian interference in the internal affairs of Arab States, of the Council of the League of Arab States, para. 27)
S/2022/891	Letter dated 29 November 2022 from the Permanent Representative of the Islamic Republic of Iran to the United Nations addressed to the Secretary-General and the President of the Security Council	Consequently, as long as the National Regulation Governing Landing Rights Regarding Provisions of Satellite Services in the Islamic Republic of Iran is not compiled by SpaceX as a legal person under the domestic jurisdiction of the United States Government, its satellite Internet services in the territory of the Islamic Republic of Iran are illegal and considered as intervening in the internal affairs of Iran in accordance with Article 2, paragraph 7, of the Charter of the United Nations, which must be observed by all States Members of the United Nations.

Part IV
Relations with other United Nations organs

Contents

Introductory note

Part IV of the present supplement covers the practice of the Security Council with regard to Articles 4 to 6, 10 to 12, 15 (1), 20, 23, 24 (3), 65, 93, 94, 96 and 97 of the Charter of the United Nations concerning the relations of the Council with other principal organs of the United Nations, namely, the General Assembly, the Economic and Social Council and the International Court of Justice. Material relating to the relations of the Council with the Secretariat is featured in part II, section V, which deals with the administrative functions and powers of the Secretary-General in connection with meetings of the Council pursuant to rules 21 to 26 of its provisional rules of procedure. The Trusteeship Council continued to be inactive during the period under review.[1]

During the period under review, the General Assembly continued to address recommendations to the Council regarding the general principles of cooperation in the maintenance of international peace and security. The Council and the Assembly, in parallel and within the limitations imposed by the Charter, considered the situation of human rights in the Democratic People's Republic of Korea and in the Syrian Arab Republic.

For the first time since 1982, by its resolution 2623 (2022) of 27 February, the Council decided to call an emergency special session of the General Assembly on the situation in Ukraine under the item entitled "Letter dated 28 February 2014 from the Permanent Representative of Ukraine to the United Nations addressed to the President of the Security Council (S/2014/136)". Accordingly, the eleventh emergency special session was convened by the Secretary-General at United Nations Headquarters on 28 February. During the course of the year, the Assembly reconvened the eleventh emergency special session several times, including for the adoption of five resolutions concerning the conflict in Ukraine.

In addition, on 26 April, recalling Articles 10 and 12 of the Charter, the General Assembly adopted resolution 76/262, by which it decided that its President should convene a formal meeting of the Assembly within 10 working days of the casting of a veto by one or more permanent members of the Council, to hold a debate, provided that the Assembly did not meet in an emergency special session on the same situation. In the same resolution, the Assembly also invited the Council, in accordance with Article 24 (3) of the Charter, to submit to the Assembly a special report on the use of the veto in question in advance of the relevant discussion in the Assembly. In 2022, pursuant to that resolution, the Assembly held meetings following vetoes cast on draft resolutions in connection with the items entitled "Non-proliferation/Democratic Republic of Korea" and "The situation in the Middle East". The Council submitted a special report to the Assembly in advance of each of those debates. With regard to the conflict in Ukraine, although the discussion on the veto cast on 30 September was held under the umbrella of the eleventh emergency special session convened pursuant to Council resolution 2623 (2022) and Assembly resolution 377 (V), the Council submitted a third special report pursuant to Assembly resolution 76/262.

The two organs collaborated in the election of a judge to fill a vacancy in the International Court of Justice following the death of one of the judges of the Court and, also in collaboration with the Secretary-General, in the reappointment of 25 judges of the International Residual Mechanism for Criminal Tribunals, consistent with the applicable provisions of the statute of the Mechanism, the provisional rules of procedure of the Council and the rules of procedure of the General Assembly.

During 2022, the President of the Security Council participated in and delivered statements at meetings and events of the General Assembly. On 9 June, the President for the month (Albania) participated in the plenary meeting of the Assembly to introduce the annual report of the Security Council. On 29 November, the President for the month (Ghana), at the invitation of the Committee on the Exercise of the Inalienable Rights of the Palestinian People of the General Assembly, delivered a statement at the high-level special meeting of the Assembly on the International Day of Solidarity with the Palestinian People. In addition, on 14 December, the Council heard a briefing by the President of the General Assembly during a high-level open debate held under the item entitled "Maintenance of international peace and security" and the sub-item entitled "New orientation for reformed multilateralism". The Assembly adopted

[1] The Trusteeship Council completed its mandate under the Charter in 1994 and suspended its operations on 1 November 1994. For more information see *Repertoire, Supplement 1993–1995*, chap. VI, part III.

a number of resolutions in which it referred to its relationship with the Council, and the Council, for its part, continued to refer to Assembly resolutions in its decisions. In addition, Council members continued to discuss the relations between the Council and the subsidiary organs of the Assembly, in particular the Human Rights Council and the Special Committee on Peacekeeping Operations.

In 2022, the Council did not address any requests for information or assistance to the Economic and Social Council, nor did it make recommendations or decide on measures with regard to the judgments rendered by the International Court of Justice or request the Court to give an advisory opinion on any legal question. The President of the Court gave a briefing to the Council at an open debate held on 2 June, under the item entitled "Maintenance of international peace and security", as well as at a private meeting held on 26 October, under the item entitled "Briefing by the President of the International Court of Justice".

I. Relations with the General Assembly

Note

Section I is focused on various aspects of the relationship between the Council and the General Assembly in accordance with Articles 4 to 6, 10 to 12, 15 (1), 20, 23, 24 (3), 93, 94, 96 and 97 of the Charter of the United Nations, rules 40,[2] 60 and 61 of the provisional rules of procedure of the Council and Articles 4, 8, 10 to 12 and 14 of the Statute of the International Court of Justice.

Section I is divided into eight subsections. Subsection A deals with the election by the General Assembly of the non-permanent members of the Council, in accordance with Article 23 of the Charter. Subsections B and C concern the functions and powers of the Assembly vis-à-vis Articles 10 to 12, with a particular focus on the practice and authority of the Assembly to make recommendations to the Council. Subsection D covers instances in which a decision by the Council must be taken prior to that of the Assembly under Articles 4 to 6, 93 and 97, such as the admission of new Members or the appointment of the Secretary-General and of judges to the International Residual Mechanism for Criminal Tribunals. Subsection E concerns the practices for the election of members of the International Court of Justice, requiring concurrent action by the Council and the Assembly. Subsection F covers the annual and special reports of the Council to the Assembly, in accordance with Articles 15 and 24 (3). Subsection G concerns Council relations with the subsidiary organs established by the Assembly that have played a part in the work of the Council during 2022. Subsection H features other Council practice bearing on relations with the Assembly.

A. Election by the General Assembly of the non-permanent members of the Security Council

Article 23

1. The Security Council shall consist of fifteen Members of the United Nations. The Republic of China, France, the Union of Soviet Socialist Republics, the United Kingdom of Great Britain and Northern Ireland, and the United States of America shall be permanent members of the Security Council. The General Assembly shall elect ten other Members of the United Nations to be non-permanent members of the Security Council, due regard being specially paid, in the first instance to the contribution of Members of the United Nations to the maintenance of international peace and security and to the other purposes of the Organization, and also to equitable geographical distribution.

2. The non-permanent members of the Security Council shall be elected for a term of two years. In the first election of the non-permanent members after the increase of the membership of the Security Council from eleven to fifteen, two of the four additional members shall be chosen for a term of one year. A retiring member shall not be eligible for immediate re-election.

3. Each member of the Security Council shall have one representative.

During the period under review, at its seventy-sixth regular session, the General Assembly elected five non-permanent members to the Council, in accordance with Article 23 of the Charter, to replace those whose terms of office were to expire on 31 December 2022 (see table 1).

Table 1
Election by the General Assembly of non-permanent members of the Security Council

Term	*General Assembly decision*	*Plenary meeting record and date*	*Members elected for the term*
2023–2024	76/422	A/76/PV.79 9 June 2022	Ecuador, Japan, Malta, Mozambique, Switzerland

[2] Rule 40 of the provisional rules of procedure is also covered in part II, sect. VIII.

B. Recommendations made by the General Assembly to the Security Council under Articles 10 and 11 of the Charter

Article 10

The General Assembly may discuss any questions or any matters within the scope of the present Charter or relating to the powers and functions of any organs provided for in the present Charter, and except as provided in Article 12, may make recommendations to the Members of the United Nations or to the Security Council or to both on any such questions or matters.

Article 11

1. The General Assembly may consider the general principles of cooperation in the maintenance of international peace and security, including the principles governing disarmament and the regulation of armaments, and may make recommendations with regard to such principles to the Members or to the Security Council or to both.

2. The General Assembly may discuss any questions relating to the maintenance of international peace and security brought before it by any Member of the United Nations, or by the Security Council or by a state which is not a Member of the United Nations in accordance with Article 35, paragraph 2, and, except as provided in Article 12, may make recommendations with regard to any such questions to the state or states concerned or to the Security Council or to both. Any such question on which action is necessary shall be referred to the Security Council by the General Assembly either before or after discussion.

3. The General Assembly may call the attention of the Security Council to situations which are likely to endanger international peace and security.

4. The powers of the General Assembly set forth in this Article shall not limit the general scope of Article 10.

During the period under review, the General Assembly addressed recommendations to the Council regarding the general principles of cooperation in the maintenance of international peace and security. Several of these recommendations concerned the powers and functions of the Council under Articles 10 and 11 (1) of the Charter. The relevant provisions of the resolutions of the Assembly are set out in table 2. In addition, in Assembly resolution 77/83, adopted under the item entitled "United Nations Regional Centre for Peace and Disarmament in Africa", Member States continued to explicitly recall the provisions of Article 11 (1), in which it is stipulated that a function of the Assembly is to consider the general principles of cooperation in the maintenance of international peace and security, including the principles governing disarmament and arms limitation.[3]

In connection with Article 11 (2) of the Charter, the General Assembly made recommendations to the Council with regard to specific questions relating to the maintenance of international peace and security or requesting action by the Council concerning those questions. In its recommendations, in reference to matters of which the Council was already seized, the Assembly continued to call upon the Council to ensure accountability, including through the consideration of a referral of the situation in the Democratic People's Republic of Korea to the International Criminal Court and to consider the further development of sanctions in order to effectively target those who appeared to be most responsible for human rights violations. The Assembly continued to encourage the Council to immediately resume discussion on the situation in the Democratic People's Republic of Korea, including the country's human rights situation. Concerning the humanitarian situation in the Syrian Arab Republic, the Assembly continued to urge the Council to reauthorize the use of the border crossings of Bab al-Salam and Ya'rubiyah for the delivery of humanitarian assistance to the country. The Assembly also continued to call upon the Council to ensure accountability of those responsible for violations and abuses of international humanitarian law or human rights law in the Syrian Arab Republic. The relevant provisions of the resolutions of the Assembly are set out in table 3.

[3] General Assembly resolution 77/83, first preambular paragraph.

On 26 April, the General Assembly adopted resolution 76/262, in which it recalled its authority under Article 10 of the Charter, as well as under Article 12, and decided that its President would convene a formal meeting of the Assembly within 10 working days of the casting of a veto by one or more permanent members of the Council, to hold a debate on the situation as to which the veto was cast, provided that the Assembly did not meet in an emergency special session on the same situation.[4] By the same resolution, the Assembly decided, on an exceptional basis, to accord precedence in the list of speakers to the permanent member or permanent members of the Council having cast a veto.[5] Pursuant to the resolution and following the casting of vetoes by permanent members of the Council,[6] the Assembly convened formal meetings to discuss the vetoes in question, which concerned situations connected with the items entitled "Non-proliferation/Democratic People's Republic of Korea"[7] and "The situation in the Middle East".[8] With regard to the conflict in Ukraine, the discussion on the veto cast on 30 September in connection with a draft resolution proposed under the item entitled "Maintenance of peace and security of Ukraine" was held on 10 October, under the umbrella of the eleventh emergency special session launched pursuant to resolution 2623 (2022) and Assembly resolution 377 (V).[9]

In 2022, the General Assembly did not draw the attention of the Council to any situations likely to endanger international peace and security pursuant to Article 11 (3) of the Charter.[10]

Table 2
Recommendations to the Security Council in resolutions of the General Assembly regarding the general principles of cooperation in the maintenance of international peace and security, 2022

General Assembly resolution and date	*Provisions*
Comprehensive review of special political missions	
77/127 12 December	Encouraging enhanced exchanges of information, in an appropriate manner, among the General Assembly, the Security Council and the Secretariat, making use of the advisory role of the Peacebuilding Commission, when relevant, on overall policy matters pertaining to special political missions (tenth preambular paragraph)
	Acknowledges the importance of strong coordination, coherence and cooperation of the Security Council and the General Assembly with the Peacebuilding Commission, and in this regard encourages the Security Council to continue to regularly request, deliberate and draw upon the specific, strategic and targeted advice of the Commission, including to assist with the longer-term perspective required for sustaining peace being reflected in the formation, review and drawdown of peacekeeping operations and special political missions mandates, in line with General Assembly resolution 70/262 and Security Council resolution 2282 (2016) (para. 4)
Report of the International Criminal Court	
77/6 2 November	Encourages further dialogue between the United Nations and the International Criminal Court, and welcomes in this regard the increased interaction of the Security Council with the Court under various formats, including the holding of open debates on peace and justice and working methods, with a special focus on the role of the Court (para. 20)

[4] General Assembly resolution 76/262, para. 1.

[5] Ibid., para. 2. See also rule 68 of the rules of procedure of the General Assembly.

[6] See S/PV.9048 and S/PV.9087.

[7] See A/76/PV.77, A/76/PV.78, A/76/PV.81 and A/76/PV.82.

[8] See A/76/PV.95 and A/76/PV.96.

[9] See A/ES-11/PV.12. A special report was submitted following the veto cast at the 9143rd meeting of the Council held on 30 September (see S/PV.9143), under the item entitled "Maintenance of peace and security of Ukraine". For more information see sect. I.F below.

[10] For information on other referrals to the Security Council, see part VI, sect. I.

General Assembly resolution and date	*Provisions*
Standing mandate for a General Assembly debate when a veto is cast in the Security Council	
76/262 26 April	Invites the Security Council, in accordance with Article 24 (3) of the Charter of the United Nations, to submit a special report on the veto in question to the General Assembly at least 72 hours before the relevant discussion in the Assembly (para. 3)

Table 3

Recommendations to the Security Council in resolutions of the General Assembly with regard to specific questions relating to the maintenance of international peace and security, 2022

General Assembly resolution and date	*Provisions*
Situation of human rights in the Democratic People' Republic of Korea	
77/226 15 December	Encourages the Security Council to continue its consideration of the relevant conclusions and recommendations of the commission of inquiry and take appropriate action to ensure accountability, including through consideration of referral of the situation in the Democratic People's Republic of Korea to the International Criminal Court and consideration of further sanctions in order to target effectively those who appear to be most responsible for human rights violations that the commission has said may constitute crimes against humanity (para. 12)
	Also encourages the Security Council to immediately resume discussion on the situation in the Democratic People's Republic of Korea and invite the Office of the United Nations High Commissioner for Human Rights to give a briefing to the Council, including on the country's human rights situation, in the light of the serious concerns expressed in the present resolution, and looks forward to its continued and more active engagement on this matter (para. 13)
Situation of human rights in the Syrian Arab Republic	
77/230 15 December	Deplores the continued closure of the Bab al-Salam and Ya'rubiyah border crossings for the purpose of cross-border humanitarian aid, expresses its concern regarding the limited renewal of the cross-border resolution for only six months, which is considered unsustainable and insufficient, considering growing humanitarian needs as winter approaches, noting that needs have increased to the highest levels since 2011, with more than 14.6 million Syrians in need, according to the United Nations, and urges the Security Council to renew the cross-border mechanism by January 2023 and to reauthorize the use of these border crossings for at least 12 months, emphasizes that more than 6.9 million people live in areas not under the control of the Syrian regime and 5.3 million require humanitarian assistance in the north-east and north-west, and considers with great concern the serious threats posed by the recent outbreak of cholera, which disproportionately affects those who are already most vulnerable, and that the cross-border mechanism remains an indispensable tool to address the humanitarian needs of the population, including to deliver vaccines and supplies to combat the coronavirus disease (COVID-19) pandemic, which cannot be adequately reached through existing operations within the Syrian Arab Republic (para. 17)
	Emphasizes the need to ensure that all those responsible for violations of international humanitarian law or violations and abuses of human rights law are held to account through appropriate, fair and independent domestic or international criminal justice mechanisms, stresses the need to pursue practical steps towards this goal, and for that reason encourages the Security Council to take appropriate action to ensure accountability, noting the important role that the International Criminal Court can play in this regard in accordance with complementarity (para. 35)

Concerning the deliberations in the Council, during the period under review, no explicit references were made to Articles 10 or 11 of the Charter. Nonetheless, Council members and non-Council members alike continued to address issues that may be considered of relevance for the application and interpretation of Articles 10 and 11 in the context of Council meetings.

At a high-level open debate held on 2 June at the initiative of Albania, which held the presidency of the Council for the month,[11] under the item entitled “Maintenance of international peace and security” and the sub-item entitled “Strengthening accountability and justice for serious violations of international law”,[12] participants discussed the convening of formal meetings of the General Assembly following the casting of a veto at a Council meeting, pursuant to Assembly resolution 76/262 of 26 April. The representative of Ireland indicated that any permanent member using the veto would have to account for that use to all members of the United Nations; he added that his delegation looked forward to the Assembly’s first debate under that resolution the following week.[13] The representative of Malaysia, expressing support for the recent adoption of the resolution by the Assembly, recalled that the text provided a standing mandate to hold a debate whenever a veto was cast in the Council. The representative of Latvia underlined that the use of its power of veto by the Russian Federation to block Council resolutions denouncing its invasion of Ukraine had compelled the Organization’s membership to enhance the role of the Assembly, in accordance with its mandate under the Charter, in order to prevent deadlock in the Council and maintain the rules-based international order.[14] The representatives of Denmark (also on behalf of Finland, Iceland, Norway and Sweden), Estonia, Türkiye and Switzerland welcomed the adoption of the Assembly resolution, which provided for the convening of a formal meeting of the Assembly to hold a debate following the casting of a veto in the Council.

The implementation of General Assembly resolution 76/262 was the subject of further discussion at the annual open debate on working methods, held under the item entitled “Implementation of the note by the President of the Security Council (S/2017/507)” (see case 1).

Case 1
Implementation of the note by the President of the Security Council (S/2017/507)

On 28 June, at the initiative of Albania, which held the presidency of the Security Council for the month,[15] the Council held its annual open debate on its working methods under the item entitled “Implementation of the note by the President of the Security Council (S/2017/507)”.[16] During the meeting, Council members heard briefings by the Director of Security Council Procedure and co-author of the fourth edition of *The Procedure of the UN Security Council* and by the Executive Director of Security Council Report.[17] The representative of former Council member Saint Vincent and the Grenadines, who had served as Chair of the Informal Working Group on Documentation and Other Procedural Questions in 2020 and 2021, submitted a statement in writing.[18]

During the debate, many participants underlined the importance of the adoption and implementation of General Assembly resolution 76/262 of 26 April 2022 for enhancing the accountability of the Council towards the wider membership.[19] The representative of the United States was pleased to see the smooth implementation of the Assembly resolution following a double veto on the draft resolution submitted by her delegation under the item entitled “Non-proliferation/The Democratic Republic of Korea”, adding that the Assembly meeting had provided an opportunity for those casting a veto to explain themselves and for the States Members of the United Nations to react to the veto.[20] On behalf of the Accountability, Coherence and Transparency Group, the representative of Switzerland emphasized that the new accountability mechanism provided for in the Assembly resolution mobilized the broader United Nations membership whenever the Council was unable to fulfil its duties because of the use of the veto

---

[11] A concept note was circulated by a letter dated 24 May (S/2022/418/Rev.1).

[12] See S/PV.9052 and S/PV.9052 (Resumption 1).

[13] See S/PV.9052.

[14] See S/PV.9052 (Resumption 1).

[15] A concept note was circulated by a letter dated 21 June (S/2022/499).

[16] See S/PV.9079 and S/PV.9079 (Resumption 1).

[17] See S/PV.9079.

[18] See S/2022/519. For more information on the procedures and working methods developed since the onset of the coronavirus disease (COVID-19) pandemic, see part II.

[19] See S/PV.9079 (United States, United Kingdom, Switzerland (on behalf of the Accountability, Coherence and Transparency Group), Luxembourg (also on behalf of Belgium and the Netherlands), Republic of Korea, Poland, Liechtenstein, Austria, Portugal and Slovenia); and S/PV.9079 (Resumption 1) (Slovakia).

[20] See S/PV.9079.

by a permanent member. The representative of Poland expressed the belief that the new practice of convening a plenary meeting of the Assembly following the use of the veto would contribute to improving the United Nations system and translate into strengthening international peace and stability. The representative of Kuwait indicated that resolution 76/262 would promote the role of the Assembly and enable it to strengthen transparency and effectiveness in its relationship with the Council.

Many participants discussed the relationship between the two organs more broadly. The representative of Ireland (on behalf of the 10 elected members of the Council) stressed that the Council should strengthen its engagement with the wider United Nations membership, including by being more transparent and by creating more opportunities for the members of the General Assembly to interact with the work of the Council, while preserving the various tools at the command of the Council to ensure its effectiveness. The representative of China emphasized that the Council belonged to all Member States and should strive to work in greater coordination and synergy with the President of the General Assembly, the Secretary-General, the Economic and Social Council and the Peacebuilding Commission. The representative of Ecuador insisted on the need to deepen the relationship between the Council and the Assembly. The representative of Luxembourg (also on behalf of Belgium and the Netherlands) emphasized that it was crucial that cooperation be strengthened between the Council and the Assembly. The representative of the Republic of Korea encouraged the Council to strengthen its interaction and engagement with other United Nations organs, including the Assembly. The representative of Thailand underlined that, given the strong interlinkages between the various global crises affecting humankind and the inherent peace-development-governance nexus in most conflict situations, it was more important than ever that the Council work in increased coordination, cooperation and interaction with other United Nations organs, including the Assembly. The representative of Malta stressed that the interaction between the Council and the Assembly should be strengthened wherever possible, as the Council could not work in isolation.

Some participants focused their interventions on the need to preserve the distinctive mandates of the Council and the General Assembly to avoid encroachment and prevent the duplication of work among the two organs. In that connection, the representative of the Islamic Republic of Iran underscored that, in order to avoid duplicating efforts and encroaching on the Assembly's mandate, the Council needed to improve communication and cooperation with the Assembly and other United Nations organs on cross-cutting issues. The representative of Cuba called for the Council to abide by its mandate and respect the functions of other United Nations organs, adding that the Council needed to stop expanding the scope of its interpretation of international peace and security and infringing on the functions and responsibilities of the Assembly. The representative of the Syrian Arab Republic similarly emphasized the importance of respecting individual mandates, indicating that the Council should work within its own mandate and not encroach on those of other United Nations bodies such as the Assembly.[21] The representative of the Sudan noted that there had been a debate in recent years about the Council's encroachment on the powers of other organs of the Organization, in particular the Assembly, and indicated that a quick glance at the list of matters of which the Council was seized revealed that its agenda was rapidly expanding, necessitating a pause for reflection and meaningful review.

C. Practice in relation to Article 12 of the Charter

Article 12

1. While the Security Council is exercising in respect of any dispute or situation the functions assigned to it in the present Charter, the General Assembly shall not make any recommendation with regard to that dispute or situation unless the Security Council so requests.

2. The Secretary-General, with the consent of the Security Council, shall notify the General Assembly at each session of any matters relative to the maintenance of international peace and security which are being dealt with by the Security Council and shall similarly notify the General Assembly, or the Members of the United Nations if the General Assembly is not in session, immediately the Security Council ceases to deal with such matters.

[21] See S/PV.9079 (Resumption 1).

Subsection C covers the practice of the Council in relation to Article 12 of the Charter. Article 12 (1) limits the authority of the General Assembly with regard to any dispute or situation in respect of which the Council is exercising its functions under the Charter. Article 14 of the Charter provides further that, subject to the provisions of Article 12, the Assembly may recommend measures for the peaceful adjustment of any situation, regardless of origin, which it deems likely to impair the general welfare or friendly relations among nations, including situations resulting from a violation of the provisions of the Charter setting forth the purposes and principles of the United Nations.

During the period under review, no reference was made to Article 12 (1) of the Charter in decisions of the Council, nor did the Council request the General Assembly to make a recommendation with regard to any dispute or situation. However, for the first time since 1982, at a meeting held on 27 February under the item entitled "Letter dated 28 February 2014 from the Permanent Representative of Ukraine to the United Nations addressed to the President of the Security Council (S/2014/136)", the Council adopted a resolution to call an emergency special session of the Assembly consistent with Assembly resolution 377 (V) of 3 November 1950. Taking into account that the lack of unanimity of its permanent members at the 8979th meeting had prevented it from exercising its primary responsibility for the maintenance of international peace and security, the Council decided, by its resolution 2623 (2022), to call an emergency special session of the General Assembly to examine the question contained in document S/Agenda/8979.[22] The Council resolution had been adopted following the use of the veto by the Russian Federation on 25 February on a draft resolution that would have condemned the 23 February declaration by the Russian Federation of a special military operation in Ukraine.[23] Immediately following the adoption of resolution 2623 (2022), some Council members discussed the Council's accountability vis-à-vis the Assembly regarding the use of the veto (see case 2).

Table 4
Action taken by the Security Council, the Secretary-General and the General Assembly in connection with the eleventh emergency special session, 2022

Council resolution and date	*Note by the Secretary-General and date*	*Request for resumption by Member States*	*Assembly meeting records and dates*	*Assembly resolution and date*
2623 (2022) 27 February	A/ES-11/1 27 February		A/ES-11/PV.1 A/ES-11/PV.2 A/ES-11/PV.3 A/ES-11/PV.4 A/ES-11/PV.5 A/ES-11/PV.6 28 February–2 March	ES-11/1 2 March
		A/ES-11/4 21 March	A/ES-11/PV.7 A/ES-11/PV.8 A/ES-11/PV.9 23 and 24 March	ES-11/2 24 March
		A/ES-11/6 5 April	A/ES-11/PV.10 A/ES-11/PV.11 7 April	ES-11/3 7 April
		A/ES-11/8 3 October	A/ES-11/PV.12 A/ES-11/PV.13 A/ES-11/PV.14 10 and 12 October	ES-11/4 12 October

[22] Prior to 2022, the last time the Council had decided to convoke an emergency special session of the General Assembly was in 1982, by its resolution 500 (1982), in connection with the item entitled "The situation in the occupied Arab territories". For more information on that session, see *Repertoire*, *Supplement 1981–1984*.

[23] At the Council's meeting of 25 February (S/PV.8979), draft resolution S/2022/155 was not adopted owing to the negative vote cast by the Russian Federation.

Council resolution and date	*Note by the Secretary-General and date*	*Request for resumption by Member States*	*Assembly meeting records and dates*	*Assembly resolution and date*
		A/ES-11/10 7 November	A/ES-11/PV.15 A/ES-11/PV.16 14 November	ES-11/5 14 November

In Council discussions, speakers at various meetings exchanged views on the scope of the action of the General Assembly and the Council. Article 12 of the Charter was explicitly referred to once, during the annual open debate on working methods of the Council, held on 28 June under the item entitled "Implementation of the note by the President of the Security Council (S/2017/507)".[24] At the meeting, the representative of the Syrian Arab Republic emphasized the importance of respecting the working methods of the Council, as well as the individual mandates of the principal bodies of the United Nations.[25] In that context, he stated that the Council should not encroach on the mandate of other United Nations bodies, nor should the Assembly violate Article 12, which contained the stipulation that the Assembly should not make any recommendations with regard to a situation being discussed by the Council.

Aside from explicit references, speakers also discussed issues that might be of relevance for the implementation and interpretation of Article 12 of the Charter. On 23 March, at a meeting held under the item entitled "Letter dated 13 April 2014 from the Permanent Representative of the Russian Federation to the United Nations addressed to the President of the Security Council" (S/2014/264),[26] the representative of France indicated that, because the Russian Federation had obstructed a draft resolution that had been negotiated by France and Mexico with the objective of obtaining an immediate cessation of hostilities and of providing a concrete response to the humanitarian catastrophe unfolding in Ukraine, the penholders had decided to take that initiative to the General Assembly. France emphasized that the Assembly must play its role and call for an immediate cessation of hostilities and an end to the war and demand full respect for international humanitarian law. The representative of the United Kingdom also acknowledged that the Assembly would soon take action on a draft resolution on the humanitarian crisis in Ukraine.

On 30 September, at a meeting held under the item entitled "Maintenance of peace and security of Ukraine",[27] owing to the negative vote of the Russian Federation, the Council failed to adopt a draft resolution in which it would have indicated that it had determined that attempts by the Russian Federation to annex the territory of Ukraine constituted a threat to international peace and security and would have condemned the "organization of illegal so-called referenda" by the Russian Federation in regions within the internationally recognized borders of Ukraine.[28] Before the vote, the representative of the United States emphasized that if the Russian Federation chose to shield itself from accountability, then the United States would take further steps in the General Assembly.[29] In turn, the representative of the Russian Federation criticized the negotiation process on the draft resolution and stated that the penholders were prepared to devalue the efforts of the Council as the principal organ for the maintenance of peace and security and to brazenly use the forum of the Council as a dress rehearsal before their main performance in the Assembly. After the vote, the representative of Albania asserted that her country would continue the fight in the Assembly and call upon the Assembly to defend the Charter. The representative of Norway emphasized that it was unacceptable that the Council had again been blocked from taking action on a significant threat to international peace and security, adding that Norway was, however, assured that the Assembly would have an opportunity to take up that grave and important issue. She urged the speedy production of a special report on the use of the veto. The representative of Ireland similarly called upon the Council to submit a special report on the use of the veto in that instance. The representative of Kenya underscored that the draft resolution, whether adopted in the Council or in the Assembly, would not solve

[24] See S/PV.9079 and S/PV.9079 (Resumption 1).
[25] See S/PV.9079 (Resumption 1).
[26] See S/PV.9002.
[27] See S/PV.9143.
[28] See S/2022/720.
[29] See S/PV.9143.

the crisis, and explained that his delegation's affirmative vote was based on his country's principled defence of the Charter.

In 2022, in meetings under items related to the situation in Ukraine, Council members and other participants invoked some of the resolutions adopted at the eleventh emergency special session of the General Assembly.[30] In addition, and consistent with past practice, Council members and other Member States continued to address the prerogatives of the Assembly and the Council at meetings held under the items entitled "The situation in Myanmar" and "Women and peace and security".[31]

Under Article 12 (2) of the Charter, the Secretary-General is required to notify the General Assembly of the matters relating to the maintenance of international peace and security being dealt with by the Council or with which the Council has ceased to deal. During the period under review, in accordance with that provision, the Secretary-General continued to notify the Assembly of the matters relating to the maintenance of international peace and security that were being dealt with by the Security Council or with which the Council had ceased to deal.[32] The notification was prepared on the basis of the summary statements of matters of which the Council was seized and the stage reached in their consideration, which were circulated weekly to Council members in accordance with rule 11 of its provisional rules of procedure.[33] The consent of the Council, required under Article 12 (2), is obtained through the circulation of the draft notification by the Secretary-General to the members of the Council. Following receipt of the notification, the Assembly formally takes note of it.[34]

Case 2
Letter dated 28 February 2014 from the Permanent Representative of Ukraine to the United Nations addressed to the President of the Security Council (S/2014/136)

On 27 February, the Security Council adopted resolution 2623 (2022), in which it decided to call an emergency special session of the General Assembly to examine the question contained in document S/Agenda/8979. The resolution was adopted with 11 votes in favour (Albania, Brazil, France, Gabon, Ghana, Ireland, Kenya, Mexico, Norway, United Kingdom and United States), 1 vote against (Russian Federation) and 3 abstentions (China, India and the United Arab Emirates).[35] After the vote, some Council members discussed the decision to call for an emergency special session of the Assembly pursuant to the veto by the Russian Federation of a draft resolution in which the Council would have condemned the 23 February declaration by the Russian Federation of a special military operation in Ukraine.[36]

The representative of the United States noted that, with the adoption of resolution 2623 (2022), the Council had taken an important step forward towards accountability concerning the aggression against Ukraine.[37] She added that the conflict in Ukraine affected all Member States and that, pursuant to that resolution, the Assembly could make their voices heard concerning the conflict. She expressed her delegation's intention to vote at the emergency special session on a draft resolution intended to hold the Russian Federation to account for its indefensible actions and for its violations of the Charter. The representative of Albania underscored that the five lines of the text that had just been adopted opened the doors of the General Assembly to speak out and condemn an unprovoked and unjustified pure act of aggression. The representative of Ireland indicated that the veto by the Russian Federation of the draft

---

[30] See, for example, S/PV.9008 (France, Mexico, Ghana, United Kingdom, Brazil, United States and Ukraine); S/PV.9011, (Brazil and Mexico); S/PV.9013 (United Kingdom and Ukraine); S/PV.9161 (France, Ireland, Albania, Ukraine, Slovakia, Germany and Poland); and S/PV.9195, (Albania, France, United Kingdom, Russian Federation, Ukraine, Poland, European Union and Slovakia).

[31] See, for example, under the item entitled "The situation in Myanmar", S/PV.9231 (Russian Federation); and, under the item entitled "Women and peace and security", S/PV.8989 (Resumption 1) (Islamic Republic of Iran) and S/PV.9016 (Resumption 1) (Islamic Republic of Iran). For more information on the mandate of the Council, see part V, sect. I.

[32] See A/77/300.

[33] For more information on matters of which the Council was seized, see part II, sect. II.B.

[34] See General Assembly decision 76/566, in which the Assembly took note of the notification by the Secretary-General under Article 12 (2) dated 1 September 2021 (A/76/300); see also *Repertoire*, *Supplement 2021*, part IV, sect. I.C. As at 31 December 2022, the Assembly had not yet taken note of the notification by the Secretary-General under Article 12 (2) dated 1 September 2022 (A/77/300)).

[35] For more information on decision-making and voting, see part II, sect. VIII.

[36] See S/PV.8980. See also S/2022/155.

[37] See S/PV.8980.

resolution in which the Council would have condemned that country's aggression in Ukraine would not prevent the international community from responding to the blatant breaches of international law by the Russian Federation or deter it from holding the country accountable for its actions. He called upon the members of the Assembly to step up where the Council had failed. The representative of Mexico stated that, in response to the paralysis of the Council, its members had invoked Assembly resolution 377 (V), entitled "Uniting for peace", to convene an emergency special session of the Assembly with the urgency that the situation warranted. The representative of Norway noted that the Council's response to the breach of the peace and the act of aggression had failed because of the veto by the aggressor itself, which had made it necessary to reconvene and to decide to call an emergency special session of the Assembly on the issue. She added that the matter would be taken to the Assembly for the purpose of making appropriate recommendations to Members for collective measures. The representative of Brazil indicated that the urgency of the situation had convinced Council members of the need to add the voice of the Assembly to that of the Council in seeking solutions to the crisis in and around Ukraine. He clarified that such action in no way detracted from his country's firm belief that the Council had not yet exhausted the instruments and mechanisms at its disposal to contribute to a negotiated and diplomatic solution towards peace. He emphasized the need for the Council and the Assembly to work together. The representative of Ghana recalled that, at its previous meeting,[38] the Council had been unable to assume its primary responsibility to act on a threat to international peace and security following the aggression by the Russian Federation against Ukraine; he indicated that it was time for the Assembly to assume its residual responsibility and to pronounce itself on the matter.[39]

D. Practice in relation to provisions of the Charter involving recommendations made by the Security Council to the General Assembly

Article 4

1. Membership in the United Nations is open to all other peace-loving states which accept the obligations contained in the present Charter and, in the judgment of the Organization, are able and willing to carry out these obligations.

2. The admission of any such state to membership in the United Nations will be effected by a decision of the General Assembly upon the recommendation of the Security Council.

Article 5

A Member of the United Nations against which preventive or enforcement action has been taken by the Security Council may be suspended from the exercise of the rights and privileges of membership by the General Assembly upon the recommendation of the Security Council. The exercise of these rights and privileges may be restored by the Security Council.

Article 6

A Member of the United Nations which has persistently violated the Principles contained in the present Charter may be expelled from the Organization by the General Assembly upon the recommendation of the Security Council.

Article 93, paragraph 2

A state which is not a Member of the United Nations may become a party to the Statute of the International Court of Justice on conditions to be determined in each case by the General Assembly upon the recommendation of the Security Council.

[38] See S/PV.8979.
[39] See S/PV.8980.

Article 97

The Secretariat shall comprise a Secretary-General and such staff as the Organization may require. The Secretary-General shall be appointed by the General Assembly upon the recommendation of the Security Council. He shall be the chief administrative officer of the Organization.

Rule 60

The Security Council shall decide whether in its judgement the applicant is a peace-loving State and is able and willing to carry out the obligations contained in the Charter and, accordingly, whether to recommend the applicant State for membership.

If the Security Council recommends the applicant State for membership, it shall forward to the General Assembly the recommendation with a complete record of the discussion.

If the Security Council does not recommend the applicant State for membership or postpones the consideration of the application, it shall submit a special report to the General Assembly with a complete record of the discussion.

In order to ensure the consideration of its recommendation at the next session of the General Assembly following the receipt of the application, the Security Council shall make its recommendation not less than twenty-five days in advance of a regular session of the General Assembly, nor less than four days in advance of a special session ...

The Charter provides for joint decision-making by the Council and the General Assembly in relation to a number of matters, but requires a decision by the Council to be taken first. This is the case with respect to the admission, suspension or expulsion of Members (Articles 4 to 6), the appointment of the Secretary-General (Article 97) and the conditions under which a State that is not a Member of the United Nations may become a party to the Statute of the International Court of Justice (Article 93 (2)).[40] In addition, the statute of the International Residual Mechanism for Criminal Tribunals provides that the judges of the Mechanism shall be elected by the Assembly from a list submitted by the Council.[41]

During the period under review, no questions arose concerning the conditions of accession to the Statute of the International Court of Justice. There was no reference to Articles 4, 5 or 6 and no activity with regard to the admission of new Members or the suspension or expulsion of any Member State. With regard to the International Residual Mechanism for Criminal Tribunals, the Council and the General Assembly collaborated on the election of judges to fill vacancies on the roster of the Mechanism.

Membership in the United Nations: references to Articles 4 and 6

The admission of a State to membership in the United Nations and the suspension or expulsion of a Member State from the Organization are effected by the General Assembly upon the recommendation of the Council (Articles 4 (2), 5 and 6 of the Charter). In accordance with rule 60 of its provisional rules of procedure, the Council submits to the Assembly, within specified time limits, its recommendations concerning each application for membership, together with a record of its discussions in relation to the application.

During the period under review, the Council did not recommend the admission of any State for membership in the United Nations. It made no negative recommendations, which would have required the submission of a special report to the General Assembly. In addition, the Council did not recommend the suspension or expulsion of any Member State. Nonetheless, consistent with previous years, at meetings held under the item entitled “The situation in the Middle East, including the Palestinian question”, participants expressed support for the admission of the State of Palestine as a full Member of

[40] Articles 4 (3) and 69 of the Statute of the International Court of Justice provide for the Council to make recommendations to the General Assembly regarding the conditions under which a State that is a party to the Statute but is not a Member of the United Nations may participate in electing members of the Court and in making amendments to the Statute.

[41] Article 10 of the statute of the Mechanism (resolution 1966 (2010), annex 1).

the Organization.[42] Furthermore, at a meeting held on 23 February under the item entitled "Letter dated 28 February 2014 from the Permanent Representative of Ukraine to the United Nations addressed to the President of the Security Council (S/2014/136)", the representative of Ukraine cited paragraphs 1 and 2 of Article 4 of the Charter and asserted that the Russian Federation was unable to carry out any of its obligations under Article 4, as its President had declared war on Ukraine.[43] In addition, at a meeting held on 28 June under the item entitled "Maintenance of peace and security of Ukraine", the President of Ukraine cited the text of Article 6 and noted that, even though the Russian Federation was violating fundamental principles of the United Nations and the international legal order, it was still not being held to account at the global level and continued to enjoy the privileges of the seat it occupied as a permanent member of the Council.[44]

Procedure for the selection and appointment of the Secretary-General

In a letter dated 8 September,[45] the representative of Costa Rica transmitted, on behalf of 27 members[46] of the cross-regional Accountability, Coherence and Transparency Group, a position paper on the selection and appointment process of the Secretary-General and expressed the hope that the paper would serve as reference and encourage timely discussion on future selection processes.

Appointment of judges to the International Residual Mechanism for Criminal Tribunals

By its resolution 1966 (2010) of 22 December 2010, the Council established the International Residual Mechanism for Criminal Tribunals to carry out residual functions of the International Tribunal for the Prosecution of Persons Responsible for Serious Violations of International Humanitarian Law Committed in the Territory of the Former Yugoslavia since 1991 and the International Criminal Tribunal for the Prosecution of Persons Responsible for Genocide and Other Serious Violations of International Humanitarian Law Committed in the Territory of Rwanda and Rwandan Citizens Responsible for Genocide and Other Such Violations Committed in the Territory of Neighbouring States between 1 January and 31 December 1994.[47] According to article 10 of the statute of the Mechanism, the judges of the Mechanism are elected by the General Assembly from a list submitted by the Council. In the event of a vacancy in the roster of judges of the Mechanism, the Secretary-General appoints judges after consultation with the Presidents of the Council and of the Assembly, for the remainder of the term of office concerned.[48]

During the period under review, the Council took note of the intention of the Secretary-General to reappoint the 25 judges of the Mechanism and to appoint a new President, as well as of his nomination of the Prosecutor of the Mechanism for reappointment for a new term of office.[49] Thereafter, by its resolution 2637 (2022) of 22 June, pursuant to article 14 (4) of the statute of the Mechanism, the Council appointed the Prosecutor of the International Mechanism for Criminal Tribunals, with effect from 1 July 2022 until 30 June 2024.[50]

---

[42] See, for example, S/PV.9174 (Resumption 1) (Türkiye, Tunisia, Malaysia, Venezuela (Bolivarian Republic of), League of Arab States, Syrian Arab Republic, Iraq and Brunei Darussalam, Committee on the Exercise of the Inalienable Rights of the Palestinian People and Cuba).

[43] See S/PV.8974.

[44] See S/PV.9080.

[45] A/76/950-S/2022/695.

[46] Austria, Chile, Costa Rica, Denmark, Ecuador, Estonia, Finland, Gabon, Ghana, Hungary, Ireland, Jordan, Latvia, Liechtenstein, Luxembourg, Maldives, New Zealand, Norway, Papua New Guinea, Peru, Portugal, Rwanda, Saudi Arabia, Slovenia, Sweden, Switzerland and Uruguay.

[47] Resolution 1966 (2010), para. 1.

[48] Ibid., annex 1.

[49] See S/2022/487. Concerning the President of the Mechanism, the Secretary-General informed the Council that the sitting President was not seeking to be reappointed and, pursuant to article 11 (1) of the statute and after consultation with the judges of the Mechanism, he intended to appoint a different judge, who had served the Mechanism since 2012, as President for a term of office from 1 July 2022 to 30 June 2024 (S/2022/486).

[50] Resolution 2637 (2022), para. 1.

For additional details on the actions taken by the Secretary-General, the Council and the General Assembly, see table 5.[51]

Table 5
Actions taken by the Security Council and the General Assembly concerning judges of the International Residual Mechanism for Criminal Tribunals, 2022

Letter from the Secretary-General	*Letter from the President of the Security Council*	*Council resolution and date*
S/2022/486, transmitting information on the intention of the Secretary General to reappoint 25 judges and to appoint a new President of the Mechanism and on the nomination of the Prosecutor for reappointment	S/2022/487, taking note of the intention of the Secretary-General to reappoint 25 judges and to appoint a new President of the Mechanism and his nomination of the Prosecutor for reappointment	2637 (2022), para. 1 22 June
S/2022/511, transmitting a letter from the President of the Assembly reflecting his concurrence with the reappointment of the 25 judges		

E. Election of members of the International Court of Justice

Rule 40

Voting in the Security Council shall be in accordance with the relevant Articles of the Charter and of the Statute of the International Court of Justice.

Rule 61

Any meeting of the Security Council held in pursuance of the Statute of the International Court of Justice for the purpose of the election of members of the Court shall continue until as many candidates as are required for all the seats to be filled have obtained in one or more ballots an absolute majority of votes.

The election of members of the International Court of Justice requires action by the Council in conjunction with the General Assembly, with the two organs proceeding independently of one another. The procedure for the election is set out in rules 40[52] and 61 of the provisional rules of procedure of the Council; Articles 4, 8, 10 to 12, 14 and 15 of the Statute of the International Court of Justice;[53] and rules 150 and 151 of the rules of procedure of the Assembly.[54]

During the period under review, the Council held an election to fill a vacancy resulting from the death of one of the judges of the International Court of Justice.[55] On 22 June, the Council held a meeting

[51] For more information concerning the Mechanism, see part I, sect. 25.

[52] Rule 40 of the provisional rules of procedure is also covered in part II, sect. VIII.

[53] Articles 4, 10–12, 14 and 15 of the Statute of the International Court of Justice establish the procedure for the following: (a) the nomination of the judges by the national groups in the Permanent Court of Arbitration; (b) the majority necessary for the election of judges; (c) the number of meetings to be held for the purpose of the election of judges; (d) the holding of the joint conference in the event of more than three meetings of the Council and the General Assembly; (e) the procedure for the filling of vacancies; and (f) the term of office applied to elected judges filling out a vacancy. Article 8 provides that the two organs proceed independently.

[54] Rules 150 and 151 of the General Assembly provide that the election of the members of the International Court of Justice take place in accordance with the Statute of the Court and that any meeting of the Assembly held in pursuance of the Statute of the Court for the purpose of electing members of the Court continue until as many candidates as are required for all the seats to be filled have obtained in one or more ballots an absolute majority of votes.

[55] See S/2022/453.

under the item entitled "Date of election to fill a vacancy in the International Court of Justice".[56] At the meeting, the Council adopted, without a vote, resolution 2638 (2022), by which it decided, in accordance with Article 14 of the Statute of the Court, that the election to fill the vacancy would take place on 4 November, at a meeting of the Council and at a meeting of the General Assembly at its seventy-seventh session.[57]

On 4 November, the Council and the General Assembly proceeded with the concurrent votes.[58] On the first ballot, at the 9182nd meeting of the Council and the 29th plenary meeting of the Assembly, Leonardo Nemer Caldeira Brant, a candidate from Brazil, obtained the requisite absolute majority of votes in both bodies and was, therefore, elected as a member of the Court for a term of office from 4 November 2022 until 5 February 2027, in accordance with Articles 2 to 4, 7 to 12, 14 and 15 of the Statute of the Court, rules 150 and 151 of the rules of procedure of the Assembly and rules 40 and 61 of the provisional rules of procedure of the Council.[59]

For details of the procedure of the election of the new member of the Court, see table 6.

Table 6
Concurrent election of a member of the International Court of Justice to fill an expiring vacancy, 2022

Notes by the Secretary-General	*Record of Council meeting setting the date of the election*	*Council resolution deciding the election date*	*Record of Council meeting for the election*	*Record of General Assembly plenary meeting for the election*
S/2022/453	S/PV.9073	2638 (2022)	S/PV.9182	A/77/PV.29
A/77/481-S/2022/722				
A/77/482-S/2022/723				
A/77/483-S/2022/724				

F. Annual and special reports of the Security Council to the General Assembly

Article 15, paragraph 1

The General Assembly shall receive and consider annual and special reports from the Security Council; these reports shall include an account of the measures that the Security Council has decided upon or taken to maintain international peace and security.

Article 24, paragraph 3

The Security Council shall submit annual and, when necessary, special reports to the General Assembly for its consideration.

Rule 60, paragraph 3

If the Security Council does not recommend the applicant State for membership or postpones the consideration of the application, it shall submit a special report to the General Assembly with a complete record of the discussion.

During 2022, the Council maintained its practice of submitting annual reports to the General Assembly pursuant to Article 24 (3) of the Charter. The annual report submitted to the Assembly covered the period from 1 January to 31 December 2021.[60] The note by the President of the Security Council

[56] See S/PV.9073.
[57] See resolution 2638 (2022).
[58] See S/PV.9182 and A/77/PV.29.
[59] See General Assembly decision 77/404.
[60] A/76/2.

dated 30 August 2017 provides that the report would consist of an introduction, containing an agreed concise summary prepared on behalf of the Council under the coordination of the President for the month of July.[61] However, in accordance with the same note, in the case of the member holding the presidency for the month of July ending its tenure on the Council that year, that task devolves on the member of the Council next in English alphabetical order and who will not be leaving the Council at the end of that calendar year. In 2022, the introduction of the annual report for 2021 was therefore prepared by the delegation of France, as the member of the Council that had held the presidency of the Council for the month of July 2021. In accordance with the note by the President dated 27 December 2019,[62] the report was adopted before 30 May 2022. The content of and procedure concerning the annual report were discussed in connection with the annual open debate on working methods held under the item entitled, "Implementation of the note by the President of the Security Council (S/2017/507)" (see case 3).

The Council considered and adopted its draft annual report, without a vote, at a meeting held on 20 May.[63] During the meeting, the representative of France emphasized that the drafting of the annual report was not only a mandatory task enshrined in the Charter, but also an important document for reviewing the activities of the Council over the previous year and opening a discussion with all Member States on how the Council had implemented its mandate.

The General Assembly considered the annual report of the Council at the 79th plenary meeting of its seventy-sixth session, held on 9 June, under the item entitled "Report of the Security Council".[64] The President of the Security Council for the month (Albania) participated in the meeting to introduce the report. During the discussions in the Assembly, many Member States[65] acknowledged or expressed appreciation for the improved timeline regarding the adoption and submission of the annual report of the Council in accordance with the note by the President dated 27 December 2019,[66] by which Member States were to be allowed time for a more careful consideration and discussion of the work of the Council for the year under review. Numerous Member States also called for future annual reports of the Council to be more analytical.[67] At the same meeting, the Assembly took note of the report of the Council.[68]

Case 3
Implementation of the note by the President of the Security Council (S/2017/507)

On 28 June, at the initiative of Albania, which held the presidency of the Security Council for the month,[69] the Council held its annual open debate on its working methods under the item entitled "Implementation of the note by the President of the Security Council (S/2017/507)".[70] During the meeting, Council members heard briefings by the Director of Security Council Procedure and co-author of the fourth edition of *The Procedure of the UN Security Council* and by the Executive Director of Security Council Report.[71] The representative of former Council member Saint Vincent and the Grenadines, who had served as Chair of the Informal Working Group on Documentation and Other Procedural Questions in 2020 and 2021, submitted a statement in writing.[72]

During the debate, Member States discussed the consideration of annual and special reports of the Council by the General Assembly in the context of the relationship between the two bodies. The representative of Costa Rica called for greater transparency in preparing the annual report of the Council

---

[61] S/2017/507, annex, para. 127.
[62] S/2019/997, para. (c).
[63] See S/PV.9037.
[64] See A/76/PV.79.
[65] Albania, Ecuador (on behalf of the Accountability, Coherence and Transparency Group), Portugal, Austria, Mexico, Singapore, Poland, Argentina, Indonesia and Slovenia.
[66] S/2019/997.
[67] See A/76/PV.79 (Ecuador (on behalf of the Accountability, Coherence and Transparency Group), Portugal, Austria, Malaysia, Singapore, Cyprus, Luxembourg, Islamic Republic of Iran, Malta, Cuba, South Africa, Argentina, Georgia, Indonesia, Italy, Slovenia, Ukraine and Costa Rica).
[68] See General Assembly decision 76/567.
[69] A concept note was circulated by a letter dated 21 June (S/2022/499).
[70] See S/PV.9079 and S/PV.9079 (Resumption 1).
[71] See S/PV.9079.
[72] See S/2022/519.

to the Assembly.[73] The representative of Cuba noted that the lack of special reports on measures to maintain international peace and security, as provided for in Articles 15 and 24 of the Charter, was a gap to be overcome. He expressed support for the proposal to hold the debate in the Assembly on the annual reports of the Security Council at a date nearer to the year-end, which would allow for a more contextualized analysis of the organ's work during the review period.

Multiple delegations[74] stressed that the annual report of the Council should be more substantive, analytical, detailed and comprehensive. The representative of the Islamic Republic of Iran underscored that the annual reports of the Council should contribute to the much-needed transparency and accountability of decisions and measures taken by the Council. He recalled that, during recent discussions on the issue in the General Assembly, the vast majority of Member States had renewed their call upon the Council to present an annual report that went beyond a simple compilation of its activities. While the representatives of France and Kuwait both welcomed the timely submission of the annual report on the activities of the Council to the Assembly, the latter also emphasized that the substance of the report could be more analytical and detailed. The representative of Pakistan welcomed the improved timeline in the submission of the report of the Council to the Assembly, but expressed disappointment in the contents of the report itself, noting that it provided a compendium of the Council's deliberations on various issues, but did not shed any light on how the Council considered specific situations and the ways in which it reached its decisions.

In addition, participants addressed the Council's implementation of the General Assembly's invitation in its resolution 76/262 of 26 April 2022, concerning the submission of a special report to the Assembly following the casting of a veto in the Council.[75] The representative of the United States indicated that, while her country had been disappointed with the double veto cast on 26 May on the draft resolution submitted in response to the ballistic missiles launched by the Democratic People's Republic of Korea,[76] the Council had been able to reach consensus on a fact-based special report to the Assembly at the latter's invitation.[77] Several participants also welcomed the timely transmission of the special report by the Council in the first application of the Assembly resolution.[78] Citing Article 24 of the Charter, the representative of Switzerland, on behalf of the Accountability, Coherence and Transparency Group, welcomed the timely transmission of the special report. The representative of Liechtenstein noted that the Council had been able to agree swiftly on the special report, highlighting its importance, given that no such document had been produced in 46 years. Similarly, and also on behalf of Belgium and the Netherlands, the representative of Luxembourg welcomed the submission of the report in good time by the Council, as well as the participation of a large number of Member States during the Assembly debate.[79] The representative of Thailand underlined that the debate on the working methods of the Council, together with the debate in the Assembly on the special report of the Council, reinforced the dialogue between the two bodies, with a view to supporting the effective workings of the Council.[80] The representative of Portugal encouraged Council members to enclose a special report in the next annual report of the Council, together with a summary of the related debate in the Assembly.

Special reports by the Security Council to the General Assembly on the use of the veto

On 26 April, the General Assembly adopted resolution 76/262, in which it invited the Council, in accordance with Article 24 (3) of the Charter, to submit a special report to it at least 72 hours before the relevant discussion in the Assembly on the use of the veto by one or more permanent members of the Council.[81]

---

[73] See S/PV.9079.

[74] Switzerland (on behalf of the Accountability, Coherence and Transparency Group), Islamic Republic of Iran, Kuwait, Portugal and Cuba.

[75] General Assembly resolution 76/262, para. 3.

[76] See S/PV.9048. See also S/2022/431.

[77] See S/PV.9079. For the special report on the use of the veto in connection with the item entitled "Non-proliferation/Democratic People's Republic of Korea, see A/76/853, annex.

[78] See S/PV.9079 (Switzerland (on behalf of the Accountability, Coherence and Transparency Group), Luxembourg (also on behalf of Belgium and the Netherlands) and Liechtenstein).

[79] See A/76/PV.77 and A/76/PV.78. See also S/PV.9048.

[80] See S/PV.9079.

[81] General Assembly resolution 76/262, paras. 1 and 3.

During the reporting period, the Council submitted three special reports to the General Assembly pursuant to resolution 76/262 on the use of the veto, in connection with the items entitled "Non-proliferation/Democratic People's Republic of Korea", "The situation in the Middle East" and "Maintenance of peace and security of Ukraine.[82] Following the submission of the reports, the Assembly met to discuss the use of the veto in each of the three instances; for the third instance, the meeting was held under the umbrella of the eleventh emergency special session pursuant to resolution 2623 (2022) and Assembly resolution 377 (V).[83]

In that regard, on 10 October, the representative of Switzerland submitted a letter to the President of the Security Council on behalf of 26 members of the Accountability, Coherence and Transparency Group, in which she recalled paragraph 3 of General Assembly resolution 76/262 concerning the submission by the Council of a special report on the use of the veto to the Assembly, and welcomed the Council's continuation of the practice with regard to the veto cast on 30 September in producing a special report in advance of the meeting of the eleventh emergency special session of the Assembly on that same day.[84] In accordance with the terms of the Assembly resolution, the Group considered the meeting of the emergency special session to be the "relevant discussion" mandated in paragraph 1 of resolution 76/262, for which the special report was to be submitted. The Group also welcomed the fact that the Council had established a consistent practice with respect to the implementation of the resolution.

During Council meetings in 2022, Council members underscored the importance of General Assembly resolution 76/262 and its implementation, in particular the submission of special reports to the Assembly. On 26 May, following the negative vote by China and the Russian Federation on a draft resolution concerning the item entitled "Non-proliferation/Democratic People's Republic of Korea",[85] the representative of Mexico indicated that, in the light of the recent adoption of resolution 76/262, her delegation was looking forward to the convening of a meeting of the Assembly, as well as the special report to be prepared by the Council, in order for the highest international organ to hear those permanent members discuss the issue and take the decisions that it deemed appropriate.[86] The representative of Ireland expressed similar anticipation for the swift issuance of a special report by the Council, in accordance with Article 24 (3) of the Charter. The representative of Norway said that her delegation recognized that, in accordance with its consensus resolution 76/262, the Assembly would be taking up the issue for discussion, in line with its own responsibilities with regard to international peace and security. She added that Norway expected the Council to comply with the provision of the resolution inviting it to submit a special report on the issue for the Assembly's consideration. On 8 July, following the negative vote by the Russian Federation of a draft resolution concerning the item entitled "The situation in the Middle East",[87] the representative of Mexico indicated that the Assembly could now turn to discussing the use of the veto pursuant to resolution 76/262, for which his delegation asked the holder of the presidency to prepare a corresponding special report.[88]

G. Relations with subsidiary organs established by the General Assembly

During the period under review, the Council continued to develop its relations with various subsidiary organs established by the General Assembly, namely, the Committee on the Exercise of the Inalienable Rights of the Palestinian People, the Human Rights Council and the Special Committee on Peacekeeping Operations.

[82] A/76/853, annex; A/76/905, annex; and A/77/551, annex.

[83] For the first instance, see A/76/PV.77, A/76/PV.78, A/76/PV.81 and A/76/PV.82; for the second, see A/76/PV.95 and A/76/PV.96; for the third, see A/ES-11/PV.12.

[84] See S/2022/752.

[85] S/2022/431.

[86] See S/PV.9048.

[87] S/2022/538.

[88] See S/PV.9087.

Committee on the Exercise of the Inalienable Rights of the Palestinian People

In 2022, the Committee on the Exercise of the Inalienable Rights of the Palestinian People continued to participate in the work of the Council. The Vice-Chair of the Committee delivered statements at four Council meetings concerning the situation in the Middle East, including the Palestinian question.[89] On 29 November, on the occasion of the International Day of Solidarity with the Palestinian People, the President of the Security Council participated in a meeting of the Committee.[90]

Human Rights Council

One decision adopted by the Security Council contained a reference to the Human Rights Council. In its resolution 2654 (2022) of 27 October, the Security Council welcomed the interaction between Morocco and the special procedures of the Human Rights Council in the context of enhancing the promotion and protection of human rights in Western Sahara and the Tindouf refugee camps.[91]

Relations between the Security Council and the Human Rights Council were also addressed during Council meetings. At an open debate held on 18 January under the item entitled "Women and peace and security" and the sub-item entitled "Protecting participation: addressing violence targeting women in peace and security processes", the representative of Italy expressed the hope that increased cooperation between the two Councils could decisively help to prevent targeted violence against women and make sure that women could play a full role in peace and security processes.[92] At a meeting held on 13 April under the same item and the sub-items entitled "Accountability as prevention" and "Ending cycles of sexual violence in conflict", the representative of Malaysia asserted that his country saw merits in broadening networking and coordination between the two Councils with a view to ensuring accountability for human rights violations, including sexual assault and violence against women and children.[93]

At the open debate on working methods of the Council held on 28 June under the item entitled "Implementation of the note by the President of the Security Council (S/2017/507)", the representative of the Republic of Korea encouraged the Council to continue to strengthen its interaction and engagement with other United Nations organs and bodies, including the General Assembly and the Human Rights Council.[94] At the same meeting, however, the representative of the Syrian Arab Republic stressed the importance of respecting individual mandates, adding that the Council should work within its own mandate and not encroach on those of other United Nations bodies such as the Assembly and the Human Rights Council.[95]

On 3 November, at an open debate held under the item entitled "Peacebuilding and sustaining peace" and the sub-item entitled "Integrating effective resilience-building in peace operations for sustainable peace", the representative of Norway stated that there was no better way of preventing conflict than protecting human rights.[96] She emphasized the need for greater interaction between the Security Council and its peacekeeping operations, together with the United Nations High Commissioner for Human Rights and the Human Rights Council, to facilitate early engagement and prevention.

Special Committee on Peacekeeping Operations

In 2022, the Security Council did not refer to the Special Committee on Peacekeeping Operations in any of its decisions. On 6 September, however, at a meeting held under the item entitled "United Nations peacekeeping operations" concerning the safety of peacekeepers, the representative of the Russian Federation expressed the belief that the main thrusts of United Nations peacekeeping activities should be determined in an intergovernmental format.[97] In that regard, he added, the Special Committee

---

[89] See S/PV.8950 (Resumption 1), S/PV.9021 (Resumption 1), S/PV.9099 (Resumption 1) and S/PV.9174 (Resumption 1).
[90] See A/AC.183/PV.409.
[91] Resolution 2654 (2022), twentieth preambular paragraph.
[92] See S/PV.8949.
[93] See S/PV.9016 (Resumption 1).
[94] See S/PV.9079.
[95] See S/PV.9079 (Resumption 1).
[96] See S/PV.9181.
[97] See S/PV.9123.

of the General Assembly was a unique platform, in which a majority of the States Members of the Organization, including troop-contributing countries and host States, had an opportunity to develop common approaches to the parameters for peacekeeping activities to guide the Secretariat and missions on the ground. On 21 December, during an explanation of vote following the adoption of a resolution concerning the mental health of peacekeepers and the personnel of peacekeeping operations and special political missions,[98] the same representative explained that, although his country supported the resolution, it considered that there had been a violation of the principle of the division of labour and expressed the view that, when putting forward initiatives, Member States should take into account the prerogatives of the principal organs as enshrined in the Charter.[99] He emphasized that there was a specialized platform to discuss general peacekeeping issues, namely, the Special Committee on Peacekeeping Operations, which was where all interested parties, including troop contributors and Secretariat experts, came together for a comprehensive review of all aspects concerning peacekeeping operations. Similarly, the representative of India, who had also voted in favour of the resolution, expressed the belief that the Special Committee was the right forum in which to deliberate the issue and that it had been giving due consideration to the issue of the mental health of United Nations personnel in peace operations. She added that, as a result, there had been consistent improvement in recent years. She expressed the hope that future deliberations on the issue of mental health and the well-being of United Nations peace operations personnel would be addressed in a systemic and holistic manner and through all relevant and mandated organs of the United Nations.

H. Other Security Council practice bearing on relations with the General Assembly

General Assembly decisions concerning relations with the Security Council

The General Assembly also made reference to its relations with the Council in several other decisions. In its decision 76/572, adopted on 12 July under the item entitled "Question of equitable representation on and increase in the membership of the Security Council and other matters related to the Security Council", the Assembly decided to reaffirm its central role concerning the question of equitable representation on and increase in the membership of the Council and other matters related to the Council.[100] The Assembly also decided to immediately continue intergovernmental negotiations on Council reform in informal plenary meetings at its seventy-seventh session, building on the informal meetings held during its seventy-sixth session, as reflected in the letter dated 16 May from the Co-Chairs, and on the document entitled "Co-Chairs' Revised Elements Paper on Convergences and Divergences on the question of equitable representation on and increase in the membership of the Security Council and related matters", circulated on 19 May, as well as the positions of and proposals made by Member States, reflected in the text and its annex circulated on 31 July 2015.

On the situation of human rights of the Rohingya Muslims and other minorities in Myanmar, on 15 December, the General Assembly adopted resolution 77/227, in which it reiterated the urgent need to ensure that all those responsible for crimes related to violations and abuses of international law throughout Myanmar, including international human rights law, international humanitarian law and international criminal law, were held to account through credible and independent national, regional or international justice mechanisms, while recalling the authority of the Council in that regard.[101]

With respect to the situation of human rights in the Syrian Arab Republic, in its resolution 77/230 of 15 December, the General Assembly expressed continued support for the work carried out by the Independent International Commission of Inquiry on the Syrian Arab Republic, welcomed its reports, and reiterated its decision to transmit those reports to the Council.[102]

---

[98] Resolution 2668 (2022).
[99] See S/PV.9229.
[100] See General Assembly decision 76/572.
[101] General Assembly resolution 77/227, thirty-seventh preambular paragraph.
[102] General Assembly resolution 77/230, twenty-fourth preambular paragraph.

Security Council decisions concerning relations with the General Assembly

A number of resolutions and presidential statements adopted by the Council during 2022 contained specific references to the General Assembly in connection with policy and implementation issues other than those covered in subsections A, D, E and G above, as set out in tables 7 and 8.

Table 7
Security Council decisions containing specific references to the General Assembly in connection with policy and implementation issues other than those covered in subsections A, D, E and G (thematic items), 2022

Decision and date	*Provision*
General issues relating to sanctions	
Resolution 2664 (2022) 9 December	Encouraging the United Nations, where appropriate, to take an active role in coordinating humanitarian activities in situations where its sanctions are applicable, recalling the United Nations guiding principles of General Assembly resolution 46/182 of 19 December 1991, on humanitarian emergency assistance, including humanity, neutrality, impartiality and independence, and noting that the intention of this resolution is to provide clarity to ensure the continuation of humanitarian activities in the future (ninth preambular paragraph)
International Residual Mechanism for Criminal Tribunals	
Resolution 2637 (2022) 22 June	Recalling the strong need for States to cooperate with the Mechanism to achieve the arrest and surrender of those remaining fugitives indicted by the International Criminal Tribunal for the Prosecution of Persons Responsible for Genocide and Other Serious Violations of International Humanitarian Law Committed in the Territory of Rwanda and Rwandan Citizens Responsible for Genocide and Other Such Violations Committed in the Territory of Neighbouring States between 1 January and 31 December 1994, and, in this regard, recalling also General Assembly resolution 74/273 of 21 April 2020 (sixth preambular paragraph)

Table 8
Security Council decisions containing specific references to the General Assembly in connection with policy and implementation issues other than those covered in subsections A, D, E and G (country and region-specific items), 2022

Decision and date	*Provision*
The situation in the Central African Republic	
Resolution 2659 (2022) 14 November	Requests the United Nations Multidimensional Integrated Stabilization Mission in the Central African Republic to consider the environmental impacts of its operations when fulfilling its mandated tasks and, in this context, to manage them as appropriate and in accordance with applicable and relevant General Assembly resolutions and United Nations rules and regulations (para. 45)
The situation in Mali	
Resolution 2640 (2022) 29 June	Requests the United Nations Multidimensional Integrated Stabilization Mission in Mali to consider the environmental impacts of its operations when fulfilling its mandated tasks and, in this context, to manage them as appropriate and in accordance with applicable and relevant General Assembly resolutions and United Nations rules and regulations (para. 53)
The situation in Somalia	
Resolution 2628 (2022) 31 March	Expressing serious concern about the humanitarian situation in Somalia, and calling for all parties to the conflict to allow and facilitate, in accordance with relevant provisions of international law, including applicable international humanitarian law, and in a manner consistent with the United Nations guiding principles of humanitarian emergency assistance

Decision and date	*Provision*
	(General Assembly resolution 46/182), including humanity, neutrality, impartiality and independence, the provision of humanitarian assistance necessary to support Somalia (twenty-fourth preambular paragraph)
	See also resolution 2657 (2022), twelfth preambular paragraph, and resolution 2662 (2022), eleventh preambular paragraph

Security Council discussions concerning relations with the General Assembly

In 2022, Council members and other participants in meetings continued to address the Council's coordination and interaction with the General Assembly. On 14 December, at a high-level open debate held under the item entitled "Maintenance of international peace and security" and the sub-item entitled "New orientation for reform multilateralism", at which Council members heard briefings by the Secretary-General and the President of the General Assembly, Council members and other participants discussed the relationship between the Council and the Assembly (see case 4).

Case 4
Maintenance of international peace and security

On 14 December, at the initiative of India, which held the presidency of the Security Council for the month,[103] the Council held a high-level open debate under the item entitled "Maintenance of international peace and security" and the sub-item entitled "New orientation for reformed multilateralism".[104] During the open debate, Council members heard briefings by the Secretary-General and the President of the General Assembly.[105]

The Secretary-General, citing calls by Member States for the revitalization of the work of the General Assembly in the framework of a reformed multilateralism, stated that the Assembly had showed that it played a valuable role and had adopted many important resolutions during the year, in particular on the war in Ukraine, the right to a healthy environment and the use of the veto by members of the Council. The President of the General Assembly emphasized that multilateralism could work, but must work better. He added that the 193 Member States of the Assembly had placed their trust in the 15 Council members and expected each Council member to act for the good of all and uphold the Charter. He further stated that collaboration across bodies, organs and processes made sense and highlighted the so-called veto initiative as having opened an important door for a new form of collaboration and accountability. In that context, he noted that the Assembly had been obliged to step up when decisions by the Council had been blocked.

Several participants highlighted the importance of strengthened cooperation among the principal organs of the United Nations, including the Council and the General Assembly. The representative of Albania underscored that the decisive response of the Assembly to the aggression in Ukraine, in the face of a Council paralysed by a blatant conflict of interest, together with the veto initiative, had confirmed the necessity of such strengthened cooperation among the two organs and had contributed to revitalizing and empowering the Assembly, while also revealing the imperative of improving the functioning of the Council and its ability to take action, remain credible and act on behalf of the entire United Nations membership. The representative of Norway emphasized that the Council must be more connected to the rest of the multilateral system and welcomed the vital role that the Assembly had played that year through Uniting for peace and by adopting and successfully implementing the veto initiative. The representative of Bangladesh emphasized the importance of bridging the power gap between the Assembly and the Council as a matter of priority and expressed support for the initiative aimed at ensuring the proper implementation of the Charter with respect to the functional relationship between its main organs, in particular the Assembly and the Economic and Social Council.[106] In that regard, he stated that the interaction with the Security Council must be improved. The representative of Thailand stressed that, in

[103] A concept note was circulated by a letter dated 25 November (S/2022/880).
[104] See S/PV.9220 and S/PV.9220 (Resumption 1).
[105] See S/PV.9220.
[106] See S/PV.9220 (Resumption 1).

order to achieve the strategic goals of maintaining international peace, security and stability, promoting sustainable development and growth and preventing the violation, abuse and disregard of universal human rights, it was absolutely essential that the United Nations work across organizations and silos, linking the work of the Council with that of other United Nations bodies and agencies, including the General Assembly.

During the discussion, many participants welcomed the adoption of General Assembly resolution 76/262 on 26 April. Some speakers explained how the adoption of the resolution had changed the dynamics between the Council and the Assembly. The representative of Switzerland stated that resolution 76/262 promoted complementarity between the United Nations organs in the event of blockages created by the use of the veto. Emphasizing that a robust multilateral system required a strengthened role for the Assembly, the representative of Singapore indicated that the Assembly had shown clearly that it had the capacity and will to act when the Council was unable or unwilling to make decisions. In that regard, he added that the adoption of resolution 76/262, in which the Assembly had stipulated that it would meet whenever a veto was cast in the Council, was a significant decision. The representative of Estonia also highlighted the importance of the resolution, stating that it had enabled the Assembly to take a more active stance on international peace and security issues in cases where the Council was paralysed, as well as increasing the Council's accountability and transparency. The representative of Ecuador stressed the need to strengthen the Council's synergy with every entity in the United Nations system, including the Assembly, and added that resolution 76/262 had revitalized the dynamics of the Assembly's efforts in that area by enabling a discussion among Member States every time a veto was cast in the Council. The representative of Malta expressed the belief that the new mechanism established under resolution 76/262 strengthened the link between the Assembly and the Council and brought more transparency, accountability and relevance on veto use to the wider membership. The representative of the European Union similarly indicated that the adoption of a standing mandate for a debate in the Assembly when a veto was cast in the Council had contributed to the efforts aimed at revitalizing and empowering the Assembly, ensuring that the United Nations was not voiceless when the Council was deadlocked, a position that was echoed by the representative of Latvia. The representative of Liechtenstein noted that the Assembly resolution was a key measure for recalibrating the balance between the Council and the Assembly and a prompt to empower the Assembly to make full use of the authority conferred on it by the Charter and to step in when the Council was unable to act.

II. Relations with the Economic and Social Council

Article 65

The Economic and Social Council may furnish information to the Security Council and shall assist the Security Council upon its request.

Note

Section II concerns the relationship between the Security Council and the Economic and Social Council, with a particular focus on the practice of the Security Council in relation to Article 65 of the Charter of the United Nations. In 2022, the decisions of the Council contained no references to the relations with the Economic and Social Council nor to Article 65. Subsection A therefore covers the deliberations of the Security Council concerning relations with the Economic and Social Council. Subsection B features communications of the Security Council concerning its relationship with the Economic and Social Council.

A. Discussions concerning relations with the Economic and Social Council

During the period under review, several references were made in meetings of the Council to its relations with the Economic and Social Council, including one explicit reference to Article 65 of the

Charter.[107] In addition, Council members and other participants at its meetings discussed the interaction with the Economic and Social Council in the context of both region-specific and thematic items.

Discussions in relation to country- or region-specific items

At a meeting held on 18 February, under the item entitled "The question concerning Haiti", the representative of Brazil stated that Haiti needed to break the perverse, reinforcing cycle of poverty, criminality and political violence, which could only be achieved through a system-wide strategy that enabled enhanced cooperation between the Council and other United Nations entities primarily responsible for economic and social development.[108] He suggested exploring mechanisms to strengthen cooperation and coordination with the Economic and Social Council, as well as with the Peacebuilding Commission. At a meeting held on 16 June under the same item, the representative of Brazil again encouraged enhanced cooperation between the Security Council and other United Nations bodies, such as the Economic and Social Council and the Peacebuilding Commission.[109] At a meeting held on 21 December, also under the same item, the representative of the United Arab Emirates underscored the need to achieve progress on the political level in order to put Haiti on the path to peace and improve the humanitarian, economic and security situations in the country, including by working closely with other stakeholders in all efforts.[110] In that connection, she indicated that the Caribbean Community and the Ad Hoc Advisory Group on Haiti of the Economic and Social Council had played a critical role in promoting development and stability in Haiti, while ensuring consistent and sustained regional and international support. At the same meeting, the representative of Canada, speaking on behalf of the Ad Hoc Advisory Group on Haiti, informed the Council about the activities of the Advisory Group since the beginning of the multifaceted crisis in Haiti that emerged following the assassination of its President, Jovenel Moïse, the previous summer. He stressed, while that the Advisory Group understood that it had no specific mandate on peace, the nexus between peace, security, economic growth and development was nonetheless real. He indicated that the Advisory Group was committed to addressing security as a precondition for democratic development and political solidarity.

In addition, during an open debate held on 9 August in connection with the item entitled "Peace and security in Africa", the representative of Thailand stated that, as a member of the Peacebuilding Commission, his country would continue to play its part in supporting global-regional endeavours for Africa, including by encouraging greater consultations and coordination between the Security Council, the Peacebuilding Commission and the Economic and Social Council to better mobilize capacity-building assistance and resources to support African countries in conflict settings.[111]

Discussions in relation to thematic items

At an open debate held on 8 March, under the item entitled "Women and peace and security" and the sub-item entitled "Women's economic inclusion and participation as a key to building peace", the representative of Switzerland emphasized that synergies between the Security Council, the Economic and Social Council and the Peacebuilding Commission must be intensified.[112]

During an open debate held on 28 June, under the item entitled "Implementation of the note by the President of the Security Council (S/2017/507)", concerning the working methods of the Council,[113] the representative of China suggested that the Security Council should listen to wide-ranging views in the course of its work, taking the concerns of States and regional organizations seriously and striving to work in greater coordination and synergy with the President of the General Assembly, the Secretary-General, the Economic and Social Council and the Peacebuilding Commission. The representative of Thailand emphasized that, given the strong interlinkages between the various global crises affecting humankind and the inherent peace-development-governance nexus in most conflict situations, it was more important

[107] See S/PV.9079 (Pakistan).
[108] See S/PV.8969.
[109] See S/PV.9066.
[110] See S/PV.9233.
[111] See S/PV.9106 (Resumption 1).
[112] See S/PV.8989.
[113] See S/PV.9079.

than ever that the Council work in increased coordination, cooperation and interaction with other United Nations organs and bodies, in particular the Assembly, the Economic and Social Council and the Peacebuilding Commission. He added that such interaction could be mutually reinforcing and complementary and should be in accordance with the Charter of the United Nations. The representative of Pakistan underscored that the Security Council's relationships with the Assembly and the Economic and Social Council should also be brought into conformity with the letter and the spirit of the Charter. He recalled that Article 65 of the Charter provided that the Economic and Social Council "may furnish information to the Security Council and shall assist the Security Council upon its request". He added that it was rare that the Economic and Social Council had been requested to play that role and noted that, apart from creating the Peacebuilding Commission, there had been no serious effort to develop a practice of inviting the Economic and Social Council to work with the Security Council in areas and on issues where their mandates overlapped.

During an open debate held on 14 December under the item entitled "Maintenance of international peace and security" and the sub-item entitled "New orientation for reformed multilateralism", the representative of Mexico noted that, although the Security Council was the organ tasked with dealing with threats to international peace and security, the United Nations system as a whole had a direct and indirect impact on the maintenance of peace.[114] He added that the success of the Security Council in discharging its responsibilities in accordance with its mandate largely depended not only on the non-abuse of the veto by its members, but also on the success of the other main United Nations organs in fulfilling their own mandates, including the Economic and Social Council. The representative of Pakistan emphasized that, in a complex world confronted by multiple threats and challenges, empowering and efficiently utilizing all the main organs of the United Nations, including the Economic and Social Council, was of vital importance. The representative of Bangladesh affirmed that his country subscribed to the initiative aimed at ensuring the proper implementation of the Charter with respect to the functional relationship between its main organs, in particular the General Assembly and the Economic and Social Council, adding that interaction with the Security Council must also be improved.[115] The representative of Thailand stressed that, in order to address, both effectively and in an integrated and holistic manner, the trinity of key strategic goals – maintaining international peace, security and stability, promoting sustainable development and growth and preventing the violation, abuse and disregard of universal human rights – while reinforcing human security for all, it was absolutely essential that the United Nations work across organizations and silos, linking the work of the Security Council with that of the Economic and Social Council and the other main organs, bodies and specialized agencies of the Organization.

B. Communications concerning relations with the Economic and Social Council

Communications of the Council did not contain any references to its relations with the Economic and Social Council. Nonetheless, on 12 July, the representative of Canada, in his capacity as Chair of the Ad Hoc Advisory Group on Haiti of the Economic and Social Council, transmitted to the President of the Security Council a statement on behalf of the Advisory Group, in which it called upon the Security Council to renew the mandate of the United Nations Integrated Office in Haiti for a period of 12 months.[116] In addition, on 14 December, the representative of Kenya informed the President that Kenya was planning to hold an Arria-formula meeting on the theme "Transitioning from protracted conflict and fragility into peace through sustainable development", with the Vice-President of the Economic and Social Council as one of the briefers.[117]

[114] See S/PV.9220.
[115] See S/PV.9220 (Resumption 1).
[116] S/2022/552, annex.
[117] See S/2022/949.

III. Relations with the International Court of Justice

Article 94

1. Each Member of the United Nations undertakes to comply with the decision of the International Court of Justice in any case to which it is a party.

2. If any party to a case fails to perform the obligations incumbent upon it under a judgment rendered by the Court, the other party may have recourse to the Security Council, which may, if it deems necessary, make recommendations or decide upon measures to be taken to give effect to the judgment.

Article 96

1. The General Assembly or the Security Council may request the International Court of Justice to give an advisory opinion on any legal question.

2. Other organs of the United Nations and specialized agencies, which may at any time be so authorized by the General Assembly, may also request advisory opinions of the Court on legal questions arising within the scope of their activities.

Note

Section III concerns the relationship between the Council and the International Court of Justice. In accordance with Article 94 of the Charter of the United Nations, the Council may make recommendations or decide upon measures to be taken to give effect to the judgment rendered by the Court if a party to a case fails to perform its obligations under that judgment. Pursuant to Article 96, the Council may also request the Court to give an advisory opinion on any legal question. In addition, pursuant to Article 41 of the Statute of the International Court of Justice, notice of any provisional measures to be taken to preserve the rights of parties may be given by the Court to the parties and to the Council.

During the reporting period, the Council did not make any recommendations or decide on any measures with regard to the judgements rendered by the Court, nor did it request the Court to give an advisory opinion on any legal question.

In line with prior practice, in 2022, the President of the International Court of Justice was invited to participate in a private meeting of the Council, held on 26 October, under the item entitled "Briefing by the President of the International Court of Justice".[118] In addition, the President of the Court participated in an open debate of the Council held on 2 June, under the item entitled "Maintenance of international peace and security" and the sub-item entitled "Strengthening accountability and justice for serious violations of international law".[119] The election of a member of the Court held concurrently by the Council and the Assembly during the reporting period is covered in section I.E. During the review period, no explicit references to Articles 94 or 96 of the Charter were made in decisions of the Council.

Subsection A covers the discussions held among Council members and other participants at Council meetings during the reporting period on the relations between the Council and the Court. Subsection B features the communications of the Council concerning the relationship between the two organs.

A. Discussion concerning relations with the International Court of Justice

During the period under review, reference was made in the deliberations of the Council to the role of the International Court of Justice in connection with the peaceful settlement of disputes and to the relationship between the Council and the Court, including one explicit reference to Article 94 of the Charter. At a meeting held on 17 March under the item entitled "Threats to international peace and security", the representative of Ukraine encouraged Council members to exercise their duty envisaged in

[118] See S/PV.9166.

[119] See S/PV.9052 and S/PV.9052 (Resumption 1).

Article 94 (2) of the Charter, to make recommendations or decide upon measures to be taken in the case of the failure by the Russian Federation to comply with the obligations incumbent upon it under the judgment rendered by the Court in the case concerning *Allegations of genocide under the Convention on the Prevention and Punishment of the Crime of Genocide (Ukraine v. Russian Federation)*.[120]

In addition, at a meeting held on 25 May under the item entitled "Protection of civilians in armed conflict", the representative of Bangladesh, recalling resolution 2601 (2021) on "protecting the protectors", underscored that, while it was critically important to strengthen national judicial institutions in host countries, the Council should also support international accountability mechanisms, including the International Court of Justice, and thereby send the right message to perpetrators.[121]

On 2 June, the Council held an open debate under the item entitled "Maintenance of international peace and security" and the sub-item entitled "Strengthening accountability and justice for serious violations of international law",[122] at which the President of the International Court of Justice was one of the briefers. During the debate, the representative of Ireland urged all members of the United Nations, and especially Council members, to accept the Court's compulsory jurisdiction and called upon the Council to strengthen its cooperation with the Court.[123] The representative of Norway, underlining the important role of the Court in the peaceful resolution of disputes and deploring the blatant examples of disregard of the Court's rulings, stated that Council members had a special responsibility to do what they could to ensure that parties faithfully abided by binding decisions rendered by the Court. The representative of Austria, on behalf of the Group of Friends of the Rule of Law, emphasized that the Council must take clear and decisive action to stop violations of international law that threatened international peace and security if a violation was ongoing, including by enforcing judgments of the Court, and to ensure that States and individuals were held accountable.[124] The representative of the Philippines suggested that Member States could consider making greater use of the fact-finding capacity of the Council, in accordance with the Charter, and that the Council could also request advisory opinions of the Court on legal questions arising within the scope of its activities, including on the issue of institutionalizing international legal principles of accountability and the related accountability mechanisms, in order to have an impact in practice.

At a meeting held on 22 August under the same item and on the topic of promoting common security through dialogue and cooperation, the representative of Mexico stated that the United Nations must strengthen coordination between its main organs in order to conduct genuine and effective diplomacy.[125] He added that collaboration among all United Nations organs, agencies, programmes and funds, including the International Court of Justice, was essential.

B. Communications concerning relations with the International Court of Justice

During the period under review, the Council continued to exchange letters[126] with the Secretary-General and to receive his reports[127] on the progress of the Cameroon-Nigeria Mixed Commission established to facilitate the implementation of the ruling of the International Court of Justice of 10 October 2002 on the land and maritime boundary dispute between the two countries. In addition, in a letter dated 17 March addressed to the President of the Security Council. the Secretary-General, pursuant to paragraph 2 of Article 41 of the Statute of the Court, transmitted the order indicating provisional measures in the case concerning *Allegations of Genocide under the Convention on the Prevention and Punishment of the Crime of Genocide (Ukraine v. Russian Federation)*.[128]

---

[120] See S/PV.8998.

[121] See S/PV.9042 (Resumption 1).

[122] See S/PV.9052 and S/PV.9052 (Resumption 1).

[123] See S/PV.9052.

[124] See S/PV.9052 (Resumption 1).

[125] See S/PV.9112.

[126] S/2022/832 and S/2022/833.

[127] See S/2022/521 and S/2022/1019.

[128] S/2022/246, annex.

Part V

Functions and powers of the Security Council

Contents

Introductory note

Part V of the present Supplement covers the functions and powers of the Security Council, as defined in Articles 24, 25 and 26 of the Charter of the United Nations, and is accordingly divided into three sections. Explicit and implicit references made to those Articles in decisions, meetings and communications of the Council during 2022 are described under each of the three sections. Case studies in sections I and II provide an overview of specific instances in which Articles 24 and 25, respectively, were discussed in meetings of the Council, or which otherwise illustrate how the Council has applied or interpreted those provisions. Consistent with previous supplements, section III does not include any case studies since there were no examples of substantive discussions on Article 26 in 2022.

As outlined in section I, in 2022, the Council made no explicit reference to Article 24 of the Charter in its decisions, instead referring to its "primary responsibility for the maintenance of international peace and security" in six decisions, adopted under both country-specific and thematic items. Article 24 was invoked explicitly in 13 instances at seven Council meetings, held under both thematic and country-specific items. In addition, Council members and other participants in the meetings discussed the primary responsibility of the Council for the maintenance of international peace and security in connection with a broad range of topics. The most salient deliberations took place under thematic items, such as those entitled "Maintenance of international peace and security", "Implementation of the note by the President of the Security Council (S/2017/507)" and "Threats to international peace and security", as well as under country-specific items relating to Ukraine. Six communications of the Council also contained explicit references to Article 24.

As featured in section II, in 2022, the Council made an explicit reference to Article 25 of the Charter in one decision, adopted under the item entitled "The situation in the Middle East". Article 25 was also explicitly invoked eight times during Council meetings held under thematic items. The obligation of Member States to accept and carry out Council decisions was extensively referenced during meetings held in connection with the items entitled "The situation in the Middle East" and "The situation in the Middle East, including the Palestinian question", while the most salient deliberations took place under the items entitled "Protection of civilians in armed conflict" and "Non-proliferation/Democratic People's Republic of Korea". In addition, three communications of the Council contained explicit references to Article 25.

As described in section III, in 2022, the Council did not refer to its responsibility to formulate plans for the establishment of a system for the regulation of armaments pursuant to Article 26 of the Charter in any of its decisions. One speaker at a Council meeting, however, made two explicit references to Article 26. No communications addressed to the Council in 2022 explicitly featured the Article.

I. Primary responsibility of the Security Council for the maintenance of international peace and security under Article 24

Article 24

1. In order to ensure prompt and effective action by the United Nations, its Members confer on the Security Council primary responsibility for the maintenance of international peace and security, and agree that in carrying out its duties under this responsibility the Security Council acts on their behalf.

2. In discharging these duties the Security Council shall act in accordance with the Purposes and Principles of the United Nations. The specific powers granted to the Security Council for the discharge of these duties are laid down in Chapters VI, VII, VIII and XII.

3. The Security Council shall submit annual and, when necessary, special reports to the General Assembly for its consideration.

Note

Section I covers the practice of the Council concerning its primary responsibility for the maintenance of international peace and security under Article 24 of the Charter of the United Nations,[1] and is divided into three subsections. Subsection A deals with decisions adopted in 2022 that refer to the primary responsibility of the Council pursuant to Article 24. Subsection B contains an examination of explicit and implicit references to Article 24 made in discussions held during the meetings of the Council. Subsection C features explicit references to Article 24 contained in communications of the Council.

During the period under review, the Council did not adopt any decision explicitly referring to Article 24 of the Charter. Consistent with recent practice, in its decisions adopted in 2022, the Council referred to its primary responsibility for the maintenance of international peace and security while taking a broad range of actions. The provision was also directly invoked in several instances during the meetings of the Council, notably in connection with items relating to Ukraine, the maintenance of international peace and security, the working methods of the Council and the situation in the Middle East. Explicit references to Article 24 were also made in six communications of the Council in 2022, more details on which are provided below.

A. Decisions referring to Article 24

During the period under review, the Council did not refer explicitly to Article 24 of the Charter in its decisions. Instead, in four resolutions and two presidential statements, the Council referred to its primary responsibility for the maintenance of international peace and security while taking a broad range of actions. Implicit references to Article 24 were featured mainly in preambular paragraphs of resolutions and initial paragraphs of presidential statements in connection with both country-specific and thematic items on the agenda of the Council.

Resolutions

In 2022, the Council implicitly invoked Article 24 of the Charter in four resolutions, in which it reaffirmed, recalled, bore in mind or indicated that it was mindful of its primary responsibility for the maintenance of international peace and security while taking a variety of actions. One resolution concerned Ukraine, two resolutions, in which the Council acted explicitly under Chapter VII of the Charter, were adopted in connection with Libya under the items entitled "The situation in Libya" and "Maintenance of international peace and security", while one was adopted under the item entitled "United Nations

[1] Article 24 (3), under which the Council is required to submit annual and special reports to the General Assembly, is covered in part IV, sect. I.F.

peacekeeping operations" in relation to mental health and psychosocial support for peace operations personnel. Additional information about the resolutions is provided in the table below.

Presidential statements

During the year under review, the Council adopted two presidential statements containing implicit references to Article 24 of the Charter, in which it reaffirmed its primary responsibility for the maintenance of international peace and security. The two statements concerned items relating to the cooperation between the United Nations and the League of Arab States in maintaining international peace and security and the role of strategic communications for efficient peacekeeping, respectively. Further details about the statements are provided in the table below.

Decisions containing implicit references to Article 24 (1) of the Charter, 2022

Decision and date	*Paragraph*	*Item*	*Sub-item*
Resolution 2623 (2022) 27 February	Second preambular paragraph	Letter dated 28 February 2014 from the Permanent Representative of Ukraine to the United Nations addressed to the President of the Security Council (S/2014/136)	
S/PRST/2022/1 23 March	First paragraph	Cooperation between the United Nations and regional and subregional organizations in maintaining international peace and security	League of Arab States
Resolution 2635 (2022) 3 June	Fifth preambular paragraph	The situation in Libya	
S/PRST/2022/5 12 July	First paragraph	United Nations peacekeeping operations	The key role of strategic communications for efficient peacekeeping
Resolution 2652 (2022) 29 September	Fourth preambular paragraph	Maintenance of international peace and security	Report of the Secretary-General on the implementation of Security Council resolution 2598 (2021) (S/2022/655)
Resolution 2668 (2022) 21 December	First preambular paragraph	United Nations peacekeeping operations	

B. Discussions relating to Article 24

During the period under review, Article 24 of the Charter was invoked both explicitly and implicitly at numerous meetings of the Council. Speakers made 13 explicit references to Article 24 at seven meetings, held under the items entitled "Letter dated 13 April 2014 from the Permanent Representative of the Russian Federation to the United Nations addressed to the President of the Security Council (S/2014/264)",[2] "Letter dated 28 February 2014 from the Permanent Representative of Ukraine to the United Nations addressed to the President of the Security Council (S/2014/136)",[3] "Maintenance of international peace and security",[4]

[2] See S/PV.8968 (Ukraine).

[3] See S/PV.8970 (Ukraine).

[4] See S/PV.9052 (Brazil); S/PV.9052 (Resumption 1) (Pakistan and Sierra Leone); and S/PV.9220 (Mexico).

"Implementation of the note by the President of the Security Council (S/2017/507)",[5] "The situation in the Middle East"[6] and "Threats to international peace and security".[7]

The following case studies illustrate the nature of some of the issues discussed in 2022 with regard to the interpretation of the primary responsibility of the Council for the maintenance of international peace and security pursuant to Article 24 of the Charter. The cases capture discussions held in connection with items relating to Ukraine (case 1), the maintenance of international peace and security (cases 2 and 5), the working methods of the Council (case 3) and climate change in the context of threats to international peace and security (case 4).

Case 1
Letter dated 28 February 2014 from the Permanent Representative of Ukraine to the United Nations addressed to the President of the Security Council (S/2014/136)

On 27 February, the Security Council held a meeting under the item entitled "Letter dated 28 February 2014 from the Permanent Representative of Ukraine to the United Nations addressed to the President of the Security Council (S/2014/136)",[8] at which it adopted resolution 2623 (2022).[9] By the resolution, taking into account that the lack of unanimity of its permanent members at the 8979th meeting had prevented it from exercising its primary responsibility for the maintenance of international peace and security, the Council decided to call an emergency special session of the General Assembly to examine the question contained in document S/Agenda/8979.

In explaining their votes, Council members deliberated on the primary responsibility of the Council for the maintenance of international peace and security. The representative of France noted that his country would remain poised within the Council to ensure that the Council assumed its primary responsibility for the maintenance of international peace and security.[10] The representative of Ireland affirmed that the Council had failed to exercise its responsibility and had been rendered powerless to do so by the use of the veto by the Russian Federation, which undermined the legitimacy of the Council. Similarly, the representative of Mexico expressed the view that the Council had been unable to fulfil its primary responsibility for the maintenance of international peace and security on 25 February as a result of the exercise of the veto. The representative of Norway also noted that the Council had failed to uphold its primary responsibility for the maintenance of international peace and security, as its response to the breach of the peace and the act of aggression had failed because of the veto by the aggressor itself. In a similar vein, the representative of Ghana asserted that, because of the exercise of the veto, the Council had been unable to assume its primary responsibility to act on a threat to international peace and security following the aggression of the Russian Federation against Ukraine.

The representative of Brazil stated that the urgency of the situation had convinced his delegation of the need to add the voice of the General Assembly to that of the Council in seeking solutions to the crisis in and around Ukraine. However, in no way did that detract from his delegation's firm belief that the Council, with its primary responsibility for the maintenance of international peace and security, had not yet exhausted the instruments and mechanisms at its disposal to contribute to a negotiated and diplomatic solution towards peace.

In explaining his vote, the representative of the Russian Federation noted that his country had voted against resolution 2623 (2022) because its authors had proposed that it be placed on record that the Council was unable to uphold its primary responsibility for the maintenance of international peace and security. He added that there was no hint in the text of any attempt to find a constructive solution in the Council.

---

[5] See S/PV.9079 (Ecuador and Cuba); and S/PV.9079 (Resumption 1) (Algeria and Sudan).

[6] See S/PV.9097 (United Kingdom).

[7] See S/PV.9127 (Mexico).

[8] See S/PV.8980.

[9] The draft resolution received 11 votes in favour (Albania, Brazil, France, Gabon, Ghana, Ireland, Kenya, Mexico, Norway, United Kingdom and United States), 1 against (Russian Federation) and 3 abstentions (China, India and United Arab Emirates). For more information about decision-making and voting, see part II, sect. VIII.

[10] For more information about the discussions relating to Ukraine, see part I, sects. 19 and 36.

Case 2
Maintenance of international peace and security

On 2 June, at the initiative of Albania, which held the presidency for the month,[11] the Security Council held a high-level open debate under the item entitled "Maintenance of international peace and security", focused on the sub-item entitled "Strengthening accountability and justice for serious violations of international law".[12] At the meeting, speakers made four explicit references to Article 24 of the Charter of the United Nations and numerous implicit references to the primary responsibility of the Council for the maintenance of international peace and security in the context of accountability for violations of international law.

In his briefing to the Council about the measures to strengthen its accountability, a professor of public international law at the University of Oxford noted that the Council had a special role to play, given its primary responsibility for the maintenance of international peace and security.[13]

In their discussion, Council members also discussed the primary responsibility of the Council for the maintenance of international peace and security. The Minister of State for External Affairs of India stated that, given its primary responsibility for the maintenance of international peace and security, the Council had acted a number of times in the past to address serious violations of international law. The representative of Brazil recalled the leading role that Article 24 of the Charter had bestowed on the Council in the maintenance of international peace and security and added that there could be no peace and security where perpetrators of serious violations of international law felt free to continue carrying out atrocities. The representative of Mexico expressed the view that the power of veto of the five permanent members was an obstacle to achieving the objective of the Council to fulfil its important responsibility to maintain international peace and security. In that regard, he noted that Mexico, together with France, would continue to promote its joint initiative for the permanent members to commit themselves, on a voluntary basis, to refraining from the use of veto in situations of mass atrocities. Noting that peace and justice were what humankind strove to uphold and were the primary responsibility of the Council, the representative of China expressed the view that the process of maintaining peace and achieving justice was an intersectional, interdisciplinary enterprise. Accountability was an important means of serving justice, and the role it played in restoring and maintaining peace defied oversimplification, as it hinged on specific circumstances and conditions.

Non-Council members also reflected on the role of the Council in fulfilling its primary responsibility for the maintenance of international peace and security in the context of ensuring accountability for the crimes committed during the war in Ukraine. The representative of Liechtenstein recalled that, since July 2018, the Council had had the power to refer situations involving the crime of aggression to the International Criminal Court and underscored that that tool had the tremendous potential to deter aggression and support the Council's mandate to maintain international peace and security. He expressed the view that, in that context, the brazen aggression against Ukraine was an obvious case for the Council to make use of that tool. The representative of Poland stated that the Council should play a significant role in the process of assuring justice and accountability for the crimes and serious violations of international law committed in Ukraine and added that a special duty within the Council lay with its permanent members. While pursuing the main goal of the United Nations to maintain international peace and security, the Council also had a track record of strengthening justice and accountability for serious violations of international law.

Case 3
Implementation of the note by the President of the Security Council (S/2017/507)

On 28 June, at the initiative of Albania, which held the presidency of the Security Council for the month and whose representative held the Chair of the Informal Working Group on Documentation and

[11] A concept note was circulated by a letter dated 24 May (S/2022/418/Rev.1).

[12] See S/PV.9052 and S/PV.9052 (Resumption 1). For more information about the item entitled "Maintenance of international peace and security", see part I, sect. 37.

[13] See S/PV.9052.

Other Procedural Questions,[14] the Council held an open debate under the item entitled "Implementation of the note by the President of the Security Council (S/2017/507)" and the sub-item entitled "Working methods of the Security Council".[15] During the meeting, speakers made four explicit references to Article 24 of the Charter of the United Nations and numerous implicit references in connection with the core mandate of the Council to maintain international peace and security, the challenges it faced in discharging its duties and its obligation to act on behalf of the wider United Nations membership.

The representative of the Russian Federation expressed the view that any reforms must be focused on a genuine increase in the effectiveness and efficiency of the implementation by the Council of its primary functions of maintaining international peace and security.[16] She further asserted that the practice of individual members using the Council to, inter alia, expand the Council's agenda through domestic, political, human rights, climate or other questions had recently increased, which absolutely ignored the fact that not only was the Council, under the Charter, not supposed to deal with those subjects, but also that it could not help with the resolution of those problems. The representative of China noted that Council members must always bear in mind that the sole agenda of the Council was the common agenda of international peace and security. He added that, however multifarious and complicated the challenges confronting the Council might be, standing together in solidarity and unity for the maintenance of international peace and security was always the Council's primary responsibility. He said that the Council had seen a steady increase in the number of emerging issues and a continuous proliferation of cross-cutting issues, some of which were clearly beyond its core mandate, and noted that the Council should focus on the major pressing issues that threatened international peace and security and avoid taking on new topics without due consideration. The representative of France underscored that the Council needed to regain the ability to make decisions, which was its role and the mandate assigned to it by the Charter, recalling that the Council was primarily an executive body, not a forum for discussion. She further stated that the Council must be able to assume its responsibilities and address situations that might constitute threats to international peace and security. The representative of Cuba called upon the Council to abide by its mandate and respect the functions of other United Nations organs. The Council must stop expanding the scope of its interpretation of international peace and security and cease the selective manipulation of its methods and practices to suit political and imperialist agendas. In his view, such strategies undermined the role of the Council in maintaining international peace and security, further exacerbated conflicts and divisions and undermined the multilateralism, credibility and legitimacy of the United Nations. The representative of Argentina affirmed that dialogue with other bodies, whether within the United Nations system or not, was essential to enabling the Council to carry out its functions and noted that the Council's job was to maintain international peace and security and that Argentina did not want to see it absorbing the functions of other bodies.[17] The representative of the Sudan underscored that the reform of the Council's working methods under Article 24 of the Charter required the Council to adhere to its Charter-mandated functions, adding that a quick glance at the list of matters of which the Council's was seized revealed that its agenda was rapidly expanding, necessitating a pause for reflection and meaningful review.

Several speakers discussed the challenges faced by the Council in discharging its duties and the extent to which its working methods contributed to the ability of the Council to fulfil its mandate. The representative of the United Kingdom stated that all Council members had a responsibility to uphold the Charter and added that General Assembly resolution 76/262 of 26 April 2022, on the veto, was a welcome step towards ensuring transparency and accountability when a member of the Council blocked action to maintain international peace and security.[18] He further noted that there was a need to do more to ensure that the Council used its time efficiently, which meant respecting the Council's mandate and not using it as a platform for propaganda and misinformation. The representative of Switzerland, speaking on behalf of 26 members of the Accountability, Coherence and Transparency Group, stated that the ability of the Council to deliver on its primary responsibility to maintain international peace and security was put to

[14] A concept note was circulated by a letter dated 21 June (S/2022/499).

[15] See S/PV.9079 and S/PV.9079 (Resumption 1).

[16] See S/PV.9079.

[17] See S/PV.9079 (Resumption 1).

[18] See S/PV.9079.

the test by the disrespect of the Charter and the lack of compliance with international law. Recalling that States Members of the United Nations had conferred upon the Council the primary responsibility for the maintenance of international peace and security, she called upon the members of the Council to fulfil all obligations to enable the Council to discharge its responsibilities, to uphold the purposes and principles of the Charter and to act in the collective interest of maintaining international peace and security. The representative of Luxembourg noted that it was more vital than ever that the Council be able to fulfil its primary responsibility for the maintenance of international peace and security and deplored the impasse in which the Council found itself, as it was not able to fully discharge its mandate, notably owing to the use of the veto. Similarly, the representative of Poland affirmed that the Council was often stuck in a deadlock, making it unable to properly carry out its primary responsibility to maintain international peace and security, citing the unprovoked aggression against Ukraine as the most recent example in that regard. Noting that, in recent weeks, many Member States had referred to the Council's responsibility for upholding international peace and security, the representative of Austria stated that in a situation that constituted a blatant breach of international law, the Council should not remain blocked by one Member State. The representative of Singapore said that, since the previous open debate on working methods held in June 2021, the geopolitical climate had darkened and the Council had yet to exercise its mandate to maintain international peace and security in response, which had made the need to improve the Council's working methods even more pressing. According to the representative of Kuwait, developing and improving the working methods of the Council constituted a critical factor in its ability to assume its responsibility for maintaining international peace and security. In a similar vein, the representative of Bahrain noted that it was of vital importance that the Council's role as the main organ responsible for maintaining international peace and security be pivotal and concrete under all circumstances, and in that regard, he attached great importance to developing its working methods. The representative of Cuba noted that it was imperative that the Council adopt its rules of procedures in order to put an end to their provisional status, which was essential for transparency and the necessary accountability to all Member States, on behalf of which the Council must act, in accordance with Article 24 of the Charter. The representative of Slovenia expressed the view that the quality of the working methods and their implementation alone could not offset the effects of geopolitical realities on the ability of the Council to fulfil its mandate to maintain international peace and security.

Some speakers recalled that the Council had a responsibility to act on behalf of the wider membership of the United Nations in line with Article 24 of the Charter. The representative of Ecuador noted that the Council acted on behalf of the States Members of the United Nations pursuant to Article 24, but that the counterpart of that representation was the obligation to ensure prompt and effective action by the United Nations. According to the representative of Algeria, it was important to maintain interaction with States that were not members of the Council, in accordance with Article 24, which stated that the Council acted on their behalf.[19] That required full transparency in dealings between the Council and Member States. The representative of the Sudan noted that the Council was entrusted by the Charter with the primary responsibility for maintaining international peace and security and that, to carry out that task effectively, the Council's work must be transparent, objective and resilient for the benefit of the greater international community as a whole rather than a specific group of elite countries.

Case 4
Threats to international peace and security

On 12 October, at the initiative of Gabon, which held the presidency for the month,[20] the Security Council held a high-level open debate under the item entitled "Threats to international peace and security" and the sub-item entitled "Climate and security in Africa".[21] During the debate, there were no explicit references to Article 24 of the Charter of the United Nations. However, Council members and other speakers discussed the extent to which the topic of the meeting fell within the purview of the Council's primary responsibility for the maintenance of international peace and security.

---

[19] See S/PV.9079 (Resumption 1).

[20] A concept note was circulated by a letter dated 3 October (S/2022/737).

[21] See S/PV.9150. For more information about the item entitled "Threats to international peace and security", see part I, sect. 36.

Many Council members expressed the view that addressing the nexus between climate change and security was part of the mandate of the Council in maintaining international peace and security. The Minister for Foreign Affairs of Gabon urged the Council to stop looking the other way and to recognize climate change as a factor that was inherently fuelling political instability and crises in many countries in Africa. He added that the Council was facing its responsibilities and had the choice between denial or scepticism, on the one hand, and action, on the other. The Minister for Foreign Affairs of Norway stated that climate change and environmental degradation were drivers of instability and conflict, which clearly made climate and security an issue for the Council, and that such an issue should not be controversial. The Permanent Representative of the United States to the United Nations and member of the President's Cabinet expressed the view that climate and security were connected and must be at the top of the agenda of the Council. She stated that some Council members continued to argue that the Council was not the place to address climate-induced security threats and had worked to defeat efforts during the previous year by the representative of the Niger to recognize that in a Council product.[22] She added that it was not possible to pretend that the Council, which was charged with maintaining international peace and security, was somehow not the right forum to tackle the security issues that stemmed from climate change.[23] The representative of the United Arab Emirates noted that the statement by the Minister for Foreign Affairs of Gabon, who was presiding the meeting, starkly highlighted the link between climate change and peace and security, adding that the Council had been discussing that nexus since 2007. She concurred with the statement that the Council had thus far failed to address it, as outlined by the Permanent Representative of the United States and member of the President's Cabinet. She also noted that, while there might not yet be agreement within the Council on a framework to address the links between climate change and security, there could be an acknowledgement of the urgency and wisdom of raising investments to prevent climate impacts from escalating into security situations. The representative of Ghana noted that the Council should not be prevented from dealing with relevant aspects of the climate question, adding that there was a sufficient link between the climate and security crises and that the Council, as the primary organ for maintaining international peace and security, must embrace climate action in the resolution of conflicts where it was relevant and/or useful to do so. That was not to suggest that the Council was to engage in norm-setting for climate action, but rather that it should not be made to shy away from applying norms universally agreed under the United Nations Framework Convention on Climate Change. The representative of Ghana, therefore, encouraged the Council to continue the existing practice of including language relating to climate security in resolutions on country situations and peacekeeping missions, where necessary. According to the representative of France, the Council must fully assume its responsibilities in addressing threats related to climate change and must be able to better assess, anticipate and prevent the impact of climate change on international peace and security and to draw conclusions from it. The representative of Mexico expressed the view that the Council should systematically consider how the effects of climate change were undermining efforts to prevent and address threats to international peace and security. The representative of Kenya stated that the Council could not remain on the sidelines when major threats to regional and international peace and security were made much worse by climate crises. The representative of Albania reiterated that the definition of security must include the threat posed by climate change for the Council to devise appropriate security policies. The representative of Ireland shared the view of the representative of Kenya in that history would judge the Council harshly if it failed to address the issue and noted that his delegation was not asking the Council to address or tackle climate change, which he believed must rightly be addressed through the United Nations Framework Convention on Climate Change. He did, however, believe that the Council should analyse and understand the effects of climate change on peace and security. The representative of the United Kingdom stated that his delegation saw an undeniable link between climate, nature, peace and security in Africa and around the world and recalled that the United Kingdom was the first to bring climate security to the Council in 2007.[24]

Other Council members expressed the view that the Council was not the appropriate body to discuss the topic of climate change.[25] The representative of Brazil expressed the view that the Council was not the adequate forum in which to address climate change and pointed to the need to preserve the

---

[22] See also *Repertoire*, *Supplement 2021*, part V, sect. I.

[23] See S/PV.9150.

[24] For more details on the proceedings in 2007, see *Repertoire*, *Supplement 2004–2007*, chap. VIII, sect. 54.

[25] See S/PV.9150.

primary responsibilities, mandates and tools of the Council and to avoid a duplication of work. He explained that, while the adverse effects of climate change were a matter of great concern, climate change was not in itself a direct cause of armed conflicts, nor did it constitute a direct threat to peace and security in the sense underscored in the Charter. He added that, while the Council might be effective in performing its functions in peacekeeping missions on the ground by supporting efforts of host countries, at their request, that did not imply that the Council had, or should have, a mandate to thematically address climate change. He further stated that proper forums, tools and mechanisms for mobilizing those resources already existed within the United Nations Framework Convention on Climate Change and the wider United Nations system and that none of them required the direct involvement of the Council. The representative of India stated that her country would continue to oppose any attempt to take climate change out of the United Nations Framework Convention on Climate Change and discuss it separately without such principles and provisions, which is why India did not subscribe to the idea of the Council as a place to discuss that issue. In fact, her delegation viewed such efforts as an attempt to evade responsibility under the United Nations Framework Convention on Climate Change and divert the world's attention from an unwillingness to deliver where it counted. The representative of the Russian Federation expressed the view that the division of labour enshrined in the Charter must be preserved for the effective functioning of the United Nations system, adding that the Council could not and should not duplicate the work of other United Nations entities. Combating climate change and its negative social and economic consequences fell exclusively within the framework of sustainable development.

During the debate, other speakers also shared their views on the role of the Council in dealing with climate change. The representative of Germany, speaking on behalf of the Group of Friends on Climate and Security, affirmed that the Council had the primary responsibility for the maintenance of international peace and security and welcomed the progress made in that regard, including the recognition of the effects of climate change in its consideration of the growing number of mandates for peacekeeping and special political missions. He added that African States and others particularly affected by the dramatic effects of climate change deserved the full support of the international community and, when climate change threatened peace, of the Council. The representative of Egypt noted his country's steadfast commitment to addressing the challenges posed by climate change and expressed the view that the General Assembly, the Economic and Social Council and the relevant international conventions remained the platforms with an original mandate to bring about the necessary solutions to address the climate crisis in all its manifestations. However, climate change was widely recognized as a threat multiplier and a driver of conflict that was affecting the peace and stability of several regions globally, especially Africa, which was why it was important to address the increasing connection between climate change and security. The representative of Morocco observed that the African continent and especially the Sahel and the Congo basin were unduly and disproportionately penalized by the consequences of global warming, unfairly suffering the drastic effects of climate change, a situation that should be of concern to the Council. He added that, as long as the international community's climate targets were not sufficient to reduce global warming to an acceptable level, the impact of climate change would be on the agenda of the Council. The representative of Namibia stated that, when debating the security dimension of climate change, the Council had not always been forthcoming in establishing a direct link between desertification, land degradation and drought and ongoing violent conflicts in Africa. He noted, however, that climate change and its threat to peace and security were no longer a far-fetched tale of a fictional dystopian world and called upon the Council to maintain the momentum regarding discussions relating to climate and security, as that nexus posed the next frontier of emerging threats for the world. The representative of the Niger noted that his understanding of the principle of unity of action at the United Nations meant that the fact that it had one organ with the principal mandate for an issue should not exclude another of its organs from dealing with an aspect of that issue relevant to its own mandate.[26] It was on the basis of that belief that in December 2021, the Niger, which held the presidency for that month, had submitted, together with Ireland, draft resolution S/2021/990, on the link between the effects of climate change and security, which had not been adopted. The representative of South Africa said that scientific evidence to support a more generalized conclusion of a direct causality between climate change and threats to international peace

[26] For more information about the relations between the Council and other principal organs of the United Nations, see part IV.

and security was still minimal and maintained that the United Nations Framework Convention on Climate Change was a fit-for-purpose United Nations body specifically created to tackle climate change. Unlike the Council, it was representative of all Member States and abided by important principles, which included equity and common but differentiated responsibilities and respective capabilities.

Case 5
Maintenance of international peace and security

On 14 December, at the initiative of India, which held the presidency for the month,[27] the Security Council held a high-level open debate under the item entitled "Maintenance of international peace and security" and the sub-item entitled "New orientation for reformed multilateralism".[28] At the meeting, the Council heard briefings by the Secretary-General and the President of the General Assembly. In his briefing, the President of the General Assembly noted that too often, sharp geopolitical divides had prevented responses by and progress in the Council and asked the members of the Council whether those rifts would continue to upstage their collective ability to maintain international peace and security.[29]

During the debate, only one explicit reference was made to Article 24 of the Charter of the United Nations. Several Council members referred, however, to the primary responsibility of the Council for the maintenance of international peace and security. Council members also shared their views on the impact of the veto on the ability of the Council to discharge its functions. Noting that the Council, charged with the critical mandate to maintain international peace and security, was too often unable to rise to that challenge, the representative of Ireland said that the veto and the absence of trust had prevented the Council from effectively implementing its mandate. The representative of France stated that, while a permanent member of the Council was waging a war of annexation in violation of the Charter, many were calling for a framework for the veto to strengthen the ability of the Council to fully assume its responsibilities. In that spirit, France, along with Mexico, had proposed, as early as 2013, that the five permanent members of the Council voluntarily and collectively suspend the use of the veto in the case of mass atrocities. The representative of China noted that it was the shared expectation of the general membership of the United Nations that the Council better fulfil the mandate entrusted to it by the Charter, adding that, no matter how complicated the challenges, it was always the greatest responsibility of the Council to stay united and work together to maintain international peace and security. The representative of Mexico said that it was naive to think that merely adding more Member States to the Council, and consequently more permanent members, would magically generate the consensus that the Council needed to fully discharge its mandate. Although the Council was the organ tasked with dealing with threats to international peace and security, the United Nations system as a whole had a direct and indirect impact on the maintenance of peace. It was clear that the success of the Council in discharging its responsibilities in accordance with its mandate depended largely not only on members not abusing the veto, but also on the success of other principal organs in fulfilling their own mandates, in conjunction with the work of the Secretary-General.[30] The representative of Mexico added that, if the Council were to remain similar to what it was today but with more members and perhaps more vetoes, it would not be capable of truly acting on behalf of all Member States, as stipulated in Article 24 (1) of the Charter. The representative of Albania noted that multilateralism was not always synonymous with success, as could be seen when self-centred, narrow interests prevented the Council from acting and discharging its responsibilities. That was why, in the face of a Council paralysed by a blatant conflict of interest, it had been crucial for the General Assembly to respond decisively by confirming the sound moral ground of a world that was not ready to condone aggression or accept the annexation of territory by force. That response, together with the veto initiative, had confirmed the necessity for strengthened cooperation among the main organs of the Organization and had contributed to revitalizing and empowering the Assembly, which clearly showed that it was imperative to improve the functioning of the Council and its ability to take action, remain credible and act on behalf of the entire United Nations membership.

[27] A concept note was circulated by a letter dated 25 November (S/2022/880).
[28] See S/PV.9220 and S/PV.9220 (Resumption 1).
[29] See S/PV.9220.
[30] For more information about the relations between the Council and other principal organs of the United Nations, see part IV.

During the debate, several other speakers also referred more broadly to the need for a reform of the Council with a view to safeguarding its effectiveness in maintaining international peace and security,[31] with some focusing on the impact of the use of veto on the ability of the Council to discharge its duties.[32] Some participants also noted that, in exercising its primary responsibility for the maintenance of international peace and security, the Council was expected to act on behalf of all Member States.[33]

C. Communications featuring Article 24

In 2022, six explicit references to Article 24 of the Charter were made in communications of the Council submitted in connection with a broad range of issues.

In the annex to a letter dated 25 January addressed to the President of the Security Council,[34] the representative of Saint Vincent and the Grenadines shared reflections on her two-year term as the Chair of the Informal Working Group on Documentation and Other Procedural Questions. The annex included an index of key words and phrases, including "Article 24 of the Charter", contained in the note by the President of the Council dated 30 August 2017[35] and subsequently adopted notes.

In the annex to a letter dated 7 February addressed to the President of the Security Council,[36] in reference to the meeting held on the same date under the item entitled "General issues relating to sanctions" and the sub-item entitled "Preventing their humanitarian and unintended consequences", the representative of the Islamic Republic of Iran submitted his country's position on the matter and noted that the mandate of the Council was limited by Article 24 of the Charter, which stated that, in discharging its duties, the Council was to act in accordance with the purposes and principles of the United Nations.

In a concept note for a high-level open debate on "Strengthening accountability and justice for serious violations of international law" under the item entitled "Maintenance of international peace and security", which was annexed to a letter dated 24 May addressed to the Secretary-General,[37] the representative of Albania noted that Article 24 of the Charter granted the Council primary responsibility for the maintenance of international peace and security, which included taking collective measures to prevent and counter threats to peace and suppressing acts of aggression.

In a concept note for an open debate on the working methods of the Council in connection with the item entitled "Implementation of the note by the President of the Security Council (S/2017/507)", which was annexed to a letter dated 21 June addressed to the Secretary-General,[38] the representative of Albania stated that such annual open debates on the working methods of the Council had served to engage with the wider membership on behalf of which the Council acted, pursuant to Article 24 of the Charter.

In a letter dated 29 July addressed to the President of the Security Council,[39] the representative of Egypt conveyed a letter from the Minister for Foreign Affairs of Egypt regarding the third consecutive unilateral filling of the Grand Ethiopian Renaissance Dam, in which the Minister noted that it was incumbent upon the Council to discharge its obligations under Article 24 of the Charter by taking appropriate measures to ensure that the question of the dam was settled amicably, which would ensure the preservation of peace and security throughout the region.

Finally, in a letter dated 8 December addressed to the Secretary-General and the President of the Security Council,[40] the representative of the Russian Federation transmitted a letter from the Board Chairman of the Donetsk public organization Fair Protection regarding the rapidly deteriorating

[31] See S/PV.9220 (Poland); and S/PV.9220 (Resumption 1) (Philippines, Slovenia, Argentina, Liechtenstein, Indonesia, Spain and Georgia).

[32] See S/PV.9220 (Poland); and S/PV.9220 (Resumption 1) (Italy, Switzerland, Bulgaria, European Union (also on behalf of Albania, Bosnia and Herzegovina, Montenegro and the Republic of Moldova) and Lithuania).

[33] See S/PV.9220 (Resumption 1) (Austria, Ecuador, Liechtenstein and Türkiye).

[34] S/2022/88.

[35] S/2017/507.

[36] S/2022/98.

[37] S/2022/418.

[38] S/2022/499.

[39] S/2022/587.

[40] S/2022/927.

humanitarian situation in the Donbass region, in which the Board Chairman called upon the Council, in the light of its primary responsibility under Article 24 of the Charter for the maintenance of international peace and security, in order to end the suffering of civilians in the Donbass, to consider immediate measures to stop Ukrainian armed formations from committing war crimes, as well as to prohibit the supply to Ukraine of the types of heavy weaponry that had led to that.

II. Obligation of Member States to accept and carry out decisions of the Security Council under Article 25

Article 25

The Members of the United Nations agree to accept and carry out the decisions of the Security Council in accordance with the present Charter.

Note

Section II outlines the practice of the Council in relation to Article 25 of the Charter of the United Nations, which concerns the obligation of Member States to accept and carry out the decisions of the Council. It is divided into three subsections: subsection A, which encompasses the references to Article 25 contained in decisions of the Council; subsection B, which contains an examination of how the principle of Article 25 was dealt with in deliberations during the meetings of the Council; and subsection C, which features explicit references to Article 25 in communications of the Council.

In 2022, the Council adopted one decision containing an explicit reference to Article 25 of the Charter, in connection with the situation in the Middle East. Speakers also made eight explicit references to Article 25 during meetings of the Council held under thematic items. More information is provided in subsection B, which covers the most salient discussions relating to the Article, including case studies on the Council's interpretation of Member States' obligations stemming from its decisions concerning the protection of civilians in armed conflict and in connection with the item entitled "Non-proliferation/ Democratic People's Republic of Korea". In addition, during the year under review, three explicit references to Article 25 were made in three communications of the Council, more details on which are provided in subsection C.

A. Decisions referring to Article 25

In 2022, the Council adopted one decision containing an explicit reference to Article 25 of the Charter, under the item entitled "The situation in the Middle East", in relation to the Syrian Arab Republic. In the resolution, the Council underscored that Member States were obligated under Article 25 of the Charter of the United Nations to accept and carry out the Council's decisions.[41] By the resolution, the Council also demanded the full and immediate implementation of all provisions of all relevant Council resolutions on the humanitarian situation in the Syrian Arab Republic and extended the authorization, until 10 January 2023, for United Nations humanitarian agencies and their implementing parties to provide cross-border humanitarian assistance for the border crossing at Bab al-Hawa, with an extension of an additional six months, until 10 July 2023, which would require a separate resolution confirming the extension.[42]

In addition, two draft resolutions submitted in connection with the above-mentioned item, and which were not adopted, contained explicit references to Article 25 of the Charter. In both draft resolutions, the Council would have underscored that Member States were obligated under Article 25 of the Charter of the United Nations to accept and carry out the Council's decisions.[43]

---

[41] Resolution 2642 (2022), final preambular paragraph.

[42] Ibid., paras. 1 and 2.

[43] See S/2022/538, final preambular paragraph, and S/2022/541, final preambular paragraph. For further information about the item entitled "The situation in the Middle East", see part I, sect. 20.

B. Discussions relating to Article 25

In 2022, Article 25 of the Charter was explicitly invoked eight times during Council meetings held under the items entitled "Protection of civilians in armed conflict",[44] "General issues relating to sanctions",[45] "Maintenance of international peace and security"[46] and "Children and armed conflict".[47] In addition, speakers implicitly referred to the obligation of Member States to accept and carry out the decisions of the Council, as well as to their binding nature, at multiple meetings held under a broad range of items. For example, during meetings convened under the item entitled "The situation in the Middle East", several speakers referred to the obligation of the Syrian Arab Republic to comply with or abide by Council decisions, in particular resolution 2118 (2013), on the use of chemical weapons.[48] Similar references were made during meetings held under the item entitled "The situation in the Middle East, including the Palestinian question", with several participants urging Israel to abide by or comply with the relevant Council decisions, in particular resolution 2334 (2016).[49]

The case studies below feature some of the most salient discussions in 2022 with respect to the Council's interpretation of the obligation of Member States to implement its decisions, notably in the context of deliberations on the protection of civilians in armed conflict (case 6) and in connection with the item entitled "Non-proliferation/Democratic People's Republic of Korea" (case 7).

Case 6
Protection of civilians in armed conflict

On 25 May, the Security Council held an open debate under the item entitled "Protection of civilians in armed conflict",[50] during which it heard briefings by the Director of Coordination in the Office for the Coordination of Humanitarian Affairs, the Director-General of the International Committee of the Red Cross, the President and Chief Executive Officer of the International Rescue Committee and the Country Director for the Democratic Republic of the Congo of Women for Women International.

During the discussion, speakers made one explicit reference to Article 25 of the Charter of the United Nations,[51] with several Council members also citing various Council resolutions adopted in connection with the protection of civilians and reflecting on their binding nature and the need for their implementation. In that regard, the representative of Gabon pointed to the obligation to fulfil commitments and the need to ensure compliance with international conventions and Council resolutions with regard to the protection of civilians in the context of human rights abuses.[52] The representative of the United Kingdom stated that the Council had adopted many resolutions in which it had called for accountability for attacks on humanitarian workers and civilians and pointed to the need to turn those words into action and ensure that those responsible for such attacks were held accountable. According to the representative of Ireland, to protect civilians, the Council needed to keep its promises and implement

---

[44] See S/PV.8953 (Resumption 1) (Pakistan); and S/PV.9042 (Resumption 1) (Pakistan).

[45] See S/PV.8962 (Ghana).

[46] See S/PV.9036 (Resumption 1) (Pakistan); S/PV.9052 (Resumption 1) (Pakistan); and S/PV.9220 (Pakistan and Azerbaijan).

[47] See S/PV.9096 (Resumption 1) (Pakistan).

[48] See, for example, S/PV.8943 (United States, Ireland, France, United Kingdom, Norway and Türkiye); S/PV.8982 (United States, Norway, Ireland, United Kingdom and France); S/PV.8990 (United States, Norway and Mexico); S/PV.9026 (United States, Ireland, Norway and United Kingdom); S/PV.9097 (United States, Ireland, Mexico, United Kingdom, Ghana (also on behalf of Gabon and Kenya) and Norway); S/PV.9141 (Albania, Norway, Ireland and United Kingdom); S/PV.9184 (United States, Mexico, Norway and Ireland); and S/PV.9207 (United States, Ireland, Mexico and Norway).

[49] See, for example, S/PV.9021 (State of Palestine, Mexico, India, Gabon, China and Algeria); S/PV.9021 (Resumption 1) (Syrian Arab Republic, Malaysia, League of Arab States, Peru, Maldives, Pakistan, Qatar, Bolivarian Republic of Venezuela, Kuwait, Committee on the Exercise of the Inalienable Rights of the Palestinian People and Oman); and S/PV.9224 (France, Mexico, China, Gabon, Kenya and Ireland).

[50] See S/PV.9042 and S/PV.9042 (Resumption 1). For more information about the item entitled "Protection of civilians in armed conflict", see part I, sect. 27.

[51] See S/PV.9042 (Resumption 1) (Pakistan).

[52] See S/PV.9042.

what it had agreed, including resolution 2222 (2015), concerning the protection of journalists, and resolution 2417 (2018), on conflict and hunger. Noting that the Council had adopted resolutions in which it had called for accountability for those who targeted health-care and humanitarian workers and critical infrastructure, the representative of Albania stated that it was the responsibility of the Council to uphold its decisions. Similarly, in the context of attacks on medical and humanitarian personnel, the representative of Mexico stated that it was undeniable that there was a crisis in the implementation of the obligations derived from the norms of international humanitarian law and the resolutions of the Council. He expressed the view that it was not enough to make calls for compliance and added that it was necessary to reinforce measures at the internal level to ensure their implementation, such as through the adoption of national legislation, military manuals and ongoing training, as well as by working hand in hand with civil society organizations. The representative of Brazil encouraged the Council to continue its work to adjust the sanctions framework to effectively minimize the suffering of the civilian population and added that humanitarian actors should not be impeded from performing humanitarian and impartial relief efforts because of overcompliance or the possibility of the criminalization of their activities. The representative of France said that it was necessary to create, in the texts adopted in the Council or in national legislation, an environment conducive to the operations of neutral and impartial humanitarian actors, in accordance with international law, for example, by combating overcompliance with bank practices and by ensuring that humanitarian actors could not be sanctioned or prosecuted for the sole reason of having carried out humanitarian activities in accordance with international humanitarian law and humanitarian principles.

During the debate, many other speakers underscored the need to implement the relevant Council resolutions relating to the protection of civilians.[53] In addition, the representative of Malta noted that the Council had developed a strong framework for the protection of civilians and that it was time to fully implement the relevant resolutions.[54] She added that the challenges illustrated in the annual report of the Secretary-General[55] were not due to an absence of laws and norms, but to the inability to enforce existing laws and norms. Similarly, the representative of Argentina expressed the view that the problem lay not in the current normative framework, but in the translation and implementation of those norms in practice.[56] In order to translate the normative advances of the past 20 years into demonstrable results, the Council, together with the international community as a whole, must advocate for a more robust implementation of the existing normative framework. The representative of New Zealand affirmed that the erosion of international rules must not be allowed to become the new normal and that Council resolutions that had been agreed on in order to protect civilians must not become rhetorical commitments. The representative of Austria stated that it was necessary to ensure and enable the full, continuous and effective implementation of Council resolutions by all Member States and noted that if those resolutions were violated, decisive and swift responses by the Council were needed to immediately counter such violations. The representative of Yemen expressed the view that the efforts of the Council to end the conflict in that country and protect civilians must be translated into the implementation of its resolutions and the adoption of a decisive approach to deterring and holding accountable the violators of those resolutions. The representative of Italy referred to the many times that agreement had been reached on universal principles to protect civilians and save lives and noted that important resolutions could not be allowed to remain empty words.

Case 7
Non-proliferation/Democratic People's Republic of Korea

At a meeting held on 21 November, the Security Council heard a briefing by the Under-Secretary-General for Political and Peacebuilding Affairs under the item entitled "Non-proliferation/Democratic People's Republic of Korea",[57] during which she asserted that the continued pursuit by the Democratic People's Republic of Korea of its nuclear weapons programme and launches of ballistic missiles blatantly

[53] See S/PV.9042 (Norway, China and Switzerland (on behalf of the Group of Friends on the Protection of Civilians in Armed Conflict)); and S/PV.9042 (Resumption 1) (Luxembourg, Portugal, Spain, South Africa, Japan, Morocco, Nepal, State of Palestine, Bangladesh, Indonesia, Republic of Korea and Belgium).

[54] See S/PV.9042 (Resumption 1).

[55] S/2022/381.

[56] See S/PV.9042 (Resumption 1).

[57] See S/PV.9197.

violated relevant Council resolutions and reiterated calls upon the Democratic People's Republic of Korea to desist from taking further provocative actions and to fully comply with its international obligations under relevant Council resolutions.

During the discussion, many members of the Council,[58] as well as the representatives of the Republic of Korea and Japan, expressed the view that those launches constituted a violation of Council resolutions and called for the full implementation of the resolutions.

In addition, several Council members reflected on the impact of the Council's lack of response to the breach of its decisions. The representative of the United States stated that the Democratic People's Republic of Korea had flagrantly violated Council resolutions 63 times in 2022 and that it was time for the Council to make the same call as that made by the Secretary-General upon the Democratic People's Republic of Korea to fully comply with its international obligations under all relevant Council resolutions. The representative of Albania stated that he wondered what message was being sent to those who believed in the United Nations and its role when the Council proved unable to deal with a regime that flouted without distinction every Council resolution on the matter. He, therefore, called upon all Council members to respond unanimously with a strong, action-oriented Council product proportional to the gravity of actions of the Democratic People's Republic of Korea and its ballistic missile programme and weapons-of-mass-destruction proliferation regime, adding that failing to do so eroded the credibility of the Council. The representative of France expressed the view that each ballistic missile launch was a challenge to the authority of the Council and a violation of its unanimously adopted resolutions. The representative of Ireland stated that it was a matter of the deepest concern that each of those launches had not received any Council response and that the silence of the Council suggested that it was unwilling, or unable, to uphold its own resolutions. He added that the Democratic People's Republic of Korea, by stating that it would not abide by Council resolutions, had rejected its obligations under the Charter of the United Nations. The actions of the Democratic People's Republic of Korea were a flagrant violation of the decisions and authority of the Council, and the Council had to, finally, be clear in its response. The representative of the United Kingdom condemned the further serious breach of Council resolutions by the Democratic People's Republic of Korea and noted that, despite the egregious violation of Council resolutions, two Council members had prevented the Council from fulfilling its role. The representative of Mexico further noted that the silence of the Council had sent the wrong signal, with the launches continuing in open defiance of the Council and its prior resolutions.

Other speakers at the meeting also referred to the binding nature of Council decisions. The representative of the Republic of Korea stated that, if the Council did not respond firmly to the continued illegal behaviour of the Democratic People's Republic of Korea, it would inevitably lead to more Member States deliberately ignoring their obligations under Council resolutions. The representative of Japan recalled that the Charter was clear in that all Member States had agreed to carry out the decisions of the Council, adding that violations should not go unchecked.

C. Communications featuring Article 25

In 2022, three explicit references to Article 25 of the Charter were made in the communications of the Council.

In a letter dated 13 April addressed to the Secretary-General,[59] pointing to the alleged violations of the national airspace of Cyprus, the infringements of international air traffic regulations in the country's flight information region, the violations of the territorial waters of Cyprus and the illegal use of closed ports and airports in Cyprus, by the air and naval forces of Türkiye, between September and December 2021, the representative of Cyprus stated that Türkiye was openly declaring that it would continue violating Council resolutions, in total disregard for Article 25 of the Charter. He further called

[58] United States, Albania, France, Ireland, Norway, United Kingdom, Gabon, Mexico, India, Kenya, Brazil, United Arab Emirates and Ghana.

[59] S/2022/317.

upon the Council to stand behind its resolutions and ensure they had meaning, adding that, otherwise, there was a risk that the credibility of the international system would be undermined.

In a letter dated 5 August addressed to the President of the Security Council,[60] the representative of Pakistan transmitted a letter from the Minister for Foreign Affairs of Pakistan, in which the Minister stated that both India and Pakistan had accepted that the only legal basis for the resolution of the dispute over Jammu and Kashmir was the Council's decision, contained in resolution 47 (1948) and several subsequent Council resolutions, stipulating that the final disposition of the State of Jammu and Kashmir was to be decided by its people through the democratic method of a free and impartial plebiscite conducted under the auspices of the United Nations. He further noted that, in accordance with Article 25 of the Charter, both parties were obligated to implement those Council resolutions.

In a letter dated 13 December addressed to the Secretary-General,[61] pointing to the alleged violations of the national airspace of Cyprus, the infringements of international air traffic regulations in the country's flight information region, the violations of the territorial waters of Cyprus and the illegal use of closed ports and airports in Cyprus, by the air and naval forces of Türkiye, between January and August 2022, the representative of Cyprus stated that, through its actions, Türkiye was openly declaring that it would continue violating Council resolutions, in total disregard for Article 25 of the Charter. Furthermore, he called upon the Council to stand behind its resolutions and ensure that they had meaning.

III. Responsibility of the Security Council to formulate plans to regulate armaments under Article 26

Article 26

In order to promote the establishment and maintenance of international peace and security with the least diversion for armaments of the world's human and economic resources, the Security Council shall be responsible for formulating, with the assistance of the Military Staff Committee referred to in Article 47, plans to be submitted to the Members of the United Nations for the establishment of a system for the regulation of armaments.

Note

Section III covers the practice of the Council concerning its responsibility for formulating plans for the establishment of a system for the regulation of armaments, as stipulated in Article 26 of the Charter of the United Nations.

In 2022, consistent with past practice, the Council did not refer explicitly to Article 26 of the Charter in any of its decisions. However, Article 26 was expressly invoked twice during a meeting held on 25 May in connection with the item entitled "Protection of civilians in armed conflict".[62] At the meeting, the representative of Costa Rica expressed regret that the Council continued to fall short in fulfilling its mandate under Article 26. Noting that in 2021 global military spending had exceeded $2 trillion for the first time in history, she stated that it could be expected that, without a corresponding regulatory effort, there would be increases in the expansion of armaments that Article 26 had been intended to prevent, and a consequent impact on conflict and armed violence. It was therefore more urgent than ever that the Council, with the assistance of the Military Staff Committee, propose plans for a system for regulating arms. She added that, similarly, United Nations actors such as peacekeeping missions and their troop-contributing countries must also play a central role in monitoring arms and ammunition and related information-sharing with the sanctions committees, in line with their mandates.[63] In 2022, there were no explicit references to Article 26 in any of the communications addressed to the Council.

[60] S/2022/600.
[61] S/2022/944.
[62] See S/PV.9042 (Resumption 1).
[63] For more information about the mandates of the committees established by the Council, see part IX, sect. I.

Part VI
Consideration of the provisions of Chapter VI of the Charter

Contents

Introductory note

Part VI of the present Supplement covers the practice of the Security Council with regard to the peaceful settlement of disputes within the framework of Chapter VI (Articles 33 to 38) and Articles 11 and 99 of the Charter of the United Nations. It is divided into four main sections.

Section I provides an illustration of how States brought disputes or situations to the attention of the Council during the period under review, pursuant to Article 35 of the Charter. It also provides a survey of the practice of the General Assembly and the Secretary-General, under Articles 11 (3) and 99, respectively, in drawing the attention of the Council to situations which are likely to threaten the maintenance of international peace and security. Section II contains a description of investigative and fact-finding activities performed by the Council and other bodies that may be deemed to fall under the scope of Article 34, including Council missions. Section III provides an overview of the decisions of the Council taken with regard to the pacific settlement of disputes, specifically illustrating recommendations of the Council to parties to a conflict and its support for the efforts of the Secretary-General in the peaceful settlement of disputes. Section IV contains a reflection of constitutional discussions on the interpretation or application of the provisions of Chapter VI and Article 99.

As in previous supplements, the practice of the Council with respect to the pacific settlement of disputes is not discussed in an exhaustive manner in part VI, which is focused instead on selected materials aimed at highlighting the interpretation and application of the provisions of Chapter VI of the Charter in the decisions and deliberations of the Council. Actions with regard to the pacific settlement of disputes in the context of the United Nations field missions authorized under Chapter VII are covered in the relevant sections of parts VII and X. Joint or parallel efforts undertaken by the Council and regional arrangements or agencies in the pacific settlement of disputes are covered in part VIII.

In 2022, as described in section I, Member States brought various matters to the attention of the Council, including matters of which the Council had not been seized. In response to a communication from a Member State, the Council convened a public meeting under a new item entitled "Letter dated 13 September 2022 from the Permanent Representative of Armenia to the United Nations addressed to the President of the Security Council (S/2022/688)". In addition, the Council convened eight meetings under existing items further to communications submitted by Member States, notably with regard to developments concerning the Democratic People's Republic of Korea, Iraq and Ukraine. The Secretary-General and the Secretariat continued to draw the attention of the Council to situations that were deteriorating, including with respect to Ukraine, and the risk of famine in Ethiopia, north-east Nigeria, Somalia, South Sudan and Yemen.

As featured in section II, the Council did not dispatch any missions in 2022. The Council acknowledged and deliberated on the investigative functions of the Secretary-General and the work of the United Nations High Commissioner for Human Rights, the Human Rights Council, the Organisation for the Prohibition of Chemical Weapons in connection with the situations concerning the Central African Republic, the Democratic Republic of the Congo, Iraq, Libya, Mali, South Sudan, the Sudan, the Syrian Arab Republic and Ukraine, as well as the investigation of the International Civil Aviation Organization into the landing of a civilian aircraft in Belarus.

As described in section III, the Council reiterated its demand for a general and immediate cessation of hostilities in all conflict situations before the Council and encouraged multilateral dialogue, the advancement of the political settlement of disputes and a comprehensive approach to sustaining peace. The Council stressed the need for the inclusion of women and youth in the prevention and resolution of conflicts, peacebuilding and sustaining peace. The Council called on parties to conflicts to cease hostilities and establish permanent ceasefires, fully implement peace agreements, ensure peaceful and inclusive political dialogue and transitions and engage in dialogue for the resolution of outstanding disputes. The Council recognized the good offices work of the Secretary-General, as well as that of his special representatives and envoys, in support of the implementation of peace agreements, political dialogue, transitions, the resolution of outstanding disputes and efforts to end violence in conflict.

As outlined in section IV, during 2022, the discussions in the Council were focused on the obligation of parties vis-à-vis the peaceful settlement of disputes, as provided for in Chapter VI of the Charter, and the role of the Council in that regard, including specifically in relation to the conflicts in Ukraine and between Armenia and Azerbaijan. Council members also discussed how to ensure the safe and meaningful participation of women in political processes and the respective roles and cooperation with the Council of the International Court of Justice and the Secretary-General in the peaceful settlement of disputes.

I. Referral of disputes or situations to the Security Council

Article 11

...

3. The General Assembly may call the attention of the Security Council to situations which are likely to endanger international peace and security.

Article 35

1. Any Member of the United Nations may bring any dispute, or any situation of the nature referred to in Article 34, to the attention of the Security Council or of the General Assembly.

2. A state which is not a Member of the United Nations may bring to the attention of the Security Council or of the General Assembly any dispute to which it is a party if it accepts in advance, for the purposes of the dispute, the obligations of pacific settlement provided in the present Charter.

3. The proceedings of the General Assembly in respect of matters brought to its attention under this Article will be subject to the provisions of Articles 11 and 12.

Article 99

The Secretary-General may bring to the attention of the Security Council any matter which in his opinion may threaten the maintenance of international peace and security.

Note

Within the framework of the Charter of the United Nations, Articles 35 (1) and (2) are generally regarded as the basis on which Member States and States that are not members of the United Nations may refer disputes to the Council. Under Articles 11 (3) and 99, the General Assembly and the Secretary-General, respectively, may also bring to the attention of the Council situations that are likely to threaten the maintenance of international peace and security.

The practice of the Council in this regard is described below in three subsections. Subsection A provides an overview of the referrals of disputes or situations by States to the Council pursuant to Article 35 of the Charter. Subsections B and C deal with referrals to the Council by the Secretary-General and the General Assembly, respectively, of matters likely to endanger international peace and security.

In 2022, pursuant to a communication from a Member State, the Council convened a meeting under a new item on its agenda entitled "Letter dated 13 September 2022 from the Permanent Representative of Armenia to the United Nations addressed to the President of the Security Council (S/2022/688)". The Council convened another seven meetings further to communications submitted by Member States under existing items, five of which were in connection with the Democratic People's Republic of Korea and one each in connection with Iraq and Ukraine. Council members also held informal consultations of the whole pursuant to a letter from a member of the Council in connection with the Houthi attacks on civilian infrastructure in the United Arab Emirates.

No State that was not a member of the United Nations brought any dispute or situation to the attention of the Council during the period under review. Neither the General Assembly nor the Secretary-General explicitly referred to the Council any matters likely to endanger international peace and security.

A. Referrals by States

During the period under review, certain situations were referred to the Council pursuant to Article 35 (1) of the Charter by affected or concerned Member States. Most of those situations were referred to the Council by Member States without an explicit reference to Article 35. This notwithstanding, in 2022, Article 35 was explicitly mentioned in four communications from Member States, namely from

Albania[1] and the United States[2] concerning the convening of a meeting by the President of the Security Council further to rule 3 of the provisional rules of procedure and Article 35, from Egypt[3] concerning the filling of the Grand Ethiopian Renaissance Dam and from Armenia[4] concerning the situation on the border between Armenia and Azerbaijan.

Specifically, in a letter dated 18 July addressed to the President of the Council,[5] the representative of Albania responded to a letter dated 29 June from the representative of the Russian Federation,[6] questioning the decision of the President of the Security Council to call an emergency meeting of the Council on 28 June under the item entitled "Maintenance of peace and security of Ukraine" following a request from Ukraine. The representative of Albania pointed out that rule 3 of the provisional rules of procedure, if read in full, mandated the President to call a meeting of the Council if a dispute or a situation was brought to the attention of the Council under Article 35 of the Charter.[7] Similarly, and in connection with the same matter, the representative of the United States, by letter dated 19 July,[8] stated that the provision of rule 3 was mandatory and that, as provided in Article 35, the Council was there for all Members of the United Nations to bring their disputes and situations to the Council.

In a letter dated 29 July addressed to the President of the Security Council,[9] the representative of Egypt conveyed a letter from the Minister for Foreign Affairs of Egypt stating that Ethiopia had informed his country that it had resumed, for the third consecutive year, the unilateral filling of the Grand Ethiopian Renaissance Dam, a process that was being undertaken in the absence of an agreement with Egypt and the Sudan to ensure that riparian States and communities were protected against potential adverse effects. The Minister also stated that, accordingly, Egypt had elected to inform the Council, pursuant to Article 35 of the Charter, that the question of the dam and the persistent Ethiopian policy of unilateralism in that regard constituted a situation that, as stipulated in Article 34, was causing international friction, the continuance of which could endanger international peace and security. He added that it was incumbent upon the Council to discharge its obligations under Article 24 by taking appropriate measures to ensure that the question was settled amicably. In a letter dated 2 August,[10] the representative of Ethiopia conveyed a letter from the Deputy Prime Minister and Minister for Foreign Affairs of Ethiopia in which he stated that, as provided under Article 33, Ethiopia, Egypt and the Sudan were pursuing a negotiated peaceful resolution regarding the dam and that, consistent with Article 52, the negotiations were being held under the auspices of the African Union. He therefore argued that there was no justification for bringing the matter to the attention of the Council.

With regard to Armenia and Azerbaijan, by letter dated 13 September addressed to the President of the Security Council,[11] the representative of Armenia transmitted a letter from the Minister for Foreign Affairs of Armenia, bringing to the attention of the Council the situation on the border between Armenia and Azerbaijan, which posed an imminent threat to international peace and security. Describing the situation in the lead-up to and surrounding the launching by Azerbaijan of "open large-scale aggression" against Armenia, the Minister stated that the actions of Azerbaijan were in violation of Articles 2 and 33 of the Charter, which provided that all Members should refrain in their international relations from the threat or use of force against the territorial integrity or political independence of any State, or in any other manner inconsistent with the purposes of the United Nations, and that the parties to any dispute should seek solutions exclusively by peaceful means. Noting that the unilateral actions of Azerbaijan constituted a real threat to international peace and security, the Minister requested an emergency meeting of the Council, on the basis of Article 35.

---

[1] See S/2022/565.
[2] See S/2022/567.
[3] See S/2022/587.
[4] See S/2022/688.
[5] See S/2022/565.
[6] See S/2022/528.
[7] For more information on the application of rule 3 of the provisional rules of procedure, see part II.
[8] See S/2022/567.
[9] See S/2022/587.
[10] See S/2022/598.
[11] See S/2022/688.

In 2022, the Council convened eight meetings pursuant to communications from Member States, seven of which were held under existing items and one under a new item on its agenda.[12] With regard to existing items, five meetings were held in connection with the Democratic People's Republic of Korea and one each concerning Iraq and Ukraine. Moreover, further to the letter from the representative of Armenia described above,[13] the Council convened a meeting under a new item entitled "Letter dated 13 September 2022 from the Permanent Representative of Armenia to the United Nations addressed to the President of the Security Council (S/2022/688)".

In addition to the five formal meetings, Council members also held informal consultations on 21 January further to a letter dated 18 January[14] from the representative of the United Arab Emirates addressed to the President of the Security Council to discuss the Houthi attacks on civilian infrastructure in the United Arab Emirates. More information is provided in table 1.

Table 1
Communications bringing disputes or situations to the attention of the Security Council that resulted in a Council meeting and/or informal consultations of the whole, 2022

Communication	*Action requested of the Security Council*	*Meeting record and date*
Threats to international peace and security		
Letter dated 18 January 2022 from the Permanent Representative of the United Arab Emirates to the United Nations addressed to the President of the Security Council (S/2022/35)	To hold a meeting on the Houthi attacks on civilian infrastructure in the United Arab Emirates	Informal consultations of the whole 21 January[a]
Letter dated 28 February 2014 from the Permanent Representative of Ukraine to the United Nations addressed to the President of the Security Council (S/2014/136)		
Letter dated 19 February 2022 from the Permanent Representative of Ukraine to the United Nations addressed to the Secretary-General (S/2022/133)	To hold an urgent meeting on the escalation of the conflict on the State border of Ukraine	S/PV.8970 21 February
Non-proliferation/Democratic People's Republic of Korea		
Letter dated 24 March 2022 from the Permanent Representative of Japan to the United Nations addressed to the President of the Security Council (S/2022/261)	To convene an urgent meeting to consider the ballistic missile launch by the Democratic People's Republic of Korea	S/PV.9004 25 March
Letter dated 9 May 2022 from the Permanent Representative of Japan to the United Nations addressed to the President of the Security Council (S/2022/379)	To convene an urgent meeting to consider the ballistic missile launch by the Democratic People's Republic of Korea	S/PV.9030 11 May
Letter dated 4 October 2022 from the Chargé d'affaires a.i. of the Permanent Mission of Japan to the United Nations addressed to the President of the Security Council (S/2022/742)	To convene an urgent meeting to consider the ballistic missile launch by the Democratic People's Republic of Korea	S/PV.9146 5 October

[12] For more information on the applicable provisional rules of procedure concerning the convening of Council meetings, see part II, sect. II.

[13] See S/2022/688. See also S/2022/729.

[14] See S/2022/35.

Communication	*Action requested of the Security Council*	*Meeting record and date*
Letter dated 3 November 2022 from the Permanent Representative of Japan to the United Nations addressed to the President of the Security Council (S/2022/829)	To convene an urgent meeting to consider the ballistic missile launches by the Democratic People's Republic of Korea	S/PV.9183 4 November
Letter dated 18 November 2022 from the Permanent Representative of Japan to the United Nations addressed to the President of the Security Council (S/2022/870)	To convene an urgent meeting to consider the ballistic missile launch by the Democratic People's Republic of Korea	S/PV.9197 21 November
Letter dated 18 November 2022 from the Permanent Representative of the Republic of Korea to the United Nations addressed to the President of the Security Council (S/2022/871)	To promptly hold a meeting to consult on and respond to the intercontinental ballistic missile launch by the Democratic People's Republic of Korea	S/PV.9197 21 November
The situation concerning Iraq		
Letter dated 22 July 2022 from the Permanent Representative of Iraq to the United Nations addressed to the President of the Security Council (S/2022/574)	To hold an emergency meeting to discuss the artillery bombardment by Türkiye in Dahuk Governorate in the Kurdistan Region of Iraq	S/PV.9100 26 July
Letter dated 13 September 2022 from the Permanent Representative of Armenia to the United Nations addressed to the President of the Security Council (S/2022/688)		
Letter dated 13 September 2022 from the Permanent Representative of Armenia to the United Nations addressed to the President of the Security Council (S/2022/688)	To convene an emergency meeting in relation to the large-scale aggression of Azerbaijan against Armenia	S/PV.9132 15 September

[a] See A/77/2, chap. 29.

Other communications from Member States

Member States also brought other matters to the attention of the Council that did not result in a meeting. For example, in a letter dated 5 August addressed to the President of the Council,[15] the representative of Pakistan transmitted a letter from the Minister for Foreign Affairs of Pakistan concerning what he described as the continuing worsening situation in Jammu and Kashmir. The Minister noted that 5 August 2022 marked the completion of three years of Indian "unilateral and illegal actions aimed at consolidating its occupation of Jammu and Kashmir", which he described as violations of international law. He concluded by underlining the strong desire of Pakistan to have the Council and the Secretary-General make concerted efforts to promote a peaceful settlement of the Jammu and Kashmir dispute in accordance with the relevant Council resolutions and the wishes of the Kashmiri people, by fully utilizing the modalities provided for in Chapter VI of the Charter, including Articles 33 and 34, as well as Article 99.

In a letter dated 10 August addressed to the President of the Security Council,[16] the representative of the Democratic Republic of the Congo transmitted a note from the Deputy Prime Minister and Minister for Foreign Affairs of the Democratic Republic of the Congo, noting that his Government had been informed on the basis of media sources that the Group of Experts on the Democratic Republic of the

[15] See S/2022/600.
[16] See S/2022/610.

Congo had stated in a report that it had "solid evidence" that Rwandan troops had carried out military operations in the eastern part of the country by participating directly in attacks against Congolese military personnel and by equipping and providing reinforcements to the "terrorist group" Mouvement du 23 mars ("M23"). In that regard, the Government of the Democratic Republic of the Congo requested the Council, among other things, to urgently convene an open meeting to consider the report.[17]

By letter dated 15 August,[18] the representative of Mali transmitted a letter from the Minister for Foreign Affairs and International Cooperation of Mali concerning violations of the country's airspace by the Barkhane force of France. The Minister invited the Council, as the guarantor of international peace and security, to take action to ensure that France immediately cease its acts of aggression against Mali, and requested the Council to hold an emergency meeting on the matter.

In a letter dated 9 December addressed to the Secretary-General and the President of the Security Council,[19] the representatives of Libya and Türkiye noted their rejection of the arguments and allegations contained in the letter dated 17 November from the representative of Greece[20] with respect to the signing of a memorandum of understanding between the Government of National Unity of Libya and the Government of Türkiye on 3 October on cooperation in the field of hydrocarbons. Among other points, the representatives of Libya and Türkiye underscored that they did not accept the objection of Greece to the memorandum on the ground that it violated Greek sovereign rights, and stated that Greece was not entitled to such rights in the maritime areas delimited between Libya and Türkiye. Moreover, the representatives asserted that their Governments, guided by the principles of the Charter, reiterated that conflicts in the Eastern Mediterranean and the Aegean were best resolved through the peaceful means as stipulated in Article 33 of the Charter, on the basis of the mutual consent of the parties.

B. Referrals by the Secretary-General

Article 99 of the Charter provides that the Secretary-General may bring to the attention of the Council any matter which in his or her opinion may threaten the maintenance of international peace and security. Like Article 35, Article 99 does not specify the means by which the Secretary-General may bring such a matter to the attention of the Council. During the period under review, the Secretary-General did not invoke Article 99, either directly or by implication. That notwithstanding, the Secretary-General continued to draw the attention of the Council to situations on its agenda that were deteriorating or with respect to which he requested the Council to take urgent action.

In his letters transmitting the monthly reports of the Director General of the Organisation for the Prohibition of Chemical Weapons submitted pursuant to paragraph 12 of resolution 2118 (2013) on the elimination of the chemical weapons programme of the Syrian Arab Republic,[21] the Secretary-General continued to note that the use of chemical weapons was intolerable and impunity for their use equally unacceptable. He pointed to unity in the Council as being essential to fulfilling the urgent obligation of accountability.

During meetings, the Secretary-General and other senior Secretariat officials also drew the attention of the Council to the deterioration of situations on the Council's agenda that threatened international peace and security.

In connection with Ukraine, the Secretary-General, the Under-Secretary-General for Political and Peacebuilding Affairs and other senior Secretariat officials gave briefings to the Council on events in the lead-up to and following the escalation of the conflict.[22] For example, at a meeting held on 31 January

---

[17] For more information about the sanctions measures concerning the Democratic Republic of the Congo, see part VII, sect. III. For more information about the work of the Committee established pursuant to resolution 1533 (2004) concerning the Democratic Republic of the Congo, see part IX, sect. I.

[18] See S/2022/622.

[19] See S/2022/936.

[20] See A/77/604.

[21] See S/2022/76, S/2022/181, S/2022/281, S/2022/365, S/2022/441, S/2022/530, S/2022/585, S/2022/658, S/2022/727, S/2022/828, S/2022/897 and S/2022/1016.

[22] For more information on items relating to Ukraine, see part I, sects. 19 and 34.

under the item entitled "Threats to international peace and security",[23] the Under-Secretary-General noted reports that more than 100,000 troops and heavy weaponry from the Russian Federation were positioned along the border with Ukraine and that unspecified numbers were also reportedly being deployed to Belarus ahead of large-scale joint military exercises in February on the borders with Ukraine, Poland and the Baltic States. She added that any escalation or new conflict would deal another serious blow to the architecture so painstakingly built up over the past 75 years to maintain international peace and security. At a meeting held on 21 February under the item entitled "Letter dated 28 February 2014 from the Permanent Representative of Ukraine to the United Nations addressed to the President of the Security Council (S/2014/136)",[24] the Under-Secretary-General expressed concern about the escalating shelling across the contact line in Ukraine, reportedly leading to a number of casualties. Noting that the risk of major conflict was real and needed to be prevented at all costs, she assured the Council of the full commitment of the Secretary-General to working towards a diplomatic resolution of the crisis.

At a meeting held on 15 September under the item entitled "Protection of civilians in armed conflict",[25] the Under-Secretary-General for Humanitarian Affairs and Emergency Relief Coordinator, recalling the request of the Council to be swiftly informed when the risk of conflict-induced famine and widespread food insecurity occurred, noted the white note of the Secretariat shared with Council members highlighting four contexts in which that risk was clear, namely Ethiopia, north-east Nigeria, South Sudan and Yemen. He stated that more than 200,000 people were already at risk of famine. In that regard, he called on Member States to pursue peaceful and negotiated resolutions to conflicts and other situations of violence, remind and encourage States and armed groups to abide by their obligations under international humanitarian law and international human rights law, support an integrated response to address the underlying drivers of acute food insecurity and sustain humanitarian financing for those crises. He also highlighted the impact of climate change on famine in Somalia and pointed to the need for the attention of the climate community and the money pledged by Member States.

C. Referrals by the General Assembly

Under Article 11 (3) of the Charter, the General Assembly may call the attention of the Council to situations that are likely to endanger international peace and security. During the period under review, the Assembly did not refer any such situations to the Council pursuant to that Article.[26]

II. Investigation of disputes and fact-finding

Article 34

The Security Council may investigate any dispute, or any situation which might lead to international friction or give rise to a dispute, in order to determine whether the continuance of the dispute or situation is likely to endanger the maintenance of international peace and security.

Note

Article 34 of the Charter of the United Nations provides that the Council may investigate any dispute or any situation which might lead to international friction or give rise to a dispute. On that basis, the Council may determine whether the continuation of the dispute or situation is likely to endanger the maintenance of international peace and security. Article 34 does not prevent the Secretary-General or other organs from performing investigative functions, nor does it limit the Council's general competence to obtain knowledge of the relevant facts of any dispute or situation by dispatching a fact-finding or investigative mission.

[23] See S/PV.8960.
[24] See S/PV.8970.
[25] See S/PV.9133.
[26] For more information regarding the relations between the Council and the General Assembly, see part IV, sect. I.

Section II provides an overview of the practice of the Council relating to fact-finding and investigation in accordance with Article 34 of the Charter, in three subsections. Subsection A relates to Council missions; subsection B to investigative and fact-finding functions of the Secretary-General; and subsection C to other instances of investigative functions acknowledged by the Council.

During the reporting period, the Council did not make any explicit reference to Article 34 of the Charter in its decisions, nor did any speaker explicitly invoke that Charter provision during Council meetings. However, Article 34 was explicitly referred to in two communications addressed to the Council concerning the operation of the Grand Ethiopian Renaissance Dam[27] and the situation in Jammu and Kashmir.[28]

During the year under review, the Council did not dispatch any mission to the field. In its decisions, the Council acknowledged the investigative functions of the Secretary-General in connection with the situations in the Central African Republic, the Democratic Republic of the Congo, Iraq, Mali and South Sudan. Consistent with recent practice, the Council renewed the mandate of the United Nations Investigative Team to Promote Accountability for Crimes Committed by Da'esh/Islamic State in Iraq and the Levant, established pursuant to resolution 2379 (2017). The Council also recognized the investigative work of the International Civil Aviation Organization in connection with the landing of a civilian aircraft in Belarus and the Office of the United Nations High Commissioner for Human Rights on the situations in the Central African Republic, the Democratic Republic of the Congo, Mali and South Sudan. In addition, Council members deliberated on the investigative functions of the Secretary-General, the Human Rights Council and the Organisation for the Prohibition of Chemical Weapons (OPCW) concerning Libya, the Syrian Arab Republic, Ukraine and the implementation of resolution 2231 (2015) concerning the Islamic Republic of Iran.

A. Security Council missions

In 2022, the Council did not dispatch any missions to the field. Council missions were, however, referenced in a communication submitted to the Council by Member States and discussed in Council meetings during the period under review.

In a letter dated 16 February addressed to the President of the Security Council,[29] the representative of Finland transmitted the report of the nineteenth annual workshop for the newly elected members of the Council, held in New York on 18 and 19 November 2021. According to the report, several outgoing members of the Council emphasized the importance of visiting missions to the work of the Council, with one member expressing regret that there had been only one visiting mission during that member's term because of the coronavirus disease (COVID-19) pandemic, and others imploring the incoming members to visit the field as often as they could. It was also indicated in the report that several speakers had noted that diplomats gained a better understanding of situations addressed by the Council when witnessing them first-hand.

The role of Council missions was also raised in several Council meetings. For example, in an open debate held on 3 November under the item entitled "Peacebuilding and sustaining peace",[30] the Executive Director of Security Council Report stated that, to signal the Council's strong interest in sustained peace, and in tandem with the work of the Peacebuilding Commission, Council members could check back in with the country concerned from time to time. In that regard, she suggested that the Council could conduct visiting missions to Sierra Leone, Côte d'Ivoire and Liberia, countries whose United Nations peace operations had closed in 2014, 2017 and 2018, respectively. Furthermore, in an open debate held on 14 December under the item entitled "Maintenance of international peace and security",[31] the representative of Norway stated that the Council had to be more in touch with the direct impact of its decisions on the lives of people on the ground. In that regard, she noted that the Council would benefit from more informal situational-awareness briefings from the Secretariat and more visiting missions by the Council and that

[27] See S/2022/587.
[28] See S/2022/600.
[29] See S/2022/128.
[30] See S/PV.9181.
[31] See S/PV.9220.

there was great potential for impact through joint visiting missions, including with the Peace and Security Council of the African Union.

The Council also discussed the value of Council missions during the annual open debate on the working methods of the Council held under the item entitled "Implementation of the note by the President of the Security Council (S/2017/507)" (case 1).

Case 1
Implementation of the note by the President of the Security Council (S/2017/507)

On 28 June, at the initiative of Albania, which held the presidency of the Council for the month and whose representative held the Chair of the Informal Working Group on Documentation and Other Procedural Questions,[32] the Council held the annual open debate on its working methods under the item entitled "Implementation of the note by the President of the Security Council (S/2017/507)".[33] The Council heard briefings by the Director of Security Council Procedure and co-author of the fourth edition of *The Procedure of the UN Security Council* and the Executive Director of Security Council Report.[34]

In her statement, the Executive Director of Security Council Report noted that Council visiting missions offered a chance for members to engage with one another less formally, as well as to be exposed, together, to facts on the ground. Recalling the impact of visiting missions, she cited the examples of missions to the Lake Chad basin in March 2017, which led to the adoption of resolution 2349 (2017) addressing the negative security, humanitarian and environmental dimensions of the Boko Haram crisis in the region, as well as the missions to Colombia in May 2017 and July 2019, which signalled the Council's political support for the implementation of the Final Agreement for Ending the Conflict and Building a Stable and Lasting Peace of 2016. The Executive Director expressed the view that the Council might also prioritize visits with regional and subregional organizations to engage with them on conflict prevention and step-up engagement with the field through virtual reality headsets and mini-missions. Suggesting a more systematic way of deciding on visiting missions, she noted that one possibility would be to have the Informal Working Group on Documentation and Other Procedural Questions, at the start of the year, consult and select three possible situations that could benefit from a Council visit, which could then be supplemented by other trips.

In the subsequent discussion, the representative of Switzerland, speaking on behalf of the members of the Accountability, Coherence and Transparency Group, said that visiting missions by the Council were an important means to gather the views of a broad range of stakeholders and gain first-hand understanding of dynamics on the ground. She encouraged the Council to continue that practice and to provide a debriefing to the wider membership upon its return. The representative of Luxembourg also encouraged the Council to resume its practice of field visits, which allowed for discussions with a broad range of actors and allowed the Council to get a direct understanding of dynamics on the ground and provide a debriefing to all Member States upon its return. The representative of Egypt also noted that Member States should be informed about the Council's visits.[35]

The representative of Portugal recommended the inclusion of the Chair of the Peacebuilding Commission – and the Chairs of the country-specific configurations, where applicable – in the Council's field visits.[36] In the view of Portugal, that would allow for a more holistic approach to the whole of the peace continuum and could be useful even if the country or countries visited had not yet engaged with the Commission.

The representative of Cyprus expressed the view that technology could not substitute for the knowledge of local circumstances that the Council needed to have to deal with a situation effectively, adding that such knowledge was best gained through visits on the ground.[37]

---

[32] A concept note was circulated by letter dated 21 June 2022 (S/2022/499).
[33] See S/PV.9079 and S/PV.9079 (Resumption 1). An analytical summary of the debate was circulated after the meeting in a letter dated 10 November 2022 (S/2022/842).
[34] See S/PV.9079.
[35] See S/PV.9079 (Resumption 1).
[36] See S/PV.9079.
[37] See S/PV.9079 (Resumption 1).

B. Investigative and fact-finding functions of the Secretary-General

In 2022, the investigative and fact-finding functions of the Secretary-General were acknowledged and referred to in decisions of the Council, as well as during its deliberations and in communications addressed to it, as detailed below.

Decisions of the Council

In its decisions adopted in 2022, the Council acknowledged the investigative and fact-finding functions of the Secretary-General in connection with the situations in the Central African Republic, the Democratic Republic of the Congo, Iraq, Mali and South Sudan, and with the thematic item entitled "Threats to international peace and security". The relevant provisions of those decisions are set out in table 2 below.

Table 2
Decisions relating to investigative and/or fact-finding activities by the Secretary-General, 2022

Decision and date	*Provision*
The situation in the Central African Republic	
Resolution 2659 (2022) 14 November	Calls upon the Central African Republic authorities to follow up on the recommendations of the report of the mapping project describing serious violations and abuses of international human rights and violations of international humanitarian law committed within the territory of the Central African Republic between January 2003 and December 2015 (para. 24)
The situation concerning the Democratic Republic of the Congo	
Resolution 2641 (2022) 30 June	Taking note of the verdict rendered on 29 January 2022 by the Military Court of Ex-Kasai Occidental and of efforts towards ensuring accountability, reiterating the need for the Government of the Democratic Republic of the Congo to fully investigate the killing of the two members of the Group of Experts and the four Congolese nationals accompanying them and bring those responsible to justice, welcoming the work of the United Nations team, known as the Follow-On Mechanism, deployed to assist the Congolese authorities in their investigations, in agreement with the Congolese authorities, and further welcoming their continued cooperation (fifth preambular paragraph) Recalls the Secretary General's commitment that the United Nations will do everything possible to ensure that the perpetrators of the killing of the two members of the Group of Experts and the four Congolese nationals accompanying them are brought to justice and stresses the importance of a continued deployment by the Secretary-General of the Follow-on Mechanism, currently comprising a senior United Nations official, four technical experts and support staff, to the Democratic Republic of the Congo to assist with the national investigation, within existing resources (para. 12)
The situation concerning Iraq	
Resolution 2631 (2022) 26 May	Requests that the Special Representative of the Secretary-General and the United Nations Assistance Mission for Iraq, at the request of the Government of Iraq, shall: ... (d) promote accountability and the protection of human rights, and judicial and legal reform, with full respect for the sovereignty of Iraq, in order to strengthen the rule of law and improve governance in Iraq, in addition to supporting the work of the United Nations Investigative Team to Promote Accountability for Crimes Committed by Da'esh/Islamic State in Iraq and the Levant established in resolution 2379 (2017) (para. 2 (d))

Decision and date	Provision
The situation in Mali	
Resolution 2640 (2022) 29 June	Reiterating, in this regard, the importance of holding accountable all those responsible for such acts and that some of such acts referred to in the paragraph above may amount to crimes under the Rome Statute, taking note that, acting upon the referral of the transitional authorities of Mali dated 13 July 2012, the Prosecutor of the International Criminal Court opened on 16 January 2013 an investigation into alleged crimes committed on the territory of Mali since January 2012, and further taking note of the finalization of the work of the International Commission of Inquiry established in accordance with the Agreement and as requested by resolution 2364 (2017) (fifteenth preambular paragraph) Calls upon the Malian parties to agree on and set up a national mechanism to follow up on the recommendations of the International Commission of Inquiry (para. 10) Decides that the mandate of the United Nations Multidimensional Integrated Stabilization Mission in Mali shall include the following priority tasks: (a) *Support to the implementation of the Agreement on Peace and Reconciliation in Mali and to the full realization of the Political Transition* .... (iv) To support the implementation of the reconciliation and justice measures of the Agreement, especially in its part V, including to support the operations of the Truth, Justice and Reconciliation Commission and the follow-up of the recommendations of the International Commission of Inquiry, and to help ensuring the effectiveness of justice and corrections officials as well as Malian judicial institutions, particularly regarding the detention, investigation and prosecution of individuals suspected of, and sentencing of those found responsible for terrorism-related crimes, mass atrocities and transnational organized crime activities (including trafficking in persons, arms, drugs and natural resources, and the smuggling of migrants) (para. 26 (a) (iv))
Reports of the Secretary-General on Sudan and South Sudan	
Resolution 2625 (2022) 15 March	Expressing grave concern at ongoing reports of sexual and gender-based violence, including the findings of the report of the Secretary-General on conflict-related sexual violence to the Security Council (S/2021/312) of the use of sexual violence as a tactic by parties to the conflict against the civilian population in South Sudan, including use of rape and sexual slavery for the purpose of intimidation and punishment, based on perceived political affiliation, and employed as part of a strategy targeting members of ethnic groups, and where conflict-related sexual violence and other forms of violence against women and girls has persisted after the signing of the Revitalized Agreement, as documented in the February 2021 report published by the Office of the United Nations High Commissioner for Human Rights on "Access to Health for Survivors of Conflict-Related Sexual Violence in South Sudan", noting that some progress was observed by South Sudanese parties through implementation of action plans to address sexual violence in conflict, and underlining the urgency and importance of timely investigations to support accountability and the provision of assistance and protection to survivors and victims of sexual and gender-based violence (eleventh preambular paragraph) Expressing grave concern regarding the reports on the human rights situation in South Sudan issued by the United Nations Mission in South Sudan and the Secretary-General, including deeply disturbing reports of cases of extra-judicial executions reported in Warrap and Lakes States, further expressing grave concern that according to the African Union Commission of Inquiry report on South Sudan, released on 27 October 2015, and the reports of the Commission on Human Rights in South Sudan, released on 23 February 2018, 20 February 2019, 20 February 2020, and 19 February 2021 that war crimes and crimes against humanity may have been committed, emphasizing its expectation that these and other credible reports will be duly considered by any transitional justice mechanisms for South Sudan including those established pursuant to the Revitalized Agreement, stressing the importance of collection and preservation of evidence for eventual use by the Hybrid Court for South Sudan and other accountability mechanisms, and encouraging efforts in this regard (sixteenth preambular paragraph)

Decision and date	*Provision*
Threats to international peace and security	
Resolution 2651 (2022) 15 September	Underscoring the importance of sharing evidence collected by the Investigative Team established by resolution 2379 (2017) with the relevant Iraqi authorities, in a timely manner, for eventual use in fair and independent criminal proceedings, consistent with applicable international law and the Investigative Team's terms of reference (seventh preambular paragraph)
	Reaffirms its resolution 2379 (2017), by which the Investigative Team, headed by a Special Adviser, was established; and recalls the terms of reference approved by the Council (S/2018/119) (para. 1)
	Takes note of the request from the Government of Iraq contained in its letter dated 12 September 2022 (S/2022/687) and decides to extend until 17 September 2023 the mandate of the Special Adviser and the Team, with any further extension to be decided at the request of the Government of Iraq, or any other government that has requested the Team to collect evidence of acts that may amount to war crimes, crimes against humanity, or genocide, committed by Islamic State in Iraq and the Levant (ISIL/Da'esh) in its territory, in accordance with its resolution 2379 (2017) (para. 2)
	Requests the Special Adviser to continue to submit and present reports to the Council on the Team's activities every 180 days (para. 3)

Meetings of the Council

In 2022, speakers referred to the investigative authority of the Council and the role of the Secretary-General in several meetings of the Council. For example, during the meetings held under items relating to Ukraine, participants referred to the fact-finding mission launched by the Secretary-General concerning the incident at a detention facility in Olenivka on 29 July.[38] Similarly, consistent with prior practice, the Council held two meetings in 2022 to discuss the work of UNITAD.[39]

The most in-depth discussions concerning the investigative functions of the Council and the Secretary-General took place during meetings held under the items entitled "Maintenance of peace and security of Ukraine" (case 2), "Maintenance of international peace and security" (case 3) and "Threats to international peace and security" (case 4).

Case 2
Maintenance of peace and security of Ukraine

At a meeting held on 24 August under the item entitled "Maintenance of peace and security of Ukraine",[40] the Council heard a briefing by the Secretary-General on his trip to Ukraine and by the Under-Secretary-General for Political Affairs and Peacebuilding on the impact of the armed conflict over the previous six months. During the meeting, several speakers discussed the fact-finding mission established by the Secretary-General to investigate an incident involving the death of prisoners at the Olenivka detention facility on 29 July, as requested by the Russian Federation and Ukraine.

The Secretary-General stated that he was deeply disturbed by the allegations of violations of international humanitarian law and violations and abuses of human rights related to the armed conflict. He reported that work was ongoing to deploy the fact-finding mission, which he maintained had to be able to freely conduct its work, gather and analyse necessary information and find the facts. He added that it was imperative that the mission had safe, secure and unfettered access to all relevant places, people and evidence without any limitation, impediment or interference.

[38] See S/PV.9115 (European Union); S/PV.9126 (Norway and Latvia); S/PV.9135 (Czechia); and S/PV.9167 (United States).

[39] See S/PV.9059 and S/PV.9206.

[40] See S/PV.9115.

Addressing the Council via videoconference, the President of Ukraine said that the deliberate killing of Ukrainian prisoners of war in Olenivka had become one of the most terrible pages in the history of Europe and noted the need for a United Nations fact-finding mission, with a mandate covering all Ukrainian prisoners of war held by the forces of the Russian Federation. The representative of France stated that the reports about extrajudicial killings and acts of torture against Ukrainian prisoners, in particular in the village of Olenivka, were shocking, and added that the Russian Federation had to comply with international humanitarian law and international human rights law, which applied in all international armed conflicts. The representative of Mexico expressed support for the establishment of a fact-finding mission on the alleged war crimes committed in Olenivka. He noted that accountability was a fundamental pillar of the multilateral system and that those responsible for the crimes that had been and were being committed in Ukraine – or would be committed in future – had to be brought to justice. Welcoming the active involvement of the Secretary-General, the representative of the European Union also welcomed the establishment of a fact-finding mission to investigate the incident at Olenivka.

Case 3
Maintenance of international peace and security

At a meeting held on 26 October under the item entitled "Maintenance of international peace and security",[41] the Council heard a briefing by the Under-Secretary-General for Legal Affairs and United Nations Legal Counsel in connection with the nature of the work performed by the Secretary-General and the Secretariat with respect to resolution 2231 (2015). The meeting took place against the backdrop of the letters submitted by the representatives of, France, Germany and the United Kingdom[42] and the United States[43] concerning their requests for a technical and impartial investigation concerning the transfer of unmanned aerial vehicles from the Islamic Republic of Iran to the Russian Federation by the Secretariat team responsible for monitoring the implementation of resolution 2231 (2015).

Opening the meeting, the Under-Secretary-General recalled that the note by the President of the Security Council dated 16 January 2016 (S/2016/44), in which were set forth practical arrangements and procedures for the Council for carrying out tasks related to the implementation of resolution 2231 (2015), in particular with respect to the provisions specified in paragraphs 2 to 7 of annex B to that resolution, and required the Secretariat to report to the Council every six months on the implementation of the resolution.[44] Furthermore, he pointed out that in paragraph 7 of the note it was anticipated that the report would include findings and recommendations and that, consistent with that, the Secretariat reported on the implementation of the restrictive measures in annex B that were in force during the reporting period. The Under-Secretary-General concluded by noting that the Secretary-General had not received any request that supplemented or modified the nature and scope of the work done in preparation for his report to the Council and that, absent further guidance by the Council, he would continue to prepare the reports in the manner in which they had been prepared to date.

Following the briefing, Council members deliberated on the investigative functions of the Secretary-General. Specifically, citing the note by the President of the Security Council of 16 January 2016 (S/2016/44), the representative of the Russian Federation expressed the view that the Council had not given the Secretariat any mandate to conduct an investigation. He asserted that the demand by Western delegations for the Secretariat to investigate the drone issue set an extremely dangerous precedent for the work of the United Nations and that, from the legal perspective, they were seeking to expand the powers of the Secretariat and give it inappropriate functions by infringing on the prerogatives of the Council. The representative of the Russian Federation stressed that the fact that Secretary-General had been tasked with preparing reports on the implementation of resolution 2231 (2015) did not mean that the Secretariat had been, by default, authorized to collect data and respond to reports from Member States about possible violations of the resolution. Moreover, according to the representative, the only thing that the Secretariat could do after receiving the letters from France, Germany, the United Kingdom and the United States, was to transmit them to the Facilitator for the implementation of resolution 2231 (2015) for circulation

[41] See S/PV.9167.
[42] See S/2022/781.
[43] See S/2022/782.
[44] See S/PV.9167.

among Council members and the report of the Secretary-General could only reflect the fact that those letters had been received. Expressing a similar view, the representative of the Islamic Republic of Iran stated that resolution 2231 (2015) provided no legal basis for such an investigation and that any misuse of the functions described in the note by the President of the Security Council of 16 January 2016 (S/2016/44) would be illegal and in clear violation of the Secretariat's mandate.

In contrast, the representative of the United States stated that the request of his delegation and those of other Council members had not been instructions, but rather requests to take appropriate action. He added that many Member States, including the Russian Federation, had made such requests to the Secretary-General, such as in August 2022 when the Russian Federation had requested that an investigation into killings at a prison in eastern Ukraine and, in response to which, the Secretary-General had decided to conduct a fact-finding mission. According to the representative of the United States, far from constituting instructions to the Secretary-General, such requests for investigations were common and appropriate. He held the view that it was well within the authority of the Secretary-General to investigate violations of resolution 2231 (2015) by the Russian Federation and the Islamic Republic of Iran, referring in that regard to the 13 reports of the Secretary-General summarizing the investigations of the Secretariat and its findings on non-compliance over the past seven years. Similarly, the representative of Norway noted that many of the findings of the 13 reports of the Secretary-General had been based on first-hand assessments of evidence collected on the ground and that many of the assessments had been initiated on the basis of letters from Member States with information concerning potential violations and actions inconsistent with the provisions of annex B to resolution 2231 (2015). The representative of the United Arab Emirates recalled that her country had welcomed the Secretariat's team on resolution 2231 (2015) to the United Arab Emirates to inspect the weapons of the Houthis and their debris or remnants, and added that, on all occasions, the Secretariat had conducted independent and impartial inspections that the United Arab Emirates believed were important to the findings and recommendations that it then submitted to the Council.

The representative of France stated that his delegation would like the Secretariat to investigate the issue of the provision of drones by the Islamic Republic of Iran to the Russian Federation and inform the members of the Council so that the Secretary-General could report accurately on the implementation of resolution 2231 (2015). Similarly, the representative of the United Kingdom recalled that his delegation expressed support for an impartial expert investigation to be conducted by the Secretariat, which he viewed entirely in line with precedent and normal practice. The representative of Ireland welcomed the invitation of Ukraine to the Secretariat to visit the country to inspect recovered unmanned aerial vehicles with regard to the implementation of resolution 2231 (2015) by the parties, and expressed the expectation that the Secretariat would keep the Council informed as appropriate on the matter. She held the view that the necessary technical investigations that the Secretariat conducted were an integral part of preparing the findings of the Secretary-General and that no further decision by the Council was necessary in that regard.

The representative of Mexico noted that, since there had been a request to the Secretariat to investigate the origin of the drones used in attacks on the civilian population in Ukraine and since their possible Iranian manufacture had been highlighted, his delegation considered the request to be in accord with the provisions of resolution 2231 (2015). He further stated that the Secretary-General also had the authority under the Charter to undertake investigations resulting from the requests made by Member States through the competent organs, as a result of established practice, based on Article 99 of the Charter, which defined the role of the Secretary-General in matters of prevention in relation to situations with the potential to endanger international peace and security.

The representative of Kenya proposed several ways to renew the utilization of and to strengthen the Secretary-General's good offices for the prevention and resolution of conflicts. Specifically, she stressed the need to redefine the impartiality and protect the independence of the Secretariat and stated that the Secretary-General must be fully partial to the Charter and should fully exercise Article 99 without regard for the approval or disapproval of any State. Furthermore, she recalled that in its resolution 46/59 the General Assembly had recognized the need for the Council to have knowledge of all relevant facts in performing the functions relevant to its mandate and for the fact-finding capabilities of the Secretary-General, as well as the requirement for him to monitor the state of international peace and security in order to provide early warning and to share relevant information with the Council, while making use of his information-gathering capabilities. The representative of Kenya underscored that, in the situation in Ukraine, rather than argue about the facts on the ground, where most members of the Council had no independent means to ascertain their veracity, Council members should challenge the parties to agree to United Nations fact-finding and verification, which was key to preventing and minimizing actions that were contrary to the Charter and international law.

The representative of Ukraine condemned the unacceptable pressure and threats to reconsider cooperation with the United Nations if the Secretariat used its authority to investigate the implementation of resolution 2231 (2015). She recalled that Ukraine had officially addressed the Council to request that the relevant independent investigation into the matter be started,[45] and expressed the belief that the findings of the Secretariat's investigations would significantly contribute to assessing the implementation of resolution 2231 (2015).

Case 4
Threats to international peace and security

At a meeting held on 2 November under the item entitled "Threats to international peace and security",[46] the Council had before it a draft resolution submitted by the Russian Federation,[47] in which it was proposed that the Council set up a commission consisting of all members of the Council to investigate the claims against the United States and Ukraine contained in the complaint of the Russian Federation regarding the compliance with obligations under the Convention on the Prohibition of the Development, Production and Stockpiling of Bacteriological (Biological) and Toxin Weapons and on their Destruction, in the context of the activities of biological laboratories in the territory of Ukraine. The draft resolution was not adopted, having failed to obtain the required number of votes.[48]

Following the vote, Council members exchanged views on the proposed investigative commission. The representative of the Russian Federation recalled that, according to section 2 of article VI of the Convention, each State party undertook to cooperate in carrying out any investigation which the Council might initiate, in accordance with the provisions of the Charter, on the basis of the complaint received by the Council.[49] He added that, regardless of the outcome of the vote, the Russian Federation retained its questions for the United States and Ukraine to answer and would continue to act within the framework of the Convention and make efforts to establish all the facts having to do with the violations by the United States and Ukraine of their obligations under the Convention. Also expressing regret that the series of questions raised by the Russian Federation had not been fully answered, the representative of China held the view that a fair and transparent investigation by the Council could effectively address compliance concerns and help to uphold the authority and effectiveness of the Convention.

The representative of Mexico noted that his delegation was not opposed to the Council being seized of a situation covered by article VI of the Convention and that the absence of a precedent in the Council's practice was not a reason to dismiss a priori the request contained in the draft resolution. However, according to the representative, the condition set forth in article VI of the Convention, namely, that the party alleging violations of the Convention must provide credible evidence to trigger an investigation at a later stage, had not been met. He held the view that it was unrealistic to think that a commission such as the one proposed could have been set up, granted a mandate to carry out an investigation and submit a report with recommendations to the Council within 28 days. He also stated that no State could be "judge and jury" of any commission that claimed to be independent and objective and that the Russian Federation should be excluded, as it was one of the parties involved in the armed conflict in Ukraine. Lastly, the representative of Mexico cited the establishment of the United Nations Monitoring, Verification and Inspection Commission in Iraq pursuant to resolution 1284 (1999) as a good example of the Council's experience in investigating alleged programmes of weapons of mass destruction.[50]

---

[45] See S/2022/771.

[46] See S/PV.9180.

[47] See S/2022/821.

[48] The draft resolution received 2 votes in favour (China, Russian Federation), 3 against (France, United Kingdom, United States) and 10 abstentions (Albania, Brazil, Gabon, Ghana, India, Ireland, Kenya, Mexico, Norway, United Arab Emirates).

[49] See S/PV.9180.

[50] For more information on the establishment of the United Nations Monitoring, Verification and Inspection Commission, see *Repertoire*, *Supplement 1996–1999*, chap. V.

Several other Council members that had abstained in the vote expressed similar views to those of the representative of Mexico. Specifically, the representative of Ireland stated that her country did not see the proposed investigation by the Council as either justifiable or useful.[51] The representative of Albania said that the Russian Federation had yet to provide credible evidence to justify its requests for an investigation under article VI of the Convention. The representative of Norway concluded that the Russian Federation had failed to demonstrate probable cause for further investigative steps and that its allegations did not justify a request for consideration by the Council under article VI.

The representative of Kenya held the view that any credible allegations of the use of any weapon of mass destruction should be treated with the seriousness that they deserved and be duly, transparently and impartially investigated. Such an investigation would require that all parties concerned had confidence and faith in the Secretariat to conduct it in an independent, transparent and professional manner. The representative of Brazil noted that his delegation believed that, at the moment, the necessary conditions for the initiation of investigations under article VI of the Convention had not been met. The representative of Ghana held the view that a necessary condition for the invocation of article VI for a formal investigation into a complaint should be a compelling prima facie case.

Communications submitted to the Council

In 2022, the Secretary-General undertook one new investigative action by establishing the fact-finding mission to look into the incident at the Olenivka detention facility in Ukraine on 29 July.[52] In that connection, by a letter dated 29 July addressed to the Secretary-General,[53] the representative of Ukraine transmitted a statement by the Ministry of Foreign Affairs of Ukraine, which contained a reference to the "shelling of a correctional facility in the occupied Olenivka, where Ukrainian prisoners of war [were] believed to be held". Furthermore, by letter dated 24 August addressed to the President of the Security Council,[54] the representative of Estonia transmitted a joint statement by the Baltic States (Estonia, Latvia and Lithuania) in connection with the Council meeting held on 24 August under the item entitled "Maintenance of peace and security of Ukraine",[55] in which they underlined the importance of continued United Nations monitoring, documenting and reporting on violations against civilians through its established mechanisms. In that regard, Estonia, Latvia and Lithuania indicated that they supported and welcomed the decision of the Secretary-General to establish a fact-finding mission with regard to the attack against the Olenivka detention facility on 29 July.

With respect to ongoing investigations, in accordance with the existing practice, by his letters dated 26 May and 7 November addressed to the President of the Security Council,[56] the Special Adviser of the Secretary-General and Head of UNITAD transmitted to the Council the eighth and ninth reports on the activities of the Investigative Team.

With respect to the International Commission of Inquiry for Mali, established by the Secretary-General in 2018 and mandated to investigate allegations of abuses and serious violations of international human rights law and international humanitarian law, including allegations of conflict-related sexual violence, committed throughout the territory of Mali between 2012 and 2018, in his report on the situation in Mali of 2 June 2022, the Secretary-General noted that there had been no tangible progress by the authorities to implement the recommendations put forward by the Commission.[57]

Concerning the investigative activities relating to the implementation of resolution 2231 (2015), Member States addressed several communications to the Council in which they expressed their positions on the matter, including, in some instances, on the investigatory actions taken by the Secretariat.[58]

[51] See S/PV.9180.
[52] See S/PV.9115.
[53] See S/2022/590.
[54] See S/2022/640.
[55] See S/PV.9115.
[56] See S/2022/434 and S/2022/836. For more information, see also part I, sect. 34 on "Threats to international peace and security".
[57] See S/2022/446.
[58] See S/2022/3, S/2022/15, S/2022/34, S/2022/415, S/2022/464, S/2022/514, S/2022/544, S/2022/771, S/2022/776, S/2022/781, S/2022/782, S/2022/783, S/2022/796, S/2022/878, S/2022/882, S/2022/889, S/2022/908, S/2022/911, S/2022/914, S/2022/915, S/2022/922, S/2022/923, S/2022/962. See also case 3 above.

C. Other instances of investigative functions acknowledged by the Security Council

During the year under review, the investigative functions of other bodies of the United Nations were also recognized and acknowledged in decisions, deliberations and communications of the Council, as detailed below.

Decisions of the Council

In 2022, the Council recognized the investigative functions of OHCHR and the Human Rights Council, in relation to the situations in the Central African Republic, Mali and South Sudan.[59] Table 3 contains the provisions of Council decisions referring to such functions.

Table 3
Decisions relating to investigation and inquiry by United Nations bodies and related organizations, 2022

Decision and date	*Provision*
The situation in the Central African Republic	
Resolution 2659 (2022) 14 November	Taking note of the joint United Nations Multidimensional Integrated Stabilization Mission in the Central African Republic-Office of the United Nations High Commissioner for Human Rights annual report to the Security Council on violations and abuses of human rights and violations of international humanitarian law committed in the Central African Republic, and noting with concern that violations and abuses were committed by all parties to the conflict, including armed groups, welcoming the response submitted by the Central African Republic authorities to address the report's findings, and expressing support for the implementation of the preventive and corrective measures proposed by the government (ninth preambular paragraph)
	Calls on the Central African Republic authorities to follow up on the recommendations of the report of the mapping project describing serious violations and abuses of international human rights and violations of international humanitarian law committed within the territory of the Central African Republic between January 2003 and December 2015 (para. 24)
The situation in Mali	
Resolution 2640 (2022) 29 June	Expresses serious concerns about repeated and increased allegations of violations and abuses of international human rights law and violations of international humanitarian law by the Malian Defence and Security Forces in the conduct of counterterrorism operations, as documented by the United Nations Multidimensional Integrated Stabilization Mission in Mali, including in the quarterly note published on 30 May 2022, takes note of the measures announced in response to these allegations, and urges the Transition Government of Mali to continue implementing such measures, notably by carrying out transparent, credible and timely investigations and holding accountable those responsible, and further urges the Transition Government to take measures to prevent further violations and abuses (para. 31)
Reports of the Secretary-General on Sudan and South Sudan	
Resolution 2625 (2022) 15 March	Expressing grave concern at ongoing reports of sexual and gender-based violence, including the findings of the report of the Secretary-General on Conflict Related Sexual Violence to the Security Council (S/2021/312) of the use of sexual violence as a tactic by parties to the conflict against the civilian population in South Sudan, including use of rape and sexual slavery for the purpose of intimidation and punishment, based on perceived political affiliation, and employed as part of a strategy targeting members of ethnic groups, and where conflict-related sexual violence and other forms of violence against women and girls has persisted after the signing of the Revitalized Agreement, as documented in the February 2021 report published by the Office

[59] For further information on relations with other United Nations organs, see part IV.

Decision and date	Provision
	of the United Nations High Commissioner for Human Rights on "Access to Health for Survivors of Conflict-Related Sexual Violence in South Sudan", noting that some progress was observed by South Sudanese parties through implementation of action plans to address sexual violence in conflict, and underlining the urgency and importance of timely investigations to support accountability and the provision of assistance and protection to survivors and victims of sexual and gender-based violence (eleventh preambular paragraph) Expressing grave concern regarding the reports on the human rights situation in South Sudan issued by the United Nations Mission in South Sudan and the Secretary-General, including deeply disturbing reports of cases of extra-judicial executions reported in Warrap and Lakes States, further expressing grave concern that according to the African Union Commission of Inquiry report on South Sudan, released on 27 October 2015, and the reports of the Commission on Human Rights in South Sudan, released on 23 February 2018, 20 February 2019, 20 February 2020, and 19 February 2021 that war crimes and crimes against humanity may have been committed, emphasizing its expectation that these and other credible reports will be duly considered by any transitional justice mechanisms for South Sudan including those established pursuant to the Revitalized Agreement, stressing the importance of collection and preservation of evidence for eventual use by the Hybrid Court for South Sudan and other accountability mechanisms, and encouraging efforts in this regard (sixteenth preambular paragraph)

Meetings of the Council

In 2022, the Council discussed the investigations of other bodies of the United Nations and related organizations such as the work of the OPCW Investigation and Identification Team and fact-finding mission in the Syrian Arab Republic,[60] as well as the Independent Fact-Finding Mission on Libya established by the Human Rights Council.[61] The most in-depth discussions were held in connection with the Independent International Commission of Inquiry on Ukraine established by the Human Rights Council to investigate violations of human rights and international humanitarian law since the outbreak of the war on 24 February 2022 and the Fact-Finding Investigation Team instituted by the International Civil Aviation Organization to investigate the forced landing of Ryanair flight FR-4978 in Minsk on 23 May 2021. The discussions were held, respectively, under the items entitled "Maintenance of peace and security of Ukraine" (case 5) and "Threats to international peace and security" (case 6).

Case 5
Maintenance of peace and security of Ukraine

On 21 October, at a meeting held under the item entitled "Maintenance of peace and security of Ukraine",[62] as part of their discussions, Council members and other speakers referred to the work of the Independent International Commission of Inquiry on Ukraine, established by the Human Rights Council on 4 March,[63] to investigate violations of human rights and international humanitarian law since the outbreak of the war on 24 February.

In her briefing to the Council, the Under-Secretary-General for Political and Peacebuilding Affairs noted that the Independent International Commission of Inquiry on Ukraine had submitted its report to the General Assembly,[64] in which the Commission had stated that there were grounds to conclude that war crimes and violations of human rights and international humanitarian law had been committed in Ukraine since 24 February. She said that the Commission had also indicated in its report that troops of the Russian Federation had been responsible for the vast majority of the violations identified, while Ukrainian armed forces had also committed international humanitarian law violations in some cases, including two incidents that qualified as war crimes.[65] According to the Commission, the relentless use of explosive weapons with wide-area effects in populated areas had killed and injured scores of civilians

[60] See S/PV.9097, S/PV.9141, S/PV.9164, S/PV.9184 and S/PV.9207.

[61] See S/PV.9098 and S/PV.9187.

[62] See S/PV.9161.

[63] See Human Rights Council resolution 49/1.

[64] See A/77/533.

[65] See S/PV.9161.

and devastated entire neighbourhoods. In addition, the Commission had documented patterns of summary executions, unlawful confinement, torture, ill-treatment, rape and other sexual violence committed in areas occupied by forces of the Russian Federation. The Under-Secretary-General noted that the Commission had called for a sound coordination of the multiple national and international accountability initiatives in Ukraine. She concluded by underlining that accountability remained crucial as new allegations of atrocities had emerged in areas that had recently returned to control by the Government of Ukraine.

During the discussion, the representative of Norway recalled that the Commission had concluded that violations of human rights and international humanitarian law amounting to war crimes had been committed by armed forces of the Russian Federation, which included the killing of civilians, the discovery of mass graves, incidents of rape and other forms of sexual violence, forced disappearance and torture, along with reports of deportations to the Russian Federation and adjustments to procedures to allow Russians to adopt Ukrainian children without the consent of their parents, among other things. She stressed that the victims deserved justice, survivors had to be cared for and those responsible had to be held accountable. The representative of Albania pointed out that the Commission had reported that family members, including children, had sometimes been forced to witness those crimes.

The representative of Ukraine asserted that the attempts by the Russian Federation to avoid responsibility for the Bucha massacre had failed almost immediately owing to numerous eyewitness accounts, findings and investigations. He added that the most recent contribution to revealing the truth about Russian war crimes and crimes against humanity had been made by the Commission. The representative of the European Union noted the decision of the Commission, based on the evidence gathered in the regions of Kyiv, Chernihiv, Kharkiv and Sumy, that atrocities to be classified as war crimes had been committed in Ukraine.

Case 6
Threats to international peace and security

At a meeting held on 31 October under the item entitled "Threats to international peace and security",[66] the Council heard a briefing by the President of the ICAO Council on the forced landing of Ryanair flight FR-4978 in Belarus on 23 May 2021. In his briefing, he noted the decision of the ICAO Council of 27 May 2021 to undertake a fact-finding investigation of the event, in which it had requested that the ICAO secretariat prepare a report that would present the available facts and relevant legal instruments and identify any gaps in order to safeguard international civil aviation and had called upon States to collaborate with the investigation. He added that pursuant to that decision, the Secretary-General of ICAO had instituted a Fact-Finding Investigation Team, which had concluded that Belarus senior officials had orchestrated the deliberate diversion of the flight under the false pretext of a bomb threat. In the light of that report, the ICAO Assembly, at its forty-first session, from 27 September to 7 October, had adopted a resolution condemning the actions of the Government of Belarus in committing an act of unlawful interference that had deliberately endangered the safety and security of Ryanair flight FR-4978 and the lives of those on board.

During the discussion, Council members and other Member States reflected on the work of the Fact-Finding Investigation Team and the findings in its report. Multiple speakers[67] expressed concern regarding the findings in the report or expressly condemned what the report described as violations of the Convention on International Civil Aviation, also known as the Chicago Convention, by the Belarusian authorities. The representative of the United Kingdom stated that the use of a spurious terrorist threat to divert an airliner also had served to undermine measures put in place by the international community to counter real aviation threats, including those addressed by the Council in resolution 2309 (2016). The representative of Ireland called on Belarus to take all appropriate action, as requested by the ICAO Assembly, and added that the facts were clear and based on a detailed and thorough fact-finding investigation that had gathered incontrovertible evidence of State-led breaches of international aviation law. The representative of Norway said that, while Belarus had pointed to missing information in the investigation, the conclusions of ICAO made it clear that it was in large part due to a lack of full

[66] See S/PV.9175.

[67] Albania, United Kingdom, United States, France, Ireland, Norway, Brazil, Kenya, Mexico, Ghana, Lithuania, Poland, Latvia (also on behalf of Czechia and Estonia), Greece and Germany.

cooperation in good faith on the part of the Belarusian authorities themselves. The representative of the United States stated that the Council had to send a clear message that such actions were unacceptable and that there had to be consequences for those responsible. The representative of Lithuania called on the Council to recognize the responsibility of Belarus for the breaches of international law and for it to be held accountable for them. He also called on the Council to demand from the authorities of Belarus that they provide all critical information that had been requested but not made available to the investigators and to remain seized of the issue. The representative of Latvia, speaking also on behalf of Czechia and Estonia, stated that the investigation by ICAO had established the facts and provided trustworthy and reliable information, which constituted a good basis for further actions of the Council and the United Nations, and called on the Council to maintain close attention to the safety of international aviation and full accountability for those responsible. The representative of Ghana reminded all States parties of their commitments not to use international civil aviation for purposes that were inconsistent with the aims of the Convention, and stressed the urgent need for enhanced cooperation among them and ICAO to secure the aviation environment from all forms of threats. In view of the seriousness of the facts reported, the representative of Gabon called on all States concerned to participate constructively in the investigations by providing all the information required to establish the facts.

The representative of India said that his delegation had always maintained that such incidents should be subject to independent investigations conducted by ICAO and, in that regard, took note of the conclusions of the investigation related to Ryanair flight FR-4978. He added that the conclusions of any such investigation should be established on the basis of facts and free of any political considerations. Furthermore, noting that actions that led to isolation or exclusion would not only impinge on cooperation in the civilian aviation sector but would also cause delays in determining circumstances that put the safety and security of the passengers in jeopardy, he stressed the need to encourage concerned Member States to extend their cooperation to those investigations. Viewing the issue as one related to human rights and the safety of international civil aviation, the representative of Brazil questioned whether the Council was the most appropriate forum for discussing the matter and expressed support for the submission of the report to the Office of the United Nations High Commissioner for Human Rights. Similarly, the representative of Mexico stated that the incident should be addressed within the framework of the competent civil aviation and human rights forums. The representative of the United Arab Emirates opined that, when there was an incident affecting the safe functioning of civil aviation, it was important to establish the facts professionally and impartially, and that the fact-finding investigation of the ICAO Council had therefore served a valuable purpose. At the same time, while expressing appreciation for the consideration given to the issue by both the Council and Assembly of ICAO, the United Arab Emirates expressed the view that international civil aviation rules and standards should continue to be dealt with as a technical matter.

The representative of the Russian Federation stated that his delegation had reason to believe that the so-called "fact-finding process" was nothing more than the settling of scores by Western countries with countries that they disliked. He questioned why the investigation was continued after the ICAO Council had, on 31 January, discussed what was said to have been the final report on the incident, in which the Fact-Finding Investigation Team had concluded that the decision to land in Minsk had been made independently by the crew, and the alleged guilt of the Belarusian side had not been established. He asserted that Western countries had taken advantage of their majority in the ICAO Council to force the Team to continue the investigation and, after considering the revised report, to reach a completely different decision. Stating that the revised report carried little credibility in terms of its objectiveness, the representative of the Russian Federation expressed serious doubts about the impartiality of ICAO and noted that the inability to properly respond to civil aviation issues led to those topics being addressed in a non-specialized forum – the Security Council – to whose mandate such topics bore no relation. The representative of Belarus stated that the report, which had been written hastily and under pressure brought to bear by certain Western countries, was not a consensus report, was biased and lacked objectivity. He added that Belarus would never accept the conclusions of the report, which was based on incomplete information and lacked the necessary international cooperation. While acknowledging the role of ICAO in handling the matter of the forced landing of the Ryanair flight, in accordance with the division of labour and its responsibility, the representative of China stated that different parties had different views on the report and concerns about the source and authenticity of some key information. He added that ICAO should eliminate interference from political factors, fully listen to the views of relevant parties, seek to fully grasp the situation, treat the concerns of all parties equally, conduct independent, professional and serious analysis and draw conclusions that could stand the test of time.

Communications of the Council

The investigative functions of other bodies of the United Nations and related organizations were also raised in several communications submitted to the Council in 2022, primarily in relation to the Independent International Commission of Inquiry on Ukraine.

By letter dated 11 April addressed to the President of the Security Council,[68] the representative of Latvia transmitted a statement on behalf of Latvia, Estonia and Lithuania in relation to the Council meeting held the same day under the item entitled "Maintenance of peace and security of Ukraine",[69] in which the representatives of the three Baltic States noted that the gender and intersectional dimensions of war crimes, crimes against humanity and other violations of international humanitarian law and international criminal law perpetrated by the Russian military needed to guide the work of the Independent International Commission of Inquiry on Ukraine.

By a letter dated 26 April addressed to the President of the Security Council,[70] the representative of Albania transmitted a concept note for an Arria-formula meeting on the theme "Ensuring accountability for atrocities committed in Ukraine", held on 27 April, in which it was noted that the Human Rights Council had established the Independent International Commission of Inquiry on Ukraine with a mandate to investigate violations of human rights and of international humanitarian law. It was also stated in the concept note that one of the objectives of the Arria-formula meeting was to mobilize and welcome all efforts, including those of the Commission. Subsequently, by a letter dated 6 May addressed to the President of the Council,[71] the representative of Albania circulated the statements delivered during the above-mentioned Arria-formula meeting, many of which referred to the work of the Commission, including the statement by the Chair of that body.

By a letter dated 27 September addressed to the President of the Security Council,[72] the representative of Estonia transmitted a joint statement by Estonia, Latvia and Lithuania in connection with the Council briefing held on 27 September under the item entitled "Maintenance of peace and security of Ukraine",[73] in which the representative of Estonia, on behalf of the Baltic States, noted that on 23 September, the Independent International Commission of Inquiry on Ukraine had concluded that Russian Federation forces had committed war crimes in Ukraine, including torture, executions and sexual violence committed against civilians. In addition, by note verbale dated 21 October addressed to the President,[74] the representative of Romania transmitted the statement made by Romania in connection with a meeting held on 21 October under the same item,[75] in which he expressed appalment with the disturbing conclusion of the report of the Commission regarding the wide range of war crimes and violations of human rights and international humanitarian law committed in Ukraine since 24 February.

The Secretary-General continued to transmit the monthly reports of the Director General of OPCW, submitted pursuant to paragraph 12 of resolution 2118 (2013), on the elimination of the chemical weapons programme of the Syrian Arab Republic.[76] In addition, by letter dated 1 February addressed to the President of the Security Council,[77] the Secretary-General transmitted to the Council the report of the OPCW Fact-Finding Mission regarding the incidents of the alleged use of chemicals as a weapon in Marea on 1 and 3 September 2015. In addition, by letter dated 14 February addressed to the President,[78]

[68] See S/2022/305.
[69] See S/PV.9013.
[70] See S/2022/352.
[71] See S/2022/375.
[72] See S/2022/717.
[73] See S/PV.9138.
[74] See S/2022/792.
[75] See S/PV.9161.
[76] See S/2022/76, S/2022/181, S/2022/281, S/2022/365, S/2022/441, S/2022/530, S/2022/585, S/2022/658, S/2022/727, S/2022/828, S/2022/897 and S/2022/1016.
[77] See S/2022/85.
[78] See S/2022/116.

he transmitted to the Council the report of the OPCW Fact-Finding Mission regarding the incident of the alleged use of chemicals as a weapon in Kafr Zeita on 1 October 2016.

III. Decisions of the Security Council concerning the pacific settlement of disputes

Article 33

1. The parties to any dispute, the continuance of which is likely to endanger the maintenance of international peace and security, shall, first of all, seek a solution by negotiation, enquiry, mediation, conciliation, arbitration, judicial settlement, resort to regional agencies or arrangements, or other peaceful means of their own choice.

2. The Security Council shall, when it deems necessary, call upon the parties to settle their dispute by such means.

Article 36

1. The Security Council may, at any stage of a dispute of the nature referred to in Article 33 or of a situation of like nature, recommend appropriate procedures or methods of adjustment.

2. The Security Council should take into consideration any procedures for the settlement of the dispute which have already been adopted by the parties.

3. In making recommendations under this Article the Security Council should also take into consideration that legal disputes should as a general rule be referred by the parties to the International Court of Justice in accordance with the provisions of the Statute of the Court.

Article 37

1. Should the parties to a dispute of the nature referred to in Article 33 fail to settle it by the means indicated in that Article, they shall refer it to the Security Council.

2. If the Security Council deems that the continuance of the dispute is in fact likely to endanger the maintenance of international peace and security, it shall decide whether to take action under Article 36 or to recommend such terms of settlement as it may consider appropriate.

Article 38

Without prejudice to the provisions of Articles 33 to 37, the Security Council may, if all the parties to any dispute so request, make recommendations to the parties with a view to a pacific settlement of the dispute.

Note

Article 33 (1) of the Charter of the United Nations expressly provides the framework for parties to settle their disputes by peaceful means. According to Article 33 (2), the Council shall call upon the parties to settle their disputes by such peaceful means as provided for in Article 33 (1). The Council may recommend appropriate procedures or methods of adjustment for the settlement of disputes under Article 36 (1). According to Article 36 (2) and (3), the Council should take into consideration procedures for the settlement of the dispute already adopted by the parties and that legal disputes should, as a general rule, be referred by the parties to the International Court of Justice. Under Article 37 (2), following a referral, the Council is to decide whether to take action under Article 36 or to recommend such terms of settlement as it may consider appropriate. Article 38 provides that the Council may make recommendations to the parties with a view to a pacific settlement of the dispute.

In section III, the decisions of the Council in 2022 are examined in connection with the peaceful settlement of disputes within the framework of Chapter VI of the Charter. Decisions explicitly adopted under Chapter VII have not been considered for the purposes of the present section. Subsections A to C feature decisions of the Council in which the pacific settlement of disputes was addressed in the context of, respectively: thematic issues; country-specific and regional situations; and the settlement of disputes involving the Secretary-General. In subsection D, reference is made to decisions of the Council in support of the pacific settlement of disputes by regional and subregional organizations which are covered in detail in part VIII.

A. Decisions of the Security Council concerning thematic issues

The present subsection provides an overview of the decisions adopted by the Council on thematic issues that relate to the pacific settlement of disputes. In 2022, in a presidential statement adopted on 23 March on the cooperation between the United Nations and the League of Arab States in the maintenance of international peace and security in the Arab region,[79] while recognizing the efforts undertaken by both organizations in response to the impact of the coronavirus disease (COVID-19) pandemic, especially in conflict-affected contexts, the Council reiterated its demand, in line with resolutions 2532 (2020) and 2565 (2021), for a general and immediate cessation of hostilities and a humanitarian pause in all conflict situations before the Council, including in the Arab region. The Council also stressed the urgent need for the intensification and acceleration of international and regional efforts to prevent the escalation of tensions, encourage multilateral dialogue, advance the political settlement of disputes, foster collective security and promote just and lasting peace in all conflict situations in the Arab region.[80] Moreover, the Council reaffirmed the important and positive contribution of youth to the efforts for the maintenance and promotion of peace and security and the role that young people played in the prevention and resolution of conflicts in the Arab region and stressed the importance of creating policies for youth that would positively contribute to peacebuilding efforts.[81] The Council also reaffirmed the important role of women's full, equal and meaningful participation in the prevention and resolution of conflicts and in peacebuilding, as recognized in resolution 1325 (2000) and other relevant Council resolutions, highlighting the importance of women's participation, empowerment, leadership and inclusion for peacebuilding and sustaining peace, and encouraged enhanced efforts to promote women's economic empowerment and the elimination of poverty in the Arab region.[82]

In a presidential statement adopted on 12 July in connection with the role of strategic communications in United Nations peacekeeping operations,[83] the Council reaffirmed that lasting peace was neither achieved nor sustained by military and technical engagements alone, but through political solutions and a comprehensive approach to sustaining peace. In that regard, the Council stressed that the pursuit of sustainable political solutions should guide the design and deployment of peacekeeping operations.[84] The Council also reaffirmed the importance of the full, equal and meaningful participation of women in all stages of peace and political processes and in United Nations peacekeeping operations.[85]

[79] S/PRST/2022/1, eleventh paragraph, in connection with the item entitled "Cooperation between the United Nations and regional and subregional organizations in maintaining international peace and security". For more information on the item, see part I, sect. 36.

[80] S/PRST/2022/1, twelfth paragraph.

[81] Ibid., sixth paragraph.

[82] Ibid., fifteenth paragraph.

[83] S/PRST/2022/5, third paragraph, in connection with the item entitled "United Nations peacekeeping operations". For more information on the item, see part I, sect. 24.

[84] S/PRST/2022/5, third paragraph.

[85] Ibid., eighth paragraph.

B. Recommendations of the Security Council concerning country-specific and regional situations

Article 33 (2) of the Charter provides that the Council call upon the parties to settle disputes by the means established in Article 33 (1), when deemed necessary. In addition, Article 36 (1) provides that the Council may recommend appropriate procedures or methods of adjustment. In Article 37 (2), it is further established that, if the Council deems that the continuance of the dispute is in fact likely to endanger the maintenance of international peace and security, it shall decide whether to take action under Article 36 or to recommend such terms of settlement as it may consider appropriate. Article 38 provides that, without prejudice to Articles 33 to 37, the Council may make recommendations to the parties with a view to a pacific settlement of the dispute, if all the parties so request.

The present subsection provides an overview of the practice of the Council relating to the pacific settlement of disputes in situations specific to a country or region. In dealing with complex situations in which the Council determined the existence of a threat to international peace and security, the Council utilized the tools available under Chapter VII of the Charter in parallel with those available under Chapter VI, with a view to restoring peace and to recommending procedures or methods for the pacific settlement of disputes. The decisions featured in the present overview do not include those adopted expressly under Chapter VII, which are covered in parts VII and X. The section also does not include the wide variety of good offices, mediation and political support tasks of peacekeeping operations and special political missions specifically mandated by the Council in 2022, which are covered in part X.

During the period under review, the Council made a wide range of recommendations with regard to the peaceful settlement of conflicts and disputes that were both inter- and intra-State in nature. As described in the overview below, the Council called for the cessation of hostilities and engagement on the establishment of durable ceasefires; the full implementation of peace agreements, peaceful and inclusive political dialogue, transitions and elections; and dialogue for the resolution of longer-term outstanding disputes.

Cessation of hostilities and permanent ceasefire

In 2022, the Council called for the cessation of violence by armed groups in the eastern part of the Democratic Republic of the Congo. In addition, while expressing deep concern regarding the maintenance of peace and security of Ukraine, the Council recalled the obligation of all Member States to settle their international disputes by peaceful means. The Council also called for the full implementation of the Libyan ceasefire agreement and the withdrawal of all foreign fighters from the country and for a strengthened truce in Yemen to be translated into a durable ceasefire and political settlement. Furthermore, the Council reiterated its call upon Israel and the Syrian Arab Republic to prevent any further breaches of the ceasefire in the Golan Heights and on Israel and Lebanon to respect the cessation of hostilities, support a permanent ceasefire and find a long-term solution to their dispute.

More specifically, the Council welcomed the recent positive political developments in the Democratic Republic of the Congo and the region and the convening of the second regional Heads of State conclave in Nairobi on 21 April and their commitment to implement a two track approach aimed at finding lasting peace in the country.[86] The Council expressed concern over the increase of armed group activity in the eastern provinces of the country and called on all armed groups operating in the area to participate unconditionally in the inter-Democratic Republic of the Congo dialogue initiated by the President of the Democratic Republic of the Congo and the President of Kenya.[87] The Council also urged all domestic armed groups to immediately cease all forms of violence, permanently disband and lay down their arms and participate in the demobilization, disarmament, community recovery and stabilization programme.[88] Furthermore, while recognizing the progress made in the implementation of national and regional commitments under the Peace, Security and Cooperation Framework for the Democratic Republic of the

[86] S/PRST/2022/4, first paragraph, in connection with the item entitled "The situation concerning the Democratic Republic of the Congo". For more information on the item, see part I, sect. 4.

[87] S/PRST/2022/4, second and third paragraphs.

[88] Ibid., third paragraph.

Congo and the Region, the Council encouraged regional countries to seize the momentum to make further progress in overcoming challenges to peace and sustainable development and to de-escalate tensions.[89]

With respect to the situation in the Golan Heights, the Council stressed the obligation of both Israel and the Syrian Arab Republic to scrupulously and fully respect the terms of the Agreement on Disengagement between Israeli and Syrian Forces of 1974.[90] The parties were called upon to exercise maximum restraint and prevent any breaches of the ceasefire and the area of separation and to take full advantage of the liaison function of the United Nations Disengagement Observer Force (UNDOF) to address issues of mutual concern and to prevent any escalation of the situation across the ceasefire line.[91] Furthermore, with respect to the situation in the Syrian Arab Republic, the Council called upon all parties to the domestic conflict in that country to cease military actions throughout the country, including in the UNDOF area of operations.[92]

In relation to the situation in Lebanon, the Council reiterated its call upon Israel and Lebanon to support a permanent ceasefire and a long-term solution based on the principles and elements set out in paragraph 8 of resolution 1701 (2006).[93] The Council condemned all violations of the Blue Line, both by air and ground, and strongly called upon all parties to respect the cessation of hostilities, to prevent any violation of the Blue Line and to respect it in its entirety and to cooperate fully with the United Nations and the United Nations Interim Force in Lebanon (UNIFIL).[94]

In connection with the situation in Libya, the Council called on all parties to implement the ceasefire agreement of 23 October 2020 in full, including the action plan agreed by the 5+5 Joint Military Commission, and urged Member States to respect and support its full implementation, including through the withdrawal of all foreign forces, fighters and mercenaries from the country without further delay.[95] The Council also emphasized that there could be no military solution in Libya and called on all parties to refrain from violence or any other actions that could escalate tensions, exacerbate conflicts and undermine the political process or the ceasefire.[96]

In relation to the situation in Yemen, the Council welcomed the announcement on 1 April 2022 of a two-month truce and its extension on 2 June 2022.[97] The Council called for a strengthened truce to be translated into a durable ceasefire and an inclusive, comprehensive political settlement under the auspices of the United Nations.[98] The Council also reaffirmed its endorsement of the Agreement on the City of Hudaydah and the Ports of Hudaydah, Salif and Ra's Isa of 2018 and reiterated its call on the Government of Yemen and the Houthis to work cooperatively to implement all its provisions.[99]

Peace agreements, peaceful and inclusive political dialogue, transitions and elections

During the period under review, the Council called for an end to the violence in Haiti and Myanmar and the engagement of relevant stakeholders in political dialogue and reconciliation. The Council urged political stakeholders in Libya to engage in dialogue to create an environment and pathway for the conduct of elections. Following the conclusion of the elections in Somalia, the Council called on the Federal Government and the federal member states to focus on the implementation of the national priorities, including with respect to the reform of the Somali security sector. In addition, the Council

---

[89] Ibid., seventh paragraph.

[90] Resolutions 2639 (2022) and 2671 (2022), para. 2, in connection with the item entitled "The situation in the Middle East". For more information on the item, see part I, sect. 20.

[91] Resolutions 2639 (2022) and 2671 (2022), para. 2.

[92] Ibid., ninth preambular paragraph.

[93] Resolution 2650 (2022), para. 4, in connection with the item entitled "The situation in the Middle East".

[94] Ibid., para. 12.

[95] Resolution 2656 (2022), para. 10, in connection with the item entitled "The situation in Libya". For more information on the item, see part I, sect. 10.

[96] Resolution 2656 (2022), para. 7.

[97] Resolution 2643 (2022), third preambular paragraph, in connection with the item entitled "The situation in the Middle East".

[98] Resolution 2643 (2022), third preambular paragraph.

[99] Ibid., sixth preambular paragraph.

recognized the achievements made in the implementation of the peace agreement in Colombia and called for further progress in that regard.

Welcoming the progress made towards peace across Colombia since the adoption of the Final Agreement for Ending the Conflict and Building a Stable and Lasting Peace, the Council urged the parties to work together to build upon the progress and address challenges, in particular the continued violence in conflict-affected areas, through comprehensive implementation of the peace agreement.[100]

In connection with the question concerning Haiti, the Council noted with deep concern the protracted and deteriorating political, economic, security, human rights, humanitarian and food security crises in the country and demanded an immediate cessation of gang violence and criminal activities.[101] The Council reiterated the need for all Haitian stakeholders, including with the support of the United Nations Integrated Office in Haiti (BINUH), to reach an urgent agreement on a sustainable, time-bound and commonly accepted framework for a political process led by Haitians to permit the organization of inclusive, peaceful, free, fair and transparent legislative and presidential elections, through an inclusive inter-Haitian national dialogue.[102]

Addressing the political transition in Libya, the Council recalled the Libyan Political Dialogue Forum road map, regretted that a number of its deliverables had yet to be achieved, rejected actions that could lead to violence or greater divisions and urged the political institutions and key stakeholders to agree a pathway to deliver elections as soon as possible across the country through dialogue, compromise and constructive engagement, in a transparent and inclusive manner.[103] The Council called upon relevant Libyan institutions and authorities to implement confidence-building measures to create an environment conducive for successful national presidential and parliamentary elections.[104]

Expressing its deep concern at the ongoing state of emergency imposed by the military in Myanmar on 1 February 2021 and its impact on the people of Myanmar, the Council demanded an immediate end to all forms of violence throughout the country and urged restraint and a de-escalation of tensions.[105] The Council urged the Myanmar military to immediately release all arbitrarily detained prisoners, including the President, Win Myint, and the State Counsellor, Aung San Suu Kyi, and reiterated its call to uphold democratic institutions and processes and to pursue dialogue and reconciliation.[106] The Council called for concrete and immediate actions, noting the military commitment to leaders of the Association of Southeast Asian Nations (ASEAN) to effectively and fully implement the five-point consensus agreed on 24 April 2021 by all members of ASEAN.[107]

Addressing the situation in Somalia, the Council welcomed the conclusion of the electoral process, which allowed for the peaceful transition of power, and underscored that the swift formation of an inclusive federal government, with the full, equal and meaningful participation of women, would help critical national priorities, promote national reconciliation, security and support transition from international security support in line with the Somalia Transition Plan and national security architecture.[108] Following the formation of the Government, the Council encouraged Somalia to seize the opportunity it had to make renewed progress in implementing its national priorities.[109] In that regard, the Council emphasized the importance of the Federal Government and the federal member states working

[100] Resolution 2655 (2022), third preambular paragraph, in connection with the item entitled "Identical letters dated 19 January 2016 from the Permanent Representative of Colombia to the United Nations addressed to the Secretary-General and the President of the Security Council (S/2016/53)". For more information on the item, see part I, sect. 13.

[101] Resolution 2645 (2022), seventh preambular paragraph and para. 5, in connection with the item entitled "The question concerning Haiti". For more information on the item, see part I, sect. 12.

[102] Resolution 2645 (2022), para. 3.

[103] Resolution 2647 (2022), para. 3, in connection with the item entitled "The situation in Libya".

[104] Resolution 2647 (2022), para. 4.

[105] Resolution 2669 (2022), first preambular paragraph and para. 1, in connection with the item entitled "The situation in Myanmar". For more information on the item, see part I, sect. 15.

[106] Resolution 2669 (2022), paras. 2 and 3.

[107] Ibid., para. 6.

[108] Resolution 2632 (2022), third preambular paragraph, in connection with the item entitled "The situation in Somalia". For more information on the item, see part I, sect. 2.

[109] Resolution 2657 (2022), third preambular paragraph, in connection with the item entitled "The situation in Somalia".

together to achieve that and reiterated the importance of inclusive dialogue and local reconciliation processes for stability.[110] The Council also encouraged the resumption of dialogue between the Federal Government and "Somaliland" to build confidence and strengthen political coordination.[111]

Peaceful settlement of disputes

In 2022, the Council reiterated its call for the peaceful resolution of disputes related to the situations in Cyprus, relations between South Sudan and the Sudan, Ukraine and Western Sahara.

Regarding Cyprus, the Council reiterated the importance of the Greek Cypriot and Turkish Cypriot sides and all involved participants approaching the engagement by the Secretary-General in the spirit of openness, flexibility and compromise and to show the necessary political will and commitment to freely negotiate a mutually acceptable settlement under the auspices of the United Nations.[112] The Council urged the sides to engage actively and with an increased sense of urgency with the Secretary-General and his team to that end, including by reaching an agreement regarding the proposal of the Secretary-General to appoint a United Nations envoy.[113] In connection with the situation in Varosha, the Council recalled its presidential statement of 23 July 2021,[114] in which it condemned the announcement by Turkish and Turkish Cypriot leaders on 20 July 2021 on the further reopening of a part of the fenced-off area of Varosha, and continued to stress the need to avoid any unilateral actions that could raise tensions on the island and undermine the prospects for a peaceful settlement.[115] The Council expressed concern at the continuing tensions in the Eastern Mediterranean and underlined that disputes should be resolved peacefully in accordance with applicable international law.[116] The Council also called upon the leaders of the two communities and all involved parties to refrain from any actions and rhetoric that might damage the settlement process and that could raise tensions on the island.[117]

With respect to relations between South Sudan and the Sudan, the Council noted the efforts of both Governments to support each other's peace processes, encouraged meetings of the Joint Political and Security Mechanism and those of other joint mechanisms to take place on a consistent basis and urged the parties to make progress in establishing temporary administrative and security arrangements for Abyei.[118] The Council reiterated that any territorial disputes between States had to be settled exclusively by peaceful means and underscored that the final status of Abyei should be resolved by negotiations between the two countries in a manner consistent with the Comprehensive Peace Agreement of 2005.[119]

The Council expressed deep concern regarding the maintenance of peace and security of Ukraine and recalled that all Member States had undertaken, under the Charter, the obligation to settle their international disputes by peaceful means.[120]

With regard to the situation concerning Western Sahara, the Council emphasized the need to achieve a realistic, practicable, enduring and mutually acceptable political solution based on compromise.[121] The Council called upon the parties to resume negotiations under the auspices of the Secretary-General without preconditions and in good faith with a view to achieving a just, lasting and mutually acceptable political solution that would provide for the self-determination of the people of Western Sahara in the context of arrangements consistent with the principles and purposes of the Charter.[122] The Council also

---

[110] Resolution 2657 (2022), third preambular paragraph.
[111] Ibid., fourth preambular paragraph.
[112] Resolutions 2618 (2022) and 2646 (2022), para. 2, in connection with the item entitled, "The situation in Cyprus". For more information on the item, see part I, sect. 17.
[113] Resolutions 2618 (2022) and 2646 (2022), para. 2.
[114] See S/PRST/2021/13, in connection with the item entitled, "The situation in Cyprus".
[115] Resolutions 2618 (2022) and 2646 (2022), para. 3.
[116] Ibid., para. 4.
[117] Ibid.
[118] Resolution 2630 (2022), fourth preambular paragraph, in connection with the item entitled "Reports of the Secretary-General on the Sudan and South Sudan". For more information on the item, see part I, sect. 7.
[119] Resolution 2630 (2022), third preambular paragraph.
[120] S/PRST/2022/3, first and second paragraphs, in connection with the item entitled "Maintenance of peace and security of Ukraine". For more information on the item, see part I, sect. 19.
[121] Resolution 2654 (2022), para. 2, in connection with the item entitled, "The situation concerning Western Sahara". For more information on the item, see part I, sect. 1.
[122] Resolution 2654 (2022), para. 4.

called on the parties to comply fully with the military agreements reached with the United Nations Mission for the Referendum in Western Sahara with regard to the ceasefire, implement their commitments to the former Personal Envoy of the Secretary-General for Western Sahara and refrain from any actions that could undermine United Nations-facilitated negotiations or further destabilize the situation in Western Sahara.[123]

C. Decisions involving the Secretary-General in the Council's efforts at the pacific settlement of disputes

While Article 99 of the Charter provides that the Secretary-General may bring to the attention of the Council any matter which, in his opinion, may threaten the maintenance of international peace and security, the Charter does not specifically define the role of the Secretary-General in relation to matters of peace and security. The work of the Council regarding conflict prevention and the peaceful settlement of disputes has, however, required the involvement of the Secretary-General in all relevant aspects of that agenda.

During the period under review, the Council recognized the good offices work of the Secretary-General, as well as that of his special representatives and envoys, in support of efforts to end violent conflict, of peace agreements, political dialogue and political transitions, and of the resolution of outstanding disputes.

Good offices to end violence

In connection with the violence in the eastern Democratic Republic of the Congo, the Council welcomed the support of the United Nations Organization Stabilization Mission in the Democratic Republic of the Congo (MONUSCO) and the Office of the Special Envoy of the Secretary-General for the Great Lakes Region to the two-track approach adopted at the second regional Heads of State conclave on 21 April.[124]

Regarding Haiti, the Council emphasized the importance of empowering BINUH to carry out its good offices role, to engage all sectors of Haitian society, in particular political actors, civil society, women and religious leaders, including communities living in areas controlled by gangs, in support of political consensus, as well as in the necessary reforms to scale up advisory police support to the Haitian National Police and reopen police commissariats in response to armed gang violence.[125]

In connection with the situation in Lebanon, the Council expressed its strong support for the continued efforts of UNIFIL to engage with Israel and Lebanon to facilitate liaison, coordination and practical arrangements on the ground.[126] The Council urged the parties to make systematic, constructive and expanded use of the tripartite mechanism and to accelerate efforts to delineate and visibly mark the Blue Line in its entirety.[127] The Council also urged all parties to cooperate fully with the Council and the Secretary-General to make tangible progress towards a permanent ceasefire and a long-term solution as envisioned in resolution 1701 (2006).[128]

Regarding the Golan Heights, the Council encouraged Israel and the Syrian Arab Republic to take full advantage of the UNDOF liaison function regularly to address issues of mutual concern and to prevent any escalation across the ceasefire line.[129]

Regarding the conflict in Ukraine, the Council expressed strong support of the efforts of the Secretary-General in the search of a peaceful solution.[130]

---

[123] Ibid., para. 6.

[124] S/PRST/2022/4, first paragraph. For more information on the mandate of MONUSCO, see part X, sect. I.

[125] Resolution 2645 (2022), sixth preambular paragraph. For more information on the mandate on BINUH, see part X, sect. II.

[126] Resolution 2650 (2022), para. 13. For more information on the mandate of UNIFIL, see part X, sect. I.

[127] Resolution 2650 (2022), para. 13.

[128] Ibid., para. 19.

[129] Resolutions 2639 (2022) and 2671 (2022), para. 2. For more information on the mandate of UNDOF, see part X, sect. I.

[130] S/PRST/2022/3, third paragraph.

Good offices in support of peace agreements, political dialogue and transitions

Addressing the situation in Libya, the Council welcomed the appointment of Abdoulaye Bathily as Special Representative of the Secretary-General for Libya and Head of the United Nations Support Mission in Libya (UNSMIL) and urged all Libyan parties and key stakeholders to engage constructively and fully with him in the fulfilment of his mandate.[131] The Council expressed support for the efforts of UNSMIL to facilitate wider engagement and participation of women from across the spectrum of Libyan society in the political process and public institutions and recognized that the process should be inclusive of all Libyans, including youth and civil society.[132]

With regard to the situation in Myanmar, the Council encouraged close coordination between the ASEAN Special Envoy for Myanmar and the Special Envoy of the Secretary-General on Myanmar in pursuit of promoting fully inclusive and representative dialogue, to achieve an end to the violence and to support the path to democracy.[133] The Council also urged all parties to work constructively with the ASEAN Special Envoy and the Special Envoy of the Secretary-General to commence dialogue to seek a peaceful solution in the interests of the people of Myanmar.[134]

Regarding the situation in Somalia, the Council emphasized the essential role of the United Nations Assistance Mission in Somalia in supporting the Federal Government and the federal member states and other relevant actors through the provision of strategic advice and good offices, capacity-building and the coordination of international partners' support, including with respect to elections support.[135]

Good offices in support of the resolution of outstanding disputes

Regarding Cyprus, the Council expressed full support for the ongoing engagement of the Secretary-General with the Greek Cypriot and Turkish Cypriot sides and encouraged further rounds of informal talks.[136] The Council urged the sides to engage actively and with an increased sense of urgency with the Secretary-General and his team, including by reaching an agreement regarding the proposal of the Secretary-General to appoint a United Nations envoy.[137] The Council expressed deep regret for the lack of progress on an effective mechanism for direct military contacts between the sides and the relevant involved parties and urged their flexibility and engagement, facilitated by the United Nations Peacekeeping Force in Cyprus (UNFICYP), to develop a suitably acceptable proposal on the establishment of such a mechanism and its timely implementation.[138] The Council called upon the two leaders urgently to consider the advice of the good offices mission of the Secretary-General regarding further ways to empower the technical committees and improve their performance.[139]

With respect to relations between South Sudan and the Sudan, the Council encouraged the African Union, the African Union High-level Implementation Panel and the Special Envoy of the Secretary-General for the Horn of Africa to intensify mediation roles with the Governments of South Sudan and the Sudan to strongly encourage them to establish temporary administrative and security arrangements for Abyei and achieve a political solution for its final status.[140] The Council also stressed the importance of the United Nations Interim Security Force for Abyei (UNISFA) initiatives to support community dialogue to strengthen intercommunal relationships and facilitate stability and reconciliation in the Abyei Area.[141]

The Council expressed its full support for the Secretary-General and his Personal Envoy for Western Sahara to facilitate the negotiations process to achieve a solution to the Western Sahara question.[142]

[131] Resolution 2656 (2022), para. 2. For more information on the mandate of UNSMIL, see part X, sect. I.
[132] Resolution 2656 (2022), eighth preambular paragraph.
[133] Resolution 2669 (2022), para. 7.
[134] Ibid., para. 8.
[135] Resolution 2632 (2022), fourth preambular paragraph, in connection with the item entitled "The situation in Somalia".
[136] Resolutions 2618 (2022) and 2646 (2022), para. 2, in connection with the item entitled "The situation in Cyprus".
[137] Resolutions 2618 (2022) and 2646 (2022), para. 2.
[138] Ibid., para. 7. For more information on the mandate of UNFICYP, see part X, sect. I.
[139] Resolutions 2618 (2022) and 2646 (2022), para. 5 (a).
[140] Resolution 2630 (2022), fifth preambular paragraph.
[141] Ibid., sixth preambular paragraph. For more information on the mandate of UNISFA, see part X, sect. I.
[142] Resolution 2654 (2022), para. 3.

The Council called upon the parties to resume negotiations under the auspices of the Secretary-General without preconditions and in good faith, and to refrain from any actions that could undermine United Nations-facilitated negotiations or further destabilize the situation in Western Sahara.[143]

D. Decisions involving regional arrangements or agencies

During the period under review, pursuant to Article 52 of the Charter, the Council expressed support for the crucial role of regional and subregional organizations and other arrangements in the pacific settlement of disputes and encouraged them to continue with those efforts and to enhance their cooperation and coordination with the United Nations in that regard. The Council's decisions regarding joint or parallel efforts undertaken by the Council and regional organizations, arrangements or agencies in the pacific settlement of disputes during the period under review are covered in part VIII.

IV. Discussions on the interpretation or application of the provisions of Chapter VI of the Charter

Note

Section IV features the main discussions in the Council in 2022 with regard to the interpretation of specific provisions of Chapter VI of the Charter of the United Nations concerning the role of the Council and the Secretary-General in the peaceful settlement of disputes. It excludes those that concern regional organizations, which are covered in part VIII.

During the period under review, explicit references were made to Article 33,[144] Article 37,[145] Article 99[146] and Chapter VI[147] of the Charter during the Council's deliberations, although not all cases resulted in a constitutional discussion. No explicit references were made to Articles 36 or 38.

The section is divided into three subsections: A. Reference to peaceful means of settlement in the light of Article 33 of the Charter; B. Referral of legal disputes to the International Court of Justice in the light of Article 36 (3); and C. Utilization of Article 99 by the Secretary-General for the pacific settlement of disputes. The section features cases in which there were relevant constitutional discussions during the period under review.

A. Reference to peaceful means of settlement in the light of Article 33 of the Charter

Article 33 of the Charter stipulates that any dispute that is likely to endanger the maintenance of international peace and security should first be addressed through negotiation, mediation or other peaceful means and that the Council can call upon the parties to settle their disputes by such means.

---

[143] Ibid., paras. 4 and 6.

[144] In connection with the maintenance of international peace and security, see S/PV.9167 (Kenya); and, in connection with threats to international peace and security, see S/PV.9216 (Brazil).

[145] In connection with the implementation of the note by the President of the Security Council (S/2017/507), see S/PV.9079 (Peru).

[146] In connection with the implementation of the note by the President of the Security Council (S/2017/507), see S/PV.9079 (Austria); in connection with the maintenance of international peace and security, see S/PV.9167 (Kenya and Mexico), S/PV.9220 (Kenya and Pakistan) and S/PV.9220 (Resumption 1) (Singapore).

[147] In connection with threats to international peace and security, see S/PV.8960 (Gabon and Ukraine) and S/PV.9206 (Brazil); in connection with general issues relating to sanctions, see S/PV.8962 (Ghana); in connection with the situation concerning Iraq, see S/PV.8975 (Iraq) and S/PV.9145 (Brazil); in connection with the letter dated 28 February 2014 from the Permanent Representative of Ukraine to the United Nations addressed to the President of the Security Council (S/2014/136), see S/PV.8986 (Brazil); in connection with the maintenance of international peace and security, see S/PV.9052 (Resumption 1) (Italy), S/PV.9112 (Secretary-General and Brazil); and, in connection with the reports of the Secretary-General on the Sudan and South Sudan, see S/PV.9054 (China).

During the period under review, discussions with respect to Article 33 were held under the items entitled "Women and peace and security" (case 7), "Threats to international peace and security" (case 8), "Maintenance of international peace and security" (case 9) and "Letter dated 13 September 2022 from the Permanent Representative of Armenia to the United Nations addressed to the President of the Security Council (S/2022/688)" (case 10).

Case 7
Women and peace and security

On 18 January, at the initiative of Norway, which held the presidency for the month,[148] the Council held a high-level open debate under the item entitled "Women and peace and security" and the sub-item entitled "Protecting participation: addressing violence targeting women in peace and security processes", during which it heard briefings by the United Nations High Commissioner for Human Rights, the Executive Director of the Women and Children Legal Research Foundation and the Executive Director of the NGO Working Group on Women, Peace and Security.[149]

In her briefing, the United Nations High Commissioner for Human Rights stated that the Council had played a vital role in the drive to ensure that peace was built by and for women, but noted that between 1992 and 2019, only 13 per cent of negotiators, 6 per cent of mediators and 6 per cent of signatories in major peace processes worldwide had been women.[150] She noted that human rights violations against women significantly undermined global efforts to prevent conflict and sustain peace because they deterred women from participation and leadership. She expressed the view that it would be valuable for the Council to consider harmonizing approaches to ensure the safe involvement of women in peace processes, as well as their participation in the Council's work, and added that decisions on peace that did not reflect women's voices, realities and rights were not sustainable.

During the subsequent discussion, Council members and other speakers exchanged views on the importance of, and how to ensure the meaningful and safe inclusion of, women in political processes and the peaceful settlement of disputes. In their remarks, many speakers recalled that resolution 1325 (2000) and overall practice demonstrated the importance of inclusivity, including that of women, for conflict prevention and sustaining peace. Several speakers echoed that view by noting the role of women and the unique perspective that women brought to peace processes, including an understanding of local communities and dynamics.[151] For example, the Minister for Foreign Affairs and Regional Integration of Ghana noted that women's voices brought real gender perspectives to peace discourses, which led to better policies and more equitable, gender-sensitive and sustainable peace deals.[152] The representative of the Russian Federation stated that the engagement of women was of vital importance as it helped, among other things, to build trust and trust-based relations with local populations. The Minister for Foreign Affairs of Norway opined that women's participation was the long-term game-changer in that women could directly influence decisions about peace and security and thereby shape protection measures that worked for them and their families and communities. While noting that resolution 1325 (2000) placed women's issues at the centre of global conflict prevention, the representative of Rwanda emphasized that the full, equal and meaningful participation of women in peace and security processes helped to minimize the chances of conflict and community confrontation and provided a larger sense of security to local populations, including women and children.

Despite its clear significance, both members and non-members of the Council recognized that the effective participation of women in conflict prevention and resolution remained hindered by a lack of protection. In that regard, many speakers referred to the responsibility of States for fostering and developing the necessary mechanisms and institutions to promote accountability for threats and violence

---

[148] A concept note was circulated by a letter dated 10 January (S/2022/22).

[149] See S/PV.8949 and S/PV.8949 (Resumption 1). For more information on the briefings, see part I, sect. 29.

[150] See S/PV.8949.

[151] Ibid. (Ghana, United Arab Emirates, United States, Russian Federation, Norway and Rwanda); and S/PV.8949 (Resumption 1) (Jordan).

[152] See S/PV.8949.

against women and to protect their participation.[153] The representative of Belgium, speaking also on behalf of the Netherlands and Luxembourg, stated that it was necessary to apply a gender perspective in peace and security processes, consider the specific risks faced by different groups of women human rights defenders and integrate appropriate risk mitigation where possible.[154] The representative of Argentina stated that normalizing the participation of women in peace processes and shining a light on the important role that they played, together with increasing the cost of attacks on them through accountability measures, were vital to broadening the space for their participation.

Taking a broader view, the representative of China stated that nothing could provide more basic protection for women than a holistic approach to conflict prevention and resolution that addressed both the symptoms and root causes of violence and conflict.[155] The representative of the Russian Federation called for greater focus on the specific development issues faced by women, including poverty eradication and access for women to education in conflict-affected countries. The representative of India called on Member States to create a conducive political environment for the meaningful participation of women based on the principles of democracy, pluralism and the rule of law and to equally focus in a holistic manner on their socioeconomic empowerment. The representative of Rwanda stated that the protection of women should be part of the inclusive process of developing a policy framework seeking to provide equal rights and opportunities.

The representative of the Russian Federation expressed the view that creating preferential processes for the protection of certain categories of participants in conflict resolution was not only counterproductive but also dangerous, as it could foment additional social tensions, set off new waves of conflict and exacerbate existing conflicts. He added that it was evident that creating safe conditions for women's participation required that the safety and security of all participants was established and that that was the only way to ensure meaningful, robust and sustained peace. The representative of China stressed the need to strengthen the protection of women in conflict areas without exception and that all women were entitled to protection, regardless of whether or not they were part of the peace process. The representative of the United Arab Emirates highlighted that Member States had to take serious steps to tackle structural gender inequality as a main root cause of violence against women.

Speakers also recognized the need for measures for the protection of women's political participation to be taken across the United Nations system. For example, speaking on behalf of the Human Rights and Conflict Prevention Caucus, the representative of Switzerland stated that the wider United Nations system had a duty to prevent and respond to alleged cases of intimidation and reprisals against those who provided information or sought to engage with it and to ensure accountability when such acts occurred. The representative of Malta stressed that the participation and protection pillars of the women and peace and security agenda were closely related and that there could not be participation without protection. The representative of Ireland stated that her delegation would continue to insist on the safe participation of women in peace processes led by the United Nations. The Minister for Foreign Affairs and Regional Integration of Ghana stated that the Council should urge the Secretary-General to ensure the allocation of targeted, practical and rapid resources to facilitate responses to threat against women peacebuilders and to use his good offices to build the capacity of United Nations staff in conflict zones, with the objective of increasing their understanding of the work of women in peace processes. She also suggested that United Nations sanctions committees should be utilized to bring to justice those guilty of intimidation, threats and reprisals against women in peacebuilding and encouraged the active participation of women on panels of experts.

Some speakers specifically addressed strengthening the work of United Nations peace operations in this domain through the inclusion of the protection of women's political participation in their mandates

[153] Ibid. (Ghana, United States, India, France, Kenya, Mexico, Japan, Malta, Canada (on behalf of the Group of Friends of Women, Peace and Security), New Zealand, Estonia and Rwanda); and S/PV.8949 (Resumption 1) (Portugal, Slovakia, Argentina, Lithuania, Indonesia, Malaysia and Denmark (on behalf of the Nordic countries)).

[154] See S/PV.8949 (Resumption 1).

[155] See S/PV.8949.

and the deployment of more women peacekeepers and women's protection advisers.[156] The representative of Japan suggested that United Nations agencies, such as the United Nations Entity for Gender Equality and the Empowerment of Women (UN-Women), and local non-governmental agencies could play a key role in supporting and protecting women in engaging in peace and security processes, adding that the full, equal and meaningful participation of women human rights defenders and peacebuilders required long-term collective efforts.[157] The Minister for Europe and Foreign Affairs of Albania, as subsequently echoed by other delegations, underscored the need to support and resource relevant United Nations entities to enable them to provide protection and described the launch of the funding window for women human rights defenders as a positive development. Similarly, speaking on behalf of the Group of Friends of Women, Peace and Security, the representative of Canada encouraged the United Nations, its Member States, international financial institutions and other relevant stakeholders to provide rapid, flexible and real funding for the protection of women peacebuilders, human rights defenders and gender equality advocates.

Multiple speakers highlighted the responsibility and role of the Council in the protection of women's political participation, including with respect to women civil society briefers at its meetings.[158] In that regard, the representative of Brazil stated that the Council must work not only to bring women to peace negotiation tables but also to find ways to protect those invited from direct violence and intimidation.[159] He added that normalizing the participation of women in peace processes and upgrading their role, including as briefers to the Council, was a very concrete way to implement the women and peace and security agenda. Several speakers expressed support for the work of the Office of the United Nations High Commissioner for Human Rights on addressing and mitigating the risk of reprisals against women engaged with the Council and the United Nations.[160] The representative of the United Kingdom opined that the Council could operate effectively only when it received honest briefings about situations on the ground, in particular from women human rights defenders and peacebuilders.[161] Underlining the crucial nature of the engagement of women human rights defenders with the Council, the representative of Belgium pointed to a collective responsibility to protect people with the courage to come to the Council Chamber, including by taking precautions to mitigate risks and, in cases of reprisals, to ensure accountability and protection.[162] Multiple delegations agreed that the Council had to clearly condemn threats or the use of violence against women peacebuilders, in particular against women peacebuilders who engaged with it.[163]

Case 8
Threats to international peace and security

At a meeting held on 31 January under the item entitled "Threats to international peace and security",[164] the Under-Secretary-General for Political and Peacebuilding Affairs gave a briefing to the Council on reports regarding the deployment of troops and heavy weaponry by the Russian Federation and mounting tensions along the border with Ukraine. During the subsequent discussion, several speakers

---

[156] Ibid. (United Arab Emirates, United States, India, Brazil, Mexico, Canada (on behalf of the Group of Friends of Women, Peace and Security) and Poland); and S/PV.8949 (Resumption 1) (Portugal, Ecuador, Argentina, Indonesia, Fiji, Malaysia and Denmark (on behalf of the Nordic countries)).

[157] See S/PV.8949.

[158] Ibid. (Albania, United Arab Emirates, Ireland, Brazil, Mexico, Norway, Slovenia, Canada (on behalf of the Group of Friends of Women, Peace and Security), New Zealand, European Union, Estonia and Switzerland (on behalf of the Human Rights and Conflict Prevention Caucus)); and S/PV.8949 (Resumption 1) (Portugal, Belgium, Ecuador, Denmark (on behalf of the Nordic countries)).

[159] See S/PV.8949.

[160] Ibid. (United Kingdom, France, Mexico, European Union, Italy and Switzerland (on behalf of the Human Rights and Conflict Prevention Caucus)); and S/PV.8949 (Resumption 1) (Portugal, Belgium and Slovakia).

[161] See S/PV.8949.

[162] See S/PV.8949 (Resumption 1).

[163] See S/PV.8949 (Ghana, France, Mexico, Malta, Slovenia, Canada, New Zealand, Estonia and Switzerland (on behalf of the Human Rights and Conflict Prevention Caucus)); and S/PV.8949 (Resumption 1) (Portugal, Belgium (on behalf of the Benelux countries), Ecuador, Liechtenstein, Australia, Latvia and Denmark (on behalf of the Nordic countries)).

[164] See S/PV.8960.

referred to the obligation of the parties to peacefully settle their dispute in accordance with Chapter VI of the Charter.

For example, while calling on all stakeholders to show restraint and turn to dialogue and negotiations in order to preserve stability and peace in the region, the representative of Gabon underscored that this was the moment for the international community and its members to activate the channels of preventive diplomacy, in accordance with Chapter VI of the Charter. The representative of Mexico recalled that States had the duty to resolve their disputes by peaceful means, as established by international law, and underlined the responsibility of the Council to carry out its preventive work and measure up to dealing with what the circumstances demanded. He added that his country had defended and would continue to defend the use of diplomacy over force and that diplomatic channels with regard to the issue facing the Council remained open and had not been exhausted. The representative of Kenya stated that where there were disputes regarding territorial jurisdiction or security interests, his country strongly supported patient diplomacy as the "first, second and third options". The representative of Ghana stated that differences between Member States should be resolved only through peaceful means, in conformity with the Charter. The representative of Brazil called for consistency in the application of the principles enshrined in the Charter in a non-selective manner and recalled that the prohibition on the use of force, the peaceful resolution of disputes and the principles of sovereignty, territorial integrity and the protection of human rights were pillars of the collective security system. He further highlighted the need for good faith to address the legitimate security concerns of all parties, including the Russian Federation and Ukraine, and encouraged the parties to pursue genuine talks on the implementation of the Minsk agreements.

In his statement, the representative of Ukraine noted that the members of the Council had received very important information at the meeting which they needed to take into account so as to make an informed decision, when appropriate, on acting swiftly and decisively in employing preventive diplomacy under Chapter VI of the Charter, which, as he pointed out, enshrined the Council's responsibility to investigate any dispute that might lead to international friction or give rise to a dispute.

Case 9
Maintenance of international peace and security

On 22 August, at the initiative of China, which held the presidency for the month,[165] the Council held a meeting under the item entitled "Maintenance of international peace and security" and the sub-item entitled "Promote common security through dialogue and cooperation", during which it heard briefings by the Secretary-General and the President of the tenth Review Conference of the Parties to the Treaty on the Non-Proliferation of Nuclear Weapons.[166]

In his briefing, the Secretary-General stated that the collective security system was being tested like never before and that the world was riven by geopolitical divides, conflicts and instability, from military coups to inter-State conflicts, invasions and wars, adding that lingering differences between the great powers, including in the Council, continued to limit the ability of the international community to respond collectively.[167] He stressed that the tools that had kept the world from a catastrophic world war were more important than ever, but that they had to be fit for today's rapidly deteriorating international peace and security environment, and that there was a need to reforge a global consensus around the cooperation required to ensure collective security, including the work of the United Nations. The Secretary-General noted that, through his proposal for a New Agenda for Peace, as contained in the report entitled "Our Common Agenda",[168] the diplomatic toolbox of the Charter to end conflicts was being explored, especially the provisions of Chapter VI on negotiation, enquiry, mediation, conciliation, arbitration and judicial settlement. Focus was also being placed on prevention and peacebuilding, which included strengthening the foresight of future threats, anticipating flashpoints and long-standing conditions that could explode into violence and exploring new and expanded roles for regional actors and groups, in

---

[165] A concept note was circulated by a letter dated 12 August (see S/2022/617).
[166] See S/PV.9112. For more information on the briefings, see part I, sect. 35.
[167] See S/PV.9112.
[168] See A/75/982.

particular as cross-border threats to peace and security emerged.[169] It also included putting human rights first in political and financial investments that could address the root causes of conflict, from social protection and education to programming to end violence and discrimination and to increase women's participation across civic and political life.

Noting that not all members of the Council were parties to the Non-Proliferation Treaty, the President of its tenth Review Conference expressed the hope that Council members could appreciate the important role played by the Treaty as a contribution to the betterment of the international security environment, adding that there were few issues more vital to common security than preventing the use of nuclear weapons.

On the state of the multilateral system and nuclear non-proliferation, Council members discussed ways to strengthen the implementation of Chapter VI of the Charter on the pacific settlement of disputes. In his statement, the representative of Brazil expressed the view that the international community should make more frequent use of preventive diplomacy and mediation and focus more on Chapter VI rather than Chapter VII. Noting that the law of action and reaction was especially applicable to the use of force, he underscored that insisting on the peaceful settlement of disputes was the only way to get out of that vicious circle. The representative of Gabon stated that international cooperation implied acting together, consulting with one another regularly, in times of peace as in times of war, and easing the differences. According to the representative, that also meant considering or taking into account each other's expectations and easing tensions with a view to seeking a peaceful settlement of disputes. The representative of the United Kingdom asserted that dialogue and cooperation were essential components in settling disputes and building peace and security. The representative of Ghana expressed the view that, in the present circumstances, it might be necessary to initiate a consensual process for Member States to formally recommit to the purposes and principles of the Charter, especially its key purpose to ensure international peace and security based on the pacific settlement of disputes, the non-use of force in international relations, except under very limited and defined conditions, the development of friendly relations and the pursuit of international cooperation in resolving international problems. The representative of Mexico noted that his country had always promoted dialogue and the peaceful settlement of disputes in order to address conflicts early and prevent their escalation. He added that preventive diplomacy and recourse to means for the peaceful settlement of disputes were key to maintaining peace and that, in order to conduct genuine and effective diplomacy, the United Nations had to strengthen coordination between its main organs. The representative of China stated that the only way to achieve common security was to find the highest common denominator through dialogue and cooperation and settling disputes by peaceful means. He added that Council members should make greater efforts to promote the political settlement of disputes and create synergies with the mediation efforts of the Secretary-General to better meet the current challenges and safeguard the common security.

The representative of Brazil stated that durable peace required comprehensive approaches, which could benefit significantly from the support of the Peacebuilding Commission as a platform to promote greater coordination among relevant partners of a particular country at risk of lapsing or relapsing into conflict. The representative of Ireland called for moving away from a default position of responding after a crisis had happened and being more proactive with regard to prevention. Ireland joined the call of the Secretary-General, as outlined in the report entitled "Our Common Agenda", for enhancing support for the Commission and ensuring that peacebuilding was adequately and sustainably financed. She also noted that the Commission continued to advance its civil society engagement, increase its advice to the Council and, as part of the wider United Nations peacebuilding architecture, had contributed to discussions on peacebuilding financing. Expressing support for the New Agenda for Peace, with its heightened focus on reinforcing human rights and freedoms and international law through a comprehensive and integrated approach to peace and security, the representative of Albania noted that it would be possible to do better and achieve more by investing in prevention rather than always addressing symptoms, and that dialogue and cooperation were crucial to that.

The representative of Norway expressed the view that it was necessary to improve the Council's situational awareness. In that regard, she added, there was a key role for the Secretariat and United Nations

[169] See S/PV.9112.

briefers to play in using their interactions with the Council to bring emerging issues to its attention and sound the alarm. To achieve sustainable peace, Norway strongly believed that it was necessary to talk to all actors involved in any conflict, and the full and meaningful inclusion of women was crucial in that regard. The representative of Ireland stressed the need to ensure that the approach to peace and security took a human rights-based approach that was inclusive, in particular of the most vulnerable. Moreover, she stated that it was vital to pay heed to women, young people, human rights defenders and civil society representatives in the Council Chamber and essential that they could speak freely about the stark realities of conflict without fear of reprisals or intimidation. She added that support for local peacebuilders, in particular women and youth, was key to finding local sustainable solutions to conflict.

Case 10
Letter dated 13 September 2022 from the Permanent Representative of Armenia to the United Nations addressed to the President of the Security Council (S/2022/688)

At a meeting held on 15 September under the item entitled "Letter dated 13 September 2022 from the Permanent Representative of Armenia to the United Nations addressed to the President of the Security Council (S/2022/688)",[170] the Council heard a briefing by the Assistant Secretary-General for Europe, Central Asia and the Americas, in the Department of Political and Peacebuilding Affairs and the Department of Peace Operations, regarding the situation on the border between Armenia and Azerbaijan.

During the meeting, several speakers underscored the importance of settling the dispute between the two countries peacefully, called for the cessation of hostilities and noted that the use of violence or force was not acceptable. The representative of Gabon condemned the use of armed force to settle disputes between States and reiterated that there could be no viable military solution to the conflict. The representative of India said that disputes such as the one between Armenia and Azerbaijan should be settled through diplomacy and dialogue and underscored that there could be no military or violent solution to any conflict. She encouraged both sides to pursue diplomatic pathways to arrive at a lasting and peaceful solution. Noting that the use of military force to settle disputes was unacceptable, the representative of Norway stated that her delegation was encouraged by the news about an agreement on a cessation of hostilities, welcomed that initiative and called on both sides to take immediate steps to de-escalate tensions and to exercise maximum restraint. She added that any outstanding issues had to be resolved peacefully through dialogue and within existing formats. The representative of Ghana welcomed the meeting as an opportunity for the Council to focus its attention on how the conflict could be peacefully resolved on the basis of established international principles that were mutually acceptable to the parties and expressed the view that the use of violence could not be the final arbiter for the settlement of the dispute. He also urged Armenia and Azerbaijan to sustain the truce and renewed his country's call for the complete cessation of hostilities and the de-escalation of tensions. The representative of Brazil called on the parties to respect international law and the Charter and to resolve their disputes through dialogue and diplomacy. He also urged both sides to avoid actions that could escalate tensions and threaten the security of the civilian population. The representative of France noted that everyone was bound by the Charter to settle their disputes peacefully and that the parties had to resume dialogue to resolve all outstanding issues through negotiations.

Furthermore, at a meeting held on 20 December under the same item,[171] the Council heard another briefing by the Assistant Secretary-General for Europe, Central Asia and the Americas, in which he commended various ongoing engagements and mediation efforts and encouraged their close coordination to ensure maximum effectiveness. He also recalled that the Secretary-General had urged progress towards a peaceful settlement during his bilateral meetings with the Prime Minister of Armenia and the Minister for Foreign Affairs of Azerbaijan.

During the discussion, Council members called for the de-escalation of tensions and settling of outstanding issues through dialogue and negotiations. The representative of the United Arab Emirates urged the parties to resolve their differences through peaceful and diplomatic means, in line with international law and the Charter, and encouraged them to engage constructively and in good faith with

[170] See S/PV.9132.
[171] See S/PV.9228.

mediation efforts. The representative of Albania stated that there was no alternative to a peaceful negotiated solution through the path of diplomacy. The representative of China expressed the view that the disputes surrounding the Lachin corridor should be resolved through dialogue and consultations and encouraged Armenia and Azerbaijan, on the basis of the trilateral statements that they had issued with the Russian Federation and with the good offices of the Russian Federation and other parties concerned, to meet each other half way and properly resolve disputes on the basis of universally recognized international law and norms governing international relations. The representative of the United States said that outstanding grievances between the two countries had to be solved through peaceful negotiations, adding that the international community had to do its part and remain engaged in efforts to diplomatically broker a lasting peace. Calling upon Azerbaijan and Armenia to exercise restraint and to refrain from the kinds of steps that could increase tensions, the representative of the Russian Federation held the view that all disputes between the two countries should be resolved exclusively through political and diplomatic means. According to the representative of Kenya, the deployment of tools available in the Charter for the pacific settlement of disputes, including consultations and negotiations, offered the best chances for a sustainable outcome. The representative of Mexico called on international actors with the capacity to engage in dialogue with the parties to urge them to resolve their differences through diplomatic channels. The representative of Ghana noted, inter alia, that it was important for the process of delineation and delimitation of borders to be undertaken on the basis of international law and the Charter, with particular regard to the principles such as the pacific settlement of disputes. The representative of India reaffirmed his country's support for the ongoing mediation efforts in the region and pointed to the consistent position of India that such disputes should be settled through diplomacy and dialogue.

B. Referral of legal disputes to the International Court of Justice in the light of Article 36 (3) of the Charter

Article 36 (3) of the Charter provides that, in making recommendations under Article 36, the Council should also take into consideration that legal disputes should, as a general rule, be referred by the parties to the International Court of Justice in accordance with the provisions of the Statute of the Court. During the period under review, a discussion with respect to Article 36 (3) was held in connection with the item entitled "Maintenance of international peace and security" (case 11).

Case 11
Maintenance of international peace and security

On 2 June, at the initiative of Albania, which held the presidency for the month,[172] the Council held a high-level open debate under the item entitled "Maintenance of international peace and security" and the sub-item entitled "Strengthening accountability and justice for serious violations of international law".[173] During the meeting, the Council heard briefings by the President of the International Court of Justice, the United Nations High Commissioner for Human Rights and Professor Dapo Akande of the University of Oxford.[174]

In her briefing, the President of the International Court of Justice highlighted the contributions of the Court to the maintenance of international peace and security, in particular within the legal framework of accountability. She noted that accountability for atrocities was enhanced when the governing law was clear and agreed among States and where a mechanism was in place to ensure that inter-State disputes could be adjudicated. Those had been among the concerns that had motivated the elaboration by the International Law Commission of draft articles on the prevention and punishment of crimes against humanity, which were under consideration by the General Assembly. The President of the Court also noted that the draft articles provided a basis for inter-State disputes to be adjudicated by the Court or in arbitration, thereby promoting the goal of State accountability in relation to crimes against humanity. The adoption of a

[172] A concept note was circulated by a letter dated 24 May (S/2022/418/Rev.1).
[173] See S/PV.9052 and S/PV.9052 (Resumption 1).
[174] See S/PV.9052. For more information on the briefings, see part I, sect. 35.

convention on crimes against humanity would be one way to promote accountability for violations of some of the most fundamental obligations found in international law. She concluded that the Court stood ready to decide any disputes over which it would have jurisdiction on the basis of such a convention.

In their statements, Council members and other speakers recognized the role played by the International Court of Justice in the pacific settlement of disputes. The representative of India said that, as the principal judicial organ of the United Nations, the Court had the role of settling, in accordance with international law, legal disputes submitted to it by States and issuing advisory opinions on legal questions referred to it by authorized United Nations organs and specialized agencies. The representative of Ireland shared the view of the President of the Court that the Court was central to the maintenance and strengthening of an international order based on the rule of law, noting that the Constitution of Ireland affirmed the country's adherence to the principle of the pacific settlement of international disputes by international arbitration or judicial determination. He also expressed a firm belief in the value of the Court's role in helping to prevent conflict between States, urged all Member States, and especially Council members, to accept its compulsory jurisdiction and called on the Council to strengthen its cooperation with the Court. The representative of Brazil noted that the Court played a vital role in preventing conflicts by providing Member States with legal and preventive means to resolve their differences.

The representative of Mexico held the view that the International Court of Justice had to be strengthened, as it was the main judicial organ of the Organization and a guarantor of accountability in cases of international responsibility of States. That could be achieved by submitting to the Court those disputes that fell within its jurisdiction. However, it was imperative that more Member States accepted the compulsory jurisdiction of the Court, without conditions. The representative of Mexico also stated that the Secretary-General had to remain a key actor in the search for dialogue and the mediation of situations of tension, and noted that it would be useful, as an additional tool, for the General Assembly to grant the Secretary-General permanent authorization to request advisory opinions from the Court, a suggestion that had already been made by the former Secretary-General, Boutros Boutros-Ghali. The representative of Norway underlined the important role of the Court in the peaceful resolution of disputes. She held the view that Council members had a special responsibility to do what they could to ensure that parties faithfully abided by binding decisions rendered by the Court.

In the context of the responsibility of States for their internationally wrongful acts, the representative of Slovakia expressed appreciation for the work of the Court and its vital role in the peaceful settlement of disputes.[175] He reiterated his country's call on all States to accept the jurisdiction of the Court and respect its legally binding decisions and called on the Council to pay closer attention to instances of non-compliance. Noting that Member States could consider making greater use of the fact-finding capacity of the Council, the representative of the Philippines stated that the Council might also request advisory opinions of the Court on legal questions arising within the scope of its activities, including on the issue of institutionalizing international legal principles of accountability and the related accountability mechanisms in order to have an impact in practice.

C. Utilization of Article 99 of the Charter by the Secretary-General for the pacific settlement of disputes

Article 99 of the Charter stipulates that the Secretary-General may bring to the attention of the Council any matter which, in his opinion, may threaten the maintenance of international peace and security. The multiple tools available to the Secretary-General under Article 99 were discussed in connection with the item entitled "Maintenance of international peace and security" (case 12).

[175] See S/PV.9052 (Resumption 1).

Case 12
Maintenance of international peace and security

On 14 December, at the initiative of India, which held the presidency for the month,[176] the Council held a high-level open debate under the item entitled "Maintenance of international peace and security" and the sub-item entitled "New orientation for reformed multilateralism".[177] At the meeting, the Council heard briefings by the Secretary-General and the President of the General Assembly.[178] During the debate, speakers referred to Article 99 of the Charter and the role of the good offices of the Secretary-General in the pacific settlement of disputes.[179]

In his briefing, the Secretary-General announced that the New Agenda for Peace, which he said he hoped to submit to Member States in 2023, would, inter alia, address the full range of new and old security challenges and examine ways to update existing tools for mediation, peacekeeping, peacebuilding and counter-terrorism, while also looking at new and emerging threats in less traditional domains, including cyberspace and outer space.[180]

Calling for adherence to Article 100 of the Charter, which protected the Secretary-General and United Nations staff from external influence and instruction, the representative of Kenya noted that the Secretary-General had to be fully on the side of the Charter and should fully observe Article 99 without regard for the approval or disapproval of any State or party. The representative of Mexico expressed the view that the success of the Council in discharging its responsibilities in accordance with its mandate depended also on the success of the General Assembly, the Economic and Social Council and the International Court of Justice in fulfilling their own mandates, in conjunction with the work of the Secretary-General. The representative of Norway stated that the Council should be more vocal in its support for the good offices of the Secretary-General.

The representative of Pakistan held the view that the Secretary-General should be more insistent in exercising his authority under Article 99 of the Charter to draw the Council's attention to impending threats to peace and security, and that no party to a conflict or dispute should be able to refuse the Secretary-General's good offices when they were offered or reject recourse to the modalities for the pacific settlement of disputes prescribed under Article 38. Noting that any United Nations reform exercise should leverage and empower the good offices of the Secretary-General, the representative of Singapore explicitly referred to Article 99 and expressed support for a greater role for the Secretary-General in mediation and conflict prevention.[181] In that connection, he cited the Black Sea Grain Initiative, to enable the international export of grain from Ukraine, which had helped to ensure food supplies and stabilize food prices globally, as a recent concrete example of the Secretary-General using his good offices. The representative of Ecuador held the view that the Council should support the efforts of the Secretary-General to promote a preventive approach that addressed the root causes of conflict and prioritized peacebuilding, accelerating disarmament and strengthening non-proliferation, as well as countering corrosive anti-institutional narratives that contributed to violent extremism.

---

[176] A concept note was circulated by a letter dated 25 November (S/2022/880).
[177] See S/PV.9220 and S/PV.9220 (Resumption 1).
[178] See S/PV.9220. For more information on the briefings, see part I, sect. 35.
[179] See S/PV.9220 and S/PV.9220 (Resumption 1).
[180] See S/PV.9220.
[181] See S/PV.9220 (Resumption 1).

Part VII

Actions with respect to threats to the peace, breaches of the peace, and acts of aggression (Chapter VII of the Charter)

Contents

Introductory note

Part VII of the present Supplement deals with action taken by the Security Council with respect to threats to the peace, breaches of the peace or acts of aggression, within the framework of Chapter VII of the Charter of the United Nations, including Articles 39 to 51. The part is divided into 10 sections, each focusing on selected material to highlight the interpretation and application of the provisions of Chapter VII by the Council in its deliberations and decisions.

Sections I to IV cover material related to Articles 39 to 42, which regulate the power of the Council to determine threats to international peace and security and to take the appropriate action in response to those threats, including the imposition of sanctions measures or the authorization of the use of force. Sections V and VI focus on Articles 43 to 47, regarding the command and deployment of military forces. Sections VII and VIII address, respectively, the obligations of Member States under Articles 48 and 49, while sections IX and X address, respectively, the practice of the Council with respect to Articles 50 and 51.

The sections contain subsections on discussions held within the Council regarding the proper interpretation and implementation of the Articles governing the Council's primary responsibility for the maintenance of international peace and security.

During the period under review, and similar to previous periods, the Council adopted 52 per cent of its resolutions (28 out of 54 resolutions) explicitly under Chapter VII of the Charter. Most of those resolutions concerned the mandates of United Nations and regional peacekeeping missions or multinational forces, and the imposition, extension, modification or termination of sanctions measures.

As discussed in section I, in 2022, while the Council did not determine the existence of any new threats to international peace and security, it reaffirmed that the situations in Afghanistan, the Central African Republic, the Democratic Republic of the Congo, Haiti, Lebanon, Libya, Mali, Somalia, South Sudan and the Sudan (including Abyei), Yemen and the former Yugoslavia constituted threats to regional and/or international peace and security.

With respect to specific countries and regions, the Council in its decisions recalled past determinations of threats to international peace and security of significance in those situations. For example, in relation to Afghanistan, the Council expressed concern over the cultivation, production, trade and trafficking of illicit drugs and acknowledged that illicit proceeds of the drug trafficking in Afghanistan were a source of financing for terrorist groups and non-State actors that threatened regional and international security. In connection with the situation in the Syrian Arab Republic, the Council determined that the devastating humanitarian situation in the country continued to constitute a threat to peace and security in the region. With regard to the situation in Somalia, the Council expressed grave concern that Al-Shabaab and its terrorist and other activities continued to pose a serious threat to the peace, security and stability of Somalia and the region.

Under thematic items, in 2022, concerning non-proliferation in the Democratic People's Republic of Korea, the Council determined that the proliferation of nuclear, chemical and biological weapons, as well as their means of delivery, continued to constitute a threat to international peace and security. With regard to the non-proliferation of weapons of mass destruction more broadly, the Council determined that the threat posed by the proliferation of nuclear, chemical and biological weapons, as well as their means of delivery, together with the threat posed by the illicit trafficking of such weapons and their means of delivery, and related materials, equipment and technology, which could be used for the design, development, production or use of nuclear, chemical and biological weapons and their means of delivery, added a new dimension to the issue of proliferation of such weapons and also posed a threat to international peace and security. The Council also recalled that Islamic State in Iraq and the Levant (ISIL/Da'esh) constituted a global threat to international peace and security.

As described in section II, in 2022, the Council adopted no decisions calling for compliance with provisional measures that might have been of relevance to the interpretation and application of Article 40 of the Charter, nor were there any discussions of relevance to the interpretation and application of Article 40.

As covered in section III, in the period under review, the Council established a new sanctions regime concerning Haiti and renamed the sanctions regime concerning Somalia to the sanctions regime concerning Al-Shabaab, underscoring the focus of the sanctions measures imposed on Al-Shabaab. In addition, by its resolution 2664 (2022), the Council introduced a standing humanitarian exemption on all asset freezes imposed by it or by its sanctions committees, with the exception of the ISIL/Da'esh and Al-Qaida sanctions regime, for which the exemption would apply for an initial period of two years, and the Taliban sanctions regime, for which the humanitarian exemption established in resolution 2615 (2021) would remain in effect. The Council renewed the existing measures concerning the Central African Republic, Libya, Mali, South Sudan, the Sudan and Yemen, as well as those concerning Al-Shabaab. It also renewed the existing measures concerning the Taliban and associated individuals and entities and ISIL/Da'esh and Al-Qaida and associates. In addition to renewing the existing measures concerning the Democratic Republic of the Congo, the Council expanded the listing criteria to include individuals and entities involved in the production, manufacture or use of improvised explosive devices and lifted the notification requirements for shipments of arms and related materiel for the Democratic Republic of the Congo. No changes were made to the measures concerning Guinea-Bissau. As far as judicial measures were concerned, no action was taken in 2022.

As described in section IV, the Council reiterated authorizations granted prior to 2022 to United Nations peacekeeping missions and multinational forces to use force under Chapter VII of the Charter, with regard to the maintenance or restoration of international peace and security in Bosnia and Herzegovina, the Central African Republic, the Democratic Republic of the Congo, Lebanon, Libya, Mali, Somalia, South Sudan and the Sudan (including Abyei). In that regard, the Council renewed the authorization to use force to discharge the protection of civilians mandate of the United Nations Interim Security Force for Abyei, the United Nations Multidimensional Integrated Stabilization Mission in the Central African Republic, the United Nations Organization Stabilization Mission in the Democratic Republic of the Congo, the United Nations Interim Force in Lebanon, the United Nations Multidimensional Integrated Stabilization Mission in Mali, the African Union Transition Mission in Somalia and the United Nations Mission in South Sudan. In relation to the situation in Libya, the Council reiterated its authorization granted to Member States to use "all measures commensurate to the specific circumstances" when confronting migrant smugglers as well as in carrying out the inspection of vessels in the implementation of the arms embargo. With regard to the situation in Bosnia and Herzegovina, the Council renewed its authorization granted to Member States, under the European Union military operation in Bosnia and Herzegovina (EUFOR-Althea) and the North Atlantic Treaty Organization (NATO) presence, to take "all necessary measures" to effect the implementation of and to ensure compliance with the General Framework Agreement for Peace in Bosnia and Herzegovina and the rules and procedures governing command and control of airspace over Bosnia and Herzegovina with respect to all civilian and military air traffic and, at the request of either EUFOR-Althea or NATO, to take "all necessary measures" in their defence.

As described in sections V to VIII, in the context of peacekeeping, the Council called upon Member States to contribute troops and other assets, including aerial force enablers. Member States also called for the Council to deepen its interaction and consultation with troop- and police-contributing countries. In addition, the Council frequently requested compliance with its decisions adopted under Chapter VII of the Charter by States and non-State actors alike, as well as by regional and subregional organizations. As featured in section IX, Council members discussed the impact of counter-terrorism measures and sanctions on the provision of humanitarian assistance. As covered in section X, Article 51 of the Charter and the principle of individual and/or collective self-defence were cited abundantly in communications addressed to the Council, as well as in its discussions concerning the conflict in Ukraine and the situation in the Syrian Arab Republic. In 2022, there was a fourfold increase in the number of references to Article 51 compared with 2021.

I. Determination of a threat to the peace, breach of the peace or act of aggression in accordance with Article 39 of the Charter

Article 39

The Security Council shall determine the existence of any threat to the peace, breach of the peace, or act of aggression and shall make recommendations, or decide what measures shall be taken in accordance with Articles 41 and 42, to maintain or restore international peace and security.

Note

Section I concerns the practice of the Council with regard to the determination of the existence of a threat to the peace, breach of the peace or act of aggression in accordance with Article 39 of the Charter of the United Nations. It provides information regarding the determination of the existence of a threat by the Council and examines instances in which a threat was debated. The section is divided into three subsections. Subsection A provides an overview of the decisions of the Council relating to the determination of a "threat to the peace". Subsection B contains a series of case studies describing some of the arguments advanced during the Council's deliberations in connection with the determination of a threat in accordance with Article 39 and the adoption of some of the resolutions mentioned in subsection A. Subsection C outlines the references to Article 39 found in communications addressed to the Council in 2022.

A. Decisions of the Security Council relating to Article 39

During the period under review, the Council did not determine the existence of any breach of the peace, act of aggression or new threat to international peace and security.

Continuing threats

In 2022, the Council continued to monitor the evolution of existing and emerging conflicts and situations and to determine, reaffirm and recognize the existence of continuing threats. The relevant provisions of decisions in which the Council referred to continuing threats to peace and security concerning country- or region-specific and thematic items during the period under review are set out in tables 1 and 2, respectively.

In that regard, the Council determined that, in and of themselves, the situations in Afghanistan, the Central African Republic, the Democratic Republic of the Congo, Haiti,[1] Lebanon, Libya, Mali, Somalia, South Sudan and the Sudan, including the Abyei Area and along the border between South Sudan and the Sudan, Yemen and the region of the former Yugoslavia continued to pose threats to international peace and security and/or threats to international peace and security in the respective regions.[2]

---

[1] The last time the Council determined that the situation in Haiti continued to pose a threat to international peace and security in the region was in 2011. See *Repertoire*, *Supplement 2010–2011*, part VII, sect. I.

[2] Resolutions 2630 (2022), last preambular paragraph, and 2660 (2022), last preambular paragraph (Abyei); 2665 (2022), penultimate preambular paragraph (Afghanistan); 2648 (2022), penultimate preambular paragraph, and 2659 (2022), penultimate preambular paragraph (Central African Republic); 2641 (2022), penultimate preambular paragraph, 2666 (2022), penultimate preambular paragraph, and 2667 (2022), second preambular paragraph (Democratic Republic of the Congo); 2653 (2022), penultimate preambular paragraph (Haiti); 2650 (2022), last preambular paragraph (Lebanon); 2619 (2022), last preambular paragraph, 2629 (2022), last preambular paragraph, 2644 (2022), penultimate preambular paragraph, 2647 (2022), last preambular paragraph, and 2656 (2022), last preambular paragraph (Libya); 2640 (2022), penultimate preambular paragraph, and 2649 (2022), penultimate preambular paragraph (Mali); 2628 (2022), penultimate preambular paragraph, and 2662 (2022), penultimate preambular paragraph (Somalia); 2625 (2022), penultimate preambular paragraph, and 2633 (2022), penultimate preambular paragraph (South Sudan); 2620 (2022), penultimate preambular paragraph (Sudan); 2624 (2022), penultimate preambular paragraph (Yemen); and 2658 (2022), first preambular paragraph (former Yugoslavia).

In relation to Asia, and in particular the situation in Afghanistan, the Council expressed concern over the cultivation, production, trade and trafficking of illicit drugs in Afghanistan, which continued to pose a threat to peace and stability in the region and beyond.[3] The Council further acknowledged that illicit proceeds of the drug trafficking in Afghanistan were a source of financing for terrorist groups and non-State actors that threatened regional and international security, and recognized the threats that terrorist groups and non-State actors involved in narcotics trade and the illicit exploitation of natural resources continued to pose to the security and stability of Afghanistan.[4] In connection with the Middle East, and specifically concerning the situation in the Syrian Arab Republic, the Council determined that the devastating humanitarian situation in the country continued to constitute a threat to peace and security in the region.[5]

In addition, in relation to Africa, and specifically the situation in Somalia, the Council expressed grave concern that Al-Shabaab and its terrorist and other activities continued to pose a serious threat to the peace, security and stability of Somalia and the region.[6] The Council also condemned in the strongest terms the attacks by Al-Shabaab targeting security forces, and its terrorist attacks against government officials, civilians and civilian infrastructure in Somalia and the wider region, as well as incidents of hostage-taking and kidnapping of civilians, and its recruitment, training and use of foreign terrorist fighters, and noted with concern that those activities constituted a threat to peace and security in Somalia, regional stability, integration and development, and exacerbated humanitarian suffering.[7]

In 2022, several decisions adopted in connection with thematic items also contained references to threats to international peace and security.

In connection with the item entitled "Non-proliferation/Democratic People's Republic of Korea", the Council determined that the proliferation of nuclear, chemical and biological weapons, as well as their means of delivery, continued to constitute a threat to international peace and security.[8]

Concerning the item entitled "Non-proliferation of weapons of mass destruction", the Council reaffirmed that the proliferation of nuclear, chemical and biological weapons, as well as their means of delivery, constituted a threat to international peace and security, and determined that, in addition to that threat, the threat posed by the illicit trafficking of such weapons and their means of delivery, and related materials, equipment and technology covered by relevant multilateral treaties and arrangements, or included on national control lists, which could be used for the design, development, production or use of nuclear, chemical and biological weapons and their means of delivery, added a new dimension to the issue of proliferation of such weapons and also posed a threat to international peace and security.[9]

With respect to the item entitled "Threats to international peace and security", the Council recalled that Islamic State in Iraq and the Levant (ISIL/Da'esh) constituted a global threat to international peace and security through its terrorist acts, its violent extremist ideology, its continued gross, systematic and widespread attacks directed against civilians, its violations of international humanitarian law and abuses of human rights, in particular those committed against women and children, and including those motivated by religious or ethnic grounds, and its recruitment and training of foreign terrorist fighters whose threat affected all regions and Member States.[10]

[3] Resolution 2626 (2022), last preambular paragraph.
[4] Resolution 2665 (2022), fifth preambular paragraph.
[5] Resolution 2642 (2022), fourth preambular paragraph.
[6] Resolutions 2628 (2022), eighth preambular paragraph; 2657 (2022), eighth preambular paragraph; and 2662 (2022), sixth preambular paragraph and para. 22.
[7] Resolution 2628 (2022), para. 18.
[8] Resolution 2627 (2022), penultimate preambular paragraph.
[9] Resolution 2663 (2022), second and fourth preambular paragraphs.
[10] Resolution 2651 (2022), third preambular paragraph.

Table 1
Decisions in which the Security Council referred to continuing threats to the peace, by region and country, 2022

Decision and date	*Provision*
Americas	
The question concerning Haiti	
Resolution 2653 (2022) 21 October	Determining that the situation in Haiti continues to constitute a threat to international peace and security in the region (penultimate preambular paragraph)
Africa	
The situation in the Central African Republic	
Resolution 2648 (2022) 29 July	Determining that the situation in the Central African Republic continues to constitute a threat to international peace and security in the region (penultimate preambular paragraph)
	See also resolution 2659 (2022) (penultimate preambular paragraph)
The situation concerning the Democratic Republic of the Congo	
Resolution 2641 (2022) 30 June	Determining that the situation in the Democratic Republic of the Congo continues to constitute a threat to international peace and security in the region (penultimate preambular paragraph)
	See also resolutions 2666 (2022) (penultimate preambular paragraph) and 2667 (2022) (second preambular paragraph)
The situation in Libya	
Resolution 2619 (2022) 31 January	Recalling its determination in its resolution 2213 (2015) that the situation in Libya continues to constitute a threat to international peace and security (last preambular paragraph)
	See also resolutions 2629 (2022), 2647 (2022) and 2656 (2022) (last preambular paragraph)
Resolution 2644 (2022) 13 July	Determining that the situation in Libya continues to constitute a threat to international peace and security (penultimate preambular paragraph)
The situation in Mali	
Resolution 2640 (2022) 29 June	Determining that the situation in Mali continues to constitute a threat to international peace and security (penultimate preambular paragraph)
Resolution 2649 (2022) 30 August	Determining that the situation in Mali continues to constitute a threat to international peace and security in the region (penultimate preambular paragraph)
Reports of the Secretary-General on the Sudan and South Sudan	
Resolution 2620 (2022) 15 February	Determining that the situation in the Sudan continues to constitute a threat to international peace and security in the region (penultimate preambular paragraph)
Resolution 2625 (2022) 15 March	Determining that the situation in South Sudan continues to constitute a threat to international peace and security in the region (penultimate preambular paragraph)
	See also resolution 2633 (2022) (penultimate preambular paragraph)

Decision and date	Provision
Resolution 2630 (2022) 12 May	Recognizing that the current situation in Abyei and along the border between the Sudan and South Sudan continues to constitute a threat to international peace and security (last preambular paragraph)
	See also resolution 2660 (2022) (last preambular paragraph)
The situation in Somalia	
Resolution 2628 (2022) 31 March	Expressing grave concern that Al-Shabaab continues to pose a serious threat to the peace, security and stability of Somalia and the region, and noting its increased use of improvised explosive devices and exploitation of the licit financial system (eighth preambular paragraph)
	Determining that the situation in Somalia continues to constitute a threat to regional and international peace and security (penultimate preambular paragraph)
	Condemns in the strongest terms the attacks by Al-Shabaab targeting security forces, and its terrorist attacks against government officials, civilians and civilian infrastructure in Somalia and the wider region, as well as incidents of hostage-taking and kidnapping of civilians, and its recruitment, training and use of foreign terrorist fighters, and notes with concern that these activities constitute a threat to peace and security in Somalia, regional stability, integration and development, and exacerbate humanitarian suffering (para. 18)
Resolution 2657 (2022) 31 October	Expressing grave concern that the terrorist group Al-Shabaab continues to pose a serious threat to the peace, security and stability of Somalia and the region, and further expressing concern at the continued presence in Somalia of affiliates linked to ISIL/Da'esh (eighth preambular paragraph)
	See also resolution 2662 (2022) (sixth preambular paragraph)
Resolution 2662 (2022) 17 November	Determining that the situation in Somalia continues to constitute a threat to international peace and security in the region (penultimate preambular paragraph)
	Reiterates that Al-Shabaab poses a threat to peace and security in Somalia, and that its terrorist and other activities pose a security threat to the region, and underscores the need to degrade Al-Shabaab through targeted sanctions and disrupting its finances, by reducing the threat posed by improvised explosive devices and by improving maritime domain awareness (para. 22)
Asia	
The situation in Afghanistan	
Resolution 2626 (2022) 17 March	Expressing concern over the cultivation, production, trade and trafficking of illicit drugs in Afghanistan, which continue to pose a threat to peace and stability in the region and beyond, calling upon States to strengthen international and regional cooperation to counter this threat and recognizing the important role of the United Nations Office on Drugs and Crime in this context (last preambular paragraph)
Europe	
The situation in Bosnia and Herzegovina	
Resolution 2658 (2022) 2 November	Determining that the situation in the region of the former Yugoslavia continues to constitute a threat to international peace and security (first preambular paragraph)
Middle East	
The situation in the Middle East	
Resolution 2624 (2022) 28 February	Determining that the situation in Yemen continues to constitute a threat to international peace and security (penultimate preambular paragraph)

Decision and date	*Provision*
Resolution 2642 (2022) 12 July	Determining that the devastating humanitarian situation in the Syrian Arab Republic continues to constitute a threat to peace and security in the region (fourth preambular paragraph)
Resolution 2650 (2022) 31 August	Determining that the situation in Lebanon continues to constitute a threat to international peace and security (last preambular paragraph)

Table 2
Decisions in which the Security Council referred to continuing threats to the peace, by thematic issue, 2022

Decision and date	*Provision*
Non-proliferation/Democratic People's Republic of Korea	
Resolution 2627 (2022) 25 March	Determining that the proliferation of nuclear, chemical and biological weapons, as well as their means of delivery, continue to constitute a threat to international peace and security (penultimate preambular paragraph)
Non-proliferation of weapons of mass destruction	
Resolution 2663 (2022) 30 November	Reaffirming that the proliferation of nuclear, chemical and biological weapons, as well as their means of delivery, constitutes a threat to international peace and security (second preambular paragraph)
	Gravely concerned by the threat of illicit trafficking in nuclear, chemical or biological weapons and their means of delivery, and related materials, equipment and technology covered by relevant multilateral treaties and arrangements, or included on national control lists, which could be used for the design, development, production or use of nuclear, chemical and biological weapons and their means of delivery, which adds a new dimension to the issue of proliferation of such weapons and also poses a threat to international peace and security (fourth preambular paragraph)
Threats to international peace and security	
Resolution 2651 (2022) 15 September	Recalling that Islamic State in Iraq and the Levant (ISIL, also known as Da'esh) constitutes a global threat to international peace and security through its terrorist acts, its violent extremist ideology, its continued gross, systematic and widespread attacks directed against civilians, its violations of international humanitarian law and abuses of human rights, particularly those committed against women and children, and including those motivated by religious or ethnic grounds, and its recruitment and training of foreign terrorist fighters whose threat affects all regions and Member States (third preambular paragraph)
Threats to international peace and security caused by terrorist acts	
Resolution 2665 (2022) 16 December	Reiterating its support for the fight against the illicit production and trafficking of drugs from, and chemical precursors to, Afghanistan, acknowledging that illicit proceeds of the drug trafficking in Afghanistan are a source of financing for terrorist groups and non-State actors that threatens regional and international security, and recognizing the threats that terrorist groups and non-State actors involved in narcotics trade and the illicit exploitation of natural resources continue to pose to the security and stability of Afghanistan (fifth preambular paragraph)
	Determining that the situation in Afghanistan continues to constitute a threat to international peace and security, and reaffirming the need to combat this threat by all means, in accordance with the Charter of the United Nations and international law, including applicable human rights, refugee and humanitarian law, stressing in this regard the important role that the United Nations plays in this effort (penultimate preambular paragraph)

B. Discussions relating to Article 39

During the period under review, four explicit references to Article 39 of the Charter were made during three meetings of the Council. First, at a meeting held on 19 January under the item entitled "The situation in the Middle East, including the Palestinian question", the co-founder and Israel Director of EcoPeace Middle East called upon the Council to recognize globally that climate change was a threat to peace within the meaning of Article 39.[11] Two further explicit references to Article 39 were made at a meeting held on 31 January under the item entitled "Threats to international peace and security", focused on the conflict in Ukraine, by the representatives of the United States and Mexico, as elaborated upon in case 1 below. Finally, at a meeting held on 21 February under the item entitled "Letter dated 28 February 2014 from the Permanent Representative of Ukraine to the United Nations addressed to the President of the Security Council (S/2014/136)", the representative of Ukraine, underlining the Council's mandate pursuant to Article 39 to make recommendations or decide on measures to be taken to maintain or restore international peace and security, called upon Council members to exercise that duty.[12]

In addition, Council members and other participants at Council meetings discussed various new and continuing threats to international peace and security in connection with both thematic and country- and region-specific items, as elaborated upon below.

Thematic items

In 2022, many of the discussions among Council members focused on the conflict in Ukraine and its potential to threaten regional and international peace and security, including during meetings held under the item entitled "Threats to international peace and security" (case 1). Under the same item, the Council also addressed climate change and its potential to pose a threat to international peace and security (case 2). In addition, on 19 May, at a high-level open debate held under the item entitled "Maintenance of international peace and security",[13] focused on conflict and food security, Council members and other Member States deliberated on whether food insecurity could pose a threat to regional or international peace and security. In that regard, the Cabinet Secretary for Foreign Affairs of Kenya underscored that the recent rise in food insecurity might lead to heightened threats to international peace and security.[14] The Minister for Foreign Affairs of Luxembourg emphasized that food insecurity, exacerbated by the negative effects of climate change, was a major threat to peace.[15] The Minister for Foreign Affairs of Guatemala pointed out that conflict and food security was an issue that could constitute a threat to international peace and security if it was not addressed in a timely manner. The representatives of Slovenia and Belgium stated that a sharp increase in global food insecurity threatened to destabilize fragile societies and further exacerbate armed conflicts and regional and global instability.

In 2022, the Council also continued to address threats to international peace and security considered by the Council in the past, including those posed by terrorism and the activities of terrorist groups,[16] the misuse of information and communications technology,[17] the proliferation of weapons of

---

[11] See S/PV.8950.

[12] See S/PV.8970.

[13] See S/PV.9036 and S/PV.9036 (Resumption 1).

[14] See S/PV.9036.

[15] See S/PV.9036 (Resumption 1).

[16] See, for example, in connection with the item entitled "Threats to international peace and security caused by terrorist acts", S/PV.8963 (Ghana, India and Brazil), S/PV.9108 (Under-Secretary-General of the Office of Counter-Terrorism, United Arab Emirates, United Kingdom, Ireland and India) and S/PV.9221 (India, Ireland, United Arab Emirates, Kenya and Ghana); in connection with the item entitled "Threats to international peace and security", S/PV.9188 (Deputy Secretary-General, United Arab Emirates, Kenya, Mexico, India and Albania); and in connection with the item entitled "Briefings by Chairs of subsidiary bodies of the Security Council", S/PV.9201 (United States, Kenya, India, United Kingdom and Ireland).

[17] See, for example, in connection with the item entitled "Maintenance of international peace and security", S/PV.9039 (France, India and Norway).

mass destruction, including nuclear weapons,[18] as well as the acquisition of those weapons by terrorist groups.[19]

Country- or region-specific items

In 2022, the Council continued to discuss threats to regional or international peace and security stemming from specific conflicts and situations. For example, Council members and other Member States discussed the threats to regional and international peace and security in relation to the conflict in Ukraine;[20] the threat posed by the proliferation and use of weapons of mass destruction, including chemical weapons, in the Syrian Arab Republic;[21] the proliferation and use of nuclear weapons by the Democratic People's Republic of Korea;[22] and threats to international peace and security posed by the Palestinian-Israeli conflict.[23]

Case 1
Threats to international peace and security

On 31 January, at the request of the United States, the Security Council held a meeting under the item entitled "Threats to international peace and security", focused on the situation in Ukraine.[24] Council members heard a briefing by the Under-Secretary-General for Political and Peacebuilding Affairs, and in accordance with rule 37 of the Council's provisional rules of procedure, the representatives of Belarus, Lithuania, Poland and Ukraine were invited to participate in the meeting.

Prior to the adoption of the agenda, the representative of the Russian Federation requested a procedural vote on the proposal to hold the meeting. He argued that the United States, in explaining its proposal to convene the meeting, had considered the deployment of Russian troops on Russian territory to be a threat to international peace and security, which was not only tantamount to unacceptable interference in the domestic affairs of the Russian Federation but also an attempt to mislead the international community on the actual situation in the region. The provisional agenda was put to a vote and was adopted.[25] After the vote, echoing the position of the Russian Federation, the representative of China also expressed opposition to the Council's holding of the meeting, stating that his country could not align itself with the point of view of the United States that the deployment of troops by the Russian Federation along the Ukrainian border posed a threat to international peace and security.

Following the adoption of the agenda, the Under-Secretary-General for Political and Peacebuilding Affairs informed the Council that reportedly more than 100,000 troops and heavy weaponry from the Russian Federation were positioned along the border with Ukraine and that unspecified numbers of Russian troops and weaponry were being deployed to Belarus ahead of large-scale joint military exercises on the borders with Ukraine, Poland and the Baltic States. During the ensuing discussion, two Council members explicitly referred to Article 39 of the Charter of the United Nations in expressing concerns regarding the escalating tensions. The representative of the United States said that the actions of the

---

[18] See, for example, in connection with the item entitled "Non-proliferation", S/PV.9085 (United Kingdom, France and United Arab Emirates).

[19] See, for example, in connection with the item entitled "Non-proliferation of weapons of mass destruction", S/PV.8993 (Mexico, India, Ireland, Brazil, Gabon, United States and United Arab Emirates).

[20] See, for example, in connection with the item entitled "Maintenance of peace and security of Ukraine", S/PV.9126 (Ghana, Russian Federation and Kenya).

[21] See, for example, in connection with the item entitled "The situation in the Middle East", S/PV.8943 (High Representative for Disarmament Affairs, Brazil, Gabon and United Arab Emirates) and S/PV.9141 (High Representative for Disarmament Affairs, Brazil and Islamic Republic of Iran).

[22] See, for example, in connection with the item entitled "Non-proliferation/Democratic People's Republic of Korea", S/PV.9004 (Ireland, France, Norway, United Kingdom and Japan) and S/PV.9030 (Ireland, United Kingdom, France, Russian Federation, Gabon, Norway, United States and Japan).

[23] See, for example, in connection with the item entitled "The situation in the Middle East, including the Palestinian question", S/PV.9021 (State of Palestine and Algeria) and S/PV.9021 (Resumption 1) (Islamic Republic of Iran).

[24] See S/PV.8960.

[25] The provisional agenda received 10 votes in favour (Albania, Brazil, France, Ghana, Ireland, Mexico, Norway, United Arab Emirates, United Kingdom and United States), 2 against (China and Russian Federation) and 3 abstentions (Gabon, India and Kenya).

Russian Federation were a clear and consequential threat to peace and security. Recalling the provisions of Article 39, she emphasized the Council's responsibility to not only address conflicts after they occurred but also prevent them from happening. Underscoring that the aggression of the Russian Federation threatened not only Ukraine but also Europe, as well as the international order that the Council was charged with upholding, she stressed that it was crucial that the Council address the risk that the destabilizing behaviour of the Russian Federation posed across the globe. In addition, the representative of Mexico underscored that the mere escalation of tensions in Eastern Europe was a potential threat to international peace and security, and that, according to Article 39, it was therefore within the purview of the Council.

Other Member States expressed concerns regarding the potential threat to international peace and security related to the military build-up by the Russian Federation at the border with Ukraine and in occupied Crimea without referring explicitly to Article 39 of the Charter. The representatives of Norway and Poland stated that the military build-up at the border with Ukraine was a clear and serious threat to international peace and security. The representative of Ukraine, underlining the Council's duty to be fully informed in the case of grave threats to international peace and security, emphasized that what was happening along the border with Ukraine – where the Russian Federation continued its military build-up – fell under that qualification. The representative of Lithuania, reaffirming his country's full commitment to the core principles of international security enshrined in the Charter, notably the sovereign equality and territorial integrity of States, the inviolability of frontiers and refraining from the use of force, underscored that the violation of such principles by the Russian Federation was an obstacle to a common and indivisible security space in Europe and threatened peace and stability on the continent.

Case 2
Threats to international peace and security

On 12 October, at the initiative of Gabon, which held the presidency for the month,[26] the Security Council held a high-level open debate under the item entitled "Threats to international peace and security", focused on climate and security in Africa.[27] During the meeting, Council members and Member States and other participants deliberated on whether and how climate change could threaten international and regional peace and security, in particular on the African continent.

Some speakers determined that climate change in itself posed a threat to international peace and security. In that regard, the representative of Germany underscored that climate change was a global threat to peace. In a similar vein, the representative of Morocco recalled that climate change was not only an environmental and economic policy issue but also a major challenge for international security and an existential threat to humankind. He further emphasized that the international community must act where climate change threatened peace and security before conflicts broke out or escalated. The Minister for Foreign Affairs of Gabon stressed the need to respond to the climate imperative as a threat to international security. The representative of Namibia said that climate change and its threat to peace and security were no longer a far-fetched tale of a fictional dystopian world, and called upon the Council to maintain the momentum regarding discussions related to climate and security, as that nexus posed the next frontier of emerging threats for the world.

Other participants discussed the ways in which climate change and its effects exacerbated other threats to international peace and security, in particular in Africa. In that regard, the representative of Ghana, underlining the link between climate change and security crises, especially on the African continent, pointed to the threat-multiplier effect of climate change in the context of peace and security, including in terms of food and water insecurity, loss of livelihoods, climate-induced displacement and the exacerbation of vulnerabilities, tensions and conflict. The representative of Egypt similarly recalled that climate change was widely recognized as a threat multiplier and driver of conflict that was affecting the peace and stability of several regions globally, in particular Africa, which was why it was important to address the increasing connection between climate change and security. Stressing that the two-way interaction between climate and security could not be ignored, the representative of Italy stated that the adverse effects of climate change, coupled with other destabilizing factors, such as extreme poverty, food

[26] A concept note was circulated by a letter dated 3 October (S/2022/737).

[27] See S/PV.9150.

insecurity, institutional fragility and terrorism, were posing a serious threat to international peace and security. He added that African States and their most vulnerable populations were often among the world's most affected by the disruptions caused by climate change, which acted as a threat multiplier for violence and instability. The representative of Mexico similarly said that the adverse effects of climate change were having a substantial impact on conflicts in Africa and underlined the need for the Council to systematically consider how the effects of climate change were undermining efforts to prevent and address threats to international peace and security. She added that the debate had made it clear how climate change could increase threats to international peace and security and called upon the Council to listen to the voices of African countries in conflict situations, which were in agreement that the adverse effects of climate change were a catalyst for threats to international peace and security. The representative of Kenya emphasized that the Council could not remain on the sidelines when major threats to regional and international peace and security were made much worse by climate crises.

In contrast, other Member States expressed the view that climate change did not threaten international peace and security. While recognizing the adverse effects of climate change as a matter of great concern and one to remain among the priorities of the international community, the representative of Brazil said that climate change was not in itself a direct cause of armed conflicts, nor did it constitute a direct threat to peace and security in the sense underscored in the Charter of the United Nations. The representative of South Africa asserted that the "ticking time bomb" that was the climate crisis was one of the most serious threats to collective security. He acknowledged that there was some evidence suggesting that, in Africa, extreme weather events, drought, water scarcity, food insecurity and desertification linked with climate change had the potential to increase the risk of violent conflict, adding that in some specific instances, climate change was a threat or risk multiplier, escalating existing tensions and conflict by placing strain on already scarce resources. He underscored, however, that while it might be intuitive to assume that climate pressures generally contributed to increasing the risk of conflict elsewhere, scientific evidence to support a more generalized conclusion of a direct causality between climate change and threats to international peace and security was still minimal.

C. References to Article 39 in communications addressed to the Security Council

During the period under review, a letter from the representative of Pakistan addressed to the President of the Council contained an explicit reference to Article 39 of the Charter.

In a letter dated 6 April,[28] the representative of Pakistan transmitted a resolution of the Council of Foreign Ministers of the Organization of Islamic Cooperation on peace and security in South Asia, concerning the violation of the airspace of Pakistan by a supersonic missile of Indian origin on 9 March 2022, which threatened peace, security and strategic stability in South Asia. In the resolution, the Council of Foreign Ministers recalled the responsibility of the Security Council under Article 39 of the Charter concerning any threat to or breach of the peace and called upon relevant international bodies, including the Security Council, to pursue, in line with their mandated duties, the matter with India to accurately establish the facts and to ensure that no such occurrence took place in the future.

II. Provisional measures to prevent an aggravation of the situation in accordance with Article 40 of the Charter

Article 40

In order to prevent an aggravation of the situation, the Security Council may, before making the recommendations or deciding upon the measures provided for in Article 39, call upon the parties concerned to comply with such provisional measures as it deems necessary or desirable. Such provisional measures shall be without prejudice to the rights, claims, or position of the parties concerned. The Security Council shall duly take account of failure to comply with such provisional measures.

[28] S/2022/294.

Note

Section II covers the practice of the Council in relation to Article 40 of the Charter of the United Nations, regarding provisional measures to prevent an aggravation of the situation. While Article 40 suggests that provisional measures to prevent the aggravation of a conflict would be adopted prior to the imposition of measures under Chapter VII (Articles 41 and 42), the practice of the Council reflects a more flexible interpretation of that provision. Given the prolonged and rapidly changing nature of conflicts dealt with by the Council, provisional measures have been imposed in parallel to the adoption of measures under Articles 41 and 42.

In 2022, the Council did not impose any measures pursuant to Article 40 of the Charter. There was also no explicit reference to Article 40 made in the decisions of the Council or during its deliberations, nor was there any discussion of constitutional significance on its interpretation. Similarly, there was no explicit reference to Article 40 in any of the communications of the Council.

III. Measures not involving the use of armed force in accordance with Article 41 of the Charter

Article 41

The Security Council may decide what measures not involving the use of armed force are to be employed to give effect to its decisions, and it may call upon the Members of the United Nations to apply such measures. These may include complete or partial interruption of economic relations and of rail, sea, air, postal, telegraphic, radio, and other means of communication, and the severance of diplomatic relations.

Note

Section III covers the decisions and deliberations of the Council related to the imposition of measures not involving the use of force, pursuant to Article 41 of the Charter of the United Nations. During the period under review, the Council imposed new such measures under Chapter VII of the Charter in connection with the question concerning Haiti, adding to the 14 existing sanctions regimes. The Council imposed no judicial measures under Article 41.[29] In 2022, the Council explicitly referred to Article 41 in the preamble of resolution 2627 (2022) in connection with the Democratic People's Republic of Korea. Article 41 was also referenced explicitly in two communications of the Council, namely, in a letter dated 7 February from the representative of the Islamic Republic of Iran addressed to the President of the Council in connection with the debate held under the item entitled "General issues relating to sanctions"[30] and in the draft resolution submitted by the United States under the item entitled "Non-proliferation/Democratic People's Republic of Korea", which was not adopted owing to the negative vote of two permanent members of the Council.[31]

The present section is divided into two subsections. Subsection A contains an outline of the decisions in which the Council imposed, modified or terminated measures under Article 41 of the Charter. It is organized under two main headings, dealing with decisions on issues of thematic and country- or region-specific nature. Subsection B covers the deliberations of the Council during 2022 and is also organized under two headings, each highlighting the salient issues that were raised in connection with Article 41, with respect to thematic and country-specific items.

---

[29] For information on the activity of the Council regarding issues pertaining to the International Residual Mechanism for Criminal Tribunals, see part IX, sect. IV.

[30] See S/2022/98, annex.

[31] See S/2022/431, last preambular paragraph. See also S/PV.9048. For more information about decision-making and voting, see part II, sect. VIII.

A. Decisions relating to Article 41

Decisions on thematic issues relating to Article 41

In 2022, the Council adopted two decisions on issues of a thematic nature concerning sanctions measures and their implementation, under the items entitled "General issues relating to sanctions"[32] and "Threats to international peace and security caused by terrorist acts".[33]

In its resolution 2664 (2022), adopted under the item entitled "General issues relating to sanctions", the Council emphasized that its sanctions were an important tool under the Charter in the maintenance and restoration of international peace and security, including in support of peace processes, countering terrorism and promoting non-proliferation. In that regard, by the resolution, the Council decided that, without prejudice to the obligations imposed on Member States to freeze the funds and other financial assets or economic resources of individuals, groups, undertakings and entities designated by the Council or its sanctions committees, the provision, processing or payment of funds, other financial assets or economic resources, or the provision of goods and services, necessary to ensure the timely delivery of humanitarian assistance or to support other activities that supported basic human needs undertaken by a range of humanitarian actors were permitted and were not a violation of the asset freezes imposed by the Council or its sanctions committees.[34] The Council further decided that the provisions introduced in paragraph 1 of resolution 2664 (2022) would apply to the Islamic State in Iraq and the Levant (ISIL/Da'esh) and Al-Qaida sanctions regime for a period of two years from the date of adoption of the resolution, and expressed its intent to make a decision on the extension of their application to that regime prior to the date on which the application would otherwise expire.[35] In addition, it requested that providers relying on paragraph 1 of the resolution use reasonable efforts to minimize the accrual of any benefits prohibited by sanctions, including by strengthening risk management and due diligence strategies and processes.[36] The Council also emphasized that where paragraph 1 of resolution 2664 (2022) conflicted with its previous resolutions, paragraph 1 would supersede the previous resolutions to the extent of such conflict, clarified in that regard that paragraph 1 would supersede and replace paragraph 37 of its resolution 2607 (2021) concerning Somalia and paragraph 10 of its resolution 2653 (2022) concerning Haiti, but that paragraph 1 of its resolution 2615 (2021) concerning the Taliban would remain in effect, and further decided that paragraph 1 of resolution 2664 (2022) would apply with respect to all future asset freezes imposed or renewed by the Council in the absence of an explicit decision by the Council to the contrary.[37] The Council requested the Emergency Relief Coordinator to brief or arrange a briefing for each relevant committee within its mandate, 11 months from the date of adoption of resolution 2664 (2022) and every 12 months afterwards, on the delivery of humanitarian assistance and other activities that supported basic human needs consistent with the resolution.[38] It also directed the committees established by the Council with respect to sanctions implementation to assist Member States in properly understanding and fully implementing paragraph 1 of the resolution by issuing implementation assistance notices to provide further guidance to give full effect to paragraph 1 and taking into account the unique context of the sanctions falling under their respective mandates, and further directed those committees, assisted by their respective panels of experts, to monitor the implementation of paragraph 1 of the resolution, including any risk of diversion.[39] Finally, it requested the Secretary-General to issue a written report on unintended adverse humanitarian consequences of Council sanctions measures, including travel ban and arms embargo measures, as well as those measures that were sui generis to particular sanctions regimes, within nine months of the adoption of the resolution, and requested that the report contain recommendations on ways to minimize and mitigate such unintended adverse consequences.[40]

---

[32] For more information on the item, see part I, sect. 28.
[33] For more information on the item, see part I, sect. 30.
[34] Resolution 2664 (2022), third preambular paragraph and para. 1.
[35] Ibid., para. 2.
[36] Ibid., para. 3.
[37] Ibid., para. 4.
[38] Ibid., para. 5.
[39] Ibid., para. 6.
[40] Ibid., para. 7. See also sect. IX below.

In its resolution 2665 (2022), adopted under the item entitled "Threats to international peace and security caused by terrorist acts", the Council reiterated the need to ensure that the sanctions regime pursuant to resolution 1988 (2011) contributed effectively to ongoing efforts to bring about sustainable and inclusive peace, stability and security in Afghanistan, and noted the importance of sanctions review when and if appropriate, while taking into account the situation on the ground, in a manner that was consistent with the overall objective of promoting peace and stability in Afghanistan.[41]

Decisions on country- and region-specific issues relating to Article 41

During the period under review, as set out in table 3 below, the Council established a new sanctions regime concerning Haiti. The Council also renamed the sanctions regime concerning Somalia to the sanctions regime concerning Al-Shabaab and expanded its listing criteria to individuals who threatened the peace, security and stability of Somalia or who were associated with Al-Shabaab. The Council renewed the existing measures concerning the Central African Republic, Libya, Mali, South Sudan, the Sudan and Yemen, as well as those concerning Al-Shabaab. It also renewed the existing measures concerning the Taliban and associated individuals and entities. In addition to renewing the existing measures concerning the Democratic Republic of the Congo, the Council expanded the listing criteria to individuals and entities involved in the production, manufacturing or use of improvised explosive devices and lifted the notification requirements for shipments of arms and related materiel for the Democratic Republic of the Congo. Concerning the ISIL/Da'esh and Al-Qaida sanctions regime, the Council decided that the standing humanitarian exemption to the asset freeze introduced in resolution 2664 (2022) would initially apply for a period of two years, while for other regimes comprising an asset freeze, the Council did not specify an expiry date for the exemption. No changes were made to the measures concerning Guinea-Bissau.

In addition, in a presidential statement adopted on 31 August under the item entitled "Peace and security in Africa", while underlining the need for the effective implementation of its sanctions measures as a tool for achieving peace and stability in Africa, the Council expressed its readiness to review, adjust and terminate, when appropriate, its sanctions regimes, taking into account the evolution of the situation on the ground and the need to minimize unintended adverse humanitarian effects.[42]

The present subsection concerning the developments in each of the sanctions regimes does not include reference to the subsidiary bodies of the Council responsible for their implementation. The decisions of the Council relating to the subsidiary bodies are described in detail in part IX, section I.B. Decisions adopted by the Council on the establishment and history of each of the sanctions regimes are covered in previous supplements.

The categories of sanctions measures used in the present subsection, such as arms embargo, asset freeze or travel ban, are for clarification purposes only and are not intended to serve as legal definitions of the measures. In addition, developments in the sanctions measures imposed by the Council during the period under review are categorized according to the following main actions taken by the Council: "establishment",[43] "modification",[44] "extension",[45] "limited extension"[46] or "termination".[47]

The sanctions regimes are discussed below in the order of their establishment.[48] Each of the following subsections consists of a narrative section describing the most significant developments in

---

[41] Resolution 2665 (2022), ninth preambular paragraph.

[42] S/PRST/2022/6, eighth paragraph.

[43] An action by the Council is categorized as an "establishment" when a sanctions measure is initially imposed by the Council.

[44] When a change is introduced to the measure, it is categorized as a "modification". A measure is modified when: (a) elements of the measure are terminated or newly introduced; (b) information on designated individuals or entities is modified; (c) exemptions to the measure are introduced, modified or terminated; and (d) elements of the measure are otherwise modified.

[45] An action by the Council is categorized as an "extension" when the sanctions measure concerned is not modified or terminated and the Council extends or restates the measure without specifying an end date.

[46] An action by the Council is categorized as a "limited extension" when the sanctions measure concerned is extended for a specific period of time, including a date upon which the measure will terminate unless further extended by the Council.

[47] An action by the Council is categorized as a "termination" when the Council ends the specific sanctions measure. However, if only an element of the measure is terminated, but other elements of that measure remain, the action will be categorized as a modification of the measure.

[48] For background and past practice, see previous supplements.

2022 and a table presenting all relevant provisions of Council decisions concerning changes to a sanctions regime, according to the categories outlined above. Tables 3 and 4 provide an overview of relevant decisions adopted in 2022 by which the Council established sanctions measures or modified ones that it had previously imposed.

Table 3
Overview of country- and region-specific decisions on measures pursuant to Article 41 of the Charter, in place or imposed in 2022

Sanctions regime	*Resolutions by which measures were established or subsequently modified*		*Resolutions adopted in 2022*
Al-Shabaab	733 (1992) 1356 (2001) 1425 (2002) 1725 (2006) 1744 (2007) 1772 (2007) 1816 (2008) 1844 (2008) 1846 (2008) 1851 (2008) 1872 (2009) 1897 (2009) 1907 (2009) 1916 (2010) 1950 (2010) 1964 (2010) 1972 (2011) 2002 (2011) 2023 (2011) 2036 (2012)	2060 (2012) 2093 (2013) 2111 (2013) 2125 (2013) 2142 (2014) 2182 (2014) 2184 (2014) 2244 (2015) 2246 (2015) 2316 (2016) 2317 (2016) 2383 (2017) 2385 (2017) 2444 (2018) 2498 (2019) 2551 (2020) 2554 (2020) 2607 (2021) 2608 (2021)	2661 (2022) 2662 (2022) 2664 (2022)
ISIL/Da'esh and Al-Qaida and associated individuals and entities	1267 (1999) 1333 (2000) 1388 (2002) 1390 (2002) 1452 (2002) 1735 (2006) 1904 (2009) 1989 (2011) 2083 (2012)	2161 (2014) 2170 (2014) 2178 (2014) 2199 (2015) 2253 (2015) 2347 (2017) 2349 (2017) 2368 (2017) 2610 (2021)	2664 (2022)
Taliban and associated individuals and entities	1988 (2011) 2082 (2012) 2160 (2014) 2255 (2015)	2501 (2019) 2557 (2020) 2611 (2021) 2615 (2021)	2665 (2022)
Iraq	661 (1990) 687 (1991) 707 (1991) 1483 (2003) 1546 (2004) 1637 (2005)	1723 (2006) 1790 (2007) 1859 (2008) 1905 (2009) 1956 (2010) 1957 (2010)	2664 (2022)
Democratic Republic of the Congo	1493 (2003) 1552 (2004) 1596 (2005) 1616 (2005) 1649 (2005) 1671 (2006) 1698 (2006) 1768 (2007)	1896 (2009) 1952 (2010) 2136 (2014) 2147 (2014) 2198 (2015) 2211 (2015) 2293 (2016) 2360 (2017)	2641 (2022) 2664 (2022) 2667 (2022)

Sanctions regime	*Resolutions by which measures were established or subsequently modified*		*Resolutions adopted in 2022*
	1771 (2007)	2424 (2018)	
	1799 (2008)	2478 (2019)	
	1807 (2008)	2528 (2020)	
	1857 (2008)	2582 (2021)	
Sudan	1556 (2004)	2265 (2016)	2620 (2022)
	1591 (2005)	2340 (2017)	2664 (2022)
	1672 (2006)	2400 (2018)	
	1945 (2010)	2455 (2019)	
	2035 (2012)	2508 (2020)	
	2138 (2014)	2562 (2021)	
	2200 (2015)		
Lebanon	1636 (2005)		2664 (2022)
Democratic People's Republic of Korea	1718 (2006)	2321 (2016)	2664 (2022)
	1874 (2009)	2356 (2017)	
	2087 (2013)	2371 (2017)	
	2094 (2013)	2375 (2017)	
	2270 (2016)	2397 (2017)	
Libya	1970 (2011)	2259 (2015)	2635 (2022)
	1973 (2011)	2278 (2016)	2644 (2022)
	2009 (2011)	2292 (2016)	2664 (2022)
	2016 (2011)	2362 (2017)	
	2040 (2012)	2441 (2018)	
	2095 (2013)	2509 (2020)	
	2146 (2014)	2510 (2020)	
	2174 (2014)	2526 (2020)	
	2208 (2015)	2542 (2020)	
	2213 (2015)	2571 (2021)	
	2238 (2015)	2578 (2021)	
Guinea-Bissau	2048 (2012)	2203 (2015)	None
	2157 (2014)		
Central African Republic	2127 (2013)	2399 (2018)	2648 (2022)
	2134 (2014)	2488 (2019)	2664 (2022)
	2196 (2015)	2507 (2020)	
	2217 (2015)	2536 (2020)	
	2262 (2016)	2588 (2021)	
	2339 (2017)		
Yemen	2140 (2014)	2511 (2020)	2624 (2022)
	2204 (2015)	2564 (2021)	2664 (2022)
	2216 (2015)		
South Sudan	2206 (2015)	2353 (2017)	2633 (2022)
	2241 (2015)	2418 (2018)	2664 (2022)
	2252 (2015)	2428 (2018)	
	2271 (2016)	2521 (2020)	
	2280 (2016)	2577 (2021)	
	2290 (2016)		
Mali	2374 (2017)	2541 (2020)	2649 (2022)
	2432 (2018)	2590 (2021)	2664 (2022)
	2484 (2019)		
Haiti	2653 (2022)		2653 (2022)
			2664 (2022)

Table 4
Overview of measures pursuant to Article 41 of the Charter, in place or imposed in 2022

Sanctions regime / *Type of measure*	*Arms embargo*	*Asset freeze*	*Travel ban or restrictions*	*Ban on arms exports by target State*	*Ban/restrictions on workers abroad*	*Ban on improvised explosive devices components*	*Business restrictions*	*Charcoal ban*	*Diplomatic/overseas representation restrictions*	*Embargo on natural resources*	*Financial restrictions*	*Luxury goods embargo*	*Natural gas embargo/restrictions*	*Non-proliferation measures*	*Oil/petroleum and petroleum products embargo/restrictions*	*Prohibition on bunkering services/port entry*	*Public financial support for trade restrictions*	*Restrictions on ballistic missiles*	*Sectoral ban*	*Specialized teaching and technical cooperation restrictions*	*Transport and aviation sanctions*	*Trade ban on cultural goods*
Al-Shabaab	X	X	X			X		X														
Taliban	X	X	X																			
ISIL/Da'esh and Al-Qaida	X	X	X																			
Iraq	X	X																				
Democratic Republic of the Congo	X	X	X																		X	
Sudan	X	X	X																			
Lebanon[a]		X	X																			
Democratic People's Republic of Korea	X	X	X	X	X		X		X	X	X	X	X	X	X	X	X	X	X	X	X	
Libya	X	X	X	X			X				X				X	X						
Guinea-Bissau			X																			
Central African Republic	X	X	X																			
Yemen	X	X	X																			
South Sudan	X	X	X																			
Mali		X	X																			
Haiti	X	X	X																			

[a] Pursuant to paragraph 15 of resolution 1701 (2006), the Council decided, inter alia, that States should take the necessary measures to prevent, by their nationals or from their territories or using their flag vessels or aircraft, the sale or supply of arms and related materiel to any entity or individual in Lebanon other than those authorized by the Government of Lebanon or by the United Nations Interim Force in Lebanon. In 2021, by its resolution 2591 (2021), the Council recalled paragraph 15 of resolution 1701 (2006) and requested the Secretary-General to continue to report to the Council on the implementation of resolution 1701 (2006) and to include in his reporting an enhanced annex on the implementation of the arms embargo.

Al-Shabaab

In 2022, the Council adopted resolution 2661 (2022), by which it extended resolution 2607 (2021) until 17 November 2022, thereby reaffirming and recalling the existing sanctions measures imposed on Somalia.[49]

By its resolution 2662 (2022), the Council decided that from the date of adoption of the resolution, the name of the Committee pursuant to resolution 751 (1992) concerning Somalia was to be henceforth known as the Committee pursuant to resolution 751 (1992) concerning Al-Shabaab.[50]

By its resolution 2662 (2022), the Council also reaffirmed the partial arms embargo and the exemptions for deliveries of weapons and military equipment or the provision of technical advice, financial and other assistance and training related to military activities intended solely for the support of or use by the Somali security and police institutions or those listed in paragraph 21.[51] It confirmed its commitment to working with Somalia to ensure that the notification procedures were lifted progressively, in the light of the progress made against the benchmarks set out in the technical assessment of the country's weapons and ammunition management capability.[52] The Council also outlined the procedures for requests for exemptions or notifications to the Committee pursuant to resolution 751 (1992).[53] It also reaffirmed the ban on the import and export of Somali charcoal as set out in paragraph 22 of resolution 2036 (2012) and paragraphs 11 to 21 of resolution 2182 (2014).[54] The Council further decided to renew until 15 November 2023 the provisions set out in paragraphs 15 and 17 of resolution 2182 (2014) concerning the maritime interdiction of charcoal and weapons or military equipment and expanded in paragraph 5 of resolution 2607 (2021) to include the components of improvised explosive devices.[55]

Recalling its decisions in resolution 1844 (2008), by which it imposed targeted sanctions, and its resolutions 2002 (2011) and 2093 (2013), by which it expanded the listing criteria, the Council decided that the arms embargo, asset freeze and travel ban measures would also apply to individuals and that the arms embargo and asset freeze measures would also apply to entities designated as: (a) having engaged in, or provided support for, acts that threatened the peace, security or stability of Somalia, including acts that threatened the peace and reconciliation process in Somalia, or threatened the Federal Government of Somalia or the African Union Transition Mission in Somalia by force; and (b) being associated with Al-Shabaab.[56] The Council further reaffirmed, in the same terms used in paragraph 37 of resolution 2607 (2021), that the asset freeze measure would not be applied to the payment of funds, other financial assets or economic resources necessary to ensure the timely delivery of humanitarian assistance.[57] Thereafter, by its resolution 2664 (2022) concerning the standing humanitarian exemption to asset freeze measures, the Council clarified that paragraph 1 of resolution 2664 (2022) would supersede and replace paragraph 37 of resolution 2607 (2021).[58]

The Council further reaffirmed that all States were to prevent the direct or indirect sale, supply or transfer of the items listed in part I of annex C to resolution 2662 (2022) to Somalia from their territories or by their nationals outside their territories, or using their flag vessels or aircraft, if there was sufficient evidence to demonstrate that the item(s) would be used, or a significant risk that they might be used, in

---

[49] Resolution 2661 (2022), para. 1.

[50] Resolution 2662 (2022), para. 24. In accordance with the change of the name of the Committee, the related sanctions regime is henceforth referred to as the "Al-Shabaab sanctions regime". For more information about the Committee and its Panel of Experts, see part IX, sect. I.B.

[51] Resolution 2662 (2022), paras. 10, 11 and 21 (a). The Council reaffirmed that weapons and military equipment sold or supplied in accordance with the exemption in paragraph 11 of the resolution were not to be resold to, transferred to, or made available for use by any individual or entity not in the service of the recipient to which it had been originally sold or supplied, or the selling or supplying State or international, regional or subregional organization (ibid., para. 12).

[52] Ibid., para. 13. See also S/2022/698.

[53] Resolution 2662 (2022), paras. 14–20.

[54] Ibid., para. 34.

[55] Ibid., para. 41.

[56] Ibid., para. 26.

[57] Ibid., para. 28.

[58] Resolution 2664 (2022), para. 4.

the manufacture in Somalia of improvised explosive devices.[59] The items in annex C to the resolution included explosive materials, explosives precursors, explosive-related equipment and related technology. The Council also decided to renew the implementation measures related to the ban on components of improvised explosive devices.[60] While noting that the security situation in Somalia continued to necessitate the measures contained in resolution 2662 (2022), including strict controls on the movement of arms, the Council affirmed that it would keep the situation in Somalia under constant review and that it would be prepared to review the appropriateness of the measures, including any modification, suspension or lifting thereof.[61] The Council also requested the Secretary-General to provide an update on progress made against each indicator set out in the benchmarks contained in the technical assessment by 15 September 2023.[62] Table 5 provides an overview of the changes to the measures authorized by the Council in 2022.

Table 5
Changes to the measures imposed pursuant to Article 41 of the Charter concerning Al-Shabaab in 2022

		Resolutions adopted during the review period (paragraph)		
Provision relating to sanctions measures	*Resolutions establishing measures*	*2661 (2022)*	*2662 (2022)*	*2664 (2022)*
Arms embargo	733 (1992), para. 5, 1425 (2002), paras. 1 and 2, 1844 (2008), para. 7	Limited extension (1) Exemption (1)	Extension (10, 26) Exemption (11, 21)	
Asset freeze	1844 (2008), para. 3	Limited extension (1) Exemption (1)	Extension (26) Exemption (28)	Exemption (1, 4)
Ban on components of improvised explosive devices	2498 (2019), para. 26	Limited extension (1)	Extension (37)	
Charcoal ban	2036 (2012), para. 22	Limited extension (1)	Extension (34)	
Travel ban	1844 (2008), para. 1	Limited extension (1)	Extension (26)	

Taliban and associated individuals and entities

In 2022, the Council adopted resolution 2665 (2022), by which it reaffirmed the asset freeze, travel ban and arms embargo measures with respect to individuals and entities designated prior to the date of adoption of resolution 1988 (2011) as the Taliban, as well as other individuals, groups, undertakings and entities associated with the Taliban in constituting a threat to the peace, stability and security of Afghanistan as designated by the Committee established pursuant to resolution 1988 (2011).[63] The Council also decided to actively review the implementation of the measures outlined in the resolution

[59] Resolution 2662 (2022), para. 37.

[60] The Council reaffirmed that where an item in part I of annex C to the resolution was directly or indirectly sold, supplied or transferred to Somalia, the State was to notify the Committee no more than 15 working days after the sale, supply or transfer had taken place, and stressed the importance that notifications contain all relevant information (ibid., para. 38). The Council also called upon Member States to undertake appropriate measures to promote the exercise of vigilance by their nationals, as well as individuals and entities subject to their jurisdiction, that were involved in the sale, supply or transfer of explosive precursors and materials to Somalia that might be used in the manufacture of improvised explosive devices, to keep records of transactions and share information with Somalia, the Committee and the Panel of Experts regarding suspicious purchases of or enquiries into those chemicals by individuals in Somalia and to ensure that Somalia was provided with adequate financial and technical assistance to establish appropriate safeguards for the storage and distribution of materials (ibid., para. 39).

[61] Ibid., fifth preambular paragraph.

[62] Ibid., para. 47 (b).

[63] Resolution 2665 (2022), para. 1. For information on the Committee established pursuant to resolution 1988 (2011) and the Analytical Support and Sanctions Monitoring Team, see part IX, sect. I.B.

and to consider adjustments, as necessary, to support peace and stability in Afghanistan.[64] The Council further recalled its decision in resolution 2615 (2021) that humanitarian assistance and other activities that supported basic human needs in Afghanistan were not a violation of paragraph 1 (a) of resolution 2255 (2015), encouraged Member States and humanitarian assistance providers to make full use of that decision and urged States, when designing and applying sanctions measures, to take into account the potential effect of those measures on exclusively humanitarian activities, including medical activities, that were carried out by impartial humanitarian actors in a manner consistent with international humanitarian law in accordance with resolution 2462 (2019).[65]

In addition, in its resolution 2664 (2022), the Council clarified that the standing humanitarian exemption to asset freeze measures established in that resolution would not apply to the sanctions regime pursuant to resolution 1988 (2011) and that instead paragraph 1 of resolution 2615 (2021) concerning the Taliban would remain in effect.[66] Table 6 provides an overview of the changes made to the measures during the period under review.

Table 6
Changes to the measures imposed pursuant to Article 41 of the Charter concerning the Taliban and associated individuals and entities in 2022

Provision relating to sanctions measures	*Resolution establishing measures*	*Resolution adopted during the review period (paragraph) 2665 (2022)*
Arms embargo	1333 (2000), para. 5	Extension (1)
Asset freeze	1267 (1999), para. 4 (b)	Extension (1)
Travel ban or restrictions	1390 (2002), para. 2 (b)	Extension (1)

ISIL/Da'esh and Al-Qaida and associated individuals and entities

During the year under review, the Council adopted one resolution concerning the sanctions measures imposed on ISIL/Da'esh, Al-Qaida and associated individuals, groups, undertakings and entities. By its resolution 2664 (2022), the Council decided that the standing humanitarian exemption to asset freeze measures, introduced in paragraph 1 of that resolution, would apply to the ISIL/Da'esh and Al-Qaida sanctions regime for a period of two years from the date of adoption of the resolution, and expressed its intent to make a decision on the extension of its application to that regime prior to the date on which the application would otherwise expire.[67] Table 7 provides an overview of the changes made to the measures during the period under review.

Table 7
Changes to the measures imposed pursuant to Article 41 of the Charter concerning ISIL/Da'esh and Al-Qaida and associates in 2022

Provision relating to sanctions measures	*Resolution establishing measures*	*Resolution adopted during the review period (paragraph) 2664 (2022)*
Arms embargo	1333 (2000), para. 5	
Asset freeze	1267 (1999), para. 4 (b)	Exemption (2)
Travel ban or restrictions	1390 (2002), para. 2 (b)	

[64] Ibid., para. 4.
[65] Ibid., seventh preambular paragraph.
[66] Resolution 2664 (2022), para. 4.
[67] Resolution 2664 (2022), para. 2.

Iraq

In 2022, the Council adopted no new resolutions concerning the remaining sanctions measures imposed on Iraq, consisting of an arms embargo, with exemptions, and an asset freeze on senior officials, State bodies, corporations and agencies of the former Iraqi regime. Pursuant to resolution 1483 (2003), the Committee established pursuant to resolution 1518 (2003) continued to oversee the implementation of the asset freeze and maintain the lists of individuals and entities.[68]

Democratic Republic of the Congo

In 2022, the Council adopted resolution 2641 (2022), by which it renewed the sanctions measures concerning the Democratic Republic of the Congo, comprising an arms embargo, a travel ban, an asset freeze and restrictions on transportation and aviation, as well as the exemptions to said measures, until 1 July 2023.[69] The Council further decided that the sanctions measures renewed in resolution 2641 (2022) would also apply to individuals and entities as designated by the Committee established pursuant to resolution 1533 (2004) concerning the Democratic Republic of the Congo for involvement in the production, manufacture or use in the country of improvised explosive devices, or in the commission, planning, ordering, aiding, abetting or otherwise assistance of attacks in the country with improvised explosive devices.[70] The Council also decided that the notification requirements set out in paragraph 5 of resolution 1807 (2008) would no longer apply to supplies of non-lethal military equipment intended solely for humanitarian or protective use, and related technical assistance or training, and to shipments of arms and related materiel for the Democratic Republic of the Congo, except in relation to items listed in annex A to the resolution, which remained subject to the applicable notification procedures.[71]

In addition, in its resolution 2667 (2022), the Council reiterated that the arms embargo measures continued to apply to all non-governmental entities and individuals operating in the territory of the Democratic Republic of the Congo and decided that the notification requirements set out in paragraph 5 of resolution 1807 (2008) would no longer apply.[72] Table 8 provides an overview of the changes made to the measures during the period under review.

Table 8
Changes to the measures imposed pursuant to Article 41 of the Charter concerning the Democratic Republic of the Congo in 2022

Provision relating to sanctions measures	*Resolution establishing measures*	*Resolutions adopted during the review period (paragraph)*		
		2641 (2022)	*2664 (2022)*	*2667 (2022)*
Arms embargo	1493 (2003), para. 20	Limited extension (1) Exemption (1)		Extension (1)
Asset freeze	1596 (2005), para. 15	Limited extension (1) Exemption (1)	Exemption (1)	
Travel ban or restrictions	1596 (2005), para. 13	Limited extension (1) Exemption (1)		
Transportation and aviation sanctions measures	1807 (2008), paras. 6 and 8	Limited extension (1)		

[68] For information on the Committee established pursuant to resolution 1518 (2003), see part IX, sect. I.B.
[69] Resolution 2641 (2022), para. 1. See also resolution 2664 (2022), para. 1
[70] Resolution 2641 (2022), para. 3.
[71] Ibid., para. 5.
[72] Resolution 2667 (2022), paras. 1 and 2.

Sudan

During the period under review, the Council adopted no new resolutions modifying the sanctions measures imposed on the Sudan. However, by its resolution 2620 (2022), the Council extended the mandate of the Panel of Experts on the Sudan until 12 March 2023, recalled the arms embargo, asset freeze and travel ban measures and the designation criteria established by previous resolutions and reaffirmed the related exemptions.[73] The Council further expressed its intention to regularly review the measures on Darfur, in the light of the reports submitted by the Panel of Experts.[74] In that regard, it took note of the report of the Secretary-General,[75] providing a review of the situation in Darfur and recommending benchmarks to assess the measures on Darfur, and expressed its intention to consider by 31 August 2022 establishing clear, well-identified and realistic key benchmarks, and its readiness to consider adjusting measures renewed in paragraph 1 to respond to the situation in Darfur in the light of the evolving situation on the ground.[76]

Lebanon

In 2022, the Council made no modifications to the sanctions measures established pursuant to resolution 1636 (2005), consisting of an asset freeze and a travel ban imposed on individuals designated by the International Independent Investigation Commission or the Government of Lebanon as being suspected of involvement in the 14 February 2005 terrorist bombing in Beirut that killed the former Prime Minister of Lebanon, Rafiq Hariri, and 22 others.[77]

Democratic People's Republic of Korea

During the period under review, the Council made no modifications to the sanctions measures concerning the Democratic People's Republic of Korea. The Committee established pursuant to resolution 1718 (2006) continued to oversee the implementation of the asset freeze, arms embargo, travel ban and other restrictions previously imposed by the Council in resolutions 1718 (2006), 1874 (2009), 2087 (2013), 2094 (2013), 2270 (2016), 2321 (2016), 2356 (2017), 2371 (2017), 2375 (2017) and 2397 (2017). By its resolution 2627 (2022), acting under Article 41 of Chapter VII of the Charter, the Council extended until 30 April 2023 the mandate of the Panel of Experts established pursuant to resolution 1874 (2009) to support the Committee.[78]

Libya

In 2022, the Council adopted six resolutions relating to the sanctions measures concerning Libya, namely, resolutions 2629 (2022), 2635 (2022), 2644 (2022), 2647 (2022), 2656 (2022) and 2664 (2022).[79]

In its resolutions 2629 (2022), 2647 (2022) and 2656 (2022) concerning the mandate of the United Nations Support Mission in Libya, the Council demanded full compliance by all Member States with the arms embargo imposed under resolution 1970 (2011), as modified in subsequent resolutions.[80] It also recalled that the measures set out in resolution 1970 (2011), as modified in subsequent resolutions, would apply to individuals and entities determined to be engaging in or providing support for acts that threatened the peace, stability or security of Libya or obstructed or undermined the successful completion of its

---

[73] Resolution 2620 (2022), paras. 1 and 2. See also resolution 2664 (2022), para. 1.

[74] Resolution 2620 (2022), para. 4. For information on the Committee established pursuant to resolution 1591 (2005) concerning the Sudan and the Panel of Experts on the Sudan, see part IX, sect. I.B.

[75] S/2021/696.

[76] Resolution 2620 (2022), para. 5. For more information on the deliberations among Council members concerning the proposed benchmarks to assess the measures on Darfur, see part II, sect. VIII.

[77] Resolution 1636 (2005), fourth preambular paragraph and para. 3. For information on the Committee established pursuant to resolution 1636 (2005), see part IX, sect. I.B.

[78] Resolution 2627 (2022), para. 1. See also resolution 2664 (2022), para. 1. For information on the Committee established pursuant to resolution 1718 (2006) and the Panel of Experts established pursuant to resolution 1874 (2009), see part IX, sect. I.B.

[79] For information on the Committee established pursuant to resolution 1970 (2011) concerning Libya and the Panel of Experts on Libya, see part IX, sect. I.B.

[80] Resolutions 2629 (2022), para. 5; 2647 (2022), para. 6; and 2656 (2022), para. 8.

political transition, including by obstructing or undermining the elections.[81] In its resolutions 2644 (2022), 2647 (2022) and 2656 (2022), the Council reaffirmed its intention to ensure that assets frozen pursuant to paragraph 17 of resolution 1970 (2011) would at a later stage be made available to and for the benefit of the Libyan people.[82]

In addition, in its resolution 2635 (2022), the Council extended the authorizations concerning the implementation of the arms embargo on the high seas off the coast of Libya for a period of 12 months and requested the Secretary-General to report within 11 months on the implementation of the resolution.[83]

By its resolution 2644 (2022), the Council extended until 30 October 2023 the authorizations and measures contained in resolution 2146 (2014), as amended in paragraph 2 of resolutions 2441 (2018) and 2509 (2020), to prevent the illicit export of petroleum, including crude oil and refined petroleum products, from Libya.[84] In addition, the Council renewed the arms embargo and travel ban.[85] The Council also affirmed its readiness to, inter alia, review the appropriateness of the measures contained in the resolution, including the strengthening, modification, suspension or lifting of the measures, as might be needed at any time in the light of developments in Libya.[86] Table 9 provides an overview of the changes made to the measures during the period under review.

In addition, in its resolution 2635 (2022), the Council extended the authorizations concerning the implementation of the arms embargo on the high seas off the coast of Libya for a period of 12 months and requested the Secretary-General to report within 11 months on the implementation of the resolution.

By its resolution 2644 (2022), the Council extended until 30 October 2023 the authorizations and measures contained in resolution 2146 (2014), as amended in paragraph 2 of resolutions 2441 (2018) and 2509 (2020), to prevent the illicit export of petroleum, including crude oil and refined petroleum products, from Libya. In addition, the Council renewed the arms embargo and travel ban. The Council also affirmed its readiness to, inter alia, review the appropriateness of the measures contained in the resolution, including the strengthening, modification, suspension or lifting of the measures, as might be needed at any time in the light of developments in Libya. Table 9 provides an overview of the changes made to the measures during the period under review.

Table 9
Changes to the measures imposed pursuant to Article 41 of the Charter concerning Libya in 2022

Provision relating to sanctions measures	*Resolution establishing measures*	*Resolutions adopted during the review period (paragraph)*				
		2629 (2022)	*2644 (2022)*	*2647 (2022)*	*2656 (2022)*	*2664 (2022)*
Arms embargo	1970 (2011), para. 9	Extension (5)	Extension (5)	Extension (6)	Extension (8)	
Asset freeze	1970 (2011), para. 17					Exemption (1)
Ban on arms exports by target State	1970 (2011), para. 10					
Business restrictions	1973 (2011), para. 21					
Financial restrictions	2146 (2014), para. 10 (d)		Limited extension (2)			

[81] Resolutions 2629 (2022), para. 4; 2647 (2022), para. 5; and 2656 (2022), para. 8.
[82] Resolutions 2644 (2022), para. 10; 2647 (2022), eighth preambular paragraph; and 2656 (2022), eleventh preambular paragraph.
[83] Resolution 2635 (2022), paras. 1 and 2.
[84] Resolution 2644 (2022), para. 2.
[85] Ibid., paras. 5 and 9.
[86] Ibid., para. 16.

Provision relating to sanctions measures	*Resolution establishing measures*	*Resolutions adopted during the review period (paragraph)*				
		2629 (2022)	*2644 (2022)*	*2647 (2022)*	*2656 (2022)*	*2664 (2022)*
Oil/petroleum embargo/ restrictions	2146 (2014), para. 10 (a), (c) and (d)		Limited extension (2)			
Prohibition on bunkering services	2146 (2014), para. 10 (c)		Limited extension (2)			
Travel ban or restrictions	1970 (2011), para. 15		Extension (9)			

Guinea-Bissau

During the period under review, the sanctions regime for Guinea-Bissau, consisting of a travel ban, continued to remain in force, without undergoing any modifications.[87]

Central African Republic

In 2022, the Council adopted resolution 2648 (2022), by which it extended until 31 July 2023 the arms embargo, asset freeze and travel ban measures concerning the Central African Republic[88] and renewed the related exemptions to those measures.[89] The Council further eased the arms embargo measures for the Central African Republic, requiring only a notification process for supplies of weapons and ammunition, military vehicles and equipment and the provision of related assistance to the Central African Republic security forces, including State civilian law enforcement institutions.[90]

The Council further requested the Secretary-General, in close consultation with the United Nations Multidimensional Integrated Stabilization Mission in the Central African Republic (MINUSCA), including the Mine Action Service, and the Panel of Experts on the Central African Republic, to report, no later than 15 May 2023, on the progress achieved by the authorities of the Central African Republic on the key benchmarks on the arms embargo established in the Council's presidential statement dated 9 April 2019.[91] The Council also affirmed that it would keep the situation in the Central African Republic under continuous review and be prepared to review the appropriateness of the measures contained in the resolution, at any time as might be necessary, in the light of the evolution of the security situation in the country, the progress achieved in relation to the security sector reform process, the disarmament, demobilization, reintegration and repatriation process and the management of weapons and ammunition.[92]

Further to the request of the Council in paragraph 13 of resolution 2588 (2021), the Secretary-General, in a letter dated 14 June addressed to the President of the Council,[93] provided a further update on the progress achieved by the authorities of the Central African Republic on the key benchmarks established in the presidential statement of 9 April 2019.

In addition, in the context of the renewal of the mandate of MINUSCA, in its resolution 2659 (2022), the Council recalled that individuals or entities that undermined peace and stability in the Central African Republic could be listed for targeted measures pursuant to resolution 2648 (2022).[94] It also

[87] For more information on the Committee established pursuant to resolution 2048 (2012) concerning Guinea-Bissau, see part IX, sect. I.B.

[88] Resolution 2648 (2022), paras. 1, 3 and 4. For information on the Committee established pursuant to resolution 2127 (2013) concerning the Central African Republic and the Panel of Experts on the Central African Republic, see part IX, sect. I.B.

[89] Resolution 2648 (2022), paras. 1 (a)–(h), 3 and 4. See also resolution 2664 (2022), para. 1.

[90] Resolution 2648 (2022), para. 1 (g).

[91] Ibid., para. 14. See also S/PRST/2019/3.

[92] Resolution 2648 (2022), para. 15.

[93] S/2022/489.

[94] Resolution 2659 (2022), para. 4.

recalled that committing acts of incitement to violence, in particular on an ethnic or religious basis, and then engaging in or providing support for acts that undermined the peace, stability or security of the Central African Republic could be a basis for sanctions designations pursuant to resolution 2648 (2022).[95] Table 10 provides an overview of the changes made to the measures during the period under review.

Table 10
Changes to the measures imposed pursuant to Article 41 of the Charter concerning the Central African Republic in 2022

Provision relating to sanctions measures	*Resolution establishing measures*	*Resolutions adopted during the review period (paragraph)*	
		2648 (2022)	*2664 (2022)*
Arms embargo	2127 (2013), para. 54	Limited extension (1, 3) Exemption (1 (a)–(h), 3)	
Asset freeze	2134 (2014), paras. 32 and 34	Limited extension (4) Exemption (4)	Exemption (1)
Travel ban or restrictions	2134 (2014), para. 30	Limited extension (4) Exemption (4)	

Yemen

In 2022, the Council adopted resolution 2624 (2022), by which it extended the asset freeze and travel ban established pursuant to resolution 2140 (2014) concerning Yemen, as well as the relevant exemptions to those measures, until 28 February 2023, and reaffirmed the arms embargo as set out in resolution 2216 (2015).[96] The Council also reaffirmed the designation criteria set out in prior resolutions[97] and decided that the entity listed in the annex to the resolution would be subject to the arms embargo as set out in resolution 2216 (2015).[98] The Council further affirmed that the designation criteria could include launches from Yemen using ballistic and cruise missile technology and attacks on merchant vessels in the Red Sea or Gulf of Aden by parties to the conflict.[99]

The Council also emphasized the importance of facilitating humanitarian assistance and facilitating commercial imports, noted that the measures imposed in resolutions 2140 (2014) and 2216 (2015) were not intended to have adverse humanitarian consequences for the civilian population of Yemen or for civilian access to humanitarian assistance, commercial imports or remittances, and reaffirmed its decision that the Committee established pursuant to resolution 2140 (2014) could, on a case-by-case basis, exempt any activity from the sanctions measures imposed by the Council in resolutions 2140 (2014) and 2216 (2015) if the Committee determined that such an exemption was necessary to facilitate the work of the United Nations and other humanitarian organizations in Yemen or for any other purpose consistent with the objectives of those resolutions.[100] The Council also reaffirmed its intention to keep the situation in Yemen under continuous review and its readiness to review the appropriateness of the sanctions measures in the light of developments in the country.[101] Table 11 provides an overview of the changes made to the measures during the period under review.

[95] Ibid., para. 22.
[96] Resolution 2624 (2022), paras. 4 and 21. See also resolution 2664 (2022), para. 1.
[97] Resolution 2624 (2022), paras. 10–12.
[98] Ibid., para. 5.
[99] Ibid., paras. 13 and 14.
[100] Ibid., para. 6.
[101] Ibid., para. 23.

Table 11
Changes to the measures imposed pursuant to Article 41 of the Charter concerning Yemen in 2022

		Resolutions adopted during the review period (paragraph)	
Provision relating to sanctions measures	*Resolution establishing measures*	*2624 (2022)*	*2664 (2022)*
Arms embargo	2216 (2015), paras. 14–16	Extension (4, 21)	
Asset freeze	2140 (2014), paras. 11 and 13	Limited extension (4) Exemption (4)	Exemption (1)
Travel ban or restrictions	2140 (2014), para. 15	Limited extension (4)	

South Sudan

In 2022, the Council adopted resolution 2633 (2022), by which it renewed the arms embargo, asset freeze and travel ban established pursuant to resolutions 2206 (2015) and 2428 (2018) concerning South Sudan, as well as the relevant exemptions to those measures, until 31 May 2023.[102] The Council further decided that the measures on arms imposed in paragraph 4 of resolution 2428 (2018) would not apply to the supply, sale or transfer of non-lethal military equipment, solely in support of the implementation of the terms of the peace agreement, as notified in advance to the Committee established pursuant to resolution 2206 (2015) concerning South Sudan.[103] By the same resolution, the Council also reaffirmed the designation criteria set out in resolution 2206 (2015) and underscored that individuals engaged in actions or policies that had the purpose or effect of expanding or extending the conflict in South Sudan could be listed for travel and financial measures.[104]

The Council also requested the Secretary-General, in close consultation with the United Nations Mission in South Sudan (UNMISS) and the Panel of Experts on South Sudan, to conduct, no later than 15 April 2023, an assessment of progress achieved on the key benchmarks established in paragraph 2 of resolution 2577 (2021).[105] The Council further reiterated its readiness to review the arms embargo measures in the light of progress achieved on the key benchmarks and decided to keep the measures concerning the asset freeze and travel ban under continuous review in the light of progress achieved in implementing all provisions of the Revitalized Agreement on the Resolution of the Conflict in the Republic of South Sudan and developments related to human rights violations and abuses, including conflict-related sexual violence.[106]

In addition, in the context of the renewal of the mandate of UNMISS, in its resolution 2625 (2022), the Council expressed its intention to consider all appropriate measures against those who took actions that undermined the peace, stability and security of South Sudan and specifically underscored that individuals or entities that were responsible for or complicit in attacks against UNMISS personnel and premises and any humanitarian personnel could meet the designation criteria. The Council further demanded that all Member States comply with their obligations to prevent the direct or indirect supply, sale or transfer of arms and related materiel of all types to the territory of South Sudan, as set out in relevant Council resolutions.[107] Table 12 provides an overview of the changes made to the measures during the period under review.

[102] Resolution 2633 (2022), paras. 1 and 12. See also resolution 2664 (2022), para. 1.
[103] Resolution 2633 (2022), para. 2.
[104] Ibid., paras. 15 and 16.
[105] Ibid., para. 5.
[106] Ibid., paras. 3 and 13.
[107] Resolution 2625 (2022), para. 18.

Table 12
Changes to the measures imposed pursuant to Article 41 of the Charter concerning South Sudan in 2022

Provision relating to sanctions measures	*Resolution establishing measures*	*Resolutions adopted during the review period (paragraph)*	
		2633 (2022)	*2664 (2022)*
Arms embargo	2428 (2018), para. 4	Limited extension (1) Exemption (1, 2)	
Asset freeze	2206 (2015), paras. 12 and 14	Limited extension (12) Exemption (12)	Exemption (1)
Travel ban or restrictions	2206 (2015), para. 9	Limited extension (12) Exemption (12)	

Mali

In 2022, the Council adopted resolution 2649 (2022), by which it renewed the asset freeze and travel ban established pursuant to resolution 2374 (2017), as well as the relevant exemptions to those measures, until 31 August 2023.[108] By the same resolution, the Council reaffirmed that those measures would apply to individuals and entities as designated by the Committee established pursuant to resolution 2374 (2017) concerning Mali, as set forth in paragraphs 8 and 9 of resolution 2374 (2017), including for involvement in planning, directing or committing acts in Mali that violated international humanitarian law, which could include attacks against medical personnel or humanitarian personnel.[109]

In the context of the renewal of the mandate of the United Nations Multidimensional Integrated Stabilization Mission in Mali, in its resolution 2640 (2022), the Council stressed that individuals or entities placed on the Mali sanctions list would not benefit from any financial, operational or logistical support from United Nations entities deployed in Mali until their removal from the list and without prejudice to the exemptions set out in paragraphs 2, 5, 6 and 7 of resolution 2374 (2017). The Council further expressed its intent, should the responsibility for actions or policies referred to in paragraph 8 of resolution 2374 (2017) be established, to respond with measures pursuant to that same resolution.[110] Table 13 provides an overview of the changes made to the measures during the period under review.

Table 13
Changes to the measures imposed pursuant to Article 41 of the Charter concerning Mali in 2022

Provision relating to sanctions measures	*Resolution establishing measures*	*Resolutions adopted during the review period (paragraph)*	
		2649 (2022)	*2664 (2022)*
Asset freeze	2374 (2017), para. 4	Limited extension (1) Exemption (1)	Exemption (1)
Travel ban or restrictions	2374 (2017), para. 1	Limited extension (1) Exemption (1)	

Haiti

In 2022, the Council established a new sanctions regime consisting of a travel ban, an asset freeze and a targeted arms embargo in connection with the question concerning Haiti.[111]

[108] Resolution 2649 (2022), para. 1. See also resolution 2664 (2022), para. 1.
[109] Resolution 2649 (2022), para. 2.
[110] Resolution 2640 (2022), para. 4.
[111] For more information about the item entitled "The question concerning Haiti", see part I, sect. 12.

On 15 July, in its resolution 2645 (2022), by which it extended the mandate of the United Nations Integrated Office in Haiti, the Council demanded an immediate cessation of gang violence and criminal activities and in that regard expressed its readiness to take appropriate measures, as necessary, that could include asset freeze or travel ban measures against those engaged in or supporting gang violence, criminal activities or human rights abuses or who otherwise took action that undermined the peace, stability and security of Haiti and the region, within 90 days from the adoption of the resolution.[112]

On 21 October, by its resolution 2653 (2022), acting under Chapter VII of the Charter, the Council decided to establish, for an initial period of one year, an asset freeze, a travel ban and a targeted arms embargo against individuals and entities designated as being responsible for or complicit in, or having engaged in, directly or indirectly, actions that threatened the peace, security or stability of Haiti.[113] The Council also established a Committee to monitor the implementation of the measures and, for an initial period of 13 months, a Panel of Experts to support the work of the Committee.[114]

In the resolution, the Council decided that the actions that threatened the peace, security or stability of Haiti included engaging in or supporting criminal activities and violence involving armed groups and criminal networks that promoted violence, including the forcible recruitment of children by such groups and networks, kidnappings, trafficking in persons and the smuggling of migrants, and homicides and sexual and gender-based violence; supporting the illicit trafficking and diversion of arms; planning, directing or committing acts that violated international human rights law or constituted human rights abuses and acts involving sexual and gender-based violence, including rape and sexual slavery; obstructing the delivery of humanitarian assistance to Haiti or access to, or the distribution of, humanitarian assistance in Haiti; and attacking personnel or premises of United Nations missions and operations in Haiti.[115]

The Council also elaborated on the exemptions to the measures. Regarding the travel ban, the Council decided that entry into or transit through the territories of Member States would be exempted from the travel ban where such travel was justified on the grounds of humanitarian need, including religious obligation, or necessary for the fulfilment of a judicial process, or where the Committee determined that an exemption would further the objectives of peace and stability in Haiti.[116] With regard to the asset freeze, the Council decided that the measure would not apply to funds, other financial assets or economic resources that had been determined by relevant Member States to be necessary for, inter alia, basic expenses, including payment for foodstuffs, rent or mortgage, medicines and medical treatment, taxes, insurance premiums and public utility charges or exclusively for the payment of reasonable professional fees and the reimbursement of incurred expenses associated with the provision of legal services in accordance with national laws, or fees or service charges.[117] Thereafter, by its resolution 2664 (2022) concerning the standing humanitarian exemption, the Council decided that paragraph 1 of that resolution would supersede and replace paragraph 10 of resolution 2653 (2022).[118] Table 14 provides an overview of the measures introduced in the period under review.

[112] Resolution 2645 (2022), paras. 1 and 5.

[113] Resolution 2653 (2022), paras. 3, 6, 11 and 15.

[114] Ibid., paras. 19 and 21. For information about the Committee established pursuant to resolution 2653 (2022) concerning Haiti and the Panel of Experts, see part IX, sect. I.B.

[115] Resolution 2653 (2022), para. 16.

[116] Ibid., para. 5.

[117] Ibid., para. 7. See also paras. 8–10.

[118] Resolution 2664 (2022), para. 4.

Table 14
Measures imposed pursuant to Article 41 of the Charter concerning Haiti in 2022

Provision relating to sanctions measures	*Resolution establishing measures*	*Resolutions adopted during the review period (paragraph)*	
		2653 (2022)	*2664 (2022)*
Arms embargo	2653 (2022), para. 11	Establishment (11)	
Asset freeze	2653 (2022), para. 6	Establishment (6) Exemption (7–10)	Exemption (1, 4)
Travel ban or restrictions	2653 (2022), para. 3	Establishment (3) Exemption (5)	

B. Discussions relating to Article 41

The present subsection covers the discussions in the Council regarding the use of sanctions and other measures pursuant to Article 41 of the Charter. In 2022, speakers made four explicit references to Article 41 in two Council meetings, both held under the item entitled "General issues relating to sanctions".[119]

During the reporting period, the use of sanctions was discussed by Council members and other speakers during deliberations held in relation to both thematic and country- or region-specific items. As outlined below, in connection with thematic items, the most salient discussions on the use of sanctions took place during the meetings held under the items entitled "General issues relating to sanctions" (case 3) and "Women and peace and security" (case 4), while the most pertinent deliberations about the measures imposed pursuant to Article 41 of the Charter in connection with country-specific items occurred during meetings focusing on South Sudan (case 5), the Democratic Republic of the Congo (case 6) and Haiti (case 7).

Case 3
General issues relating to sanctions

On 7 February, at the initiative of the Russian Federation, which held the presidency of the Security Council for the month,[120] the Council held a debate under the item entitled "General issues relating to sanctions" and the sub-item entitled "Preventing their humanitarian and unintended consequences".[121] Council members heard a briefing by the Under-Secretary-General for Political and Peacebuilding Affairs and the Under-Secretary-General for Humanitarian Affairs and Emergency Relief Coordinator. In addition, the representatives of Iraq, Mali, South Sudan, the Sudan and Venezuela (Bolivarian Republic of) participated in the meeting under rule 37 of the provisional rules of procedure. During the discussion, three speakers made explicit reference to Article 41 of the Charter of the United Nations, while many others implicitly discussed the use of measures imposed pursuant to Article 41.

In her briefing, the Under-Secretary-General for Political and Peacebuilding Affairs noted that sanctions remained a vital Charter-based tool available to the Council to ensure the maintenance of international peace and security and added that, in order to be effective, sanctions should be a part of a comprehensive political strategy, working in tandem with political dialogue, mediation, peacekeeping and special political missions. She highlighted that almost all the sanctions regimes supporting conflict resolution included designation or listing criteria intended to uphold international humanitarian law and international human rights law and had served as leverage to bring about positive outcomes for people at risk. She noted that the evolution from comprehensive to targeted sanctions had marked a sea change in that area of the work of the Council, while also acknowledging that some concerns remained about the

[119] See S/PV.8962 (Under-Secretary-General for Humanitarian Affairs and Emergency Relief Coordinator, Gabon and Ghana); and S/PV.9214 (India).

[120] A concept note was circulated by a letter dated 2 February (S/2022/86).

[121] See S/PV.8962.

unintended consequences and adverse effects of Council sanctions and that more could be done to reduce them.[122] The Under-Secretary-General for Humanitarian Affairs and Emergency Relief Coordinator similarly elaborated on the need to mitigate the humanitarian impact of sanctions while also noting that it was the Council's vital prerogative to devise measures under Article 41 of the Charter in the pursuit of international peace and security.

During the ensuing discussion, Council members deliberated on the use of sanctions as a tool in the maintenance of international peace and security. The representative of the Russian Federation said that Council sanctions, as one of the strongest forms of response to threats to peace, must be applied with extreme care and be irreproachably substantiated and nuanced. He added that leveraging sanctions as a punitive weapon was unacceptable, noting that international sanctions should reflect the situation on the ground and serve to further political processes and that sanctions regimes should be subject to regular review and modification, up to and including their full lifting, where applicable. The representative of the Russian Federation also called for the targeted and flexible nature of Council restrictions to become standard practice. It was necessary, he added, to listen more attentively to, and heed the views of, the authorities of sanctioned States, as well as to more realistically formulate so-called benchmarks to prevent their morphing into deliberately unattainable objectives. He also viewed the practice of applying unilateral coercive measures as an encroachment upon the prerogatives of the Council and thereby as hindering the maintenance of peace.

The representative of the United Kingdom affirmed that, given its unique responsibility for the maintenance of international peace and security, it was right for the Council to make full and judicious use of every tool at its disposal in the pursuit of that goal, citing targeted sanctions as one such tool, as set out in the Charter. He noted that the value of sanctions had been proven in, inter alia, helping to end conflict and supporting the transition to peace and democracy, enabling the seizure of ammunition, anti-tank guided missiles and sniper rifles, countering the threat of transnational terrorism and preventing the proliferation of weapons of mass destruction. He concluded that sanctions were an important tool of the Council to help to change the behaviour of regimes or individuals responsible for conflicts and to help the Council to fulfil its collective responsibility to maintain international peace and security.

The representative of China presented the view that sanctions were meant to create conditions conducive to a political solution and were not a substitute for diplomatic efforts. He also indicated that the Council should keep in check the impulse to resort too readily to sanctions or the threat of sanctions and should give precedence to non-compulsory measures, such as good offices, mediation and negotiation. The representative of China added that, as a basic principle, Council sanctions should not be open-ended. Instead, he suggested that all new sanctions mechanisms include a sunset clause and that, for existing sanctions, clear and actionable exit benchmarks be established.

According to the representative of Ireland, sanctions had a critical role to play in furthering accountability and deterring unacceptable behaviour, including violent repression and violations of human rights and international humanitarian law. She expressed the view that sanctions could also support peaceful transitions and deter non-constitutional changes. Underscoring that sanctions did not and should not operate in a vacuum, the representative of Ireland added that, each time the Council had taken the decision to impose sanctions, they had been applied as part of a comprehensive strategy of political dialogue, peacekeeping or peacebuilding.

The representative of the United Arab Emirates asserted that, in certain situations, sanctions could be effective at achieving the Council's objectives, such as supporting peace processes, resolving disputes, countering terrorism and promoting non-proliferation, without the Council having to resort to force. He noted that Council members had a duty to ensure that sanctions measures continued to be an effective and useful tool for the Council and that Council members must be ready to constantly readjust, suspend or terminate the measures to keep them fit for purpose and legitimate.

The representative of India stated that the sanctions regimes had served well in the fight against terrorism, preventive diplomacy, assisting Member States in implementing peace agreements and against

[122] During the meeting, many speakers expressed their concerns about the unintended consequences of sanctions imposed by the Council and how to mitigate them. For more on that discussion, see sect. IX below.

the proliferation of weapons of mass destruction. He noted that sanctions should always be used as an instrument of last resort after having exhausted all other options and in accordance with the provisions of the Charter and should not violate principles of international law. He added that the Council should remain respectful of the regional approach adopted by countries and, in collaboration with regional organizations, address challenges related to peace and security before considering the issuance of such sanctions. He also emphasized that sanctions should have a clear end goal and that a clear timeline and criteria for their phased withdrawal should be spelled out from their inception.

The representative of Norway emphasized the importance of targeted sanctions as a tool to address threats to international peace and security, adding that they could act as a deterrent against further violations of international law. She further noted that targeted and well-designed sanctions could also help to protect civilians and prevent and curb sexual violence, as well as the recruitment and use of children in armed conflict.

The representative of Gabon presented the view that, in convening the Council to discuss the topic of sanctions, the presidency was guiding Council members in making the needed self-criticism on the effectiveness of the mechanisms provided for in Article 41 of the Charter in the maintenance or restoration of peace and security. He further stated that the imposition of sanctions had proven to be a relatively inexpensive policy mechanism in comparison to armed conflicts, although it was virtually impossible to determine the exact level of action required for a sanctions regime to have an impact on the policy of the State under sanction. The representative of Gabon also noted that, nonetheless, sanctions had become a commonly used instrument and were meted out automatically and systematically in their implementation and that there was a clear tendency to apply the same tools to dissimilar situations. He concluded that regardless of the true purpose of sanctions, the result remained the same: the effectiveness of sanctions was lacking or far below expectations.

The representative of Brazil said that, when the situation on the ground called for enforcement action by the Council, sanctions were alternatives to the use of armed force and could be legitimate and effective when multilaterally created and strategically targeted. As a measure of last resort, they should follow the exhaustion of diplomatic solutions and be part of a comprehensive strategy to overcome the crisis. He underlined that sanctions should be limited in their scope and temporal elements, preferably with the inclusion of sunset clauses in their mandates, and stated that sanctions regimes that lasted for years were warning signs of either their limited effectiveness for that particular situation or the lack of additional tools to address it. He further noted that both the listing criteria and the conditions for lifting sanctions should be clearly established. Clear and well-defined benchmarks for easing sanctions were also ways to measure progress and signal the temporary nature of the restrictions.

The representative of the United States stated that sanctions were a potent tool that could, inter alia, deter and address threats to international peace and security and constrain the resources of those who would spoil peace processes, threaten United Nations peacekeepers, commit atrocities and obstruct humanitarian assistance. Outlining ways to ensure that sanctions were effective and as targeted as possible, the representative of the United States noted that the Council should continue to use sanctions, when appropriate, to improve the lives of people in conflict zones, protect civilians and promote the peaceful resolution of disputes. She added that when Member States wilfully ignored sanctions, ignored sanctions evasion activity or failed themselves to live up to the commitments made to enforce those measures, they undermined the utility of those tools and the work of the Council itself.

The representative of Albania underscored that the Charter was very clear on the necessity of using sanctions to prevent further violence and address threats to peace, breaches of peace or any act of aggression. As such, targeted sanctions represented a tool that needed to be used with the utmost care and precision as a deterrent and a means of accountability when human rights violations and gross atrocities were committed. He also noted that the strength of sanctions rested in their compatibility with international law, international humanitarian law and international human rights law as part of a comprehensive strategy and actions to preserve peace and security. In his statement, the representative of Kenya proposed, inter alia, building into sanctions regimes the automatic requirement for periodic reviews to ascertain that, at all stages, they still met their purpose.

Explicitly citing Article 41 of the Charter, the representative of Ghana stated that sanctions were not intended for extraneous objectives but were required as a tool to modify the behaviour of any State whose actions were in breach of its Charter obligations, where those actions constituted a threat to international peace and security, without resorting to the use of force. He emphasized that sanctions must be imposed only as a last resort when a threat to international peace and security existed, and that, before sanctions were imposed, serious efforts must be made to exhaust all measures of pacific settlement contained in Chapter VI of the Charter. The representative of France noted that Council sanctions regimes were an essential instrument to help to maintain international peace and security and added that sanctions were part of a political strategy aimed at preventing and resolving conflicts, combating the proliferation of nuclear weapons, countering terrorism and combating violations of international humanitarian law and human rights.

Other Member States also shared their views on the role of sanctions in addressing matters of international peace and security. The representative of the Sudan stated that peaceful avenues set out in the Charter should be preferred to sanctions and added that the conditions demanded of targeted countries or parties should be realistic and clearly defined. He added that sanctions should be reviewed periodically and should never be imposed indefinitely. The representative of South Sudan reiterated that his delegation did not support sanctions in any shape or form, especially when they did not achieve their desired or intended goal. He noted that the Council should seek a peaceful world through means other than sanctions. The representative of Iraq stressed the importance of being cautious when implementing sanctions regimes, while taking into account the achievement of the Sustainable Development Goals. Speaking on behalf of the Group of Friends in Defence of the Charter of the United Nations, the representative of the Bolivarian Republic of Venezuela stated that the measures provided for in Chapter VII of the Charter must be taken only as a last resort and in accordance with the purposes and principles enshrined in the Charter. He called for a comprehensive and exhaustive review of measures imposed by the Council to ensure that they comply with the letter and spirit of the principles enshrined in the Charter.

Case 4
Women and peace and security

On 13 April, at the initiative of the United Kingdom, which held the presidency of the Security Council for the month,[123] the Council held an open debate under the item entitled "Women and peace and security" and the sub-items entitled "Accountability as prevention" and "Ending cycles of sexual violence in conflict",[124] during which Council members and other participants discussed the role of sanctions in curtailing sexual violence in conflict situations.

In her briefing, the Special Representative of the Secretary-General on Sexual Violence in Conflict underscored that it was critical to have coherence in the practice of listing suspected perpetrators of sexual violence and the practice of imposing targeted and graduated measures by sanctions committees to improve compliance.[125] She expressed the view that leveraging the credible threat of sanctions could change the calculation of parties to conflict that operated on the assumption that rape was cost free, or even profitable, in the political economy of war, in which women and girls were trafficked, traded and sold, and recalled that eight sanctions regimes included sexual violence as part of their designation criteria.

During the discussion, several Council members reflected on the use of sanctions as a tool to address conflict-related sexual violence. The representative of the United Arab Emirates noted that a strong tool for the Council to achieve accountability for conflict-related sexual violence was to include conflict-related sexual violence as a stand-alone designation criterion for sanctions on terrorists, individuals and entities, whenever they were responsible for the commission of such acts. The representative of Albania held a similar view and stated that the Council should incorporate sexual violence as a stand-alone designation criterion for targeted sanctions. The representative of India asserted that sanctions regimes and other targeted measures by the Council needed to be strengthened in order to utilize their full potential to deter the perpetrators of sexual violence in armed conflict. According to the representative of Ireland, the use of targeted sanctions on grounds of conflict-related sexual violence was another important – but underutilized – tool at the Council's disposal. The representative of France said that, in parallel with the fight against impunity, the Council must also use all the tools at its disposal, in particular sanctions, which

[123] A concept note was circulated by a letter dated 5 April (S/2022/293).

[124] See S/PV.9016 and S/PV.9016 (Resumption 1).

[125] See S/PV.9016.

represented a deterrent measure that had not been sufficiently applied to date. The representative of Ghana reaffirmed his country's support for the Council in ensuring that conflict-related sexual violence was treated as a basis for targeted sanctions against culpable actors and that sanctions committees had the requisite expertise on conflict-related sexual violence. He added that periodic briefings to the committees by the Special Representative would be useful in sustaining their focus and reviewing progress on the implementation of such sanctions, as well as the existing challenges. The representative of Kenya urged the Council to take steps to list and sanction administrators of prisons and their chains of command if their facilities were party to systemic and systematic sexual violence against prisoners. The representative of Kenya noted that, beyond listings and the incorporation of sexual and gender-based violence as a separate listing criterion in the relevant sanctions regimes, the Council should take specific steps and deterrent measures to also increase the costs of acts of conflict-related sexual violence.

Speaking on behalf of 64 States members of the Group of Friends of Women, Peace and Security, the representative of Canada strongly encouraged the Council to incorporate and apply sexual violence as a designation criterion in United Nations sanctions regimes. Similarly, in their statements, many other speakers expressed support for the introduction of conflict-related sexual violence as a stand-alone designation criterion in sanctions regimes imposed by the Council.[126]

Case 5
Reports of the Secretary-General on the Sudan and South Sudan

At a meeting held on 26 May under the item entitled "Reports of the Secretary-General on the Sudan and South Sudan",[127] the Security Council adopted, with five abstentions, resolution 2633 (2022), concerning the sanctions measures imposed on South Sudan.[128] By the resolution, the Council renewed the sanctions measures imposed on South Sudan for one year and decided that the arms embargo would not apply to the supply, sale or transfer of non-lethal military equipment, solely in support of the implementation of the terms of the peace agreement.[129] Following the vote, several Council members and the representative of South Sudan took the floor and expressed divergent views on whether the decision by the Council to renew the sanctions regime on South Sudan would promote peace in the country.

The representative of Kenya explained that his country had abstained in the voting because the text fell short of the call by the Intergovernmental Authority on Development and the African Union to lift the arms embargo and targeted sanctions on South Sudan.[130] He added that the resolution also fell short of the Council's own commitment to progressively lift the arms embargo and targeted measures against South Sudan, which had not been effective tools in support of the South Sudan peace process. Nonetheless, he affirmed that the new resolution reflected a positive step in its attempt to exempt non-lethal military equipment from the arms embargo, but stated that more progress could have been made, including by suspending the individual targeted sanctions. He also said that more could have been done to ease restrictions on the provision of capacity-building, technical assistance and regional training programmes. According to the representative of Kenya, in essence, the Council had continued to unintentionally suppress the country's capacity to develop its security sector, thereby limiting its ability to respond effectively to security incidents such as the reported intercommunal violence and other crimes. He urged the Government and all the parties in South Sudan to redouble their efforts to expeditiously implement the pending aspects of the Revitalized Agreement on the Resolution of the Conflict in the Republic of South Sudan and all the remaining benchmarks so that it would no longer be necessary to extend the arms embargo and targeted sanctions when the resolution next came up for review.

---

[126] See S/PV.9016 (Resumption 1) (Luxembourg, Estonia, Switzerland, European Union (also on behalf of Albania, Andorra, Bosnia and Herzegovina, Georgia, Montenegro, North Macedonia, the Republic of Moldova, San Marino and Ukraine), Türkiye, Croatia, Portugal, Belgium, Bulgaria, Liechtenstein, Denmark (on behalf of the Nordic countries), Spain and Austria).

[127] See S/PV.9045.

[128] The draft resolution received 10 votes in favour (Albania, Brazil, France, Ghana, Ireland, Mexico, Norway, United Arab Emirates, United Kingdom and United States) and 5 abstentions (China, Gabon, India, Kenya and Russian Federation). For more information, see part I, sect. 7.

[129] Resolution 2633 (2022), paras. 1, 2 and 12.

[130] See S/PV.9045.

In explaining his abstention, the representative of India stressed that the international community, including the Council, must spare no effort in addressing the concerns that South Sudan had repeatedly raised regarding the sanctions, including the arms embargo and targeted measures. Echoing a view similar to that of the representative of Kenya, he added that the resolution fell short of expectations and continued to maintain the sanctions measures without giving due consideration to the positive strides made by South Sudan.

The representative of Ghana, explaining his delegation's vote in favour of the resolution, welcomed the Council's decision to exempt the supply, sale or transfer of non-lethal military equipment from the arms embargo inspections regime and expressed hope that the progressive fulfilment of the benchmarks by the Government of South Sudan would lead to a more positive consideration of the embargo in subsequent reviews.

Asserting that his country's abstention reflected the position of the African Union, the representative of Gabon expressed the view that sanctions were counterproductive with regard to the efforts made in the past few years by the Government and the people of South Sudan. While noting the progress made with regard to the sanctions regime, he also stated that the efforts of the international community must be more firmly directed towards capacity-building, post-conflict reconstruction and peacebuilding.

While asserting that Council sanctions constituted a powerful response to threats to peace, the representative of the Russian Federation, who had also abstained in the vote, expressed a firm belief that sanctions must be applied with the utmost care and be totally justified and nuanced. She noted that their use as a punitive measure was unacceptable and that the restrictions applied by the Council should reflect the situation on the ground and serve the political process. Accordingly, she added, they should also be subject to regular review and modification until they were fully lifted. In the view of the Russian Federation, many of the current Council sanctions regimes no longer corresponded to the situations on the ground and thereby hindered the plans of Governments in their State-building efforts and formation of effective security forces. The representative of the Russian Federation underlined that the situation concerning the South Sudanese sanctions regime was no exception. She further noted that while preparing the document, the penholder for the South Sudan file, the United States, had once again ignored not only Juba's calls but also the agreed position of the countries of the African continent and the views of other Council members regarding the importance of demonstrating respect for the country's opinion and willingness to ease the sanctions in order to help the country achieve even greater results in its State-building process.

According to the representative of China, who had abstained in the vote, the sanctions regime on South Sudan was the most controversial of all the Council's sanctions regimes because South Sudan needed constructive support, not sanctions pressure, from the international community, and because the African Union and the Intergovernmental Authority on Development had always taken a clear stand against Council sanctions on South Sudan. The representative of China expressed the view that sanctions pressure was not only frequently ineffective but also restricted the ability of the Government of South Sudan to build up its security capacity for the protection of civilians. Recalling that in 2021 the Council had established benchmarks for adjusting sanctions on South Sudan and that according to the report of the Secretary-General,[131] South Sudan had made progress in implementing the benchmarks, the representative of China stressed that his country and other Council members believed that the Council should take measures to gradually ease the sanctions regime on South Sudan.

The representative of South Sudan said that it was common knowledge that his country did not agree with the sanctions and the arms embargo imposed on it, because South Sudan had viewed those sanctions as ill-intended from the beginning and counterproductive since they had been imposed. He further noted that punitive measures were not effective tools in the case of South Sudan.

[131] S/2022/156.

Case 6
The situation concerning the Democratic Republic of the Congo

At a meeting held on 30 June under the item entitled "The situation concerning the Democratic Republic of the Congo",[132] the Security Council adopted, with five abstentions, resolution 2641 (2022), concerning the sanctions measures imposed on the Democratic Republic of the Congo.[133] By the resolution, the Council renewed the existing sanctions measures concerning the Democratic Republic of the Congo for one year and decided that they would also apply to individuals and entities as designated by the Committee established pursuant to resolution 1533 (2004) concerning the Democratic Republic of the Congo for involvement in the production, manufacture or use in the country of improvised explosive devices, or in the commission, planning, ordering, aiding, abetting or otherwise assistance of attacks in the country with improvised explosive devices.[134] The Council also decided that the notification requirements set out in paragraph 5 of resolution 1807 (2008) would no longer apply to supplies of non-lethal military equipment intended solely for humanitarian or protective use, and related technical assistance or training, and to shipments of arms and related materiel for the Democratic Republic of the Congo, except in relation to items listed in annex A to the resolution, which remained subject to the applicable notification procedures.[135]

Following the vote, the representative of France welcomed the adoption of the resolution and noted that the Council should be prepared to sanction those responsible for instability in the eastern part of the country.[136] He stated that the sanctions regime would now include a new designation criterion to combat the growing use of improvised explosive devices and added that France had heard the calls by the Democratic Republic of the Congo with regard to the notification procedure for providing military materials and assistance. He added that for that reason and in order to support efforts to step up the capacity and reform of the Congolese armed forces, the resolution eased that procedure significantly. The representative of France noted, however, that the resolution did not relax the embargo on weapons destined for active armed groups in the country. While expressing regret for the lack of unanimity in the Council, he expressed hope that the measures still in place would in future be adapted to national efforts to combat trafficking and the spread of weapons.

In explaining her abstention from the vote, the representative of Ghana said that the ability of armed groups in the Democratic Republic of the Congo to acquire even the most sophisticated and state-of-the-art weapons and ammunition, despite the existence of an arms embargo in the country, was a testament to the need for the Government to be better equipped to respond to the internal security threats it was facing. She added that the current notification requirement continued to impede the capacity of the country to limit armed groups and to improve its ability to safeguard its internal security. Similarly, the representative of Gabon presented the view that the current notification requirement continued to hamper the country's ability to quickly and effectively counter the activities of armed groups, which were heavily equipped and not subject to the embargo or the notification requirement. She indicated that Gabon remained in favour of a complete lifting of the notification requirement to allow the Armed Forces of the Democratic Republic of the Congo to more effectively carry out their constitutional mandate of defending the territorial integrity of their country. The representative of Kenya noted that some of the proposals made by the three African countries that were members of the Council had been taken on board, citing a modest positive step in the lifting of the notification requirement on supplies of non-lethal military equipment intended solely for humanitarian and protective use, and related technical assistance and training. However, he stated that Kenya had abstained in the voting on the resolution because the resolution fell short of the appeal made by the Democratic Republic of the Congo for a full lifting of the notification requirement on arms and the provision of assistance and training related to military activities. The representative of Kenya presented the view that the notification requirement was unnecessary, as it had not been an effective tool in addressing the illicit proliferation and supply of weapons to armed

[132] See S/PV.9084.
[133] The draft resolution received 10 votes in favour (Albania, Brazil, France, India, Ireland, Mexico, Norway, United Arab Emirates, United Kingdom and United States) and 5 abstentions (China, Gabon, Ghana, Kenya and Russian Federation).
[134] Resolution 2641 (2022), paras. 1 and 3.
[135] Ibid., para. 5.
[136] See S/PV.9084.

groups. If anything, he added, it served only to make information available that should otherwise remain privileged for a sovereign State. He further noted that the Council had continued to unintentionally suppress the capacity of the Democratic Republic of the Congo to develop its security sector, thereby limiting its ability to respond effectively to security threats. The representative of Kenya expressed hope that the notification requirement would not be necessary when resolution 2641 (2022) next came up for review.

The representative of the Russian Federation stated that Council sanctions should reflect the situation on the ground, facilitate the political process and account for the views of the host country and countries in the region. She added that restrictions needed to be regularly reviewed and modified up to the full lifting thereof. According to the assessment of the Russian Federation, many of the sanctions regimes of the Council currently in effect failed to reflect the situation on the ground and instead impeded Governments' plans in the area of State-building and the establishment of effective armed forces and security structures. The representative of the Russian Federation expressed regret that many of those sanctions regimes merely persisted for the purpose of exerting pressure.

The representative of China indicated that the Council's sanctions regime imposed on the Democratic Republic of the Congo had been designed to curb the violent activities of armed groups but that, regrettably, 18 years after its initial implementation, armed groups in the eastern part of the country remained rampant while the security capacity of the country had been constrained. The representative of China stated that during the consultations on resolution 2641 (2022), China and the African members of the Council had expressly supported the removal of the notification requirement for the Government of the Democratic Republic of the Congo, adding that France, as penholder, had tried as much, but that the Council had been unable to reach consensus owing to the opposition of some Council members. The representative of China expressed the view that the resolution would artificially complicate the process, create difficulties and affect the security-related cooperation of international partners with the Democratic Republic of the Congo and would be detrimental to the improvement of the Congolese security capacity and to efforts to find a fundamental solution to the situation in the eastern part of the country.

The representative of Brazil stressed that neither the multilateral sanctions nor the activities of the Committee and its experts were measures against the Democratic Republic of the Congo or the Congolese people. He presented the view that the measures that the Council had just renewed either targeted individuals and entities that destabilized the already dire security situation in the eastern part of the country or addressed the concerning and illicit flow of weapons and equipment to armed groups that had escalated the violence in Ituri, North Kivu and South Kivu. He noted that Brazil had supported a broader clause on the humanitarian consequences of sanctions, explaining that the International Committee of the Red Cross and other humanitarian agencies had reported and argued that instances of overcompliance with Council measures on the part of banks and financial institutions in general had made donations to humanitarian agencies and humanitarian assistance itself more difficult in the Democratic Republic of the Congo. The excerpt that Brazil had proposed had been intended to address that unintended and damaging consequence. The representative of Brazil expressed hope that Council members would address that concern in future negotiations and find constructive ways to reach a productive consensus.

The representative of the United Arab Emirates stated that his delegation had hoped to be able to achieve consensus on the text and to give greater consideration to the concerns expressed by a number of Council members, including African members, regarding notifications and the arms embargo. He further noted that the United Arab Emirates had voted in favour of the resolution as a whole and was in agreement with the general objectives contained therein.

Case 7
The question concerning Haiti

In 2022, the Security Council held several meetings under the item entitled "The question concerning Haiti", during which it discussed the imposition of sanctions in response to the persistence of violence, criminal activities and human rights abuses in Haiti,[137] culminating in the unanimous adoption of resolution 2653 (2022) on 21 October, by which the Council introduced an asset freeze, a travel ban and a targeted arms embargo against individuals and entities designated as being responsible for or

[137] For more information on the item, see part I, sect. 12.

complicit in, or having engaged in, directly or indirectly, actions that threatened the peace, security or stability of Haiti.[138]

At a meeting held on 17 October,[139] Council members and other participants discussed the Council's intention to establish a sanctions regime to address the situation in Haiti. The representative of the United States noted that her delegation had worked with Mexico to draft a resolution that would impose financial sanctions on the criminal actors who were inflicting suffering on the Haitian people and that would target those responsible for committing gang violence, trafficking arms, attacking United Nations personnel, kidnapping innocent citizens, perpetrating human rights abuses and sexual and gender-based violence, as well as the individuals blocking the country's ports and the delivery of humanitarian assistance. She added that the United Nations sanctions regime would aim to stop those criminal actors from having access to reputable financial institutions and that it would work to freeze their assets and prohibit their international travel. In addition, its arms embargo provisions would prevent the direct or indirect supply, sale or transfer of arms to criminal gangs and their leaders, as designated by the Council. Similarly, the representative of Mexico asserted that the draft resolution would seek to establish a sanctions regime focused on the actors responsible for the violence and instability and would impose an arms embargo to prevent gangs from obtaining weapons so easily and using them with such impunity. The representative of Brazil noted that developing appropriate listing criteria, conditions and mechanisms for lifting the sanctions and humanitarian exemptions and carve-outs were essential for the effectiveness of the new sanctions regime. Speaking on behalf of the African members of the Council, the representative of Kenya expressed support for the proposed sanctions resolution as an important step to cut off the flow of weapons and financing to gangs and to ensure accountability for human rights violations. The representative of Norway presented the view that sanctions, as proposed by the United States and Mexico, could be an important tool to address violence committed by armed groups and criminal networks. She added that for the sanctions regime to be efficient, it must include safeguards for due process. She noted that the Council should have a clear view on how to deal with that issue going forward, adding that one option would be to look to existing processes, such as those of the Office of the Ombudsperson. The representative of China expressed appreciation for the draft resolution and stated that he supported targeted sanctions on gang members and their supporters, adding that he hoped that those measures would be robust and effective. He noted that it was important to prevent gang members from using potential loopholes to evade sanctions on the one hand and, on the other, to avert a situation where implementation was only superficial and became a mere formality with no real impact. The representative of the Russian Federation expressed the view that his country did not share the desire of the co-penholders to mix the issue of unblocking the country's port infrastructure with the issue of introducing a sanctions regime in the country. He recalled that Council members had agreed to discuss restrictive measures on the condition that their future effectiveness, targeted nature and humanitarian consequences be carefully considered and added that Council sanctions were a serious and long-term instrument that required in-depth analysis and detailed negotiations, especially given that the last time the Council had introduced a sanctions regime had been five years before. Several other speakers also expressed support for the proposed sanctions measures,[140] with some also highlighting the importance of safeguards against any unintended consequences.[141]

At a meeting held on 21 October,[142] the Council adopted resolution 2653 (2022), by which it imposed sanctions measures concerning Haiti consisting of a targeted arms embargo, an asset freeze and a travel ban. Following the vote, the representative of the United States underscored that sanctions were at their most effective when they were targeted specifically towards bad actors and allowed humanitarian aid to reach civilian populations, adding that the adopted resolution accomplished both of those objectives. She noted the work undertaken by the penholders to incorporate clear, measurable and well-defined methods to periodically review the efficacy of those sanctions. The representative of Mexico highlighted the importance of an embargo on any transfer of arms to non-State actors who were

[138] Resolution 2653 (2022), paras. 3, 6, 11 and 15.

[139] See S/PV.9153.

[140] Ireland, United Kingdom, France, Haiti, Dominican Republic and International Organization of la Francophonie.

[141] Brazil, United Arab Emirates and Russian Federation.

[142] See S/PV.9159.

terrorizing the civilian population and destabilizing the country, adding that the resolution sent a clear signal that the Council would not stand idly by and would take action. The representative of China asserted that his country had always called for caution on the use or threat of use of sanctions in international relations, regardless of the circumstances. However, considering the urgency of the situation in Haiti and the call of its people, China had been the first in the Council to propose targeted sanctions against Haitian criminal gangs, and its proposal had been quickly echoed by other Council members and countries of the region. The representative of Norway noted that the focus had been on creating a robust and well-designed regime that would act as a constraint on and deterrence against sexual and gender-based violence, the recruitment of children to armed groups and criminal networks and human rights abuses that threatened the peace and security of Haiti and the region. The representative of the Russian Federation noted that, despite its support for the resolution, the Russian Federation was not convinced that international restrictive measures would provide an adequate response to the range of problems that were plaguing Haiti. He added that the problems of illegal arms flows and organized crime in the Caribbean were not confined to Port-au-Prince and that other actors must not be overlooked by the sanctions committee that was being established and its panel of experts. The representative of the Russian Federation further asserted that Council sanctions were not a punitive tool, but rather one of the strongest means in the Council's toolkit to respond to emerging threats, adding that international restrictions should be regularly reviewed to assess their appropriateness and be eased or completely lifted, as required. The representative of Kenya welcomed the specific and measurable benchmarks for the review of the sanctions and noted that the implementation of the sanctions would rely heavily on the cooperation and support of the international community, particularly States of the region. Welcoming the strengthened sanctions designation criteria to address the horrifying reports of sexual and gender-based violence by armed gangs, the representative of the United Arab Emirates stated that her delegation looked forward to future discussions to establish clear, well-defined and achievable benchmarks for the eventual lifting of sanctions when the time was right. Recalling that the Charter of the United Nations provided the Council with a set of instruments to maintain international peace and security, which included sanctions, the representative of Brazil affirmed that sanctions could be legitimate and effective when they were multilaterally created, strategically targeted and designed to have minimal impact on the civilian population. He added that Brazil considered monitoring mechanisms, listing criteria, humanitarian exemptions and carve-outs and conditions for lifting sanctions to be essential for applying sanctions measures in a responsible and effective manner. The representative of Ghana also welcomed the strengthened benchmarks in the resolution, which would enable the Council to make an overall assessment of the effectiveness and appropriateness of the measures contained therein. Some Council members also noted the potential role of the Ombudsperson in ensuring due process in the application of the sanctions measures concerning Haiti.[143] The representative of Haiti welcomed the unanimous adoption of resolution 2653 (2022), establishing a sanctions regime that targeted the leaders of armed gangs operating in Haiti and all who supported them, and underlined that the measures sent a powerfully deterrent political message that was likely to change the behaviour of actors operating on the ground.

IV. Measures to maintain or restore international peace and security in accordance with Article 42 of the Charter

Article 42

Should the Security Council consider that measures provided for in Article 41 would be inadequate or have proved to be inadequate, it may take such action by air, sea, or land forces as may be necessary to maintain or restore international peace and security. Such action may include demonstrations, blockade, and other operations by air, sea, or land forces of Members of the United Nations.

[143] Norway, Ireland and Brazil. See also resolution 2653 (2022), nineteenth preambular paragraph.

Note

Section IV covers the practice of the Council in relation to Article 42 of the Charter of the United Nations, regarding the authorization of the use of force by peacekeeping operations and multinational forces, as well as interventions by regional organizations.[144]

During the year under review, the Council authorized the use of force under Chapter VII of the Charter with respect to the maintenance or restoration of international peace and security by several peacekeeping missions and multinational forces in Bosnia and Herzegovina, the Central African Republic, the Democratic Republic of the Congo, Lebanon, Libya, Mali, Somalia, South Sudan and the Sudan (including Abyei).[145] In 2022, there were no communications of the Council containing explicit references to Article 42.

The present section is divided into two subsections. Subsection A outlines decisions in which the Council authorized the use of force under Chapter VII of the Charter. Subsection B covers discussions of the Council of relevance to Article 42.

A. Decisions relating to Article 42

During the reporting period, the Council made no explicit reference to Article 42 of the Charter in its decisions. That notwithstanding, the Council adopted several resolutions under Chapter VII of the Charter by which it authorized peacekeeping missions and multinational forces, including those deployed by regional organizations, to use "all necessary measures" or "all necessary means", or to take "all necessary action(s)" for the maintenance or restoration of international peace and security.

For information on the authorization of the use of force of missions in the past, including some of the missions covered below, see previous supplements. For more information on the specific mandates of each field mission, see part X of the present Supplement.

In 2022, the Council reiterated its authorization to use force in relation to various situations and disputes. In Africa, in connection with the situation in Abyei, the Council extended the tasks of the United Nations Interim Security Force for Abyei as set out in paragraph 3 of resolution 1990 (2011), which included the authorization to take "necessary actions".[146]

In relation to the situation in the Central African Republic, the Council renewed the authorization granted to the United Nations Multidimensional Integrated Stabilization Mission in the Central African Republic to take "all necessary means" to carry out its mandate within its capabilities and areas of deployment.[147]

Consistent with past practice in connection with the situation in the Democratic Republic of the Congo, the Council authorized the United Nations Organization Stabilization Mission in the Democratic Republic of the Congo to take "all necessary measures" to carry out its mandate.[148]

With regard to the flows of arms and related materiel transferred to or from Libya in violation of the arms embargo, the Council extended the authorizations first granted in paragraphs 4 and 8 of resolution 2292 (2016) to Member States, acting nationally or through regional organizations, to use "all measures commensurate to the specific circumstances" when conducting inspections of vessels and seizing of items in the course of such inspections, emphasizing that the inspections were to be carried out in compliance with international humanitarian law and international human rights law and "without causing undue delay to or undue interference with the exercise of freedom of navigation".[149] Furthermore, in connection with the smuggling of migrants into, through and from Libyan territory, the Council

---

[144] The Council's authorization of the use of force by regional organizations is covered in part VIII. The authorization of the use of force by peacekeeping operations is covered in part X in the context of the mandates of peacekeeping operations.

[145] For more information on the mandates of peacekeeping operations, see part X, sect. I.

[146] Resolutions 2630 (2022) and 2660 (2022), para. 1.

[147] Resolution 2659 (2022), para. 34.

[148] Resolution 2666 (2022), para. 22.

[149] Resolution 2635 (2022), para. 1.

renewed the authorizations granted in paragraphs 7 to 10 of resolution 2240 (2015) to Member States, acting nationally or through regional organizations, engaged in the fight against migrant smuggling and human trafficking, to use "all measures commensurate to the specific circumstances" in confronting migrant smugglers or human traffickers when carrying out inspections of vessels on the high seas off the coast of Libya that they had reasonable grounds to suspect were being used for migrant smuggling or human trafficking and to seize such vessels that were confirmed as being used for such activities. The Council also reaffirmed paragraph 11 of resolution 2240 (2015), in which it had clarified that the authorization to use force applied only when confronting migrant smugglers and human traffickers on the high seas off the Libyan coast and would not affect the rights or obligations of Member States under international law.[150]

Regarding the situation in Mali, the Council, consistent with its practice in previous years, authorized the United Nations Multidimensional Integrated Stabilization Mission in Mali to take "all necessary means" to carry out its mandate and requested it to continue to carry out its mandate with a "proactive, robust, flexible and agile posture".[151]

In connection with the situation in Somalia, the Council authorized the States members of the African Union to take "all necessary measures", in full compliance with participating States' obligations under international law, including international humanitarian and human rights law, and in full respect for the sovereignty, territorial integrity, political independence and unity of Somalia, to carry out the mandate of the African Union Transition Mission in Somalia.[152]

With regard to the situation in South Sudan, the Council reiterated the authorizations granted to the United Nations Mission in South Sudan to use "all necessary means" to perform its mandated tasks.[153]

In Europe, with regard to the situation in Bosnia and Herzegovina, the Council renewed its authorization granted to Member States, under the European Union military operation in Bosnia and Herzegovina (EUFOR-Althea) and the North Atlantic Treaty Organization (NATO) presence, to take "all necessary measures" to effect the implementation of and to ensure compliance with annexes 1-A and 2 of the General Framework Agreement for Peace in Bosnia and Herzegovina.[154] The Council also authorized Member States, at the request of either EUFOR-Althea or NATO, to take "all necessary measures" in the defence of EUFOR-Althea or the NATO presence, respectively, and recognized the right of both EUFOR-Althea and the NATO presence to take "all necessary measures" to defend themselves from attack or threat of attack.[155] The Council further authorized Member States, acting in accordance with annex 1-A of the Agreement for Peace, to take "all necessary measures" to ensure compliance with the rules and procedures governing command and control of airspace over Bosnia and Herzegovina with respect to all civilian and military air traffic.[156]

In the Middle East, in connection with the situation in Lebanon, the Council underlined the necessity that the United Nations Interim Force in Lebanon (UNIFIL) had at its disposal "all necessary means" and equipment to carry out its mandate.[157] It also recalled its authorization granted to UNIFIL to take "all necessary action" in areas of deployment of its forces, to ensure that its area of operations was not utilized for hostile activities, to resist attempts by forceful means to prevent it from discharging its duties, to protect United Nations personnel, facilities, installations and equipment, to ensure the security and freedom of movement of United Nations personnel and humanitarian workers and to protect civilians under imminent threat of physical violence.[158]

---

[150] Resolution 2652 (2022), para. 2.
[151] Resolution 2640 (2022), paras. 17 and 19.
[152] Resolution 2628 (2022), para. 22.
[153] Resolution 2625 (2022), para. 3.
[154] Resolution 2658 (2022), para. 3.
[155] Ibid., para. 4.
[156] Ibid., para. 5.
[157] Resolution 2650 (2022), twenty-fourth preambular paragraph.
[158] Ibid., para. 23. See also twenty-sixth preambular paragraph.

B. Discussions relating to Article 42

During the period under review, speakers made no explicit reference to Article 42 of the Charter at the meetings of the Council. The Council did, however, continue to discuss matters relating to the authorization of the use of force by United Nations peacekeeping operations and other multinational missions operating under Chapter VII of the Charter.

For example, at a meeting held on 12 July under the item entitled "United Nations peacekeeping operations", the representative of India referred to misplaced expectations among local communities about peacekeepers and the mandate to protect civilians, adding that such misunderstandings were further aggravated by the use of ambiguous terminology such as "robust mandate", "robust posture" or even "offensive posture" in the peacekeeping mandate resolutions of the Council, creating room for speculative and arbitrary interpretations of those mandates.[159] At a meeting held on 6 September under the same item, the representative of Ghana expressed concern about the insufficient emphasis on the primacy of politics in some peacekeeping missions, adding that, despite the fact that the mandates of some missions included the creation of rapid intervention brigades, the structure and focus of current peacekeeping arrangements made them inappropriate for counter-terrorism.[160] The representative of the Russian Federation presented the view that clear and realistic mission mandates that took into account the views of host States, the specific causes of each conflict and the current situation on the ground helped to improve the effectiveness of peacekeeping activities. He expressed the belief that it was essential to reduce peacekeepers' secondary and non-core tasks, especially those on the human rights, social and gender fronts, which distracted peacekeepers from their primary functions and required considerable funding. He also noted that one imperative was to comply with the basic principles of peacekeeping, including refraining from the use of force except in self-defence and to protect the mandate. He added that obsessing over force mandates and involving peacekeepers in offensive and counter-terrorist operations could undermine the neutral status of the blue helmets. The representative of Brazil also recalled that efficient peacekeeping must abide by the basic principles of peacekeeping, including the non-use of force except in self-defence and in defence of the mandate.

In another instance, at a meeting held on 3 November under the item entitled "Peacebuilding and sustaining peace", the Commissioner for Political Affairs, Peace and Security of the African Union asserted that one way that the Council could ensure that peace operations in Africa helped to provide a pathway to addressing the underlying causes of conflict was to adopt a whole-of-organization approach in implementing mandates.[161] He added that, since current peace support operations were multidimensional and multifunctional, with mandates that went beyond military pacification of the conflict theatre, it was imperative to ensure that the relevant United Nations and other stakeholders supported deployed missions as early as possible. The Minister for Foreign Affairs and Regional Integration of Ghana pointed to an overwhelming and urgent need for United Nations peace operations to be reconfigured to ensure a situationally determined balance between military actions aimed at restoring peace, including by defeating terrorism, and non-military measures to address the underlying causes of conflicts. The representative of India presented the view that the military component of peacekeeping could play only an enabling role but could not bring about peacebuilding on its own. According to the representative of Kenya, United Nations peacekeeping under Chapter VII of the Charter was necessary, but insufficient. It must be combined with other measures in a coordinated and sufficiently resourced manner for peace and security to be achieved in a reasonable period of time.

In addition, at a meeting held on 16 November under the item entitled "Peace and security in Africa", Zakaria Ousman Ramadan, an independent expert, noted that one weakness of the Joint Force of the Group of Five for the Sahel was that it did not have an extremely robust mandate from the Council under Chapter VII of the Charter, which would have provided guidance, more focus and much more resonance.[162]

[159] See S/PV.9090.

[160] See S/PV.9123.

[161] See S/PV.9181.

[162] See S/PV.9194.

In addition to the above, the most salient deliberations on the question of the use of force by peacekeeping operations took place under the items entitled "Protection of civilians in armed conflict" (case 8) and "The question concerning Haiti" (case 9).

Case 8
Protection of civilians in armed conflict

On 25 May, the Security Council held an open debate under the item entitled "Protection of civilians in armed conflict",[163] during which it heard briefings by the Director of Coordination in the Office for the Coordination of Humanitarian Affairs, the Director-General of the International Committee of the Red Cross, the President and Chief Executive Officer of the International Rescue Committee and the Country Director for the Democratic Republic of the Congo of Women for Women International. During the debate, several speakers discussed the mandates of United Nations peacekeeping operations in the context of the protection of civilians, including with respect to the use of force.

During the discussion, Council members focused on the core nature of the protection of civilians mandate and on the challenges faced in peacekeeping operations. The representative of Brazil stated that peacekeeping operations continued to play a role in promoting strategies for the protection of civilians, as more than 95 per cent of United Nations peacekeepers were mandated to protect civilians.[164] The representative of India emphasized that the role of United Nations peacekeeping operations was to supplement national efforts to advance peace and security, adding that peacekeepers could not and should not be a substitute for the primary responsibility of protecting civilians, which rested primarily with host Governments. He also noted that it was necessary to ensure that peacekeepers were adequately equipped and trained to take up the tasks involved in protecting civilians. He expressed concern about the fact that, with the increasingly multidimensional nature of peacekeeping missions, there was a risk of diluting the focus on protection of civilians mandates, adding that, in that regard, it was necessary to simplify peacekeeping mandates.

According to the representative of Ghana, the protection of civilians should remain a critical and integral component of all parts of peacekeeping operations and in a manner that provided for missions not only the authorization but also the capabilities to use all necessary means, including force, as required to prevent or respond to threats of physical violence against civilians, without prejudice to the responsibility of host Governments.

Regarding the challenge posed by terrorism in many States in Africa, the representative of Kenya presented the view that the piecemeal approaches by the Council would yield only failure. He also referred to the need for the Council to take bold action against terrorist groups and noted that none of the efforts of concerned Governments would come close to succeeding if there was no robust, sustained military and police pressure on those groups. He noted that the Council was in a position to act on that knowledge and referred to the need to deploy capable regional forces with access to predictable and adequate funding and to appropriate intelligence and force multipliers. The representative of Kenya further stated that it was necessary to ensure that peacekeeping mandates were fit for purpose to challenge terrorist groups, protect civilians and strengthen national military and police competencies. He also pointed to the need for peacekeeping missions to have robust public messaging and counter-narrative capabilities against terrorist groups operating in the same territory. Similarly, the representative of Norway said that the Council should adopt strong protection mandates for peacekeeping operations and political missions, including during transition phases, and should ensure adequate resourcing, including for child protection.

The representative of China said that the civilian protection mandate of United Nations peacekeeping operations should be realistic and feasible. It was important to cooperate closely with the countries concerned in the implementation process, to fully guarantee their resources and capacity, to make full use of good offices and mediation as a means of implementation and to only use force as a last resort.

---

[163] See S/PV.9042 and S/PV.9042 (Resumption 1). For more information about the item, see part I, sect. 27.

[164] See S/PV.9042.

The representative of the United Arab Emirates suggested that, in designing the mandates of peace operations, the Council should consider whether and how the mandates could foster a secure environment to enable humanitarian assistance. She also pointed to the need for the Council to give appropriate consideration to unarmed approaches to complement the fundamental physical protection provided by peacekeepers.

Other speakers also focused on the central role of the protection of civilians mandate, as well as on the means of delivering such mandate. The representative of Slovenia noted that effective and comprehensive peacebuilding and peacekeeping, with robust mandates that were flexible enough to provide protection and assistance to the civilian population, were critical.[165] The representative of Australia stated that peace operations played an important role in protecting civilians by creating more stable conditions for physical protection, intercommunal dialogue and the protection of human rights, as well as by contributing to processes of accountability within judicial systems. He expressed the view that the credibility and legitimacy of United Nations peace operations largely depended on the willingness and capability of peacekeepers to act when civilians were under threat and added that peacekeepers must be empowered and supported by both the United Nations and troop-contributing countries to protect civilians.

According to the representative of Bangladesh, peacekeeping missions should be adequately resourced and equipped to fulfil their protection of civilians mandates, including through community engagement and intelligence gathering and analysis. She added that the Council should factor in those issues when setting the mandates of peacekeeping missions.

The representative of Argentina asserted that it was necessary to continue to include and strengthen protection of civilians activities on the ground in the mandates of United Nations peacekeeping missions. In that regard, he expressed the view that the protection of civilians was an integrated mission-wide effort, requiring as an essential first step close cooperation among military, police and civilian components, in coordination with Governments, local communities and humanitarian organizations on the ground. The use of force to respond to threats of physical violence against civilians must be authorized in accordance with applicable legal obligations, the mandate established by the Council and mission-specific rules of engagement.

The representative of Malaysia pointed to the need to strengthen the capacity and mandate of peacekeepers, adding that the provision by the Council of civilian protection mandates in peacekeeping operations was vital in curbing violence against civilians. Peacekeepers must be trained appropriately and adequately to protect civilians, and operational plans and strategies to protect civilians that were used by peacekeeping missions must be informed by an analysis of the various impacts of conflict on all populations, especially vulnerable groups.

Case 9
The question concerning Haiti

At a meeting held on 17 October under the item entitled "The question concerning Haiti",[166] the Security Council heard a briefing by the Special Representative of the Secretary-General for Haiti and Head of the United Nations Integrated Office in Haiti, during which she reported that, against the backdrop of insecurity and a humanitarian crisis, on 7 October, the Council of Ministers of Haiti had authorized the Prime Minister to request the support of a specialized international armed force to help to secure the free movement of water, fuel and medical supplies to prevent the situation from deteriorating further. The Special Representative also reiterated the call of the Secretary-General upon the country's partners to consider the request as a matter of urgency for the immediate relief of those already most vulnerable.

During the discussion, the representative of the United States emphasized that the situation in Haiti required robust international cooperation and urgent action by the Council. As mandated by the Charter of the United Nations, it was necessary to mobilize the resources and power of the Council and the

[165] See S/PV.9042 (Resumption 1).

[166] See S/PV.9153. For more information about the item, see part I, sect. 12.

broader United Nations. In that context, she explained that the United States had worked with Mexico to propose a draft resolution that would authorize a non-United Nations international security assistance mission to help to improve the security situation and enable the flow of desperately needed humanitarian aid. She added that the draft resolution reflected one of the options that the Secretary-General had recommended that the Council consider and was also a direct response to the request of the Prime Minister and the Council of Ministers of Haiti for international assistance to help to restore security and alleviate the humanitarian crisis. The draft resolution would propose a limited, carefully scoped, non-United Nations mission led by a partner country with the deep, necessary experience required for such an effort to be effective. The representative of the United States further noted that the non-United Nations international security assistance mission would operate under Chapter VII of the Charter and would facilitate international support to the Haitian National Police and Coast Guard. She added that such a mission would rely on support from Member States and that the draft resolution would contain an explicit request for contributions of personnel, equipment and other resources. She also expressed awareness of the concerns about the Council's authorization of a response that could lead to an open-ended peacekeeping role and noted that the Council and the international community must look at its role differently from the way they had in the past. It was necessary to seek a different course, one that could better respond to the humanitarian and security crisis in Haiti and be able to address the needs of the Haitian people directly.

Several Council members took note of the request of the Haitian authorities to deploy an international specialized armed force and the recommendations of the Secretary-General for improving the security situation in Haiti.[167] Expressing support for the draft resolutions proposed by Mexico and the United States, the representative of Albania also expressed full support for a strong and robust security mandate in order to provide authorities and law enforcement bodies with the means necessary to guarantee safe and adequate conditions of life. The representative of the United Kingdom welcomed further Council discussion on the authorization of an international security assistance mission, as proposed by the Secretary-General, adding that the international community, led by Haitian needs, should help to restore effective governance and combat endemic gang violence.

The representative of China posed the question of whether sending a rapid reaction force to Haiti, at a time when the Government lacked legitimacy and was unable to govern, would be met with the understanding, support and cooperation of the parties in Haiti, or whether it would face resistance from or even trigger violent confrontation among the population. He asserted that the United Nations had deployed several missions to Haiti since the 1990s, none of which had achieved their objectives. He added that a rapid solution brought from the outside would yield only temporary results, with no lasting impact. The representative of the Russian Federation noted the varying opinions within Haitian society on the matter of an international response to the request made by the Prime Minister of Haiti, adding that many opposition groups had called for not allowing foreign intervention. He called for taking into account such opinions and carefully considering all possible implications of bringing foreign international and regional contingents to the island.

V. Consideration of Articles 43 to 45 of the Charter

Article 43

1. All Members of the United Nations, in order to contribute to the maintenance of international peace and security, undertake to make available to the Security Council, on its call and in accordance with a special agreement or agreements, armed forces, assistance, and facilities, including rights of passage, necessary for the purpose of maintaining international peace and security.

2. Such agreement or agreements shall govern the numbers and types of forces, their degree of readiness and general location, and the nature of the facilities and assistance to be provided.

[167] India, Brazil, Kenya (also on behalf of Gabon and Ghana), Norway, United Kingdom, United Arab Emirates, China, Russian Federation and France.

3. The agreement or agreements shall be negotiated as soon as possible on the initiative of the Security Council. They shall be concluded between the Security Council and Members or between the Security Council and groups of Members and shall be subject to ratification by the signatory states in accordance with their respective constitutional processes.

Article 44

When the Security Council has decided to use force it shall, before calling upon a Member not represented on it to provide armed forces in fulfilment of the obligations assumed under Article 43, invite that Member, if the Member so desires, to participate in the decisions of the Security Council concerning the employment of contingents of that Member's armed forces.

Article 45

In order to enable the United Nations to take urgent military measures, Members shall hold immediately available national air-force contingents for combined international enforcement action. The strength and degree of readiness of these contingents and plans for their combined action shall be determined within the limits laid down in the special agreement or agreements referred to in Article 43, by the Security Council with the assistance of the Military Staff Committee.

Note

Under Article 43 of the Charter of the United Nations, all Member States undertake to make available to the Council, for the maintenance of international peace and security, armed forces, assistance and facilities in accordance with special agreements. Such agreements, to be entered into by the Council and Member States, were conceived to regulate the numbers and types of troops, their readiness and location and the nature of facilities to be provided.

No agreements under Article 43 of the Charter were ever concluded, however, and in the absence of such agreements, there is therefore no practice in application of Article 43. The United Nations has developed practical arrangements to carry out military operations in the absence of such agreements. In that context, the Council authorizes peacekeeping forces (under the command and control of the Secretary-General and assembled pursuant to ad hoc agreements entered into by the United Nations and Member States) and national or regional forces (under national or regional command and control) to conduct military action. Peacekeeping operations, as well as their mandates, are covered in detail in part X of the present Supplement, and peacekeeping operations led by regional arrangements are featured in part VIII of the present Supplement.

Articles 44 and 45 of the Charter contain explicit references to Article 43 and are therefore intimately linked. As with Article 43, there is no prior practice in the application of Articles 44 and 45. Nonetheless, the Council has developed, through its decisions, a practice by which to: (a) call upon Member States to contribute armed forces, assistance and facilities, including rights of passage; (b) consult with Member States contributing troops for United Nations peacekeeping activities; and (c) call upon Member States to contribute military air assets in the context of peacekeeping. Some of those decisions of the Council are also featured in section VII below, which relates to Article 48, to the extent that they concern action required to carry out decisions of the Council for the maintenance of international peace and security.

During the period under review, in its decisions, the Council called for the provision of troops and other military assistance, including air assets, to the African Union Transition Mission in Somalia (ATMIS), the United Nations Multidimensional Integrated Stabilization Mission in the Central African Republic (MINUSCA) and the United Nations Multidimensional Integrated Stabilization Mission in Mali (MINUSMA). While the Council did not engage in any constitutional discussion concerning Articles 43 and 45 during the reporting period, some speakers at Council meetings addressed the need to provide additional troops and military equipment to peacekeeping operations to ensure effective mandate implementation. Throughout 2022, the Council also adopted decisions in which it emphasized, and held meetings at which participants deliberated upon, the importance of consulting troop- and police-contributing countries on issues pertaining to the mandates of peacekeeping operations.

Set out below is an overview of the practice of the Council during 2022 concerning the need for Member States to contribute, support and provide assistance to peacekeeping operations (subsection A) and the need for consultation with troop- and police-contributing countries (subsection B).

A. Need for Member States to contribute, support and provide assistance, including military air assets, to peacekeeping operations

In 2022, the Council made no explicit reference to Articles 43 or 45 of the Charter in its decisions or discussions, but it did call upon Member States to contribute, support and provide assistance to peacekeeping operations.

In its resolution 2628 (2022), adopted on 31 March, the Council urged Member States, including new donors, to consider providing predictable, sustainable and multi-year support for ATMIS, including through the provision of additional funding for police and troop stipends, equipment and technical assistance.[168] The Council also urged Member States to support the African Union in mobilizing the required resources and equipment for ATMIS, including through financial contributions to address identified gaps in resource requirements and specific requests for resources and equipment.[169] Furthermore, the Council requested the African Union to ensure that structures were in place to provide command, control and accountability of mission enabling units, including air assets.[170]

In its resolution 2640 (2022), adopted on 29 June, expressing its full support for the continuation of the implementation of the MINUSMA adaptation plan, the Council encouraged Member States to contribute to the plan by providing the capabilities needed for its success, particularly air assets, and urged Member States to provide to MINUSMA troops and police with adequate capabilities and equipment, including enablers, specific to the operating environment.[171] The Council also noted the potential adverse effects on mandate implementation of national caveats that had not been declared and accepted by the Secretary-General prior to deployment and called upon Member States to declare all national caveats, provide troops and police with the minimum of declared caveats and fully and effectively implement the provisions of the memorandums of understanding signed with the United Nations.[172]

By its resolution 2659 (2022), adopted on 14 November, the Council reiterated its concern at the continuing lack of key capabilities for MINUSCA and the need to fill gaps, as well as the importance of current and future troop- and police-contributing countries providing troops and police with adequate capabilities, equipment and predeployment training to enhance, inter alia, the ability of MINUSCA to operate effectively in an increasingly complex security environment.[173] Recognizing that the effective implementation of peacekeeping mandates was the responsibility of all stakeholders and contingent upon several critical factors, including adequate resources and training and equipment, the Council urged Member States to provide troops and police that had adequate capabilities and mindset, predeployment and, where appropriate, in situ training, and equipment, including enablers, specific to the operating environment, and called upon Member States to declare all national caveats, prior to the contingent's deployment, provide troops and police with the minimum of declared caveats and fully and effectively implement the provisions of the memorandums of understanding signed with the United Nations.[174]

During the period under review, several discussions of the Council touched upon the importance of providing peacekeeping operations with adequate troops and equipment, including military air assets, in meetings held under country- and region-specific items. For example, at meetings held under the item entitled "The situation in Mali", speakers raised repeatedly the need for stronger support for MINUSMA, including air assets. At a meeting held on 11 January, the representative of Gabon, speaking also on behalf of Ghana and Kenya, took note of the lack of sufficient and adequate airlift capability of MINUSMA, in particular with regard to medium utility and armed helicopters, which continued to hamper the Mission's

[168] Resolution 2628 (2022), para. 45.
[169] Ibid., para. 46.
[170] Ibid., para. 29 (d).
[171] Resolution 2640 (2022), paras. 21 and 40.
[172] Ibid., para. 40.
[173] Resolution 2659 (2022), para. 40.
[174] Ibid, para. 41.

performance, and therefore urged the Council to source the Mission with outstanding air assets, which were critical enablers for MINUSMA to continue to implement its mandates across its area of operation.[175] At the same meeting, the representative of the United States noted that MINUSMA needed, following the proposal of the Secretary-General, an increase to its troop ceiling, which would help to protect civilians in central Mali with more quick-reaction forces and air assets and enhance the safety and security of peacekeepers through explosive ordnance removal teams. At a meeting held on 13 June, the Special Representative of the Secretary-General for Mali and Head of MINUSMA, honouring the memory of all the peacekeepers who had lost their lives since the inception of MINUSMA, stated that their ultimate sacrifice underscored the need to ensure that the Mission had the requisite capabilities, including armed and utility helicopters.[176] The representative of Ghana, speaking also on behalf of Gabon and Kenya, expressed the view that MINUSMA would benefit from stronger support for troop contributions, capacity-building on counter-terrorism measures and the provision of adequate logistics, including airlift assets. He urged that peacekeepers be supported to ensure that they be robust enough in their training, operational posture, force multipliers and intelligence assets in order to be able to protect civilians and fully implement the mandate. According to the representative of China, the priority was to make full use of existing resources in an effort to improve the effectiveness of peacekeeping operations, as the challenges facing the Mission in performing its duties could not be solved by raising the troop ceiling alone.

With respect to the reconfiguration of the United Nations Interim Security Force for Abyei (UNISFA), during meetings held under the item entitled "Reports of the Secretary-General on the Sudan and South Sudan", Council members also noted the importance of troop and equipment contributions. For example, at a meeting held on 21 April, the representative of Ireland echoed the Secretary-General's appreciation for the support and collaboration of the Sudan, South Sudan and the new troop-contributing countries in the reconfiguration of UNISFA and urged all involved to continue to work towards the deployment of additional enablers in the coming months.[177] The representative of the Russian Federation noted that the replacement of the Ethiopian troops in UNISFA with new peacekeepers from other countries was proceeding smoothly and underscored the importance of ensuring that the new configuration was deployed in proper succession with the work of the Ethiopian peacekeepers. The representative of China also noted the orderly manner in which the reconfiguration of the military component of UNISFA was progressing and commended the Ethiopian peacekeepers for actively fulfilling their mandates under extremely difficult conditions. He also pointed out that, as a new troop-contributing country to UNISFA, China had deployed a helicopter unit in Abyei and would deploy a rapid reaction force as soon as possible. Furthermore, at a meeting held on 27 October, the Assistant Secretary-General for Africa stated that the new force must be better equipped to cover a wider area, adding that force mobility in the context of the reduced helicopter capacity was a further challenge.[178] At the same meeting, the representative of China noted that its peacekeeping helicopter contingent had, since its deployment, actively met the needs of the peacekeeping mandate and had spared no effort to complete a range of flights and ground-support tasks.

In connection with the situation concerning the Democratic Republic of the Congo, at a meeting held on 29 June, the representative of the Democratic Republic of the Congo requested the Council to allocate sufficient resources to the United Nations Organization Stabilization Mission in the Democratic Republic of the Congo to update its weaponry and helicopters and improve the quality of its equipment in general.[179]

The need to provide peacekeeping operations with adequate troops and equipment, including digital technologies, was also discussed in meetings under thematic items. For example, at a meeting held on 23 May under the item entitled "Maintenance of international peace and security", Dirk Druet, an adjunct professor at the McGill University Centre for International Peace and Security Studies, noted that monitoring and surveillance technologies, such as unarmed unmanned aerial systems, were being used with increasingly effective integration into mission-wide qualitative and quantitative data-gathering tools

---

[175] See S/PV.8945.
[176] See S/PV.9061.
[177] See S/PV.9020.
[178] See S/PV.9170.
[179] See S/PV.9081.

and analysis systems to generate higher quality peacekeeping intelligence.[180] That translated into better-informed detection of threats and more rapid action to protect civilians. The representative of Gabon presented the view that the use of unmanned aerial vehicles and point analysis systems were increasingly becoming the preferred means of observing and anticipating movements in hard-to-reach areas, such as battlefields, in order to obtain reliable information for more timely and efficient responses. According to the representative of Ireland, technology could act as a force multiplier in peacekeeping missions, offering peacekeepers greater situational awareness and improved data analysis capabilities. He added that those critically important enablers improved safety, security and operational efficiency, thereby enhancing mandate implementation, which was why implementing the Strategy for the Digital Transformation of United Nations Peacekeeping was so important.

In addition, at a meeting held on 6 September under the item entitled "United Nations peacekeeping operations", the Under-Secretary-General for Peace Operations called for the support of Council members to fill the critical gaps faced by peace operations in the area of capacities, especially with regard to utility and armed helicopters.[181] The representative of China expressed the view that Member States and the Secretariat should work together to enhance the emergency response and early warning capabilities of missions, strengthen rescue and medical support systems and properly use new technologies to improve equipment and security. In that context, China was sending a unit of unmanned aerial vehicles to MINUSMA. Similarly, the representative of Mexico noted that his country had made progress in the contribution of equipment to operate unmanned aerial vehicles as part of its commitment to the women and peace and security agenda. Several other Council members also pointed to the need to provide peacekeepers with the necessary training and equipment.[182]

B. Recognition of the need to consult troop- and police-contributing countries

During the period under review, the Council adopted five decisions concerning the need to consult troop- and police-contributing countries on matters pertaining to peacekeeping.

On 27 June and 22 December, respectively, the Council adopted resolutions 2639 (2022) and 2671 (2022) on the situation in the Middle East. In those resolutions, the Council emphasized the importance of the Council and troop-contributing countries having access to reports and information related to the redeployment configuration of the United Nations Disengagement Observer Force (UNDOF) and reinforced that such information assisted the Council with evaluating, mandating and reviewing UNDOF and with effective consultation with troop-contributing countries.[183] The Council also urged prompt reporting by the Secretary-General to the Council and troop-contributing countries of any actions that impeded the ability of UNDOF to fulfil its mandate.[184]

On 29 June, the Council adopted resolution 2640 (2022) on the situation in Mali, in which it requested the Secretary-General to ensure that troop-contributing countries received sufficient information relevant to up-to-date tactics, techniques and procedures for reducing troop casualties in an asymmetric environment before deploying to Mali.[185]

In a presidential statement adopted on 12 July, the Council recognized the need to continue to improve the strategic communications capabilities of peacekeeping operations and encouraged the Secretariat and Member States, including troop- and police-contributing countries, to work together in that regard.[186]

On 31 August, the Council adopted resolution 2650 (2022) on the situation in the Middle East, in which it welcomed the report of the Secretary-General on the assessment of the continued relevance of the resources and options of the United Nations Interim Force in Lebanon (UNIFIL) for improving the

[180] See S/PV.9039.
[181] See S/PV.9123.
[182] Norway, United Kingdom, United States and Albania.
[183] Resolutions 2639 (2022) and 2671 (2022), thirteenth preambular paragraph.
[184] Ibid., para. 6.
[185] Resolution 2640 (2022), para. 42.
[186] S/PRST/2022/5, fourteenth paragraph.

efficiency and effectiveness between UNIFIL and the Office of the United Nations Special Coordinator for Lebanon, requested the Secretary-General to continue the implementation of his detailed plan, with timelines and specific modalities, in full and close consultation with the parties, including Lebanon, the troop-contributing countries and the members of the Council, to implement recommendations, and further requested him to periodically update the Council on that process.[187]

During 2022, no explicit references to Article 44 of the Charter were made during discussions of the Council. Nonetheless, consistent with recent practice, during the annual open debate on the working methods of the Council, held on 28 June under the item entitled "Implementation of the note by the President of the Security Council (S/2017/507)", several participants highlighted the importance of cooperation and consultation by the Council with troop- and police-contributing countries, including on matters pertaining to the formulation and implementation of mandates.[188]

The importance of consulting troop- and police-contributing countries on matters relating to the mandates of peacekeeping operations continued to be discussed at meetings held under the item entitled "United Nations peacekeeping operations". For example, at a meeting held on 6 September, the representative of the Russian Federation stated that triangular cooperation between the Council, troop-contributing countries and the Secretariat was important in strengthening a spirit of partnership, collaboration and mutual trust.[189] The representative of the United Arab Emirates expressed the view that designing better mandates required strengthened triangular cooperation between the Council, troop-contributing countries and the Secretariat on the one hand, and improved cooperation between missions and host communities on the other, in addition to enhanced cooperation between those actors and regional organizations, especially in Africa.

VI. Role and composition of the Military Staff Committee in accordance with Articles 46 and 47 of the Charter

Article 46

Plans for the application of armed force shall be made by the Security Council with the assistance of the Military Staff Committee.

Article 47

1. There shall be established a Military Staff Committee to advise and assist the Security Council on all questions relating to the Security Council's military requirements for the maintenance of international peace and security, the employment and command of forces placed at its disposal, the regulation of armaments, and possible disarmament.

2. The Military Staff Committee shall consist of the Chiefs of Staff of the permanent members of the Security Council or their representatives. Any Member of the United Nations not permanently represented on the Committee shall be invited by the Committee to be associated with it when the efficient discharge of the Committee's responsibilities requires the participation of that Member in its work.

3. The Military Staff Committee shall be responsible under the Security Council for the strategic direction of any armed forces placed at the disposal of the Security Council. Questions relating to the command of such forces shall be worked out subsequently.

4. The Military Staff Committee, with the authorization of the Security Council and after consultation with appropriate regional agencies, may establish regional subcommittees.

[187] Resolution 2650 (2022), para. 8.

[188] See S/PV.9079 (Guatemala, Morocco and Indonesia); and S/PV.9079 (Resumption 1) (Argentina, Slovakia and Egypt).

[189] See S/PV.9123.

Note

Section VI covers the practice of the Council under Articles 46 and 47 of the Charter of the United Nations regarding the Military Staff Committee, including instances in which the Council considered the role of the Committee in planning the application of armed force and in advising and assisting the Council on the military requirements for the maintenance of international peace and security.

During the period under review, the Council did not explicitly refer to either Article 46 or Article 47 of the Charter in any of its decisions. Articles 46 and 47 were also not explicitly referred to in any of the Council's discussions. Nonetheless, at an open debate held on 25 May under the item entitled "Protection of civilians in armed conflict", the representative of Costa Rica emphasized that it was more urgent than ever that the Council, with the assistance of the Military Staff Committee, propose plans for a system for regulating arms, including a more robust effort to monitor and enforce Council arms embargoes at the national and regional levels.[190]

In 2022, the Military Staff Committee introduced a new practice by issuing its first annual report in the form of a communication addressed to the Council. By a letter dated 16 December addressed to the President of the Council,[191] the Chair of the Military Staff Committee conveyed its annual report, which contained two explicit references to Article 47 of the Charter. In the report, the Committee recalled that it had been established in accordance with Article 47 and Council resolution 1 (1946) and stated that it remained prepared to carry out the functions assigned to it under the terms of Article 47.

As customary, the annual report of the Council to the General Assembly covering the reporting period also referred to the activities of the Military Staff Committee.[192]

VII. Action required of Member States under Article 48 of the Charter

Article 48

1. The action required to carry out the decisions of the Security Council for the maintenance of international peace and security shall be taken by all the Members of the United Nations or by some of them, as the Security Council may determine.

2. Such decisions shall be carried out by the Members of the United Nations directly and through their action in the appropriate international agencies of which they are members.

Note

Section VII covers the practice of the Council in relation to Article 48 of the Charter of the United Nations, regarding the obligation of all or some Member States to carry out the decisions of the Council for the maintenance of international peace and security. Under Article 48 (2), Member States shall carry out the decisions directly, or through international organizations of which they are members. The section is focused on the types of obligations imposed on Member States pursuant to Article 48 and on the range of addressees designated by the Council to implement, or comply with, decisions adopted.

While Article 48 of the Charter relates to requests to Member States to carry out action decided upon by the Council, during 2022, as in previous periods, the Council also addressed some of its pleas to "actors" or "parties", reflecting the intra-State and increasingly complex nature of many contemporary conflicts dealt with by the Council. In its requests to carry out actions, the Council also addressed "regional and subregional organizations", signalling the importance of such entities in tackling disputes

[190] See S/PV.9042 (Resumption 1).
[191] S/2022/1036.
[192] See A/77/2, part IV.

and situations before the Council. Additional information on the engagement of regional arrangements in the maintenance of international peace and security is provided in part VIII of the present Supplement.

During the year under review, the Council did not explicitly invoke Article 48 of the Charter in any of its decisions. The Council, however, adopted resolutions in which it underlined the obligation of Member States and other entities concerned to comply with the measures imposed under Chapter VII of the Charter pursuant to Article 48. The present section is divided into two subsections: subsection A, covering decisions of the Council requiring Member States to carry out actions in relation to measures under Article 41; and subsection B, covering decisions of the Council requiring Member States to carry out action in relation to measures under Article 42. During 2022, no explicit references to Article 48 were made in communications to the Council, nor was there any discussion held in relation to the interpretation or application of that Article.

A. Decisions in which the Security Council required Member States to carry out action in relation to measures under Article 41 of the Charter

In 2022, the Council adopted no decisions concerning judicial measures taken under Article 41 of the Charter. The Council, however, adopted a number of decisions under Article 41 concerning sanctions, in which it frequently requested or stressed the importance of specific measures being implemented by all Member States or all States, as well as regional organizations. The Council requested the countries specifically targeted by the measures to carry out the actions required.

In relation to the Central African Republic, the Council urged all parties and all Member States, as well as international, regional and subregional organizations, to ensure cooperation with the Panel of Experts on the Central African Republic and the safety of its members.[193] It further urged all Member States and all relevant United Nations bodies to ensure unhindered access, in particular to persons, documents and sites in order for the Panel to execute its mandate, and recalled the value of information-sharing between the United Nations Multidimensional Integrated Stabilization Mission in the Central African Republic (MINUSCA) and the Panel.[194] The Council also requested the Central African Republic authorities to report, by 15 May 2023, to the Committee established pursuant to resolution 2127 (2013) concerning the Central African Republic on the progress achieved regarding security sector reform; the implementation of the disarmament, demobilization, reintegration and repatriation process in line with the Political Agreement for Peace and Reconciliation in the Central African Republic via the road map adopted by the International Conference on the Great Lakes Region; and the management of weapons and ammunition.[195] In addition, the Council decided that all Member States were to continue to take the necessary measures to prevent the direct or indirect supply, sale or transfer to the Central African Republic of arms and related materiel of all types.[196]

Concerning the Democratic People's Republic of Korea, the Council urged all States, relevant United Nations bodies and other interested parties to cooperate fully with the Committee established pursuant to resolution 1718 (2006) and the Panel of Experts established pursuant to resolution 1874 (2009), in particular by supplying any information at their disposal on the implementation of the measures imposed by the Council in its relevant resolutions.[197]

With respect to the Democratic Republic of the Congo, the Council called for enhanced cooperation between all States, particularly those in the region, and the Group of Experts on the Democratic Republic of the Congo.[198]

In connection with Lebanon, the Council recalled paragraph 15 of resolution 1701 (2006), according to which all States were to take the necessary measures to prevent, by their nationals or from their

[193] Resolution 2648 (2022), para. 10.
[194] Ibid., para. 11.
[195] Ibid., para. 13.
[196] Ibid., para. 1.
[197] Resolution 2627 (2022), para. 6.
[198] Resolution 2641 (2022), para. 9.

territories or using flag vessels or aircraft, the sale or supply of arms and related materiel to any entity or individual in Lebanon other than those authorized by the Government of Lebanon or the United Nations Interim Force in Lebanon (UNIFIL).[199]

With regard to Libya, the Council demanded full compliance by all Member States with the arms embargo imposed under resolution 1970 (2011), as modified by the Council in subsequent resolutions.[200] Concerning the other sanctions measures, the Council called upon Member States, particularly those in which designated individuals and entities were based, as well as those in which their assets frozen under the measures were suspected to be present, to report to the Committee established pursuant to resolution 1970 (2011) concerning Libya on the actions taken to implement effectively the travel ban and asset freeze measures in relation to all individuals on the sanctions list.[201] It also reiterated that all States were to take the necessary measures to prevent entry into or transit through their territories of all persons designated by the Committee and called upon the Government of Libya to enhance cooperation and information-sharing with other States in that regard.[202] Furthermore, the Council urged all States, relevant United Nations bodies, including the United Nations Support Mission in Libya (UNSMIL), and other interested parties to cooperate fully with the Committee and the Panel of Experts on Libya, in particular by supplying any information at their disposal on the implementation of the measures decided by the Council in its relevant resolutions, in particular on incidents of non-compliance, and called upon UNSMIL and the Government of Libya to support the Panel's investigatory work inside Libya, including by sharing information, facilitating transit and granting access to weapons storage facilities.[203] The Council also called upon all parties and all States to ensure the safety of the Panel's members and further called upon all parties and all States, including Libya and countries of the region, to provide unhindered and immediate access, in particular to persons, documents and sites that the Panel deemed relevant to the execution of its mandate.[204]

Concerning Somalia, the Council decided that all States were to take the necessary measures to prevent all deliveries of weapons and military equipment to Somalia, including prohibiting the financing of all acquisitions and deliveries of weapons and military equipment and the direct or indirect supply of technical advice, financial and other assistance, and training related to military activities, except where the beneficiaries were the country's security and police institutions at the national and local level or where the recipient was exempt pursuant to paragraph 21 of resolution 2662 (2022).[205] The Council reiterated its request for Member States to assist the Panel of Experts on Somalia in its investigations, and for Somali Government authorities, the African Union Transition Mission in Somalia (ATMIS) and partners to share information with the Panel regarding conduct or activities, in particular by Al-Shabaab and other actors intent on undermining peace and security in Somalia, where covered by listing criteria.[206]

The Council also called upon the Federal Government of Somalia to continue working with Somali financial authorities, private sector financial institutions and the international community to: (a) identify, assess and mitigate money-laundering and terrorist financing risks; (b) improve compliance; (c) strengthen supervision and enforcement; (d) prioritize the continued development of a secure national identification system to improve financial access and compliance and counter the financing of terrorism; (e) improve monitoring, reporting and investigations into money-laundering and terrorist financing; and (f) develop a plan to mitigate the risks posed by Al-Shabaab to personnel working in anti-money-laundering and counter-terrorist financing roles within national competent authorities and the private sector.[207] The Council requested the Federal Government of Somalia, the United Nations Office on Drugs and Crime and the Panel of Experts to continue exchanging information about Al-Shabaab's operations and to continue working with stakeholders to develop a plan to disrupt Al-Shabaab's operations and exploitation

[199] Resolution 2650 (2022), para. 22.
[200] Resolution 2629 (2022), para. 5.
[201] Resolution 2644 (2022), para. 8.
[202] Ibid., para. 9.
[203] Ibid., para. 14.
[204] Ibid., para. 15.
[205] Resolution 2662 (2022), para. 10.
[206] Ibid., para. 27.
[207] Ibid., para. 30.

of the licit financial system.[208] The Council also requested the Federal Government of Somalia to strengthen cooperation and coordination with other States, particularly those in the region, and with international partners to prevent and counter the financing of terrorism.[209] The Council reaffirmed that all States were to prevent the direct or indirect sale, supply or transfer of the items specified in part I of annex C to resolution 2662 (2022) to Somalia from their territories or by their nationals outside their territories, or using their flag vessels or aircraft, if there was sufficient evidence to demonstrate that the item(s) would be used, or a significant risk they might be used, in the manufacture in Somalia of improvised explosive devices.[210] In addition, the Council called upon Member States to undertake appropriate measures to promote the exercise of vigilance by their nationals, persons subject to their jurisdiction and firms incorporated in their territory or subject to their jurisdiction that were involved in the sale, supply or transfer of explosive precursors and materials to Somalia that might be used in the manufacture of improvised explosive devices.[211] The Council also recalled the importance of full cooperation between Somalia and the Panel and requested the Somali Government authorities to facilitate for the Panel interviews with suspected members of Al-Shabaab and other persons of interest held in custody.[212] Finally, the Council reiterated its request for Somalia, States and ATMIS to provide information to the Panel and to assist them in their investigations.[213]

Regarding South Sudan, and in particular the arms embargo, underscoring that arms shipments in violation of the measures contained in resolution 2633 (2022) risked fuelling conflict and contributing to further instability, the Council strongly urged all Member States to take urgent action to identify and prevent such shipments within their territory.[214] The Council called upon all Member States, in particular States neighbouring South Sudan, to inspect, in accordance with their national authorities and legislation and consistent with international law, all cargo to South Sudan, in their territory, including seaports and airports, if the State concerned had information providing reasonable grounds to believe that the cargo contained items of which the supply, sale or transfer was prohibited, and decided that all Member States were to seize and dispose of such items upon discovery.[215] The Council also called upon all parties and all Member States, as well as international, regional and subregional organizations, to ensure cooperation with the Panel of Experts on South Sudan, and further urged all Member States involved to ensure the safety of the members of the Panel and unhindered access, in particular to persons, documents and sites in order for the Panel to execute its mandate.[216]

In relation to Yemen, recalling the provisions of paragraph 14 of resolution 2216 (2015), the Council called upon all Member States and other actors to comply with their obligations under the targeted arms embargo.[217] Furthermore, the Council urged all parties and all Member States, as well as international, regional and subregional organizations, to ensure cooperation with the Panel of Experts on Yemen and further urged all Member States involved to ensure the safety of the members of the Panel and unhindered access, in particular to persons, documents and sites, in order for the Panel to execute its mandate.[218]

More broadly, with respect to measures adopted under Article 41 of the Charter for the purpose of preventing and suppressing the financing of terrorism, the Council called upon all States to cooperate fully with the Committee pursuant to resolutions 1267 (1999), 1989 (2011) and 2253 (2015) concerning Islamic State in Iraq and the Levant (Da'esh), Al-Qaida and associated individuals, groups, undertakings and entities, and its Analytical Support and Sanctions Monitoring Team in the fulfilment of its tasks, including supplying such information as might be required by the Committee in that respect.[219] The Council also recalled the ability of the Committee to engage with Member States to ensure the effective

[208] Ibid., para. 32.
[209] Ibid., para. 33.
[210] Ibid., para. 37.
[211] Ibid., para. 39.
[212] Ibid., para. 45.
[213] Ibid., para. 46.
[214] Resolution 2633 (2022), para. 8.
[215] Ibid., paras. 9 and 10.
[216] Ibid., para. 20.
[217] Resolution 2624 (2022), twenty-third preambular paragraph.
[218] Ibid., para. 18.
[219] Resolution 2664 (2022), para. 2.

implementation of Council decisions, including by requesting additional information from such Member States, including with respect to providers under their jurisdiction, as needed to support such implementation.[220]

B. Decisions in which the Security Council required Member States to carry out action in relation to measures under Article 42 of the Charter

During the period under review, the Council urged, called upon and requested action by a particular Member State, a designated group of Member States, all Member States or all parties in relation to measures adopted under Article 42 of the Charter.

With respect to the situation in Abyei, the Council urged the Governments of the Sudan and South Sudan to provide full support to the United Nations Interim Security Force for Abyei (UNISFA) in the implementation of its mandate and deployment of its personnel, including by removing any obstacles that hindered its mandate to protect civilians in Abyei.[221] The Council also urged the two Governments and the local communities to take all necessary steps to ensure that Abyei was effectively demilitarized and to extend full cooperation to UNISFA in that regard.[222] The Council reiterated that the Abyei Area was to be demilitarized from any forces, as well as armed elements of the local communities, other than UNISFA and the Abyei Police Service, and urged the Governments of the Sudan and South Sudan and the local communities to take all necessary steps in that regard.[223]

Concerning the situation in the Central African Republic, the Council urged all parties in the country to cooperate fully in the deployment and activities of MINUSCA, in particular by ensuring its safety, security and freedom of movement, with unhindered and immediate access throughout the territory of the Central African Republic, to enable MINUSCA to carry out fully its mandate.[224] The Council also called upon Member States, especially those in the region, to ensure the free, unhindered and expeditious movement to and from the Central African Republic of all personnel, as well as equipment, provisions, supplies and other goods that were for the exclusive and official use of MINUSCA.[225]

In connection with the situation concerning the Democratic Republic of the Congo, the Council reiterated its call upon all parties to cooperate fully with the United Nations Organization Stabilization Mission in the Democratic Republic of the Congo and to remain committed to the full and objective implementation of the Mission's mandate, and further reiterated the importance of continued compliance with the status-of-forces agreement.[226]

With regard to the situation in Lebanon, the Council called upon all parties to respect the cessation of hostilities, to prevent any violation of the Blue Line and to respect it in its entirety, and to cooperate fully with UNIFIL.[227] The Council also urged all parties to abide scrupulously by their obligation to respect the safety of UNIFIL and other United Nations personnel and to ensure that the freedom of movement of UNIFIL in all its operations and its access to the Blue Line in all its parts were fully respected and unimpeded, in conformity with its mandate and its rules of engagement.[228] The Council called upon the Government of Lebanon to facilitate prompt and full access to sites requested by UNIFIL, including all relevant locations north of the Blue Line related to the discovery of tunnels crossing the Blue Line that UNIFIL had reported as a violation of resolution 1701 (2006).[229] In addition, the Council demanded that the parties cease any restrictions and hindrances to the movement of UNIFIL personnel

[220] Ibid., para. 5.
[221] Resolutions 2630 (2022) and 2660 (2022), para. 4.
[222] Resolution 2630 (2022), para. 6.
[223] Resolution 2660 (2022), para. 4.
[224] Resolution 2659 (2022), para. 52.
[225] Ibid., para. 53.
[226] Resolution 2666 (2022), seventeenth preambular paragraph.
[227] Resolution 2650 (2022), para. 12.
[228] Ibid., paras. 15 and 16.
[229] Ibid., para. 16.

and guarantee the freedom of movement of UNIFIL.[230] The Council reaffirmed its call upon all States to fully support and respect the establishment between the Blue Line and the Litani River of an area free of any armed personnel, assets and weapons other than those of the Government of Lebanon and UNIFIL.[231] The Council also urged the Government of Israel to expedite the withdrawal of its army from northern Ghajar without further delay in coordination with UNIFIL.[232]

In connection with the situation in Mali, the Council called upon Member States, especially those in the region, to ensure the free, unhindered and expeditious movement to and from Mali of all personnel, as well as equipment, provisions, supplies and other goods, which were for the exclusive and official use of the United Nations Multidimensional Integrated Stabilization Mission in Mali (MINUSMA), in order to facilitate the timely and cost-effective delivery of the logistical supply of MINUSMA.[233] The Council also urged all parties in Mali to cooperate fully with the Special Representative of the Secretary-General for Mali and MINUSMA in the implementation of the Agreement on Peace and Reconciliation in Mali, as well as to ensure the safety, security and freedom of movement of MINUSMA personnel, with unhindered and immediate access throughout the territory of Mali.[234]

In connection with the situation in South Sudan, the Council called upon the Government of South Sudan and all relevant actors to end all obstructions to the United Nations Mission in South Sudan (UNMISS)[235] and reiterated its call upon the Government of South Sudan to comply with the obligations set out in the status-of-forces agreement between the Government and the United Nations and to immediately cease obstructing UNMISS in the performance of its mandate.[236]

VIII. Mutual assistance pursuant to Article 49 of the Charter

Article 49

The Members of the United Nations shall join in affording mutual assistance in carrying out the measures decided upon by the Security Council.

Note

Section VIII covers the practice of the Council in relation to Article 49 of the Charter of the United Nations, concerning mutual assistance among Member States in carrying out the measures decided upon by the Council.

In 2022, the Council did not explicitly invoke Article 49 of the Charter in any of its decisions. However, in its decisions adopted during the reporting period, the Council called upon Member States to cooperate with one another or to assist specific States in the implementation of measures imposed under Chapter VII of the Charter. The present section is divided into two subsections. Subsection A covers decisions in which the Council urged cooperation among Member States with respect to measures under Article 41. Subsection B covers decisions in which the Council requested mutual assistance in relation to measures under Article 42.

In 2022, there was no constitutional discussion in the Council relating to the interpretation or application of Article 49 of the Charter. No reference to Article 49 was made in the communications received by the Council.

---

[230] Ibid., para. 17.
[231] Ibid., para. 21.
[232] Ibid., para. 20.
[233] Resolution 2640 (2022), para. 43.
[234] Ibid., para. 6.
[235] Resolution 2625 (2022), para. 9.
[236] Ibid., para. 10.

A. Decisions in which the Security Council requested mutual assistance in the implementation of measures under Article 41 of the Charter

During the period under review, the Council called upon Member States to enhance their cooperation in implementing specific sanctions measures. The addressees of the Council's calls for mutual assistance ranged from individual Member States, in particular concerned and neighbouring States, to "all Member States", as well as regional and subregional organizations. The types of assistance requested of Member States varied greatly, from requests to share information and requests for the provision of technical assistance to requests for cooperation in carrying out inspections.

For example, with regard to the situation concerning the Democratic Republic of the Congo, the Council called for enhanced cooperation between all States, particularly those in the region, and the Group of Experts on the Democratic Republic of the Congo.[237]

In connection with the situation in Libya, the Council called upon the Government of Libya to improve the implementation of the arms embargo and called upon all Member States to cooperate in such efforts.[238] The Council further called upon the Government of Libya to enhance cooperation and information-sharing with other States regarding measures taken to prevent entry into or transit through their territories of all persons designated by the Committee established pursuant to resolution 1970 (2011) concerning Libya.[239]

With respect to the situation in Somalia, the Council requested the Federal Government of Somalia to strengthen cooperation and coordination with other States, particularly other States in the region, and with international partners to prevent and counter the financing of terrorism, including through compliance with resolutions 1373 (2001), 2178 (2014) and 2462 (2019) and relevant domestic and international law.[240]

Concerning the situation in South Sudan, the Council decided that all Member States were to cooperate in efforts to seize and dispose of items of which the supply, sale or transfer was prohibited by the Council in paragraph 4 of resolution 2428 (2018).[241]

B. Decisions in which the Security Council requested mutual assistance in the implementation of measures under Article 42 of the Charter

During the period under review, the Council also adopted several resolutions in which it requested cooperation among Member States in carrying out measures under Article 42 of the Charter, under which the use of force is authorized. The types of assistance requested included sharing information and capacity-building to deter various criminal acts, and coordination among Member States to deter such acts.

For example, concerning the situation in Lebanon, the Council called upon Member States to urgently assist the Lebanese Armed Forces as needed to enable them to perform their duties in line with resolution 1701 (2006).[242]

With respect to the situation in Libya and the question of migration, the Council reiterated its calls made in previous resolutions to "all flag States involved" to cooperate in efforts aimed at inspecting vessels suspected of being used for migrant smuggling or human trafficking from Libya.[243] The Council also reiterated its calls made in previous resolutions upon Member States, acting nationally or through regional organizations, including the European Union, to cooperate with the Government of Libya and with each other, including by sharing information to assist Libya in building capacity to secure its borders

[237] Resolution 2641 (2022), para. 9.
[238] Resolution 2644 (2022), para. 7.
[239] Ibid., para. 9.
[240] Resolution 2662 (2022), para. 33.
[241] Resolution 2633 (2022), para. 10.
[242] Resolution 2650 (2022), twenty-seventh preambular paragraph.
[243] Resolution 2652 (2022), para. 2.

and to prevent, investigate and prosecute acts of smuggling of migrants and human trafficking through its territory and in its territorial sea.[244]

Concerning the situation in Somalia and efforts aimed at countering and suppressing acts of piracy and armed robbery off the coast of Somalia, the Council commended the role played by the Federal Government of Somalia, Member States and regional organizations in that regard and urged the continued development of a Somalia-led, coordinated approach in developing the country's maritime governance sector, including through the formation of the Somali Navy and Coast Guard Working Group, and support for the country's maritime institutions.[245]

IX. Special economic problems of the nature described in Article 50 of the Charter

Article 50

If preventive or enforcement measures against any state are taken by the Security Council, any other state, whether a Member of the United Nations or not, which finds itself confronted with special economic problems arising from the carrying out of those measures shall have the right to consult the Security Council with regard to a solution of those problems.

Note

Section IX covers the practice of the Council in relation to Article 50 of the Charter of the United Nations, regarding the right of States to consult the Council with a view to resolving economic problems arising from the implementation of preventive or enforcement measures, such as sanctions, imposed by the Council.

During the period under review, the Council continued its practice of imposing targeted instead of comprehensive economic sanctions, thereby minimizing the unintended adverse impact on third States.[246] In 2022, none of the Council-mandated sanctions committees received formal requests for assistance under Article 50 of the Charter. While the Council did not explicitly invoke Article 50 in any of its decisions during the reporting period, in its resolution 2664 (2022), the Council urged States, when designing and applying measures to counter the financing of terrorism, to take into account the potential effect of those measures on exclusively humanitarian activities, including medical activities, that were carried out by impartial humanitarian actors in a manner consistent with international humanitarian law.[247] In the same resolution, the Council expressed its readiness to review, adjust and terminate, when appropriate, its sanctions regimes taking into account the evolution of the situation on the ground and the need to minimize unintended adverse humanitarian effects,[248] requested the Secretary-General to issue a written report on unintended adverse humanitarian consequences of Council sanctions measures within nine months of the adoption of the resolution, requested that the report contain recommendations on ways to minimize and mitigate such unintended adverse consequences, including through the promulgation of additional standing exemptions to the sanctions measures, and expressed its intent to consider further steps, as necessary, to further minimize and mitigate such unintended adverse consequences.[249]

During Council meetings in 2022, in addition to one explicit reference to Article 50 of the Charter, which is featured in case 10 below,[250] speakers made numerous implicit references to the unintended consequences of sanctions that are of relevance to the interpretation and application of Article 50. For example, at a meeting held on 28 February under the item entitled "The situation in the Middle East",

---

[244] Ibid.
[245] Resolution 2662 (2022), tenth preambular paragraph.
[246] For more information on sanctions measures, see sect. III above.
[247] Resolution 2664 (2022), fifth preambular paragraph.
[248] Ibid., eighth preambular paragraph.
[249] Ibid., para. 7.
[250] See S/PV.8962 (Ghana).

several speakers expressed concern about the possible unintended consequences of sanctions imposed on Yemen, in particular as they concerned humanitarian assistance and the country's economy.[251] At a meeting held on 7 March under the item entitled "Reports of the Secretary-General on the Sudan and South Sudan", the representative of Kenya, speaking also on behalf of Gabon and Ghana, reiterated the call for the lifting of sanctions and the arms embargo against South Sudan, noting that they were counterproductive to the peace efforts and had had the unintended consequence of undermining the country's potential for economic investments.[252] At a meeting held on 30 June under the item entitled "The situation concerning the Democratic Republic of the Congo", following the adoption of resolution 2641 (2022) concerning the sanctions regime on the Democratic Republic of the Congo, the representative of Brazil noted that his country had supported a broader clause on the humanitarian consequences of sanctions in the resolution, adding that the International Committee of the Red Cross and other humanitarian agencies had reported and argued that instances of overcompliance with Council measures on the part of banks and financial institutions in general had made donations to humanitarian agencies and humanitarian assistance itself more difficult in the country.[253] The excerpt that Brazil had proposed had been intended to address that unintended and damaging consequence. In addition, during meetings held under the item entitled "The question concerning Haiti", some speakers also referred to the unintended damage or consequences of sanctions measures on humanitarian efforts in Haiti.[254]

Concerns about the unintended impact of Council-mandated sanctions and counter-terrorism measures were also raised in thematic meetings of the Council, notably in connection with the items entitled "Briefings by Chairs of subsidiary bodies of the Security Council",[255] "Briefing by the United Nations High Commissioner for Refugees",[256] "Protection of civilians in armed conflict",[257] "Threats to international peace and security"[258] and "Threats to international peace and security caused by terrorist acts".[259]

Featured below is the most salient discussion concerning the interpretation and application of Article 50 of the Charter, which took place during meetings held under the item entitled "General issues relating to sanctions" (case 10).

Case 10
General issues relating to sanctions

On 7 February, at the initiative of the Russian Federation, which held the presidency for the month,[260] the Security Council held a debate under the item entitled "General issues relating to sanctions" and the sub-item entitled "Preventing their humanitarian and unintended consequences".[261] During the meeting, the Council heard briefings by the Under-Secretary-General for Political and Peacebuilding Affairs and the Under-Secretary-General for Humanitarian Affairs and Emergency Relief Coordinator.

In her briefing, the Under-Secretary-General for Political and Peacebuilding Affairs noted that United Nations sanctions had undergone considerable changes since the 1990s to minimize their possible adverse consequences on civilian populations and third States. She added that the Council and its sanctions committees had increasingly sought in recent years to obtain first-hand information on possible adverse consequences and indicated that sanctions were continually adjusted in response to changes on the ground, with due regard for their impact on civilian populations. The Under-Secretary-General also noted that, in the past decade, only one Member State had reported facing special economic problems arising from Council sanctions. The evolution from comprehensive to targeted sanctions had marked a sea change in that

[251] See S/PV.8981(Ghana, Ireland, Mexico, Norway and Russian Federation).
[252] See S/PV.8987.
[253] See S/PV.9084.
[254] See, for example, S/PV.9153 (United Arab Emirates); and S/PV.9159 (Brazil).
[255] See, for example, S/PV.9218 (Norway).
[256] See, for example, S/PV.9178 (Brazil and Ireland).
[257] See, for example, S/PV.9042 (Brazil, Norway and Switzerland (on behalf of the Group of Friends on the Protection of Civilians in Armed Conflict)).
[258] See, for example, S/PV.9188 (Ireland).
[259] See, for example, S/PV.9221 (Norway).
[260] A concept note was circulated by a letter dated 2 February (S/2022/86).
[261] See S/PV.8962.

area of the Council's work, but some concerns remained about unintended consequences and adverse effects of Council sanctions. According to the Under-Secretary-General, de-risking policies and overcompliance were probably two of the most important problems facing humanitarian actors. Financial actors and other service providers might impose additional conditions, increase their costs or simply refuse to provide the requested goods and services, thereby inhibiting the delivery of humanitarian assistance. Noting that the humanitarian community, and much of the world, had welcomed resolution 2615 (2021), which carved out a humanitarian exemption to the sanctions regime imposed on Afghanistan, the Under-Secretary-General asserted that similar standing exemptions in other sanctions regimes could go a long way to respond to the critical needs of civilian populations.

The Under-Secretary-General for Humanitarian Affairs and Emergency Relief Coordinator noted that sanctions affected humanitarian relief operations directly and indirectly, as well as civilians, even when those impacts were unintended. However smart and targeted they were, compliance with sanctions was a daily element in the work of humanitarian agencies. He added that sanctions could have an impact on the humanitarian agencies' logistics, finances and ability to deliver and could lead to humanitarian projects being delayed or stalling, while some could threaten the well-being of a wider section of the population in a civilian society. The Emergency Relief Coordinator noted that United Nations sanctions were designed to limit unintended consequences and welcomed the Council's clear consistent signals that they were not intended to have adverse humanitarian consequences. Listing some of his concerns over the use of sanctions in countries already affected by humanitarian crises, he highlighted, inter alia, that banks and other commercial operators, aiming to avoid any risk of penalty or prosecution, could effectively deny services to humanitarian customers and that commercial operators that traded food, fuel and other necessities could also decide to err on the side of caution or overcomply, leading to shortages and price rises. That was especially disastrous in fragile countries already heavily dependent on food imports and experiencing a humanitarian crisis. Addressing some of the ways to mitigate the humanitarian impact of sanctions, the Emergency Relief Coordinator urged the Council and Member States to ensure that sanctions applicable in armed conflict did not impede the assistance and protection activities of impartial humanitarian organizations for persons who were not fighting, irrespective of their allegiance or designation. In all contexts, they should ensure that sanctions did not restrict the enjoyment of economic, social and cultural rights, including the right to food, water, shelter and health. He added that sanctions should not have cascading secondary implications that went beyond the focus of the action.

During the debate, Council members and other speakers presented their views on how to mitigate the possible unintended consequences of sanctions imposed by the Council, including with regard to humanitarian assistance. In that context, one explicit reference to Article 50 of the Charter of the United Nations was made by the representative of Ghana, who underscored the need to enhance humanitarian exemption mechanisms to safeguard the livelihoods of populations and noted that the existing exemptions did not appear to fully tackle the humanitarian problem, especially when comprehensive sanctions had been imposed.

The representative of the Russian Federation stated that many of the active Council sanctions regimes no longer corresponded to the situation on the ground, hindering the plans of Governments in terms of State-building and socioeconomic development, and called for the collateral damage resulting from sanctions measures to be taken seriously, as it manifested in detrimental impacts on the national economy and the lives and well-being of the population. He expressed the view that, despite declarations that restrictive Council measures should not affect the lives of ordinary people, in practice, international restrictions often led to a deterioration in the socioeconomic situation of countries under sanctions.

The representative of the United Kingdom stated that his country was committed to minimizing any unintended consequences of sanctions, including on the delivery of humanitarian assistance. To achieve that, his country advocated carefully targeted sanctions, aimed at specific goals, as part of a comprehensive approach to conflict resolution. He noted that the adoption of resolution 2615 (2021) concerning Afghanistan had been a good demonstration of how sanctions regimes could be tailored to address any unintended consequences as they emerged and ensure that they did not hinder the delivery of urgently needed humanitarian assistance.

According to the representative of China, for over twenty years, there had been a trend of expanding the Council's sanctions regimes, whose adverse impacts on humanitarian issues and livelihoods could not be ignored and increasingly caused disruptions to normal economic and social activities of ordinary citizens and third countries. Emphasizing the importance of designing targeted sanctions mechanisms, he noted that the intensity and scope of compulsory measures should be carefully calibrated, with clear and unequivocal provisions to minimize collateral damage. The representative of China added that the Council should closely monitor and comprehensively assess the humanitarian, economic and social impacts of sanctions and that the Office for the Coordination of Humanitarian Affairs and the United Nations missions deployed in the sanctioned countries should be requested to monitor any adverse impact of sanctions and report it to the Council in a timely manner so that the Council could make timely arrangements and adjustments.

The representative of Ireland expressed the view that carefully targeted sanctions, particularly where due process was respected, could serve to reduce unintended consequences. Highlighting recommendations to minimize any potential humanitarian or other unintended consequence of sanctions, the representative of the United Arab Emirates noted that the potential humanitarian consequences of sanctions should systematically be considered in the design of each and every sanctions regime and addressed wherever applicable. He added that constant re-evaluation and adaptation of sanctions throughout their lifespan was necessary to protect affected populations from unintended adverse consequences.

The representative of India noted that the unintended consequences of sanctions measures were being increasingly emphasized by Member States and other stakeholders and that there was an urgent need to credibly address those concerns to ease the sufferings of the people. It was also necessary to ensure that the legitimate trade and economic activities of the concerned State and its regional partners were not adversely affected. He added that, while it was imperative that sanctions not impede legitimate humanitarian requirements, it was also important to exercise due diligence while providing humanitarian carveouts, especially in cases where terrorism found safe haven. The representative of Norway expressed concern about reports from humanitarian non-governmental organizations that sanctions might negatively impact their work but stated that her country was pleased that the Council, over the past year, had adopted clear language stressing that sanctions were not intended to have negative humanitarian consequences.

The representative of Gabon noted, inter alia, that while most sanctions regimes provided for exemptions to meet the basic needs of those targeted, the fact remained that their goal was clearly to financially drain or harm the key economic sectors of the targeted entities. Such measures often affected the budgetary revenues of the States on which sanctions had been imposed and inevitably affected the overall economy and people's standard of living. The representative of Brazil asserted that, despite the progress made to minimize the negative impact of sanctions, there were still many reports of their unintended consequences on humanitarian assistance, which was why Brazil encouraged the Council to continue its work to adjust the sanctions framework so that sanctions would effectively minimize human suffering rather than accentuate it. He further noted that there should be better monitoring of the socioeconomic and humanitarian consequences of sanctions.

The representative of the United States underscored the importance of ensuring that sanctions were effective and targeted and minimized unintended consequences. Referring to humanitarian exemptions, she further noted that in certain cases, they could strengthen sanctions by ensuring that their economic costs were more effectively targeted. Expressing full support for targeted sanctions that responded to specific situations, the representative of Albania noted that they needed to be measured and proportional in order to be effective and should avoid any eventual collateral damage or unintended consequences. He presented the view that targeted sanctions did not harm the economy, nor did they hurt populations or affect essential needs, such as food and medicine. In contrast, according to the representative of Kenya, when applied with insufficient care for civilian suffering and lacking a sense of proportion, sanctions could have the same debilitating impact on a country as kinetic warfare.

The representative of France stated that sanctions had undergone significant changes in recent years, particularly to take into account their potential negative effects on the delivery of humanitarian and medical assistance. The representative of Mexico expressed the view that the Council had moved from the debate on whether or not sanctions produced undesirable humanitarian consequences to a stage of action in which it was trying to prevent or mitigate their impact, citing in that regard the examples of Somalia, the Democratic Republic of the Congo and Afghanistan.

At the same meeting, representatives of non-Council members also voiced their concerns about the unintended impact of sanctions on their countries and regions.[262]

Further to the above discussion, Council members met again under the same item at the end of the year, on 9 December,[263] to adopt resolution 2664 (2022), under Chapter VII of the Charter. Adopted not unanimously,[264] the resolution provided for a standing humanitarian exemption to all asset freeze measures imposed by the Council or any of its committees with the exception of the sanctions regime pursuant to resolution 1988 (2011) concerning the Taliban, which had its own humanitarian carveout pursuant to resolution 2615 (2021) and which would remain in effect.[265]

Following the vote, Council members reflected on the importance of minimizing the negative unintended effects of sanctions, including their humanitarian consequences.[266] In that regard, the representative of Ireland stated that with the adoption of the resolution, Council members diminished the unintended consequences of sanctions without diminishing United Nations sanctions themselves. He indicated that it was clear that Council members shared the desire to mitigate any inadvertent effects that sanctions might have on humanitarian activity. Noting that the humanitarian community had consistently documented and called attention to the unintended negative consequences of sanctions for principled humanitarian action, the representative of Norway said that her country attached great importance to ensuring that sanctions were well designed and that it was pleased that the practices of the Council had developed on the issue of broad humanitarian exemptions in the past few years. The representative of the Russian Federation pointed out that the adopted resolution included provisions proposed by her delegation in relation to: assessing the potential humanitarian consequences prior to the Council taking a decision about imposing a sanctions regime; the readiness to conduct a review to correct or stop sanctions regimes when it became necessary to do so; and emphasizing the fact that sanctions were temporary in nature. She noted that the resolution also contained a request to the Secretary-General to prepare a written report about unintended adverse humanitarian consequences of Council sanctions. Welcoming the adoption of resolution 2664 (2022), the representative of Albania referred to it as a milestone development of the Council in making the sanctions regime more effective by minimizing its potential unintended consequences and by strengthening its legitimacy.

Explaining the abstention of her delegation, the representative of India expressed the view that, in implementing sanctions regimes, it was important to ensure that they had the intended impact and did not further exacerbate the suffering of the populations at the receiving end. She added that the legitimate trade and economic activities of the State concerned and its regional partners could not be ignored and that the unintended consequences of sanctions measures, including the humanitarian consequences, required effective redress. The representative of India reiterated that under no circumstances should the garb of humanitarian cover intended to be provided by the exemptions be misused by proscribed terrorist groups to expand their terror activities and called for due diligence and extreme caution in the implementation of the resolution.

---

[262] Sudan, South Sudan, Mali, Iraq and Bolivarian Republic of Venezuela (on behalf of the Group of Friends in Defence of the Charter of the United Nations).

[263] See S/PV.9214.

[264] The draft resolution received 14 votes in favour (Albania, Brazil, China, France, Gabon, Ghana, Ireland, Kenya, Mexico, Norway, Russian Federation, United Arab Emirates, United Kingdom and United States) and 1 abstention (India).

[265] Resolution 2664 (2022), paras. 1 and 4.

[266] See S/PV.9214.

X. Right of individual or collective self-defence in accordance with Article 51 of the Charter

Article 51

Nothing in the present Charter shall impair the inherent right of individual or collective self-defence if an armed attack occurs against a Member of the United Nations, until the Security Council has taken measures necessary to maintain international peace and security. Measures taken by Members in the exercise of this right of self-defence shall be immediately reported to the Security Council and shall not in any way affect the authority and responsibility of the Security Council under the present Charter to take at any time such action as it deems necessary in order to maintain or restore international peace and security.

Note

Section X deals with the practice of the Council in relation to Article 51 of the Charter of the United Nations, regarding the "inherent right of individual or collective self-defence" in the event of an armed attack against a Member State. The section is divided into two subsections. Subsection A covers the discussions of the Council of relevance to the interpretation and application of Article 51, and subsection B covers references to Article 51 and the right to self-defence in communications addressed to the Council. The Council did not refer to Article 51 or the right of self-defence in its decisions during the reporting period.

A. Discussions relating to Article 51

In 2022, Article 51 of the Charter was explicitly invoked 49 times during the deliberations of the Council at 27 Council meetings,[267] representing a fourfold increase compared with the previous year.[268] Moreover, the right of self-defence was discussed at several meetings of the Council held under thematic and country- and region-specific items.

---

[267] See, in connection with the item entitled "Children and armed conflict", S/PV.9096 (Resumption 1) (Türkiye); in connection with the item entitled "Cooperation between the United Nations and regional and subregional organizations in maintaining international peace and security", S/PV.8967 (Belarus); in connection with the item entitled "Letter dated 13 September 2022 from the Permanent Representative of Armenia to the United Nations addressed to the President of the Security Council (S/2022/688)", S/PV.9132 (Armenia); in connection with the item entitled "Letter dated 28 February 2014 from the Permanent Representative of Ukraine to the United Nations addressed to the President of the Security Council (S/2014/136)", S/PV.8970 (Ukraine), S/PV.8974 (Russian Federation) and S/PV.8979 (United Kingdom and Ukraine); in connection with the item entitled "Maintenance of international peace and security", S/PV.9052 (Mexico and Russian Federation) and S/PV.9220 (Azerbaijan); in connection with the item entitled "Maintenance of peace and security of Ukraine", S/PV.9104 (Mexico); S/PV.9135 (United States and Ukraine) and S/PV.9195 (Estonia (also on behalf of Latvia and Lithuania)); in connection with the item entitled "Protection of civilians in armed conflict", S/PV.9042 (Resumption 1) (Canada); in connection with the item entitled "The situation concerning Iraq", S/PV.8975 (Mexico); S/PV.9034 (Mexico and Iraq); and S/PV.9100 (Iraq and Türkiye); in connection with the item entitled "The situation in Mali", S/PV.9154 (Mali); in connection with the item entitled "The situation in the Middle East", S/PV.8958 (Syrian Arab Republic), S/PV.9083 (Mexico and Türkiye), S/PV.9117 (United States, Mexico, China, Syrian Arab Republic and Türkiye), S/PV.9130 (Syrian Arab Republic, Islamic Republic of Iran and Türkiye), S/PV.9163 (Türkiye) and S/PV.9204 (Mexico and Türkiye); in connection with the item entitled "Threats to international peace and security", S/PV.9127 (Russian Federation, United States, Albania, Ireland, Norway and Ukraine) and S/PV.9216 (Norway, Albania, Mexico, Ireland and Ukraine); and in connection with the item entitled "Threats to international peace and security caused by terrorist acts", S/PV.8963 (Mexico), S/PV.9108 (Mexico) and S/PV.9221 (Mexico).

[268] For more information, see *Repertoire, Supplement 2021*, part VII, sect. X.

Discussions on thematic items

At a meeting held on 9 February under the item entitled "Threats to international peace and security caused by terrorist acts" and specifically focused on counter-terrorism operations, the representative of Mexico underscored that the collective security system must not be violated under the pretext of the need to address terrorism and that violations of Article 51 of the Charter were inadmissible.[269] Furthermore, at a meeting held on 9 August under the same item, the representative of Mexico again reiterated that abuses of the invocation of Article 51 in order to use force against terrorists were inadmissible and in violation of international law.[270] Again at a meeting held on 15 December under the same item, the representative of Mexico expressed similar concerns about the ongoing invocation of legitimate self-defence when using force against non-State actors in a third State, under the so-called unwilling and unable doctrine, reiterating that those interpretations went beyond the provisions of Article 51.[271]

At a meeting held on 16 February, in relation to the item entitled "Cooperation between the United Nations and regional and subregional organizations in maintaining international peace and security", the representative of Belarus stated that the principles of the United Nations, including the right to collective self-defence enshrined in Article 51 of the Charter, formed the basis of the Collective Security Treaty Organization.[272] At the same meeting, the representative of Kazakhstan referred to a series of coordinated, violent armed riots carried out by criminal elements and religious extremists, including foreign terrorist fighters, in January 2022 throughout Kazakhstan, which had been qualified as a terrorist threat to national security and an act of aggression. Recalling that the Charter recognized the right of every State to individual or collective self-defence in such events, he informed the Council that the President of Kazakhstan had officially requested the Collective Security Treaty Organization to provide peacekeeping assistance in order to maintain stability in the country and the United Nations had been properly informed in a timely manner about the intention of the Collective Security Treaty Organization to send a peacekeeping contingent composed of all five member States to Kazakhstan to the deal with the situation.

At a meeting held on 25 May, in connection with the item entitled "Protection of civilians in armed conflict", the representative of Canada pointed out that when parties to armed conflict committed serious violations, they must be held accountable – diplomatically, through collective sanctions; militarily, by supporting Governments, such as Ukraine, that were defending themselves under Article 51 of the Charter; and legally, through prosecution at the International Criminal Court, the International Court of Justice and other bodies.[273]

At a meeting held on 2 June under the item entitled "Maintenance of international peace and security", the representative of Mexico stressed that interpretations of the fundamental norms of international law that were not supported by the jurisprudence of the International Court of Justice should be avoided, as they endangered the integrity of the Charter, as was the case of the abusive invocations of Article 51 of the Charter to justify the use of force.[274] He added that the misuse and abuse of the right to legitimate defence only caused violence to escalate and recalled that his country had repeatedly objected to such interpretations both in the Council and the General Assembly. During the same meeting, the representative of the Russian Federation recalled that its special military operation in Ukraine had been launched on the basis of Article 51 and the corresponding notification had been submitted in writing to the Council on 24 February in the manner prescribed by Article 51.[275] He underscored that the issue of abolishing certain provisions of the Charter, including its Article 51, or of depriving a Member State of the right to exercise its inalienable right to collective or individual self-defence had not been considered by the International Court of Justice.[276] At a meeting held on 14 December under the same item, the representative of Azerbaijan informed the Council that, as a result of a large-scale armed provocation in September 2020, Azerbaijan had been obliged to launch a counter-offensive operation fully in line with

[269] See S/PV.8963.
[270] See S/PV.9108.
[271] See S/PV.9221.
[272] See S/PV.8967.
[273] See S/PV.9042 (Resumption 1).
[274] See S/PV.9052.
[275] See S/2022/154.
[276] See S/PV.9052.

Article 51 and Council resolutions adopted in 1993, resulting in the liberation of its territories from the long-term unlawful foreign military occupation.[277]

On 19 July, at a meeting held under the item entitled "Children and armed conflict", the representative of Türkiye categorized the references made in the report of the Secretary-General on children and armed conflict with regard to the country's counter-terrorism operations in the Syrian Arab Republic and Iraq as incorrect, and underlined that all those operations had been conducted as part of its legitimate right to self-defence, in full compliance with international law and international humanitarian law and in line with Article 51 of the Charter.[278]

In 2022 and under the item entitled "Threats to international peace and security", the Council also discussed the right to self-defence in the context of the situation in Ukraine, as further elaborated upon in case 13 below.

Discussions on country- and region-specific items

During its deliberations, the Council also addressed issues relevant to the interpretation and application of Article 51 of the Charter and/or the right to self-defence under a number of country- and region-specific items, relating to the Middle East, Ukraine, Iraq, Armenia and Azerbaijan, and Mali, which are featured below in descending order based on the volume of references to Article 51.

Middle East

The Council addressed the interpretation and application of Article 51 of the Charter and the right to self-defence under the item entitled "The situation in the Middle East" in relation to the military activities conducted in the territory of the Syrian Arab Republic in meetings held on 27 January, 29 June, 29 August, 14 September, 25 October and 29 November. At a meeting held on 27 January, the representative of the Syrian Arab Republic referred to a series of events in Hasakah city, which had started with the explosion of a car bomb by Da'esh.[279] He added that what the city had gone through in the preceding days was the inevitable result of an erroneous and hostile approach adopted by some Western countries towards his country since 2011 and the product of a number of serious violations of the principles of international law by successive United States Administrations and their allies, who had bypassed the Council by erroneously interpreting Article 51 to form their own illegitimate coalition, without the approval of, or coordination with, the Government of the Syrian Arab Republic. At a meeting held on 29 June, the representative of Mexico expressed concern about the announcement of a new military intervention in northern Syrian Arab Republic, in particular the attempt to justify it under Article 51, stressing that it would be totally contrary to the provisions of international law, specifically with respect to the use of force and self-defence, and that if it were to occur it would undermine the country's sovereignty, independence, unity and territorial integrity.[280] At that same meeting, in reference to the terrorist organization Kurdistan Workers' Party/People's Protection Units, the representative of Türkiye stressed his country's commitment to combating all terrorist organizations that threatened its security, in line with Article 51 and the relevant Council resolutions. He added that Türkiye would not hesitate to continue to take all the necessary measures to deal with all threats against its vital security interests. At meetings held on 29 August and 14 September,[281] a detailed discussion was held on the letter submitted to the Council on 26 August by the United States,[282] in which the United States had informed the Council that it had undertaken precision strikes against a facility in eastern Syrian Arab Republic used by militia groups affiliated with the Islamic Revolutionary Guard Corps of the Islamic Republic of Iran (case 12). At the meeting held on 14 September, the representative of Türkiye also reiterated that his country would continue its resolute fight against all terrorist organizations threatening its national security, in the exercise of its inherent right of self-defence, as reflected in Article 51 and in accordance with the relevant Council resolutions on the fight against terrorism.[283] Similarly, at a meeting held on 25 October, the

[277] See S/PV.9220.
[278] See S/PV.9096 (Resumption 1). For the report of the Secretary-General, see S/2022/493.
[279] See S/PV.8958.
[280] See S/PV.9083.
[281] See S/PV.9117 and S/PV.9130.
[282] S/2022/647.
[283] See S/PV.9130.

representative of Türkiye reiterated that Turkish counter-terrorism operations were carried out to combat all terrorist organizations that threatened the nation's security, in the exercise of its inherent right of self-defence, as reflected in Article 51 and in accordance with Council resolutions on the fight against terrorism.[284] At a meeting held on 29 November, the representative of Mexico, stressing that any action in the fight against terrorism must comply with international law, including international humanitarian law and international human rights law, reiterated his country's alarm at the abuse of invocations of Article 51, which were supposedly justified in the name of the fight against terrorism.[285] At the same meeting, the representative of Türkiye underscored that the fact that the obligations stemming from the agreements of October 2019 with the United States and the Russian Federation had not been fully implemented resulted in an increased terrorist threat against the borders of Türkiye, and asserted that Türkiye would continue to carry out counter-terrorism operations to protect its people and ensure its border security, in the exercise of its inherent right of self-defence, as reflected in Article 51.

Ukraine

In 2022, the right of self-defence of Ukraine was discussed during multiple meetings held under the item entitled "Letter dated 28 February 2014 from the Permanent Representative of Ukraine to the United Nations addressed to the President of the Security Council (S/2014/136)" (case 11). At a meeting held on 21 February under the item and in response to the decision by the Russian Federation to recognize the independence of certain areas of the Donetsk and Luhansk regions, the representative of Ukraine underscored that, in accordance with Article 51 of the Charter, Ukraine had the inherent right to individual and collective self-defence.[286] At a subsequent meeting held under the same item on 23 February, the representative of the Russian Federation informed the Council that the President of the Russian Federation had decided to launch a special military operation in Donbas, a decision that had been made in accordance with Article 51, the approval of the Federation Council of the Russian Federation and pursuant to the Treaty of Friendship, Cooperation and Mutual Assistance signed with the Donetsk and Luhansk People's Republics.[287]

Also in relation to the situation in Ukraine, on 29 July, at a meeting held under the item entitled "Maintenance of peace and security of Ukraine", the representative of Mexico recalled that for more than five months, various interpretations had been heard of a confusing narrative that failed to justify the war in Ukraine.[288] In that context, he recalled his country's position with regard to upholding Article 2 (4) of the Charter, which stated that all Members were to refrain from the threat or use of force against the territorial integrity or political independence of any State.[289] He emphasized that what was happening in Ukraine was a flagrant violation of the Charter and that the free and self-serving interpretations of the right to self-defence set out in Article 51, which set a dangerous precedent, were also very worrisome. At a meeting held on 22 September under the same item, the Secretary of State of the United States expressed support for the range of national and international efforts to collect and examine the mounting evidence of war crimes perpetrated by Russian forces in Ukraine and stressed that the perpetrators must be held accountable for those crimes.[290] He further recalled that more than 40 nations had come together to help the Ukrainian people to defend themselves, which was a right enshrined in Article 51. At the same meeting, the Minister for Foreign Affairs of Ukraine said that the President of Ukraine had proposed a peace formula, which included not only accountability but also a mechanism of security guarantees based on Article 51. At a meeting held on 16 November under the same item, the representative of Estonia, speaking also on behalf of Latvia and Lithuania, stated that the territories occupied by the Russian Federation within the internationally recognized borders of Ukraine were Ukrainian and that Ukraine had every right to defend them in full accordance with Article 51.[291]

---

[284] See S/PV.9163.
[285] See S/PV.9204.
[286] See S/PV.8970.
[287] See S/PV.8974.
[288] See S/PV.9104.
[289] For more information on discussions concerning the item in the context of Article 2 (4) of the Charter, see part III, sect. II.B, case 4.
[290] See S/PV.9135.
[291] See S/PV.9195.

Iraq

At a meeting held on 24 February under the item entitled "The situation concerning Iraq", the representative of Mexico reiterated his country's concern about wrongly invoking Article 51 of the Charter in the context of combating terrorism, while urging regional and international partners to continue to support the efforts of Iraq, particularly in the area of capacity-building of the security forces.[292] The representative of Mexico voiced similar concerns at the meeting held on 17 May under the same item.[293] During that meeting, the representative of Iraq noted that the use of Article 51 in the acts of aggression carried out by Turkish forces was without legal basis and that the Article did not authorize acts that undermined an independent country's sovereignty. At a subsequent meeting held under the same item on 26 July, the Minister for Foreign Affairs of Iraq said that Türkiye would try to justify its military presence in Iraq by presenting many illegal arguments and would claim that there was an agreement with Iraq that would allow for a Turkish military presence in Iraq so that it could resolve its Turkish problem.[294] He further asserted that Türkiye would once again refer illegally to Article 51 to justify its actions, which were in violation of the sovereignty of Iraq. He underscored that the same Article compelled Türkiye to inform the Council of military violations carried out in Iraq and added that Türkiye was failing to uphold the Article, in violation of the Charter. At the same meeting, the representative of Türkiye highlighted the obligation of Iraqi authorities under both international law and the Constitution of Iraq to stop the Kurdistan Workers' Party from using the territory of Iraq. He recalled that Iraq had so far proven to be either unable or unwilling to fight the terrorists and indicated that if a country could not control its own territory, was unwilling to fight against terrorists and could not stop terrorists from using its territory to kill the citizens of a neighbouring State, then it was siding, either directly or indirectly, with the terrorists, and could not castigate its neighbour for using the right to self-defence. He further underscored that, in the absence of the ability and willingness of Iraq to deal with the presence of terrorist organizations in its own country, Türkiye was obliged to take appropriate measures and would continue to exercise its inherent right to self-defence as outlined in Article 51.

Armenia-Azerbaijan

In connection with the increase in violence at the border between Armenia and Azerbaijan, at a meeting held on 15 September under the newly introduced item entitled "Letter dated 13 September 2022 from the Permanent Representative of Armenia to the United Nations addressed to the President of the Security Council (S/2022/688)", the representative of Armenia recalled that, over the past year, his delegation had repeatedly brought to the attention of the Council the fact that Azerbaijan had been engaging in the illegal practice of acquisition of territories by force and had duly reported such acts of aggression under Article 51 of the Charter.[295] He underscored that the representative of Azerbaijan would offer justifications for his country's predatory conduct but that there was no such justification under international law.[296]

Mali

At a meeting held on 18 October under the item entitled "The situation in Mali", the Minister for Foreign Affairs and International Cooperation of Mali emphasized that the Government of Mali reserved the right to resort to self-defence in accordance with Article 51 of the Charter if France continued to undermine the sovereignty, territorial integrity and national security of Mali.[297]

[292] See S/PV.8975.
[293] See S/PV.9034.
[294] See S/PV.9100.
[295] See S/PV.9132. For more information on the introduction of new items, see part II, sect. II.
[296] For more information on the developments under the item, see part I, sect. 16.
[297] See S/PV.9154.

Case 11
Letter dated 28 February 2014 from the Permanent Representative of Ukraine to the United Nations addressed to the President of the Security Council (S/2014/136)

At a meeting held on 25 February under the item entitled "Letter dated 28 February 2014 from the Permanent Representative of Ukraine to the United Nations addressed to the President of the Security Council (S/2014/136)",[298] the Security Council voted on a draft resolution submitted by 82 Member States.[299] The Council failed to adopt the draft resolution owing to the negative vote of the Russian Federation.[300] Under the draft resolution, the Council would have condemned the 23 February declaration by the Russian Federation of a special military operation in Ukraine and would have decided that the Russian Federation must immediately cease its use of force against Ukraine, refrain from any further unlawful threat or use of force and immediately, completely and unconditionally withdraw all of its military forces from the territory of Ukraine within its internationally recognized borders.[301]

Speaking before the vote, the representative of the United Kingdom stated that the President of the Russian Federation had launched a massive invasion of Ukraine with the aim of removing its Government and subjugating its people.[302] She stressed that such an act was not self-defence under Article 51 of the Charter of the United Nations; rather, it was naked aggression and an unprovoked, unjustified war that the Council must condemn. Following the vote, the representative of the United Kingdom took the floor again and underscored that the claim of the Russian Federation that its invasion of Ukraine was in self-defence was absurd and indicated that the only act of self-defence of the Russian Federation was the vote that it had cast against the draft resolution. The representative of Ghana, also speaking after the vote, took note of the letter from the Russian Federation submitted to the Council,[303] in which the Russian Federation had sought to indicate that its use of force against Ukraine was in self-defence while dismissing its all-out military action against Ukraine. The representative of Ghana said that his country was pained by the unnecessary and rising number of deaths that had been occasioned by the invasion and called upon the Russian Federation to immediately withdraw its forces from Ukraine and to recommit to dialogue and diplomacy.[304] The representative of Ukraine recalled that his country had been exercising its right to self-defence under Article 51. He stressed that the Russian Federation did not have that excuse and that calling occupying troops peacekeepers and claiming the right of self-defence was lunacy.

The representative of the Russian Federation explained that the main reason for his country's negative vote was that the draft resolution had left out issues that could not be overlooked in the context of the Ukrainian problem and emphasized that the Russian Federation was not waging a war against Ukraine or the Ukrainian people but was instead carrying out a special operation against nationalists to protect the residents of Donbas and for the purposes of denazification and demilitarization.

Case 12
The situation in the Middle East

On 29 August, at a meeting held under the item entitled "The situation in the Middle East" and focused on the situation in the Syrian Arab Republic,[305] the representative of the United States referred to a letter that it had submitted to the Security Council on 26 August,[306] in which it had informed the Council that it had undertaken precision strikes against a facility in eastern Syrian Arab Republic used by militia groups affiliated with the Islamic Revolutionary Guard Corps of the Islamic Republic of Iran.

---

[298] See S/PV.8979.
[299] See S/2022/155.
[300] The draft resolution received 11 votes in favour (Albania, Brazil, France, Gabon, Ghana, Ireland, Kenya, Mexico, Norway, United Kingdom and United States), 1 against (Russian Federation) and 3 abstentions (China, India and United Arab Emirates). For more information on decision-making and voting, see part II, sect. VIII.
[301] S/2022/155, sixth preambular paragraph and paras. 3 and 4. For more information on discussions concerning the item in the context of Article 2 (4) of the Charter, see part III, sect. II.B, case 3.
[302] See S/PV.8979.
[303] S/2022/154.
[304] See S/PV.8979.
[305] See S/PV.9117.
[306] S/2022/647.

The representative of the United States recalled that, as specified in the letter, the action had been in response to armed attacks against the United States and had been taken in the exercise of its inherent right to self-defence, as reflected in Article 51 of the Charter of the United Nations.[307] The representative of Mexico took note of the military actions in eastern Syrian Arab Republic for which Article 51 had been invoked and reiterated her country's position that, based on that provision, invocations of self-defence justifying the use of force against non-State actors in a third State under the so-called unwilling and unable doctrine were contrary to the Charter and customary international law. The representative of China underscored that there was no doubt that the military operations in eastern Syrian Arab Republic carried out by the United States constituted a violation of the country's sovereignty and territorial integrity and had nothing to do with the right to self-defence under Article 51. He called for an end to the unlawful presence of foreign forces and illegal military operations in the Syrian Arab Republic. The representative of the Syrian Arab Republic clarified that the presence of United States forces on Syrian territory was illegal and had been carried out without the request or consent of the Government of the Syrian Arab Republic and, therefore, was also a violation of the Charter. He added that the justification made by the representative of the United States and the use of Article 51 and what he had called the right to self-defence as a pretext was a legal misrepresentation, political insolence and an excuse, which was worse than the action itself.

Concerning other regional dynamics, the representative of Türkiye stated that his country would continue its resolute fight against all terrorist organizations threatening its national security, in the exercise of its inherent right of self-defence, as embodied in Article 51 of the Charter and in accordance with Council resolutions on the fight against terrorism. He recalled that his country's past operations against the Kurdistan Workers' Party/People's Protection Units terrorist organization had made it ready to cooperate with all actors that had a genuine interest in and the determination to preserve the unity of the Syrian Arab Republic, as well as an interest in the fight against terrorism. The representative of the Islamic Republic of Iran condemned the Israeli military attacks in the Syrian Arab Republic, including on civilian infrastructure, and stated that his delegation recognized the legitimate right to self-defence of the Syrian Arab Republic under international law and the Charter.

At a subsequent meeting held on 14 September under the same item,[308] the representative of the Syrian Arab Republic recalled that certain Western countries, including what was called the international coalition, had been misinterpreting and wrongly applying Article 51 of the Charter as they used unfounded pretexts and misleading interpretations to justify attacks on the sovereignty, independence and territorial integrity of other countries. In that regard, he referred to a letter dated 6 September from the Syrian Arab Republic addressed to the Council, in which the Syrian Arab Republic had responded to the statement of the Permanent Representative of the United States justifying her country's aggression against the Syrian Arab Republic on the pretext of Article 51.[309] He recalled that in the letter, the Syrian Arab Republic had stressed that the only de facto and de jure description of the actions and activities of the illegitimate United States troops present in the Syrian Arab Republic was the crime of aggression.[310] The representative of the Islamic Republic of Iran stressed that the illegal presence of foreign forces in parts of the Syrian Arab Republic, which had created ideal conditions for terrorist activities, must be ended. He also underlined that the recent air strikes in north-eastern Syrian Arab Republic by illegal foreign forces could not be justified under Article 51 or through an arbitrary interpretation of self-defence, adding that the attacks constituted a flagrant violation of international law and the Charter.

Case 13
Threats to international peace and security

On 8 September, the Security Council held a meeting under the item entitled "Threats to international peace and security" focused on the situation in Ukraine.[311] During the meeting, the representative of the Russian Federation stated that his country had launched a special operation to protect

[307] See S/PV.9117.
[308] See S/PV.9130.
[309] See S/2022/647 and S/2022/675.
[310] See S/PV.9130.
[311] See S/PV.9127.

the people of Donbas, in accordance with Article 51 of the Charter of the United Nations, after the Kyiv regime, with the approval of its Western sponsors, had publicly "killed" the Minsk process. He added that it had been a difficult but necessary decision after it had become clear that the military action of Ukraine against the Donetsk and Luhansk People's Republics was inevitable. He further explained that one of the goals of the special military operation was the denazification and demilitarization of Ukraine, with a view to ensuring that there would no longer be any threats to the Donbas or to the Russian Federation from its territory.

Several speakers referred to the right of Ukraine to self-defence under Article 51 of the Charter against the aggression of the Russian Federation, including in reference to the acquisition of arms for the purpose of self-defence. In that regard, the representative of the United States stated that all countries had an inherent right to self-defence, consistent with Article 51, adding that every Member of the United Nations had a right to its sovereignty and territorial integrity. The representative of Albania underscored that Article 51 was clear and provided an unquestionable legal basis for individual States to offer any assistance to a country exercising its inherent rights to self-defence and the defence of its sovereignty and territorial integrity. The representative of Ireland expressed his country's commitment to the core principles enshrined in the Charter, which included the sovereign equality and territorial integrity of States, underscoring that Ukraine had the same fundamental right as every other sovereign and independent State to choose its own foreign policy and to ensure the security and defence of its own territory. He stressed that the principles of the Charter were not an à la carte menu and that Articles 2 (4) and 51 applied to all Members of the United Nations, with no exceptions or waiving of those principles.[312] The representative of Ireland further pointed out that Ukraine had not committed or threatened to commit an armed attack against the Russian Federation; rather, it was the Russian Federation that had attacked Ukraine and had sought to justify its invasion by invoking Article 51, and it was the Russian Federation that then sought to deny a fellow Member of the United Nations that same right to self-defence. He added that the European Union was providing military support to help Ukraine to exercise its inherent right of self-defence and defend its territorial integrity and sovereignty. The representative of Norway emphasized that Ukraine had a right to defend itself against the armed attack of the Russian Federation, as enshrined in Article 51, and other States were entitled to respond positively to the call of Ukraine for assistance in the exercise of its legitimate right to self-defence. The representative of Ukraine underscored that international law guarded the sovereignty and territorial integrity of Ukraine and conferred upon it the inherent right to self-defence, enshrined in particular in Article 51. He added that Ukraine was defending itself, Europe, the world and the Charter and would keep on fighting in strict accordance with the provisions of Article 51 until every inch of the sovereign territory of Ukraine, including Crimea, was liberated.

Other speakers referred to the right of Ukraine to self-defence without explicitly invoking Article 51 of the Charter. In that regard, the representative of the United Kingdom stressed that Ukraine had every right to defend itself under the Charter, legally and morally. The representative of Mexico expressed concern regarding arms transfers that had been occurring since the beginning of the conflict in eastern Ukraine in 2013. He said that as long as the Council did not shoulder its responsibility to address a situation involving an invasion such as the one that Ukraine was confronting, Mexico acknowledged the natural right to legitimate self-defence and to acquire arms to that end. He stressed, however, the need for protections and safeguards to minimize risks and prevent diversions of weapons or their use to commit grave and systematic violations of human rights or international humanitarian law. The representative of France recalled that his country furnished military support, which helped to provide Ukraine with a way to defend itself, because it had resolved to help Ukraine to defend its sovereignty and territorial integrity. He also recalled that the European Union had similarly made a collective decision to fund weaponry to ensure that Ukraine could withstand the aggression of the Russian Federation and added that the military assistance provided by France and the European Union would continue for so long as the armed aggression of the Russian Federation persisted.

At a subsequent meeting held on 9 December under the same item,[313] Council members continued the discussion on the right to self-defence in the context of the acquisition of arms by Ukraine. The representative of the Russian Federation explained that the reason for calling the meeting was to cover

[312] For more information on discussions concerning the item in the context of Article 2 (4) of the Charter, see part III, sect. II.B, case 2.

[313] See S/PV.9216.

two topics, namely, the consequences for international peace and security of the growing smuggling of arms supplied to Ukraine and the impact that the ongoing massive pumping of Ukraine with Western weapons was having on the prospects for ending the Ukrainian conflict. Condemning the war of the Russian Federation against Ukraine in the strongest possible terms and reiterating her country's unwavering support for the sovereignty and territorial integrity of Ukraine within its internationally recognized borders, the representative of Norway underlined the right of Ukraine to self-defence, as enshrined in Article 51 of the Charter, as well as the sovereign right to ask for and receive support from other States in the exercise of that right. The representative of Albania underscored that international law was crystal clear on the fact that a country under attack had every right to defend itself, under Article 51. She stated that, having been under attack for 10 months, Ukraine was simply defending itself, and that the sovereignty, territorial integrity and political independence of Ukraine had been assaulted, which made self-defence not only a natural right but also an existential imperative. She added that, for that reason, whoever was helping Ukraine, in whatever way legally and openly, was not only helping a nation in need, a nation in danger and a nation under threat but also upholding the law and protecting the Charter. The representative of Ireland stressed that Ukraine had not committed or threatened to commit an armed attack against the Russian Federation; rather, it was the Russian Federation that had attacked Ukraine and had cynically sought to justify its invasion by invoking Article 51. He further pointed out that the Russian Federation then sought to deny Ukraine its entirely legitimate right of self-defence, as enshrined in the Charter. The representative of Ukraine said that Ukraine would continue to de-occupy its sovereign territories in strict accordance with Article 51 and expressed gratitude to all friends and allies who supported Ukraine in that noble endeavour, including by supplying modern weapons. He stressed that the use of those weapons had been an element of Ukraine exercising the inherent right to self-defence under Article 51.

Other Council members expressed support for the right of Ukraine to self-defence without explicitly referring to Article 51 of the Charter. Affirming the inherent right of Ukraine to self-defence under customary international law, codified in Chapter VII of the Charter, the representative of Ghana stated that Ukraine had deployed its military and strategic capabilities in asserting its inherent right to self-defence against the armed attack of the Russian Federation and in a courageous endeavour to preserve its national interests, stressing that there was no prohibition on such action, and that neither the rules of international law nor the Charter prohibited the supply of conventional weapons to a State under armed attack by another. The representative of France explained that, by providing military support to Ukraine, both nationally and at the European level, his country continued to give the Ukrainian people all the support they needed to exercise their right to legitimate self-defence and to preserve their freedom, sovereignty and independence. The representative of the United Kingdom said that in the face of the relentless efforts of the Russian Federation to seize the territory of Ukraine, in violation of the Charter, and to dehumanize, kill and subjugate its people, Ukraine had no choice but to exercise its right to defend itself, for if it did not, it would cease to exist.

Taking note of the right of Ukraine to self-defence, other speakers expressed concerns regarding the proliferation of weapons resulting from the conflict. The representative of Mexico recalled that his country's concern regarding arms transfers and their impact on civilians, in the light of Article 51 of the Charter, was not limited to the current situation but dated back to the beginning of the conflict in eastern Ukraine in 2014. The representative of Kenya, acknowledging the heavy responsibility that Ukraine bore in defending its internationally recognized borders, underscored that while conscripting for, training and equipping one's army in times of war was expected, the proliferation of weapons was bound to have a significant impact not only in the country in conflict but also beyond. The representative of Brazil stated that while it should be recognized that the supply of arms and ammunition to the parties to the conflict in Ukraine could result in prolonging it and in more suffering for the civilian population, it was undeniable that States had a right to self-defence, as enshrined in the Charter, in cases of violations of their sovereignty and territorial integrity and, consequently, the right to acquire arms for their security, including from outside sources. The representative of the United States said that, although his country had seen no credible evidence of Ukraine diverting United States-origin arms and munitions, the inherent risk of weapons' capture and diversion on the battlefield in any armed conflict must be recognized.

B. References to Article 51 and the right of self-defence in communications addressed to the Security Council

In 2022, Article 51 of the Charter was explicitly referenced in 17 communications from Member States addressed to the President of the Council or circulated as a document of the Council. Those communications concerned a variety of disputes and situations. A complete list of letters from Member States containing explicit references to Article 51 is provided in table 15 below. Explicit references to Article 51 were also found in the reports of the Secretary-General on the implementation of resolutions 2576 (2021) and 2631 (2022),[314] concerning the mandate of the United Nations Assistance Mission for Iraq, as well as in the report of the Informal Working Group on Documentation and Other Procedural Questions,[315] containing an account of the Informal Working Group's activities from 1 January to 31 December 2022. In addition, references to the principle of self-defence continued to be found in other communications from several Member States, listed in table 16 below, as well as in communications from the Permanent Observer of the State of Palestine.[316]

Table 15
Communications from Member States containing explicit references to Article 51 of the Charter, 2022

Document symbol	*Document title*
S/2022/112	Letter dated 11 February 2022 from the Permanent Representative of Turkey to the United Nations addressed to the President of the Security Council
S/2022/154	Letter dated 24 February 2022 from the Permanent Representative of the Russian Federation to the United Nations addressed to the Secretary-General
S/2022/179	Letter dated 3 March 2022 from the Permanent Representative of the Russian Federation to the United Nations addressed to the Secretary-General
S/2022/206	Letter dated 10 March 2022 from the Permanent Representative of the Islamic Republic of Iran to the United Nations addressed to the Secretary-General and the President of the Security Council
S/2022/363	Letter dated 28 April 2022 from the Permanent Representative of the Russian Federation to the United Nations addressed to the President of the Security Council
S/2022/372	Identical letters dated 28 April 2022 from the Permanent Representative of Lebanon to the United Nations addressed to the Secretary-General and the President of the Security Council
S/2022/515	Letter dated 16 June 2022 from the Permanent Representative of Türkiye to the United Nations addressed to the President of the Security Council
S/2022/574	Letter dated 22 July 2022 from the Permanent Representative of Iraq to the United Nations addressed to the President of the Security Council
S/2022/622	Letter dated 15 August 2022 from the Chargé d'affaires a.i. of the Permanent Mission of Mali to the United Nations addressed to the President of the Security Council
S/2022/647	Letter dated 26 August 2022 from the Permanent Representative of the United States of America to the United Nations addressed to the President of the Security Council
S/2022/675	Letter dated 6 September 2022 from the Permanent Representative of the Syrian Arab Republic to the United Nations addressed to the President of the Security Council
S/2022/680	Letter dated 7 September 2022 from the Permanent Representative of the Islamic Republic of Iran to the United Nations addressed to the President of the Security Council
S/2022/694	Letter dated 13 September 2022 from the Permanent Representative of Armenia to the United Nations addressed to the Secretary-General

[314] S/2022/103 and S/2022/714.
[315] S/2022/1032.
[316] S/2022/236, S/2022/283, S/2022/361, S/2022/377, S/2022/603 and S/2022/758.

Document symbol	*Document title*
S/2022/717	Letter dated 27 September 2022 from the Permanent Representative of Estonia to the United Nations addressed to the President of the Security Council
S/2022/790	Letter dated 21 October 2022 from the Permanent Representative of Lithuania to the United Nations addressed to the President of the Security Council
S/2022/808	Letter dated 27 October 2022 from the Permanent Representative of Azerbaijan to the United Nations addressed to the Secretary-General
S/2022/837	Letter dated 8 November 2022 from the Permanent Representative of Türkiye to the United Nations addressed to the President of the Security Council

Table 16
Communications from Member States containing references to the principle of self-defence, 2022

Document symbol	*Document title*
S/2022/61	Letter dated 27 January 2022 from the Permanent Representative of Azerbaijan to the United Nations addressed to the Secretary-General
S/2022/90	Letter dated 3 February 2022 from the Permanent Representative of Pakistan to the United Nations addressed to the President of the Security Council
S/2022/223	Letter dated 14 March 2022 from the Permanent Representative of Pakistan to the United Nations addressed to the President of the Security Council
S/2022/225	Letter dated 14 March 2022 from the Permanent Representative of the Islamic Republic of Iran to the United Nations addressed to the Secretary-General and the President of the Security Council
S/2022/445	Letter dated 31 May 2022 from the Permanent Representative of the Islamic Republic of Iran to the United Nations addressed to the Secretary-General and the President of the Security Council
S/2022/464	Letter dated 8 June 2022 from the Permanent Representative of the Russian Federation to the United Nations addressed to the Secretary-General and the President of the Security Council
S/2022/520	Letter dated 28 June 2022 from the Permanent Representative of Ethiopia to the United Nations addressed to the President of the Security Council
S/2022/679	Letter dated 7 September 2022 from the Permanent Representative of the Islamic Republic of Iran to the United Nations addressed to the President of the Security Council
S/2022/680	Letter dated 7 September 2022 from the Permanent Representative of the Islamic Republic of Iran to the United Nations addressed to the President of the Security Council
S/2022/748	Letter dated 10 October 2022 from the Permanent Representative of the Islamic Republic of Iran to the United Nations addressed to the President of the Security Council
S/2022/797	Letter dated 17 October 2022 from the Permanent Representative of South Africa to the United Nations addressed to the President of the Security Council

Part VIII
Regional arrangements

Contents

Introductory note

Article 52

1. Nothing in the present Charter precludes the existence of regional arrangements or agencies for dealing with such matters relating to the maintenance of international peace and security as are appropriate for regional action provided that such arrangements or agencies and their activities are consistent with the Purposes and Principles of the United Nations.

2. The Members of the United Nations entering into such arrangements or constituting such agencies shall make every effort to achieve pacific settlement of local disputes through such regional arrangements or by such regional agencies before referring them to the Security Council.

3. The Security Council shall encourage the development of pacific settlement of local disputes through such regional arrangements or by such regional agencies either on the initiative of the states concerned or by reference from the Security Council.

4. This Article in no way impairs the application of Articles 34 and 35.

Article 53

1. The Security Council shall, where appropriate, utilize such regional arrangements or agencies for enforcement action under its authority. But no enforcement action shall be taken under regional arrangements or by regional agencies without the authorization of the Security Council, with the exception of measures against any enemy state, as defined in paragraph 2 of this Article, provided for pursuant to Article 107 or in regional arrangements directed against renewal of aggressive policy on the part of any such state, until such time as the Organization may, on request of the Governments concerned, be charged with the responsibility for preventing further aggression by such a state.

2. The term enemy state as used in paragraph 1 of this Article applies to any state which during the Second World War has been an enemy of any signatory of the present Charter.

Article 54

The Security Council shall at all times be kept fully informed of activities undertaken or in contemplation under regional arrangements or by regional agencies for the maintenance of international peace and security.

Chapter VIII of the Charter of the United Nations provides the constitutional basis for the involvement of regional arrangements in the maintenance of international peace and security.[1] While Article 52 encourages the engagement of regional arrangements in the pacific settlement of disputes prior to their referral to the Security Council, Article 53 allows the Council to utilize regional arrangements for enforcement action under its authority and with its explicit authorization. Article 54 stipulates that regional arrangements should inform the Council of their activities at all times.

During the period under review, in its decisions, the Council reiterated that cooperation with regional and subregional organizations in matters relating to the maintenance of international peace and security, consistent with Chapter VIII of the Charter, was significant to improving collective security. The Council recognized that regional organizations were well positioned to understand the root causes of armed conflicts, owing to their knowledge of the region, which could be of benefit for their efforts to influence the prevention or resolution of conflicts. In particular, the Council welcomed the strong cooperation between the United Nations and the League of Arab States and reiterated its intention to consider further steps to promote closer cooperation between them in a variety of fields. The Council emphasized the importance of strengthening trilateral cooperation and coordination between the United Nations, the African Union and the League on cross-regional peace and security issues. In addition, the

[1] Chapter VIII of the Charter refers to “regional arrangements or agencies”. For the purposes of the *Repertoire*, the term “regional arrangements” is understood to encompass regional and subregional organizations as well as other international organizations.

Council recognized the role that regional and subregional organizations played in the implementation of resolution 1540 (2004) on the non-proliferation of weapons of mass destruction and acknowledged their perspectives on the need to minimize the adverse humanitarian effects of sanctions regimes.

In 2022, the Security Council of the United Nations and the Peace and Security Council of the African Union held their seventh joint informal seminar and sixteenth annual joint consultative meeting in New York on 13 and 14 October, respectively, during which they discussed how to strengthen African Union and United Nations peacekeeping in Africa, the situation in West Africa and the Sahel, the situation in the Great Lakes region and the application of sanctions in conflict situations in Africa.[2] In addition to the African Union and the League of Arab States, engagement with other regional organizations, such as the Association of Southeast Asian Nations, the Collective Security Treaty Organization, the Economic Community of Central African States, the Economic Community of West African States, the European Union, the Intergovernmental Authority on Development and the Organization for Security and Cooperation in Europe, featured prominently in Council discussions.

Discussions in the Council were focused on various aspects of the cooperation between the United Nations and regional and subregional organizations, including on the role of regional organizations in conflict prevention, peacekeeping, peace enforcement, counter-terrorism and peacebuilding. Council members and other Member States exchanged views on the principles underlying that cooperation, including complementarity, subsidiarity and the comparative advantage of regional organizations in the maintenance of international peace and security, practical modalities for joint engagement and the need for predictable, sustainable and flexible funding for African Union-led peace support operations.

In connection with the pacific settlement of disputes, the Council highlighted in its decisions the important role played by regional and subregional organizations, including the African Union, the Association of Southeast Asian Nations, the Caribbean Community, the East African Community, the Economic Community of Central African States, the Economic Community of West African States, the Gulf Cooperation Council, the Intergovernmental Authority on Development, the International Conference on the Great Lakes Region, the League of Arab States and the Southern African Development Community, in the prevention and mediation of conflicts and the promotion of inclusive peace processes and reconciliation. During their discussions, Council members exchanged views on the engagement of regional and subregional organizations in addressing the situations in the Central African Republic and the Central African region, the Democratic Republic of the Congo, the Great Lakes region, Mali, West Africa and the Sahel, and the Sudan and South Sudan. In addition, they discussed the cooperation between the United Nations and the African Union and the regional economic communities on capacity-building for sustaining peace in Africa.

Concerning peacekeeping operations led by regional organizations, the Council authorized the reconfiguration of the African Union Mission in Somalia (AMISOM) into the African Union Transition Mission in Somalia (ATMIS), and renewed the authorization of the European Union Force-Althea in Bosnia and Herzegovina. Meanwhile, the North Atlantic Treaty Organization Force in Kosovo continued to operate without any decisions taken with respect to its mandate. The Council also discussed the mandate and United Nations support for ATMIS and the Joint Force of the Group of Five for the Sahel.

As in previous periods, the Council authorized enforcement action by regional and subregional organizations beyond the framework of peacekeeping operations, such as in relation to Libya and Somalia, and continued to request reporting by regional organizations, in particular on the implementation of mandates of relevant regional peacekeeping operations and on cooperation with the United Nations.

The practice of the Council under Chapter VIII of the Charter in 2022 is set out in five sections. Each section covers both the decisions adopted by the Council and the discussions held during Council meetings. Section I contains an examination of the practice of the Council regarding cooperation with regional and subregional organizations in the maintenance of international peace and security concerning items of a thematic nature. Section II is focused on recognition by the Council of the efforts of regional

[2] See S/2022/768 and A/77/2. For more information on prior practice concerning the informal joint meetings of the Security Council and the Peace and Security Council of the African Union, see *Repertoire*, *Supplements 2008–2009* to *2021*.

organizations in the peaceful settlement of disputes, within the framework of Article 52 of the Charter. Section III covers the practice of the Council relating to its cooperation with regional organizations in the area of peacekeeping. Section IV contains a description of the practice of the Council in authorizing enforcement action by regional organizations outside the context of regional peacekeeping operations. Section V contains information on the reporting on the activities of regional organizations in the maintenance of international peace and security, in accordance with Article 54 of the Charter, and also includes reference to relevant communications of the Council.

I. Consideration of the provisions of Chapter VIII of the Charter of the United Nations under thematic items

Note

Section I contains an examination of the practice of the Security Council in 2022 in cooperating with regional organizations in the maintenance of international peace and security, within the framework of Chapter VIII of the Charter of the United Nations, in connection with items of a thematic nature. The section is divided into two subsections. Subsection A covers decisions on thematic issues relating to Chapter VIII, and subsection B covers discussions on thematic issues concerning the interpretation and application of Chapter VIII.

A. Decisions on thematic issues relating to Chapter VIII of the Charter

During the period under review, the Council explicitly referred to Chapter VIII of the Charter in one decision of a thematic nature. In a presidential statement adopted on 23 March under the item entitled "Cooperation between the United Nations and regional and subregional organizations in maintaining international peace and security", the Council reiterated that cooperation with regional and subregional organizations in matters relating to the maintenance of international peace and security, and consistent with Chapter VIII of the Charter, was significant to improving collective security.[3] The Council recognized that regional organizations were well positioned to understand the root causes of armed conflicts, owing to their knowledge of the region, which could be of benefit for their efforts to influence the prevention or resolution of conflicts.[4] The Council welcomed the strong cooperation between the United Nations and the League of Arab States and reiterated its intention to consider further steps to promote closer cooperation and strategic coordination between them in the fields of, among others, conflict early warning and prevention, peacekeeping, peacebuilding, sustaining peace, promoting respect for international law and the Charter, addressing root causes of conflict, enhancing safety and security at sea, preventing and countering terrorism and violent extremism, and building resilience to resist incitement.[5] The Council also recognized the importance of cooperation in sustainable development, comprehensive risk assessments and risk management strategies, including poverty eradication, food security and water management, disaster risk reduction, and desertification and drought management in the Arab region.[6] The Council emphasized the importance of strengthening trilateral cooperation and coordination between the United Nations, the African Union and the League of Arab States on cross-regional peace and security issues and encouraged consultations between them.[7]

In terms of the modalities of their engagement, the Council expressed support for the holding of an annual briefing by the Secretary-General of the League of Arab States, an annual informal meeting with the Council of the League and an informal meeting with representatives of the Arab Summit Troika and the Secretary-General of the League, on the margins of the General Assembly high-level segment.[8] Lastly, the Council requested the Secretary-General to provide a brief report on the implementation of the presidential statement and on further ways of strengthening institutional relations and cooperation between the two organizations.[9]

The Council also referred to the role of regional and subregional organization in the maintenance of international peace and security in two other decisions adopted under thematic items related to the non-proliferation of weapons of mass destruction and the use of sanctions. In resolution 2663 (2022), the Council welcomed efforts by regional and subregional organizations in supporting Member States in their

[3] S/PRST/2022/1, third paragraph.
[4] Ibid., fourth paragraph.
[5] Ibid., seventh paragraph.
[6] Ibid., eighth paragraph.
[7] Ibid., nineteenth paragraph.
[8] Ibid., sixteenth and seventeenth paragraphs.
[9] Ibid., twenty-first paragraph.

implementation of resolution 1540 (2004) on the non-proliferation of weapons of mass destruction and recognized the role that they could play in facilitating the implementation of the resolution by Member States in their respective regions.[10] In resolution 2664 (2022), adopted under the item entitled "General issues related to sanctions", the Council expressed its readiness to review, adjust and terminate its sanctions regimes, taking into account the evolution of the situation on the ground and the need to minimize unintended adverse humanitarian effects, and acknowledged the perspectives of regional and subregional organizations in that regard.[11]

B. Discussions on thematic issues concerning the interpretation and application of Chapter VIII of the Charter

In 2022, Council members and other Member States discussed the role of regional and subregional organizations in maintaining international peace and security under several thematic items, including "Briefing by the Chairperson-in-Office of the Organization for Security and Cooperation in Europe",[12] "Children and armed conflict",[13] "Cooperation between the United Nations and regional and subregional organizations in maintaining international peace and security",[14] "General issues relating to sanctions",[15] "Implementation of the note by the President of the Security Council (S/2017/507)",[16] "Maintenance of international peace and security",[17] "Peacebuilding and sustaining peace",[18] "Threats to international peace and security",[19] "United Nations peacekeeping operations"[20] and "Women and peace and security".[21] The most extensive discussions were held under the item entitled "Cooperation between the United Nations and regional and subregional organizations in maintaining international peace and security", in particular on cooperation with the Collective Security Treaty Organization (see case 1), the League of Arab States (see case 2) and the African Union (see case 4), as well as under the items entitled "Women and peace and security", focusing on partnerships in the implementation of the women and peace and security agenda (see case 3), and "Threats to international peace and security" regarding counter-terrorism efforts in Africa (see case 5).

Case 1
Cooperation between the United Nations and regional and subregional organizations in maintaining international peace and security

On 16 February, the Security Council held a briefing under the item entitled "Cooperation between the United Nations and regional and subregional organizations in maintaining international peace and security" to discuss relations with the Collective Security Treaty Organization (CSTO).[22] At the outset of the meeting, Council members heard a briefing by the Secretary-General of the United Nations and the Secretary-General of CSTO. In his briefing, the Secretary-General of the United Nations stated that the founders of the United Nations had understood that no single organization could alone ensure peace, security and development in a complex and rapidly changing world and that it required partnership across all levels – from the local, to the regional and global. He recalled that one of the main goals of his report entitled "Our Common Agenda"[23] was to build, by encouraging partnerships, a more inclusive and

---

[10] Resolution 2663 (2022), fifteenth and sixteenth preambular paragraphs.
[11] Resolution 2664 (2022), eighth preambular paragraph.
[12] See S/PV.8992.
[13] See S/PV.9096 and S/PV.9096 (Resumption 1).
[14] See S/PV.8967, S/PV.9001, S/PV.9065 and S/PV.9149.
[15] See S/PV.8962.
[16] See S/PV.9079 and S/PV.9079 (Resumption 1).
[17] See S/PV.9112, S/PV.9220 and S/PV.9220 (Resumption 1).
[18] See S/PV.9101, S/PV.9181 and S/PV.9181 (Resumption 1).
[19] See S/PV.9150 and S/PV.9188.
[20] See S/PV.9123.
[21] See S/PV.8989, S/PV.8989 (Resumption 1), S/PV.9064, S/PV.9064 (Resumption 1), S/PV.9158 and S/PV.9158 (Resumption 1).
[22] See S/PV.8967. For more information on the briefings, see part I, sect. 36.
[23] See A/75/982.

effective multilateralism that operated more like a network. To that end, he indicated that he planned to continue to hold annual meetings with all the leaders of regional organizations, guided by the Charter of the United Nations and other instruments of international human rights law and international humanitarian law.[24] The Secretary-General of CSTO reaffirmed the commitment of his organization to developing friendly and mutually acceptable relations with third countries and international organizations to maintain peace and stability based on the principles of international law, the rejection of confrontation and an embrace of lasting solutions reached through political and diplomatic means, in line with the provisions of the Charter.

In their statements, Council members and participating Member States expressed support for strengthening cooperation between the United Nations, including the Council, and regional and subregional organizations, in accordance with Chapter VIII of the Charter, and addressed some of the principles that should underlie such cooperation. The representative of China stated that the promotion of cooperation in the field of peace and security between the United Nations and regional and subregional organizations, under Chapter VIII, was conducive to strengthening the universality and effectiveness of collective security mechanisms and improving the maintenance of international peace and security. The representative of the Russian Federation, as echoed by the representative of Tajikistan, held the view that regional organizations had to complement United Nations efforts within their areas of responsibility, noting that they were, in most cases, more familiar with the situation on the ground. The representative of France stated that the entire point of Chapter VIII was the recognition that regional organizations were closest to the ground, the first to witness security crises and knew the deep roots involved and effective solutions to resolve and prevent them. The representative of India recalled that Article 52 of the Charter encouraged the settlement of disputes through regional arrangements and that such organizations were uniquely placed to provide better solutions to conflicts in their regions. The representative of Brazil stated that the United Nations and regional organizations should not only complement each other, but also combine efforts to develop effective tools for conflict prevention, mediation, crisis management and post-conflict peacebuilding.

Speakers also reflected on and expressed differing views on the first deployment by CSTO of a peacekeeping force following civil unrest in Kazakhstan in January 2022. Several delegations[25] expressed the view that CSTO played a decisive and positive role in stabilizing the situation in Kazakhstan. The Deputy Minister for Foreign Affairs of the Russian Federation and the representative of Kazakhstan emphasized that the operation, the objective of which was to provide peacekeeping assistance and maintain stability in the country, was conducted further to the request of the President of Kazakhstan and in accordance with Article 4 of the Treaty on Collective Security.

Other delegations[26] expressed concern about the violence in Kazakhstan and maintained that regional interventions had to be conducted in full respect of human rights, fundamental freedoms and the rule of law. The representative of the United Kingdom stressed that regional deployments had to be proportionate in any use of force and that the sovereignty of Kazakhstan had to be respected, adding that sovereignty and territorial integrity were at the very heart of the Charter and essential to the work of the Council. The representative of the United States expressed concern that the CSTO deployment had been sought before sustained efforts at national dialogue, reconciliation and the peaceful resolution of disputes had taken place. The representative of Ghana opined that closer collaboration between the United Nations and CSTO on any future deployment would enhance the Council's accountability over actions for regional peace and security.

More generally, the representatives of France and the United Kingdom underscored that regional partnerships must be based on the principles and purposes of the Charter. The representatives of Albania, France and the United Kingdom emphasized the need for cooperating with regional organizations, including their peacekeeping forces, to respect human rights and ensure the participation of women. The representative of Albania also stated that regional organizations should work in a transparent manner, follow clear rules and principles, and that any country must be able to decide in full freedom on the regional body that it wished to join, in accordance with the aims and aspirations of its people. The representative of the United Kingdom viewed the rule of law as a key component of institutional cooperation with regional organizations, consistent with the Charter of the United Nations. In addition to democracy, human rights

[24] See S/PV.8967.

[25] China, Gabon, Armenia and Kazakhstan.

[26] United Kingdom, France, United States, Ireland and Albania.

and the rule of law, as common objectives of cooperation, the representative of Brazil cited the promotion of peace, reconciliation, stability, freedom and economic prosperity. The representative of Kenya noted that, when there was good cooperation between the United Nations and regional and subregional organizations, emerging crises could be effectively contained, however, whenever organizations "read from different scripts" or took unilateral actions, conflicts became unnecessarily complex, protracted, internationalized and more destructive. He added that in a globalized world where many security threats were shared, regular exchanges between regional and subregional organizations and the United Nations contributed to building collaborative frameworks to deal with transregional threats such as terrorism, piracy and sea-based crime. The representative of the United Arab Emirates called for the enhanced inclusion of regional actors in Council discussions and for the systematic inclusion of regional perspectives in its consideration of items on its agenda.

Case 2
Cooperation between the United Nations and regional subregional organizations in maintaining international peace and security

On 22 March, at the initiative of the United Arab Emirates, which held the presidency of the Security Council for the month,[27] the Council held its annual briefing on cooperation between the United Nations and the League of Arab States under the item entitled "Cooperation between the United Nations and regional and subregional organizations in maintaining international peace and security".[28] The Council heard briefings by the Secretary-General of the United Nations, the Secretary-General of the League of Arab States and Razan Farhan Alaqil, a civil society representative.[29]

In the discussions that followed the briefings, Council members and the representative of Yemen, who spoke on behalf of the Group of Arab States, recognized the importance of cooperation between the United Nations and the League of Arab States in accordance with Chapter VIII of the Charter. Several speakers[30] noted that the League, with its deep knowledge and experience, possessed a comparative advantage in addressing challenges to peace and security in the Arab region. The representative of Gabon stated that regional and subregional organizations were, through their regional mechanisms, able to mobilize and deploy rapidly on the ground. The representative of Ghana encouraged greater diplomatic engagement by the League in the conflicts in the region, in collaboration with the Council, through its conflict resolution tools and strategies. The representative of Kenya stated that cooperation between the Council and the League had to be more ambitious if it was to be fit for purpose. He opined that Chapter VIII of the Charter and its embrace of the contribution of regional and subregional organizations in the maintenance of international peace and security could be what would ultimately rescue multilateralism.

Some delegations underscored the importance of regional ownership of peace and security efforts and the need to prevent foreign interference. The Minister of State of the Ministry for Foreign Affairs and International Cooperation of the United Arab Emirates stressed the need to adhere to the principle of seeking "Arab solutions to Arab issues", which required an end to foreign interference in Arab affairs. The representative of the Russian Federation stated that cooperation with the League of Arab States could contribute to the peaceful settlement of existing disputes without external interference, while respecting the interests of all parties concerned, in accordance with the norms and provisions of international law. Noting that the League had raised its voice in favour of the sovereignty and territorial integrity of its member States through moderation and the peaceful settlement of disputes, the representative of Brazil opined that it was essential for the Council to draw on the League's experience and wisdom to find balanced solutions to the problems of the region.

Participants also exchanged views on the thematic and country-specific areas of cooperation between the two organizations. Multiple delegations[31] called for closer cooperation on the implementation of the women and peace and security agenda and the youth and peace and security agenda. The representatives of Norway and the United States specifically welcomed the cooperation between the League and the United Nations Entity for Gender Equality and the Empowerment of Women (UN-Women) on the

---

[27] A concept note was circulated by a letter dated 17 March (S/2022/240).

[28] See S/PV.9001.

[29] For more information on the briefings, see part I, sect. 36.

[30] United Arab Emirates, Ghana, China, Gabon and Yemen (on behalf of the Group of Arab States).

[31] United Arab Emirates, Mexico, Norway, Albania, Brazil, United States and Yemen (on behalf of the Group of Arab States).

development and implementation of national action plans on women and peace and security. The representative of Norway called for strengthening mediation efforts that were sensitive to the issue of children and armed conflict, as well as the prevention of grave violations against children. Several representatives[32] called for increased cooperation in addressing the relationship between climate change and insecurity. The representative of Yemen underlined the need to promote cooperation between the Council and the League on early warning, peacekeeping, the peaceful settlement of disputes and post-conflict peacebuilding towards sustaining peace, which could be achieved through the development of mechanisms to exchange information and promote capabilities through training and capacity-building. Council members[33] further called for enhanced joint efforts between the United Nations and the League on settling, inter alia, the conflicts in Libya, the Syrian Arab Republic, Yemen and the State of Palestine, as well as addressing the situation in Lebanon.

In terms of specific proposals on ways to strengthen cooperation, some delegations[34] emphasized the need for regular communication and exchange of information between the Council and the League of Arab States. The Minister of State of the Ministry for Foreign Affairs and International Cooperation of the United Arab Emirates noted the need to institutionalize that relationship, which would require establishing mechanisms for the exchange of information and viewpoints on how to address regional challenges from a realistic and practical perspective.

Several representatives[35] called for the strengthening of the United Nations Liaison Office to the League of Arab States. Council members[36] also stressed the need for coordination between the special envoys of the Secretary-General and the League. The representative of China noted the holding of the first informal dialogue between the Council and the League's Troika in the margins of the General Assembly high-level segment in September 2021 and stated that such dialogue should continue in more flexible and diverse formats. In line with the presidential statements adopted on 13 June 2019 and 29 January 2021,[37] the representative of Yemen conveyed the support of the Group of Arab States for the holding of the annual high-level Council meeting on cooperation with the League, as it served to assist the Council in attaining a deeper and better understanding of Arab crises.[38] He further stressed the need to establish a mechanism that promoted bilateral cooperation and coordination between the Secretary-General and the Group in New York to discuss and address Arab priorities at the United Nations, in particular in the Council, including the holding of periodic formal meetings with the Secretary-General. Several delegations[39] also called for strengthening the trilateral cooperation between the African Union, the League of Arab States and the United Nations to address the multiple cross-regional peace and security issues that affected the Arab region in Africa.

Case 3
Women and peace and security

On 15 June, at the initiative of Albania, which held the presidency of the Security Council for the month,[40] the Council held a high-level open debate under the item entitled "Women and peace and security" and the sub-item entitled "Keeping the promises: the role of regional organizations in implementing the women and peace and security agenda in the face of political turmoil and seizures of power by force".[41] The Council heard briefings by the Secretary-General, the Executive Director of the United Nations Entity for Gender Equality and the Empowerment of Women (UN-Women), the Secretary-General of the Organization for Security and Cooperation in Europe, the Special Envoy of the Chairperson of the African Union Commission on Women, Peace and Security, the European Union Ambassador for Gender and

---

[32] Mexico, Ireland, Norway, Ghana, United States and Gabon.

[33] India, Mexico, Albania, China and Gabon.

[34] United Arab Emirates, India, Ghana, Gabon and Yemen (on behalf of the Group of Arab States).

[35] United Arab Emirates, India, Russian Federation, Mexico, Ireland, Albania, Gabon and Yemen (on behalf of the Group of Arab States).

[36] India, Russian Federation, Norway, China and Yemen.

[37] S/PRST/2019/5 and S/PRST/2021/2.

[38] See S/PV.9001.

[39] United Arab Emirates, Ghana, Albania, Kenya and Gabon.

[40] A concept note was circulated by a letter dated 4 June (S/2022/457).

[41] See S/PV.9064 and S/PV.9064 (Resumption 1).

Diversity, and the Assistant Secretary-General and Head of the Social Affairs Sector at the League of Arab States.[42]

Opening the debate, the Secretary-General stated that, when conflict erupted, neighbouring countries and regional organizations could make a significant difference to the women and peace and security agenda by ensuring that commitments were implemented. He noted that the cooperation between the United Nations and regional organizations on the agenda was reflected not only in joint statements and resolutions, but in the daily work on the ground, including in the Sudan, West and Central Africa and Myanmar. In her briefing, the Executive Director of UN-Women observed that most regional organizations had committed to action plans following the adoption of resolution 1325 (2000) and that, when Member States made such commitments on a regional level, national actions often followed. She added that regional organizations had also played a key role in the development of networks of women mediators, such as the African Women Leaders Network and the Network of African Women in Conflict Prevention and Mediation (FemWise-Africa), which regularly deployed its members to peace processes and national dialogues led by the African Union. She stressed, however, that, when regional organizations convened negotiations, they had to ensure that women were present in their own right, with their own lived experiences, knowledge and visions for their future. In their remarks, the representatives of the African Union, the European Union, the League of Arab States and the Organization for Security and Cooperation in Europe provided an overview of the contribution of their respective organizations to advancing the women and peace and security agenda and efforts to expand their cooperation with the United Nations and the Council.

Following the briefings, Council members and other Member States shared their views on the cooperation between the United Nations and regional organizations in the implementation of the women and peace and security agenda, in particular with respect to securing the safe participation of women in political processes and decision-making. The Minister for Europe and Foreign Affairs of Albania stated that regional organizations had unique and complementary capacities, which, when properly coordinated with the United Nations system, could produce good, fast and effective results in accelerating the implementation of the women and peace and security agenda, especially in contexts of political turmoil and the seizure of power by force. The State Secretary of Norway said that regional organizations carried the weight of many and diverse voices and were key actors and partners to the United Nations in translating women and peace and security ambitions into actual impact. The representative of Mexico held the view that regional organizations were crucial in promoting political dialogue and advancing respect for human rights, including gender equality and the empowerment of women and girls. The Assistant Minister for Foreign Affairs and International Cooperation for Political Affairs of the United Arab Emirates noted that, when properly empowered and supported, regional organizations could expand and complement international practices that might overlook contexts and identities of a conflict. The representative of Brazil recalled that resolution 2242 (2015) recognized the complementary role of regional organizations in the implementation of Council resolutions on women and peace and security and that, in recent years, the Council had strengthened dialogue with regional organizations by holding annual meetings and adopting outcome documents. Also noting that regional organizations and United Nations entities played an important complementary role alongside States, the representative of Türkiye stated that cooperation between the United Nations and regional and subregional organizations on women and peace and security should be seen in the context of their broader cooperation on conflict prevention and the maintenance of peace and security.

Several speakers[43] highlighted the important positive effect regional organizations had on individual Member States for advancing the women and peace and security agenda. The representative of Namibia stated that regional actions plans had a catalytic effect by encouraging the development of national action plans and that regional organizations had a convening power that had to be positively exploited. Multiple speakers further indicated that the successful implementation of the women and peace

[42] For more information on the briefings, see part I, sect. 29.

[43] United States, Ireland, Malta, Greece and Namibia.

and security agenda also required strengthening ties between regional actors themselves, including by sharing best practices.[44]

Council members and other Member States also widely agreed about the importance for the United Nations and regional organizations of supporting the work of civil society organizations that promoted the political participation of women. The representative of the United Arab Emirates stated that deepening partnerships between regional organizations and local women leaders could promote their roles in conflict resolution, preventive diplomacy, peacekeeping and peacebuilding. Similarly, speaking on behalf of the Group of Friends of Women, Peace and Security, the representative of Canada said that in conflicts and crises, including in contexts of seizures of power by force, regional organizations and networks provided much support in conflict prevention, mediation and resolution. The representative of Germany, speaking on behalf of the Group of Friends of the African Women Leaders Network, stated that, to ensure strong implementation, the women and peace and security agenda required strong partnerships between the Council, the Peacebuilding Commission and regional and subregional organizations in order to support women's organizations and peacebuilding initiatives. The representative of Kenya opined that partnerships with regional and subregional organizations implied meaningful partnerships with women's regional networks, which played a key role in contextualizing solutions, broadening action points and identifying informed and practical implementation opportunities for the women and peace and security agenda based on proximity. The representative of Gabon stated that it was important for those valuable initiatives, which included networks of women peacebuilding leaders, to receive financial, logistical and technical support that was stable and predictable.

Case 4
Cooperation between the United Nations and regional and subregional organizations in maintaining international peace and security

On 11 October, at the initiative of Gabon, which held the presidency of the Security Council for the month,[45] the Council held a briefing under the item entitled "Cooperation between the United Nations and regional and subregional organizations in maintaining international peace and security" further to the annual report of the Secretary-General on strengthening the partnership between the United Nations and the African Union on issues of peace and security in Africa, including the work of the United Nations Office to the African Union.[46] The Council heard briefings by the Secretary-General and the Chairperson of the African Union Commission.[47]

In the subsequent discussion, members and participating non-members of the Council welcomed the deepening relations between the United Nations and the African Union since the signing of the Joint United Nations-African Union Framework for Enhanced Partnership in Peace and Security in 2017 and their cooperation on the implementation of the Silencing the Guns in Africa initiative, the 2030 Agenda for Sustainable Development and Agenda 2063 of the African Union. The Minister for Foreign Affairs of Gabon stated that cooperation between the United Nations and the African Union was a standing item on the Council's agenda because it was key to the effectiveness of international peace and security and because the international community had to ensure that the necessary complementarity and subsidiarity that flowed from their partnership was enhanced. The Minister for Foreign Affairs of Gabon and the representative of India further stressed that the partnership between the two organizations was crucial given the prominence of African issues on the agenda of the Council.

More specifically, regarding the division of labour between the United Nations and the African Union, the representative of South Africa underlined that it was important that the partnership be anchored on the principles of subsidiarity, complementarity and comparative advantages. Similarly, the representative of India said that the activities of the United Nations, the African Union and subregional bodies should complement each other, while keeping their respective core mandates intact. The representative of Egypt

---

[44] Albania, Ghana, United Kingdom, France, Mexico, Canada (on behalf of the Group of Friends of Women, Peace and Security), Greece, Namibia and Indonesia.

[45] A concept note was circulated by a letter dated 3 October (S/2022/736).

[46] See S/PV.9149. See also S/2022/643.

[47] See S/PV.9149. For more information on the briefings, see part I, sect. 36.

stated that integration between the Security Council and the Peace and Security Council of the African Union required joint work and exploiting each organization's comparative advantages to address conflicts, especially emerging ones. He added that establishing a hierarchy in that context did not mean that the United Nations would relinquish its responsibility as an overarching organization under the Charter.

The representative and Assistant Minister for Foreign Affairs and International Cooperation for Political Affairs of the United Arab Emirates expressed the view that the Council should endorse the leadership of African regional and subregional organizations and in particular their efforts to resolve African conflicts. The representative of Norway stated that combining the situational awareness of the African Union with the mandates, tools and technical capacity of the United Nations improved conflict resolution and mediation. Furthermore, participants[48] highlighted a range of areas of cooperation between the United Nations and African Union such as conflict prevention, early warning, mediation, peacekeeping, peacebuilding, disarmament, counter-terrorism, countering maritime piracy and security sector reform, among others. Some speakers[49] called for the further enhancement of cooperation in addressing climate and security issues and natural disasters, countering misinformation, food security, mercenaryism, proliferation of arms and the plundering of natural resources.

Multiple speakers[50] focused on the need for stronger cooperation between the United Nations and the African Union on addressing the root causes of conflict and peacebuilding. The representative of Senegal opined that, although considerable progress had been made in the implementation of the Joint Framework in terms of mediation and technical electoral assistance, it was still lacking in terms of peacebuilding and post-conflict reconstruction. In that regard, he stated that the focus should be on addressing unconstitutional changes of government, the implementation of disarmament, demobilization and reintegration programmes, security sector reform, national reconciliation, transitional justice and judicial reform. The representatives of Ghana, Ireland and South Africa echoed that view and underscored the importance of cooperation on strengthening good governance, particularly in the light of the recent unconstitutional changes of government on the continent. The representative of Egypt called for the development of a specific United Nations programme to build the capacity of the African Union Commission and subregional organizations to implement the Silencing the Guns initiative and Agenda 2063, in line with the integration benchmarks between the United Nations and the African Union, pursuant to Chapter VIII of the Charter. Similarly, the representative of China called for more tangible assistance for Africa for capacity-building in governance, law enforcement, sustainable development and talent training and development.

With respect to the modalities of cooperation between the Security Council and the Peace and Security Council of the African Union, speakers called for the increased use of joint missions, briefings, assessments, reports and political declarations. Several of them[51] highlighted the importance of the annual joint consultative meeting for enhancing coordination. The representative of Senegal stated that the two Councils had to intensify their dialogue in order to ensure a common understanding of the security dynamics and challenges in Africa and to define the best modalities for supporting African peace and security initiatives.

Most speakers[52] agreed about the need for the international community to ensure predictable, sustainable and flexible funding for African peace support operations authorized by the Council, with some of them asserting that such support should be provided from United Nations assessed contributions. The representative of the United States, also speaking in her capacity as a member of the President's Cabinet, stated that the implementation of compliance frameworks for African peace support operations on international humanitarian law, human rights and conduct and discipline, including sexual exploitation and abuse, remained a key consideration for United Nations assessed contributions and covered any actions undertaken by regional organizations under Chapter VIII of the Charter. Moreover, the representatives of

[48] Gabon, United States, India, China, Ghana, Brazil, Mexico, Japan, Egypt, Senegal, Germany, Morocco, United Arab Emirates, Russian Federation and Norway.

[49] United Kingdom, Morocco, Albania, France, Kenya, China, Brazil, Gabon, Mexico and Namibia.

[50] Albania, Ghana, Japan and South Africa.

[51] Gabon, Albania, Kenya, Russian Federation, United Kingdom and Japan.

[52] France, Kenya, China, India, Egypt, Norway, South Africa and Morocco.

Norway and Senegal expressed support for the call of the Secretary-General for a United Nations support office for the Joint Force of the Group of Five for the Sahel. The representative of the Russian Federation recalled that the activities of regional bodies had to be consistent with the purposes and principles of the Charter and that peaceful means had to be given priority in the settlement of disputes. The representative added that, as far as funding methods were concerned, regardless of which of them was appropriate, it was important that initiating countries be able to retain the space to make their own policy decisions to counter threats, rather than having them imposed by others.

Many speakers[53] held the view that the reform of the Council to better reflect geopolitical realities and ensure that it was a more representative body was an important element for the strengthening of relations between the United Nations and the African Union. The representative of South Africa added that a partnership with a global institution without democratic composition and representation undermined the essence of such a partnership. For the representative of Kenya, pending the reform of the Council, the ability of African Member States to act as penholders on Council decisions would bring extra life to the Chapter VIII linkage to the African Union.

Case 5
Threats to international peace and security

On 10 November, at the initiative of Ghana, which held the presidency of the Security Council for the month,[54] the Council held a high-level briefing under the item entitled "Threats to international peace and security" and the sub-item entitled "Counter-terrorism in Africa: an imperative for peace, security and development".[55] The Council heard briefings by the Deputy Secretary-General, the Chairperson of the African Union Commission, the Managing Director for Common Security and Defence Policy and Crisis Response of the European External Action Service, and the President and Chief Executive Officer of the International Crisis Group.[56]

In her statement, the Deputy Secretary-General underlined that regional organizations had a critical role to play in fighting terrorism and cited several initiatives in Africa, including the Multinational Joint Task Force in the Lake Chad basin, the Joint Force of the Group of Five for the Sahel, the Accra Initiative and the Nouakchott Process. She welcomed the United Nations-African Union technical working group on preventing violent extremism and countering terrorism, which was aimed at increasing coordination and synergies between the two organizations and reiterated the appeal to the Council to ensure predictable funding for African Union peace operations. She further conveyed the need to put in place an innovative architecture that supported African peace operations in an effective and sustainable manner.

The Chairperson of the African Union Commission noted that Africa was not lacking in initiatives to counter terrorism and further mentioned the Southern African Development Community force in Mozambique and the more recently established East African Community Regional Force in eastern Democratic Republic of the Congo. While noting that the African Union had set up a peace fund to work on prevention and to support the efforts of countries that were victims of terrorist violence, he pointed to a pressing need for sustainable financial resources and technical and logistical support to sustain its efforts. He expressed the view that traditional mechanisms for responding to threats to peace, peacebuilding and peacekeeping were no longer entirely consistent with new circumstances and threats. In that regard, he stated that the mandates of United Nations peacekeeping operations needed to be urgently revised to make them real actors in the fight against terrorist groups. He further stated that the African Union was ready to work with the United Nations, including the Secretariat and the Council, to bring about an innovative approach at the doctrinal and operational levels.

Expressing a similar view, the President and Chief Executive Officer of the International Crisis Group noted that the Security Council and the Peace and Security Council of the African Union had been

[53] Gabon, United States, France, Kenya, India, Ghana, Brazil, Mexico, Norway, Egypt, Japan, South Africa, Senegal, Namibia, Germany and Morocco.

[54] A concept note was circulated by a letter dated 1 November (S/2022/822).

[55] See S/PV.9188.

[56] For more information on the briefings, see part I, sect. 34.

debating how to provide African Union missions with reliable funds for years. She observed that many studies concluded that the only credible option in that regard was a mechanism that enabled the Security Council to direct United Nations assessed contributions to African-led stabilization missions. Moreover, she added that the United Nations and the African Union would also have to define the rules that would govern the political oversight of future United Nations-funded, African-led operations, as well as the mechanisms for assessing their operational performance and accounting procedures to oversee their finances.

In the discussion that followed, multiple speakers stressed that the African Union and subregional organizations were central to countering violent extremism and terrorism in Africa. The representative of Brazil commended these efforts within the framework of the African Peace and Security Architecture, in accordance with Chapter VIII of the Charter. Council members agreed that African-led peace operations should not carry the counter-terrorism burden alone. The President of Ghana, together with the representatives of China and Kenya, underscored that it was the responsibility of the Council to support Africa and its regional organizations in that regard. Most speakers expressed support for the establishment of a mechanism to provide African-led peace operations with predictable, sustainable and flexible funding, in particular through United Nations assessed contributions. The representative of France called for using either mandatory United Nations contributions or establishing an innovative mechanism that would combine United Nations with bilateral contributions. She also encouraged the members of the Peace and Security Council of the African Union and the African Union Commission to redouble their efforts to arrive at a common position on financing African Union-mandated operations. The representative of Norway reiterated her delegation's support for the establishment of a United Nations support office for the Joint Force of the Group of Five for the Sahel. At the same time, she underscored that it was necessary for United Nations funding to be matched by sufficient human rights due diligence and African Union compliance frameworks.

Several speakers underscored that United Nations peacekeeping operations were not the appropriate tool to address terrorism in Africa. Specifically, the representative of Kenya stated that United Nations peacekeeping was not innovating enough to address terrorist groups and called upon the Council to learn from the situations in Somalia and Mozambique, in particular citing the operations of the African Union Transition Mission in Somalia (ATMIS) and the forces of the Southern African Development Community. The representative of the Russian Federation argued against imposing additional counter-terrorism obligations on United Nations missions in Africa, stating that that would not be in line with the nature of the Organization's presence and divert valuable resources from other forms of assistance. The representative of India opined that regional and subregional organizations enjoyed advantages in combating terrorism with regard to language and situational awareness and could respond more quickly and effectively based on a better understanding of the complexities involved. The representative of Norway stated that, working side by side with counter-terrorism operations, United Nations missions could contribute to the protection of civilians, use of good offices, capacity-building for governance, service delivery and human rights protection. The representative of China noted that African countries had certain expectations regarding the support of United Nations peacekeeping operations for counter-terrorism and called upon the Secretariat to take those concerns into consideration and present solutions that conformed to peacekeeping mandates and met the needs of African countries.

More broadly, in his statement, the President of Ghana welcomed the launch of the joint strategic assessment of security and development in the Sahel, encouraged the high-level panel led by former the President of the Niger, Mahamadou Issoufou, to leverage the best elements of the Joint Force of the Group of Five for the Sahel, the Accra Initiative, the Nouakchott Process and the Multinational Joint Task Force, consider recommendations for a unified and restructured regional force, and urged the Council to be supportive of such efforts. The representative of Ireland expressed the view that overly militarized counter-terrorism efforts could be ineffective or even counterproductive in the long term and stressed the need for the Council to work with the African Union, African subregional organizations and African Member States on addressing the drivers of terrorism and violent extremism in a more holistic manner, as part of a One United Nations approach.

II. Recognition of the efforts of regional arrangements in the pacific settlement of disputes

Note

Section II is focused on recognition by the Security Council of the efforts by regional and subregional organizations in the pacific settlement of local disputes, within the framework of Article 52 of the Charter. The section is divided into two subsections. Subsection A covers decisions concerning efforts of regional arrangements in the pacific settlement of disputes, and subsection B covers discussions concerning the pacific settlement of disputes by regional arrangements.

A. Decisions concerning efforts of regional arrangements in the pacific settlement of disputes

During the period under review, the Council did not explicitly refer to Article 52 of the Charter in any of its decisions. The Council, however, acknowledged and expressed support for the engagement of regional and subregional arrangements in the peaceful settlement of disputes, conflict prevention, resolution and sustaining peace, as well as the implementation of peace agreements, political dialogue and transitions, reconciliation processes and addressing the root causes of conflict. The Council did so in relation to a variety of items on its agenda, as featured in more detail in table 1. The decisions are organized in alphabetical order by item.

Table 1
Decisions concerning the pacific settlement of disputes by regional arrangements, 2022

Item	*Decision and date*	*Paragraphs*	*Regional organizations mentioned*
Peace and security in Africa	S/PRST/2022/6 31 August	Second, sixth and twenty-first paragraphs	African Union
The situation in the Central African Republic	Resolution 2648 (2022) 29 July	Third preambular paragraph	International Conference on the Great Lakes Region
	Resolution 2659 (2022) 14 November	Sixth and twelfth preambular paragraphs and para. 5	African Union, ECCAS, International Conference on the Great Lakes Region
The situation concerning the Democratic Republic of the Congo	Resolution 2666 (2022) 20 December	Paras. 10, 15 and 16	African Union, East African Community, International Conference on the Great Lakes Region, SADC
The question concerning Haiti	Resolution 2645 (2022) 15 July	Sixteenth and seventeenth preambular paragraphs	CARICOM
The situation in Libya	Resolution 2647 (2022) 28 July	Para. 4	African Union, European Union, League of Arab States
	Resolution 2656 (2022) 28 October	Para. 6	African Union, European Union, League of Arab States
The situation in Mali	Resolution 2640 (2022) 29 June	Sixth and eleventh preambular paragraphs and para. 14	African Union, ECOWAS
	Resolution 2649 (2022) 30 August	Fourth and sixth preambular paragraphs	ECOWAS

Item	*Decision and date*	*Paragraphs*	*Regional organizations mentioned*
The situation in the Middle East	Resolution 2624 (2022) 28 February	Para. 2	Gulf Cooperation Council
The situation in Myanmar	Resolution 2669 (2022) 21 December	Tenth to thirteenth preambular paragraphs and paras. 5–8	ASEAN
Reports of the Secretary-General on the Sudan and South Sudan	Resolution 2625 (2022) 15 March	Sixth preambular paragraph and paras. 21 and 22	IGAD
	Resolution 2630 (2022) 12 May	Fifth preambular paragraph	African Union
	Resolution 2633 (2022) 26 May	Third preambular paragraph	IGAD

Abbreviations: ASEAN, Association of Southeast Asian Nations; CARICOM, Caribbean Community; ECCAS, Economic Community of Central African States; ECOWAS, Economic Community of West African States; IGAD, Intergovernmental Authority on Development; SADC, Southern African Development Community.

B. Discussions concerning the pacific settlement of disputes by regional arrangements

During the period under review, Council members discussed the role of multiple regional and subregional organizations in the peaceful settlement of disputes. For example, in relation to the Central African region, Council members highlighted the support provided by the Economic Community of Central African States (ECCAS) to Member States for advancing inclusive political processes and electoral reforms, addressing cross-cutting issues such as climate-related security risks, implementing the youth, peace and security agenda, and promoting the political participation of women.[57] Specifically in relation to the situation in the Central African Republic, Council discussions referred to the good offices and mediation efforts of the African Union, ECCAS and the International Conference on the Great Lakes Region to support the implementation of the 2019 Political Agreement for Peace and Reconciliation and the 2021 joint road map, as well as the engagement of the African Union and ECCAS on the ongoing transition process in Chad.[58]

Regarding the situation concerning the Democratic Republic of the Congo and the Great Lakes region, Council members exchanged views on the work of the International Conference on the Great Lakes Region in support of the implementation of the Peace, Security and Cooperation Framework for the Democratic Republic of the Congo and the Region.[59] Further to the escalation of violence in the eastern part of the Democratic Republic of the Congo, they also discussed the regional mediation efforts, including the engagement of the East African Community, to achieve a cessation of hostilities and disarmament of armed groups through the Nairobi and Luanda Processes. Regarding Mali and the West Africa and Sahel region, Council discussions were focused on the engagement of the Economic Community of West African States (ECOWAS) with transitional authorities in Burkina Faso, Guinea and Mali to ensure the holding of elections and a return to constitutional order.[60]

In relation to the Sudan, Council members discussed the work of the African Union, Intergovernmental Authority on Development (IGAD) and United Nations trilateral mechanism in support of the Sudanese-owned and Sudanese-led political dialogue to restore the political transition, which resulted in the signing of a political framework agreement on 5 December 2022.[61] They also

[57] For more information, see part I, sect. 6.

[58] For more information, see part I, sect. 5.

[59] For more information, see part I, sects. 3 and 4.

[60] For more information, see part I, sects. 8 and 11.

[61] For more information, see part I, sect. 7.

continued to express support for the work of the African Union, IGAD and the reconstituted Joint Monitoring and Evaluation Commission on the implementation of the 2018 Revitalized Agreement on the Resolution of the Conflict in the Republic of South Sudan and the 4 August 2022 road map for the completion of the political transition. Council members further highlighted the European Union-facilitated dialogue between Serbia and Kosovo.[62]

In addition, discussions held under the item entitled "Peace and security in Africa" were focused on the cooperation of the United Nations with the African Union and the regional economic communities in capacity-building for sustaining peace in Africa (see case 6).

Case 6
Peace and security in Africa

On 8 August, at the initiative of China, which held the presidency of the Security Council for the month,[63] the Council held an open debate under the item entitled "Peace and security in Africa" and the sub-item entitled "Capacity-building for sustaining peace".[64] The Council heard briefings by the African Union Commissioner for Political Affairs, Peace and Security, the Special Adviser of the Secretary-General on Africa and the Permanent Representative of Bangladesh, in his capacity as Chair of the Peacebuilding Commission.[65]

In his briefing, the African Union Commissioner for Political Affairs, Peace and Security stated that, in a very concerning continental and global security context, it was necessary to redouble efforts to develop capacities to sustain peace in Africa. He called for strengthening the linkages between the African Governance Architecture and the African Peace and Security Architecture to provide a springboard for engagement in improving the effectiveness of governance, peace and security. In addition, he noted that the African Union Silencing the Guns initiative and Agenda 2063 set out the areas in which attention had to be focused and that the nexus between those two frameworks was critical. He concluded his remarks by offering three recommendations. First, he emphasized the need for demonstrable joint transformative leadership between the Security Council and the Peace and Security Council of the African Union, which, for Africa, would require building an integrated capacity for peace enforcement operations, based on both a military and a whole-of-society approach. Second, he informed Council members that the African Union was ready to recommit to the implementation of Sustainable Development Goal 16 on building peace, justice and strong institutions, which he noted was of the utmost importance in the quest for inclusive, effective and accountable institutions in the peace sector. Lastly, the Commissioner underscored the importance of building capacity for political transitions that was inclusive and fully participatory.

In his statement, the President of the Peacebuilding Commission stressed the importance of the African Union and other regional and subregional organizations in Africa in addressing peacebuilding challenges and fostering regional strategies in support of regional capacities to sustain peace. He further noted the Peacebuilding Commission's commitment to work more closely with the African Union and its Peace and Security Council in support of those strategies and in mobilizing peacebuilding tools to sustain peace.

In the ensuing discussion, Council members and other participants exchanged views on the key capacities necessary for sustaining peace in Africa. In that regard, they addressed how cooperation could be enhanced between the United Nations, including the Security Council, the African Union and subregional organizations in Africa on conflict prevention, peacekeeping, peacebuilding and the promotion of good governance.

Participants widely recognized the efforts made by the African Union and subregional organizations in developing capacities for sustaining peace, including through Agenda 2063, the African Peace and Security Architecture, the African Peace Fund and the African Governance Architecture. Speakers[66] underscored the critical importance of partnership with regional organizations in sustaining peace and the need for an alignment of their respective strategic objectives, in particular with the African

[62] For more information, see part I, sect. 18.B.
[63] A concept note was circulated by a letter dated 1 August (S/2022/592).
[64] See S/PV.9106 and S/PV.9106 (Resumption 1).
[65] For more information on the briefings, see part I, sect. 9.
[66] Gabon, Norway, Algeria and Italy.

Union. Several delegations[67] also noted that the Joint United Nations-African Union Framework for Enhanced Partnership in Peace and Security of 2017 was the appropriate strategic framework for building capacity to address peace and security challenges and promote peacebuilding in Africa.

A number of speakers reflected on the practical aspects of cooperation. The representative of Senegal maintained that the Security Council and the Peace and Security Council of the African Union had to intensify their dialogue in order to ensure a common understanding of security dynamics and challenges in Africa and to define the best modalities for supporting African initiatives in that area. In addition to the Joint Framework, the representative of Ghana stated that the annual joint consultative meetings between the Security Council and the Peace and Security Council of the African Union should be enhanced through a more regular exchange of information, joint briefings by special representatives and envoys and joint field visits by senior officials. The representative of Malta said that the relationship between the Security Council and the African Union, in particular through the African Peace and Security Architecture, enabled the Council to facilitate peace agreements and strengthen regional cooperation on the ground. The representative of Equatorial Guinea expressed the view that strengthened cooperation and coordination between the two councils would help to promote peace infrastructure and risk management, and enable the exploration of further solutions for the allocation of resources and capacity-building for African countries. The representative of South Africa opined that cooperation between the African Union and the United Nations could be further streamlined and strengthened with the harmonization of activities between the African Union Post-Conflict Reconstruction and Development Framework and the Peacebuilding Commission, as well as the African Union liaison offices and the United Nations missions in Africa.

Speakers paid particular attention to the role of the African Union and subregional organizations in promoting good governance and preventing conflict in Africa. Specifically, the representative of Ireland noted their role in responding to coups d'état and particularly commended the preventive diplomacy of the Economic Community of West African States (ECOWAS) and its efforts to promote dialogue, democracy, good governance and regional stability. The representative of Germany called for strengthening the vital role of the African Union in preventive diplomacy and fostering democratic resilience and encouraged Member States to follow its call for increased support to African-owned regional conflict prevention, mediation, peacekeeping and peacebuilding. The representative of Denmark stated that regional and subregional organizations were instrumental in developing context-specific and tailor-made approaches, often the first to react in crisis response and to engage with the parties concerned to ensure the protection of civilians, and uniquely placed to build trust and promote dialogue among the parties concerned and offer support in mediation and reconciliation. He further recognized that conflict prevention and enduring peace could not be sustained without addressing the root causes of insecurity and conflict and, in that regard, called for a comprehensive whole-of-system response by the United Nations, in cooperation with regional actors, to work preventively to address the factors that caused and exacerbated conflict.

Participants also discussed the responsibility of the Council to provide sufficient support for increasing capacity for sustaining peace in Africa, in particular through the creation of predictable, sustainable and flexible funding for African peace support operations authorized by the Council, including through assessed contributions. The representative of Ethiopia stated that, given that the African Peace and Security Architecture had been established in compliance with the Charter of the United Nations and that African peace operations were endorsed by the Council, it was legitimate and practical for the United Nations to allocate the resources necessary for them. The representative of Ireland said that United Nations peacekeeping operations, in addition to European Union missions and operations, played a key role in strengthening the national security defence capacities of African partners and called upon the Council to ensure that human rights due diligence policies were implemented. The representatives of Norway and Senegal expressed support for the establishment of a United Nations support office for the Joint Force of the Group of Five for the Sahel. The representative of Ghana stressed the need for the Council to determine the conditions under which African regional forces acting under Chapter VII of the Charter could meet the requirements for financing, especially from assessed contributions. The representative of the Russian Federation asserted that discussions on financing had been going on in the United Nations for many years and that, as a pretext for opposing such support,

[67] Ghana, Senegal, Switzerland, Algeria, Mozambique, Thailand and Argentina.

distrust of African efforts was often mentioned, and special demands related to human rights were often put forward. He added that agreeing on a common African position on the modalities for financing operations and the use of the African Union Peace Fund was key. The representative of Senegal stated that the revitalization of the Peace Fund, as a mechanism for the operationalization of the African Standby Force, was essential to provide Africa with a collective, autonomous and fully operational security system.

On 31 August 2022, in connection with the same item, the Council adopted a presidential statement in which it welcomed the progress made by African countries, the African Union and subregional organizations in conflict prevention, peacemaking, peacekeeping, peacebuilding and development.[68] The Council called for intensified efforts, support and a more coordinated approach to improve capacity-building in addressing these challenges.[69] The Council encouraged the continued development and application of mechanisms for the peaceful settlement of disputes through regional and subregional arrangements and commended the efforts of the African Union to strengthen its capacity, including through the advancement of the African Peace and Security Architecture.[70] The Council recognized that a major constraint facing the African Union in effectively carrying out African Union-led operations was the need to secure predictable, sustainable and flexible resources for its operations that were authorized by the Council and, consistent with Chapter VIII of the Charter, encouraged further dialogue on options, including using United Nations assessed contributions in accordance with resolution 2378 (2017).[71]

III. Peacekeeping operations led by regional arrangements

Note

Section III contains a description of the practice of the Security Council in connection with the cooperation between the United Nations and regional organizations pursuant to Chapter VIII of the Charter in the area of peacekeeping. The section is divided into two subsections. Subsection A covers decisions concerning peacekeeping operations led by regional arrangements, and subsection B covers discussions concerning peacekeeping operations led by regional arrangements.

A. Decisions concerning peacekeeping operations led by regional arrangements

Subsection A covers decisions concerning peacekeeping operations led by regional arrangements and is organized into three separate subheadings covering peacekeeping operations led by regional arrangements and authorized by the Council, other peacekeeping operations led by regional arrangements and other regional missions and security forces.

1. Peacekeeping operations led by regional arrangements authorized by the Security Council

In 2022, the Council renewed the authorization of the European Union military operation in Bosnia and Herzegovina (EUFOR-Althea)[72] and endorsed the decision of the Peace and Security Council of the African Union to reconfigure the African Union Mission in Somalia (AMISOM) into the African Union Transition Mission in Somalia (ATMIS) and authorized its mandate as detailed below.[73] The North Atlantic Treaty Organization (NATO)-led Kosovo Force, established by resolution 1244 (1999), continued to operate and no decisions were taken with respect to its mandate.[74]

[68] S/PRST/2022/6, second paragraph.

[69] Ibid.

[70] Ibid., nineteenth paragraph.

[71] Ibid., twentieth paragraph.

[72] Resolution 2658 (2022), para. 1. In addition to the authorization of EUFOR-Althea, the Council renewed its authorization provided by paragraph 11 of resolution 2183 (2014) to maintain a presence in Bosnia and Herzegovina in the form of a NATO headquarters (see resolution 2658 (2022), para. 2).

[73] Resolution 2628 (2022) paras. 22–24, 26 and 27.

[74] For more information on the international security presence in Kosovo, see *Repertoire*, *Supplement 1996–1999*, chap. VIII, sect. F.

African Union Transition Mission in Somalia

In 2022, the Council adopted resolutions 2628 (2022) of 31 March, 2657 (2022) of 31 October, 2662 (2022) of 17 November and 2670 (2022) of 21 December 2022 addressing the mandate and reconfiguration of AMISOM into ATMIS.

In resolution 2628 (2022), acting under Chapter VII of the Charter, the Council endorsed the decision of the Peace and Security Council of the African Union to reconfigure AMISOM into ATMIS and authorized, for an initial period of 12 months, the member States of the African Union to take all necessary measures to: (a) carry out its mandate to reduce the threat posed by Al-Shabaab; (b) support the capacity-building of the integrated Somali security and police forces; (c) conduct a phased handover of security responsibilities to Somalia; and (d) support peace and reconciliation efforts in Somalia, in line with the Somalia Transition Plan and National Security Architecture, in support of the development of a stable, federal, sovereign and united Somalia.[75]

The Council authorized the member States of the African Union to deploy up to 19,626 uniformed ATMIS personnel, inclusive of a minimum of 1,040 police personnel, including five formed police units, until 31 December 2022, and endorsed the decision of the Peace and Security Council of the African Union to draw down 2,000 personnel by that date.[76] The Council further authorized the member States of the African Union, between 1 January and 31 March 2023, to deploy up to 17,626 uniformed personnel, inclusive of a minimum of 1,040 police personnel and five formed police units.[77] The Council noted that the joint proposal and concept of operations submitted by the Secretary-General, together with the African Union, envisaged further reductions to 14,626 uniformed personnel, inclusive of a minimum number of 1,040 police, by the end of phase 2 (September 2023), 10,626 uniformed personnel, inclusive of a minimum number of 1,040 police personnel by the end of phase 3 (June 2024), and zero personnel by the end of phase 4 (December 2024), and expressed its intention to authorize those reductions, taking into account the situation in Somalia and the regular joint technical assessments as outlined in the resolution.[78]

Further to the joint proposal, the Council decided that ATMIS would pursue the following strategic objectives: (a) to conduct jointly planned operations with Somali security forces to degrade Al-Shabaab and affiliates linked to the Islamic State in the Levant/Da'esh; (b) to support Somali security forces by jointly holding priority population centres and providing protection to local communities and United Nations personnel and installations, while coordinating to support the implementation of the Somalia National Stabilization Strategy and State Stabilization Plans; (c) to assist the Federal Government of Somalia in the implementation of stabilization efforts for all recovered areas; (d) to support the capacity development of the Somali security forces to facilitate the progressive takeover of security responsibilities; (e) to support the Somali security forces across the clear, hold and build phases, in line with the Somalia Transition Plan and, in collaboration with institutions of the Federal Government, by facilitating humanitarian liaison, community engagement, as well as assisting Somali security forces with complying with international humanitarian law and international human rights law and holding accountable those responsible for violations thereof.[79]

The Council underlined the need for Somalia and its partners to take a coordinated approach towards supporting Somali-led political and security reforms to enable a progressive transition of security responsibility to Somalia and requested the United Nations to establish a technical partnership coordination function to increase coordination and collaboration between the Federal Government of Somalia, federal member states, ATMIS, the United Nations Support Mission in Somalia (UNSOM), the United Nations Support Office in Somalia (UNSOS), the United Nations country team and other partners.[80] In addition, the Council requested the United Nations, jointly with the African Union, the Federal Government of Somalia, the European Union and other donors to identify relevant, clear and realistic benchmarks in order to assess the implementation of the security transition by 30 September 2022, taking

[75] Resolution 2628 (2022), para. 22.
[76] Ibid., para. 26.
[77] Ibid., para. 27.
[78] Ibid., para. 28.
[79] Ibid., para. 23.
[80] Ibid., para. 48.

into account resolution 2594 (2021), while also requesting these actors to undertake regular, joint technical assessments of progress made to guide the Council as it further decided on the next steps of the phased drawdown of ATMIS and support provided by UNSOS, reporting to the Council by 15 February 2023.[81] Furthermore, underlining the need to enhance the predictability, sustainability and flexibility of financing for African Union-led peace support operations authorized by the Council and under the Council's authority consistent with Chapter VIII of the Charter, the Council encouraged the Secretary-General, the African Union and Member States to continue efforts to explore in earnest funding arrangements for ATMIS, bearing in mind the full range of options available to the United Nations, the African Union, the European Union and other partners, and considering the limitations of voluntary funding, in order to establish secure future funding arrangements for ATMIS.[82]

Lastly, the Council underlined the importance of ATMIS forces continuing to cooperate with UNSOM and UNSOS in implementing the human rights due diligence policy, including in the context of joint or coordinated operations with Somali security and police forces, and recognized the role that the African Union compliance framework and its operationalization in ATMIS could play in enhancing compliance with international human rights law and international humanitarian law.[83] The Council also encouraged efforts to ensure female uniformed personnel were deployed to ATMIS by troop- and police-contributing countries and urged the Mission to ensure the full, effective and meaningful participation of women across its operations and to integrate a gender perspective throughout the delivery of its mandate.[84]

In resolution 2657 (2022), the Council recalled its authorization of ATMIS in resolution 2628 (2022) and commended the renewed cooperation between all stakeholders to implement its mandate in support of the Somalia Transition Plan and National Security Architecture and to empower Somalia to progressively assume greater responsibility for its own security.[85] By resolution 2662 (2022), acting under Chapter VII of the Charter, the Council reiterated its request to the Government of Somalia, ATMIS and other partners to share information with the Panel of Experts on Somalia regarding the conduct or activities, in particular by Al-Shabaab and other actors intent on undermining peace and security in Somalia.[86] The Council further reiterated its request for ATMIS to support and assist Somalia in implementing the charcoal ban and facilitate regular access for the Panel to charcoal exporting ports.[87]

Lastly, by resolution 2670 (2022), acting under Chapter VII of the Charter, the Council exceptionally extended its authorizations under resolution 2628 (2022) until 30 June 2023, and affirmed that paragraph 27 of that resolution, which provided for the deployment of up to 17,626 uniformed personnel from 1 January to 31 March 2023, was annulled.[88] The Council recalled the revision of the operational timeline requested by Somalia, which was supported by the Peace and Security Council of the African Union in its communiqué of 11 November 2022,[89] to complete the drawdown of 2,000 ATMIS personnel by 30 June 2023.[90] The Council further noted that the Peace and Security Council of the African Union had reconfirmed the commitment to maintain the exit date for ATMIS of 31 December 2024.[91] The Council requested the Secretary-General to provide the report initially requested by 15 February 2023 under paragraph 51 of resolution 2628 (2022), by 30 April 2023 instead, and decided to convene a formal meeting on the transition in Somalia no later than 31 March 2023.[92]

---

[81] Ibid., paras. 50 and 51.
[82] Ibid., para. 49.
[83] Ibid., para. 31.
[84] Ibid., para. 35.
[85] Resolution 2657 (2022), para. 1
[86] Resolution 2662 (2022), paras. 27 and 46.
[87] Ibid., para. 35.
[88] Resolution 2670 (2022), para. 1 (a).
[89] See S/2022/939.
[90] Resolution 2670 (2022), second preambular paragraph.
[91] Ibid., para. 1 (b).
[92] Resolution 2670 (2022), paras. 1 (c) and 3.

Operation Althea of the European Union Force in Bosnia and Herzegovina

By resolution 2658 (2022) of 2 November, acting under Chapter VII of the Charter, the Council renewed its authorization of EUFOR-Althea for a period of 12 months.[93] The Council reiterated its authorization to Member States to take all necessary measures to effect the implementation of and to ensure compliance with annexes 1-A and 2 of the General Framework Agreement for Peace in Bosnia and Herzegovina, and stressed that the parties would be held equally responsible for compliance with those annexes and would be subject to such enforcement action by EUFOR-Althea and the NATO presence as might be necessary.[94] The Council also authorized Member States to take all necessary measures, at the request of either EUFOR-Althea or NATO Headquarters, in defence of EUFOR-Althea or the NATO presence, respectively, and to assist both organizations in carrying out their missions. In addition, the Council recognized the right of EUFOR-Althea and the NATO presence to take all necessary measures to defend themselves from attack or threat of attack.[95]

2. Other peacekeeping operations led by regional arrangements

The Council also addressed the role and mandates of other peacekeeping operations led by regional arrangements, namely, the Joint Force of the Group of Five for the Sahel and the European Union Training Missions in the Central African Republic and Mali, and expressed support for the development and deployment of the African Standby Force and the East African Community force in the eastern Democratic Republic of the Congo.

Joint Force of the Group of Five for the Sahel

In resolution 2640 (2022) of 29 June 2022, acting under Chapter VII of the Charter, the Council expressed support for the support provided by the United Nations Multidimensional Integrated Stabilization Mission in Mali (MINUSMA) to the Joint Force of the Group of Five for the Sahel, as per the conditions set out in resolutions 2391 (2017) and 2531 (2020), and in the technical agreement between the United Nations, the European Union and the Group of Five for the Sahel, through emergency evacuation of the sick or wounded and casualty evacuation, access to life support consumables, and the use of engineering plant equipment, material and enabling units.[96] The Council recalled that that support had always been considered as a temporary measure provided in strict compliance with the human rights due diligence policy.[97] The Council further reiterated its call upon the Joint Force to continue to develop its own capacity to support itself, while noting that the European Union had decided to suspend temporarily and reversibly some of its funding.[98]

Going forward, the Council requested that the next report by the Secretary-General on the Joint Force contain updates on the independent high-level panel strategic assessment on security and development in the Sahel, as well as a section assessing how the decision of Mali to withdraw from the Group of Five for the Sahel had impacted the support being provided by MINUSMA.[99] The Council also expressed its intent to make a decision on the continuation of such support, while noting the views and decisions of the Group of Five for the Sahel and the European Union.[100] The Council further requested the Secretary-General to continue to ensure close coordination and information-sharing, where appropriate, between MINUSMA, the United Nations Office for West Africa and the Sahel (UNOWAS) and subregional organizations, including the Economic Community of West African States (ECOWAS) and the Group of Five for the Sahel, as well as to ensure adequate coordination, exchange of information and, when applicable, support within their respective mandates and through existing mechanisms, between MINUSMA, the Malian Defence and Security Forces, the Joint Force of the Group of Five for

---

[93] Resolution 2658 (2022), para. 1. For information on the establishment of EUFOR-Althea, see *Repertoire, Supplement 2004–2007*, chap. XII, part III.C.

[94] Resolution 2658 (2022), para. 3.

[95] Ibid., para. 4. For further information on the authorization of the use of force in accordance with Chapter VII of the Charter, see part VII, sect. IV.

[96] Resolution 2640 (2022), para. 34. For more information on the mandate of MINUSMA, see part X, sect. I.

[97] Resolution 2640 (2022), para. 34.

[98] Ibid.

[99] Ibid., para. 35.

[100] Ibid.

the Sahel, the French forces, until the planned end of their presence in Mali, and the European Union missions in Mali.[101]

European Union Training Missions in the Central African Republic and Mali

By resolution 2659 (2022) of 14 November 2022, acting under Chapter VII of the Charter, the Council maintained the mandate of the United Nations Multidimensional Integrated Stabilization Mission in the Central African Republic (MINUSCA) to provide strategic and technical advice to the authorities of the Central African Republic to implement the National Strategy on Security Sector Reform and the National Defence Plan, in close coordination with, inter alia, the European Union Training Mission in the Central African Republic, the European Union Advisory Mission in the Central African Republic, the African Union Observer Mission in the Central African Republic and other international partners.[102] The Council also decided that the mandate of MINUSCA included taking a leading role in supporting the Central African Republic authorities in enhancing the capacities of the Internal Security Forces, in particular its command and control structures and oversight mechanisms, and to coordinate the provision of technical assistance and training between the international partners in the Central African Republic, in particular with the European Union Training Mission and the European Union Advisory Mission, in order to ensure a clear distribution of tasks in the field of security sector reform.[103]

In resolution 2640 (2022), acting under Chapter VII of the Charter, the Council encouraged the European Union, notably its Special Representative for the Sahel and its European Union training mission in Mali and European Union capacity-building Mission Sahel Mali, to continue its efforts to support Malian authorities in security sector reform and the re-establishment of State authority and presence throughout the Malian territory.[104] The Council further encouraged close coordination of these efforts with MINUSMA and requested the Secretary-General to enhance cooperation between MINUSMA and the European Union Training Mission in Mali and the European Union Capacity-Building Mission in Mali, including by developing further complementarity between the missions and by exploring modalities for potential mutual support.[105]

African Standby Force and the East African Community Regional Force

In a presidential statement adopted on 31 August 2022, the Council emphasized that the presence of terrorism and violent extremism conducive to terrorism could exacerbate conflicts, and contribute to undermining affected States, specifically their security, stability, governance and social and economic development.[106] The Council stressed the need for strengthened support to African countries, including through capacity support and institutional training, to address the underlying conditions conducive to the spread of terrorism and violent extremism conducive to terrorism at the national, subregional and regional levels, including through supporting the full operation of the African Standby Force, the delivery of effective and targeted capacity-building, sharing of information and best practices, and mobilizing more sustainable and predicable resources and expertise.[107]

In connection with the situation concerning the Democratic Republic of the Congo, in resolution 2666 (2022), acting under Chapter VII of the Charter, the Council encouraged support to the East African Community Regional Force and stressed the importance of the protection of civilians, close coordination and information-sharing between the Regional Force, the Armed Forces of the Democratic Republic of the Congo, the Burundi National Defence Forces, the Uganda Peoples' Defence Forces and MONUSCO, including to deconflict operations and to ensure MONUSCO mandate implementation and the need to carry out all operations in strict compliance with international law and the African Union compliance framework.[108]

---

[101] Ibid., paras. 24, 28 and 36.

[102] Resolution 2659 (2022), para. 36 (d) (i). For more information on the mandate of MINUSCA, see part X, sect. I.

[103] Resolution 2659 (2022), para. 36 (d) (iii).

[104] Resolution 2640 (2022), para. 38.

[105] Ibid.

[106] S/PRST/2022/6, sixteenth paragraph.

[107] Ibid.

[108] Resolution 2666 (2022), para. 17.

B. Discussions concerning peacekeeping operations led by regional arrangements

During the period under review, the Council discussed the role of peacekeeping operations led by regional arrangements such as EUFOR-Althea,[109] ATMIS,[110] the Collective Peacekeeping Forces of the Collective Security and Treaty Organization (CSTO),[111] the East African Community Regional Force in the Democratic Republic of the Congo,[112] the Joint Force of the Group of Five for the Sahel[113] and the NATO-led Kosovo Force.[114] Discussions of relevance for the interpretation of Chapter VIII of the Charter in the context of the cooperation between the United Nations and regional organizations in the area of peacekeeping were held under the following items: "Peace and security in Africa", specifically focused on the counter-terrorism efforts of the Joint Force of the Group of Five for the Sahel (see case 7); and "The situation in Somalia" in relation to the reconfiguration of the African Union Mission in Somalia (AMISOM) into the African Union Transition Mission in Somalia (ATMIS) and the transition of its security responsibilities to the Somali national authorities (see case 8).

Case 7
Peace and security in Africa

At a meeting held on 18 May under the item entitled "Peace and security in Africa", the Security Council discussed the mandate and operations of the Joint Force of the Group of Five for the Sahel and its cooperation with the United Nations Multidimensional Integrated Stabilization Mission in Mali (MINUSMA) further to the report of the Secretary-General.[115] The Council heard briefings by the Assistant Secretary-General for Africa in the Departments of Political and Peacebuilding Affairs and Peace Operations, the Executive Secretary of the Group of Five for the Sahel, and the Coordinator and President of the Rights and Resources Initiative, a civil society organization.

In her remarks, the Assistant Secretary-General stated that, against the backdrop of a deteriorating security situation in the Sahel, the decision of the Malian transitional authorities to withdraw from the Group of Five for the Sahel and its Joint Force was regrettable. She noted that the current challenging political and security dynamics in the Sahel, including the uncertain outcomes of the transitions in Mali and Burkina Faso, affected the operationalization of the Joint Force, which had slowed down significantly. In the light of the growing complexity of the crisis, she noted that the Secretary-General and the Chairperson of the African Union Commission would jointly carry out a strategic assessment of security and governance initiatives in the Sahel, with the objective of strengthening support to the Group of Five for the Sahel, its Joint Force and other security and governance initiatives in the region. The Assistant Secretary-General further noted that the assessment, which would be overseen by an independent high-level panel chaired by the former President of the Niger, Mahamadou Issoufou, would also focus on innovative ways to mobilize sustainable resourcing for those regional initiatives.

In his remarks, the Executive Secretary of the Group of Five for the Sahel recalled that the Heads of State of the organization's members had always appealed to the United Nations to support the Joint Force because their countries were fighting against terrorism, not only in their own interests, but also in the interest of international peace and security. He also noted that the three African members of the Council had always advocated for a positive stance towards the Joint Force that would allow it to meet the challenges, as the support provided by MINUSMA remained below expectations. Nevertheless, the Executive Security added that, since the end of 2019, the Joint Force had been able to carry out numerous operations and put in place a compliance framework to ensure respect for international human rights law and international humanitarian law.

---

[109] See S/PV.9029, S/PV.9065 and S/PV.9179.
[110] See S/PV.8965, S/PV.9009, S/PV.9040, S/PV.9125, S/PV.9188 and S/PV.9232.
[111] See S/PV.8967.
[112] See S/PV.9081, S/PV.9142 and S/PV.9165.
[113] See S/PV.8944, S/PV.8945, S/PV.9035, S/PV.9061, S/PV.9188 and S/PV.9194.
[114] See S/PV.9019 and S/PV.9155.
[115] See S/PV.9035. See also S/2022/382.

In the discussion that followed the briefings, Council members underscored the importance of the Joint Force of the Group of Five for the Sahel as a regional effort to address the threat of terrorism. The representative of Ghana, who also spoke on behalf of Gabon and Kenya, stated that continuous support for regionally led and complementary initiatives, including through bilateral and multilateral support for the Joint Force, remained one of the most effective ways to counter the security challenges in the Sahel. Most delegations expressed concern and disappointment about the decision of Mali to withdraw from the Group of Five for the Sahel. In that regard, most Council members also expressed concern about the impact of the withdrawal, as well as the recent unconstitutional changes of government in Burkina Faso, Chad and Mali, on the operations of the Joint Force. Several delegations[116] underscored the need for continued engagement by member States of the Group of Five for the Sahel to ensure the necessary coordination of their efforts in the fight against terrorism.

Council members exchanged views on the operational difficulties faced by the Joint Force and the need for support from the United Nations. The representative of China stated that MINUSMA should continue to improve its logistical support and that the United Nations should explore more solutions. The representative of India stressed the importance for traditional peacekeeping to be complemented by regional operations in order to neutralize terrorist groups and entities and called for sustainable and predictable support to the Joint Force. While expressing regret that the Council had not reached an agreement on the creation of a United Nations support office for the Joint Force, the representative of France stated that increased support from the Council and Member States for robust African operations was vital and that, without it, there was a risk of more countries turning to harmful solutions, such as the use of mercenaries. The representative of Ghana maintained that the withdrawal of Mali from the Joint Force required the Council and other partners to speak with one voice on the appropriate support mechanisms to fill security gaps for other regionally led initiatives, such as for the Nouakchott Process, the African Peace and Security Architecture in the Sahel-Saharan region, the Accra Initiative and the mobilization of an Economic Community of West African States standby force, while also finding the much-needed support mechanism to strengthen the Joint Force itself.

Several speakers highlighted the importance of the human rights compliance framework for the Joint Force endorsed by the Group of Five for the Sahel. The representative of Albania expressed concern about reports of sexual and gender-based violence committed by Joint Force personnel, encouraged better monitoring of such cases and urged the force to comply with the framework. The representative of Brazil, as echoed by the representative of Norway, urged the Joint Force to pay particular attention to the elements related to child protection in its compliance framework. The representative of Ireland opined that it was not possible to effectively address terrorism if the fundamental principles of international human rights law and international humanitarian law were ignored.

Several Council members[117] welcomed the launching of the high-level assessment of security and development in the Sahel, in particular in the context of changing political and security dynamics in the region. The representative of China expressed the view that the assessment should focus on the challenges faced by countries of the region with regard to logistics, funding and capacity-building and put forward realistic solutions. The representative of Mexico opined that, without a clear, solid political agreement among the countries of the region regarding the strategy to be followed, it would be difficult for the Council to make progress in its discussions on how the United Nations could increase its support for combating terrorism in the Sahel, including the financing of the Joint Force.

Case 8
The situation in Somalia

At a meeting held on 23 May under the item entitled "The situation in Somalia", Security Council members discussed the reconfiguration of the African Union Mission in Somalia (AMISOM) into the African Union Transition Mission in Somalia (ATMIS) further to resolution 2628 (2022).[118] In his statement

[116] Albania, China, India, Mexico and Ghana (also speaking on behalf of Gabon and Kenya).

[117] Albania, Brazil, China, Mexico, Ireland, Norway, Ghana (also on behalf of Gabon and Kenya) and United Arab Emirates.

[118] See S/PV.9040.

to the Council, the Special Representative of the Secretary-General for Somalia and Head of the United Nations Mission in Somalia (UNSOM) noted that, since the formal transition from AMISOM to ATMIS on 1 April 2022, Somali and African Union security officials had been heavily focused on electoral security. He also noted that the United Nations had taken steps to engage both the Federal Government of Somalia and ATMIS on the way forward in the implementation of the Somalia Transition Plan and the Mission's mandate. Moreover, he recalled that the United Nations Support Office for Somalia (UNSOS) had continued to provide support under its mandate to ATMIS and established a transition cell to ensure that it was well postured to meet the needs of the new Mission.

In his briefing, the Special Representative of the African Union Commission for Somalia and Head of ATMIS stated that the establishment of the Mission had been followed by transition activities in close collaboration with the Somali Federal Government, primarily focused on joint security forces disruption operations, securing main population centres and supply routes, mentoring and training of Somali security forces and joint planning and coordination. He added that force generation and adequate and predictable funding and equipment were key to degrading Al-Shabaab and ensuring the success of the transition within the 2024 timeline for the handing over of security responsibilities to the Somali security forces, as defined under resolution 2628 (2022).

Council members commended ATMIS for the support that it had provided for the Somali electoral process and noted the casualties among its personnel during that time. The representative of China expressed his delegation's expectation that the United Nations, the Government of Somalia, the African Union and other relevant parties would discuss and define the sharing of responsibilities and the assessment benchmarks during the transition period, in accordance with the requirements of Council resolutions. Multiple delegations[119] underscored that the successful implementation of the ATMIS mandate and the transition of responsibilities to the Somali security forces under the Somalia Transition Plan depended on the provision of adequate, sustainable and predictable funding for the Mission. The representative of Gabon, who also spoke on behalf of Ghana and Kenya, and the representative of the United Arab Emirates stated that a careful and effective transition from ATMIS to the Somali security forces was required to prevent the creation of a security vacuum which would enable Al-Shabaab to expand its operations. By contrast, the representative of France stated that no new funding, regardless of the amount, would suffice without Somali efforts to generate armed forces or without strong support from ATMIS to help Somali forces and conduct offensive operations with them. She added that France therefore encouraged the Government and ATMIS to resolutely commit to the security transition in order to achieve the objectives as outlined in resolution 2628 (2022).

IV. Authorization of enforcement action by regional arrangements

Note

Section IV concerns the practice of the Security Council in utilizing regional and subregional arrangements for enforcement action under its authority, as provided for in Article 53 of the Charter. The present section is focused on the authorization of enforcement action by regional and other organizations, with the exception of authorizations to use force for regional peacekeeping operations, which are covered in section III above. Cooperation with regional arrangements in the implementation of measures adopted by the Council under Chapter VII not involving the use of force is also covered in the present section. The section is divided into two subsections. Subsection A covers decisions concerning the authorization of enforcement action by regional arrangements, and subsection B covers discussions concerning the authorization of enforcement action and the implementation of other Chapter VII measures by regional arrangements.

[119] China, Gabon (also on behalf of Ghana and Kenya), Russian Federation and India.

A. Decisions concerning the authorization of enforcement action by regional arrangements

In 2022, the Council did not explicitly refer to Article 53 of the Charter in its decisions. It did, however, authorize the use of force by regional arrangements beyond the context of regional peacekeeping operations.

Concerning the situation in Libya, in resolution 2635 (2022), acting under Chapter VII of the Charter, the Council extended the authorizations as set out in resolution 2578 (2021) for Member States, acting nationally or through regional organizations, to inspect vessels they had reasonable grounds to believe were carrying arms or related materiel to or from Libya in order to ensure implementation of the arms embargo on the high seas off the coast of Libya, and to use all measures commensurate to the specific circumstances to carry out such inspections.[120] By resolution 2652 (2022), acting under Chapter VII, the Council renewed the authorizations to Member States, acting nationally or through regional organizations, set out in paragraphs 7 to 10 of resolution 2240 (2015), to inspect on the high seas off the coast of Libya vessels believed to be used for migrant smuggling and human trafficking from Libya, seize those that were confirmed as being used for those purposes, and authorized Member States to use all measures commensurate to the specific circumstances in confronting migrant smugglers or human traffickers in carrying out the aforementioned activities.[121]

Also acting under Chapter VII, the Council adopted several decisions not involving the use of force, such as requesting the support of regional and subregional organizations in the implementation of sanctions measures or calling for their cooperation with sanctions committees and panels of experts, in particular those concerning the Central African Republic, Haiti, South Sudan and Yemen, as outlined in table 2. The Council further requested the support of regional and subregional organizations for the work of the Committee established pursuant to resolution 1540 (2004) on the non-proliferation of weapons of mass destruction.

Table 2
Decisions by which the Security Council requested the cooperation of regional arrangements in the implementation of enforcement action, 2022

Item	*Decision and date*	*Paragraphs*
The situation in the Central African Republic	Resolution 2648 (2022) 29 July	Para. 10
The question concerning Haiti	Resolution 2653 (2022) 21 October	Para. 23
The situation in the Middle East	Resolution 2624 (2022) 28 February	Para. 18
Non-proliferation of weapons of mass destruction	Resolution 2663 (2022) 30 November	Para. 23
Reports of the Secretary-General on the Sudan and South Sudan	Resolution 2625 (2022) 15 March	Twentieth preambular paragraph and para. 23
	Resolution 2633 (2022) 26 May	Paras. 17 and 20

[120] Resolution 2635 (2022), para. 1.
[121] Resolution 2652 (2022), para. 2.

B. Discussions concerning the authorization of enforcement action and implementation of other Chapter VII measures by regional arrangements

In 2022, the Council heard two semi-annual briefings under the item entitled "Reports of the Secretary-General on the Sudan and South Sudan" by the Prosecutor of the International Criminal Court on the implementation of resolution 1593 (2005), by which the Council, acting under Chapter VII of the Charter, had referred the situation in Darfur to the Court.[122] At the meeting held on 17 January,[123] the representative of Kenya recalled that, in resolution 1593 (2005), the Council had invited the International Criminal Court and the African Union to discuss practical arrangements to facilitate the Court's work, including the possibility of conducting proceedings in the region. Further to the statement of the representative of Kenya, the Prosecutor highlighted his engagement with the African Union and underscored that the Darfur case had to be properly investigated and put before an appropriate tribunal, whether it be the International Criminal Court, a tribunal in the Sudan or a hybrid option, including with support from the African Union. Similarly, at the second meeting held on 23 August,[124] the representative of Ghana noted the steps taken by the Court to increase avenues of accountability through cooperation with third States and international and regional organizations, adding that increased cooperation with the African Union could help address the lack of cooperation between the Court and the Sudanese authorities and garner support for other cases that the Prosecutor was investigating.

In 2022, discussions in the context of meetings of the Council were also focused on the activities and mandate of Operation IRINI in Libya, under the items entitled "The situation in Libya" and "Cooperation between the United Nations and regional and subregional organizations in maintaining international peace and security",[125] and Operation Atalanta of the European Union Naval Force off the coast of Somalia, under the item entitled "The situation in Somalia".[126] In both cases, participants discussed the roles of these operations in support of the arms embargoes imposed by the Council concerning Libya and Somalia, respectively.[127]

At a meeting held on 3 June under the item entitled "The situation in Libya", acting under Chapter VII of the Charter, the Council adopted resolution 2635 (2022), by which it extended the authorizations for Member States, acting nationally or through regional organizations to inspect vessels in support of the arms embargo off the coast of Libya.[128] Following the adoption of the resolution, having abstained in the vote, the representative of the Russian Federation expressed regret that Operation IRINI had over recent years demonstrated very low levels of effectiveness in assisting the implementation of the provisions of the Libyan arms embargo.[129] In that regard, the representative pointed to a lack of successful seizures of contraband goods, lack of transparency and a selective approach to vessels flying flags of particular States. He further stated that, for the upcoming year, the Russian Federation would continue to closely monitor the work of Operation IRINI to ensure full compliance with the arms embargo, in particular whether it was effective in combating flows of illegal weapons and whether it was in line with the mandate stipulated in resolution 2292 (2016).

Subsequently, at a meeting held on 25 July under the same item, the representative of Mexico expressed concern about reports of possible shipments of military equipment to Libya in contravention

---

[122] See S/PV.8948 and S/PV.9113. For more information, see part I, sect. 7, and *Repertoire*, *Supplements 2004–2007* to *2021*.

[123] See S/PV.8948.

[124] See S/PV.9113.

[125] See, in connection with cooperation between the United Nations and regional and subregional organizations in maintaining international peace and security, S/PV.9065; and, in connection with the situation in Libya, S/PV.9047, S/PV.9053 and S/PV.9098. For more information on the establishment of Operation Irini in Libya, see *Repertoire*, *Supplement 2020*, part VIII, sect. IV.

[126] See S/PV.8965. For more information on the establishment of Operation Atalanta off the coast of Somalia, see *Repertoire*, *Supplement 2008–2009*, part VIII, sect. IV.

[127] For more information, see sect. III above, part I, sects. 2 and 10, and part IX, sect. I.B.

[128] See S/PV.9053. The draft resolution received 14 votes in favour (Albania, Brazil, China, France, Gabon, Ghana, India, Ireland, Kenya, Mexico, Norway, United Arab Emirates, United Kingdom and United States) and 1 abstention (Russian Federation).

[129] Ibid.

of Council resolutions.[130] He called upon all States to cooperate with Operation IRINI in order to prevent weapons from continuing to fuel violence in the country. He also recalled that the authorization by the Council could be used by any State or regional organization to monitor compliance with the arms embargo. Several representatives stated that the interception of a vessel that was in violation of the arms embargo demonstrated the importance of Operation IRINI for its implementation.[131]

At a meeting held on 15 February under the item entitled "The situation in Somalia" and further to the report of the Secretary-General,[132] Council members discussed the mandate of Operation Atalanta of the European Union, for which the Council's authorization was due to expire on 2 March 2022.[133] At the meeting, Council members heard briefings by the Special Representative of the Secretary-General and Head of the United Nations Assistance Mission in Somalia, the Special Representative of the Chairperson of the African Union Commission for Somalia and Head of the African Union Mission in Somalia, and the Head of the Delegation of the European Union to the United Nations. The representative of the European Union held the view that Operation Atalanta had successfully contributed to the suppression of piracy off the coast of Somalia. While noting the readiness of the European Union to work with the Somali authorities to support their efforts on maritime security, the representative expressed hope that the Council would be able to agree on a revised resolution that better reflected Somali priorities, while also renewing the legal provisions necessary for the continuation of Operation Atalanta for at least the remainder of the year. He further cautioned that, if the resolution was not extended beyond 3 March 2022, Operation Atalanta would not have the authorization to fight piracy or to protect the deliveries of the World Food Programme and other vulnerable vessels in the Somali territorial waters.[134]

During the discussion, the representative of the United Kingdom noted that her delegation had no objection in principle to the desire of the Federal Government of Somalia to move to a bilateral maritime cooperation framework,[135] while at the same time expressing support for an extension of resolution 2608 (2021) until such a framework was in place in order to avoid any operational gaps, which included ensuring that Operation Atalanta could continue to function.

Council members and other delegations also discussed the role of regional organizations in support of the implementation of sanctions measures on the Central African Republic and South Sudan. On 26 May, at a meeting held under the item entitled "Reports of the Secretary-General on the Sudan and South Sudan", acting under Chapter VII of the Charter, the Council adopted resolution 2633 (2022), by which it renewed sanctions measures on South Sudan.[136] In his remarks after the vote, the representative of Kenya noted that his country had abstained in the voting because the text fell short of the call by the Intergovernmental Authority on Development and the African Union for the lifting of the arms embargo and targeted sanctions on South Sudan. Echoing that view, the representative of China noted that the Peace and Security Council of the African Union had taken that position on the sanctions measures in order to allow South Sudan to build the security capacity necessary to maintain national security and stability. He further recommended that the Council adopt measures to gradually ease the sanctions regime, which would help South Sudan to respond positively to the concerns of the African Union.

At a meeting held on 29 July under the item entitled "The situation in the Central African Republic", acting under Chapter VII of the Charter, the Council adopted resolution 2648 (2022).[137] As a result, the Council extended the sanctions measures on the Central African Republic. Speaking after the vote, the representative of Kenya explained that his delegation had abstained in the voting because

[130] See S/PV.9098.

[131] United Kingdom, France, Ireland, Norway and Albania.

[132] See S/2022/101.

[133] See S/PV.8965. For more information on the establishment of Operation Atalanta of the European Union, see *Repertoire*, *Supplement 2020*, part VIII, sect. IV.

[134] During the period under review, the authorizations for Operation Atalanta were not renewed upon their expiry on 3 March 2022.

[135] See S/2022/162.

[136] See S/PV.9045. The draft resolution received 10 votes in favour (Albania, Brazil, France, Ghana, Ireland, Mexico, Norway, United Arab Emirates, United Kingdom and United States) and 5 abstentions (China, Gabon, India, Kenya and Russian Federation).

[137] See S/PV.9105. The draft resolution received 10 votes in favour (Albania, Brazil, France, India, Ireland, Mexico, Norway, United Arab Emirates, United Kingdom and United States) and 5 abstentions (China, Gabon, Ghana, Kenya and Russian Federation).

resolution 2648 (2022) fell short of the full lifting of the arms embargo, as advocated by the Government of the Central African Republic, the African Union, the Economic Community of Central African States and the International Conference on the Great Lakes Region. The representative further maintained that, in line with the provisions of Chapter VIII of the Charter, the least the Council could do was to give those regional organizations a more respectful hearing. The representative of the Russian Federation echoed that view and stated that the voices of African States had again gone unheard, despite the frequent promises in the Council to take into account the views of regional organizations. While noting that the resolution had replaced the arms embargo with a notification regime, the representative of Gabon also stated that the text did not take into account the recommendations of the Peace and Security Council of the African Union, which had requested the lifting of the arms embargo to enable the national defence and security forces of the Central African Republic to fully carry out their constitutional mandate to protect their country and citizens. Acknowledging that the resolution partially addressed the assessments and claims of the Central African authorities, the African Union and other regional organizations, the representative of Brazil stated that the voices of these stakeholders could made a meaningful contribution, not only because of their legitimacy, but also primarily because they offered a perspective that considered the peace and security situation in the Central African Republic on its own merits. The representative of the Central African Republic recalled the communiqué issued by the Peace and Security Council, in which it reiterated its call upon the African members of the Security Council, namely, Gabon, Ghana and Kenya, to show solidarity in accordance with the principles of the African Union Charter, which opposed unjust sanctions against African States.

V. Reporting by regional arrangements on their activities in the maintenance of international peace and security

Note

Section V contains an examination of the reporting by regional arrangements on their activities in the maintenance of international peace and security within the framework of Article 54 of the Charter of the United Nations. The section is divided into three subsections. Subsection A covers decisions concerning reporting by regional arrangements, subsection B covers discussions concerning reporting by regional arrangements, and subsection C covers communications concerning reporting by regional arrangements.

A. Decisions concerning the reporting by regional arrangements

During the period under review, the Security Council made no explicit reference to Article 54 of the Charter in its decisions. The Council did, however, request reporting from regional organizations on peacekeeping operations led by them, either directly or through the Secretary-General, as well as on maritime enforcement actions undertaken further to relevant resolutions of the Council, as described in further detail and summarized in table 3.

Concerning Libya, in resolution 2635 (2022), the Council requested the Secretary-General to report in six and 11 months on the implementation of the authorizations set out in resolution 2578 (2021) for Member States acting nationally or through regional organizations concerning the implementation of the arms embargo on the high seas off the coast of Libya.[138] In addition, in resolution 2652 (2022), the Council renewed the reporting requests set out in paragraph 17 of resolution 2240 (2015), requiring Member States acting nationally or through regional organizations, to inspect on the high seas off the coast of Libya vessels believed to be used for migrant smuggling and human trafficking from Libya.[139]

[138] Resolution 2635 (2022), para. 2. See also the reports of the Secretary-General on the implementation of resolutions 2578 (2021) and 2635 (2022) (S/2022/360 and S/2022/910).

[139] Resolution 2652 (2022), para. 2. See also the report of the Secretary-General on the implementation of resolution 2598 (2021) (S/2022/655).

The Council further requested the Secretary-General to report 11 months after the adoption of the resolution on its implementation.[140]

With regard to the situation in Mali, the Council requested the Secretary-General to report, every three months after the adoption of resolution 2640 (2022), on the coordination, exchange of information and mutual operational and logistical support between the United Nations Multidimensional Integrated Stabilization Mission in Mali (MINUSMA), the Malian Defence and Security Forces, the Joint Force of the Group of Five for the Sahel, the French forces until the planned end of their presence in Mali, and the European Union missions in Mali.[141]

In relation to Somalia, in resolution 2628 (2022), the Council requested the African Union to keep it informed through the Secretary-General on the implementation of the mandate of the newly-established African Union Transition Mission in Somalia (ATMIS) and defined specific timelines for the submission of its reports, as well as matters on which specific reporting was required.[142] In addition, the Council requested the United Nations, jointly with the African Union, Federal Government of Somalia, European Union and other donors, to undertake regular, joint technical assessments made against the benchmarks requested under the resolution to guide the Council on the next steps of the drawdown of ATMIS and support provided by the United Nations Support Office in Somalia (UNSOS).[143] In resolution 2662 (2022), the Council requested the African Union to provide an update on its preparations for the planned drawdown of 2,000 ATMIS personnel by 31 December 2022 in accordance with resolution 2628 (2022).[144]

In connection with the item entitled "Reports of the Secretary-General on the Sudan and South Sudan", in resolution 2625 (2022), the Council encouraged the Intergovernmental Authority on Development to share reports of fighting and violations of the 2017 Agreement on the Cessation of Hostilities and the permanent ceasefire provisions of the Revitalized Agreement on the Resolution of the Conflict in the Republic of South Sudan.[145] In the same resolution, the Council invited the African Union to share information on progress made in the establishment of the Hybrid Court for South Sudan with the Secretary-General.[146] Similarly, in resolution 2633 (2022), the Council invited the reconstituted Joint Monitoring and Evaluation Commission to share relevant information with the Council on its assessment of the implementation by the parties of the Revitalized Agreement, adherence to the cessation of hostilities and the facilitation of unhindered and secure humanitarian access.[147]

Lastly, in a presidential statement adopted on 31 August in connection with the item entitled "Peace and security in Africa", the Council recognized that one major constraint facing the African Union in effectively carrying out peace operations was the need to secure predictable, sustainable and flexible resources that were authorized by the Council and consistent with Chapter VIII of the Charter. In that regard, the Council encouraged further dialogue on options, including using United Nations assessed contributions for addressing the issue and requested the Secretary-General to provide a report on the progress made by the United Nations and the African Union to fulfil the commitments as set out in resolution 2320 (2016) and resolution 2378 (2017) and recommendations on moving forward that reflected good practices and lessons learned with a view to securing predictable, sustainable and flexible resources.[148]

In 2022, the Council also continued to receive reports on the activities of the European Union military operation in Bosnia and Herzegovina,[149] Operation Atalanta of the European Union Naval Force,[150] the Joint Force of the Group of Five for the Sahel[151] and the North Atlantic Treaty Organization (NATO)-led Kosovo Force.[152]

---

[140] Resolution 2652 (2022), para. 3.
[141] Resolution 2640 (2022), para. 57 (ii).
[142] Resolution 2628 (2022), para. 53.
[143] Ibid., para. 51.
[144] Resolution 2662 (2022), para. 47 (f).
[145] Resolution 2625 (2022), ninth preambular paragraph.
[146] Ibid., para. 24.
[147] Resolution 2633 (2022), para. 23.
[148] S/PRST/2022/6, twentieth paragraph.
[149] See resolution 1575 (2004) and S/2022/591.
[150] See resolution 2608 (2021) and S/2022/819.
[151] See resolution 2391 (2017), S/2022/382 and S/2022/838.
[152] See resolution 1244 (1999) and S/2022/208.

Table 3
Decisions concerning the reporting of activities by regional arrangements, 2022

Item	*Decisions*	*Paragraphs*	*Reporting from*
The situation in Libya	Resolution 2635 (2022) 3 June	Para. 2	Secretary-General
Peace and security in Africa	S/PRST/2022/6 31 August	Twentieth paragraph	Secretary-General
Maintenance of international peace and security	Resolution 2652 (2022) 29 September	Para. 3	Secretary-General
The situation in Mali	Resolution 2640 (2022) 29 June	Paras. 35 and 57 (ii)	Secretary-General
The situation in Myanmar	Resolution 2669 (2022) 21 December	Para. 6	Secretary-General, Association of Southeast Asian Nations
The situation in Somalia	Resolution 2628 (2022) 31 March	Paras. 51, 53 and 54	Secretary-General, African Union, European Union
	Resolution 2662 (2022) 17 November	Para. 47 (f)	African Union
	Resolution 2670 (2022) 21 December	Para. 1 (c) and (d)	Secretary-General, African Union, European Union
Reports of the Secretary-General on the Sudan and South Sudan	Resolution 2625 (2022) 15 March	Ninth preambular paragraph and para. 24	Secretary-General, African Union, Intergovernmental Authority on Development
	Resolution 2633 (2022) 26 May	Para. 23	Reconstituted Joint Monitoring and Evaluation Commission

B. Discussions concerning the reporting by regional arrangements

During the period under review, Article 54 of the Charter was explicitly mentioned in a meeting of the Council held on 16 February under the item entitled “Cooperation between the United Nations and regional and subregional organizations in maintaining international peace and security”, during which Council members discussed the cooperation between the United Nations and the Collective Security Treaty Organization (CSTO).[153] In his briefing to the Council, the Secretary-General of CSTO noted the deployment of a CSTO peacekeeping force following civil unrest in Kazakhstan in January 2022 and stated that, in line with the requirements under Article 54 of the Charter and Article 4 of the Treaty on Collective Security, CSTO had swiftly informed the Secretary-General of the United Nations about the operation by letter.[154] Similarly, the representative of the Russian Federation stated that, following the decision of CSTO to deploy the force further to the request of Kazakhstan, the Council and the Secretary-General of the United Nations had been immediately informed of the operation. The representative of Kazakhstan added that the United Nations had been properly informed in a timely manner about the intention of CSTO to deploy the force.

[153] See S/PV.8967. For more information on the discussion, see sect. I.
[154] See S/PV.8967.

C. Communications concerning the reporting by regional arrangements

In five letters addressed to the President of the Council, the representatives of Kuwait[155] and Lebanon,[156] in their respective capacities as Chairs of the Council of the League of Arab States, and citing Article 54 of the Charter, transmitted the decisions of the Council of the League on a variety of peace and security issues affecting the Arab region. Furthermore, in a letter dated 17 March 2022 addressed to the Secretary-General, the representative of the United Arab Emirates circulated a concept note for a Council briefing held on 23 March 2022 under the item entitled "Cooperation between the United Nations and regional and subregional organizations in maintaining international peace and security" and the sub-item entitled "Cooperation between the Security Council and the League of Arab States", noting that Article 54 required regional organizations to keep the Council informed of their activities pertaining to international peace and security.[157]

[155] S/2022/57, S/2022/169 and S/2022/394.

[156] S/2022/349 and S/2022/372.

[157] See S/2022/240. For more information on the discussion at that meeting, see sect. I.

Part IX
Subsidiary organs of the Security Council: committees, tribunals and other bodies

Contents

Introductory note

Article 29

The Security Council may establish such subsidiary organs as it deems necessary for the performance of its functions.

Rule 28

The Security Council may appoint a commission or committee or a rapporteur for a specified question.

The power of the Security Council to establish subsidiary organs is set out in Article 29 of the Charter of the United Nations and rule 28 of its provisional rules of procedure. Part IX of the present Supplement covers the practice of the Council relating to committees, working groups, investigative bodies, tribunals, ad hoc commissions, and special advisers, envoys and representatives, as well as the Peacebuilding Commission. It also includes instances of subsidiary organs that were proposed but not established, where applicable. Field-based missions, including United Nations peacekeeping and political missions, are covered in part X. Field-based missions led by regional organizations are covered in part VIII. Each subsection below provides a summary of the major developments relating to each subsidiary organ during the period covered by this Supplement.

I. Committees

Note

Section I focuses on the decisions of the Council adopted during 2022 concerning the establishment of committees and the implementation of and changes to their mandates, as well as their termination. Subsection A covers standing committees and subsection B covers committees established under Chapter VII of the Charter of the United Nations. The description of each committee includes the tasks of the committee, as mandated by the Council in the context of the implementation of sanctions measures, such as an arms embargo, an asset freeze and/or a travel ban. Information on measures mandated by the Council pursuant to Article 41 of the Charter is provided in part VII, section III. The committees are discussed within each subsection below in the order of their establishment.

The committees of the Council consist of all 15 members of the Council. Their meetings are held in private, unless a committee itself decides otherwise, and decisions are reached by consensus. The Council has both standing committees that meet only when issues under their purview are being considered and committees established on an ad hoc basis in response to specific requirements of the Council, such as counter-terrorism or sanctions committees.

The Bureau of each committee generally consists of a Chair and a Vice-Chair, who are elected by the Council on an annual basis.[1] Since the issuance in 2012 of a note by the President of the Security Council on the matter, the process for the appointment of Chairs and Vice-Chairs is conducted with the participation of all Council members.[2] According to the note by the President of the Council dated 31 August 2017, the informal process would be undertaken in a balanced, transparent, efficient and inclusive way "so as to facilitate an exchange of information related to the work of the subsidiary bodies involved" and would be "facilitated jointly by two members of the Security Council working in full cooperation".[3] On 27 December 2019, a new note by the President was issued, according to which the Council members stressed that the "informal consultation process should take into account the need for a shared responsibility and a fair distribution of work for the selection of the Chairs among all members of the Council, bearing in mind the capacities and resources of members".[4]

A. Standing committees

During 2022, the standing committees, namely, the Committee of Experts on Rules of Procedure, the Committee of Experts established by the Council at its 1506th meeting to study the question of associate membership, the Committee on the Admission of New Members and the Committee on Council Meetings away from Headquarters, continued to exist but did not meet.

B. Committees established under Chapter VII of the Charter

Subsection 1 deals with the committees and associated monitoring teams, groups or panels of experts (expert groups) that oversaw specific sanctions measures in 2022.[5] Subsection 2 deals with subsidiary organs with a thematic scope, namely the Committee established pursuant to resolution 1373 (2001) concerning counter-terrorism and the Committee established pursuant to resolution 1540 (2004), which have broader mandates relating to terrorism and non-proliferation. Other subsidiary bodies,

---

[1] For the Bureaux of the committees during the period covered in the present Supplement, see S/2022/2, S/2022/2/Rev.1, S/2022/2/Rev.2, S/2022/2/Rev.3 and S/2022/2/Rev.4.

[2] See S/2012/937.

[3] S/2017/507, annex, paras. 111–114. It was also indicated in the note that the Council should make every effort to agree on the appointment of the Chairs for the following year no later than 1 October. Previous notes of this nature were S/2006/507 and S/2010/507.

[4] See S/2019/991.

[5] For information concerning the sanctions measures relevant to each of the committees, see part VII, sect. III.

including the Office of the Ombudsperson, the Counter-Terrorism Committee Executive Directorate and expert groups, are discussed together with the relevant committees.

In 2022, the committees carried out their mandate of, inter alia, listing and delisting individuals and entities, granting exemptions and processing notifications, monitoring and assessing implementation and reporting to the Council. In addition to reporting by means of written reports, some Committee Chairs delivered briefings to the Council in open meetings and closed consultations. As outlined in table 1, briefings by Chairs of subsidiary organs took place under both thematic and country- and region-specific items and were delivered as joint or individual briefings, in the context of which Chairs reported at varying intervals on a variety of aspects of the work of the subsidiary organs, including their mandates and/or any visits conducted by the Chairs.

Table 1
Briefings by Chairs of Security Council subsidiary organs, 2022

Item	*Briefing by the Chair*	*Meeting record and date*
Country- and region-specific		
The situation in Afghanistan	Committee established pursuant to resolution 1988 (2011)	S/PV.8954 26 January
		S/PV.9227 20 December
The situation concerning the Democratic Republic of the Congo	Committee established pursuant to resolution 1533 (2004)	S/PV.9142 30 September
		S/PV.9215 9 December
The question concerning Haiti	Committee established pursuant to resolution 2653 (2022)	S/PV.9233 21 December
The situation in Libya	Committee established pursuant to resolution 1970 (2011)	S/PV.8952 24 January
		S/PV.8996 16 March
		S/PV.9047 26 May
		S/PV.9120 30 August
		S/PV.9223 16 December
The situation in Mali	Committee established pursuant to resolution 2374 (2017)	S/PV.9200 23 November
The situation in the Middle East	Committee established pursuant to resolution 2140 (2014)	S/PV.8966 15 February
The situation in Somalia	Committee pursuant to resolution 751 (1992)	S/PV.8976 24 February
		S/PV.9071 21 June

Item	*Briefing by the Chair*	*Meeting record and date*
Reports of the Secretary-General on the Sudan and South Sudan	Committee established pursuant to resolution 1591 (2005)	S/PV.9005 28 March
		S/PV.9070 21 June
		S/PV.9128 13 September
		S/PV.9210 7 December
	Committee established pursuant to resolution 2206 (2015)	S/PV.9219 13 December
Thematic		
Briefings by Chairs of subsidiary bodies of the Security Council	Committee pursuant to resolutions 1267 (1999), 1989 (2011) and 2253 (2015)	S/PV.9201 23 November
	Committee established pursuant to resolution 1373 (2001)	S/PV.9218 12 December
	Committee established pursuant to resolution 1540 (2004)	
	Committee pursuant to resolution 751 (1992)	
	Committee established pursuant to resolution 1718 (2006)	
	Committee established pursuant to resolution 1373 (2001)	
	Committee established pursuant to resolution 1988 (2011)	
	Committee established pursuant to resolution 1970 (2011)	
	Committee established pursuant to resolution 1540 (2004)	
	Committee established pursuant to resolution 2374 (2017)	
	Committee pursuant to resolutions 1267 (1999), 1989 (2011) and 2253 (2015)	
Non-proliferation of weapons of mass destruction	Committee established pursuant to resolution 1540 (2004)	S/PV.8993 14 March

1. Committees overseeing specific sanctions measures

In 2022, the Council established one new committee to oversee the implementation of measures adopted under Chapter VII of the Charter, namely, the Committee established pursuant to resolution 2653 (2022) concerning Haiti. The Council also amended the name of the Committee pursuant to resolution 751 (1992) concerning Somalia to the "Security Council Committee pursuant to resolution 751 (1992) concerning Al-Shabaab". The total number of committees overseeing specific sanctions measures had increased from 14 to 15 by the end of 2022.

As described in more detail below, while most of the mandates of the committees remained largely unchanged, the Council modified some aspects of the mandates of certain committees or requested committees or expert panels to carry out specific tasks. For example, noting the increasing use of explosive ordnance, including improvised explosive devices and landmines, the Council expanded the mandate of the Panel of Experts on the Central African Republic by requesting the Panel to devote special attention to the analysis of threats relating to explosive ordnance, in cooperation with other panels or groups of experts established by the Council.[6] The Council also strongly condemned attacks committed

[6] Resolution 2648 (2022), para. 9.

by armed groups of the Coalition des patriotes pour le changement and requested the Panel to consider proposing or updating further statements of cases for possible designation.[7]

In addition, during the period under review, the Council adopted, not unanimously, resolution 2664 (2022), in which it directed all committees established by it with respect to sanctions implementation to assist Member States in properly understanding and fully implementing the standing humanitarian exemption to all asset freeze measures imposed by the Council or any of its committees, with the exception of the Committee established pursuant to resolution 1988 (2011), as decided by the Council in the same resolution, and further directed those committees, assisted by their respective panels of experts, to monitor the implementation of the humanitarian carve out, including any risk of diversion.[8] In that regard, the Council emphasized the role of the Committee pursuant to resolutions 1267 (1999), 1989 (2011) and 2253 (2015) concerning Islamic State in Iraq and the Levant (Da'esh), Al-Qaida and associated individuals, groups, undertakings and entities.[9]

Table 2 provides an overview of the committees, including selected categories of the main mandatory measures that they oversaw during 2022.

Table 2
Security Council committees responsible for oversight of specific sanctions measures, 2022

Type of measure / *Sanctions committee*	*Arms embargo*	*Asset freeze*	*Travel ban or restrictions*	*Non-proliferation measures/ restrictions on ballistic missiles*	*Economic and financial restrictions*	*Petroleum-related (including bunkering services)*	*Natural resources*[a]	*Other*[b]
Committee pursuant to resolution 751 (1992)	X	X	X				X	X
Committee pursuant to resolutions 1267 (1999), 1989 (2011) and 2253 (2015)	X	X	X					
Committee established pursuant to resolution 1518 (2003)	X	X						
Committee established pursuant to resolution 1533 (2004)	X	X	X					X
Committee established pursuant to resolution 1591 (2005)	X	X	X					
Committee established pursuant to resolution 1636 (2005)		X	X					
Committee established pursuant to resolution 1718 (2006)	X	X	X	X	X	X	X	X
Committee established pursuant to resolution 1970 (2011)	X	X	X		X	X		
Committee established pursuant to resolution 1988 (2011)	X	X	X					
Committee established pursuant to resolution 2048 (2012)			X					

[7] Ibid., para. 8.
[8] Resolution 2664 (2022), paras. 1, 4 and 6.
[9] Ibid., paras. 2 and 5.

Sanctions committee / *Type of measure*	*Arms embargo*	*Asset freeze*	*Travel ban or restrictions*	*Non-proliferation measures/ restrictions on ballistic missiles*	*Economic and financial restrictions*	*Petroleum-related (including bunkering services)*	*Natural resources*[a]	*Other*[b]
Committee established pursuant to resolution 2127 (2013)	X	X	X					
Committee established pursuant to resolution 2140 (2014)	X	X	X					
Committee established pursuant to resolution 2206 (2015)	X	X	X					
Committee established pursuant to resolution 2374 (2017)		X	X					
Committee established pursuant to resolution 2653 (2022)	X	X	X					

[a] This category refers to a variety of measures on natural resources, including charcoal, coal, iron, gold, titanium, copper, nickel, silver and zinc.

[b] Includes measures relating to, inter alia, transport and aviation, the ban on components of improvised explosive devices, trade restrictions and/or diplomatic restrictions.

Committee pursuant to resolution 751 (1992) concerning Al-Shabaab

In 2022, while the mandate of the Committee pursuant to resolution 751 (1992) remained largely unaltered,[10] its name was changed to the "Security Council Committee pursuant to resolution 751 (1992) concerning Al-Shabaab".[11] More information about the work of the Committee can be found in its annual report.[12]

By its resolution 2661 (2022), the Council provided for a two-day extension of the existing mandate of the Panel of Experts on Somalia, until 17 November 2022.[13] Subsequently, the Council adopted, not unanimously, resolution 2662 (2022), by which it renewed the mandate of the Panel of Experts until 15 December 2023.[14] Consistent with prior decisions, the Council also requested the Secretary-General to include dedicated gender expertise, in line with paragraph 11 of its resolution 2467 (2019), further requested the Panel to include gender as a cross-cutting issue in its investigations and reporting, and expressed its intention to review the mandate and to take appropriate action regarding any extension and modification of the mandate, including restrictions on the import of weapons and ammunition by the Federal Government of Somalia, no later than 15 November 2023.[15]

The Council further requested the Panel to provide regular updates to the Committee, including a minimum of four different thematic reports, a comprehensive midterm update, and a final report by 1 October 2023.[16]

[10] The mandate of the Committee included, inter alia, designating individuals and entities subject to the sanctions measures adopted by the Council, which comprise an arms embargo, an asset freeze, a travel ban, a charcoal ban and a ban on components of improvised explosive devices, monitoring the implementation of the measures and deciding on requests for exemptions.

[11] Resolution 2662 (2022), para. 24.

[12] S/2022/995.

[13] Resolution 2661 (2022), para. 1. The mandate of the Panel of Experts included supporting the Committee, gathering and analysing information on compliance, monitoring implementation, making recommendations to improve the implementation of the relevant measures and providing periodic reports.

[14] Resolution 2662 (2022), para. 44.

[15] Ibid.

[16] Ibid., para. 47 (c).

Committee pursuant to resolutions 1267 (1999), 1989 (2011) and 2253 (2015) concerning Islamic State in Iraq and the Levant (Da'esh), Al-Qaida and associated individuals, groups, undertakings and entities

In 2022, the Council addressed matters relating to the Committee pursuant to resolutions 1267 (1999), 1989 (2011) and 2253 (2015) under the item entitled "Threats to international peace and security caused by terrorist acts".[17] The mandates of the Committee, the Analytical Support and Sanctions Monitoring Team and the Office of the Ombudsperson remained largely unchanged in 2022.[18] For more information on the work of the Committee, see its annual report for 2022.[19] More information on the work of the Monitoring Team can be found in its reports.[20] More information on the work of the Office of the Ombudsperson can be found in its reports for 2022.[21]

By its resolution 2664 (2022), the Council created a standing humanitarian exemption to all asset freeze measures imposed by the Council or any of its committees[22] and decided that the exemption would apply to the Islamic State in Iraq and the Levant (ISIL/Da'esh) and Al-Qaida sanctions regime for a period of two years, while expressing its intent to make a decision on the further extension of the exemption's application to that regime prior to its expiration. The Council further emphasized the role of the Committee in monitoring the implementation of the humanitarian carve out, in particular by assisting Member States in properly understanding and fully implementing the humanitarian carve out and monitoring its implementation, including any risk of diversion.[23]

Committee established pursuant to resolution 1518 (2003)

In 2022, there were no modifications to the mandate of the Committee established pursuant to resolution 1518 (2003). By its resolution 1518 (2003), the Council established the Committee and mandated it to continue to identify individuals and entities whose funds, other financial assets and economic resources should be frozen and transferred to the Development Fund for Iraq, in accordance with paragraphs 19 and 23 of resolution 1483 (2003).[24] For more information on the work of the Committee, see its annual report for 2022.[25]

Committee established pursuant to resolution 1533 (2004) concerning the Democratic Republic of the Congo

In 2022, the mandate of the Committee established pursuant to resolution 1533 (2004) remained largely unaltered.[26] The Chair and several members of the Committee conducted a visit to the Democratic Republic of the Congo, Rwanda and Uganda from 7 to 18 November, regarding which the Chair provided

---

[17] For more information, see part I, sect. 30.

[18] The mandate of the Committee included, inter alia, monitoring the implementation of the sanctions measures, which comprise an arms embargo, an asset freeze and a travel ban; deciding on requests for exemptions; designating individuals and entities subject to the sanctions measures; and conducting periodic and specialized reviews of the entries on the ISIL/Da'esh and Al-Qaida sanctions list. The mandate of the Analytical Support and Sanctions Monitoring Team included, inter alia, supporting the Committee, gathering and analysing information on compliance with the sanctions measures, providing to the Committee information relevant to the listing of individuals and entities subject to the sanctions measures, assisting the Committee in regularly reviewing names on the sanctions list, assisting the Ombudsperson to the Committee in carrying out its mandate, and providing periodic reports. The mandate of the Office of the Ombudsperson included, inter alia, reviewing requests from individuals and entities seeking to be removed from the sanctions list and making a recommendation to the Committee on those requests.

[19] S/2022/963.

[20] S/2022/547 and S/2023/95.

[21] S/2022/608 and S/2023/133.

[22] With the exception of the Committee established pursuant to resolution 1988 (2011).

[23] Resolution 2664 (2022), paras. 1, 2, 5 and 6.

[24] For background information, see *Repertoire*, *Supplement 2000–2003*, chap. V, part I.B.2.

[25] S/2022/968.

[26] The mandate of the Committee included, inter alia, designating individuals and entities subject to the sanctions measures adopted by the Council, which comprise an arms embargo, an asset freeze, transport and customs controls and a travel ban, monitoring implementation and deciding on requests for exemptions.

a briefing to the Council.[27] For more information on the work of the Committee, see its annual report for 2022.[28]

During the period under review, the Council adopted, not unanimously, resolution 2641 (2022), by which it extended the mandate of the Group of Experts established pursuant to resolution 1533 (2004) until 1 August 2023 and expressed its intention to review the mandate and to take appropriate action regarding its further extension no later than 1 July 2023.[29] In addition, the Council called for enhanced cooperation between all States, in particular those in the region, and the Group of Experts, and requested the Group of Experts to provide a midterm report and a final report.[30] The Council also reaffirmed the reporting provisions set out in resolutions 2360 (2017) and 2478 (2019).[31] The Council recalled the Secretary-General's commitment that the United Nations would do everything possible to ensure that the perpetrators of the killing of the two members of the Group of Experts and the four Congolese nationals accompanying them were brought to justice and stressed the importance of a continued deployment by the Secretary-General of the follow-up mechanism to the Democratic Republic of the Congo to assist with the national investigation, within existing resources.[32]

In its resolution 2666 (2022), by which the mandate of the United Nations Organization Stabilization Mission in the Democratic Republic of the Congo (MONUSCO) was extended, the Council requested MONUSCO to monitor the implementation of the arms embargo as described in paragraph 1 of resolution 2293 (2016) in cooperation with the Group of Experts and to assist and exchange relevant information with the Group of Experts.[33]

Committee established pursuant to resolution 1591 (2005) concerning the Sudan

In 2022, the mandate of the Committee established pursuant to resolution 1591 (2005) remained unchanged.[34] For more information on the work of the Committee, see its annual report for 2022.[35]

In its resolution 2620 (2022), by which the mandate of the Panel of Experts on the Sudan was extended until 12 March 2023, the Council requested the Panel to provide periodic reports and expressed its intention to review the mandate of the Panel and to take appropriate action regarding its further extension no later than 12 February 2023.[36]

Committee established pursuant to resolution 1636 (2005)

During the period under review, there were no changes to the mandate of the Committee established pursuant to resolution 1636 (2005) to register and oversee the travel ban and asset freeze on individuals designated by the International Independent Investigation Commission or by the Government of Lebanon as being suspected of involvement in the terrorist bombing in Beirut on 14 February 2005 that killed the former Prime Minister of Lebanon, Rafiq Hariri, and 22 others.[37] The Committee held no meetings during 2022. As at 31 December 2022, no individual had been registered.

---

[27] See S/PV.9215.

[28] S/2022/971.

[29] Resolution 2641 (2022), para. 8. The mandate of the Group of Experts included, inter alia, supporting the Committee, gathering and analysing information on compliance, providing information relevant to the listing of individuals and entities subject to the sanctions measures and providing periodic reports.

[30] Resolution 2641 (2022), para. 9.

[31] Ibid., para. 10.

[32] Ibid., para. 12.

[33] Resolution 2666 (2022), para. 34. For more information on the mandate of MONUSCO, see part X, sect. I.

[34] The mandate of the Committee included monitoring the implementation of the measures adopted by the Council, which comprise an arms embargo, an asset freeze and a travel ban, deciding on requests for exemptions and designating individuals and entities subject to the sanctions measures.

[35] S/2022/961.

[36] Resolution 2620 (2022), para. 2. The mandate of the Panel of Experts included supporting the Committee, gathering and analyzing information on compliance, providing information relevant to the listing of individuals and entities subject to the sanctions measures and providing periodic reports.

[37] For more information, see *Repertoire*, *Supplement 2004–2007*, chap. V, part I.B.10.

Committee established pursuant to resolution 1718 (2006)

During the period under review, there were no modifications to the mandate of the Committee established pursuant to resolution 1718 (2006).[38] For more information on the work of the Committee, see its annual report for 2022.[39]

In its resolution 2627 (2022), by which the mandate of the Panel of Experts established pursuant to resolution 1874 (2009) was extended until 30 April 2023, the Council requested the Panel to provide periodic reports and expressed its intent to review the mandate of the Panel and to take appropriate action regarding its further extension no later than 25 March 2023.[40] The Council also requested the Panel of Experts to provide to the Committee a planned programme of work no later than 30 days after the Panel's reappointment and encouraged the Committee to engage in regular discussions with the Panel about its programme of work and its work.[41]

Committee established pursuant to resolution 1970 (2011) concerning Libya

In 2022, the mandate of the Committee established pursuant to resolution 1970 (2011) remained unchanged.[42] For more information on the work of the Committee, see its annual report for 2022.[43]

During the period under review, the Council adopted resolution 2644 (2022), by which it extended the mandate of the Panel of Experts on Libya until 15 November 2023 and decided that the mandated tasks of the Panel as defined in resolution 2213 (2015) were also to apply with respect to the measures updated in resolution 2644 (2022), namely, the measures aimed at preventing the illicit export of petroleum, including crude oil and refined petroleum products.[44] In the same resolution, the Council expressed its intent to review the mandate of the Panel and to take appropriate action regarding its further extension no later than 15 October 2023 and requested the Panel to provide periodic reports.[45] The Council also requested that the Panel closely follow and report to the Committee any information relating to the illicit export from or illicit import to Libya of petroleum and directed the Committee to immediately inform all relevant Member States about notifications to the Committee from the focal point of the Government of Libya regarding vessels transporting petroleum, including crude oil and refined petroleum products, illicitly exported from Libya.[46]

---

[38] The mandate of the Committee included, inter alia, monitoring implementation, deciding on requests for exemptions and designating individuals, entities and vessels subject to the sanctions measures adopted by the Council, which comprise, inter alia, an arms embargo, an embargo relating to nuclear, ballistic missile and other weapons of mass destruction programmes, sectoral bans on coal, minerals and fuel, a ban on the export of luxury goods, a travel ban, an asset freeze, a ban on the provision of financial services and a ban on specialized teaching and training in disciplines that could contribute to prohibited activities and programmes.

[39] S/2022/1001.

[40] Resolution 2627 (2022), paras. 1 and 2. The mandate of the Panel of Experts included, inter alia, supporting the Committee, gathering and analysing information on compliance, making recommendations on actions that the Council, the Committee or Member States might consider to improve the implementation of the measures and providing periodic reports.

[41] Resolution 2627 (2022), para. 3.

[42] The mandate of the Committee included monitoring implementation, gathering and analysing information on compliance, deciding on requests for exemptions and designating individuals, entities and vessels subject to the sanctions measures adopted by the Council, which comprise an arms embargo, a travel ban, an asset freeze and measures aimed at preventing illicit exports of petroleum.

[43] S/2022/970.

[44] Resolution 2644 (2022), paras. 2 and 12. The mandate of the Panel of Experts included supporting the Committee, gathering and analysing information on compliance, monitoring implementation, making recommendations on actions that the Council, the Committee, the Government of Libya or other States might consider to improve the implementation of the relevant measures and providing periodic reports.

[45] Resolution 2644 (2022), paras. 12 and 13.

[46] Ibid., paras. 3 and 4.

Committee established pursuant to resolution 1988 (2011)

In 2022, the Council addressed matters related to the Committee established pursuant to resolution 1988 (2011) under two different items, namely, "The situation in Afghanistan" and "Threats to international peace and security caused by terrorist acts".[47]

The mandate of the Committee remained largely unchanged.[48] The Council adopted one resolution in relation to the mandate of the Committee and the Analytical Support and Sanctions Monitoring Team. By its resolution 2665 (2022), the Council extended for a period of 12 months, until December 2023, the mandate of the Monitoring Team in support of the Committee established pursuant to resolution 1988 (2011), with further details on the mandate set forth in the annex to the resolution.[49] The Council also directed the Monitoring Team to gather information on instances of non-compliance with the measures imposed by resolution 2255 (2015) and to keep the Committee informed of such instances, as well as to facilitate, upon request by Member States, assistance on capacity-building. In addition, the Council encouraged Committee members to address issues of non-compliance and bring them to the attention of the Monitoring Team or the Committee and directed the Monitoring Team to provide recommendations to the Committee on actions taken to respond to non-compliance.[50] For more information on the work of the Committee, see its annual report for 2022.[51] More information on the work of the Monitoring Team can be found in its thirteenth report.[52]

Committee established pursuant to resolution 2048 (2012) concerning Guinea-Bissau

During 2022, no changes were made to the mandate of the Committee established pursuant to resolution 2048 (2012). The Committee continued to oversee the implementation of the travel ban, designate individuals who met the listing criteria contained in resolution 2048 (2012) and consider and decide on requests for exemptions from the sanctions measures. For more information on the work of the Committee, see its annual report for 2022.[53]

Committee established pursuant to resolution 2127 (2013) concerning the Central African Republic

In 2022, the mandate of the Committee established pursuant to resolution 2127 (2013) remained unchanged.[54] For more information on the work of the Committee, see its annual report for 2022.[55]

During the period under review, the Council adopted, not unanimously, resolution 2648 (2022), by which it extended the mandate of the Panel of Experts on the Central African Republic until 31 August 2023, requested the Panel to provide periodic reports and expressed its intention to review the mandate of the Panel and to take appropriate action regarding its further extension no later than 31 July 2023.[56]

---

[47] For more information, see part I, sects. 14 and 30.

[48] The mandate of the Committee included, inter alia, monitoring implementation, deciding on requests for exemptions and designating individuals and entities subject to the sanctions measures adopted by the Council, which comprise an arms embargo, an asset freeze and a travel ban, and conducting periodic and specialized reviews of the entries on the sanctions list. The Committee was supported by the Analytical Support and Sanctions Monitoring Team.

[49] Resolution 2665 (2022), para. 2. See the annex to the resolution for a comprehensive overview of the mandate of the Monitoring Team, which included, inter alia, supporting the Committee, gathering and analysing information on compliance with the sanctions measures, providing to the Committee information relevant to the listing of individuals and entities subject to the sanctions measures, assisting the Committee in regularly reviewing names on the sanctions list and providing periodic reports.

[50] Resolution 2665 (2022), para. 3.

[51] S/2022/969.

[52] S/2022/419.

[53] S/2022/996.

[54] The mandate of the Committee included, inter alia, monitoring and discussing implementation, processing notifications, deciding on exemptions, gathering and analysing information on compliance and designating individuals and entities subject to the sanctions measures adopted by the Council, which comprise an arms embargo, an asset freeze and a travel ban.

[55] S/2022/987.

[56] Resolution 2648 (2022), paras. 6 and 7. The mandate of the Panel of Experts included supporting the Committee, gathering and analysing information on compliance, monitoring implementation, providing information relevant to listing and providing periodic reports.

Expressing concern about reports of illicit transnational trafficking networks that continued to fund and supply armed groups in the Central African Republic, and noting the increasing use of explosive ordnance, including improvised explosive devices and landmines, the Council reiterated its request to the Panel to devote special attention to the analysis of such networks and to threats relating to explosive ordnance, in cooperation with other panels or groups of experts established by the Council.[57] The Council also strongly condemned attacks committed by armed groups of the Coalition des patriotes pour le changement and requested the Panel to consider proposing or updating further statements of cases for possible designation.[58] The Council further reaffirmed the Committee provisions and the reporting and review provisions as set out in resolution 2399 (2018) and extended by resolution 2588 (2021).[59]

In its resolution 2659 (2022), by which it extended the mandate of United Nations Multidimensional Integrated Stabilization Mission in the Central African Republic (MINUSCA), the Council reiterated the Mission's tasks to assist the Committee and the Panel of Experts, including by monitoring the implementation of sanctions measures, supporting the Panel in the collection of information on acts of incitement to violence, in particular on religious or ethnic grounds, and ensuring unhindered access and safety for the Panel of Experts.[60]

Committee established pursuant to resolution 2140 (2014)

In 2022, the mandate of the Committee established pursuant to resolution 2140 (2014) remained largely unchanged.[61] For more information on the work of the Committee, see its annual report for 2022.[62]

During the period under review, the Council adopted, not unanimously, resolution 2624 (2022), in which it reaffirmed its decision that the Committee might, on a case-by-case basis, exempt any activity from the sanctions measures imposed by the Council if the Committee determined that such exemption was necessary to facilitate the work of the United Nations and other humanitarian organizations in Yemen.[63] By the same resolution, the Council also extended the mandate of the Panel of Experts on Yemen until 28 March 2023, requested the Panel to provide periodic reports and expressed its intention to review the mandate of the Panel and to take appropriate action regarding its further extension no later than 28 February 2023.[64] The Council further directed the Panel to cooperate with other relevant expert groups established by the Council to support the work of its sanctions committees, in particular the Analytical Support and Sanctions Monitoring Team.[65]

Committee established pursuant to resolution 2206 (2015) concerning South Sudan

In 2022, the mandate of the Committee established pursuant to resolution 2206 (2015) remained unchanged.[66] For more information on the work of the Committee, see its annual report for 2022.[67]

During the period under review, the Council adopted, not unanimously, resolution 2633 (2022), by which it extended the mandate of the Panel of Experts on South Sudan until 1 July 2023 and requested

[57] Resolution 2648 (2022), para. 9.
[58] Ibid., para. 8.
[59] Ibid., para. 12. See also resolution 2399 (2018), paras. 26 and 41, and resolution 2588 (2021), para. 11.
[60] Resolution 2659 (2022), para. 37 (a)–(d). For more information on the mandate of MINUSCA, see part X, sect. I.
[61] The mandate of the Committee included, inter alia, monitoring and discussing implementation, deciding on exemptions, gathering and analysing information on compliance and designating individuals and entities subject to the sanctions measures adopted by the Council, which comprise an arms embargo, an asset freeze and a travel ban.
[62] S/2022/1006.
[63] Resolution 2624 (2022), para. 6.
[64] Ibid., paras. 15 and 16. The mandate of the Panel of Experts included supporting the Committee, gathering and analysing information on compliance, monitoring implementation, providing information relevant to listing and providing periodic reports.
[65] Resolution 2624 (2022), para. 17.
[66] The mandate of the Committee included monitoring implementation, deciding on requests for exemptions and designating individuals and entities subject to the sanctions measures adopted by the Council, which comprise an arms embargo, an asset freeze and a travel ban.
[67] S/2022/965.

the Panel to provide periodic reports.[68] The Council reiterated its request to the Secretariat to include the necessary gender expertise on the Panel and encouraged the Panel to integrate gender as a cross-cutting issue across its investigations and reporting.[69] The Council also encouraged the Committee to consider, where and when appropriate, visits to selected countries by the Chair and/or Committee members.[70]

In its resolutions 2625 (2022) and 2633 (2022), the Council encouraged the timely exchange of information between the United Nations Mission in South Sudan (UNMISS) and the Panel of Experts and requested the Mission to assist the Committee and the Panel regarding the measures adopted in relation to South Sudan.[71]

Committee established pursuant to resolution 2374 (2017) concerning Mali

In 2022, the mandate of the Committee established pursuant to resolution 2374 (2017) remained unchanged.[72] For more information on the work of the Committee, see its annual report for 2022.[73]

In its resolution 2649 (2022), by which the mandate of the Panel of Experts on Mali was extended until 30 September 2023, the Council requested the Panel to provide periodic reports and expressed its intention to review the mandate of the Panel and to take appropriate action regarding its further extension no later than 31 August 2023.[74] The Council also reiterated its request to the United Nations Multidimensional Integrated Stabilization Mission in Mali (MINUSMA) to assist and exchange information with the Committee and the Panel of Experts.[75]

In its resolution 2640 (2022), by which the mandate of MINUSMA was extended, the Council encouraged the Panel of Experts to identify parties responsible for engaging, directly or indirectly, in actions or policies referred to in paragraph 8 of resolution 2374 (2017), through its regular reporting and interim updates.[76] The Council also tasked MINUSMA with assisting and exchanging information with the Committee and the Panel and to assist in raising awareness on their roles and mandates.[77]

Committee established pursuant to resolution 2653 (2022) concerning Haiti

In July, in its resolution 2645 (2022), the Council expressed its readiness to take, within 90 days from the adoption of the resolution, appropriate measures that could include asset freeze or travel ban measures against those who engaged in or supported gang violence, criminal activities or human rights abuses or who otherwise took action that undermined the peace, stability and security of Haiti and the region.[78]

In October, by its resolution 2653 (2022), the Council imposed, for an initial period of one year, a travel ban, an asset freeze and a targeted arms embargo against individuals and entities designated as responsible for or complicit in, or having engaged in, directly or indirectly, actions that threatened the peace, security or stability of Haiti.[79] By the same resolution, the Council established a Committee,

---

[68] Resolution 2633 (2022), para. 18. The mandate of the Panel of Experts included supporting the Committee, gathering, examining and analysing information on compliance and, as of 2018, information regarding the supply, sale or transfer of arms and related materiel and related military or other assistance, providing information relevant to the listing of individuals and entities subject to the sanctions measures and providing periodic reports.

[69] Resolution 2633 (2022), para. 19.

[70] Ibid., para. 17.

[71] Resolution 2625 (2022), para. 20 (i), and resolution 2633 (2022), para. 22. For more information on the mandate of UNMISS, see part X, sect. I.

[72] The mandate of the Committee included, inter alia, monitoring implementation, deciding on requests for exemptions and designating individuals and entities subject to the sanctions measures adopted by the Council, which comprise an asset freeze and a travel ban.

[73] S/2022/978.

[74] Resolution 2649 (2022), paras. 4 and 5. The mandate of the Panel of Experts included, inter alia, supporting the Committee, gathering and analysing information, in particular on non-compliance, providing information relevant to the listing of individuals and entities subject to the sanctions measures and providing periodic reports.

[75] Resolution 2649 (2022), para. 4. For more information on the mandate of MINUSMA, see part X, sect. I.

[76] Resolution 2640 (2022), paras. 4 and 15.

[77] Ibid., para. 27 (b).

[78] Resolution 2645 (2022), para. 5.

[79] Resolution 2653 (2022), paras. 3, 6, 11 and 15.

consisting of all the members of the Council, mandated to designate those individuals and entities to be subject to the sanctions measures and to consider and decide on requests for exemptions.[80] The Council also mandated the Committee to monitor the implementation of the sanctions measures and to examine and take appropriate action on information regarding alleged violations of or non-compliance with the measures.[81] Finally, the Committee was tasked with encouraging a dialogue with interested Member States, in particular those in the region, and to cooperate with other relevant sanctions committees.[82]

By the same resolution, the Council established a Panel of Experts, for an initial period of 13 months, to support the work of the Committee.[83] The Panel was mandated to provide the Committee with information relevant to the designation of individuals who might be responsible for or complicit in, or having engaged in, directly or indirectly, actions that threatened the peace, security or stability of Haiti. Furthermore, the Council tasked the Panel with assisting the Committee in refining and updating information on the list of individuals and entities subject to the sanctions measures imposed by the resolution, and also tasked the Panel with gathering, examining and analysing information regarding the implementation of the sanctions measures.[84] The Council also directed the Panel to cooperate with the United Nations Integrated Office in Haiti, the United Nations Office on Drugs and Crime, the Caribbean Community and relevant expert groups established by the Council.[85] The Council requested the Panel to provide periodic reports, and a final report no later than 15 September 2023.[86] In addition, in December 2022, the Council appointed the Chair of the Committee, and the Secretary-General appointed the four members of the Panel of Experts.[87]

2. Other committees

During the period under review, both the Committee established pursuant to resolution 1373 (2001) concerning counter-terrorism and the Counter-Terrorism Committee Executive Directorate established by resolution 1535 (2004) to support the Counter-Terrorism Committee remained active. On 28 and 29 October, the Counter-Terrorism Committee held a special meeting in Mumbai and New Delhi, India, on countering the use of new and emerging technologies for terrorist purposes. At the conclusion of the meeting, the Counter-Terrorism Committee adopted the Delhi Declaration on countering the use of new and emerging technologies for terrorist purposes. On 15 December, the Council adopted a presidential statement, in which it welcomed the adoption of the Delhi Declaration by the Counter-Terrorism Committee and called upon the Committee to consider developing, with the support of the Counter-Terrorism Committee Executive Directorate, within a reasonable period, a set of non-binding guiding principles, as provided in the Declaration.[88]

The Committee established pursuant to resolution 1540 (2004) also remained active in 2022, holding seven in-person meetings during the year. The Council adopted resolutions 2622 (2022) and 2663 (2022) in relation to the mandate of the Committee.

Committee established pursuant to resolution 1373 (2001) concerning counter-terrorism

On 30 June, the Chair of the Committee established pursuant to resolution 1373 (2001) transmitted to the President of the Security Council, pursuant to resolution 2395 (2017), the report of the Counter-Terrorism Committee Executive Directorate on the activities and achievements of the Counter-Terrorism Committee and the Executive Directorate for the period 2018 to 2021 and the observations of the Executive Director on the way forward to enhance the support of the Executive Directorate for the Counter-Terrorism Committee, the Council and Member States.[89]

On 28 and 29 October, the Counter-Terrorism Committee held a special meeting in Mumbai and New Delhi, India, on countering the use of new and emerging technologies for terrorist purposes. At the

[80] Ibid., paras. 19 (a) and (c).
[81] Ibid., paras. 19 (a) and (h).
[82] Ibid., paras. 19 (f) and 20.
[83] Ibid., para. 21.
[84] Ibid., paras. 21 (a), (b) and (d).
[85] Ibid., para. 22.
[86] Ibid., paras. 4 and 21 (c).
[87] See S/2022/2/Rev.4 and S/2022/1033.
[88] S/PRST/2022/7, penultimate paragraph.
[89] S/2022/529, annexes I and II.

conclusion of the meeting, the Committee adopted the Delhi Declaration on countering the use of new and emerging technologies for terrorist purposes, in which the Committee reaffirmed that terrorism in all forms and manifestations constituted one of the most serious threats to international peace and security and noted with concern the increased use by terrorists and their supporters of the Internet and other information and communications technologies, including social media platforms, for terrorist purposes, such as for recruitment and incitement to commit terrorist acts, as well as for the financing, planning and preparation of their activities.[90] The Committee also noted with additional concern the increasing global misuse of unmanned aerial systems by terrorists to conduct attacks against and incursions into critical infrastructure and soft targets or public places, and to traffic drugs and arms.[91] The Committee further decided to work on recommendations on the three themes of the special meeting, namely, countering terrorist exploitation of information and communications technologies and emerging technologies; threats and opportunities related to new payment technologies and fundraising methods; and threats posed by the misuse of unmanned aerial systems by terrorists, after the conclusion of the special meeting.[92] The Committee also resolved to continue to assist Member States, with the support of the Counter-Terrorism Committee Executive Directorate, to achieve the full implementation of all relevant Council resolutions that pertained to countering the use of new and emerging technologies for terrorist purposes, while respecting human rights and fundamental freedoms.[93] The Committee also expressed its intention to develop, with the support of the Executive Directorate, a set of non-binding guiding principles, with a view to assisting Member States in countering the threat posed by the use of new and emerging technologies for terrorist purposes, including by compiling good practices on the opportunities offered by the same set of technologies to counter the threat, consistent with international human rights and international humanitarian law.[94] In addition, the Committee requested the Executive Directorate to produce a gap analysis, for consideration by the Committee, on the capacities of Member States to counter the use of new and emerging technologies for terrorist purposes.[95]

In a letter dated 30 November addressed to the Secretary-General, the Council took note of the intention of the Secretary-General in his letter dated 10 August,[96] to appoint Natalia Gherman of the Republic of Moldova as the Executive Director of the Counter-Terrorism Committee Executive Directorate.[97]

On 15 December, the Council adopted a presidential statement, in which it welcomed the adoption of the Delhi Declaration by the Counter-Terrorism Committee and called upon the Committee to consider developing, with the support of the Counter-Terrorism Committee Executive Directorate, within a reasonable period, a set of non-binding guiding principles, as provided in the Declaration.[98]

On 23 December, the Chair of the Counter-Terrorism Committee transmitted to the President of the Security Council the joint report of the Counter-Terrorism Committee Executive Directorate and the Office of Counter-Terrorism, prepared pursuant to paragraph 24 of resolution 2617 (2021).[99] The Chair indicated that, following consideration of the report at its 366th meeting, the Committee had agreed to recommend that the report be issued as a document of the Security Council and that the President of the Council address a letter to the President of the General Assembly annexing the report, to be brought to the attention of the Assembly in the context of the United Nations Global Counter-Terrorism Strategy review.

Committee established pursuant to resolution 1540 (2004)

In 2022, the Council adopted resolutions 2622 (2022) and 2663 (2022), related to the mandate of the Committee established pursuant to resolution 1540 (2004).

---

[90] S/2022/998, paras. 1 and 5.
[91] Ibid., para. 7.
[92] Ibid., para. 30.
[93] Ibid., para. 31.
[94] Ibid., para. 32.
[95] Ibid., para. 35.
[96] S/2022/900.
[97] S/2022/901.
[98] S/PRST/2022/7, penultimate paragraph.
[99] S/2022/1002.

At a meeting held on 14 March,[100] in connection with the item entitled "Non-proliferation of weapons of mass destruction", the Council heard a briefing by the Chair of the Committee on the activities of the Committee in promoting the full and effective implementation of resolution 1540 (2004) and on the role of the Committee in facilitating assistance to Member States to fulfil their obligations pursuant to the resolution The Chair noted that, as one of its main priorities, the Committee continued to conduct the comprehensive review of resolution 1540 (2004), in accordance with the provisions of resolution 1977 (2011). The Chair informed the Council that a central theme of the comprehensive review was the status of the implementation of resolution 1540 (2004) by Member States. In addition, he indicated that the Committee had been addressing its role in facilitating assistance matchmaking, its collaboration with relevant international, regional and subregional organizations and other United Nations bodies and its outreach activities.

In 2022, the Council adopted two resolutions related to the mandate of the Committee. In its resolution 2622 (2022) of 25 February, the Council noted that the comprehensive review on the status of implementation of resolution 1540 (2004) had been postponed due to the coronavirus disease (COVID-19) pandemic, and, acting under Chapter VII of the Charter, decided to extend the mandate of the Committee until 30 November 2022, with the continued assistance of its Group of Experts.[101] In the same resolution, the Council further decided that the Committee, while continuing its work pursuant to its mandate, was to continue to conduct and complete the comprehensive review and submit to the Council a report on the conclusion of the review.[102]

In its resolution 2663 (2022) of 30 November, the Council endorsed the 2022 comprehensive review of the status of implementation of resolution 1540 (2004) and took note of the results as contained in the final report.[103] Acting under Chapter VII of the Charter, the Council decided to extend the mandate of the Committee for a period of 10 years, until 30 November 2032, and further decided that the Committee would conduct comprehensive reviews on the status of implementation of resolution 1540 (2004) both after five years and prior to the renewal of its mandate and would submit to the Council a report upon the conclusion of each of the reviews, with the first review to be held before December 2027.[104] The Council also decided to continue to provide the Committee with the assistance of its Group of Experts to assist the Committee in carrying out its mandate.[105] To facilitate the implementation of resolution 1540 (2004), the Council encouraged the Committee to continue to actively engage in dialogue with Member States on the implementation of the resolution, and reiterated that the Committee was to continue to intensify its efforts to promote full implementation by all States of the resolution, through its programme of work, which included the compilation and general examination of information on the status of implementation.[106] The Council also encouraged the Committee to develop and review, as appropriate, voluntary technical reference guides, which Member States could take into consideration in their implementation of resolution 1540 (2004), reiterating also its request that the Committee take note in its work of the continually evolving nature of the risks of proliferation, including those posed by non-State actors.[107] To facilitate technical assistance to Member States, the Council directed the Committee to periodically review, as appropriate, the role, efficiency and effectiveness of the Committee's mechanism for matching offers and requests for assistance, as well as the status of assistance matters, and in that connection requested the Committee to maintain an updated comprehensive list of assistance providers.[108] Moreover, the Council requested the Committee to continue to organize and participate in outreach events on the implementation of resolution 1540 (2004) and to convene regular open briefings at least once a year, or as needed, for Member States and international, regional and subregional organizations.[109] The Council further requested the Committee to make information and assistance-related programmes

---

[100] See S/PV.8993.
[101] Resolution 2622 (2022), third preambular paragraph and para. 1.
[102] Ibid., para. 2.
[103] Resolution 2663 (2022), penultimate preambular paragraph. See also S/2022/899.
[104] Resolution 2663 (2022), paras. 2 and 3.
[105] Ibid., para. 5.
[106] Ibid., paras. 9 and 12.
[107] Ibid., paras. 13 and 15.
[108] Ibid., paras. 17 and 18.
[109] Ibid., paras. 25 and 26.

relevant to the implementation of resolution 1540 (2004) widely available to and easily accessible for Member States.[110]

At year end, the Committee had not agreed on its programme of work, covering the period from 1 February 2022 to 31 January 2023, as requested by resolutions 1540 (2004), 1673 (2006), 1810 (2008), 1977 (2011), 2325 (2016) and 2663 (2022). On 31 December, the Committee submitted the 2022 review of the implementation of resolution 1540 (2004), pursuant to paragraph 9 of resolution 1977 (2011), paragraph 2 of resolution 2325 (2016) and paragraph 4 of resolution 2663 (2022).[111]

II. Working groups

Note

During the period under review, working groups of the Council continued to meet. As in the case of the committees, the working groups were composed of all 15 members of the Council and meetings were held in private unless otherwise decided. Decisions were reached by consensus. In 2022, four of the six existing working groups of the Council held regular meetings.[112]

Table 4 provides information on the establishment, mandate, key provisions and chairmanship and vice-chairmanship of the informal and ad hoc working groups of the Council in 2022.

Table 3
Working groups of the Security Council, 2022

Establishment	*Mandate*	*Chair (Vice-Chair)*
Working Group on Peacekeeping Operations		
Established on 31 January 2001 (S/PRST/2001/3)	To address both generic peacekeeping issues relevant to the responsibilities of the Council, and technical aspects of individual peacekeeping operations, without prejudice to the competence of the Special Committee on Peacekeeping Operations Where appropriate, to seek the views of the troop-contributing countries, including through meetings between the Working Group and the troop-contributing countries, so that their views are taken into account by the Council	Ghana (United Kingdom)
Ad Hoc Working Group on Conflict Prevention and Resolution in Africa		
Established in March 2002 (S/2002/207)[a]	To monitor the implementation of recommendations contained in the presidential statement S/PRST/2002/2 and previous presidential statements and resolutions regarding conflict prevention and resolution in Africa To propose recommendations on the enhancement of cooperation between the Security Council and the Economic and Social Council as well as with other United Nations agencies dealing with Africa To examine, in particular, regional and cross-conflict issues that affect the Council's work on African conflict prevention and resolution To propose recommendations to the Security Council to enhance cooperation in conflict prevention and resolution, between the United Nations and regional (Organization of African Unity [now African Union]) and subregional organizations	Kenya (Gabon)

[110] Ibid., para. 27.
[111] S/2022/1034, annex.
[112] Eighteen meetings were held. The Working Group on Peacekeeping Operations and the Working Group established pursuant to resolution 1566 (2004) did not meet during the period under review.

Establishment	Mandate	Chair (Vice-Chair)
Working Group established pursuant to resolution 1566 (2004)		
Established on 8 October 2004 (resolution 1566 (2004))	To consider and submit recommendations to the Council on practical measures to be imposed upon individuals, groups or entities involved in or associated with terrorist activities, other than those designated by the Committee established pursuant to resolution 1267 (1999) concerning Al-Qaida and the Taliban and associated individuals and entities, including more effective procedures considered to be appropriate for bringing them to justice through prosecution or extradition, freezing their financial assets, preventing their movement through the territories of Member States, and preventing supply to them of all types of arms and related material, and on the procedures for implementing these measures To consider the possibility of establishing an international fund to compensate victims of terrorist acts and their families, which might be financed through voluntary contributions, which could consist in part of assets seized from terrorist organizations, their members and sponsors, and submit its recommendations to the Council	United Arab Emirates (France, India, Russian Federation)
Working Group on Children and Armed Conflict		
Established on 26 July 2005 (resolution 1612 (2005))	To review the reports of the monitoring and reporting mechanism on children and armed conflict To review progress in the development and implementation of the action plans called for in resolutions 1539 (2004) and 1612 (2005) To consider other relevant information presented to it To make recommendations to the Council on possible measures to promote the protection of children affected by armed conflict, including through recommendations on appropriate mandates for peacekeeping missions and recommendations with respect to the parties to the conflict To address requests, as appropriate, to other bodies within the United Nations system for action to support the implementation of resolution 1612 (2005) in accordance with their respective mandates	Norway (Mexico)
Informal Working Group on Documentation and Other Procedural Questions		
Established in June 1993 (no formal decision was taken)	To deal with issues related to documentation and other procedural questions	Albania (United Arab Emirates)
Informal Working Group on International Tribunals		
Established in June 2000 pursuant to a proposal made by some Council members at the 4161st meeting (no formal decision was taken)[b]	To deal with a specific issue pertaining to the statute of the International Tribunal for the Former Yugoslavia and subsequently mandated to deal with other (legal) issues pertaining to the Tribunals	Gabon (Kenya)

[a] In notes by the President of the Security Council, the Council renewed the mandate of the Working Group for periods of one year until 31 December 2011 (see S/2003/1138, S/2004/1031, S/2005/814, S/2007/6, S/2008/795, S/2009/650 and S/2010/654). From that date onward, the Ad Hoc Working Group has continued to meet without the annual renewal of its mandate.

[b] See S/PV.4161.

III. Investigative bodies

Note

During the period under review, the Council extended the mandate of the United Nations Investigative Team to Promote Accountability for Crimes Committed by Da'esh/Islamic State in Iraq and the Levant (UNITAD) for 12 months, until 17 September 2023.[113] The Council did not authorize the establishment of any new investigative bodies.

United Nations Investigative Team to Promote Accountability for Crimes Committed by Da'esh/Islamic State in Iraq and the Levant

UNITAD formally commenced its activities on 20 August 2018.[114] On 26 May and 7 November 2022, the Special Adviser and Head of UNITAD submitted to the Council the eighth and ninth reports on the activities of the Team,[115] which were marked by progress on all investigative lines of inquiry, including the completion of an initial case assessment on the use of chemical and biological weapons by Islamic State in Iraq and the Levant (ISIL/Da'esh) in Iraq, as well as constructive collaboration with Iraqi authorities, including Kurdish entities and other Member States engaged in investigating and prosecuting ISIL/Da'esh perpetrators for their involvement in war crimes, crimes against humanity and genocide.[116] In 2022, the Council held two meetings to hear briefings by the Special Adviser on the activities of UNITAD and its progress in implementing its mandate further to its reports.[117]

In addition, on 15 September, the Council unanimously adopted resolution 2651 (2022), reaffirming resolution 2379 (2017), by which UNITAD had been established, and recalling the terms of reference approved by the Council.[118] By the same resolution, the Council extended the mandate of the Special Adviser and UNITAD until 17 September 2023.[119] As with previous extensions, the Council noted that any further extension of the mandate would be decided at the request of the Government of Iraq, or any other Government that had requested UNITAD to collect evidence of acts that might amount to war crimes, crimes against humanity or genocide committed by ISIL/Da'esh in its territory.[120] In addition, the Special Adviser was requested to continue to submit and present reports to the Council on the activities of the Team every 180 days.[121]

IV. Tribunals

Note

In a note by the President of the Security Council dated 2 February 2018,[122] the Council agreed that issues pertaining to the International Residual Mechanism for Criminal Tribunals would be

---

[113] Resolution 2651 (2022), para. 2.

[114] S/2018/1031, para. 4. For more information on the establishment and history of UNITAD, see *Repertoire, Supplement 2016–2017* to *Supplement 2021*.

[115] S/2022/434 and S/2022/836.

[116] For more information on the investigative priorities, see the previous reports of the Special Adviser and Head of UNITAD (S/2018/1031, S/2019/407, S/2019/878, S/2020/386, S/2020/1107, S/2021/419 and S/2021/974).

[117] See S/PV.9059 and S/PV.9206. For additional information, see part I, sect. 34.

[118] Resolution 2651 (2022), para. 1. For the terms of reference approved by the Council for UNITAD, see S/2018/118, annex.

[119] Resolution 2651 (2022), para. 2.

[120] Ibid. See also resolution 2379 (2017), paras. 2 and 3, and letter dated 12 September 2022 from the representative of Iraq addressed to the Secretary-General (S/2022/687).

[121] Resolution 2651 (2022), para. 3.

[122] S/2018/90.

considered under an item entitled "International Residual Mechanism for Criminal Tribunals",[123] under which would be subsumed the earlier consideration by the Council of issues pertaining to the International Tribunal for the Former Yugoslavia and the International Criminal Tribunal for Rwanda.[124] During the period under review, the Council adopted one presidential statement and one resolution under Chapter VII of the Charter of the United Nations concerning, inter alia, the reappointment of the Prosecutor of the Mechanism and other aspects regarding the management, reporting and completion of functions of the Mechanism. The Council also took note of the intention of the Secretary-General to reappoint 25 judges, including the President of the Mechanism.[125]

Developments in 2022

On 31 March, the Council adopted a presidential statement, in which it recalled its decision that the Mechanism was to operate for an initial period of four years starting from 1 July 2012 and its decision to review the progress of the work of the Mechanism, including in completing its functions, before the end of that initial period and every two years thereafter. The Council also recalled its decision that the Mechanism was to continue to operate for subsequent periods of two years following each such review, unless the Council decided otherwise, and that the Mechanism should be a small, temporary and efficient structure, whose functions and size would diminish over time, with a small number of staff commensurate with its reduced functions.[126]

By its resolution 2637 (2022), adopted under Chapter VII of the Charter, the Council appointed the Prosecutor of the Mechanism, with effect from 1 July 2022 until 30 June 2024.[127] In the resolution, the Council once again emphasized that, in view of the substantially reduced nature of the residual functions, the Mechanism was established to be a small, temporary and efficient structure, whose functions and size would diminish over time, with a small number of staff commensurate with its reduced functions, and requested the Mechanism to continue to be guided in its activities by those elements.[128] In addition, the Council welcomed the report submitted by the Mechanism to the Council pursuant to its presidential statement of 31 March for the purposes of the review of the progress of the work of the Mechanism, including in completing its functions, as required by paragraph 17 of resolution 1966 (2010), and the report of the Office of Internal Oversight Services (OIOS) on the evaluation of the methods and work of the Mechanism.[129] The Council also took note of the conclusions of OIOS on the Mechanism's implementation of the OIOS recommendations and paragraph 9 of resolution 2529 (2020).[130] The Council further noted the views and recommendations made with regard to the Mechanism's work by the Informal Working Group on International Tribunals, requested the Mechanism to take into account those views and implement the recommendations, and listed a series of steps the Mechanism should continue to take to further enhance efficiency and effective and transparent management.[131]

---

[123] By its resolution 1966 (2010), the Council established the Mechanism to carry out the residual functions of the International Tribunal for the Prosecution of Persons Responsible for Serious Violations of International Humanitarian Law Committed in the Territory of the Former Yugoslavia since 1991 (International Tribunal for the Former Yugoslavia) and the International Criminal Tribunal for the Prosecution of Persons Responsible for Genocide and Other Serious Violations of International Humanitarian Law Committed in the Territory of Rwanda and Rwandan Citizens Responsible for Genocide and Other Such Violations Committed in the Territory of Neighbouring States between 1 January and 31 December 1994 (International Criminal Tribunal for Rwanda) after the completion of their mandates. For more information on the activities of the Council during 2022 in connection with the Mechanism, see part I, sect. 25.

[124] See *Repertoire*, *Supplement 2014–2015* to *Supplement 2021*.

[125] For more information on the appointment procedure, see part IV, sect. I.D.

[126] S/PRST/2022/2, second and third paragraphs.

[127] Resolution 2637 (2022), para. 1.

[128] Ibid., para. 7.

[129] Ibid., para. 8. For the report submitted by the Mechanism to the Council pursuant to its presidential statement of 31 March (S/PRST/2022/2, fifth paragraph), see S/2022/319. For the report of OIOS, see S/2022/148.

[130] Resolution 2637 (2022), para. 8.

[131] Ibid., para. 10.

V. Ad hoc commissions

Note

No new commissions were created during 2022. The United Nations Compensation Commission, established pursuant to resolutions 687 (1991) and 692 (1991) to process claims and pay compensation for losses and damage suffered as a direct result of the invasion and occupation of Kuwait by Iraq in 1990 and 1991, fulfilled its mandate in 2022. In a letter dated 10 February,[132] the President of the Governing Council of the Compensation Commission reported that in January 2022 the $52.4 billion in compensation awarded by the Commission had been paid in full and that the sixteenth special session of the Governing Council had been held on 9 February to mark the fulfilment of the mandate of the Commission, after nearly 31 years, and transmitted the final report on the work of the Commission. The President also reported that the Governing Council had adopted decision 277 (2022), in which it had declared that the Government of Iraq had fulfilled its international obligations to compensate all claimants awarded compensation by the Commission for losses and damages suffered as a direct result of the invasion of Kuwait by Iraq. In the same decision, the Governing Council had invited the Security Council to take the necessary action to note that the mandate of the Commission had been fulfilled and that the Commission would be winding down all activities in 2022.

On 22 February, the Council held a meeting under the item entitled "The situation between Iraq and Kuwait",[133] at which the President of the Governing Council presented the final report on the work of the Commission.[134] At the meeting, the Council unanimously adopted resolution 2621 (2022) under Chapter VII of the Charter of the United Nations, in which it decided that the Commission had fulfilled its mandate under resolutions 687 (1991) and 692 (1991) and other relevant resolutions of the Council and reaffirmed that Iraq had fulfilled its international obligations to compensate all claimants awarded compensation by the Commission for direct loss, damage – including environmental damage and the depletion of natural resources – or injury to foreign Governments, nationals and corporations as a result of its unlawful invasion and occupation of Kuwait.[135] By the same resolution, the Council decided to terminate the mandate of the Commission, and, in accordance with decision 277 (2022) of the Governing Council, directed the Commission to conclude the outstanding matters necessary for its closure and for the dissolution of the United Nations Compensation Fund by the end of 2022, and to return to the Government of Iraq any amounts remaining in the Fund at the point of dissolution.[136] The Council also decided to conclude its consideration of compensation by the Commission and that upon completion of outstanding matters, the Commission was to be closed and the Fund was to be dissolved.[137]

In a letter dated 12 December, the President of the Governing Council reported on the outcome of the eighty-ninth and final session of the Governing Council, held in Geneva on 9 December.[138] The President of the Governing Council announced that the Compensation Fund had been closed as at 30 June and that the amount that remained in the Fund had been returned to the Government of Iraq on 2 December. She also indicated that transition arrangements had been made for the Department of Political and Peacebuilding Affairs to receive, beginning in 2023, the progress reports by Jordan, Kuwait and Saudi Arabia, on their environmental remediation and restoration projects being undertaken with compensation awarded by the Commission. She further confirmed that the work of the Governing Council had ended and that the Commission would formally close on 31 December 2022.

---

[132] S/2022/104.

[133] See S/PV.8972. For further details on the Council meeting to consider the final report of the Compensation Commission, see part I, sect. 23.

[134] S/2022/104, annex.

[135] Resolution 2621 (2022), paras. 1 and 2.

[136] Ibid., para. 7.

[137] Ibid., para. 8.

[138] S/2022/941.

VI. Special advisers, envoys and representatives

Note

Section VI provides a list of special advisers, envoys and representatives in whose appointment the Council has been involved and whose mandates relate to the Council's responsibility for the maintenance of international peace and security. Special representatives appointed as heads of peacekeeping or special political missions are covered in part X and those authorized by the General Assembly are covered in part IV. Previous supplements should be consulted for information concerning special advisers, envoys and representatives whose functions have ceased.

During the period under review, the following envoys, advisers and representatives of the Secretary-General continued to exercise their functions:

- Personal Envoy of the Secretary-General for Western Sahara
- Special Adviser to the Secretary-General on Cyprus[139]
- Special Adviser to the Secretary-General on the Prevention of Genocide
- Special Envoy of the Secretary-General for the implementation of Security Council resolution 1559 (2004)[140]
- Special Adviser to the Secretary-General on the Responsibility to Protect
- Special Representative of the Secretary-General on Sexual Violence in Conflict
- Special Envoy of the Secretary-General for the Horn of Africa
- Special Envoy of the Secretary-General for Yemen
- Special Envoy of the Secretary-General for the Great Lakes Region
- Special Adviser and Head of the United Nations Investigative Team to Promote Accountability for Crimes Committed by Da'esh/Islamic State in Iraq and the Levant

In February, through an exchange of letters between the Secretary-General and the President of the Security Council, the Secretary-General appointed a new Special Envoy for the Horn of Africa.[141] In addition, in its resolutions 2618 (2022) and 2646 (2022), the Council welcomed the continuing personal engagement of the Secretary-General and that of his team on the situation in Cyprus, including his proposal for a United Nations envoy to lead further engagement which could provide critical support in the search for common ground with the goal of returning to formal negotiations, and urged the two sides of the conflict to engage actively and with an increased sense of urgency with the Secretary-General and his team towards a mutually acceptable settlement under the auspices of the United Nations, including by reaching an agreement regarding the proposal of the Secretary-General to appoint a United Nations envoy.[142]

Decisions of the Council acknowledging the appointment of special envoys, advisers and representatives of the Secretary-General, their mandate and any developments that occurred during the period under review are listed in table 4.

---

[139] In 2022, the Secretary-General proposed the appointment of a United Nations envoy (see S/2022/534).

[140] The Under-Secretary-General for Political and Peacebuilding Affairs has fulfilled the reporting functions of the Secretary-General to the Security Council regarding resolution 1559 (2004) since the former Special Envoy ended his functions in May 2016.

[141] S/2022/141 and S/2022/142.

[142] Resolutions 2618 (2022) and 2646 (2022), third preambular paragraph and para. 2.

Table 4
Developments relating to special advisers, envoys and representatives, 2022

Establishment/appointment	*Decisions*
Personal Envoy of the Secretary-General for Western Sahara	
S/1997/236 19 March 1997	Resolution 2654 (2022), second, third, fourth, fifth, twelfth and fourteenth preambular paragraphs and paras. 3 and 5
Special Adviser to the Secretary-General on Cyprus	
S/1997/320 17 April 1997	There were no developments in 2022
S/1997/321 21 April 1997	
Special Adviser to the Secretary-General on the Prevention of Genocide	
S/2004/567 12 July 2004	Resolution 2625 (2022), para. 3 (d) (iii)
S/2004/568 13 July 2004	
Special Envoy of the Secretary-General for the implementation of Security Council resolution 1559 (2004)	
S/PRST/2004/36 19 October 2004	There were no developments in 2022
S/2004/974 14 December 2004	
S/2004/975 16 December 2004	
Special Adviser to the Secretary-General on the Responsibility to Protect	
S/2007/721 31 August 2007	There were no developments in 2022
S/2007/722 7 December 2007	
Special Representative of the Secretary-General on Sexual Violence in Conflict	
Resolution 1888 (2009) 30 September 2009	Resolution 2633 (2022), para. 21 Resolution 2659 (2022), nineteenth preambular paragraph and para. 35 (a) (vi)
S/2010/62 29 January 2010	Resolution 2662 (2022), para. 48 Resolution 2666 (2022), para. 7
S/2010/63 2 February 2010	
Special Envoy of the Secretary-General for the Horn of Africa	
S/2018/955 24 October 2018	Resolution 2630 (2022), fifth preambular paragraph
S/2018/979 31 October 2018	

Establishment/appointment	*Decisions*
Special Envoy of the Secretary-General for Yemen	
S/2012/469 18 June 2012 S/2012/470 21 June 2012	Resolution 2624 (2022), seventh and thirteenth preambular paragraphs Resolution 2643 (2022), paras. 3 and 4
Special Envoy of the Secretary-General for the Great Lakes Region	
S/2013/166 15 March 2013 S/2013/167 18 March 2013	S/PRST/2022/4, first paragraph Resolution 2666 (2022), paras. 16, 18, 24 (ii) (j) and 45
Special Adviser and Head of the United Nations Investigative Team to Promote Accountability for Crimes Committed by Da'esh/Islamic State in Iraq and the Levant	
Resolution 2379 (2017) 21 September 2017 S/2018/118 9 February 2018 S/2018/119 13 February 2018	Resolution 2631 (2022), para. 2 (d) Resolution 2651 (2022), paras. 1–3

VII. Peacebuilding Commission

Note

The Peacebuilding Commission was established by the Council in resolution 1645 (2005) of 20 December 2005.[143] During the period under review, the Commission held a total of 27 meetings and produced a total of 65 outcome documents, with a sharp increase in the number of times the Commission submitted advice to the Council (17 times, compared with 9 in the previous session), including in the form of letters and formal briefings.[144] The Commission also undertook two field visits: one to South Sudan by the Chair and Vice-Chairs, and one to Liberia by the Chair of the Commission's Liberia configuration. In 2022, the Commission addressed the situations in Burkina Faso, Burundi, the Central African Republic, Colombia, the Gambia, Guinea-Bissau, Liberia and, for the first time, South Sudan and Timor-Leste. The Commission was also engaged on the regional situations in the Great Lakes region, the Gulf of Guinea, the Lake Chad basin, the Pacific islands, the Sahel and, for the first time, Central Asia.[145]

Appointments to the Organizational Committee

In 2022, Kenya and Mexico were the two elected members of the Council that were selected to participate in the Organizational Committee of the Peacebuilding Commission for a term of one year, until the end of 2022.[146]

[143] In its resolution 1645 (2005), the Council, acting concurrently with the General Assembly, decided that the main purposes of the Peacebuilding Commission would be to, inter alia, bring together all relevant actors within and outside the United Nations involved in peacekeeping and peacebuilding to marshal the resources and advise on and propose integrated strategies for post-conflict peacebuilding and recovery, to focus attention on the reconstruction and institution-building efforts necessary for recovery from conflict, and to provide recommendations and information to improve the coordination of all relevant actors within and outside the United Nations. For more information, see part I, sect. 33.

[144] For the report of the Peacebuilding Commission on its sixteenth session, see S/2023/86, in particular paras. 3, 5 and 29.

[145] Ibid., paras. 6–21.

[146] See S/2022/29.

Developments in 2022

In 2022, consistent with past practice, the Council invited the Chair of the Peacebuilding Commission to provide briefings on the activities of the Commission as described below.[147] In addition, the Chair of the Peacebuilding Commission transmitted written advice from the Commission to the Council in the form of letters addressed to the President of the Security Council on eight occasions (see table 5 below).

In 2022, the Council did not hear briefings by the Chairs of the country-specific configurations of the Commission on the situations that were also on the agenda of the Council. However, the Chair of the Central African Republic configuration addressed a letter to the President of the Security Council transmitting the Commission's advice pertaining to the renewal of the mandate of the United Nations Multidimensional Integrated Stabilization Mission in the Central African Republic.[148] In the letter, the Chair expressed his readiness to provide further information and clarifications, as required, adding that the Peacebuilding Commission, through its Central African Republic configuration, would continue to accompany the Central African Republic and inform the Council on peacebuilding-related developments, as appropriate.

Table 5
Written advice by the Peacebuilding Commission transmitted by means of letters addressed to the President of the Security Council, 2022

Date	*Topic*	*Related Council meeting or document*
11 April	Implementation of resolutions 2532 (2020) and 2565 (2021)	S/2022/307
25 April	The situation in the Great Lakes region	S/2022/353
8 June	The Central African region	S/2022/461
10 October	Cooperation between the United Nations and the African Union	S/2022/750
21 October	The situation in the Great Lakes region	S/2022/789
3 November	Integrating effective resilience-building in peace operations for sustainable peace	S/2022/827
15 November	Peace and security in Africa (Group of Five for the Sahel)	S/2022/860
18 November	Peace and security in Africa: piracy and armed robbery in the Gulf of Guinea	S/2022/872

(i) Briefings and discussions

During a meeting held on 7 July, under the item entitled "Peace consolidation in West Africa",[149] the representative of Bangladesh, in her capacity as Chair of the Peacebuilding Commission, shared the perspective of the Commission on the situation in West Africa and the Sahel. She expressed concern about recent military takeovers in the region and about the persistence of violent incidents perpetrated by non-State armed groups and terrorist groups. She also expressed worry over the expansion of the terrorist groups to the coastal countries, notably in the Gulf of Guinea, and their growing nexus with organized criminal networks and pirates. In that connection, she reiterated the support of th e Commission for the efforts to strengthen the regional maritime security architecture. Concerning the Sahel region, she encouraged greater support for the objectives of the priority investment plan of the Group of Five for the

[147] The practice of inviting the Chairs of country-specific configurations of the Peacebuilding Commission to participate in formal Council meetings was established in the note by the President of the Security Council dated 26 July 2010 (S/2010/507, para. 61) and was reaffirmed in the note by the President dated 30 August 2017 (S/2017/507, para. 95).

[148] S/2022/840.

[149] See S/PV.9086.

Sahel, which incorporated climate change adaptation and governance reform, and called for enhanced efforts to combat terrorism and the prevalent violent extremism that was conducive to terrorism. Regarding the Lake Chad basin region, she stressed the need to increase support for the implementation of the Regional Stabilization, Recovery and Resilience Strategy for Areas Affected by Boko Haram in the Lake Chad Basin Region, with a focus on the critical role of the territorial action plans. She also elaborated on the Commission's country-specific engagements in the Gambia, Liberia and Sierra Leone.

At a meeting held on 27 July, under the item entitled "Peacebuilding and sustaining peace",[150] the Council heard briefings by the representative of Egypt in his capacity as Chair of the Peacebuilding Commission for 2021 and by the representative of Bangladesh in his capacity as Chair of the Peacebuilding Commission for 2022.

The Chair of the Peacebuilding Commission for 2021 gave a briefing to the Council on the annual report of the Commission on its fifteenth session.[151] He reported on efforts by the Commission to operationalize the outcome of the review set forth in the 2020 twin resolutions on the review of the United Nations peacebuilding architecture (General Assembly resolution 75/201 and Security Council resolution 2558 (2020)), including by exploring avenues to strengthen the advisory, bridging and convening roles of the Commission.[152] In that regard, the Commission had further expanded and strengthened its relations with the General Assembly, the Security Council and the Economic and Social Council through the designation of informal coordinators for the Commission's relations with those organs. The Chair of the Peacebuilding Commission for 2022 gave a briefing to the Council on the Commission's programme of work for 2022 and its implementation status over the previous six months. The Chair informed the Council that the Commission had continued its efforts to enhance its advisory and bridging roles with the other main United Nations organs, including by sharing its programme of work with the General Assembly and the Security Council through formal communications from the Chair. He also highlighted an exchange of letters between the Chair of the Peacebuilding Commission and the President of the Security Council[153] in which the Secretary-General was requested to liaise with the Commission in advance of relevant reporting to the Council.

During a meeting held on 8 and 9 August, under the item entitled "Peace and security in Africa",[154] the representative of Bangladesh, in his capacity as Chair of the Peacebuilding Commission, provided updates on the Commission's engagement in the Central African Republic, Liberia, Burundi and the Lake Chad basin in the field of capacity-building. On the basis of those engagements, the Chair shared several observations, including the recognition of the need to increase collective efforts to strengthen effective, accountable and inclusive public service institutions, within the framework of the rule of law, and the importance of ensuring that women, youth and those in vulnerable situations were included in capacity-building efforts at the local, national and regional levels.[155] He further noted that the Commission promoted the role of regional, South-South and triangular cooperation and the sharing of best practices in addressing common challenges to peacebuilding and advancing economic recovery and sustainable development in Africa, and emphasized the commitment of the Commission to work more closely with the African Union and its Peace and Security Council in support of regional strategies and in mobilizing peacebuilding tools to sustain peace.

At a meeting held on 12 October, under the item entitled "Identical letters dated 19 January 2016 from the Permanent Representative of Colombia to the United Nations addressed to the Secretary-General and the President of the Security Council (S/2016/53)",[156] the representative of Bangladesh, in his capacity as Chair of the Peacebuilding Commission, drawing on the Commission's engagements with Colombia, shared the views of the Commission on peacebuilding efforts in the country following the ratification of the Final Agreement for Ending the Conflict and Building a Stable and Lasting Peace in 2016. He expressed the Commission's recognition of the Government's determination to reactivate the

---

[150] See S/PV.9101.
[151] S/2022/89.
[152] See S/PV.9101.
[153] S/2022/202 and S/2022/250.
[154] See S/PV.9106 and S/PV.9106 (Resumption 1).
[155] See S/PV.9106.
[156] See S/PV.9151.

dialogue between the signatory parties and civil society, adding that the Commission welcomed the Government's commitment to reduce inequality and that it underlined the importance of inclusive approaches to addressing inequalities as drivers of conflict. He added that the Commission encouraged the full and effective use of mechanisms that drew on the inputs of Colombian civil society actors, victims and former combatants to build consensus towards the success of peace efforts, and that it welcomed the invaluable and complementary support provided by the United Nations Verification Mission in Colombia and the United Nations country team. He added that the Commission welcomed the decision by the Government and the Ejército de Liberación Nacional to resume peace dialogues and reiterated the commitment of the Commission, within its mandate, to continue to accompany Colombia in its peacebuilding efforts.

The Chair of the Peacebuilding Commission did not participate in informal interactive dialogues of Council members in 2022, departing from recent practice.[157]

(ii) Decisions

The Council referred to the Peacebuilding Commission and its mandate in several decisions adopted under country- and region-specific items. No decisions of the Council adopted under thematic items contained references to the Peacebuilding Commission.

On 31 May, under the item entitled "Peace and security in Africa", the Council adopted resolution 2634 (2022), in which it welcomed the interest given by the Peacebuilding Commission to the issue of piracy and its cost to States in the region through economic impacts on trade, investments, development and growth, and encouraged the Commission to continue to support, upon request and within its mandate, efforts by States of the Gulf of Guinea and regional and subregional organizations to consolidate peace in and around the Gulf of Guinea.[158]

On 31 August, under the same item, the Council adopted a presidential statement, in which it reiterated its support for the work of the Peacebuilding Commission, acknowledged the importance of strong coordination, coherence and cooperation with the Commission and commended the Commission's continued engagement with the countries and regions in Africa in enhancing capacity in the areas of inclusive peacebuilding; socioeconomic development; disarmament, demobilization and reintegration; security sector reform; institutions of justice; and national reconciliation, in line with national peacebuilding priorities. The Council also emphasized that such engagement should continue to be guided by the principles of national ownership and meaningful partnerships with subregional and regional organizations.[159]

On 27 October, under the item entitled "Identical letters dated 19 January 2016 from the Permanent Representative of Colombia to the United Nations addressed to the Secretary-General and the President of the Security Council (S/2016/53)", the Council adopted resolution 2655 (2022), in which it took note of the engagement of the Peacebuilding Commission with the Government of Colombia and looked forward to further cooperation, including with relevant United Nations agencies, in order to ensure an integrated and coherent approach to the comprehensive implementation of the Final Agreement for Ending the Conflict and Building a Stable and Lasting Peace.[160]

On 28 October, under the item entitled "The situation in Libya", the Council adopted resolution 2656 (2022), in which it encouraged further international support and regional cooperation between Libya, neighbouring countries and relevant United Nations bodies, including the Peacebuilding Commission, in support of peacebuilding and sustaining peace in the country and the region.[161]

---

[157] For further information on informal interactive dialogues in which the Chair of the Peacebuilding Commission has participated, see *Repertoire*, *Supplement 2012–2013* to *Supplement 2021*. The Chair also gave a briefing at an Arria-formula meeting on transitioning from conflict and fragility into peace through sustainable development, held on 20 December (S/2023/86, para. 29). For more information on Arria-formula meetings, see part II, sect. I.C.

[158] Resolution 2634 (2022), tenth preambular paragraph and para. 14.

[159] S/PRST/2022/6, seventh paragraph.

[160] Resolution 2655 (2022), fourth preambular paragraph.

[161] Resolution 2656 (2022), fifth preambular paragraph.

On 14 November, under the item entitled "The situation in the Central African Republic", the Council adopted resolution 2659 (2022), in which it stressed the valuable role of the Commission in offering strategic advice, providing observations for the Council's consideration and fostering a more coherent, coordinated and integrated approach to international peacebuilding efforts.[162]

VIII. Subsidiary organs of the Security Council proposed but not established

During the period under review, there was one instance of a subsidiary organ of the Council being proposed but not established.

On 2 November, at a meeting held under the item entitled "Threats to international peace and security",[163] the Council considered a draft resolution submitted by the Russian Federation concerning the claims against the United States and Ukraine contained in the complaint of the Russian Federation regarding the compliance with obligations under the Convention on the Prohibition of the Development, Production and Stockpiling of Bacteriological (Biological) and Toxin Weapons and on their Destruction in the context of the activities of biological laboratories in the territory of Ukraine.[164]

The draft resolution was not adopted, owing to the negative vote of 3 permanent members of the Council and the abstention of 10 non-permanent members.[165] By the draft resolution, the Council would have set up a commission consisting of all members of the Council to investigate the claims against the United States and Ukraine contained in the complaint of the Russian Federation regarding the compliance with obligations under the Convention in the context of the activities of biological laboratories in the territory of Ukraine. The commission would have presented a report to the Council containing recommendations by 30 November 2022 and would have informed the States parties to the Convention at the ninth Review Conference of the results of the investigation.

Speaking before the vote as penholder of the draft resolution, the representative of the Russian Federation noted that it was a considerable milestone for the Council and that it would show whether the Council was ready to act in line with the Convention.[166] He also made reference to a prior discussion held on 27 October, during which the Russian Federation had explained the contents of the complaint lodged on 24 October under the Convention.[167] He also denounced the derailing of the negotiations, noting that Western countries were simply fearful of establishing the kind of commission that would consider the materials presented by the Russian Federation and adding that objections had also been raised with regard to the fact that the commission would consist of all members of the Council.[168] After the vote, the representative of the Russian Federation affirmed that, regardless of the outcome of the vote, his delegation retained the questions for the United States and Ukraine and would continue to further act within the framework of the Convention and make the efforts needed to establish all the facts having to do with the violations by the United States and Ukraine of their obligations thereunder.

After the vote, other Council members also intervened to explain their votes. In explaining their abstentions, several representatives[169] noted that the condition set forth in article VI of the Convention, namely, that the party alleging violations of the Convention must provide credible evidence to trigger an investigation, had not been met. The representative of Mexico explained that no State could be judge and jury of any commission that claimed to be independent and objective, adding that the Russian Federation

[162] Resolution 2659 (2022), para. 18.
[163] See S/PV.9180.
[164] S/2022/821.
[165] The draft resolution received 2 votes in favour (China and Russian Federation), 3 against (France, United Kingdom and United States) and 10 abstentions (Albania, Brazil, Gabon, Ghana, India, Ireland, Kenya, Mexico, Norway and United Arab Emirates).
[166] See S/PV.9180.
[167] See S/PV.9171. See also S/2022/796.
[168] See S/PV.9180.
[169] Mexico, Ireland, Albania, Norway, Brazil and Ghana.

should be excluded, as it was one of the parties involved in the armed conflict. The representative of India explained his abstention by referring to his country's position at the consultative meeting under article V of the Convention held in Geneva in September, adding that any matter relating to the obligations under the Convention should be addressed in accordance with its provisions and through consultations and cooperation between the relevant parties. The representative of the United Arab Emirates explained that, in the absence of a broad agreement on the triggers and modalities for proceeding under article VI, his country chose to abstain in the voting on the draft resolution.

Explaining her vote against, the representative of the United States said that the draft was based on disinformation, dishonesty, bad faith and a total lack of respect for the Council, noting that the Russian Federation had failed to provide any credible evidence to support the false allegations. The representative of the United Kingdom, who had also voted against, explained that the allegations by the Russian Federation of United States and Ukrainian biological activities had been given a full hearing in Geneva in September, adding that the allegations had no credible basis in fact. Similarly, the representative of France stated that the allegations by the Russian Federation were completely groundless and supplemented his explanation of his country's negative vote by noting that the so-called evidence had already been assessed in detail and that it did not merit further consideration.

Explaining his country's vote in favour, the representative of China said that the Russian Federation had submitted its complaint to the Council and had requested that the Council initiate an investigation, which was reasonable and legitimate and should not be blocked. He also expressed his delegation's belief that a fair and transparent investigation by the Council could effectively address compliance concerns and help to uphold the authority and effectiveness of the Convention.

Part X

Subsidiary organs of the Security Council: peacekeeping operations and special political missions

Contents

Introductory note

Article 29

The Security Council may establish such subsidiary organs as it deems necessary for the performance of its functions.

Rule 28

The Security Council may appoint a commission or committee or a rapporteur for a specified question.

The powers of the Security Council to establish subsidiary organs are set out in Article 29 of the Charter of the United Nations and reflected in rule 28 of its provisional rules of procedure. Part X of the present Supplement covers decisions of the Council relating to field-based subsidiary organs that the Council established for the performance of its functions under the Charter and that were active during 2022. These field-based subsidiary organs are divided into two categories: peacekeeping operations (covered in section I); and special political missions (covered in section II).

Other subsidiary organs, such as committees, working groups, investigative bodies, tribunals, ad hoc commissions, special advisers, envoys, representatives and coordinators, and the Peacebuilding Commission, are covered in part IX. Peace operations led by regional organizations are covered in part VIII, which also covers the Council's cooperation with regional organizations.

Peacekeeping operations and special political missions covered in part X are presented by region and in the order in which they were established. Successor missions are listed immediately after their predecessors. The introduction to each main section includes overview tables identifying the mandates assigned to each mission (tables 1, 2, 4 and 5) and provides an analysis of the key trends and developments during the reporting period. The mandates of the missions are presented in those tables according to 21 categories of mandated tasks, which are based exclusively on the language of the decisions of the Council and do not necessarily reflect the specific structure or activities of the mission. The categories are provided only as a convenience for readers and do not reflect any practice or position of the Council. The introduction to section I includes an overview table of changes to the composition of peacekeeping operations during the reporting period (table 3).

Subsections provide a summary of major developments concerning the mandate and composition of each mission, reflecting the decisions of the Council adopted during the period under review. For information on the mandate and composition of missions in the past, see previous supplements to the *Repertoire*.

I. Peacekeeping operations

Note

Section I is focused on the decisions adopted by the Council during the period under review concerning the establishment and termination of peacekeeping operations, as well as changes to their mandates and composition.

Overview of peacekeeping operations during 2022

During the period under review, the Council oversaw 12 peacekeeping operations.[1] Six of the operations were in Africa, three in the Middle East, two in Europe and one in Asia. The Council did not establish or terminate any operations in 2022.

Extensions of mandates

The Council extended the mandates of the following nine peacekeeping operations:

- United Nations Mission for the Referendum in Western Sahara (MINURSO)
- United Nations Organization Stabilization Mission in the Democratic Republic of the Congo (MONUSCO)
- United Nations Interim Security Force for Abyei (UNISFA)
- United Nations Mission in South Sudan (UNMISS)
- United Nations Multidimensional Integrated Stabilization Mission in Mali (MINUSMA)
- United Nations Multidimensional Integrated Stabilization Mission in the Central African Republic (MINUSCA)
- United Nations Peacekeeping Force in Cyprus (UNFICYP)
- United Nations Disengagement Observer Force (UNDOF)
- United Nations Interim Force in Lebanon (UNIFIL)

The resolutions concerning the mandate of four peacekeeping operations that were extended by the Council in 2022, namely, MINUSCA, MINUSMA, MINURSO and UNMISS, were not adopted unanimously. The mandates of the United Nations Military Observer Group in India and Pakistan (UNMOGIP), the United Nations Interim Administration Mission in Kosovo (UNMIK) and the United Nations Truce Supervision Organization (UNTSO) remained open-ended.

Mandates of peacekeeping operations: differences in scope

In 2022, the mandates of peacekeeping operations continued to vary considerably depending on their scope and complexity. In that regard, the Council reauthorized the four largest missions, MINUSCA, MINUSMA, MONUSCO and UNMISS, to use all necessary means to implement their mandates, which covered a broad array of tasks.[2] The mandates of all four missions continued to include the protection of civilians, the protection and promotion of human rights, the facilitation of humanitarian assistance and the protection of United Nations personnel and equipment. The Council retained the implementation of peace agreements and political transitions as priorities for MINUSCA, MINUSMA and UNMISS, while

[1] For Council decisions and deliberations relating to the item entitled "United Nations peacekeeping operations", see part I, sect. 24. For Council discussions concerning individual peacekeeping operations, see the respective country-specific studies in part I.

[2] In connection with MINUSCA, resolution 2659 (2022), para. 34; in connection with MINUSMA, resolution 2640 (2022), para. 17; in connection with MONUSCO, resolution 2666 (2022), para. 22; and, in connection with UNMISS, resolution 2625 (2022), para. 3.

MINUSCA, MINUSMA and MONUSCO remained focused on supporting the stabilization and the extension of State authority.

The mandates of the remaining eight peacekeeping operations remained relatively narrow by comparison. UNIFIL and UNISFA, as interim security forces, remained focused on observing the redeployment of forces and maintaining security within their areas of responsibility. Both missions were reauthorized to use force in fulfilling only specific tasks such as the protection of civilians, United Nations personnel and equipment, the protection of their freedom of movement and that of humanitarian workers, and the protection of the mission's area of responsibility.[3] UNFICYP continued to support the maintenance of the ceasefire and bicommunal contacts in Cyprus, while longstanding observer missions such as MINURSO, UNDOF, UNMOGIP and UNTSO concentrated on the monitoring of ceasefires and the implementation of armistice and disengagement agreements.[4]

Mandates of peacekeeping operations: modifications

During the period under review, the Council modified the mandates of 5 of the 12 existing peacekeeping operations. The most significant changes concerned provisions on the protection of civilians, human rights in joint operations with national security forces, electoral support, gender- and conflict-sensitive analysis in the work of missions and the use of strategic communications.

In the light of the deteriorating security situations in north and central Mali and the eastern Democratic Republic of the Congo and intercommunal violence in South Sudan in 2022, the Council modified the tasks relating to the protection of civilians and support to national security forces by MINUSMA, MONUSCO and UNMISS. Specifically, the Council added new language to the protection mandate of MONUSCO by requesting the Mission to take all necessary measures to ensure effective, timely, dynamic and integrated protection of civilians by preventing, deterring and stopping all armed groups and local militias from inflicting violence on the populations.[5] Furthermore, the Council introduced new language on the obligation of MINUSMA and MONUSCO to ensure that their security support was provided in strict compliance with the United Nations human rights due diligence policy.[6] Similarly, the Council stressed the requirement for UNMISS to operate at all times consistent with the policy in its coordination with police services, security and government institutions and civil society actors in relevant and protection-focused activities.[7]

The Council expanded the human rights mandate of UNMISS to include two new elements. First, UNMISS was requested to ensure that monitoring, analysis and reporting arrangements relating to conflict-related sexual violence served to promote action to deter, prevent and respond to such violence.[8] Second, the Council requested UNMISS to include capacity-building in its coordination, information-sharing and technical support for international, regional and national mechanisms and relevant stakeholders engaged in monitoring, investigating and reporting on violations of international humanitarian law and human rights violations and abuses.[9]

In the Democratic Republic of the Congo, the Council tasked MONUSCO with providing support for the 2023 electoral process, including limited logistical support.[10] In Mali, as part of its support for the implementation of the peace agreement and the full realization of the political transition, the Council requested MINUSMA to assist the transitional Government in the holding of free and fair elections and

---

[3] In connection with UNIFIL, resolution 2650 (2022), para. 23; and, in connection with UNISFA, resolutions 2630 (2022) and 2660 (2022), para. 1.

[4] In connection with MINURSO, resolution 2654 (2022), para. 1; in connection with UNDOF, resolutions 2639 (2022) and 2671 (2022), para. 15; and, in connection with UNFICYP, resolutions 2618 (2022) and 2646 (2022), para. 10. See also, in connection with UNMOGIP, resolutions 47 (1948) and 91 (1951); and, in connection with UNTSO, resolution 48 (1948).

[5] Resolution 2666 (2022), para. 24 (a).

[6] In connection with MINUSMA, resolution 2640 (2022), para. 32; and, in connection with MONUSCO, resolution 2666 (2022), para. 24 (c).

[7] Resolution 2625 (2022), para. 3 (a) (viii).

[8] Ibid., para. 3 (d) (ii).

[9] Ibid., para. 3 (d) (iv).

[10] Resolution 2666 (2022), para. 26 (a).

a constitutional referendum, in cooperation with the Economic Community of West African States.[11] In South Sudan, UNMISS was requested to provide technical assistance, capacity-building and logistical support for the electoral process, as well as to protect civilians under the threat of physical violence in the context of the elections and to mitigate the potential for tensions throughout the electoral period.[12] Furthermore, the Council requested UNMISS to use technical assistance, including capacity-building, to support the constitutional drafting process, transitional security arrangements and the development of a sound regulatory framework.[13]

Lastly, the Council newly emphasized the importance of gender- and conflict-sensitive analysis in various aspects of the mandate of UNMISS, including in the implementation of its early warning and response strategy, support to community-led peace dialogue processes and capacity-building support for the rule of law and justice sector.[14] Furthermore, UNMISS was also requested to provide gender-sensitive risk assessments on the adverse effects of climate change as part of its mandate to support the creation of conditions conducive to the delivery of humanitarian assistance.[15]

Strategic communications

On 12 July 2022, the Council adopted a presidential statement in which it underscored the importance of the use of strategic communications by peacekeeping operations for the effective implementation of their mandates.[16] In that context, many of the mandates renewed during the reporting period included new tasks related to the use of strategic communications. For example, the Council requested MONUSCO to enhance its use of strategic communications, including through joint communications with the Government of the Democratic Republic of the Congo, to raise awareness and understanding about its mandate and activities to protect civilians, to strengthen its early warning mechanism, including to prevent disinformation campaigns and misinformation.[17] Similarly, the Council requested MINUSCA and UNIFIL to improve communication efforts in support of their mandates through strategic communications strategies and strategies to counter disinformation and misinformation.[18] In relation to the mandate of UNISFA, the Council requested the Secretary-General to ensure the Mission's use of strategic communications to counter disinformation and misinformation that might hinder its ability to implement its mandate and the mandate of the Joint Border Verification and Monitoring Mechanism.[19]

Effectiveness of peacekeeping operations

As a means of enhancing effectiveness, the Council continued to request the Secretary-General to implement existing obligations and utilize capacities in the planning and conduct of the operations of MINUSCA, MINUSMA, MONUSCO, UNFICYP and UNMISS.[20] In 2022, the Council added new obligations, such as implementing more effective casualty and medical evacuation procedures, taking measures to improve the planning and functioning of safety and security facilities and arrangements, improving intelligence and analysis capacities, including intelligence processes specific to explosive ordnance disposal and strengthened forensics exploitation, and strengthening capacities to monitor and counter disinformation and misinformation. With regard to MONUSCO, the Council underscored that the primary responsibility for the safety and security of United Nations personnel and assets rested with the host State and requested the Secretary-General to implement the provisions of resolution 2589 (2021) to establish accountability for crimes against peacekeepers.[21]

---

[11] Resolution 2640 (2022), para. 26 (a) (vi).

[12] Resolution 2625 (2022), para. 3 (a) (i) and (c) (v).

[13] Ibid., para. 3 (c) (iv).

[14] Resolution 2625 (2022), para. 3 (a) (ii), (v) and (vii).

[15] Ibid., para. 3 (b) (i).

[16] See S/PRST/2022/5.

[17] Resolution 2666 (2022), para. 24 (f).

[18] In connection with MINUSCA, resolution 2659 (2022), para. 32; and, in connection with UNIFIL, resolution 2650 (2022), para. 24.

[19] Resolution 2630 (2022), para. 5.

[20] In connection with MINUSCA, resolution 2659 (2022), para. 43; in connection with MINUSMA, resolution 2640 (2022), para. 41; in connection with MONUSCO, resolution 2666 (2022), para. 36; in connection with UNFICYP, resolution 2618 (2022), para. 16; and, in connection with UNMISS, resolution 2625 (2022), para. 20.

[21] Resolution 2666 (2022), para. 35.

Furthermore, the Council requested the Secretary-General to report on the implementation of the mandates of MINUSCA, MINUSMA, MONUSCO, UNFICYP and UNMISS using the data collected and analysed through the Comprehensive Planning and Performance Assessment System, the implementation of the integrated peacekeeping performance and accountability framework and through other strategic planning and performance measurement tools to describe impact and overall performance, as well as information on the actions and impact of strategic communications for mandated activities.[22]

Tables 1 and 2 provide an overview of the mandates of peacekeeping operations in 2022 and show the wide range of tasks mandated by the Council. The mandates reflected in the tables include: (a) tasks mandated by the Council in decisions adopted during the reporting period; and (b) tasks mandated in previous periods and reiterated by the Council during the reporting period. The tables include the tasks of peacekeeping operations with open-ended mandates adopted in decisions during previous periods. The tables are provided for information purposes only and do not reflect any position or view of the Council with regard to the status of the mandates of the operations concerned.

Table 1
Mandates of peacekeeping operations, 2022: Africa

Mandate	*MINURSO*	*MONUSCO*	*UNISFA*	*UNMISS*	*MINUSMA*	*MINUSCA*
Chapter VII		X	X	X	X	X
Authorization of the use of force		X	X	X	X	X
Ceasefire monitoring	X			X	X	X
Civil-military coordination		X		X	X	X
Demilitarization and arms management	X	X	X	X	X	X
Electoral assistance	X	X		X	X	X
Human rights-related[a]		X	X	X	X	X
Humanitarian support	X	X	X	X	X	X
International cooperation and coordination	X	X	X	X	X	X
Mission impact assessment		X			X	X
Political process		X	X	X	X	X
Protection of civilians		X	X	X	X	X
Protection of humanitarian/United Nations personnel and facilities; ensuring free movement of personnel and equipment		X	X	X	X	X
Public information		X		X	X	X
Rule of law/judicial matters		X	X	X	X	X
Security monitoring, patrolling and deterrence		X	X	X	X	X
Security sector reform		X			X	X
Support to military		X			X	X
Support to police	X	X	X	X	X	X

[22] In connection with MINUSCA, resolution 2659 (2022), para. 58; in connection with MINUSMA, resolution 2640 (2022), para. 57; in connection with MONUSCO, resolution 2666 (2022), para. 43; in connection with UNFICYP, resolutions 2618 (2022), para. 19, and 2646 (2022), para. 20; and, in connection with UNMISS, resolution 2625 (2022), para. 30.

Mandate	*MINURSO*	*MONUSCO*	*UNISFA*	*UNMISS*	*MINUSMA*	*MINUSCA*
Support to sanctions regimes		X		X	X	X
Support to State institutions		X		X	X	X

Abbreviations: MINURSO, United Nations Mission for the Referendum in Western Sahara; MINUSCA, United Nations Multidimensional Integrated Stabilization Mission in the Central African Republic; MINUSMA, United Nations Multidimensional Integrated Stabilization Mission in Mali; MONUSCO, United Nations Organization Stabilization Mission in the Democratic Republic of the Congo; UNISFA, United Nations Interim Security Force for Abyei; UNMISS, United Nations Mission in South Sudan.

[a] Includes tasks related to human rights; children and armed conflict; women and peace and security; and youth and peace and security.

Table 2

Mandates of peacekeeping operations, 2022: Asia, Europe and Middle East

Mandate	*UNMOGIP*	*UNFICYP*	*UNMIK*	*UNTSO*	*UNDOF*	*UNIFIL*
Chapter VII			X			
Authorization of the use of force						X
Ceasefire monitoring	X	X		X	X	X
Civil-military coordination			X			
Demilitarization and arms management						X
Electoral assistance						
Human rights-related[a]		X	X			X
Humanitarian support		X	X			
International cooperation and coordination		X	X	X	X	X
Political process		X	X			
Protection of civilians						X
Protection of humanitarian/United Nations personnel and facilities; ensuring free movement of personnel and equipment						X
Public information						X
Rule of law/judicial matters						
Security monitoring, patrolling and deterrence						X
Security sector reform						
Support to military						X
Support to police		X	X			
Support to sanctions regimes						
Support to State institutions			X			X

Abbreviations: UNDOF, United Nations Disengagement Observer Force; UNFICYP, United Nations Peacekeeping Force in Cyprus; UNIFIL, United Nations Interim Force in Lebanon; UNMIK, United Nations Interim Administration Mission in Kosovo; UNMOGIP, United Nations Military Observer Group in India and Pakistan; UNTSO, United Nations Truce Supervision Organization.

[a] Includes tasks related to human rights; children and armed conflict; women and peace and security; and youth and peace and security.

Authorized strength of peacekeeping operations

As illustrated in table 3, during the period under review, the Council modified the composition of MONUSCO by authorizing an increase from 1,050 to 1,410 personnel of formed police units, which encompassed the previous temporary deployment of up to 360 formed police unit personnel.

Table 3
Changes in composition of peacekeeping operations, 2022

Mission	*Changes in composition*	*Decision*
MONUSCO	The Council decided to increase the number of formed police unit personnel from 1,050 to 1,410 personnel, while maintaining 13,500 military personnel, 660 military observers and staff officers and 591 police personnel	Resolution 2666 (2022)

Abbreviation: MONUSCO, United Nations Organization Stabilization Mission in the Democratic Republic of the Congo.

Africa

United Nations Mission for the Referendum in Western Sahara

The Council established the United Nations Mission for the Referendum in Western Sahara (MINURSO) by resolution 690 (1991) of 29 April 1991, in accordance with the settlement proposals accepted by Morocco and the Frente Popular para la Liberación de Saguia el-Hamra y de Río de Oro (Frente POLISARIO). MINURSO was mandated to monitor the ceasefire, provide security for the repatriation of refugees and support the organization of a free and fair referendum.[23]

In 2022, by resolution 2654 (2022) of 27 October, the Council extended the mandate of MINURSO for one year, until 31 October 2023.[24] The resolution was adopted with 13 votes in favour and 2 abstentions.[25] The Council did not modify the mandate or composition of MINURSO during the period under review.

United Nations Organization Stabilization Mission in the Democratic Republic of the Congo

The Council established the United Nations Organization Stabilization Mission in the Democratic Republic of the Congo (MONUSCO) by resolution 1925 (2010) of 28 May 2010, acting under Chapter VII of the Charter of the United Nations, to succeed the United Nations Organization Mission in the Democratic Republic of the Congo. MONUSCO was authorized to use all necessary means to carry out its protection mandate as set out in the resolution and was tasked with, inter alia, ensuring the effective

[23] For more information on the history of the mandate of MINURSO, see previous supplements covering the period 1991 to 2021. For more information on the situation concerning Western Sahara, see part I, sect. 1.

[24] Resolution 2654 (2022), para. 1. See also the report of the Secretary-General on the situation concerning Western Sahara dated 3 October 2022 (S/2022/733).

[25] See S/PV.9168. Explaining his delegation's abstention, the representative of Kenya expressed concern that the resolution did not substantively reflect the Council's commitment, as had been previously reflected in resolution 2602 (2021) and other resolutions, to provide for the self-determination of the people of Western Sahara in the context of arrangements consistent with the principles and purposes of the Charter of the United Nations, noting the role and responsibilities of the parties in that respect. The representative of the Russian Federation stated that, in the previous few years, the resolutions on the renewal of the mandate of MINURSO had included amendments that harmed the unbiased and impartial approach needed to resolve the issue of Western Sahara. He added that the resolution did not reflect the real situation on the ground with regard to the settlement of the question and was unlikely to facilitate the efforts of the Personal Envoy of the Secretary-General for Western Sahara to resume the direct negotiation process in order to reach a mutually acceptable solution.

protection of civilians and supporting the efforts of the Government of the Democratic Republic of the Congo with stabilization and peace consolidation.[26]

By resolution 2666 (2022) of 20 December, acting under Chapter VII of the Charter, the Council unanimously extended the mandate of MONUSCO for one year, until 20 December 2023.[27] In the resolution, the Council reiterated the two strategic priorities of MONUSCO, namely, to protect civilians and to support the stabilization and strengthening of State institutions and key governance and security reforms, as well as the decision that the Mission's mandate should be implemented on the basis of a prioritization of tasks, with the protection of civilians to be given priority.[28] In addition to modifying the content of the mandate, the Council defined the order of priority of the tasks of MONUSCO as follows: (a) protection of civilians; (b) disarmament, demobilization, reintegration and stabilization; and (c) security sector reform.

Against the backdrop of the deteriorating security situation in the east of the country following the resurgence of the Mouvement du 23 mars and the continued attacks by other armed groups, the Council adjusted the Mission's protection of civilians mandate. Specifically, the Council provided that MONUSCO should take all necessary measures to ensure effective, timely, dynamic and integrated protection of civilians by preventing, deterring and stopping all armed groups and local militias from invading, attacking or surrounding major population centres, including in support of the Congolese authorities, by disarming them, using good offices and supporting and undertaking local mediation efforts and national level advocacy to prevent the escalation of violence and to counter hate speech, disinformation and misinformation.[29] The Council decided that MONUSCO should conduct increased and effective joint operations with the Congolese security forces in accordance with its mandate and in strict compliance with the human rights due diligence policy, and enhance its community engagement with civilians and use of strategic communications.[30] Furthermore, the Council encouraged support to the East African Community Regional Force (deployed in August 2022 to counter armed groups in the east of the country), stressing the importance of the protection of civilians and close coordination and information-sharing between the Force and MONUSCO, among other actors.[31]

With respect to the second priority task, the Council expanded the disarmament, demobilization, reintegration and stabilization mandate of MONUSCO to include the provision of good offices, advice and assistance, in close cooperation with international and local partners, including the East African Community-led Nairobi process.[32] Regarding security sector reform, the Council underlined the role of MONUSCO in supporting women's full, equal, effective and meaningful participation and safety and tasked the Mission with enhancing the capacities of the Congolese security forces on basic investigation and forensics exploitation related to improvised explosive devices.[33]

By resolution 2666 (2022), the Council further authorized MONUSCO to provide support for the 2023 electoral process in the three provinces where the Mission was still deployed, including limited logistical support.[34] Among the Mission's other tasks, the Council included human rights monitoring and reporting, support for the national judicial system and the fight against impunity, the protection and freedom of movement of United Nations and associated personnel, child protection and the cross-cutting issues of gender and sexual violence.[35]

Regarding the effectiveness of the Mission and the safety and security of peacekeepers, the Council requested the Secretary-General to provide MONUSCO with the necessary capacities to fulfil

---

[26] For more information on the history of the mandate of MONUSCO, see previous supplements covering the period 2010 to 2021. For more information on the situation concerning the Democratic Republic of the Congo, see part I, sect. 4.

[27] Resolution 2666 (2022), para. 19. See also the reports of the Secretary-General on MONUSCO submitted during the period under review (S/2022/252, S/2022/503, S/2022/709 and S/2022/892).

[28] Resolution 2666 (2022), paras. 21 and 24.

[29] Ibid., para. 24 (a).

[30] Ibid., para. 24 (c) and (f).

[31] Ibid., para. 17.

[32] Ibid., para. 24 (g).

[33] Ibid., para. 24 (l).

[34] Ibid., para. 26 (a).

[35] Ibid., paras. 26 (b) and (c) and 27–30.

its mandate in a complex security environment.[36] The Council also reiterated its request to the Secretary-General to implement the activities set out in paragraph 42 of resolution 2612 (2021) in the planning and conduct of the operations of MONUSCO.[37]

With regard to the exit strategy, the Council took note of the call by the Government to review the transition plan for MONUSCO and encouraged the United Nations and the Government, in liaison with civil society, to identify concrete and realistic steps to create the minimum security conditions to enable the responsible and sustainable exit of MONUSCO.[38] In addition, the Council called upon MONUSCO to work closely with the United Nations country team to identify ways to address gaps in capabilities to prepare for the exit and to clarify roles and responsibilities for all relevant United Nations stakeholders in line with resolution 2594 (2021).[39]

By resolution 2666 (2022), the Council maintained the Mission's authorized troop ceiling of 13,500 military personnel, 660 military observers and staff officers, and 591 police personnel.[40] The Council also authorized a ceiling of 1,410 personnel of formed police units, which encompassed the previous temporary deployment of up to 360 formed police unit personnel.[41] Lastly, the Council requested the Secretary-General to provide, once the joint review of the transition plan had been concluded and no later than July 2023, options for adapting the Mission's configuration of its civilian, police and military components and on the future configuration of the United Nations in the Democratic Republic of the Congo beyond the current mandate of MONUSCO.[42]

United Nations Interim Security Force for Abyei

The Council established the United Nations Interim Security Force for Abyei (UNISFA) by resolution 1990 (2011) of 27 June 2011, taking into account the Agreement between the Government of the Republic of the Sudan and the Sudan People's Liberation Movement on temporary arrangements for the administration and security of the Abyei Area of 20 June 2011. The Council mandated UNISFA to, inter alia, monitor and verify the redeployment of the Sudanese Armed Forces and the Sudan People's Liberation Army or its successor from the Abyei Area, participate in relevant bodies as stipulated in the Agreement, facilitate the delivery of humanitarian aid and strengthen the capacity of the Abyei Police Service. By the same resolution, acting under Chapter VII of the Charter, the Council authorized UNISFA to take the actions necessary to, inter alia, protect United Nations and humanitarian personnel and property, protect civilians under imminent threat of physical violence and ensure security in the Abyei Area. By resolution 2024 (2011) of 14 December 2011, the Council expanded the mandate of UNISFA to include assisting the Sudan and South Sudan in ensuring the observance of their agreement on border security and supporting the operational activities of the Joint Border Verification and Monitoring Mechanism.[43]

In 2022, the Council unanimously adopted resolutions 2630 (2022) of 12 May and 2660 (2022) of 14 November, by which it extended the mandate of UNISFA for periods of six months and one year, respectively, on the latter occasion until 15 November 2023.[44]

The Council did not modify the mandate of UNISFA during the period under review. By resolution 2630 (2022), the Council requested the Secretary-General, consistent with resolution 2609 (2021), to

---

[36] Ibid., para. 35.
[37] Ibid., para. 36.
[38] Ibid., para. 38.
[39] Ibid., para. 40.
[40] Ibid., para. 20.
[41] Ibid.
[42] Ibid., para. 44.
[43] For more information on the history of the mandate of UNISFA, see previous supplements covering the period 2011 to 2021. For more information on the item entitled "Reports of the Secretary-General on the Sudan and South Sudan", see part I, sect. 7.
[44] Resolutions 2630 (2022) and 2660 (2022), para. 1. See also the reports of the Secretary-General on the situation in Abyei submitted during the period under review (S/2022/316 and S/2022/760).

ensure the mission's use of confidence-building, facilitation, mediation, community engagement and strategic communications to support the implementation of its mandate and its protection, information-gathering, and situational awareness activities, as well as to counter disinformation and misinformation that might hinder its ability to implement its mandate and the mandate of the Joint Border Verification and Monitoring Mechanism.[45]

By resolutions 2630 (2022) and 2660 (2022), while maintaining the authorized troop and police ceilings as set out in resolution 2609 (2021), the Council expressed its intention to remain seized of the recommendations of the strategic review as contained in the letter dated 17 September 2021 from the Secretary-General addressed to the President of the Council.[46]

By an exchange of letters dated 26 January and 1 February 2022,[47] the Secretary-General appointed Major General Benjamin Olufemi Sawyerr as Force Commander of UNISFA.

United Nations Mission in South Sudan

By resolution 1996 (2011) of 8 July 2011, acting under Chapter VII of the Charter, the Council established the United Nations Mission in South Sudan (UNMISS) with a mandate to support peace consolidation and foster longer-term State-building and economic development; support the Government of South Sudan in exercising its responsibilities for conflict prevention, mitigation and resolution and protect civilians; and support the Government, in cooperation with the United Nations country team and other international partners, in developing its capacity to provide security, establish the rule of law and strengthen the security and justice sectors. UNMISS was authorized to use all necessary means to carry out its protection of civilians mandate.[48]

In 2022, acting under Chapter VII of the Charter, the Council adopted resolutions 2625 (2022) of 15 March and 2633 (2022) of 26 May in connection with UNMISS. By resolution 2625 (2022), the Council extended the mandate of UNMISS for one year, until 15 March 2023.[49] The resolution was adopted with 13 votes in favour and 2 abstentions.[50]

By resolution 2625 (2022), the Council reiterated that the mandate of UNMISS was designed to advance the three-year strategic vision defined in resolution 2567 (2021) to prevent a return to civil war in South Sudan, build durable peace at the local and national levels and support inclusive and accountable governance and free, fair and peaceful elections in accordance with the Revitalized Agreement on the Resolution of the Conflict in the Republic of South Sudan.[51] Within the framework of the strategic vision, the Council introduced several modifications to the tasks of UNMISS related to the following (a) protection of civilians; (b) creating the conditions conducive to the delivery of humanitarian assistance; (c) supporting the implementation of the Revitalized Agreement and the peace process; and (d) monitoring, investigating and reporting on violations of international humanitarian law and violations and abuses of human rights.

---

[45] Resolution 2630 (2022), para. 5.

[46] Resolutions 2630 (2022) and 2660 (2022), para. 3. See also S/2021/805.

[47] S/2022/78 and S/2022/79.

[48] For more information on the history of the mandate of UNMISS, see previous supplements covering the period 2011 to 2021. For more information on the item entitled "Reports of the Secretary-General on the Sudan and South Sudan", see part I, sect. 7.

[49] Resolution 2625 (2022), para. 1. See also the reports of the Secretary-General on the situation in South Sudan submitted during the period under review (S/2022/156, S/2022/468, S/2022/689 and S/2022/918).

[50] See S/PV.8994. In her statement after the vote, the representative of the Russian Federation asserted that the Council and UNMISS did not have the appropriate resources to assist in capacity-building to resolve problems related to the protection of human rights, combating sexual violence, defending the rights of women and fighting corruption, which were, first and foremost, internal matters for the country. She added that, while the Mission could, at the request of the host country, provide technical and logistical assistance for the conduct of elections, its core function was to stabilize the security situation and assist in the implementation of the Revitalized Agreement on the Resolution of the Conflict in the Republic of South Sudan. The representative of China objected to the inclusion of human rights-related provisions in the draft resolution and the assignment of climate change-related mandates to a peacekeeping operation. For more information on the discussion, see part I, sect. 7.

[51] Resolution 2625 (2022), para. 2.

Specifically, regarding the protection of civilians, the Council indicated that the Mission would be responsible for the protection of civilians under threat of physical violence, which would include protection against violence in the context of elections, and that the best practices in this context should be shared with relevant local stakeholders for the purpose of capacity-building.[52] Furthermore, the Council called for the continued and consistent use and deployment of the Mission's child protection, women protection and uniformed and civilian gender advisers.[53] The Council adjusted the mandate of UNMISS to deter, prevent and respond to sexual and gender-based violence by adding the task of facilitating access to organizations that provided services and support to survivors.[54] The Council also placed particular emphasis on the Mission's use of conflict-sensitive and gender-based analysis in the implementation of its early warning and response strategy, support to community-led peace dialogue processes and capacity-building in connection with rule of law and justice sector reform.[55] Furthermore, UNMISS was requested to provide support for the development and implementation of gender-responsive community violence reduction programmes to help to de-escalate intercommunal violence, with a particular focus on members of armed groups ineligible or unwilling to be integrated into the Necessary Unified Forces.[56] The Council also stressed the requirement for UNMISS to operate at all times consistent with the human rights due diligence policy in its coordination with police services, security and government institutions and civil society actors in relevant and protection-focused activities.[57] Moreover, as part of the group of tasks related to the creation of conditions conducive to the delivery of humanitarian assistance, the Council requested UNMISS to provide gender-sensitive risk assessments on the adverse effects of climate change.[58]

With respect to the Mission's support for the implementation of the Revitalized Agreement, taking note of the needs assessment transmitted by the Secretary-General in his letter dated 15 July 2021, the Council requested UNMISS to provide technical assistance, including capacity-building, and logistical support for the electoral process, in coordination with the United Nations country team and regional and international partners, as well as security support.[59] The Council also requested UNMISS, using technical assistance, to include capacity-building, to support mechanisms of the Revitalized Agreement, including with regard to the constitution drafting process, transitional security arrangements and the development of a sound regulatory framework.[60] Furthermore, UNMISS was tasked with assisting all parties to ensure the participation of women and the inclusion of youth, faith groups and civil society in the transitional justice and constitution-making process.[61]

The Council expanded the human rights mandate of UNMISS to include ensuring that monitoring, analysis and reporting arrangements relating to conflict-related sexual violence served to promote action to deter, prevent and respond to such violence.[62] In addition, the Mission was requested to include capacity-building in its coordination, information-sharing and technical support for international, regional and national mechanisms and relevant stakeholders engaged in monitoring, investigating and reporting on violations of international humanitarian law and human rights violations and abuses.[63] Lastly, with respect to the Mission's operations, the Council requested the Secretary-General to fully implement 18 substantive and operational capacities and existing obligations in the planning and conduct of UNMISS operations.[64]

By resolution 2633 (2022), the Council reiterated its request to UNMISS to assist the Committee established pursuant to resolution 2206 (2015) concerning South Sudan and the Panel of Experts.[65]

---

[52] Ibid., para. 3 (a) (i).
[53] Ibid.
[54] Ibid., para. 3 (a) (iv).
[55] Ibid., para. 3 (a) (ii), (v) and (vii).
[56] Ibid., para. 3 (a) (vi).
[57] Ibid., para. 3 (a) (viii).
[58] Ibid., para. 3 (b) (i).
[59] Ibid., para. 3 (c) (v). See also S/2021/661.
[60] Resolution 2625 (2022), para. 3 (c) (iv).
[61] Ibid., para. 3 (c) (ii).
[62] Ibid., para. 3 (d) (ii).
[63] Ibid., para. 3 (d) (iv).
[64] Ibid., para. 20.
[65] Resolution 2633 (2022), paras. 18 and 22. For more information on the Committee established pursuant to resolution 2206 (2015) concerning South Sudan, see part IX, sect. I. For more information on the sanctions measures concerning South Sudan, see part VII, sect. III.

By resolution 2625 (2022), the Council decided to maintain the overall force levels of UNMISS with a troop ceiling of 17,000 personnel and a police ceiling of 2,101 personnel, including 88 corrections officers.[66] The Council expressed its readiness to consider adjustment to UNMISS force levels and capacity-building tasks based on security conditions on the ground and implementation of priority measures by the Government of South Sudan and all relevant stakeholders, as set out in the resolution.[67]

United Nations Multidimensional Integrated Stabilization Mission in Mali

The Council established the United Nations Multidimensional Integrated Stabilization Mission in Mali (MINUSMA) by resolution 2100 (2013) of 25 April 2013, acting under Chapter VII of the Charter. The Council authorized MINUSMA to use all necessary means to stabilize population centres and support the re-establishment of State authority, support the implementation of a transitional road map, protect civilians and United Nations personnel and property, assist the Malian authorities in promoting and protecting human rights, and support humanitarian assistance, national and international justice and cultural preservation.[68]

In 2022, by resolution 2640 (2022) of 29 June, acting under Chapter VII of the Charter, the Council extended the mandate of MINUSMA by one year, until 30 June 2023.[69] The Council maintained the strategic priorities of MINUSMA, first, to support the implementation of the Agreement on Peace and Reconciliation in Mali and the political transition and, second, to facilitate the implementation by Malian actors of a comprehensive, inclusive, politically focused strategy that addressed the root causes and drivers of conflict, protected civilians, reduced intercommunal violence and re-established State presence and authority, as well as basic social services in central Mali.[70] Furthermore, while requesting MINUSMA to continue to carry out its peacekeeping mandate with a proactive, robust, flexible and agile posture, the Council emphasized that this should be done with a clear understanding and interpretation of roles and responsibilities among its civilian and uniformed personnel.[71] Resolution 2640 (2022) was adopted with 13 votes in favour and 2 abstentions.[72]

The Council largely maintained the priority tasks of MINUSMA, with a few adjustments. As part of its first priority task, to support the implementation of the peace agreement and the full realization of the political transition, the Council requested the Mission to assist the transitional Government, together with the United Nations country team, in the holding of free and fair elections and of a constitutional referendum, in cooperation with the Economic Community of West African States.[73] Within the framework of the second priority task, to support the stabilization and restoration of State authority in central Mali, MINUSMA was requested to support the authorities in agreeing on and implementing a comprehensive, inclusive, politically focused strategy that addressed the root causes and drivers of violent conflict.[74] Under the third priority task, to protect civilians, the Council requested MINUSMA to strengthen community engagement and protection mechanisms, including through the use of quick-impact

---

[66] Resolution 2625 (2022), para. 4.

[67] Ibid.

[68] For more information on the history of the mandate of MINUSMA, see previous supplements covering the period 2012 to 2021. For more information on the situation in Mali, see part I, sect. 11.

[69] Resolution 2640 (2022), para. 15. See also the reports of the Secretary-General on the situation in Mali submitted during the period under review (S/2021/1117, S/2022/278/Rev.1, S/2022/446 and S/2022/731) and the letter dated 1 June 2022 from the Secretary-General addressed to the President of the Council (S/2022/448) on the progress in Mission operations, Mission performance and the implementation of the force adaptation plan, submitted pursuant to resolution 2584 (2021).

[70] Resolution 2640 (2022), para. 18.

[71] Ibid., para. 19.

[72] See S/PV.9082. In explaining their decision to abstain in the vote, the representatives of China and the Russian Federation expressed disagreement with the addition in the resolution of new language on human rights, particularly with respect to the support of MINUSMA to the Malian Defence and Security Forces. For further detail on the discussion, see part I, sect. 14.

[73] Resolution 2640 (2022), para. 26 (a) (vi).

[74] Ibid., para. 26 (b) (i).

projects.[75] Lastly, regarding the fourth priority task, to promote and protect human rights, MINUSMA was requested to report publicly and quarterly to the Council on violations of international humanitarian law and violations and abuses of human rights.[76]

Beyond the priority tasks, the Council made several adjustments to the responsibilities of MINUSMA regarding its support of the Malian Defence and Security Forces. The Council urged MINUSMA to ensure that its support was provided in compliance with the human rights due diligence policy across all phases of operations.[77] The Council further urged MINUSMA to ensure that such support was subject to appropriate oversight.[78]

With regard to the effectiveness of MINUSMA, the Council encouraged the Mission to implement the integrated peacekeeping performance and accountability framework and the Comprehensive Planning and Performance Assessment System to ensure that the whole-of-mission performance was assessed against the delivery of the mandate.[79] The Council also reiterated its request to the Secretary-General, originally outlined in resolution 2584 (2021), to fully implement a number of capacities and existing obligations in the planning and conduct of the operations of MINUSMA.[80] In that regard, the Council added new requirements to improve explosive ordnance disposal specific intelligence, to verify that contingents were trained and equipped to counter explosive devices and to strengthen capacities to monitor and counter disinformation and misinformation.

Regarding the Mission's configuration, the Council decided that MINUSMA would continue to comprise up to 13,289 military personnel and 1,920 police personnel.[81] Lastly, the Council expressed its support for the proposal of the Secretary-General to conduct an internal review of MINUSMA, to be conveyed no later than 13 January 2023.[82]

United Nations Multidimensional Integrated Stabilization Mission in the Central African Republic

The Council established the United Nations Multidimensional Integrated Stabilization Mission in the Central African Republic (MINUSCA) by resolution 2149 (2014) of 10 April 2014, acting under Chapter VII of the Charter. MINUSCA was authorized to use all necessary means to, inter alia, protect civilians and United Nations personnel and property; support the implementation of the transition process; facilitate the delivery of humanitarian assistance; promote and protect human rights; support justice and the rule of law; and support the implementation of disarmament, demobilization, reintegration, and repatriation strategies.[83]

In 2022, acting under Chapter VII of the Charter, the Council adopted resolutions 2648 (2022) of 29 July and 2659 (2022) of 14 November concerning MINUSCA. By resolution 2659 (2022), the Council

---

[75] Ibid., para. 26 (c) (ii).
[76] Ibid., para. 26 (d) (ii).
[77] Ibid., para. 32.
[78] Ibid.
[79] Ibid., para. 40.
[80] Ibid., para. 41.
[81] Ibid., para. 16.
[82] Ibid., para. 58. In his report on the situation in Mali dated 2 June (S/2022/446), the Secretary-General underscored that the increasingly complex and fluid security situation was such that it would be difficult for the Mission to cope with the related challenges in the northern part of Mali within the currently authorized strength. He further expressed his intention to conduct a thorough analysis of the situation, with a view to presenting recommendations to the Council on how best MINUSMA could continue to deliver on its priorities.
[83] For more information on the history of the mandate of MINUSCA, see previous supplements covering the period 2014 to 2021. For more information on the situation in the Central African Republic, see part I, sect. 5.

extended the mandate of MINUSCA for one year, until 15 November 2023.[84] The resolution was adopted with 12 votes in favour and 3 abstentions.[85]

The Council did not make major changes to the mandate of MINUSCA during the period under review. By resolution 2659 (2022), the Council reiterated that the mandate was designed to advance a multi-year strategic vision to create the political, security and institutional conditions conducive to national reconciliation through the implementation of the Political Agreement for Peace and Reconciliation in the Central African Republic and the elimination of the threat posed by armed groups through a comprehensive approach and proactive and robust posture without prejudice to the basic principles of peacekeeping.[86] The Council requested MINUSCA to improve its communication efforts to support the implementation of its mandate and enhance its protection and raise awareness on its mandate and its role.[87]

Furthermore, the Council recalled that the mandate of MINUSCA should be implemented on the basis of a prioritization of tasks and, when relevant, in a sequenced manner, and reiterated, with some modifications, that the Mission's priority tasks were: (a) to protect civilians; (b) to provide good offices and support to the peace process; (c) to facilitate the immediate, full, safe and unhindered delivery of humanitarian assistance; and (d) to protect United Nations personnel, installations, equipment, goods and associated personnel.[88]

Beyond the priority tasks, the Council reiterated, with one addition, the other tasks of MINUSCA, namely: (a) support for the extension of State authority, the deployment of security forces, and the preservation of territorial integrity; (b) promotion and protection of human rights; (c) assistance in the follow-up to the republican dialogue and with the 2023 elections; (d) security sector reform; (e) disarmament, demobilization, reintegration and repatriation; and (f) support for national and international justice, the fight against impunity, and the rule of law.[89] Specifically, with respect to reintegration, the Council requested MINUSCA to support the Government in providing security and appropriate protection to demobilized ex-combatants.[90] The Council reiterated the additional tasks of MINUSCA to support the Committee established pursuant to resolution 2127 (2013) concerning the Central African Republic and its Panel of Experts.[91] By resolution 2648 (2022), the Council further reiterated the task of MINUSCA to report to the Committee on the contribution to security sector reform of the sanctions exemption related to supplies and assistance intended solely for this purpose.[92]

Regarding the Mission's operations, in its resolution 2659 (2022), the Council recognized that the effective implementation of peacekeeping mandates was contingent upon several critical factors, including strategic communications and integration across mission components.[93] The Council further reiterated its request to the Secretary-General, originally outlined in resolution 2605 (2021), to fully implement a number of capacities and existing obligations in the planning and conduct of the operations

---

[84] Resolution 2659 (2022), para. 29. See also the reports of the Secretary-General on the situation in the Central African Republic submitted during the period under review (S/2022/119, S/2022/491 and S/2022/762) and the letter dated 1 June 2022 from the Secretary-General addressed to the President of the Council (S/2022/449) on the logistical support provided by MINUSCA to the Central African Republic defence and security forces submitted pursuant to resolution 2605 (2021).

[85] See S/PV.9190. In explaining the vote of their delegations, the representatives of China, Gabon and the Russian Federation expressed the view that the new mandate of MINUSCA should have included, among other tasks, stronger support for the restoration of State authority. The representatives of Gabon and the Russian Federation further objected to a lack of differentiated treatment in the resolution between the national authorities and armed groups in the Central African Republic. For further detail on the discussion, see part I, sect. 5.

[86] Resolution 2659 (2022), para. 31.

[87] Ibid., para. 32.

[88] Ibid., paras. 33 and 35.

[89] Ibid., para. 36.

[90] Ibid., para. 36 (e) (i).

[91] Ibid., para. 37 (a)–(d). For more information on the Committee established pursuant to resolution 2127 (2013), see part IX, sect. I. For more information on the sanctions measures concerning the Central African Republic, see part VII, sect. III.

[92] Resolution 2648 (2022), para. 1 (b).

[93] Resolution 2659 (2022), para. 41.

of MINUSCA and, in this regard, added improving explosive ordnance disposal specific intelligence processes and strengthened forensics exploitation capacity and verifying that contingents were trained and equipped to counter explosive devices in accordance with United Nations standards.[94]

The Council recalled its decision in resolution 2566 (2021) to increase the authorized size of the Mission's military and police components and stressed the need for the rest of those reinforcements, especially quick reaction forces, to be deployed as quickly as possible and sequenced through a phased approach.[95] Lastly, the Council expressed its intention to request an independent strategic review of MINUSCA, assessing the challenges to peace and security in the Central African Republic, including constraints on the Mission's operations and providing detailed recommendations on the continued relevance of all mandate tasks, priorities and related resources, realistic, relevant and clearly measurable benchmarks and options for adapting the configuration of its civilian, police and military components.[96]

By an exchange of letters dated 17 and 22 February 2022 with the President of the Council,[97] the Secretary-General appointed Valentine Rugwabiza as his Special Representative for the Central African Republic and Head of MINUSCA.

Asia

United Nations Military Observer Group in India and Pakistan

The Council established the United Nations Military Observer Group in India and Pakistan (UNMOGIP) by resolution 47 (1948) of 21 April 1948. The first team of military observers, who eventually formed the nucleus of UNMOGIP, was deployed in January 1949 to the United Nations Commission for India and Pakistan established by resolution 39 (1948). Following the termination of the Commission, the Council, by resolution 91 (1951), decided that UNMOGIP would continue to supervise the ceasefire in the State of Jammu and Kashmir. Since the renewed hostilities in 1971, the task of UNMOGIP has been to monitor developments pertaining to the strict observance of the ceasefire of 17 December 1971. In 2021, the Council did not discuss UNMOGIP or make changes to its composition or mandate, which remained open-ended.[98]

By an exchange of letters dated 8 and 10 August 2022 with the President of the Council,[99] the Secretary-General appointed Rear Admiral Guillermo Pablo Ríos as Head of Mission and Chief Military Observer of UNMOGIP.

Europe

United Nations Peacekeeping Force in Cyprus

The Council established the United Nations Peacekeeping Force in Cyprus (UNFICYP) by resolution 186 (1964) of 4 March 1964. In the interest of preserving international peace and security, UNFICYP was mandated to use its best efforts to prevent a recurrence of fighting and, as necessary, to contribute to the maintenance and restoration of law and order and a return to normal conditions.[100]

---

[94] Ibid., para. 43.
[95] Ibid., para. 39.
[96] Ibid., para. 58 (c).
[97] S/2022/149 and S/2022/150.
[98] For more information on the history of the mandate of UNMOGIP, see *Repertoire, Supplement 1946–1951*, and subsequent supplements covering the period 1952 to 2021.
[99] S/2022/612 and S/2022/613.
[100] For further information on the history of the mandate of UNFICYP, see previous supplements covering the period 1964 to 2021. For more information on the situation in Cyprus, see part I, sect. 17.

In 2022, the Council unanimously adopted resolutions 2618 (2022) of 27 January and 2646 (2022) of 28 July in relation to UNFICYP. The Council extended the mandate of the mission twice, for a period of six months each time, the second time until 31 January 2023.[101]

During the period under review, the Council did not modify the mandate or composition of UNFICYP. By resolution 2618 (2022), regarding the mission's operations, the Council stressed that the mandated authority of UNFICYP extended throughout Cyprus and requested the Secretary-General, Member States and all parties to continue to take all appropriate measures to ensure the safety and security and freedom of movement of its personnel in line with resolution 2518 (2020).[102] The Council further requested the Secretary-General to implement six activities and existing obligations in the planning and conduct of the operations of UNFICYP within the limits of the mandate and area of operations, including: (a) women and peace and security requirements under resolution 1325 (2000); (b) peacekeeping performance requirements under resolutions 2378 (2017) and 2436 (2018); (c) the United Nations zero-tolerance policy on serious misconduct, sexual exploitation and abuse and sexual harassment; (d) more effective casualty and medical evacuation procedures; (e) active and effective measures to improve the planning and functioning of safety and security facilities and arrangements; and (f) youth and peace and security requirements under resolutions 2250 (2015), 2419 (2018) and 2535 (2020).[103]

United Nations Interim Administration Mission in Kosovo

The United Nations Interim Administration Mission in Kosovo (UNMIK) was established by the Council on 10 June 1999, by resolution 1244 (1999), under Chapter VII of the Charter. The Council mandated UNMIK to carry out a range of tasks, including promoting the establishment of substantial autonomy and self-government in Kosovo, performing basic civilian administrative functions, and organizing and overseeing the development of provisional institutions for democratic and autonomous self-government.[104] In 2022, the Council did not adopt any decisions relating to UNMIK and made no change to its composition or to its mandate, which remained open-ended.[105]

Middle East

United Nations Truce Supervision Organization

The United Nations Truce Supervision Organization (UNTSO) was established by the Council on 29 May 1948, by resolution 50 (1948), to assist the United Nations Mediator and the Truce Commission in supervising the observance of the truce following the end of the 1948 Arab-Israeli conflict. Since the establishment of UNTSO, the Council has assigned it different tasks without formally changing its mandate, including the supervision of the General Armistice, the supervision of the armistice following the Suez war, the supervision of the armistice between Egypt and Israel in the Sinai, and the supervision of the truce between Israel and Lebanon and Israel and the Syrian Arab Republic, in collaboration with the United Nations Interim Force in Lebanon (UNIFIL) and the United Nations Disengagement Observer Force (UNDOF), respectively.[106]

---

[101] Resolutions 2618 (2022) and 2646 (2022), para. 10. See also the report of the Secretary-General dated 5 July 2022 on the United Nations operation in Cyprus (S/2022/533).

[102] Resolution 2618 (2022), para. 13.

[103] Ibid., paras. 16.

[104] For more information on the history of the mandate of UNMIK, see previous supplements covering the period 1996 to 2021.

[105] For more information on Security Council resolutions 1160 (1998), 1199 (1998), 1203 (1998), 1239 (1999) and 1244 (1999), see part I, sect. 18.B. See also the reports of the Secretary-General on UNMIK submitted during the period under review (S/2022/313 and S/2022/739).

[106] For more information on the history of the mandate of UNTSO, see *Repertoire*, *Supplement 1946–1951*, and subsequent supplements covering the period 1952 to 2021. For more information on the situation in the Middle East, see part I, sect. 20.

In 2022, the Council did not make changes to the composition or mandate of UNTSO, which remained open-ended. By resolutions 2639 (2022) of 27 June and 2671 (2022) of 22 December, the Council encouraged the Department of Peace Operations, UNDOF and UNTSO to continue relevant discussions on recommendations from the 2018 independent review of UNDOF to improve that mission's performance and the implementation of its mandate.[107]

United Nations Disengagement Observer Force

The United Nations Disengagement Observer Force (UNDOF) was established by the Council on 31 May 1974, by resolution 350 (1974), following the Agreement on Disengagement between Israeli and Syrian forces in the Golan Heights. Since then, UNDOF has remained in the area to maintain the ceasefire between Israel and the Syrian Arab Republic and to supervise the implementation of the Agreement and the areas of separation and limitation.[108]

In 2022, the Council did not make changes to the mandate or composition of UNDOF. By resolutions 2639 (2022) of 27 June and 2671 (2022) of 22 December, the Council unanimously extended the mandate of the Mission twice, for a period of six months each time, the second time until 30 June 2023.[109]

In resolutions 2639 (2022) and 2671 (2022), the Council reiterated its request to UNDOF, within existing capacities and resources, to take all appropriate steps to protect the safety, security and health of all mission personnel, in line with resolution 2518 (2020), taking into account the impact of the coronavirus disease (COVID-19) pandemic.[110] The Council further requested the Department of Peace Operations, UNDOF and UNTSO to continue relevant discussions on recommendations from the 2018 independent review of UNDOF to improve mission performance and implementation of the mandate of UNDOF.[111]

By an exchange of letters dated 7 and 12 July 2022 with the President of the Council,[112] the Secretary-General appointed Major General Nirmal Kumar Thapa as Head of Mission and Force Commander of UNDOF.

United Nations Interim Force in Lebanon

The United Nations Interim Force in Lebanon (UNIFIL) was established by the Council on 19 March 1978, by resolutions 425 (1978) and 426 (1978), to confirm the withdrawal of Israeli forces from southern Lebanon, restore international peace and security, and assist the Government of Lebanon in ensuring the return of its effective authority in the area. By resolution 1701 (2006), to address the continuing hostilities in Lebanon, the Council expanded the mandate of UNIFIL to include monitoring the cessation of hostilities; accompanying and supporting the Lebanese Armed Forces; extending its assistance to help to ensure humanitarian access to civilian populations and the voluntary and safe return of displaced persons; and assisting the Government of Lebanon in securing its borders and other entry points to prevent the entry of arms or related materiel.[113]

---

[107] Resolutions 2639 (2022) and 2671 (2022), para. 12.

[108] For more information on the history of the mandate of UNDOF, see previous supplements covering the period 1972 to 2021.

[109] Resolutions 2639 (2022) and 2671 (2022), para. 15. See also the reports of the Secretary-General on UNDOF submitted during the period under review (S/2022/247, S/2022/447, S/2022/711 and S/2022/887).

[110] Resolutions 2639 (2022) and 2671 (2022), para. 8.

[111] Ibid., para. 12. See also S/2018/1088, in which the Secretary-General provided an overview of the recommendations of the independent review of the mission's mandate.

[112] S/2022/558 and S/2022/559.

[113] For more information on the history of the mandate of UNIFIL, see previous supplements covering the period 1975 to 2021. For more information on the situation in the Middle East, including the Palestinian question and the situation in the Middle East, see part I, sects. 19 and 20.

In 2022, by resolution 2650 (2022) of 31 August, the Council unanimously extended the mandate of UNIFIL for one year, until 31 August 2023.[114] The resolution was adopted in accordance with the recommendation of the Secretary-General contained in his letter dated 9 August 2022 addressed to the President of the Council.[115]

By resolution 2650 (2022), the Council reiterated the mandate of UNIFIL, with one addition. Specifically, the Council requested UNIFIL to improve its communication efforts to support the implementation of its mandate, enhance its protection and raise awareness on its mandate, role and authority to operate independently, as well as to underscore the role and responsibilities of the Lebanese authorities in line with resolution 1701 (2006).[116] Moreover, the Council requested UNIFIL to prioritize the development of a strategic communications strategy outlining how it would improve those efforts and requested it to strengthen its efforts to monitor and counter disinformation and misinformation that might hinder its ability to implement its mandate or threaten the safety and security of peacekeepers and to develop a strategy to counter disinformation and misinformation.[117]

The Council requested UNIFIL, in line with resolution 1701 (2006) and following the letter dated 15 March 2022 from the Government of Lebanon addressed to the President of the Council, as well as in accordance with the recommendations of the Secretary-General, to exceptionally extend the temporary and special measures to support and assist the Lebanese Armed Forces with the provision of relevant additional non-lethal material (fuel, food and medicine) and logistical support.[118] The support would be provided for a period of six months, until 28 February 2023, within existing resources, for the Lebanese Armed Forces-UNIFIL joint activities and in compliance with the human rights due diligence policy.[119]

Lastly, the Council reiterated the tasks of UNIFIL to support and cooperate with the Lebanese Armed Forces and the tripartite mechanism, ensure enhanced cooperation with the Office of the United Nations Special Coordinator for Lebanon, to take all necessary action in areas of deployment to ensure that its area of operations was not utilized for hostile activities, protect United Nations personnel, facilities, installations and equipment, and take fully into account gender considerations as a cross-cutting issue throughout its mandate.[120]

The Council maintained the composition of UNIFIL during the reporting period.

II. Special political missions

Note

Section II is focused on the decisions adopted by the Council during the period under review concerning the establishment and termination of special political missions,[121] as well as the changes to their mandates.[122]

---

[114] Resolution 2650 (2022), para. 1.

[115] Ibid., fifth preambular paragraph. See letter dated 9 August 2022 from the Secretary-General addressed to the President of the Council regarding the renewal of the mandate of UNIFIL (S/2022/607) and the reports of the Secretary-General on the implementation of resolution 1701 (2006) submitted during the period under review (S/2022/214, S/2022/556 and S/2022/858).

[116] Resolution 2650 (2022), para. 24.

[117] Ibid.

[118] Ibid., para. 11. See also S/2022/235 and S/2022/556.

[119] Resolution 2650 (2022), para. 11.

[120] Ibid., paras. 2, 5, 13–15, 23 and 27.

[121] Special political missions described in the present part include regional offices and offices in support of political processes. Other types of special political missions, such as offices of special and personal envoys, advisers or representatives of the Secretary-General, sanctions monitoring teams, groups and panels and other entities and mechanisms, are covered in parts VII and IX of the present Supplement.

[122] For information on the envoys, advisers and representatives of the Secretary-General whose mandates relate to the Council's responsibility for the maintenance of international peace and security, other than those appointed as heads of peacekeeping operations or special political missions, see part IX, sect. VI.

Overview of special political missions during 2022

In 2022, the Council oversaw 12 special political missions. Five were based in Africa, three in the Middle East and two each in the Americas and Asia. Their nature varied from regional offices such as the United Nations Regional Office for Central Africa (UNOCA) and the United Nations Office for West Africa and the Sahel (UNOWAS), missions with limited mandates to monitor and support the implementation of ceasefires and peace agreements such as the United Nations Verification Mission in Colombia and the United Nations Mission to Support the Hudaydah Agreement (UNMHA), to larger assistance missions such as the United Nations Assistance Mission in Afghanistan (UNAMA), the United Nations Assistance Mission for Iraq (UNAMI), the United Nations Integrated Transition Assistance Mission in the Sudan (UNITAMS), the United Nations Assistance Mission in Somalia (UNSOM) and the United Nations Support Mission in Libya (UNSMIL).

Newly established special political missions, terminations and extensions of mandates

The Council did not establish new or terminate existing special political missions during the period under review. The Council extended the mandates of the United Nations Integrated Office in Haiti (BINUH), UNAMA, UNAMI, UNITAMS, UNMHA, UNSMIL, UNSOM and the United Nations Verification Mission in Colombia. The mandates of UNOCA and UNOWAS were renewed in 2020 and 2021, respectively, for periods of three years, until 31 January 2023 and 31 August 2024.[123] The mandates of the United Nations Regional Centre for Preventive Diplomacy for Central Asia and the Office of the Special Coordinator for Lebanon remained open-ended.

Mandates of special political missions: differences in scope

In 2022, for most special political missions, the Council reiterated without significant modification existing mandates that prioritized good offices and technical support for the implementation of peace agreements, political dialogue and national and local-level reconciliation, and political transitions involving elections and constitutional review processes. The Council underlined the importance of strengthening good governance and the capacity of national institutions to deliver basic services and implement reform agendas, including justice and security sector reform, as well as of providing support for the promotion and protection of human rights and of ensuring accountability. As part of those priorities, most missions were mandated to coordinate and support the mobilization of humanitarian and development assistance among a broad spectrum of United Nations, international, regional, and subregional partners and stakeholders. Moreover, gender mainstreaming, including ensuring the full, equal, meaningful and effective participation of women in political decision-making, as well as the protection of children, were the most common cross-cutting element of mandates.

Regional offices, namely, UNOCA and UNOWAS, continued to monitor and analyse emerging threats to peace and security, support conflict prevention and management and early warning, promote inclusive political dialogue and reform processes and provide electoral support. The two missions also continued to help to address cross-border and cross-cutting issues and challenges, such as transnational organized crime, terrorism and violent extremism, illicit trafficking, transhumance and conflicts between farmers and herders, and the security implications of climate change. The mandates of BINUH and the United Nations Verification Mission in Colombia continued to place particular emphasis on, respectively, capacity-building of national justice and rule of law institutions and the political, economic and social reincorporation of former members of armed groups. UNMHA further retained its relatively narrow mandate to oversee and facilitate the implementation of ceasefire arrangements.

Mandates of special political missions: modifications

In 2022, the Council defined new priorities for the mandate of UNAMA and made modifications to the mandates of BINUH, UNAMI, UNSMIL and UNSOM. The mandates of UNITAMS, UNMHA and the United Nations Verification Mission in Colombia, which were also extended during the period under review, were not modified.

[123] See S/2019/1009, S/2020/85, S/2021/719 and S/2021/720. See also *Repertoire*, *Supplements 2020* and *2021*.

With regard to the mandate of UNAMA, for the first time since the takeover of the country by the Taliban in August 2021, the Council introduced new priorities for the Mission, including the coordination and facilitation of humanitarian assistance, the protection and promotion of human rights, gender mainstreaming and supporting and promoting the full protection of the human rights of women and girls, monitoring and supporting the protection of children, and providing outreach and good offices with a focus on inclusive governance.[124]

In amending the mandate of UNAMI and focusing on its humanitarian support, the Council requested the Mission to support the transition of humanitarian services to government systems and the timely access to legal assistance and civil documentations for internally displaced persons and displaced Iraqis in the Syrian Arab Republic.[125]

Changes to the mandates of BINUH and UNSOM were focused primarily on strengthening their support for State institutions and stabilization. In the context of the deteriorating security situation in Haiti resulting from the activities of armed gangs, the Council amended the mandate of BINUH to include working with the United Nations Office on Drugs and Crime and other relevant United Nations agencies in support of combating illicit financial flows and trafficking and diversion of arms and in enhancing the management and control of borders and ports.[126] In Somalia, the Council encouraged UNSOM to support the national authorities to ensure that plans were in place to protect civilians, accelerate the implementation of national stabilization plans and promote expansion of governance and service delivery.[127] Following the reconfiguration of the African Union Mission in Somalia (AMISOM) into the African Union Transition Mission in Somalia (ATMIS), the Council requested the United Nations to increase coordination and collaboration between the Federal Government of Somalia, the federal member states, ATMIS, UNSOM, the United Nations Support Office for Somalia (UNSOS), the United Nations country team and the country's other partners.[128]

Furthermore, the Council continued to introduce new tasks related to addressing the impact of climate change in the mandates of special political missions. Specifically, the Council provided that UNAMI should support the Government of Iraq with facilitating regional dialogue and cooperation on the adverse impacts of climate change, in particular those that contributed to desertification and drought.[129] In relation to UNSOM, the Council, requested the United Nations, the Federal Government of Somalia and federal member states to consider the adverse implications of climate change, environmental degradation, other ecological changes and natural disasters, among other factors, in their programmes in Somalia, including by undertaking comprehensive risk assessments and risk management strategies.[130] Lastly, consistent with its approach to the mandates of peacekeeping operations as described above in section 1, the Council requested BINUH and UNSMIL to strengthen and enhance the use of strategic communications in support of their mandates and activities.[131]

Tables 4 and 5 provide an overview of the mandates of special political missions in 2022, showing the range of tasks mandated by the Council. The mandates reflected in the tables include: (a) tasks mandated by the Council in decisions adopted during the period under review; (b) tasks mandated in previous periods and specifically reiterated by the Council during the period under review; and (c) tasks of missions with open-ended or multi-year mandates adopted in previous periods. The tables are provided for information purposes only and do not reflect any position or view of the Council with regard to the status of the mandates of the field missions concerned.

---

[124] Resolution 2626 (2022), para. 5.
[125] Resolution 2631 (2022), para. 2 (c) (i) and (ii).
[126] Resolution 2645 (2022), para. 8.
[127] Resolution 2657 (2022), para. 7 (a), (b) and (d).
[128] Resolution 2628 (2022), para. 48 (c).
[129] Resolution 2631 (2022), para. 2 (b) (iv).
[130] Resolution 2657 (2022), para. 14.
[131] In connection with BINUH, resolution 2645 (2022), para. 6; and, in connection with UNSMIL, resolution 2656 (2022), para. 3.

Table 4
Mandates of special political missions, 2022: Africa

Mandate	*UNOCA*	*UNSMIL*	*UNSOM*	*UNOWAS*	*UNITAMS*
Chapter VII					
Ceasefire monitoring		X			X
Civil-military coordination					
Demilitarization and arms management	X	X	X		X
Electoral assistance	X	X	X	X	X
Human rights-related[a]	X	X	X	X	X
Humanitarian support		X		X	X
International cooperation and coordination	X	X	X	X	X
Maritime security	X		X	X	
Mission impact assessment					
Political process	X	X	X	X	X
Protection of civilians			X		X
Public information		X		X	X
Rule of law/judicial matters	X	X	X	X	X
Security sector reform			X	X	X
Support to military			X		X
Support to police			X		X
Support to sanctions regimes		X			X
Support to State institutions		X	X		X

Abbreviations: UNITAMS, United Nations Integrated Transition Assistance Mission in the Sudan; UNOCA, United Nations Regional Office for Central Africa; UNOWAS, United Nations Office for West Africa and the Sahel; UNSMIL, United Nations Support Mission in Libya; UNSOM, United Nations Assistance Mission in Somalia.

[a] Includes tasks related to human rights; children and armed conflict; women and peace and security; and youth and peace and security.

Table 5
Mandates of special political missions, 2022: Americas, Asia and Middle East

Mandate	*UNVMC*	*BINUH*	*UNAMA*	*UNRCCA*	*UNAMI*	*UNSCOL*	*UNMHA*
Chapter VII							
Ceasefire monitoring	X						X
Civil-military coordination			X				
Demilitarization and arms management	X	X	X		X		X
Electoral assistance		X	X		X		
Human rights-related[a]		X	X		X		

Mandate	*UNVMC*	*BINUH*	*UNAMA*	*UNRCCA*	*UNAMI*	*UNSCOL*	*UNMHA*
Humanitarian support			X		X		
International cooperation and coordination	X	X	X	X	X	X	X
Political process	X	X	X	X	X	X	
Protection of civilians			X				
Public information		X			X		
Rule of law/judicial matters	X	X	X		X		
Security monitoring, patrolling and deterrence							X
Security sector reform					X		
Support to police		X					
Support to sanctions regimes			X				
Support to State institutions		X	X		X		

Abbreviations: BINUH, United Nations Integrated Office in Haiti; UNAMA, United Nations Assistance Mission in Afghanistan; UNAMI, United Nations Assistance Mission for Iraq; UNMHA, United Nations Mission to Support the Hudaydah Agreement; UNRCCA, United Nations Regional Centre for Preventive Diplomacy for Central Asia; UNSCOL, Office of the United Nations Special Coordinator for Lebanon; UNVMC, United Nations Verification Mission in Colombia.

[a] Includes tasks related to human rights; children and armed conflict; women and peace and security; and youth and peace and security.

Africa

United Nations Regional Office for Central Africa

The United Nations Regional Office for Central Africa (UNOCA) was established by an exchange of letters dated 11 December 2009 and 30 August 2010 between the Secretary-General and the President of the Council.[132] The functions of UNOCA included cooperating with the Economic Community of Central African States and other regional partners in the promotion of peace and stability in the broader subregion, to carry out good offices roles in the areas of conflict prevention and peacebuilding, to strengthen the capacity of the Department of Political Affairs to advise the Secretary-General on matters relating to peace and security in the region, to promote an integrated subregional approach and facilitate coordination and information exchange among United Nations organizations and partners in the subregion, and to report to Headquarters on developments of subregional significance. UNOCA was subsequently mandated to promote efforts to address emerging security and cross-border threats, to incorporate gender perspectives in the implementation of its mandate and to take into consideration in its activities the adverse implications of climate and ecological change and natural disasters on the stability of the Central African region.[133]

In 2022, the Council did not adopt any decisions concerning UNOCA, including with regard to its mandate, which had been renewed from 1 September 2021 to 31 August 2024 by an exchange of letters between the Secretary-General and the President of the Council.[134]

[132] S/2009/697 and S/2010/457.

[133] For more information on the history of the mandate of UNOCA, see previous supplements covering the period 2008 to 2021. For more information on the situation in the Central African region, see part I, sect. 6.

[134] S/2021/719 and S/2021/720. See also the reports of the Secretary-General on the situation in Central Africa and the activities of UNOCA submitted during the period under review (S/2022/436 and S/2022/896).

In a letter dated 28 July 2022 addressed to the President of the Council,[135] the Secretary-General informed the Council of his decision to appoint Abdou Abarry as his Special Representative for Central Africa and Head of UNOCA.

United Nations Support Mission in Libya

By resolution 2009 (2011) of 16 September 2011, acting under Chapter VII of the Charter, the Council established the United Nations Support Mission in Libya (UNSMIL), with a mandate to support Libyan national efforts to restore public security and order and promote the rule of law, undertake inclusive political dialogue and promote national reconciliation, extend State authority, promote and protect human rights and support transitional justice, initiate economic recovery and coordinate international support.[136]

In 2022, the Council adopted resolutions 2619 (2022) of 31 January, 2629 (2022) of 29 April, 2644 (2022) of 13 July, 2647 (2022) of 28 July and 2656 (2022) of 28 October concerning the mandate of UNSMIL. By resolutions 2619 (2022), 2629 (2022) and 2647 (2022), the Council extended the mandate of UNSMIL, as set out in resolution 2542 (2020) and paragraph 16 of 2570 (2021), three times, for a period of three months each time.[137] Resolution 2647 (2022) was adopted with 12 votes in favour and 3 abstentions.[138] By resolution 2656 (2022), the Council unanimously extended the mandate for one year, until 31 October 2023.[139]

By resolution 2629 (2022), the Council took note of the independent strategic review of UNSMIL, requested the Mission to implement its recommendations and decided that it should be led by a Special Representative of the Secretary-General for Libya and Head of UNSMIL in Tripoli, supported by two Deputy Special Representatives of the Secretary-General.[140] The Council further called upon the Secretary-General to appoint his Special Representative promptly.[141] In the implementation of the recommendations of the strategic review, UNSMIL was requested to explore all avenues to increase efficiency and redeploy existing resources, including through prioritization and the reconfiguration of tasks and resources, as needed and where appropriate.[142]

By resolution 2644 (2022), acting under Chapter VII of the Charter, the Council reiterated the mandate of UNSMIL to cooperate fully with the Committee established pursuant to resolution 1970 (2011) concerning Libya and its Panel of Experts and called upon UNSMIL and the Government of Libya to support the Panel's investigatory work inside Libya.[143]

---

[135] S/2022/582.

[136] For more information on the history of the mandate of UNSMIL, see previous supplements covering the period 2010 to 2021. For more information on the situation in Libya, see part I, sect. 10.

[137] Resolutions 2619 (2022), 2629 (2022) and 2647 (2022), paras. 1.

[138] See S/PV.9103. After the vote, the representatives of Gabon, Ghana and Kenya expressed regret regarding the Council's decision to again extend the mandate of UNSMIL for a short period of time and underscored the need for progress on the appointment of the Special Representative of the Secretary-General for Libya and Head of the Mission.

[139] Resolution 2656 (2022), para. 1. See also the reports of the Secretary-General on UNSMIL submitted during the period under review (S/2022/31, S/2022/409, S/2022/632 and S/2022/932).

[140] Resolution 2629 (2022), para. 2. See also S/2021/716, annex, in which the independent expert who conducted the independent strategic review recommended, inter alia, that the good offices of the Mission be intensified; that the Head of Mission be relocated to Tripoli from Geneva; that the Mission return to its previous configuration consisting of a Special Representative instead of a Special Envoy, to be supported by two Deputy Special Representatives; that an immediate surge capacity be put in place to reinforce the Mission; and that women and child protection advisers be deployed swiftly.

[141] Resolution 2629 (2022), para. 2.

[142] Ibid., para. 3.

[143] Resolution 2644 (2022), para. 14. For more information on the Committee established pursuant to resolution 1970 (2011) concerning Libya, see part IX, sect. I. For more information on the sanctions measures concerning Libya, see part VII, sect. III.

By resolution 2656 (2022), the Council welcomed the appointment of Abdoulaye Bathily as Special Representative of the Secretary-General for Libya and Head of UNSMIL.[144] Furthermore, the Council reiterated its request for UNSMIL to implement the recommendations of the independent strategic review, including by strengthening the use of strategic communications to support the Mission's activities.[145] The Council requested the Secretary-General to update it on the implementation of the recommendations in his reporting pursuant to the resolution.[146]

United Nations Assistance Mission in Somalia

By resolution 2102 (2013) of 2 May 2013, the Council established the United Nations Assistance Mission in Somalia (UNSOM) with the mandate, inter alia, to provide good offices functions to support the Federal Government of Somalia in the peace and reconciliation process and to provide strategic policy advice on peacebuilding and State-building; to assist in the coordination of international donor support, in particular on security sector assistance and maritime security; to help to build the capacity of the Federal Government to promote respect for human rights, women's empowerment, child protection, the prevention of conflict-related sexual and gender-based violence and the strengthening of justice institutions; and to monitor, help to investigate and report on abuses or violations of human rights.[147]

In 2022, the Council adopted resolutions 2628 (2022) of 31 March, 2632 (2022) of 26 May and 2657 (2022) of 31 October regarding UNSOM. By resolutions 2632 (2022) and 2657 (2022), the Council unanimously extended the mandate of UNSOM, as set out in resolution 2158 (2014), twice, for a period of five months and one year, respectively, on the latter occasion until 31 October 2023.[148]

By resolution 2628 (2022), acting under Chapter VII of the Charter, the Council endorsed the decision of the Peace and Security Council of the African Union to reconfigure AMISOM into ATMIS and authorized its deployment for an initial period of 12 months.[149] With regard to UNSOM, the Council requested the United Nations, in coordination with the Federal Government, the African Union and the European Union, to establish a technical partnership coordination function to increase coordination and collaboration between the Federal Government, federal member states, ATMIS, UNSOM, UNSOS, the United Nations country team and the country's other multilateral, regional and bilateral partners.[150]

By resolution 2632 (2022), the Council decided that UNSOM was to continue to implement its mandate in accordance with resolution 2592 (2021).[151] The Council requested the Secretary-General, following consultations with the Federal Government of Somalia, to undertake a strategic review of UNSOM to include recommendations for clearly defined, measurable and realistic benchmarks to track the Mission's timely execution and achievement of its mandate and to report to the Council by 30 September 2022.[152]

By resolution 2657 (2022), the Council welcomed the strategic review of UNSOM, endorsed the proposed benchmarks set out in the annex to the report on the strategic review and modified the Mission's

[144] Resolution 2656 (2022), para. 2. See also the exchange of letters dated 31 August and 2 September 2022 between the Secretary-General and the President of the Council (S/2022/669 and S/2022/670).

[145] Resolution 2656 (2022), para. 3.

[146] Ibid.

[147] For more information on the history of the mandate of UNSOM, see previous supplements covering the period 2013 to 2021. For more information on the situation in Somalia, see part I, sect. 2.

[148] Resolutions 2632 (2022), para. 1, and 2657 (2022), para. 4. See also the reports of the Secretary-General on the situation in Somalia submitted during the period under review (S/2022/101, S/2022/392 and S/2022/665).

[149] Resolution 2628 (2022), para. 22.

[150] Ibid., para. 48 (c).

[151] Resolution 2632 (2022), para. 1.

[152] Ibid., para. 3.

mandate.[153] The Council encouraged UNSOM to support Somalia to ensure that plans were in place to protect civilians and communities in areas which were the focus of military operations; accelerate implementation of the national stabilization strategy and state-level stabilizations plans; promote expansion of governance and service delivery to areas and districts where fragility persisted; and ensure timely, balanced support to areas newly or recently recovered from Al-Shabaab.[154] Lastly, the Council requested the Secretary-General to provide an update in due course on progress made in implementing the recommendations set out in the strategic review.[155]

United Nations Office for West Africa and the Sahel

The United Nations Office for West Africa and the Sahel (UNOWAS) was established by an exchange of letters dated 14 and 28 January 2016 between the Secretary-General and the President of the Council, merging the Office of the Special Envoy for the Sahel with the United Nations Office for West Africa.[156] The Council mandated UNOWAS to, inter alia, monitor political developments in West Africa and the Sahel and carry out good offices on behalf of the Secretary-General to assist in peacebuilding, sustaining peace efforts and enhancing subregional capacities for conflict prevention and mediation; enhance subregional capacities to address cross-border and cross-cutting threats to peace and security; support the implementation of the United Nations integrated strategy for the Sahel and the coordination of international and regional engagements; and promote good governance, respect for the rule of law, and human rights and the mainstreaming of gender into conflict prevention and management initiatives. The mandate of UNOWAS was subsequently modified and was most recently extended for a period of three years, from 1 February 2020 to 31 January 2023.[157]

In 2022, the Council did not adopt any decisions related to UNOWAS or modify its mandate.[158]

United Nations Integrated Transition Assistance Mission in the Sudan

By resolution 2524 (2020) of 3 June 2020, the Council established the United Nations Integrated Transition Assistance Mission in the Sudan (UNITAMS) for an initial period of 12 months, in the context of the drawdown and exit of the African Union-United Nations Hybrid Operation in Darfur.[159] The Council decided that UNITAMS, as part of an integrated and unified United Nations structure in the Sudan, would have four strategic objectives, namely, to assist the political transition in the Sudan, progress towards democratic governance, in the protection and promotion of human rights, and sustainable peace; to support peace processes and the implementation of future peace agreements; to assist peacebuilding, civilian protection and the rule of law, in particular in Darfur and in Blue Nile and

---

[153] Resolution 2657 (2022), para. 2. See also S/2022/716, annex, in which the independent expert who conducted the independent strategic review recommended, inter alia, that UNSOM accord top priority to providing support for an agreement between the Federal Government of Somalia and the leaders of the federal member states regarding the federal model to be implemented in Somalia and to ensuring that the agreement was codified in the Constitution. Other priorities included support for reconciliation, democratic participation, security sector reform and the implementation of the Somalia Transition Plan with respect to human rights, the rule of law and the women and peace and security agenda. It was recommended that the partnership with ATMIS be further strengthened by engaging in joint analysis and establishing joint co-located teams in overlapping mandate areas. Emphasis was placed on the importance of commencing planning for the security transition and the withdrawal of ATMIS. It was also recommended that a review of UNSOM staffing and configuration be carried out following the renewal of its mandate.

[154] Resolution 2657 (2022), para. 7 (a), (b), (d) and (e).

[155] Ibid., para. 15 (b).

[156] S/2016/88 and S/2016/89.

[157] For more information on the mandate of UNOWAS, see previous supplements covering the period 2016 to 2021. For more information on peace consolidation in West Africa, see part I, sect. 8.

[158] See the reports of the Secretary-General on the activities of UNOWAS submitted during the period under review (S/2022/521 and S/2022/1019).

[159] Resolution 2524 (2020), para. 1. For more information on the mandate of UNITAMS, see previous supplements covering the period 2020 to 2021. For more information on the item entitled "Reports of the Secretary-General on the Sudan and South Sudan", see part I, sect. 7.

South Kordofan (the Two Areas); and to support the mobilization of economic and development assistance and coordination of humanitarian assistance.

In 2022, by resolution 2636 (2022) of 3 June, the Council unanimously extended the mandate of UNITAMS, as contained in resolution 2579 (2021), for one year, until 3 June 2023, without any modifications.[160]

Americas

United Nations Verification Mission in Colombia

The Council established the United Nations Verification Mission in Colombia by resolution 2366 (2017) of 10 July 2017 after the completion of the mandate of the United Nations Mission in Colombia. The Verification Mission was mandated to, inter alia, verify the implementation of the process of political, economic and social reincorporation of the Revolutionary Armed Forces of Colombia-People's Army (FARC-EP) and of the personal and collective security guarantees provided under the Final Agreement for Ending the Conflict and Building a Stable and Lasting Peace of 24 November 2016 between the Government of Colombia and FARC-EP.[161]

In 2022, by resolution 2655 (2022) of 27 October, the Council unanimously extended the mandate of the Verification Mission for one year, until 31 October 2023, without any modification.[162] The Council acknowledged the request from the Minister for Foreign Affairs of Colombia for the extension of the Mission's mandate and for the Council to consider tasking it with verifying the implementation of section 1, on comprehensive rural reform, and section 6.2, on ethnic perspectives, of the Final Agreement as a shared request from the Government of Colombia and the party of the former FARC-EP.[163] In that regard, the Council requested the Secretary-General to provide detailed recommendations on how those additional tasks would be carried out and to confirm any implications for the configuration of the Mission and expressed its intent to consider those recommendations swiftly.[164]

United Nations Integrated Office in Haiti

By resolution 2476 (2019) of 25 June 2019, the Council established the United Nations Integrated Office in Haiti (BINUH), subsequent to the closure of the United Nations Mission for Justice Support in Haiti. BINUH was mandated to advise the Government of Haiti in promoting and strengthening political stability and good governance, including the rule of law; preserving and advancing a peaceful and stable environment, including through supporting an inclusive inter-Haitian national dialogue; and promoting and protecting human rights. BINUH was further tasked with assisting the Government in planning and executing free, fair and transparent elections; reinforcing the capacity of the Haitian National Police;

---

[160] Resolution 2636 (2022), para. 1. See also the reports of the Secretary-General on the situation in the Sudan and the activities of UNITAMS submitted during the period under review (S/2022/172, S/2022/400, S/2022/667 and S/2022/898).

[161] For more information on the mandate of the United Nations Verification Mission in Colombia, see previous supplements covering the period 2016 to 2021. For more information on the item entitled "Identical letters dated 19 January 2016 from the Permanent Representative of Colombia to the United Nations addressed to the Secretary-General and the President of the Security Council (S/2016/53)", see part I, sect. 13.

[162] Resolution 2655 (2022), para. 1. See also the reports of the Secretary-General on the United Nations Verification Mission in Colombia submitted during the period under review (S/2022/267, S/2022/513, S/2022/715 and S/2022/1004).

[163] Resolution 2655 (2022), ninth preambular paragraph.

[164] Ibid., para. 2. See also the letter dated 9 December 2022 (S/2022/940), in which the Secretary-General presented his recommendations regarding the additional tasks of the Verification Mission, focusing, among other issues, on access to land and its adequate use, national plans for comprehensive rural reform, the functioning of dialogue mechanisms to resolve conflicts in the implementation of ethnic priorities and the linkages between the ethnic chapter and the gender provisions of the Agreement, factoring an ethnic perspective into rural reform and strengthened engagement with Indigenous and Afro-Colombian representatives in the Congress.

developing an inclusive approach to reduce community violence; addressing human rights abuses and violations and complying with international human rights obligations; improving penitentiary administration management and oversight of prison facilities; and strengthening the justice sector.[165]

In 2022, by resolution 2645 (2022) of 15 July, the Council unanimously extended the mandate of BINUH, in accordance with resolution 2476 (2019), for one year, until 15 July 2023.[166] The Council acknowledged the letter of the Secretary-General of 29 April 2022 providing recommendations, as requested in resolution 2600 (2021), for adjustments to the mandate and resources of BINUH to increase its effectiveness and made several changes to the Mission's mandate and configuration.[167]

Specifically, the Council encouraged continued close collaboration and enhanced coordination between BINUH, the United Nations country team in Haiti, regional organizations and international financial institutions with a view to helping the Government of Haiti to take responsibility to realize the long-term stability, sustainable development and economic self-sufficiency of the country.[168] The Council further encouraged enhanced public strategic communication regarding the mandate and specific role of BINUH.[169] The Council requested BINUH to work with the United Nations Office on Drugs and Crime and other relevant United Nations agencies to support Haitian authorities in combating illicit financial flows as well as trafficking and diversion of arms and related materiel and in enhancing management and control of borders and ports.[170]

The Council adjusted the Mission's configuration by increasing the number of civilian and seconded personnel serving as police and corrections advisers in the police and corrections unit from 30 to 42 and decided that the human rights unit would include dedicated capacity to address sexual and gender-based violence, including the identification of women's protection advisers, as applicable.[171] Lastly, the Council requested the Secretary-General to consult with the Government of Haiti, relevant countries and regional organizations regarding possible options for enhanced security support for the efforts of the Haitian National Police to combat high levels of gang violence, and to submit a written report to the Council regarding those consultations by 15 October 2022.[172]

Asia

United Nations Assistance Mission in Afghanistan

The United Nations Assistance Mission in Afghanistan (UNAMA) was established by the Council by resolution 1401 (2002) of 28 March 2002 with the core mandate to fulfil the tasks and responsibilities, including those related to human rights, the rule of law and gender issues, entrusted to the United Nations under the Agreement on Provisional Arrangements in Afghanistan Pending the Re-establishment of Permanent Government Institutions, signed in Bonn on 5 December 2001, as well as to promote national reconciliation and rapprochement through its good offices and manage all United Nations humanitarian relief, recovery and reconstruction activities in Afghanistan.[173]

---

[165] For more information on the mandate of BINUH, see previous supplements covering the period 2019 to 2021. For more information on the situation concerning Haiti, see part I, sect. 12.

[166] Resolution 2645 (2022), para. 1. See also the reports of the Secretary-General on BINUH submitted during the period under review (S/2022/117 and S/2022/481).

[167] See S/2022/369.

[168] Resolution 2645 (2022), para. 6.

[169] Ibid.

[170] Ibid., para. 8.

[171] Ibid., para. 2.

[172] Ibid., para. 10. See letter dated 8 October 2022 from the Secretary-General addressed to the President of the Council, transmitting the report on possible options for enhanced security support for the Haitian National Police (S/2022/747).

[173] For more information on the history of the mandate of UNAMA, see previous supplements covering the period 2000 to 2021. For more information on the situation in Afghanistan, see part I, sect. 14.

In 2022, by resolution 2626 (2022) of 17 March, the Council extended the mandate of UNAMA for one year, until 17 March 2023.[174] The resolution was adopted with 14 votes in favour and 1 abstention.[175]

By the resolution, the Council decided that UNAMA and the Special Representative of the Secretary-General for Afghanistan and Head of the Mission were to continue to carry out their mandate in close consultation with all relevant Afghan political actors and stakeholders, including relevant authorities, as needed, in support of the people of Afghanistan in a manner consistent with Afghan sovereignty, leadership and ownership.[176] Taking note of the report of the Secretary-General on the situation in Afghanistan and its implications for international peace and security, the Council defined 10 new priorities for the Mission.[177]

Specifically, the Council requested UNAMA to coordinate and facilitate the provision of humanitarian assistance and financial resources to support humanitarian activities, taking into account resolution 2615 (2021), as well as to coordinate international donors and organizations in relation to basic human needs, support efforts to increase accountability, transparency and the effective use of aid without discrimination, support community-based systems for meeting basic human needs and increasing resilience, and support the provision of essential services to the Afghan population.[178] Furthermore, the Council requested UNAMA to provide outreach and good offices with a focus on promoting inclusive, representative, participatory and responsive governance at the national and subnational levels, without any discrimination based on gender, religion or ethnicity, with the full, equal and meaningful participation of women and the meaningful participation of minorities and persons with disabilities.[179] UNAMA was also requested to promote responsible governance and the rule of law, including transitional justice, monitor and report on political, security and economic developments, including the adverse impacts of the drought in Afghanistan, provide assistance, as appropriate, to the Analytical Support and Sanctions Monitoring Team, monitor and analyse security dynamics, the political economy and developments relating to the rule of law, and liaise with all relevant political actors, civil society representatives and other stakeholders to promote political inclusion and broad participation in the conduct of public affairs.[180]

Regarding human rights, the Council tasked UNAMA with engaging with all stakeholders at the national and subnational levels and civil society and international non-governmental organizations in the protection and promotion of the human rights of all Afghans, monitoring, reporting and advocating with regard to the situation for civilians, the prevention and elimination of violence, the prevention of torture, monitoring of places of detention and the promotion of the rights of detainees, monitoring and reporting on civil, political, social, economic and cultural rights, supporting and advising on the implementation of instruments concerning human rights and fundamental freedoms to which Afghanistan was a State party, including the Convention on the Elimination of all Forms of Discrimination against Women, and, as appropriate, providing technical advice to duty bearers on international human rights standards.[181] UNAMA was also requested to integrate gender mainstreaming as a cross-cutting issue throughout the implementation of its mandate, support and promote gender equality, the empowerment and the full protection of the human rights of women and girls, including education, and engage with diverse Afghan women's organizations and networks, as well as to monitor and report specifically on violations, abuses

[174] Resolution 2626 (2022), para. 4. See also the reports of the Secretary-General on the situation in Afghanistan and its implications for international peace and security (S/2022/64, S/2022/485, S/2022/692 and S/2022/916).

[175] See S/PV.8997. In the explanation of his delegation's vote, the representative of the Russian Federation expressed regret that the resolution did not mention the importance of ensuring more substantive cooperation between the Mission and the Taliban authorities, as a result of which its effectiveness in achieving its mandate and international efforts to stabilize the situation could be undermined.

[176] Resolution 2626 (2022), para. 5.

[177] Ibid. In his report (S/2022/64), submitted pursuant to resolution 2596 (2021), the Secretary-General set out strategic and operational recommendations for the mandate of UNAMA in the light of recent political, security and social developments.

[178] Resolution 2626 (2022), para. 5 (a) and (b).

[179] Ibid., para. 5 (c).

[180] Ibid., para. 5 (d).

[181] Ibid., para. 5 (e).

and reprisals committed against women, including those who are journalists or health-care and humanitarian workers.[182] The Council further requested UNAMA to monitor and report on violations and abuses against children and support efforts to strengthen the protection of children.[183]

As part of the efforts of UNAMA to support regional cooperation, the Council added the task of facilitating coordinated approaches by countries and organizations in the region to contribute to a stable and prosperous Afghanistan.[184] Moreover, the Council requested UNAMA to support, within its mandate, existing mechanisms to improve the overall security situation in Afghanistan, provide assessments of the explosive ordnance threat and its impact on civilians, including children, advise and coordinate explosive ordnance threat mitigation measures, and support regional and international efforts to prevent and address the illicit trade in and destabilizing accumulation of small arms and light weapons.[185] Lastly, the Council requested UNAMA to coordinate the overall risk management approach of the United Nations in Afghanistan, including the risk of aid diversion.[186]

The Council also stressed in the resolution the critical importance of a continued presence of UNAMA and other United Nations agencies, funds and programmes across Afghanistan, and called upon all relevant Afghan political actors and stakeholders, including relevant authorities, as needed, as well as international actors to coordinate with the Mission in the implementation of its mandate and to ensure the safety, security and freedom of movement of United Nations and associated personnel throughout the country.[187]

Lastly, by an exchange of letters dated 31 August and 2 September 2022 with the President of the Council,[188] the Secretary-General appointed Roza Otunbayeva as his Special Representative for Afghanistan and Head of UNAMA.

United Nations Regional Centre for Preventive Diplomacy for Central Asia

The United Nations Regional Centre for Preventive Diplomacy for Central Asia was authorized by the Council through an exchange of letters dated 7 and 15 May 2007 between the Secretary-General and the President of the Council,[189] at the initiative of the Governments of the region. With a view to strengthening the United Nations capacity for conflict prevention in Central Asia, the Centre was assigned a number of tasks, including liaising with the Governments of the region on issues relevant to preventive diplomacy; monitoring and analysing the situation on the ground; and maintaining contact with regional organizations such as the Organization for Security and Cooperation in Europe and the Shanghai Cooperation Organization. The Centre was established with an open-ended mandate. During the period under review, the Council made no changes to its mandate.[190]

Middle East

United Nations Assistance Mission for Iraq

The Council established the United Nations Assistance Mission for Iraq (UNAMI) on 14 August 2003 by resolution 1500 (2003) to support the Secretary-General in the fulfilment of his mandate under resolution 1483 (2003) in accordance with the structure and responsibilities set out in his report of 17 July 2003.[191] Those responsibilities included coordinating activities of the United Nations in post-conflict

[182] Ibid., para. 5 (f).
[183] Ibid., para. 5 (g).
[184] Ibid., para. 5 (h).
[185] Ibid., para. 5 (j).
[186] Ibid., para. 5 (i).
[187] Ibid., para. 6.
[188] S/2022/671 and S/2022/672.
[189] S/2007/279 and S/2007/280.
[190] For more information on the history of the mandate of the United Nations Regional Centre for Preventive Diplomacy for Central Asia, see previous supplements covering the period 2007 to 2021.
[191] S/2003/715.

processes in Iraq and humanitarian and reconstruction assistance; promoting the return of refugees and displaced persons, economic reconstruction and the conditions for sustainable development; and supporting efforts to restore and establish national and local institutions.[192]

In 2022, by resolution 2631 (2022) of 26 May, the Council unanimously extended the mandate of UNAMI for one year, until 31 May 2023.[193] By the resolution, the Council commended the Government of Iraq and the Independent High Electoral Commission for executing a technically well-managed and generally peaceful election on 10 October 2021 and called for the swift and peaceful formation of a new government.[194] The Council reiterated that the Special Representative of the Secretary-General for Iraq and UNAMI, at the request of the Government, were to continue to prioritize the provision of advice, support and assistance to the Government and people of Iraq on advancing inclusive political dialogue and national and community-level reconciliation, taking into account civil society input, with the full, equal and meaningful participation of women.[195]

Furthermore, the Council made several modifications to the mandate of UNAMI with regard to electoral preparation, humanitarian support, gender mainstreaming and support for regional dialogue and dialogue between the national Government and the Kurdistan Regional Government. Specifically, the Council tasked the Mission with advising, supporting and assisting the Government, the Independent High Electoral Commission and other Iraqi institutions with efforts to strengthen electoral preparation and processes.[196] The Council provided that, in its support for regional dialogue and cooperation, the Mission should include dialogue on the adverse impacts of climate change, in particular those contributing to desertification and drought.[197] Furthermore, the Council requested UNAMI to promote, support and facilitate the transition of humanitarian services to government systems and timely access to legal assistance and civil documentation for internally displaced persons and displaced Iraqis in the Syrian Arab Republic.[198] Regarding gender mainstreaming, the Council requested UNAMI to advise and assist the Government to ensure the full, equal and meaningful participation and involvement of women at all levels of decision-making.[199] The Council further requested UNAMI to actively support the Government of Iraq and the Kurdistan Regional Government to work together and engage in regular and structured dialogue in order to resolve outstanding issues, including security provisions, budgetary arrangements and the management of the country's oil and gas resources, and to implement existing agreements, including the 2020 Sinjar Agreement.[200] The Council also reiterated the remaining tasks of UNAMI concerning the support for constitutional review, security sector reform, the provision of basic services, economic reform, capacity-building and the coordination of humanitarian assistance, promoting human rights and child protection, as outlined in resolution 2576 (2021).[201]

Lastly, the Council expressed its intention to review the mandate and reporting cycle of UNAMI by 31 May 2023, or sooner, if requested by the Government of Iraq.[202]

Office of the United Nations Special Coordinator for Lebanon

The establishment of the Office of the United Nations Special Coordinator for Lebanon was authorized by the Council by means of an exchange of letters dated 8 and 13 February 2007 between the Secretary-General and the President of the Council.[203] The Office was established with an open-ended

---

[192] or more information on the history of the mandate of UNAMI, see previous supplements covering the period 2003 to 2021. For more information on the situation concerning Iraq, see part I, sect. 22.

[193] Resolution 2631 (2022), para. 1. See also the reports of the Secretary-General on UNAMI submitted during the period under review (S/2022/103, S/2022/368 and S/2022/714).

[194] Resolution 2631 (2022), sixth and seventh preambular paragraphs.

[195] Ibid., para. 2 (a).

[196] Ibid., para. 2 (b) (i).

[197] Ibid., para. 2 (b) (iv).

[198] Ibid., para. 2 (c) (i) and (ii).

[199] Ibid., para. 2 (e).

[200] Ibid., para. 2 (g).

[201] Ibid., para. 2 (b) (ii) and (iii), (c) (iii)–(v), (d) and (f).

[202] Ibid., para. 4.

[203] S/2007/85 and S/2007/86.

mandate. The position of Special Coordinator was created to replace the position of Personal Representative of the Secretary-General for Southern Lebanon, which had been created in 2000.[204] The Special Coordinator was tasked with coordinating the work of the United Nations in the country and representing the Secretary-General on all political aspects of the Organization's work. The Special Coordinator was also responsible to ensure that the activities of the United Nations country team in Lebanon were well coordinated with the Government of Lebanon, donors and international financial institutions. During the period under review, the Council made no changes to the mandate of the Office.[205]

United Nations Mission to Support the Hudaydah Agreement

The Council established the United Nations Mission to Support the Hudaydah Agreement (UNMHA) by resolution 2452 (2019) of 16 January 2019 to support the implementation of the Agreement on the City of Hudaydah and the Ports of Hudaydah, Salif and Ra's Isa as set out in the Stockholm Agreement. UNMHA succeeded the work of an advance team that was established by resolution 2451 (2018) of 21 December 2018 and deployed to begin monitoring and to support and facilitate the immediate implementation of the Stockholm Agreement.[206] UNMHA was mandated to oversee the governorate-wide ceasefire, redeployment of forces and mine action operations; to monitor the compliance of the parties with the ceasefire and the mutual redeployment of forces; to work with the parties so that security was assured by local security forces; and to facilitate and coordinate United Nations support to assist the parties in fully implementing the Hudaydah Agreement.[207]

In 2022, by resolution 2643 (2022) of 13 July, the Council unanimously extended the mandate of UNMHA for one year, until 14 July 2023.[208]

By the resolution, the Council reiterated the existing mandate of the Mission without any modifications. The Council requested the Secretary-General to fully deploy UNMHA expeditiously and reiterated its call upon the parties to the Hudaydah Agreement to support the United Nations.[209] In that connection, the Council demanded an end to the hindrances to the movement of UNMHA personnel in Hudaydah Governorate, particularly in conflict-affected districts, and expressed support for the efforts by UNMHA to reactivate the Redeployment Coordination Committee and its joint mechanisms to implement the Hudaydah Agreement and to meet the access needs of all parties and be equally responsive to their requests.[210] Lastly, the Council requested the Secretary-General to present to the Council a further review of UNMHA at least one month before its mandate was due to expire.[211]

---

[204] See S/2000/718.

[205] For more information on the history of the mandate of the Office of the United Nations Special Coordinator for Lebanon, see previous supplements covering the period 2004 to 2021. For more information on the situation in the Middle East, see part I, sect. 20. For more information on the situation in the Middle East, including the Palestinian question, see part I, sect. 21.

[206] See resolution 2452 (2019), para. 1.

[207] For more information on the mandate of UNMHA, see previous supplements covering the period 2019 to 2021. For more information on the situation in the Middle East, see part I, sect. 20.

[208] Resolution 2643 (2022), para. 1.

[209] Ibid., para. 5.

[210] Ibid.

[211] Ibid., para. 9. See also S/2022/484 containing the review of UNMHA requested by the Council in resolution 2586 (2021), prior to the extension of the Mission's mandate by resolution 2643 (2022).

Index

ARTICLES OF THE UNITED NATIONS CHARTER

PROVISIONAL RULES OF PROCEDURE OF THE SECURITY COUNCIL

SUBJECT INDEX

23-100